W9-AUD-359

International Directory of

COMPANY HISTORIES

International Directory of COMPANY HISTORIES

VOLUME 38

Editor
Jay P. Pederson

ST. JAMES PRESS
AN IMPRINT OF THE GALE GROUP
DETROIT • NEW YORK • SAN FRANCISCO
LONDON • BOSTON • WOODBRIDGE, CT

STAFF

Jay P. Pederson, *Editor*

Miranda H. Ferrara, *Project Manager*

Erin Bealmear, Christa Brelin, Joann Cerrito, Steve Cusack,
Kristin Hart, Melissa Hill, Margaret Mazurkiewicz, Carol Schwartz,
Christine Tomassini, Michael J. Tyrkus, *St. James Press Editorial Staff*

Peter M. Gareffa, *Managing Editor, St. James Press*

Library of Congress Catalog Number: 89-190943

British Library Cataloguing in Publication Data

International directory of company histories. Vol. 38
I. Jay P. Pederson
338.7409

ISBN 1-55862-443-0

Printed in the United States of America
Published simultaneously in the United Kingdom

St. James Press is an imprint of The Gale Group

Cover photograph: NASDAQ Market Site
(courtesy: NASDAQ)

10 9 8 7 6 5 4 3 2 1

CONTENTS

Company Histories

PREFACE

The St. James Press series *The International Directory of Company Histories (IDCH)* is intended for reference use by students, business people, librarians, historians, economists, investors, job candidates, and others who seek to learn more about the historical development of the world's most important companies. To date, *IDCH* has covered over 4,900 companies in 38 volumes.

Inclusion Criteria

Most companies chosen for inclusion in *IDCH* have achieved a minimum of US$25 million in annual sales and are leading influences in their industries or geographical locations. Companies may be publicly held, private, or nonprofit. State-owned companies that are important in their industries and that may operate much like public or private companies also are included. Wholly owned subsidiaries and divisions are profiled if they meet the requirements for inclusion. Entries on companies that have had major changes since they were last profiled may be selected for updating.

The *IDCH* series highlights 10% private and nonprofit companies, and features updated entries on approximately 45 companies per volume.

Entry Format

Each entry begins with the company's legal name, the address of its headquarters, its telephone, toll-free, and fax numbers, and its web site. A statement of public, private, state, or parent ownership follows. A company with a legal name in both English and the language of its headquarters country is listed by the English name, with the native-language name in parentheses.

The company's founding or earliest incorporation date, the number of employees, and the most recent available sales figures follow. Sales figures are given in local currencies with equivalents in U.S. dollars. For some private companies, sales figures are estimates and indicated by the abbreviation *est.* The entry lists the exchanges on which a company's stock is traded and its ticker symbol, as well as the company's NAIC codes.

Entries generally contain a *Company Perspectives* box which provides a short summary of the company's mission, goals, and ideals, a *Key Dates* box highlighting milestones in the company's history, lists of *Principal Subsidiaries, Principal Divisions, Principal Operating Units, Principal Competitors,* and articles for *Further Reading.*

American spelling is used throughout *IDCH*, and the word "billion" is used in its U.S. sense of one thousand million.

Sources

Entries have been compiled from publicly accessible sources both in print and on the Internet such as general and academic periodicals, books, annual reports, and material supplied by the companies themselves.

Cumulative Indexes

IDCH contains three indexes: the **Index to Companies**, which provides an alphabetical index to companies discussed in the text as well as to companies profiled, the **Index to Industries**, which allows researchers to locate companies by their principal industry, and the **Geographic Index**, which lists companies alphabetically by the country of their headquarters. The indexes are cumulative and specific instructions for using them are found immediately preceding each index.

Suggestions Welcome

Comments and suggestions from users of *IDCH* on any aspect of the product as well as suggestions for companies to be included or updated are cordially invited. Please write:

The Editor
International Directory of Company Histories
St. James Press
27500 Drake Rd.
Farmington Hills, Michigan 48331-3535

St. James Press does not endorse any of the companies or products mentioned in this series. Companies appearing in the *International Directory of Company Histories* were selected without reference to their wishes and have in no way endorsed their entries.

ABBREVIATIONS FOR FORMS OF COMPANY INCORPORATION

A.B.	Aktiebolaget (Sweden)
A.G.	Aktiengesellschaft (Germany, Switzerland)
A.S.	Atieselskab (Denmark)
A.S.	Aksjeselskap (Denmark, Norway)
A.Ş.	Anomin Şirket (Turkey)
B.V.	Besloten Vennootschap met beperkte, Aansprakelijkheid (The Netherlands)
Co.	Company (United Kingdom, United States)
Corp.	Corporation (United States)
G.I.E.	Groupement d'Intérêt Economique (France)
GmbH	Gesellschaft mit beschränkter Haftung (Germany)
H.B.	Handelsbolaget (Sweden)
Inc.	Incorporated (United States)
KGaA	Kommanditgesellschaft auf Aktien (Germany)
K.K.	Kabushiki Kaisha (Japan)
LLC	Limited Liability Company (Middle East)
Ltd.	Limited (Canada, Japan, United Kingdom, United States)
N.V.	Naamloze Vennootschap (The Netherlands)
OY	Osakeyhtiöt (Finland)
PLC	Public Limited Company (United Kingdom)
PTY.	Proprietary (Australia, Hong Kong, South Africa)
S.A.	Société Anonyme (Belgium, France, Switzerland)
SpA	Società per Azioni (Italy)

ABBREVIATIONS FOR CURRENCY

DA	Algerian dinar
A$	Australian dollar
Sch	Austrian schilling
BFr	Belgian franc
Cr	Brazilian cruzado
R	Brazilian Real
C$	Canadian dollar
RMB	Chinese renminbi
COL	Colombian Peso
DKr	Danish krone
E£	Egyptian pound
EUR	Euro Dollars
Fmk	Finnish markka
FFr	French franc
DM	German mark
HK$	Hong Kong dollar
HUF	Hungarian forint
Rs	Indian rupee
Rp	Indonesian rupiah
IR£	Irish pound
L	Italian lira
¥	Japanese yen
W	Korean won
KD	Kuwaiti dinar
LuxFr	Luxembourgian franc
M$	Malaysian ringgit
Dfl	Netherlands florin
Nfl	Netherlands florin
NZ$	New Zealand dollar
N	Nigerian naira
NKr	Norwegian krone
RO	Omani rial
P	Philippine peso
PLN	Polish Zloty
Esc	Portuguese escudo
Ru	Russian ruble
SRls	Saudi Arabian riyal
S$	Singapore dollar
R	South African rand
W	South Korean won
Pta	Spanish peseta
SKr	Swedish krona
SFr	Swiss franc
NT$	Taiwanese dollar
B	Thai baht
£	United Kingdom pound
$	United States dollar
B	Venezuelan bolivar
K	Zambian kwacha

International Directory of

COMPANY HISTORIES

Aceto Corp.

One Hollow Lane
Lake Success, New York 11042
U.S.A.
Telephone: (516) 627-6000
Fax: (516) 627-6093
Web site: http://www.aceto.com

Public Company
Incorporated: 1947 as Aceto Chemical Co.
Employees: 125
Sales: $184.79 million (2000)
Stock Exchanges: NASDAQ
Ticker Symbol: ACET
NAIC: 325612 Polish and Other Sanitation Good Manufacturing; 42269 Other Chemical and Allied Products Wholesalers

Aceto Corp. is engaged in the marketing of chemicals used primarily by the agricultural, color-producing, pharmaceutical, nutraceutical, and surface-coating industries. The company sells about 1,000 chemicals used in these and other fields. Most are purchased in Europe or Asia for sale throughout the United States, but some are sold abroad as well. A small segment of Aceto's business is the manufacture of industrial sanitary supplies.

Growing Importer and Manufacturer: 1947–80

The company was founded by Arnold Frankel and Seymour Mann and incorporated in 1947 as Aceto Chemical Co. with initial capital of $4,000. Sons of immigrants, Frankel and Mann met while studying chemical engineering at the City College of New York, which Frankel later described to Anne Bagamery of *Business Week* as "a traditional route for poor boys in New York to enter the middle class." They were employed by TNT plants in World War II. After the war, Mann was working for a consultant when he saw barrels of aniline chemicals outside the plant of a client who had no use for this byproduct. He knew it could be used in dyes, so he bought it for $200, refined it, and resold it for a $200 profit. Mann and Frankel then borrowed from their parents to found Aceto, opening an office in Flushing, a community in New York City's borough of Queens.

The surplus chemicals business, as Frankel later described it to Rhonda Brammer of *Barron's*, was then "a dirty word—garbage! Now it's called 'recycling-environmental enhancement.' " Since American companies, for the most part, had their own sales outlets, the two young men traveled to Europe to purchase chemicals otherwise unavailable to them. There they bought off-grade aniline, paying for it by purchasing surplus solvents and chemicals from paint and varnish makers in Brooklyn and Queens and shipping these products to their European clients. The two also bought methyl alcohol produced by drug companies in the manufacture of penicillin and sold it as off-grade antifreeze. The Korean War boosted demand for Aceto's chemical stocks, and by war's end in 1953 the fledgling company had a net worth of $100,000, plus contacts with hundreds of buyers and sellers in the United States and Europe.

Beginning in 1956, Aceto ran off a streak of 27 consecutive years of increased sales and profits. By 1961 Aceto had raised its annual sales to $1 million and its net worth to about $200,000. The company made its initial public offering the following year and, for $50,000, leased its first manufacturing plant, in Long Island City, another Queens community. Net sales grew from $2.38 million in fiscal 1964 (the year ended June 30, 1964) to $7.41 million in fiscal 1968. Net income increased from $40,000 to $184,000 over this period. Aceto raised an additional $250,000 by selling more stock in 1969 and purchased a larger plant in Carlstadt, New Jersey, from Inmont Corp. Production there was aimed at organic chemicals for the pharmaceutical, cosmetic, and veterinary fields.

The company also included Pfaltz & Bauer, Inc., a research subsidiary purchased in 1965 that was maintaining one of the world's largest "libraries" of rare chemicals, with 40,000 listings. Pfaltz & Bauer moved into Stamford, Connecticut quarters in fiscal 1974. In 1975 Mann told a group of securities analysts, "During the last 10 years we have made 10 acquisitions . . . [including] divisions of major companies. We are proud of the fact that all 10 of these acquisitions were losing money at the time we acquired them and all 10 are running profitably now."

Key Dates:

1947: Arnold Frankel and Seymour Mann found Aceto Chemical Co.
1956: Aceto begins 27 consecutive years of increasing sales and profits.
1969: The company purchases a New Jersey manufacturing plant (closed in 1993).
1975: Aceto believes itself to be the world's leading producer of phenylpropanolamine, a synthetic drug (ultimately banned by the FDA in 2000) used in nasal decongestants, cough medicines, and diet pills.
1990: Company annual net income reaches $5 million for the first time.
1999: China is supplying Aceto with about 29 percent of its supplies.

Aceto was, in 1970, supplying its clients with pharmaceutical, cosmetic, and veterinary chemicals; chemicals for the color and photographic fields; textile and rubber chemicals; plastics and paint chemicals; agricultural chemicals; and industrial organic acids. Arsynco, Inc., the Carlstadt-based manufacturing subsidiary, was making about 50 products that, in fiscal 1971, accounted for about one-third of company sales (compared with three percent before the purchase of the Carlstadt facility). Among these products was phenylpropanolamine, a substance used in cold tablets such as Contac (and banned by the Food and Drug Administration in 2000). By 1975 Aceto believed itself to be the world's largest manufacturer of phenylpropanolamine. Other products included homomenthyl salicylate, principally used as a sunscreen agent; trimellitic anhydride monoacid chloride, used for polymers that were highly resistant insulations for electric motors; dyes used in Clairol hair-coloring products; and synthetic penicillin intermediates.

By 1975 Aceto was importing industrial chemicals from about 25 countries, with Japanese and European (mainly English) companies each accounting for about one-third of the total. These foreign companies, for the most part, were doing such business with Aceto on an exclusive basis. The Roehr Chemicals division in Long Island City was complementing Arsynco by supplying raw materials to it as well as finished fine (as opposed to bulk) chemicals for pharmaceutical and other uses. Two subsidiaries—one of them in the Bahamas—were handling export and other sales to the approximately five percent of customers outside the United States. Another one—Hyde Petrochemical Corp.—was marketing petrochemicals and related products.

Continued Prosperity: 1980–97

Aceto's net sales reached $89.12 million in fiscal 1980, compared with $14.19 million in fiscal 1970, and its net income was $2.92 million, compared with $362,582 a decade earlier. Frankel and Mann owned 35 percent of the common stock at this time. During fiscal 1983 sales dipped for the first time since 1955, but income continued to rise until fiscal 1985. In that calendar year the company changed its name to Aceto Corp. Among the profitable niches Aceto was exploiting at this time was as a supplier of amino anthraquinone, the orange dye in auto taillights and in the amines that allow paint to stick to auto bodies. Such chemicals were required only in minute quantities, but the markup made them lucrative for Aceto to import, working through its established network of overseas suppliers. Sales and income advanced in fiscal 1986 but dropped the following year, a decline the company attributed to the poor performance of the agricultural sector. Growth then resumed, and in fiscal 1990 sales reached $121.59 million. Net income reached $5 million for the first time that year.

In 1991 Aceto shut down its Long Island City plant and shifted its production to Arsynco. By this time manufacturing was accounting for only ten percent of the parent company's revenue. In that year an accident at the Carlstadt plant released a yellow dye used in Clairol hair coloring (a Bristol-Myers Squibb brand) into the neighborhood. This substance was not toxic, but it discolored cars and houses and cost the company about $500,000 in damages. Also in 1991, Aceto moved its headquarters from Flushing to suburban Lake Success, New York. Aceto continued to prosper despite the 1990–92 national recession, and in the latter year had $18 million in cash in its coffers, offset by only $3 million in long-term debt. Its customers included Eli Lilly & Co., Eastman Kodak Corp., and Celanese Corp. Frankel still held about 15 percent of the shares, while the heirs of Mann, who died in 1989, held about ten percent. Aceto closed the Arsynco plant in 1993. The only U.S. producer of phenylpropanolamine hydrochloride at this time, it reached an agreement by which Dixie Chemical Co. began manufacturing the substance and other specialty organic chemicals produced at Carlstadt, while Aceto retained exclusive marketing rights for the products.

Frankel retired in 1997 and was replaced as Aceto's chief executive by Leonard Schwartz. At this time—the company's 50th anniversary year—its specialty chemicals included ones for clarifying beer, keeping potatoes from sprouting, and providing pain relievers, antihypertensives, and antidepressants. The company continued to buy more than half of its chemicals from Europe, but another 35 to 40 percent were being purchased from Asia. Schwartz, who first traveled to China in 1976, compared the country to California during the gold rush because of cheap labor and the thousands of chemical factories being opened in the absence of stringent environmental laws. China, where the company established an office in Shanghai, also had become a lucrative market for Aceto's sales. Schwartz also opened sales offices in Bombay, Frankfurt, Sao Paulo, Tokyo, and Toronto.

Aceto was maintaining 34 warehouses of chemicals to assure quick delivery to its clients. Speaking to Gregory Morris of *Chemical Week,* Schwartz pointed out that the company's sources of supply were only as good as its own personnel made them. Referring to China and India, he said, "When you're buying 200 tons of the 500-ton worldwide market, they have to listen to you. [But] when raw materials are tight, or when domestic sales are strong, sometimes the factories just won't ship. That's why we're over there with the people at the factory every two weeks if necessary, making sure we get the first stuff." Aceto's assets included the average 28-year tenure of its nine top executives, since, as Schwartz also said, "Our strength is sourcing, even more than selling. We know markets."

Aceto in 1999–2000

Aceto continued to emphasize its Chinese market in 1999, when this country provided the company with about 29 percent of its supplies. A full-time Food and Drug Administration employee was hired to work in its Shanghai sales and sourcing office to help customers meet federal regulatory issues. Following the signing of a trade agreement between the United States and China, Schwartz said he would upgrade the Shanghai office to a wholly owned enterprise. To develop another potential growth area, Aceto began manufacturing and distributing institutional sanitary products, including biocides and odor counteractants. Leased space was acquired in an industrial park in New Hyde Park, Long Island, for this purpose. The acquisition of Queens-based CDC Products Corp., a manufacturer of janitorial supply products, presented a legal problem after Aceto fired the company's president and chief executive. In January 2000 Aceto acquired the aroma/flavor, nutraceuticals, and industrial chemicals distribution business of Schweizerhall Holding AG of Switzerland for about $6.4 million. Together these activities represented $32 million in annual sales.

Aceto's fiscal 2000 sales of $184.8 million was divided into six segments. Organic intermediates and colorants, whose products included dye and pigment intermediates used in color-producing industries such as textiles, inks, paper, and coatings, accounted for 27 percent. Industrial chemicals, including a variety of specialty chemicals in adhesives, coatings, foods, fragrances, cosmetics, and many other areas, comprised another 27 percent. Pharmaceutical biochemicals and nutritionals products, including the active ingredients for generic pharmaceuticals, vitamins, and nutritional supplements, accounted for 19 percent. Pharmaceuticals intermediates and custom manufacturing products, used in the preparation of pharmaceuticals, primarily by major ethical drug companies, accounted for 18 percent. Agrochemicals, including herbicides, fungicides, insecticides, and the potato-sprout inhibitor, comprised six percent. Institutional sanitary supplies and other products, including cleaning solutions, fragrances, and deodorants, accounted for the remaining three percent.

In terms of profit, industrial chemicals accounted for 29 percent in fiscal 2000; organic intermediates and colorants, 23 percent; pharmaceutical biochemicals and nutritionals, 20 percent; agrochemicals, 12 percent; pharmaceutical intermediates and custom manufacturing, eight percent; and institutional sanitary supplies and other, eight percent. During fiscal 2000 about 45 percent of the company's purchases of chemicals came from Asia and about 40 percent from Europe. The company had foreign offices in Frankfurt, Mumbai (Bombay), Paris, Sao Paulo, Shanghai, Tokyo, Toronto, and Derby, England.

Aceto's net sales fell 7.5 percent in fiscal 1999 but rebounded nine percent to a new high of $184.79 million in fiscal 2000. Net income dipped 19 percent in fiscal 1999 from the previous year's record $7.56 million but rose four percent in fiscal 2000, to $6.34 million. The company's long-term liabilities came to only $908,000 at the end of fiscal 2000. Some 20 to 40 percent of net profits were being applied on an annual basis to a stock repurchase program. During fiscal years 1997–99 the company repurchased at least 1.13 million shares for this purpose, and at the end of fiscal 2000 it held 4.9 million of its own shares. Another 6.17 million shares were outstanding in fiscal 1999.

Principal Subsidiaries

Acci Realty Corp.; Aceto Chemicals Inc.; Aceto Industrial Chemical Corp.; Arsynco, Inc.; Arsynco International Corp.; Platz & Bauer, Inc.; Roehr Chemicals, Inc.; VGF Corp.

Principal Competitors

Ajinomoto USA Inc.; OSCA Inc.; RS Hughes Co. Inc.; Waxie Sanitary Supply.

Further Reading

Bagamery, Anne, "I Could Retire, But . . . ," *Forbes,* December 5, 1983, pp. 223, 226.

Bary, Andrew, "The Right Chemistry," *Barron's,* May 14, 1992, pp. 20, 22.

Brammer, Rhonda, "Clever Formula," *Barron's,* April 7, 1997, p. 18.

——, "Special Delivery," *Barron's,* November 16, 1998, p. 22.

Carroll, Susan, "Aceto Forges Ahead Despite Hurdles in International Marketplace," *Chemical Market Reporter,* June 14, 1999, p. 37.

Ernst M. Fuller & Co., "Aceto Chemical Co., Inc.," *Wall Street Transcript,* August 11, 1975, pp. 41099, 41115-16.

Mann, Seymour, "Aceto Chemical Company, Inc.," *Wall Street Transcript,* November 24, 1975, p. 42063.

Morris, Gregory D.L., "Aceto Trades on Market Savvy," *Chemical Week,* August 13, 1997, p. 52.

——, "Dixie, Aceto in Strategic Moves," *Chemical Week,* January 20, 1993, p. 9.

"Top 100 on LI," *Newsday,* June 8, 2000, p. C45.

Walzer, Robert, "Firms Get Prepped for China Biz," *Long Island Business News,* November 19, 1999, p. 5A.

—Robert Halasz

ACNielsen Corporation

177 Broad Street
Stamford, Connecticut 06901
U.S.A.
Telephone: (203) 961-3000
Fax: (203) 961-3190
Web site: http://www.acnielsen.com

Public Company
Incorporated: 1929 as A.C. Nielsen Company
Employees: 21,000
Sales: $1.52 billion (1999)
Stock Exchanges: New York
Ticker Symbol: ART
NAIC: 54191 Marketing Research and Public Opinion Polling

ACNielsen Corporation is the global leader in consumer research, offering comprehensive information that tracks sales, volume, shares, trends, pricing, promotions, distribution, and inventory levels for corporate clients in a variety of industries worldwide. The company was originally founded in 1923. In 1996, while under the ownership of The Dun & Bradstreet Corporation, the research firm was split off into two separate entities: ACNielsen and Nielsen Media Research. However, in December 2000 Netherlands-based VNU N.V. announced that it would be acquiring ACNielsen and reuniting it with Nielsen Media, which the information powerhouse had purchased the previous year.

The Growth of the Market Research Industry: 1920–60

The company's origins date back to 1923, when an engineer by the name of Arthur C. Nielsen borrowed $45,000 to start a business running quality tests and offering buying suggestions on conveyor belts, turbine generators, and other machine-related parts. After that business was nearly bowled over by the Depression, Nielsen shifted to measuring consumer sales. In 1933, Nielsen introduced measurements for drugstore and retail store sales. A year later, similar measurements were introduced for grocery and department store sales. By going beyond conventional consumer questionnaires and having auditors actually survey store shelves and accounting books to determine sales patterns, Nielsen helped pioneer key market research tools—including the concept of market share in 1935.

While he was shaping the discipline of marketing research, Nielsen faced the difficult task of drumming up demand for his services. The labor required to gather and tabulate useful data was expensive, and many businesses were skeptical about paying top dollar for data that they thought they could gather almost as effectively themselves. "For years my father would go around and try and explain that his work was worth something. He'd quote the price. And he couldn't get any takers," Arthur C. Nielsen, Jr., told Barry Stavro of *Forbes* in 1984. Nielsen recalled that his father's attempts to sell his services to Kellogg Co. were rebuffed on the grounds that the cereal giant already had its own, cheaper alternative: "a guy stationed outside the gates trying to see how many carloads General Foods shipped out."

Though sales did not always come easily to the budding leader in marketing research, A.C. Nielsen Company enjoyed continued growth into the 1950s. That decade saw the emergence of new industries in mass media through radio and television—areas that called for new forms of marketing measurement that Nielsen was equipped to provide. Indeed, as early as 1942, Nielsen began measurement of radio audiences on a national scale. In radio's heyday following World War II, determining radio ratings was a labor-intensive endeavor: listeners would send cards to advertisers, who would actually weigh the mailbags to determine which shows were most popular. Improving upon this technique, Nielsen attached meters to radios in sample households and, eventually, installed cameras that took pictures of the meter readings. The heads of the households then mailed the pictures in to the rating company on a regular basis. In the 1950s, the advent of television and the need for ever-quicker rating techniques spurred the development of meter readers that Nielsen attached to telephone lines for "overnight" TV ratings. This method saved time over past techniques, but costs were extremely high. Still, the relatively young company persisted, driven by the belief that the TV market would grow—and communications technology along with it—enough to compensate for the high costs of tracking market trends.

Nielsen's projections were right on the mark, and the rapid growth of television worked to the overwhelming advantage of

Company Perspectives:

ACNielsen Corporation is the world's leading provider of market research, information and analysis to the consumer products and services industries. More than 9,000 clients in more than 100 countries rely on ACNielsen's dedicated professionals to measure competitive marketplace dynamics, to understand consumer attitudes and behavior, and to develop advanced analytical insights that generate increased sales and profits.

the marketing research company. By the mid-1980s, more than $19 billion was spent on national TV advertising; Nielsen metered more than 5,500 homes and generated approximately $100 million in revenue from that business segment alone. Encouraged by the continued success of its media rating service, the company established a separate division to manage it. Nielsen Media Research provided television advertisers, advertising agencies, syndicates, cable operators, networks, and stations with TV-rating information to increase the effectiveness of television advertising and programming into the 21st century.

A.C. Nielsen, Sr.'s efforts gained momentum in 1945 when his son, A.C. Nielsen, Jr., joined the firm, bringing new energy and ideas. The time-consuming tasks of sorting through data cards and doing calculations on slide rules prompted the younger Nielsen to consider emerging computer technology as a way to reduce the time and costs involved in managing the data so crucial to their business. In 1952, the company acquired one of the first computers manufactured by IBM. Although it was unwieldy in size and function compared to later models, it nonetheless marked a milestone in efficiency. Nielsen, Jr., also helped implement a training program that allowed the company to disseminate its expertise in cutting-edge marketing research tools to its growing employee base.

New Research Technologies: 1960s to Early 1980s

Such technological and administrative advances helped position A.C. Nielsen Company for decades of growth and diversification. From the 1960s through the early 1980s, the company developed new information-management systems and attracted a broader client base. In 1963, Nielsen introduced measurement of sales at mass merchandisers, providing a bulk of consumer-related information that would have been virtually unmanageable just a decade earlier. Three years later, a system of warehouse withdrawal reporting was introduced. In addition, the company established a coupon clearinghouse segment that would top $91 million in volume by the mid-1980s, with no sign of slowing down.

A momentous advancement for Nielsen was the development of scanning technology, which allowed the company to collect accurate and instantaneous data on consumer purchases as they occurred. Scanning of universal product codes at retail stores was introduced in 1977. By 1979, Nielsen offered local SCANTRACK service, which gave clients proprietary means of tracking specific market trends and producing custom reports to develop better marketing and distribution plans. A year later, such services were available on the national level. Scanning technology and data processing software continued to improve, and by the mid-1990s Nielsen considered retail scanning information "the nerve center of the changes now underway," according to the company's promotional literature. "Not only do scanning databases bring a speed and precision never previously possible, they also provide the foundation for a range of diagnostic and analytical applications which can help clients find and implement solutions that grow their revenues and minimize the cost of delivering their products to their consumers." In 1993, Nielsen became the first in the industry to offer scanning-based information from warehouse clubs with the introduction of the Nielsen Warehouse Club Service.

Corporate Restructuring, Rapid Growth in the 1980s

Nielsen's unparalleled status as a marketing research leader drew the attention of The Dun & Bradstreet Corporation, and Arthur C. Nielsen, Jr., sold A.C. Nielsen Company to the financial data giant for $1.3 billion in stock, a remarkable 26 times earnings, in May 1984. In fact, the two companies had been considering such a merger for over 15 years, as Nielsen, Jr., and Harrington Drake, chairman and CEO of Dun & Bradstreet, told the *New York Times.* "We both have the ability to collect a lot of data and deliver it efficiently to clients," Nielsen, Jr., explained. "I'm sure Nielsen will take advantage of our technology as well as our data bases," Drake added.

With the backing of its powerful parent, Nielsen continued to grow rapidly, entering several alliances and introducing new products in the late 1980s. In June 1987, Nielsen Marketing Research and The NPD Group signed a contract to establish electronic household panel services through a joint venture, NPD/Nielsen Inc. The venture had three main objectives: to measure all marketing stimuli received by sample households, including TV commercials and product purchases; to measure consumer response to promotions at the local market level; and to provide profiles by product category and brand by integrating facts from store, retail-promotion, TV-commercial, coupon distribution, and household databases. The scope of the project was enormous, offering detail and complexity unprecedented in the marketing research industry. By 1991—just three years after its inception—the National Electronic Household Panel announced coverage of 40,000 homes.

Nielsen also formed other key alliances. In August 1987, Dun & Bradstreet acquired Information Resources Inc. (IRI), bringing the market research "wonderkid" together with its rival, Nielsen. IRI's flagship product, BehaviorScan, provided a highly effective method for analyzing the effectiveness of TV commercials. Under the auspices of the same parent, IRI and Nielsen were freed from the "upward battle" of head-on competition and were better positioned to focus on new product development, according to David Snyder in *Crain's Chicago Business.* A similar collaboration of formerly competitive forces occurred in 1988, when Nielsen acquired Logistics Data Systems, the market leader whose software product, SPACEMAN, helped retailers profitably manage shelf space and display areas.

Market Research in the Information Age

Capitalizing on new developments in networking, information modeling, and forecasting, Nielsen was able to introduce a

Key Dates:

1923: Arthur Charles Nielsen, Sr., founds the A.C. Nielsen Company.
1935: A.C. Nielsen creates ''market share'' concept.
1939: A.C. Nielsen opens office in United Kingdom.
1984: A.C. Nielsen is acquired by Dun & Bradstreet.
1987: Nielsen Media Research enters into joint venture with NPD Group, forming NPD/Nielsen Inc.
1988: NPD/Nielsen Inc. launches National Electronic Household Panel.
1996: Dun & Bradstreet spins off A.C. Nielsen Company; ACNielsen Corporation is formed.
1999: ACNielsen Media International is launched.
2000: VNU announces plans to acquire ACNielsen Corporation.

wave of new products in the early 1990s. The company's decision-support and software services enabled customers to retrieve data and analyze information via terminals and personal computers installed in their offices. Such information was accessible in a number of ways, including online connection to mainframes or permanent downloading of information into customers' in-house information systems. In 1990 alone, new product introductions included: a national Convenience Store Service representing all major U.S. chains; the SCANTRACK Food/Drug Combo Retail Outlet Service, representing all major U.S. chains; the Discount Drug Service for health and beauty aids (HBA) customers; WealthWise, a modeling tool for consumer-oriented financial services firms; and ScorePlus, which provided demographic and product-use data applicable to specific trading areas.

New product introductions kept pace with rapid growth in demand, as ever more powerful computer processing systems were made available to Nielsen's customer base. In 1991, the company introduced Spotlight, a system that enabled users to locate and account for volume and share changes for given brands. That system would win an award for outstanding artificial intelligence application from the American Association for Artificial Intelligence in 1992. Other products introduced that year included: Nielsen Sales Advisor, SCANTRACK Category Manager, and ScanQuick. In addition, PROCISION provided a single source for tracking all components of HBA marketing, and the Nielsen Workstation provided Windows-based support for marketers. In 1993, the company introduced Nielsen Opportunity Explorer to help marketing and sales professionals understand category dynamics and pinpoint sales opportunities. Along with Nielsen Promotion Simulator, that product placed first in the software applications category at the Information Industry Association's Product Achievement Awards in 1993.

Responding to overwhelming demand for its efficiency-related solutions in the consumer packaged goods industry, in 1993 Nielsen created a separate division for Efficient Consumer Response (ECR) and began forging ties within the industry to enhance its capabilities. The key objectives of ECR were to streamline distribution and sales processes, eliminate waste, and deliver product to consumers faster and at a lower cost. One example was the 1993 implementation of a Micro-Marketing system—Nielsen's Eagle Eye—to help the Anheuser-Busch Company work with its retailers to organize space plans, marketing, and distribution for maximum sales. One retail chain that implemented the system saw an annual potential increase in beer category sales of $3.2 million, according to Nielsen literature.

In a joint effort aimed at ECR implementation around the globe, the company worked together with suppliers and distributors to form the Nielsen Solution Partners program in 1994. The program was designed to align the ''best practices'' of industry leaders, such as NON-STOP Logistics, a state-of-the-art cross-docking network focused on reducing warehouse inventory and speeding the delivery process from plants to stores. Heading into the 21st century, one of Nielsen's key objectives was to strengthen that partnership and thereby contribute innovative solutions to ECR in general.

Nielsen also continued to increase its global presence. Indeed, the company's international reach grew steadily after its first overseas office was opened in England in 1939. By 1991, the company had opened an office in its 28th country, Hungary. In 1993, the company was looking into a subsidiary office in Israel. In April 1994, Nielsen expanded into South Africa through a partnership with Integrated Business Information Services (IBIS), the premier market research company in that country. Serge Olun, President and CEO of A.C. Nielsen, told *Business Wire* in 1994 that ''Nielsen is moving aggressively today to negotiate further partnerships in South America, Africa, Eastern Europe, the Middle East and elsewhere.'' He cited plans to increase the company's coverage to 70 countries worldwide by 1995. In April 1995, the company made significant progress toward achieving that goal when it extended its global coverage to six countries in Central America: Costa Rica, Guatemala, Honduras, Nicaragua, El Salvador, and Panama. Since its origin as a strictly American concern in the 1920s, Nielsen branched out until 70 percent of its business came from outside the United States in the 1990s.

By the mid-1990s, Nielsen had asserted its dominance in the marketing information industry by successfully consolidating or winning back 26 consumer packaged goods clients, such as Dole Foods, Tambrands, Johnson & Johnson, Bristol Myers Squibb, and Clairol. It also remained king of the hill in media rating services—especially since its main TV-rating competitor, The Arbitron Company, stopped providing local TV ratings at the end of 1993. Nielsen, a company that started as a rating service for conveyor belts, became a global success story by gathering information from an ever-increasing variety of sources and turning it into valuable products.

Corporate Spinoff Trends in the Late 1990s

Unfortunately, intense competition and prolonged pricing wars with market research rivals like Information Resources, Inc. (IRI), particularly in the supermarket scanner information sector, began to have a significantly negative impact on A.C. Nielsen's earnings by the mid-1990s. In January 1996 Dun & Bradstreet, intent on unloading its less profitable divisions, announced a plan to split into three separate public companies: Dun & Bradstreet; Cognizant, which was to be comprised of Dun & Bradstreet's three fastest growing units, including Nielsen Media Research; and ACNielsen Corporation. The demerger, which was completed by November of that year, left the struggling ACNielsen to fend for itself.

However, the company's new chairman and CEO, Nicholas L. Trivisonno, was determined to turn things around. Promising to reinvigorate Nielsen's focus on customer service and to streamline company operations, Trivisonno was able to restore the company to profitability almost immediately. Increased efficiency and improved services in Nielsen's U.S. and European operations resulted in a strong fourth quarter for fiscal 1996, and by April 1998 the company was enjoying a profitable first quarter for the first time in five years.

A series of strategic acquisitions further strengthened the newly independent company's position. In 1997 Nielsen merged with Entertainment Data, Inc. to form ACNielsen EDI, a new division dedicated to providing up-to-the-minute box office returns to the motion picture industry. In 1998 the company acquired The BASES Group, an international provider of simulated test marketing services and proprietary products, to create ACNielsen BASES, and the following year it purchased Media Monitoring Services Ltd., one of Britain's leading advertising measurement services. Throughout this period Nielsen also entered into a number of new partnerships with major consumer goods companies, including Safeway, Quaker Oats, and Nestlé USA.

The company also emphasized global expansion in the latter half of the 1990s. In 1999 it launched ACNielsen Media International, with the aim of consolidating the company's diverse broadcast and print capabilities worldwide. Aiming to increase its overall client base, Nielsen actively pursued new audience measurement contracts in a number of emerging international markets, including China, where it quickly situated its Peoplemeter audience measurement service in ten major cities. In September 1998 the company increased its ownership in AMER Nielsen Research to 100 percent, in order to strengthen its hold on consumer data markets in Eastern Europe, the former Soviet Union, Sub-Sahara Africa, and India; in the same month the company also acquired a 49 percent stake in AMER World Research Ltd.—which charted consumer trends in the Middle East and North Africa—with an option to purchase the remaining 51 percent by 2003.

Adapting to the rapid proliferation of new technologies in the late 1990s was a crucial process for any company devoted to studying audience information, and the challenges created by e-commerce and interactive media largely dictated the direction of Nielsen's international growth during this time. In 1999 the company entered into a joint partnership with NetRatings to form ACNielsen eRatings.com, the world's first global Internet data measurement service. By July 2000, the new division had expanded its client base to 520 worldwide, solidifying its position as the leading provider of consumer e-commerce information in the world.

This continued financial success and rapid growth sparked the interest of Dutch media and marketing giant VNU, and in December 2000 a merger agreement was announced, making ACNielsen a wholly owned subsidiary once again. The deal reunited the company with Nielsen Media Research, which VNU had acquired the previous year. Working together, the two market research leaders clearly enjoyed a competitive advantage as they moved forward into the information age.

Principal Subsidiaries

AC Nielsen EDI; AC Nielsen eRatings.com; AC Nielsen Bases; AC Nielsen International Research.

Principal Competitors

The Arbitron Company; Information Resources, Inc.; Taylor Nelson Sofres plc; WPP Group plc.

Further Reading

"A. C. Nielsen Extends Global Reach to Six Countries in Central America," *Canada News Wire,* April 18, 1995.

"A. C. Nielsen Signs Pan-European Contract with Reckitt & Colman; Global Expansion Continues at Record Pace," *PR Newswire,* March 14, 1994.

"A.C. Nielsen to Israel; Plans Subsidiary," *Israel Business Today,* July 2, 1993, p. 5.

Alexander, Keith L., "Dutch Firm VNU to Buy ACNielsen in $2.3B Deal," *USA TODAY,* December 19, 2000.

Clark, Kenneth R., "CBS Taps 2nd Ratings Firm in Jab at Nielsen," *Chicago Tribune,* November 5, 1991, p. C1.

——, "Maxwell Firm to Challenge Nielsen," *Chicago Tribune,* June 20, 1990, p. C3.

——, "Nielsen Acts to Upgrade TV Monitoring System," *Chicago Tribune,* June 6, 1990, p. C1.

"Dun & Bradstreet to Link Nielsen and IMS Data with Manugistics' Supply Chain Management Software to Provide Integrated ECR Solution," *PR Newswire,* August 8, 1994.

Farhi, Paul, "Maryland-Based 'Peoplemeter' Firm Is Suspending Its Operation; Demise Leaves Nielsen As Only TV Ratings Firm in U.S.," *Washington Post,* July 30, 1988, p. D10.

"GTE Interactive Services and Nielsen to Conduct Market Test," *PR Newswire,* May 6, 1992.

Haire, Kevlin C., "TV Stations Rate Need for Nielsen," *Baltimore Business Journal,* October 22, 1993, p. 5.

Jackovics, Ted, "Eye to the Future," *Tampa Tribune,* January 25, 1999.

Jackson, Tony, "Dun & Bradstreet to Split into Three," *Financial Times* (London), January 11, 1996.

Koranteng, Juliana, "ACNielsen Shoots for Global Growth," *Advertising Age International,* June 1, 1999.

Millenson, Michael L., "Arbitron Leaves TV to Nielsen," *Chicago Tribune,* October 19, 1993, p. N1.

"Nielsen Expands into South Africa Through Partnership with IBIS," *PR Newswire,* April 6, 1994.

"Nielsen Marketing Research Announces Joint Venture with the NPD Group," *Business Wire,* June 15, 1987.

"Nielsen's New Magazine Measurement Service a Boon to Marketers and Advertisers," *PR Newswire,* March 25, 1991.

"Revlon Signs Agreement with Nielsen; Significantly Expands Current Relationship," *PR Newswire,* July 26, 1994.

Salibian, Catherine E., "Marketing Firm Lodges Action Against Nielsen," *Rochester Business Journal,* July 24, 1989, p. 1.

Salmans, Sandra, "Dun and Nielsen: Compatible Goals," *New York Times,* May 21, 1984, p. D1.

Snyder, David, "Why Archrivals IRI, A.C. Nielsen Merged," *Crain's Chicago Business,* August 31, 1987, p. 1.

Stavro, Barry, "Rating Nielsen," *Forbes,* December 17, 1984, p. 100.

—Kerstan Cohen
—updated by Stephen Meyer

Advanta Corporation

Welsh & McKean Roads
P.O. Box 844
Spring House, Pennsylvania 19477-0844
U.S.A.
Telephone: (215) 657-4000
Fax: (215) 444-6121
Web site: http://www.advanta.com

Public Company
Incorporated: 1974 as Teachers Service Organization, Inc.
Employees: 2,643
Sales: $572.6 million (1999)
Stock Exchanges: NASDAQ
Ticker Symbols: ADVNB; ADVNA
NAIC: 52221 Credit Card Issuing (pt); 52222 Sales Financing (pt); 52231 Mortgage and Nonmortgage Loan Brokers; 52391 Miscellaneous Intermediation (pt); 53242 Office Machinery and Equipment Rental and Leasing (pt); 522110 Commercial Banking; 522120 Savings Institutions; 522292 Real Estate Credit (pt); 522298 All Other Nondepository Credit Intermediation (pt); 522320 Financial Transactions Processing, Reserve, and Clearinghouse Activities (pt); 524126 Direct Property and Casualty Insurance Carriers

Advanta Corporation originates, services, and sells small business credit card and home equity loans. It also provides equipment leasing for small businesses and offers credit life, disability, and unemployment insurance. From a family-run credit union issuing loans primarily to nurses and teachers, the company pioneered the no-fee credit card in the 1980s and moved into the 1990s as a relatively small but highly profitable niche business, depending on gold cards for the bulk of its success. After a significant rise in consumer bankruptcies and debt chargeoffs in the late 1990s forced Advanta to sell off its credit card operations, the company restructured itself to focus more intently on the subprime mortgage and small business credit card markets. By 2000 Advanta had narrowed its core business even further, announcing an imminent deal to sell its mortgage operations.

A Loan Company for the Education Community: 1950s–60s

Advanta's roots reach back to a family business that financed educational programs. In 1951 J.R. Alter, a former Philadelphia schoolteacher, founded the Philadelphia Teachers Service Organization, Inc., in the Olney section of Philadelphia. The example of J.R. Alter and his wife, also a schoolteacher, influenced their son, Dennis Alter, who also became a schoolteacher and eventually served as chairman and CEO of the much-expanded family business. In the 1960s Dennis Alter taught English at Benjamin Franklin High School for three years while moonlighting as executive vice-president and director of TSO. J.R. Alter retired in 1971. His son finished graduate school and assumed the post of president and chief executive officer of the company.

After 20 years in business, TSO maintained a modest profile, with a net worth of $300,000 in 1971. The bulk of business consisted of loans by mail, primarily to schoolteachers, nurses, and other affinity groups via endorsements by their professional and trade organizations. Its lending activities included second mortgage loans, unsecured installment loans, and home equity installment loans. The company also operated consumer finance subsidiaries in Pennsylvania, New Jersey, and Florida.

Dennis Alter worked quickly to change TSO from a sleepy credit union into a national consumer finance company. One of his first steps was to lure James T. Dimond, a former Fidelity Bank of Philadelphia senior vice-president, to TSO as president and chief operating officer. Dimond's banking expertise contributed to TSO's next strategic move: its 1982 acquisition of Colonial National Bank in Wilmington, Delaware, for $2.1 million. With its $9 million in assets, Colonial became TSO's primary resource for lending and funding management.

As part of the acquisition transaction, Colonial divested its commercial loan portfolio and thus moved outside the Bank Holding Company Act's definition of a bank, becoming what

Company Perspectives:

Advanta is a highly focused financial services company, well positioned in sizable and growing markets. We offer diverse and innovative financial solutions to consumers and small businesses nationwide. Our principal objectives are to use our information based strategy to continue to grow each of our businesses for the benefit of our customers while increasing profitability and improving cash flow.

Banking Expansion Reporter called a ''Nonbank Bank'' in a September 1982 article. Although Colonial no longer made commercial loans, it serviced 30,000 depositors from all 50 states, accounting for $525 million in deposits by 1986. Even as a so-called nonbank, Colonial drew new customers to TSO because of banking benefits such as FDIC-insured deposits. In addition, exploitation of communications technology enabled clients to reap the benefits of Colonial's banking without ever going near the bank. Loans and deposits were managed via WATS long-distance telephone lines, wire transfers, mail, nationwide automated teller machines, debit and credit cards, and checks. With such branchless banking, Colonial could potentially provide TSO customers with more personalized service than traditional bank service. ''The corner branch of a local bank may seem far more distant and less responsive than our customer service personnel,'' said Alter in an August 4, 1986 *American Banker* article.

TSO also developed a special unit, Colonial National Leasing, Inc., to lease computers, telephone and medical equipment, industrial machinery, and other tools to professionals and small businesses. In 1987 TSO acquired Leasetech Inc., an Atlanta-based equipment leasing organization.

The 1980s: Diversification and Rapid Growth

With its unusual features—a ''nonbank bank'' organizing ''branchless banking''—Colonial helped TSO realize unusual growth. From 1982 to 1986, TSO's net income grew at a compound annual rate of 113 percent, while assets grew at a compound annual rate of 63 percent. Gross revenue for 1985 was $67.8 million, representing an 87 percent increase over the previous year's.

Success in the early 1980s, however, was only a preface to the virtual explosion of growth that was set in motion by the 1983 introduction of credit cards. By 1985, card receivables topped installment loans—$169 million versus $167 million at year end. Whereas installment loans grew 25 percent in 1985, card balances jumped by more than 250 percent. In 1986 *Money* magazine, *USA Today,* and the Consumer Credit Card Rating Service all rated TSO's premium cards in their top categories. TSO, in turn, put 350,000 cards in circulation, assuming 89th place on the national charts. By 1991 the company derived 70 percent of its revenues from its Visa and MasterCard customers.

TSO's credit card strategy involved loans to the general public, as opposed to its previous practice of lending to select affinity groups. At year end, the general public accounted for 67 percent of card receivables in 1985, up from 17 percent the year before; they also accounted for 22 percent of installment loans, up from less than one percent. Driven by aggressive marketing to foster nationwide deposits and loans, the company relied on direct mail, telemarketing, newspaper ads, and radio and television spots. Institutional deposits were promoted by telephone marketing and certificate of deposit quotes on the Telerate Service. With high rates to attract deposits, longer-term loans to draw installment loan borrowers, and very competitive rates on premium credit cards, TSO expanded operations at a hefty rate.

Lending to the general public, however, represented substantial credit risk as well as quick growth. In order to best protect itself, the company invested in sophisticated marketing research, enlisting several services to provide in-depth demographic data on precise areas of the country. The company only targeted potential customers of a very specific profile: usually college-educated, ages 20 to 44, with above-average incomes. ''You cannot apply to Advanta [TSO's name after 1988]. They have to pick you as a customer who has these two characteristics: high credit quality and high usage patterns,'' said First Boston's Allerton Smith in a September 15, 1992, article for *Financial World.* Once a potential customer was selected, however, the offer was unusually attractive. It often consisted of mostly no-fee credit cards with better-than-average interest rates and attractive credit lines, according to company spokeswoman Deborah Dove in a January 31, 1992 *Investor's Business Daily* article. By 1992, 80 percent of the company's credit card offerings were gold cards, reflecting the high-end emphasis of the company's marketing research efforts.

Even with the support of extensive market research, credit card lending proved a risky business in the mid-1980s, giving rise to some skepticism regarding TSO's stability. Not only was the company portfolio relatively new and untested, but mounting consumer debt had reached frightening heights. Credit card defaults doubled during 1986, to 4.2 percent of charges outstanding. ''Consumers cannot continue to carry the debt they have, and if we have an economic slowdown early next year, which I think we will, we could see a lot of problems,'' said Nancy Bush, analyst with Butcher & Singer, Inc., in a December 8, 1986 *Philadelphia Business Journal* article. That year, Moody's graded a BA3 to $50 million in subordinated debentures offered by TSO, and Standard & Poor's ranked them B+. Likewise, TSO's common stock fell from an $18.50 high in April to $13.50 in December.

One buffer against credit card risks was TSO's involvement in other financial services, including consumer installment loans, equipment leasing, credit life and disability insurance, and residential mortgage services. Such a wide range of services was responsible, in part, for the company's 1985 name change from Teachers Service Organization, Inc. (TSO) to the more inclusive TSO Financial Corp. In 1986 the company acquired Advanta Mortgage Corp. USA (formerly Apex Financial Corp.) for $7.5 million. TSO's mortgage banking rapidly expanded nationwide and capitalized on home equity loans, which grew in popularity after mid-1980s tax reform cut the personal deductions allowed on credit card charges.

Starting in 1988, TSO began securitizing its growing home equity loan assets and credit card receivables, pooling the loan balances into securities for sale to investors. Over the years, that

Key Dates:

1951: J.R. Alter founds Philadelphia Teachers Service Organization, Inc.
1971: J.R. Alter retires; Dennis Alter becomes company president and CEO.
1982: Teacher's Service Organization, Inc. acquires Colonial National Bank.
1983: Teacher's Service Organization introduces its first credit cards.
1985: Teacher's Service Organization becomes TSO Financial Corp.
1986: TSO Financial Corp. acquires Advanta Mortgage Corp., USA.
1988: TSO Financial Corp. becomes Advanta Corporation.
1995: Advanta National Bank is chartered.
1998: Fleet Financial Group acquires Advanta's credit card operations.
2000: Advanta announces tentative agreement to sell mortgage operations.

financial strategy became one of Advanta's (TSO's name as of 1988) fundraising specialties. In May 1989, for example, the company announced that Colonial National and Advanta Mortgage had placed with institutional investors $31.1 million of Class A certificates representing fractional ownership interests in Advanta Second Mortgage Trust. The certificates were insured by Financial Guaranty Insurance Corp. and were rated ''AAA'' by Standard & Poor's and ''Aaa'' by Moody's. On August 29, 1990, Colonial sold $250 million in credit card-backed notes, marking its tenth asset securitization deal. William Kaiser, senior vice-president of Advanta Mortgage, estimated in a June 12, 1991 *Business Wire* article that the company had securitized more than $550 million in home equity loans since 1988 and intended to pursue the practice on a regular basis. In May 1992 Advanta continued funding its credit portfolio by tapping the securitization market, completing two private placements with a combined value of about $332 million. In June of that same year, the company issued certificates in a $100 million home equity loan securitization deal. The announcement was notable on several accounts: it was Advanta's first transaction insured by MBIA, and it employed an innovative form of securitization with both fixed and variable components, increasing the company's funding flexibility and broadening its investor base, according to a June 1992 article in *Global Guaranty.* Advanta not only applied, but broadened securitization techniques.

In the late 1980s the company continued to grow. In August 1987 it delved back into familiar territory, acquiring Educational Credit Corporation (ECC) from Pacific Financial Asset Management Corp. ECC loan programs included competitive rates and long-term repayment plans to accommodate escalating costs of education aggravated by reductions in federal tuition assistance. That same year, the company acquired the remaining stock of LeaseComm Financial Corp., of which it previously held 21 percent equity interest. By 1988, since its primary focus was no longer on educators, TSO stockholders voted to change the company name to Advanta Corporation.

In addition to a change of name, 1988 brought a change of fortune, as Advanta posted its first loss—$9 million—since it was founded in 1951. After an initial loss of $6.1 million in the fourth quarter of 1987, Dennis Alter commented in a February 10, 1988 *PR Newswire* report that ''the decline in earnings . . . is due, in large part, to an earlier decision to restructure the company's balance sheet to achieve a more balanced asset portfolio. We believe this restructuring will significantly strengthen Advanta.''

Along with financial restructuring, Chairman and CEO Dennis Alter recruited a new management team to help refocus the company. In June 1987 James T. Dimond resigned as chief operating officer, to be replaced by Richard A. Greenawalt, former president of Transamerica Financial Corporation in Los Angeles. Before that he had been with Citicorp for 15 years, as chairman and chief executive of Citicorp Person-to-Person Inc., and president and chief executive of Citicorp Retail Services Inc., New York. In March 1988 Dennis R. Eickhoff joined the company as president of its Advanta Mortgage Corp. USA subsidiary. Eickhoff had served since 1983 as president and chief executive officer of Gibraltar MoneyCenter, Inc., the San Diego-based $1 billion second mortgage subsidiary of Gibraltar Financial Corporation. With the expertise of its new management, Advanta exited the installment loan business and focused on credit cards and secured lending products.

Advanta also began more aggressively promoting its stock, undertaking a new investor relations campaign in the early 1990s. Convincing investors to buy into high stock prices proved challenging, as 50 percent of the company's 9.13 million outstanding shares were controlled by insiders. Dennis Alter himself held 41 percent of the company's outstanding stock, or 3.8 million shares. Consequently, the float—the number and value of shares tradable—was small. Advanta enlisted the help of Prudential-Bache Securities and First Boston Corp., two of Wall Street's big players, to provide analyst coverage and consulting services. In September 1990 Hambrecht & Quist analyst Dirk Godsey valued Advanta stock at $18 to $23 a share, with strong potential for the future, according to a September 17, 1990 article in *Philadelphia Business Journal.* His assessment was confirmed in July 1991, when Prudential Securities Research, Inc. analyst Larry Eckenfelder named Advanta Corp. his ''single best idea'' in the financial services industry and repeated his buy recommendation on the stock.

Eckenfelder almost proved mistaken when the stock price of Advanta and other credit card companies fell on worries over a November 1991 Senate vote to cap interest rates on consumer credit cards. After a 52-week high of $38.50 on November 13, Advanta dropped 25 percent over the next two days. Even after the Senate's quick shelving of the rate ceiling, Advanta shares remained well below their November peak. Nevertheless, Advanta's outstanding growth record—the company registered 40 percent compound growth in cards outstanding between 1987 and 1990—made its shares a good investment, according to Gordon Matthews in a December 17, 1991 feature for the *American Banker.*

With its experienced management team and focus on a profitable niche business, Advanta moved into the 1990s with excellent prospects. By January 30, 1992, its stock had more than recovered from the 1991 scare, closing at $39.375. The company also had realized a broad portfolio, with a 1991 revenue breakdown of 70 percent from credit cards, 20 percent from home equity loans, five percent from equipment leasing, and five percent from its credit insurance business. To expand its leasing program, Advanta introduced the Access to Capital Equipment (ACE) card in January 1993. The service was designed to augment leasing services with such features as deferred payment, adjustable payment schedules, and a simplified application process.

With roughly one percent of the U.S. credit card market in 1991, Advanta had plenty of room for continued growth. In April 1992 its board approved a share-for-share dividend of Class B common for each old common (now Class A common) share outstanding, doubling the number of common shares outstanding to 22.2 million and increasing the float for new investors. ''This plan is designed to increase the company's flexibility in financing future growth and to promote management continuity,'' said Dennis Alter in an April 13, 1992 *National Mortgage News* article. Indeed, Advanta Corp. appeared to be entering the latter half of the 1990s in healthy condition, as it announced a company record $17.2 million in net income for the second quarter of 1993.

The Specialized Credit Card Industry in the Late 1990s

The bulk of Advanta's profits in the mid-1990s came from its credit card operations. By 1995 cards accounted for 80 percent of earnings. The company was attracting new customers at a record pace, issuing more than 1.5 million new cards in 1994, 700,000 of those in the fourth quarter alone—compared with 310,000 in the fourth quarter of 1993. Net income in 1994 rose to $106.1 million, a 36 percent increase from the previous year (marking Advanta's sixth consecutive year of record earnings), while total managed assets climbed to $8.6 billion.

Encouraged by this rapid growth, Advanta began focusing on marketing new card products in previously unexplored markets. In June 1995 the company struck a deal with Royal Bank of Scotland, one of the leading credit card issuers in the United Kingdom, to create RBS Advanta, a joint venture geared toward marketing a new low-interest credit card in the United Kingdom. The card was launched the following February with an APR of 15.9 percent, which was significantly lower than rates offered by other major card companies in England. It marked the beginning of an American invasion of the British credit card industry, with People's Bank of Connecticut following suit in April 1996, when it launched a card offering 14.4 percent financing.

By the end of 1995 Advanta and three other specialized card companies—Capital One, First USA, and MBNA—had seized a 20 percent market share of a credit card industry that had swelled to $305 billion. Between 1995 and early 1997 Advanta's cardmember base doubled; 1995 earnings rose to $136 million, and in 1996 the company began developing a wider range of products, including a Platinum Edge MasterCard. In November 1996 it reached an agreement with American Express to market the Rewards Accelerator Card, which would allow customers who made charges on Advanta MasterCard and Visa cards to accrue Membership Rewards points in their American Express accounts. Visa and MasterCard were quick to cry foul, however, and in the midst of the ensuing litigation the project was eventually scrapped.

During this period of expansion, however, the red flags were already beginning to fly. In addition to unprecedented profits, 1995 also saw a significant rise in credit card delinquency. In the third quarter of 1994, companies were reporting that 2.9 percent of cardholders were more than 30 days late with payments; by the third quarter of 1995 that number rose to 4.2 percent. In June 1996 the Bank of New York established a $350 million provision as insurance against potential credit card losses, causing Advanta's stock to drop 13.8 percent in one week. At around the same time, Advanta relaxed its charge-off accounting policy, raising the time allowed for reporting from 30 to 90 days—a move that raised more than a few eyebrows in the financial world.

The bottom fell out on March 17, 1997, when Advanta reported a quarterly loss of $20 million. Rumors that the company would be sold were rampant in the industry. After a period of aggressive restructuring—which primarily involved turning increased attention to its subprime mortgage business—Advanta managed to get back on an even keel, however, and was once again reporting strong earnings by the third quarter. In October 1997, the company reached an agreement with Fleet Financial Corporation to sell its credit card operations for $500 million.

The year 1998 was dedicated to rebuilding, with a new emphasis on nonconforming mortgages and credit cards for small businesses. By the end of 1999 Advanta was the fourth leading subprime lender in the United States, and the company saw increased earnings into the first quarter of 2000. In spite of these gains, however, the company's stock valuation continued to fall. Advanta's new focus failed to restore investor confidence, and by May 2000 the company's stock had dropped to $17.50 a share—compared with a peak value of $57.50 a share in May 1996. Regulatory changes in the home mortgage industry, which imposed stricter limitations on lending, resulted in a second quarter loss of $192.7 million and drove the company's stock down to $8.56 a share. By the end of the year the company announced it had reached an agreement to sell its home mortgage operations—although it declined to identify the buyer at the time of the announcement—and that it would begin to devote most of its marketing resources to building a reputation as a leading provider of credit cards for small businesses. At this time Advanta also was facing a potentially disastrous legal battle with Fleet Financial Corporation, over alleged misappropriations of funds and misrepresentation of portfolio value relating to the sale of its credit card business, with a trial date set for 2001.

Principal Subsidiaries

Advanta National Bank; Advanta Bank Corp.; Advanta Partners LP; Advanta Mortgage Corp.; Advanta Leasing Services; Advanta Insurance Companies; Advanta Business Cards.

Principal Competitors

Aames Financial Corporation; Citigroup Inc.; Household International, Inc.

Further Reading

''Advanta Sells ABS Debt, Will Service Daiwa Placement,'' *American Banker-Bond Buyer,* May 25, 1992, p. 3.

Authers, John, ''Change on the Cards at Advanta: Credit-Card Issuer May Abandon Its Low-Price Strategy,'' *Financial Times* (London), March 18, 1997.

Chesler, Caren, ''Advanta's Alter and Greenawalt: Turning Technology into Credit Card Marketing Machine,'' *Investor's Business Daily,* January 14, 1993.

Foust, Dan, ''TSO Gets Credit for Three-Year's Rapid Growth,'' *Philadelphia Business Journal,* December 8, 1986, p. 5.

Gregory, Michael, ''OCC Wallops Advanta: Who's Next?,'' *Asset Sales Report,* August 7, 2000.

Groc, Isabelle, ''Advanta: Credit Where Credit Is Due,'' *Financial World,* September 15, 1992, p. 16.

Hansell, Saul, ''A Shaky House of Plastic with No Quick Fix in Sight,'' *New York Times,* December 28, 1995.

Hornblass, Jonathan S., ''Advanta Reinventing Itself in Low-Key Way,'' *American Banker,* March 20, 1995.

Jones, John A., ''Advanta Picks Its Prospects in No-Fee Credit Card Market,'' *Investor's Business Daily,* November 3, 1992, p. 32.

Julavits, Robert, ''Advanta Says It May Sell Mortgage, Leasing Divisions to Focus on Cards,'' *American Banker,* May 18, 2000.

Kramer, Farrell, ''Advanta Rebounds from Rate-Cap Scare,'' *Investor's Business Daily,* January 31, 1992, p. 1.

Mandzy, Orest, ''TSO Unit Buys Leasetech,'' *American Banker,* August 3, 1987, p. 3.

Matthews, Gordon, ''STOCKS: Advanta Gets Thumbs Up Despite a Brief Downturn,'' *American Banker,* December 17, 1991, p. 16.

''MBIA to Insure $100 Million Advanta Securitization Deal,'' *American Banker-Bond Buyer,* June 15, 1992, p. 7.

Newman, Joseph A., Jr., ''Greenawalt Named President of TSO,'' *American Banker,* October 7, 1987, p. 18.

——, ''TSO Welcomes Long-Distance/Nationwide Customer with System That Could Make Walk-in Banking Passe,'' *American Banker,* August 4, 1986, p. 24.

'' 'Nonbank Banks' Continue to Attract Interest,'' *Banking Expansion Reporter,* November 15, 1982, p. 4.

Pae, Peter, ''Advanta Finds Edge with Careful Customer Screening,'' *Wall Street Journal,* April 8, 1993.

Roberts, William L., '' 'Proactive' Advanta Trumpets Value of Stock,'' *Philadelphia Business Journal,* September 17, 1990, p. 14.

Stein, Charles, ''Fleet Financial Group Buys Advanta Corp.'s Credit Card Business,'' *Boston Globe,* October 29, 1997.

Timmons, Heather, ''Bruised Advanta Wins Wary Support for Its Strategy,'' *American Banker,* November 17, 1998.

Warner, Susan, ''Spring House, Pa.-Based Investment Firm May Sell Off Parts of Itself,'' *Philadelphia Inquirer,* May 18, 2000.

—Kerstan Cohen
—updated by Stephen Meyer

AFLAC Incorporated

1932 Wynnton Road
Columbus, Georgia 31999
U.S.A.
Telephone: (706) 323-3431
Toll Free: (800) 992-3522
Fax: (706) 323-1448
Web site: http://www.aflac.com

Public Company
Incorporated: 1973
Employees: 4,927
Total Assets: $37.04 billion (1999)
Stock Exchanges: New York Pacific Tokyo
Ticker Symbol: AFL
NAIC: 524113 Direct Life Insurance Carriers (pt); 524114 Direct Health and Medical Insurance Carriers (pt)

Established in April 1973 as the holding company for a specialized insurance subsidiary, AFLAC Incorporated now insures more than 40 million people worldwide. The company's chief subsidiaries in Columbus, Georgia, and Japan have developed a number of unique marketing techniques to sell a product that they introduced more than 40 years ago: supplementary cancer expense insurance. The company has been one of the fastest-growing companies in the health insurance industry and is a leader in supplemental insurance sold at workplaces in the United States. AFLAC was founded in 1955 with about $300,000 in capital. The company now has assets in excess of $37 billion.

1958: Finding a Niche in the Insurance Industry

In 1955 a young lawyer named John B. Amos moved to Columbus, Georgia, and with his two brothers founded the American Family Life Assurance Company of Columbus, Georgia. After struggling for three years selling life, health, and accident insurance door-to-door in Georgia and Alabama, Amos decided that AFLAC would do better if it could find a specific market niche. In 1958 he developed a cancer insurance policy based on the polio policies of previous decades, and AFLAC's 150 licensed agents sold 5,810 cancer care policies in the first year.

AFLAC's cancer care policy was intended to cover the expenses not covered by comprehensive health insurance. John Amos's research reckoned that most comprehensive policies covered only about 70 percent of the costs of cancer treatment. The early policies were designed to cover up to 50 percent of the average cost of cancer treatment, with the extra coverage to help protect against such expenses as travel and loss of income. The increase of cancer incidence and the high cost of its treatment made the policies popular. By the end of 1959, AFLAC was writing $900,000 in premiums and had begun to operate in Florida.

The company continually looked for new ways to market its policies. In 1964 it began making presentations to groups rather than to individuals and developed the ''cluster-selling'' technique, which was very successful. Agents first approached a company or organization for permission to make a presentation to its employees or members. The agent made a group sales pitch with the implicit endorsement of the company. This method allowed agents to reach more prospects at a given time, and the cooperation of the organization was a selling point. In addition, many companies implemented a payroll deduction plan for the premiums, reducing AFLAC's processing costs. Cluster-selling boosted the company's premiums to $7 million by 1967.

Cluster-selling proved a very effective way to sell cancer insurance. AFLAC built up an aggressive, well-paid sales force that would typically sell to five percent of a group's members immediately. The salesman would return later and usually sign up the rest. Years later John Amos explained the technique's success: ''Sooner or later, there's going to be a cancer in the group. If he's insured, he's satisfied, and the word gets around to the rest of them. And if he's not insured, he's sorry, and we get the rest of them.''

During the late 1960s AFLAC greatly increased the number of states in which it did business. An agreement with the Globe Life Insurance Company of Chicago, which was licensed to sell

Company Perspectives:

AFLAC insures more than 40 million people in the United States and Japan with a variety of supplemental insurance products. Our mission is to provide the best supplemental insurance value in the marketplace. Although AFLAC is the leading provider of individual insurance at the worksite in the United States and the largest foreign insurance company in Japan, we continue to look for even more ways to widen our reach into both markets. This effort is AFLAC's way of improving a business that most observers would say doesn't need improving.

We believe the way to maintain our leadership in the supplemental insurance market is to fix it, even if it isn't broken.

insurance throughout the country, resulted in AFLAC's policies being sold nationwide; Globe sold the policies and AFLAC reinsured them, so that when AFLAC wanted to be licensed itself, it could show state insurance commissioners that its policies were already available in their state and that the company was already making good on claims. Between 1969 and 1971 AFLAC increased the number of states in which it operated from 11 to 42.

In 1973 American Family Corporation was formed as a holding company for AFLAC. A year later the company's headquarters moved from a modest collection of houses into the new 18-story American Family Center. In June 1974, American Family's shares were listed on the New York Stock Exchange.

The 1970s: Breaking into the Japanese Insurance Market

During the 1970s a number of companies, seeing AFLAC's success, introduced cancer policies of their own. By the end of the decade there were about 300 insurers selling cancer coverage. AFLAC, however, handily controlled the market, having sold about 60 percent of all cancer policies. The company, in fact, claimed to be the world's fastest-growing insurance company. Between 1972 and 1977 annual premium income rose 294 percent to $205 million, while earnings jumped to $25 million—a 181 percent increase.

Much of AFLAC's success in the mid-1970s was the result of its entry into the rapidly expanding Japanese market. When Chairman John Amos visited Japan in 1970, he was convinced that it would be an excellent market for his cancer care policies. The Japanese industry, however, was well entrenched, and foreign companies found it virtually impossible to get licensing. Amos was not deterred and quickly formulated a plan to gain acceptance for his company's product in Japan.

When AFLAC was licensed by Japan's Ministry of Finance to sell insurance in 1974, it was only the second U.S. company to be allowed to do so in more than two decades. Part of AFLAC's success came from the fact that it offered a product that was not yet available from Japanese insurers, at a time when cancer awareness was expanding. Another factor was AFLAC's decision to employ retired workers as its agents, a move that impressed both former coworkers—potential policyholders—and the Ministry of Finance. In addition, Amos's choice of company officers was truly inspired: it included many luminaries of the Japanese insurance industry. Furthermore, these executives enlisted the support of the medical community even before AFLAC applied for its license.

Once AFLAC received permission to sell its product, it further moved to insure its own success by signing up large Japanese industrial and financial groups as agents, a variation on the cluster-selling theme. AFLAC paid commissions to the companies, which made the presentations themselves. Huge conglomerates including the Mitsui and Mitsubishi groups and the Dai-Ichi Kangyo and Sanwa banks tapped thousands of their own employees before having to search for customers. The plan was an unprecedented success. Japanese consumers had the money to buy coverage, meticulously paid their premiums, and had a very high rate of policy renewal. By 1987 the Japanese market accounted for two-thirds of AFLAC's total revenues and 70 percent of after-tax earnings.

Just as AFLAC's cancer insurance began taking off in Japan, the cancer insurance industry came under close scrutiny from a number of consumer groups in the United States. Two congressional committees investigated the product. The major complaints were that cancer insurance had limited value because it did not cover the entire cost of the disease and that the companies selling it, including AFLAC, used hard-sell tactics that exploited fear of cancer, particularly in elderly people.

John Amos was characteristically aggressive in defense of his company and its product. In 1979 AFLAC sued American Broadcasting Company (ABC) for alleged damages that resulted from a segment on insurance fraud on the network's ''World News Tonight'' program. A similar lawsuit was filed against *Changing Times* magazine several months later.

In June 1980 John Amos appeared before the Senate Subcommittee on Antitrust and Monopoly. A Senate aide described the scene to *Barron's* (July 28, 1980): ''Amos sat with an attorney on each side of him and four corporate vice-presidents behind. There were public relations people handing out press kits by the door. They brought their own easels to display a bunch of charts. The hearing room was packed with sales agents and satisfied policyholders from every state. There were four senators there—Hatch, Laxalt, Leahy, and Thurmond—to introduce their satisfied constituents. There was applause and cheers from the audience at every statement Amos made, and groans every time [Senator] Metzenbaum spoke.''

The Metzenbaum committee's report, a study from the Federal Trade Commission, another from the Massachusetts Department of Insurance, and several independent reports all suggested that cancer insurance was not a good buy because it covered only about a third of the actual costs of the disease, left a policyholder uncovered if struck by any other disease, and had a high premium relative to benefits.

AFLAC pointed out that in spite of all the controversy millions of informed customers wanted the coverage and continued to buy it. On the subject of fear being used to make sales, John Amos commented, ''All insurance is sold on fear.'' By the time the controversy began to die down in 1982, Missouri, New

Key Dates:

1955: American Family Life Assurance Company (AFLAC) is formed.
1958: AFLAC introduces cancer insurance policy.
1973: American Family Corporation is formed.
1974: AFLAC earns license to sell insurance in Japan.
1978: AFLAC acquires WYEA-TV in Columbus, Georgia.
1985: AFLAC introduces universal life insurance policy.
1990: Super Cancer policy is launched in Japan.
1992: American Family Corporation is renamed AFLAC, Inc.; John Amos dies of cancer.
1997: AFLAC completes divestment of television broadcasting unit.
2000: AFLAC enters strategic partnership with Dai-Ichi Mutual Life Insurance Co.

York, New Jersey, and Connecticut had all placed restrictions on the sale of dread-disease policies.

Diversification in the 1980s and 1990s

AFLAC had, meanwhile, been building a chain of television and radio stations in the southern United States. In 1978, as the company passed the $1 billion mark in assets, AFLAC acquired WYEA-TV in Columbus, Georgia, and an NBC affiliate in Huntsville, Alabama. In 1979 two CBS affiliates were acquired, in Cape Girardeau, Missouri, and in Savannah, Georgia. A year later the Black Hawk Broadcasting Group, which consisted of two Iowa NBC affiliates, was purchased for $34.2 million.

Throughout the 1980s AFLAC continued to deal in media-oriented companies. In 1981 the group sold WYEA-TV to remain flexible within FCC regulations at a gain of about $1 million. Communicorp, an advertising and print media subsidiary, also was formed that year. In 1982 the cable franchises acquired in the Black Hawk Broadcasting deal were sold to CBS for a profit. In 1984 the Howard Printing Company was purchased for 56,952 shares and merged into Communicorp. Several more television stations were acquired in the latter half of the decade: WITN-TV in Washington-New Bern, North Carolina, for $25 million, in 1985; a Baton Rouge, Louisiana, CBS station for $59 million, in 1988; and an ABC station in Columbus, Georgia, in 1989, for $45 million. By the end of the 1980s, the broadcasting group was contributing about five percent of AFLAC's total revenues.

In 1983 several executive changes took place at AFLAC. Paul Amos, John Amos's brother, was moved up from president—a position he had held since his brother Bill's retirement in 1978—to vice-chairman. Sal Diaz-Verson became president of the holding company, and Daniel P. Amos was elected president of AFLAC. Daniel Amos, John Amos's nephew, became deputy CEO in 1988, in preparation for his eventual promotion to CEO.

AFLAC's business in Japan became more significant throughout the 1980s. By 1986 AFLAC Japan's policies increased to 5.4 million, compared with 731,000 a decade earlier. In 1981 cancer became the leading cause of death in Japan, and while cancer insurance was criticized in the United States, it was welcomed by the Japanese, whose general health insurance picture was very different. Health insurance was written under the country's nationalized medicine program, and certain diseases were not covered. A co-payment of at least ten percent was also a standard feature. Supplemental dread-disease policies, therefore, became extremely popular, particularly with cancer, where many costs are nonmedical. Cancer insurance was widely accepted, and AFLAC Japan controlled 88 percent of the market by 1988.

Although AFLAC's success in Japan was stunning, there were certain pitfalls. Japanese regulations prevented the repatriation of Japanese earnings to the United States. The company was earning 70 percent of its revenues in Japan, but could not invest that money outside the country. In addition, with such a large percentage of its income earned in yen, AFLAC's bottom line was continually threatened by fluctuations in the value of the foreign currency.

Although the overwhelming majority of AFLAC's revenues were generated by cancer insurance, the company also introduced a number of other products over the years. In 1970 intensive care coverage was introduced. Supplemental senility policies were introduced in Japan in 1984, providing coverage for Alzheimer's disease and three other forms of senility. In 1985 a universal life insurance policy was introduced, followed by a Medicare supplemental policy a year later. In 1988 two new lines were introduced: accident insurance and advance life insurance, which allowed a policyholder to receive 25 percent of death benefits upon diagnosis of heart attack, internal cancer, or stroke, leaving 75 percent for beneficiaries. In 1990 AFLAC launched Super Cancer, a new upgraded policy for Japanese customers. Super Cancer offered a higher daily benefit than did the previously available product, as well as an additional lump sum payment for first occurrences. The policy also covered outpatient services.

AFLAC's earnings grew from $117 million on $2.7 billion in revenue in 1990 to $149 million on revenues of $3.3 billion in 1991. By that time, the company's share of the Japanese market for cancer insurance had grown to 90 percent, with 9.9 million policies covering 25 million people (one fifth of Japan's population) in force. On the first day of 1992, holding company American Family Corporation changed its name officially to AFLAC Inc. The company turned in record performances again that year, as total revenue reached the $4 billion mark for the first time. In May 1992 AFLAC introduced a new product called Super Care, designed to meet the long-term needs of Japan's rapidly growing elderly population. Super Care was AFLAC's first noncancer product offered in Japan. Among Super Care's benefits were nursing home coverage and a death benefit. Meanwhile, AFLAC's market share for supplemental cancer policies in Japan continued to creep up steadily, reaching 94 percent in 1992. During that year, 88 percent of AFLAC's new cancer policy sales in Japan were made through corporate-sponsored payroll deduction plans.

In spite of the popularity of cancer policies in Japan, cancer policies accounted for less than a third of the new AFLAC policies sold in the United States in 1992. The balance of U.S.

sales came from supplemental healthcare protection for diseases other than cancer. One new market that AFLAC began attempting to tap in the United States around this time was HMO members. As employers started asking workers to contribute as much as 30 percent of the cost of their HMO membership, AFLAC began approaching HMOs about offering AFLAC's supplemental policies to their subscribers.

Preliminary figures for 1993 showed another big gain in company revenue, as much as 25 percent from the previous year. Toward the end of the year, AFLAC initiated a joint marketing agreement with CIGNA Corporation. Under the agreement, the two companies would cooperate in the development of group long-term disability products, which would then be marketed under the AFLAC name.

During the late 1980s founder John Amos himself suffered from cancer. Amos died in 1990 and was succeeded as chairman by his brother, Paul Amos. Paul Amos's son, Daniel P. Amos, acquired the duties of CEO and COO of AFLAC.

Into the 21st Century: New Challenges in Japan, New Opportunities at Home

AFLAC continued to experience rapid growth throughout the late 1990s. By decade's end the company controlled more than $37 billion in assets, and total sales for 1999 topped $8.6 billion. Much of this success came in the face of major changes in the Japanese insurance industry—which by the mid-1990s had reached a staggering $362.2 billion in value. The single most significant development for AFLAC was the completion of a far-reaching new trade agreement between the United States and Japan in December 1996. Three years in the making, the deal made the Japanese insurance market more vulnerable to increased penetration by foreign companies, by opening up "mainstream" insurance sectors like life, auto, and fire, which had previously been subject to regulations that favored domestic companies, to outside competition. Perhaps more important for AFLAC, the deal also provided protection to companies that were already firmly established in so-called "niche" markets, effectively making the cancer insurance sector off-limits to Japanese firms until 2001.

Whereas AFLAC was obviously pleased with the new regulations, the company's Japanese competitors were extremely critical, claiming that the agreement's bias toward foreign corporations could prove potentially devastating to domestic insurers. Indeed, there was some substance to these allegations, as a number of prominent Japanese insurance companies found themselves out of business by decade's end. AFLAC, meanwhile, thrived under the new conditions, in spite of the recent downturn in the Asian economy. In June 1997 the company became the first foreign insurer in Japan to exceed ¥2 trillion in gross assets, and by 1999 it had established policies with employees at 95 percent of the companies on the Tokyo stock exchange.

It was its solid presence as a major insurer in Japan that helped AFLAC weather the economic storm that hit Asia in the late 1990s. The steady decline of the yen throughout the decade ultimately took a bite out of AFLAC's share value, and in 1997 the company saw its new sales rate in Japan drop 20 percent. AFLAC was saved, however, by the strong persistency rate—the percentage of policy renewals—of its established Japanese clients, a rate that held steady at 96 percent throughout the mid-1990s. The company's ability to exceed analysts' expectations, while other U.S. companies doing business in Asia were floundering, caused its stock to begin rising again in early 1998; by December, the company's share value had increased 75 percent for the year. In 1999 the company finally was able to exceed its 1996 sales figures for new policies in Japan, achieving revenues of ¥87 million, an increase of almost ¥8 million.

AFLAC's domestic business also underwent dramatic changes during the late 1990s, beginning with the sale of its broadcasting unit to Raycom for $485 million—approximately 14 times the unit's annual cash flow. This money went directly into strengthening the company's insurance operations, which included expanding its advertising budget. In October 1996 the company reached an agreement with Fox Sports to run ads during the baseball playoffs and World Series. In December 1999 AFLAC took a significant step toward establishing national brand-name recognition when it launched a humorous new advertising campaign, which featured a digitally animated duck that quacked the word "AFLAC."

Facing the further deregulation of the Japanese insurance industry in 2001, AFLAC CEO Dan Amos met repeatedly with Japanese regulators throughout 2000 in the hope of easing the company's transition to a more competitive marketplace. In 2000 AFLAC still controlled 90 percent of Japan's cancer insurance coverage; to help secure this market share it established a marketing agreement with Dai-Ichi Mutual Life Insurance Co. in September 2000, wherein the companies would begin selling each other's products. AFLAC also began to turn its focus toward small businesses in Japan, a market where it held only a 20 percent share by the end of 1999.

As it entered the 21st century, AFLAC had no reason to feel anything but confident about its prospects for success. *Forbes Global* named AFLAC the world's Top Insurer in 1999, and the company was one of only 23 American companies listed in Andrew Leckey's *Global Investing 1999: A Guide to the 50 Best Stocks in the World.* That same year, Dan Amos was one of 16 CEOs from major corporations invited to participate in President Bill Clinton's New Markets Initiative, a program designed to explore business opportunities in America's rural and inner city areas.

Principal Subsidiaries

AFLAC U.S.; AFLAC Japan; AFLAC International, Inc.

Principal Competitors

American International Group, Inc.; Conseco, Inc.; UNUMProvident.

Further Reading

"American Family: Big Profits from Cancer Insurance," *Dun's Review,* March 1978.

Brach, Abby, "Insurer Aflac Tries Lighter Approach in New Ad Campaign," *Columbus Ledger-Enquirer* (Georgia), December 29, 1999.

Englade, Kenneth F., "The First American Family of Japan," *Across the Board,* March 1987.

Groeller, Greg, ''Asia's Economic Turmoil Hits Stocks in Columbus, Ga., Companies,'' *Columbus Ledger-Enquirer* (Georgia), January 13, 1998.

Hardman, Adrienne, ''American Sumo,'' *Financial World,* August 3, 1993, pp. 42–43.

Lohr, Steve, ''Under the Wing of Japan Inc., A Fledgling Enterprise Soared,'' *New York Times,* January 15, 1992, p. A1.

McMennamin, Breeze, ''A Heck of a Sales Force,'' *Forbes,* March 1, 1977.

Montgomery, Leland, ''AFLAC: Good Book, Bad Chapter,'' *Financial World,* October 13, 1992, p. 16.

Quinn, Matthew C., ''Deregulation in Japan Keeps AFLAC Chief Busy,'' *Atlanta Journal and Constitution,* April 13, 2000.

——, ''Japanese Insurance Market Trade Deal Protects AFLAC; Columbus-Based Firm Already Has Large Share,'' *Atlanta Journal and Constitution,* December 17, 1996.

Tett, Gillian, ''Aflac Forms Life Link with Dai-Ichi Mutual,'' *Financial Times* (London), September 8, 2000.

Wells, Garrison, ''Companies Take Proactive Actions to Cut Soaring Health Care Costs,'' *Columbus Ledger-Enquirer* (Georgia), March 15, 1996.

—Robert R. Jacobson
—updated by Stephen Meyer

Agilent Technologies Inc.

395 Page Mill Road
P.O. Box 10395
Palo Alto, California 94303
U.S.A.
Telephone: (650) 752-5000
Fax: (650) 752-5633
Web site: http://www.agilent.com

Public Company
Incorporated: 1999
Employees: 46,000
Sales: $10.77 billion (2000)
Stock Exchanges: New York
Ticker Symbol: A
NAIC: 334413 Semiconductor and Related Device Manufacturing; 334290 Other Communications Equipment Manufacturing; 334513 Instruments and Related Products Manufacturing for Measuring, Displaying, and Controlling Industrial Process Variables

Agilent Technologies Inc. began business in November 1999 as a company with $8 billion in annual revenue and 43,000 employees. It was spun off by Hewlett-Packard Company, which wanted to concentrate on its computer, printing, and software businesses. Agilent's principal businesses include test and measurement, semiconductors, healthcare products, and chemical analysis products. Historically, Agilent's roots go back to the founding of Hewlett-Packard Company in 1939. Toward the end of 2000 Agilent announced it would divest its unprofitable healthcare products business for $1.7 billion.

Agilent's Roots in Hewlett-Packard: 1938–98

In 1938 Dave Packard and Bill Hewlett, both electrical engineers who graduated from Stanford University, created their first product, an audio oscillator used to test sound equipment. The product was used by Walt Disney's studios to test sound equipment in the production of the animated movie *Fantasia.* The next year Packard and Hewlett formed the Hewlett-Packard (HP) partnership on January 1, 1939.

During the 1940s, HP's test and measurement equipment won acceptance among engineers and scientists. With the advent of World War II, the trickle of government orders quickly became a flood. In 1942 HP constructed its first company-owned building, a 10,000-square-foot facility at 395 Page Mill Road in Palo Alto that combined office, laboratory, and factory space. Among the products that HP produced were a voltmeter designed by Dave Packard and microwave products, including signal generators developed for the Naval Research Laboratory and a radar-jamming device. After World War II HP developed a complete line of microwave test products, and HP became the acknowledged leader in signal generators. Hewlett-Packard was incorporated on August 18, 1947.

The 1950s saw HP develop its corporate objectives and a management style that became known as "The HP Way." In 1957 the company had its first public stock offering. Toward the end of the decade HP built its first manufacturing plant outside of Palo Alto in Boeblingen, West Germany. The company also established a European marketing organization based in Geneva, Switzerland.

During the 1960s HP continued to grow its test and measurement business, branching out into related fields such as medical electronics and analytical instrumentation. In 1960 HP established its first U.S. manufacturing plant outside of Palo Alto in Loveland, Colorado. In 1961 the company was listed on the New York and Pacific Stock Exchanges, and in 1962 it joined the *Fortune* 500 as the 460th largest U.S. corporation. HP celebrated its 25th anniversary in 1964, with Dave Packard being elected chairman, and Bill Hewlett, president. In 1966 the company established HP Laboratories as the company's central research facility. In 1969 Dave Packard was appointed U.S. Deputy Secretary of Defense, where he served until 1971.

For HP the 1970s was a decade of significant growth in earnings and employment. Net revenue grew from $365 million in 1970 to $3 billion in 1980, and the company's workforce grew from 16,000 to 57,000 employees. Toward the end of the decade Dave Packard and Bill Hewlett delegated day-to-day

Company Perspectives:

Dreams made real. Agilent provides solutions and technologies that revolutionize the way people live and work . . . to make dreams real.

management of the company to John Young, who was named president in 1977 and CEO in 1978.

In the 1980s HP, like many other companies, was impacted by globalization, rapid economic change, and computer technology. Revenue more than doubled in the first half of the decade to $6.5 billion and reached $13.2 billion by 1990, when the company had 91,500 employees.

The rate of change accelerated even more in the 1990s, as web-based information and applications became more pervasive toward the end of the decade. Competition intensified, and time-to-market cycles were greatly reduced. In 1992 Lewis E. Platt became HP's president and CEO. In 1994 revenue reached $25 billion, and by 1997 the company had $42.9 billion in revenue and 121,900 employees.

Agilent Spun Off from HP: 1999

In 1999 HP announced a strategic realignment and the creation of a separate company, Agilent Technologies Inc., which consisted of HP's test and measurement, semiconductor, chemical analysis, and healthcare businesses. Hewlett-Packard would continue as a computing and imaging company that included all of HP's computing, printing, and imaging businesses. Edward W. (Ned) Barnholt was named Agilent's president and CEO. HP announced the formation of the new company on March 2, 1999, and on July 28 Agilent Technologies was given its name, a combination of ''agile'' with the popular ''ent'' ending that suggested high technology (compare, for example, Lucent, Scient, and Teligent).

The split went into effect on November 1—the beginning of Agilent's and HP's fiscal year—and Agilent had its initial public offering (IPO) on November 18, 1999. Some 65 million shares were sold at $30 each. The IPO involved 15 percent of Agilent's stock, with HP retaining 85 percent. HP planned to spin off the rest of its Agilent stock to HP shareholders in 2000. Wall Street reacted favorably to the IPO, sending the stock up from its initial offering price of $30 a share to $42.44 on the first day. HP stock also rose from $81 to $94.31.

Agilent began business with about 43,000 employees, approximately one-third of HP's workforce, and revenue of about $8 billion, the equivalent of about 15 percent of HP's revenue. It also took with it about one-third of HP Laboratories, which would be called Agilent Technologies Laboratories. After the split, HP would have about 80,000 employees and $40 billion in annual revenue.

Agilent's four businesses consisted of test and measurement, semiconductor products, healthcare solutions, and chemical analysis. In the area of test and measurement, Agilent provided companies in the communications, electronics, semiconductor, and related industries with standard and customized test and measurement solutions, including instruments and systems, automated test equipment, communications network monitoring and management tools, and software design tools. Customers included communications and network equipment manufacturers, providers of communications services, designers and manufacturers of semiconductor products, and designers and manufacturers of electronic equipment.

In the field of semiconductors, Agilent was a supplier of semiconductor components, modules, and assemblies for high-performance communications infrastructure, computing devices, and mobile information appliances. Products included fiber-optic communication devices, components, and assemblies; integrated circuits for high-speed local area networks (LANs) and storage area networks (SANs); devices and integrated circuits for microwave and radio frequency (RF) mobile wireless devices and infrastructure; infrared components for short-range communications; ASICs (application specific integrated circuits) for workstations, servers, and laser and inkjet printers; LEDs for electronic image and information display; and more. These products were sold to original equipment manufacturers (OEMs) and contract manufacturers in the communications and computing industries.

Agilent's healthcare solutions were focused on electro-medical clinical measurement and diagnostic solutions. Products and services included patient monitoring systems, imaging systems, external defibrillators, cardiology products, and related services and support. These products enabled medical professionals to gather and analyze information in a variety of settings, from intensive care units to doctors' offices.

In the field of chemical analysis, Agilent provided analytical instrument systems that enabled customers to identify, quantify, analyze, and test the properties of substances and products down to the atomic level. The company's main product lines in this area were chromatography, spectroscopy, bio-instrumentation, and related consumables. These products were used by scientists, engineers, and technicians mainly in the hydrocarbon-processing, environmental, pharmaceutical, and bioscience markets.

Approximately 75 to 80 percent of Agilent's revenue came from its test and measurement business and its semiconductor business, with healthcare solutions and chemical analysis accounting for about 20–25 percent. Realizing that Agilent's future was tied to the growth of the communications industry, and specifically to the Internet, where networks and devices required more and more test equipment, Wall Street sent Agilent's stock to a 52-week high of $79.25 on December 31, 1999.

An Independent Company: 2000

In 2000 Agilent continued to introduce new products, form strategic partnerships, and make acquisitions. One key partnership was formed with wireless chipmaker Qualcomm Inc., which included the incorporation of Agilent's RFIC (radio frequency integrated circuit) test equipment with Qualcomm's RF chips. Other alliances were formed with Alcatel, Rosetta Inpharmatics Inc., PE Biosystems Group, Xilinx Inc., American Healthways, STMicroelectronics, Extended Systems Inc., and Adeptec Inc.

Key Dates:

1938: Dave Packard and Bill Hewlett, former Stanford classmates, create their first product, an audio oscillator used to test sound equipment.
1939: Packard and Hewlett form the Hewlett-Packard partnership on January 1.
1942: The first HP-owned building is constructed at 395 Page Mill Road in Palo Alto, California.
1947: Hewlett-Packard Company is incorporated on August 18.
1957: Hewlett-Packard makes its first public stock offering on November 6.
1962: Hewlett-Packard is listed on the *Fortune* 500 for the first time.
1966: HP Laboratories is established.
1999: Hewlett-Packard announces a strategic realignment and the creation of a separate company, to be named Agilent Technologies Inc., consisting of HP's test and measurement, semiconductor, chemical analysis, and healthcare businesses; Agilent holds its initial public offering (IPO) on November 18.
2000: Hewlett-Packard distributes its shares of Agilent to HP shareholders on June 2, making Agilent a fully independent company; Agilent divests its healthcare products group for $1.7 billion.

Acquisitions in the first half of 2000 included the Silicon Valley Networking Lab, Inc., which provided a range of testing services and products to network equipment manufacturers, communications service providers, and system integrators. The acquisition helped boost Agilent into a leadership position as a provider of third-party testing services. Agilent also acquired J&W Scientific, which became part of its chemical analysis business; American Holographic Inc., a manufacturer of holographic diffraction gratings and spectral sensor modules; Zymed Inc., a provider of cardiac analysis solutions; and SAFCO Technologies, a subsidiary of Salient 3 Communications Inc. and a supplier of planning, measurement, analysis, and predictive software systems for the wireless industry.

At the Optic Fiber Communications show in March 2000, Agilent introduced its photonic switching platform, which eliminated the need for electronics and moving parts. The technology allowed voice, video, and data to be switched as optical signals without converting them from photons to electrons. The photonic switching platform was designed to improve the provisioning and management of wavelengths across networks as well as to speed the time-to-market for optical devices. Agilent entered into a partnership with Alcatel to develop optical network switching products based on the platform for delivery by the end of 2000.

On June 2, 2000, Hewlett-Packard distributed its shares of Agilent to HP shareholders, making Agilent a fully independent company. For the rest of the year Agilent would execute its strategy of selling off its unprofitable businesses to focus on faster-growing markets for communications and measurement equipment. In August 2000 Agilent announced the acquisition of the eCamera business unit of PhotoAccess.com Corp. Agilent also acquired Digital Technology Inc., a developer of network-protocol test solutions.

For its fiscal fourth quarter ending October 31, 2000, Agilent reported that quarterly net income more than doubled to $305 million, compared to $146 million in the previous year's fourth quarter. Quarterly revenue rose 38 percent from $2.45 billion in fiscal 1999 to $3.37 billion in fiscal 2000. For the year, revenue increased to $10.77 billion, compared to $8.33 billion in fiscal 1999. Net income increased from $512 million in fiscal 1999 to $757 million in fiscal 2000.

In November 2000 Agilent agreed to buy Objective Systems Integrators for about $665 million. Based in Folsom, California, Objective Systems Integrators had about 400 employees and specialized in communications test software. Its software helped communications providers, such as Internet sites and e-commerce systems, provide more reliable service. For fiscal 2000 ending October 31, Agilent's sales of communications test equipment rose 55 percent, making it the company's fastest growing business. Companies such as Cisco Systems Inc. and AT&T Corp. used Agilent products to test their communications network equipment.

Earlier in the month Agilent announced it would sell its healthcare products business to Royal Philips Electronics NV for about $1.7 billion. Agilent had experienced falling orders for its healthcare products during fiscal 2000 and had laid off about 650 workers in its Healthcare Solutions Group. Quarterly operational losses for the healthcare products business were about $40 million. The sale of the healthcare products group, which was headquartered in Andover, Massachusetts, was expected to close by mid-2001.

In December 2000 Agilent signed an agreement to acquire ATN Microwave Inc., which specialized in microwave measurement solutions for wireless and high-speed data communication applications. The acquisition gave Agilent products, engineering expertise, and intellectual property related to the measurement of multiport devices, balanced circuits, signal integrity, large-signal characterization, and noise, as well as the electronic calibration of test instruments. HP planned to integrate ATN into its test component business headquartered in Santa Rosa, California. Also in December 2000 Agilent sold its Automation Integration Software (AIS) business to Verano. AIS was a division of Agilent Technologies Canada Inc.

For the future Agilent planned to focus on achieving strong growth in its communications and life sciences businesses. Earlier in 2000 the company had created a new Life Sciences Business Unit as part of its Chemical Analysis Group to focus on the demand for its life sciences products. In addition, the company had added manufacturing capacity in both communications and life sciences to address the strong demand for its products in those areas.

Principal Subsidiaries

Agilent Technologies World Trade, Inc.; Microsensor Technology, Inc.; Pete Inc.; Qos-Effective Systems Ltd.; Rockland Technologies, Inc.; Security Force Software, Inc.; Scope Communications, Inc.; Telegra Corp.; Versatest, Inc.

Principal Divisions

Chemical Analysis Group; Semiconductor Group; Test and Measurement Group.

Principal Competitors

General Electric Co.; International Business Machines Corporation; Lucent Technologies Inc.; Siemens AG; Anritsu Co.; Marconi Communications Ltd., Network Associates Inc.; Emulex Corporation; LSI Logic Corporation; QLogic Corporation; Vitesse Semiconductor Corporation; Motorola Inc.; NEC Inc.; EG&G Inc.; PE Biosystems Group; Shimadzu Corporation; Thermo Instrument Systems Inc.; Waters Corporation.

Further Reading

''Agilent Acquires Camera Unit,'' *Business Journal,* August 25, 2000, p. 24.

''Agilent and Adaptec Partner to Deliver Fibre Channel for NT,'' *ENT,* February 23, 2000, p. 30.

''Agilent Buys Communications Software Firm,'' *Bloomberg News,* November 27, 2000, http://news.cnet.com/news/0-1003-200-3873281.html?tag = st.ne.1430735.

''Agilent Sees Profits Double,'' *Bloomberg News,* November 20, 2000, http://news.cnet.com/news/0-1003-200-3785202.html?tag = st .ne.1430735.

''Agilent Technologies Reports Strong First-Year Results,'' *Canadian Corporate News,* November 21, 2000.

''The Antenna,'' *Electronic News (1991),* November 1, 1999, p. 4.

Cassell, Jonathan, ''Unlikely Superstars,'' *Electronic News (1991),* January 10, 2000, p. 8.

Chappell, Jeff, ''Agilent Rides Wireless Wave,'' *Electronic News (1991),* January 24, 2000, p. 26.

''Download: Vendor Neutral, Agilent Becomes a Lab Rat,'' *Telephony,* February 14, 2000.

Greenberg, Ilan, ''Hewlett-Packard Reveals Name of New Scientific Instrument Spinoff,'' *Knight-Ridder/Tribune Business News,* July 29, 1999.

Haber, Carol, ''Agilent Gains Ground Despite Health Bind,'' *Electronic News (1991),* September 4, 2000, p. 54.

——, ''HP Posts Results on Eve of Spin-Off,'' *Electronic News (1991),* August 23, 1999, p. 32.

Harris, Pat Lopes, ''Palo Alto, Calif.-Based Test Equipment Maker Plans to Sell Medical Supply Unit,'' *Knight-Ridder/Tribune Business News,* November 17, 2000.

Hirschman, Dave, ''Colorado Springs, Colo., Tech Firm Is Finally Independent from Hewlett-Packard,'' *Knight-Ridder/Tribune Business News,* June 7, 2000.

Kane, John, ''A 60-Year-Old Startup?,'' *Business Journal,* April 2000, p. 45.

Kong, Deborah, ''Hewlett-Packard Spinoff Shows Strong Opening on Wall Street,'' *Knight-Ridder/Tribune Business News,* November 18, 1999.

Kwan, Joshua L., ''Hewlett-Packard Spin-Off Flourishes in Independent Existence,'' *Knight-Ridder/Tribune Business News,* April 16, 2000.

——, ''Palo Alto, Calif.-Based Hewlett-Packard Spin-Off to Cut 650 Jobs,'' *Knight-Ridder/Tribune Business News,* August 14, 2000.

LaBarba, Liane H., ''Bubbling Over: Can Road to All-Optical Lead Through Inkjet Technology?,'' *Telephony,* March 13, 2000.

Meade, Peter, ''The '$8B Start-Up' Starts Out,'' *Communications News,* July 2000, p. 14.

Moore, Cathleen, ''Agilent Raises the Optical Bar,'' *InfoWorld,* March 13, 2000, p. 8.

''Photonic Switching Platform,'' *Telecommunications,* May 2000, p. 94.

Poletti, Therese, ''Palo Alto, Calif.-Based Technology Firms' Earnings Beat Forecasts,'' *Knight-Ridder/Tribune Business News,* November 20, 2000.

Rosenberg, Ronald, ''Palo Alto, Calif.-Based Medical Supplier Announces 450 Firings,'' *Knight-Ridder/Tribune Business News,* August 14, 2000.

Shankland, Stephen, ''Agilent Shares Leap on Earnings Surprise,'' *CNET News.com,* August 18, 2000, http://news.cnet.com/news/0-1003-200-2549296.html?tag = st.ne.ni.rnbot.rn.ni.

Smokler, Jeff, ''Philips Snapping up Agilent HSG Unit, Broadening Ultrasound Portfolio,'' *Health News Daily,* November 20, 2000, p. 1.

Strassberg, Dan, ''HP Reveals Name of New T&M Company,'' *EDN,* August 19, 1999, p. 24.

Swett, Clint, ''Palo Alto, Calif.-Based Telecom Firm to Acquire Folsom, Calif., Company,'' *Knight-Ridder/Tribune Business News,* November 28, 2000.

Wilcox, Joe, ''Agilent Cuts 450 Employees, 200 Temps,'' *CNET News.com,* August 14, 2000, http://news.cnet.com/news/0-1003-200-2517979.html?tag = st.ne.ni.rnbot.rn.ni.

—David P. Bianco

Air New Zealand Limited

Quay Tower
29 Customs Street West
Auckland
New Zealand
Telephone: 64-9-366-2400
Toll Free: 0800-737-000
Fax: 64-9-336-2764
Web site: http://www.airnewzealand.com

Public Company
Incorporated: 1940 as Tasman Empire Airways Limited
Employees: 23,000
Sales: NZ$3.72 billion (2000)
Stock Exchanges: New Zealand Australian
Ticker Symbols: AIRVA; AIRVB
NAIC: 481111 Scheduled Passenger Air Transportation; 481112 Scheduled Freight Air Transportation; 488999 All Other Support Activities for Transportation; 56152 Tour Operators

Air New Zealand Limited (ANZ) is New Zealand's largest airline. The acquisition of Ansett Holdings has made ANZ one of the 20 largest air carriers in the world. Marketing alliances with numerous airlines, including United Airlines, Lufthansa, and British Midland, bring it traffic from around the globe; ANZ carries approximately eight million passengers a year. In addition, the company operates subsidiaries involved in a range of businesses, including cargo services, travel agencies, terminal services, and engineering services.

Operated as a government-owned airline until the mid-1980s, Air New Zealand established itself as the dominant national carrier, although its profit record was spotty. After bottoming out in the early 1980s, Air New Zealand was privatized beginning in the mid-1980s; healthy sales and profit gains ensued and even accelerated after the company became fully private in 1989. ANZ took on considerable debt in acquiring Australia's Ansett Holdings in the 1990s, and faces a well-funded and well-organized rival in Qantas.

Tasman Origins

Tasman Empire Airways Limited, the company that became Air New Zealand, was registered on April 26, 1940, as a limited liability company in Wellington, the capital of New Zealand. Its first flight occurred just four days later.

New Zealand's government originally owned 20 percent of the enterprise, while the remainder was held by regional airlines BOAC (38 percent) and Qantas (23 percent), and Union Airways of New Zealand (19 percent). The company started out as a specialty carrier, providing air service across the Tasman Sea (between New Zealand, Australia, and Tasmania) with "flying boats."

F.M. Clarke was the first general manager of Tasman Empire Airways. However, it was Sir Geoffrey Roberts, who joined the company in 1946, who became known as the "Father of Air New Zealand." Roberts served as general manager until 1958, and then as a director and chairman of the company during the 1960s and 1970s.

In 1953 the governments of New Zealand and Australia became the sole owners of Tasman Empire Airways, each with a 50 percent share. The New Zealand government bought out Australia's half in 1961, though, and became the sole owner of the operation. In 1965 the name of the company was changed to Air New Zealand Limited to reflect its status as a national air service provider. Throughout the 1960s and 1970s, in fact, the government invested heavily to make Air New Zealand a leading airline in the South Pacific. The company expanded with destinations throughout the New Zealand/Australia region and South Pacific Islands, but also to other locales in Asia and the West. During that period, the company logged millions of miles flying over water and forged a worthy reputation in the global airline industry as a safe and competent carrier.

Air New Zealand benefited during the 1960s and 1970s from government ownership. Besides having easy access to investment capital, the airline enjoyed protection from competing carriers in its domestic market. Despite deep pockets and protected markets, however, Air New Zealand eventually began to suffer from limitations imposed by the vast bureaucracy that

Company Perspectives:

The Air New Zealand—Ansett Australia Group operates a competitive network serving key gateway airports of the Asia-Pacific region. The Group flies to more destinations in Australia, New Zealand and the South West Pacific than any other airline.

engulfed the enterprise. High operating costs and a stifling management environment were hurting the company's performance. Intensifying the strain was the government decision to merge Air New Zealand and National Airways Corporation. The government had created National Airways in 1947, a few years after Tasman Empire was formed. That government-owned operation was initiated to provide domestic air service, as well as regional services to other South Pacific Islands. The two airlines were merged into a single entity called Air New Zealand (ANZ).

1980s Turnaround

The operations of National Airways burdened the resultant organization with even higher operating costs, such as big wages paid to union workers. The airline was losing money and, by the early 1980s, even the government recognized that something needed to be done to turn it around. To that end, in 1982 it brought in Norman Geary to serve as chief executive of the company and to whip the organization into shape. Geary succeeded Morrie Davis, who had been with Air New Zealand since the 1940s and had served as chief executive since 1975. Under Geary's direction, ANZ's financial performance began to improve. In fact, the company started posting profits in 1982 and continued to do so throughout the 1980s and into the early 1990s.

Geary was able to achieve gains at ANZ by reducing operating costs and boosting revenues. He accomplished that by convincing the government to back him up in key efforts, particularly related to labor negotiations, and by breathing new life into the company's marketing strategy. Soon after taking the helm, for example, he launched a route from Auckland to Los Angeles to London. He also purchased a new fleet of Boeing 747s and initiated an effort to boost ANZ's share of the Pacific tourist market. The government had sponsored studies that suggested that those moves would fail. Nevertheless, Geary was committed to the new strategy and was even able to persuade doubting bureaucrats to give him a chance.

As a result of Geary's efforts, ANZ rapidly improved. The new route to London, for example, sold out quickly, and Geary's efforts to boost profits from tourism paid off. Indeed, during the 1980s New Zealand became an increasingly popular destination for leisure travelers around the world. New routes, upgraded equipment, elimination of unnecessary overhead, and improved marketing helped the company to boost its number of passengers to more than four million annually by the mid-1980s. Meanwhile, operating profits rose to more than NZ$100 million. Geary was eventually credited with turning ANZ into an efficient, profitable carrier. In 1987, the last full year that Geary was in charge, ANZ's revenues increased to about US$800 million and total passengers served climbed to about 4.7 million (about 3.3 million international passengers and 1.4 million domestic).

Geary departed in June 1988 and was succeeded by R. James Scott. Scott was brought in to usher ANZ into a new era of privatization. Indeed, New Zealand's government had started privatizing much of the nation's air transport system in the mid-1980s, including airports and air traffic control systems. It also started moving ANZ toward privatization and preparing to open the New Zealand market to competition. To that end, it allowed a new air carrier called Ansett New Zealand (renamed Qantas New Zealand in 2000) to begin operating in July 1987. From modest beginnings, the start-up expanded rapidly into other routes dominated by ANZ. It initially managed to snap up as much as 30 percent of the market in some of those routes and threatened to pose a formidable long-term challenge to ANZ's domestic operations; some observers speculated that the government's decision to allow Ansett to compete eventually played a role in Scott's leaving ANZ.

Private and Public in the 1990s

ANZ completed its privatization in 1989. Its new owners included Australian rival Qantas, as well as Japan Air Lines and American Airlines. Those three companies owned 35 percent of the company, and Brierley, a New Zealand investment firm, controlled about 65 percent of the stock, much of which it had agreed to sell to the public. Thus, Air New Zealand was effectively free from government interference. With the domestic market increasingly open to competition and offering few growth opportunities, Scott planned to focus the newly private ANZ on international business. Tourism had been surging in New Zealand and surrounding areas, and Scott planned to boost the share of ANZ's revenues attributable to international traffic from about 60 percent in 1988 to 90 percent by 1993.

Specifically, Scott wanted to turn ANZ into a ''quality niche carrier'' that dominated the markets and routes that it was most able to serve, rather than trying to compete with major international airlines in the most popular routes. ANZ's financial performance and passenger volume declined in 1990 and 1991, primarily as a result of diminished international traffic during the global economic downturn. But management undertook a number of new initiatives that buoyed the company. For instance, ANZ reached marketing agreements with major airlines that strengthened its commitment to the North American and South Pacific market; for example, services were added or augmented in Dallas, Honolulu, Toronto, and Vancouver. Those agreements, according to Scott, represented ANZ's intent to double in size by the year 2000.

James McCrea replaced Scott as chief executive of ANZ in August 1991. McCrea had joined the airline in 1956, in the engineering division, and worked his way up to general manager of airline operations by 1982 and then to deputy chief executive in 1989. He worked closely with Scott to ensure that ANZ operated profitably and efficiently. As chief executive, McCrea continued to pursue many of his predecessor's goals, although he reduced ANZ's growth forecasts. Instead, he planned to steer ANZ on a course toward steady passenger growth and healthy profitability, largely by cultivating interna-

Key Dates:

1940: Tasman Empire Airways connects New Zealand and Australia with "flying boats."
1953: Governments of New Zealand and Australia become sole owners of Tasman.
1961: The New Zealand government buys out Australia's share.
1965: Air New Zealand (ANZ) name is adopted.
1982: Norman Geary is hired to turn around ANZ.
1989: ANZ is privatized.
1996: ANZ acquires 50 percent of regional competitor Ansett.
2000: Remainder of Ansett is acquired; Singapore Airlines invests in ANZ.

tional tourism traffic. Importantly, the company began to promote what it termed "multidestinational regional tourism." In other words, it focused on encouraging leisure travelers to fly ANZ into New Zealand or some other South Pacific destination, and then on to other locations along ANZ's South Pacific network—Hawaii, Fiji, Tahiti, Western Samoa, the Cook Islands—during the same vacation.

ANZ prospered under new management during the early 1990s and into the mid-1990s. Passenger volume rose from about 4.8 million in 1991 to 6.4 million in 1995. During the same period, sales rose 30 percent, approaching the US$1.5 billion mark for the fiscal year ended June 1995. More importantly, operating profits rebounded and vaulted to roughly US$150 million annually by 1995. The gains were primarily the result of increased leisure traffic, particularly in Asia, and new programs designed to take advantage of tourism growth. In 1992, for example, the Australian government allowed ANZ to establish a minor hub in Brisbane, feeding traffic from Asian gateways to New Zealand. In 1993 ANZ initiated service to South Korea. In 1994 and 1995, moreover, ANZ boosted the number of direct flights from Los Angeles to Sydney to five per week.

On a typical weekday in 1995, ANZ made 528 flights between 60 airports and 19 countries. In addition to its thriving airline business, ANZ managed to rack up profit gains from its diverse assemblage of subsidiaries and operating units. Among the most important of those entities was Air New Zealand Engineering Services, which alone generated about US$176 million in sales for 1994. Additional profit centers included a pilot training center, travel agency, information systems services, and catering and cargo operations. Other operations included ANZ's domestic airline operations, which continued to face challenges prompted by deregulation and increased competition. For the mid- and late 1990s, ANZ management was planning to continue building its international leisure business with a focus on Asia, as well as to pursue its strategy of multidestinational regional tourism.

New Alliances in the Late 1990s

In May 1996, ANZ unleashed an A$45 million "Pacific Wave" marketing campaign, designed to position the airline as a leading Pacific Rim carrier. The next month, it was due to acquire a 50 percent stake in Ansett Australia Holdings. This acquisition seemed to alienate Qantas, which sold its 19.4 percent stake in Air New Zealand for NZ$426 million (A$373 million) in March 1997. A couple of months later, ANZ took full ownership of its Jetset Travel venture, which had lost millions in the hands of its former management.

Strategic alliances helped supply ANZ with traffic during the Asian financial crisis. However, ANZ was still forced to cut back its flights in Korea, a particularly hard-hit area, in early 1998. The crisis allowed the carrier to step up delivery of several new Boeing 737s as other buyers reneged on purchase agreements.

By this time, Singapore Airlines (SIA) had been making overtures towards an alliance with both ANZ and Ansett. In early 1999, ANZ and SIA struggled for control of a half interest in Ansett. During this time, Brierley increased its ownership in ANZ to 47 percent, near the 49 percent limit for foreign ownership (whereas foreign airlines could together hold no more than 35 percent). Brierley had moved its headquarters from Wellington to Singapore (and changed its country of incorporation to Bermuda), transferring some of its ANZ shares to local subsidiaries, which had local and independent directors on their corporate boards, making them sufficiently "ring-fenced" for the satisfaction of the New Zealand government. However, it did raise some controversy; Alliance party leader Jim Anderton maintained "ANZ should be renamed Air Asia because it is no longer a New Zealand airline in any meaningful sense."

In February 2000, ANZ agreed to pay News Ltd. A$580 million plus 10.5 percent of its shares for the remaining half of Ansett Holdings. The impending arrival of Richard Branson's Virgin Express discount airline in the Australasian skies sped up the deal. Singapore Airlines had bought a 49 percent interest in Virgin Atlantic the year before. There had also been a management buyout offer on the table for Ansett. Yet another factor precipitating the sale was the appointment of Brierley's new CEO, Greg Terry, who felt his firm should begin to divest its ANZ holdings. Together, ANZ and Ansett had A$6.7 billion in assets and 24,000 employees, and likely much room for combining operations between them. ANZ management anticipated saving NZ$250 to NZ$350 million annually as a result of the merger.

SIA then aimed to ultimately increase its ownership of ANZ from eight percent to 40 percent and to gain board control of the airline. New Zealand's prime minister, Helen Clark, opposed the sale since it would have the appearance of giving control of ANZ to the government of Singapore (which owned 54 percent of SIA). Brierley took its 47 percent stake in ANZ off the market when ANZ's board discovered Qantas was also interested in it.

SIA bought an initial 8.4 percent stake in ANZ in April 2000 for NZ$140 million (A$116 million). The New Zealand government soon cleared SIA to increase its shareholdings to 25 percent, the maximum any single foreign airline was allowed to hold.

ANZ CEO Jim McCrea resigned in July 2000, a sign of SIA's growing control over the airline. By one count, annual profits had risen by a third to NZ$177.9 million (A$134.7

million) due to rising passenger counts. However, ANZ reported a NZ$600 million loss for the 1999/2000 fiscal year due to a change to international accounting standards. ANZ continued to show an interest in regional air services in Australia, bidding A$15 million for Hazelton Airlines Ltd., based in New South Wales, mostly because it needed Hazelton's slots at Sydney Airport to compete for its share of the lucrative business market.

Although ANZ executives had initially forecast good results for the 2000/2001 fiscal year, partly due to the Olympics, in the end higher fuel costs, unfavorable exchange rates, and increased competition pointed towards a substantial revenue drop. Gary Toomey, taking over as CEO in early 2001, faced a debt load of NZ$3.9 billion (A$3.05 billion), devalued share price, and formidable competition from well-funded Qantas. Toomey had been finance director at Qantas, where he was known for slashing costs; it was hoped he could apply some of the same winning formulas at ANZ.

Principal Subsidiaries

Aeropelican Air Services Pty Limited (Australia); Air Nelson Limited; Air New Zealand (Australia) Pty Limited; Air New Zealand Destinations Limited; Ansett Australia Limited; Ansett Australia & Air New Zealand Engineering Services Limited; Ansett Holdings Limited; Ansett International Limited (Australia; 49%); Blue Pacific Tours Limited (Japan); Eagle Aviation Limited; Jetset Travel & Technology Holdings Pty Limited (Australia); Kendell Airlines (Australia) Pty Limited; New Zealand International Airlines Limited; Safe Air Limited; Show Group Pty Limited (Australia); Skywest Airlines Pty Limited; Tasman Aviation Enterprises (Queensland) Pty Limited (Australia); The Mount Cook Group Limited; Traveland International Pty Limited (Australia).

Principal Divisions

Air NZ Domestic/Trans-Tasman & SW Pacific; Air NZ International; Ansett Domestic; Ansett International; Australian Regionals; Terminal Services; Cargo; ANNZES (Ansett Australia and Air New Zealand Engineering Services).

Principal Operating Units

Corporate; Commercial; Airline; Service.

Principal Competitors

Qantas Airways Limited.

Further Reading

"Air New Zealand: Flying in the Face of Disaster Warnings," *Business Week,* September 13, 1982, pp. 80, 84.

Air New Zealand's First 30 Years, Auckland: Air New Zealand Limited, 1970.

Bartholomeusz, Stephen, "Virgin Adversary Forces Parties to the Table on Ansett," *The Age* (Melbourne), February 17, 2000, p. 3.

Brady, Diane, "In Wellington: ANZ Appears Prepared to Weather Asian Storm," *Asian Wall Street Journal,* January 6, 1998, p. J13.

Dabkowski, Stephen, "Air NZ Vows to Make Ansett Fly," *Sydney Morning Herald,* Bus. Sec., August 30, 2000, p. 27.

——, "Ansett Disappoints Air NZ," *The Age* (Melbourne), August 30, 2000, p. 2.

Davidson, Brian, "Air New Zealand's Prickly Path to Privatisation," *Interavia,* February 1989, p. 130.

Driscoll, Ian, *Airline: The Making of a National Flag Carrier,* Auckland: Shortland Publications, 1979.

Espiner, Colin, "Air NZ Job Losses to Hurt Aust.," *The Press,* December 20, 2000, p. 9.

Fang, Nicholas, "SIA Gets Go-Ahead for 25 Percent of Air NZ," *Straits Times* (Singapore), Money Sec., April 18, 2000, p. 64.

Hill, Leonard, "Kiwis Widen the Niche," *Air Transport World,* November 1994, p. 87.

Holmes, Noel, *To Fly a Desk: Sir Geoffrey Roberts, Father of Air New Zealand,* Wellington: Reed, 1982.

Hosking, Patrick, "Ansett to Forge Closer Air NZ Links," *The Age* (Melbourne), May 1, 1997, p. 1.

——, "Qantas Ends Tie with Air NZ," *The Age* (Melbourne), March 20, 1997, p. 1.

Knight, Elizabeth, "Flying in a Different Direction," *Sydney Morning Herald,* Bus. Sec., November 2, 2000, p. 25.

Mooney, Timothy, "Air New Zealand Expands Its Role As Leading Carrier to Australia, New Zealand and South Pacific Island," *Business Wire,* January 25, 1991.

Morris, Kathleen, "Air New Zealand: Friendlier Skies," *Financial World,* April 11, 1995, p. 15.

O'Toole, Kevin, "ANZ Ownership Debate Hots Up," *Airline Business,* December 1, 1999, p. 28.

Ries, Ivor, "Piloting Ansett: Toomey's Big Test," *Australian Financial Review,* December 16, 2000, p. 25.

Stone, David, "Air New Zealand Slams 'Indefensible' US Airline Rules," *Independent Business Weekly,* December 20, 2000, p. 8.

——, "Who Owns National Airlines Is Not Just a Question for Air NZ," *Independent Business Weekly,* February 9, 1999, p. 10.

Tan, Tammy, "Shake of S'pore Inc. Image Fast," *Straits Times* (Singapore), Money Sec., March 18, 2000, p. 79.

Thomas, Geoffrey, "Air NZ Chief Bundled Out," *Sydney Morning Herald,* Bus. Sec., July 8, 2000, p. 47.

——, "Qantas Grounded As SIA Makes Its Move," *Sydney Morning Herald,* Bus. Sec., April 12, 2000, p. 25.

Thomas, Geoffrey, and Mark Todd, "Brierley in Pilot's Seat Over Air NZ," *Sydney Morning Herald,* Bus. Sec., March 20, 2000, p. 39.

Thomas, Ian, "The Elusive Prize," *Air Transport World,* May 1, 2000, p. 87.

Todd, Mark, "Brierley Withdraws Air NZ Stake from Sale," *Sydney Morning Herald,* Bus. Sec., March 29, 2000, p. 25.

Webb, Christopher, "Leiblers Leave the Jetset Crowd Behind," *The Age* (Melbourne), June 20, 1997, p. 1.

Wood, Leonie, "Air NZ Takes Control at Ansett," *The Age* (Melbourne), February 19, 2000, p. 1.

Woolsey, James P., "Air New Zealand Sets Sights to Be Quality Niche Carrier," *Air Transport World,* July 1989, p. 66.

—Dave Mote
—updated by Frederick C. Ingram

Aktiebolaget SKF

S-415 50 Göteborg
Sweden
Telephone: (31) 337 1000
Fax: (31) 337 2832
Web site: http://www.skf.com

Public Company
Incorporated: 1907
Employees: 40,637
Sales: SKr 36.69 billion (US$4.31 billion) (1999)
Stock Exchanges: Stockholm London Paris Zürich NASDAQ
Ticker Symbol: SKFR
NAIC: 332991 Ball and Roller Bearing Manufacturing; 325520 Adhesive Manufacturing; 331513 Steel Foundries (Except Investment)

Aktiebolaget SKF is the acknowledged leader of the world's rolling bearing industry. The company also produces seals for bearings and for other applications and the steel from which rolling bearings are produced, as well as offering its customers service and maintenance solutions. SKF's main customers are in the automotive, general machinery, aerospace, electrical, and customized engineering industries. Geographically, sales break down as follows: Sweden, five percent; western Europe, 48 percent; North America, 26 percent; Asia, 11 percent; Latin America, five percent; central and eastern Europe, three percent; and the Middle East and Africa, two percent. The company has about 80 manufacturing facilities in 22 countries. Investor AB, the investment vehicle for the Wallenberg family business empire, holds nearly 29 percent of the voting rights in SKF stock.

Early Decades

SKF was established in 1907 in Göteborg, Sweden, by the textile company Gamlestadens Fabriker. Its founder was Sven Wingquist, a maintenance engineer at the Gamlestadens factory who had become increasingly disillusioned with the poor performance and high cost of the imported bearings used in the factory's overhead shafts. These latter also tended to misalignment, causing additional functional difficulties in the bearings.

Granted facilities for research by an unusually farsighted management, Wingquist developed a superior single-row deep-groove ball bearing. Gamlestadens decided to set up a new company named Svenska Kullagerfabriken (SKF) to sell the new product. Initially SKF production took place in Wingquist's own workshop, but soon a separate factory was built in Göteborg.

Wingquist went on to develop a bearing capable of diminishing the effects of misalignment between shaft and housing. This, the double-row self-aligning ball bearing, established SKF's fortunes and helped propel it to the forefront of the industry.

Wingquist's talents, however, extended beyond pure engineering. From an early stage, he appears to have recognized that Sweden's domestic market was far too small to underwrite the expansion in sales which alone could generate sufficient profits to keep SKF in business and capable of competing with its major European, particularly German, rivals. Wingquist therefore undertook a series of sales trips across Europe and subsequently set up sales offices and appointed agents. Subsidiary companies were established in France and the United Kingdom and factories were built.

From the start, SKF's fortunes were closely bound up with those of the automotive industry, which in the first decades of the 20th century had a growing requirement for SKF's quality bearings. SKF therefore chose to locate its plants close to major established motor plants—for example, in the United Kingdom at Luton, near the large Vauxhall/Bedford plants. In the years immediately preceding World War I, automotive manufacturers were enjoying a boom period, and by 1912 SKF found itself unable to meet demand for its bearings due to supply problems with the foreign balls used in its bearing products. SKF therefore decided to produce its own balls in Göteborg. In 1913 the company could literally afford to strengthen its position in the crucial German market by the acquisition of a half share in Norma Compagnie GmbH at Cannstatt. SKF, in common with most

Company Perspectives:

SKF's overall financial objective is to create value for its shareholders. Over time, the return on the shareholders' investment in SKF should exceed the risk-free interest rate by some 5–6 percentage points. This is the basis for SKF's financial objectives in its operations.

Swedish businesses, derived considerable advantage from Sweden's declaration of neutrality in 1914, trading with both the Allied and Central powers and successfully increasing its market share, particularly outside Europe, at the expense of its German, British, and French competitors whose countries were at war.

The year 1916 was a significant one for the company. A steel works at Hofors Bruk in central southern Sweden was bought to provide SKF's bearings plants with a dedicated supply of high quality steel. The size of SKF's research laboratory at Göteborg was doubled, testifying to the company's recognition of the importance of innovative technology in maintaining market share. SKF also acquired one of the few remaining independent Swedish producers of ball bearings and converted its factory to the production of axle boxes and bearings housings. Finally, in order to avoid the hazards and high insurance costs of wartime transatlantic shipment, SKF established a plant at Hartford, Connecticut, for the supply of bearings to a U.S. motor and armaments industry rapidly expanding under the stimulus of the wartime requirements of the Allied powers in Europe. The next year a second French factory was opened on the outskirts of Paris.

Nevertheless, there were occasional setbacks. The Russian installation, set up in 1914 and expanded during the next three years, was nationalized without compensation in the wake of the 1917 revolution. The second decade of the century, however, was in general a period of continuous expansion for SKF. By 1919 it had 12 plants in full operation, a worldwide sales network, and a staff of almost 12,000.

Profits in the first years of the 1920s were blighted by the onset of economic depression. This onset was SKF's first experience of an economic pattern that to a large extent determined its fortunes ever since—the level of consumer spending influencing the level of purchase of consumer durables, in its turn determining the level of capital investment by manufacturers in new machinery.

Nonetheless, the early and middle years of the decade saw SKF enhance its reputation for innovation with the introduction of spherical and taper roller bearings. By 1925, steel production at the Hofors mill had reached 24,000 tons and in the next year it doubled in response to improving economic conditions in Western Europe. In 1926 SKF decided that its AB Volvo subsidiary should enter the car and truck manufacturing industry. SKF used Volvo as a practical testing ground for its bearings until 1935 when Volvo became an independent company. SKF retained close links with its former subsidiary. In 1927, SKF again displayed its eminence in the field of technological innovation when an employee patented a series of bearing measuring devices and established a set of measuring standards for use in the industry at large.

The Great Depression, which began in 1929, enabled SKF to buy a number of rival German bearings companies, giving the company a leading position in the important German market. These separate operations were concentrated at Schweinfurt and Cannstatt. In that year, SKF was quoted for the first time on the international stock exchange, and acquired the Swedish engineering firm Lidköpings Mekaniska Verkstad AB, thus incorporating machine tools in its product range.

As in the early 1920s, so in the opening years of the 1930s, SKF's profits suffered during the worst years of the Depression. Special emphasis was placed on the development of new bearing types, leading in 1932 to the patenting of the "narrow type" spherical roller bearing and the self-aligning spherical roller bearing. The premium on efficiency in the production process caused SKF to introduce automation at about this time.

By 1935 the effects of the Depression had begun to recede in Europe and the United States. The ensuing rise in capital expenditure on new plant and machinery and the increasing pace of rearmament in Europe made the next five-year period up to the outbreak of World War II one of great prosperity for SKF.

Although Sweden once again chose neutrality in 1939, conditions for its export-dependent industries were not as generally favorable as they had been during World War I. During this time, SKF factories were taken over and headed by local governments. Swedish companies took advantage of their nation's neutral position to trade actively with both Allied and Axis powers, but the Nazi occupation of Denmark and Norway, Germany's unrestricted submarine warfare, and British naval blockades deprived SKF and other companies of their traditional sea-routes out of Scandinavia. From 1942 large-scale British and American bombing raids over France and Germany sought to achieve the wholesale destruction of Nazi Germany's industrial base and thus Germany's capacity to continue the war. Realizing how crucial efficient and large-scale bearings production was to the Axis war effort, Allied bombers paid close attention to bearings plants, in particular those at Schweinfurt and Cannstatt. By the end of hostilities in 1945, the SKF plants lay in ruins. As in the previous conflict and the Depression of the early 1930s, SKF used the war years to good effect for the development of new products. In 1943 the company introduced its revolutionary OK oil-injection shaft coupling, enabling rolling bearings to function efficiently in marine propeller shafts.

Postwar Rebuilding, Expansion, and Increased Competition

Postwar reconstruction of the German and French plants was paralleled by new building of factories in countries formerly outside SKF's traditional manufacturing area—for example in Spain, Canada, and Holland. In Sweden itself, new facilities for the continuous annealing and tube-rolling of steel were added to the Hofors mill. In answer to the requirement for steel in a postwar Europe rebuilding its shattered industries, SKF increased its production capacity by acquiring Hellefors Jernverk, and in 1957 a new ball and roller factory was completed on the original Göteborg site. A notable feature of the immediate postwar decades was the rate of increase of automation in SKF's bearings production, facilitating the introduction in 1953 of SKF's first high-precision bearings.

Key Dates:

1907: Svenska Kullagerfabriken (SKF) is founded to make ball bearings.
1916: SKF acquires its first steel works.
1926: Production of cars is begun by AB Volvo, a subsidiary of SKF.
1935: Volvo becomes independent of SKF.
1957: Hellefors Jernverk is acquired.
1975: Company purchases a 66 percent stake in SARMA of France.
1986: Steel division is merged into Ovako Oy to form Ovako Steel AB, 50 percent owned by SKF.
1988: Austria-based Steyr Wälzlager and AMPEP plc of the United Kingdom are acquired.
1990: Company acquires Chicago Rawhide, U.S. maker of oil seals.
1991: The Ovako Steel venture is divided between the two partners, with SKF gaining full control of the Swedish operations, which take the name Ovako Steel AB.
1995: The CARB, or compact aligning roller bearing, is unveiled.

SKF expanded beyond Europe and the United States to two newly industrializing countries of the Third World, Brazil and India, both engaged in the rapid expansion of their automotive and textile industries and therefore requiring large quantities of bearings. SKF started activities in these countries at their behest. Brazil and India represented vast potential markets for SKF products and offered in addition the important advantage of labor costs cheap by European and U.S. standards.

Meanwhile in Europe the creation of the European Economic Community (EEC) and the growing penetration of the European bearings market by cheap Japanese imports presented SKF with new opportunities and difficulties. Sweden had successfully negotiated with the EEC in 1972 for the free entry of its industrial products into the community, but of more importance to SKF, with its particularly high level of plant investment in EEC member states, was management's growing awareness that the new trading conditions created by the establishment of the EEC trading block could be turned to the group's advantage in helping it fight its Japanese competitors—NTN, NSK, and Koyo Seiko.

SKF's plan involved concentrating production of particular products in specific plants, treating Europe as if it were a single nation in economic terms rather than a collection of six—and later nine—separate states. This would prevent wasteful duplication of production, allowing economies of scale by permitting longer runs of fewer types of bearings or tools at each individual factory. Finished products could then be transported across EEC boundaries progressively being freed from import duties and quotas.

SKF restructured itself in the early 1970s. SKF's bearings and related products were formed into three new divisions—a European bearings division, an overseas bearings division, and SKF Industries Inc. The overseas bearings section became responsible for the group's non-European production and sales companies outside North and Central America while SKF Industries handled the United States, Canadian, and Mexican operations. Also created were cutting tools, steel, and engineering products divisions. Lidköping—manufacturing grinding machines—was preserved as a separate profit center.

Pursuing its niche strategy—establishing a dominant position in particular segments of the bearings and precision tools industries—SKF in the late 1960s and early 1970s took steps to become the leading supplier of bearings to Europe's, particularly France's, newly revitalized aerospace industry. It acquired Les Applications du Roulement (ADR) for the manufacture of airframe bearings and in 1975 bought a 66 percent shareholding in Société Anonyme de Recherches de Mécanique Appliquée (SARMA), a French aerospace engineering research company. During this period it became increasingly apparent that the highest rates of growth were being recorded in some of the group's non-bearing activities—for example, cutting and machine tools—although these still accounted for only a small proportion of the value of total group sales. Consequently SKF chose to strengthen its position in these areas by acquiring some leading manufacturers, including the Swedish engineering firm Malcus Industri in 1969 and the large British cutting-tool manufacturer Sheffield Twist Drill & Steel Company in 1975. This strategy of buying into positions of dominance in particular sectors of the bearings and precision engineering industries was characteristic of SKF.

The mature nature of the European bearings market in the 1970s and its penetration by the Japanese—especially worrying in the large volume markets such as the motor industry—placed a premium on retaining existing customer loyalty and on emphasizing the quality of SKF products over those of its rivals.

In order to make full use of the opportunities created by the new EEC trading conditions, SKF instituted a global forecasting and supply system (GFSS) in 1974 to improve coordination of the type and quantity of bearings produced at its five major European plants. GFSS became an integral part of SKF's strategy of refusing to cede any product to its Japanese competitors.

SKF's decision not to surrender any part of its home European market to the Japanese led to a period of further cost-cutting and rationalization in the late 1970s and early 1980s and served to reduce the groups' overall profit levels during this time. SKF also redefined itself, its goals, and the best means to achieve them.

In essence SKF saw the need to transform itself from a primarily manufacturing-oriented business into a group of companies much more responsive to its customers' changing requirements. In 1968 SKF had centralized control of its activities by setting up its group headquarters in Göteborg. Hand in hand with this change went renewed emphasis on closer collaboration between its research and development and its marketing staff. This arrangement, combined with continuing technical innovation and improvement, made possible by the establishment of the SKF Engineering & Research Center (ERC), enabled SKF to stay ahead of its Japanese competitors despite their lower production costs and greater production efficiency.

Surviving the Recessionary 1980s

Such restructurings and shifts of emphasis could not alleviate the effects of the recession that afflicted the bearings industry in the early 1980s, largely caused by overcapacity. By 1983, overall employment in the industry had fallen by about 15 percent and several manufacturers had gone out of business altogether. Demand was especially depressed in Europe, a factor that affected SKF severely because of its heavy dependence on European sales. SKF was compelled to reduce the size of its workforce at several plants with sometimes divisive results. The prospect of 600 redundancies at SKF's Luton plant in the United Kingdom caused the 1,700-strong workforce to walk out on strike in early 1983, and lowered both morale and productivity. The closure of the Ivry plant near Paris in the same year triggered a lengthy protest occupation by Confédération Générale du Travail militants, resulting in a series of violent confrontations with the police.

Although the group had to resort to a policy of severe cost-cutting, redundancy, and plant closure, it is significant that SKF did not waver in its commitment to the research and development of new technology. One object of research at this time was the so-called "plasma" steel-making process, a method of recovering the base metal from metal wastes by means of an ionized superheated gas stream. The economic rationale for plasma technology was its potential for reducing the cost of producing special steels. By the mid-1980s, SKF had invested SKr 200 million in the commissioning of plasma plants at Landskrona and Malmo—all this at a time of recession in the metals and metals recovery industries. During the early 1980s, SARMA had expanded production on the basis of a substantial involvement in the European Airbus program, but cuts in the program in 1983, combined with a state of general depression in the aerospace industry, forced the closure of SARMA's Champigny plant in 1984. It is worth noting, however, the use of SARMA's special carbon-fiber rods in the European Space Agency's satellite launcher Ariane 4.

In the middle of the decade, SKF benefited from a general economic upturn in Europe, but its overall profit level was dented by a sharp deterioration in the performance of its U.S. operation, SKF Industries Inc. Sales of bearings dropped almost 15 percent in volume, mainly due to the penetration of Japanese imports. Additionally losses at SKF Steel amounted to some SKr 65 million, caused by overcapacity in the world's steel industry and the unexpectedly high cost of the two new plasma plants. Nonetheless SKF made important acquisitions in 1985: SKF Española, which became a fully owned subsidiary after SKF bought 99 percent of its shares, and Waldes Truarc Inc., a U.S. maker of fasteners, evidence of SKF's desire to strengthen its presence both in this field and, as the 1986 acquisition of aerospace bearings manufacturer MRC showed, in the U.S. market generally. Also important was the formation of SKF Miniature Bearings, reflecting the group's keenness to penetrate this high growth area of the bearings business.

In Europe too SKF had increased its strength in fastening systems and linear motion products. The German SKF subsidiary Seeger-Orbis had bought the British company Anderton in 1983 for £1.4 million, thereby placing SKF in a leading position in the European market and providing the group with another valuable bridgehead into the United States. Between 1983 and 1985, the group's components business registered a near 40 percent growth in sales. SKF's steel division was not so successful. SKF decided to pull out of this loss-making area of its business, and from October 1986 steel operations ceased to be part of its activities. Instead, SKF merged its steel subsidiary with the Finnish steel manufacturer Ovako Oy, forming a new steel company named Ovako Steel AB—in which SKF had a 50 percent shareholding—to concentrate on the production of special steel. Significantly, Ovako Steel did not take on SKF's plasma projects.

In that year SKF announced the formation of a 50–50 joint venture with the Japanese bearings producer Koyo Seiko, the first foreign bearings company to gain a foothold in the Japanese home market. SKF was attracted by the 20 percent stake held in Koyo by Toyota, and Koyo, by the prospect of access to SKF's advanced technology. Recognizing in Southeast Asia the fastest growing market for bearings in the world, SKF began to increase productive capacity in the region, culminating in the decision four years later to build a new plant in Malaysia.

In 1987 the bearings operations were once again restructured, this time around product types and functions, forming SKF Bearing Industries, SKF Bearing Services, and SKF Specialty Bearings. The tools and component systems divisions—engineering products—remained unaltered. Each of the new bearings groupings assumed worldwide total responsibility for its own products and services.

Simultaneously SKF decided to withdraw from its involvement in plasma technology. A West German industrial waste company, Berzelius Umwelt-Service, was allowed to acquire a 25 percent holding in ScanDust, SKF's wholly owned subsidiary at Landskrona, while in January 1990 SKF and the other owners of SwedeChrome, based in Malmo, decided to close down the company after a slump in the price of ferrochrome proved the plant's inability to operate at a profit. This step may have led SKF to regret its decision in the early 1980s not to build smaller and more efficient plants. With the acquisition in 1988 of the Austrian bearings manufacturer Steyr Wälzlager Ges.m.b.H. and the British aerospace engineering firm AMPEP plc, the group increased its presence in the European bearings market and in bearings for aerospace purposes. However, SKF's dependence on free trading conditions was illustrated in that year by an anti-dumping investigation in the United States in which SKF and other European and Asian manufacturers were accused of unfair price-cutting. In May 1989 the U.S. Commerce Department began imposing import duties as high as 50 percent and demanding a security deposit against every import shipment. This requirement, combined with a rise in U.S. demand, led SKF to strip out production lines in Europe and ship them to the United States. There was a certain irony in the accusation of an unfair pricing policy, since SKF and other European bearings manufacturers had themselves called for an EEC investigation of Japanese pricing in the European market. Meanwhile, in 1988 the company opened the SKF College of Engineering, a testament to its long tradition of technical innovation.

Fortunately the overcapacity that had dogged the world's bearing industry for almost a decade had begun to recede in 1988, and by 1989 the better balance between supply and demand had begun to show in SKF's profits. SKF, so often the predator, found itself under threat from the Swedish industrial group Trelleborg when the latter acquired a 10.1 percent equity holding in the group in 1988. Trelleborg claimed the stake was for investment purposes only, but some industry analysts believed the move could herald a full bid for SKF in the future. The stake was sold by Trelleborg in 1989. SKF started its own tender of $107 million for the U.S. bearings manufacturer McGill Manufacturing. This move clearly demonstrated SKF's wish to build up its U.S. manufacturing base and thereby avoid burdensome import duties. McGill, however, was acquired by Emerson.

Restructuring in the 1990s

SKF completed the acquisition of a different U.S. company in 1990: Chicago Rawhide (CR), a leading U.S. maker of fluid sealing devices for automotive and machinery applications. Founded in 1879, CR soon became one of the top suppliers of seals to the burgeoning U.S. automobile industry. For SKF, the purchase of CR represented the addition of a new but bearing-related product line since one of CR's key product areas was that of bearing seals. Another important development in the early 1990s was the failure of the Ovako Steel joint venture. In 1991 SKF reluctantly reacquired the Swedish portion of the venture, which became a wholly owned SKF subsidiary under the name Ovako Steel AB.

Unfortunately for SKF, the economic turnaround at the end of the 1980s quickly evaporated in 1990 with the beginning of the crisis in the Persian Gulf and the resultant worldwide recession. From 1990 through 1993, worldwide bearing sales fell 20 percent, leading SKF to cut its workforce by 10,000 from 1990 to 1993 and to suspend payment of its dividend in 1992 and 1993, the first such suspensions in company history. The company posted three consecutive years of losses starting in 1991. SKF finally returned to the black in 1994, posting net profits of SKr 1.28 billion (US$167.9 million) on sales of SKr 33.27 billion (US$4.48 billion). In the midst of this latest turnaround, SKF's chief executive, Mauritz Sahlin, stepped down from his position in April 1995 and was replaced by Peter Augustsson, who had been a senior vice-president in charge of European operations. Also in 1995, SKF unveiled what it considered its most significant technical achievement in 25 years, a new rolling bearing dubbed the CARB, or compact aligning roller bearing. The CARB offered lower friction and a higher load capacity and tolerated misalignment.

Augustsson quickly set out to reduce SKF's continued dependence on Europe, where the company still derived about 60 percent of its sales. The company had only 12 percent of the bearing market in North America, with the United States alone accounting for one-third of world bearing demand. In addition to seeking to boost U.S. sales, Augustsson targeted fast-growing emerging economies in Asia as well, including India, Malaysia, South Korea, and Indonesia. In the mid-1990s, SKF established five joint ventures in China. Augustsson also moved to make the company more competitive by cutting costs and increasing productivity at the company's factories worldwide.

As it entered the late 1990s, SKF was under increasing pressure from the Wallenberg empire, which through its Investor AB investment arm was the largest SKF shareholder, to improve its profitability. Percy Barnevik in particular demanded better results from a number of Wallenberg companies, including SKF, after becoming chairman of Investor in 1997. Augustsson attempted to turn around SKF's fortunes with two restructurings—an October 1997 plan to cut more than 2,000 jobs and a June 1998 program involving 4,000 job losses. But with the economic crisis wreaking havoc in Asia and the SKF's core European market in a slump, Augustsson was evidently not producing results fast enough and was replaced as chief executive in August 1998 by Sune Carlsson, who had been a top executive at another Wallenberg company, ABB, where he had worked closely with Barnevik in Barnevik's other role as ABB chairman.

Carlsson stepped up the pace of restructuring, announcing an additional 1,000 job cuts and the beginning of a program to divest a number of noncore businesses. Restructuring charges during 1998 totaled SKr 3.1 billion (US$383 million), leading to a net loss for the year of SKr 1.64 billion (US$202.6 million). Among SKF's divestments was the 2000 sale of Lidköping Machine Tools AB to Karolin Machine Tool AB, marking SKF's exit from the manufacturing of machine tools. SKF also planned to unload its steel division. On the acquisition side, SKF was focusing in part on building up its service division, which offered mechanical services, maintenance services, and monitoring solutions. Overall, Carlsson's restructuring program appeared to be bearing fruit as operating margins improved from less than four percent in late 1998 to nine percent by mid-2000. SKF was aiming to increase margins to ten percent by 2002 and was well on its way to meeting this target.

Principal Subsidiaries

MANUFACTURING COMPANIES: SKF Sverige AB; SKF USA Inc. (99.8%); SKF Österreich AG (Austria); SKF Pozna_ S.A. (Poland; 99.8%); Lutsk Bearing Plant (Ukraine; 93.7%); SKF Actuators AB; SKF AutoBalance Systems AB (91%); SKF de Mexico S.A. de C.V.; SKF do Brasil Limitada (Brazil; 99.9%); SKF Argentina S.A. (99.9%); SKF Bearings India Ltd. (42.4%); SKF Mekan AB; Anhui Zhongding CR Seals Ltd. (China; 60%); Beijing Nankou SKF Railway Bearings Company Limited (China; 51%); SKF Automotive Components Corporation (Korea); CR Korea Co., Ltd. (50%); PT. SKF Indonesia (60%). SALES COMPANIES: SKF Danmark A/S (Denmark); SKF Norge A/S (Norway); Oy SKF Ab (Finland); SKF Portugal Rolamentos, Limitada (95%); SKF Loziska, a.s. (Czech Republic); SKF Svéd Golyóscsapágy Részvenytársaság (Hungary); SKF Hellas S.A. (Greece); SKF Canada Limited (62.5%); SKF del Peru S.A.; SKF Chilena S.A.I.C. (Chile); SKF Venezolana S.A. (Venezuela); SKF South East Asia (Pte) Ltd. (Singapore); SKF Australia Pty Ltd.; SKF New Zealand Limited; SKF South Africa (Proprietary) Ltd.; SKF Eurotrade AB; SKF Multitec AB. OTHER COMPANIES: SKF Bearings Ltd. (U.K.); SKF Holding Maatschappij Holland B.V. (Netherlands); SKF Verwaltungs AG (Switzerland); SKF Holding Mexicana, S.A. de C.V. (Mexico; 98%); Immobiliaria Nicolás Arriola S.A.C. (Peru); SKF (China) Investment Co. Ltd. (China); Barseco (Pty) Ltd. (South Africa); SKF Australia (Manufacturing) Pty. Ltd.; Compania SKF Nicaragua S.A.; Latinoamericana de Administracion S.A. (Panama); SKF Lager AB; SKF Vehicle Parts AB; Nordiska Kullager Aktiebolaget; AB SKF-Agenturer; SKF Logistic Services AB; AB Compania Sudamericana SKF; AB S.A. des Roulements à Billes Suédois SKF; SKF International AB; SKF Reinsurance Co. Ltd.; SKF Fondförvaltning AB; AB Svenska Kullagerfabriken; SKF Data-service AB; SKF Nova AB; Bagaregården 16:7 KB (99.9%); KB Nya Kulan (99%); SKF Fastighetsförvaltning AB; SKF Support AB; Ovako Couplings Holding AB; Ovako Tube AB; Ovako Steel Holding AB.

Principal Divisions

SKF Automotive Division; SKF Electrical Division; SKF Industrial Division; SKF Service Division; SKF Seals Division; SKF Steel Division.

Principal Competitors

Applied Industrial Technologies, Inc.; FAG Kugelfischer Georg Schäfer AG; Kaydon Corporation; Koyo Seiko Co., Ltd.; NSK Ltd.; NTN Corporation; The Timken Company.

Further Reading

Arbose, Jules, "SKF's U.S. Strategy to Counter the Japanese," *International Management,* June 1986, pp. 40+.

Banks, Howard, "Good Bearings," *Forbes,* September 23, 1996, p. 52.

Brown-Humes, Christopher, "SKF Aims for Smoother Global Performance: The Bearings Maker Is Stressing Marketing and R&D," *Financial Times,* July 20, 1995, p. 27.

Burt, Tim, "A Tough Regime in Anyone's Language: SKF's New Chief Is Imposing Brutal Measures to Achieve His Aims," *Financial Times,* December 4, 1998, p. 25.

Madslien, Jorn, "SKF Finds Its Bearings with a Plan of Action," *Corporate Finance,* October 1998, pp. 7-8.

Marsh, Peter, "Change of Culture at SKF: Ball-Bearings Maker Switches from Europe in Search of Growth," *Financial Times,* August 25, 1997, p. 17.

Shipman, Alan, "Sweden's High Roller," *International Management,* March 1994, pp. 22–24.

Steckzéén, Birger, *SKF, Svenska Kullagerfabriken: En svensk exportindustris historia, 1907–1957,* Göteborg: Svenska Kullagerfabriken, 1957, 884 p.

The Story of SKF, Göteborg: Aktiebolaget SKF, 1982.

Webster, Mark, "Bearing Up After 10 Hard Years," *Financial Times,* May 14, 1982, p. 19.

The World of SKF, Göteborg: Aktiebolaget SKF, 1988.

—D.H. O'Leary
—updated by David E. Salamie

All Nippon Airways Co., Ltd.

3-5-10 Haneda Airport, Ota-ku
Tokyo 144-0041
Japan
Telephone: +81-3-5756-5665
Fax: +81-3-5756-5659
Web site: http://www.ana.co.jp

Public Company
Incorporated: 1952 as Nippon Helicopter & Aeroplane Transport Co., Ltd.
Employees: 15,000
Sales: ¥1.21 trillion (US$11.40 billion) (2000)
Stock Exchanges: OTC Tokyo Osaka London Frankfurt
Ticker Symbol: ALNPY
NAIC: 481111 Scheduled Passenger Air Transportation; 481112 Scheduled Freight Air Transportation; 481211 Nonscheduled Chartered Passenger Air Transportation; 481212 Nonscheduled Chartered Freight Air Transportation; 488119 Other Airport Operations; 488999 All Other Support Activities for Transportation; 56152 Tour Operators; 561599 All Other Travel Arrangement and Reservation Services; 72111 Hotels (Except Casino Hotels) and Motels

All Nippon Airways Co., Ltd. (ANA) operates Japan's second largest airline in terms of revenue, behind the now privatized national carrier Japan Air Lines (JAL). However, in terms of passengers carried, ANA ranks in the world's top ten and is Japan's leading airline. ANA has traditionally been engaged primarily in domestic operations but is now competing aggressively with JAL on the lucrative international routes. ANA started regular flights to the United States in 1986, and flights to Europe and other destinations in the succeeding five years. ANA also has an extensive cargo business and, through a number of subsidiaries, is engaged in hotel and resort operation, travel agencies, trading, and restaurants. Nonetheless, All Nippon Airways' namesake airline contributes about two-thirds of the parent company's total revenue.

Founded in the 1950s

The foundation of ANA's success as an international airline lies in the rapid growth of Japan's domestic travel market in the 1950s and 1960s. ANA was originally formed in Tokyo in 1952 as Nippon Helicopter & Aeroplane Transport Co., Ltd. The formation came after the signing of the San Francisco Peace Treaty of April 1952, which effectively ended the American occupation of Japan. A new law was passed by the Japanese government that subsequently allowed for the establishment of private airlines, administered by JDAC, the country's air transport regulatory body.

The founder of Nippon Helicopter and its first president was Masuichi Midoro. At the time of its establishment the company had 28 employees, 12 of whom were board members. The new airline began operations in February 1953 using Japanese pilots and a De Havilland Dove on the busy Tokyo-Osaka route. Initially limited to cargo, the flight began passenger service early the next year.

Other private domestic airlines were beginning to form within Japan, and by 1953 nine had been granted permission by the government. Notable among these was the Osaka-based Far East Airlines, which gained its operating license in 1953. Far East Airlines was founded by Choichi Inoue, who recognized a market for private air travel and began operations in 1953 between Tokyo and Osaka.

Both Nippon Helicopter and Far East Airlines enjoyed success in the following five years with the expansion of networks in eastern and western Japan based around Japan's two main cities, Tokyo and Osaka. At the end of 1956 the two airlines agreed to merge to create Japan's largest private airline. The merged company was called All Nippon Airways Co., Ltd., and the president was Midoro from Nippon Helicopter, the larger of the two companies. Respective networks were combined, and Nippon Helicopter's logo was adopted on all planes. In 1958 eight DC-3s were put into service and stewardesses' uniforms were redesigned and standardized. ANA was rapidly proving

Company Perspectives:

A superior company is one that customers choose first. Committed to our highest priorities of safety and reliability, our goal is to be the First Choice of customers on the strength of personal service and world-class performance.

to be strong competition for Japan's national carrier JAL on domestic routes.

Jets in the 1960s

In 1962 Midoro became chairman of ANA, making way for incoming President Kaheito Okazaki, whose first move was to acquire the much smaller Fujita Airways in 1963. ANA entered the jet age in 1964 when it purchased three Boeing 727s for use on its Tokyo to Sapporo route and for charter flights.

In 1964 Japan National Railways unveiled the ''bullet train'' for operation between Tokyo, Osaka, and other destinations, providing a cheap alternative to air as a means of business travel between Japan's major cities. Japan's economy was encountering explosive growth at the time, with the widespread use of the automobile as a means of transport. ANA realized that it was competing for passengers with rail and road as well as other airlines and embarked on a program of expanding both the size and number of jets it operated. ANA was also eyeing JAL's monopoly on international services from Japan and began lobbying the government to gain access to this lucrative market. A department was formed with the task of preparing for the airline's eventual debut into international air travel.

New Horizons in the 1970s

The foundation of regular international service was laid in 1971 when ANA operated a Boeing 727 charter flight to Hong Kong, its first foray into the market. In 1973, after 20 years of service, ANA carried its 50 millionth passenger.

In 1973 ANA embarked on a diversification strategy that attempted to exploit the growing tourist trade in Japan. ANA Enterprises, Ltd. was formed to operate hotels around the country. The hotel business would come to provide an integral part of the ANA Group's total revenues. Another ANA subsidiary was set up in 1974 with the formation of Air Nippon Co., Ltd. The new airline was intended to serve regional destinations with smaller planes and thus link many remote islands and towns with ANA's network. At this point ANA had the most extensive domestic network in Japan and was seeking to expand. In 1978 ANA took a minor stake in the newly formed subsidiary Nippon Cargo Airlines, on the assumption that it would have access to international freight markets in the near future.

Both ANA and JAL were at the center of a scandal in the 1970s in which it was alleged that the airlines were influenced by leading Japanese politicians, notably Japanese Prime Minister Tanaka, in their decision to purchase aircraft from U.S. manufacturer Lockheed. The scandal led to the resignation of the Japanese government and investigation of the airlines by authorities. Scandal aside, ANA introduced the new Lockheed Tristar on its Tokyo to Okinawa route in 1974. Boeing 747s were introduced five years later on the Tokyo to Sapporo and Tokyo to Fukuoka routes. The problem of severe crowding at Tokyo's Haneda airport was alleviated in 1978 with the opening of the new Tokyo International Airport. From this point on all international travel, which was increasing rapidly, would originate from the new airport at Narita, near Tokyo. By 1980 ANA was the world's sixth largest airline, although it was virtually unknown outside Japan, with its international services limited to charter flights within Asia.

Deregulated in the 1980s

The Japanese government was, however, preparing to deregulate its international air transport market. This was partly in response to international pressure and partly due to market demand for more flights. Foreign airlines such as TWA had enjoyed access to Japan for years, but the majority of outbound passengers traveled on Japan's national airline, JAL. Government doubts about the management of JAL began to surface after the crash of a 747 en route to Osaka from Tokyo in 1984. Over 500 lives were lost in the packed jet and negligent maintenance by JAL was shown to be the cause. JAL was privatized in 1985, and ANA was allowed to compete on international routes. This came after United Air Lines of the United States took over Pan Am's Pacific network. The Japanese government was concerned that Japanese airlines were losing out on the international market and nominated ANA as the second Japanese carrier allowed to fly on overseas routes. ANA was well prepared for this and began cargo service in 1985 and international passenger travel in 1986, with flights first to Guam and then to Washington, D.C., and Los Angeles. (The airline became the only carrier to travel between the U.S. and Japanese capital cities.) ANA initiated its overseas expansion with a huge publicity campaign and a change of logo to the now familiar blue ANA letters on the tailfin of each plane.

With a firm hold on the slowly growing domestic market (a 50 percent market share), ANA embarked on a huge expansion of its international network. Demand for international air travel was booming as the Japanese economy invested heavily overseas. This demand far outstripped supply, with existing landing slots at the main international airports in Tokyo and Osaka inadequate for the traffic. As a result, the government began construction on three major airport projects, including the New Kansai International Airport near Osaka. To meet the huge growth in passenger volume, ANA initiated its ABLE computerized reservation and ticketing system. In 1987 ANA added Beijing, Hong Kong, Sydney, and Dalian to its list of overseas destinations and in the following year Stockholm, Bangkok, Vienna, London, Moscow, and Saipan. This expansion of overseas routes, although meticulously planned, required significant logistical effort. ANA obtained listings on the London and Frankfurt stock exchanges in 1991 in order to raise funds for expansion. Training and recruitment were emphasized to such an extent that a 1991 poll of university graduates revealed that ANA was Japan's most popular company among young graduates. In 1990 ANA established World Air Network, Ltd. (WAC), offering charter flights to destinations in Asia from regional Japanese airports, thus opening up international travel to a larger segment of the population. ANA upgraded its computer reservation system in 1990 with the formation of INFINI, the world's first reservation system to be operated

Key Dates:

1952: Company is formed as Nippon Helicopter & Aeroplane Transport Co., Ltd.
1953: Far East Airlines begins operations.
1956: Nippon Helicopter and Far East Airlines merge to form All Nippon Airways Co., Ltd. (ANA).
1973: Diversification program begins.
1986: ANA begins flying from Tokyo to Washington, D.C.
1994: ANA posts its first loss.
1997: A new bilateral agreement gives ANA more access to the U.S. market.

by a consortium of airlines. ANA's partners in the venture were Cathay Pacific Airways, China Airlines, Malaysian Airlines, and several others.

Struggling in the 1990s

As of 1991, ANA was Japan's largest airline and the eighth largest in the world. *Air Transport World* magazine pronounced it "Airline of the Year." With a high standard of passenger service, ANA served some 30 cities in Japan and 19 overseas, operating approximately 500 flights per day.

Japan was one of the most expensive places in the world to operate an airline. ANA created a low-cost, Singapore-based charter subsidiary, World Air Network, in March 1991. ANA leased some aircraft from World Air Network to fly on certain scheduled routes.

The fiscal year ending March 31, 1993, was the worst in Japanese history. JAL lost ¥44 billion (US$404 million) and ANA maintained its profitability only through shrewd aircraft sales. The two airlines soon struck a deal to jointly warehouse parts for the two dozen new Boeing 777s they had ordered.

Both ANA and JAL were constrained in their efforts to cut labor costs due to the job-for-life culture in Japan. However, by late 1994, ANA was planning to reduce its workforce of 14,800 by ten percent within a year and a half, mostly through attrition. It would continue to announce impending staff cuts throughout the decade.

In 1994, ANA finally posted its first loss (¥2.9 billion or US$28 million) in 27 years. Revenues were about $7.5 billion, $1 billion from international service. This area was an important part of the airline's recovery plan; it planned to increase its international business by nearly a third in fiscal 1995. Several new, leased Boeing and Airbus aircraft arrived during the year to meet the projected demand. In contrast, JAL saw its opportunities for growth in the domestic market dominated by ANA.

Domestic traffic, which accounted for three-quarters of ANA's revenues, continued to decline. To counter this, ANA introduced its Hayawari fares in 1995, advance tickets priced less than the bullet trains.

ANA continued to expand its international service. In the fall of 1994, it launched routes to Korea, Singapore, China, Hong Kong, and Australia from the new Osaka Kansai International Airport. The United States was served from Tokyo. ANA was also developing marketing agreements with Air Canada, Austrian Airlines, and Delta. Code share arrangements with Sabena and SAS had collapsed due to cultural differences.

"We do more" was ANA's new slogan. However, what it could not do was turn back the clock to 1952, when the original U.S.-Japan air agreement gave JAL, Northwest, and United Lines incumbent status. Gaining comparable access to the U.S.-Japan market took years of extended negotiations. ANA was also limited in its control of needed take-off and landing slots at Japan's crowded and notoriously inefficient airports. The installation of new runways offered some relief, but this was another process that took years. When finally sealed in February 1997, the new bilateral agreement gave ANA more access to the U.S. market, while giving the U.S. carriers nearly free reign to pick up passengers in Japan and carry them to other points in Asia.

In April 1997, ANA agreed to provide operational support for Skymark Airlines, a new budget carrier in the domestic market. The previous month, JAL announced the formation of its own low-cost domestic unit, JAL Express.

Seiji Fukatsu, a new president brought in to administer ANA's recovery, resigned in May 1997 over resistance to change from former transport ministry bureaucrats on the company's board.

Although ANA's domestic business helped cushion it from the Asian financial crisis, and the continent was slow to recover, ANA's SPEED21 five-year plan aimed to further increase its international business, an area of operations that had never shown a profit. Cost reductions and productivity increases were also made part of the plan.

In the late 1990s, ANA's dominance in the domestic market was threatened by weakening demand and heavy competition from two new start-up airlines, Skymark and Hokkaido International Airlines, "Air Do" for short. ANA cut routes and reduced the size of its domestic fleet as a result. It also slashed the salaries of its highest-paid employees by as much as 25 percent.

Pilots staged a two-week strike in April 1998 that cost ANA ¥1.7 billion (US$12.5 million). More misfortune lay ahead. On July 23, 1999, an enthusiast of flight simulation games hijacked an ANA Boeing 747, killing the pilot with a knife he had smuggled on board.

By 2000, ANA had joined the Star Alliance and formed a low-cost domestic subsidiary, Air Nippon (ANK), slated to begin operations with a single Boeing 767. It stimulated the domestic market by promotions such as a complimentary ¥10,000 fare between any two points in Japan.

At the end of the 2000 calendar year, the cost-cutting measures seemed to be working. Profits for the fiscal half-year were more than double that of the year before, and the trend was expected to continue.

Principal Subsidiaries

Air Nippon Co., Ltd.; Air Hokkaido Co., Ltd.; All Nippon Airways Co., Ltd.; All Nippon Airways Travel Co., Ltd.; All

Nippon Airways World Tours Co., Ltd.; ANA Aircraft Maintenance Co., Ltd.; ANA Enterprises, Ltd.; ANA Information Systems Planning Co., Ltd.; ANA Real Estate Co., Ltd.; ANA Sky Holiday Tours Co., Ltd.; ANA TELEMART Co., Ltd.; ANK Trading Co., Ltd.; Infini Travel Information, Inc.; International Airport Utility Co., Ltd.; Nippon Cargo Airlines Co., Ltd.

Principal Divisions

Air Transportation; Travel Services; Hotel Operations; Other Businesses.

Principal Competitors

Hokkaido International Airlines; Japan Air Lines Company, Ltd.; Japan Air System; Skymark Airlines.

Further Reading

Barth, Steve, ''Blue Skies for Air Cargo,'' *World Trade*, May 1998, pp. 60–62.

Jane's Aviation Yearbook, 1991.

Jones, Dominic, ''Home Sweet Home,'' *Airfinance Journal*, April 2000, pp. 38–40.

Mecham, Michael, ''ANA Reacts to Shifts in Domestic Demand,'' *Aviation Week & Space Technology*, June 7, 1999, p. 40.

Moorman, Robert W., ''Domestic Bliss?'' *Air Transport World*, October 1999, pp. 91–94.

——, ''Growing with Less,'' *Air Transport World*, November 1994, pp. 115+.

O'Connor, Anthony, ''Caught in the Headlines,'' *Airfinance Journal*, March 1996, pp. 24+.

''Risky Take-Off,'' *Economist*, October 25, 1997, pp. 74–75.

Sekigawa, Eiichiro, ''ANA Helps Low-Cost Airline Get Started,'' *Aviation Week & Space Technology*, April 21, 1997, p. 33.

——, ''Bizarre Tokyo Hijacking Leaves ANA Pilot Dead,'' *Aviation Week & Space Technology*, August 2, 1999, p. 39.

''The Skies in 1992,'' *Airline Business*, 1992.

Snelling, Mark, ''When Asia Catches Cold,'' *Airfinance Journal*, December 1993, pp. 28ff.

''Travel and Tourism Analyst 1992,'' *Business International*, 1992.

Woolsey, James P., ''Don't Fence Me In,'' *Air Transport World*, May 1997, pp. 65–66.

—Dylan Tanner
—updated by Frederick C. Ingram

Allegheny Energy, Inc.

10435 Downsville Pike
Hagerstown, Maryland 21740-1766
U.S.A.
Telephone: (301) 790-3400
Toll Free: (800) 255-3443
Fax: (301) 790-3400
Web site: http://www.alleghenyenergy.com

Public Company
Incorporated: 1925 as West Penn Electric Company
Employees: 4,923
Sales: $2.81 billion (1999)
Stock Exchanges: New York Midwest Pacific Amsterdam
Ticker Symbol: AYE
NAIC: 221111 Hydroelectric Power Generation; 221112 Fossil Fuel Electric Power Generation; 221119 Other Electric Power Generation; 221121 Electric Bulk Power Transmission and Control; 221122 Electric Power Distribution; 22121 Natural Gas Distribution; 51331 Wired Telecommunications Carriers; 51333 Telecommunications Resellers

Allegheny Energy, Inc. controls both regulated and unregulated generation facilities and owns 8,593 megawatts of power. It provides electricity to markets in several mid-Atlantic states, primarily Pennsylvania and West Virginia, as well as parts of Maryland, Ohio, and Virginia. The decline of the steel industry since the 1950s has changed the revenue mix at Allegheny significantly. To supplement its shrinking base of industrial customers, Allegheny increased sales to the residential and commercial sectors, while also taking advantage of its low-cost, coal-fired generators to sell large amounts of electricity to other utilities. This latter source of revenue, however, was threatened by the 1990 Clean Air Act Amendments, which forced Allegheny to spend in the neighborhood of $2 billion for new pollution control devices, mainly scrubbers for its high-sulfur coal plants. In answer to this new challenge, Allegheny diversified its holdings to include natural gas facilities in West Virginia and several Midwestern states. The company reorganized in 1997 in response to deregulation, with the goal of taking advantage of the newly opened energy markets.

Utility Holding Companies in the Early 1900s

The history of Allegheny Power is interwoven with the controversial history of utility holding companies in the United States. From the beginnings of centralized power generation in the 1880s, ownership of the nation's electric companies was concentrated increasingly in the hands of financiers such as J.P. Morgan and Samuel Insull. The power industry required more capital per dollar of operating revenue than any other business and thus became controlled in large part by a small number of men with intimate connections on Wall Street and in the banking community. The early power magnates found it useful to unite many small generating companies under the umbrella of a single holding company. Such a holding company, with a far larger asset base than any of its constituents, was more likely to impress investors as a reasonable gamble than were the individual companies, thus providing a means of generating the immense capital needed to expand in the power industry.

One of these holding companies was the New York-based American Water Works & Electric Company, which in the first decades of the 20th century began to acquire control of both water facilities and power plants in the northeastern part of the United States. Among the companies it controlled were the 53 Pennsylvania light and power companies that in 1916 had been united to form the West Penn Power Company. Included in the purchase of these small power companies was their former parent, West Penn Traction Company—later known as West Penn Railways—a minor operator of electric railways. West Penn Power served much of Pennsylvania's southwest corner, with the important exception of Pittsburgh proper, as well as a chunk of the state's north-central region and most of its border with Maryland. The company's generators were a mix of water turbines and coal-fired steam, the percentage of the latter growing rapidly as the area's electrical needs outstripped its limited hydroelectric capacity. Much of West Penn Power's revenue was derived from industrial sales, primarily to the region's iron, steel, and coal mining operations.

Company Perspectives:

Allegheny Energy, Inc. is a strong, diversified energy company on the leading edge of change. We are excited by the challenge of deregulation and dedicated to the goals of increasing shareholder value, becoming a national supplier of energy and value-added energy-related services, and diversifying into other ventures related to our core business which enhance value.

Another of American Water Works' major investments was Washington County Light & Power Company, based in Marietta, Ohio, but with most of its customers in neighboring West Virginia. Washington County served a predominantly rural area that, like West Penn's, was rich in both coal and in rivers suitable for hydroelectric damming. Farther to the east lay a number of electric companies amalgamated in 1923 into The Potomac Edison Company, doing most of its business in western Maryland along the Potomac River. Potomac Edison, like Washington County Light & Power, was a relatively small, rural electric system that also controlled several local bus lines and electric railways.

By assembling these three regional companies, American Water Works had succeeded in gaining control of the power generation in a sizable portion of land in five states. Nearly all of the plants involved were tiny, pioneering outfits that, given the economic and engineering realities of the utility industry, were certain one day to be unified in one form or another. In 1925 American Water Works took a second step toward doing so by consolidating all of its electrical, bus, rail, and natural gas companies under the name of West Penn Electric Company. West Penn Electric, a Maryland corporation, took charge of the three operating companies—West Penn Power, Washington County Light & Power, and Potomac Edison—and began the gradual integration of the system's complex array of power plants, transformers, and transmission lines. The area served by West Penn Electric's companies in 1925 was very nearly identical to that served by the Allegheny Power System in 1991; further expansion evidently was blocked by other, more powerful utilities busy consolidating their own holdings. West Penn Electric officially incorporated in 1925.

The Challenges of Independence: 1920–60

In the 1920s the formation of public utility holding companies reached its zenith. Amid growing public concern, people such as Samuel Insull put together enormous pyramids of interlocking corporations, many of them widely overcapitalized and all difficult to police with the existing regulatory resources. When the stock market crash of 1929 brought many of these holding companies to bankruptcy, thousands of stock and bond holders were ruined and the outcry prompted a series of congressional investigations of the power industry. In 1935 Congress enacted the Public Utility Holding Company Act, a comprehensive piece of legislation designed to restrict the concentration of ownership in the power industry to those instances where it clearly resulted in greater efficiency and lower consumer costs. In particular, power companies serving noncontiguous areas were not to be held in common ownership unless such benefits could be shown, which was not likely; hence, under the aegis of the Securities and Exchange Commission (SEC), a long series of dissolution proceedings was instituted against the leading utility holding companies.

Among the targets of the SEC was American Water Works & Electric Company. Although the latter's electric holdings under the direction of West Penn Electric were all within a single geographic area, American Water Works also owned water works in other parts of the country. The SEC objected to this arrangement and ordered American Water Works to propose a plan for segregation of its water and electric holdings, which was forwarded and accepted in January 1948. Under the American Water Works plan, equity in West Penn Electric owned by American Water Works would be distributed to American Water Works shareholders, the water works firms would be similarly spun off, and American Water Works itself would cease to exist. Accordingly, as of January 1948, West Penn Electric became the independent owner of its three operating companies, whose territories and facilities were not otherwise affected. West Penn Electric's headquarters remained in New York City.

The newly independent power company faced an ambiguous economic situation. Use of electricity was growing as never before, the U.S. postwar boom adding daily to the applications of electricity in the home and in the factory. Yet, the steel industry was moving away from Pittsburgh. Within a scant ten years the Pittsburgh area would lose its position as the world's leading steel center, and steel production provided West Penn Electric with the largest portion of its industrial sales. A third, even more crucial, factor was the price of fuel. In this respect, West Penn Electric was extremely fortunate. Since the earliest years of power generation, utilities in the eastern part of the country had been shifting from hydroelectric energy to coal-fired steam turbines, with capacity far greater than that offered by Appalachian rivers. West Penn Electric was located in the midst of one of the richest coal regions in the United States, which meant that its fuel costs would remain low as long as coal remained its primary fuel. West Penn Electric always had owned a number of minor coal deposits as an emergency reserve but for the most part had relied on long-term contracts with the region's large mining companies for its supply.

Guaranteed a secure and inexpensive source of fuel, West Penn Electric was able to compile an admirable record of unbroken growth in the postwar decades. With the exception of 1958, the company increased its dividend payments every year from 1948 to 1990. By the mid-1950s West Penn Electric had divested itself of all interests outside the utility business, selling off the various minor bus and rail lines inherited from the company's early years. The company also became interested in the newly emerging field of nuclear power, which it considered as an alternative energy source for the coming years despite its ready access to coal. West Penn Electric joined a number of other utilities in forming the East Central Nuclear Group to study further the possibilities of nuclear power, but in the end decided that the expense and risk inherent in nuclear generation could not be justified given the company's coal resources. West Penn Electric thus was spared the increasingly severe problems faced by the nuclear power industry. The company's total reli-

Key Dates:

1916: American Water Works & Electric Co. creates West Penn Power Company.
1923: Potomac Edison is formed.
1925: West Penn Electric Company is incorporated.
1948: West Penn Electric assumes independent ownership of its operating companies.
1960: West Penn Electric is renamed Allegheny Power System, Inc.
1985: Klaus Bergman becomes president and CEO.
1992: Energy Policy Act inaugurates age of deregulation.
1997: Allegheny Power System is reorganized as Allegheny Energy, Inc.
1998: Pennsylvania Public Utility Commission approves restructuring of West Penn Power Company.
1999: Allegheny Energy Supply, LLC is formed.

ance on coal-fired plants, however, had left it vulnerable to national concern about acid rain and air pollution in general.

The Energy Crisis of the 1970s

In 1960 West Penn Electric adopted its present name of Allegheny Power System, Inc. Its three principal subsidiaries, then as in the early 1990s, were West Penn Power, Potomac Edison, and Monongahela Power, the latter formerly Washington County Light & Power. The 1960s continued the postwar trend toward a decreasing industrial revenue offset by general population growth and by increased per capita use of electricity. With the U.S. economy generally in robust health, Allegheny Power System faced few problems more serious than the occasional wind storm or system overload. This pleasant scenario changed abruptly in 1973, when the OPEC oil embargo changed forever the economics of energy. Almost overnight the price of coal tripled, a jump that would have spelled disaster for Allegheny if it had been forced to rely on the usual laborious procedure for rate adjustments. State and federal regulatory agencies, however, agreed to let Allegheny and most other utilities establish a special fuel index as part of their rate structure, passing on to the consumer such wholesale leaps in the cost of doing business. Despite the turmoil, Allegheny did not suffer any significant reverses.

In the early 1980s, Allegheny agreed to purchase 40 percent of the output of Virginia Electric and Power Company's pumped storage project, forming Allegheny Generating Company to act as its representative in the partnership. Pumped storage is a type of hydroelectric generation that adds to output capacity. The pumped storage project provided about ten percent of Allegheny's 1990 total of 7,991 megawatts of power, with the remainder generated almost entirely by coal.

Deregulation in the 1990s

In 1985 Klaus Bergman assumed the titles of president and chief executive at Allegheny, from which vantage he prepared for the difficulties awaiting the company in the 1990s, in particular the cost of compliance with the Clean Air Act Amendments of 1990. The new amendments were aimed squarely at owners of coal-fired generators such as Allegheny's operating companies, setting new, more stringent limits on sulfur dioxide emissions that were to become fully effective in the year 2000. Thus Allegheny faced the downside of its decision in the 1950s not to pursue nuclear power; with 90 percent of its electricity from coal, the company estimated that compliance with the new standards would cost as much as $2 billion. Allegheny planned to lower emissions by installing scrubbers—equipment that cleans up the emissions from smoke stacks—at its coal plants, rather than abandoning its local suppliers of high-sulfur coal in favor of more distant sources of low-sulfur coal. The company concluded that scrubbers were more cost-effective in the long run and would obviate the need for fuel purchasing changes that would hurt the local economy.

Allegheny's focus shifted toward new opportunities in 1992, when the Energy Policy Act opened the door for deregulation of the nation's regional utilities. Pennsylvania became one of the first states to encourage competition in the energy business with the Electricity Generation Customer Choice and Competition Act of 1996. This new law declared that all customers in the state would be free to sign up with the power provider of their choice by January 1, 2001. In 1997 Allegheny Power Supply became Allegheny Energy, Inc. and formed a new subsidiary, Allegheny Energy Solutions, for the purpose of marketing electricity to a broader base of retail customers. That same year the company signed a deal to acquire Pennsylvania utility DQE for $10.6 billion. After the Pennsylvania Public Utilities Commission (PUC) ruled that Allegheny Energy would be responsible for two-thirds of its overall stranded costs after the transition to the competitive market, however, DQE elected to withdraw from the deal. Later that year the PUC approved a restructuring of West Penn Power Company, Allegheny's utility subsidiary in Pennsylvania. This agreement allowed Allegheny to offer two-thirds of its customers the right to choose their electricity providers beginning in January 1999. It also authorized the transfer of West Penn's generating capacity of 3,778 megawatts to Allegheny's new subsidiary, Allegheny Energy Supply, LLC, for sale in unregulated markets.

Allegheny Energy Supply was formed in November 1999. One of the new company's priorities was to diversify Allegheny's energy interests to include natural gas. This move not only opened up a wider range of opportunities for growth, but, more importantly, provided Allegheny with a means of making the transition to cleaner fuel alternatives. Although Allegheny had maintained strict compliance with the Clean Air Act Amendments throughout the decade, in 1999 almost 90 percent of its power generation still came from coal-burning generators. At the end of 1999 Allegheny finally became a player in the natural gas industry with the purchase of West Virginia Power. The deal gave Allegheny 26,000 new electricity customers and 24,000 new natural gas customers. In 2000 the company announced its plan to acquire Mountaineer Gas Company, adding an additional 200,000 natural gas customers.

The year 2000 was one of significant growth for Allegheny Energy. In August the company transferred Potomac Edison's generating assets from three states into Allegheny Energy Supply, increasing its unregulated megawatt capacity by 2,100. This transaction gave Allegheny Energy Supply more than half of the company's total electricity. In November the company expanded its natural gas holdings, as well as its geographical scope, with the purchase of three natural gas-fired generators in Tennessee, Indiana, and Illinois. This followed the announcement in October that the company planned to build a 1,080-megawatt capacity natural gas generator outside of Phoenix, Arizona, with construction scheduled to begin in 2002. Closer to home, the company also began building a 540-megawatt combined-cycle generating plant in Springdale, Pennsylvania. The new plant featured two gas-fired turbines and one steam turbine and was expected to be operational by 2003. This diversification of the company's holdings, along with its plans to introduce competition into the Ohio and Virginia markets in 2001 and 2002, has placed Allegheny in a leadership position in the deregulated energy industry.

Principal Subsidiaries

Allegheny Energy Supply LLC; Allegheny Power; Allegheny Ventures; Allegheny Energy SVC Corp.; Allegheny Energy Solutions; Allegheny Communications Connect; Monongahela Power Company; The Potomac Edison Company; West Penn Power Company; Allegheny Generating Company.

Principal Competitors

American Electric Power Company, Inc.; DQE, Inc.; PPL Corporation.

Further Reading

Bauer, John, and Costello, Peter, *Public Organization of Electric Power: Conditions, Policies, and Program,* New York: Harper, 1949.

Reeves, Frank, ''Executive in the Spotlight: Chief of Allegheny Energy's New Business Venture Sees Opportunity in Electric Choice,'' *Pittsburgh Post-Gazette,* February 13, 2000.

Zapinski, Ken, ''DQE Ends Allegheny Energy Merger,'' *Pittsburgh Post-Gazette,* July 29, 1998.

—Jonathan Martin
—updated by Stephen Meyer

American Express Company

American Express Tower
World Financial Center
200 Vesey St.
New York, New York 10285
U.S.A.
Telephone: (212) 640-2000
Fax: (212) 619-9743
Web site: http://www.americanexpress.com

Public Company
Incorporated: 1965
Employees: 88,378
Total Assets: $148.51 billion (1999)
Stock Exchanges: New York Chicago Pacific London Paris
Ticker Symbol: AXP
NAIC: 52211 Commercial Banking; 52221 Credit Card Issuing; 52222 Sales Financing; 52232 Financial Transactions Processing, Reserve, and Clearinghouse Activities; 52311 Investment Banking and Securities Dealing; 52312 Securities Brokerage; 52313 Commodity Contracts Dealing; 52314 Commodity Contracts Brokerage; 52321 Securities and Commodity Exchange; 52391 Miscellaneous Intermediation; 522291 Consumer Lending; 522293 International Trade Financing; 522298 All Other Nondepository Credit Intermediation; 523999 Miscellaneous Financial Investment Activities

American Express Company, a multibillion-dollar holding company whose subsidiaries provide travel and financial services worldwide, traces its roots to a New York express business founded by Henry Wells in 1841. From the safe transport of valuables it grew naturally into money orders and traveler's checks; from there its travel service operations, including its credit card services, also grew naturally. In the 1980s, American Express expanded into financial planning through Investors Diversified Services, Inc. (IDS) to merger and acquisition advice from Shearson Lehman Hutton. Faced with intensifying competition and poor public relations in the early 1990s, American Express divested itself from many of the businesses it had acquired in the previous decade. Throughout its history, American Express has enjoyed a reputation for innovation, profitability, and integrity.

Westward Expansion in 19th-Century America

Henry Wells began his expressman career as an agent for William Harnden, who had founded the first express company in the United States in 1839. Express companies were in the business of transporting money and other valuables safely. Wells was an ambitious man who repeatedly proposed expanding the business westward—to Buffalo, New York; the Midwest; and the far West. When Harnden refused to leave the East Coast, Wells struck out on his own, organizing Wells & Co. in 1841.

At first Wells and his associate, Crawford Livingston, served only New York City and Buffalo, then an arduous route by five rickety shortline railroads and wagon or stagecoach for the last 65 miles into or out of Buffalo. A few years later, Wells and William G. Fargo launched an express service from Buffalo to major Midwestern cities. Although appreciated by the Midwestern business community, the new express service simply did not pay. In 1846, Wells decided to retrench and focus his energies on the growing routes serving New York City, Buffalo, Boston, and Albany, leaving the express business west of Buffalo to Fargo's company, Livingston, Fargo and Co.

In 1849 John Butterfield, a wealthy and experienced transportation mogul, entered the express business with Butterfield, Wasson & Co., a direct competitor to Wells & Company on New York state routes. Later that year, Butterfield proposed that he, Fargo, and Wells eliminate their wasteful competition by joining forces. On March 18, 1850, the three companies consolidated to form the American Express Company, a joint-stock company with initial capital of $150,000. Wells was elected the new company's first president; Fargo became vice-president.

Under Wells's leadership American Express was immediately and unexpectedly profitable, expanding rapidly and acquiring small competitors in the Midwest, negotiating contracts

Company Perspectives:

Reinvention. For 150 years, American Express has continuously transformed itself to meet changing customer needs. What began as a rough-and-tumble freight forwarding company in 1850, later became a travel company, and today, a leading global financial and travel services company.

What remains constant are the hallmarks of the American Express brand—trust, integrity, security, quality and customer service.

In many ways, the history of our company and the evolution of the American Express brand over 150 years have shaped the actions we take today. Our commitment to providing extraordinary service to our customers around the world is unwavering and now extends to the Internet.

The attributes on which American Express was built are key competitive advantages that we continue to bring to bear with every product and service we offer.

with the first railroads, and running packet boats on the Illinois Canal to connect Ohio, Illinois, and Iowa with steamship lines on the Illinois River. In 1851, American Express reached an amicable agreement with its major rival, Adams and Co. (reorganized as Adams Express Co. in 1854). American Express was to expand north and west of New York while Adams was free to grow south and east. This agreement was kept and renewed over the next 70 years, buying American Express time to establish its business solidly.

Despite the agreement with Adams and Co., Wells and Fargo still distrusted its rival and feared the company would gain a monopoly in the California gold fields. When Wells proposed his old dream of a transcontinental express service to the American Express board of directors, they rejected his idea. But in 1852 Wells and Fargo got the board's blessing to launch an independent venture, Wells Fargo & Company, to provide express and banking services in California.

In 1854, trouble developed with the New York, Lake Erie & Western Railroad (American Express's link to the Midwest) when Daniel Drew, the railroad's owner, became outraged that American Express had picked off the Erie's most profitable freight business by shipping light, high-rate freight on the Erie under its express contract. Drew was determined to award the express rights to others. In response, American Express created an affiliate and presented it as a bona fide competitor. American Express loaned the funds to start a new company to Danforth Barney, then president of Wells Fargo. Barney's new company, United States Express Co., then acquired the Erie express rights from Drew and split the lucrative Midwestern business with American Express.

American Express's first decade saw two other noteworthy accomplishments. In 1857, American Express launched the Overland Mail Co. as a joint venture with Wells Fargo, Adams Express Co., and United States Express Co. The Overland Mail Co. (later controlled by Wells Fargo) won the first transcontinental mail contract from the United States Postal Service, which led to its involvement with the *Pony Express.* Also, James C. Fargo, William's younger brother, proposed the establishment of a fast, bulk freight express service for merchants. Merchants Dispatch, created in 1858, proved immediately successful.

The Civil War was enormously profitable for American Express, as it was for the express industry generally. American Express shipped supplies to army depots, took election ballots to soldiers, and delivered parcels to parts of the Confederacy taken by Union forces. During this period, American Express distributed huge dividends to its shareholders.

Competition After the Civil War

After the war, the express industry attracted the attention of financial raiders. The first raid, by National Bankers Express Co. in 1866, was thwarted at relatively low cost. American Express quickly reached an agreement with Adams Express and United States Express to neutralize the threat by giving National Bankers Express shares of the established companies and a seat on the American Express board of directors.

The second raid had much more serious consequences. Late in 1866, a group of New York merchants established Merchants Union Express Co., to both get into the express business and destroy the three largest express lines—Adams, American, and United States. Merchants Union first hired away the older companies' experienced agents and then invaded their territories. American Express suffered such losses in 1867 that for the first and only time in its history it failed to pay a dividend. On December 21, 1868, the four express companies reached a peace agreement, dividing the express and fast-freight business and pooling and distributing net earnings. American Express got the worst of the deal; Merchants Union acquired rights on railways that had been its bread-and-butter lines (the Hudson River and New York Central railroads) and lost its supremacy in the express business. In 1868, American Express was forced to merge with Merchants Union to form the American Merchants Union Express Company (shortened in 1873 back to the American Express Company). Also in 1868 Wells retired and was replaced as president by William G. Fargo.

Fargo's tenure saw the beginning of two trends that would later prove significant. First, Fargo's brother, James, expanded Merchants Dispatch operations to Europe. Soon Merchants Dispatch was transporting more than half the first-class tonnage from New York City to over a dozen European cities, making international operations a lucrative sideline for American Express. Second, high express rates set after the Panic of 1873 created public demand for a government operated parcel post. In 1874, the U.S. Postal Service began to deliver packages at a new, low rate. The following year, Congress set the parcel rate at a half-cent per ounce, far below cost. This cut deeply into express company profits. Express industry lobbying and the post office's substantial operating loss soon persuaded Congress to raise rates to a more reasonable level, but the precedent for governmental involvement in the express business had been established.

Late 19th-Century Innovations

William Fargo's death in 1881 and James's succession to the presidency began a new era for American Express. Although James Fargo was often described as autocratic, aloof, and old-

Key Dates:

1841: Henry Wells founds Wells & Co.
1850: Wells, William G. Fargo, and John Butterfield form the American Express Company.
1852: Wells Fargo & Company is founded.
1868: American Express Company merges with Merchants Union to form the American Merchants Union Express Co.; Henry Wells retires.
1881: William Fargo dies.
1891: The American Express Traveler's Cheque is introduced.
1910: Mann-Elkins Act makes express companies subject to the scrutiny of the Interstate Commerce Commission.
1914: George C. Taylor becomes company president.
1915: American Express opens its Travel Department.
1919: The American Express Co. is established to expand the company's international banking operations.
1958: The American Express travel-and-entertainment card (the "green card") is introduced.
1981: American Express acquires Shearson Loeb Rhoades Inc.
1982: American Express is reorganized under American Express Corp.
1987: The Optima Card is introduced.
1993: Harvey Golub becomes CEO; American Express wins federal government's travel and transportation system contract.
1999: American Express launches Blue, the first "smart card" offered in the United States.

fashioned, he was also remarkably innovative. During his term of office, American Express first diversified into the financial services industry with the introduction of two instruments—the American Express Money Order in 1882 and the American Express Travelers Cheque in 1891.

The post office first introduced the postal money order in 1864. This immediately threatened the express industry because it reduced the demand by banks and merchants for the transport of money and other valuables. The postal money order, however, had a serious flaw: its face value could be altered without detection. Although American Express directors had discussed introducing a money order since the end of the Civil War, it took James Fargo to galvanize the company into action. At his direction Marcellus Berry, an American Express employee, designed a safer money order. American Express's money order was an immediate hit; it could be used to settle charges on express shipments, was more readily available than the postal money order, and was simpler, cheaper, and easier to negotiate. Not only did the money order provide a new source of revenue (over 250,000 were issued the first year), but for the first time American Express had a credit balance (or "float"—funds from instruments that had been paid for but were not yet cashed) that could be safely invested to bring in additional income.

The traveler's check filled a similar financial niche. Before 1891, tourists and business travelers could transfer funds from the United States to Europe only via a letter of credit, a time-consuming and cumbersome method: only specified correspondents of the issuing United States bank could negotiate letters of credit, and then only during banking hours and after an appreciable delay. Fargo, annoyed by his own experience with the procedure, again directed Marcellus Berry to find a solution. The American Express Travelers Cheque was a marked improvement over the letter of credit in several respects: its simple signature and countersignature provision made the instrument very secure; it could easily be converted into foreign currency at any American Express freight office; and, if lost or stolen, American Express would refund the owner's money. The value and convenience of the traveler's check was recognized at once, and its popularity again provided American Express with additional revenues and float.

After the traveler's check was introduced in 1891, travelers began making American Express freight offices their informal headquarters—places to convert funds, to seek information about hotels and travel arrangements, and simply to congregate. American Express officers saw the opportunities offered by the travel industry and urged diversification in that direction. James Fargo, however, was absolutely opposed to the idea. He allowed American Express agents to offer travel information purely as a service to customers, but drew the line there. American Express's official entry into the travel industry, which became one of its best-known and most lucrative businesses, was delayed until after Fargo's retirement in 1914.

After the turn of the century, the express industry came under attack from a number of quarters. The railroads had steadily eroded express profits by raising their rates from 40 percent of gross receipts to more than 55 percent by 1910. Also in 1910, long-overdue government regulation of the express industry began with passage of the Mann-Elkins Act, which made express companies common carriers subject to the scrutiny of the Interstate Commerce Commission (ICC). In 1912, New York express company drivers and their helpers went on strike for higher wages and fewer working hours (they were underpaid and overworked, even in an era of low pay and long hours), exciting highly unfavorable press and public reaction. In 1913, the U.S. Post Office again expanded parcel delivery services at reduced rates, while the ICC set express rates that the industry feared were prohibitively low.

International Growth Between the Wars

When George C. Taylor, a longtime American Express employee, was elected the company's fourth president after Fargo's retirement in 1914, the end of the laissez-faire express industry was in sight. Taylor's first actions, to expand foreign remittance operations and to officially inaugurate travel services by opening a travel department in 1915, saved the company when its domestic express division was nationalized in 1918 and became part of the American Railway Express Co. as a wartime measure. Another of Taylor's accomplishments was to establish the American Express Co. This wholly owned subsidiary was created in 1919 primarily to expand international banking operations (which had been conducted sporadically through foreign remittance offices since 1904). Although American Express was slow to gain a foothold in Europe, its international banking operations flourished in Asia during the 1920s and 1930s, especially in Hong Kong and Shanghai.

In the late 1920s, American Express again changed hands. The express industry was targeted for takeovers during this period because most express companies had been organized prior to antitrust legislation, raising the possibility of their exemption from antitrust regulations. American Express was especially attractive because its net income had more than doubled in the six years ending in 1928. In 1927 Albert H. Wiggin, chairman of the Chase National Bank, started buying American Express stock through dummies. By July, Wiggin had acquired two seats on the board and 42 percent of the stock, at a bargain price. In 1929, Chase Securities Corp., an affiliate of Chase National Bank, acquired control of American Express in a stock exchange and Wiggin was elected first chairman of the American Express board.

In May 1930 Chase National merged with the giant Equitable Trust Co. to become the largest bank in the world. John D. Rockefeller supplanted Wiggin as largest shareholder and Winthrop W. Aldrich, Rockefeller's brother-in-law, became chairman of both the Chase Securities and the American Express boards.

This was a difficult time for American Express management, headed by Frederick P. Small (who became president on Taylor's death in 1923). Not only were the directors preoccupied with their power struggles, but the financial climate was steadily worsening. Then the Great Depression hit. Between 1930 and 1932, roughly a third of all American banks failed. In early 1933, President Franklin D. Roosevelt announced a national bank holiday to allow banks to recover from the panic. The bank holiday brought commerce to a virtual standstill. During this period American Express, since it was not a bank and thus not required to close, enjoyed a tremendous advantage: it remained open and redeemed traveler's checks, providing the only financial services available to individuals and merchants while the nation's assets were frozen. The traveler's check business ultimately allowed American Express to remain profitable throughout the Depression and World War II.

The Card Revolution of the 1950s

In 1944 Ralph T. Reed replaced Small as president. Under Reed's management, the late 1940s and the 1950s were a period of expansion, primarily in the booming travel industry. Within seven years the number of American Express offices increased by 400 percent and international operations surpassed their prewar level.

When Diners Club introduced the first credit card in the mid-1950s, American Express executives proposed investigating this new line of business. Reed, who thought the company should improve existing business and feared a credit card would threaten its traveler's check business, opposed the proposal. In 1958, Reed reversed himself and the American Express travel-and-entertainment card (the American Express green card) was introduced virtually overnight. The company had 250,000 to 300,000 applications for cards on hand the day the card went on the market, and 500,000 cardmembers within three months. Introduction of the green card began an era of unprecedented growth: earnings rose from $8.4 million in 1959 to $85 million in 1970.

Diversification in the 1960s

A new era of management began when Howard L. Clark was elected president and CEO on April 26, 1960. Clark transformed American Express from a renowned but fairly small company to a corporate giant with diverse interests. Clark's goal was to establish a balanced earnings base dependent on multiple sources and thus more resistant to economic fluctuations. His strategy was to expand American Express's business within its areas of expertise—travel and financial services.

However, before Clark could put his plan in operation, the company had to be streamlined and modernized. Management had long been centralized and the chain of command obscure. Clark gave each division room to innovate and made each directly responsible for its own performance. Also, the company had no uniform identity. The now famous "blue box" logo was developed at Clark's direction and adopted by all the divisions.

Next, the company's accounting system had to be overhauled, since the system then in place was obsolete and unable to handle the high volume of charge card transactions. Moreover, the travel division (the glue that held the various divisions together and gave the company its identity) had to improve its profitability. By the time the jet airline industry made an impact on commercial travel, American Express was ready.

Also, the charge card had yet to show a profit, in large part because American Express had no experience dealing directly with merchants and consumers or with credit controls. Clark brought in George Waters, formerly of IBM and the Colonial Stores supermarket chain, to put the charge card division on a sounder footing. Waters used two simple strategies: first, he raised the card fee and merchant discount; next, he persuaded merchants to think of American Express as their marketing partner by dedicating .05 percent of gross sales to retail advertising. By the end of 1962 more than 900,000 cards had been issued, and by the end of 1963 the card division had shown a profit.

Finally, marginal operations had to be divested. Ridding the company of one subsidiary, American Express Field Warehousing Co., proved to be a nightmare. When the field warehousing division was sold to Lawrence Warehouse Co. in 1963, Clark withheld the two most profitable accounts, Allied Crude Vegetable Oil Refining Co. and Freezer House (both owned by Anthony "Tino" De Angelis), pending an investigation of other field warehousing opportunities. Late that year, Clark decided to sell the two accounts to Lawrence Warehouse. An independent audit conducted prior to closing revealed that about 800 million tons of vegetable oil was missing. Holders of some $150 million in security interests and notes (some forged by De Angelis) were understandably upset. The American Express board realized the company's reputation was at stake and quickly issued a statement to the effect that American Express assumed moral responsibility for the losses caused by its subsidiary. American Express's assurances did little to appease those defrauded. The "salad oil swindle," as it was dubbed by the press, involved American Express in complex and protracted litigation that was settled in 1965 (although a final case lingered until 1970) at a cost to American Express of $60 million, excluding attorneys' fees.

With the salad oil episode behind it and reorganization of the divisions completed, the late 1960s and early 1970s were good years for American Express. Consolidated net income grew steadily, and Clark concentrated on expanding the company's financial services. In 1966, American Express acquired W.H. Morton & Co., an investment banking house with an excellent reputation for underwriting municipal and government bonds. Two years later, American Express made the most important purchase yet in its diversification strategy: the Fireman's Fund Insurance Company, one of the largest property and casualty insurers in the nation.

Even the international monetary crisis of 1971, culminating in the devaluation of the dollar and the suspension of almost all dollar transactions, did not phase American Express. The company honored its traveler's checks at the exchange rate posted before trading was suspended and its card continued to be accepted internationally. American Express extended emergency funds to thousands of tourists caught short abroad, and its international banking subsidiary advised corporate clients on how to protect their foreign assets and import-export payments during the crisis.

During the late 1970s, however, American Express seemed to lose its direction, and its integrity and soundness were challenged on many fronts. In 1975, the *Washington Post* suggested that American Express was successful only because it was not regulated as banks and other financial institutions were. When Visa and MasterCard started competing in the traveler's check market, Citicorp, a major issuer of bank credit cards, took out a full-page advertisement accusing American Express of false and deceptive advertising of its traveler's checks. American Express also received unfavorable publicity when four acquisition attempts in a row failed.

The last of these attempts, a bid for the McGraw-Hill Publishing Co. in 1979, produced the worst repercussions. Roger Morley (who had replaced James D. Robinson III to become American Express's tenth president when Clark resigned in 1977 and Robinson became chairman and CEO) was a member of the McGraw-Hill board at the time. After American Express bid for the publisher, McGraw-Hill sued the company and Morley, accusing them of breach of trust and corporate immorality.

But in 1981 American Express made the big acquisition it had been looking for when it bought Shearson Loeb Rhoades Inc., one of the nation's leading brokerage houses, which became an independently operated subsidiary. Shearson in short order acquired Robinson-Humphrey, an Atlanta-based brokerage firm; Foster & Marshall, a well-respected securities firm; and Balcor, Inc., the largest real estate syndicator in the United States.

In 1982, American Express was reorganized under a holding company called American Express Corp.; its travel services became a wholly owned subsidiary, American Express Travel Related Services.

Sanford I. Weill, formerly of Shearson Loeb Rhoades Inc., was elected the 12th president of American Express in early 1983. Under Weill, American Express continued to expand. That same year, American Express acquired Ayco Corp., a financial counseling firm, and in 1984 it bought Allegheny Corporation's principal subsidiary, the financial planning company Investors Diversified Services, Inc. (IDS). Also in 1984, Shearson acquired Lehman Bros. Kuhn Loeb, one of the most respected Wall Street brokerage firms, to form Shearson Lehman Brothers Holdings Inc.

In 1985 American Express announced that it would spin off Fireman's Fund Insurance Company, the property and casualty insurer it had purchased in 1968. Stiff competition in the insurance industry during the early 1980s had led to price wars, and the subsidiary's profits had been declining since 1983. In addition, in 1983 and 1984, American Express had to spend $430 million strengthening Fireman's reserves. The first public offering of Fireman's Fund stock was made in October 1985; by December 1987, American Express retained only 31 percent of the company. In 1988 its holding was reduced to 20 percent and American Express formally exited the insurance business.

Also in 1985 the American Express International Banking Corp., established in 1919 to help American Express expand internationally, became simply American Express Bank, Ltd. In the mid-1990s, American Express was a thoroughly international company; its bank, with a presence in more than 40 countries, completed the range of financial services the company offered, focusing on private banking for wealthy individuals.

Credit Card Wars: 1980s–90s

The year 1987 was a dramatic—and difficult—one at most financial companies, and American Express was no exception. The stock market crash in October shook Shearson Lehman, and fears about Third World debt forced American Express Bank to add nearly $1 billion to its loan-loss reserves. But American Express's core business, Travel Related Services, continued to prosper. That year it introduced its Optima Card, American Express's first credit card (regular American Express cards are charge cards; the balance must be paid in full each month). By late 1989, Optima had garnered some 2.5 million members.

In the 1980s, as competition in the card industry intensified, American Express pursued both an increased customer and merchant base. At the beginning of the decade, American Express had ten million cardmembers who had roughly 400,000 places to use their cards. By the end of the decade those numbers had grown to 33 million cardholders around the world whose cards were accepted at 2.7 million places. But sheer size was not the objective: American Express emphatically positioned its services as "premium"—its card cost much more than credit cards, like Visa and MasterCard, offered by banks, and it charged merchants a higher percentage of the bills charged to the card than its competitors did. These higher fees to merchants were warranted, the company told them, by the business its generally high-income cardmembers generated; the higher card dues bought better services. Nevertheless, American Express ran into heavy competition, especially abroad, where its greatest hopes for expansion lay.

At the beginning of 1988, Shearson made another dramatic acquisition when it bought E.F. Hutton and became Shearson Lehman Hutton. Such growth in so short a time added up to a second year of decreased earnings—a five percent drop on top of 1987's 70 percent drop. At the end of 1989 Shearson was still struggling to cut costs and raise profits. American Express announced plans, in December 1989, to pump an additional $900 million into its ailing subsidiary. The recapitalization included $350 million of American Express's own money. The rest was to come from notes.

American Express toppled from its perch as the preeminent charge card due to a number of serious problems in the early 1990s. The flagship charge card suffered fading customer loyalty, intense competition from lower-priced bank cards, and loss of service establishments accepting the card because of high fees to the merchants. Some observers blamed advertising for a public relations fiasco that damaged the company's image. But the company's 1991 revelation that its Optima revolving credit card—which analysts and investors had previously regarded as one of American Express's biggest successes—lost $300 million in write-offs, also eroded its credibility. At the same time, the Travel Related Services unit was battered by competition from no-fee bank cards and debit cards. As a recession deepened, merchants dropped the high-fee American Express card in droves. Profits plummeted from $1.16 billion in 1989 to $461 million in 1992.

In 1993, Harvey Golub advanced to American Express's chief executive office upon the resignation of Robinson, who had served in that capacity since 1977. He instituted several recovery strategies at the firm, including retrenchment to core businesses, new product launches, cost-cutting, and brand-building.

Part of American Express's recovery strategy involved aggressive brand promotion, launching what were derisively called ''guerrilla'' or ''ambush'' marketing campaigns. In response to a Visa advertising campaign tied to the 1988 Olympic Games, American Express engaged in a campaign in which it ran television and space ads featuring those cities where the Olympics were held, trying to affiliate itself with the games without directly sponsoring them. American Express also launched a legal battle with Visa, claiming that the rival's ''But they don't take American Express'' commercials implied broader exclusivity than existed. Visa retorted that its ad claims were valid, and that American Express was simply using legal maneuvers, public relations, and newspaper ads to blunt its advertising effectiveness. Early in 1994, Gary Levin, of *Advertising Age,* declared that ''neither is entirely blameless, and both are unlikely to surrender.'' In 1994, American Express's promotional efforts were extended internationally, with a global advertising campaign targeting Italy, Germany, Japan, and the United Kingdom. The company planned to take 60 new ads to 30 countries around the world.

American Express's new products included Cheques for Two, introduced in 1992; a Senior Member card featuring special services and benefits; and a corporate purchasing card. American Express hoped to capture a significant share of the prospective $300 billion market segment, only one percent of which had been put on plastic by 1994. In 1993, American Express won the federal government's travel and transportation payment system contract—the largest corporate card account in the world. Some industry analysts interpreted the introduction of these new products as a sign of ''renewed vigor'' at American Express.

Golub aimed to cut $1 billion in costs by 1995, and planned to use those savings to finance the rate cutting necessary to attract the nearly 200,000 new merchant locations he expected to sign up. He also made several divestments that brought funds to the company and helped refocus on core businesses. Early in 1993, American Express sold its Shearson brokerage operations to Primerica Corp.'s Smith Barney, Inc. for $859 million in cash and about $275 million in Primerica stock. American Express netted $1.1 billion on the 1993 sale of 32 million shares of First Data Corp. to the public. In January 1994, American Express announced that it would contribute over $1 billion to Lehman Brothers, then spin the subsidiary off to shareholders. The capital injection enabled Lehman Brothers to sustain an ''A'' credit rating as an independent venture.

Credit Card Management magazine named American Express its ''1993 Turnaround of the Year,'' praising Golub's recovery plan. That year, American Express's worldwide charge volume increased 5.5 percent to $117.5 billion, discount revenues from merchants increased 3.2 percent, and merchant locations grew 4.5 percent. American Express's net income made a dramatic comeback as well, tripling from $461 million to $1.48 billion.

One of Golub's main objectives was to expand American Express's foreign operations, to the point where international revenues accounted for 50 percent of the company's total earnings. In 1997 American Express signed ten new agreements with overseas partners and introduced 20 new card products into foreign markets, including cobranded corporate cards with France's Credit Lyonnais and Qantas Airlines in Australia. Although disturbances in the Asian economy during this period caused American Express to fall far short of its desired annual international growth rate of 25–30 percent, the company continued to carve a niche in developing foreign markets. In early 1999 it formed a branch of American Express Financial Advisors in Japan, and in 2000 it established a strategic position in the burgeoning Chinese economy by opening a headquarters in Beijing.

American Express's range of financial services demonstrated consistent growth throughout the late 1990s. American Express Financial Advisors enjoyed particularly strong performances, with total client assets climbing from $182 billion in 1997, to $212 billion in 1998, to $262.5 billion in 1999. In 1996 the company launched American Express Financial Direct, which offered financial products directly to its customers. American Express Bank also saw gains in its overall client holdings during this period, with an increase from $6 billion in 1997 to $9 billion in 1999.

The Internet revolution provided American Express with the opportunity to explore new avenues for its banking and travel interests. In January 1995 the company launched ExpressNet, a web site dedicated to online cardmember and travel services. In April 1996 it formed American Express Travel on the Web, and later that year it created InvestDirect, an extensive online securities trading service. In 1997, InvestDirect was recognized by *Financial Service ONLINE Magazine* as the year's most innovative online brokerage. That same year, a new member web site gave American Express cardholders complete access to their accounts online.

With increased electronic traffic came concerns over Internet security and privacy. In July 1995 American Express joined forces with four leading technology firms to develop a means of ensuring secure online business transactions, through sophisticated encryption codes and a digital signature authentication system. In February 1996 American Express signed a licensing agreement with Microsoft to develop a software that employed secure electronic transactions (SET) protocol, and in 1997 the company partnered with Hewlett-Packard to create ExpressVault, which combined Hewlett-Packard's security and computing expertise with the American Express payment processing network.

The battle over the credit and charge card market intensified in 1998, when the federal government filed an antitrust lawsuit against Visa and MasterCard. The Justice Department's findings focused on the competitors' policy of prohibiting member banks from issuing cards of rival companies, most notably American Express and Discover. Charging that this practice was anticompetitive, the Justice Department accused Visa and MasterCard of discouraging product innovation and ultimately hurting consumers.

Another intriguing development in the card wars came in September 1999, when American Express launched Blue, the first "smart card" offered in the United States. Embedded with a computer chip in addition to the traditional magnetic strip, Blue made it possible for consumers to consolidate their credit and debit information in a single card. As more and more computer manufacturers began including smart card "readers" as standard features on personal computers by decade's end, Blue's design made it ideal for e-commerce. While it remained to be seen whether smart cards would become the industry standard, by the end of 2000 there were approximately four million Blue cardholders. In addition, Visa launched its own smart card during the 2000 Olympics, ensuring that the new market would be competitive.

By the year 2000 American Express had climbed back into a position of leadership within the industry, with record net earnings throughout the late 1990s and the emergence of an extensive line of new products and services. The company continued its pursuit of a strong e-commerce presence with the introduction of a number of web sites in 1999 and 2000, including American Express Brokerage, Express B@nking, and American Express Mortgage. In 2000 the company joined the Worldwide E-commerce Fraud Protection Network, a coalition dedicated to guaranteeing the security of online transactions, and subsequently building consumer confidence in the Internet as a preferred place to shop. Although Visa and MasterCard still controlled 75 percent of the overall card market in 2000, innovations in the function of the traditional credit card put American Express in a position to remain very competitive in the 21st century.

Principal Subsidiaries

American Express Travel Related Services; American Express Financial Advisors, Inc.; American Express Bank, Ltd.; American Express Bank S.A. (France); American Express Bank International; American Express Centurion Bank; American Express Bank GMBH (Germany); American Express Bank (Luxembourg) S.A.; American Express Bank (Switzerland) S.A.; American Express Bank (Uruguay) S.A.; Banco Inter American Express (Brazil; 49%); Amex International Trust (Cayman) Ltd. (Cayman Islands); Egyptian American Bank (Egypt; 40%).

Principal Operating Units

Global Corporate Services; Global Financial Services; Global Establishment Services and Traveler's Cheques; U.S. Consumer and Small Business Services.

Principal Competitors

Carlson Wagonlit Travel; Japan Travel Bureau, Inc.; Visa International.

Further Reading

Burrough, Bryan, *Vendetta: American Express and the Smearing of Edmond Safra,* New York: HarperCollins, 1992.

Carrington, Tim, *The Year They Sold Wall Street,* Boston: Houghton Mifflin, 1985.

Friedman, Jon, *House of Cards: Inside the Troubled Empire of American Express,* New York: Putnam, 1992.

Grossman, Peter Z., *American Express: The Unofficial History of the People Who Built the Great Financial Empire,* New York: Crown, 1987.

Hatch, Alden, *American Express: A Century of Service,* Garden City, N.Y.: Doubleday, 1950.

O'Brien, Timothy, "Foreign Economic Warning Hurts American Express," *New York Times,* August 7, 1998.

Promises to Pay, New York: American Express Company, 1977.

Reed, Ralph Thomas, *American Express: Its Origin and Growth,* New York: Newcomen Society in North America, 1952.

Wahl, Melissa, "Justice Department Says Lack of Credit Card Competition Stifles Innovation," *Chicago Tribune,* July 17, 2000.

—April Dougal Gasbarre
—updated by Stephen Meyer

American Water Works Company, Inc.

1025 Laurel Oak Road
Voorhees, New Jersey 08043
U.S.A.
Telephone: (856) 346-8200
Fax: (856) 346-8360
Web site: http://www.amwater.com

Public Company
Incorporated: 1936
Employees: 4,970
Sales: $1.26 billion (1999)
Stock Exchanges: New York
Ticker Symbol: AWK
NAIC: 22131 Water Supply and Irrigation Systems (pt); 22132 Sewage Treatment Facilities

American Water Works Company, Inc. is the largest investor-owned water supply company in the United States. With 25 utility subsidiaries operating in 23 states, the massive utility company services more than 1,000 communities nationwide and has served more than ten million customers through its 300 water production facilities. Bringing water to residential, commercial, industrial, and public clients, American Water Works continues to broaden both the size and scope of its business through acquisitions and construction projects to ensure its viability in the 21st century and beyond.

Collision of Two Forces: The 1930s to 1947

John H. Ware, Jr., was an eighth grade dropout and self-made millionaire who, during the 1930s, had begun acquiring small U.S. water utilities. While much of the country was still struggling from the devastation of the Great Depression, Ware had managed to amass a small fortune. He was particularly interested in one of President Franklin D. Roosevelt's New Deal policies, the Public Utility Holding Act of 1935, which required that multilayered holding companies owning or operating utilities be broken up into smaller, independent companies. Among those targeted was the American Water Works & Electric Company, a prime example of the type of company the 1935 law was intended to abolish. Originally founded in 1886 as the American Water Works and Guarantee Company, the company was renamed in 1917 as American Water Works & Electric and owned several utility operating companies in western Pennsylvania, West Virginia, Maryland, and Virginia, and about 80 local water companies in the eastern, southern, and Midwestern states.

Ware was determined to add the water utility assets of American Water Works & Electric to his expanding empire. The company unsuccessfully lobbied the Roosevelt administration to fight the Public Utility Holding Act of 1935, but the act was passed by Congress and signed into law. American Water Works and Guarantee then joined with the North American Company, another huge public utility holding company, in an action before the U.S. Supreme Court to have the law declared unconstitutional. The suit notwithstanding, American Water Works & Electric was the first utility holding company to file a plan of reorganization with the federal government, as the law required. As it was approved in 1937, the plan called for a simple reorganization to reduce its layers and required the company to divest itself of real estate holdings in California. The reorganization was to cost about $60 million and was viewed as a milestone when approved by the U.S. Securities and Exchange Commission, because it demonstrated that the federal regulatory agency could act benevolently when utility holding companies cooperated.

Despite complying with the restructuring and divestment plan, the company, newly renamed American Water Works Company, Inc., bitterly fought in the courts for the next nine years. The end came in 1946 when the Supreme Court found that the 11-year-old Public Utility Holding Act Law was, indeed, constitutional. The same year, American Water Works was forced to revise its reorganization plan when it realized that its inability to pay stock dividends for the previous eight years would make the investment community reluctant to put its money into the company. The reorganization plan had the company selling its cash cow, its water works business, to finance the restructuring. The company's management thought that its existing shareholders would bid on the company's stock through sealed bids and nothing would change; they also

Company Perspectives:

The core business of American Water Works Company, Inc. is the ownership of common stock of utility companies providing water service. The combination of American Water Works with its subsidiaries constitutes the American Water System—a system that has functioned well for over 50 years. Each subsidiary functions independently, yet shares in the benefits of size and identity afforded by the American Water System.

expected its stock to be sold at $10 or more a share in the sealed bidding process.

Ware, meanwhile, had been waiting in the wings and raising funds. He had not only pursued his interest in buying water companies, but had invested in a series of successful smaller ventures, including several electrical contracting companies, and had been able to raise $13 million in capital. Although an unknown entity to American Water Works' managers, Ware submitted the only bid for the company, at $8 per share. He invested the entire $13 million and won a company with assets of $183 million, though some of the company's water works facilities and pipelines were broken down and decrepit. The once mighty holding company had become an aging vestige of a bygone era; American Water Works, with operating revenues of $24 million for the year, joined Ware's burgeoning resources with little fanfare in 1947.

In New Hands: 1948 Through the 1960s

The previous managers at American Water Works left with Ware's purchase of the company, and he brought in his own management team, including Lawrence T. (Bill) Reinicker and John J. (Jack) Barr. Reinicker was skilled as an operations manager, and Barr was Ware's financial expert. Both had joined Ware in his earlier ventures in the late 1930s and had been named vice-presidents. The company Ware, Reinicker, and Barr took over included electrical utilities, but Ware was primarily interested in the water utility operating units. He bid on the entire company to gain a 51 percent ownership share when his financial advisers warned that his $13 million in cash would not be enough to buy the company or its water works assets outright, and he consolidated his ownership in the ensuing years. Within a few years Ware spun off the electrical power business.

The company moved six times in the eight years between 1942 and 1950, to various office buildings in New York City, in Camden, New Jersey, and back to New York City, before finally moving to new headquarters at Three Penn Center in Philadelphia in 1955, where it remained for the next 21 years.

Ware bought and sold smaller water companies at a fast pace during his first few years of owning American Water Works Company. Where cities wanted to own and operate their own water systems, he divested, sometimes after bitter feuds; where municipal utility operations were too small to grow or to remain afloat on their own, he acquired them, and, where new projects were needed, Ware stepped in with his company's deep financial pockets to establish viable water systems.

Ware scored a major coup in 1948 when he contracted to build a dam and reservoir on the Occoquan River in Alexandria, Virginia. The huge project also called for pumping and treatment stations, but before the ink was dry American Water Works found itself in another bitterly contested court fight. In a move proving all too common, the city wanted to acquire the Alexandria water company and operate it as a community-owned utility. This spurred the court actions, which ended with Ware's loss of the Alexandria system after a protracted legal battle. Despite the legal wrangles, American Water Works, with its economy of scale and Ware's inimitable drive, was able to afford the costly improvements and maintenance of water systems taxed by the growing demands of development in the United States' boom years.

In the executive offices, Bill Reinicker had been named president in 1953 and vice-chairman in 1954; he retired at the age of 61 in 1955. When Reinicker became vice-chairman, Jack Barr was named president of the company and effectively became its CEO and COO, while Ware continued as chairman. Barr oversaw the company's growth through the turbulence of the 1960s, a period when American Water Works continued its acquisitions of smaller companies while spending huge amounts of money to renovate and build new water treatment, pumping, and storage facilities. It was in 1963 that American Water Works and Ware's company, Northeastern Water Company, officially merged into one nationwide utility giant. The new company's size and clout helped make possible one of its largest acquisitions, that of International Utilities (later known as UI International), another sizable water utility operating company.

The 1970s and 1980s

The dawn of the 1970s brought a new era of environmental awareness and, along with it, increasing environmental legislation. In 1975 Barr retired and was succeeded as president by John A. Gubanich. Ware, too, retired as chairman of the company and his son, John H. Ware III, became chairman. Gubanich, former treasurer of the company, was given credit for greatly increasing the company's profit throughout the decade. During his eight-year term as president of the company, Gubanich continued consolidating the company's smaller water companies, installing a uniform and centralized management system and merging many of the smaller companies into larger, regional operations. By the end of Gubanich's presidential term, American Water Works Company had only 33 operating units, a drastic reduction from the 151 companies the company had owned or acquired since its founding.

The stagnant growth and high inflation of the late 1970s left the company strapped for cash. To meet the challenge, Gubanich ushered in a series of cost-cutting moves that included merging several operating units and relocating, in 1976, the corporation's headquarters from Philadelphia to Voorhees, New Jersey. Gubanich also worked to broaden the American Water Works board to include outside directors, bringing in a fresh perspective and business acumen previously lacking. One of these new directors was Philadelphia banker Sam Ballam, who became the first outside chief executive of the company in 1984 when he replaced the retiring John Ware III as chairman of the board. At the same time, Gubanich was succeeded by James V. LaFrankie as president of the company. LaFrankie had been

Key Dates:

1886: American Water Works and Guarantee Company is founded.
1917: The company is renamed American Water Works & Electric Company.
1935: The Public Utility Holding Act Law is passed.
1936: The company is incorporated and newly named American Water Works Company, Inc.
1946: The U.S. Supreme Court rules that the Public Utility Holding Act Law is constitutional.
1947: American Water Works is acquired by John H. Ware, Jr.
1963: American Water Works merges with Northeastern Water Company.
1976: Corporation headquarters relocates from Philadelphia to Voorhees, New Jersey.
1993: A joint venture with the United Kingdom's Anglian Water Plc forms AmericanAnglian Environmental Technologies.
1996: The company's Pennsylvania unit purchases the water holdings of Pennsylvania Gas and Water Company for $409 million, the industry's largest asset acquisition.
1998: The company surpasses the billion dollar mark, with operating revenues of $1.02 billion.

with American Water Works Company almost from the day John Ware bought it, and he rose through the ranks of various operating units. LaFrankie was the first president of the company from the operations side since Bill Reinicker, and he continued the Herculean task of consolidating the company's dozens of operating units.

Marilyn Ware Lewis, daughter of John Ware III and granddaughter of John Ware, Jr., was named chairman of American Water Works Company, Inc. in 1987. In a 1989 interview with the *Lancaster (Pennsylvania) New Era,* she recalled that when she was a little girl her grandfather had told her the availability of water would be one of the most significant issues faced by her generation. Lewis was convinced at an early age that water was the single most essential commodity in a household and she, like her grandfather, had come to believe a company that efficiently treated and supplied clean drinking water to its customers would be a very profitable enterprise. She was right: as the 1980s came to a close American Water Works Company's utility subsidiaries crisscrossed the country. By 1989 operating revenues had reached $528 million, with the company having sold more than 211 million gallons of water to 1.5 million customers in the residential, commercial, industrial, and public sectors.

A Veritable Giant: 1990–97

The last decade of the 20th century brought further expansion for American Water Works in the Midwest, as well as on both the East and West Coasts. The earliest years, 1990 and 1991, saw unprecedented growth, with operating revenues climbing from $573 million to $636 million and income leaping 30 percent to $74 million. Much of the increase in revenue and income came from the company's widening scope within the wastewater treatment sector, led by new President and CEO George W. Johnstone, who had been with the company for 25 years. A new water carbon regeneration plant was in operation in Columbus, Ohio, supplying filtered water to other subsidiaries as well as nonaffiliated companies; this was followed by a joint venture in 1993 with the United Kingdom's Anglian Water Plc to form AmericanAnglian Environmental Technologies (AAET), as an advisor to wastewater treatment plants offering both technical and financial aid. Other acquisitions during the year included water utility companies in Indiana, Michigan, Missouri, and Ohio.

In addition to buying utility holdings throughout the United States, American Water Works maintained its edge by extensive renovations to its subsidiaries as well as undertaking massive building projects. One such plan was the $200 million Tri-County Water Supply Project to augment the existing New Jersey water supply by tapping into the Delaware River; another included adding 26 miles of new pipeline and a wastewater treatment plant to its West Virginia utility. By 1995 the company's expansion projects were forging ahead to the tune of more than $331 million invested for that year alone and operating revenues at year end were a robust $803 million. In addition, American Water Works executives were delighted when the company was included in Standard & Poor's well-known MidCap 400 Index.

In 1996 the New Jersey/Delaware River project was completed and put into use while the company's Pennsylvania unit executed the industry's largest asset acquisition, for $409 million, to buy Pennsylvania Gas and Water Company's water holdings, supplying water to Scranton, Wilkes-Barre, and the surrounding areas. American Water Works Company's utility assets, spread over 21 states, were now worth more than $3.4 billion, and operating revenues had climbed to $895 million. The next year, 1997, marked the end of an era as John Ware III passed away and the company's president and CEO, George W. Johnstone, retired after more than three decades of service. Taking the helm as CEO was J. James Barr, who had been CFO since the beginning of the decade, and who had held various executive positions in the interim. Marilyn Ware Lewis continued as chairman of the board.

Plans for the Future: 1998 Onward

A new kind of history began in 1998 when American Water Works broke the billion dollar mark with operating revenues of $1.02 billion. The United States' largest regulated water utility business was not content to rest on its laurels; during the last two years of the century came several sizable acquisitions, including National Enterprises Inc. (for $458 million), SJW Corp. ($390 million), and the water and wastewater assets of Citizens Utilities Company ($745 million). The company's joint venture with Anglian Water Plc, however, had not lived up to expectations. In an effort to salvage the operation, American Water Works bought out Anglian's interest and restructured AAET into a new company. Operating revenues for 1999 surpassed $1.26 billion, while stock performance ranged from a low of $17 to a high of more than $34 per share.

Whereas American Water Works Company's predecessor was broken up by the Public Utilities Act of 1935 because of its size and stranglehold on the market, the younger behemoth followed in the footsteps of its elder. Although regulated and publicly owned, American Water Works certainly dominated its market, operating two dozen subsidiaries throughout the United States in 23 states, producing some 345 billion gallons of water in 1999 to serve more than ten million customers. The company's weakness, however, was none other than its client base, which had proven fickle throughout its colorful history. As had happened time and again, communities large and small often decided to obtain and supply their own water; these demands were generally settled in court. American Water Works had had more than its share of legal skirmishes, and to keep its customers happy, had invested millions of dollars to maintain what it touted as the best water utilities and treatment plants in the nation. With the EPA projecting upgrades and maintenance of the nation's more than 50,000 water systems costing upward of $1.35 billion during the next two decades, American Water Works was already way ahead in the game. In 2000 and beyond, the company's continued prosperity was a relatively safe bet, and customer service was given a higher priority with plans for a new national service facility to open in Alton, Illinois, in 2001.

Principal Subsidiaries

American Commonwealth Management Services Company; Arizona-American Water Company; California-American Water Company; Connecticut-American Water Company; Hampton Water Works Company; Hawaii-American Water Company; Illinois-American Water Company; Indiana-American Water Company; Iowa-American Water Company; Kentucky-American Water Company; Long Island-American Water Company; Maryland-American Water Company; Massachusetts-American Water Company; Michigan-American Water Company; New Jersey-American Water Company; New Mexico-American Water Company; New York-American Water Company; Ohio-American Water Company; Pennsylvania-American Water Company; St. Louis County Water Company and Missouri-American Water Company; Salisbury Water Supply Company; Tennessee-American Water Company; Virginia-American Water Company; West Virginia-American Water Company.

Principal Competitors

Philadelphia Suburban Corporation; Suez Lyonnaise des Eaux; United Water Resources Inc.; Vivendi.

Further Reading

Cross, Gilbert, *A Dynasty of Water: The Story of The American Water Works Company,* Voorhees, N.J.: American Water Works Company, 1991.

Jaffe, Thomas, ''Ring of Bright Water,'' *Forbes,* November 2, 1987, p. 247.

Sullivan, Allanna, ''American Water Agrees to Acquire Utility for Stock,'' *Wall Street Journal,* October 14, 1998, p. B2.

——, ''American Water Works Navigates Acquisition Course—Utility Benefits from New Federal Rules to Buy and Fix Ailing Systems,'' *Wall Street Journal,* December 7, 1998, p. B10.

Welsh, Jonathan, ''Deal Reached to Buy Firm's Water Assets,'' *Wall Street Journal,* October 19, 1999, p. C22.

—Bruce Vernyi
—updated by Nelson Rhodes

Applied Micro Circuits Corporation

6290 Sequence Drive
San Diego, California 92121
U.S.A.
Telephone: (858) 450-9333
Fax: (858) 535-6500
Web site: http://www.amcc.com

Public Company
Incorporated: 1979
Employees: 920
Sales: $172.4 million (2000)
Stock Exchanges: NASDAQ
Ticker Symbol: AMCC
NAIC: 334413 Semiconductor and Related Device Manufacturing

Originally established to provide integrated circuits (ICs) to the military, Applied Micro Circuits Corporation (AMCC) has become a leading provider of silicon solutions for high-speed voice and data fiber-optic networks in the 1990s. Following AMCC's initial public offering (IPO) in 1997, the company's market capitalization rose to some $13 billion by 2000. That enabled the company to acquire several companies in 1999 and 2000, which would allow AMCC to offer a complete range of silicon IC solutions for fiber-optic networks. The company's largest acquisition involved MMC Networks Inc., which it acquired in 2000 for $4.5 billion.

Diversifying into Nonmilitary Markets: 1980s

AMCC was founded in California in 1979 as a private company to produce ASICs (application specific integrated circuits)—also known as chips or semiconductors—primarily for the military market. In the early 1980s sales to the military accounted for 70 percent of AMCC's revenue. Over the next several years the company would diversify, so that by 1987 approximately 65 percent of its chips went to nonmilitary markets.

In 1982 Roger Smullen, one of the cofounders of National Semiconductor Corporation in 1967, was named chairman of the board of AMCC. He served as CEO from April 1983 to April 1987 and would remain chairman until August 31, 2000, when he was named vice-chairman. Under Smullen's leadership AMCC would diversify and produce semicustom logic chips for engineering workstations. AMCC's chips were primarily designed for specific customer applications and were not standard production chips that could be used by several different customers. AMCC was producing chips for the aerospace, industrial, and automotive chip markets. In many cases, AMCC was the only source for particular chips.

During the mid-1980s, when most chip makers were struggling, AMCC had 11 straight profitable quarters. Sales for fiscal 1986 ending March 31 were $20.3 million. One analyst called AMCC ''a model start up.'' In addition to its profitability, AMCC had technical agreements with nine companies that provided it with an inflow of technology. The companies also provided AMCC with a built-in customer base. Then in fiscal 1987 ending March 31, AMCC's sales dropped to $18 million. It was the first time in three years the company posted a net loss.

In July 1987 Al Martinez joined AMCC as president and CEO. He was formerly vice-president of the LSI Products Division at TRW Inc. His previous experience included 14 years with Motorola's semiconductor division. At the time Martinez joined AMCC, the company was in the process of moving to its new Pacific Corporate Center, expanding its total space from 43,000 to 120,000 square feet. The move would triple the company's manufacturing space, all of which was located in San Diego.

Introducing Products for Data Communications: 1990–97

During the early 1990s AMCC had two failed attempts to go public. It was a time when the entire semiconductor industry was in a slump. In 1996 AMCC overhauled its top management. David Rickey, who was AMCC's vice-president of operations from August 1993 to May 1995, was brought back as the new president and CEO. Rickey had left the company in 1995 to serve as vice-president of operations for semiconductor manufacturer NexGen Inc. NexGen was subsequently acquired by Advanced

Company Perspectives:

In the face of unprecedented demand, capacity expansion and industry activity, AMCC has continued to deliver on time, on target and on budget. In fact, our lead times have improved over the past several years. This ability to deliver on our promises has earned us the highest level of credibility—as well as several awards—from customers, investors and the industry as a whole.

Micro Devices. Rickey's mission was to return the company to profitability, provide strategic focus, revitalize product development, and position AMCC for a successful public offering.

AMCC returned to profitability in fiscal 1997 ending March 31. The company reported net income of $6.3 million on revenue of $57.5 million, compared with a net loss of $3.7 million on revenue of $50.3 million in fiscal 1996. The company's good results enabled it to embark on a two-phase capital investment program. Over the next three years AMCC planned to invest $70 million to expand manufacturing capacity and advance its process technology. The first phase, to be completed by the end of calendar 1997, involved a $15 million investment to retool its bipolar wafer fabrication plant to handle new processes. The retooling was expected to enable the facility to produce network and interface chips with transmission speeds up to ten gigabits per second.

Phase 2 of the program would require additional financing. AMCC went public in November 1997 with an initial public offering (IPO). Approximately 5.5 million shares were offered at $8 a share. Of those, about 2.7 million were sold by the company and 2.8 million by stockholders.

In recent years the company had shifted its focus from producing ASICs to producing ASSPs (application specific standard parts). ASICs were custom products that were designed by or for only one customer and could be sold only to that one customer. ASSPs, on the other hand, were standardized products that could be designed for and used by several customers. For fiscal 1998 ASSPs were expected to account for more than half of the company's revenue. The company's products included ATM, SONET, and Fibre Channel physical layer chips, which were first introduced in 1995; PCI bus interface chips; precision clock and timing chips, which AMCC introduced in 1993; and its BiCMOS and bipolar logic array product lines.

Under Rickey's leadership the company focused its development efforts on the high-speed data communications market and discontinued several other product lines. In fiscal 1997 telecommunications already accounted for about 38 percent of sales. The company's bipolar CMOS (BiCMOS) circuitry was optimized for analog technologies. It allowed higher data transfer speeds and lower power consumption than mainstream CMOS circuits. While expanding its fabrication facility to handle the next generation of high-performance chips, AMCC was looking at more complex silicon germanium (SiGe) technology to achieve even faster switching speeds. At the time SiGe technology was being developed by industry leaders such as IBM and Analog Devices Inc. AMCC's BiCMOS products also were competing with GaAs (gallium arsenide) technology at switching speeds in the range of one gigabit per second.

Expanding Technology Through Acquisitions: 1998–2000

In March 1998 AMCC announced a secondary offering of about 3.5 million shares of stock, of which about two million were being sold by stockholders in the company. None of the selling shareholders was an officer or director of the company. The offering price was $19.375 per share, and the company realized net proceeds of $29.1 million.

In mid-1998 AMCC signed a long-term agreement with IBM to gain access to IBM's SiGe (silicon germanium) BiCMOS processes and libraries. IBM had been developing SiGe technology for a decade. SiGe process technologies were expected to accelerate AMCC's development of high-speed, SONET OC-192, ten gigabit-per-second chips with optoelectronic capability for manipulating fiber-optic signals. AMCC expected to introduce OC-192 products in calendar 1999. For fiscal 1999 ending March 31 AMCC reported revenue of $76.6 million, an increase of 33 percent over fiscal 1998. Net income more than doubled to $15.2 million.

In March 1999 AMCC acquired Cimaron Communications Corp., a developer of circuits and ASIC cores for high-speed SONET networking systems, for about $115 million in stock. The acquisition would enable AMCC to move beyond its analog physical media devices (PMDs) and mixed-signal physical-layer devices up to the next layer of network protocol, the digital layer. The acquisition was part of AMCC's strategy to strengthen its position in the telecommunications market and provide IC solutions for the high-bandwidth marketplace. Cimaron's president and CEO, Ram Sudireddy, became AMCC's vice-president in charge of digital products. Also joining AMCC was Dr. Gary Martin, a cofounder of Cimaron in 1998 and its chief technology officer (CTO), who became AMCC's CTO for digital products. Within a few months AMCC announced new products based on NILE technology acquired from Cimaron. NILE took the place of five chips and integrated them into a single device. Principal applications of the products were for high-speed data transmission networks.

In September 1999 AMCC rolled out a series of products based on the SiGe process technology acquired through its agreement with IBM. A spokesperson for AMCC explained in *Electronic News,* ''We believe that the market for silicon germanium will move quite rapidly. We're the first to prove that this technology is acceptable and we're now at a point where we're helping to define our customers' next-generation products.''

In December 1999 AMCC was added to the NASDAQ 100, and in January 2000 it broke ground on a new 62,000-square-foot engineering office complex on the three acres adjacent to its corporate headquarters in San Diego. For fiscal 2000 (ending March 31) AMCC reported $172.4 million in revenue, a 64 percent increase over fiscal 1999. Net income rose 184 percent to $48.6 million. Since going public in November 1997 at $8 a share, the company's stock had split twice and was trading around $150 a share. The firm had a market capitalization of

Key Dates:

1979: Applied Micro Circuits Corporation (AMCC) is founded in California and begins operations.
1982: Roger Smullen, a cofounder of National Semiconductor Corporation, is named chairman of the board.
1996: David Rickey is hired as president and CEO.
1997: AMCC goes public.
1999: AMCC acquires Cimaron Communications Corp. for $115 million.
2000: AMCC completes its acquisition of MMC Networks Inc. for $4.5 billion.

some $13 billion. During the year AMCC completed a secondary stock offering of approximately 12 million shares that realized net proceeds of about $816 million. Rickey noted, "Our growth is very indicative of an inflection point in the industry's optical revolution . . . providing further affirmation of our strategy to become the premier supplier of high-bandwidth silicon for the world's optical networks."

AMCC's acquisition of MMC Networks Inc. for $4.5 billion in stock was finalized on October 25, 2000. It was the second largest semiconductor merger in history. MMC, based in Mountain View, California, had developed Internet and cellular applications. The Israeli founder of MMC received about $520 million worth of AMCC's stock, making him one of the largest single shareholders in the company. MMC also had a development center in Israel.

MMC was considered a market leader in network processing platforms and services; it was producing second and third generation products, while other companies were struggling to get their initial products to market. In 1999, though, it lost business from two major customers, Cisco Systems and IBM, and half its revenue.

AMCC's revenue more than doubled during the first two quarters of fiscal 2001. First quarter revenue was $74.2 million, up 134 percent over the same period in fiscal 2000. Second quarter revenue increased 156 percent to $97 million. During the first quarter AMCC expanded its digital design capabilities with the acquisition of three companies: YuniNetworks, Inc.; Chameleon Technologies, Inc.; and pBaud Logic, Inc. In the second quarter the company established a design center in Bedford, New Hampshire, that would focus on ten gigabit Ethernet designs. It also completed the acquisition of SiLUTIA, Inc., a company with digital and mixed-signal products for the broadband communications market.

Having led AMCC into high-bandwidth silicon connectivity solutions for fiber-optic networks, David Rickey was elected chairman of the board on August 31, 2000. He also would continue as the firm's president and CEO. Former Chairman Roger Smullen was elected vice-chairman.

With the acquisition of MMC Networks, AMCC was strongly positioned to provide complete system solutions for the emerging intelligent optical network, including AMCC's fiber-to-switch connectivity portfolio and MMC's network processor, traffic management, and switch fabric capabilities. Having also strengthened its digital design capabilities, AMCC could look forward to offering products utilizing a combination of high-frequency analog, mixed-signal, and digital design capabilities. With more companies becoming involved in building fiber-optic networks for the high-speed transmission of voice and data, AMCC was positioned to become a leader in providing them with enabling IC products.

Principal Subsidiaries

MMC Networks Inc.

Principal Competitors

Broadcom Corp.; PMC-Sierra Inc.; Cree Inc.; Exar Corp.; Motorola Inc.; Vitesse Semiconductor Corp.; Conexant Systems Inc.; Agilent Technologies Inc.; Giga-Tronics Inc.; Infineon Technologies AG; Lucent Technologies Inc.; Maxim Integrated Products Inc.; Philips N.V.; TriQuint Semiconductor Inc.; Analog Devices Inc.

Further Reading

Allen, Mike, "AMCC's Rickey Driving Firm's Successful Ride," *San Diego Business Journal,* September 25, 2000, p. 4.

——, "A New Level of Success," *San Diego Business Journal,* May 15, 2000, p. 63.

"AMCC in Pact for SiGe Tech," *Electronic News (1991),* July 27, 1998, p. 24.

"AMCC Plans to Acquire Cimaron in $115M Deal," *Electronic News (1991),* March 8, 1999, p. 45.

"Applied Micro Circuits Buys MMC Networks for $4.5 Billion," *Israel Business Today,* September 2000, p. 24.

Ascierto, Jerry, "AMCC's SiGe Surge," *Electronic News (1991),* September 13, 1999, p. 18.

Brown, Peter, "AMCC's Sonet," *Electronic News (1991),* June 14, 1999, p. 34.

——, "NILE: No Longer Just a River in Egypt," *Electronic News (1991),* June 14, 1999, p. 34.

"From $8.00 to $281.75 Per Share in Two Years," *San Diego Business Journal,* March 27, 2000, p. B4.

Hill, Martin, "AMCC Breaks Ground on New Expansion," *San Diego Business Journal,* January 24, 2000, p. 28.

Levine, Daniel S., "Fast, Savvy High-Techers Can Continue Huge Gains," *Sacramento Business Journal,* September 1, 2000, p. 8.

Malik, Om, "Cyberbargain," *Forbes,* August 24, 1998, p. 259.

Murphy, Tom, and Kallender, Paul, "AMCC Joins the Major Leagues," *Electronic News (1991),* September 4, 2000, p. 1.

Rowe, Bruce, "Martinez Leaves TRW to Become AMCC President," *San Diego Business Journal,* July 27, 1987, p. 1.

——, "Weathering Uncertainty," *San Diego Business Journal,* November 9, 1987, p. 13.

"Semiconductors—Atiq Raza," *Electronic News (1991),* September 27, 1999, p. 14.

Siedsma, Andrea, "Applied Micro Circuits Plans $70M Expansion," *San Diego Business Journal,* June 16, 1997, p. 15.

Souza, Crista Hardie, "AMCC Readies $70M for High Volume Push," *Electronic News (1991),* June 9, 1997, p. 14.

Weiss, Ray, "Engineering Workstations Aid Designers, Spur Development of Semicustom Logic Chips," *Electronic Design,* April 4, 1985, p. 69.

—David P. Bianco

The Arbitron Company

142 West 57th Street
New York, New York 10019-3300
U.S.A.
Telephone: (212) 887-1300
Fax: (212) 887-1390
Web site: http://www.arbitron.com

Public Company (IPO pending)
Incorporated: 1949 as American Research Bureau
Employees: 530
Sales: $215 million (1999)
NAIC: 541910 Marketing Research and Public Opinion Polling

The Arbitron Company is a market research firm that gathers information about broadcast media and consumer spending for use by client broadcast media, advertisers, and advertising agencies. The company's principal method of gathering information is through diaries that are filled out by television viewers or radio listeners. Initially the company surveyed the television viewing habits of American consumers in the 1950s. In the 1960s it began surveying radio audiences as well. In the 1990s the firm abandoned TV ratings to its rival, Nielsen Media Research Inc. (eventually renamed ACNielsen Corporation), and began monitoring Internet radio usage.

Early History: 1940s–70s

In the late 1940s, a George Washington University student named Jim Seiler wrote a thesis that described a method using personal diaries to survey television audiences to find out what they were watching. Only one household in ten had a television set then. Seiler, who lived in Laurel, Maryland, was subsequently hired by the National Broadcasting Company (NBC) to survey its audiences. NBC soon developed a business that marketed such information to other broadcasters and advertisers.

Seiler set out on his own in 1949 and founded the American Research Bureau, which later became Arbitron Ratings Co. and then The Arbitron Company. Initially focused on the Baltimore-Washington, D.C. area, the company eventually spread nationally. In 1960 it became a subsidiary of Control Data Corporation, and in 1964 Arbitron entered into radio audience research.

Measuring Radio and TV Audiences: 1980s

In the early 1980s Arbitron had about $80 million in revenue. It was not as well known as its rival, ACNielsen. The two companies were involved in a controversy over measuring cable homes. Nielsen surveyed cable homes four times a year, while Arbitron only did it annually. Arbitron also measured radio ratings and local TV ratings. Only Nielsen measured national network TV ratings, although Arbitron was planning to mount a challenge in that area. Over the past several years Arbitron had spent more than $23 million to meter eight cities electronically in addition to New York, Los Angeles, and Chicago. With 11 metered markets and 5,700 machines, it had more than Nielsen, making it attractive to the networks. In addition, the company planned to add six more cities in 1984 for a total of 7,200 meters. For Nielsen, broadcast ratings accounted for about 11 percent of its $644 million in 1982 revenue.

Arbitron used its Area of Dominant Influence (ADI) to classify its ratings, while Nielsen used its Designated Market Area (DMA). Arbitron provided annual rankings of ADIs in terms of number of TV households; it would also add or combine ADIs each year. In smaller markets, where it was important for a television station to be identified with an ADI, changes made in ADIs could result in complaints and even litigation. Usually Arbitron's and Nielsen's respective rankings of television markets would not be in complete agreement.

For radio ratings, Arbitron issued quarterly market rating reports with such information as audience trends, discrete demographics, audience composition, demographic buyers, hour-by-hour average quarter-hour listening estimates, listening locations, loyal and exclusive audience, overnight listening, and ethnic composition. The company used an Arbitron Radio Advisory Council, which channeled feedback from the radio community back to the company.

Radio stations typically entered into one-, three-, or five-year contracts with Arbitron to provide monitoring and rating

Company Perspectives:

Arbitron has three core businesses: measuring radio audiences in local markets across the United States; surveying the retail, media and product patterns of local market consumers; and providing software applications that give its customers access to Arbitron's media and consumer information via proprietary databases, and enable them to more effectively analyze and understand that information.

services. In 1986 Arbitron had about 1,750 radio station customers. It was facing new competition from Birch Radio, established in 1978, which had grown to cover 230 radio markets. Birch's clients were primarily advertising agencies, advertisers, and smaller market radio stations, but it was planning to go after contracts with major market radio stations as well. While Arbitron used its diary system to measure listening habits, Birch employed a telephone recall system in which respondents were interviewed about what they had listened to the previous day. Birch was undercutting Arbitron's pricing by about half and was also battling for acceptance of its methodology. In 1987 Birch merged with Scarborough Research Inc.

Arbitron introduced its people meter, ScanAmerica, in late 1986, by testing it in Denver. It was planning to introduce people meters for the 1988–89 TV season. Meters were expected to provide more accurate information, as television viewership was becoming fragmented between broadcast network, independent, syndication, and cable television. Arbitron's ScanAmerica was designed to package national TV audience ratings with household purchase data. The service would require participants to scan the bar codes on purchased products with a wand. Primary customers were expected to be packaged goods advertisers. Critics argued that ScanAmerica was too ambitious, and that it would be too difficult to collect both household product purchase information and national TV ratings. Arbitron committed $125 million to develop ScanAmerica.

Introducing New Services, Discontinuing Others: 1990s

By 1990 Arbitron had nearly 2,000 full-time employees and more than 1,000 part-time employees nationwide. It introduced a new electronic monitoring system called MediaWatch in the spring of 1990. Targeted to advertisers who wanted to monitor their commercials and those of their competition, MediaWatch would enable more accurate identification and classification of TV ads on a full-time basis in most of Arbitron's 75 markets.

Arbitron was one of three firms that provided single source data that tracked consumer behavior to determine the influence of advertising exposure among individual consumers or groups of consumers. ACNielsen and Information Resources Inc. were the other two. All of the systems were scanner-based, generating a database at the store level to determine the effectiveness of marketing promotions. Arbitron planned to expand its ScanAmerica service from its initial test in Denver to provide local coverage for the top 25 markets by 1995.

During the 1990s sample size would be a controversial issue for Arbitron's radio ratings. The company announced in the fall of 1990 that it would increase the sample size of its radio audience in all markets. A ten percent increase would be included at no charge, with customers having the opportunity to purchase extra samples in addition to the ten percent increase in standard markets. The company had been advised by the Arbitron Radio Advisory Council to increase its sample size by 33 percent over a three-year period.

Arbitron also faced strong competition for its TV rating services from ACNielsen. A 1990 survey by Petry Television indicated that stations were discontinuing the common practice of using both Nielsen and Arbitron ratings services. In the top 50 markets, more than 40 percent of TV stations subscribed to just one service for the November 1989 ratings book, double what it was three years ago. Cancellations were estimated to cost Arbitron and Nielsen between $12 and $15 million annually in lost revenue.

In October 1990 Arbitron dissolved its supermarket tracking unit, Sales Area Marketing Information (SAMI), and entered into a cross-licensing arrangement with Information Resources Inc. of Chicago. SAMI had tracked supermarket sales data through warehouse withdrawals. Now, Arbitron would use IRI's data, which was gathered through the use of scanners at retail checkout counters. IRI would pay Arbitron $7 million over four years and receive any revenue from Arbitron's clients for the service. IRI also got access to Arbitron's broadcast tracking data.

Arbitron's 1990 revenue was estimated at $187 million by *Marketing News*. The company's principal businesses were TV audience measurement services in 209 local markets and radio audience measurement services in 262 local markets. In addition, two ScanAmerica markets were in operation, namely, Denver and Phoenix. The firm's MediaWatch system recorded TV commercial exposure primarily for advertisers and their agencies. Additional revenue came from the publication of specialized reports on TV and radio usage.

After testing and fine-tuning its ScanAmerica service in Denver for three years, Arbitron was prepared to install ScanAmerica in 1,000 households in Atlanta, Chicago, Dallas, Los Angeles, and New York in the spring of 1991. At the time Arbitron, like many other broadcast industry-related services, was undergoing financial difficulties. Arbitron announced company-wide layoffs in early 1991, eliminating 52 positions.

In 1991 the company's advisory board continued to press Arbitron to increase its sample size, this time by 20 percent over the next two years. It also wanted the company to reduce the reporting service from four books to three books a year. Arbitron had about 1,800 radio station clients at this time. Radio subscribers were given the opportunity to vote on reducing the number of ratings periods from four to three. Ultimately, the radio and advertising subscribers voted to continue the four 12-week audience surveys. However, the company vowed to continue to try to find ways to increase the sample size and, thus, the reliability of its surveys.

TV stations continued the trend of opting for only one ratings service. CBS chose Nielsen over Arbitron for its five

Key Dates:

1949: The company is founded by Jim Seiler as American Research Bureau; it eventually is renamed The Arbitron Company.
1960: Arbitron becomes subsidiary of Control Data Corporation.
1992: Control Data splits into two companies, one of which, Ceridian Corporation, becomes Arbitron's parent.
2000: Ceridian announces plans to spin off Arbitron as a publicly traded company in early 2001.

owned and operated stations. Out of a total of 811 TV stations, 54 percent subscribed to a single ratings service, with only 43 percent subscribing to both Nielsen and Arbitron. Of the 811 stations, 592 (73 percent) subscribed to Nielsen and 543 (67 percent) to Arbitron.

Later in 1991 CBS contracted with Arbitron for its ScanAmerica service for network ratings as well as for local market ratings for its owned and operated TV stations and its seven AM and 11 FM radio stations. The ScanAmerica service would consist of 1,000 households in five markets: New York, Los Angeles, Chicago, Dallas, and Atlanta. CBS was the first network to sign up for ScanAmerica, which Arbitron rolled out on November 4, 1991, as a result of the contract with CBS. CBS had just recently gained the number one spot among broadcast television networks and would also continue to use the Nielsen ratings service. Within a week Arbitron signed a multi-year contract to provide all seven Fox-owned TV stations with local ratings services.

At the end of 1991 radio stations were applying pressure to Arbitron to improve its radio ratings system. They wanted Arbitron to broaden the sample size, improve diary reporting, and make the system more economical. Arbitron identified its top priority to improve the ratings system as improving response rates from diary-keepers. Weak reporting was especially prevalent among Hispanics and young males.

Starting in 1989, Arbitron began holding a consultants fly-in every December. At the 1991 meeting major issues involved ways to improve reporting among 18- to 24-year-old males. Arbitron's policy at the time was to exclude group quarters, such as college dormitories and the military, from its samples. The company planned to introduce two new services in January 1992. One was a radio version of MediaWatch, that would monitor radio advertising. The other was a disc-supplied version of Radio Fingerprint, which broke down raw diary data into age, sex, zip code, and format preferences.

Arbitron's main competitor in radio ratings, Birch Radio Inc., ceased operations at the end of 1991. The ratings service was shut down by its parent company, VNU Business Information Services Inc. Arbitron and VNU signed a five-year contract that made Arbitron the exclusive marketer of VNU's Scarborough report to radio and television stations. The demise of Birch left Arbitron as the sole company providing data on local radio audiences.

In March 1992 the Federal Communications Commission (FCC) announced it would use data supplied by Arbitron to determine radio station ownership limits. The new limits would prevent broadcasters from purchasing a new station if it would give a broadcaster more than 25 percent of the total market, based on audience share, in markets with 15 or more stations.

The National Association of Broadcasters (NAB) announced it would hold a summit in November 1992 to discuss problems with Arbitron's rating system for radio. The chief complaint seemed to be that audience samples were too small, due largely to low response rates from some audience segments. Arbitron had consistently rejected increasing the sample size as being too expensive. Instead, it wanted to lengthen the current three-month reporting periods. Some hoped that new technology would provide a solution.

In television, Nielsen continued to gain market share at Arbitron's expense. Between May 1991 and May 1992, Nielsen increased the number of exclusive clients from 286 to 323, an increase of 13 percent. Arbitron lost 8 percent of its exclusive clients, dropping from 199 to 184 during the same period. Nielsen served a total of 641 commercial stations, up from 626, while Arbitron served 502 stations, down from 539 stations. With the addition of Lifetime and TNT cable networks to its MediaWatch service, Arbitron was monitoring about 80 percent of all cable TV advertising, including CNN, ESPN, Family Channel, MTV, USA Networks, and WTBS.

Focusing on Radio Audiences: 1992–2000

After four years of research and ten months of operation, Arbitron dropped its ScanAmerica service for lack of a viable subscriber base. The company said it planned to continue to offer local ratings service in six markets using ScanAmerica technology. The move left Nielsen as the only company measuring national network TV audiences.

Control Data split into two companies in 1992, Control Data Systems Inc. and Ceridian Corporation. Ceridian would become Arbitron's parent company. In anticipation of becoming a public company, Arbitron released revenue figures indicating that annual revenue from radio was $94 million out of total revenue of $194 million. The ratings company had 1,900 radio station customers.

In September 1992 another rating service entered the radio market. Strategic Radio Research's AccuRatings service used weekly telephone calls to survey radio listeners. At first it targeted radio stations rather than advertisers for clients. In 1993 AccuRatings was introduced to New York City. The company offered the service free of charge for one year to advertising agencies. The AccuRatings service was currently available in 14 markets representing about 20 percent of the national radio audience. By March 1994 AccuRatings was available in 25 markets, including eight of the top ten metropolitan areas.

In December 1992 President and CEO Anthony ''Rick'' Aurichio was replaced by Stephen Morris. Morris was formerly president and CEO of VidCode, a media company that tracked broadcast commercials, and head of the Maxwell House division of General Foods. As president and CEO of Arbitron, Morris would report to Lawrence Perlman, chairman, president, and

CEO of Ceridian Corporation, the successor to Control Data. Aurichio's sudden departure was clouded by concurrent setbacks at Arbitron, including the end of ScanAmerica. In addition, several radio station groups, including Hearst, Westinghouse, and Post-Newsweek, had cut back on Arbitron service.

In December 1992 Arbitron announced it would test a new passive measurement system using a device called a portable people meter. The device would pick up inaudible codes etched into radio or TV soundtracks to record viewing and listening habits. Pretesting Co. already had a patent on a wristwatch device that used an audible code and was watching Arbitron closely. Arbitron planned on introducing its people meter in two markets in late 1994. The device utilized technology developed by Martin Marietta Corporation, as well as the BBM Bureau of Management of Canada, AGB McNair of Australia, and Intellisys Automation, in addition to Arbitron.

In April 1993 Arbitron presented another plan to increase the sample size of its radio rating service. The company proposed replacing the current system of 12-week surveys with 18-week rolling average reports that would be distributed every six weeks. Thus, the new system would have eight ratings periods instead of only four per year. Although the new system would involve additional costs, Arbitron did not plan to charge more under the new system.

Arbitron revised its plan to increase sample sizes after receiving negative feedback from broadcasters. The company scrapped the concept of 18-week rolling averages, which was not well-received by radio stations, and announced it would increase sample sizes by distributing more diaries. By the end of 1994 the number of diaries in continuously metered metro areas would increase by 30 percent. Then, the sample size would be increased another 40 percent in 1995 to achieve a 70 percent increase over 1993 levels. In noncontinuously metered markets, the sample size would be increased by a total of 40 percent through the introduction of new diaries. As part of the plan, radio stations would be charged an additional four percent and Arbitron would begin using a computer imaging system for diary storage and retrieval in the fall of 1994. Developed jointly by Arbitron and IBM, the system captured exact images of every diary page and sorted it on CD-ROMs for retrieval during processing and review.

Arbitron announced it would terminate its broadcast and cable TV ratings services effective December 31, 1993. A company spokesperson noted that competition from Nielsen resulted in fewer contracts and declining price per contract. Arbitron had lost money for several years in the television ratings part of its business. It would cut more than 700 positions from its workforce, leaving the company with about 550 employees. The company planned to continue developing information tools for TV and cable stations to work with advertisers, and it planned to continue development of its people meter for radio and TV. In May 1994 Arbitron joined with GE Capital and investment banker Veronis, Suhler to make a multimillion-dollar equity investment in ADcom Information Services. ADcom used a technology that combined pay-per-view with passive measurement to install household meters for cable TV ratings.

In November 1994 Arbitron acquired a 50 percent interest in Scarborough Research Corporation from VNU Business Information Services. In exchange, VNU received a 50 percent interest in Competitive Media Reporting, a subsidiary of Ceridian Corporation. Scarborough conducted qualitative research on the habits and media usage of consumers in 58 markets. It was expected that a joint venture between Arbitron and Scarborough would bring new research techniques to Arbitron's radio ratings service.

In March 1995 Arbitron released its first study of new media preferences. The company collected information about consumer electronic and entertainment preferences from 4,000 U.S. consumers. Among the technologies studied were home entertainment media, online services, and CD-ROMs. The company also entered into a joint venture with ASI Market Research and Next Century Research to create the Interactive Information Index, which would rate interactive media in terms of consumer preferences.

Arbitron was plagued with data collection errors in 1994, when books from nine markets had to be reissued. To address this problem the company created a new position, director of data collection, and rehired Pierre Bouvard as general manager. Beginning with its spring 1995 radio survey, Arbitron began calling college and military residences that were equipped with private phones in an effort to better measure the traditionally hard-to-measure 18-to-34-year-old male group. More than 400,000 such numbers were added to the sample base in 51 markets.

In 1996 Arbitron won a patent infringement lawsuit brought against it by Pretesting Co. in 1993. The suit centered on Arbitron's portable people meter, which Pretesting claimed violated its portable sound-technology patents. Because of the lawsuit, Arbitron had only developed a working prototype of the people meter, which was a passive measuring device that recorded inaudible sound signals encoded in radio and television programs. Arbitron's revenue for 1996 was $153.1 million.

At the end of 1997 Arbitron acquired Continental Research, located in London, England. It was the first step in Arbitron's plan to expand outside of North America. The company planned to bid on the official U.K. radio ratings contract when it came up in 1998. However, it was unsuccessful in its bid, but still planned to develop a presence in the United Kingdom. In a related acquisition, Arbitron purchased the overseas TV and cable software products of Tapscan Inc., a software developer based in Birmingham, Alabama. Later in 1998 Arbitron began testing its personal portable meters in Manchester, England.

In 1999 Arbitron released a study on Internet radio habits. By the end of 1999 the company had released its first monthly report on Internet radio usage. By 2000 the monthly reports covered nearly 400 channels on the Internet. Arbitron would form an alliance with Lariat Software in mid-2000 to use its MediaReports software to collect data directly from servers to report the number of unique listeners to an audio channel on the Internet. A competitor, MeasureCast Inc. of Portland, Oregon, began its streaming audience measurement service in August 2000.

In 1999 low response rates became a crisis of sorts for the diary method of tracking radio and television audiences. As a result, both Arbitron and Nielsen were under pressure to develop alternatives to the diary method. Arbitron's average response rate on its radio listener surveys was 35.9 percent, compared to 39.1 percent in 1998. The lowest response rate in any single market dropped to 26.3 percent. Among the steps Arbitron took to boost response rates was to offer higher cash payments, make more telephone calls to survey participants, and repackage the diaries. Advertising buyers were disgruntled at the start of 2000 when Arbitron had to delay the release of its fall 1999 ratings report by 21 days. The company explained that the delay was due to its new diary-processing system and issues related to Y2K compliance.

In mid-2000 Nielsen and Arbitron announced they would cooperate in testing Arbitron's new portable people meter. The test would take place in the Philadelphia-Wilmington, Delaware, market with 300 people during the fourth quarter of 2000. For the test, Nielsen would contribute its expertise in TV surveys.

In July 2000 it was announced that parent company Ceridian Corporation would spin off Arbitron in 2001. Ceridian and Arbitron would split off into two publicly traded companies. In 1999 Arbitron's $215 million in revenue was about 15 percent of Ceridian's $1.3 billion in revenue. Arbitron consistently had annual profit margins of 30 percent or more, making it a cash cow for its parent company. It was speculated that once it became a public company, Arbitron would be acquired by another media firm, possibly the Dutch-based VNU, which acquired Nielsen one year after Nielsen went public. Taylor Nelson Sofres of the United Kingdom was mentioned as another possible buyer.

As Arbitron prepared to become a publicly traded company, it held a near monopolistic leadership position in radio ratings. The company had also established itself in rating Internet radio usage. During the 1990s it nudged along new technologies to improve audience measurement, culminating in its portable people meter being tested in 2000. In the new millennium, Arbitron would likely continue as the most reliable radio ratings service in the industry.

Principal Subsidiaries

Tapscan WorldWide; Continental Research (U.K.).

Principal Competitors

ACNielsen Corporation; Strategic Radio Research Inc.; MeasureCast Inc.; Information Resources Inc.

Further Reading

''Ailing Oligopoly,'' *Broadcasting,* April 23, 1990, p. 63.

''Arbitron,'' *Regardie's Magazine,* August 1990, p. 219.

''Arbitron Begins Network Ratings Competition,'' *Television Digest,* November 4, 1991, p. 2.

''Arbitron, Birch Lock Horns in Audience Measurement Battle,'' *Broadcasting,* February 9, 1987, p. 96.

''Arbitron Braces for Round Two,'' *Marketing & Media Decisions,* November 1986, p. 52.

''Arbitron Buys Radio Software Developer,'' *Broadcasting & Cable,* May 25, 1998, p. 41.

''The Arbitron Co. Has Signed a Multiyear Contract with the Fox Television Stations,'' *Broadcasting,* November 11, 1991, p. 96.

''Arbitron Drops ScanAmerica,'' *Television Digest,* September 7, 1992, p. 3.

''Arbitron, GE Capital,'' *Television Digest,* May 16, 1994, p. 4.

''Arbitron Gets Help on Meter Test,'' *Mediaweek,* October 2, 2000, p. 5.

''Arbitron in Court Battle over ADI Move,'' *Broadcasting,* June 30, 1986, p. 56.

''Arbitron Increases Its Sample Size,'' *Broadcasting,* December 18, 1989, p. 89.

''Arbitron Is Adding,'' *Television Digest,* August 31, 1992, p. 5.

''Arbitron Plans to Test,'' *Television Digest,* December 14, 1992, p. 10.

''Arbitron Throws in Towel,'' *Television Digest,* October 25, 1993, p. 4.

Bachman, Katy, ''Arbitron Delays Fall '99 Ratings Book,'' *Mediaweek,* January 10, 2000, p. 16.

——, ''Arbitron Goes It Alone,'' *Mediaweek,* July 24, 2000, p. 8.

Bachman, Katy, ''Arbitron Goes Portable,'' *Mediaweek,* October 19, 1998, p. 10.

——, ''Diaries: Not So Dear,'' *Mediaweek,* November 29, 1999, p. 4.

——, ''A New Ratings Stream,'' *Mediaweek,* December 13, 1999, p. 8.

——, ''Nielsen, Arbitron Agree to Agree,'' *Mediaweek,* June 5, 2000, p. 6.

Berniker, Mark, and Chris McConnell, ''Arbitron Moves Toward Tracking Interactive Media,'' *Broadcasting & Cable,* March 20, 1995, p. 32.

Blyskal, Jeff, ''Rating War,'' *Forbes,* August 1983, p. 158.

Brunelli, Richard, ''New Radio Ratings Research Service to Be Introduced to Agencies in New York,'' *Mediaweek,* July 26, 1993, p. 9.

Bunzel, Reed E., and Joe Flint, ''Birch Radio to Cease Operations Dec. 31,'' *Broadcasting,* December 23, 1991, p. 11.

Bunzel, Reed E., and Peter Viles, ''New Ownership Limits,'' *Broadcasting,* March 23, 1992, p. 75.

''CBS Puts No. 1 Ranking to Arbitron Test,'' *Mediaweek,* November 4, 1991, p. 34.

''Ceridian Spins off Arbitron,'' *Billboard,* July 29, 2000, p. 95.

Del Prete, Dom, ''Advances in Scanner Research Yield Better Data,'' *Marketing News,* January 7, 1991, p. 54.

Fannin, Rebecca, and Joe Mandese, ''Adding to the Vocabulary,'' *Marketing & Media Decisions,* October 1988, p. 69.

''The First Results,'' *Mediaweek,* March 13, 1995, p. 14.

Flint, Joe, ''Scanamerica Signs CBS,'' *Broadcasting,* November 4, 1991, p. 65.

——, ''Stations Opting for Only One Ratings Service,'' *Broadcasting,* June 3, 1991, p. 39.

Flint, Joe, and Lucia Cobo, ''Arbitron, Advisory Council Contemplate Changes,'' *Broadcasting,* July 29, 1991, p. 62.

Hill, Julianne, ''Reality Media Hit Back Shop,'' *Advertising Age,* July 31, 2000, p. S18.

Honomichi, Jack, ''Top 50 Research Firms Profiled,'' *Marketing News,* May 27, 1991, p. H2.

McCusker, Tom, ''Ceridian Corp.,'' *Datamation,* June 15, 1993, p. 87.

McGeever, Mike, ''Arbitron Acquires U.K. Research Firm,'' *Billboard,* December 20, 1997, p. 94.

——, ''Arbitron Still Eyeing European Growth,'' *Billboard,* July 18, 1998, p. 73.

McManus, John, ''Arbitron, Nielsen Announce Expanded Tracking Services,'' *Adweek's Marketing Week,* August 14, 1989, p. 34.

Miles, Laureen, ''More Diaries for Listeners,'' *Mediaweek,* August 16, 1993, p. 12.

Moshavi, Sharon D., ''Arbitron Ends ScanAmerica Network Service,'' *Broadcasting,* September 7, 1992, p. 37.

——, ''Arbitron: New Ratings Service, New President,'' *Broadcasting,* December 7, 1992, p. 68.

——, ''Nielsen Gains Ground in Rating War,'' *Broadcasting,* July 27, 1992, p. 34.

——, ''Room for Two? AccuRatings Hopes So,'' *Broadcasting,* September 7, 1992, p. 54.

Muirhead, Greg, "Arbitron Is Dissolving SAMI," *Supermarket News,* October 8, 1990, p. 16.
"New Arbitron Rating Books in the Works," *Broadcasting,* December 17, 1984, p. 100.
"Nielsen, Arbitron Set New TV Market Rankings," *Broadcasting,* October 6, 1986, p. 64.
"1987 Ushers in the People Meter Era," *Broadcasting,* January 5, 1987, p. 59.
Ozemhoya, Carol U., "Birch/Scarborough Research Inc. Turns into Ratings Giant," *South Florida Business Journal,* December 3, 1990, p. 15.
Paskowski, Marianne, "Invasion of the People Meters," *Marketing & Media Decisions,* May 1987, p. 36.
Petrozzello, Donna, "Arbitron Acquires 50% of Scarborough," *Broadcasting & Cable,* November 14, 1994, p. 54.
——, "Arbitron Moves to Offer Audio Measuring," *Broadcasting & Cable,* August 26, 1996, p. 38.
Riche, Martha Farnsworth, "Scanning for Dollars," *American Demographics,* November 1998, p. 8.
Saxe, Frank, "Arbitron Study Details Net Radio Usage," *Billboard,* July 17, 1999, p. 99.
Schlossberg, Harold, "Radio Stations Pressure Arbitron to Fine-Tune Its Ratings Service," *Marketing News,* December 9, 1991, p. 1.
Schmuckler, Eric, "New Arbitron Passive People Meter Described As 'Affordable'," *Mediaweek,* December 14, 1992, p. 3.
——, "Questions Focus on Readiness of Arbitron's New System," *Mediaweek,* December 7, 1992, p. 3.
Stark, Phyllis, "AccuRatings Gaining Quickly on Arbitron," *Billboard,* March 5, 1994, p. 78.
——, "Arbitron Council Seeks Sample Boost," *Billboard,* March 30, 1991, p. 19.
——, "Arbitron Plan Gets Mixed Ratings," *Billboard,* May 29, 1993, p. 86.
——, "Arbitron Plans to Increase Sample Size in 85 Markets," *Billboard,* January 29, 1994, p. 95.
——, "Arbitron Refocuses on Radio After Leaving TV Race," *Billboard,* October 30, 1993, p. 4.
——, "Arbitron to Use Military and College Area Phone Nos.," *Billboard,* April 22, 1995, p. 94.
——, "Arbitron Users Divided over 3-Book Plan," *Billboard,* June 15, 1991, p. 1.
——, "Arb Subscribers Vote to Reject 3-Book Plan," *Billboard,* August 17, 1991, p. 1.
——, "Birch Radio Folds; Arbitron to Market Scarborough Data," *Billboard,* January 4, 1992, p. 1.
——, "Consultants Network with Arbitron," *Billboard,* December 21, 1991, p. 10.
——, "New Arbitron Prez Outlines Plan for Success," *Billboard,* January 9, 1993, p. 67.
——, "Radio Endorses New Arbitron Sampling Plan," *Billboard,* August 21, 1993, p. 7.
Stark, Phyllis, and Chuck Taylor, "1995: The Year of the Arbitron Snafu," *Billboard,* January 6, 1996, p. 81.
Sukow, Randall M., "NAB Plans Summit to Study Arbitron Problem," *Broadcasting,* July 13, 1992, p. 25.
"Survey Cut Voted Down," *Broadcasting,* August 12, 1991, p. 43.
Sussman, Stephen L., "Radio's Research Ratings," *Marketing & Media Decisions,* September 1988, p. 136.
Tedesco, Richard, "Ratings Services Take a Walk," *Broadcasting & Cable,* June 5, 2000, p. 11.
Torpey-Kemph, Anne, "Arbitron Forms Alliance with Lariat," *Mediaweek,* July 31, 2000, p. 51.
Viles, Peter, "Arbitron Proposes Doubling of Sample Sizes," *Broadcasting & Cable,* April 26, 1993, p. 36.
——, "Arbitron Revises Ratings Redesign," *Broadcasting & Cable,* July 5, 1993, p. 24.
——, "Arbitron Solution: Paid Sample Increases in 117 Markets," *Broadcasting & Cable,* January 24, 1994, p. 153.
——, "Criticism Mounts Against Arbitron Changes," *Broadcasting & Cable,* June 7, 1993, p. 83.
——, "RAB Votes for Arbitron Task Force," *Broadcasting,* October 26, 1992, p. 51.
"Web Ratings Challenger Emerges," *Billboard,* September 2, 2000, p. 87.

—David P. Bianco

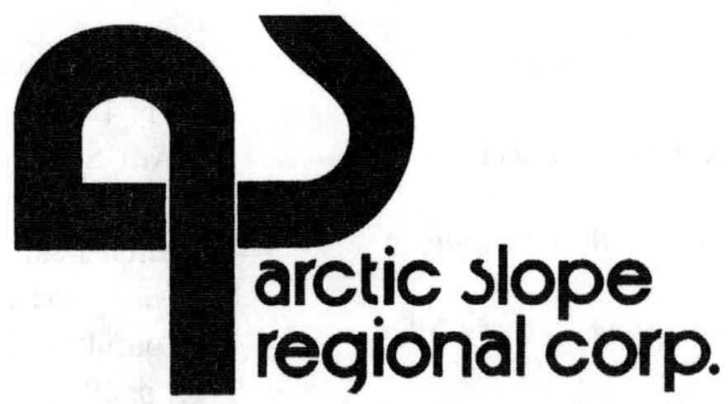

Arctic Slope Regional Corporation

1230 Agvik Street
Barrow, Alaska 99723
U.S.A.
Telephone: (907) 852-8633
Fax: (907) 852-5733
Web site: http://www.asrc.com

Private Company
Incorporated: 1972
Employees: 3,000
Sales: $887.51 million (1998)
NAIC: 211111 Crude Petroleum and Natural Gas Extraction; 32411 Petroleum Refineries; 213112 Support Activities for Oil and Gas Operations

Arctic Slope Regional Corporation (ASRC) was established following the passage of the Alaska Native Claims Settlement Act in 1971 as one of 13 regional corporations created to administer and to manage settlement benefits to native Alaskans. Owned by the Inupiat Eskimos, Arctic Slope controls dozens of subsidiaries involved in aerospace, construction, manufacturing, engineering, communications, oilfield services, capital financing, and petroleum refining and distribution businesses. The northernmost and the largest of the 13 regional corporations, ASRC obtains 40 percent of its revenues from oilfield services, a business managed by the company's subsidiary, Natchiq Inc., the largest oilfield service contractor in Alaska.

Origins

Statehood for Alaska in 1959 promised to usher in a host of changes, marking a momentous transition for its citizens. Some of the changes would be welcomed, but for the Native Alaskan groups who had occupied the land for countless generations, the change in status was accompanied by one overriding fear. The Native Alaskan groups feared state and federal encroachment upon their traditional lands, anxiously aware that they lacked the legal documentation to support their claims of ownership. When U.S. Secretary of State William Seward purchased Alaska from Russia in 1867, the transaction failed to acknowledge the ownership rights of those who had lived there for 4,000 years, largely because Native Alaskans' concept of land ownership had nothing in common with the shared precepts of ownership observed by Russia and the United States. The issue, begging an inevitable confrontation, festered for years, eventually becoming a matter that required resolution once federal and state legislators assumed their seats of influence.

In 1966, Native leaders banded together and formed a statewide organization named the Alaska Federation of Natives, or AFN. As an organized body, the AFN lobbied the U.S. Congress, seeking a resolution to the thorny issue of land ownership. The struggle to find a solution endured for five years after the formation of the AFN, as the clash of two contrasting cultures and the interests of oil companies and environmental groups combined to create a complicated debate. Negotiations ended on December 18, 1971, when President Richard Nixon signed into law the Alaska Native Claims Settlement Act (ANCSA). Under the terms of ANCSA, Native Alaskans exchanged their claims to land ownership for roughly one-ninth of the state's land and $962.5 million in compensation. Approximately 80,000 Natives were enrolled under ANCSA, entitling them to settlement benefits that would be administered by 13 regional corporations. The northernmost of the regional corporations, formed in 1972, was Arctic Slope Regional Corporation, owned by the Inupiat people.

Through ANCSA, the Inupiat were given five million acres on Alaska's North Slope, including 92,000 acres on the Arctic National Wildlife Refuge Coastal Plain. Arctic Slope was established to manage the Inupiat's land, a corporation formed to develop the land and its natural resources according to Inupiat beliefs. As a commercial concern, ASRC pursued the usual corporate objective of generating a profit for shareholders, but it also pursued another, equally important objective: employing its shareholders. As ASRC developed through the years, it would prove to be adept at performing both functions, perhaps better than any of the other regional corporations established after the promulgation of ANCSA. Initially, however, the re-

Company Perspectives:

Inupiat values have enabled our ancestors to survive successfully in the harsh Arctic environment for many centuries. ASRC embraces both Inupiat and Western cultural values to compete successfully in tomorrow's global business environment. The Corporation, our subsidiaries, all our employees, and shareholders are part of the Inupiat extended family. We respect our rich history, culture, and language and instill in our growing family of business enterprises such traditional Inupiat Values as: respecting the knowledge, wisdom, and guidance of our Elders; honoring the philosophy of cooperation and sharing; developing our lands and resources by means that respect Inupiat subsistence values and ensure proper care of the environment, habitat, and wildlife.

gional corporation's executive officers were charged with administering the provisions laid out in ANCSA.

With few exceptions, ASRC's activities during its first months in operation were related to the interpretation, dispensation, and implementation of the conditions included within ANCSA. The company was involved in the organization of village corporations, providing assistance to village corporations, and determining which businesses could best engender profit and shareholder employment. Considering that the regional corporation was based in the oil-rich North Slope Borough, its foray into oil and into businesses that supported the local oil industry was not surprising. At first, ASRC delved into construction activity geared toward developing North Slope infrastructure for oil-related activities, an ideal business area because company shareholders could immediately be put to work without much preliminary training.

In its pursuit of business opportunities, ASRC had to strike a balance between profitability and shareholder employment. The company could not create employment at the expense of entering into money-losing ventures and neither could it forsake its obligation to employ shareholders. Pursuing these twin objectives presented the company with a perennial challenge, but during the early 1970s a more difficult task loomed as ASRC directors had to decide which businesses to enter. They lacked the expertise to plunge headlong into one business area through an acquisition, which forced them to employ a different strategy. During its formative years, the company developed its business interests by forming a joint venture with an experienced partner in a particular business. As an organization, ASRC then gradually learned how to manage and operate the business in question, using its joint venture partner as a tutor. Once the company learned the nuances of a joint venture, it bought out its partner, creating a wholly owned subsidiary that management had the confidence to operate on its own.

ASRC's development strategy became a pattern during the company's formative years. In one of the company's early deals, a joint venture was formed with an established construction firm named SKW Clinton. Along with SKW Clinton, ASRC pursued public works projects beginning in the mid-1970s. After several years, ASRC gained the confidence and talent to run the business on its own, leading to the buyout of SKW Clinton and to the formation of a wholly owned subsidiary named SKW/Eskimos, Inc. in the early 1980s. There were exceptions, however. One of the first business ventures undertaken by ASRC occurred through a direct acquisition. In the early 1970s, the company purchased a Barrow, Alaska-based fuel company. The acquisition eventually steered the company into oil-field service work, performed under the name Eskimo Oilfield Services. From there, Arctic Slop entered into the construction of state-owned facilities under the banner Inupiat Builders.

Although the company did enter into businesses on its own, the tendency to establish a joint venture first and take over the business on its own at a later date was unmistakable. ASRC adopted this approach when it entered the oil patch construction business. The company formed a joint venture with Alaska General and later bought out its partner, creating a new wholly owned subsidiary named Arctic Slope/Alaska General. A similar path was taken to develop interests in design consulting. Beginning in 1977, Arctic Slope formed alliances with companies specializing in petroleum and cold region design, then used the management experience it gained from the joint ventures to form a wholly owned subsidiary, Arctic Slope Consulting Engineers, in 1982.

Development in the 1980s

Eventually, the company gained the expertise to make decisive moves into particular businesses on its own. None was more important than the acquisition of Houston Contracting Company. In 1985, Arctic Slope purchased the established pipeline construction firm and formed Natchiq Inc., which would rank as the largest Arctic Slop subsidiary a quarter-century later. Natchiq served as a holding company for several oilfield service and construction enterprises. Natchiq's interests included Alaska Petroleum Contractors, formed in 1987, and GSL Oilfield Service, a contractor with experience in offshore oil exploration that was acquired several years later. Other Natchiq-controlled businesses included VRCA Environmental Services, a specialist in oilfield clean-up services, and Entech, an incinerator manufacturer.

The addition of Natchiq helped spur robust growth for ASRC. Between 1985 and 1989, ASRC both doubled its revenues and its number of employees, aided by a 20 percent increase in revenues that pushed the company past the $100-million-in-sales mark to $112.8 million in 1989. Growth became decidedly more vigorous as the company entered the 1990s. In 1990, revenues leaped 94 percent, reaching $218.3 million, while earnings shot up 76 percent to $25.5 million. The increase in profitability, one half of ASRC's success equation, was coupled by a 50 percent increase in employees, as the company's payroll swelled to 1,500.

By all measures, ASRC entered the 1990s as the prime example of the benefits a regional corporation could deliver to its shareholders. It ranked as the largest of the 13 regional corporations, comprising 14 wholly owned subsidiaries and 20

Key Dates:

1971: President Richard Nixon signs into law the Alaska Native Claims Settlement Act.
1972: Arctic Slope is created.
1985: Houston Contracting Co. is acquired.
1990: Company declares goal of reaching $1 billion in annual revenues by the decade's end.
2001: Revenues expected to eclipse $1 billion.

operating divisions. After establishing itself in the northern reaches of Alaska, the company expanded throughout the state and into the contiguous United States. Geographic expansion was coupled with diversification, as ASRC branched out into tourism, engineering, architectural design, lodging, transportation, communications, environmental services, and petroleum refining. Behind these businesses were more than 3,700 Inupiat Eskimo shareholders whose ranks were expected to swell by 2,500 in 1991, when ASRC was scheduled to issue new stock to children born to shareholders since the signing of ANCSA in 1971.

Pursuit of $1 Billion in Revenues in the 1990s

The company's success was not lost on its leaders, whose confidence and expertise had grown enormously during the company's first 20 years. "We've gained the experience needed to make direct acquisitions," ASRC's vice-president of international business declared in an October 1990 interview with *Alaska Business Monthly.* No longer forced to forge alliances to make its way in the business world, the company had developed the organizational structure and managerial acumen to act as the conglomerate it was, enabling an aggressive corporation to emerge. As the company's leaders set their course at the start of the 1990s, their aim was to reach $1 billion in revenues by the decade's end. The pursuit of this lofty goal transformed an experimental commercial concern into one of the largest privately held corporations in the United States.

During the 1990s, one of ASRC's primary objectives was to develop an oil producing arm to its operations, the one missing facet of an otherwise fully vertically integrated oil company. One likely source, reputed to contain the last remaining substantial oil field in North America, was on the Arctic National Wildlife Refuge Coastal Plain, abutting 92,000 acres of ASRC-owned village land. The U.S. Congress, however, forbade all exploration and development on the land, diminishing the chances that the company would find oil on its land. ASRC was forced to look elsewhere to complete its portfolio of properties, but even without an oil production subsidiary to its name, the company recorded robust growth as it pursed its aim of $1 billion in revenues by the decade's end. Led by Natchiq and its two operating subsidiaries, Houston Contracting and Alaska Petroleum Contractors, which accounted for a third of ASRC's revenues, the company generated $468 million in revenues in 1995. The total was nearly twice the amount recorded two years earlier, making ASRC the largest Alaska-owned company in the state.

The company's progress during the latter half of the 1990s was marked by the need to broaden its operations beyond Alaska and to secure a presence in global markets. Although the company continued to add to its operations in Alaska, the state's oil exploration activity began to subside as companies moved elsewhere to develop oil fields, particularly to South America. ASRC's geographic expansion included the addition of Omega Service Industries, a Louisiana-based oilfield construction and fabrications company that became part of Natchiq. The company also acquired Oregon-based Puget Plastics Corp., a leader in injection-molded plastic parts, a diversification that was complemented by the formation of a Mexican manufacturer of plastic injection molding components. Additionally, the company acquired Correa Enterprises, a telecommunication and systems engineering company based in Albuquerque, New Mexico, and formed a subsidiary to seek contract work in Venezuelan oil fields.

The extension of ASRC's geographic base helped contribute to animated financial growth during the late 1990s, driving the company closer toward its goal. In 1998, revenues increased from $700 million to $887 million, while earnings swelled 77 percent. Natchiq and its oilfield services companies, which accounted for 40 percent of total sales, accounted for much of the growth, but another important factor contributing to the company's success was its astute and stable management. Individuals such as ASRC's president and chairman, Jacob Adams, and its first vice-president, Lands Oliver Leavitt, had held leadership positions since the company's inception in 1972. Other members of the company's top management had been with the company for more than 20 years. Thanks largely to management's ability to successfully diversify while fulfilling the company's commitment to shareholder training and hiring programs, ASRC exited the 1990s tantalizingly close to the goal it had been pursuing for a decade. The anticipated date for reaching $1 billion in revenue was pushed back to 2001, by which time the company expected to generate $60 million in annual profits and have 10,000 shareholders on record.

Principal Subsidiaries

Alaska Growth Capital Bidco Inc.; Arctic Slope Construction, Inc.; Arctic Slope World Services, Incorporated; ASRC Aerospace Corp.; ASRC Parsons Engineering, LLC; Entech Corporation; Kodak Oil Sales Inc.; Natchiq Sakhalin, Inc.; Petro Star Inc.; SKW/Eskimos, Inc.; Tundra Tours, Inc.; APC/Wood, LLC; Arctic Slope Native Association, Ltd.; ASCG Incorporated; ASRCCommunications, LTD.; Barrow Cable TV; Alaska Lube and Fuel; Arctic Education Foundation; Arctic Slope Technical Services, Inc.; ASCG Inspection Services; ASRC Contracting Company, Inc.; Correa Enterprises, Inc.; Houston Contracting Company-Alaska, LTD.; Natchiq, Inc.; Omega Service Industries, Inc.; Puget Plastics Corp.; SPN de Venzuela C.A.; Western Arctic Coal.

Principal Competitors

Nobel Drilling Corporation; Nabors Industries, Inc.; Halliburton Company.

Further Reading

Berger, Michael, ''Arctic Slope Regional Corporation,'' *Alaska Business Monthly,* November 1993, p. 29.

Griffin, Judith Fuerst, ''Arctic Slope Regional Corp.,'' *Alaska Business Monthly,* October 1990, p. 59.

''Latin American Deals Appeal to Alaska's Arctic Slope,'' *Knight-Ridder/Tribune Business News,* February 14, 1998, p. 214B0934.

Patkotak, Elise, ''Still No. 1—Still Growing,'' *Alaska Business Monthly,* October 1996, p. 72.

Ragsdale, Rose, ''Aggressive Alaska Native Corporations Take Investments Out-of-State,'' *Knight-Ridder/Tribune Business News,* August 17, 1998, p. OKRB98229088.

Stricker, Lulie, ''The 13 Regional Native Corporations,'' *Alaska Business Monthly,* September 1999, p. 70.

Tyson, Ray, ''Slippery Slopes: Native Firms Adapt to Changing Oil Industry,'' *Alaska Business Monthly,* November 1992, p. 34.

—Jeffrey L. Covell

Avedis Zildjian Co.

22 Longwater Drive
Norwell, Massachusetts 02061
U.S.A.
Telephone: (781) 871-2200
Fax: (781) 871-3984
Web site: http://www.zildjian.com

Private Company
Incorporated: 1929
Employees: 95
Sales: $34 million (1999 est.)
NAIC: 339992 Musical Instrument Manufacturing

Avedis Zildjian Co. is the world's leading producer of cymbals. The company traces its origin back to 1623, when a formula for making an alloy that produced superior cymbals was discovered by a forebear of the Zildjian family. The name Zildjian in fact means "cymbal maker" in Armenian. The formula for the alloy has been passed down through generations, always remaining in the hands of Zildjian family members. The company has been responsible for many of the advances in cymbal playing. It has worked closely with musicians, especially early jazz drummers, to develop new products. Cymbal types, such as the Ride, Crash, and Ping, which are used as generic designations, were actually invented and named by the Avedis Zildjian Company. The company produces cymbals in a full range of sizes and prices, from inexpensive sets for amateur musicians to the top-quality instruments used by premier symphony orchestras. Zildjian also produces cymbals specifically for marching bands and drum corps, and sells gongs and crotales. Zildjian manufactures drumsticks at a facility it owns in Alabama as well.

Ancient Roots

Avedis Zildjian Co. was officially recognized in 1988 as the U.S. firm with the longest history. The company was incorporated in Massachusetts in 1929, but it has been run by members of the Zildjian family in Turkey since 1623. In that year, an alchemist named Avedis was experimenting with metal alloys, and came up with a recipe that lent itself to cymbal manufacturing. Cymbals had been in existence since at least 1200 B.C. They are mentioned in the Old Testament and were known in ancient China. Ancient cymbals, like today's, were made of bronze, an alloy of copper and tin. Cymbals had religious uses in various cultures, and in China and elsewhere were used in war to make a terrifying sound. Cymbals were made by skilled metal workers who could cast and beat bronze.

Avedis's innovation was in formulating an alloy that gave a good sound but was not so brittle that the instrument would crack. His fame grew, so that his family was given the name Zildjian—"zil" is Turkish for cymbal, "ji" is maker, and "ian" is the Armenian suffix for son of. The Zildjian family guarded its secret, passing it down through succeeding generations. The cymbals the Zildjian family business manufactured were mostly sold to military bands and to churches, which used them in religious processions. Cymbals appeared sporadically in orchestral music in the late 18th century, but by the end of the 19th century, they were increasingly specified in the scores of leading composers such as Hector Berlioz and Richard Wagner.

The Zildjian company began marketing its cymbals outside of Turkey in 1851. The company at the time was led by another Avedis Zildjian, who apparently had more zest for marketing than some of his forebears. He made a trip to London and Paris in 1851 to display Zildjian's wares, and continued to travel and advertise abroad until his death in 1865. The firm's leadership then passed to Kerope Zildjian, and then in 1910 passed to Kerope's nephew Aram Zildjian. Aram was temporarily in exile in Bucharest, where he set up a cymbal factory. He eventually returned to Turkey, and built up the business so that it made significant exports to the United States, a growing market.

Launch of U.S. Company During the Depression

When Aram was ready to retire, he needed to pass the family secret on to his oldest male descendant, who was his nephew, Avedis. Avedis had immigrated to the United States around 1908. He had worked in a candy factory, and then set up his own confectionary business near Boston. Armenian immigrants had a large share of the Boston confectionary market, and Avedis

Company Perspectives:

Following his father's philosophy, Armand Zildjian and the Zildjian Sound Lab technicians maintain a close relationship with today's leading drummers like Steve Gadd, Neil Peart, Vinnie Colaiuta, Dave Weckl, Dennis Chambers, Gregg Bissonette and Lars Ulrich; leading orchestral percussionists like Frank Epstein and Anthony Cirone; major universities; and top Drum Corps like the Blue Devils, Cavaliers and the Cadets. They listen to their music and turn their ideas into sounds. It's no wonder so many professional drummers and percussionists choose their cymbals by name—Zildjian. Because if it doesn't say Zildjian, it's not an authentic Zildjian Cymbal.

had married and was doing well. When his uncle contacted him around 1928, asking him to come back to Turkey and take over the family cymbal factory, Avedis was not interested. Oppression of Armenians in Turkey had led to Aram's own, earlier flight from the country, and Avedis simply did not want to return there. Instead he convinced his uncle to bring the Zildjian company to the United States. It was the world's leading market for musical instruments at the time, and jazz was just taking off. Musicians were experimenting with new sounds and new ways of playing. Consequently, Aram came over to Boston and supervised the building of a factory in Norfolk Downs, Massachusetts. This first factory was a small, dirt-floored garage. It was exposed to salt air and had ready access to salt water, duplicating the conditions of the Turkish factory near Istanbul. Leaving nothing to chance, the company also imported the coal for its smelting furnace from Cardiff, as the Turkish factory did. Avedis Zildjian Co. opened for business in 1929. The factory had three employees.

The year 1929 was not the greatest one during which to start a business. The stock market crash plunged the country into the worst economic depression it had ever seen, leaving many people unemployed and leisure industries such as music drastically cut back. The end of the silent picture era had also put many musicians out of work. Yet jazz was just emerging in the late 1920s, and its growth continued in the 1930s. Avedis Zildjian courted jazz musicians, traveling to jazz hotspots such as the Savoy Ballroom and Dicky Wells' in Harlem, and the many clubs springing up in Chicago and Kansas City. Because he was manufacturing domestically and in small batches, Zildjian could respond to musicians' needs. He made friends with many leading jazz drummers, including Gene Krupa and Dave Tough, and made new cymbals according to their specifications. One of the inventions of the jazz bands of the 1930s was the hi-hat cymbal. This was a device that held two cymbals suspended over each other horizontally. The drummer activated it with a foot pedal, causing the cymbals to clap together. Drummers in the 1920s had come up with various ways to clap their cymbals using boards and springs. Early versions were the "snow shoe," the "low sock," and then the "high sock." Avedis helped perfect technology that let drummers operate the cymbals with the foot, while mounting them high enough so that the drummer could also hit them with a stick. Zildjian followed jazz trends, making hi-hats, thinner cymbals, various sizes, and generally responding to what musicians wanted as the music evolved.

By working closely with cutting-edge percussionists, the Avedis Zildjian Company was able to prosper despite the lean conditions of the Great Depression. The original factory burned down in 1939, but Zildjian replaced it with a more modern facility, forsaking the dirt floor and Cardiff coal Uncle Aram had thought essential. The company began producing cymbals for school marching bands, and Avedis Zildjian again consulted with music directors and worked with them to supply the kinds of cymbals their bands needed.

World War II and After

During World War II, copper and tin were rationed by the government, and so the amount of metal Zildjian could use was curtailed. Yet the company made cymbals for military bands, and these orders were enough to keep Zildjian's factory going. After the war, Zildjian continued to respond to the demands of contemporary musicians. With the advent of Bebop in the 1940s, the cymbal became an even more important member of the drummer's kit, because Bebop percussionists kept the beat on the cymbal instead of the drum. Zildjian developed larger, thicker cymbals in response to Bebop. These were known as the Bop ride and Ping ride cymbals. Through the 1950s, bass drums grew smaller and cymbals larger. Zildjian made ride cymbals in the large diameters drummers demanded, and developed smaller, lighter cymbals—the "crash" cymbal—to provide a contrasting accent sound.

The 1960s brought the Beatles. The enormous popularity of the group, and in particular Ringo Starr's charismatic drumming, caused a surge in amateur drumming in the United States. Demand for Zildjian's cymbals blossomed, growing fourfold in a very short amount of time. By 1968, Zildjian needed to expand its manufacturing facilities to keep up with orders. Though Aram Zildjian had brought the Zildjian family business over to the United States when Avedis Zildjian Co. was founded in 1929, Zildjian cymbals continued to be made in Turkey by a branch of the Zildjian family. Avedis Zildjian Co. had been working since the early 1950s to buy back the rights to certain cymbal lines from the Turkish company. In 1968, Avedis Zildjian Co. bought back all the remaining rights to the Zildjian cymbals made in Turkey. Then Avedis Zildjian opened a new cymbal finishing factory in New Brunswick, Canada. For a time, cymbals made in Turkey were finished in Canada. Eventually though, the Turkish factory closed, and cymbals were made from start to finish by the Canadian subsidiary, which was called Azco Ltd.

In 1972, the U.S. plant was upgraded significantly. The new facility in Norwell, Massachusetts, was as mechanized and technologically advanced as possible, reducing the amount of hand labor required to make the cymbals. The reject rate had always been high in the old manufacturing process. With new machinery, plant managers endeavored to make a more consistent product. Zildjian's line continued to change to meet the needs of popular musicians. The company developed louder, brighter, or dryer sounding cymbals for rock musicians. Zildjians were the choice of many percussionists with major

Key Dates:

1623: Secret formula for cymbal alloy is discovered by a Turkish alchemist named Avedis.
1851: Zildjian cymbals are marketed at trade fairs in London and Paris.
1910: Aram Zildjian is in charge of family business.
1929: Aram passes Zildjian legacy on to his nephew Avedis in the United States.
1981: Company splits; Robert Zildjian founds Canadian company Sabian Ltd.
1999: Craigie Zildjian is appointed first female CEO in company's history.

rock groups, including Ginger Baker of Cream, and Mitch Mitchell, Jimi Hendrix's drummer.

Division of Company Following Avedis Zildjian's Death in 1979

Avedis Zildjian ran the company that bore his name until his death at age 90 in 1979. He left the company to his two sons, Armand and Robert. Though the secret alloy the first Avedis had invented in1623 probably was not much of a secret in the era of modern metallurgy, still the family business had moved through generations by transmission of this recipe to one individual. Armand and Robert Zildjian had both been involved in Avedis Zildjian Co. for years, and when the company was bequeathed to both of them, they had to take to the courts to determine how to proceed. The major problem was that they had extremely different views on how to run the company. Armand, the older brother, was in favor of modern technology and modern business management techniques. Robert apparently had more of a hands-on approach to running the business, and did not want outside consultants giving him advice. Robert also advocated making a lower-priced line of cymbals to appeal to young amateurs. Armand did not want to. Resentment between the brothers escalated to ferocious animosity. In 1981, the company split, with Robert taking the Canadian subsidiary. He renamed it Sabian.

Sabian continued to make cymbals in an old-fashioned process, with a large amount of skilled hand work. Zildjian moved in the opposite direction, filling its factory with computerized controls so that hand-work was at a minimum. Sabian agreed not to compete with Zildjian in the U.S. market until 1983. It entered the market in a fiercely antagonistic mode, claiming that Sabian cymbals were the true Zildjians, made by the ancient recipe. Both companies innovated, following the ideas of professional drummers and using well-known musicians to endorse their products. By the mid-1980s, Zildjian was still the leading cymbal manufacturer in the world, with a market share of about 40 percent worldwide. Sabian was in second place or close to second place, sharing the spot with a Swiss company, Paiste A.G.

1990s and Beyond

In the following decade, Zildjian continued to lead the world cymbal market, despite competition from Sabian. Sales stood at around $34 million by the late 1990s, with the total worldwide market for cymbals valued at only about $50 million. The company entered a new line of business beginning in 1989, when it purchased a drumstick manufacturing plant in Alabama. In the 1990s Zildjian grew to become one of the world's leading drumstick manufacturers. When Zildjian celebrated its 375th anniversary in 1998, it was endorsed by many of the leading jazz drummers in the United States. Zildjian also courted symphonic talent, working with a percussionist from the Boston Symphony to come up with a new line of cymbals for orchestral use. In the late 1990s, Zildjian's product line ran from tiny finger cymbals and low-priced cymbals for beginners to handcrafted Ride cymbals retailing for over $600. In 1999, Armand Zildjian named his daughter Craigie as vice-president and CEO. He remained president and chairman, but it seemed clear that she would be his successor, the first woman in such a position in the firm's history.

Principal Competitors

Sabian Ltd.; Paiste A.G.

Further Reading

Blades, James, *Percussion Instruments and Their History,* New York: Frederick A. Praeger, 1970.
Brewer, Margot, "Status Cymbals," *Canadian Business*, September 1985, p. 67.
Pinksterboer, Hugo, *The Cymbal Book,* Milwaukee, Wis.: Hal Leonard Publishing Corp., 1992.
Plazonja, Jonathan, "Avedis Zildjian, the Father of Cymbals," *Modern Drummer*, November 1995.
Stiff, David, "Cymbaling Rivalry: Two Brothers Clash in the Music Business," *Wall Street Journal*, April 21, 1995, pp. A1, A12.

—A. Woodward

Avid Technology Inc.

Avid Technology Park
1 Park West
Tewkesbury, Massachusetts 01876
U.S.A.
Telephone: (978) 640-6789
Fax: (978) 640-1366
Web site: http://www.avid.com

Public Company
Incorporated: 1987
Employees: 1,550
Sales: $452.6 million (1999)
Stock Exchanges: NASDAQ
Ticker Symbol: AVID
NAIC: 511210 Software Publishers

Avid Technology Inc. is a pioneer in the development of digital video editing systems and provides the tools to help Hollywood studios, post-production houses, and newsrooms make the transition from analog film to digital video. Through acquisitions the company has acquired the technology to provide digital audio and newsroom automation systems. In addition to professional-level systems, Avid also publishes video editing software for amateurs and novices for use on Macintosh and Windows operating systems. With the growth of streaming media on the Internet, Avid has dedicated itself to providing Internet-based solutions for video, audio, and other high-bandwidth streaming media.

Revolutionizing Film and Video Editing: 1987–93

Avid Technology Inc. was founded in 1987 by William J Warner. He developed a system to copy video footage in real time to digital hard disks to allow editors to more easily view shots and quickly make trial cuts and changes. Warner originally designed the system on an Apollo computer. When Warner's preliminary system came to the attention of Apple Computer Inc. in the fall of 1988, he was persuaded to switch to a Macintosh computer. Avid and Apple became informal partners, with Avid receiving marketing help, technical support, and distribution matching from Apple. At the time the Apple Development Group was working with some 10,000 similar companies that were developing hardware and software for the Macintosh.

In 1989 Avid introduced its Media Composer system, a digital nonlinear editing system that revolutionized the film and video post-production process by providing editors with faster, more intuitive, and more creative ways to work than was possible with traditional analog linear methods. In linear editing, the editor starts at the beginning and continues chronologically to the end. Nonlinear video editing, on the other hand, is not necessarily chronological; it depends on the rapid recall and utilization of any segment of the original video sequences. Avid's Media Composer system, priced between $50,000 and $80,000, integrated all of the monitors and tape recorders that were previously needed to get from one place to the next in the video editing process. Avid did it on a PC-based platform and in a visual way that let editors click directly on an image.

Warner served as president and CEO of Avid until May 1991, when Curt A. Rawley was hired as president and COO. Warner retained his CEO title until September 1991, when Rawley was promoted to president and CEO. In 1992 Warner established and became chairman of Wildfire Communications, Inc., a developer of personal communications products. He remained a part-time employee of Avid.

In April 1992 Avid released its Open Media Framework (OMF) into the public domain. According to *PC Week,* "Industry analysts describe OMF as a high-end version of Apple Computer Inc.'s QuickTime, which synchronizes video and audio." Later in the year Silicon Graphics Inc. (SGI) and Avid announced an agreement whereby SGI would bundle OMF with its Iris RISC workstations to provide users with a multimedia platform. Upon its release OMF received support from some 20 companies, among them Eastman Kodak Co., Polaroid Corp., and C-Cube Microsystems Inc. By this time Avid's Media Composer system for professional TV and film post-production was in use at nearly 1,000 sites.

In 1993 Avid's Media Suite Pro was described by *Computer Graphics World* as "in a class by itself" and "the closest thing

Company Perspectives:

Today, Avid offers a broad range of products and solutions to multiple markets that vary dramatically in terms of user requirements, applications, and budgets. All of Avid's products stem from the company's core philosophy: provide customers with innovative, computer-based content creation tools that will allow them to work faster, more productively, and with greater creative freedom—and, in many cases, do things that simply were not possible before. Avid is also extending its business of providing industry-leading client tools for audio and video creation and production into Internet infrastructure technology that helps customers exploit opportunities created by the Internet. Avid is helping content creators and distributors leverage the full power of the Internet by providing them with new, complete, connected, and collaborative solutions.

to real-time, non-linear video production available.'' The turnkey system for Apple's QuickTime consisted of the Media Suite Pro software, a NuVista video board, a CD-quality audio board, and an SCSI accelerator board for pre-approved hard drives. In its review of the Media Suite Pro 1.1 digital video editing system, priced at $9,995, *PC Week* said it ''offers sophisticated editing tools for both novices and experienced users and sets a new standard for desktop video post-production.''

Also in 1993 Avid entered into a six-year partnership with Lucasfilm Ltd. to develop a better nonlinear editor. The project would involve combining features developed by *Star Wars* producer George Lucas with Avid's existing editors. The new editor would be based on Silicon Graphics computers, which indicated Avid's commitment to serve a variety of computer platforms. During 1993 Avid and SGI continued to work together to create Open Media Framework Interchange standards for computer graphic and editing products, which would become a key enabling technology for all-digital post-production. This industry-standard file format permitted the exchange of digital media among different platforms and applications.

Meanwhile, Media Suite Pro 2.0 was scheduled to ship in the fall of 1993. From 1989 to 1993, when the company went public, Avid's revenue jumped from $1 million to $112 million. The company was positioned to provide the broadcast industry with tools to help it make the transition from analog to digital. Avid's latest system would allow a video image to exist as a digital computer signal, from the time it entered a studio, through editing, and finally through a transmitter, thus virtually eliminating the need for video tape. Hollywood studios could purchase an Avid editing system for less than $100,000, compared with about $1 million for a fully equipped film-editing studio. In addition to saving money, the Avid film editing system gave film editors more creative freedom and the ability to edit quickly.

For home video enthusiasts, Avid introduced VideoShop 2.0 for $499. This QuickTime movie-editing program was originally produced by DiVA Corp., which Avid acquired in 1993. For TV stations, Avid offered the AirPlay playback system. Other products included NewsCutter, a news editing system; Media Recorder, a VCR replacement; and AvidNet, a networking system for sending video between different programs. Together, AvidNet and MediaServer created an integrated, networked audio, video, and film environment.

Developing Newsroom Automation and Other New Technologies: 1994–96

In 1994 Avid acquired the news division of BASYS Automation Systems, based in Langley, England, and SofTECH Systems Inc. of Maryland, two leading providers of newsroom computer systems for broadcasters, for a total of $5.5 million. The acquisition gave Avid an installed customer base of 500 firms, including CNN and NBC, for the newsroom automation equipment.

Along with increased demand for Avid's Media Composer nonlinear editing system came a demand for training on the system. Avid set up a program to designate selected companies as Avid Authorized Education Centers. Media Composer was used by post-production companies, advertising agencies, and other corporations.

At the November 1994 Comdex trade show and exhibition, Avid announced Media Suite Pro for Windows, one of the first nonlinear professional video production tools for Windows. The product was scheduled to ship in April 1995 through resellers, with the software priced at $15,000 and $35–$40,000 for hardware and software combined. Included in the system were video-capture, compression, and audio boards and an SCSI-2 disk controller. The system would run on a 486-based PC with 20 megabytes of RAM, a three-gigabyte or larger hard drive, and a pair of speakers.

In 1995 Avid completed its $200 million merger with Digidesign Inc., a pioneering developer of digital audio production software based in Menlo Park, California. The acquisition formed the basis for Avid's new professional audio products group, which would be headed by Digidesign President and CEO Peter Gotcher. Avid also acquired Parallax Software Inc. and Elastic Reality Inc., two leading developers of paint, compositions, effects, and image manipulation software, in 1995.

Avid introduced its disk-based camera technology at the April 1995 convention of the National Association of Broadcasters. Following the introduction, Avid's stock jumped nearly six points, an increase of about 20 percent. The company also announced plans for its new nonlinear online suite called Media Spectrum. The system provided full-resolution, uncompressed digital image quality and was based on SGI's Onyx platform. Although individual components of the system were available separately, a complete package with SGI's Onyx supercomputer would be priced at $450,000. Other new products introduced in 1995 included Avid's CamCutter camera for TV and cable news reporting that recorded images on a computer disk rather than on film. Later in the year Avid released its 32-bit Real Impact for Windows NT package, which let users create digital video content for multimedia presentations, CD-ROMs, information kiosks, interactive training, and Internet distribution, as well as for videotapes. Real Impact was priced at $2,995 and ran on a 486- or Pentium-based PC running Windows NT 3.51. It replaced the company's Media Suite Pro for Windows.

Key Dates:

1987: William J. Warner founds Avid Technology Inc.
1989: Avid introduces the Media Composer system.
1994: Avid acquires the news division of BASYS Automation Systems and SofTECH Systems Inc.
1995: Avid merges with Digidesign Inc. and acquires Parallax Software Inc. and Elastic Reality Inc.
1997: Intel Corporation invests $14.75 million in Avid.
1998: Avid acquires Softimage Inc. from Microsoft Corporation.

Avid and SGI formalized their alliance in September 1995 and announced they would jointly develop a complete newsroom system to be priced between $1 million and $3 million. The prototype for the alliance was the Avid/SGI system being installed in CNN's new digital production facility for the CNN Financial Network. In December Hearst Broadcasting placed a $1.5 million order for three Avid NewsView newsroom automation systems. CBS News also purchased multiple Avid Media Composers for work on the network's news magazines.

The year 1995 was difficult financially for Avid. Although revenue nearly doubled from $203.7 million in 1994 to $406.6 million in 1995, the company reported a 22 percent drop in earnings to $15.4 million, with fourth quarter net income dropping 77 percent despite a 46 percent increase in quarterly revenue. In January 1996 the firm announced that Daniel Keshian, vice-president and general manager of Avid's post-production division, would be promoted to president of Avid. Curt Rawley would remain as CEO and take on the new position of vice-chairman of the board. The company also was looking for a permanent head for its broadcast division, following the departure of Tony Mark in May 1995. In April 1996 William Miller, former chairman of Quantum Corp., was named CEO and chairman, with Rawley remaining as vice-chairman. The company hoped to improve its financial performance in 1996 by cutting back on research and development and eliminating 100 jobs. Development of the disk-based camera, a joint venture with Tokyo-based Ikegami, had proved extremely costly. By the end of 1996 Keshian had resigned as president, leaving William Miller as chairman, CEO, and president of Avid.

Avid introduced Beyond Reality 1.0 in the spring of 1996. Priced at $9,995, Beyond Reality was based on Elastic Reality, a special effects technology that Avid acquired in 1995. It enabled users to create special effects in two- and three-dimensional graphics, including morphs, composites, and warps. Avid continued to form alliances with other companies, announcing joint development partnerships with Hewlett-Packard and Panasonic Broadcast Television Systems at the NAB convention in April 1996.

Later in 1996 Avid postponed launching its Media Spectrum system with SGI's Onyx supercomputer. During 1996 Avid had released Fusion and Illusion, two standalone products for editing and graphics effects, that were to be portions of Spectrum. After extensive beta testing of Media Spectrum at ten sites worldwide, Avid determined that it did not deliver on price performance when coupled with the SGI Onyx. As an alternative, Fusion and Illusion could be networked together to run on the same workstation or two separate ones.

Other new products included the first release of AvidNews, the company's next-generation newsroom automation system. AvidNews would allow journalists to browse low-resolution video feeds and build a shot list, compose text scripts, create spreadsheet-style rundowns for on-air playout, and publish finished stories to the Web in HTML (hypertext markup language). AvidNews was directly accessible to Avid's NewsCutter nonlinear editing system and was scheduled for beta testing in Europe in January 1997, with shipping to begin in June 1997. In August 1998 the CNN News Group selected AvidNews to replace 150 existing Avid NetStations for CNN Headline News. If the Headline News installation proved successful, CNN would roll out AvidNews throughout CNN, CNNfn, CNN International, and all CNN domestic and international bureaus.

For fiscal 1996 Avid reported revenue of $429 million and a net loss of $38 million. Contributing to the loss were a one-time charge of $29 million, an increase of $15.6 million in R&D, a nearly $25 million increase in selling and general administrative expenses, and an additional $40 million attributed to cost of sales.

Strengthening Ties with Microsoft and Intel: 1997–98

In March 1997 it was announced that Intel Corporation would invest $14.75 million in Avid by purchasing a 6.75 percent interest in the company's common stock. Although Avid's customers tended to be loyal Macintosh users, an Intel spokesperson noted that Intel's next-generation Pentium processors would be well suited for high-end video editing work. It was expected that future and current Avid products would be tailored for use on both Intel-based PCs and Macintoshes.

Avid enjoyed a financial comeback in 1997, showing strong first-half revenue and overall revenue of $471.3 million for fiscal 1997, an increase of 9.9 percent. After trimming operating costs, the company returned to profitability with net income of $26.4 million.

In mid-1998 Avid acquired Softimage Inc. from Microsoft Corporation for $285 million in stock and cash to strengthen its television finishing and 3-D product lines. Based in Montreal, Softimage developed high-end software for all areas of professional visual content production, including tools for 3-D and 2-D animation and for creating, editing, and finishing graphics and effects-centric video programs. Softimage had an installed base of more than 21,000 products used by more than 6,000 customers. As a result of the acquisition, Microsoft owned about 9.1 percent of Avid's shares of common stock then outstanding and received warrants to purchase up to 12 percent of Avid's stock over the next three years.

Later in 1998 Avid entered into a technology alliance with competitor Tektronix, which subsequently announced that it would exit the nonlinear editing business following the release of its Lightworks VIP 4500 3.0 in 1999. The alliance combined Avid's newsroom nonlinear editing systems with Tektronix's playback servers, storage, routing, and networking products to create a "production-to-air digital broadcast solution." Effective October 1, 1998, Tektronix became the exclusive distributor of Avid's broadcast products in the United States and Canada and could also sell Avid's professional products to broadcast customers in both countries on a nonexclusive basis.

Before the end of 1998 Avid shipped Symphony, a nonlinear noncompressed editing system for Windows NT that was priced at $150,000 for a basic turnkey system. Employing the familiar Avid Media Composer interface, Symphony was essentially a noncompressed version of Media Composer. For 1998 the company reported revenue of $482.2 million and a net loss of $3.6 million. Contributing to the loss were a one-time charge of $28.4 million and an amortization/depreciation charge of $34.2 million.

New Management Addressing Company's Financial Concerns: 1999–2000

The Avid Film Composer won an Academy Award for its concept, design, and engineering, with the Oscar being awarded February 27, 1999. For novice editors, Avid released Avid Cinema for Windows. Priced at $140, Avid Cinema supported Web, CD-ROM, and tape-based distribution.

Avid's revenue in 1999 was affected by broadcasters' reluctance to adopt high-definition TV (HDTV), which required digital editing systems. After third-quarter results failed to meet expectations, CEO William Miller and President and COO Clifford Jenks resigned. Contributing to Avid's poor financial performance was its 50 percent discount promotion for its new ABVB (Avid Broadcast Video Board)-based Media Composer, which hurt margins. In October 1999 David Krall was named president and COO. He was formerly COO of Avid's Digidesign division. Krall would become Avid's president and CEO in April 2000. As part of its restructuring Avid laid off nearly 200 employees, or 11 percent of its workforce, in November 1999. For fiscal 1999 Avid reported a six percent decline in revenue to $452.6 million and a net loss of $137.5 million.

For 2000 Avid intended to focus on Internet-based products. In June 2000 its new Internet infrastructure division, Edgestreme Systems, introduced the Edgestreme Cluster, a turnkey streaming media server platform. The server platform employed new Internet infrastructure technology that allowed corporate communicators as well as the entertainment industry to deliver streaming media and other high bandwidth content over the Internet. Another Internet-based product introduced in 2000 was Avid ePublisher, a streaming media publishing tool for Web-enabled video production that began shipping in November 2000.

Avid acquired The Motion Factory, Inc. in June 2000. Based in Fremont, California, the company specialized in applications for the creation, delivery, and playback of interactive-rich 3-D media for character-driven games and the Web. The Motion Factory's former president and CEO, David Pritchard, was named general manager of Softimage Co., a subsidiary of Avid Technology.

In September 2000 Avid acquired Pluto Technologies International Inc. Pluto was a video-server vendor that provided video storage and networking solutions for broadcast news, post-production, and other bandwidth-intensive markets. Avid, together with Grass Valley Group and Pluto Technologies, jointly owned Avstar, which marketed newsroom automation equipment.

As 2000 drew to an end, Avid was still in the process of putting its financial house in order. For the first half of the year Avid enjoyed two modestly profitable quarters exclusive of acquisition-related charges. Acquisitions made during the year reinforced Avid's commitment to develop Internet-based products, although its core businesses remained its popular video and film editing systems, professional audio systems, and newsroom automation systems.

Principal Subsidiaries

Softimage Co.; Avstar (50%).

Principal Divisions

Avid Internet Solutions; Edgestreme Systems; Broadcast Media Solutions; Digidesign.

Principal Competitors

FutureTel Inc.; Adobe Systems Inc.; Macromedia Inc.; Pinnacle Systems Inc.; Ulead Systems Inc.; MGI Software Corp.; Grass Valley Group; Quantel Inc.; Autodesk Inc.

Further Reading

Anderson, Karen, "Avid's Shares Take a Spill," *Broadcasting & Cable,* April 5, 1999, p. 14.

"Avid Cinema," *PC Magazine,* May 4, 1999, p. 42.

"Avid Supports Open Framework and Process-Oriented Products," *Shoot,* April 8, 1994, p. 8.

"Avid Technology," *Broadcasting & Cable,* April 17, 1995, p. 80.

Barney, Doug, "Digital Technology Makes Video Easy," *InfoWorld,* August 2, 1993, p. 17.

Bethonet, Herb, "Avid Media Suite Pro Video Editor's Non-Linear Capabilities Eclipse Traditional Editing Systems," *PC Week,* April 5, 1993, p. 97.

"The Boston Globe Fast Track Column," *Knight-Ridder/Tribune Business News,* January 12, 1999.

Bray, Hiawatha, "Intel Invests in Massachusetts' Avid Technology," *Knight-Ridder/Tribune Business News,* March 25, 1997.

Brokaw, Leslie, et al., "Avid Technology: Apple Connection," *Inc.,* November 1989, p. 70.

Churbuck, David C., "The Digital Splice," *Forbes,* June 6, 1994, p. 100.

Clancey, Heather, "Solutions Providers Answer Casting Call," *Computer Reseller News,* April 17, 1995, p. 41.

Coe, Steve, "Lucas, Avid Join Forces," *Broadcasting & Cable,* April 26, 1993, p. 32.

"Curt A. Rawley," *Broadcasting,* September 23, 1991, p. 78.

"Curt Arnold Rawley," *Broadcasting & Cable,* August 9, 1993, p. 63.

DeSalvo, Kathy, "Avid Begins Restructuring," *Shoot,* November 26, 1999, p. 4.

——, "Miller and Jenks Resign from Avid," *Shoot,* November 5, 1999, p. 1.

Dickson, Glen, "Avid Acquires Another 3-D Firm," *Broadcasting & Cable,* July 10, 2000, p. 73.

——, "Avid and Silicon Graphics Announce Team Effort," *Broadcasting & Cable,* October 30, 1995, p. 63.

——, "Avid Has Introduced the First Release of AvidNews," *Broadcasting & Cable,* October 7, 1996, p. 96.

——, ''Avid Makes New Friends in Las Vegas,'' *Broadcasting & Cable,* April 17, 1996, p. 12.
——, ''Avid Picks Miller As New CEO,'' *Broadcasting & Cable,* April 15, 1996, p. 86.
——, ''Avid Reaffirms News Commitment,'' *Broadcasting & Cable,* November 22, 1999, p. 42.
——, ''Avid's Turnaround Man,'' *Broadcasting & Cable,* October 9, 2000, p. 81.
——, ''Avid Technology Makes a Management Edit,'' *Broadcasting & Cable,* January 15, 1996, p. 132.
——, ''Avid Tightens Ship After Leaky 4th Quarter,'' *Broadcasting & Cable,* February 26, 1996, p. 58.
——, ''Headline News Newsroom Chooses Avid,'' *Broadcasting & Cable,* August 3, 1998, p. 41.
——, ''Hearst Makes Big Newsroom Buy,'' *Broadcasting & Cable,* December 11, 1995, p. 90.
——, ''Pluto in Avid's Orbit,'' *Broadcasting & Cable,* September 18, 2000, p. 47.
Dillon, Nancy, ''Avid Posts Vigorous Gains,'' *Computerworld,* August 18, 1997, p. 113.
Donelan, Jenny, ''In Brief,'' *Computer Graphics World,* August 2000, p. 11.
''Fortune Visits 25 Cool Companies,'' *Fortune,* Autumn 1993, p. 56.
Giardina, Carolyn, ''Avid, Digidesign Plan Merger,'' *Shoot,* November 4, 1994, p. 1.
——, ''Avid Shifts from Spectrum,'' *Shoot,* September 6, 1996, p. 1.
——, ''Increased Use of Nonlinear Edit Systems Elicits Need for Training,'' *Shoot,* September 2, 1994, p. 7.
——, ''Making Overtures,'' *Shoot,* March 12, 1999, p. 36.
——, ''NAB: Avid Premieres D1 Nonlinear Editor,'' *Shoot,* April 21, 1995, p. 1.
——, ''Tektronix to Exit Nonlinear Editing Business,'' *Shoot,* September 11, 1998, p. 8.
Hirsch, Evan, ''Avid Takes Users Beyond Reality,'' *Computer Graphics World,* March 1996, p. 72.
Hwang, Diana, ''Multimedia: A Hotbed for Small ISVs Whets Appetite of Software Giants,'' *Computer Reseller News,* April 24, 1995, p. 98.
Jessell, Harry A., ''Avid Avidly Exploring Digital World,'' *Broadcasting & Cable,* February 21, 1994, p. 66.
Kilcollins, Tony, ''Easy Streaming from Avid,'' *Videomaker,* July 2000, p. 10.
Kim, Jeanhee, ''Get into the Movies with This Innovator,'' *Money,* July 1995, p. 72.
Leland, Jon, ''The Full Picture,'' *Computer Graphics World,* March 1993, p. 47.
Linsmayer, Anne, ''The Customer Knows Best,'' *Forbes,* August 24, 1998, p. 92.
MacNicol, Gregory, ''Video Meets PC,'' *Computer Graphics World,* February 1991, p. 55.
McCabe, Kathy, ''The Boston Globe Business Notebook Column,'' *Knight-Ridder/Tribune Business News,* May 1, 2000.
McConnell, Chris, ''Avid Technology,'' *Broadcasting & Cable,* October 10, 1994, p. 102.
——, ''Avid Technology Merging with Digidesign,'' *Broadcasting & Cable,* October 31, 1994, p. 51.
——, ''Curt Rawley: Avid Advocate for a Disk-Based Future,'' *Broadcasting & Cable,* April 3, 1995, p. 63.
——, ''Multimedia Merging into News Production,'' *Broadcasting & Cable,* September 5, 1994, p. 38.
''Measuring the Market,'' *Broadcasting & Cable,* August 21, 2000, p. 26.
Mulqueen, John T., ''Avid Trades Stock and Cash for Microsoft Unit,'' *InternetWeek,* June 22, 1998, p. 65.
Negrino, Tom, ''Avid VideoShop 2.0,'' *Macworld,* February 1994, p. 75.
Ozer, Jan, ''Your Videos—Online,'' *PC Magazine,* May 4, 1999, p. 41.
Schroeder, Erica, ''Avid Aims to Make Real Impact with NT Package,'' *PC Week,* October 9, 1995, p. 34.
——, ''Avid Editing Tool to Offer Professional-Quality Video,'' *PC Week,* November 14, 1994, p. 70.
Scully, Sean, ''Standards Are Operating Procedure for Computer Graphic, Editing Companies,'' *Broadcasting & Cable,* May 10, 1993, p. 45.
Sullivan, Kristina B., ''SGI to Offer Avid's Multimedia Wares on Iris Workstations,'' *PC Week,* July 6, 1992, p. 22.
''Top Executives Out at Avid,'' *Broadcasting & Cable,* October 25, 1999, p. 93.
Vadlamudi, Pardhu, ''Real Impact Converts Video to Digital for Multimedia Apps,'' *InfoWorld,* October 9, 1995, p. 26.

—David P. Bianco

▲Bass

Bass PLC

20 North Audley Street
London W1Y 1WE
United Kingdom
Telephone: (020) 7409 1919
Fax: (020) 7409 8503
Web site: http://www.bass.com

Public Company
Incorporated: 1967 as Bass Charrington Ltd.
Employees: 74,451
Sales: £4.69 billion (US$7.72 billion) (1999)
Stock Exchanges: London New York
Ticker Symbol: BAS
NAIC: 721110 Hotels (Except Casino Hotels) and Motels; 722110 Full-Service Restaurants; 722410 Drinking Places (Alcoholic Beverages); 713120 Amusement Arcades; 713950 Bowling Centers; 312111 Soft Drink Manufacturing

Conceived as a single brewery in the late 18th century, Bass PLC was in the process of a historic transition at the turn of the millennium. Entering 2000, Bass was an international group operating in four main areas: hotels and resorts; pubs, restaurants, and entertainment venues; brewing; and soft drinks. The company, however, was in the process of divesting its two oldest businesses: brewing and pubs. Bass Brewing, the number two brewer in the United Kingdom with two leading brands, Carling Black Label and Tennent's Lager, was being sold to Interbrew S.A.; the pub operations were placed up for sale late in 2000. The remaining company, which would need to adopt a new name, included Bass Hotels & Resorts, one of the largest international hotel groups, owning, operating, or franchising more than 2,900 hotels in more than 95 countries under several names, including Inter-Continental, Crowne Plaza, Holiday Inn, Holiday Inn Express, and Staybridge Suites. In soft drinks, Bass has a 50 percent stake in Britvic Soft Drinks, which holds the U.K. license for Pepsi and 7Up and also makes several other brands, including Robinsons, Tango, and Britvic.

A Steadily Growing Concern in the 18th and 19th Centuries

The founding of Bass dates back to 1777 in the ancient town of Burton-on-Trent in Staffordshire. Although monks had been brewing beer in this town since the 12th century, it was William Bass who laid the foundation for securing Burton's status as the focal point of Britain's brewing activities. William Bass inhabited the house next to the gateway of his brewery; it was here that his son and grandson, both future company leaders, were born. By 1791 Michael Bass, William's son, was actively engaged in his father's business.

By the turn of the century the increased volume of brewing, now 2,000 barrels per year, compelled the family to expand the High Street brewery to twice its original size. In 1821 the company became one of the first brewers to export ale to India after discovering that it was a suitable product for warm climates. Thus was born the "East India Pale Ale," which many other brewers soon imitated.

Michael Thomas Bass, William's grandson, assumed control of the brewery in 1827 when brewing capacity had reached nearly 10,000 barrels per year. By 1837 the company was known by the name of Bass, Ratcliffe & Gretton, after two fellow businessmen—John Gretton and Richard Ratcliffe—who had formed a partnership with Bass. The expansion of the railways greatly benefited the growing business; Burton ales, transported across the nation, became widely recognized as premier brands. With Bass's output surpassing 140,000 barrels a year by 1853, a second brewery was needed. By 1860 volume had increased threefold; a third brewery was constructed.

Michael Thomas Bass became not only an important figure in the industry but also a widely recognized civic leader. He financed the construction of several churches, recreation facilities, and a public library. Moreover, he served in Parliament for 33 years as a member for Derby.

By 1876 Bass was recognized; it was now Britain's largest brewing company. Its bottled ale was so popular that the company was forced to become the first firm in England to make use of the Trade Marks Registration Act of 1875 to protect its red

Company Perspectives:

Our strategy is to be the leading player in each of our businesses, in our chosen geographical areas.

Across our businesses, we continue to build the quality, scale and range of our brands for our customers and in so doing, we create value for our shareholders.

pyramid trademark. A few years prior to Michael Bass's death in 1884, the business was organized as a private limited company. The old brewery on High Street was renovated, but now the Bass empire covered 145 acres of land, the largest ale and bitter beer brewery in the world.

In 1888, under the leadership of Michael Bass's eldest son, Michael A. Bass, later Lord Burton, the company was incorporated as Bass, Ratcliffe & Gretton Ltd. with a share capital of £2.7 million. Output neared one million barrels a year; more than 2,500 men and boys were employed at the breweries.

In the same year that Lord Burton incorporated the company, Gretton's son, John Gretton, Jr., joined the firm. After assuming control of the malting department in 1893, Gretton went on to join the board of directors. Gretton also served as a Conservative MP between 1895 and 1943. Among his many political causes, Gretton opposed the Licensing Bill of 1908 and trade restrictions on the brewing industry during World War I. Upon Lord Burton's death in 1908, Gretton assumed the title of Bass's chairman.

Failing to Modernize in the First Half of the 20th Century

During the next decades Bass's management, unlike that of many competitors, adhered to the free trade system whereby the company relied on small traders to bottle and stock its products. Increasingly, the more common practice for British brewers was to run their own ''public houses'' as outlets to retail their beer. Bass did own a few public houses, but preferred to depend on the continuing national popularity of its brands to achieve expansion. As long as Bass remained in such high demand, the retailing could be left to the free trade customers. While competitors chose to invest money in the improvement of their public houses, Gretton ignored the trend and neglected his properties.

During World War I overall consumption of beer decreased. The brewing industry (through taxation) was used by the government as a source of income. This led to an increase in the price of beer. The advent of radio, cinema, and other modern leisure activities drew patrons away from the public houses. These changes in social attitudes gave further impetus to the brewers to improve their properties. Public houses were increasingly converted to comfortable places where customers could enjoy an evening of food, drink, and conversation.

Yet Gretton chose to continue rejecting the general trend toward improved public houses. Instead, his company spent the decade of the 1920s acquiring several other breweries. In 1926 Bass purchased control of Worthington & Company Ltd., a long-established competitor also located in Burton-on-Trent. The Worthington label, like that of Bass, enjoyed a national reputation. This acquisition, however, did not lead to the kind of merger common in today's market; Worthington remained virtually an autonomous operation.

While Bass continued making acquisitions, including the purchase of a wine and spirit operation, further changes in the industry occurred that were at odds with Bass's traditional approach. The small but growing firm of Mitchells & Butler not only set an industry example by improving its public house properties, but also led a trend in initiating a policy of direct brewery management. Formerly, most brewery-owned houses were run by tenants who were given a free hand to operate the business. Mitchells & Butler imposed new regulations on the tenant managers; it compelled them to sell more of the firm's own beer rather than national brands such as Bass and Worthington. This policy ensured higher earnings and, therefore, a greater return on their investment. Such actions undercut Bass's market position.

Bass's continuing reliance on the free trade system became increasingly anachronistic. But it was not only changing social attitudes and industry trends that contributed to Bass's declining sales in the postwar years; the economic conditions of the early 1930s created further obstacles. As a result of worldwide depression, factories shut down and unemployment increased, and Bass was forced to cut back production.

Gretton had become preoccupied with his nonbusiness activities. He was deeply involved in political life, a vocal advocate of conservative causes. Bass management was not entirely asleep, however. When awareness of hygiene and quality drew consumers to pasteurized and bottled products, Bass capitalized on the trend: it introduced its ''Blue Triangle'' brand in 1934. Sales of this bottled version of the older ''Red Triangle'' grew steadily.

After Gretton died in 1947, Arthur Manners, a longtime Bass executive, assumed the title of chairman. Like Gretton's, his management style was conservative. Yet between the late 1940s and the late 1950s Bass's net profits increased by 123 percent. Expansion took the form of share acquisitions in the equity of fellow brewers. Bass acquired holdings in William Hancock & Company and Wenlock Brewery Company.

Over the next few years, however, Bass's failure to adopt a more modern business approach helped to create competition that previously did not exist. Because of the ''tied house'' system, Bass beer lost popularity to more aggressively marketed national brands and regionally brewed pale ales. The company refused to update its pricing system or adjust to changing public tastes toward milder beers. Even Bass's holdings in other companies were mismanaged; integration was nonexistent and redundant operations put a strain on profits. Although Bass operated an extensive trading network, controlled 17 subsidiaries across the United Kingdom, and still manufactured a venerated beer, a major change was in order.

When Arthur Manners retired as chairman in 1952, his position was filled by C.A. Ball, a 65-year-old executive who had started his career as Manners's typist. Although Ball recognized the need to modernize by hiring professional managers, Bass's

Key Dates:

1777: William Bass begins brewing beer in Burton-on-Trent, Staffordshire.
1888: Company is incorporated as Bass, Ratcliffe & Gretton Ltd.
1926: Bass purchases control of rival beermaker, Worthington & Company.
1961: Bass merges with Mitchells & Butler to form Bass, Mitchells & Butler.
1967: Bass merges with Charrington United Breweries, maker of Carling Lager, to form Bass Charrington Ltd.
1969: Company launches the Crest Hotel chain, marking entry into the lodging sector.
1983: Company is renamed Bass PLC.
1989: Bass acquires the Holiday Inn lodging chain.
1991: The Holiday Inn Express budget lodging chain is launched.
1995: Company acquires Robinsons Soft Drinks.
1997: Company launches the Staybridge Suites lodging chain.
1998: Bass purchases the Inter-Continental Hotels and Resorts chain; the company's remaining gambling-related operations are divested.
2000: Bass reaches agreement to sell its brewing operations to Interbrew.

decline had progressed too far. Ball died in 1959 and was succeeded by the nearly 70-year-old Sir James Grigg, a former cabinet minister under Churchill. Grigg's first action as chairman was to find a suitable merger to help the company solve growing financial difficulties.

Modernizing and Merging in the 1960s and 1970s

H. Alan Walker, the dynamic chief executive director of Mitchells & Butler, approached Grigg, and an agreement was soon completed. Walker had built Mitchells & Butler into one of the most efficient and financially successful breweries in the industry. By closing down unprofitable operations, by modernizing marketing and production, and by acquiring other breweries, he had significantly improved the company's performance. Yet Walker's company was not large enough to protect itself against any potential takeover bid; he was looking for a merger of his own choosing. Bass, Ratcliffe & Gretton merged with Mitchells & Butler in 1961.

At virtually the same time, another industry merger occurred that would play an important role in Bass's future. In 1962 Charrington & Company Ltd., a London brewery with a history dating back to 1766, merged with United Breweries, the brewers of the national brands of Carling Lager and Jubilee Stout. Whereas Charrington functioned in many ways as a family concern, United was a new consortium of medium-sized brewers from various parts of the United Kingdom.

The formation of Charrington United Breweries created a well-balanced national company with strong ties to London and an established distribution network across the United Kingdom. Almost the exact same thing could be said of the Bass, Mitchells & Butler merger. With Walker assuming the title of chief executive and Grigg maintaining his position as chairman, the management began a program of rationalization to integrate and modernize the companies' operations.

By the late 1960s, however, the management of both newly formed companies recognized the unfulfilled potential in their firms' performance. Although Charrington United Breweries controlled a variety of regional brands, the company lacked a premium draft beer such as Bass or Worthington. Bass, Mitchells & Butler lacked a spirit and soft drinks business as successful as that of Charrington United Breweries' Canada Dry subsidiary. Although the mergers improved the two companies' national distribution networks, areas of weakness existed for both firms. In 1967 a new merger was arranged between Charrington United Breweries and Bass, Mitchells & Butler.

Bass Charrington Ltd. was an immediate success. The easy integration process was followed by years of effort to improve market position. This improvement slowed for a short time between 1973 and 1974 as a result of rising inflation and economic recession. By 1975, however, company performance once again improved, and Bass Charrington began to garner the benefits from its investments and expansion.

Diversifying: 1980s Through Mid-1990s

By the early 1980s the newly renamed Bass PLC had registered an 18 percent increase in its earnings. Under the leadership of Chairman Derek Palmar, Bass now managed more pubs in the United Kingdom than any other industry competitor. Furthermore, the company successfully capitalized on the growing market for lager. Yet in many ways Bass maintained its conservative management policies. A ''Bass package'' of regional ales continued to be distributed by the free trade system. Similarly, Bass's property improvements, though generous, were more concerned with promoting family establishments than catering to younger clients. A program of diversification led Bass to create a leisure division. Although mostly profitable, their subsidiaries, which included a hotel business and betting shops, contributed less than 20 percent to profits. Bass remained one of the least diversified of the major brewers.

In the late 1980s, however, Bass's leisure activities assumed a greater role in the company, particularly after Ian Prosser took over as chairman and chief executive in 1987. The hotel division, through its Coral and Crest subsidiaries, enjoyed healthy financial gains. Indeed, Crest became one of the fastest-growing British companies in Europe. In May 1987 Bass announced an agreement with the U.S.-based Holiday Corporation to purchase eight European Holiday Inn hotels for £152 million. Two years later, Bass dramatically increased its hotel holdings when it acquired the full Holiday Inn chain from Holiday Corporation in 1989 for US$2.23 billion. Bass gained 55 company-owned Holiday Inn hotels, the Holiday Inn brand name, and franchise rights to the more than 1,400 Holiday Inn hotels that were franchised or based on joint ventures. The remainder of Holiday Corporation—which included Embassy Suites, Hampton Inns, and Homewood Suites properties and Harrah's casinos—was spun off to shareholders as Promus Companies Inc.

The initial years under Bass were difficult ones for Holiday Inn. Founded in Memphis in 1952 and named after the film *Holiday Inn,* the chain grew rapidly in the United States, mainly along the burgeoning highways of the 1950s and 1960s. By the time of its acquisition by Bass, Holiday Inns could be found in nearly 50 countries, but were beginning to show their age back home in the United States. Holiday Inn had built its empire in the middle of the lodging market, attracting both business customers and vacationers. As its properties aged and its service declined, the chain was being squeezed by a drop-off in business customers dissatisfied with the service and travelers not willing to pay rates that had crept higher and were ever more uncompetitive given the rise of newer, cut-rate chains such as Hampton Inn. To counter these trends, Bass in 1990 initiated a US$1 billion renovation of the Holiday Inn chain to be completed over the course of several years. Bass also began to expand its top-of-the-line Crowne Plaza hotels to gain market share on the high end, while it simultaneously launched its own cut-rate chain called Holiday Inn Express in 1991 to win back budget-conscious customers. By 1995 Bass had more than doubled the number of Crowne Plaza properties to over 100, while Holiday Inn Express reached the 350 mark. Another part of Bass's strategy was to aggressively expand all three of the chains outside North America, concentrating primarily on Europe and the Asia/Pacific region. During 1995, the number of countries with Holiday Inn properties exceeded 60 and the total number of Bass lodging properties passed 2,000. Finally, Bass in 1992 invested US$60 million in technology upgrades, including a new Holiday Inn Reservation Optimization system to improve its reservations capability.

None of these moves paid off immediately, however, and the Holiday Inn division dragged down Bass's overall operating results with decreases in profits for the hotel operations in 1991 and 1992. Meanwhile, evidence of Bass's displeasure with its acquisition became evident from a 1992 lawsuit it filed against Promus. The suit alleged that Promus had intentionally withheld important information from Bass during the acquisition negotiations, thus inflating the price Bass paid. Wishing to free itself from the suit in order to move forward with a split of the company, Promus settled with Bass in 1995 without admitting guilt and agreed to pay US$49 million. While the suit was being contested, Holiday Inn seemed to turn the corner with an 18 percent increase in profits in 1993, followed by more modest four percent and 2.4 percent profit increases in 1994 and 1995.

The turnaround in lodging came just in time as Bass experienced difficulties in its brewery unit in the 1990s stemming from a decline in beer drinking in England. Beer sales for Bass declined 0.8 percent in 1994, then fell 5.1 percent in 1995. With the English beer market soft, Bass continued to expand its soft drink holdings with the 1995 acquisition of Robinsons Soft Drinks from Reckitt & Colman plc for £103 million. This was an indirect acquisition in that Robinsons became a subsidiary of Britannia Soft Drinks Limited, which was 50 percent owned by Bass (with 25 percent shares for both Whitbread and Company PLC and Allied-Domecq PLC); Britannia, in turn, held a 90 percent stake in Britvic Soft Drinks Limited, with the other ten percent belonging to Pepsico Holdings Limited. The leisure retailing sector was bolstered through the purchase in 1995 of 78 Harvester pub restaurants and the Harvester brand from Forte Plc for £165 million. The brewery sector was not left out of the 1995 spending spree, however, as Bass increased its holdings in the Czech Republic with the purchase of majority stakes in the Czech brewing companies Vratislavice A.S. and Ostravar A.S. and established a joint venture in China—the world's second largest beer market—with the Ginsber Beer Group.

Focusing on Hotels in the Late 1990s and Beyond

In 1996 Bass reached an agreement to acquire 50 percent of Carlsberg-Tetley for £200 million. The intention was to merge the rival brewer into Bass Brewers (the company's beer subsidiary), with Bass PLC owning 80 percent of the resultant business and Carlsberg A/S owning 20 percent. Bass Brewers would have become the number one brewery firm in the United Kingdom, with a 37 percent market share, but the deal was blocked for antitrust reasons in mid-1997 by the country's secretary of trade and industry. Bass suffered a further blow to its expansion efforts in October 1997 when it was outbid for William Hill, a chain of betting shops, by the Nomura Securities Co., Ltd. Meanwhile, in April 1997 Bass reduced its presence in the mid-market hotel sector by selling 60 company-managed Holiday Inns in the United States and Canada to Bristol Hotel Company for US$391 million and a minority stake in Bristol that initially stood at 36 percent. In October of that same year, Bass launched its fourth hotel brand, Staybridge Suites, a new entry into the growing extended-stay niche.

While continuing to seek out acquisition targets, Bass from December 1997 to August 1998 disposed of a host of businesses, raising £1.3 billion in the process. These included all of the company's gambling-related operations: the Coral chain of betting shops, the Gala bingo chain, and the subsidiaries that focused on manufacturing electronic entertainment and gaming machines. Also sold off were the firm's leased pub business and more than 300 smaller managed pubs. Following the divestments, Bass created a new pub and restaurant division called Bass Leisure Retail.

As its cash horde was growing through the portfolio pruning, Bass finally completed, in March 1998, a long-awaited major acquisition. That month the company bought the Inter-Continental Hotels and Resorts chain from the Saison Group of Japan for £1.8 billion (US$2.9 billion), besting Marriott International, Inc. in an intense bidding war. The addition of Inter-Continental's 117 upscale hotels provided Bass with a bolstered presence in the high end of the hotel market, particularly in Latin America and Europe—where it had a weak position compared with its core U.S. market. Inter-Continental became part of the newly named Bass Hotels & Resorts division.

In mid-1999 Bass Hotels launched a two-year, £900 million (US$1.4 billion) expansion program as the first step in a five-year plan to quadruple the size of its upscale Inter-Continental and Crowne Plaza brands. Expansion in the North American market was particularly targeted for these brands. At the same time, the Holiday Inn and Holiday Inn Express chains were to be expanded in the United Kingdom, Germany, Italy, and China. Further growth of the lodging unit came in January 2000 through the purchase of Southern Pacific Hotels Corporation, operator of 59 hotels in the Asia-Pacific region, for about £128 million.

By early 2000 Bass operated the world's second largest hotel group, with nearly 3,000 properties and 480,000 rooms. The hospitality businesses, which included both Bass Hotels & Resorts and Bass Leisure Retail, were driving growth at the company, particularly compared with the continuing doldrums of the brewing operation. With the additional impetus of an ongoing consolidation drive in the world beer industry, Bass made the historic decision to sell Bass Brewers, reaching an agreement with Interbrew S.A. of Belgium in June 2000 on a £2.3 billion (US$3.5 billion) deal. Provided that the deal passed antitrust muster, Bass would be able to use the proceeds to further expand its lodging empire, including a planned entrance into the timeshare market. The fragmented hotel industry was ripe for global consolidation. The company also hoped that its stock would rise in value with the jettisoning of the now albatross-like brewing operations. Later in 2000, Bass also placed up for sale its pub operations, with Japan's Nomura understood to be a likely buyer. It was speculated that Bass might eventually sell off all of Bass Leisure Retail, transforming itself into a pure hotel company. In any event, it was clear that in his 13 years at the helm of Bass, Prosser had thoroughly transformed the company. In October 2000 Prosser stepped down as chief executive but remained chairman; Tim Clarke, who had headed Bass Leisure Retail, stepped up to the chief executive slot.

Principal Subsidiaries

CORPORATE ACTIVITIES: Bass America Inc. (U.S.A.); Bass Holdings Limited; Bass International Holdings N.V. (Netherlands); Bass Investments Limited; Bass Overseas Holdings Limited. BASS HOTELS & RESORTS: BHR Holdings BV (Netherlands); BHR Luxembourg SA; Holiday Hospitality Corporation (U.S.A.); Holiday Inns Franchising Inc. (U.S.A.). BASS LEISURE RETAIL: Bass Leisure Entertainments Limited; Bass Taverns Limited; Toby Restaurants Limited. BRITVIC SOFT DRINKS: Britannia Soft Drinks Limited (50%); Britvic Soft Drinks Limited (90%); Robinsons Soft Drinks Limited. OTHER ACTIVITIES: Bass Developments Limited; Société Viticole de Château Lascombes SA (France; 97.5%); White Shield Insurance Company Limited (Gibraltar).

Principal Divisions

Bass Hotels & Resorts; Bass Leisure Retail; Britvic Soft Drinks.

Principal Competitors

Accor; Best Western International Inc.; De Vere Group PLC; Enterprise Inns PLC; Greene King plc; Hilton Hotels Corporation; J D Wetherspoon plc; Marriott International, Inc.; The Nomura Securities Co., Ltd.; Punch Taverns Group Ltd.; Scottish & Newcastle plc; Starwood Hotels & Resorts Worldwide, Inc.; Whitbread PLC; The Wolverhampton & Dudley Breweries, PLC.

Further Reading

Bass: The Story of the World's Most Famous Ale, Burton-on-Trent: Bass, 1927.

Beck, Ernest, ''Bass Wins Battle for Inter-Continental,'' *Wall Street Journal,* February 23, 1998, p. A19.

Carreyrou, John, and Beck, Ernest, ''Interbrew to Acquire Bass's Beer Operations,'' *Wall Street Journal,* June 15, 2000, p. A20.

Clark, Jack J., ''Holiday Inn: New Rooms in the Inn,'' *Cornell Hotel and Restaurant Administration Quarterly,* October 1993, p. 59.

Daneshkhu, Scheherazade, and Voyle, Susanna, ''Brewing Sale Positions Bass to Open Doors Overseas,'' *Financial Times,* June 13, 2000, p. 33.

DeMarco, Edward, ''Holiday Inn's Profits Surged in '94, Helping Bass,'' *Atlanta Business Chronicle,* February 24, 1995, p. 18B.

Hawkins, Chuck, Maremont, Mark, and Cuneo, Alice, ''Bass Can't Get Comfortable at Holiday Inns,'' *Business Week,* March 2, 1992, p. 42.

Nozar, Robert A., ''Acquisition Adds to Bass' Global Umbrella,'' *Hotel and Motel Management,* March 16, 1998, pp. 1, 9.

Oram, Roderick, ''Bass Options Make Heady Cocktail for Investors,'' *Financial Times,* February 28, 1996, p. 23.

''Room for Reservations,'' *Economist,* July 1, 2000, p. 64.

Rowe, Megan, ''Holiday Inn: From Fat and Sassy to Lean and Mean,'' *Lodging Hospitality,* July 1992, pp. 24–26.

Tieman, Ross, ''Brewer in Search of a Strategy: Bass Must Look at Alternative Ways to Expand Its Profits,'' *Financial Times,* August 27, 1997, p. 15.

Willman, John, ''A Heady Brew of Hotels and Leisure But the Shares Have a Hangover,'' *Financial Times,* December 11, 1999, p. 12.

—updated by David E. Salamie

Bay State Gas Company

300 Friberg Pkwy.
Westborough, Massachusetts 01581-5039
U.S.A.
Telephone: (508) 836-7000
Fax: (508) 836-7070
Web site: http://www.baystategas.com

Wholly Owned Subsidiary of NiSource, Inc.
Incorporated: 1974
Employees: 1,244
Sales: $450.0 million (1998)
NAIC: 221210 Natural Gas Distribution

Bay State Gas Company is a wholly owned subsidiary of NiSource, Inc., acquired in a 1999 merger that created the tenth largest U.S. natural gas distribution company. With headquarters located in Westborough, Bay State serves its home state of Massachusetts as well as New Hampshire and Maine. Although its primary business remains the distribution of natural gas to more than 300,000 customers, Bay State was making efforts even before the merger with NiSource to take advantage of the movement to deregulate utilities in order to create a new business model for the company. Bay State sees itself not so much as a gas company but as an evolving retail energy marketer, providing a variety of energy products and solutions.

The 19th Century and the Advent of Gas Lighting

The roots of Bay State reach back to the first half of the 19th century and the rise of the gas lighting industry. Scientists had experimented throughout the 1700s with the concept of creating an illuminant from gas distilled from coal that could potentially replace candles and oil lamps, but it was not until 1798 that the technology was ready to be applied in a commercial way. William Murdock distributed coal gas through pipes in the Boulton and Watt Soho Works in Birmingham, England. In 1807 Frederick Winsor used gas to light the Pall Mall section of London, and in 1812 he was granted a charter from Parliament to create The London and Westminster Chartered Gas Light and Coke Company. By 1823 some 23 English cities had gas street lighting. Paris had gas lights in 1816, and Vienna in 1818.

In Colonial America the lighting of city streets was the responsibility of citizens. In New York in 1697, every seven householders were required to share the expense of a candle to burn in a lantern suspended on a pole from the window of every seventh house. It was not until 1762 that New York erected wooden public lampposts from which oil lamps burned dimly. A small army of lamp lighters maintained the system. In the evening the lamps were lit by torch, and the next morning the flames would be blown out, the wicks trimmed, and the supply of oil replenished. Across the East River in Brooklyn, candles in the front windows of houses would serve as street lighting until 1820, when oil lamps on public lampposts were finally introduced. By then gas illumination was already making serious inroads in the United States.

The country's first gas company to be chartered was located in Baltimore in 1817, followed by Boston in 1822, and New York a year later. New York replaced its wooden lampposts with cast-iron lamps in 1827, when in June of that year gas streetlights were first lit. Even then, for the next 30 years the lamps would be dark on nights when it was determined by the calendar that there should be sufficient moonlight, despite any overcast conditions that might arise.

One of the earliest companies created to provide street lighting in the United States was an ancestor of Bay State: the Springfield Gas Light Company, formed in 1847 and chartered in 1848. It is not known when the Massachusetts company moved beyond street lighting to begin providing residential service for illumination, but according to its records Springfield Gas ran steam lines in order to provide gas heat to buildings in 1878. The company began heating homes in 1916.

Although electric lighting was made practical by Thomas Edison in the early 1880s, gas lighting maintained its dominance for many more years to come. Electric lights with their intense white light were not as accommodating as gas lighting, and generally only appropriate for theaters, factories, stores, and other large settings. Competition from electric lights, however, forced gas to be innovative in order to maintain its position as a cheap

Company Perspectives:

Understanding customer needs has led to success in introducing energy products and services that provide value to our customers.

alternative. The invention of the Auer or Welsbach lamp, using a process that involved bringing a mantle to incandescence with a non-luminous flame, provided softer illumination while providing three times the amount of light and consuming only half as much gas. One method to make gas affordable to customers that was employed by many companies, including Springfield Gas, was the ''prepayment meter,'' also known as the ''quarter meter.'' A meter with a coin slot allowed the customer to purchase a measured volume of gas. This pay-as-you-go system was used by Springfield Gas from 1893 to 1929.

It was not until the years following World War I that electric lighting finally superseded gas. The use of gas as a fuel for heating and cooking, however, remained quite viable. In the beginning of the 19th century, wood was the most common fuel used by households, replaced later by coal ranges. Early in the 20th century, gas ranges began superseding coal for a variety of reasons. In essence, gas was more efficient in cooking, with no wasted fuel, therefore making it cheaper; and unlike coal, gas required no hauling or cleanup. Gas heat enjoyed similar advantages: units were smaller, were quicker to heat a room, and required little maintenance.

The United States was served by a multitude of small companies such as Springfield Gas, that produced their product in local plants. Typically, gas was made by reducing coal to coke in a retort house, then piped to another facility where it was purified by lime. The gas was then piped to an immense tank called a gasholder or ''gasometer.'' This method of producing gas would remain essentially unchanged and predominant until the 1930s and the advent of natural gas, which is found, like other petroleum products, trapped within the Earth's strata. Used for centuries, natural gas was not a widely available energy source until the improvement of pipeline technology. In the 1950s natural gas provided by wells in the southwestern United States began to be distributed throughout the country by thousands of miles of pipeline. Customers, thus, were gradually converted from ''town gas'' to natural gas.

Formation of Bay State Gas Company: 1974

Local gas plants were no longer necessary and gradually closed in the 1960s. (The property on which the plants were located, however, would remain a source of concern for gas companies for the next 30 years, as local governments forced them to clean up contaminated sites.) Gas companies were now essentially distributors only. It was not surprising when these small companies began to consolidate into regional concerns. In 1974 the Bay State Gas Company was formed when Springfield Gas merged with the Brockton Taunton Gas Company, the Northampton Gas Light Company, and the Lawrence Gas Company. Several of Bay State's partners, like Springfield Gas, dated their origins back to the mid-19th century.

In 1979 Bay State acquired Northern Utilities, Inc., as well as Granite State Gas Transmission, Inc., an interstate natural gas pipeline company. In 1987 Bay State gained direct access to Canadian natural gas via the Portland Gas Pipeline Project. Granite State and Shell Canada worked together to convert a crude-oil pipeline to natural gas, primarily to serve customers in Maine and coastal New Hampshire.

Bay State operated as a public utility, because states assumed that creating a duplicate piping system in a local community was cost prohibitive. Since it was granted a partial monopoly, Bay State was subject to state regulation and control over the rates it could charge. In general, utilities can only charge customers operating costs plus a reasonable return to shareholders. In 1987 Massachusetts ordered Bay State and other utilities to lower their rates due to a cut in federal corporate tax rates. A year later the company requested a 7.6 percent rate increase, the first sought since 1983. Bay State cited the increase in its operating costs as a justification for the hike. The state Department of Public Utilities maintained that Bay State overstated its costs and finally settled on a 4.5 percent increase.

Bay State's request for a 7.2 percent rate increase in 1992 was contested by the Massachusetts attorney general. The company maintained that the increase was justified by the expense incurred with the expansion and maintenance of its distribution system, as well as the effects of a recession and an increase in retiree benefit costs. The attorney general's office asked that Bay State's rates actually be reduced by one percent. A major area of contention was Bay State's attempt to recover the costs of programs that tried to attract new customers, in particular through advertising. For years gas companies were the target of negative ads produced by oil dealers that insinuated that gas heating was dangerous. Bay State in Massachusetts and its subsidiary Northern Utilities in Maine fought back with their own ad campaign. According to Massachusetts law, however, gas and electric utilities were generally prohibited from recovering promotional advertising costs from its ratepayers.

In 1996 the trend of deregulation that changed the airline, trucking, and telephone industries came to electric and gas utilities. It was expected that consumers would eventually be given options on companies from which to buy power. Because of the complexity of such a fundamental shift in how energy was to be provided to people, only pilot programs were planned at first. Although unforeseen effects were anticipated, it was also widely assumed that the industry was likely to see consolidation and a possible spree of mergers similar to what occurred in other deregulated industries.

Under the leadership of a new CEO, Joel Singer, Bay State entered the new deregulated world. Singer had been involved with helping companies adapt to deregulation when he worked at Arthur D. Little, Inc., a management consultant firm. He was quick to impose a new vision: Bay State should become a retail energy marketer, essentially a consumer-product business, not merely a gas distributor. His priority was to acquire as many customers as quickly as possible and through low price and excellent customer service create brand loyalty, so that when electric power became open to competition in the future, customers would see no reason to change energy suppliers. Bay State, through its subsidiary EnergyUSA, was also becoming

Key Dates:

1847: Springfield Gas Light Company is formed.
1916: Heating is offered to residential customers.
1974: Bay State Gas Company is formed.
1979: Bay State acquires Northern Utilities, Inc. and Granite State Gas Transmission, Inc.
1987: Bay State gains direct access to Canadian natural gas via the Portland Gas Pipeline Project.
1996: Deregulation of gas industry allows Bay State to initiate pilot program to offer customers choice of gas suppliers.
1997: NIPSCO Industries, Inc. announces that it will acquire Bay State.
1999: NIPSCO changes its name to NiSource, Inc.

involved in a diversity of products that included water heater sales and rentals, insurance programs for heating system maintenance, energy-related project loans, carbon monoxide detectors, as well as home security systems and satellite television. To help make the transition to a new kind of business model, Singer felt the need to change the company culture. He instituted a three-month transition plan to involve key middle-management. In order to get the rank and file to buy into the program, he also introduced a ''gain-sharing'' plan that would reward workers for increases in productivity.

In July 1996 Massachusetts regulators approved a two-year Bay State pilot program called Pioneer Valley Customer Choice, the first of its kind in New England. On a first-come, first-serve basis, 83,000 residential gas customers in 16 western Massachusetts towns and cities would be eligible to enroll in the program that would allow them to buy gas from participating marketers other than Bay State, which would continue to maintain the delivery infrastructure. The purpose was to learn how competition could benefit customers, as well as helping utilities and marketers to determine what areas they would need to address in order to serve the customers and make a profit. Regulators would also be able to analyze the ramifications of allowing such freedom of choice. By the time the program was set to begin in November 1996, 6,300 residential customers had signed up, three times the number that Bay State had expected. Nine suppliers of gas also qualified for the program. One benefit immediately apparent to Singer was that allied marketers could help create new gas users. About 30 of the households that signed up for the program actually converted to gas heating from oil.

Merger with NIPSCO Industries: 1997–99

Industry consolidation—one of the anticipated effects of deregulation—would have a major impact on Bay State in December 1997 when the company announced a merger with Indiana-based NIPSCO Industries Inc, in a $780 million deal. NIPSCO would pay Bay State shareholders $40 per share and assume $240 million in Bay State debt and preferred stock under terms of the deal. NIPSCO had an ancestry similar to Bay State, its oldest component being the Fort Wayne Gas Light Company that was formed in 1853 and chartered in 1858. An 1886 discovery of natural gas in northern Indiana created an early market for that form of gas in the area. A number of small Indiana gas and electric companies were combined in 1926 under the name of Northern Indiana Public Service Company (NIPSCO).

It would take more than a year for the Bay State-NIPSCO transaction to be finalized. The Massachusetts attorney general voiced concerns that the terms of the deal could result in higher rates for customers. NIPSCO's offer of $40 per share was higher than the book value of Bay State's stock, the difference of which the attorney general feared would end up being financed by consumers. In response, Bay State proposed a rate freeze until 2005, as well as to share profits with customers if the company exceeded an authorized rate of return. In February 1999 the deal received final approval from the U.S. Securities and Exchange Commission. A month later NIPSCO changed its name to NiSource, Inc.

With the NiSource acquisition of Columbia Energy Group in 2000, Bay State found itself a part of a network of utility companies that spanned nine states, serving 3.6 million customers. In New England there remained considerable room for growth. Whereas gas supplied 24 percent of the nation's energy needs, in New England that amount was only 17 percent. With increased pipeline capacity and the company positioned through its pilot program to take advantage of the deregulation of the electric industry, Bay State was ready to continue a business evolution that started with the simple task of lighting the streets of a quiet New England town.

Principal Competitors

KeySpan Corporation; National Grid USA; NSTAR.

Further Reading

Ackerman, Jerry, ''Bay State Gas Will Sell Stake in Springfield Electric Plant,'' *Boston Globe,* March 30, 1996, p. 63.

——, ''Utilities Prepare to Enter World of Competition,'' *Boston Globe,* January 7, 1996, p. 57.

''Bay State Gas Co.: Massachusetts Regulators Urged to Deny Rate Increase,'' *Wall Street Journal,* September 16, 1992.

''Bay State Gas Residential Project,'' *Wall Street Journal,* July 17, 1992.

''Bay State Gas Seeks 7.6 Percent Rate Hike,'' *Boston Globe,* April 16, 1989, p. 36.

Cassidy, Tina, ''Indiana Utility Will Buy Bay State Gas,'' *Boston Globe,* December 19, 1997, p. C4.

Crawford, Alan Pell, ''And the Survey Says . . . ,'' *American Gas,* October 1994, p. 42.

Gerhard, Wm. Paul, *American Practice of Gas Piping and Gas Lighting in Buildings,* New York: McGraw Publishing Company, 1908, 306 p.

''Harshberger Seeks to Block Acquisition of Bay State Gas,'' *Boston Globe,* June 24, 1998, p. D5.

Krasner, Jeffrey, ''Fight Looms Over Savings in Gas Deal,'' *Wall Street Journal,* July 29, 1998, p. NE1.

''Massachusetts Orders Utilities to Reduce Rates Effective July 1,'' *Wall Street Journal,* June 3, 1987, p 1.

''More Utilities Plan Residential Unbundling Experiments,'' *American Gas,* August 1996, p. 12.

Myers, Denys Peter, *Gaslighting in America,* Washington, D.C.: U.S. Department of Interior, 1978, 279 p.

Nagelhout, Mary, "Promotional Practices at Energy Utilities: An Update on Recent State Action," *Public Utilities Fortnightly,* May 1, 1993, p. 44.

"Natural Gas Flow Begins," *Boston Globe,* December 17, 1987, p. 64.

"NIPSCO Pays $780 Million for Bay State Gas," *Buffalo News,* December 18, 1997, p. B7.

"Nipsco Plans to Change Name," *Wall Street Journal,* March 3, 1999, p. B4.

"OGJ Newsletter," *Oil & Gas Journal,* October 28, 1996, p. 2.

"On the Street Where You Live," *American Gas,* April 1997, pp. 76–79.

Schular, Joseph F., Jr., "Bay State Rolls up Its Sleeves," *Public Utilities Fortnightly,* April 1, 1996, p. 16.

"SEC Approves Bay State, Nipsco Merger," *Boston Globe,* February 12, 1999, p. C5.

Suo, Steve, "Bay State Gas Will Net $9.5M from Rate Hike," *Boston Globe,* July 14, 1989, p. 25.

True, Warren R., "Canadian Gas Imports to New York, New England Surging in 1992," *Oil & Gas Journal,* March 2, 1992, p. 33.

Zitner, Aaron, "Cleanup of Contaminated Site Nears Completions," *Boston Globe,* November 1, 1992, p. 3.

—Ed Dinger

Bayerische Motoren Werke AG

Petuelring 130
Munich D-80788
Germany
Telephone: +49-893-822-4272
Fax: +49-893-822-4418
Web site: http://www.bmw.com

Public Company
Incorporated: 1917
Employees: 114,874
Sales: US$34.64 billion (1999)
Stock Exchanges: OTC
Ticker Symbol: BAMXF
NAIC: 336111 Automobile Manufacturing; 42111 Automobile and Other Vehicle Wholesalers; 336991 Motorcycles

Bayerische Motoren Werke AG, popularly known as BMW, is a global manufacturer and marketer of luxury automobiles and motorcycles. In addition to its BMW brand, the company owns Rover Cars' Mini brand of cars, a vestige of its failed ownership of Rover Group Ltd. In an era of rapid consolidation within the global car industry, BMW is one of the few independent companies in operation. The Quandt family, the company's largest shareholder for more than 40 years, owns more than 45 percent of BMW.

Origins As an Aircraft-Engine Builder

Although not officially established until 1917, BMW can trace its heritage back to 1913 when Karl Rapp started to build aircraft engines for Austria in anticipation of World War I. Rapp-Motorenwerke's top customer was Franz Josef Popp, general inspector of Emperor Franz Josef's army. Popp hired Max Friz, an aircraft engine designer from Austro-Daimler; together in Munich they established Bayerische Motoren Werke based on the engineering ideas of Rapp.

Popp, an engineer, took charge of administration while Friz served as senior designer. A third associate, Camillo Castiglioni from Vienna, looked after the accounts. The trio began their enterprise at the old Rapp factory, then moved to the Moosacher Strasse factory, also in Munich, in 1918. There, Friz designed and built the company's first aircraft engine.

At the end of the war, Bayerische Motoren turned to the production of train brakes, and when in 1922 the Moosacher Strasse factory was sold to Knorr-Bremse, BMW employees moved to another Munich location, the former Ottowerke plant on the Lerchenauer Strasse. (Ottowerke had been founded by Gustav Otto, son of Nikolaus August Otto, inventor of the four-stroke internal combustion engine.)

Despite the 1923 Treaty of Versailles' ban on aircraft production in Germany, Bayerische Motoren continued to operate and thrive. Its 12-cylinder engines were used on international flights by ace pilots such as Lpuschow, Gronau, and Mittelholzer, and more than a thousand BMW VI engines were sold to the Soviet Union. Production continued to rise steadily through the 1930s.

The company's interests in motorcycle manufacture developed rapidly in the early 1920s. The first model, the R32, consisted of a flat twin engine and drive shaft housed in a double-tube frame, with valves in an inverted arrangement to keep the oil clean. Ernst Henne, riding an R32, broke the world motorcycle speed record at 279.5 kph (173.35 mph) in 1929; his record held until 1937.

In 1928, Bayerische Motoren acquired the ailing Fahrzeugwerke Eisenach, and a year later the Dixi, BMW's first luxury car, was produced at the Eisenach site. The Dixi won the 1929 International Alpine Rally, covering the mountain route in five days. But despite its success, the Dixi created major financial problems for BMW, and a merger with Daimler-Benz was discussed in detail. Meanwhile, a partnership contract was agreed upon; Dr. Wilhelm Kissel, Daimler-Benz's chairperson, and Popp, at Bayerische Motoren, joined each other's supervisory boards. A smaller 6-cylinder model of the Dixi proved to be a most effective competitor in the Daimler-Benz market, however, and Popp dropped the merger plans.

Another Dixi, the DA2, based on the 6-cylinder model, was introduced in Berlin in July 1929. It featured improved han-

Company Perspectives:

It has always been the desire of BMW to create automobiles of unmistakable identity. As you can see, this has posed no problem to us over the last eight decades. But what you cannot see is the one thing that has always been true about BMW automobiles both in the past as well as in the present: a BMW is always the ultimate driving machine.

dling, better brakes, and a more attractive interior. Despite the stock market crash in October 1929 and the subsequent depression (17,000 German firms were forced into bankruptcy, including one of Bayerische Motoren's shareholders, the Danat-Bank), the company avoided financial disaster. A total of 5,390 DA2s, the "mini car at a mini price," were sold in 1929; this was increased the following year to 6,792 cars.

When Hitler assumed power in 1933, Bayerische Motoren, along with other German automotive companies, was required to manufacture airplane engines for the new air force, the Luftwaffe. In the same year, BMW acquired licenses to produce the 525 horsepower Hornet engine and to develop small radial engines for sports planes. The company also launched its 300 automobile series with the 303, the first car to feature the long-familiar "kidney" shape. Lighter than comparable models, the 303 was 50 percent more powerful. Its success encouraged BMW to introduce two popular compact sports models, the 315 and the 319. Early in 1936, the 326 model was launched in both sedan and convertible versions. The all-steel bodied 327 was also introduced that year, and in September Popp unveiled the standard-production 328, which proved to be the fastest sports car of its time; it won the Italian Mille Miglia race in 1938.

The company's rising production of aircraft engines and armored motorcycles resulted in an expansion of facilities at the Milbertshofen plant on the Lerchenauer Strasse, which previously had been devoted to motorcycle manufacturing. A 1939 edict of the German Ministry of Aviation required Brandenburgische Motorenwerke to merge with Bayerische Motoren, and a new factory, Allach, was constructed with government money. The Allach buildings, tucked away in woods near Munich, were constructed at a distance from one another to minimize damage in the event of an air raid.

BMW played an important role in the German war effort and at the height of Nazi domination the company operated plants as far afield as Vienna and Paris. In two crucial areas of military technology, BMW was in the vanguard: with the guidance of Dr. Hermann Oestrich of the German aviation test center, the company developed the 003, the first jet engine to enter standard production; and under conditions of intense secrecy, it opened a rocket testing and production plant at Zuhlsdorf.

Intent on maintaining a plentiful supply of military aircraft, the Nazi government instructed Bayerische Motoren in 1941 to halt all motor car production. Popp, who had been at the company helm for 25 years, refused. He was forced to resign and narrowly avoided internment in a concentration camp. It was left to his successor, Fritz Hille, to institute Bayerische Motoren's automatic system of monitoring production—a mechanical forerunner of the computer.

After the defeat of the Nazis, Allied Command ordered the dismantling of many BMW facilities; at the same time, reconstruction of the now divided Germany got underway. In the immediate postwar years, few West Germans were in a position to buy cars, but by 1948, the year of German currency reform, there was a substantial need for motorcycles. BMW produced a new model out of spare parts provided by dealers. Known as the R24, this motorcycle was put into production and in 1949 almost 10,000 machines came off the assembly line. Production in 1950 increased to 17,000, 18 percent of which was exported.

Post-World War II: The Emergence of a Luxury Car Maker

Bayerische Motoren's return to car manufacturing in 1951 proved to be a disappointment. The 501 model, a 6-cylinder conservatively styled car with few technical innovations, was not well received; neither was its successor, the 502, which featured a V8 engine. The company pinned its hopes on the 503 and 507 models, highlights of the 1955 Frankfurt Motor Show. Both cars were designed by Albrecht Graf Goertz and were powered by Alex von Falkenhausen engines. They proved to be too expensive, however, for the majority of West German motorists. To add to BMW's woes, its motorcycle sales dropped drastically, and the Allach factory had to be sold.

The company's fortunes revived a little in the late 1950s during the era of the "bubble car." Its Isetta mini-car, a mere 2.29 meters (7.51 feet) in length and fitted with motorcycle engines, reached a speed of 53 mph. Customer interest in the machine was short-lived, but it enabled BMW to recoup some of its recent losses.

To capitalize on the increasing market for cars—albeit inexpensive ones—Bayerische Motoren introduced the rear-engined 700 LS model in August 1959. Available as a coupe or convertible, and powered by motorcycle engines, the 700 LS was initially unprofitable. By 1965, however, when annual sales reached 18,000 units, the car had become the company's first long-term success of the postwar years.

BMW's fortunes further improved with the launching of its 1500 model. Indeed, this first "sports sedan" secured the company's prominence in the automotive market for the foreseeable future. The balance sheet showed a profit of DM 3.82 million in 1963 and a six percent dividend was paid. By the end of the decade, the company's long-suffering shareholders were much happier. Nine more models had been introduced, sales for 1969 set a new record of 144,788 cars, and turnover was up to DM 1.4 billion.

The 1970s, a period of dramatic growth in Western Europe, proved to be a time of significant reorganization and development at BMW. All motorcycle production was moved to West Berlin, a new plant was opened, the popular 520 sports sedan was launched (1972), the Dingolfing plant in Lower Bavaria was further expanded (providing jobs for 15,000 farmworkers), and following the establishment of the European Economic Community, BMW subsidiaries were set up in member countries. Halfway through the decade, a U.S. importing, marketing,

Key Dates:

1913: Inventor Karl Rapp opens an aircraft design shop.
1917: Rapp's original business leads to the formation of Bayerische Motoren Werke AG, under the direction of Franz Josef Popp and Max Friz.
1918: First BMW aircraft engine is built.
1929: First BMW car is built.
1959: Herbert Quandt becomes BMW's dominant shareholder.
1962: Introduction of the 1500 model creates a lasting market niche for BMW.
1994: British-based Rover Group Ltd. is acquired for US$1.2 billion.
2000: After years of losses due to an unsuccessful assimilation of the Rover brand, Rover Group Ltd. is divested.

distribution, and support subsidiary was formed in Montvale, New Jersey, and later in the 1970s the company built a car plant at Steyr in Austria.

Early in the 1970s, it appeared that Bayerische Motoren's interests in motor racing, operated by BMW Motorsport GmbH, might be curtailed; in fact, however, the company was able to expand its racing activities. For some years, BMW had been the leading producer of racing car engines in the classification known as Formula 2; the company now decided to compete in the Formula 1 market as well. Success was swift. In 1975, Nelson Piquet won the Formula 1 World Championship in a BMW-powered Brabham. This was the first turbo-charged engine to win in the 34-year history of Formula 1 racing.

The Steyr plant in Austria commenced operation in the early 1980s as a producer of turbo-charged diesel engines. By the mid-1980s, the factory was a major petrol engine manufacturer and at full capacity could turn out 150,000 engines a year. Another factory, at Spandau in West Berlin, opened in the spring of 1984 to make BMW's new four-cylinder, water-cooled K series of motorcycles. This machine won the January 1985 Paris-Dakar Rally, the world's toughest and longest off-road race. The company's motorcycles won this rally four times in its first six years.

BMW's car sales during the 1970s and 1980s increased along with the demand for higher-priced models, and healthy domestic sales were enhanced by the successes of foreign subsidiaries. In 1984, for example, BMW of North America sold 71,000 cars. On the other hand, motorcycle sales suffered. High unemployment, high interest rates, and loan restrictions decreased the purchasing power of a crucial motorcycle market—young Europeans; and competition from Japan became fierce.

As the company entered the 1990s, competition from Japanese car manufacturers represented perhaps the greatest threat to BMW's future growth, although high German labor costs continued to be a perennial problem. Adopting design characteristics from European luxury models, the Japanese produced cars of similar quality, yet sold the cars at substantially lower prices than those offered by European manufacturers, including BMW. Exacerbating BMW's woes, economic conditions in Europe soured during the early 1990s, portending dismal financial results for the coming years. Despite these ominous developments, however, BMW entered the decade in sound shape. BMW exhibited a vitality few other European car manufacturers could muster, thanks to robust sales during the 1980s and comparatively small debt. In this regard, BMW was the exception rather than the norm in a troubled European automobile industry. But the 1990s promised to be quite different from the 1980s, when luxury items and luxury cars sold extremely well, and as the company charted its future it braced itself for less profitable times.

1990s: The Rover Saga

As the recession increased in intensity, BMW's financial performance suffered, but not to the extent that other European manufacturers exhibited. The most glaring decline in the company's growth took place at its U.S. operations, where the Japanese struck their first blow in the luxury car market, and the German mark's strength against the dollar slowed sales and squeezed profit margins. By 1992, BMW of North America was recording a 50 percent decline in sales from the subsidiary's peak years in the mid-1980s. BMW management regarded the American situation as boding ill for its European operations. To strengthen its position in the United States, the company announced plans that year to construct an approximately US$300 million assembly plant near Spartanburg, South Carolina, which, through the plant's state-of-the-art equipment, was designed to produce 72,000 cars a year. Half of this annual production volume the company planned to export overseas, which lessened BMW's dependence on its domestic production facilities and the associated high labor costs of German workers.

In 1993, von Kuenheim ended his 23-year reign at BMW and was replaced by Bernd Pischetsrieder, who had spent his entire career at BMW. Under Pischetsrieder's stewardship, BMW concluded a momentous acquisition that promised to dramatically change the company's future and bolster its position worldwide. In January 1994, less than a year after gaining control of BMW, Pischetsrieder announced the acquisition by BMW of Rover Group Ltd., the esteemed British manufacturer of sport utility vehicles (SUVs) and Rover Cars. The purchase, a US$1.2 billion deal, immediately doubled BMW's share of the European market to 6.4 percent and gave the company a prestigious presence in the SUV market, which was growing exponentially during the early 1990s. The purchase of Rover Group stunned the industry, particularly Honda Motor Company, which held the remaining 20 percent interest in the British car manufacturer and did not learn of BMW's purchase until three days before Pischetsrieder's announcement.

BMW's prospects after the acquisition of Rover Group were exceedingly brighter. With the addition of Rover Group, BMW gained not only an entry into the fast-growing SUV market, but also the high-volume business of Rover Cars. Pischetsrieder's bold move, made less than a year after he took the helm, was designed to usher BMW into the mainstream with a product line geared toward the mass market. One line of thinking held that BMW was too large to compete as a niche player catering exclusively to the premium segment of the car market and too small to compete as one of the major global concerns. The acquisition of Rover Group, when viewed from this perspective, represented a solution to the company's dilemma, giving it a product line that stretched from entry level models all the way through to the high-priced, luxury end of the market. Pischetsrieder's formidable task was to make the strategy work. If he succeeded, the BMW of the late 1990s and beyond would figure as a full-bodied car manufacturer, competing model against model with global heavyweights such as Ford Motor Co. and General Motors Corp.

As Pischetsreider set out to incorporate Rover Group into BMW's fold, a change of command occurred in the backdrop. The publicity-shy Quandt family, which owned nearly 50 percent of BMW, had controlled the company since Herbert Quandt became its dominant shareholder in 1959. Johanna Quandt sat on BMW's supervisory board when the Rover Group acquisition was made, but in 1997 she relinquished her post to the fourth generation of Quandt leadership, sister and brother Susanne and Stefan Quandt. When the Quandt siblings assumed control, they, like the industry analysts who were charting Pischetsrieder's progress, wanted to know why Rover Group was continuing to lose money three years after its acquisition.

The marriage between BMW and Rover Group was failing miserably, leading one BMW shareholder to describe the acquisition as the worst investment deal in German corporate history, according to the May 17, 2000 issue of the *Financial Times*. The financial losses incurred by Rover Group were numbing. As BMW poured billions of dollars into the company, all it received in exchange were successive years of financial losses, punctuated by a staggering US$1 billion loss in 1998. Critics charged that BMW never properly assimilated Rover Group into its fold and that the company gave U.K. managers too much control. Consequently, the branding of BMW cars and Rover Cars never came together to form a cohesive strategy. Instead of using Rover Cars to gain entry into the mainstream market, BMW marketed the British cars as a premium brand, despite the fact that the cars were distinctly midmarket models. What BMW was left with was two premium brands that competed against one another and no solution to the dilemma that had precipitated the purchase of Rover Group in the first place.

Disaster loomed as BMW entered the last year of the 1990s, a year that would end with another US$1 billion loss recorded by Rover Cars. In February 1999, a board meeting was held to determine the fate of Rover Group. By the end of the meeting Pischetsrieder had resigned, as had his deputy and heir apparent, Wolfgang Reitzle, leaving a leadership vacuum that was filled by little-known Joachim Milberg, an academic who had joined BMW a mere six years earlier. With Milberg in charge, BMW continued to suffer both from the losses incurred by Rover Cars and from the distraction the British subsidiary caused, which adversely affected the progress of BMW's luxury car business. Sales of Rover Cars fell approximately 25 percent in 1999, a year in which the launch of Rover 75, a US$30,000 luxury sedan, was delayed by six months. In response, increasing numbers of BMW's research and development staff were dispatched to develop new models and improve production quality at Rover, but the rescue efforts occurred at a time when the company was under great pressure to develop new BMW models. BMW's luxury sedan business began to suffer from the distraction, as Mercedes eclipsed BMW in the lucrative U.S. market in 1999. In Europe, the company's market share fell to 3.1 percent, dropping from the 3.4 percent the company held in 1996.

As BMW entered the 21st century, the struggle to resuscitate Rover Cars continued. Milberg promised to improve quality standards and to turn Rover Cars into a profitable enterprise by 2002. To show his commitment to the ailing British subsidiary, which the German business press had dubbed ''The English Patient,'' Milberg announced plans to invest roughly US$5.3 billion in Rover Cars between 2000 and 2005, an investment that represented one-third of BMW's total projected spending during the period. By March 2000, however, the company had conceded defeat and announced it would abandon its efforts at Rover Cars. During BMW's six years of ownership it spent an estimated US$4.4 billion on Rover Cars. The decision to dispose of Rover Group led to a US$2.85 billion restructuring charge and left Milberg with the daunting task of formulating a future for BMW in the post-Rover era.

Rover Cars was sold to Phoenix Consortium, a loose alliance of English businessmen who paid a nominal fee of US$15 for the beleaguered carmaker. Ford Motor Co. acquired Rover Group's Land Rover SUV operations. BMW retained ownership of Rover Group's Mini brand. Milberg planned to release an entirely revamped line of Mini cars in 2001. Milberg also planned to develop an entry-level BMW in the midprice segment to take on Volkswagen's US$14,000 Golf, which dominated the midprice segment in Europe. The company's plans also called for the development of the luxury brand Rolls-Royce, which was set to come under BMW's control in 2003. As the company pushed forward, amid speculation that it would be acquired by a larger competitor, few certainties about its future existed, making the first years of the 21st century a critical period in BMW's history.

Principal Subsidiaries

BMW Ingenieur-Zentrum GmbH; BMW Rolls-Royce GmbH (50.5%); BMW Bank GmbH; BMW Maschinenfabrik Spandau GmbH; KONTRON GmbH; BMW Leasing GmbH; BMW Motorrad GmbH; BMW Fahrzeugtechnik GmbH; BMW INTEC Beteiligungs GmbH; BMW M GmbH; KONTRON Elektronik GmbH; BMW Motoren Gesellschaft m.b.H. (Austria); BMW Coordination Center N.V. (Belgium); BMW France S.A.; BMW (South Africa) (Pty) Ltd.; BMW Finance N.V. (Netherlands); BMW Austria Gesellschaft m.b.H.; BMW Overseas Enterprises N.V. (Curacao); BMW Holding AG (Switzerland); BMW (Schweiz) AG (Switzerland); BMW Holding AG (Switzerland); BMW Japan Corp.; BMW Holding Corporation (U.S.A.); BMW Ltd. (Great Britain); BMW Italia S.p.A.; BMW Iberica S.A. (Spain); BMW Australia Ltd.; BMW Belgium S.A.; BMW Canada Inc.; BMW Nederland B.V.; BMW Sverige AB (Sweden); BMW New Zealand Ltd.

Principal Competitors

DaimlerChrysler AG; General Motors Corporation; Ford Motor Company; Toyota Motor Corporation; Volkswagen AG.

Further Reading

''BMW Board Set to Decide Chief's Future,'' *Financial Times,* February 5, 1999, p. 24.

''BMW Could Use a Little Skid Control,'' *Business Week,* January 24, 2000, p. 134.

''BMW: Unloading Rover May Not Win the Race,'' *Business Week,* April 3, 2000, p. 59.

Burt, Tim, ''Europ,'' *Financial Times,* September 1, 2000, p. 24.

Flynn, Julia, ''How BMW Zipped In—And Called Rover Right Over,'' *Business Week,* February 14, 1994, p. 44.

Kay, John, ''A Takeover That Missed Its Marque,'' *Financial Times,* February 18, 1999, p. 18.

Kurylko, Diana T., ''Profit Fell, BMW Discloses,'' *Automotive News,* January 31, 1994, p. 2.

——, ''10 Years of BMW Growth Stalling Now,'' *Automotive News,* March 29, 1993, p. 4.

Loeffelholz, Suzanne, ''Kuenheim's Complaint; The BMW CEO Spurns the Japanese and Berates Washington, Wall Street and Detroit,'' *FW,* January 9, 1990, p. 26.

Marquardt, Stephan, ''BMW's Bold Gamble: Buying Rover Makes BMW Twice As Big As Mercedes,'' *Automotive Industries,* April 1994, p. 44.

McElroy, John, ''Why Can't Germany Compete?,'' *Automotive Industries,* August 1992, p. 22.

''Then There Were Seven,'' *Economist,* February 5, 1994, p. 19.

—updated by Jeffrey L. Covell

BBAG Osterreichische Brau-Beteiligungs-AG

Poschacherstrasse 35
A-4020 Linz
Austria
Telephone: (+43) 732 69 51 2566
Fax: +43-732-69-51-2568
Web site: http://www.bbag.com

Public Company
Incorporated: 1988
Employees: 6,913
Sales: EUR 845 million (US$851.9 million) (1999)
Stock Exchanges: Vienna
Ticker Symbol: OBRG
NAIC: 312120 Breweries

Linz, Austria's BBAG Österreichische Brau-Beteiligungs AG has been slaking its thirst for growth through a series of acquisitions that has made it Central Europe's leading brewer—with more than 65 percent of the beer market. The company's majority holding in publicly listed Brau-Union AG gives it a strong portfolio of both national and regional brands, as well as a number of brands—including its best-selling Gösser, one of Russia's top beers—that enjoy strong sales internationally. The company's focus is primarily on beer brands. However, through its subsidiary Pago Fruchtsäfte the company manufactures a line of fruit drinks to the Central European and Spanish markets, and the company also produces natural spring waters under the Gussinger and Gassteiner brands. Led by Karl Büche, the company is a product of the rapid consolidation of the Austrian and Central European beer markets—itself spurred on by the declining beer consumption in Austria and elsewhere. The company's primary subsidiary, Brau Union Österreich, was itself formed by the 1998 merger of two of Austria's leading brewers, Brau AG and Steirerbrau AG. In 1999, BBAG posted sales of EUR 845 million.

Merging Beer Histories in 1921

BBAG Österreichische Brau-Beteiligungs was formed through a long series of mergers that began with the 1921 association of five major Austrian breweries. The economic collapse of what remained of Austria after World War I had placed its beer industry in dire straits. In order to offset the high cost of beer-making, the five brewers—Wieselburger Aktienbrauerei, Poschacher Brauerei Linz AG, Linzer Aktienbrauerei und Malzfabrik, Salzkammergut-Brauerei, and Kaltenhausen Brauerei—joined together to create the Braubank AG brewery. That company went public in 1923.

The five companies remained independent bodies until 1926, when they agreed to merge completely into Braubank AG. The newly expanded company then changed its name to Österreichische Brau AG. Three years later, Brau AG was joined by another brewer, Burgerbrau Innsbruck.

If Brau AG itself was new, its founding members could lay claim to more than 500 years of brewing expertise. The Kaltenhausen brewery, which gave the group its best-selling Kaiser Bier, had been first established in 1475 by Johann Elsenhaimer. The brewery was originally known as the ''Kälte Brau-haus'' because of its mountainside location, where cracks in the rock layers gave the brewery a naturally occurring cooling and ventilation system. The brewery remained under Elsenhaimer's leadership until his death in 1498, when the brewer was taken over for the next 300 years by the court exchequer to the royal Austrian government. The Kaltenhausen brewery was later to have such notable owners as the French government, the royal house in Bavaria, and even the Archduke Ferdinand, before being bought up by Deutsche Bank in 1898. The brewery was incorporated as a private company in 1901, taking the name of Aktiengesellschaft Brauerei Kaltenhausen.

Another of the founding Brau AG companies was that of Wieselburger Aktienbrauerei, which traced its origins to the 18th century—although brewing had been performed on its Wieselburg site since as early as the 13th century. In the 1770s, the property surrounding the brewery, as well as the brewery itself, was registered under the ownership of Joseph Schauer, who subsequently added a neighboring parcel. The Schauer family remained in possession of the brewery and property until 1823, when it was sold to Nepomuk Mutzer, who operated the brewery until his death in 1860. In that year, the brewery was bought by Josef Riedmüller, whose family already operated a number of nearby breweries. Riedmüller's widow remarried another brewer, Caspar Bartenstein, then working for another

Company Perspectives:

What makes a group strong? Is it the clout that comes from a sheer accumulation of resources and market positions?

We think differently at BBAG, Austria's largest brewery group. This has to do with the manner in which the group came into being. Taking Austrian history as an example, its own progress has been one of growth through astute marriages. Again and again, since the mid-1920s, successful, long established Austrian brewing companies have been added by mergers or acquisitions. However, instead of pressing these newcomers into the mould of a unified, ''streamlined'' group, BBAG has allowed them to retain their individual identity.

We believe that the muscle of a group is the sum of the individual forces supplied by its component companies. BBAG has a simple formula for finding the right balance between common features and individuality among its forty or so consolidated companies: the closer to the market they operate, the greater is the need for an individual brand image. The more generalized the activities are—as, say, is the case of logistics—the greater the effort that should be made to leverage the advantages of a common approach.

Riedmüller-family brewery. Bartenstein expanded the Wieselburg brewery's operations and gave it his own name. By the turn of the century, the Bartenstein-Wieselburg brewery had bought up a number of other breweries, including that of his former employer, before joining Brau AG in 1921. By then Bartenstein's operations had grown to regional importance, producing more than 75,000 hectoliters (hl) of beer per year. The Wieselburg brewery became one of Brau AG's principal sites, and saw a number of expansion and modernization improvements that accelerated production to more than 100,000 hl by the mid-1950s, then doubling to more than 200,000 by the mid-1960s. The Wieselburg brewery moved to a new location in the early 1970s after Brau AG built a new brewery, the most modern in Europe for the period.

Building Brau Union in the 1970s

At that time, Brau AG itself had begun to grow. At the end of the 1960s, the company took a major step and diversified beyond its brewery operations for the first time, when it acquired a license to bottle and distribute Coca-Cola for the Austrian market, a franchise the company would hold until the mid-1990s. But Brau AG was also expanding in its core beer market as well. In 1970 the company acquired Brauerei Zipf AG. The Zipf brewery had originally been named after Franz Schaup, who had bought the property in the mid-1850s. At that time, the brewery produced less than 2,000 hl per year. Under Schaup, however, who eagerly adopted the new production techniques being developed at the time, the brewery topped 20,000 hl by the 1860s. The company later added artificial refrigeration techniques, necessary for the production of lager beer, and then constructed Austria's first electric railroad in 1894. By the end of the century, production had neared 100,000 hl per year, then rose to nearly 150,000 hl before the outbreak of World War I. During World War II, the brewery was taken over and converted to an armaments factory. But the Zipf brewery was returned to the Schaup family—to great-grandson Fritz Kretz, who modernized its facilities and brought production past 200,000 hl by the end of the 1950s. The Zipf brewery continued to expand through the 1960s, notably with the introduction of its Zipf Utryp pilsener-type beer. By the time of its merger with Brau AG, Zipf's production had topped 500,000 hl. The Zipf label was to remain one of Brau AG's top sellers, topping 800,000 hl (half of which were accounted for by its Zipf Utryp brand) by the 1990s.

In the late 1970s, Brau AG made new moves to expand its businesses. In 1977, the company acquired a majority share of Pago Fruchtsäfe GmbH, adding a new fruit juice component to Brau's non-alcoholic beverages production. Pago had originally been founded in 1888 by the brothers Pagitz, but the company had achieved its biggest success with the introduction of the Pago brand—named after the founders, with the ''O'' for obst (German for fruit) added on to the end. Pago was fully acquired by Brau AG in 1979.

By then, Brau AG had completed a number of new expansion moves. After a new series of diversification efforts—including the acquisition of a mineral water component, Gussinger Mineralwasser GmbH, and the acquisitions of Lembacher Restaurationsbetriebe, a catering company, and the label printers, Printa—Brau AG expanded its beer label offerings through a merger with the Schwechat Brewery, maker of the famous Schwechater Lager. That company had been founded in 1632, but achieved its fame after it came into the possession of the Dreher family near the turn of the 19th century. The Dreher family—particularly Anton Dreher, born in 1810—was credited with the creation of a new type of beer, the ''lager,'' named for its process of bottom-fermenting. In 1841, Dreher realized that the key to lager brewing was in the cooling process, giving birth to the modern lager. Dreher built cooling cellars and ice storage facilities, before turning to refrigeration machines in 1877. Dreher gave his name to the company, and Anton Dreher Brauerei AG became one of Austria-Hungary's most prominent brewers. A series of mergers in the early decades of the 20th century built the brewery, renamed for its home Schwechat location into one of Austria's brewing leaders.

Central European Leader in the 21st Century

The merger with Schwechat had helped to transform Brau AG's brewing arm. Meanwhile, its non-alcoholic beverages and its other diversified interests led the company to a reorganization in the late 1980s. In 1988, the company spun off its brewing and malt businesses into a separate publicly listed company, which kept the Österreichische Brau for itself, while the new parent company—which maintained majority control of the newly created company—was renamed as BBAG Österreichische Brau-Beteiligungs-AG.

BBAG began an ambitious expansion program in the 1990s that transformed it into the leading Central European brewer by the end of the decade. Driving the company were a number of factors, including the increasing consolidation of the European brewing industry, which in turn was responding to steadily declining consumption levels in its core markets. BBAG reacted early and quickly to stake a claim to the newly liberated Central European states, while also protecting its position in Austria.

Key Dates:

1921: Association of five brewers forms Braubank AG.
1923: Braubank takes public listing.
1926: Five founding companies merge with Braubank to form Österreische Brau AG.
1929: Burgerbrau Innsbruck merges with Brau AG.
1968: Bottling and distribution agreement is signed with Coca Cola.
1970: Company merges with Zipf Brewery.
1977: Company acquires Pago fruit drinks.
1978: Company merges with Schwechat Brewery; acquires Gussinger mineral waters, Lembach catering.
1988: Brewing operations are spun off as a public subsidiary named Österreische Brau AG; parent company changes name to BBAG Österreichische Brau-Beteiligungs AG.
1991: BBAG acquires first brewery in Hungary; company also acquires rival Austrian brewer Steierbrau AG.
1992: BBAG acquires second brewery in Hungary.
1993: Company regroups all brewing activity under Brau Union AG subsidiary.
1994: BBAG acquires brewery in Czech Republic.
1997: BBAG acquires interests in three Romanian breweries.
1998: Company mergers Brau Union with Steierbrau AG.
2000: Company acquires Polish brewer Van Pur.

The company entered Hungary in 1991, with the purchase of the Martfu brewery, a position comforted by its acquisition of another Hungarian brewer, Sopron, in 1992. At the same time, BBAG also greatly expanded its Austrian holdings when it bought up the holding company for rival brewer Steierbrau AG and its stable of historic Austrian beers. Among the Steierbrau breweries was that of the Göss Brewery, built on the site of a nunnery-brewery originally founded in 1020. The modern Göss brewing operations had been set up by Max Kober in the late 19th century. By the end of the century, the Göss brewery had become one of the largest in its region, and by the beginning of World War I the company had achieved an annual output of some 300,000 hl. This figure was to rise to 400,000 hl before World War II cut short the company's production. Rebuilding after the war, the Göss brewery once again became one of Austria's most prominent. After its acquisition by Steierbrau in 1977, the Göss brewery continued to invest in modernizing its facilities, increasing production to more than one million hl by 1983 and topping 1.3 million hl by 1991, making it Austria's largest single beer production facility.

Despite the acquisition of the Steierbrau holding, Brau AG and Steierbrau were operated as separated companies until late in the decade. In the meantime, BBAG moved to restructure its brewing operations in light of its increased international growth. In 1993, the company regrouped all of its brewing operations in both Austria and Hungary under its Brau-Union AG subsidiary.

Brau-Union moved into new international territory in 1994 when the company acquired the Czech Republic's Starobrno Brewery. The company next eyed nearby Romania, and in 1997 purchased interests in three breweries—Craiova Brewery in Craiova, Malbera Brewery in Constanta, and Arbema Brewery in Arad—in that country. As with its other Central European acquisitions, BBAG promptly invested in modernizing its acquisition's facilities. At the same time, BBAG remained committed to its long-held tradition of maintaining its acquisitions' individual identities and regional labels.

The following year, as BBAG faced the declining consumption, falling prices, and over-production that marked the beer industry throughout Europe, the company moved to consolidate its own holdings, merging the Steierbrau and Brau AG operations under the single Brau Union Österreich subsidiary. The new entity instantly became Austria's largest brewer, with more than 57 percent of the total Austrian beer market.

After acquiring another Romanian brewery, the Silva Brewery in Reghin, BBAG turned its attention to another important domestic market, that of Poland. In 1999, the company entered a cooperation and licensing agreement with Van Pur Brewery. In that same year, BBAG boosted its Russian presence, reaching a licensing agreement with the Ostmark Brewery in Kaliningrad to distribute the Gösser label, already a popular brand in the vast Russian market. The company then moved to sell off its non-beverage operations, including its Lembacher catering arm.

In 2000, BBAG went ahead and acquired 100 percent control of the Van Pur Brewery, before acquiring stakes in two more Polish breweries, those of Warsawskie Krolewskie, and Kujawiak, in Bydgoszcz. These acquisitions melded with the company's ambition to capture ten percent of the Polish brewing market, a move which in turn would help propel the company closer to taking the firm lead among the Central European market. BBAG's annual production of ten million hectoliters of beer remained small compared to such European leaders as Heineken and Guinness. Nonetheless, the company's focus on the Central European market gave it a solid position among the ranks of Europe's leading brewers.

Principal Subsidiaries

Austrian Breweries International Gesellschaft mbH; Bier & Mehr Heimservice Ges.mbH; Brau-Union AG; Brau Union Österreich AG; Gasteiner Mineralwasser G.m.b.H.; Österreichische Brau-Gesellschaft mbH; Innsbrucker Gastwirte Getränke Service Gesellschaft mbH; Pago Fruchtsäfte Ges.m.b.H.; Steierbrau Gesellschaft mbH.

Principal Competitors

Aachener und Munchener; Guinness Ltd.; Anheuser-Busch Companies, Inc.; Heineken N.V.; Bass PLC; Interbrew S.A.; Brau und Brunnen; Nestlé S.A.; Brauerei Beck & Co.; Paulaner Salvator Beteiligungs; Budvar; PepsiCo, Inc.; Carlsberg A/s; Plzensky Prazdroj; Central European Distribution; The South African Breweries Limited; The Coca-Cola Company; Tucher Bräu; Danone SA.

Further Reading

''Brau-Union Buys Stake in Polish Brewery,'' *Reuters*, April 21, 2000.

—M.L. Cohen

BEAR CREEK
CORPORATION

Bear Creek Corporation

2518 South Pacific Highway
Medford, Oregon 97501
U.S.A.
Telephone: (541) 776-2121
Toll Free: (800) 547-3033
Fax: (541) 864-2194
Web sites: http://www.harryanddavid.com;
http://www.jacksonperkins.com;
http://www.northwestexpress.com

Wholly Owned Subsidiary of Shaklee Corporation
Incorporated: 1972
Employees: 1,600
Sales: $368.9 million (1999)
NAIC: 454110 Electronic Shopping and Mail-Order Houses; 111339 Other Non-Citrus Fruit Farming; 111422 Floriculture Production; 111421 Nursery and Tree Production; 44411 Nursery and Garden Center–Retail

Bear Creek Corporation is one of the nation's leading direct-mail marketers with facilities in Oregon's Rogue River valley; Wasco and Somis, California; and Hebron, Ohio. The company includes Harry and David, a direct marketer of fruit and gift foods; the Harry and David Stores division; Jackson & Perkins, a mail-order supplier of roses and other plants; Bear Creek Gardens, a nursery and wholesale distributor of roses and other plants, marketing products under the Jackson & Perkins, Armstrong Rose, and Heritage labels; and Northwest Express, a products lifestyle mail-order business focusing on the styles and trends of the Pacific Northwest. The company owns nearly 2,000 acres of land throughout the fertile Rogue River valley, where Harry and David Rosenberg first tended their peach and pear orchards, and rose growing fields in the San Joaquin valley.

Bear Creek Orchards: 1910s

The story of family-run Bear Creek Corporation traces its roots back to Sam Rosenberg, a prosperous clothier and hotel owner, who built the luxury Seattle Hotel Sorrento in Seattle in the early 1900s and traded it in 1910 for 240 acres of pear trees in southern Oregon's Rogue River valley. The orchard cost $300,000; the pears were Doyenne du Comice, a thin-skinned, easily bruised fruit hybridized in France in the 1700s and renowned for its fine texture and flavor. The Rogue River valley, with its rich volcanic soils and sunny microclimate free of frost, proved better suited to the Comice pear than its birthplace in France. Under Rosenberg's management, the pears took first place twice at the annual New York pear show.

After Rosenberg died in 1916, his sons, David and Harry, 27 and 26, who had studied agriculture at Cornell University, took over the family business. Bear Creek Orchards flourished. The Rosenberg growers were able to raise larger-than-average pears, weighing approximately one pound apiece. They sold their pears—renamed Royal Riviera to set them apart from similar varieties grown in Oregon, California, and France—to the grand hotels and restaurants of Europe. Their harvesters were migrant workers, who lived in tents in the orchards and drove carts pulled by mules. Local women labored as packers, hired seasonally to fill the wooden boxes of fruit and ice that were transported by rail to the East Coast and to San Francisco, and, ultimately, to Europe.

Throughout the 1920s, the fame of the Royal Riviera pear grew. Harry and David increased their land holdings and planted more pear trees. They built the first cold storage warehouse in their river valley in 1924 to reduce fruit spoilage and extend the selling season. After the stock market crash in 1929, however, and the subsequent worldwide depression, the brothers' business slumped. But when other pear growers in the region began to rip out their Comice orchards in favor of more mainstream crops such as apples, corn, and potatoes, Harry and David Rosenberg, instead, took samples of their pears to business acquaintances in Seattle and San Francisco. They hoped to offset the loss of their export business with increased sales closer to home.

By 1934, the brothers were enjoying a modest success with their fruit baskets, mailed "right from the orchard," and Harry set off for New York City with 15 boxes of his prized pears. He checked into the Waldorf-Astoria, but after one week had sold

Company Perspectives:

To be as successful as we have—for as long as we have—a company has to be based on some pretty sound, basic rules: Start with the world's finest, freshest ingredients. From fruit to nuts and everything in between, don't cut corners and don't make compromises, because just when you think no one will notice the difference, someone will. Pack each gift with pride and personal attention to detail. In short, you need to be a stickler for perfection, every step of the way. Treat the customer the way you'd want to be treated. The people who answer our phones are a helpful lot—friendly, informative, never in a hurry. Guarantee satisfaction 100 percent. Not just the condition of the package. Not just on-time arrival. Our guarantee goes one step further to cover the unconditional satisfaction of everyone involved. If the giver and the receiver aren't delighted, we'll make it right with either a replacement gift or a full refund—whichever you think best. No delays. No questions asked.

nothing. Not certain what to do with his ripening pears, he consulted an advertising executive, G. Lynn Sumner, who wrote out 15 letters from Harry and David Rosenberg on hotel stationery and sent each one, accompanied by a box of pears, to a top Manhattan business executive. Recipients included Walter Chrysler, David Sarnoff, and Alfred Sloan. This first direct-mail effort yielded orders for 489 boxes of pears.

The 1930s: Launching a Mail-Order Business

Back home, the brothers worked up a four-page flyer, which they themselves mailed. Their strategy worked and, all in all, the business sold 6,000 boxes of pears in 1934. By 1935, shipments surpassed 15,000 boxes. In May 1936, David Rosenberg traveled to New York to discuss further marketing plans with Sumner. This trip produced a full-page ad in *Fortune* magazine, which played on the theme of making a ''royal'' delicacy available to the common man. The award-winning ad set the tone that identified Harry and David for years to come: ''Imagine Harry and me advertising our pears in *Fortune*!'' read the headline for the ad, which went on to say, ''Out here on the ranch we don't know much about advertising, and maybe we're foolish to spend the price of a tractor on this space, but . . . we believe you folks who read *Fortune* are the kind of folks who'd like to know . . . our story.''

With similar ads in *National Geographic*, *Time*, the *New York Times*, and other publications, Harry and David reached a broad consumer base, and sales really took off. To satisfy the flood of mail orders, Harry and David had to increase pear production, and enlarge their storage and order processing facilities. In 1937, they began construction of a large, modern packing plant, and in 1938, they bought the Hollywood Orchard, nearly doubling their acreage. That year, the brothers also started their Fruit-of-the Month Club, which soon became their best-known offering. For $14.95, customers could sign up to send or receive a different fruit gift six times a year: pears in December, apples in January, preserves in April, nectarines in August, peaches in September, and grapes in October. The response to the club yielded a further increase in business; orders shot up to 87,000 in 1938.

Business remained surprisingly strong throughout World War II. However, it was a challenge to find the labor to harvest the hundreds of acres of pears each October, and Harry and David, themselves the target of anti-Semitism, decided to change their last name to Holmes to hide their identity as Jews. One year, Harry and David convinced Congressional and military authorities to allow 600 soldiers from nearby Camp White to bring in the crop. Another year, they relied upon the help of German prisoners of war to pick the fruit. Women and children also became part of the wartime labor force.

Following the war, business blossomed. The brothers built a new warehouse, packing house, cold storage, and office, and invested in IBM's latest data processing technology, the punch card, to handle mail orders, mailing lists, and the payroll. The company expanded its product offerings as sales continued to climb, and fruit cakes, fruit preserves, ceramic candy-filled Santas, miniature Christmas trees, dried flowers, and holly came to grace the pages of the Harry and David catalog.

The company's attention to quality and detail became a well-publicized part of their business. Glenn Harrison, later executive vice-president, ''would look for things,'' according to one company publication, ''like crooked labels or the square knots on ribbons. If they weren't right, he'd rip them out . . . they did not want fingerprints on the [preserve] jars, so we all learned to handle them by the lids,'' said one retiree. When express shipping charges climbed to prohibitive amounts in 1947, the firm began a system of loading straight cars for a given city, then delivering the packages directly to the post office to avoid delays en route.

The Next Generation of Leadership: 1950s–80s

Glenn Harrison took over the day-to-day decision making for the $5 million business, along with David Holmes, Jr., in 1953, after Harry Holmes withdrew from active participation in the business because of a heart condition. David Holmes had died in a fatal car accident in 1950. When David Holmes, Jr., assumed leadership of the company in 1959, he shifted corporate headquarters to Newport Beach, California, where he cultivated an entrpreneurial bent, creating a number of subsidiaries—selling jewelry, toys, clothing, travel trailers—which met with only modest success. However, the company's core business continued growing; by 1961, the company was bringing in $8 million. Two years later it had its own fleet of refrigerated cars and trucks to carry Harry and David fruit packages to 39 mailing points throughout the United States.

In 1966, Bear Creek Corporation acquired Jackson & Perkins, one of the world's largest suppliers of new rose varieties. A.E. Jackson and Charles Perkins had begun their business in Newark in 1872, wholesaling strawberry and grape plants. The duo also sold directly to customers who stopped by their farm. Later the partners also began growing roses and, by the early 20th century, roses had become Jackson & Perkins' main product.

Jackson & Perkins, like Bear Creek Corporation, was a family-run business, and, in the early days, Charles Perkins himself sold and personally guaranteed all his roses. In time, the

Key Dates:

1910: Samuel Rosenberg purchases Bear Creek Orchards.
1916: Sons Harry and David (who eventually adopt the surname Holmes to avoid anti-Semitism) take over the family business.
1934: The company begins selling pears by mail.
1936: The brothers debut Harry and David's Fruit-of-the Month Club.
1939: Jackson & Perkins becomes the nation's first mail-order rose nursery.
1950: David Holmes dies.
1959: Harry Holmes dies; David Holmes, Jr., assumes leadership of the company.
1966: Bear Creek Orchards acquires Jackson & Perkins.
1968: John Holmes heads the family business.
1972: The company forms Bear Creek Corporation.
1976: Bear Creek Corporation goes public.
1986: Shaklee Corporation acquires Bear Creek.
1988: Jackson & Perkins merges with Armstrong Roses and Bear Creek Gardens is born; William B. Williams becomes CEO of the company.
1989: Yamanouchi Pharmaceutical Co., Ltd. acquires Shaklee Corporation, including Bear Creek; Bear Creek acquires Orchids Only, Inc.
1991: Harry and David opens its first outlet store in Oregon.
1992: Harry and David debuts its stores division.
1993: Bear Creek Corporation founds Northwest Express.
1996: Company begins online marketing.

company ventured into breeding new roses, and in 1901, it introduced its first hybrid, the Dorothy Perkins Climber. Under the continuing direction of hybridizer Dr. J.H. Nicolas and, later, Eugene Boerner, Jackson & Perkins became one of the foremost producers of new roses worldwide. Boerner especially gained a reputation for hybridizing many of the early varieties in the class of floribunda, so-named by a cousin of Charles.

In 1939, quite by accident, Jackson & Perkins became the world's first mail-order rose nursery. At that year's New York World's Fair, the company set up a garden display called ''A Parade of Modern Roses.'' When a number of out-of-state visitors wanted to buy roses, but did not want to carry the plants home themselves, Jackson & Perkins agreed to mail them the plants. The following season, the same customers and others returned to order more roses by mail. Over the next several years, the mail-order portion of the company grew so much that Jackson & Perkins began publishing a spring catalog of roses.

By the early 1960s, the very successful company had outgrown its New York location. It headed west, relocating its growing fields first to Pleasanton, California, for the long growing season, and then, in 1966, to the San Joaquin valley of California where the loamy soil, abundant water, and 262-day growing season made it ideal for rose cultivation. The company's headquarters relocated to Medford, Oregon, at the time of the acquisition, so that the company's storage, packaging, and order processing facilities could be shared with Bear Creek Orchards. Jackson & Perkins' research facility was also moved to California, where hybridizers William Warriner and then Keith Zary continued to manufacture new varieties of rose.

In 1968, David Holmes, Jr., stepped down from active management of Harry and David and John Holmes, Harry Holmes's son, took over the business. He formed Bear Creek Corporation as an umbrella organization for the company's several functions in 1972, and, in 1976, took the corporation public. Although considered a ''reluctant'' president, according to company literature, John Holmes led his company through a time of exponential growth. He invested in completely computerizing Bear Creek, not only for processing orders and bookkeeping, but to develop the practice of direct mail.

Throughout the 1980s, Harry and David continued to publish its ''honest-to-gosh'' full color catalogues. The company still had a country store, produce stand, and flower market at its compound gate, but within those gates the business was very much of its time. Under the direction of John Holmes, Harry and David now transported its food to major cities in temperature-controlled trucks and railway cars. Jackson & Perkins dominated American rose production with its approximately 24 million roses per year.

The 1990s: Continued Growth As a Bouncing Subsidiary

As a result of its success, Bear Creek began to attract offers from interested buyers, and in January 1984, R.J. Reynolds Development Corporation acquired Bear Creek Corporation for $74 million as part of its own effort to generate growth through acquisition. Nearly three years later, in November 1986, Shaklee Corporation, a vitamin, household goods, and personal care products company, purchased Bear Creek from R.J. Reynolds for $123 million. Bear Creek earned between $12 million and $13 million in 1986, and $11.4 million in 1987, helping out the stalled Shaklee. In 1988, Shaklee named William B. Williams president and chief executive officer of Bear Creek Corporation and senior vice-president of the parent corporation. Williams brought with him nearly 20 years of general retailing and mail-order experience at Neiman-Marcus, Inc. He remained in charge of Bear Creek when, in 1989, Yamanouchi Pharmaceutical Co., Ltd. acquired Shaklee Corporation.

During Williams's early years at Bear Creek, the company achieved growth through the acquisition of related businesses. In 1988, Jackson & Perkins merged with Armstrong Roses and the wholesale operations of both companies were combined into a single marketing, sales, and administrative unit called Bear Creek Gardens. In 1989, Bear Creek Corporation acquired Orchids Only Inc., a Portland, Oregon-based direct marketer of orchids and other floral gifts. Williams viewed this acquisition as part of Bear Creek's commitment to expand the company's direct marketing business.

The 1990s spawned new ventures from within at Bear Creek. In 1991, the company opened its first Harry and David outlet store near Medford, Oregon, featuring catalog items plus frozen foods and picnic and kitchen accessories. By 1994, the company's store division oversaw 11 outlet stores. In 1993, Bear Creek founded a separate business, Northwest Express, a catalog company offering apparel, lifestyle accessories, and home accessories "in the spirit of the outdoors" with golf-themed items, fishing accessories, and decorative items featuring the flora and fauna of the Pacific Northwest.

The family-run business had grown into a sophisticated operation. By 1997, Harry and David achieved $300 million in sales. By 1998, that number had reached $325 million. Gone were the original pear trees, replaced with dwarf Comice stock, easier to spray, prune, and harvest. Harry and David stores numbered 50 and had achieved a national presence, and Harry and David's award-winning web site was chosen by *Catalog Age* for its first Gold Award. Bear Creek's other ventures were successful as well. In 1998, Jackson & Perkins won top prize in international rose competitions in England, Germany, and The Netherlands. The business in Medford was still fronted by a fruit stand and the fruitcake recipe was still the 1957 original, but behind all this stood a hangar-sized packing house, a huge cold-storage facility, a network of kitchens, machines shops, and offices, and several hundred acres of orchards.

True to its homespun beginnings, Bear Creek Corporation still engaged in little traditional advertising, relying on its award-winning catalogs to spur sales, but the company had developed a knack for capturing media moments by designing products that were "newsworthy," for example, the Jackson & Perkins' Veterans' Honor Hybrid Tea Rose, unveiled at Arlington National Cemetery in 1999, or the Princess Diana Memorial Rose, promoted in 1997, a few months after the princess's death. When the *Wall Street Journal* picked Harry and David's truffle heart as the best Valentine's Day box of chocolates, the company sold its entire supply of hearts on the day that story appeared in print.

Building on more than a half century of direct marketing experience, the move to the Internet was a natural extension of the company's catalog sales, although Bear Creek waited until 1996 to go on the Web. In 1999, e-commerce sales topped $25 million, and the company created a new Internet division. The company's web site offered services in addition to products—gift reminder services and electronic gift certificates as well as gift suggestions, an online gift registry, real-time inventory, verification of shipment, and package tracking.

The Internet also introduced Bear Creek Corporation to a younger customer base and posed the challenge of "jazzing up" the company's brand appeal, according to the editorial director of *Catalog Age*. By the year 2000, with an expected $400 million in sales, Bear Creek was looking to add "an element of fashion," according to CEO Williams, overhauling its catalog to include more appetizing shots of prepared foods. Looking to the future, it aimed to make a quarter of its sales online by 2005, and was opening stores at the rate of about 75 a year.

Principal Divisions

Bear Creek Development Corporation; Bear Creek Gardens; Harry and David; Jackson & Perkins; Northwest Express; Orchids Only Inc.

Principal Competitors

1-800-FLOWERS, Inc.; Garden.com; Martha Stewart Living.

Further Reading

Alley, Bill, "Story of a Century: 1935–1939," *Southern Oregon Historical Society*, July 15, 1999, p. B2.

"Bear Creek: Twelve Oranges for $11.95," *New York Times*, December 7, 1980, Section 3, p. 5.

Horovitz, Bruce, "Selling Pears at $5 a Pound," *USA Today*, December 3, 1999, p. 1B.

Preszler, David, "Marketer Gains Worldwide Attention with Catalogs Aimed at Media," *Associated Press*, August 7, 1999.

Shaw, Diana, "Have Pears, Will Ship," *USA Weekend*, December 1, 1991, p. 20.

Streeper, Dick, "A Picture of U.S. Rose Industry Is Gradually Coming into Focus," *San Diego Union-Tribune*, November 5, 1989, p. F31.

—Carrie Rothburd

Benjamin Moore & Co.

51 Chestnut Ridge Road
Montvale, New Jersey 07645
U.S.A.
Telephone: (201) 573-9600
Toll Free: (800) 344-0400
Fax: (201) 573-0046
Web site: http://www.benjaminmoore.com

Wholly Owned Subsidiary of Berkshire Hathaway Inc.
Incorporated: 1883
Employees: 2,274
Sales: $779.5 million (1999)
NAIC: 32551 Paint and Coating Manufacturing (pt)

Benjamin Moore & Co. is a leading manufacturer of high-quality paints, stains, and protective coatings, with operations in both the United States and Canada. From its origins as a family-run paint business, the firm grew into an industry leader, ranking as the fourth largest U.S. paint company and seventh top brand, with a seven percent market share by 1992, according to *Chemical Business,* an industry periodical. By the 1990s, approximately 3,500 independent dealers in the United States and 1,500 in Canada distributed Benjamin Moore products, ranging from interior and exterior latex and oil-based paints to industrial maintenance coatings, safety-coated industrial enamels, porch and floor enamels, wood stains and finishes, and swimming pool paint, in a broad spectrum of colors.

The 1880s: Quality from the Start

The company's origins date back to 1883, when Benjamin Moore and his brother, Robert Moore, started a family-run paint business in Brooklyn, New York. At the time, the paint and coatings industry was still in its infancy; not until the mid-1880s did paint producers move decisively toward bulk production and distribution of their products. Chemical advances in such areas as film-forming compounds, emulsions, and inorganic pigment production helped the growing industry cover more and more ground—and surface area—with increasingly durable and adhesive products. Benjamin Moore rode the wave, growing rapidly beyond the regional market of New York and, within years, across the border into Canada and beyond.

From the outset, the Moore brothers distinguished themselves from the competition by stringently adhering to their slogan: "quality, start to finish." Most other paint manufacturers laid claim to products of comparable quality, but the Moores were unique in their willingness to risk market share by charging premium dollar for truly premium paints. This strategy would eventually pay off; once the company had cornered the market niche that was willing and able to distinguish truly premium quality paints—by such criteria as greater durability, broader color spectrums and pigment quality, and easier application—they could depend on their reputation for continued success. Indeed, the numbers demonstrated that consumers were willing to pay top dollar to invest in protective—and beautifying—coatings for their homes and equipment.

From the outset, Benjamin Moore implemented a distribution strategy that helped maintain its niche appeal to premium-quality paint users and helped separate it from the competition. Into the 1990s, the company sold its products only through independent Benjamin Moore paint dealers. Generally, paint reaches the consumer in one of three ways: Companies can make private-label paints for retailers; they can sell their own brands in hardware stores, home centers, and decorating stores; or they can operate their own retail stores, selling to consumers and painting contractors. While most companies employ a combination of these methods, Benjamin Moore has adhered to its strict system of certifying specific dealers and selling its products only through them.

Benjamin Moore's other characteristic trademark was the closely guarded nature of its business operations. Two generations after its founding brothers plied their trade, the company continued to guard the details of its internal workings and history. In a 1983 celebration of its centennial anniversary, Benjamin Moore made exception to its administrative secrecy, compiling an in-house brochure titled "100 Years of Progress," which included biographical information on the founders and accounts of the company's early history. Unfortunately, by the 1990s, the company was no longer making this brochure available to the public. Nevertheless, the success of Moore products has delineated a historical narrative for itself.

Company Perspectives:

The heirs of the original founders and directors continue among those who guide the company today. And while product offerings have expanded and changed, Mr. Benjamin Moore's original philosophy for guiding the company remains in effect to this day: "First . . . a fair deal for everyone. Second . . . the giving of value received without any graft or chicanery. Third . . . a recognition of the value of truth in the representation of our products and an effort at all times to keep the standard of our goods up to the highest mark. And last . . . the practice of strict economy without the spirit of parsimony, and the exercise of intelligent industry in the spirit of integrity."

That narrative described continued growth for the company through World War I, the difficult Depression years, and into the World War II era. In the mid-1940s, the research and development of latex-based paint products proved beneficial to the paint industry in general. As legislation in various states increasingly controlled solvent-thinned paint products, water-based latex paints became more attractive and more environmentally welcome. Moreover, they were noted for ease of application and cleanup, a beautiful finish, durability, and outstanding protective qualities. Benjamin Moore capitalized on consumer demand for the new product by introducing its own latex line, which grew into several more specialized lines in the decades that followed. By the 1990s, Benjamin Moore offered a latex product for virtually every application. For exterior finishing, the products included: MoorGlo Latex House & Trim Paint, MoorGard Latex House Paint, Moore's Flat Exterior Latex House Paint, Moore's Latex Floor & Patio Enamel, Moore's Latex Exterior Primer, Impervex Enamel, and Moorwood Vinyl Acrylic Latex Stain. The Moore line of interior latex products included: Regal Wall Stain, Regal AquaGlo, Impervex Enamel, Latex Enamel Underbody, Latex Quick Dry Prime Seal, Latex Urethane Acrylic Finish High Gloss, and Latex Urethane Acrylic Finish Low Lustre.

Paint Products for the Postwar Era

Having focused efforts on numerous industrial coatings for the war effort, Benjamin Moore was positioned to market related products for civilian and industrial use in the postwar era. In 1948, the company founded its Technical Coatings Co. to formulate and manufacture a complete line of primers and topcoats for general industrial coatings as well as coatings used for both rigid and flexible packaging, vacuum metallizing, wood finishing, and coil stock. Five decades later, that division retained its high standing in the industry and continued to grow, acquiring the general industrial coating business of Cook Paint and Varnish Co. of Kansas City, Missouri, in late 1991.

Moore's move into industrial coatings was just one example of how the company accommodated new trends with its marketing strategies and product lines. The passage of the Occupational Safety and Health Act (OSHA) in 1971 helped set up a whole new niche market of industrial operations seeking quality color-coded coatings to meet the new safety standards. OSHA required that all industries color mark physical hazards, safety equipment locations, and fire and other protective equipment, according to the American National Standards Institute (ANSI) code. Moore transformed those legal restrictions into business opportunities, including OSHA/ANSI-compatible colors in its IronClad Quick Dry Industrial Enamel line of paints.

With the rise of computer technology in the everyday affairs of the 1980s, Benjamin Moore once again adapted to the times, introducing computerized color analysis systems to help its dealers match precise pigments to customers' needs. Previously, dealers had depended on the company's proprietary Moor-O-Matic color matching system, using charts, gradation sheets, and a good measure of eye expertise to match up to 1,600 colors to particular projects. The new computerized system, introduced in the early 1980s, analyzed color specimens to provide a formula indicating the base and the precise types and amounts of colorants to match the sample. The system could match virtually any color, with the exception of certain intense or fluorescent colors beyond the paint pigment spectrum. The computerized system was developed over a seven-year period by Benjamin Moore and Digital Equipment Corp. and consisted of a spectrophotometer (color analyzer) and a minicomputer loaded with color-matching software fine-tuned to Moore's paint products.

In 1985, Benjamin Moore also organized a financing plan that would bring the $24,900 computerized system within the budgets of interested dealers. After making an initial ten percent deposit on a system, Benjamin Moore dealers were offered a four-year payment plan by the company. Maurice Workman, Moore's president at the time, told the *Business Journal of New Jersey* on June 13, 1985 that the computer sales were not income producing for the paint company, but were offered as a means of increasing paint sales for its dealers. The bottom line, however, was beneficial to both Benjamin Moore and those dealers that saw improved sales from the technological sales assistant.

Financial assistance to its certified dealers was nothing new to Benjamin Moore. In the 1960s, the company initiated its Temporary Co-Ownership (TCO) program, which provided minority entrepreneurs with the initial funding needed to open a neighborhood paint store—usually approximately $200,000. As the budding businesses turned profitable, the plan called for them to begin buying back their stock, until they fully owned the operation. After the 1992 Los Angeles riots and the media focus on neighborhood reinvestment projects, Benjamin Moore's longstanding program drew considerable attention—and praise. Moreover, in mid-1992, the company announced that Triad Systems Corp. would provide automated business and inventory management systems for the outlets participating in its TCO program. The system would permit maximum efficiency and productivity at the store level and also would use a telecommunications package to transmit data—inventory, sales figures, etc.—to a centralized collection point. Still, the main objective remained the bottom line: "This is not an altruistic move on our part; this is good business for Benjamin Moore," said Billy Sutton, western division vice-president for the company, in an August 31, 1993 *Los Angeles Times* article.

Environmental Awareness in the 1980s and 1990s

Benjamin Moore had expanded its coverage through thousands of independent dealers in the United States and Canada

Key Dates:

1883: Brothers Benjamin and Robert Moore launch painting business in Brooklyn, New York.
1892: Benjamin Moore introduces Muresco white paint.
1907: Sani-Flat interior paint debuts.
1929: Benjamin Moore establishes home decorating department.
1948: Technical Coatings Company is formed.
1959: Moor-O-Matic Color System Debuts.
1968: Benjamin Moore removes lead from paint formulations.
1993: *A Stroke of Brilliance* is published.
2000: Berkshire Hathaway announces acquisition of Benjamin Moore.

from the 1950s onward. In the late 1980s and early 1990s, however, the company took more aggressive steps not only to expand its national market share, but to position itself for international growth potential. In 1985, the company opened a new plant in Pell City, Alabama, followed in 1991 by another in Johnstown, New York. In order to develop markets in British Columbia and, eventually, the northwestern United States, the company opened its facility in Aldergrove's Gloucester Industrial Estates (western Canada), replacing the plant it opened in Burnaby in 1964. The plant, outfitted for production of both latex and alkyd trade sales paints, nearly doubled the company's production capacity on the West Coast. ''The plant is designed as a completely closed loop system, for both water-bornes and solvent-bornes. Nothing will be released to either the sewers or the air,'' said Ron Hoare, senior vice-president of the plant, in a November 1991 *Coatings* article.

Such environmental conscientiousness, though not new to Benjamin Moore, saw more stringent implementation in response to new Volatile Organic Compounds (VOC) rules and regulations issued by the Environmental Protection Agency and other agencies since the 1980s. As such rules shifted according to region, Benjamin Moore and other paint producers tailored paint formulations to fit VOC standards for the various jurisdictions, making compliance more difficult, though no less prioritized, for the company. ''Paint is really a very small part of the emissions problem,'' Walt Gozden, technical director of Rohm & Haas' Paint Quality Institute, told *Building Supply Home Centers* in a July 1990 article. ''But whether that is fair or not, paint manufacturers and retailers are going to have to comply with existing laws,'' he added.

Benjamin Moore not only complied with environmental laws, but continued to stand out as a particularly ''environmentally friendly'' paint manufacturer. When the Technical Coatings subsidiary set up a new facility at its Burlington, Canada site in 1992, for example, VOC considerations were a top priority. Alastair MacDonald, the plant's technical director, explained in a May 1992 *Coatings* article that the entire industry had moved in the direction of waterborne and powder coatings to meet environmental regulations. In mid-1995, Benjamin Moore received a Pollution Prevention Award for its Milford, Massachusetts facility's source reduction and recycling activities, which had been in operation since the 1970s.

Along with moves toward environmental efficiency, Benjamin Moore prepared for the 21st century by implementing state-of-the-art computerized management tools at all its facilities. In August 1992, the company began a transition from mainframe-based data processing to client-server computing by installing a nationwide network of 17 IBM AS/400s and 150 PCs. The company began using the software to automate its entire manufacturing operations, from order entry and inventory management to formula management and invoicing.

That same year, Benjamin Moore invested approximately $3.5 million in a state-of-the art technical and administrative center in Flanders, New Jersey. The facility housed the company's central laboratories and data processing and engineering departments, as well as a model store for sales training and a ''paint farm'' for rigorous testing of paint products. ''The growth of these organizations, along with our desire to create a corporate training center called for a central facility which could accommodate several interrelated departments,'' Benjamin Belcher, Jr., executive vice-president, noted in the *New York Times* on July 5, 1992.

As both consumers and retailers started looking at painting as a system and not just a product, Benjamin Moore developed increasingly sophisticated marketing solutions. One particularly resourceful marketing tool was a 1993 company publication entitled *A Stroke of Brilliance,* a book packed with information and tips on how consumers could apply color and paints to their decorating needs. Interior designer Leslie Harrington presented her expertise in a readable and, not surprisingly, colorful format. The book addressed common questions about how colors match or complement one another, as well as suggestions for painting projects, which ranged from applying matching paint to shower curtains and bathroom walls, to making painted rugs, decorated stairs, stenciled floors, and achieving specialty wall finishes. The book was distributed nationwide at all authorized Benjamin Moore dealers at a cover price of $11.95.

The company also produced ''Fantasy Finishes and Beyond,'' a videotape, also featuring Leslie Harrington, providing step-by-step instructions and lists of tools, techniques, and types of paint for various finishes and design projects. Video technology also was used to develop the Video Color Planner, a color visualization video system that allowed consumers to experiment with the entire selection of Benjamin Moore paints on a video screen. After selecting from a wide variety of pre-programmed interiors or exteriors—or even scanning in images of their own homes—consumers could use a trackball and mouse to apply test colors and finishes on screen before actually rolling up their sleeves onsite.

Benjamin Moore also moved into aggressive television advertising, airing the 1993 ''Stroke of Brilliance'' campaign comprised of spots featuring Myrna Loy in a scene from ''Mr. Blandings Builds His Dreamhouse.'' The following year, the company adopted a new theme, ''We Decorate Your Life,'' with ads featuring the popular Kenny Rogers tune ''You Decorated My Life.'' Print ads reflecting the TV spots also appeared in national lifestyle publications, including *Better Homes & Gardens.*

Realigning its expanding advertising program, the company discontinued all regional agencies—such as an estimated $2 million to $2.5 million account with Chicago-based Keroff & Rosenberg, which closed in late 1994—and consolidated its advertising with Gianettino & Meredith in New Jersey. Although Keroff & Rosenberg had helped make Chicago the number one market for the paintmaker, Benjamin Moore preferred to centralize its advertising efforts as much as possible into the 1990s.

In a similar vein, the company's Canadian subsidiary launched an aggressive customized flier campaign to aid in the development of a database and a centralized marketing program. Following up on a similar campaign the previous year, in April 1994 Benjamin Moore Canada mailed four million customized sweepstakes promotion fliers to retailers for customer distribution onsite or through the mail. It marked the first step toward collecting names for loyalty programs planned for 1995, according to President Charles deGruchy of Salter deGruchy Christenson, the agency in charge of the campaign. In addition, the data compiled by the campaign was used for profiling the creation of models for prospecting, according to deGruchy in an April 18, 1994 *DM News* article.

In the mid-1990s, Benjamin Moore continued to expand its global coverage as well. In April 1994, the company announced the formation of a joint venture with Southern Cross Paints, a paint manufacturer headquartered in Auckland, New Zealand, and its existing subsidiary, Benjamin Moore & Co. (NZ) Ltd. The new company, Benjamin Moore Pacific Limited, manufactured both decorative and industrial maintenance coatings. "This joint venture will enable us to meet the growing demands of our existing customer base as well as provide the newest technologies being developed in the coatings industry," stated David Arnold, sales and marketing director of Southern Cross Paints, in *American Paint & Coatings Journal* on May 9, 1994. For Benjamin Moore, the venture extended the company's growing global presence and added to the list of manufacturing locations that it already boasted in the early 1990s: Newark, Boston, Richmond, Jacksonville, Johnstown, Cleveland, Chicago, St. Louis, Houston, Dallas, Birmingham, Denver, Los Angeles, Santa Clara, Toronto, Montreal, and Vancouver, as well as thousands of dealers across North America.

Into the 21st Century

As it approached the year 2000, Benjamin Moore had positioned itself as one of the leading paint manufacturers in North America and one of the top 500 private companies. Net sales increased steadily in the last five years of the decade, rising from $564 million in 1995 to $779 million in 1999. By 1999 there were 73 company-owned stores nationwide, along with more than 3,700 authorized retailers in the United States and Canada. The company continued to make strategic acquisitions designed to enlarge its share of the retail paint outlet market, purchasing Janovics/Plaza Inc. in 1999 and Virginia Paint Company the following year. In 1999 it also implemented its Banner Store Program in Canada, to establish uniform standards for advertising and store displays among its sellers north of the border. By the end of the year more than 120 dealers had converted their storefronts to the new system, and another 100 were expected to comply in 2000.

The company also undertook significant restructuring measures in the late 1990s, in the hope of consolidating its operations and ceasing production at its more antiquated, inefficient manufacturing plants. The plan necessitated the closing of four facilities nationwide, as well as the cessation of manufacturing operations at an additional four plants—effectively cutting the total number of the company's manufacturing facilities from 16 to eight. At the same time, distribution centers in Cleveland, Newark, and Melrose Park, Illinois, were relocated into larger, more modern facilities. The company also instituted an early retirement plan, which reduced its workforce by 300 employees. In 1999 the company terminated its ownership interests in Australia and New Zealand.

In 1996 Benjamin Moore extended its commitment to environmental concerns when it joined the Coatings Care Program, a project spearheaded by the National Paints & Coatings Association. The goal of the program was to adopt the highest environmental, health, and safety standards in the industry. As a member of the program, the company was able to anticipate the stricter standards imposed by the revised Volatile Organic Compounds (VOC) regulations, which went into effect in September 1999.

The company also was able to apply its environmental awareness to product development in the late 1990s. In 1999 it introduced its Pristine Eco-Spec line of acrylic latex interior paints. In addition to drying very quickly, the innovative new paint contained no solvents and, therefore, released no harmful VOCs—a particularly important quality for painters who worked indoors. At around the same time the company improved its color selection system with the launching of the Color Preview Studio, a revolutionary interactive store display that enabled customers to preview what colors would look like in a home environment. The Studio, which featured a three-dimensional "Room with a View" and more than 1,400 colors, debuted in Benjamin Moore retail locations in January 2000.

The most radical development, however, occurred near the end of the year. On November 8, 2000, after more than a century as a major independent paint manufacturer and retailer, Benjamin Moore entered into a merger agreement with Berkshire Hathaway, the Omaha, Nebraska-based holding company led by Warren Buffett. The deal, worth approximately $1 billion, made the paint company a wholly owned subsidiary of Berkshire Hathaway. The buyout, however, was not expected to affect the management structure or operations of Benjamin Moore in any meaningful way, and company officials remained extremely optimistic about the company's future as the acquisition moved forward.

Principal Subsidiaries

Benjamin Moore & Co., Ltd. (Canada); Technical Coatings, Inc.

Principal Competitors

Imperial Chemical Industries PLC (U.K.); PPG Industries, Inc.; The Sherwin-Williams Company.

Further Reading

Applegate, Jane, "Minority Businesses Get a Head Start on Ownership," *Washington Post*, September 20, 1993.

——, ''Moore's Program Lays the Base Coat for Minority-Owned Paint Stores,'' *Los Angeles Times,* August 31, 1993, p. D3.

Ballinger, Jerrold, ''Benjamin Moore Moves into Retail Loyalty Programs Via Sweeps Mail,'' *DM News,* April 18, 1994, p. 21.

''Benjamin Moore and Co. Celebrating Success,'' *BC Business,* July 1993, p. 51.

Berger, Amy, ''Benjamin Moore Uses Computers to Analyze Colors,'' *Business Journal of New Jersey,* June 13, 1985, p. 20.

Casson, Clarence, ''Environmental Issues Cloud Paint Strategies,'' *Building Supply Home Centers,* July 1990, p. 138.

Harrington, Leslie, *Color: A Stroke of Brilliance; A Guide to Color & Decorating with Paint,* Montvale, N.J.: Benjamin Moore & Co., 1993.

Jackson, Lily, ''Paint Comes in a Rainbow of Good Choices Today,'' *Times-Picayune* (La.), April 9, 1993.

Larson, Mark, ''Benjamin Moore to Build Paint Factory in Dixon,'' *Business Journal-Sacramento,* February 4, 1991, p. 3.

Louie, Elaine, ''Paints in Crayon Hues,'' *New York Times,* September 19, 1996.

McComb, Eileen, ''Technical Coatings Announces Acquisition of Cook Paint and Varnish of Kansas City, Mo.,'' *Business Wire,* December 12, 1991, p. 1.

''Moore Enters Joint Venture with New Zealand Producer,'' *American Paint & Coatings Journal,* May 9, 1994, p. 9.

Moran, Robert, ''Benjamin Moore: A New Coat of IS—Paint Maker Moves Away from Traditional DP Model,'' *Information Week,* June 8, 1992.

''New B.C. Plant Might Sell Paint to Northwest United States; Benjamin Moore and Co.; British Columbia,'' *Coatings,* November 1991, p. 25.

Randel, Susan, ''The Countertrend of House Paints; Chemical Focus,'' *Chemical Business,* October 1992, p. 6.

Scianna, Mary, ''MacDonald: Thirty-Five Year Veteran Proud of Company He's Grown With,'' *Coatings,* May 1992, p. 35.

Stancavish, Don, ''Omaha, Neb., Investor to Buy Montvale, N.J.-Based Paint Company,'' *Record* (N.J.), November 12, 2000.

Wedlock, Sara, ''Paint and Coatings Manufacturers Go for the Green,'' *Modern Paint and Coatings,* March 1995, p. 8.

—Kerstan Cohen
—updated by Stephen Meyer

Brinker International, Inc.

6820 LBJ Freeway
Dallas, Texas 75240-6515
U.S.A.
Telephone: (972) 980-9917
Fax: (972) 770-9593
Web site: http://www.brinker.com

Public Company
Incorporated: 1975 as Chili's Bar & Grill, Inc.
Employees: 71,000
Sales: $2.16 billion (2000)
Stock Exchanges: New York
Ticker Symbol: EAT
NAIC: 53311 Lessors of Nonfinancial Intangible Assets (Except Copyrighted Works) (pt); 72211 Full-Service Restaurants

Brinker International, Inc. operates several popular American restaurant chains: Chili's Grill & Bar, Romano's Macaroni Grill, Cozymel's Coastal Mexican Grill, On the Border Mexican Grill & Cantina, Maggiano's Little Italy, Big Bowl, Wildfire, Corner Bakery Cafe, and Eatzi's Market and Bakery. The mainstay of the company is Chili's, a chain of more than 1,000 eateries featuring Southwest decor and inexpensive meals. Under the direction of Norman E. Brinker, for whom the company is named, Brinker has expanded the Chili's chain and opened similar restaurants with different themes.

1975: The Birth of the Chili's Concept

Brinker traces its origins to the first Chili's Grill & Bar, opened on Greenville Street in Dallas in March 1975. Chili's was established by Dallas restaurateur Larry Levine, who sought to provide an informal full-service dining atmosphere with a menu that focused on different varieties of hamburgers offered at reasonable prices. Levine's concept proved successful, and 22 more Chili's restaurants, featuring similar Southwest decor, were opened in the late 1970s and early 1980s. In 1983, Levine's restaurant chain was taken over by Norman E. Brinker.

Brinker had a long and illustrious history in the restaurant business. He had begun his career in 1957 working for the Jack-in-the-Box fast-food chain, which then had just seven outlets. Nine years later, Brinker left the greatly expanded Jack-in-the-Box operation to found Steak & Ale, an informal, full-service restaurant chain with a menu that emphasized inexpensive steak dinners and friendly service. Responsible for introducing the salad bar, an innovation that soon swept the restaurant industry, this new, casual dining concept became a favorite among the baby boomer generation.

By the 1970s, Brinker's nearly 200 restaurants, including the Steak & Ale and Bennigan's chains, were overseen by his S&A Restaurant Corporation. When S&A was sold to the Pillsbury Company in 1976, Brinker became an executive at Pillsbury, in charge of that company's restaurant group, which now had four chains, including Burger King and Pillsbury's Poppin' Fresh Restaurants. Together, the operations of this group represented the second largest restaurant company in the world.

By 1983, however, Brinker had decided to leave Pillsbury to strike out again on his own. "I wanted to see if I could take a very small company and develop it against the big chains," Brinker recalled in a 1992 article in *Food & Service* magazine. Toward this end, Brinker purchased a significant share in the Chili's chain, becoming its chairperson and chief executive officer. At this time, Chili's had less than $1 million in equity, was $8.5 million in debt, and was earning less than $1 million a year. Planning to expand, Brinker took Chili's public in 1984, selling stock under the ticker symbol EAT. On the basis of Brinker's strong reputation in the restaurant industry, Chili's stock offering received strong support from the investment community.

Franchise Expansion in the 1980s

In 1984, Chili's 23 restaurants were generating $40 million in sales from their menu of gourmet burgers, french fries, and margaritas. To improve the chain's profitability and thereby allow for expansion, Brinker began the process of fine-tuning Chili's operations. Seeking input from Chili's customers, as well as from customers of competing restaurants, Brinker made

Company Perspectives:

To be the very best in the business. Our game plan is status go . . . we are constantly looking ahead, building on our strengths, and reaching for new goals. In our quest of these goals, we look at the three stars of the Brinker logo and are reminded of the basic values that are the strength of this company . . . People, Quality and Profitability. Everything we do at Brinker must support these core values. We also look at the eight golden flames depicted in our logo, and are reminded of the fire that ignites our mission and makes up the heart and soul of this incredible company. These flames are: Customers, Food, Team, Concepts, Culture, Partners, Community and Shareholders. As keeper of these flames, we will continue to build on our strengths and work together to be the best in the business.

a practice of strolling around the parking lots of eating establishments, informally asking customers how they liked their meals and what changes they would like made. On the basis of this feedback, he began to shift the focus of Chili's menu away from burgers to include a broader array of salads and chicken and fish entrees.

Throughout the mid-1980s, Brinker and his associates expanded Chili's steadily, opening new restaurants across the country and further adapting the eatery's offerings. By the end of the decade, burgers accounted for just ten percent of the company's sales, as new items, such as ribs and fajitas, proved more popular. The company counted on its loyal customers, dubbed ''chiliheads,'' to keep revenues high, while also striving to maintain its rapid rate of customer turnover; the average length of time a customer spent in a Chili's restaurant was just 35 minutes, which allowed for more profitable and efficient use of space and wait staff.

By the late 1980s, the company was ready to branch out into new restaurants and began to consider several different acquisitions. A plan to attempt regaining control of Brinker's former S&A Restaurant Corporation was vetoed, as was an idea to take on several fast-food chains, such as Taco Cabana and Flyer's Island Express. Chili's eventually decided to focus on the casual, low-priced restaurant niche, in which it was already a strong player. In February 1989, the company purchased Grady's Goodtimes, a Knoxville, Tennessee-based restaurant chain owned by a family named Regas, who had been in the restaurant business in Tennessee since 1919. In 1982, the Regas family had opened the first of its Grady's Goodtimes outlets, which served primarily beef, seafood, salads, and sandwiches.

Since the Dallas restaurant market already had a chain called Grady's, Chili's executives decided to call their new chain ''Regas.'' This new name eventually proved unsuccessful, however, as some customers expressed confusion over its pronunciation and others associated it with ''regal,'' leading them to suspect that it was an expensive restaurant. Moreover, Regas faced tough competition from established steakhouse chains in Texas. As a result, Chili's faced unexpected difficulties in expanding the acquisition.

Nine months after purchasing Regas, Chili's acquired another restaurant concept, which it also planned to expand into a chain. With $41 million in capital obtained through a stock sale, Chili's purchased the rights to the Romano's Macaroni Grill concept. Texas restaurateur Phil Romano had opened the prototype restaurant in 1988 in a location north of San Antonio, Texas. He based the eatery's atmosphere and menu on the communal style of dining that he remembered from growing up in an Italian family. Just as his grandfather had always kept a four-liter jug of wine on the dinner table, patrons in Romano's restaurant were provided with casks of house red wine. Customers were invited to serve themselves throughout the meal and then to inform their waiter of how much they had consumed; the waiter would then charge them accordingly. This ''honor system'' for wine was modified in areas where liquor laws forbid patrons to serve themselves, but on the whole, it helped to keep sales high at Romano's.

Other innovations at Romano's restaurants included glass walls through which patrons could see kitchen workers creating the evening's meals. The unique interior design of Romano's created a cavernous effect, with strings of bare light bulbs illuminating high, wooden, vaulted ceilings and tables placed between fieldstone arches. Daily specials were displayed in deli cases near the restaurant's front door, and crates of wine and canned tomato products were hung on the walls, serving as decoration and storage space.

Chili's planned for Romano's to compete with the extremely successful Olive Garden chain of Italian restaurants owned by General Mills. Rapid expansion of Romano's and Regas was anticipated, and Brinker set a goal for the Chili's company to earn annual revenues of $1 billion by 1995. Brinker planned to pattern the growth of the new acquisitions after the Chili's chain expansion. In just seven years under Brinker's leadership, Chili's had grown to include 215 restaurants; although a large percentage of these were directly owned by the company, a franchising program also had proved useful in opening new restaurants.

The Early 1990s: New Challenges

To help Romano's and Regas achieve similar growth, Brinker decided to keep the identities and priorities, even the administration, of its three restaurant chains distinct. Each restaurant was designed to appeal to a middle-class customer, between the ages of 25 and 55, and prices were kept reasonable: the average bill for a Chili's customer was $7.50; the average for a Regas customer was $9.50; and at Romano's, a slightly more upscale property, average bills per customer were $13.50. By the end of 1990, Chili's was operating 240 Chili's outlets, 14 Regas Grill restaurants, and three Romano's Macaroni Grill eateries. Together, these operations reported $438 million in revenues.

In May 1991, Chili's announced that it was changing its corporate name, to better reflect the newly diversified nature of its operations. The company's name became Brinker International, Inc., and Brinker told the *Dallas Morning News* that ''this new name is a way to bridge our past with our future as a multi-concept corporation in the midst of international expansion.'' The first foreign countries targeted for Chili's operations were Canada and Mexico, where the company planned for restaurants to open in 1992.

Key Dates:

1975: Larry Levine opens first Chili's Grill & Bar in Dallas, Texas.
1983: Norman Brinker takes over Chili's restaurant chain.
1988: First Romano's Macaroni Grill opens in San Antonio, Texas.
1991: Chili's is renamed Brinker International, Inc.
1992: Brinker reaches an agreement with Pac-Am Food Concepts to expand Chili's franchise to the Far East.
1995: Brinker establishes a strategic partnership with Lettuce Entertain You Enterprises.
2000: Norman Brinker steps down as company chairman.

Again, Brinker undertook extensive market research to adapt restaurant offerings to suit customer preferences. As U.S. demographic studies and customer feedback began to suggest that the average age of a Chili's customer had increased, the restaurant took steps to make itself more appealing to this segment of the public. The volume of music played over restaurant loudspeakers was lowered, the size of the print on Chili's menus was enlarged, sizes of some portions were reduced, and more low-fat entrees were added. At the same time, the company promoted Chili's as a friendly place for younger couples with children, providing fast and efficient service and low prices. ''You have to stay in the energetic group of customers, but you try to tone it down enough so that you don't turn off the older group,'' Brinker explained to *Food & Service* magazine.

To keep the company's operations as efficient and cost-effective as possible, Brinker also invested in an elaborate computer system. Computers were used to schedule workers' shifts and to help company headquarters determine the amount of supplies each restaurant needed. In addition, Brinker invested in extensive kitchen staff training programs, which were designed to minimize waste in company operations.

By the end of 1991, Brinker's had sales totaling $426.8 million and earnings of $26.1 million, a 44 percent increase over the previous year. Already operating a total of 271 restaurants by the spring of 1992, Brinker was opening one new restaurant a week, as the company chalked up a 23 percent rate of growth in sales, despite a general recession in the restaurant industry. Many of the Chili's restaurants opened in early 1992 showed a higher rate of sales than older properties, reflecting the company's growing expertise in the industry. Moreover, Brinker established Chili's restaurants in less populous areas, reflecting the widespread popularity of the Chili's concept.

Despite these strong signs of continuing financial health, Brinker executives estimated that the market for its Chili's chains would mature by the late 1990s. To take the pressure off the Chili's concept, and lessen the number of new restaurant openings needed to maintain brisk growth in corporate profits, Brinker looked for expansion in its newer properties.

By mid-1992, Brinker had opened 17 Regas restaurants, and, in response to the problems surrounding the chain's name, he had rechristened all of these outlets as Grady's American Grill. The company continued to experiment with different formats for the eatery, redesigning its interiors as more casual and being careful to distinguish Grady's from Chili's. As part of this effort, Grady's menu was centered on beef, seafood, and pasta, rather than the Mexican-based entrees that had become popular at Chili's.

Brinker also looked to Romano's to bolster corporate earnings. By May 1992, eight of these restaurants were in operation, contributing about $3 million a year in sales each, up from $2.4 million the year before. A Romano's restaurant cost no more to build than a Chili's and brought in revenues that were twice as high, since its menu featured higher-priced items, and Brinker planned to nearly triple the number of Romano eateries over the next 12 months. The company's strategy was to enter as many markets as soon as possible, reap the rewards of novelty in areas without moderately priced Italian eateries, and then decide on which markets could support two or more Romano's outlets.

The success of Romano's prompted Brinker to test a second, less expensive Italian eatery concept, also developed by restaurateur Phil Romano. In July 1992, Spageddie's, a low-priced, casual pasta restaurant, was opened at a test location in Plano, Texas. The prototype restaurant seated 216 patrons, had a decor featuring bright colors, decorative canned goods, and colorful billboards, and included two bocce ball courts to keep customers amused while they waited for seats. As in Romano's restaurants, exhibition kitchens at Spageddie's allowed patrons to watch their food being prepared. With the two chains, Brinker hoped to flank its competitor Olive Garden, with Spageddies engaging a slightly less expensive niche and Romano's occupying a more costly segment of the market.

At the end of June 1992, Brinker posted annual revenues of $519.3 million, with earnings of $26.1 million; 300 Chili's Bar & Grills, 20 Grady's American Grills, and 17 Romano's outlets were in operation. Later that year, Brinker announced plans for further foreign expansion, signing an agreement with Pac-Am Food Concepts, based in Hong Kong, to franchise 25 Chili's restaurants in the Far East over the next 15 years. Pac-Am planned to duplicate the Chili's decor and menu in locations such as Jakarta, Indonesia, and Seoul, South Korea, with some changes to satisfy local tastes.

Brinker also began to test another theme restaurant, Kona Ranch Steakhouse, in Oklahoma City. A small Tex-Mex restaurant in San Antonio, called Nacho Mama's, also was considered a possible avenue for expansion, although Brinker's executives vowed to change that restaurant's name in the event of an acquisition. In the midst of its aggressive plans to expand all four of its principal restaurant chains, the company encountered an unexpected obstacle on January 21, 1993, when Norman Brinker suffered a serious head injury while playing polo. Brinker was comatose for two weeks, during which time he was temporarily replaced at the company by his second in command. Despite an initially unfavorable prognosis, Brinker made a rapid recovery and returned to resume his positions of chairperson and CEO in May 1993.

Shortly thereafter, Brinker International moved to expand its Spageddies property, buying out the interest of its partner Romano in the prototype Spageddie's restaurant and announcing that two more Texas locations, in Tyler and Mesquite, would be opened. To provide a corporate structure that would enhance growth in all areas of the company, Brinker reorganized its headquarters staff into concept teams, which were designed to act as small companies within the framework of the larger corporation. As Brinker approached the mid-1990s, it appeared well positioned for strong growth, enhanced by an experienced management team and a track record of success with a variety of different restaurant concepts.

Restaurant Concepts for the Millennium

The year 1995 was pivotal for Brinker. By mid-decade it had become clear that the traditional casual dining concept was losing momentum, while other, more specialized niches, in particular Italian and Mexican cuisine, promised a much larger potential for growth. Observing the success of The Olive Garden, which remained the only major chain of Italian restaurants in the United States, Brinker recognized the need to retool its own Italian concept. In July 1995 the company announced a strategic partnership with Lettuce Entertain You Enterprises, a restaurant developer in the Chicago area. The joint venture enabled Brinker to acquire three of Lettuce's Maggiano's Little Italy restaurants and five of its Corner Bakeries, in addition to establishing a creative development deal between the two companies. Dubbed the ''Dream Team'' by executives from both sides, this arrangement brought together two men who were widely considered to be the best creative talents in the restaurant industry: Brinker's Phil Romano, ''an oracle'' in the restaurant business, according to the *Dallas Morning News,* with Lettuce's Rich Melman, whom Business Week had called the ''Andrew Lloyd Weber of the Industry.'' The two companies agreed to come up with at least one new concept within the first year, over which Lettuce would retain control. The company also created an Italian Concepts Division in 1996, naming Gerard Centioli as president.

In the meantime, Brinker also made some strategic changes in its holdings. In December 1995 the company sold Grady's and Spageddie's to Quality Dining Inc.; then, in January 1996 it opened its first Eatzi's in Dallas. Catering to the public's demand for restaurants that also featured prepared foods and groceries, Eatzi's was an immediate success, earning $12 million in the first year, more than double its predicted sales. By November 1997 a second location had opened in Houston, and a third opened in Atlanta the following February. During this same period, the company set out to modify its Romano's Macaroni Grill concept, with the aim of transforming it into a more casual, less expensive restaurant in order to attract a broader clientele. The new Romano's opened in November 1998 and promptly showed increased sales. In March 1999 Romano's debuted in the United Kingdom, the first of a projected 20 restaurants to be established in England through a joint venture with Queensborough Holdings PLC of London.

Brinker was equally determined in carving out its niche in the Mexican cuisine market. In February 1994 it acquired the On the Border restaurant chain, comprised of 21 units, and in May it opened the first Cozymel's Coastal Mexican Grill. The success of Cozymel's in Texas led to the announcement in May 1995 of the opening of an additional 12 locations nationwide. The following March the company embarked on an aggressive marketing campaign to promote the franchising of On the Border, and by early 1997 it announced the opening of two new On the Border locations in Columbus, Ohio.

By the end of the decade Brinker had nearly doubled its sales over a five-year period, from $1.2 billion in 1996 to nearly $2.2 billion in 2000, and increased its restaurant total to more than 1,000. Although economic indicators suggested a decline in the casual restaurant market in the future, the prognosis for the industry in general remained encouraging, and Brinker's proven talent for adaptation and innovation promised that the company would be able to confront its future challenges head on.

Principal Competitors

Carlson Restaurants Worldwide Inc.; Darden Restaurants, Inc.; Outback Steakhouse, Inc.

Further Reading

Bell, Sally, ''Norm!,'' *Food & Service,* January, 1992.

Bernstein, Charles, ''Brinker's Three-Way Combination: A Bid for Full-Service Dominance,'' *Nation's Restaurant News,* October 29, 1990.

Chaudhry, Rajan, ''Ron McDougall's Winning Ways,'' *Restaurants & Institutions,* July 1, 1993.

Fairbank, Katie, ''Eating Profits: Home-style Restaurants Losing Out in the Battle for Dining Dollars,'' *Dallas Morning News,* November 5, 2000.

Fox, Valerie, and Taylor, Lisa Y., ''Chili's Makes 1,000,'' *Dallas Business Journal,* February 11, 2000.

Gutner, Toddi, ''Norman Brinker Scores Again,'' *Forbes,* January 6, 1992.

Hall, Cheryl, ''Brinker International Runs on Good Game Plan,'' *Dallas Morning News,* February 21, 1993.

——, ''The Brinker Touch,'' *Dallas Morning News,* May 10, 1992.

Oppel, Richard A., Jr., ''A Return Performance,'' *Dallas Morning News,* May 5, 1993.

Rigsby, G.G., ''Analysts Predict Slowdown in Casual-Dining Earnings,'' *Tampa Bay Business Journal,* August 4, 2000.

Ruggless, Ron, ''Brinker Inks Deal for Chili's Units in Asia,'' *Nation's Restaurant News,* November 16, 1992.

——, ''Norman Brinker Hits the Comeback Trail,'' *Nation's Restaurant News,* March 29, 1993.

Sherbert, Felicia M., ''Beyond Chili's,'' *Market Watch,* July/August, 1992.

—Elizabeth Rourke
—updated by Stephen Meyer

BM British Midland

British Midland plc

Donington Hall, Castle Donington
Derby DE742SB
United Kingdom
Telephone: +44-1332-854-687
Fax: +44-1332-854-255
Web site: http://www.iflybritishmidland.com

Private Company
Incorporated: 1938 as Air Schools Limited
Employees: 6,400
Sales: £613.3 million (1999)
NAIC: 481111 Scheduled Passenger Air Transportation; 481112 Scheduled Freight Air Transportation; 481212 Nonscheduled Chartered Freight Air Transportation; 48819 Other Support Activities for Air Transportation

British Midland plc, the second largest airline in the United Kingdom, flies more than six million passengers a year to more than 30 cities in Europe. It is a member of the Lufthansa/SAS/United Airlines-led STAR Alliance. From his headquarters in an 18th-century castle, its chairman, Michael Bishop, has worked to keep European airfares in check for more than three decades.

Early Development

Air Schools Limited was formed in 1938 at Burnaston in Derby to train pilots of the Royal Air Force. Air Schools stopped training RAF pilots in 1953. After the war, the company diversified into passenger and freight charters, aircraft maintenance, and aircraft sales. It carried its first passengers in 1949 as Derby Aviation.

Derby Aviation launched its first international route, to the Belgian city of Ostend, in 1956. It soon began to offer holiday vacation packages. This operation was renamed Derby Airways in 1959. At this time, its U.K. route network connected 15 cities.

Derby Aviation was renamed British Midland Airways (BMA) in 1964. The company's future chairman, Michael Bishop, joined British Midland the same year at the age of 24 after working at Manchester Airport. BMA had bought the aircraft-handling company he had set up just a year earlier for locally based Mercury Airlines.

Bishop learned his values, work ethic, and people skills from his father, who ran a business of his own. He advanced rapidly through the ranks, becoming general manager in 1969, director in 1970, managing director in 1972, and chairman in 1978. A BMA Argonaut crashed near Stockport in 1967, killing 72. At the age of 25, Bishop had to address the victims' family members, which he told *Management Today* was a life-changing experience.

The booming long-haul charter market had taken BMA across the Atlantic by the early 1970s. BMA abandoned the holiday tours in 1972, however, instead devoting its fleet and staff to developing nations eager to operate their own ''instant airlines.''

Bishop and his partners John Wolfe and Stuart Balmforth bought BMA for £1.8 million in 1978. It was one of Britain's first management buyouts, according to *Management Today*. By 1979, BMA was carrying a million passengers a year.

New Freedom in the 1980s

British Midland acquired its distinctive headquarters building, Donington Hall, in 1980. Formerly owned by the Earl of Huntingdon, this late 18th-century manor built in gothic revival style gave BMA a unique space to grow. The building's 72-foot-long library housed BMA's reservations department, while bedrooms were converted to executive offices.

The company acquired slots at London's Heathrow Airport and, soon, Margaret Thatcher's government allowed BMA to compete with British Airways on Britain's major trunk routes, linking London with Glasgow, Edinburgh, and Belfast. The national carrier, British Airways, had had a monopoly on these routes. The new competition, British Midland boasted, immediately brought passengers better service in addition to lower fares. BMA was not competing as a low-fare, low-service airline, however. As *Forbes* described later, early morning travelers were served breakfast on china rather than plastic plates.

Company Perspectives:

Our Mission: To be the airline of choice. Our Vision: We will ensure that every moment spent with British Midland is time well spent by delivering the outstanding service of a world-class airline. Our Value: Speed and efficiency. Charm and hospitality. Style in service delivery. Innovation. Honesty in communication.

BMA began operating the first trunk route, Heathrow-Glasgow, in 1982. The company competed with lower fares, but improved in-flight amenities. Service to Edinburgh followed in 1983, when *Executive Travel* voted BMA ''Best Domestic Airline.'' In 1984, BMA began flying to Belfast and opened its own departure lounge at Heathrow.

In 1985, BMA became simply ''British Midland'' (BM) and introduced a new red, white, and blue livery for its planes. An open skies agreement between the United Kingdom and the Netherlands allowed British Midland to launch service to its first continental destination, Amsterdam, in 1986. The same year, BM introduced its Diamond Service one-class cabin, which plied passengers with free drinks and better food. The Diamond Club frequent flyer program followed in 1987.

British Midland continued to expand its network throughout Europe, bringing a new alternative to Europe's state-supported airlines. Dublin and Paris were among the first European destinations added. By the late 1980s, BM was aiming for a 50–50 split between domestic and international flights. It began to refleet with Boeing 737s, while continuing to use existing McDonnell Douglas DC-9 aircraft on international routes.

In 1987, BM established London City Airways to fly out of London City Airport, near the docklands. The venture ultimately failed, however, costing the group £10 million.

BM's parent company, Airlines of Britain Holdings, included the much smaller Loganair (Scotland) and Manx Airlines (Isle of Man). The group was recapitalized in December 1988, when Scandinavian Airlines System (SAS) bought a 24.9 percent stake for £25 million. SAS became a significant source of international feeder traffic and performed heavy maintenance on BM's DC-9 aircraft. BM posted a profit of £14.3 million for 1988.

The triumphant year was followed closely by tragedy. British Midland lost a Boeing 737 at Kegworth, England, a few miles from its headquarters, in January 1989. It crashed on the edge of the M1 motorway, killing 47 people.

The airline continued to expand, although at a faster pace than it desired: BM opened a London-Paris route in 1989 to avoid giving up slots it had been awarded at Heathrow. Besides the increased competition from British Airways, British Midland faced rising fuel prices and reduced passenger counts as a result of the Gulf War in January 1990. After losing millions, BM cut a tenth of its workforce, or 300 people.

Meanwhile, British Airways was increasing frequencies on its domestic trunk routes. BM alleged BA was dumping capacity at home to capture feeder traffic for its international routes. British Midland was already the second largest operator at Heathrow Airport, though British Airways still moved more than twice as many flights through it. Many of BM's low-fare competitors fell away, as Air Europe had done in 1990. Eurostar, the passenger train service using the Chunnel, was beginning, however, to take the profits out of BM's cross-channel business. Otherwise, BM's international growth plans were ahead of schedule.

Michael Bishop was knighted by the Queen in 1991. (The chessboard was rounded out by his counterpart, Lord King, British Airways chairman until 1993.) Bishop credited the success of British Midland with its careful, incremental expansion. He told *Director* his guiding principle was ''not to take risks disproportionate to the size of the business,'' explaining that he had always paced himself for a long career. ''We don't want to pay the price of being a pioneer,'' he told *Aviation Week.* He told *Director* he wanted this epitaph: ''Je ne regrette rien.''

New Frontiers in the 1990s

SAS increased its shareholding in BM parent Airlines of Britain to 40 percent in 1992. As Europe prepared for a theoretically open air travel market in 1993, BM continued to upgrade its product. It pioneered vegetarian meal service on domestic and European flights, and in March 1993 introduced business class seating on its European routes that was priced less than its competitors' economy class seats. That September, British Midland introduced a unique pass, good for five international business class return flights within three months of purchase. It was refleeting with Boeing 737 airliners and smaller Fokker aircraft. BM carried more than four million passengers in 1993 and managed a profit of more than £1 million.

In 1994, Bishop called for European countries to end subsidies to their respective national airlines: Air France, for example, had received a massive US$3.7 billion bailout. Mile for mile, Europe had some of the highest airfares in the world. There were some signs of progress: Lufthansa was being partially privatized.

British Midland continued to add new routes in Europe in the mid-1990s, as its cargo unit partnered with Federal Express. Another unit, International Cargo Marketing, installed a new computer system allowing it to process more inquiries. In 1995, BM claimed to be the first airline to offer Internet flight reservations. The company carried five million passengers in that year.

A fleet renewal program completed in 1996 at a cost of £225 million (US$350 million) gave BM the youngest fleet of jets in Europe, with an average age of less than four years. The airline was already considering buying larger aircraft, however, to leverage its limited slots at Heathrow. It had been leasing most of its aircraft. To accompany the new planes, BM updated the livery on its planes and redesigned its uniforms. It also unveiled business class lounges in several European airports and automatic ticketing machines.

BM's international traffic accounted for 60 percent of its business. It had more than a dozen code share partners, including United Airlines and American Airlines, which also had a strategic partnership with British Airways. BM declined for the moment,

Key Dates:

1938: Air Schools Limited is founded.
1949: Air Schools carries first passengers as Derby Aviation.
1956: Derby Aviation launches first international service, to Belgium.
1964: Michael Bishop joins Derby Aviation, renamed British Midland Airways.
1978: Bishop and partners buy British Midland.
1982: BM begins competing with British Airways on London-Glasgow.
1988: SAS buys a stake in BM parent Airlines of Britain.
1997: Lufthansa buys half of SAS's shares; BM orders US$1 billion worth of Airbus planes.
1998: BM lobbies to "Make the Air Fair" at Heathrow.
2001: Service to the United States is planned.

however, the opportunity to join a global alliance such as STAR or the British Airways/American Airlines-led oneworld.

In March 1997, British Midland placed a US$1 billion order for 20 Airbus Industrie A321 and A320 jetliners. It was Airbus's largest British order to date. A dozen of the planes were to be leased from International Lease Finance Corporation; the rest were bought outright.

BM had a banner year in 1997: income of more than £17 million on revenues of £529 million. Traffic to Ireland in particular was booming. The carrier competed with a wave of budget start-ups such as easyJet. BM aimed for the business traveler, pitching itself as "the airline for Europe." It focused on shorter routes than those of its most visible private sector counterpart, Richard Branson's Virgin Airways.

With an open skies agreement between the United States and the United Kingdom pending in March 1998, British Midlands applied for permission to fly to ten U.S. destinations from Heathrow. BM had not flown to the United States since 1983. Its competitors, American Airlines and British Airways, were being pressured to give up 350 slots at Heathrow to allay regulators' antitrust concerns regarding their close alliance. BM flew into the last remaining British Airways domestic monopoly route, Heathrow-Manchester, in March 1998. Bishop bemoaned the difficulty of keeping up with pacesetting British Airways in the area of information technology.

Although European skies ostensibly began to be liberalized (deregulated) in the early 1990s, access to airport landing slots and ground services proved a practical barrier to new entrants hoping to challenge state airlines on their own turf. The chief constraint on BM's growth was the lack of capacity at Heathrow Airport, the largest international airport in the world. Nearly half of BM's employees were based there.

In September 1998, British Midland launched a public relations campaign called "Make the Air Fair." It attacked the lack of competition on the transatlantic market from Heathrow Airport, whose business fares to the United States were nearly double those from Amsterdam. BM claimed this differential was costing U.K. businesses £2.4 billion a year.

Half of SAS's shareholding (20 percent) was sold to Lufthansa in 1999. BM finally joined the STAR Alliance, led by Lufthansa and United Airlines. Austin Reid, who had arranged for the SAS share purchase, was named CEO in November 1999. A former executive at Hertz Rent-A-Car Europe, Reid had joined Airlines of Britain in 1985 and previously served as finance director and managing director. BM posted profits of £13.7 million on sales of £613.3 million in 1999.

Services from Heathrow to Rome, Milan, and Madrid were launched in May 2000. British Midland operated these in cooperation with Lufthansa and SAS. BM planned to begin service from Manchester to Washington (Dulles) and Chicago (O'Hare) in the spring of 2001, with United Airlines as a code share partner.

Principal Divisions

BM Commuter; Cargo; Commercial; Engineering; Handling; Marketing; Operational Sales.

Principal Competitors

British Airways plc; easyJet; Virgin Group PLC.

Further Reading

Banks, Howard, "Friendlier Skies," *Forbes,* November 21, 1994, p. 140.
Bright, Julia, "The Pilot for the Long Haul," *Director,* December 1994, p. 90.
Brown, Malcolm, "Flights, Ferries and the Fairer Sex," *Management Today,* April 1993, p. 76.
——, "Michael Bishop's Obsession," *Management Today,* July 1991, p. 50.
Feldman, Joan M., "Code-Sharing Promiscuity Pays," *Air Transport World,* February 1997, pp. 37–40.
Goldsmith, Charles, "Airbus Wins British Midland Order for Twenty Jetliners Valued at $1 Billion," *Wall Street Journal,* April 3, 1997.
Lennane, Alexandra, "BM's Changing Market Measures," *Airfinance Journal,* July/August 1997, pp. 20–21.
Meller, Paul, "Price War for Business Fliers," *Marketing,* September 16, 1993, p. 8.
Morrocco, John D., "British Midland Eyes Larger Aircraft," *Aviation Week & Space Technology,* September 23, 1996, p. 44.
——, "British Midland in Transatlantic Bid," *Aviation Week & Space Technology,* March 2, 1998, p. 44.
"Pontiff of the Skies," *Economist,* June 14, 1997, p. 74.
Reed, Arthur, "Getting There—Tortoise Style," *Air Transport World,* June 1991, p. 54.
Stone, Mark, "BM Outlook Optimistic," *Global Trade & Transportation,* September 1994, p. 33.

—Frederick C. Ingram

Broder Bros.

Broder Bros. Co.

45555 Port Street
Plymouth, Michigan 48170
U.S.A.
Telephone: (734) 454-4800
Toll Free: (800) 521-0850
Fax: (734) 454-8971
Web site: http://www.broderbros.com

Private Company
Incorporated: 1919
Employees: 675
Sales: $344.2 million (1999)
NAIC: 42232 Men's and Boys' Clothing and Furnishings Wholesalers; 42233 Women's, Children's, and Infants' Clothing and Accessories Wholesalers

Broder Bros. Co. is the leading wholesaler of imprintable sportswear in the United States. The company's clients are businesses that imprint or embroider names, logos, or designs on clothing for sale to corporations, organizations, teams, and so on. Broder Bros. maintains seven regional branches, each of which carries its full line of products. The company places an emphasis on service: orders received by 6:00 p.m. are shipped the same day, and customer service representatives are given extensive training before they handle actual orders. Owned by two successive families since its founding in 1919, the company was acquired in 2000 by Bain Capital, Inc., a private investment firm.

Early Years

Broder Bros. was founded in 1919 by siblings Max and Louis Broder. The Detroit, Michigan company started as a wholesaler of haberdashery items and successfully operated in this field for the next several decades, gradually coming to specialize in hosiery. In the early 1950s Jack Brode, similarly named but not related, bought one of the brothers' stakes in the company upon his death. Brode himself had extensive experience in the hosiery business as a partner in Robbins & Brode, which also had been founded in 1919. Robbins & Brode recently had ceased operations when the building it occupied was sold to make way for a new highway, and Brode was happy to continue in the business as a partner in Broder Bros.

In 1955 the remaining Broder brother passed away, and Jack Brode bought the rest of the company from the Broder estate. After giving the idea some consideration, Brode decided against changing the company's name to his own to avoid confusing the firm's customers. Soon after taking full control he expanded the company's offerings into dry goods, and in 1959 he moved the business to a new location, a building that had previously housed a draft board during World War II.

Business was good during the 1960s, but the company's fortunes began to decline during the early 1970s when leading hosiery makers such as L'eggs began handling distribution themselves, cutting out middlemen like Broder Bros. Jack Brode, seeing the writing on the wall, began to look for other types of clothing to distribute. Noticing the growing popularity of imprinted t-shirts, he decided to concentrate on handling this line while phasing out hosiery and dry goods. Brode's gamble paid off, and the company soon found it was shipping new stock as fast as it came in the door. The company's clients were generally small businesses that silk-screened or embroidered designs and names on shirts for teams, school groups, businesses, and the like.

A key factor in Broder's success was its maintenance of a large backstock of goods, which led to a higher order fulfillment ratio and happier customers. The company's clients also benefited in that they were able, essentially, to use Broder Bros. as their own warehousing service, freeing them from having to maintain extensive stock onsite. To find new customers Broder Bros. maintained a traveling sales staff and also advertised in industry publications.

Beginning in the mid-1970s Jack Brode began to hand over control of the company to his son Harold, who eventually was named president and CEO. Harold's son Michael also joined the

Company Perspectives:

Broder Bros. is the largest imprintable sportswear wholesaler in the country. As we move forward as a leader in the industry, we continue to grow and improve the way we do things—from the way we take an order to the way we ship an order—dedicated to providing our customers with the best product selection and customer service.

family business as an assistant buyer. Tragically, Jack Brode and his wife both died in an automobile accident in 1981.

A Successful Formula Fueling Rapid Growth in the 1980s

The company grew by leaps and bounds during the late 1970s and early 1980s, and in 1983 it moved into a 20,000-square-foot location in the Detroit suburb of Oak Park. Growth at this time was topping 100 percent per year, and the new facility was itself soon bursting at the seams, requiring acquisition of an adjacent structure as well as the construction of an addition. Annual revenues were now topping $5 million.

A catalog was started in 1984 that could be imprinted with the logo of a small business that bought from Broder, giving the latter a useful marketing tool. The professionally designed full-color catalog did not mention its source, making the company's clients seem more substantial than they might appear otherwise. The successful introduction of the catalog helped the company's customer base double during this period, as did increased advertising and reduced prices.

By the late 1980s Broder Bros. had expanded its offerings well beyond t-shirts, encompassing a broad range of clothing that also included sweatshirts and pants, sport jerseys, golf shirts, coaches' shirts, and jackets. The company continued to distribute only imprintable garments. To differentiate itself from its competitors, Broder Bros. focused on setting high standards for customer service. The company filled all orders that came in before 1:00 p.m. by the close of business that same day and used an automated telephone routing system and an extensively trained staff to make sure that all of its customers' needs were met.

The company also continued to keep its full line of goods in stock at all times. To keep up inventory of items that were in higher demand, Broder Bros. purchased them in the off-season when they were easier to obtain. This policy proved its worth in the mid-1980s when a fleece shortage occurred. Customers who called imprintables distributors for fleece products were told they were unobtainable . . . until they reached Broder Bros. Competitors and even clothing manufacturers also began to contact the company, which, wisely, had procured stock before the heaviest sales season began. For its foresight, Broder Bros. was rewarded with further growth to its customer base.

New Quarters in 1989, Surging Growth in the 1990s

Broder's rapid expansion continued to strain the limits of its Oak Park warehouse, and in 1989 the company again moved to a new location. This time it built an 80,000-square-foot warehouse and corporate headquarters building in Plymouth, Michigan, which was designed from the ground up with the company's needs in mind. Automated stock handling machines, conveyer belts, and a computerized barcode scanning system were all installed. The computer programs were written by Broder's own in-house computer programming department. The company was taking an average of 1,000 phone calls per day, up to 7,000 during peak periods, with an average order consisting of more than $300 worth of merchandise. Industry sources now ranked it as one of the top five imprintables distributors in the United States.

With growth still surging, the company opened its first branch warehouse in Orlando, Florida, in 1991. During the decade new branches were added every two years, with locations following in Dallas, Albany, Fresno, and Charlotte, North Carolina, respectively. Broder Bros. also created its own line of golf shirts and caps, Luna Pier, which was manufactured by outside contractors. The company was now distributing familiar names such as Fruit of the Loom, Lee, Jerzees, and Cross Creek. The lineup of clothing had expanded to include corporate casual ware, which was a new and rapidly growing segment of the market. This category included a variety of outerwear, sweaters, and woven and denim goods. Ratcheting up its service commitment, the company now offered same-day shipping on orders received before 6:00 p.m. Eastern Standard Time. This virtually guaranteed one- or two-day service to 98 percent of the United States. President and CEO Harold Brode told *Distributor Showcase* magazine in 1995, ''From the beginning we set service standards as our goal—not necessarily dollar volumes or profit margins. We believed that if we could meet certain goals from service and productivity standpoints, the money part would take care of itself. It has.''

Annual sales had leapt to an estimated $160 million by 1995, more than double the figure of just four years earlier. Employees at the company were treated well and were paid better than average for the industry. Broder Bros. adhered to the philosophy that higher wages attracted a better quality staff, a policy that paid for itself through increased productivity.

With the rise of the Internet Broder Bros. also went online, creating an attractive web site that described its products, gave information on industry trends, and offered bulletin boards where customers could place their own classified ads. Online ordering and stock-checking functions were to be phased in later.

In 2000 majority ownership of Broder Bros. was purchased by Bain Capital, Inc. The 16-year-old private investment firm owned sizable stakes in more than 120 companies, including 93 percent of Michigan-based Domino's Pizza, Inc. Bain invested in a wide range of businesses that spanned the manufacturing, distribution, retail, information, and healthcare industries. After selling control of their company, CEO Harold Brode and his son Michael, now president, stepped back to take vice-president posts. Twenty-year company veteran and executive vice-president Todd Turkin took over as president, and newcomer Vince Tyra was named CEO. Tyra's experience in the field was considerable, as he had served previously as president of Fruit of the Loom and executive vice-president for T-Shirts & More,

Key Dates:

1919: Max and Louis Broder found a haberdashery goods wholesaling company.
1955: Jack Brode (his similar surname purely coincidental) buys the company from the Broder family.
1984: The company begins printing a catalog.
1991: First branch location opens, in Orlando, Florida.
1993: Dallas, Texas branch opens.
1995: New branch opens in Albany, New York.
1997: Fresno, California branch opens.
1999: Charlotte, North Carolina branch is added.
2000: Broder Bros. is purchased by Bain Capital, Inc.; St. Louis T's is acquired.

Inc., a Louisville, Kentucky imprintables wholesaler. Following the acquisition by Bain, Broder Bros. purchased a St. Louis, Missouri company named St. Louis T's, which was converted into the company's seventh branch. Revenues of more than $344 million for 1999 were expected to rise another ten percent during 2000.

The growth of Broder Bros. since its entrance into the imprintables market in the early 1970s had been explosive, and the company was continuing its expansion in the new millennium. With seven warehouses that gave it coast-to-coast coverage of the United States, an expanding Web-based ordering service, and guaranteed same-day shipping, Broder's dominance of the imprintables marketplace seemed unlikely to diminish. The financial resources of new owner Bain Capital would give it further opportunity for acquisitions and expansion.

Principal Competitors

Alpha; Bodek & Rhodes; Full Line Distributors, Inc.; NES; Premium Wear, Inc.; Sanmar; Staton Wholesale.

Further Reading

Fridstein, Stan, ''Silver Award: Wholesale and Dealer: Broder Bros.,'' *Catalog Age,* September 15, 1995, p. 126.
''The Golden Rule—Dedication and Service Drive Operations at Broder Bros.,'' *Distributor Showcase,* 1995, p. A12.
Haldane, Neal, ''Domino's Owner Buys Sportswear Wholesaler,'' *Detroit News,* May 26, 2000, p. O2.
''Harold Brode: Selling Service,'' *Corporate Detroit Magazine,* August 1, 1991, p. 4.
''If You Haven't Got Service, What Have You Got?,'' *Printwear Magazine,* April 1989, pp. 86–87.
Serwach, Joseph, ''Broder: Bain Deal Provides Fuel for Growth,'' *Crain's Detroit Business,* May 15, 2000, p. 41.
Slater, Deborah M., ''Broder Brothers: Wholesaler on the Go,'' *T-Shirt Retailer and Screen Printer,* June 1986, pp. 31–34.

—Frank Uhle

Brown-Forman Corporation

850 Dixie Highway
Louisville, Kentucky 40210
U.S.A.
Telephone: (502) 585-1100
Fax: (502) 774-7876
Web site: http://www.brown-forman.com

Public Company
Founded: 1870 as Brown-Forman Distillery
Employees: 7,400
Sales: $2.13 billion (2000)
Stock Exchanges: New York
Ticker Symbol: BFB
NAIC: 312130 Wineries; 312140 Distilleries; 316991 Luggage Manufacturing; 316993 Personal Leather Good (Except Women's Handbag and Purse) Manufacturing; 327112 Vitreous China, Fine Earthenware, and Other Pottery Product Manufacturing; 327212 Other Pressed and Blown Glass and Glassware Manufacturing; 339912 Silverware and Hollowware Manufacturing

Brown-Forman Corporation is a diversified producer, marketer, and exporter of alcoholic beverage and consumer products. The full-line distiller markets Jack Daniel's whiskey, Southern Comfort liqueur, Canadian Mist Canadian whiskey, Early Times and Old Forester bourbon, Glenmorangie Scotch, Finlandia vodka, Korbel champagne and brandy, and Fetzer, Bolla, and Sonoma-Cutrer wines. Brown-Forman also produces and markets crystal, china, silverware, giftware, and collectibles under the Lenox, Gorham, Dansk, and Kirk Stieff brands; as well as Hartmann luggage and leather goods.

Early History

George Garvin Brown and John Forman founded the Brown-Forman Distillery in Louisville, Kentucky, in 1870. At the outset, Brown-Forman marketed Old Forester bourbon. Before Brown and Forman marketed their own brand, bourbon had been sold to taverns in barrels, and bartenders decanted the alcohol into special bottles with the name of the tavern on the label. Brown poured the bourbon into bottles at the distillery, corked and sealed the bottles, labeled them, and warned taverns not to buy the bourbon if the seals were broken. As an additional innovation, all of the labels were handwritten and included a guarantee on the quality of the bourbon. Old Forester sold well as a result of these innovations—but Forman was dubious: in 1902 he sold his interest in the Brown-Forman Distillery because he believed that Brown-Forman's success would diminish as soon as the novelty of packaging began to fade. The Brown family purchased all of Forman's interest in the company.

In 1905 Brown-Forman continued its packaging innovations by bottling Old Forester in pear-shaped bottles. Old Forester's tavern sales increased significantly as a result. These increased sales led to a certain amount of bitterness among other distillers in Kentucky. Some competitors went so far as to slip iron nails into barrels of Brown-Forman whiskey to make it turn black.

Brown-Forman's bourbon was aged in barrels in large warehouses. At that time, warehouses were not heated, and labels on bourbon bore the expression "summers old," a reference to the fact that bourbon can age only in a warm climate. As a result, during the early decades of the 20th century it took many years for the bourbon to be prepared for the market. Consequently, the word "old" became a common prefix in any brand name of bourbon.

Old Forester, produced, marketed, and distributed by Brown-Forman, continued to be very successful under the private ownership of the Brown family, which had no plans to diversify. All the company's advertising concentrated on marketing Old Forester, which it promoted as a product that would restore health: "Many, many times a day, eminent physicians say, Old Forester will life prolong and make old age hale and strong." Although this advertising was effective, Prohibition threatened to close Brown-Forman. To prevent this from happening, Brown-Forman went public just prior to Prohibition (1920–33), but the Browns maintained control of the majority of shares.

The pre-Prohibition advertising had been valuable: the Brown-Forman company was one of four distillers permitted by

Company Perspectives:

Our business philosophy is straightforward. We believe that by investing in our people and brands, and by always trying to improve the quality of our products while also controlling costs, we will succeed in providing premium brands to our consumers and superior returns for our shareholders.

We demonstrate this philosophy in a variety of ways across a broad spectrum of activities within our company, including employee training and development, investments in brand-building programs and production improvements, and carefully managing our assets. All of these activities, and many others, are like pieces of a puzzle that, when connected, reveal the entire picture of how our company succeeds.

the government to sell alcohol for medicinal purposes during Prohibition. The marketing of Old Forester had saved the company from the kind of downfall that other distillers suffered as a result of Prohibition.

Brown-Forman spent the decade between the end of Prohibition and World War II readjusting to the fact that it could now legally sell Old Forester as bourbon. The bourbon now needed to be advertised as an alcoholic beverage rather than as a health tonic, in order to change the image it had acquired during Prohibition. The extensive advertising of the late 1930s and early 1940s, however, was largely futile; the production of alcoholic beverages was once again severely curtailed during World War II. This time Old Forester could not be advertised as a health tonic since even this type of alcohol was now illegal. In spite of this development, the Brown family was not pessimistic about the future of their distillery. They investigated ways in which their alcohol could be used to help the war effort, and during the war Brown-Forman produced alcohol that was used in making both gunpowder and rubber. The Browns also continued to plan for the end of World War II and the future of the Brown-Forman company. They wanted their bourbon to have a head start in the postwar market.

During World War II Brown-Forman's executive committee considered the fact that it took at least four years to age a marketable bourbon. They attempted to predict when the war would end and correctly decided on 1945. By starting the aging in 1941, they could have Old Forester ready for sale immediately following the war. As the competition's bourbon would not be marketable until 1949, Brown-Forman could monopolize the bourbon market for the first four postwar years.

Because the executive committee's predictions were correct and resulted in impressive sales, Brown-Forman management decided to create a committee system of management. Finance, marketing, and production committees were created, in addition to the executive committee, to discuss and implement policies that could lead to the future success of the company.

In 1945 the management at Brown-Forman implemented an annual training course for ten to 20 selected individuals from outside the firm. These individuals worked in all areas of the company, from the lowest to the highest positions. Approximately half of them were then hired by other companies, and half continued with Brown-Forman in management positions. In this way, Brown-Forman created for itself an adequate supply of employees for management positions from outside the company itself. The remaining other employees, however, were hired according to a policy of "planned nepotism."

Since George Garvin Brown founded Brown-Forman in 1870, the Browns supported this type of company nepotism. In 1945 the executives at Brown-Forman publicly stated that nepotism was good for their business and would be encouraged. They believed that if a father enjoyed working at Brown-Forman, his son would feel just as comfortable working there. Brown-Forman executives, as a policy, encouraged the children and grandchildren of good employees to work for the company.

Postwar Diversification

One of the effects of the limited production of alcohol during World War II was that postwar consumers favored whiskey blends that did not have a strong alcohol taste. The executives at Brown-Forman, however, did not pay attention to this new trend. They continued to sell bourbon with high alcohol content. In 1956 Brown-Forman diversified into the premium rye whiskey business by purchasing the Jack Daniel Distillery in Lynchburg, Tennessee. Jack Daniel's had been founded in 1866 and enjoyed a popular, "down-home" image. The label of the "Tennessee sipping whiskey" featured men in overalls, coonhounds, and scenes from Lynchburg. Brown-Forman's confidence in the value of the Jack Daniel's franchise was evinced by the fact that the acquisition cost $20 million, a debt that exceeded the company's net worth. The deal also confirmed Brown-Forman's movement away from being a company that produced only bourbon.

At the beginning of the 1960s, Brown-Forman continued its diversification program by purchasing the Joseph Garneau Co., an importer of scotch whiskeys and European wines. Although Brown-Forman had not followed consumer trends after World War II when blends were popular, the company succumbed to the high demand for scotch in the 1960s. By 1962 scotch held nine percent of the liquor market, and the popularity of wine was increasing steadily.

Despite the diversifications, Brown-Forman portrayed itself as a medium-sized company. This stance worked in favor of the company during the 1960s. Before 1963, 80 percent of all hard liquor in the United States was sold by the four largest distilling companies, and the remaining 20 percent was sold by Brown-Forman, Heublein, James B. Beam Distilling Co., and the American Distilling Co. In 1963, however, these smaller companies increased their sales by 70 percent while the larger companies did not increase their sales at all. Consumer tastes during the 1960s favored the small, independent distilling companies. One reason for this change was that consumers in increasing numbers were switching from blended whiskey, popular after World War II, to straight whiskey.

In 1964, in order to continue its expansion in the broader market for alcoholic beverages, Brown-Forman purchased all outstanding stock of the Oertel Brewing Co., a small Louisville brewery. This company produced beer that was distributed in Kentucky, Tennessee, Indiana, Ohio, and Alabama. The brewery later became unprofitable, and Brown-Forman sold its inter-

Key Dates:

1870: George Garvin Brown and John Forman found the Brown-Forman Distillery, marketing Old Forester bourbon.
1920: Prohibition is adopted; Brown-Forman receives a license to sell alcohol for medicinal purposes.
1933: Prohibition is repealed.
1956: Company purchases the Jack Daniel Distillery.
1971: The Canadian Mist brand is acquired.
1979: Company purchases Southern Comfort.
1983: Company acquires Lenox, maker of crystal, china, and giftware, as well as Hartmann luggage.
1984: The company's name is changed to Brown-Forman Corporation.
1991: Dansk International, maker of premium giftware, is acquired.
1992: Fetzer Vineyards is acquired.
1994: Company creates Brown-Forman Beverages Worldwide, a combination of previously separate U.S. and overseas divisions.
1999: An 80 percent interest in Sonoma-Cutrer Vineyards is acquired.
2000: A 45 percent stake in Finlandia Vodka Worldwide is acquired.

est in the company during the late 1960s. Yet the purchase of Oertel was proof of Brown-Forman's willingness to diversify into new areas of the alcohol market.

In 1966 Daniel L. Street was appointed president of Brown-Forman, the first time that a man outside the Brown family had been president of the company. Street joined Brown-Forman as a lawyer in 1938 and advanced to the position of executive vice-president in 1953. He continued Brown-Forman's program of diversification while president. In 1967 he authorized a merger with Quality Importers, which provided Brown-Forman with a "top scotch and good gin," according to Street. Quality Importers produced Ambassador scotch, Ambassador gin, and Old Bushmills Irish whiskey. By 1968 sales had risen to $180 million as Brown-Forman continued to expand under the direction of Street.

Although Street effectively diversified Brown-Forman, William F. Lucas replaced him as president in 1969. Lucas was also not part of the Brown family. He had joined Brown-Forman as an engineer in 1935 and advanced through the ranks. Lucas concentrated on marketing Brown-Forman's premium-priced products—President's Choice, Jack Daniel's, Old Forester, and Early Times. Lucas did not spend large sums advertising Brown-Forman's low profit brands, because he felt that, as higher quality whiskey could be made for pennies more per fifth, and could be sold at a much higher price, only the expensive brands merited increased advertising expenditures.

Adding Canadian Mist and Southern Comfort in the 1970s

In 1969 Lucas purchased the Bols line of liqueurs and Korbel champagne and brandy. These purchases expanded Brown-Forman's premium product line. In the early 1970s, as the demand for wine soared, Lucas initiated the purchase of Bolla and Cella Italian wines. This purchase was followed by the company's development of another product called Gold Pennant Canadian Whiskey. This whiskey was marketed specifically to women. Each bottle sold was accompanied by a horoscope pamphlet with "love potion" recipes for each astrological sign.

Lucas then bought six-year-old barrel-stored whiskey from Publicker Industries Inc. In the 1960s Publicker had decided to make light whiskey but had later, when it was unsuccessful, reversed this decision. Lucas used Publicker's misfortune to Brown-Forman's advantage by purchasing their light whiskey, triple filtering it, and marketing the clear 80 proof product. Light whiskey is a clear beverage because it is aged in used barrels that have already given color to the whiskey previously stored in them. The clear whiskey is then distilled at a higher proof so it is lighter in taste. The term "light whiskey" actually refers to the type or body of the whiskey and not to its color.

In December 1970 Schenley Industries, National Distillers and Chemical Corporation, and American Distilling Co. filed an injunction against Brown-Forman to bar introduction and further distribution of Brown-Forman's light whiskey called Frost 8/80. Under government restrictions light whiskey was not permitted to be marketed until July 1972. Although Brown-Forman's light whiskey was distributed before it was allowed to be, Brown-Forman's competition dropped its suit because Frost 8/80 was already on the market. As a result, Brown-Forman was free to advertise its new product as a "dry, white whiskey" with which "the possibilities are endless." By advertising the whiskey as easily combining with any mixers, Brown-Forman tried to capture a share of the vodka and lighter Canadian whiskey market. The difficulty was that consumers did not buy Frost 8/80; they were used to drinking whiskey with color and, moreover, they could not associate Frost 8/80 with identically colored vodka: the flavors were different.

By 1973, $6 million had been invested in Frost 8/80 without a profitable return. Brown-Forman had extensively researched the popularity of a white whiskey and had received positive consumer response in various areas of the United States. Consumers, however, were confused by the company's advertising promotions and did not purchase the product. The extensive market research that Lucas had consulted before distributing Frost 8/80 had been incorrect.

Although light whiskey was not successful, Lucas still believed that American tastes were turning to lighter alcoholic drinks. For this reason, in 1971, Lucas contacted Lester Abdson and Oscar Getz who owned Barton Brands of Canada. Barton Brands bottled Canadian Mist, a blended whiskey. Brown-Forman could not purchase the entire company because of strict antitrust laws, so Lucas negotiated an agreement with Getz and Abdson to buy Canadian Mist and its distillery without buying the entire company. (This was the first time that a major brand of liquor was sold separately from the remainder of the company.) Lucas's determination to satisfy the American taste for lighter drinks was not diminished by the strict antitrust laws or the failure of Frost 8/80. By 1973 sales of such products had significantly increased.

Brown-Forman's success dwindled in the late 1970s as the bourbon market declined. Lucas moved aggressively to concentrate on faster growing segments of the alcoholic beverage market. In 1979 Brown-Forman spent $35 million to advertise its full line of alcoholic products. Lucas significantly increased Brown-Forman's wine and liqueur revenue to 22 percent of total sales. Most importantly, in 1979 Lucas purchased privately held Southern Comfort for $90 million. This purchase provided Brown-Forman with greater access to foreign markets since one-fifth of Southern Comfort sales were overseas.

The acquisitions of Southern Comfort and Jack Daniel's were similar because both companies were small and privately held. Also, each company had developed a distinctive character for their single product. Unlike Jack Daniel's, Southern Comfort is a liqueur and does not need to be aged. It can be produced and sold at a much faster rate. Before the Brown-Forman acquisition, Southern Comfort was already the number one selling liqueur. Brown-Forman simply enhanced its success. The company was equally successful with Jack Daniel's: from 1970 to 1979 Brown-Forman tripled Jack Daniel's sales to 1.7 million cases by popularizing the image of a quaint distillery nestled in a Tennessee hollow.

In 1979, W.L. Lyons Brown, Jr., was appointed president of Brown-Forman. He was the great grandson of George Garvin Brown who founded Brown-Forman in 1870. After two presidents who were not related to the Brown family, W.L. Lyons Brown, Jr., reestablished the tradition of a Brown at the head of the business. The restoration of the family was a good omen: Brown-Forman advanced to sixth in the alcohol industry and became the fastest growing full-line distiller.

Expanding Beyond Alcoholic Beverages in the 1980s and Early 1990s

Despite overall growth, the company experienced a setback with Southern Comfort in 1982; as competition increased, the share held by Southern Comfort in the market decreased. Brown-Forman responded to this weakening market share with another innovative idea, one and three-quarter liter plastic bottles to replace the one-half gallon glass bottles. After petitioning the Bureau of Alcohol, Tobacco, and Firearms, the company was granted permission to begin using the plastic bottle in 1983. However, later tests indicated that a loose molecule of plastic could contaminate the alcohol, and the container was soon prohibited.

In 1983, Brown-Forman acquired Lenox Inc., even though Lenox fervently fought the acquisition. Lenox made crystal, china, and giftware, and Hartmann luggage, products that presented special problems for Brown-Forman. Drastically different methods of distribution were needed to market the Lenox products. Yet management at Brown-Forman understood the need for a transition. This was apparent in the name change from Brown-Forman Distillers Corp., under which it had been known for decades, to Brown-Forman Corporation in 1984.

Subsidiary shuffling continued in the late 1980s and early 1990s, as the company worked to solidify its position in giftware. Brown-Forman sold Lenox's ArtCarved jewelry division to SGI Acquisition Corporation for $120 million cash in 1989, and sold the related Lenox Awards division to Jostens in 1990. The Lenox subsidiary acquired the Kirk-Stieff Co., a manufacturer and marketer of silver tableware, and Wings Luggage, Inc., in 1990 and 1991, respectively. Brown-Forman purchased Denver's Athalon Products Ltd., a manufacturer of travel and leisure products, in 1989, and supplemented its Lenox operations with the $70 million acquisition of premium giftware maker Dansk International Designs Ltd. in 1991.

Nevertheless, the company's realignment did not exclude the rearrangement of other alcoholic products; Brown-Forman bought California Cooler Inc. in 1985 for $63 million, and sold Cella Italian Wines to Cosorzio Interprovinciale Vini, an Italian firm, at the end of the decade.

Unfortunately, a recession in the late 1980s—in combination with price and tax hikes—brought a halt to a burgeoning trend toward premium liquors, as consumers traded down to cheaper brands. Unit sales in the liquor industry fell 5.6 percent in 1991, which was widely characterized as "one of the worst years since Prohibition." The decline continued in 1992, when total sales dropped about three percent.

Brown-Forman launched several ready-to-serve cocktails as extensions of its primary brands in the early 1990s. Jack Daniel's Country Cocktails, which were introduced nationally in 1992, soon became one of America's top 20 spirit brands. Southern Comfort Cocktails and Pepe Lopez Margaritas were introduced soon afterward. It was hoped that these products would serve as an alternative to beer, rather than erode or cannibalize their parent brands. In August 1992, Brown-Forman acquired Fetzer Vineyards, an important producer of premium California wines, for about $80 million. In the process, Brown-Forman became the fifth largest player in the U.S. wine market.

W.L. Lyons Brown, Jr., retired as CEO in 1993 and younger brother Owsley Brown II assumed the position. The new leader helped boost his company's stock through a Dutch auction wherein the company repurchased over 4.5 million shares.

Expanding Internationally in the Mid-to-Late 1990s

In the mid-to-late 1990s, Brown-Forman made a concerted effort to bolster its non-U.S. sales. In 1994, Brown-Forman Beverages Worldwide was created through a reorganization that combined the previously separate U.S. and overseas divisions. Among the subsequent overseas initiatives was the 1995 formation of a joint venture with Jagatijit Industries, Limited of India to distribute Brown-Forman alcoholic products in India. Southern Comfort was introduced into that country the following year. In South Africa, a blended whiskey called BlueGrass Kentucky Whiskey was successfully introduced. Worldwide sales of Jack Daniel's increased rapidly, with the brand becoming the world's seventh best-selling spirits brand by decade's end. During this period, Brown-Forman also gained a presence in the hot super-premium vodka category through a 1996 agreement whereby it became the exclusive U.S. importer of the Finlandia brand. Brown-Forman helped increase U.S. sales of Finlandia by nearly 50 percent by 1999, and in August 2000 the company acquired a 45 percent stake in Finlandia Vodka Worldwide Ltd., with the balance of the ownership remaining with Altia Group Ltd., a distiller and marketer owned by the government of Finland. Also in 2000, Brown-Forman expanded its distribution of Glenmorangie Scotch, which the company had been marketing in the United States since 1991. Brown-Forman agreed to take over sales and marketing of the brand in continental Europe, the Far East, Australia, and South America. On the wine front, meantime, Brown-Forman acquired an 80 percent interest in Sonoma-Cutrer Vineyards, Inc. in April 1999, then one year later acquired most of the remaining stake. Sonoma-Cutrer was one of the leading U.S. makers of premium Chardonnay.

While the spirits and wine operations were being steadily expanded, Brown-Forman's consumer durables business—the Lenox, Gorham, Dansk, Kirk Stieff, and Hartmann brands—were not performing as well. At the turn of the millennium, durables accounted for more than one-quarter of overall sales but only ten percent of the profits. A number of analysts called for the divestment of these brands but Brown-Forman resisted such pleas and company officials pointed instead to such positives as the cash flow generated by the brands. The company also attempted to revive the brands' flagging fortunes through a number of initiatives. Lenox, known for its fine china, began selling lines of casual dinnerware. The same brand also found success with a number of millennium-themed products and, in a departure from its traditional department store sales, garnered increasing revenue from catalog, direct mail, and Internet channels. Dansk, meantime, was successfully reintroduced into department stores.

After net sales surpassed the $2 billion mark for the first time in fiscal 1999, the following year marked Brown-Forman's 55th consecutive year of paying regular dividends, a testament to a consistently successful company. Prospects for the early 21st century appeared bright as it was anticipated that the echo boomers—the children of baby boomers—would reach their prime drinking ages (21 to 34 years of age) between 2000 and 2014 and that aging baby boomers would at the same time be reaching their prime wine-consuming years, age 50 and beyond. Brown-Forman's strength in both liquor and wine positioned the company to benefit from both of these demographic trends.

Principal Subsidiaries

Brown-Forman Beverages Australia Pty. Ltd.; Brown-Forman Beverages North Asia, L.L.C.; Brown-Forman International FSC, Ltd. (U.S. Virgin Islands); B-F Korea, L.L.C. (U.S.A.); Brown-Forman Beverages Poland; Brown-Forman Relocation Corp.; Brown-Forman Travel, Inc.; Canadian Mist Distillers, Limited (Canada); Early Times Distillers Company; Fetzer Vineyards; Fratelli Bolla International Wines, Inc.; Hartmann Incorporated; Heddon's Gate Investments, L.L.C.; Jack Daniel's Properties, Inc.; Lenox, Incorporated; Mt. Eagle Corporation; Sonoma-Cutrer Vineyards, Inc.; Southern Comfort Properties, Inc.; Washington Investments, L.L.C.; West Main Interactive, L.L.C.; Longnorth Limited (Ireland); Chissick Limited (Ireland); Clintock Limited (Ireland); Brooks & Bentley Limited (U.K.); Dansk International Designs Ltd.; Norfolk Investments, Inc.; Voldgade Investment Holdings A/S (Denmark); Brown-Forman Mauritius Limited; Pitts Bay Trading Limited (Bermuda; 75%); BFC Tequila Limited (Ireland; 67%); Ireland Drake Investments, Inc.; Jack Daniel Distillery, Lem Motlow, Prop., Inc.; Brown-Forman Korea Ltd.; Fratelli Bolla, S.p.A. (Italy); Brown-Forman Beverages Worldwide, Comercio de Bebidas Ltda. (Brazil); Brown-Forman Worldwide, L.L.C.; JDPI Investments, L.L.C.; Amercain Investments C.V. (Netherlands); Brown-Forman Beverages Africa, Ltd. (Bermuda).

Principal Competitors

Allied Domecq PLC; Bacardi Limited; Beringer Wine Estates Holdings, Inc.; Constellation Brands, Inc.; Diageo plc; Fortune Brands, Inc.; E. & J. Gallo Winery; Kendall-Jackson Wine Estates, Ltd.; LVMH Moet Hennessy Louis Vuitton SA; The Robert Mondavi Corporation; The Seagram Company Ltd.; Tattinger S.A.

Further Reading

Benoit, Ellen, ''Brown-Forman: Wall Street vs. the Family,'' *Financial World,* February 23, 1988, p. 14.

Branch, Shelly, ''Brown-Forman Siphons Market Share from Its Rivals,'' *Wall Street Journal,* February 22, 2000, p. B4.

Fromson, Brett Duval, ''Keeping It All in the Family,'' *Fortune,* September 25, 1989, pp. 86–87+.

Goetz, David, ''Brown-Forman Cashes in on International Tastes,'' *Louisville Courier-Journal,* August 17, 1997, p. 1E.

——, ''Brown-Forman Realigning Lenox Casual Line,'' *Louisville Courier-Journal,* September 8, 1996, p. 1E.

——, ''Brown-Forman Sees Growth in Duty-Free Liquor Market,'' *Louisville Courier-Journal,* April 8, 1999, p. 10B.

——, ''Brown-Forman Toasts Payoff of Global Push,'' *Louisville Courier-Journal,* July 23, 1999, p. 1E.

——, ''Cost-Cutting, New Products Help Lenox Collection Profits Rebound,'' *Louisville Courier-Journal,* October 7, 1997, p. 1C.

——, ''Wine Venture Bears Fruit: When Brown-Forman Acquired Fetzer Vineyards, Both Cultures Profited,'' *Louisville Courier-Journal,* December 25, 1998, p. 22B.

Heath, David, ''BF Adding Dansk to Tableware Collection,'' *Louisville Courier-Journal,* May 21, 1991, p. 8C.

Levin, Gary, ''New Coolers Pouring It On,'' *Advertising Age,* August 3, 1992, pp. 3, 26.

''Liquor Sales Go Dry: Recession, Taxes Blamed for 5.6% Decrease,'' *Advertising Age,* February 10, 1992, p. 44.

Lucas, William F., *Nothing Better in the Market: Brown-Forman's Century of Quality, 1870–1970,* New York: Newcomen Society, 1970, 32 p.

McGinty, David, ''Brown-Forman Corp. Brings Good Tidings to Shareholders,'' *Louisville Courier-Journal,* July 28, 2000, p. 1C.

Pitturro, Marlene C., ''Bottoms Up!,'' *World Trade,* December 1991, pp. 60–64.

Song, Kyung M., ''Brown-Forman Plans to Tap into Developing Spirits Markets,'' *Louisville Courier-Journal,* May 11, 1994, p. 8B.

——, ''Jack Daniel's Country Cousins Are Helping to Bolster Brown-Forman's Whiskey Sales,'' *Louisville Courier-Journal,* September 1, 1992, p. 8D.

——, ''Lee Brown Hands Top Post at Brown-Forman to Brother,'' *Louisville Courier-Journal,* July 23, 1993, p. 1A.

—April Dougal Gasbarre
—updated by David E. Salamie

Buca, Inc.

1300 Nicollet Mall, Suite 5003
Minneapolis, Minnesota 55403
U.S.A.
Telephone: (612) 288-2382
Fax: (612) 827-6446
Web site: http://www.bucadibeppo.com

Public Company
Incorporated: 1994 as Buca di Beppo
Employees: 2,500
Sales: $71.5 million (1999)
Stock Exchanges: NASDAQ
Ticker Symbol: BUCA
NAIC: 722110 Full Service Restaurants

Buca, Inc. is an industry leader in terms of growth in the number of restaurants it oversees. The company owns and operates 51 full service, dinner-only restaurants under the name Buca di Beppo. Its restaurants are located in 18 states as well as the District of Columbia. Buca ranked third in *Restaurant Business Magazine*'s year 2000 ranking of 50 top growth chains and ninth in *Corporate Report*'s performance rankings for 2000. Industry analysts ranked Buca among the ten best restaurant stocks for 2000, and the chain was recognized as one of 17 ''best of'' designations in a variety of readers' polls across the United States and in numerous restaurant publications, including *Bon Appetit*. Buca di Beppo (meaning ''Joe's basement'') restaurants differentiate from other Italian restaurant chains by providing distinctive oversized Southern Italian family style portions in a casual, festive, humorous, socially interactive atmosphere. Appealing to nostalgic trends, the décor at each of Buca's restaurants irreverently exaggerates the clichés of traditional postwar neighborhood Italian/American restaurants. In terms of scale, Buca thinks big: large food portions, large tables, and large restaurant size with an average seating capacity of 300.

Founding a Concept: 1993

In 1993 Philip A. Roberts and cofounders Don W. Hays and Peter J. Mihajlov launched Buca di Beppo. The following year Parasole Restaurant Holdings, Inc., established following the merger of several privately held restaurant companies that had been cofounded by Roberts and Mihajlov, acquired Buca and took over its operations. Roberts, Hays, and Mihajlov each had extensive industry experience leading up to their collaborative venture. Prior to his involvement in Parasole, Mihajlov served in a variety of marketing and business management positions within the Pillsbury Company. Don Hays had been involved in the restaurant industry since 1964, working as director of operations for Dayton's restaurant division; and Roberts had worked in several privately held restaurant companies since 1977.

The founders agreed to pay homage to the bygone era when waves of immigrants from southern Italy sailed to the United States ''with little more than a rich culinary heritage and a zest for life.'' The concept, as envisioned by Phil Roberts, evolved as an attempt to imitate the family-run restaurants established by immigrants in urban centers throughout the country. Roberts, a non-Italian, said he had originally been inspired by a restaurant in Florence, Italy, commenting that he was impressed with its ''communal quality, people laughing and talking, pouring wine, sharing the meal,'' according to *Nation's Restaurant News*. He decided to replicate that type of dining atmosphere.

The first Buca restaurant opened in a crowded Minneapolis basement adorned with mementos of Italian heritage: posters, statues, colorfully painted murals, and photos of Dean Martin, Joe DiMaggio, Sophia Loren, and Frank Sinatra—among scores of others. Despite the difficult-to-find location, Buca's memorable menu, large portions, and colorful ambiance caught on. Crowds withstood Minnesota's sub-freezing temperatures to wait in lines outside the restaurant.

Once inside, customers read from large menus on the walls that included a broad selection of antipasti (appetizers), salads, pizzas, pastas, and entrees that included chicken cacciatore, fried calamari, veal lemone, and eggplant parmigiana. Buca's spaghetti and meatball dish included 2½ pounds of pasta and three baseball-sized meatballs that weighed ½ pound each. Each platter was intended to serve from three to five guests. The desert menu included ''chocolate drenched cannoli, spumoni ice cream, or a quart-sized bowl of rum and espresso-soaked tiramisu.'' According to a *Minneapolis Star-Tribune* article, the

Company Perspectives:

BUCA's mission is to provide a real immigrant, Southern Italian neighborhood-dining experience. Only the freshest high-quality ingredients will be used in our restaurants. Our food will be as expressive as our Italian heritage. We will search for, and retain, only the most sincere and enthusiastic team members. The quality and integrity of our staff will be the catalyst for our commitment to the service of our guests and the profitability of our company. Our teamwork and humor will create tremendous loyalty among our team and guests, making us sought after by each. Our long-term growth strategy is to continue expanding into markets of 400,000 people or more across the U.S. To that end, the company intends to select appropriate restaurant sites, effectively manage development risks, recruit qualified personnel and raise additional capital as necessary.

Buca concept worked because in addition to offering quantities of flavorful Italian food, it "feeds an American hunger for community."

Before long, a second Buca opened in suburban St. Paul. It catered to a different demographic, but proved equally successful. Ivy and bottles of wine hung from ceilings, and a large "Pope's Table" provided seating for 14 to 18 guests. The Pope's Table featured a centerpiece bust of Pope John Paul II on a lazy susan, an apt symbol for the cultural reverence surrounding food and mealtime—and a provocative conversation piece. By 1995, a third Buca opened in the Twin Cities suburb of Eden Prairie, followed by the first out-of-state Buca, which opened in Milwaukee, Wisconsin. Buca restaurants soon expanded from Minnesota and Wisconsin to Washington, Indiana, California, and Illinois.

1996: Recruiting Proven Leadership

In 1996 Joseph P. Micatrotto, a second-generation Italian immigrant, was hired by Buca to lead the company's national expansion by taking on the positions of chairman, president, and CEO. Micatrotto had spent much of his youth working in his family's Italian restaurant business. He had earned an M.B.A. from Miami University in Ohio, and decided by 1975 that his future would embrace the hospitality industry. Micatrotto began his career with a three-store, 24-hour family restaurant chain, Hall's Waffles, located in the southern Ohio area. Seeking an opportunity for more formalized training, Micatrotto embarked on a new venture as managing partner and general manager for Steak and Ale Restaurants Corporation—then considered the leading "premier restaurant" chain in the nation. Next, Micatrotto undertook a position as franchise general manager of Chi-Chi's Mexican Restaurants, where he played an instrumental role in the company's expansion from 26 units to a 270-store chain with sales in excess of $500 million. His performance led him to become Chi-Chi's president and CEO, where he remained until accepting a position as president and CEO of Panda Management Company, Inc. in 1995. Micatrotto expanded Panda from 85 to 225 units in 29 states, increasing sales from $85 million to $150 million, making the company the country's largest and fastest growing privately held Chinese foodservice company. Commenting on his move to Buca, Micatrotto said that assuming leadership of Buca di Beppo restaurants "felt like coming home."

Under Micatrotto's leadership, Buca began preparations for major expansion. In 1997, Buca surprised analysts by raising $16.3 million in venture capital, the largest investment sum received by a Minnesota company for that year, according to the accounting firm Coopers & Lybrand. Ralph Weinberger, a partner in Coopers & Lybrand who tracked the venture capital industry for the firm, commented, "If you ask somebody what a venture capitalist invests in, the first words out of their mouth wouldn't be restaurant." Venture capital firms typically put money into technology, healthcare and communications rather than retail concepts and restaurants. However, the company promised investors that it would initiate rapid growth on a tight schedule. Micatrotto told a *City Business* writer that "all the money goes right back into the business," including excess money generated by the restaurants. Micatrotto reasoned that the newer the company, the "more susceptible we are to making a mistake," and that as a private concern, any mistakes will not drive down share prices. Honoring its promise, Buca management was operating 11 restaurants by the end of 1997 and planned to open an additional eight in 1998, scattered from middle America to the Pacific Northwest and southern California.

Buca developed its "Paisano Partners Program" as part of its marketing strategy, one that revolves around the local partner. It was a way to lure dedicated talent into the enterprise. The program, which includes a training period, stipulates that restaurant general managers purchase Buca stock, receive stock options, and share in the company's profits. According to Micatrotto, "When you tie in value creators—the general managers—and make them shareholders, that's the definition of capitalism." Partners are encouraged to make appearances on local morning TV programs or cooking shows in lieu of most other forms of advertising. The chain does only a small amount of print advertising and uses direct mail primarily to establish a presence when it opens a new location.

Micatrotto and Phil Roberts make regular visits to villages south of Rome and sample from mom-and-pop restaurants. Buca's executive chef, Vittorio Renda, a native of Calabria, Italy, has sometimes spent up to two months adapting the recipes for the Buca menu. As a traditional accompaniment to its food offerings, Buca began importing an Italian white wine from Tuscany, a blend of 80 percent chardonnay grapes and 20 percent Malvasia grapes, shipped in basket bottles, under the Buca private label. The first shipments debuted in Buca's restaurants in December 1998. Within a year the company was daily serving more than 1,000 liters of its white wine. By 2000, it sold more Chianti than any other restaurant chain in the country.

Expanding Revenues: 1999

Following Buca's initial public offering in April 1999, the company's stock jumped by more than 50 percent on its first day. New restaurant openings and a 7.3 percent same-store sales increase for the 12-month period ending in July 2000 boosted total revenues 88 percent to $56.52 million, up from $30.01 million (representing a $2.49 million loss) for the comparable

Key Dates:

1993: Buca di Beppo opens its first restaurant in a Minneapolis basement.
1994: Parasole Restaurant Holdings, Inc. acquires Buca di Beppo.
1996: Buca spins off from Parasole through a share dividend of common stock.
1997: Buca launches a period of rapid expansion.
1999: The company completes its initial public offering.

period of the previous year. Buca executives named an improvement in operating margins as the major reason for the positive turn in earnings. Operating margins were 16.9 percent for the first half of 2000, compared to 15.3 percent for the same period of the prior year. According to *Nation's Restaurant News*, Micatrotto explained, "Our ability to negotiate stronger purchasing contracts in a number of key products has impacted product costs favorably in 2000." The company showed steady, continuous growth but did not make the mistake of too aggressive expansion, which often encumbered chains. Buca opened 17 restaurants in the year 2000 with plans to open another 17 in 2001, bringing the grand total to 68. The new restaurants averaged $56,000 per week in sales for the year, 25 percent higher than what was projected. Its market strategy following the IPO targeted metropolitan areas with 800,000 or more people that could support multiple Buca restaurants. The plan called for 32 restaurants to open in at least 17 markets by year's end.

Buca's marketing strategy also involved planning so that new sites opened ahead of the lucrative holiday season, since the restaurants were suited to celebratory gatherings. Fourth quarter earnings for the company had consistently been the highest. Most restaurant openings occurred prior to November to enable the company to take full advantage of the holidays. Buca reported strongest startups in markets where it already had a presence and an established reputation. The 49th restaurant opened in Cincinnati, Ohio, and recorded record-breaking sales volume of over $92,000 in its first week.

Buca announced in May 2000 that it was restructuring its real estate organization in order to separate site selection and construction operations. The intent was to allow the real estate function to focus exclusively on finding optimum sites for new Buca restaurants. Micatrotto reported in a press release that tremendous progress had been made in reducing construction costs for new restaurants. He said, "This management realignment will strengthen the ties between the construction and financial functions and enable us to further reduce our building costs by taking advantage of the economies of scale of multiple construction projects." In addition to the 17 new restaurants starting up according to schedule in 2000, the company negotiated deals for opening another ten for 2001.

For the long term, the company envisioned at least 450 restaurants spread across the country. Micatrotto said in a *Minneapolis-St. Paul City Business* interview that he believed that this was a very reasonable, probably even conservative, estimate. Buca planned to maintain control of the company's direction by keeping nearly two-thirds of the stock in the hands of its directors and early investors. John Waley, venture capitalist and partner at Norwest Equity Partners of Minneapolis, remained the largest shareholder with 1.4 million shares, or 14.5 percent of the company. According to Micatrotto, "When you have a great concept and people have a proprietorship mentality, that is the formula for success." He added, "Our vision is to be the dominant immigrant Southern Italian restaurant in the United States."

Principal Divisions

Midwest; Central; Texas; Northeast; Florida; Southern California; West.

Principal Competitors

Brinker International, Inc.; Carlson Restaurants Worldwide Inc.; Darden Restaurants, Inc.; Spaghetti Warehouse, Inc.; Applebee's International Inc.

Further Reading

Berta, Dina, "Restaurants Focus on Importance of Culture to Recruit and Retain Staff," *Nation's Restaurant News*, December 11, 2000, p. 16.

Cebrzynski, Gregg, "Buca di Beppo: To Grandmother's House We Go," *Nation's Restaurant News,* May 11, 1998, pp. 90–92.

Crumm, David, "Italian Eatery Serves Up Fun, Food," *Detroit Free Press*, July 9, 1999.

Farkas, David, "Italian Stallion," *Chain Leader*, July 2000, pp. 52–60.

Huber, Tim, "Buca Gets Big Venture Helping," *CityBusiness: The Business Journal of the Twin Cities*, April 17, 1998, p.20.

Montgomery, Christine, "Buca di Beppo Adds Extra Touch," *Washington Times,* June 3, 1999.

Rosengren, John, "Gluttons for Growth," *Corporate Report Minnesota*, June 1999, p. 21.

Tellijohn, Andrew, "Beaucoup Open Nationwide," *Minneapolis-St. Paul City Business*, September 29, 2000, p. 5.

—Terri Mozzone

C-COR.net Corp.

60 Decibel Road
State College, Pennsylvania 16801
U.S.A.
Telephone: (814) 238-2461
Toll Free: (800) 233-2267
Fax: (814) 238-4065
Web site: http://www.c-cor.com

Public Company
Incorporated: 1953 as Community Engineering Corporation
Employees: 2,200
Sales: $281.1 million (2000)
Stock Exchanges: NASDAQ
Ticker Symbol: CCBL
NAIC: 334220 Radio and Television Broadcasting and Wireless Communications Equipment Manufacturing; 513330 Telecommunications Resellers

Based in State College, Pennsylvania, C-COR.net Corp. has been involved with the cable television industry from the very beginning. The company, originally incorporated as Community Engineering, ran a number of small cable systems in the 1950s and pioneered the development of the equipment necessary to amplify and distribute signals to cable subscribers. It earned a well-deserved reputation for making products of the highest quality. C-COR sold off its cable operations to TCI in 1970 to concentrate on manufacturing. As cable has moved into two-way communications via the Internet, C-COR has rapidly expanded through mergers and acquisitions to become a leading provider of the technologies and services necessary to create and manage a broadband delivery system of voice, video, and high-speed data. The bulk of its customers, however, remain cable TV operators. Time Warner accounts for 28 percent of sales, and AT&T another 17 percent. C-COR is now a worldwide company with a presence in South America, Europe, and the Pacific Rim.

Postwar Rise of Television and Birth of Cable TV

Although the technology of television was available before World War II, it was not until the late 1940s that the public began to embrace the new medium. In 1946, 6,000 television sets were sold. By 1948, sales neared one million. Transmitting stations were few and limited to urban areas. Signals could travel about 50 miles, and only then if the terrain allowed. People located in more mountainous regions saw little chance that television would be available to them in the foreseeable future, especially when the Federal Communications Commission in 1948 put a freeze on the licensing of new TV stations. Nevertheless, the desire for television existed just as much in remote regions as in big cities, and appliance dealers were eager to meet the demand. But in order to sell televisions, dealers had to provide something to watch. The answer would be Community Antenna TV, or CATV. Today it is simply known as cable.

Although simultaneous efforts were underway across the country to provide television signals to secluded areas, the father of cable TV is generally regarded as Ed Parsons, who ran a radio station in Astoria, Oregon, located 125 miles from Seattle and KRSC-TV, channel 5. In 1948, using frequency-survey equipment, Parsons discovered that KRSC's signal reached Astoria in fingerlike bands, one of which extended to a nearby hotel. He received permission to set up an antenna on the hotel's roof, then ran a line to his apartment. Using his own "booster equipment," Parsons was able to deliver a signal to a television in his living room, which quickly became crowded with guests every time that KRSC was on the air. To regain his privacy as much as any reason, Parsons devised a way to distribute the television signal to others. A makeshift web of coaxial cable spread throughout Astoria. Parsons turned the system into a profit-making venture by charging $100 per installation, as well as through the sale of television sets.

Similar efforts were underway in Pennsylvania. John Wilson of Mahoney City also has a claim to having built the first commercial CATV system. In 1948 he owned an interest in an appliance store. He set up an antenna on one of the mountains that surrounded Mahoney City and offered to connect anyone who would buy a television. By June 1948 he claimed to have had 727 subscribers. A year later he upgraded his system to

Company Perspectives:

C-COR.net is dedicated to responsive customer service, innovative technology, and the manufacture of quality products. We will be a leader in communication technology. The company will research and develop market opportunities within our expertise to enhance profitable growth.

coaxial cable and began charging $100 for installation and $2 per-month per-connection fee.

In 1947 in another mountainous area, State College, Pennsylvania, Dr. Walter Brown (a Penn State University professor) and a group of investors organized a company called Central Pennsylvania Corporation with the goal of building a television broadcasting station. Unable to obtain a license from the Federal Communications Commission (FCC), the group in 1951 built a CATV system in Bellefonte, a dozen miles away. A second system for State College was added later. The investors created yet another venture, Centre Video Corporation to distribute equipment of Jerrold Electronics, an early developer of master antenna configurations. Because of poor relations with Jerrold, Dr. Brown and his investors in 1953 formed Community Engineering Corporation, which they called CECO, in order to build their own equipment. Dr. Brown was in charge of these wide-ranging television operations, as well as being a partner in an earlier and more prominent venture, HRB (Haller, Raymond, and Brown), a military electronics research and development company. In December 1954 he convinced Jim Palmer, who had been hired by HRB a year earlier, to ''look after'' CECO in addition to his regular work. His payment would be in the form of stock in the corporation.

Looking after CECO turned out to be a second full-time job for Palmer. After a year he was exhausted, and Dr. Brown had died in a drowning accident. Palmer and other CECO principals then sold stock in the company to friends and neighbors in order to allow Palmer to devote himself exclusively to CECO. On August 1, 1956 Palmer became president of the company. Two days later CECO took over Centre Video Corporation, which brought with it control of the cable TV operations in Bellefonte and State College. In this way Palmer, trained as an electrical engineer, would become involved in the cable television industry for the next 30 years.

A company called Century Lighting had trademarked CECO for a lighting system and forced Palmer to change his company's name. At first he tried ''C-CO,'' a simple typographical alteration, only to discover another electronics outfit was using that name as well. In order to maintain the company's position in the alphabet, the beginning of the ''C''s, Palmer and his colleagues decided to call the company ''C-COR,'' a name that was then properly trademarked. In 1964 the company would change its name to C-COR Electronics, Inc.

Divesting Cable Systems Business: 1970

For a number of years C-COR continued to build and operate cable TV systems as well as manufacture the equipment that made the systems run. When Palmer first became president, the State College system only had 280 subscribers and Bellefonte another 500. None of them were overly pleased with the quality of the service of this one channel operation. By 1965, under the auspices of Centre Video and the management of Robert Tudek, cable operations had expanded to surrounding areas, subscribers totaled 9,000, and the number of television stations offered increased to three. Tudek wanted to grow further. He requested permission to build a cable system in his hometown of Glassport, located a few miles south of Pittsburgh. Although the city was easily within range of the five Pittsburgh television stations, Tudek recognized that the area's topography prevented people from receiving clear reception on all of the channels. By 1970 Centre Video had 69 cable franchises, located mostly in the mountainous areas around Pittsburgh. Despite this success with cable operations, Palmer wanted to concentrate on engineering and manufacturing. Furthermore, to build and activate all the franchises that the company had won would require a great deal of capital. It was decided to either sell or merge Centre Video with a company that could take on that financial burden. On February 16, 1971 Centre Video was merged into Tele-Communications, Inc. (TCI) in a tax-free exchange of stock. What Palmer and his colleagues did not realize at the time was that their company was actually in a much stronger position than TCI, the future cable giant.

On the manufacturing side of its business, C-COR had been steadily gaining a reputation for innovation and quality. Palmer's military background—he had been an electronics officer on a destroyer in World War II—and subsequent training with General Electric, led him to focus on a conservative approach to development and manufacture. The goal was product reliability; cutting corners was not acceptable. C-COR, although profitable, never attempted to compete with Jerrold for a greater share of the cable equipment business. It was a company run by a professional engineer, not a marketer. He did not have to claim that C-COR's products were of the highest quality. His customers, as well as rivals, knew it. C-COR did not offer financing to customers, nor did it have the resources to do so. A discount schedule based on dollar volume of purchases was established and never compromised in order to make a sale.

C-COR made a number of advances in its field of electronics. In 1965 the company introduced the use of integrated circuits in amplifiers. It was the first to offer 220 MHz (megahertz) amplifiers. It did pioneering research on heat dissipation for solid-state amplifiers, which led to the first use of fins on amplifiers in 1969. In 1979 C-COR became the first to market amplifiers with a bandwidth greater than 300 MHz, in order to meet the demand of cable systems that were, in turn, trying to meet consumer demand for more and more channels.

By 1965 C-COR had moved into new facilities on the outskirts of State College. But the company suffered a setback in the early 1970s when federal regulations hampered the cable industry by requiring that systems offer 20 or more channels and provide studios for public access programming. Employment at C-COR, which had reached 219, fell to 35. The company slowly made its way back, and was doing so well that by 1981 C-COR made a public offering of its stock on the Nasdaq.

Bolstered with additional funding, the company in the early 1980s became involved in digital fiber optics as well as network

Key Dates:

1951: A group of State College, Pennsylvania, investors establish CATV system.
1953: Community Engineering Corporation (CECO) is created to provide equipment for the investors' CATV operations.
1956: Jim Palmer, an electrical engineer, becomes president of CECO.
1964: To avoid trademark violation, CECO is renamed C-COR Electronics, Inc.
1970: Cable TV systems are sold to Tele-Communications, Inc. (TCI).
1981: C-COR becomes a publicly traded company.
1999: Company changes name to C-COR.net Corp.

management software systems. The company, however, suffered another slump, forcing it to lay off 361 employees. In 1985 Palmer retired as president and CEO of C-COR, and in July of that year was replaced by Richard Perry, who had worked for Northwestern Bell Telephone Co. for 32 years. In 1983 he became CEO of a subsidiary of U S West, one of the seven regional phone companies that emerged from the AT&T breakup.

Deregulation of cable TV led to the upgrading of local cable systems, spurring demand for C-COR's products. Perry hoped to diversify the company, which was heavily reliant on the state of the cable industry, with 65 percent of all sales coming from that sector. C-COR looked to the new technology of fiber optics, which had the potential of replacing coaxial cable by using beams of light rather than electrical pulses to deliver a much greater volume of TV signals, as well as other kinds of data. Perry considered opting out of the cable business to focus on data transmission and local area networks (LAN), but when that market slumped, C-COR became even more dependent on cable, now accounting for 85 percent of its sales. The company was then rocked by the uncertainty in the cable industry in 1990, when Congress was considering reregulation. C-COR was one of the first companies to suffer. The company posted four consecutive quarters of significant losses. Sales in the fiscal year ending in June 1991 were only half of what they had been the previous year. When cable regained its feet in 1991, coupled with the industry's expansion overseas, C-COR began to recover as well.

The 1990s Bring Another Media Revolution

C-COR, which had been a part of the technology revolution of television, now found itself unexpectedly poised to play a role in a new technology revolution: the Internet. Two-way communications over a wire that could encompass voice, video, and data would require a wide highway, or bandwidth, and an amplification of the signal. C-COR's reputation for producing the highest quality amplifiers in the world made it a prime choice for forward-looking investors.

Positioning itself to take advantage of the Internet was not without pain for C-COR. In July 1996 Perry stepped down as president and CEO, though continued to serve as chairman of the board. He was replaced by Scott Chandler, a U S West executive, who in 1997 would discontinue C-COR's digital fiber optics business. He also shifted production of radio-frequency amplifiers to a new plant in Mexico, in turn downsizing a Reedsville, Pennsylvania facility. But less than two years into running the company, Chandler abruptly resigned to accept another position in the communications industry, forcing Perry to again assume day-to-day control. Almost immediately he was forced to make a difficult decision. To further cut costs he closed the Reedsville plant, eliminating 145 employees, or 12 percent of the company's workforce.

In July 1998 a new CEO took over for Perry: David Woodle, who had been general manager at another State College electronics company, Raytheon, and whose focus had been on real-time information systems integration. He also brought with him considerable involvement in mergers, start-ups, international partnerships, and acquisitions. Less than a year later, in May 1999, Woodle would make his first deal to help C-COR position itself in the Internet business. For $46 million in stock C-COR acquired Convergence.com, an Atlanta-based company that serviced cable lines to prepare small to midsized cable TV operators to provide high-speed Internet access. In addition to the transaction, C-COR announced it would change its name to C-COR.net Corp. Later in the month, Woodle announced that C-COR had signed a letter of intent to acquire Silicon Valley Communications (SVCI), a company that supplied high quality fiber optic technology for hybrid fiber/coax (HFC) networks. To fuel its growth, in November 1999 C-COR offered an additional 2.8 million shares of stock at a price of $44 per share; and to make the stock more broadly accessible, the board of directors approved a two-for-one stock split of its common shares.

Early in 2000 C-COR made two more acquisitions to further enhance its position. It acquired Advanced Communications Services Incorporated (ACSI), a Riverside, California, company that provided engineering services for HFC system rebuilds and upgrades. Its customer base complemented C-COR's, as well as added a presence in the West and the South. In addition, C-COR acquired Worldbridge Broadband Services, Inc., a Colorado company that provided full-system field operations as an outsourcing option for broadband cable operators. Worldbridge's 230 technicians worked out of eight regional offices that covered the Southeast, Midwest, Mountain, Southwest, and Western states.

Also in 2000 C-COR made strategic alliances with other companies. It announced an agreement with Finisar Corporation to co-develop fiber optics-based products for HFC networks. C-COR also invested in Fortress Technologies, Inc., one of the leading security networking companies. With more and more businesses and individuals connected to the Internet via broadband conduits, the need for easy-to-use security products was certain to grow.

Woodle made clear in an August 2000 interview what was driving C-COR's aggressive acquisition strategy and where he hoped to take the company in the future: "We have been known over our forty-seven-year history for providing high-quality products. Building on that, we have added capabilities in the technical services and network management areas through four acquisitions. We are now providing a full life cycle of support to our customers, from designing and building the network, through management and maintenance of the network. We provide products, services and solutions for the entire life cycle of that network, to help our customers have a high quality, high integrity network for delivering advanced services to their customers.''

Principal Subsidiaries

Convergence Systems; Silicon Valley Communications; Worldbridge Broadband Services.

Principal Competitors

ADC Telecommunications, Inc.; ANTEC; Motorola, Inc.

Further Reading

''C-COR Announces Restructuring, Plant Consolidation,'' *PR Newswire,* June 26, 1998, p. 1.

''C-COR Announces Scott Chandler Resigns As President and CEO,'' *PR Newswire,* March 25, 1998, p. 1.

''C-COR Electronics Closes Plant,'' *Wall Street Journal,* June 29, 1998.

''C-COR Electronics Inc,: Convergence.com Takeover for $42 Million Is Planned,'' *Wall Street Journal,* May 17, 1999, p. B6.

''C-COR.net and Finisar Corporation Announce Agreement to Co-Develop Advanced Fiber Optic Products,'' *PR Newswire,* March 15, 2000, p. 1.

''C-COR.net and Fortress Technologies Announce Agreement to Provide Data Security Solution for Internet Over Cable,'' *PR Newswire,* January 12, 2000, p. 1.

''C-COR.net and Silicon Valley Communications (SVCI) Agree to Merge; Follows May 1999 Signing of Letter of Intent to Acquire SVCI,'' *PR Newswire,* July 14, 1999, p. 1.

''C-COR.net and Worldbridge Broadband Services, Inc. Agree to Merge,'' *PR Newswire,* January 20, 2000, p. 1.

''C-COR.net Announces Completion of Merger with Worldbridge Broadband Services, Inc.,'' *PR Newswire,* February 21, 2000, p. 1.

''C-COR.net Announces Offering of 2.8 Million Shares of Common Stock,'' *PR Newswire,* November 9, 1999, p. 1.

''C-COR Pre-Announces Record Fiscal Year 1999 Bookings and Revenues,'' *PR Newswire,* July 1, 1999, p. 1.

''C-COR Signs Letter of Intent to Acquire Silicon Valley Communications (SVCI),'' *PR Newswire,* May 25, 1999, p. 1.

Chesworth, Jo, ''The C-COR Family,'' *T&G,* April 1990, pp. 26–34.

''David A. Woodle,'' *Wall Street Transcript,* August 28, 2000.

Galant, Debbie, ''Home-Run Hitters of 1994,'' *Institutional Investor,* March 1995, p. 93.

Katz, Frances, and Charles Haddad, ''Local Internet Firm to Be Purchased,'' *Atlanta Constitution,* May 19, 1999, p. D6.

Palmer, Jay, ''Brighter Picture: Cable Revives and So Does C-COR Electronics,'' *Barron's National Business and Financial Weekly,* June 1, 1992, p. 17.

Phillips, Mary Alice Mayer, *CATV: A History of Community Antenna Television,* Evanston: Northwestern University Press, 1972, 209 p.

Taylor, Archer S., *History Between Their Ears,* Denver: The Cable Center, 2000, 320 p.

Thiel, Sally O., ''C-COR Names Former US West Executive As New President and CEO,'' *PR Newswire,* July 18, 1996, p. 1.

—Ed Dinger

Carter-Wallace, Inc.

1345 Avenue of the Americas
New York, New York 10105
U.S.A.
Telephone: (212) 339-5000
Fax: (212) 339-5100
Web site: http://www.carterwallace.com

Public Company
Incorporated: 1880 as Carter Medicine Company
Employees: 3,320
Sales: $747.7 million (2000)
Stock Exchanges: New York
Ticker Symbol: CAR
NAIC: 32562 Toilet Preparation Manufacturing; 325412 Pharmaceutical Preparation Manufacturing (pt); 422990 Other Miscellaneous Nondurable Goods Wholesalers

Carter-Wallace, Inc. is a diversified healthcare company that has exhibited a consistent knack for anticipating business trends. The company markets and makes toiletries, proprietary drugs, diagnostic specialties, pharmaceuticals, and pet products. Best known for such products as Arrid deodorant and Trojan condoms, Carter-Wallace has more recently emphasized its laboratories division, where work on various medications points the way to future profits.

The Late 1800s: Carter's Little Liver Pills

Carter-Wallace's roots can be traced back to the 1800s and a modest pill compounded by an Erie, Pennsylvania doctor for folks suffering from digestive distress. ''Carter's Little Liver Pills'' first were advertised by a sign placed in Dr. John Samuel Carter's pharmacy window, but the pills' popularity soon spread beyond the capacity of the pharmacy's back room. By 1859 a four-floor plant had been built to produce the liver pills. Dr. Carter also had created other products, but it was the sales of the liver pills that led New York businessman Brent Good to suggest a merger to make a nationwide business. In 1880 Carter Medicine Company was born.

In its first year of business, the company spent a third of its revenues on advertising. Coupled with all the other start-up expenses, plus the move to New York, the first year ended in the red, but belief in the product remained strong. By its second year Carter was exporting to Canada and England and enjoying vigorous sales in the United States. By 1890 the company had already outgrown its new quarters and moved to larger ones. Soon imitators were popping up everywhere and an attorney was retained to battle the counterfeiters. With the loss in 1884 of Samuel Carter—the company's president and the son of the pill's inventor—Carter Medicine Company entered a new era.

The 1890s was a time of uncertainty and financial panic in the United States and Carter Medicine Company suffered along with nearly every other business. It was just recovering when another economic crash rattled the country in 1907. Companies stabilized again just in time for World War I to alter the global economy. What sustained the Carter Medicine Company through these times was the fact that Carter's Little Liver Pills had become such a staple household item. Meanwhile, the company continued to operate like many family-owned corporations. Brent Good passed the presidency on to his son Harry Good; Harry's brother-in-law, Charles Orcutt, later succeeded him. Another new era for the company was ushered in when Harry Hoyt, Sr., who was Orcutt's son-in-law, became managing director in 1929. Hoyt bought controlling interest in the company and instilled Carter-Wallace with his axiom that ''a business cannot stand still.''

Product Diversification Between the Wars

Hoyt's first order of business was to expand beyond the company's one profitable product, the liver pills. Creating new products meant risk and investment. It was difficult at first to convince trustees of his vision. Hoyt wanted to cut dividend payments and spend the money on the development of new products. While this struggle for change was taking place, the government dropped a blow: the Department of Agriculture contested the use of the word ''liver'' on the pills' labels, since the pills were not really targeted for liver ailments. This was catastrophic for a product whose brand name had been familiar to households for more than half a century. In light of all the money it had invested in advertising and brand recognition, the

Key Dates:

1880: Carter Medicine Company is formed.
1929: Harry Hoyt, Sr., becomes company's managing director.
1935: Arrid antiperspirant is launched.
1937: Carter Medicine Company becomes Carter Products, Inc.
1940: Carter Products introduces Nair depilatory.
1949: Carter launches Rise, the first pressurized shave cream.
1961: Harry Hoyt, Sr., becomes company chairman.
1965: Carter Products is renamed Carter-Wallace, Inc.
1985: Carter-Wallace acquires Youngs Drug Products Corporation.
1989: Carter-Wallace acquires Hygeia Sciences, Inc.
1993: Carter-Wallace launches Felbatol, a medication for epileptics; serious complications with the drug eventually led to lawsuits.
1999: The first polyurethane condom, Trojan Supra, is introduced.
2000: Henry Hoyt, Jr., retires.

company decided to fight to retain its brand name and, eventually, it won.

The Federal Trade Commission brought similar charges against the company in 1943. For 17 years the company battled in the courts to retain its name. The decision came back in 1959: ''liver'' had to be dropped from all advertising. The product, whose name was known in every home and painted on the sides of barns across the country, was renamed Carter's Little Pills.

Meanwhile, Hoyt was pioneering research for new products even through the hardships of the 1930s. With so many Americans living hand-to-mouth during the Depression, few could afford liver pills, and sales sank. This only fueled Hoyt's determination to diversify. Research pointed to deodorants and antiperspirants. At the time there were two dominant brands in the United States, and each had a weakness: one was a stainless dry cream that was a deodorant only; the other a liquid antiperspirant that often stained clothes and irritated skin. The challenge became how to find a dry, stainless cream that could stop perspiration while deodorizing, yet not irritate the skin. A research chemist from Princeton, John H. Wallace, was tapped for the task. In 1935 the company launched the product that would soon outstrip its liver pills in sales and brand name recognition: Arrid.

Between an ad campaign that saturated the public and a product that really did meet consumer needs, Arrid became the largest selling deodorant in the United States. These two characteristics of the Arrid product became Carter-Wallace trademarks: the effective use of advertising, combined with a product that was developed instead of copied. To keep ahead of its many imitators and competitors, Arrid was constantly improved. The success of the deodorant soon led to the construction of a new plant in New Brunswick. Carter's sales topped the $1 million mark for the first time in 1935. To reflect its new direction, the company's name was changed to Carter Products, Inc., in 1937. For ten years, the original formula of Arrid was a top-seller. After that, various improvements were used to further boost sales.

Another innovation was a new depilatory product introduced in 1940. Designed primarily as a hair remover for women, Nair became another company success. During World War II Carter Products also produced foot powders for the armed forces. Indeed, through 1945, war work absorbed much of the company's attention.

The Prescription Drug Market in the 1950s

In 1949 another product innovation was unveiled: an aerosol shaving product named Rise that was the first pressurized shaving cream. The product's explosive popularity prompted many imitations, including a Colgate product so similar that Carter sued for infringement of patent rights. This case was won by Carter more than ten years later.

Attention turned to ethical drugs as the newest market. The company began to look at the development of prescription drugs. This led to another Carter-Wallace cornerstone, Miltown, a tranquilizer that was the first of its kind. It relaxed muscles and also relieved mental stress. Following its introduction in 1955, Miltown's sales doubled and tripled each of the subsequent five months. By 1958 Carter was again constructing a new plant to handle production demands.

Celebrating its 75th anniversary in 1955, Carter Products looked back on a remarkable record of growth. Its products were selling in 54 countries. Two years later, the company listed stock on the New York Stock Exchange. The company served as a sponsor of such radio programs as ''Amos 'n Andy'' and ''Fibber McGee and Mollie'' and was a pioneer among television advertisers, thus making Carter products familiar to millions.

When sales and profits took a plunge in the 1960–61 fiscal year, Carter claimed that one contributor was the fact that the company's patented meprobamate tablets—commercially known as Miltown—were being purchased abroad in violation of patent laws. When the United States brought antitrust charges against Carter Products, accusing it of creating a monopoly on meprobamate, the company contested the charge. After a year of hearings, the case was concluded and Carter won the patented right to be sole manufacturer of meprobamate. This victory was significant as it secured one of Carter's steady sources of income. Sales rebounded in the following year.

In 1961 Harry Hoyt, Sr., was named chairman of the board. A new product was released that same year, a muscle relaxant with the generic name carisoprodol and the brand name Soma. Although a success, Soma was no rival for Miltown. It did, however, signal further diversification. Carter soon purchased a majority interest in Frank W. Horner, Ltd., a Canadian drug company with sales of more than $5 million. Horner—a leader in drugs that dealt with diabetes, nausea, and antibiotics—would become one of Carter's most profitable outlets. About the same time, Carter acquired a 50 percent interest in Millmaster Chemical Corporation, a company with more than $10 million in sales.

The Wallace Laboratory division of Carter Products had compiled more than 13 product innovations by the mid-1960s.

In 1965 the company name was changed to Carter-Wallace, Inc., a reflection of this division's importance to the firm. Arrid Extra Dry Anti-Perspirant Spray Deodorant was introduced in 1968. It was the only aerosol spray of its kind, another product revolution, and it quickly shot to the head of its market in sales, serving as a mainstay for the company in ensuing decades.

Having outgrown its executive offices, Carter-Wallace moved in 1968. Lambert Kay Company, a manufacturer of pharmaceutical and nutritional products for pets, was acquired around that time. By 1970 company sales topped $125 million. Although toiletries and proprietary drugs represented the largest percentage of sales, prescription drugs were becoming an increasingly substantial segment. At this juncture, the company was marketing 32 products at home and abroad and Wallace Laboratories was concentrating on three major groups of therapeutic agents: anti-inflammatory compounds, anti-arteriosclerotic compounds, and antihistamines. The company obviously had come a long way from the days when its staple product was Carter's Little Liver Pills. To keep ahead in the competitive pharmaceutical industry, Carter acquired majority interest in two research organizations: Industrial Biological Laboratories and the Laboratory for Analytical Blood Studies.

With the patent on meprobamate set to expire in 1972, Carter-Wallace concentrated on new income sources. As a result of a licensing agreement with Cameo, Inc. of Ohio, Carter-Wallace received the rights to manufacture and sell Pearl Drops. This liquid tooth polish was another one-of-a-kind product at the time. Sales were solid enough to prompt the company to purchase the product outright within three years.

Still, the many economic uncertainties of the 1970s had an impact on Carter-Wallace. A record profit drop came in 1974. Inflation, high energy and labor costs, and wary consumers all contributed to the downturn. During this period Carter-Wallace bought Princeton Laboratories Products Company, a manufacturer of diagnostic kits, for $10 million. This seemed a promising new field at the time. It proved to be even more lucrative than expected. One of Princeton's primary customers was the Wampole Division of Denver Chemical Company. Wampole led the country in sales of pregnancy tests, as well as diagnostic tests for rheumatoid arthritis, streptococcal infections, and mononucleosis. Adding Wampole to the Carter-Wallace roster required that Denver Chemical be acquired. Carter-Wallace made the purchase for $25 million.

While Hoyt, Sr., was chairman of the executive committee, his son, Harry Hoyt, Jr., became chairman of the board and CEO. Hoyt, Jr., had by that time been with the company for 25 years; his brother Charles had worked alongside him for 22 of those years.

A New Business: The Rise of Condom Sales in the 1980s

In 1976 earnings again fell dramatically. The plunge was, in large part, the result of publicity regarding the dangers of aerosol emissions. Carter-Wallace fought back with aggressive advertising and promotional expenditures. Closing in on its 100th birthday, the company began to feel an improvement in its financial health. In 1979 it purchased the Pharmaceutical Products Division of Mallinckrodt, Inc., which specialized in cough and cold medications, antihypertensives, and diuretics.

The 1980s were another era of explosive growth for the company. In 1985 Carter-Wallace acquired Youngs Drug Products Corporation, the privately held maker of Trojan-brand condoms. It was Carter-Wallace's first foray into that industry. With the advent of the contraceptive pill and IUDs in the 1960s, condoms had become a relic of a method of pregnancy prevention. During the 1970s the pill and penicillin were the preferred guardians against pregnancy and venereal disease. When Carter-Wallace began manufacturing Trojans, condom sales had dropped to half of what they had been in the previous ten years. But within less than a year of the acquisition, condoms were being cited as the only known protection against the sexual transmission of AIDS. Condoms quickly became an omnipresent topic in the media. Sales soared and Trojan—a longtime brand on the market—accounted for about 55 percent of the sales.

It was a revolution both in the country and for the company. Condoms had long been associated with illicit sex and prostitution, relegated to vending machines or beneath-the-counter sales in pharmacies. By 1986, however, condoms were widely available, displayed openly in retail stores and even supermarkets. First-time buyers accounted for a great amount of the increase; in fact, women were buying about 50 percent of condoms sold in 1986. With the AIDS epidemic dominating the public's attention, condom sales were assured even without advertising, but Carter-Wallace took an early lead in magazine advertising anyway, committing itself to a multimillion-dollar ad campaign early in the AIDS information explosion. In an industry where brand loyalty is high, the Trojan brand led the way in sales, followed by Ramses and Sheik brands, both made by the same company, Schmid. In 1988 Carter-Wallace bought Mentor's condom business, which, combined with Trojan, gave it about 62 percent of the market. Carter-Wallace claimed that its condom products accounted for about ten percent of its sales and 15 percent of its earnings in 1987.

The bulk of the company's revenue at that time was derived from the sale of deodorants and prescription drugs. Drug sales were growing at four percent a year, increasing from $152 million in 1983 to $209 million in 1987. This division accounted for nearly half of company sales in 1987. Although the lucrative patent protection of Miltown had expired, Carter-Wallace had established an effective strategy of licensing foreign drugs and bringing them into U.S. markets. Dwarfed in size by some of its competitors in this field, Carter-Wallace focused more on solid products with steady sales than on the discovery of cutting-edge drugs.

Antiperspirants were still the company's largest consumer division in 1987. While sales of Rise and Pearl Drops fell in the face of increased competition from rivals, sales of Sea & Ski suntan lotion and Answer pregnancy tests bloomed. Sea & Ski was another example of the company's ability to spot growth industries before they became unaffordable. Pregnancy testing kits also became a boom product in the late 1980s. By 1990 home pregnancy test manufacturing had become a $100 million industry. The year prior, Carter-Wallace had acquired Hygeia Sciences, Inc., a subsidiary of Tambrands Inc. and the producer of First Response, the number one selling brand of home pregnancy tests. Carter-Wallace's own Answer product was at that time the fourth ranked kit in terms of market share; coupled with First Response, Carter-Wallace was able to secure a 31 percent share of the market. In 1989 drugstore sales of tests rose nearly 30 percent, and supermarket sales were on the rise as well. The trend was attributed to the increased interest in self-healthcare, plus the increased reliability of the tests. With First Response, Carter-Wallace shifted the product's pitch for the first time to young women who might not want to be pregnant, especially college students, while also maintaining traditional ads aimed at the 50 percent of test users who, according to market research, wanted to be pregnant. With a new market niche within an expanding market, Carter-Wallace was again just ahead of the trends.

By the end of 1990, the company had shifted its strategy slightly and increased its research and development spending by 20 percent over the previous year; the company further claimed that it would increase spending in this area by another 20 percent in 1991. Carter-Wallace tested drugs for the treatment of such ailments as epilepsy, asthma, and angina. Consumer goods and drugs are fairly recession-proof industries. The company seemed on solid footing. Carter-Wallace purchased Dramamine, a motion sickness product, from Procter & Gamble Company in 1991. Sales of the well-established brand were then about $13 million.

Earnings declined despite a rise in sales in early 1992, because of R&D outlays. Meanwhile, Trojan condoms increased its stranglehold on the condom industry; it gained 60 percent of market share, with sales still on the increase. In July 1991 the FDA seized 1.2 million Trojan brand natural-membrane condoms, contending that the lambskin condoms were not effective protection against sexually transmitted diseases and that the condom labels did not note this. Carter-Wallace argued, however, that it was in the process of complying with relabeling the condoms in the wake of the discovery that only latex condoms had pores small enough to prevent transmission of diseases.

In November 1991 Fox Broadcasting Company broadcast an advertisement for the Trojan brand, thus becoming the first national broadcast television network to run a condom commercial. Condom spots had run on some local and cable stations, but this national ad was a ground-breaker. It came on the heels of basketball great Magic Johnson's announcement that he would retire after testing positive for HIV, the virus associated with AIDS. Just when ad and sales plateaus had seemed to be reached in this area, the news of Johnson's test results triggered another jump in condom sales. Between 1985 and 1991, condom sales worldwide more than doubled.

Buyout Scares in the Late 1990s

In late 1991 there was much speculation about Carter-Wallace's soon-to-be released drug felbamate, a drug that controlled epileptic seizures. Sales were projected to be $100 to $200 million annually. In 1992 Schering-Plough Corporation signed an agreement with Carter-Wallace for marketing rights for felbamate outside of North America. The drug, known by the brand name Felbatol, received FDA approval in the summer of 1993 and was introduced into the marketplace in August of that year. An aggressive marketing campaign followed, with claims that the new drug eliminated the need for epileptics to monitor their blood on a regular basis. Initial reviews of the drug's efficacy were extremely positive, and by mid-1994 more than 100,000 patients had converted to Felbatol.

During this same period, however, Carter-Wallace began to receive reports of serious problems relating to the use of the drug. Data revealed that a number of Felbatol patients were contracting aplastic anemia, a rare blood disease, and that there were several cases of serious liver damage arising from use of the drug. The first Felbatol-related death occurred in January 1994; by August a total of ten deaths had been reported, and the company, along with the FDA, was compelled to issue a warning letter to more than 240,000 physicians nationwide, recommending that they cease administering the drug to the majority of their patients. Although the overall effectiveness of the drug, particularly with patients who had failed to respond to other treatments, remained undisputed, the news of the side effects significantly curtailed the product's market growth, and by the end of 1995 only 10,000 patients were still using it. In December 1995, a class action lawsuit was filed against Carter-Wallace, on behalf of everyone who had ever taken Felbatol. This litigation followed two other lawsuits filed by shareholders of the company in 1994, charging that Carter-Wallace had deliberately made false claims about both Felbatol's medical value and its sales potential.

In March 1995 the company reported a net loss of $56.3 million for the previous fiscal year, and its stock dropped to $14 a share, a more than 50 percent drop from a high of $31 posted in 1993. The setbacks could be traced to the large scale of the company's investment in Felbatol, coupled with inadequate marketing for its other products during the period of the new drug's development. By the following year a massive restructuring of the company became inevitable. Carter-Wallace reduced its workforce by more than a thousand employees in early 1996, in addition to announcing plans to shut down its condom manufacturing operations in Trenton, New Jersey, which would cut an additional 625 jobs. With its drastically reduced stock prices, the company became a target for a takeover; in October 1996, businessman Marvin Davis made a bid of $835 million for the company.

Chairman Henry Hoyt, Jr., however, was bitterly opposed to selling Carter-Wallace, and he used his leverage as a majority stakeholder to block the deal. The company then turned its attention to gaining substantial market share for a number of its new products. In 1996 Wallace Laboratories introduced ASTELIN, a prescription nasal spray that treated seasonal allergic rhinitis. The antihistamine received FDA approval in November 1996 and hit the market the following March. In June 1999 Wampole laboratories launched a new diagnostic that aimed to become the first rapid response testing method for Lyme's disease. The company was buoyed further by an appeals court ruling in July 1998 that determined that no investor fraud had taken place in connection with the marketing of Felbatol.

The company's most successful product development, however, arrived with the introduction of the Trojan Supra condom in September 1999. The first polyurethane condom, the Trojan

Supra brand contributed to record condom sales in the fiscal year ending March 31, 2000, when Carter-Wallace was able to claim a 68 percent market share of the domestic condom business. Overall, the company saw its earnings rise 55 percent in 1999, with net income surpassing $43.3 million. It was in the midst of this resurgence that, in December 2000, Henry Hoyt, Jr., stepped down from his position as chairman of Carter-Wallace, after more than 50 years with the company.

Principal Subsidiaries

Laboratoires Fumouze S.A. (France); Carter-Horner Inc. (Canada); Carter-Wallace Limited (U.K.); Carter-Wallace (Australia) Pty. Limited; S.p.A. Italiana Laboratori Bouty (Italy); Carter-Wallace, S.A. (Mexico); Icart S.A. (Spain).

Principal Divisions

Carter Products; Carter-Wallace International; Lambert Kay; Wallace Laboratories; Wampole Laboratories; Carter-Wallace Manufacturing.

Principal Competitors

Colgate-Palmolive Company; SSL International plc (U.K.); Unilever (U.K.).

Further Reading

Appelbaum, Cara, ''Carter-Wallace Buys a New Strategy for Pregnancy Tests,'' *Adweek's Marketing Week,* May 28, 1990, p. 10.

''Barriers to Entry,'' *Economist,* November 30, 1991, p. 71.

''Carter-Wallace Ends Bid to Buy P&G's Dramamine,'' *Wall Street Journal,* May 28, 1987, p. B3.

''Carter-Wallace Inc.,'' *New York Times,* May 18, 1991, p. 37.

''Carter-Wallace Intends to Buy Line from P&G,'' *Wall Street Journal,* May 20, 1991, p. A12B.

''Carter-Wallace Net Fell in Fourth Period; Stock Drops Sharply,'' *Wall Street Journal,* May 7, 1991, p. C21.

Cutler, Blayne, ''Condom Mania,'' *American Demographics,* June 1989, p. 17.

Elliott, Stuart, ''The Sponsor Is the Surprise in Fox's First Condom Ad,'' *New York Times,* November 19, 1991, p. D19.

''FDA Panel Supports Approval of 2 Drugs for Treating Epilepsy,'' *Wall Street Journal,* December 16, 1992, p. B8.

Ferraro, Cathleen, ''Condom Maker's Television Ads Will Stress Romance,'' *Sacramento Bee,* August 21, 1998.

Hamilton, Patricia, ''Corporate Dynasties,'' *D&B Reports,* March-April 1992, p. 16.

Hawng, Suein, ''Carter-Wallace Discontinues Sales of Diabetes Device,'' *Wall Street Journal,* October 7, 1991, p. A7D.

Horowitz, Bruce, ''Trojan Gets a Condom Ad on Network TV,'' *Los Angeles Times,* November 19, 1991, p. D1.

Katz, Donald, ''The Investor: Counting on a Cure,'' *Esquire,* November 1987, p. 71.

Lazo, Shirley, ''Speaking of Dividends,'' *Barron's,* July 27, 1987, p. 45.

Leinster, Colin, ''The Rubber Barons,'' *Fortune,* November 24, 1986, pp. 105–18.

Marcial, Gene [G.], ''Be Cautious with Carter-Wallace,'' *Business Week,* February 23, 1987, p. 116.

——, ''Nice Dovetail for Carter-Wallace?,'' *Business Week,* May 26, 1997.

McFadden, Michael, ''AIDS Stock Worth the Gamble,'' *Fortune,* April 13, 1987, pp. 113–14.

Palmer, Jay, ''Who Needs Hype?,'' *Barron's,* February 29, 1988, pp. 13, 60.

''Protection Money,'' *Forbes,* February 23, 1987, p. 8.

Shaw, Donna, ''FDA, Drug Company Urge Physicians to Withdraw Patients from Epilepsy Medicine,'' *Philadelphia Inquirer,* August 1, 1994.

Squires, Sally, ''Warning on Epilepsy Drug Poses Dilemma: Risk of Fatal Blood Disease Must Be Balanced Against Felbamate's Effectiveness Against Seizures,'' *Washington Post,* August 16, 1994.

Sullivan, Joseph, ''Condoms Seized by U.S. Agents in a Label Case,'' *New York Times,* July 27, 1991, p. 26.

Teitelbaum, Richard, ''Prescription: More R&D,'' *Fortune,* December 17, 1990, p. 128.

''Too Far, Too Soon?,'' *Forbes,* September 16, 1992, p. 209.

Valeriano, Lourdes Lee, ''Carter-Wallace Inc. Agrees to Relabel Lambskin Condoms,'' *Wall Street Journal,* October 14, 1991, p. B6.

—Carol Keeley
—updated by Stephen Meyer

CHARMING SHOPPES, INC.

Charming Shoppes, Inc.

450 Winks Lane
Bensalem, Pennsylvania 19020
U.S.A.
Telephone: (215) 245-9100
Fax: (215) 633-4640

Public Company
Incorporated: 1969 as Fashion Bug, Inc.
Employees: 18,000
Sales: $1.2 billion (2000)
Stock Exchanges: NASDAQ
Ticker Symbol: CHRS
NAIC: 44812 Women's Clothing Stores

Charming Shoppes, Inc. is a leading retailer, specializing in women's apparel. Founded in 1940 with a single store in Philadelphia, Charming now operates over 1,200 stores in more than 40 states. The stores are large by apparel industry standards (averaging 8,000 square feet) and are usually located in strip malls rather than major shopping centers. The stores target middle income shoppers and specialize in junior, misses', and large-size women's apparel, including sportswear, outerwear, intimate apparel, and accessories. A public company since 1971, Charming Shoppes is a member of the *Fortune* 500.

The 1940s and 1950s: A New Kind of Women's Clothing Store

On September 13, 1940, Morris and Arthur Sidewater opened the first Charm Shoppes store, in Philadelphia. In the 1930s, Morris (Moe) had been a buyer for Associated Merchandising in New York and Arthur (Artie) performed as a dancer on tour with Red Skelton. Apparently, Moe and Artie had long talked about opening up a women's clothing store and, with borrowed money, opened up Charm Shoppes. The two ambitious businessmen had rough going in the beginning, bringing in only $480 in sales in the first week of business. In addition, they received legal notice that very same week that they had to change their store's name because the name "Charm" was already registered. Rather than give up the business completely, the Sidewaters agreed to add "ing" to their name.

Shortly thereafter, the new store became a thriving business. By the end of the decade the Sidewater brothers were discussing expansion. In order to open up and manage the new stores, Moe and Artie took on additional partners, with each partner managing his/her own store. In these early days, the two Sidewater brothers did their own advertising, a task at which they proved quite effective; with his previous experience as a buyer, Moe Sidewater displayed a keen understanding of fashion trends.

In 1950 the Sidewaters began a lifelong business relationship with Artie's good friend, David Wachs, and David's brother, Ellis. The four formed the Sidewater/Wachs alliance and opened stores in Norristown, Pennsylvania, and Woodbury, New Jersey. Both stores were promoted with grand openings that featured local celebrities. The Woodbury store was the largest retail establishment in the town at that time.

Expanding into the Suburbs: The 1960s and 1970s

By 1960 the four partners were ready to open the first Charming Shoppes store in a large suburban shopping center. Sensing that suburban shopping would be the wave of the future, Sidewater/Wachs felt the new stores should operate under a new name. The first Fashion Bug was introduced into the Black Horse Pike Shopping Center in Audubon, New Jersey, that year. This sparked a period of tremendous growth for the company as it added Fashion Bug stores to an additional eight shopping centers throughout Pennsylvania, New Jersey, and New York.

In 1971 the four primary partners decided to take Charming Shoppes public. By this time the company had 21 stores, 18 partners, and accelerated growth rates in sales, with further potential yet untapped. Moe had taken over the primary tasks of management and systems control and, in looking toward cost cutting, had begun to computerize the operations; all credit charges and payments were consolidated onto a computer system installed in the company headquarters. The company centralized its bookkeeping and credit operations, in addition to centralizing the Fashion Bug charge accounts, thus making it possible to

Company Perspectives:

Guided by our customers and our own expertise as a fashion specialist for women, we will continue to provide a shopping experience that generates sales and profitability.

charge merchandise in any store. The company became a pioneer in the use of computerized cash register (point-of-sale) terminals that offered direct control over inventory.

After the computerization of much of the company's operations the company experienced its highest growth rates in its history. By the late 1970s, Charming Shoppes had 60 stores. To accommodate this accelerated growth, the company opened an additional buying office in Bensalem, Pennsylvania, that housed offices and a distribution center. The distribution center, innovative for its time, gave Charming greater control over its inventory and was soon imitated by Charming's competitors.

The centralization of operations also included a reorganization of the buying operations. Up until this time, each store manager acted as the buyer for that store. But due to the more complicated and diverse clothing markets, buyers now had to become specialists, individuals trained to select a particular type of clothing. To accommodate this trend, Charming centralized buyers into one buying division, with each buyer reporting to a specific clothing department and helping the distribution center ship out new merchandise to the stores. The larger stores also led the company to expand its display and interior design staff.

The company continued to grow during this period of reorganization. By the end of the 1970s the number of stores increased from 60 to 100 and the company again moved its headquarters to a larger location, its present Bensalem offices, a 400,000-square-foot facility. Growth continued unabated into the 1980s, as the number of stores increased sixfold in comparison with the previous decade. The company streamlined its distribution process in order to improve the flow of merchandise.

Changing Fashions in the 1980s

The increasing complexity associated with managing the Charming Shoppes network of stores led to a management overhaul. For its first 30 years of existence, the entire 900-store network was essentially managed by the partnership of the four brothers from two families, the Wachs and the Sidewaters. By 1987, however, the company leadership saw the need to reevaluate its management and decision-making strategy for the future. This involved a reorganization of the managerial hierarchy.

In an attempt to remedy the perceived stagnation of management, David Wachs took over in 1987 as chairman and CEO and implemented a restructuring geared toward attracting professional expertise and recapturing the company's core market constituency: middle income women, aged 25 to 45, seeking a range of apparel, from dresswear to sportswear.

Wachs, according to the *Wall Street Journal,* ''took over at the opportune time for change. Like other women's apparel retailers, Charming Shoppes ... saw demand plunge for its once-popular sportswear, leaving it laden with costly inventories. Accompanying this consumer turnoff to tired fashions and miniskirts were other pesky problems: price rises from overseas suppliers hurt by the falling U.S. dollar, and uncertainty of supplies from abroad.'' The *Journal* went on to laud the company's efforts at reorganization, asserting that the Charming Shoppes ''merchandising prowess faltered as too many chefs played with its marketing recipe.''

The management ''revolution'' was also viewed as necessary since management expertise was crucial to future growth. This shakeup, referred to by the *Wall Street Journal* as a ''blood transfusion,'' broke up the family control that had previously determined long-term marketing strategy.

Charming Shoppes remained in a solid competitive position, in spite of its difficulties. The company's fiscal 1993 sales were up by more than 15 percent. According to a report in *Women's Wear Daily,* the company ended fiscal 1993 with net income of $81.1 million on sales of more than $1.1 billion, a marked improvement from just ten years before, when net income was just $12.1 million on sales of $174.3 million.

According to some industry analysts, Charming's success was largely a function of its strip mall locations, its direct control over its distribution and sourcing, and its private label credit card program. These factors remained crucial: Developers were projected to build more strip malls; the company sourced 75 percent of its own goods, eliminating the need for middlemen; and its credit card program promoted customer loyalty and multiple purchases.

Most importantly, in the words of Charming Shoppes CEO and Chairman David Wachs, in the women's retail market, ''we are the low-cost operator.'' In the end, for a given quality level, the lowest cost producer continued to have the competitive advantage. The low cost strategy depended heavily on the strip mall sites; rents were historically about 40 percent lower at strip malls than large shopping centers, and the strip mall sites offered greater growth potential, according to some analysts. Further, the company's reliance on strips, which often included exclusive rental contracts, excluded much of the competition in the women's apparel industry.

Another way in which Charming Shoppes was able to maintain its competitive cost structure was via its vertical integration. The company, which already sourced a high percentage of its own goods in the early 1990s, planned on increasing this figure to 75 to 80 percent over the next few years. In pursuit of this increased efficiency, which further contributed to the low cost strategy, Charming capitalized its operations, investing in the latest electronics technology for clothing pattern design, computerized inventory control, and design.

Investors' analysis of the expected future earnings were optimistic in the early 1990s, and Charming planned to expand to 2,000 stores, according to Wachs. This expansion would include new merchandising efforts into the sportswear and ready-to-wear departments, with special emphasis on men's wear.

Key Dates:

1940: Morris and Arthur Sidewater open first Charm Shoppes in Philadelphia.
1950: Sidewater brothers enter business partnership with David and Ellis Wachs; Charming Shoppes stores open in Norristown, Pennsylvania, and Woodbury, New Jersey.
1960: Fashion Bug opens in Audubon, New Jersey.
1971: Charming Shoppes goes public.
1987: David Wachs becomes company chairman and CEO.
1995: Dorrit J. Bern becomes president and CEO.
1999: Charming Shoppes acquires Catherine Stores Corp.

Recovering from the Retail Disaster of the Mid-1990s

Unfortunately, Wachs's ambitions never bore fruit. The year 1993 marked the beginning of a serious decline in sales for the retail industry, and Charming Shoppes was not immune to the economic slump. A general decrease in spending on women's clothing, combined with tighter competition, resulted in a drop in the company's sales of over 18 percent for the first seven months of 1995. Reports in October of operating losses of 20–30 cents a share caused Charming Shoppes stock to plummet, and by year's end the company had suffered a total loss of $139 million.

The company took steps to turn things around in August, when it hired Dorrit J. Bern as its new president and CEO. Bern had already made a name for herself in the industry as a vice-president at Sears, where she had played an integral role in revamping the women's clothing line. One of her first major actions as head of Charming Shoppes came in December, when she closed 290 of the company's most unprofitable stores. After the dust settled, in February 1996 Bern initiated a major restructuring project. Up to that time, the company had relied on overseas sourcing for 70 percent of its total purchases. Bern proposed that this proportion be reduced to 50 percent, and redirected the company's ''timely fashion'' purchases—clothes that reflected the most current styles—to the domestic market, allowing its merchants more time to anticipate trends, and subsequently reducing the volume of ''unfashionable'' items left over in inventory. Meanwhile, the foreign sourcing operations began focusing exclusively on basic purchases.

The initial blow to the company was hard. The restructuring resulted in the layoff of more than 2,500 employees and the closing of several factories overseas. Store closures continued throughout the following year, with over 270 retail locations going out of business in 1996. However, while total sales continued to decline over the course of the year, sales-per-store actually rose five percent in 1996. Also, while total sales showed no appreciable improvement in 1997, the company did enjoy a net gain of almost $20 million, its first profit in three years.

Bern immediately directed these earnings toward the creation of new business opportunities for the company. In January 1998 Charming Shoppes purchased 28 stores in Texas and Louisiana from Petric Retail, Inc. In 1999 the company completed two key acquisitions that would help ensure its role as a major player in the women's large size apparel niche. The first came in July, when it purchased the Modern Woman chain, comprised of 137 stores in 25 states, for $10 million. In November Charming Shoppes acquired Catherine Store Corp. for $150 million, bringing in an additional 436 stores. By January 2000 Charming Shoppes owned 1,740 retail stores nationwide. The company continued to maintain an aggressive growth strategy for the future, with plans to open 106 new stores in 2000, followed by an additional 140 stores in 2001 and 160 in 2002; the ultimate goal was to open 1,000 new stores within five years. The company reported record earnings for the second quarter of 2000, and sales for the year were projected to exceed $1.6 billion, an increase of 33 percent over the previous year. Considering the company's dramatic turnaround since 1995, it appeared that with Dorrit Bern, Charming Shoppes was in very good hands heading into the 21st century.

Principal Operating Units

Fashion Bug; Catherine's Plus Sizes; Added Dimensions.

Principal Competitors

The Limited, Inc.; Target Corporation; Wal-Mart Stores, Inc.

Further Reading

Dobrzynski, Judith H., ''Small Companies, Big Problems,'' *New York Times*, February 6, 1996.
''The History of Charming Shoppes,'' *In Touch,* Charming Shoppes, August, 1986.
Hymowitz, Carol, ''At Charming Shoppes, A Blood Transfusion,'' *Wall Street Journal,* October 10, 1988.
Klein, Alec Matthew, ''Area Losing Two Fashion Bug Stores; Apparel Industry Still in Doldrums,'' *Baltimore Sun*, September 26, 1995.
Macintosh, Jeane, ''Charming Shoppes' Fashion Bug Flies High,'' *Women's Wear Daily,* November 25, 1992.
Marcial, Gene G., ''All Gussied Up at Charming Shoppes,'' *Business Week*, May 19, 1997.
Neuborne, Ellen, ''Charming Shoppes Falls on Earnings News,'' *USA Today*, October 3, 1995.
Von Bergen, Jane M., ''Bensalem, Pa.-Based Women's Clothing Retailer to Acquire Tennessee Chain,'' *Philadelphia Inquirer*, November 16, 1999.
Woolley, Suzanne, ''In the Bargain Basement of Retail Stocks,'' *Business Week*, November 27, 1995.

—John A. Sarich
—updated by Stephen Meyer

Chautauqua Airlines, Inc.

2500 S. High School Road, Suite 160
Indianapolis, Indiana 46241-4943
U.S.A.
Telephone: (317) 484-6000
Fax: (317) 484-6040
Web site: http://www.flychautauqua.com

Wholly Owned Subsidiary of Wexford Management, LLC
Incorporated: 1973
Employees: 800
Sales: $84 million (1998 est.)
NAIC: 481111 Scheduled Passenger Air Transportation

Chautauqua Airlines, Inc. is one of a dozen obscure airlines flying as US Airways Express. It tries to differentiate itself from the others by improved passenger amenities such as increased legroom. In November 1999, Chautauqua sealed an agreement to fly regional jets for Trans World Airlines, only the second client in its history. It carries about 750,000 passengers a year on 240 daily flights around 26 points in the Northeast and Midwest. Chautauqua is about a tenth the size of American Trans Air, a publicly traded airline also based in Indianapolis.

Upstate Origins

Joel and Gloria Hall started Chautauqua Airlines in Jamestown, New York, in 1973. Joel had previously been a chief pilot for Mohawk Airlines, which had merged with Allegheny Airlines in 1972.

Chautauqua's sole raison d'être was to take over routes from Allegheny (later called USAir and US Airways). This relationship pioneered code-share arrangements between major airlines and contract carriers.

In 1974, Chautauqua began flying two new, leased Beech 99s under the Allegheny Commuter name. The first destinations were Pittsburgh and Buffalo. Canton/Akron, Ohio was connected to Pittsburgh in 1979, when the company began operating a couple of Shorts 3-30 aircraft. Allegheny changed its name to USAir in 1979, and Chautauqua added flights between Orlando and three other cities (Ocala, Lakeland, and Vero Beach) following its expansion into Florida.

Routes between Pittsburgh and Lynchburg, Roanoke, and Charlottesville, Virginia, were added in 1984, along with the Fairchild Metro III to operate them. Chautauqua replaced its Shorts Brothers aircraft with the Saab 340 in 1986. The 30-passenger Saab aircraft cost several million dollars each.

In 1988, an affiliate of Guarantee Security Life Insurance Company of Jacksonville, Florida, bought Chautauqua Airlines from Joel Hall. Guarantee Security was oriented towards junk bonds but also bought several operating businesses, including a Cleveland amusement park and a Toronto women's clothing chain. Chautauqua Airlines employed about 250 people in the early 1990s. Revenues for 1991 exceeded $30 million.

Florida's Department of Insurance took over Guarantee Security Life in 1991 after it was declared insolvent, or actuarially unsound. The state then spent the first seven months of 1992 trying to find a suitable buyer for Chautauqua Airlines. Bidders included former USAir Express Allegheny Commuter President Fred Arnold and then current Chautauqua Airlines President Tom Hall (no relation to founders Joel and Gloria Hall).

Tom Hall resigned when the Department of Insurance stopped accepting bids in August 1992. According to *Commuter Regional Airline News,* he had offered $7 million for Chautauqua. A $10 million bid by Fred Arnold was also rejected, even though one analyst valued the company at just $5 million. British Airways' plans to invest $750 million in USAir supported the state's higher valuation.

A consultant for the State of Florida, I. Edward London, took over as CEO and president after Hall's resignation. London was a licensed private pilot but had never worked in the airline industry. He was an experienced entrepreneur and consultant, however.

In 1993, the insurance industry established the Guaranty Reassurance Corp. (GRC) to sell the assets of the Guarantee Security Life Insurance Company, including Chautauqua Air-

Company Perspectives:

At Chautauqua Airlines, serving our customers with the highest possible degree of safety, comfort, and convenience are our #1 goals. Our 26-year history of continued commitment to these goals along with a flawless safety record has ensured our success and enabled us to become one of the 20 largest scheduled regional airlines in the United States. We currently operate service to 34 cities in the United States, and 3 cities in Canada.

lines. GRC was given the next five years to increase the value of the airline, after which Chautauqua would either be sold or taken public.

Company founder Joel Hall died in December 1993 at the age of 59. By this time, Chautauqua had become the 24th largest scheduled commuter airline in the United States. Revenues were more than $40 million in 1993, when the company employed 265 people. Its 16 planes (nine of them leased) were constantly busy, flying between 18 cities in seven states and the Canadian province of Ontario. Although most of the flights fed USAir's largest hub in Pittsburgh, Chautauqua Airlines kept its headquarters in Jamestown, New York. Maintenance facilities had been established in Akron/Canton, Ohio, and Lynchburg, Virginia.

Switching Seats in 1994

The early 1990s were notoriously difficult for Chautauqua's sole client, USAir, which lost $2.6 billion from 1991 to 1994. They were also hard for Chautauqua, which saw revenue fall considerably when USAir began flying jets on routes serving Pittsburgh. Another negative factor was the 1994 crash of an American Eagle commuter plane flying from Chicago to Indianapolis. Imprecise media coverage spread the stigma of the crash to Chautauqua by association, and passengers stayed away in droves. The airline posted its first loss in 20 years in 1994, but returned to profitability the next year.

In the midst of these hard times came a dramatic change that would give Chautauqua a launching pad for another few years of vigorous growth. On May 8, 1994, Chautauqua Airlines exchanged routes with Jetstream International, literally overnight. Jetstream was owned by USAir and had been providing Indianapolis with commuter service.

After the swap, Chautauqua moved about three dozen maintenance personnel to Ohio and relocated two dozen flight crews to the Midwest. It added 15 flights a day to the 44 Jetstream had been operating from Indianapolis, where USAir was the leading carrier. Chautauqua also eventually moved its headquarters to Indianapolis. (Liberty Express, a subsidiary of Mesa Airlines which flew non-pressurized Beech 1900 aircraft, picked up Chautauqua's old routes out of Chautauqua County Airport.)

In 1995, Chautauqua arranged to buy all of Jetstream's British Aerospace Jetstream 31 aircraft. It also picked up several routes in Pennsylvania, Maryland, and Ontario. Jetstream International subsequently changed its name to PSA Airlines. In the fall of 1995, Chautauqua took over PSA's flights out of Pittsburgh which used 19-passenger planes. This allowed PSA to reduce its diverse fleet to just one type, and gave USAir increased scheduling flexibility in mixing its jets with its subsidiary's turboprops.

USAir also stopped using Indianapolis as a mini-hub in 1995. In several cases, Chautauqua benefited by replacing canceled jet service with its own turboprop flights.

Chautauqua had 470 employees in 1996. It had doubled in size in the two years since moving from Pittsburgh to Indianapolis.

Chautauqua's customers could receive USAir frequent flyer miles and other amenities. Although its affiliation with a major airline gave it certain selling points like these, Chautauqua began to try to differentiate itself among USAir Express carriers. It served ''bagel buttons,'' cheese, and champagne and outfitted some planes with leather seats. Chautauqua configured its Saab 340s for 30 passengers, not 34, giving each more legroom.

Half of Chautauqua's passengers connected with other USAir flights. This ratio increased to 90 percent on shorter flights such as Evansville-Indianapolis. Longer routes like Indianapolis-Nashville generated mostly point-to-point traffic, where Chautauqua's own efforts in keeping passengers were vital.

Officials from Chautauqua County, New York, met with Chautauqua Airlines President Tim Coon in October 1996, trying to entice the carrier to return to its former home. Liberty Express had scaled back service to the area when it took over Chautauqua's routes in May 1994.

USAir became known as US Airways in February 1997. Chautauqua, flying as US Airways Express, began flying between Columbus and Toronto nonstop in June 1997. It had been connecting them via Port Columbus for two years; now that city was at the end of the last leg. Air Ontario, a subsidiary of Air Canada, competed on the route. Revenues were about $80 million in 1997.

Sold in 1998

Wexford Management, LLC, a diversified Greenwich, Connecticut-based investment company, bought Chautauqua Airlines on May 15, 1998. It installed Edward Wegel as president and CEO. Wegel was a cofounder of Atlantic Coast Airlines, a publicly traded commuter operator for United Air Lines. By July the company had launched an advertising campaign aimed at the many local business people who were driving instead of flying to Chautauqua's destinations.

Wexford soon ordered 60 new 37- and 50-seat Embraer regional jets, which were enough in demand that it could probably easily lease whatever planes it could not use itself or in its newly acquired airline (Wexford also owned part of Las Vegas-based National Airlines and a leasing service in Switzerland). Chautauqua was operating 30 turboprops at the time of the order.

US Airways Express was slow to utilize regional jets, while competitors Continental Express and Delta Connection Comair were already stocking their entire fleets with jets. Out of ten US

Key Dates:

1973: Chautauqua Airlines founded to take over regional routes for Allegheny Airlines.
1986: Fleet is upgraded with purchase os Saab 340 aircraft.
1988: Guarantee Security Life buys Chautauqua.
1991: Florida's Department of Insurance takes over Chautauqua after placing its parent in receivership.
1993: An insurance industry group begins managing Chautauqua.
1994: Chautauqua exchanges routes with Jetstream International.
1999: Chautauqua lands its second client ever, TWA.

Airways affiliates, only Mesa Air Group was flying regional jets in 1998. The contract US Airways had with its pilots' union restricted the total number of regional jets that could be flown by its regional affiliates. They were permitted just one dozen in 1998, rising to 25 two years later. One analyst concluded the late switchover could only be effective as a move to defend market share, not add it as the other airlines had done.

The addition of jets to their fleets was what helped regional airlines outpace the majors in terms of earnings growth, making them attractive to investors. An initial public offering was tentatively scheduled for October 1998, but a stock market slump in the fall of 1998 resulted in Chautauqua deferring it. Revenues reached $84 million for the year, when Chautauqua Airlines had 500 employees.

Bryan Bedford, the 37-year-old CEO of Mesaba Holdings, Inc., was picked to head Chautauqua in June 1999. He had restructured Mesaba's contract with Northwest Airlines. Before that, he had led Business Express Airlines. One observer described him as the perfect choice for an airline planning to go public.

Chautauqua received permission to operate ten Embraer ERJ-145 regional jets for US Airways Express in June 1999. The recall of furloughed US Airways pilots earlier in the year cleared the way for the deal with the US Airways pilots' union.

Chautauqua Airlines, which had always been identified with US Airways, was looking for other areas in which to develop its business. Officials considered marketing flights out of Indianapolis under its own name, or partnering with another major airline in addition to US Airways.

TWA agreed to become Chautauqua's second client airline in November 1999. TWA was growing quickly after repairing a faltering reputation. It was, however, the last major airline to introduce regional jets on its feeder routes due to restrictive agreements with its unions. The machinists' union had signed a new contract in July 1999.

TWA already had agreements with two other contract carriers, but this was the first arrangement to use regional jets, rather than turboprops, to feed TWA regional traffic. The contract was good for ten years.

In September 1999, Chautauqua announced plans to relocate 60 flight and maintenance personnel to Fort Wayne, Indiana concurrent with the relocation of its maintenance center.

Principal Competitors

Air Ontario; American Trans Air.

Further Reading

Anderson, Manley J., ''Chautauqua Airlines' Business Soars,'' *Post-Journal* (Jamestown, New York), January 16, 1994.
Andrews, Greg, and Chris O'Malley, ''Pair of Local Firms Delay IPOs: Volatility in Market Shelves Stocks Offerings by Chautauqua Airlines and Monument Realty,'' *Indianapolis Star,* Bus. Sec., October 3, 1998.
Ball, Brian R., ''US Airways Affiliate Offers Columbus-Toronto Nonstops,'' *Business First,* June 30, 1997.
''Chautauqua Airlines to Move 70 Employees from Jamestown,'' *Buffalo News,* Bus. Sec., February 12, 1994, p. B11.
''Chautauqua Future Could Be Brightened by BA,'' *Aviation Daily,* October 30, 1992.
''Chautauqua Tackles Cost and Pilot Problems,'' *Flight International,* August 4, 1999.
''Chautauqua Taken Off the Market; Tom Hall Resigns,'' *Commuter/Regional Airline News,* August 31, 1992.
''Chautauqua to Operate ERJ-145s,'' *Air Transport World,* June 1999, pp. 135–36.
Culbertson, Katie, ''Chautauqua Chases Lofty Goals,'' *Indianapolis Business Journal,* August 24, 1998, p. 1.
Dinnen, S.P., ''Indy Carrier Builds a Quiet Following,'' *Indianapolis Star,* March 27, 1996, p. E1.
Horgan, Sean, ''Chautauqua Embraces Embraer Jets,'' *Indianapolis Star,* May 5, 1999.
''Joel Hall, Founder of Chautauqua Airlines, Dies,'' *Aviation Daily,* December 17, 1993.
LeDuc, Doug, and Lynne McKenna Frazier, ''Commuter Airline to Move Crews, Repair Operations to Fort Wayne, Ind.,'' *News-Sentinel,* September 30, 1999.
Lewis, Arnold, ''Chautauqua Prepped for Sale,'' *Regional Airline Observer,* May 1, 1996.
——, ''Displaced, Profitable, and Available,'' *Business & Commercial Aviation,* July 1, 1996.
McCarthy, Sheila, ''County Hoping to Bring Chautauqua Airlines Back to Area,'' *Buffalo News,* October 29, 1996.
Moorman, Robert W., ''Playing Catch-Up,'' *Air Transport World,* September 1998, pp. 131–35.
O'Malley, Chris, ''Airline Considers Moving Here,'' *Indianapolis News,* March 9, 1994, p. B6.
——, ''Local Airline Weighs Public Stock Offering,'' *Indianapolis Star,* June 12, 1998.
Schoettle, Anthony, ''Chautauqua Growth Takes Wing,'' *Indianapolis Business Journal,* November 15, 1999, p. 3.
Wilson, Benet J., ''Chautauqua Takes on ERJ-145s from Parent's Fleet,'' *Commuter/Regional Airline News,* May 10, 1999.

—Frederick C. Ingram

Chupa Chups S.A.

Avda. Diagonal, 662
08034 Barcelona
Spain
Telephone: (+34) 93 495 27 27
Fax: (+34) 93 495 27 07
Web site: http://www.chupachups.com

Private Company
Incorporated: 1946 as Granja Asturias S.A.
Employees: 2,000
Sales: Pta 73 billion (US$445 million) (1998 est.)
NAIC: 311340 Nonchocolate Confectionery Manufacturing

Spain's Chupa Chups S.A. (pronounced ''shoopa shoop,'' it comes from the Spanish verb ''chupar,'' to lick) is the world's leading manufacturer and distributor of lollipops. The company's famed logo—designed by Salvador Dali—adorns the company extensive line of lollipops, featuring more than 50 different flavors and flavor combinations and sold in a variety of packaging, from traditional lollipops, to motorized lollipops and tubes, cans and other specially designed packaging, such as the Mobile Pop shaped like a cellular phone and featuring a functional calculator, or the Chupa + Surprise, introduced in 2000, which bundles snap-together toys with the company's lollipops. In the 1990s, Chupa Chups, which takes credit for providing the well-known prop for famous 1970s television detective Kojak, branched out from its long-held lollipop specialty to introduce products directed at new markets. The company's Crazy Planet subsidiary creates a line of value-added candy, lollipop, and toy products, geared particularly to the children's and adolescent markets, including Crazy Zoo, which features a toy inside a chocolate egg, and the Gum Watch, a wristwatch chewing gum dispenser. Chupa Chups has also launched its first line of products targeting the adult market, the Smint range of flavored breath mints. Chupa Chups sells its products in more than 160 countries, with production facilities in Spain, France, Russia, Mexico, and China. Some 93 percent of its sales, which reached Pta 73 billion (US$445 million) in 1999, are generated outside of Spain. A privately held company, Chupa Chups is led by founder, President, and CEO Xavier Bernat.

Sticking to Success

The predecessor company to Chupa Chups S.A. was founded in 1946 as Granja Asturias S.A. Originally specializing in apple-based sweets, the small Asturias-based company nearly folded in the early 1950s. That was when Enrique Bernat—the grandson of a Barcelona candymaker—joined the company and set to work transforming the artisan operation into a production giant capable of manufacturing and distributing its products across the world. By the late 1950s, Bernat had succeeding in turning the company around—and received 50 percent of the company for his efforts in 1958. Bernat decided to buy out the rest of the company, and then transform it entirely.

During the decade, Bernat had begun investigating a new product idea. Recognizing the majority of Spain's candies were being consumed by children, Bernat sought to create a product specifically for this market. Most candies at the time were traditional sugar-based drops—which tended to produce a sticky mess in children's hands. Bernat's idea was simple: he began inserting sticks into the candies—originally a piece of metal—to function as a handle, or, as Bernat himself said, ''like eating a sweet on a fork.'' Bernat eventually named his candy the Chups, after the Spanish verb ''chupar,'' or ''to lick.''

The candy quickly became all the rage among Asturias's children, and its success encouraged Bernat to take a drastic step. After gaining full control of the company, Bernat decided to eliminate the company's range of some 200 different candies to concentrate solely on its lollipop. The first Chups were launched in 1958, available in seven flavors, and selling for one peseta apiece—considered expensive for the time.

Expensive or not, the Chups took off across the country. Bernat had quickly industrialized the company's production, enabling the company to meet the rising demand for the lollipops. Already by the end of the 1950s the company was delivering up to 200,000 lollipops per day, using its own fleet of trucks. Meanwhile, the company continued to refine its sole product, replacing the metal sticks with wooden sticks, which were in

Company Perspectives:

Chupa Chups, as a Spanish company with an international outlook, operates in a frontier-free global market. Its effectiveness is based on the go-getting character of its staff combined with a deep-rooted commercial attitude inherited from the Catalan, Spanish and pan-European cultures. Its aim is to stand out as the leader in all the product lines in which it participates. To do this it centers its efforts on new markets where the areas of marketing and commercial and industrial know-how are key competitive angles.

turn replaced with plastic in the early 1960s. An important refinement came in 1961, when the company changed the lollipop's name to the more musical-sounding Chupa Chups, and it was under this name that the lollipop was to achieve international domination.

The success of the Chupa Chups brand led Bernat to change the company's name to that of its flagship line in 1964. Rising sales, and preparations to take the company international, encouraged Bernat to open a second factory, in Sant Esteve de Sesrovires, outside of Barcelona, in 1967. That factory helped support the company's launch of its first subsidiary, in Perpignan, France, in that same year.

A major moment in the Chupa Chups brand history came in 1969 when the company adopted a new logo. For this, Bernat turned to friend—and world-renowned surrealist painter—Salvador Dali, who quickly devised the company's daisy-shaped logo and bright colors. The association of Dali's name with the still small Chupa Chups company gave it a great deal of international attention, enabling the company to penetrate new markets. In that same year, the company built its first foreign production facility, in Bayonne, France. The company's sales still remained predominantly Spanish, however; in 1970, just ten percent of the company's lollipops were sold outside of Spain.

Ten years later, the company had entirely transformed itself and its sales—by 1980, some 90 percent of all sales were made outside of Spain. The company could also celebrate the sale of its ten billionth lollipop sold. Supporting the booming growth in the company's sales was its rollout in Japan in 1977. The 1970s had also given the company an enormous boost in publicity when its lollipops were adopted by actor Telly Savalas as a prop for his character Kojak. Worldwide television audiences watched Kojak's ever-present Chupa Chups every week. The company was to continue to benefit from such public relations coups, as a means to compete against the mammoth advertising budgets of its large-scale competitors, such as Nestlé, Hershey, Cadbury, Haribo, and others.

Meanwhile, the company maintained a small but steady advertising strategy, begun during the 1960s, beginning with radio, then adding television, but also carefully targeting the children's listening and viewing audience. At the same time, the company continued introducing new flavors—often created to appeal to the tastes of specific national markets. Chupa Chups also led the industry in the creation of ''value-added'' candies, such as the world's first ''motorized'' lollipop, lollipops that painted the tongue and other technical and marketing innovations.

In 1980, Chupa Chups moved to boost its presence in the U.S. market, setting up its Chupa Chups USA subsidiary. This was the start of a string of foreign forays as the company opened distribution subsidiaries in a number of countries during the decade, including Germany and the United Kingdom. At the end of the 1980s, Chupa Chups entered a new, and potentially vast market, when it created its Russian subsidiary, Zao Neva Chupa Chups. This subsidiary promptly included its own production facility, opened in St. Petersburg, which began production in 1991.

Soaring into the New Century

The St. Petersburg facility gave Chupa Chups the opportunity for yet another marketing coup. In 1995 the company sent a number of lollipops made in St. Petersburg into space, to the Mir space station. During live broadcasts, a worldwide audience watched the Russian cosmonauts enjoying their Chupa Chups. Closer to home, the mid-1990s had already marked two new expansion moves for the company. In 1994, Chupa Chups opened a new production facility in Villamayor, Spain, and created a new subsidiary, Shanghai Chupa Chups Food Co. Ltd., bringing its production and distribution reach to the vast Chinese market.

Central to the company's expansion had been its willingness to form partnership agreements with local companies—even with its competition—enabling Chupa Chups to enter a country without requiring heavy investments in setting up a distribution network. As such, the company sealed a distribution agreement in the United States with the wholesaling firm Maclean, later acquired by Wal-Mart. In the Italian market, the company's lollipops were being distributed by Haribo; and in Australia, Cadbury agreed to handle the company's distribution.

After decades of single product focus, Chupa Chups began to look for ways to diversify its product range. In the early 1990s, the company moved into chocolate production, producing chocolate eggs for the Italian market. It also bought up France's Bêtises de Cambrai, a regional maker of specialty hard candies, in 1992. Chupa Chups success in its attempt to turn this product into an international brand remained limited, however. In the mid-1990s, the company had better luck with a new product, the Smint breath mint, the first of the company's products to be targeted at an entirely new market—adults.

By then Enrique Bernat had stepped down from the company's leadership, turning over the president and CEO's chair to son Xavier Bernat. The younger Bernat quickly proved his father's student, arranging the Mir space station publicity coup, but also continuing both the company's international expansion and its eagerness to diversify its product range. In 1996, Chupa Chups entered the Mexican market, building a new production facility there to provide not only for the North American market but for the South American market as well. This market was soon to be served by its own Chupa Chups subsidiary, when Chupa Chups do Brasil Ltda. was formed in 1998. Construction began on a production facility in that country, with a production launch scheduled for 2001.

Key Dates:

1946: Company starts as Granja Asturias S.A.
1954: Enrique Bernat joins company, begins development of the lollipop.
1958: Bernat acquires full control of company, launches Chups brand lollipop.
1961: Lollipop name is changed to Chupa Chups.
1964: Company's name is changed to Chupa Chups.
1967: Chupa Chups forms French subsidiary, opens second production plant in Spain.
1969: Salvador Dali designs logo; French production facility is constructed.
1977: Chupa Chups enters the Japanese market.
1980: Company creates Chupa Chups USA subsidiary.
1982: Chupa Chups launches German subsidiary.
1983: Company creates U.K. subsidiary.
1989: Chupa Chups enters Russian market.
1991: Company establishes St. Petersburg production facility.
1992: Chupa Chups unveils Smint line of breath mints for adult market.
1994: Company creates Chinese subsidiary and production plant.
1996: Company opens Mexican subsidiary and production plant.
1998: Brazilian subsidiary is launched.
1999: Chupa Chups establishes Japanese, Canadian, and Korean sales offices.
2000: Crazy Planet subsidiary is formed to develop and market non-lollipop products.

By then, Chupa Chups—celebrating its 40 billionth lollipop—was receiving a boost from somewhat unexpected places. The late 1990s saw the emergence of a new trend—that of the lollipop as a fashion accessory, and the Chupa Chups was quickly adopted as the candy of choice by such international celebrities as Madonna, Michael Jackson, Uma Thurman, George Clooney, as well as supermodels and others. The suddenly fashionable lollipop quickly expanded far beyond its traditional children's market.

As the end of the century neared, Chupa Chups also continued to reinforce its international distribution activities, opening sales offices in Japan, Korea, and Canada. The new subsidiaries gave the company more direct access to those markets and support for its rollout of its Smint products in those regions.

Chupa Chups was also preparing a diversification drive for the new century, launching a new brand and subsidiary, Crazy Planet. This subsidiary enabled the company to launch a new range of non-lollipop confectionery products. Meanwhile, after reaching a German distribution partnership agreement with Van Melle, Chupa Chups continued to roll out new value-added products built around its global brand name. Among the products launched at the end of the century and the start of the new century were a range of so-called ''cocktail'' Chupa Chups, featuring alcohol-free cocktail inspired flavors such as Pina Colada; a line of Chupa + Surprise, adding a line of snap-together toys to its lollipop package; and the Mobile Pop—designed to resemble a portable phone, complete with belt-clip, the product came complete with a calculator and, of course, a compartment for storing Chupa Chups lollipops. Such innovative product offerings were expected to keep Chupa Chups at the top of the lollipop world into the 21st century.

Principal Subsidiaries

Chupa Chups USA Corp.; Chupa Chups France S.A.; Chupa Chups Diversificacion S.A.; Chupa Chups GmbH (Germany); Chupa Chups UK Ltd; ZAO Neva Chupa Chups (Russia); Shanghai Chupa Chups Food Co. Ltd. (China); Chupa Chups Invest Mexico S.A. de C.V.; Chupa Chups Do Brasil Ltda.; Chupa Chups Japan KK; Chupa Chups Canada Inc.; Crazy Planet S.A.

Principal Competitors

Brach's Confections, Inc.; Herman Goelitz, Inc.; Hershey Foods Corporation; Grupo Industrial Bimbo, S.A. de C.V.; Mars, Inc.; Nabisco Holdings Corp.; Nestlé S.A.; Tootsie Roll Industries, Inc.; UIS Inc.; Wm. Wrigley Jr. Company.

Further Reading

''Chupa Chups Lures a New Generation to Suck,'' *Ad News*, July 14, 2000.
De la Rocque, Jean-Pierre, ''Chupa Chups régale le monde,'' *Capital*, February 1996, p. 38.
Kitov, Vladimir, ''Chupa Chups on Sweet Road to Recovery,'' *Russia Journal*, April 2000.
Warner, Melanie, ''Killer Companies—How to Win Big Quietly,'' *Fortune*, November 25, 1996, p. 170.

—M.L. Cohen

CLIFFORD CHANCE

Clifford Chance LLP

200 Aldersgate Street
London EC1A 4JJ
United Kingdom
Telephone: +44 (0)20 7600 1000
Fax: +44 (0)20 7600 5555
Web site: http://www.cliffordchance.com

Partnership
Founded: 1802 as Anthony Brown
Employees: 3,000
Sales: $1 billion (2000 est.)
NAIC: 54111 Offices of Lawyers

Clifford Chance LLP is the world's largest law firm, based on its approximately 3,000 lawyers operating in some 30 offices. That status is based on two events. First, in 1987 it became England's largest law firm with the merger of Coward Chance and Clifford-Turner. Then in 2000 it merged with New York City's Rogers & Wells and Germany's Punder, Volhard, Weber & Axster. This unprecedented consolidation of law firms is one approach to globalization and the increasing number and size of multinational corporations. Clifford Chance's predecessor firms that dated back to 1802 served corporate, individual, and government clients throughout the British Empire, including India, Africa, Australia, and the Middle East. In 2000 some of its long-term clients included Citibank, Midland Bank, Fujitsu Europe, Panasonic UK, and Sumitomo Bank. Although smaller law firms remain competitive with this consolidated colossus, only time will tell if bigger is better. In any case, Clifford Chance is breaking new ground in the history of the legal profession.

Coward Chance: Predecessor Firms in the 1800s

In 1802 Anthony Brown became the first lawyer in his family when he started a solo law practice in London. In 1809 Parliament passed a bill that Anthony Brown wrote to incorporate the Kent Water Works Company (until 1844, Parliament had to approve all incorporation requests.)

Brown became one of the city's most prominent solicitors and community leaders and, in 1826, was elected London's Lord Mayor. Meanwhile his firm was growing by representing railroads after the English first invented that new form of transportation in the early 1800s. In the 1830s the Brown law firm also represented some banks that financed the growing business community and continued to get regular work from the Kent Water Works Company.

After Parliament passed The Joint Stock Companies Act in 1844, many more businesses incorporated because they could simply file papers with the government and no act of Parliament was required. That of course stimulated the growth of the nation's banks and law firms. For example, in1863 the partnership then known as Thomas & Hollams helped establish the East London Bank, later renamed the Central Bank of London that in 1891 merged with the Birmingham & Midland Bank to become the Midland Bank. Other banking and financial clients included William Brandt's Sons & Co. formed in 1805, Frederick Huth & Co. started in 1809, Schroders, the National Discount Company organized in 1856, and the Imperial Bank of Persia, the firm's major overseas banking client that was formed in 1889.

As a leading London law firm, the predecessor to Coward Chance played an important role in serving the nation's growing international interests. The United Kingdom in the 19th century ran the world's largest empire, with colonies such as Canada, Hong Kong, India, Australia, and New Zealand.

In 1888 the firm then known as Hollams, Son & Coward represented the London Produce Clearing House (LPCH) formed by several of the city's brokers to trade sugar and coffee. The following year tea, wheat, and maize (corn) were added. The Hollams before 1888 had counseled some of the backers of the LPCH, including Carey & Brown, Rucker & Bencraft, and William Brandt's Sons & Co. Other founding sponsors of LPCH included Barings, Hambros, and the Rothschilds, probably Europe's wealthiest family based on its international system of banks in Frankfurt, London, Paris, Vienna, and Naples, Italy. Since 1953 the LPCH has been known as the International Commodities Clearing House.

Key Dates:

1802: Anthony Brown begins his law practice, the predecessor of Coward Chance, in London.
1824: Brown & Marten is formed.
1830: Brown & Marten is renamed Brown, Marten & Brown.
1833: The firm becomes known as Brown, Marten & Thomas.
1844: The firm is renamed Brown, Thomas & Hollams.
1862: Thomas & Hollams becomes the new firm name.
1873: Hollams, Son & Coward is formed.
1889: Hollams, Sons, Coward & Hawksley is organized.
1900: H. Clifford Turner & Co., the second predecessor firm, is founded in London.
1905: The Clifford Turner firm adopts the new name Clifford Turner & Hopton.
1910: Hollams, Sons, Coward & Hawksley is renamed Coward & Hawksley, Sons & Chance.
1924: The Coward firm is renamed Coward, Chance & Co.
1926: The Clifford Turner firm is renamed Clifford-Turner, Hopton & Lawrence.
1934: Clifford-Turner becomes Clifford-Turner & Co.
1971: The Coward firm's name is simplified to Coward Chance.
1973: Coward Chance opens its first overseas office, in Brussels.
1975: Clifford-Turner & Co. is simplified to Clifford-Turner.
1987: Coward Chance and Clifford-Turner merge to create Clifford Chance.
2000: Clifford Chance becomes the world's largest law firm after mergers with New York's Rogers & Wells and Germany's Punder, Volhard, Weber & Axster.

Other clients with international ties included David Sassoon & Sons and also E.D. Sassoon & Sons. Started in Bombay, India, these companies later had offices or operations in London, Shanghai, Baghdad, and Japan to buy and sell tea, spices, silk, dried fruit, opium, and Indian cotton. Insurance clients in the late 1800s included the Universal Marine Insurance Company, the Marine Insurance Company, and the Commercial Union Assurance Company. Such insurance companies protected trading and shipping companies against losses from theft, fires, natural disasters, and shipwrecks.

In South Africa the law firm represented Cecil Rhodes and his many companies that dominated the diamond mining industry in that area, including the De Beers Consolidated Mines Ltd. and the British South Africa Company. The firm assisted Rhodes when he was investigated by the House of Commons, administered Rhodes's estate after he died in 1902, helped set up the famous Rhodes Scholarships, and then continued in the years ahead to counsel the Rhodes Trust.

Another prominent client around the turn of the century was Guglielmo Marconi and his companies. After the Italian government rejected Marconi's newly invented wireless telegraphy using radio waves, the inventor moved to England in 1895. In 1897 the law firm accepted him as a new client and soon helped him with his Wireless Telegraph and Signal Company and the Marconi International Marine Communication Company.

Coward Chance in the 20th Century

The law firm continued to represent the Midland Bank in the early 20th century. For example, its client opened a branch bank in St. Petersburg, Russia, in 1917. After the new Communist government took over Russian banks, the London law firm helped Midland as several persons filed lawsuits to get their money back. Midland Bank was one of the world's largest banks before World War II.

Meanwhile, the firm began representing the Commonwealth of Australia during World War I. During the 1930s and even after World War II, the state government of Hyderabad used the firm for legal advice as India prepared for independence. Unfortunately, Nazi bombers in 1941 destroyed almost all firm records.

Coward Chance in the early 1950s began representing the Standard Oil Company of California that later became Chevron. In the 1950s the firm worked on agreements that facilitated oil exports from Iran, and in the 1960s it provided legal counsel for companies extracting oil just discovered in the North Sea. In addition to serving the Midland Bank as it expanded after World War II, Coward Chance began representing American and Japanese banks that either started or restarted London operations.

In the postwar era Coward Chance continued to serve trade associations such as the National Association of British and Irish Millers as they dealt with the Restrictive Trade Practice Act of 1956 and also the United Kingdom's 1973 entry into the European Economic Community (EEC). In 1973 the law firm opened its branch office in Brussels, the headquarters of the EEC.

Meanwhile, the general trend of decolonization brought more legal challenges to Coward Chance lawyers. For example, when Zambia became independent in October 1964, the firm's client the British South Africa Company still had not negotiated an agreement. Finally, in December 1964 the company agreed to give up its mineral rights in Zambia in return for compensation from both the Zambian and British governments.

Clifford-Turner: Origins and 20th-Century Practice

Harry Clifford Turner in 1900 was admitted as a solicitor in London, where his firm was named H. Clifford Turner & Co. In 1906 the firm was the solicitor for the Amalgamated Motor Bus Company, Limited, when it issued its first public stock offering. During World War I, the partnership began serving the Dunlop Rubber Company, which remained a client into the 1980s.

In the 1920s the firm prospered, with profits peaking in 1927 at £60,000. At the time the firm had just three partners. Major clients before World War II included the British Foreign & Colonial Corporation (BFC), and the British General Insurance Company. Imperial Airways, Limited used Clifford Turner from its formation in 1924 to the time it was acquired in 1940.

Although the firm's corporate practice declined during the 1930s depression, the firm's profits and number of partners increased. It received vital cash flow from its workmen's compensation cases and its work with various other accident victims. Representing businesses that were forced into receivership was a mainstay of the firm's work during the 1930s.

In the early post-World War II era, Clifford Chance received considerable work from the Labour Party's fulfillment of its promise to nationalize several private industries. For example, the government used the law firm in 1948 to acquire the National Omnibus and Transport Company. New merchant banking client S.G. Warburg & Company kept the firm busy. With its practice increasing, the firm in 1950 approved a more formal structure with five departments: company, conveyancing, trust and probate, taxation, and litigation. By 1961 the firm had 16 partners, and the following year it opened its first overseas branch in Paris. In 1972 Clifford Chance opened an Amsterdam office in cooperation with a well-known Dutch law firm.

The 1987 Merger: Clifford Chance in the Late 20th Century

In 1987 Coward Chance with 358 lawyers merged with 278-lawyer Clifford-Turner to create the new firm of Clifford Chance. This union brought together two firms with different strengths. Coward Chance had a strong banking practice, while Clifford-Turner's forte was in the corporate field. In spite of wagging tongues and critics who doubted the merger would work, legal journalists in the early 1990s agreed it was a successful amalgamation.

Because the newly merged firm had offices in eight London buildings, making shuttle buses necessary, it decided to lease a new headquarters. In the fall of 1992 the firm moved to new offices that Karen Dillon in the June 1993 *Legal Business* described as ''spectacular'' by London's traditional standards. The new facility, with towers of 17 and 7 floors, featured 74 meeting rooms to serve the firm's 2,000 employees and its clients.

The 1987 merger stimulated the firm to increase its international competitiveness. By May 1993 the firm had almost doubled its number of attorneys to 1,192, making it the world's second largest law firm, following Chicago's Baker & McKenzie with 1,642 lawyers. Just two years earlier, based on annual revenues, Clifford Chance ranked fourth in the world with about $315 million.

In March 1992 Clifford Chance made a major decision that received considerable attention in both British and American legal periodicals. The firm hired Nancy Jacklin to work in its New York office, ''the first American partner hired by Clifford Chance,'' wrote Karen Dillon in the *American Lawyer* in May 1993. That move ''broke an unofficial understanding between some of the top U.S. and British firms. They would not directly challenge each other on their home territories by setting up offices to represent local clients on matters involving local law. That way British and American firms could refer work to one another without having to worry that clients would be poached.''

That angered some lawyers in top New York law firms, while others welcomed the new competition on their home turf. Some New York law firms, of course, were already operating in the same manner. For example, New York's Coudert Brothers law firm employed several lawyers in its London office to practice British law.

Meanwhile, Clifford Chance built up its practice in continental Europe. Its Amsterdam office was that city's second largest foreign office in the early 1990s. About the same time, it opened offices in Moscow, Warsaw, Frankfurt, Barcelona, and Rome.

For its work on three of the top 12 Asian mergers and acquisitions in 1999, Clifford Chance was named ''Asia's M&A Law Firm of the Year'' by the *International Financial Law Review* in early 2000. Clifford Chance won this honor for the third straight year.

Creating the World's Largest Law Firm

Effective January 1, 2000, Clifford Chance merged with New York's Rogers & Wells and Germany's Punder, Volhard, Weber & Axster to create the world's largest law firm, known as Clifford Chance Rogers & Wells in the Americas and Clifford Chance Punder Volhard Weber & Axster in some nations of continental Europe. The merged firm included about 3,000 lawyers worldwide. It maintained offices in New York, London, Sao Paulo, Washington, D.C., and Dubai. Its continental European offices were located in Amsterdam, Barcelona, Berlin, Brussels, Budapest, Dusseldorf, Frankfurt, Leipzig, Luxembourg, Madrid, Milan, Moscow, Munich, Padua, Paris, Prague, Rome, and Warsaw. Its Asian offices were in Bangkok, Hong Kong, Shanghai, Singapore, Tokyo, and Beijing.

Rogers & Wells had been started in 1871 with the law practice of Walter S. Carter. The New York firm was named for William P. Rogers, President Eisenhower's attorney general and secretary of state under President Nixon, and the late corporate lawyer Jack Wells. The *American Lawyer* (July 1999) ranked Rogers & Wells as the 47th largest U.S. law firm, based on its 1998 gross revenue of $214 million. At that time Rogers & Wells employed 366 lawyers.

The merger between Clifford Chance and Rogers & Wells was the first transatlantic union of two major firms. For years some had speculated about the possibility of a New York and a London firm merging. ''I think it's inevitable that we're going to see a transatlantic merger of some significance—probably in the next year or two,'' said consultant Ward Bower in the *American Lawyer* of December 1996.

Intense competition among various large firms in the two cities had occurred for many years. In addition, law firms in the 1990s competed with the Big Six international accounting firms that employed thousands of tax lawyers.

The 2000 mergers that created Clifford Chance as the world's largest law firm were part of the consolidation trend occurring in an increasingly globalized economy. With the rise of multinational corporations, the European Union, the North American Free Trade Agreement, and electronic commerce conducted on the Internet, national borders lost economic significance and many firms of all kinds merged to be able to compete in the larger world markets.

However, not all big law firms chose the consolidation strategy. They argued that the quality of their lawyers was more important than the quantity found in a firm like Clifford Chance. Regardless, big law firms continued to grow, whether by mergers or internal hiring. In light of the difficulties mergers faced, including leadership challenges and differences in corporate cultures, the wisdom of the 2000 Clifford Chance mergers remained to be seen.

Principal Operating Units

Corporate; Banking and Finance; Capital Markets; Real Estate; Litigation and Dispute Resolution; Tax, Pensions and Employment.

Further Reading

Bose, Mihir, "Clifford Chance: A Very Peculiar Practice?" *Director*, March 1990, pp. 65–66, 68, 70.

Dillon, Karen, "The British Empire Strikes Back," *American Lawyer*, May 1993, pp. 52–56.

——, "Playing for Stakes: The Game of Clifford Chance," *Legal Business*, June 1993, pp. 28–31.

"Merger in the First Degree: British Law Firms Are Forging New Relationships That Could Transform the Style of Global Legal Practice," *Time International*, August 9, 1999, p. 41.

Morris, John E., "The New World Order," *American Lawyer*, August 1999, pp. 92–99.

——, "London Braces for the Big Six Invasion," *American Lawyer*, December 1996, pp. 5–6.

Page, Nigel, "Managing Nicely: Will the Real Geoffrey Howe Step Forward," *Legal Business*, June 1991, pp. 15–20.

Rice, Robert, "At the Heart of Europe," *Financial Times*, August 17, 1993.

Rose, Craig, "Clifford Chance: The Merger That Worked," *Commercial Lawyer*, Issue 15, 1997, pp. 32–34.

Scott, John, *Legibus*, London: Clifford-Turner, 1980.

Slinn, Judy, *Clifford Chance: Its Origins and Development*, Cambridge, England: Granta Editions, 1993.

Steinberger, Mike, "Is Clifford Chance/Rogers & Wells the Next Wave, or Simply Overkill? Big Transatlantic Legal Merger Sparks Fierce Debate on Global Strategy," *Investment Dealers' Digest*, August 9, 1999, pp. 12–13.

—David M. Walden

CNA Financial Corporation

CNA Plaza
333 South Wabash Avenue
Chicago, Illinois 60685
U.S.A.
Telephone: (312) 822-5000
Fax: (312) 822-6419
Web site: http://www.cna.com

Public Company, 86.9 Percent Owned by Loews Corporation
Incorporated: 1967
Employees: 18,600
Total Assets: $62.5 billion (2000)
Stock Exchanges: New York Midwest Pacific
Ticker Symbol: CNA
NAIC: 524126 Direct Property and Casualty Insurance Carriers; 524113 Direct Life Insurance Carriers; 524114 Direct Health and Medical Insurance Carriers; 524130 Reinsurance Carriers

As the unified holding company for a diverse group of insurance entities that date back to the second half of the 19th century, CNA Financial Corporation was conceived in 1967, though not born until 1975. Chicago-based CNA was among several large insurers that formed holding companies in the late 1960s to overcome state insurance regulations against diversification. CNA's foray into non-insurance ventures proved disastrous, however, and the firm was close to insolvency in 1974 when Loews Corporation acquired control late that year. The New York-based conglomerate quickly installed new management and launched a sweeping reorganization that restored CNA's financial base and set the stage for solid growth. CNA provides underwriting, marketing, and servicing for its various companies, chief among which are the Continental Casualty Company, the Continental Insurance Company, and Continental Assurance Company. With an emphasis on commercial rather than personal insurance, the CNA companies offer broad coverages, including property and casualty; life, accident, and health; and pension products and annuities.

Late 19th-/ Early 20th-Century Origins

The origins of CNA Financial trace back to the late 1800s, even before the incorporation in 1897 of what is now known as Continental Casualty Company, CNA's principal property and casualty insurance subsidiary. After the Civil War, a hospital benefit organization called the National Benefit Company was formed to provide health insurance for workers involved in construction of the Northern Pacific Railroad. Cyrus W. Field, a prominent financier who built the first transatlantic telegraph cable in 1866, was the principal investor.

In the early 1890s, National Benefit merged with its biggest competitor, the Northwest Benefit Association based in Duluth, Minnesota, and as the only provider of health insurance at the time, the newly merged company grew rapidly until the Illinois Department of Insurance ruled that it needed nearly $100,000 in additional capital. New investors were found, and it was reorganized in Milwaukee, Wisconsin, as the National Benefit and Casualty Company. With the refinancing, a large group of agent representatives in the field, and franchises to do business with nearly every railroad, the future looked bright. The firm, however, ran short of capital again and was put out of business by the Wisconsin superintendent of insurance.

Two years after that failure, a new insurance company was organized by some of National Benefit's investors. This was the founding, on November 29, 1897, of the firm that is the ''C'' in CNA: Continental Assurance Company of North America. Incorporated in Hammond, Indiana, but headquartered in Chicago, the new firm was licensed to operate in Illinois, Indiana, Michigan, and Ohio, with $100,000 in initial capital and a surplus of $60,000. The first president was C.B. Hubbard, and its general manager was B.A. Scott, who had been an executive with National Benefit.

Continental Assurance got off to a fast start by offering the same popular accident and health coverage, called disability insurance today, that had propelled National Benefit's growth, attracting many of the agents and franchises of the old company. By February 1, 1898, agencies had been set up in all four states, and gross assets had grown to $228,000, leaving surplus and capital of $205,733 after insurance reserves. At the end of

Company Perspectives:

We are committed to remaining focused on our core businesses of insurance and insurance services. We are committed to remaining financially strong and stable, so that we will be here to keep our promises to you, no matter how many years in the future those promises must be kept.

1898, assets had reached $294,527 and capital and surplus stood at $252,618.

In 1900 Gerald Bunker was elected president and the firm changed its name to Continental Casualty Company. By the end of the year, it merged with three other insurers: Metropolitan Accident Company of Chicago, the Northwestern Benevolent Society of Duluth, and the Railway Officials and Employees Accident Association of Indianapolis, Indiana. During the next year the company survived the stock market panic that was brought on by an attempt to corner the market in Northern Pacific Railroad shares. The fledgling firm successfully pursued expansion during the two-year depression that followed.

In 1902 Continental introduced the first type of accident and health policy with a monthly premium, affordable for those who could not pay quarterly or annual premiums. By 1904 the firm was doing business in 41 states and territories, and in one month nearly 15,000 policies were issued. Within a year, Continental had branch offices in nine states and territories from New York City to Honolulu, Hawaii.

Aside from a boost to its railroad-oriented business, the merger with the Railway Officials and Employees Accident Association brought a key manager into Continental, a London-born insurance executive named Herbert George Barlow Alexander. He had been a successful New York agent for the Indianapolis-based firm and was its agency superintendent at the time of the merger. H.G.B. Alexander, as he was known, joined Continental as a vice-president, soon became general manager, and was elected president in 1906, a position he held until his death in 1928.

In 1911 Continental Casualty ventured into life insurance with the organization of Continental Assurance Company. Although management of the two firms was the same, a separate, wholly owned subsidiary was required because Continental Casualty could not sell life insurance under its charter. The new firm was licensed in 11 states and the District of Columbia, with $100,000 in capital and surplus of $60,000.

Despite four business recessions between 1903 and 1912, Continental was growing rapidly, and by 1914 it had moved three times to satisfy its need for more office space. In 1915, as the prewar economy was recovering, Continental ventured into miscellaneous casualty lines, starting with workers' compensation. In the next few years, Continental sold coverage for liability, burglary, plate glass, and steam boilers, among other risks.

In 1917 Continental Casualty participated in what was the largest group insurance contract at the time. With Equitable Life providing the life insurance, Continental wrote an accident and health policy covering 35,000 employees of the Union Pacific Railroad and its affiliates. The premium for Continental's share of the business alone was $800,000 a year. The policy, however, was in danger of cancellation after the outbreak of war, with the federal government's takeover of the railroads. Unable to continue the premiums, the Union Pacific issued a termination notice effective December 31, 1918. Officials of Continental and Equitable fought hard to convince William G. McAdoo, U.S. secretary of the treasury and director general of the railroads, that cancellation would cause an uproar among Union Pacific workers. Although he was concerned about charges of favoritism, as the Union Pacific was the only railroad that provided group insurance for its employees, McAdoo agreed on December 16, 1918, to renew the contract and to assume its obligations. This action is thought to be the U.S. government's first involvement with group insurance.

By 1919 the combined assets of Continental Casualty and Continental Assurance had reached $5.8 million, with capital and surplus of nearly $1.4 million. By 1928, however, the year of H.G.B. Alexander's death, assets had soared to nearly $33.4 million, while capital and surplus stood at almost $10.9 million, making ''the Continental Companies in point of financial security by far the strongest in the entire West,'' according to the firm.

During the 1920s, the Continental Companies introduced several new products and marketing strategies that contributed to their growth. In 1921 Continental Assurance established the Bank Plan, which in cooperation with local banks allowed customers to obtain a combination of savings and life insurance, by encouraging them to save a certain amount each month. Within ten years, the Bank Plan was credited with putting $35 million of life insurance on Continental's books. Following on the success of its Bank Plan, Continental Assurance introduced in 1926 a salary investment plan, which was a payroll-deduction program for obtaining insurance through one's employer.

Continental Casualty wrote a group insurance contract for the Cleveland Teachers Association in 1923, which CNA claims to be the first association group policy written by any insurer. At about the same time, the casualty company also established surety facilities, providing bonds required in business activities such as construction and court proceedings. By 1923 Continental was operating in every U.S. state and territory, as well as every province of Canada.

Steady Mid-20th-Century Growth

After the death of H.G.B. Alexander—who oversaw the firm's evolution from a small but innovative provider of accident and health coverage to a multiline property, casualty, and life insurance company during his tenure as president—Continental's structure changed less dramatically, but the firm posted substantial growth while pursuing a number of insurance-industry innovations. Continental, for instance, was the first to offer polio insurance on a national basis, as well as group dental insurance and health insurance for senior citizens.

The Continental Companies more than doubled in size under the leadership of Alexander's successor, Herman A. Behrens, an experienced insurance executive who started with Continental as a vice-president in 1912 and became general manager in 1923. He served as president of Continental Assurance from 1928 until his

Key Dates:

1897: Continental Assurance Company of North America is founded to offer accident and health coverage.
1900: Continental Assurance is renamed Continental Casualty Company.
1911: Continental Assurance Company is formed to sell life insurance.
1956: Continental Casualty acquires 67 percent of National Fire Insurance Company, creating Continental-National Group.
1963: American Casualty Company is acquired, creating the Continental-National American Group.
1967: The group is reorganized under a new holding company, CNA Financial Corporation; a diversification drive is soon undertaken.
1974: Loews Corporation acquires 83 percent of CNA's stock; company begins selling off non-insurance operations.
1975: CNA ranks as the 17th largest insurer in the United States.
1989: CNA ranks as the eighth largest insurer in the United States.
1995: CNA acquires the Continental Corporation.
1999: Company sells the bulk of its personal lines to Allstate.

death in 1945, and served as president of Continental Casualty until 1937, when he became chairman. Assets of Continental Casualty increased from nearly $20.4 million in 1927 to more than $53.3 million in 1943, while the amount of premiums increased from $14.6 million to $31.7 million. By 1928 the Continental Companies had more than 800 employees in Chicago, and the firm paid more than 150,000 claims that year.

In 1929 the firm offered every kind of life and casualty insurance except marine and fire, which was available through an affiliation with the National Fire Insurance Company of Hartford, Connecticut, whose president, F.D. Layton, was a director of Continental Assurance. During the 1930s this relationship grew as Continental Casualty and National Fire teamed up to provide coverage for the growing number of automobile owners. At that time, insurance laws did not permit multiple-peril policies, but they did allow companies such as Continental and National Fire to combine on a joint contract. National Fire's policy covered physical damage to a customer's automobile while Continental provided liability coverage, allowing ''one-policy convenience'' for agents and insureds alike.

In 1938 Continental Casualty created a new subsidiary, Transportation Insurance Company, to provide personal-property and inland marine insurance. Accident and health carriers were not allowed to provide that kind of coverage, but it was legal to set up a subsidiary to do so. Continental also started offering hospitalization insurance that year, with a range of benefits costing from two to 15 cents per day.

In 1941 Continental established a division to provide accident, health, and hospitalization insurance for people in high-risk occupations and older age groups, and it started offering hospital and surgical benefits on a group basis at wholesale rates in 1944. In the same year, Continental became the first insurer to write all-risks aviation insurance on a worldwide basis. The firm's personal accident policies were selected by the U.S. government to insure aviators during and after World War II.

Leadership passed in 1945 to Roy Tuchbreiter, who became president of the Continental Companies after the death of Behrens, the firm's chairman since 1937. Martin P. Cornelius, the son of Continental's first cashier and a lifelong Continental executive, had served as president of Continental Casualty from 1937 until he was named general counsel in 1944. By 1952 Continental had leaped to $2 billion worth of life insurance in force, up from $420 million in 1942, according to *Business Week* of October 11, 1952, which cited Continental's growth as ''only an exaggerated example of what has taken place in life insurance as a whole during the past generation.''

After ten years of study, Continental Casualty established a special-risks division in 1953, and within a few years the firm's willingness to insure test pilots, participants in the Indianapolis 500, and other persons requiring unusual coverages earned it the nickname ''Lloyd's of Chicago,'' according to a *Newsweek* article of October 20, 1958. Patterned after the well-known London insurance exchange, the new unit was bringing in seven percent of the casualty company's $240 million in premiums by 1957.

In 1956 Continental acquired 67 percent of National Fire in an exchange of stock, forming what was then known as the Continental-National Group. In 1956 the group's combined net premiums of $414.9 million made it one of the three largest insurers in the United States offering insurance for casualty, life, and fire and allied lines, according to Continental's annual report of 1956. Despite the diversification, accident and health coverage still accounted for more than half of the premiums and most of the profits at Continental Casualty. In 1956 also, Tuchbreiter became chairman, a title he held until 1964.

With all its growth, diversifications, and acquisitions, Continental Casualty was still relying on its original business of accident and health insurance for more than 54 percent of its net premiums in 1956, with automobile coverage a distant second at 19 percent. In life insurance, Continental pioneered the concept of a quantity discount that year, in which the premiums decreased with increasing amounts of insurance.

Emergence of CNA in the 1960s

By the early 1960s Continental Assurance had caught the attention of investors as one of the fastest-growing publicly owned stock life companies, as opposed to mutual life insurers, which are owned by their policyholders. Continental was the sixth largest stock life company by then. It had by far the highest price-earnings ratio, selling at $192 or 51.8 times earnings per share.

Continental's next major insurance-company acquisition, the one that put the ''A'' in CNA, took place in 1963 when American Casualty Company of Reading, Pennsylvania, was acquired in a $40 million stock transaction. That put 529,532 shares of Continental Casualty stock into the hands of Accident and Casualty Insurance Company of Winterthur, Switzerland, a holding that became significant when CNA became embroiled in a takeover battle more than a decade later.

The firm, then known as the Continental-National American Group (CNA Group), also acquired American's subsidiaries, Valley Forge Insurance Company and Valley Forge Life Insurance Company, in the deal. American Casualty, originally founded in 1884 as the American Protective Mutual Insurance Company Against Burglary of Reading, Pennsylvania, was the first U.S. company to offer burglary insurance. In 1902 it reorganized as a publicly owned casualty and surety company and was renamed American Casualty. An affiliate formed in 1944 to write fire and property coverage, American Aviation and General Insurance Company, later became Valley Forge Insurance. In the late 1940s both American and its subsidiary expanded into property, casualty, and surety coverage when laws restricting the writing of multiple lines of insurance were lifted. Between 1945 and 1955 the firm's annual premiums increased from $11 million to $74 million, and in 1956 it formed the Valley Forge Life subsidiary. By 1963 American's premium volume had reached $165 million, making the insurance company group the third-largest fire and casualty stock company in the United States, in terms of combined premium volume. It totaled $546.8 million.

In 1964 Continental Assurance's assets reached $1 billion. In 1965 Howard C. Reeder became the CNA Group's chairman. In the mid-1960s the CNA Group was not immune to the tough times that hit the insurance industry—''skyrocketing inflation . . . ; astronomical settlements awarded by juries; spiraling medical costs; more heavily concentrated business risks; and laws in many states prohibiting insurers from revising rates quickly and effectively,'' according to an article by Jacque W. Sammet, president of Continental Casualty, in the February 1972 issue of *Nation's Business*. Between 1955 and 1970 stock liability companies suffered $1.5 billion in underwriting losses, he noted, and the 14 largest firms alone suffered $609 million in losses during the 1960s.

In 1963 Continental Casualty's underwriting losses stood at $14.6 million, and the red ink would continue to flow for the rest of the decade. The losses were more than offset by investment income, but CNA executives were still alarmed. In 1965 Continental Casualty's top echelon held a strategy session at which it pored over a huge underwriting loss of $34 million, according to Sammet, and the idea of scrapping the casualty business was discussed and rejected. The plan adopted was: more emphasis on commercial accounts and a range of cost-cutting moves. Within three years, CNA was at least breaking even on insurance underwriting.

In 1966 the CNA Group briefly flirted with a merger with the Continental Insurance Companies of New York, called Continental Corporation today. Despite the similarity in names, the insurers have always been totally unrelated. The merger of the two firms, each with about $2 billion in assets, would have made sense. Besides consolidating their overhead, the New York insurer was strong in fire and casualty business, weak in accident and health, and had no life insurance operation—the opposite of the Chicago Continental. Three weeks after acknowledging that merger ''studies'' were underway, the idea was dropped abruptly.

Reeder soon steered the company in another direction, converting the CNA Group into a holding company called CNA Financial Corporation, on December 31, 1967. At the time, many large insurance companies were doing the same thing to get around state regulations against investing in non-insurance ventures. Reeder then took CNA on an acquisition binge. By the end of 1969 he had acquired one of the country's best-known mutual funds as well as two personal-finance operations, a major West Coast homebuilding company, a nuclear-core leasing company, insurance companies in Canada and California, and a 29 percent stake in a nursing-home operator. CNA also established new subsidiaries in real estate development, hotel development, and investment services.

The move that drew the most attention on Wall Street was the payment of about $20 million in stock for New York's Tsai Management & Research Corporation, a mutual fund founded by Gerald Tsai, Jr., one of the hottest stock pickers of the mid-1960s, who became CNA's executive vice-president in charge of acquisitions and CNA's huge investment portfolio. Tsai Management ran five mutual funds, including the Manhattan Fund introduced at the bull market's peak in 1966. The Manhattan Fund reached a value of about $500 million in 1968 but slid to $380.9 million by the end of its first year under CNA's ownership. CNA widely was considered to have overpaid for the mutual fund operation, but Reeder wanted to enhance CNA's image.

Taken Over by Loews in the 1970s

At first, CNA's diversification strategy caught the fancy of investors. The stock doubled between 1968 and 1969, the year it started trading on the New York Stock Exchange. The company's profitability, however, was eroding. Several of the new acquisitions were losing money, and insurance underwriting results were still a problem, although income from the investment of premiums made up for that. Kane Financial Corporation, one of the consumer credit subsidiaries, lost $16.5 million in 1970 and 1971. CNA Nuclear Leasing was barely profitable, but it tied up $200 million in credit. The Manhattan Fund, the country's worst-performing mutual fund in 1970, lost $1.5 million, and CNA Realty had heavy losses from, among other things, developing hotels in the overbuilt Honolulu, Hawaii, market.

Breaking precedent, a divided board of directors reached outside of the company for new leadership when Reeder reached mandatory retirement age in 1971. With the six inside directors abstaining from the vote, CNA's seven outside directors picked Elmer L. ''Nick'' Nicholson, president of Fidelity Mutual Insurance Company in Philadelphia, Pennsylvania, as the new chairman. Nicholson moved quickly to dismantle Kane Financial and CNA Realty. He tried to sell CNA Nuclear Leasing but did not succeed until 1974. He also reorganized the holding company into four groups: insurance, asset management, real estate, and financial services. He started a long-range strategic planning effort and established new management-performance incentives.

The losses at non-insurance subsidiaries were trimmed to $1.1 million in 1972 from $6.5 million in the prior year, but CNA's worst problems were only beginning at Continental Casualty and Larwin Group, a West Coast homebuilding firm that CNA had acquired for $200 million in stock in 1969. Larwin was growing fast because housing was on an upswing, and between 1970 and 1972 the firm went into nine new markets, including New York, Chicago, and Washington, D.C. At the same time, Larwin ventured beyond its expertise in single family homes and got involved in apartment buildings and recreational properties. In 1973 the housing market turned sour. Eventually, Larwin was written off at a loss of more than $124 million.

Meanwhile, profits were tumbling at Continental Casualty, which was forced by unexpected underwriting losses to put $17 million into reserves in the third quarter, producing the first quarterly net loss in the company's history. CNA assured Wall Street that there would be no more earnings surprises, but the company then was forced to put another $15 million into reserves in the fourth quarter, plus yet another $29.7 million in early 1974. At the holding company level, pretax operating income went from $127 million in 1972 to $24.9 million in 1973, and then to a loss of $188.2 million in 1974.

In October 1973 CNA again tried to merge its way out of its problems by agreeing to be acquired by Gulf Oil Corporation in a proposed $850 million stock-and-debt deal. For Gulf, the non-energy diversification would have reduced its dependence on crude oil profits endangered by tension in the Middle East. CNA needed a partner with deep pockets: its surplus, the financial ''cushion'' left after deducting legally required insurance reserves from assets, was eroded to $482.4 million and would plummet to $125.8 million in the following year. Less than a month after the deal was announced, however, Gulf called it off. No reason was given. The aborted deal left CNA vulnerable to a takeover. Its stock had dropped from about $20 per share in early 1973 to less than $8 a year later.

In March Loews Corporation, a New York conglomerate headed by Laurence A. Tisch, announced that it owned more than five percent of CNA's stock, and in May it sought approval from Illinois insurance authorities to seek control. Accident and Casualty Company of Switzerland, which had a seven percent stake in CNA stemming from the sale of its American Casualty holdings to CNA, was also interested in a takeover.

CNA fought bitterly for the next five months, but in October the board accepted Loews's offer to buy 20 million common shares at $6 each, which would give it 56 percent of the stock. That same day, the company revealed that losses would total $135 million in the third quarter, including another $40 million required to increase the insurance reserves. CNA disclosed it still had need for $122 million in additional capital on top of its existing reserves of $736 million. With $85 million in stock market losses in the third quarter alone, surplus had dropped to $100 million from $277 million at the beginning of the year, and Continental Casualty was ''uncomfortably close to insolvency,'' according to a November 9, 1974, article in *Business Week*. As a result, Loews withdrew its CNA bid while it studied the insurer's financial disclosures. Within a few days, Loews cut its offer to $5 a share, which the board immediately accepted, noting that Loews planned to inject new capital into the company.

By December, Nicholson resigned and Tisch was named chairman. Loews had acquired 83 percent of a company with $4.5 billion in assets for about $206 million. When the new team from Loews moved in, what it found ''was a bloated management mess,'' said a November 1, 1976, article in *Business Week*. CNA's two-year-old headquarters building in Chicago had the top three floors reserved for lavish executive offices. Belt-tightening was the first move for Loews, a $2.7 billion conglomerate of theater, tobacco, and hotel interests whose own headquarters staff then numbered less than 20 people. The three levels of executive suites were closed down, and about 1,400 people were dismissed. Within less than a year, only five of CNA's original headquarters staff of 400 would remain.

Loews then hired a seasoned insurance industry executive to head the operation. Edward J. Noha, former executive vice-president at Allstate Insurance, took over as chairman of the insurance operations in February 1975. First he obtained a $50 million cash infusion from Loews to shore up CNA's surplus position, then he launched a massive reorganization. By June 1975, all of the insurance operations were combined under six departments reporting directly to Noha, with two of the most important—marketing and administrative services—filled by former Allstate executives. The objective was to improve sales by getting agents to sell all of CNA's insurance products at the same time. In addition, Noha's new team reviewed CNA's insurance lines and eliminated the unprofitable ones.

Noha also reversed the strategy of relying on investment income to cover underwriting losses. Noha made clear that CNA was in the insurance business, and that underwriting income produced profit. To do so meant raising rates, which is what he did. Within the first half of 1975, the Continental Casualty unit posted pretax profits of $7 million, compared to a $23 million loss in the first six months of the prior year.

Laurence Tisch and his staff took over the non-insurance operations and moved quickly to cut costs. Tisch sold 55 nursing homes CNA owned and cut the staff of its home-building subsidiary to 96 from 600 people. By the end of the first year under new management, CNA as a whole posted a $107 million profit versus a $207 million loss in 1974. By 1983, when it sold General Finance Corporation for $193 million, CNA had divested, discontinued, or written off nearly all of its non-insurance operations.

CNA continued to improve its financial stability during the 1980s, a period when the insurance industry generally was racked by underwriting losses due to severe rate competition, and to poor results on investments. In 1984, the sixth year of a decline in insurance rates, the property and casualty industry experienced an underwriting loss of about $21 billion, producing the industry's first net loss since 1906. CNA, however, did not weaken its surplus by extensive price-cutting, as many insurers did. Thus, CNA had the financial capacity to increase its volume once the soft market had turned around. As a result, in 1989 CNA was the eighth largest insurer in the United States, as measured by premium income. In 1975 it had been 17th largest.

Under Noha, CNA also moved to strengthen its business relationships with the independent agents who sell its products. Independent agents, who represent several insurers, had steadily lost market share to direct-writing agents, who sell for one company only. CNA introduced the High Performance Agency program, which permitted its agents to retain independence while enjoying many of the benefits of company personnel. Participants in this program account for one-quarter of CNA's casualty sales force while generating more than half of CNA's property and casualty premium. At year-end 1989, surplus had reached $3.1 billion on the casualty side and $786.4 million for life insurance, up from a consolidated surplus of $125.8 million in 1974. Assets stood at $31.9 billion in late 1990, up from $4.8 billion in 1974.

1990s: Acquiring Continental Corp. and Restructuring

In 1992 Noha was named chairman of CNA Financial, while Dennis H. Chookaszian took over as chairman and CEO of the insurance operations. Chookaszian, who was hired by Noha shortly after he joined CNA, initially concentrated on improving the efficiency of operations through office automation initiatives and the trimming of the workforce by the end of 1994 from 15,600 to 13,000. Meantime, in 1993, CNA agreed to pay nearly $1.5 billion to settle a decade-long product-liability lawsuit stemming from asbestos manufactured by Fibreboard Corporation from the early 1940s to the late 1960s that may have harmed as many as 325,000 people. CNA's Continental Casualty along with Pacific Indemnity Co., a unit of Chubb Corporation, had written policies for Fibreboard providing unlimited coverage. The result, at the time, was one of the biggest product-liability settlements in U.S. history.

In May 1995, CNA completed what was believed to be the largest property-casualty insurance merger in the United States in 20 years: the acquisition of the troubled Continental Corporation for $1.1 billion. New York-based Continental, the same company that had almost merged with CNA in 1966, traced its origins back to 1853, when it issued its first policy. The company in 1906 formed the Fidelity Fire Insurance Company, which merged with Phoenix Insurance Company in 1910 to create Fidelity-Phoenix Fire Insurance Company. Continental created the American Eagle Fire Insurance Company in 1915, then, three years later, the entire group adopted the name American Fore Group. After acquiring control of Fireman's Insurance Company of Newark in 1957, the group changed its name again to the American Fore Loyalty Group. Yet another name change came in 1962 when American Fore became the Continental Insurance Companies. Following a series of acquisitions in 1966, a parent holding company, the Continental Corporation, was created for the growing group of companies. During the 1970s, Continental undertook a number of overseas expansionary moves—in Japan, France, Germany, and Latin America. The 1980s ushered in a period of refocusing, with Continental exiting from the wholesale brokerage business in 1983, then divesting its life and health insurance operations from 1987 to 1989. Continental was now focused exclusively on property-casualty insurance but it suffered blows from a series of major hurricanes, paying out hundreds of millions of dollars in damage claims spawned by Hurricanes Hugo, Iniki, and Andrew in the late 1980s and early 1990s. Continental was further troubled by its potential exposure to mounting environmental pollution claims. In 1994 Continental increased its reserves covering environmental claims to $600 million. From August 1993 to December 1994, when the deal with CNA was announced, Continental's stock had fallen 60 percent.

The merger of CNA and Continental created the nation's third largest property-casualty insurance firm and the number six insurance company overall. At the end of 1995, total assets stood at $60.36 billion. Consolidating Continental into CNA was the immediate objective following the buyout, with the focus on cost-cutting and a workforce reduction of about 5,000 employees.

In the late 1990s, CNA faced a difficult operating environment, including a severe slump in commercial insurance, which accounted for more than 60 percent of the company's premium revenue. Net operating income fell slightly in 1997 to $488 million, from the $578 million figure of the previous year, but then CNA posted a net operating loss of $152 million for 1998. Certain noncore lines began to be divested, including group health, entertainment, and agriculture insurance. In 1997 the company merged its surety business into a publicly traded surety firm called Capsure Holdings Corporation, which was renamed CNA Surety Corporation. CNA Financial retained a 62 percent stake in CNA Surety. In 1998 CNA Financial cut its workforce by 2,400 and consolidated several processing centers. This restructuring aimed to cut annual operating expenses by $300–$350 million.

In the midst of the restructuring, Chookaszian retired as chairman and CEO of the insurance operations but remained on the board of directors. Replacing him in February 1999 was Bernard L. Hengesbaugh, who had been executive vice-president and chief operating officer. In October of that year, CNA sold the bulk of its personal lines—including its auto and homeowners insurance lines—to the Allstate Corporation. Hengesbaugh also launched a plan to improve the profitability of the company's commercial underwriting by asking CNA's independent agents to demand rate increases as high as 15 percent for property and casualty insurance policies. Clients that balked were dropped. In early 2000, CNA announced that it was exploring the sale of its life insurance and life reinsurance businesses, in a further move away from personal insurance. In October of that year the company announced that it would sell its life reinsurance unit to MARC, the U.S. life subsidiary of Munich Re; a deal involving the life insurance unit, however, had yet to be found. Meanwhile, CNA announced in March 2000 an offer to purchase the 38 percent of CNA Surety it did not already own, but two months later the plan was scrapped because of increasing stock prices among property-casualty insurance firms. Despite some false starts, it appeared that Hengesbaugh had a solid plan in place for an early 21st century turnaround for CNA Financial.

Principal Subsidiaries

American Casualty Company of Reading, Pennsylvania; CNA Casualty of California; CNA Reinsurance Company, Ltd. (U.K.); CNA Surety Corporation (62%); Columbia Casualty Company; Convida, Inc. (Bahamas); Continental Assurance Company; Continental Casualty Company; Continental Insurance Company of New Jersey; Firemen's Insurance Company of Newark, New Jersey; First Insurance Company of Hawaii; National Fire Insurance Company of Hartford; National-Ben Franklin Insurance Company of Illinois; Pacific Insurance Company; RSKCo Claims Services, Inc.; The Buckeye Union Insurance Company; The Continental Insurance Company; The

Fidelity and Casualty Company of New York; Transcontinental Insurance Company; Transportation Insurance Company; Valley Forge Insurance Company; Valley Forge Life Insurance Company; Western National Warranty Corporation.

Principal Competitors

American International Group, Inc.; The Allstate Corporation; CIGNA Corporation; The Chubb Corporation; GEICO Corporation; The Guardian Life Insurance Company of America; John Hancock Financial Services, Inc.; Massachusetts Mutual Life Insurance Company; Metropolitan Life Insurance Company; Nationwide; New York Life Insurance Company; The Prudential Insurance Company of America; Reliance Group Holdings, Inc.; The St. Paul Companies, Inc.; The Hartford Financial Services Group, Inc.; Travelers Property Casualty Corp.; USAA.

Further Reading

Bary, Andrew, ''A New Leaf?: Loews' Neglected Stock Could Jump If Tobacco Unit Is Spun Off,'' *Barron's,* November 30, 1998, pp. 23–24.

CNA: A Century of Commitment, 1897–1997, Chicago: CNA Financial, 1997.

Fritz, Michael, ''Way to Grow: Insurance Vet Has CNA All Chook Up,'' *Crain's Chicago Business,* September 15, 1997, p. 17.

Greenwald, Judy, ''CNA Reviews Units in Search for Edge,'' *Crain's Chicago Business,* July 27, 1998, p. 20.

''How Loews' Lean Management Fattened the Profits at CNA,'' *Business Week,* November 1, 1976.

Johnsson, Julie, ''CNA's Rookie Chief Braces for Risky Ride,'' *Crain's Chicago Business,* March 1, 1999, p. 3.

——, ''Risk-Averse CNA Takes a Chance with a New Strategy: Insurance Rate Hikes Could Anger Customers, Agents,'' *Crain's Chicago Business,* September 6, 1999, p. 4.

Lohse, Deborah, ''CNA Financial Considers Selling Two Insurance Units,'' *Wall Street Journal,* March 9, 2000, p. B17.

Merrion, Paul, ''CNA Buyout Puts New CEO on Map,'' *Crain's Chicago Business,* December 12, 1994, p. 4.

Miller, Theresa, ''Staying the Course,'' *Best's Review,* February 1999, pp. 47–49.

Scism, Leslie, and Steven Lipin, ''CNA Agrees to Acquisition of Continental,'' *Wall Street Journal,* December 7, 1994, p. A3.

''The Second Fifty,'' Chicago: The Continental Companies, 1947.

Steinmetz, Greg, and Marilyn Chase, ''Fibreboard Sets Asbestos Accord with Insurers: CNA, Chubb Agree to Pay an Estimated $3 Billion to Cover All Claims,'' *Wall Street Journal,* August 31, 1993, p. A3.

—Paul R. Merrion
—updated by David E. Salamie

CNH Global N.V.

World Trade Center
Tower B, 10th Floor
Amsterdam Airport
The Netherlands
Telephone: (20) 446-04-29
Fax: (20) 446-04-36
Web site: http://www.cnh.com

700 State Street
Racine, Wisconsin 53404
U.S.A.
Telephone: (262) 636-6011
Fax: (262) 636-6432

Public Company, 71 Percent Owned by Fiat S.p.A.
Incorporated: 1991 as N.H. Geotech
Employees: 35,000
Sales: $10.67 billion (1999)
Stock Exchanges: New York
Ticker Symbol: CNH
NAIC: 333111 Farm Machinery and Equipment Manufacturing; 333112 Lawn and Garden Tractor and Home Lawn and Garden Equipment Manufacturing; 333120 Construction Machinery Manufacturing; 333924 Industrial Truck, Tractor, Trailer, and Stacker Machinery Manufacturing

CNH Global N.V. was the name adopted by the Dutch firm New Holland N.V. following its 1999 acquisition of Case Corporation. CNH is the world's second largest maker of agricultural equipment, trailing Deere & Company, and third in construction equipment, following Caterpillar Inc. and Komatsu Ltd. The company's products are sold in 160 countries under a number of brands, including Case, Case IH, and New Holland, through a network of more than 10,000 dealers and distributors. By region, 46 percent of sales are generated in North America, 39 percent in western Europe, five percent in Latin America, and ten percent elsewhere. Fiat S.p.A., the Italian automaker, holds a stake in CNH of approximately 71 percent.

19th-Century Origins of Case

The history of Case is merged with the Industrial Revolution's impact on farming. Jerome Increase Case grew up threshing wheat by hand on his father's farmstead in the early 1800s. Wheat was cut with scythes, then beaten by hand to remove the grain. The blistering work meant that one person produced about half a dozen bushels a day, so farmers necessarily limited their acreage to prevent bottlenecks in production of their wheat. When Case was 16, he took his father to a demonstration of a crude, mechanized thresher patented around 1788 by Scotsman Andrew Meikle. His father was sufficiently impressed by the machine and applied for a franchise to sell them.

For five seasons, Jerome Case operated the machine for his father and his father's clients. During that time, Case became aware of the machine's flaws, as well as its indispensability to farming. In 1842, Jerome Case moved to Rochester, Wisconsin, then the growing heart of the wheat culture in the United States. He sold five thresher machines along the way, reserving one for himself.

Rochester was a village when Case arrived. That autumn, he did custom threshing and worked on his modifications of the machine. Case envisioned a machine that was both separator and thresher, constructed so that the straw would move to one end while grain fell underneath the machine. Such a machine had already been patented by inventors in Maine in 1837, but Case had not seen their invention. His machine differed in its operation. Case was helped by Stephen Thresher, a carpenter he met where he boarded in Rochester. The two were advised by Richard Ela, who made fanning mills and hailed from New Hampshire.

After a successful first demonstration of his new thresher-separator, Case decided to concentrate on manufacturing rather than custom threshering. When Rochester balked at his petition for water-power rights, Case moved to Racine, Wisconsin, in 1844, playing a part in that town's explosive growth. Within three years, he had gone from renting a building to constructing his own factory. First named Jerome Increase Case Machinery Company, the name was changed to Racine Threshing Machine Works. By 1848, Case was producing 100 threshers a year and

Company Perspectives:

To continue to give customers access to their preferred brands, CNH is committed to a multiple brand, multiple distribution business model. While the company will combine functional operations on a global basis, commercial and sales organizations and distribution networks will remain dedicated to specific brands.

For CNH, this strategy makes solid business sense for two reasons. Brand loyalty is strong in the equipment industry, in part due to the generations of equipment use within family businesses that are prevalent in the agricultural and construction equipment industries. Second, the Case and New Holland businesses are highly complementary, and the various brands of each business have strengths in different customer segments and geographic markets around the world. CNH will build on the existing points of differentiation between its brands. For example, in the North American agricultural equipment markets, the Case IH line has a substantial presence in the large cash grain customer segment, while the New Holland line has a strong position in multi-use farms that include livestock and dairy segments. These product lines have been developed over time to deliver the features and performance required by these distinct customer groups.

In addition, the two brands have products that address specific, sometimes specialized, market needs. New Holland, for example, is a dominant supplier of grape harvesting equipment, while Case has leading products for cotton and sugar cane harvesting.

claimed he was meeting only half of the orders received. By 1854, water power was supplanted by a steam boiler and engine within the factory.

It was difficult to deliver such cumbersome equipment in the 1800s. There were no railroads in Wisconsin until the 1850s. Most roads were widened Indian trails, and rain could make them treacherous to wheels. Timely delivery of the heavy machines was not always possible, and timing is as essential as rain to farmers. In addition, Case spent much time traveling to distant farms to collect back payments, credit being another necessity of his clients' business.

Many complementary farming products were appearing during the same period that the wheat belt of the Midwest and the Great Plains was burgeoning. While Case's business was growing, John Deere and Major Andrus were developing a steel plow in Illinois, and a reaper had been developed by Cyrus McCormick. Case purchased rights to the thresher and fanning mill invented before his, then added improvements. Acknowledging that his own strength was business and seeing the applications of machines, Case often acquired and improved upon the inventions of others. Case was established as a leading thresher manufacturer by the early 1850s.

Business was steady enough to allow Case to pursue civic interests; he was elected three times to the State Senate and served twice as Racine's mayor. The poor harvest and financial panic of 1857 did not prevent the company, then still specializing in threshers, from introducing new products. In 1862, Case began selling the "Sweepstakes," a thresher capable of producing 300 bushels of wheat a day. Pressures, including the Civil War, drove Case to create a co-partnership by 1863, established as J.I. Case & Co. The partnership included Case, Massena Erskine, and Stephen Bull until 1880.

The same year that Alexander Graham Bell won a bronze medal at the Philadelphia Centennial Exhibition, Case's new thresher, the 1869 Eclipse, also won a bronze and a commendation. The thresher took the gold medal at the World's Fair in Paris two years later. With the Homestead Act of 1862, farming burst into a new era, requiring equipment that could keep up. In 1878, Case produced its first steam traction engine, and by the following year had sold 109 of them. Sales doubled in 1878, reaching the million dollar mark by 1880. The partnership was incorporated as J.I. Case Threshing Machine Company in 1880. By 1890, Case was offering nine different horsepowers of steam traction engines, and continued improvements. Production peaked the same year the first gasoline tractor was introduced, 1911. Most steam engine products were eclipsed by the gasoline tractor by 1924. At that point, Case had built about one-third of this country's farm steam engines. But it took time for tractors to become standard farm equipment; as a power source on U.S. farms, draft animals outnumbered tractors until 1952.

Case died in 1891 at the age of 73. Leadership of the company was passed to one of his former partners, Stephen Bull, who was assisted by his son Frank. Between 1893 and 1924, the company expanded to Europe, South America, and Australia. Competition between thresher manufacturers led to the dissolution of the Thresher Manufacturers Association in 1898 and increased rivalries. A depression between 1893 and 1897, a warehouse fire, and a Great Plains drought contributed to a decline in Case profits of nearly three-quarters between 1892 and 1896. Stockholder dissatisfaction led to new ownership, which resulted in Frank Bull as president. Bull became chairman of the board in 1916 and was succeeded in presidency by Warren J. Davis. The company name was changed to J.I. Case Company after further reorganization around 1928.

Early 20th Century: Becoming a Full-Line Manufacturer

Case was advertising a full line of road machinery by 1912. The gasoline tractor became one of the company's most important products. Since 1902, many firms were fighting to produce the gasoline-powered successors to steam-powered engines. International Harvester began making them in 1905, and Ford in 1907. The design and manufacture of lighter, smaller versions of the engines made Case a major player in the gasoline tractor market by the 1920s. By the late 1920s, Case had become a full-line manufacturer, aided by its 1919 acquisition of Grand Detour, a tillage equipment company. Case also made expensive automobiles from 1912 to 1927: roadsters, coupes, and sedans in 14 different models over the years. Because of low profitability, the auto lines were phased out.

Key Dates:

1842: Jerome Increase Case builds his first thresher machine, and soon founds the Jerome Increase Case Machinery Company.
1863: Company is reformed as a co-partnership, called J.I. Case & Co.
1878: Case produces its first steam traction engine.
1880: Partnership is incorporated as J.I. Case Threshing Machine Company.
1895: New Holland Machine Company is founded.
1917: Ford Motor Company begins making the first mass-produced agricultural tractor.
1919: Fiat introduces its first mass-produced tractor to the market.
c. 1928: Case changes its name to J.I. Case Company.
1945: Case workers in Racine begin a 440-day strike—at the time, the nation's longest ever.
1947: Sperry Corporation acquires New Holland, creating the subsidiary Sperry New Holland.
1957: Case relaunches its industrial equipment line and acquires American Tractor Corp.
1964: Kern County Land Company (KCL) gains majority control of Case.
1967: Tenneco Company acquires KCL and its stake in Case.
1970: Case becomes a wholly owned subsidiary of Tenneco; Fiat creates an earthmoving equipment subsidiary, Fiat Macchine Movimento Terra.
1974: Fiat Macchine creates joint venture with Allis Chalmers Corporation, Fiat-Allis.
1984: Fiat consolidates all of its agricultural machinery manufacturing under Fiatagri unit.
1985: Case acquires International Harvester's agricultural product line.
1986: Ford acquires Sperry New Holland and merges it with Ford Tractor Operations to form Ford New Holland, Inc.
1988: Fiat-Allis and Fiatagri are merged to form FiatGeotech S.p.A., which includes all of Fiat's agricultural and earthmoving equipment.
1991: Case posts a net loss of $1.1 billion; Fiat acquires an 80 percent interest in Ford New Holland, which is merged with FiatGeotech to form N.H. Geotech.
1993: N.H. Geotech changes its name to New Holland N.V.
1994: Tenneco takes Case Corporation public.
1996: Tenneco sells its remaining stake in Case, which gains its full independence.
1999: New Holland acquires Case and changes its name to CNH Global N.V.

The depression in the American economy in the wake of World War I greatly impacted the farm equipment industry. By 1929, only 18 of the 157 manufacturers of farm equipment operating 12 years earlier remained. Case's profits fell steadily, despite the addition of a combine to its line in 1923. The company was especially challenged by the dealer network of International Harvester. Case did not keep up with competitors' improvements while it was enjoying the sales of its steam traction engines and threshers. Between 1920 and 1922, annual gross sales plunged from $34 million to less than $16 million. In 1924, Case's new president, Leon R. Clausen, assumed the reigns after leaving John Deere Company. He would remain president until 1948, and chairman of the board until 1958.

Clausen brought many ideas with him from Deere, including faith in aggressive marketing and the value of being a full-line manufacturer. He established three primary goals: improve tractor designs, establish a full line, and modernize the factories. The Model C tractor was introduced in 1929, and a tricycle tractor appeared in 1930. A line of "Motor Lift" implements arrived in 1935. Lines were expanded by acquisition as well as invention: Case purchased through the Emerson-Brantingham Company a line of farm equipment that included binders, mowers, reapers, and corn planters. The Rock Island Plow Company was acquired in 1937, adding drills, spreaders, and plows to the company's offerings.

Case also purchased that year a factory in Iowa to make small combines, sales of which had been growing steadily since they were introduced to the market. Case, Harvester, and Deere were responsible for three-quarters of the farm machinery sold in the United States by 1937. Although Case had, since 1912, offered an array of road building machinery, these products were not promoted under Clausen and it was not until the mid-1950s that Case became serious about marketing its construction equipment.

Clausen set to work on revamping the sales department and restructuring manufacturing. He is credited with building Case's dealer network. Although severe cutbacks were necessary to weather the Great Depression, Case managed to increase sales by 1936 on the strength of the company's tractor sales. In 1939, a new tractor line was introduced, as well as a small combine, hammer feed mills, and farm wagon gears.

With the start of World War II, Case's tractors were in even greater demand. More than 15,000 of its tractors went to the military between 1941 and 1945. New tractors were designed and manufactured with war needs in mind. Case was also producing items such as shells, aircraft wings, and gun mounts for the war effort. Case devoted much more wartime engineering to federal production than did Deere or Caterpillar, which left it at a disadvantage at the war's end. Nonetheless, the postwar demand for farm machinery outpaced supply and Case's lost wartime share soon seemed recoverable.

Postwar Difficulties for Case

Regaining lost market share, however, was interrupted by a strike in 1945 that lasted 440 days. It was, at that time, the nation's longest strike. Clausen's animosity for unions—first noted when he was still with Deere—was mutual. Depleted by the strike and its aftermath, Clausen stepped down as president in 1948, staying on as chairman of the board. The strike hurt Case on every level: in its relationship with dealers, customers, and its union, and in its research and development, where it was already lagging behind its competitors.

With the Marshall Plan and the lifted export restrictions, devastated Europe's hunger for working machinery became a fresh market for Case. In addition, stateside farm machinery was in disrepair. There was a shortage of manpower on farms, due to deaths in the war, which increased the need for machinery. Sales growth on the West Coast led to a plant purchase in California in 1947. This purchase expanded Case's range into a new tobacco harvester. These factors helped Case post a profit through 1949, despite its costly strike.

Profits declined between 1950 and 1953, in part because of outdated products. Competitors introduced lighter models of tractors in the late 1930s, and these units became popular after the war. Case, on the other hand, had at the end of the war roughly the same heavy series it had at the beginning. Poor engineering hurt Case during the early 1950s as well, as did a propensity to blame the dealer rather than the product. Items such as Case's hay baler, which had topped the market in 1941, lagged to less than five percent of baler sales in 1953 because Case failed to respond to a competitor's improvements.

All of these problems added up to a crisis in leadership at Case. According to Case's own published history, *J.I. Case: The First 150 Years,* Clausen consistently made decisions opposed to change: he opposed diesel engines for domestic sales; he believed farmers preferred "dependability" to changes such as a foot-operated clutch, a cab, and an oil filter—all of which a 1946 survey of farmers specified as desired. When Clausen left the presidency in 1948, Theodore Johnson took over. Johnson was 66 and had never worked outside of Case. The company continued to drift, with a lackluster response to competition, and no notable innovations. Johnson was replaced in 1953 by John T. Brown.

Under Brown's direction, Case released a multitude of new or improved implements, including the 500 series tractor, which would become a popular line. The 500 had a six-cylinder, fuel-injected, diesel engine; power steering; and a push-button start. Two manure spreaders were unveiled in 1956. That same year, however, Case reported its second loss since 1953. For the first time, bankruptcy seemed a possibility. Diversification appeared to be the only remedy.

Diversifying Case's Product Line: Late 1950s

Case launched its industrial equipment line in 1957 as though it were new, but it had been making industrial units based on agricultural models for three decades. Street and highway builders, national forests and parks, and others had come to rely on industrial tractors adapted from farm use. Case applied itself to expanding this sector of its line, and turned to Caterpillar Company for marketing assistance. To revitalize its industrial line, Case acquired American Tractor Corporation (ATC) in 1957. ATC's volume around purchase time was $10 million, but the company was in debt due to recent rapid growth. Its assets included a vigorous president, Marc Bori Rojtman; a strong line of distributors and dealers; and a sturdy line of crawler tractors and loader backhoes—the company's star product. Under Rojtman, Case's manufacturing capacity improved, new retailers were attracted, and the company moved confidently into the construction equipment business.

Rojtman's showman's personality led to dazzling regional shows to promote new product lines. Deliberate showmanship in marketing resulted, despite criticism, in huge increases in orders. New product invention and marketing and overseas expansion proved financially taxing. But sales rose 50 percent in 1957, reaching $124 million. Clausen, head of the board, strongly opposed Rojtman's presidency and his debt load, and resigned in 1958. An economic downturn in 1958 left the company in a precarious position. William Grede replaced Rojtman in 1960.

Case's debt load in 1959 was $236 million. It had become the country's fourth largest farm and construction equipment producer. Grede's first order of business was to reduce debt and consolidate manufacturing. A new offering of accessories such as batteries, oil, and hydraulic fluid proved successful. Between the new offering and special discounts, Case sales were still strong in 1960. A six-month strike occurred that same year. Unable to met a $145 million bill due on short-term notes in 1962, a bank agreement was negotiated which called for reorganization and deferment of most of the interest until 1967, so Case could focus on paying down principal. Reorganization included the ousting of Grede. He was succeeded by Merritt D. Hill, who had previously worked in Ford's Tractor and Implement Division.

Hill brought talent with him from Detroit, including a chief product engineer. He completely restructured Case. Separate divisions were created for marketing, manufacturing, and engineering. Hill also ushered in a new era of labor-management relations, being the first of Case's presidents sympathetic to issues of labor and race. Money constraints impeded the development of new product lines, but Case managed to stay in the ring with competitors such as Ford and Deere, as the new head of its engineering department insisted. In 1964, Case introduced the 1200 Traction King, a 4-wheel drive, 120-horsepower giant that marked the company's entry into the large agricultural tractor market.

Case's operating loss had declined and its production levels were up. The company seemed on solid business ground by 1964, but was still not in a position to meet the terms of the 1962 agreement and have enough left over to fuel growth. Case shopped for a cash-rich partner to whom it could offer the use of its agreement's tax loss carry-forwards.

Late 1960s: Beginning of Case's Tenneco Era

In May 1964, the Kern County Land Company (KCL) of California acquired majority stock in Case. KCL was founded in 1874 and began as a cattle-raising venture that branched into petroleum royalties after oil was discovered. It diversified into hard minerals, real estate, and businesses such as its Racine, Wisconsin-based parent company, the Walker Manufacturing Company. KCL was cash-rich and agreed not to dictate Case's growth or internal decisions. These circumstances allowed Case to expand between 1964 and 1967, in accordance with a booming demand for existing products and the itch to produce new ones. Around 1965, the 450 crawler and the 1150 dozer debuted. A new series of loader backhoes were introduced around this time also, among them Case's mainstay, the 580. By

1966, Case's income decline had been reversed. Hill became chairman of the board and Charles A. Anderson became president. Anderson had been with KCL and Walker.

Suddenly KCL, under threat of a hostile takeover by Armand Hammer, wooed a friendly buyer instead, and ended up being acquired by Tenneco Company of Houston. Gardiner Symonds, Tenneco's president, was familiar with KCL's natural resources but had no experience with manufacturing. Tenneco was a holding company. The deal closed in 1967. It was thought that Tenneco would quickly sell Case.

When investors began inquiring about Case's stock, Tenneco decided to run an analysis of the company and found it well-run, but too low on liquid assets to grow. This shifted Tenneco's plan. Case would prosper from a shift to construction equipment, so Tenneco decided not to sell it. In 1968, Tenneco acquired Drott Manufacturing Company in Wisconsin and leased it to Case. Case had been buying loader buckets from Drott for years. That same year, Tenneco also bought Davis Manufacturing Company of Wichita, Kansas, a producer of crawler and rubber-tire mounted trenchers and cable-laying equipment. Tenneco allowed Case to expand by two product lines: log skidders for timber harvesting, through Beloit Woodlands of Wisconsin, and a ''skid steer'' loader, manufactured by the Uni-Loader Division of Universal Industries.

James Ketelsen succeeded Anderson as Case's president in 1967. Tenneco deferred to Case's manufacturing experience, but both agreed that the company's future was in construction equipment. The agricultural market had slowed, with replacements and larger machinery to accommodate fewer, larger farms, reflecting the bulk of sales. Case essentially exited the farm implement business by 1970. Yet, while Case dropped its combine business in 1972, an acquisition in 1985 returned harvesting equipment to Case's line.

After dropping so many of its lines, Case thought it could survive without being a full-line company. The farm economy was dire in the early 1970s, especially for smaller farmers. Case shifted its focus not away from agricultural implements altogether, but toward the large tractor market. Tenneco ''loaned'' Case $60 million from 1969 to mid-1970, giving the company enough fiscal strength to deal with healthy competitors such as Deere. Even Deere did not have access to such resources. By 1971, Case's entire construction equipment line had replaced and that year it unveiled more new machinery than any of its competitors. Tenneco's faith was repaid, as Case led all of Tenneco's companies in earnings gains the following year. Meantime, by 1970, Tenneco had purchased the remaining stock in Case, turning Case into a wholly owned subsidiary.

In 1972, Case bought David Brown, Ltd., a British agricultural equipment firm founded in 1860. Brown had a large distribution system in Britain and Case concentrated its small tractor production in Brown. Thomas Guendel took over the company presidency in 1972 and commanded a chapter of unprecedented growth until he left Case seven years later. Sales quadrupled during that time and earnings improved more than 600 percent. The phenomenal growth was due largely to increased success in construction equipment and overseas markets.

The company reentered the military market during the 1970s. It was awarded a $55 million contract with the Army and Air Force in 1978. The economy was improving after the recession between 1974 and 1975, and Case was the country's third largest producer of construction equipment by 1975. By the late 1970s, 45 percent of Case's sales were overseas, while 80 percent of its production was domestic. France's Poclain Company, the largest manufacturer of hydraulic excavators in the world, was purchased by Case in 1977. Because Drott's excavators could not be sold in Europe due to trade restrictions, Poclain was a savvy purchase; it was a recognized worldwide market leader.

1980s and Early 1990s: Bleakest Times Yet

When Jerome K. Green replaced Guendel in 1979, Case passed the $2 billion mark in revenues. Case started the 1980s with 28,000 employees, but it did not anticipate the recession that would shatter the farming community. Shifting to the construction product line was no rescue, as that industry was equally hard hit. New general purpose tractors had been introduced in 1983 and were languishing. Four more 94 series tractors were unveiled in 1984, but by that point, farms were in a real crisis. Case cut production to 55 percent of capacity and it still exceeded demand. Although overseas sales of construction equipment remained strong during the 1980s, Case's overseas sales did not balance the wounds of the recession in the United States: in 1983, Case lost $68 million, and followed that with a deficit of $105 million in 1984.

Case acquired International Harvester's agricultural product line, production facilities, and distribution system in 1985. The history of Harvester was as long and as distinguished as Case's. (Harvester retained its trucking business, renaming it Navistar International Transportation Corp.) Case shut down its own factories for the start of 1985, reducing production to 45 percent of retail sales, and went on to close several Brown plants, and to retire the oldest and least efficient of Case's home plants. Trimming its agricultural product line to such things as tractors, tillage equipment, crop production, and combines, Case was prepared to compete head-on with John Deere, dominator of the farm equipment market.

Losses in 1986 were down to $1 million, despite the deepening farm recession. In addition, Case was among the top three farm equipment manufacturers in Germany, France, and the United Kingdom. Nevertheless, Tenneco was unhappy with Case's bad financial showing and unacceptably tardy production in 1987. Green was replaced by James K. Ashford that same year. About 35 new agricultural products were introduced in 1987, while nine factories were closed or closing. Case was assisted by *Fortune*'s listing of its combines, planters, and loader backhoes as among the best U.S. products in 1988. Ashford oversaw aggressive cutbacks and revamping, including the elimination of 300 jobs in Racine and an intended worldwide cut of 3,000 employees.

By 1989, Case had gone from a $142 million loss to a record profit of $228 million. The recovering farm economy and improved construction equipment sales were cause for celebration. Case's confidence was sufficient to announce a new headquarters complex, but the recovery was short-lived and sales began to weaken. Although John Deere was cutting back production, Ashford gambled that the recession was over and that Case would gain from a preparatory inventory.

This decision was disastrous. The market did not rebound. In the fourth quarter of 1990, Case's earnings were off by nearly $100 million and the year ended with a $42 million decline in operating profits. Part of this decline was due to a weakened dollar, which raised imported parts costs. Though Ashford was credited for Case's turnaround in 1989 and for replacing 80 percent of its divisions' managers and reviving a sluggish management, he resigned suddenly.

Losses continued in 1991 as Case scrambled to cut personnel by 5,000 and production schedules by as much as 23 percent. Sales were up, but discounts cut deeply into profits. Case ended 1991 with a $618 million operating loss.

Case had become a serious problem for Tenneco when Robert J. Carlson assumed the presidency in 1991. Carlson had spent nearly 30 years at Deere and inspired confidence at Case. The company announced extended factory shutdowns at all of its ten domestic plants and closure of some of its European facilities. Case had restructuring charges of $461 million in 1991. Added to Case's operating losses for that year, the loss was a staggering $1.1 billion. While Deere and Caterpillar had suffered from the extended recession as well, their trimmed production left them in better shape than Case. Tenneco executives, in fact, were so exasperated by the situation at Case that they offered to sell the subsidiary for $1 to anyone who was willing to assume the hefty $1 billion debt load; there were no takers.

Talk of further reducing the workforce by 4,000 employees started in 1992, when Edward J. Campbell assumed the presidency of Case. Campbell's approach to downsizing was different: he did not just slash, he reorganized and cut from the top, dismissing 21 of the company's 43 officers. Various European factories were closed or sold, including the Poclain plant at Carvin. An agreement was made with Sumitomo Heavy Industries of Japan to make midsized excavators for the North American market. Japan was an increasing presence in the agricultural and construction equipment industries.

These measures helped reduce losses for 1992, but revenues were also down. Operating losses were reduced by about 75 percent while agricultural equipment sales were down by about 30 percent. The year closed with revenues of $3.8 billion, and operating losses of $260 million, not including restructuring charges. From a high of 30,000 in 1990, Case's employees now numbered 18,600.

The farm economy appeared to have stabilized at the end of 1992, but construction equipment sales were sluggish. All manufacturers suffered from weak pricing, lower unit volume, the economic slump overseas, and cautious dealers. Caterpillar had a sales increase, but Deere and Case both reported losses. Though Case's performance improved, its progress was uneven, with profits in the second quarter of 1992 and losses in the third. Tenneco announced a $2 billion restructuring plan to revamp Case into three divisions: sales and marketing, manufacturing, and engineering. Jean-Pierre Rosso became president and chief executive of Case in 1993.

Mid-1990s: Case's Recovery and Short-Lived Return to Independence

Case launched a three-year, $920 million restructuring program in March 1993. The program involved further plant closings and consolidations, revitalizing new product development with a renewed emphasis on customer input, abandoning money-losing product lines (such as smaller tractors and heavy construction equipment), and the gradual privatization of the 250 Case dealerships owned by the company. Sales of farm equipment were up by the summer of 1993, especially large tractor sales. Most farmers had not purchased new tractors or combines since the farming boom in the 1970s. Case announced that its 1993 combine production was sold out by June, but its Racine tractor plant was closed for 17 weeks following a $17 million loss in the first quarter of that year. The heavy equipment markets were proclaimed healthy by the end of 1993. The year ended well for Case: operating income was $82 million in 1993, an improvement over its operating loss of $260 million the previous year, and revenues were $3.7 billion. Case was aided by a vast reduction in inventories, higher retail pricing, and increased demand for new products late in the year.

Case appeared to have recovered fully by 1994, as revenues increased to $4.3 billion while net income tripled to $165 million. The health of the company was also evident in Tenneco's successful sale of 56 percent of Case Corporation stock to the public during 1994, marking Case's first return to the public trading arena in nearly 30 years. During 1995 Tenneco further decreased its ownership of Case to 21 percent, then sold this remaining stake in March 1996, completing Case's return to independence.

Under Rosso's continued leadership, the revitalized Case adopted a more aggressive approach to developing new farm and construction equipment, earmarking $835 million in new product spending for 1996 through 1998, more than double the amount spent in the early 1990s. At the same time, Case also pursued growth—particularly abroad—through acquisition and joint ventures. The company in 1995 had already entered the burgeoning market in China through the establishment of a joint venture with a leading Chinese construction equipment firm, Guangxi Liugong Machinery Co. Ltd., to make and market Case loader/backhoes. In 1996 and 1997 Case completed 11 acquisitions, nine of which were of agricultural equipment companies with the others being makers of construction equipment. Among the firms purchased in 1996 were Australia-based Austoft Holdings Limited, the world-leading maker of sugar cane harvesting equipment, with annual sales of $74 million; Steyr Landmaschinentechnik GmbH, an Austrian tractor manufacturer with annual sales of $176 million; and U.K. construction equipment maker Fermec Holdings Ltd., which had annual revenues of $154 million. In 1997 Case acquired Fortschritt Erntemaschinen GmbH, a German maker of harvesting equipment, and the assets of two other German firms;

the combined annual sales of the products acquired was about $110 million. The new and acquired products helped Case increase its revenues to a record $6 billion in 1997 while the company's cost-consciousness led to record net income that year of $403 million.

By 1998, however, economic difficulties in Asia and Russia, which reduced the grain exports of U.S. farmers, coupled with three straight years of record crops, drastically reduced crop prices—to 20-year lows—and in turn sharply depressed demand for farm equipment. Agricultural equipment makers, including Case, began once again laying off workers. In 1998 Case fired or laid off 2,100 workers; then, late that year, it said that it planned to lay off 1,300 more employees by the end of 1999. The latest downturn in the agricultural equipment market also led to pressure for consolidation within the industry as one way to cut production overcapacity and lessen competition, and in May 1999 Case agreed to be acquired by New Holland N.V.

The Origins of New Holland

New Holland's roots can be traced back to 1895, when handyman Abe Zimmerman made his first feed mill at his New Holland, Pennsylvania, repair shop. Zimmerman soon began making other agricultural products as well. He called his operation the New Holland Machine Company and incorporated it in 1903, the same year Henry Ford incorporated the automobile company he had started up in Detroit. Ford came out with the prototype for the world's first mass-produced agricultural tractor in 1907, and ten years later the tractor, known as the Fordson Model F, went into actual production. Decades later, these two fledgling operations would become linked.

Meanwhile, across the Atlantic, Italian auto maker Fiat was developing a tractor of its own. That company's efforts resulted in the development of the 702, Fiat's first mass-produced tractor, which hit the market in 1919. In Belgium, another company, Claeys, was entering the picture. Founded in 1906, Claeys began manufacturing harvesting equipment in 1910. Back in the United States, Zimmerman's New Holland company was also thriving. It continued to do well until about 1930, when the Great Depression began to hit rural America hard. As farm income plummeted, so did New Holland's revenue.

Sperry Takes Over in 1947

After about a decade of struggle, New Holland was purchased by a group of four investors. The new owners were able to turn the company around quickly by introducing a new product, the world's first successful automatic pick-up, self-tying hay baler. The baler, invented by local thresherman Ed Nolt, was an instant hit among farmers. It almost singlehandedly put New Holland back on solid footing, and balers were a key company product line into the 21st century.

In 1947 New Holland Machine Company was acquired by electronics specialist Sperry Corporation, creating a subsidiary dubbed Sperry New Holland. In the years that followed, Sperry New Holland developed and manufactured a large number of agricultural machines. In particular, the company carved out a niche as a producer of high-quality harvesting equipment. Things were also developing quickly in the European agricultural equipment industry during this period. In 1952 Claeys unveiled the first European self-propelled combine harvester. By the early 1960s, Claeys was one of the biggest combine manufacturers in Europe. Sperry New Holland bought a major interest in Claeys in 1964. The same year, Sperry New Holland made a major breakthrough in hay harvesting technology with the introduction of the haybine mower-conditioner, model 460. This machine was capable of performing tasks that previously required two or three separate pieces of equipment. New Holland would go on to revolutionize harvesting equipment in 1974, with the introduction of the world's first twin rotor combine.

As the 1960s continued, Fiat became increasingly active in the manufacture of equipment for agriculture and construction. Late in the decade, that company created a Tractor and Earthmoving Machinery Division. Fiat's earthmoving segment was moved into its own subsidiary, Fiat Macchine Movimento Terra S.p.A., in 1970. Fiat continued to move further into heavy equipment through the 1970s. In 1974 Fiat Macchine Movimento Terra launched a joint venture with American manufacturer Allis Chalmers Corporation, called Fiat-Allis. That year also marked the creation of the company's Fiat Trattori S.p.A. subsidiary. Fiat finally gained entry into the North American market in 1977, with the acquisition of Hesston, a Kansas-based manufacturer of hay and forage machinery. Fiat also purchased Agrifull, a small-sized tractor manufacturer, that year. In 1984 Fiat consolidated all of its agricultural machinery manufacturing under the umbrella of Fiatagri, the new name for Fiat Trattori.

The 1980s Belong to Ford

All the while, Ford was also becoming a global force in agricultural equipment. Its Ford Tractor division had been responsible for a number of industry breakthroughs, including the use of rubber pneumatic tires, power hydraulics, diesel engines, and the three-point hitch. Ford's inexpensive tractors had been largely responsible for the replacement of horses and mules by machines on United States farms over the first several decades of the 20th century. By 1985 Ford Tractor had 9,000 employees, about one-third of them located in North America, and 5,000 dealers worldwide, again about a third of them in the United States.

In 1986 Ford purchased Sperry New Holland and merged it with its Ford Tractor Operations to create a new company, Ford New Holland, Inc. By this time New Holland had grown to become one of the best performing companies in the farm equipment business, with 2,500 dealers and more than 9,000 employees of its own, working in 100 different countries. The merger was part of an overall consolidation taking place in the farm equipment industry at the time, occurring just one year after Case took over International Harvester. With combined annual sales of $2 billion, the new company made Ford the third largest farm equipment manufacturer in the world. Most of Ford Tractor's executives and managers were moved over to New Holland's Pennsylvania offices, which became Ford New Holland's corporate headquarters.

Within months of this merger, Ford New Holland added on the agricultural division of Versatile Farm and Equipment Co., an agricultural equipment manufacturer that had been founded in Canada in 1947. The combination of Ford's tractors, New Holland's harvesters, and Versatile's large four-wheel-drive machines created a company that produced a wide spectrum of agricultural equipment, and, best of all, there was almost no overlap in what the three entities manufactured and, therefore, little pruning to be done once they were united. One of the few major changes at New Holland was the gradual elimination of its company-store system. Between 1987 and 1989, New Holland's 53 company-owned outlets were sold off or closed, in favor of a dealer development program that provided training and assistance for independent dealers.

Back in Europe, changes were also taking place at Fiat. In 1988 the activities of Fiat-Allis and Fiatagri were merged to form a new company, FiatGeotech S.p.A., which now encompassed Fiat's entire farm and earthmoving equipment sector. By the end of the 1980s, Fiat was Europe's leading manufacturer of tractors and hay and forage equipment. FiatGeotech's revenue for 1989 was $2.3 billion.

1990s: The Fiat Era

By 1990 Ford New Holland had 17,000 employees, revenue of $2.8 billion, and plants in the United States, Canada, Belgium, England, and Brazil, plus joint ventures in India, Pakistan, Japan, Mexico, and Venezuela. In 1991 Fiat purchased an 80 percent interest in Ford New Holland. Ford New Holland was merged with FiatGeotech to create a huge new industrial equipment entity dubbed N.H. Geotech—though its North American operation kept the name Ford New Holland for the time being. The purchase surprised nobody in the industry, since Ford had been looking for a buyer for its tractor operation for the better part of a decade. The new international behemoth, headquartered in London, instantly became the world's largest producer of tractors and haying equipment, the second largest producer of combines, and one of the largest producers of diesel engines.

Between 1991 and 1993, the company undertook a number of measures designed to better integrate its many pieces into a coherent whole. Among the goals of this group of projects were a reduction in the time needed to bring new products to market and to focus manufacturing operations on core components. The company's supply chain was also streamlined. N.H. Geotech changed its name to New Holland N.V. in January 1993, although the company's North American operation stuck with the Ford New Holland moniker for two more years. The year 1993 also brought the introduction of the company's Genesis line of 140- to 210-horsepower tractors. The Genesis line proved so popular that it took only a little more than two years to sell 10,000 of them.

New Holland made the completion of its integration process official at its 1994 worldwide convention, at which the company unveiled its new corporate identity and logo. For that year, the company reported net income of $355 million on sales of $4.7 billion. Fiat eventually acquired the other 20 percent of New Holland previously owned by Ford, and in 1995, the 100th anniversary of the New Holland brand name, Ford New Holland was rechristened New Holland North America.

Operating as a wholly owned subsidiary of Fiat, New Holland brought in just more than $5 billion in sales in 1995. By this time, the company controlled 21 percent of the world market for agricultural tractors, 17 percent of the world market for combines, 42 percent of the market for forage harvesters, and significant shares of the world markets for just about every other category of agricultural or construction equipment one could name.

An IPO in 1996

By 1996 New Holland was selling about 280 different products in 130 countries around the world. Globally, 5,600 dealers were selling the company's agricultural equipment and 250 were peddling its construction machinery. During the last quarter of that year, Fiat sold 31 percent of New Holland's stock, 46.5 million common shares, to the public at $21.50 per share, to raise capital to bolster its sagging core automobile business. On November 1, the first day New Holland stock was traded on the New York Stock Exchange, it was the most heavily traded stock on the market.

In addition to the stock offering, 1996 also brought a number of technological innovations and new product unveilings as well. New Holland's new E-Series backhoe-loaders were chosen by *Construction Equipment* magazine as one of the construction industry's 100 most significant products. The company also introduced several new tractor lines, four Roll-Best round balers, and two large self-propelled forage harvesters. New Holland was also active in conducting research on futuristic, driverless machines. Working with NASA and Carnegie Mellon University as part of the NASA Robotics Engineering Consortium, New Holland created a prototype of a self-propelled windrower that cuts, conditions, and puts alfalfa into windrows without requiring a human operator. One further 1996 development at New Holland was the appointment of former U.S. Treasury Secretary and Vice Presidential candidate Lloyd Bentsen as its chairman of the board.

In July 1997, the 25,000th New Holland Twin Rotor combine rolled off the company's Grand Island, Nebraska assembly line. As the year continued, the company announced the creation of a new Boomer line of light diesel tractors, including four brand new models. Building on its longstanding philosophy of manufacturing products close to where they were sold, the company moved production of the light tractors from Japan to a new facility in Dublin, Georgia. The launch of the Boomer line reflected New Holland's commitment to the production of the kind of compact but powerful machines sought by customers for a variety of off-highway uses.

New Holland + Case = CNH Global

New Holland, like Case, was buffeted by the downturn in the worldwide agricultural equipment market in the late 1990s, and cut its workforce by 1,300 during the second half of 1998. The company in early 1999 announced that it would make further job cuts, then in May agreed to acquire Case. Completed in November 1999, the $4.6 billion acquisition involved the purchase by New Holland of all of Case's stock at $55 per share. Fiat thereby maintained its 71.1 percent stake in the new New Holland, which was renamed CNH Global N.V. A symbol of globalization at the turn of the millennium, CNH was incorporated in the Netherlands, headquartered in Racine, Wisconsin (adopting Case's headquarters), had its stock traded on the New York Stock Exchange, and was majority owned by an Italian automaker. Rosso, a Frenchmen, was named cochairman and CEO, while the head of New Holland, Umberto Quadrino, an Italian, was the other cochairman.

As a condition of approval of the merger, the European Commission required CNH to divest itself of four business lines, including Fermec Holdings. CNH also began consolidating the operations of its predecessor companies, aiming to generate annual cost savings of around $500 million within three to four years. In early 2000 the company announced that it would close or sell ten of its 46 manufacturing plants around the world, cutting its 36,000-person workforce by 7,000. CNH also planned, within a few years, to reduce the number of chassis platforms used in its various products from 50 to about 35. With commodity prices remaining depressed and sales of large tractors and harvesting combines in the United States down ten to 15 percent, CNH warned in June 2000 that it was expecting to post a loss of $90 million for its first full year of operation, before restructuring charges. In July 2000 the company announced that it would close its manufacturing plants in Racine by 2004, ending production of tractors in the city most identified with the Case side of CNH. The painful nature of the integration of New Holland and Case was becoming increasingly evident and indicated that the emergence of CNH as a formidable competitor to Deere, Caterpillar, and other rivals was not likely to occur until well into the first decade of the 21st century.

Principal Competitors

AGCO Corporation; Caterpillar Inc.; Deere & Company; Komatsu Ltd.

Further Reading

Bas, Ed, "Ford New Holland's Goal: The Blue Tractor Pulling a Red Harvester," *Ward's Auto World,* June 1987, p. 72.

Deutsch, Claudia, "Former BMC Chairman Assumes Post at Case," *New York Times,* July 23, 1991, p. D4.

Eiben, Therese, "How the Industries Stack Up," *Fortune,* July 12, 1993, p. 102.

Erb, David, and Eldon Brumbaugh, *Full Steam Ahead: J.I. Case Tractors and Equipment, 1842–1955,* St. Joseph, Mich.: American Society of Agricultural Engineers, 1993, 343 p.

Fisher, Lawrence, "Tenneco Names Head of Its J.I. Case Unit," *New York Times,* December 7, 1991, p. 39.

Fogarty, Bill, "Ford New Holland: Out of the Company Store Business," *Implement and Tractor,* July 1989, p. 15.

"Ford New Holland Here to Stay," *Construction Equipment,* March 1994, p. 14.

Gaines, Sallie L., "Here's a Case of Good Results," *Chicago Tribune,* May 30, 1999.

Gilpin, Kenneth, "Chief at Troubled J.I. Case Stepping Down," *New York Times,* September 16, 1992, p. D4.

Hawkins, Lee, Jr., "Farming Trends Prompt CNH Cutbacks," *Milwaukee Journal Sentinel,* July 19, 2000, p. 15D.

Hayes, Thomas, "Head of Tenneco Unit to Quit All His Posts," *New York Times,* March 16, 1991, p. 33.

——, "J.I. Case Plans to Cut Work Force by 4,000," *New York Times,* December 5, 1991, p. D4.

Holbrook, Stewart H., *Machines of Plenty: Chronicle of an Innovator in Construction and Agricultural Equipment,* New York: Macmillan, 1955, 269 p., reprinted, 1976.

Holmes, Michael, *J.I. Case: The First 150 Years,* Racine, Wis.: Case Corporation, 1992, 200 p.

"The Impact of Ford New Holland's Buyout," *Agri Marketing,* September 1990, p. 18.

Johnson, Robert, "Tenneco Restructuring Is Over, but Doubts Remain," *Wall Street Journal,* September 8, 1992, p. B4.

——, "Tenneco's Plans to Restructure Case Unit Include $843 Million After-Tax Charge," *Wall Street Journal,* March 23, 1993, p. A3.

Kelly, Kevin, "Case Digs Out from Way Under," *Business Week,* August 14, 1995, pp. 62–63.

Krebs, Michelle, "New Holland Called a 'Natural' for Ford," *Automotive News,* October 21, 1985, p. 53.

Marsh, Peter, "Jean-Pierre Rosso Rolls Up His Sleeves at CNH," *Financial Times,* June 5, 2000, p. 23.

McKanic, Patricia Ann, "Tenneco's Ashford to Resign As Chief of Case Unit, Which He Turned Around," *Wall Street Journal,* March 18, 1991, p. B8.

McMurray, Scott, "Farm-Equipment Sales Are Running at Full Throttle," *Wall Street Journal,* June 15, 1993, p. B4.

Miller, James P., "Case Announces More Job Cuts As Demand Falls," *Wall Street Journal,* December 22, 1998, p. A3.

Nesbitt, Scott, "Ford, Fiat Merger Brings Speculation," *Implement and Tractor,* September 1990, p. 1.

"New Holland Grows As Global Leader," *Lancaster (Penn.) Sunday News,* March 23, 1997, p. 32.

"New Holland Marks 100th Anniversary," *Implement and Tractor,* May-June 1995, p. 26.

Osenga, Mike, "Case Corporation," *Diesel Progress Engines and Drives,* June 1992, p. 102.

——, "A Look at New Holland's New Tractors," *Diesel Progress,* July 1997, p. 10.

Raghavan, Anita, and Carl Quintanilla, "New Holland Agrees to Acquire Case for $4.2 Billion, Creating Rival to Deere," *Wall Street Journal,* May 17, 1999, p. A3.

Romell, Rick, "Racine Losing Its Case Tractor Plant," *Milwaukee Journal Sentinel,* July 19, 2000, p. 15A.

Savage, Mark, "Case Acquiring Global Influence," *Milwaukee Journal Sentinel,* October 12, 1997.

——, "Case to Lay Off 1,300 Workers," *Milwaukee Journal Sentinel,* December 22, 1998.

——, "Company Takes Best of All Worlds: Racine Farm Equipment Firm Has Global Look," *Milwaukee Journal Sentinel,* November 15, 1999.

——, "Deere Reaps Profits As CNH Stumbles," *Milwaukee Journal Sentinel,* August 16, 2000, p. 15D.

——, "Farm Equipment Slide Feeds Talk of Mergers," *Milwaukee Journal Sentinel,* May 16, 1999.

——, "Sale of Case Would Form Ag Giant," *Milwaukee Journal Sentinel,* May 18, 1999.

——, "Tenneco Cutting Link to Case: Move Will Leave Racine Firm Independent for the First Time Since 1964," *Milwaukee Journal Sentinel,* February 23, 1996.

Solomon, Caleb, "Tenneco Plans to Sell 35 Percent of Case Unit to Public, on Revival in Agriculture," *Wall Street Journal,* April 27, 1994, p. A2.

Stonehouse, Tom, and Eldon Brumbaugh, *J.I. Case Agricultural and Construction Equipment, 1956–1994,* St. Joseph, Mich.: American Society of Agricultural Engineers, [1996].

Sturani, Maria, ''Fiat's Offering of New Holland Shares Expected to Swell Coffers by $1 Billion,'' *Wall Street Journal,* November 4, 1996, p. B11.

Tait, Nikki, ''The Case for Working from a Platform,'' *Financial Times,* June 1, 1999, p. 27.

''Tenneco in Plan to Revamp Case,'' *New York Times,* January 23, 1992, p. D4.

Verespej, Michael A., ''An Abrupt Turnaround,'' *Industry Week,* April 15, 1996, pp. 62–64, 66.

Wyatt, Edward A., ''Case Reopened,'' *Barron's,* June 6, 1994, pp. 14–15.

—Robert R. Jacobson and Carol I. Keeley
—updated by David E. Salamie

CPI Corp.

1706 Washington Avenue
St. Louis, Missouri 63103
U.S.A.
Telephone: (314) 231-1575
Fax: (314) 621-9286
Web site: http://www.cpicorp.com

Public Company
Incorporated: 1942 as Rembrandt Studio
Employees: 8,500
Sales: $319.1 million (1999)
Stock Exchanges: New York
Ticker Symbol: CPY
NAIC: 541921 Photography Studios, Portrait

CPI Corp. is a consumer services company best known for its chain of photography studios located inside Sears stores. CPI operates close to 1,000 Sears Portrait Studios in the United States and Canada, and approximately 65 more photography studios located in malls or other non-Sears locations. The company has been an exclusive Sears concessionaire since 1973, and its chain of portrait studios grew alongside the larger retailer. About 90 percent of the U.S. population lives within 30 minutes of a Sears store, so CPI has gained vast market exposure through its Sears relationship. CPI controls a major share of the preschool portrait market in the United States. It offers professional portraiture, with pictures ranging from wallet size to 16″ by 20″. CPI also produces passport photos and photo greeting cards, and sells photographic accessories such as picture frames and albums. The company had related consumer services businesses until the late 1990s. CPI ran a chain of one-hour photofinishing labs across the country until 1997, and it also operated quick printing shops until 1996. CPI announced that a chain of poster and framing stores it owned, called Prints Plus, was up for sale in 2000. CPI has been a public company since 1982. A 1999 private buyout arrangement fell through.

Small Beginnings

The company that became CPI Corp. began as a single photography studio in St. Louis, Missouri. It was opened by Milford Bohm in 1942, and he called it Rembrandt Studio. Bohm and his family expanded the business over the next decade, opening a chain of portrait studios. By the late 1950s there were 20 Rembrandt Studios spread across the middle of the country from Wichita, Kansas, to York, Pennsylvania. Besides opening new studios, the business also expanded by sending single photographers out across the countryside to take pictures wherever people would pay for them. CEO Alyn Essman described the early business in a June 6, 1983 interview with *Forbes* magazine: "We'd hire a young guy, put him in a car with a camera and ship him out. A year later he might get home." In addition to hiring traveling cameramen and opening new shops, Rembrandt Studios established relationships with several mass merchandisers including Montgomery Ward and Sears. The portrait studio operated out of the stores, as a concession. The big chain stores pressed into numerous locations, and both the stores and the portrait studios benefited from mutual promotions.

Producing finished portraits was a laborious business, requiring the customer to make several trips. The photographer would set up the shot and take a series of pictures. After these proofs were developed, the customer had to return to the studio to decide which ones he or she wanted printed. And then the customer had to make yet another trip to pick up the portraits when they were done. Rembrandt came up with a revolutionary finishing system in 1964, allowing the company to produce finished portraits in a variety of sizes in much less time. The next year, Rembrandt also began producing color portraits for the first time. Previously, color portraits had to be hand-tinted, and this was both costly and time-consuming.

Subsidiary Company in the 1970s

Rembrandt Studios flourished, expanding across the country and increasing the sophistication of its services. But it needed greater financial backing in order to grow more. In 1968, founder Milford Bohm sold the family-owned company to a larger company called Chromalloy American Corp. Bohm continued to head the company, which was renamed Chromalloy Photographic Industries, or CPI Corp. (the acronym would ultimately be redefined as Consumer Programs Incorporated). Chromalloy American was a St. Louis-based conglomerate that

Company Perspectives:

Founded in 1942, CPI has long been the recognized market leader in preschool portrait photography. As the exclusive Sears Portrait Studio concessionaire in a continuing 40-year partnership, CPI operates over 1,000 studios—962 in all major Sears stores in the U.S. and Canada and 65 in non-Sears shopping centers. Throughout this long period, CPI and Sears have worked together in creating the mass portrait market, progressing from traveling photographers to permanent studios, developing pre-printed full-color portrait packages and introducing services based on state-of-the-art technology such as the exclusive Portrait Preview System.

had grown to own hundreds of subsidiaries in industries as diverse as metal fabrication and men's and women's clothing. The company owned barges and textile mills, made gas turbines, and offered financial services. As a subsidiary of Chromalloy American, CPI had access to its parent company's deep pockets to fund a larger rollout of products and locations. The year before the buyout, Rembrandt had established its first permanent mall studio, a store called Children's Photographer in Evergreen Plaza in Chicago. The company saw the suburban mall as the place to be, and opened more mall stores over the next few years. CPI gradually phased out its traveling photographers, and continued to work with Sears, Montgomery Ward, and other chain retailers. CPI began operating portrait studios in Canada in 1970, working again through the Sears chain.

In 1973, CPI President and CEO Milford Bohm decided to give up the company's other retail accounts and work exclusively with Sears. Sears by that time was the leading retailer in the world, and CPI had portrait studios in hundreds of Sears stores. But there were hundreds of other Sears locations that would become available to CPI if it could negotiate an exclusive deal. So CPI resigned its accounts with Montgomery Ward and other retailers, and asked Sears for approximately 300 square feet of floor space in all possible locations. In exchange, CPI agreed to pay 15 percent of each studio's gross sales to the retailer. CPI would benefit from national advertising and the prominence of the Sears name, and Sears would collect a much higher amount of sales per square foot on the space it allocated to CPI than on the rest of its store. CPI packed a lot of business into its corner of the store, and turned over about $450 per square foot on average, versus a little less than $300 per square foot on average for the rest of the store.

The new relationship with Sears worked well for CPI. Milford Bohm resigned in 1973, and Alyn Essman, a longtime accountant with the company, took over the top job. Under Essman, the CPI chain grew to include roughly 400 Sears locations by the end of the 1970s. Essman was keen to expand more. However, he ran into resistance from CPI's parent, Chromalloy American. The parent was not as eager to back its subsidiary as it had once been, and Essman and other CPI executives faced a yearly struggle to get their growth plans approved. CPI was just one facet of a sprawling business, and Chromalloy was undergoing major changes following the death of its founder in 1977. Tired of fighting for approval of its expansion, Essman decided to split from the conglomerate. In 1979 Essman and ten other CPI executives pooled their assets and raised $1 million in cash and an additional $6 million in preferred stock, and bought CPI from Chromalloy.

Expansion into Other Businesses in the 1980s

Free from the constraints of the parent company, CPI began to grow in new ways. The company had enticed customers into its portrait studios by offering a low-priced deal, and then made money when it was able to sell additional sets of prints or other services. However, many customers settled for the cheap deal alone, meaning CPI's profits were low. In 1979, the average customer spent only $14, and those taking just the loss-leader bargain spent only 99 cents. Essman eliminated the bargain, which resulted in lower costs and an actual increase in the amount of services sold. CPI also moved into selling other services, on the advice of Sears. The company began viewing itself as a customer service company rather than a photography business, and it tried to reach Sears shoppers by offering residential carpet cleaning and upholstery cleaning. CPI hoped to diversify into several complementary business lines, and in 1981 it acquired a small firm that marketed office telephone systems. The bulk of CPI's business remained its Sears portrait studios, and by the mid-1980s it had roughly 700 studios in the United States and Canada. The company went public in 1982. It was making money extravagantly, with sales tripling between 1979 and 1983, and per share earning over those four years was growing at a 78 percent compounded annual rate.

By the mid-1980s, it was clear that the market for Sears portrait studios was slowing down. There were simply not enough Sears stores left to accommodate CPI's earlier growth rate. CPI opened over 100 studios in 1980, then 60 in 1981, 36 in 1982, and then only 21 in 1983. The studios continued to be highly profitable at both old and new locations. In fact CPI was far more profitable than Sears itself. But the company seemed to need something else to shore it up, as its market matured. In 1984 CPI bought the first of several sets of photographic finishing labs, chains of ''photomats'' or ''mini-labs'' that offered consumers finished photographs in one hour. CPI had great hopes for its mini-labs. It hoped to build or acquire hundreds of the labs, looking for prime shopping mall locations. In 1985 CPI divested itself of its residential cleaning business and its office telephone business, and focused on the photofinishing labs. The labs lost money at first, not turning a profit until 1986. By that time, CPI had put together a chain of 180 labs, and was one of the biggest players in the market.

CPI entered another new market in 1988. It bought part of a chain of quick printing shops in California, acquiring 17 CopyMat stores in California for $10 million. By the end of 1988, CPI had bought more California CopyMat franchises and opened its own quick print shop in St. Louis, Copy USA. Quick printing seemed roughly analogous to the mini-lab market CPI had entered a few years earlier. The quick printing industry was growing rapidly, and it was extremely fragmented, split among thousands of small shop owners. CPI hoped to build itself into a major player in the market, just as it had with photographic finishing. The company entered into an agreement with CopyMat to open more locations, and it used CopyMat as a

Key Dates:

1942: First Rembrandt Studio is founded in St. Louis.
1968: Business is sold to Chromalloy American; corporate name is changed to CPI.
1973: CPI becomes exclusive Sears concessionaire.
1979: Chromalloy sells CPI to executive group.
1982: CPI becomes a public company.
1984: Company enters photofinishing business.
1988: Company enters quick printing business.
1997: CPI divests itself of most non-portrait photography business lines.
1999: New York investment firm withdraws from buyout agreement with CPI.

model for the stores it was operating under the Copy USA name. These stores offered high-quality photocopying and desktop publishing, binding, mailing, and other services. The industry was estimated to be worth $4.5 billion total, and it was expected to grow rapidly in the 1990s.

Meanwhile, CPI's portrait studio business continued to be highly profitable. The amount customers spent on average increased to $48 per portrait session by the end of the 1980s, up from only $14 a decade earlier. The company was so profitable that it was a potential takeover target, and CPI took pains to buy back some of its stock in 1989, to discourage an unwelcome acquisition. The company also found some new market niches. It opened a chain of portrait studios geared for upscale department stores, called Portraits of Distinction, and also embarked on a joint venture with a department store-based gift wrapping business called Tender Sender. Though these new businesses were not immediately profitable, they were illustrative of the company's attempts to diversify as it reached an inevitable plateau in the number of new Sears portrait studios it could open.

Divesting Businesses in the 1990s

By the mid-1990s, CPI was the biggest operator of one-hour photofinishing labs in the country. It had acquired Fox Photo in 1991, which gave CPI another 300 mini-labs. CPI also had a significant business in quick printing shops. The company had also moved into poster framing with its acquisition in 1993 of a 102-store chain called Prints Plus. The new businesses began contributing a larger portion of the company's earnings, bringing in around 40 percent by the mid-1990s.

The profitability of the portrait studios started to fall in the 1990s, as more and more competitors moved into the market. J.C. Penney, Kmart, and Wal-Mart all began opening their own in-store photographic studios in the late 1980s, and by 1993 there were 2,500 rival studios in the United States and Canada. CPI ran about 1,000 portrait studios at that time. Increasing competition had brought about price cuts. Though CPI had close to 30 percent of the family portrait market, its operating margins fell. Profits from its portrait studio business went from $34 million in 1990 to $23 million in 1992. In 1993 CPI vowed to invest $50 million on upgrading its studios over the next year, and planned to spend another $75 million by the end of the decade. CPI began adopting digital imaging technology in the mid-1990s, hoping to gain a technological edge over its competitors. In 1994 it announced its Portrait Preview System, a digital imaging system that let customers see what their pictures would look like before they were snapped. In 1995 CPI began further development of digital photography at its Sears studios.

Heightened competition had forced CPI into lower operating margins, and made the company spend money on technological improvements. CPI had spread itself into three major operating divisions—photography studios, photo finishing, and quick printing—in order to cushion itself against a slow-down in its portrait business. Yet by 1996, the company had changed its outlook. It now began to focus on photography studios as its core business. It sold off its quick printing operations for $4.8 million in 1996, getting the company out of that business entirely. In 1996 CPI also agreed to sell 51 percent of its Fox Photo photofinishing business to Eastman Kodak for $56 million. At the same time, CPI sold off 50 of its poorer performing photo labs. In 1997 CPI went ahead and sold the remaining 49 percent of Fox Photo to Kodak.

The sell-offs left CPI with its portrait studios and its chain of Prints Plus poster and framing stores. Seeking to mollify stockholders disappointed with the company's decreasing profitability, CPI put itself up for sale. In 1999 a New York-based investment firm called American Securities Capital Partners agreed to buy out CPI for $482 million. The deal was expected to close at the end of October, but American Securities pulled out several weeks shy of the deadline. The buyout group claimed that reported lower-than-expected third quarter earnings represented a development that would significantly hurt profits. Both American Securities and CPI sued each other over the collapse of the agreement.

In 2000, CPI announced that its Prints Plus chain was for sale. A group formed by top managers of the chain negotiated to buy the business, but talks terminated in August and CPI continued to look for other possible buyers. Meanwhile CPI concentrated on controlling its costs and implementing its new technology to bolster its portrait business. By its second quarter of 2000, the company recorded earnings higher than in any year since 1992, when competitors began to squeeze CPI badly. Though sales continued to be lackluster, the increasing level of profitability sounded a hopeful note. The company had lost money in 1999, but CPI seemed to be returning to profitability again in 2000, even without a big increase in sales.

Principal Competitors

Lifetouch Portrait Studios Inc.; PCA International Inc.; Olan Mills Inc.

Further Reading

Burgert, Philip, and Gerry Khermouth, "Chromalloy Gets in Trim for Profits," *American Metal Market*, October 3, 1983, p. 5.

Byrne, John A., "Profits from Portraits," *Forbes*, June 6, 1983, pp. 107–108.

Curley, John, "CPI to Buy 32 More One-Hour Minilabs for Photofinishing," *Wall Street Journal*, January 4, 1984, p. 30.

Derks, Sarah A., ''CPI Focuses on Sears Studios with $75 Million Spending Plan,'' *St. Louis Business Journal*, December 27, 1993, p. 1A.

''Fox Photo to Be Acquired by Concern for $62 Million,'' *Wall Street Journal*, July 19, 1991, p. C14.

Moore, Rob, ''CPI Enlarging Picture with 60 New Sites,'' *St. Louis Business Journal*, May 28, 1990, p. 15A.

——, ''CPI Ignores Skeptics, 15 Quick Print Stores Opening,'' *St. Louis Business Journal*, March 12, 1990, p. 4C.

——, ''CPI Opens Copy USA Store, Expands Franchises to 22,'' *St. Louis Business Journal*, December 26, 1988, p. 9A.

Rosenberg, Hilary, ''CPI and Sears,'' *Financial World*, August 22, 1984, p. 17.

''Sitting Pretty,'' *Barron's*, March 19, 1984, pp. 46–47.

Slovak, Julianne, ''CPI Corp.,'' *Fortune*, March 13, 1989, p. 73.

Slutsker, Gary, ''Look at the Birdie and Say 'Cash Flow',''' *Forbes*, October 25, 1993, pp. 100–02.

Stamborski, Al, ''New York-Based Investment Firm's Reversal on Takeover May Spark Suits,'' *Knight-Ridder/Tribune Business News*, October 13, 1999, p. OKRB99286187.

Troxell, Thomas N., Jr., ''Striking Pose,'' *Barron's*, February 17, 1986, pp. 88–89.

''Where Pictures Help the Earnings Picture,'' *Fortune*, June 23, 1986, pp. 132–137.

—A. Woodward

Creative Artists Agency LLC

9830 Wilshire Blvd.
Beverly Hills, California 90212
U.S.A.
Telephone: (310) 288-4545
Fax: (310) 288-4800
Web site: http://www.caa.com

Private Company
Incorporated: 1995
Employees: 400
Sales: $200 million (1999 est.)
NAIC: 71141 Agents and Managers for Artists; 711410 Literary Agents; 71132 Promoters of Performing Arts; 51224 Sound Recording Studios; 54189 Other Services Related to Advertising

As the entertainments industry's leading literary and talent agency from the mid-1970s through the mid 1990s, Creative Artists Agency LLC (CAA) represented the majority of top actors, writers, directors, producers, and performing artists in Hollywood. In the early 1990s, CAA expanded its business activities to include consulting relationships with several major U.S. and international corporations, among them Coca-Cola, for whom the agency developed a successful advertising campaign. It also brokered several entertainment mega-deals, such as the purchase of MCA by Matsushita and then Seagram, and the purchase of Columbia Pictures by Sony. CAA has divisions that oversee activities in film, television, music, new technology, and mergers and acquisitions. It has represented such well-known individuals as Meryl Streep, Tom Cruise, Dustin Hoffman, Barbra Streisand, Aaron Spelling, and David Kelley. The agency's revenues and assets are subject to considerable speculation.

Terrific Growth the First Four Years

Creative Artists Agency was founded in 1975 by five dissident talent agents employed by the William Morris Agency, the most powerful firm in ''the business'' at the time. Fed up with Morris's relatively low pay and slow pace of advancement, Michael Ovitz, Ron Meyer, William Haber, Michael Rosenfeld, and Rowland Perkins met over dinner one night after they discovered that they all had in mind creating an agency of their own. As Ovitz reminisced in a 1989 *New York Times* article, ''We all sang the same tune, and we came out of that dinner with a clear understanding of how we were going to do it.'' However, before they could obtain adequate financing for their new venture, they were fired.

By early 1975, Creative Artists Agency was in business, with a $100,000 line of credit and a $21,000 bank loan, in a small rented office outfitted with card tables and folding chairs. The five agents had only two cars among them, and their wives took turns as agency receptionist. Within about a week, according to one industry insider, they had sold their first three packages, a game show called ''Rhyme and Reason,'' the ''Rich Little Show,'' and the ''Jackson Five Show.''

At first, CAA's founders planned to form a medium-sized, full-service agency—one that was as unlike Morris as possible in approach and feel. Ovitz, who shortly assumed de facto leadership of the agency, described the company's corporate culture as a blend of Eastern philosophy and team sports. ''I liken myself to the guy running down the court with four other players and throwing the ball to the open guy,'' he once said. Theirs was a relaxed partnership based on teamwork, with proceeds shared equally. Clients enjoyed the services of a number of agents because at CAA information was pooled. There were no nameplates on doors, no formal titles, no individual agent client lists. Work practices followed the company's two ''commandments'': Be a team player and return phone calls promptly. There was an endless stream of meetings and talk. Because of this, others sometimes referred to CAA agents as the ''Moonies'' of the business, famous for ''walking in lock-step,'' according to the authors of *Hit and Run*, the bestseller Hollywood insider account by Griffin and Masters.

Four years later, CAA, still largely a television agency, was no longer a medium-sized company. It was the third largest agency in Hollywood, where it occupied a suite of offices in Century City. Competitive and hard-working, its agents carried off many former International Creative Management (ICM) clients, following a turnover in management there. CAA also

Key Dates:

1975: Michael Ovitz, Ron Meyer, Bill Haber, Rowland Perkins, and Michael Rosenfeld found Creative Artists Agency, Inc. (CAA).

1989: CAA commissions and erects a building designed by I.M. Pei; Ovitz brokers Sony Corporation's acquisition of Columbia Pictures Entertainment.

1990: Ovitz brokers Matsushita Electric Industrial Co.'s acquisition of MCA.

1991: CAA joins forces with The Coca-Cola Company as its worldwide media and communications partner.

1993: CAA teams up with Nike to create a global sports entertainment business; Credit Lyonnais hires CAA to help manage its entertainment portfolio.

1995: Ovitz brokers the sale of MCA to Seagram; Meyer and Ovitz leave CAA; Richard Lovett becomes the new president of CAA.

1996: CAA teams up with the Smithsonian to increase recognition and awareness of the museum; CAA creates a new multimedia facility in its headquarters with Intel.

1997: CAA partners with Joyce Ketay Agency in New York.

1999: CAA invests in Shephardson Stern and Kaminsky, a communications consulting and advertising company.

aggressively recruited other agencies' clients throughout the 1980s, paving the way, many later insisted, for the cutthroat atmosphere that would characterize Hollywood in the 1990s. CAA also gained ground by cutting, from ten to six percent, the price of television's packaged deals, whereby an agent supplied not only the talent, but filled all the necessary positions for producing a program and earned a share of syndication fees.

An Emerging Power in the Movie Business in the Late 1980s

With its stable full of actors and about $90 million in annual bookings in the late 1980s, the agency, led by Ovitz, decided to get into movies. Its timing again was propitious, and its approach to the business inventive: CAA used its growing leverage to apply packaging to the movies. Its letterhead, which presented it as a ''literary and talent agency,'' reminded all that CAA represented a large number of screenwriters as well as actors and directors. It was not only in a position to broker deals, but to supply material. Although the agency did not, like ICM and Morris, have an office in Manhattan, the center of the publishing industry, it was closely associated with Morton Janklow, a connection that later led to its involvement in the television miniseries format.

CAA's use of packaging changed the face of movie-making, making CAA increasingly powerful in the process. By 1989, CAA had built its own three-story building at the corner of Little Santa Monica and Wilshire Boulevards in Beverly Hills. The $25 million, 75,000-square-foot building, draped in honeyed travertine marble, tinted glass, and crisp white steel, was a paean to classical modernism. Designed by I.M. Pei and filled with works of commissioned art, it had a mural by Roy Lichtenstein in the lobby. According to Pei in a 1989 *Los Angeles Times* article, the building was designed to encourage ''the relaxed interaction that characterizes this agency, where around 200 creative people, engaged in the collective enterprise of making movies and television, can casually gather here, or cross overhead bridges that link the two halves of the building.''

By 1988, the agency pulled in revenues of an estimated $65 million and represented 146 directors, 134 actors, and 288 writers. By 1992, CAA's approximately 75 agents read scripts, suggested parts, and placed actors, writers, and directors in more than 100 titles a year. It was now in a position to control the studios, to the resentment of many studio heads, who did not like the way CAA made deals, insisting that along with desirable projects, they also had to take ''the dogs.'' Instead of the ten percent agents typically made on a contract, CAA insisted upon on a share in the product. Some, including David Geffen, blamed CAA in the press for throwing Hollywood's economy out of whack. Representing most of the major talent in the industry, CAA reputedly drove up salaries, and thus, the cost of making movies.

By the early 1990s, only three of the original five founders remained as owners—Ovitz, Meyer, and Haber. To the world, they were equal partners, but, in fact, Ovitz held a 55 percent share of the company in recognition of his having greater clout in the business. Meyer and Haber each held 22.5 percent shares. With Ovitz at the helm, CAA was now regarded as one of the most powerful presences in the industry, feared as well as respected by agents and talent alike. CAA's corporate culture was likened to everything from a Maoist camp to a fashionable frat house for its monolithic, secretive way of doing business. It expected its people to stay with the company, and both agents and talent reported being reluctant to leave CAA for fear that Ovitz and associates would hurt their future job prospects. Ovitz himself had become an industry icon, his face a familiar one in paparazzi photos.

Yet despite the fact that he repeatedly refused to be interviewed, rarely allowed himself to be quoted, and insisted that photographers sign an agreement not to sell pictures of him without his approval, much of Ovitz's private lifestyle and modus vivendi became public knowledge. He collected art, was exceptionally disciplined, always wore a tie, even after he arrived home in the evening to his wife—his former UCLA sweetheart—and their three children. He spoke in hushed tones, the better to command attention. In college, he had abandoned his pre-med studies after being introduced to ''the business'' during a stint as a summer tour guide at Universal Studios. Ovitz had joined the Morris Agency fresh out of college as a mail-room clerk in 1969 and had risen rapidly to specialize in representing television talent, despite a temporary leave to go to law school.

Ovitz started his day with an hour of aikido, followed by a working breakfast, a round of phone calls at the office, lunch at a Hollywood hangout, meetings back at the office, and a working dinner. During meetings, he frequently scribbled notes to himself. In the office, he used a headphone so that no one else could listen in to the conversation. The man, whose extreme sense of responsibility led him to abhor criticism, nonetheless was noted for a temper which he let fly at CAA's Monday and Wednesday staff meetings.

Mega-Deal Brokering in the Early 1990s

During the 1990s, Ovitz's focus expanded beyond that of Hollywood, and he carved out relationships with major New York financial figures, a move attributed in part to hard financial times in the industry, but also to his endless restlessness. After an early misstep with Archer Communications, whose QSound technology never became an industry standard, Ovitz helped negotiate Sony Corporation's $3.4 billion acquisition of Columbia Pictures Entertainment in 1989. A second blockbuster deal followed in 1990; with Ovitz as advisor to Matsushita Electric Industrial Co., the Japanese firm successfully courted and conquered MCA, owner of Universal Studios, in a $6.6 billion buyout. This deal earned CAA anywhere from $8 million to $40 million and garnered Ovitz the title of ''Mike the Manipulator'' in *Spy* magazine.

Another deal in 1990 gained CAA a ten percent interest in Mercantile National Bank, which then proceeded to lose more than half its value by 1992. In 1991, in a venture of a different sort, CAA joined forces with The Coca-Cola Company as its worldwide media and communications consultant in an effort to develop global strategies for marketing, promotion, and new technologies for the soft drink manufacturer and American icon. In 1993, CAA produced two series of commercials for Coke. Solidifying its move to Madison Avenue, CAA also teamed up with Nike in 1993 to create a global sports entertainment business, a series of events starring top athletes in live or made-for-TV specials to be broadcast by satellite. In 1995, CAA took on creative responsibility for Coke's Nestea brands.

The rest of the entertainment world watched in some awe as Ovitz expanded the reach and definition of the agency business. But in late March 1993, the industry cried ''conflict of interest'' when CAA announced that it had been hired by Crédit Lyonnais to help manage its deeply troubled $3.1 billion entertainment portfolio, which included management of its Metro-Goldwyn-Mayer studio. Observers feared that CAA would be able to use its access to the ledgers of Crédit Lyonnais's film companies to examine the deals made by rivals. CAA, for its part, insisted that it was advising Credit Lyonnais in matters of entertainment investing. The dispute ended in a compromise with the Hollywood unions.

By now, CAA divided its agents into two camps: traditional agents, who oversaw the careers of CAA's 1,000 stars, and specialists, whose expertise in investment banking and advertising made CAA into a one-stop shop for digital media. Founders Ron Meyer, in charge of CAA's film franchise, and William Haber, whose focus was on television, headed up the traditional staff, while Ray Kurtzman took on the responsibilities of CAA's chief lawyer, and Sandy Climan oversaw corporate finance. Robert Kavner, AT&T's vice-president for multimedia products and services, joined the staff to oversee new media work. CAA's first endeavor in this area was a late 1994 joint venture with three regional Bells to develop the programming and technology to allow consumers to receive video by telephone. Others in marketing and technology assisted Ovitz in brokering deals and creating new ventures, such as the 1994 association with N.S. Bienstock, which represented broadcast journalists, to blend entertainment and news, possibly launching talk shows and nonfiction projects.

The End of the Triumvirate: 1995

In 1995, Ovitz again brokered the sale of MCA, this time for $5.7 billion to Seagram Co., which offered Ovitz close to $250 million to become president of the entertainment conglomerate. When Ovitz, represented by Meyer, pushed for a better deal, Seagram turned around and offered the position to Meyer, who accepted it. Meyer moved to MCA in July 1995. Within a month, Ovitz, too, had accepted a position elsewhere, assuming the duties of Disney's number two chief executive under Michael Eisner, a longtime friend. Ovitz joined Disney's board and ran all three operating divisions of the company—its movie studio, theme parks, and consumer products/retail business, as well as television network owner Capital Cities/ABC, which Disney had just purchased.

The departure of both Meyer and Ovitz raised hope in the industry and fears in-house that CAA would lose talent to competitors. A transitional management group, representing CAA agents and management, appointed a four-person team with Richard Lovett as the new president; Lee Gabler, Rick Nicita, and Jack Rapke, all former department heads, became co-chairmen. The group also formed Creative Artists Agency LLC, whose employee shareholders, CAA's former staff, would buy out Ovitz, Meyer, and Haber over time using earned income.

W & S Properties, a partnership of CAA's principals, Ovitz, Meyer, and Haber, retained ownership of the building by I.M. Pei. The management team, which made decisions by committee, devised a four-point strategy for keeping competitors at bay during its transitional year: Make sure the 100-plus agents remain committed to the new CAA; re-sign longtime clients whose primary relationship was with Ovitz or Meyer; sign up new clients; and put together new movies.

Ovitz, Meyer, and Haber's departure led inevitably to an exodus of some of CAA's top-marquee names. CAA's television group was weakened that year, according to one network executive quoted in the *Los Angeles Times,* when two of its top agents left soon after Ovitz joined Disney. Another three agents left to join the upstart Endeavor agency in 1996. ''The balance of power is now shifting, opening the door for United Talent and Endeavor, and helping to build up the more established agencies like William Morris and ICM,'' said one industry observer in the wake of the changes, expressing the resentment many felt at CAA for its packaging prices and aggressive recruitment techniques.

Others lamented the turmoil that overtook Hollywood, describing the agency business as a free-for-all, its atmosphere more cutthroat than ever. Press reports quoted agents who admitted to spending 60 percent of their time chasing other agents' clients in the days following the shake-up at CAA. ''There's no more center of gravity around which everyone else in the business orbits,'' said one top business lawyer, quoted in the *New York Times* in May 1996. The diminishing profit margins, rising costs, the glut of movies, and flat attendance at theaters of the mid-1990s created a growing sense of distress and confusion in the movie business. Without CAA to lead the way, no one knew which way to turn.

Ovitz's departure also led to the termination of some of CAA's contracts. The Baby Bells terminated the interactive programming venture, TELE-TV, but retained CAA's Kavner and Griffiths as consultants. The CAA team of three that had been handling Coca-Cola Classic left to form an in-house ad agency for Coke in which they and Walt Disney would have minority stakes.

However, it was not long before new contracts came rolling in. In 1996, the Smithsonian and CAA forged a relationship on the occasion of the museum's 150th anniversary to increase the public's recognition and awareness of the Smithsonian through film, television, music, news media, and merchandising. Also in 1996, CAA joined with Intel Corporation to create a new multimedia facility in CAA's headquarters, an educational tool designed to teach CAA clients about new entertainment possibilities based on high-performance multimedia PCs. The lab was equipped with technology to enable users to create, distribute, and present digital entertainment.

In May 1997, CAA formed a partnership with the Joyce Ketay Agency in New York, which represented writers, directors, composers, choreographers, and designers, to offer CAA clients the chance to work with New York-based theater agents. In 1999, Shephardson Stern and Kaminsky, one of the fastest-growing communications consulting and advertising companies, formed a partnership with CAA to help corporate clients use popular culture and entertainment to differentiate brands.

From 1998 onward, the upheaval in the agency business intensified. Many artists, valuing their independence, began to reject the agency system, opting instead for representation by lawyers or personal managers. Seizing the opportunity, Ovitz, whose tenure at Disney had ended in December 1996 after only about 16 months, formed Artists Management Group (AMG) in 1999, in direct competition with CAA. CAA, which considered AMG a threat, refused to do business with Ovitz's group, forcing clients, in effect, to choose between the two. Some resisted, and left to rejoin Ovitz. Meyer personally voiced his support of CAA.

Still a force to be reckoned with in Hollywood, CAA was a very different place five years after Meyer and Ovitz's departure. No longer espousing the team approach, its agents now took on clients individually. Still powerful, with the largest stable of top talent in the business, it was yet unclear how it would fare in the years ahead. In 2000, Omnicom Group, one of the big three agency holding companies, seeking to expand its entertainment assets, targeted CAA for possible acquisition; however, no specific plans were made.

Principal Competitors

International Creative Management, Inc.; William Morris Agency, Inc.; Endeavor; United Talent; Artists Management Group.

Further Reading

Busch, Anita M., and Doug Galloway, "Philip F, Weltman," *Variety*, January 6–12, 1997, p. 184.

Citron, Alan, "Eating Hollywood Alive: The Insatiable Appetite and Other Deadly Sins of Mike Ovitz," *Los Angeles Times*, July 26, 1992, p. 12.

Davis, L.J., "Hollywood's Most Secret Agent," *New York Times*, July 9, 1989, p. 24.

Eller, Claudia, "Inheriting CAA Mantle Will Put Young Turks to the Test," *Los Angeles Times*, August 23, 1995, p. D1.

——, "Young Turks at CAA Poised to Take the Reins," *Los Angeles Times*, August 22, 1995, p. D1.

Eller, Claudia, and Sallie Hofmeister, "Company Town: Buzz Shifts to CAA Partner Bill Haber," *Los Angeles Times*, July 18, 1995, p. D4.

Grover, Ronald, "A Supporting Cast of Minimoguls," *Business Week*, August 9, 1993, p. 54.

Hirschberg, Lynn, "Michael Ovitz Is on the Line," *New York Times*, May 9, 1999, p. 46.

Wallace, Amy, "Hollywood Agents Lose the Throne," *Los Angeles Times*, December 11, 1998, p. A1.

—Carrie Rothburd

CSK Auto Corporation

645 E. Missouri Avenue, Suite 400
Phoenix, Arizona 85012-1373
U.S.A.
Telephone: (602) 265-9200
Fax: (602) 631-7231
Web site: http://www.cskauto.com

Public Company
Incorporated: 1987 as Northern Automotive
Employees: 14,810
Sales: $1.23 billion (2000)
Stock Exchanges: New York
Ticker Symbol: CAO
NAIC: 441310 Automotive Parts and Accessories Stores

CSK Auto Corporation is a holding company for CSK Auto, Inc., a subsidiary that manages all of the corporation's business from its headquarters in Phoenix, Arizona. CSK Auto is the largest retailer of automotive parts and accessories in the western United States, and the third largest in the nation. The company's more than 1,100 stores in 19 states operate primarily under three brand names, the first initials of which form the CSK in its name: Checker Auto Parts with stores located in the Southwest, Rocky Mountains, and Northern Plains region; Schuck's Auto Supply in the Pacific Northwest; and Kragen Auto Parts in California. Most of the focus of CSK Auto is on the do-it-yourself customer, accounting for approximately 85 percent of its business. The company hopes to increase its sales to auto repair professionals and fleet owners, a segment of the automotive aftermarket parts and accessories business that is considered to have a greater potential for growth. CSK Auto has also taken aggressive steps to use the Internet, combined with the delivery infrastructure it already has in place, as a way to sell even more of its products.

The Rise of Standardized Parts and the Introduction of the Model T in 1908

During the early days of the automobile there was no need for businesses specializing in spare parts. With the refinement of the internal combustion engine in the mid-1880s, inventors in Europe and the United States began to develop self-propelled vehicles. In Europe in the 1890s many familiar car makers, including Mercedes, Peugeot, Renault, and Fiat, were established. By 1898 in the United States there were more than 50 automobile companies. The first American car to sell in significant numbers was the Oldsmobile. Some 425 were purchased in 1901, a number that grew to 5,000 by 1904. This success prompted more than 240 additional companies to enter the U.S. market by 1908. These early cars—expensive to buy and expensive to maintain—were clearly intended for the wealthy. The vehicles and their parts were essentially the handmade work of craftsmen. Henry Ford revolutionized the auto industry by standardizing parts. His Model T, introduced in 1908, was the first car to be mass produced and therefore affordable to the middle class. By 1929 there were 26.7 million cars registered in the United States, and any number of businesses were established to maintain and service them.

One of the founding fathers of CSK Auto was Harry Schuck, who in 1917 opened a store in Seattle to sell motorcycle, bicycle, and automobile parts. Al Kragen got into the business in San Jose in 1947. Checker Auto Parts was not founded until 1968, when Valley Distributing Company in Phoenix converted a country-and-western dance hall into its first store. All three companies would add units until they became regional chains.

In 1987 brothers Jules and Eddie Trump, New York investors unrelated to Donald Trump, merged the Checker, Kragen, and Schuck's auto parts chains, along with AutoWorks, to form what was then known as Northern Automotive. At its peak Northern operated 750 stores, although with limited success. It sold off AutoWorks, dropping to 569 total stores, and changed its name to CSK Auto. In the first half of the 1990s the company lost money three out of five years and was just marginally profitable the other two. CSK Auto did, however, make significant investments to upgrade its information management system and build a new distribution center in Phoenix. Like most auto parts retailers, CSK Auto felt that the do-it-yourself market was shrinking because many customers lacked the equipment and training to work on the newer computer-controlled cars, and thus felt the need to shift focus to the commercial trade.

Company Perspectives:

Our operating strategy is to offer our products at everyday low prices and at conveniently located and attractively designed stores, supported by highly trained, efficient and courteous service personnel.

In 1996 CSK Auto announced that it was going to make a public offering of its stock, with the intention of raising about $100 million to pay off debt. Given the company's lackluster performance, investors showed little interest. The Trumps changed their plans and instead sold a 51 percent stake in the company to Investcorp, a London-based holding company that invested Persian Gulf oil money in European and American properties.

The automotive aftermarket parts and accessories business, traditionally highly fragmented with local stores competing with regional chains, entered a period of increased consolidation similar to what had happened in the banking, drugstore, and supermarket industries. For several years the $32 billion a year do-it-yourself market had been showing nominal growth, only one percent to two percent. In order to generate growth, chains were forced to expand, with the result that there was not enough customers to support the inflated supply of sellers, a situation that only fueled the need to get bigger. AutoZone was the most aggressive player. Even though it was growing internally by 300 stores a year, it also initiated an acquisition strategy. AutoZone in 1998 had well over 2,000 stores, with an estimated potential of 5,000, and was quickly becoming what amounted to the first true national auto parts chain.

Expanding by Acquisition: 1997

In order to maintain its position as one of the largest chains, CSK Auto had no choice but to be equally as aggressive as its chief rivals, AutoZone and Pep Boys. Late in 1997 CSK Auto paid $38 million to acquire 80 California stores from Trak Auto Corp., which opted to focus on its outlets located in the East and Midwest. Not only did the transaction bring the total number of stores in the CSK Auto chain to 685, it increased the company's presence in the highly important Los Angeles market. CSK Auto was able to use its existing warehouses and distribution system to service the new stores, which would be switched to its Kragen brand name. One of the area's major players, with 400 of its 556 stores located in California, Chief Auto Parts answered by announcing plans to pursue a public offering of its stock to finance its own expansion, then changed course and agreed to be purchased by AutoZone. The effect of these transactions was to reduce the number of auto parts chains in the Los Angeles market from five to just three.

Although CSK Auto operated under three brand names, the company had established a corporate identity and a focus. While retaining local brand recognition, every Checker, Schuck's, or Kragen store was essentially the same. The target was the 22- to 45-year-old customer who worked on his own car. The ideal outlet was located in a blue-collar or working class area. It offered free testing of starters, alternators, and batteries, as well as free battery charges. An efficient computerized distribution system linked all the stores together, so if an item was not available at one location it could be delivered from another. Centralized depots that delivered to stores throughout the day also featured call windows, should customers prefer to save time by picking up an item themselves. A satellite communications network linked the stores to the Phoenix office, where purchasing was centralized. Through the online network, individual stores could also price items in order to be competitive with their local rivals. The company also initiated what it called CSK University, a continuing education program for its sales staff. Formal classes were conducted in 26 centers. In addition to customer service and management development skills, students were trained in basic automotive systems, as well as more advanced automotive knowledge, with the goal of better serving customers who had limited knowledge about the workings of the new computer-controlled cars.

Early in 1998 CSK Auto again attempted to go public with a stock offering in order to finance the opening of new stores, remodel existing ones, and to make further acquisitions. The offering successfully raised $172.5 million. When a month later the company reported its results for fiscal 1997, it was clear that CSK Auto was on an upward trajectory. Net sales increased 6.6 percent from the previous year, to $845.8 million. The $45.4 million operating income was a significant improvement over the $3.4 million loss reported in fiscal 1996. With the integration of the Auto Trak stores and the opening of new stores that brought the total number of units to 807, CSK Auto cracked the $1 billion mark in net sales in fiscal 1998. Operating profits jumped to $81.4 million.

CSK Auto began an accelerated effort to expand its operation. In June 1999 it purchased the 86 stores of Apsco Products Company that operated as Big Wheel or Rossi outlets. The $60 million deal added new markets in Minnesota, North Dakota, and Wisconsin, bringing the total number of CSK Auto stores to 914, now spread across 13 states. The company elected to retain the Big Wheel and Rossi names for these units. In August CSK Auto made an even larger purchase, paying $143.2 million to PACCAR Inc. for 192 stores that operated under the trade names of Grand Auto Supply and Al's Auto Supply in the states of Washington, California, Idaho, Oregon, Nevada, and Alaska. The deal increased the CSK Auto chain to more than 1,100 stores.

Selling Online: 1999

In 1999 CSK Auto made an aggressive entry into the e-commerce world with the introduction of a wholly owned Internet subsidiary called CSKAUTO.COM. Although there were online sites already selling auto parts, CSK Auto became the first of the traditional auto parts retailers to offer a full assortment of parts and accessories on the web. The site was integrated with CSK Auto's order management and credit card authorization system to take advantage of the company's existing electronic infrastructure. Parts for cars, vans, and trucks dating back to 1960 were available on the site.

In August 1999 CSK Auto bolstered its Internet initiative when it acquired Automotive Information Systems (AIS) for approximately $10 million. AIS, since its inception in 1987, had been building a database of repair information, appropriate for

Key Dates:

1917: Schuck's Auto Supply is founded in Seattle, Washington.
1947: Kragen Auto Parts is founded in San Jose, California.
1969: Checker Auto Parts is founded in Phoenix, Arizona.
1987: Jules and Eddie Trump combine Schuck's, Kragen, and Checker chains to form CSK Auto, then known as Northern Automotive.
1998: CSK Auto makes public offering of stock.
1999: CSK Auto becomes first major auto parts retailer to sell products on the Internet.

do-it-yourself customers as well as experienced mechanics. Fielding more than 250,000 inquiries a year for repair information from 15,000 repair shops, the 32 master technicians working for AIS compiled a comprehensive body of vehicle-specific information, including how to diagnose problems and make repairs. Just as important to CSK Auto was AIS's role as the key content supplier to Microsoft's highly popular CarPoint web site, which boasted three million unique visitors each month. AIS provided CarPoint visitors with recommended maintenance schedules for over 1,200 vehicles and repair cost estimates based on national averages. The next step for CSK Auto was to forge a direct relationship with CarPoint. In September 1999 it became the site's exclusive auto parts web provider. Visitors to CarPoint looking for repair information would be directly linked to CSKAUTO.COM in order to easily purchase the necessary parts or accessories. In essence, this relationship was the ultimate in targeted advertising.

CSK Auto added to its online presence early in 2000 with the announcement that along with Advance Auto Parts and Sequoia Capital, a Silicon Valley venture-capital company, it was launching PartsAmerica.com. The new entity would feature a ''bricks-to-clicks'' strategy that would take advantage of the chains' 2,700 stores to offer same-day parts delivery to both repair shops and consumers. Because Advance Auto and its 1,600 outlets operated out of the East and Midwest, and CSK's 1,100 outlets were located in the West, the two chains were not direct competitors, even though both sold parts on the Internet. By combining forces via the web they would be able to create a network of stores that covered all 50 states. Moreover, because the chains already had 3,000 vehicles delivering to repair shops, an infrastructure was in place to serve consumers doing repair work at home.

In 2000 CSK Auto also continued to grow its traditional business. In May it acquired the assets of All-Car Distributors, Inc. for approximately $865,000 in cash and the assumption of approximately $3 million in debt. CSK Auto thus added 22 stores to the Checker Auto Parts roster: 21 units in Wisconsin and one in Michigan. The transaction helped CSK Auto to build its presence in the Wisconsin market without overlap. None of the AllCar stores had been in direct competition with Checker stores.

Results for fiscal 1999 reported in March 2000 showed that CSK Auto had increased its net sales from $1 billion to $1.23 billion, and operating profits jumped from $82.4 million to $119.6 million. Industry sales reached $10 billion, a significant milestone, but hardly explosive growth. The environment of the automotive aftermarket parts and accessories business remained one in which too many sellers were chasing too few buyers, and a major chain like CSK Auto had no choice but to continue to expand, either by clicks or by brick, or risk becoming the victim of a reckoning that was sure to one day visit the industry.

Principal Subsidiaries

CSK Auto, Inc.; Schuck's Distribution Company; Kragen Auto Supply Company; TRK Socal, Inc.; CSKAUTO.COM.

Principal Competitors

AutoZone, Inc.; The Pep Boys–Manny, Moe & Jack.

Further Reading

''Acquisitions Top Growth Chart,'' *Discount Store News,* August 7, 2000, p. 43.
''Aftermarket Distributors with the Shortest Lead Times Are the Winners in Competitive Industry,'' *PR Newswire,* June 22, 1998, p. 1.
''Autos,'' *Los Angeles Times,* October 9, 1996, p. 2.
Clark, Don, ''CSK, Advance Auto Form Firm to Allow Customers to Purchase Parts Online,'' *Wall Street Journal,* January 10, 2000, p. A8.
''CSK Auto Corporation Reports Fiscal 1997 Financial Results,'' *PR Newswire,* April 15, 1998, p. 1.
''CSK Auto Corporation Reports $1 Billion in Net Sales and Record Earnings for Its 1998 Fiscal Year,'' *PR Newswire,* March 17, 1999, p. 1.
''CSK Auto Corporation Reports Results for Its 1999 Fiscal Year,'' *PR Newswire,* March 21, 2000, p. 1.
''CSK Auto Corporation to Acquire All-Car Distributors, Inc.'' *PR Newswire,* March 13, 2000, p. 1.
''CSK Auto Corporation to Acquire Big Wheel/Rossi Auto Parts Stores,'' *PR Newswire,* May 18, 1999, p. 1.
''CSK Auto Corporation to Acquire Grand Auto Supply and Al's Auto Supply,'' *PR Newswire,* August 23, 1999, p. 1.
''CSK Auto Expects $100M IPO,'' *Discount Store News,* August 5, 1996, p. 6.
''CSK Auto Inc. Gears up for E-Commerce,'' *PR Newswire,* June 22, 1999, p. 1.
Greater Phoenix, Phoenix: Towery Publishing, Inc., 1999, 399 p.
Halverson, Richard, ''Auto Aftermarket Consolidates,'' *Discount Store News,* October 26, 1998, pp. 6, 126.
——, ''The Preeminent Purveyor of Parts,'' *Discount Store News,* December 14, 1998, pp. 67–68.
Howell, Debbie, ''CSK Acquires Big Wheel/Rossi,'' *Discount Store News,* July 26, 1999, p. 6.
''Investcorp: Group to Buy 51% Interest in Retailer CSK Auto Inc.,'' *Wall Street Journal,* October 9, 1996, p. A16.
Master, Greg, ''Shift into High Gear,'' *Discount Merchandiser,* April 1999, pp. 97–100.
Pelz, James F., ''Auto Parts Business Is Being Rebuilt,'' *Los Angeles Times,* May 14, 1998, p. D1.
''Specialty Watch,'' *Discount Store News,* October 21, 1996, p. 6.
''Trak Auto to Sell 80 California Stores,'' *Los Angeles Times,* October 8, 1997.

—Ed Dinger

Culligan®

Culligan Water Technologies, Inc.

1 Culligan Parkway
Northbrook, Illinois 60062
U.S.A.
Telephone: (847) 205-6000
Fax: (847) 205-6030
Web site: http://www.culliganman.com

Wholly Owned Subsidiary of United States Filter Corporation
Incorporated: 1936 as Culligan Zeolite Company
Employees: 4,578
Sales: $505.7 million (1998)
NAIC: 333319 Other Commercial and Service Industry Machinery Manufacturing

Culligan Water Technologies, Inc. became known across the United States as the father of the soft water industry. ''Hey Culligan Man!'' was an advertising mantra nationally synonymous with conditioned water. The company is a subsidiary of United States Filter Corporation (USFilter), which is itself a subsidiary of a French water treatment company, Vivendi SA. Culligan markets an array of water filtration products, including household water softeners and filtering systems, water filtering and deionizing products for commercial and industrial customers, and several brands of bottled water. The company moved into mass market retailing in the late 1990s, marketing consumer products such as faucet-mounted filter systems through nationally known merchants such as Target, Sears, and Home Depot. Culligan operates through a vast network of franchises, with Culligan dealers in more than 90 countries. Culligan owns a Canadian subsidiary, Culligan of Canada, Ltd., and has wide penetration in Latin America as well.

Early Years

Emmett J. Culligan developed a novel process for manufacturing zeolite, the man-made mineral used in water softeners, in 1936, which involved the very early use of solar drying. With a lot of confidence and a little money, Culligan approached the city council of Northbrook, Illinois, that year and offered to lease a stretch of streets. The streets had been paved, but then left unused when a real estate project went under. Several miles of empty, paved streets were just what Culligan needed for drying his zeolite in large quantities, using the sun. The council leased him the streets for $50 and a company was born: Culligan Zeolite Company.

From the start, the company was a community endeavor. Culligan's first home was a shared blacksmith's shop behind the Northbrook Garage on Shermer Avenue, run by ''Jock'' McLachlan. As the operations grew, Culligan rented a brick garage building beside the blacksmith's shop and relocated the blacksmith's building to face Walters Avenue. The garage became the first manufacturing plant for portable exchange units. The office and laboratory stayed in the blacksmith's shop. Eventually, these buildings grew together, with more manufacturing space on the ground floor and offices added onto the second.

Through franchised dealers, Culligan soon launched a campaign for soft water in every home. In 1938, the first Culligan dealer started up business in Wheaton, Illinois. Growth was swift. The number of dealers bloomed to 150 by the beginning of World War II. While the war slowed growth—no new dealers were signed on during that time—Culligan's skills were called upon for the war effort and a facility was developed in San Bernardino, California. There, Culligan manufactured silica gel, a dehydrating material that protected metals from atmospheric corrosion. Silica gel was in great demand during the war and Culligan soon became one of the largest suppliers. The company was later given an award for its contributions to the war effort.

Postwar Expansion

After the war, stateside expansion resumed. The dealer organization was growing again by 1946. Only a few years later, the Northbrook plant had become the largest producer of water softeners in the world. The San Bernardino facility had converted quickly and become—with its 34 acres of solar drying basins—the largest zeolite manufacturing plant in the world. Further plant facilities were purchased in Evanston, Illinois, not far from the Northbrook headquarters, and these also were expanding. In 1947, a two-story structure was added to the Northbrook home base.

Company Perspectives:

After being in the water treatment business for nearly 65 years, we know water. Our mission is to deliver high-quality water treatment products that will benefit every part of consumers' lives. We hope to raise the quality of life by purifying its most essential element: water.

We've seen about every water problem imaginable and we've solved these problems to deliver the refreshing, clean and pure water that's become our hallmark. Free of contaminants and minerals, water treated with Culligan softeners or filtration systems will make an impression on you and your household, and at the work place.

A mere 15 years after Emmett Culligan approached the city council with $50 and an off-kilter idea, Northbrook proclaimed a ''Culligan Day.'' On October 13, 1951, a square dance and barbecue gathered the town's residents together to celebrate Culligan's new half-million dollar plant on South Shermer Road. Soft water had become such a national mainstay that the old plant had suffered from eight major expansions. With the new facility, Culligan had more than 450,000 square feet of space to accommodate its sales growth.

The Culligan Zeolite Company became Culligan Incorporated in 1952. Over the decades, Culligan grew in scope, broadening its water-quality improvement offerings and branching out over the oceans. To reflect that expansion, the company's name was again changed in 1970 to Culligan International Company. Internationally, Culligan products were available through licensees in 85 countries.

Under Many Owners in the 1970s and 1980s

In 1978, Culligan became part of Beatrice, a food products conglomerate. Beatrice later became a privately held company as a result of a buyout, and at that time a number of brands, including Culligan, were reorganized into E-II Holdings. E-II was purchased by American Brands, Incorporated, in 1988 for $1.1 billion. American Brands, a holding company with interests in tobacco, distilled spirits, and insurance, kept five of E-II's companies and sold the rest of E-II, including Culligan and Samsonite, to the Riklis Family Corporation. American Brands had owned Culligan for about six months before it sold E-II to Riklis. About three years later, Riklis issued junk bonds and E-II fell into bankruptcy. A struggle then ensued between financiers Carl C. Icahn, who purchased senior junk bonds, and Leon Black, who purchased junior junk bonds.

Throughout this time, Culligan remained quite profitable, keeping its recipe for success basically unchanged. It had endured the bankruptcy of E-II and was still doing business and making money. In fact, Culligan did not feel many effects after the change of ownership. While junk bonds were being swapped, Culligan quietly kept at its business. In the spring of 1993, Ametek Inc. and Icahn made a bid for E-II and Culligan, but the package ultimately went to Black. After the sale, E-II became Astrum International. Culligan remained a subsidiary of Astrum, a holding company whose core businesses included American Tourister and Samsonite luggage; McGregor, a line of men's tailored clothing; and Global Licensing, which licensed trademarks.

In the summer of 1994, Culligan was an official sponsor of the Goodwill Games, which took place in St. Petersburg. At the same time, the company provided a water purification system for a group of townhomes in that city, the first American-style housing development in the Commonwealth of Independent States (CIS), formerly the Soviet Union. Culligan warmed up for this event by supplying water treatment systems for both visitors and athletes at the Olympic games in Barcelona in 1992.

Expansion and New Owners in the Mid-1990s and Beyond

In the mid-1990s, Culligan's mainstay was still water treatment, and it still operated sales and distribution franchises. In fact, Culligan had changed very little over the years. From the beginning, it was one of the few water treatment companies that offered a complete water treatment line, from homes to corporations and commercial use. Most of its competitors provided either industrial or household water treatments, but not both. Culligan was able to offer that range because of its size, history, and fiscal stability. This provided Culligan with distinct advantages, because when one side of business was up, the other was often down.

In 1995, Culligan's parent, Astrum, decided to split itself into two entities. Water purification did not have much to do with luggage, and Astrum became the Samsonite Corp., after its leading luggage brand, and spun off Culligan as Culligan Water Technologies, Inc., a public company traded on the New York Stock Exchange. Culligan immediately began to expand, acquiring smaller companies and going after new markets. Shortly after going public, Culligan bought up all or part of many small water-related companies, including Ametek, a water-filtration company; Sparkling S.A., a bottled water company located in Buenos Aires; and two different water treatment and bottled water companies in southern California. In 1998, Culligan paid approximately $132.5 million for Protean plc, a British water purification equipment maker, and then spent $4.4 million for Harmony Brook, a Minnesota-based manufacturer of consumer water purification products.

Culligan also moved aggressively into retail markets, designing new products that could be sold at mass merchandise outlets like Sears and at home improvement retailers like Home Depot. Culligan entered into joint ventures with several manufacturers to expand its product line. Culligan contracted with Moen, a major faucet manufacturer, on a joint project to sell faucet-mounted water filtration systems for home use. With General Electric, Culligan collaborated on a line of water filters installed in that company's refrigerators. Culligan also worked with Signature Brands, the parent company of the Mr. Coffee brand of coffee maker, on a new line of coffee makers using water filters. These products led Culligan into many new areas of distribution. Whereas most of its products had been available only through Culligan dealers, in the late 1990s some Culligan filter products were sold in supermarkets and drugstores. The company backed its new lines with increased advertising. Culligan upped its ad budget from $2 million in its first year as a

Key Dates:

1936: Emmett J. Culligan invents water softening process with zeolite.
1938: First Culligan franchise opens.
1951: Culligan plant completes huge expansion.
1970: Name is changed to Culligan International Company.
1978: Culligan is bought by Beatrice Foods.
1988: Culligan becomes part of Riklis Family Corporation.
1993: Culligan becomes subsidiary of Astrum International.
1995: Culligan goes public.
1998: Culligan is bought by United States Filter Corporation (USFilter) for $1.5 billion.
1999: USFilter is acquired by French firm Vivendi SA.

public company to about $10 million in 1997. The company capitalized on its wide brand recognition to push into retail markets. For fiscal 1997, Culligan reported sales of $371 million, reflecting an increase of more than 20 percent from the year previous. With more joint ventures planned, the company hoped to grow the retail side of its business by several hundred million dollars over the next few years.

But Culligan did not remain an independent company for long. It had busily bought up smaller companies in the United States and abroad to increase its business, and in 1998 a bigger company bought it. USFilter, based in Palm Desert, California, paid $1.5 billion to get Culligan. USFilter had paralleled Culligan's growth strategy in recent years, acquiring smaller players in the water products and services industry throughout the 1990s. Culligan was a much bigger target for USFilter than any of its previous purchases, but it brought the company the invaluable Culligan name.

USFilter hoped to increase Culligan's visibility, both in the United States and abroad. At the time of the acquisition, Culligan water was found in three million homes, and USFilter boasted that its target number for its new subsidiary was 300 million homes. The parent company saw itself as a global player in a world that was in growing need of filtered water. In an interview with the *Business Press,* of Ontario, California, on February 16, 1998, a USFilter vice-president claimed that his company's goal was to "have a U.S. Filter or Culligan dealer . . . in every city in the world in five to 10 years." USFilter became the largest U.S. water products company with its purchase of Culligan, but it had bigger competitors in Europe, such as the French companies Generale des Eaux and Lyonnaise des Eaux.

Given the rapid consolidation in the water industry by which Culligan and USFilter had grown, it was perhaps not surprising that USFilter was itself acquired in 1999. Its buyer was a French company, Vivendi SA. Vivendi was a water treatment conglomerate, and it paid $6.2 billion for USFilter. So Culligan became a subsidiary of that company, though it continued to maintain headquarters in Illinois. Its sales had grown handsomely in the late 1990s, to more than $505 million when last released in 1998. Culligan sold water or water products in more than 90 countries by the time of the sale to Vivendi, with a strong presence in the Middle East, in Latin America, and in Canada.

Principal Subsidiaries

Culligan of Canada, Ltd.; Everpure Inc.; Indiana Soft Water Service Inc.; Bruner Water Treatment Service Inc.

Principal Competitors

WTC Industries; Brita Products Co.; Generale des Eaux.

Further Reading

"Astrum to Separate into 2 Public Concerns," *Wall Street Journal,* April 25, 1995, p. B4.
"California's United States Filter to Make $1.5 Billion Purchase," *Knight-Ridder/Tribune Business News,* February 16, 1998, p. 216B1068.
"Culligan International," *New York Times,* June 15, 1994, p. D3.
"The Culligan Man Is Splashing into Supermarkets," *Beverage Industry,* October 1994, p. 19.
"Culligan Water Technologies," *Beverage Industry,* June 1999, p. 9.
Elliott, Stuart, "Culligan International," *New York Times,* October 7, 1994, p. C16.
"Illinois-Based Culligan Water Plans to Buy Minnesota-Based Harmony Brook," *Knight-Ridder/Tribune Business News,* January 13, 1998, p. 113B0947.
McClenahen, John, "Hey, Culligan Man," *Industry Week,* October 17, 1994, p. 21.
Oloroso, Arsenio, "Desert Calls for Culligan Man: Firm Seeks to Provide Water to U.S. Troops," *Crain's Chicago Business,* September 3, 1990, p. 3.
"Samsonite Will Spin Off Water Purification Firm," *Knight-Ridder/Tribune Business News,* September 1, 1995, p. 9010010.
Steele, Jeanette, "Caution Heard Over Palm Desert, Calif.-Based U.S. Filter's Latest Buyout," *Knight-Ridder/Tribune Business News,* June 15, 1998, p. OKRB981660E6.
Strom, Stephanie, "Ametek and Icahn Join in Bid to Control E-II," *New York Times,* May 25, 1993, p. D5(L).
Werner, Holly M., "Culligan's Building Plans," *HFN,* June 9, 1997, p. 60.

—Carol I. Keeley
—updated by A. Woodward

D.G. Yuengling & Son, Inc.

5th and Mahantongo Sts.
Pottsville, Pennsylvania 17901
U.S.A.
Telephone: (570) 622-4141
Fax: (570) 622-4011
Web site: http://www.yuengling.com

Private Company
Founded: 1829 as Eagle Brewery
Employees: 64
NAIC: 312120 Beer; Breweries

D.G. Yuengling & Son, Inc. is officially registered as America's Oldest Brewery. Located in the center of mountainous Pottsville, Pennsylvania, Yuengling (pronounced *yin-ling*) has been brewing beer since 1829. Traditionally passed down from father to son, the company has been family-owned for five generations. Yuengling was founded in 1829 by David G. Yuengling, a German immigrant, and is now run by Dick Yuengling, Jr., David's great-great grandson. Once a struggling regional beer, Yuengling has established itself as a popular, high-quality, affordable beer. The company brews five brands of beer: Yuengling Premium, Lord Chesterfield Ale, Dark Brewed Porter, Tradition Lager, and Original Black and Tan. To meet the great demand for its beer, in 1998 Yuengling purchased a former Stroh brewery in Tampa, Florida, and broke ground on a new $50 million brewery in St. Claire, Pennsylvania, near the original brewery in Pottsville, Pennsylvania. In 1999, Yuengling was ranked the eighth largest brewery in the United States; by the end of 2000, the company expected to have sold nearly 800,000 barrels of beer. Yuengling also offers tours of its historical brewery and its Yuengling Museum and Gift Shop. Nearly 50,000 visitors tour its facilities each year.

The Eagle Brewery in 1829

D.G. Yuengling & Son, Inc. began in 1829 when David G. Yuengling, an immigrant from Wurtenburg, Germany, opened a brewery on Centre Street in Pottsville, Pennsylvania. He named his new business the Eagle Brewery, ''to identify with the qualities of strength and pride, symbolic of the American eagle.'' Years later, when his son joined him in the family business, he changed the company's name to D.G. Yuengling & Son, Inc.

In 1831 a fire destroyed the plant and Yuengling built a new brewery on Mahantongo Street on the side of a mountain. At the time many small breweries were built in similar locations so tunnels could be dug in the rock. These tunnels provided natural cool temperatures suitable for aging and fermenting beer.

Pottsville itself was an ideal location for a brewery. The water was soft and clean, and it lacked the mineral taste of the water in many cities. Pottsville also had an abundance of beer drinkers. Thousands of German immigrants like Yuengling had settled in southeastern Pennsylvania, creating a unique community. ''Unlike other parts of the country where the locals preferred to drink whiskey, rum and hard cider, the Germans of this area showed a distinct preference for beer,'' reported *Ale Street News*. Pottsville also had access to railroads, so it could easily ship its beer to nearby Reading and Philadelphia. The company was an instant success, and Yuengling beer became a popular regional beer.

Prohibition in 1919

The late 1800s and early 1900s were difficult years for Yuengling. In 1899, Frederick Yuengling passed away at the age of 51. After his death, his son Frank took over the company. Then in 1919, the Eighteenth Amendment was ratified, which enacted a call for the national prohibition of alcohol. Nearly 400 breweries were forced out of business. Yuengling adapted to Prohibition by producing three different ''near beers,'' malt beverages with less than .05 percent alcohol. Its near beers were successful, but the company still struggled.

When Prohibition ended in 1933, the company celebrated by producing a brand called Winner Beer. ''We introduced Winner Beer as a salute to the repeal of Prohibition in 1933. Then to show our appreciation, we shipped a truckload to President Roosevelt at the White House,'' said Frank Yuengling.

While the company believed its troubles to be in the past, it suffered further disaster in the 1950s when area steel, coal, and

Company Perspectives:

Under Dick Yuengling's guidance, Yuengling beer has gone from a small regional brand to a well-known and sought-after entity. but that's not surprising. Throughout the company's storied history, the Yuengling family's commitment to its customers, determination and forward thinking have been the sources of its ongoing success.

railroad industries collapsed. The disaster forced many locals to quickly relocate. This meant trouble for Yuengling, since it was losing many of its loyal, local customers. Almost overnight, Pottsville's population dwindled. In the years that followed, Yuengling struggled to make its beer appealing to younger drinkers in the area—and this was no easy feat. Yuengling beer was sitting on Pennsylvania tavern tables when General Custer was leading cavalry charges on the battleground at Gettysburg. This rich history caused many younger drinkers to shun the beer. They associated the brand with old-timers, the coal miners and mill workers who once lived in the area, and wanted to distance themselves from this image.

In 1960, Yuengling hired N. Ray Norbert as head brewmaster. Hiring Norbert was a good move, for he quickly earned a reputation for meticulous brewing. In an article in the *Pottsville Republican and Evening Herald,* Norbert compared brewing beer to manufacturing cars. ''It can be a model T or a Cadillac,'' he said. ''It has four wheels and a steering wheel, but everything in between is different.''

The company changed hands again in 1963 when Frank Yuengling passed away. Yuengling was 86 and had managed the brewery as president and chairman of the board for 64 years. After his death his two sons, Richard (Dick) L. and F. Dohrman Yuengling, took the company's reigns.

In the 1960s and the 1970s the Pennsylvania legislature succumbed to pressure from large, national breweries and repealed laws that protected small breweries. Many of the smaller breweries were either swallowed up by larger breweries or forced to declare bankruptcy. Yuengling seemed destined for a similar fate—until Dick Yuengling, Jr., stepped in.

Reorganization in the 1980s

Dick Yuengling, Jr., left his own beer-distribution business to help his ailing father manage the brewery. The younger Yuengling vowed not to be the Yuengling who would close down the brewery. Instead he planned to restructure the company and capture much-needed market share. The timing was certainly right for Yuengling's revival: Micro breweries were growing in popularity, regional pride was rising, and sales for top national brands had dipped slightly. The *Philadelphia Inquirer* reported that ''it was a time when micro breweries, brew pubs, and home brewers were reintroducing porters, ales, and gourmet brews to the nation's 84 million beer drinkers.'' ''Somebody had to develop or find that taste,'' Yuengling said. ''I attribute that to people who got into the home brewing, and other small breweries like we are, that started putting out wheat and gourmet beers. And that's where we fit in, because we've been brewing porter and ale here since the brewery started 166 years ago.''

Yuengling invested all of the company's earnings into new equipment and asked Norbert and the company's other brewers to develop several new brands of Yuengling beer.

Yuengling also believed the company needed a new image. His distributors urged him to hire David Casinelli, whose father Anthony worked for L & M. Beverages Co., Yuengling's Philadelphia distributor. Yuengling made Casinelli the vice-president of marketing and sales, and later promoted him to executive vice-president.

Casinelli wanted to remake the company's image starting with the labels on its beer. He and Yuengling designed new sophisticated labels that emphasized the beer's regional appeal. The new labels even included a historic eagle, which was designed by founder David Yuengling for the original Eagle Brewery. Casinelli launched an aggressive marketing campaign that focused on the company's foothold in Pennsylvania's history.

Said Yuengling in the *Wall Street Journal:* ''I don't even want to know how much it cost. But David made me do things that built a new image for our brands.''

The company switched to more aggressive wholesalers along its eastern seaboard territory. In addition, unlike many competitors who were cutting prices to gain market share, Yuengling raised the price of its beer to above-premium levels and pushed it in high-end markets such as Philadelphia's historic district and Penn's Landing.

Casinelli also cross-marketed Yuengling beer with other campaigns that focused on tourism and Pennsylvania's history. ''He worked with a concessionaire at the Philly airport to build displays that promoted the historical significance of the nation's oldest brewery,'' reported the *Wall Street Journal.* He also launched campaigns to increase the beer's appeal among younger drinkers, who were steering away from large, national brands in a search of beer with unique flavor.

Casinelli's efforts proved worthwhile. Sales rose from approximately 127,000 barrels in 1986 to 230,000 barrels in 1993. (One barrel is equal to roughly 360, 12-ounce servings of beer.)

To help promote its historic theme, in 1991 Yuengling began offering tours of its historic brewery along with its Yuengling Museum and Gift Shop. Yuengling's onsite museum featured memorabilia and artifacts from the pre-Civil War era. ''The museum contains some amazing items we found in closets and drawers, items that hadn't been seen in a quarter century or more,'' said Dick Yuengling. ''We found the diary that my great-great grandfather brought from Germany when he founded the brewery.''

Included in the tour was the brew house ''where grain hops and water are mixed in huge ancient copper kettles, fermentation tanks, grain storage areas, and shipping docks.'' The bottling plant was a major attraction. ''You get to go right down on the factory floor so you're only a few feet away from the bottles as they zip through the washing, filling, labeling, capping and packing station,'' reported *Money* magazine.

Key Dates:

1829: German immigrant David G. Yuengling founds the Eagle Brewery in Pottsville, Pennsylvania.
1831: A fire destroys the Eagle Brewery and a new brewery is built on Mahantongo Street in Pottsville.
1873: Yuengling changes the name of the brewery to D.G. Yuengling and Son, Inc. when his son Frederick joins the business.
1919: The 18th Amendment is ratified, making it illegal to sell alcohol.
1933: Prohibition ends and Yuengling starts producing alcoholic beer once again.
1960: Frank Yuengling, Frederick's son, hires N. Ray Norbert as brewmaster.
1963: Frank Yuengling dies; his sons, Richard L. and F. Dohrman Yuengling, take over the brewery.
1985: Richard L. Yuengling, Jr., buys the company from his father .
1991: The Yuengling Museum and Gift Shop opens.
1996: Yuengling goes online.
1998: Yuengling breaks ground on a second brewery in Pennsylvania and buys a former Stroh brewery in Tampa, Florida.

A Shortage in the 1990s

By the 1990s, Yuengling had become successful—too successful. Its sales had far exceeded its expectations. The demand for its beer was so high that it could not fill all of its orders. It was forced to cut back on its advertising. The shortage in Yuengling beer also led to a public relations crisis. Rural Pennsylvanian's, Yuengling's most fervent customers, were furious about the beer shortage. They felt betrayed and accused the company of shipping too many barrels of beer to areas outside of Schuylkill County.

Yuengling listened to its customers. It stopped shipping beer to districts in Maine, Massachusetts, and Rhode Island and concentrated on meeting the demand in Pennsylvania. It also sold its beer locally at lower-than-normal prices.

By 1997, the ''brewery was running around the clock and was still unable to meet demand,'' according to an article in the *Gainesville Sun.* ''With only 150 people producing some 600,000 barrels of beer a year in a brewery designed to produce only 200,000 the risk of overproduction can run high.''

The company had to chart a new course: it could sell out or expand its facilities. Yuengling initially tried to expand the existing brewery, but this was difficult because the brewery was built on a mountainside. It added new storage and holding tanks, increased its refrigeration, and updated its electrical system. While the expansions and upgrades helped, the company was still unable to satisfy the demand for its beer.

In 1998, the company purchased a former Stroh brewery in Tampa, Florida. In addition to increasing production, the 1.6-million barrel facility opened up new markets for Yuengling.

Around the same time, Yuengling broke ground on a new $50 million brewery in nearby St. Claire. The company hoped that between the new brewery and the old brewery it could produce enough beer to satisfy its customers.

A Bright Future

The beer market promised to remain extremely competitive. In 2000 giants Anheuser-Busch, Miller Brewing, and Coors controlled 80 percent of the market. Over 500 smaller breweries battled fiercely for the remaining market share. Despite the odds, however, Yuengling continued to thrive as it entered the new millennium. In Dick Yuengling's own words, ''Yuengling is a survivor.''

Principal Competitors

Adolph Coors Company; Anheuser-Busch Companies, Inc.; Boston Beer Company, Inc.; The Gambrinus Company; Miller Brewing Company;

Further Reading

Baumgartner, Nancy E., ''For Small Brewer, A Time for Cheers,'' *Philadelphia Inquirer,* February 27, 1995.
Charlier, Marj, ''Yuengling Brews up a Transformation,'' *Wall Street Journal,* August 26, 1993.
De Hora, John, ''American's Oldest Brewery More Popular Than Ever,'' *Ale Street News,* Aug/Sept, 1997.
Hippler, Patricia A., ''Yuengling Announces Plans for New $50 Million Brewery,'' *Pottsville Republican and Evening Herald,* May 8, 1998.
Igoe, Ruth E. ''The Brewing Secrets of Yuengling,'' *Pottsville Republican and Evening Herald,* March 9–10, 1996.
Lukas, Paul, ''Ale in the Family,'' *Money,* March 2000.
Steinriede, Kent D., ''Its Sales Expanding, Brewery's Growing, Too,'' *Philadelphia Inquirer,* June 8, 1990.
Thompson, Andrew, ''A Family Thing,'' *Gainesville Sun,* August 20, 2000.

—Tracey Vasil Biscontini

DIRECTV, Inc.

2230 East Imperial Highway
El Segundo, California 90245
U.S.A.
Telephone: (310) 535-5000
Toll Free: (800) 531-5000
Fax: (310) 535-5225
Web site: http://www.directv.com

Private Subsidiary of Hughes Electronics Corporation
Incorporated: 1993
Employees: 1,400
Sales: $3.78 billion (1999)
NAIC: 51322 Cable and Other Program Distribution

DIRECTV, Inc. is the largest direct broadcast satellite service provider in the United States, delivering more than 200 channels of programming to more than nine million subscribers in the United States and to one million subscribers in Latin America. Programming includes movies, sports, music, and general interest content that subscribers receive via an 18-inch satellite dish and a set-top receiver. DIRECTV is owned by Hughes Electronics Corporation, a unit of General Motors Corporation.

Origins

Residential satellite television got its start in the early 1980s, but it would be years until the business developed into a legitimate industry. Early efforts failed largely because of poor signal quality and insufficient programming, which generally consisted of sporting events. Sports as a mainstay of programming was not at fault—the market appeal of sporting events represented an all-powerful force in the broadcast industry—but the depth and diversity of the programming offered by satellite broadcasters paled against the content provided by cable operators. One of satellite broadcasting's advantages was that it could reach markets and communities cable lines had not reached, which freed satellite operators from competing head to head with cable in some locations. However, catering to the sliver of potential customers in hard to reach areas would never be enough to cover operating costs. To develop into genuine competitors within the broadcast market, satellite operators had to steal business away from cable companies, something their meager programming offerings and scratchy picture quality could not do in the early 1980s. Consumers, by and large, opted for cable boxes on top of their television sets rather than for high-priced, massive satellite dishes in their backyards. The era of residential satellite service, it became apparent, had arrived prematurely.

Hughes Electronics Corporation, a unit of General Motors, realized the fundamental flaws of direct broadcast satellite (DBS) service when it first began to develop DBS plans in 1985. The problem of programming could be overcome by forging distribution deals, but the inherent problems of signal clarity and capacity were inescapable. Hughes's position, and with it the market feasibility of DBS service, was transformed by the development of digital compression technology. Digital compression increased the broadcast capacity of satellites by as much as eightfold. Perhaps more important, the new technology produced a much sharper image than earlier satellite broadcasting efforts, sharper, satellite operators could claim, than the picture received by cable customers. The ramifications were profound, suddenly giving DBS operators a chance to profit in a multibillion-dollar market. Hughes, as the largest satellite company in the world, wanted to dominate the market potential created by digital compression technology. Beginning in 1990, Hughes started forming DIRECTV to fulfill its objective, allocating $750 million to fund the company's start-up.

To steward Hughes's entry into DBS, the company picked Eddy W. Hartenstein, a senior project engineer for scientific, commercial, and classified satellite programs for Hughes Aircraft Co. Hartenstein, as the orchestrator of DIRECTV's formation and development, championed the cause of satellite television, acting as the industry's vocal and influential promoter. His first priority as the 1990s got underway was to forge partnerships with other companies, alliances that would give DIRECTV the hardware, software, and the programming to become operational. During the company's formative years, Hartenstein allied DIRECTV with high-profile concerns such as Sony Corporation and Digital Equipment Corporation. Thomson Consumer Electronics (a subsidiary of Thomson S.A.), for instance, entered into an agreement with DIRECTV to manufacture the satellite dishes that would

Key Dates:

1990: Hughes Electronics Corporation begins formulating plans for DIRECTV.
1993: First DIRECTV satellite is launched.
1994: DIRECTV's programming is beamed to subscribers for the first time.
1996: A record one million subscribers sign up during the year.
1999: Primestar and United States Satellite Broadcasting are acquired.

eventually be marketed to consumers. Aside from such major tasks as perfecting the home receiving equipment, getting the programming in place, and, of course, launching a satellite, there were equally important projects such as developing the software systems to control programming, scheduling, billing, and other functions. ''This is probably the single most complex television start-up in history,'' Hartenstein remarked in a March 28, 1994 interview with *Broadcasting & Cable.* ''There is an incredible amount of detail work that we need to do and make sure is working correctly before we turn this on-line and generate revenues,'' he explained.

As Hartenstein set out, only the problem of picture quality had been resolved from satellite television's previous flawed existence. The problems of programming and hardware costs incurred by the customer remained to be solved, representing two of the most important factors that would determine DIRECTV's fate. The company needed programming that would justify in the minds of consumers the expense of a $700 to $900 satellite dish, and it needed programming capable of luring customers away from cable television providers. The cost of dishes, according to Hartenstein, would fall as more and more people became DIRECTV subscribers, which left obtaining programming as the company's primary objective. Good programming would attract customers, which would drive down the cost of dishes, and, in turn, attract even more customers.

Toward this end, Hartenstein scrambled to secure the programming that would serve as the foundation for DIRECTV's success. In 1993, the company signed distribution agreements with several leading entertainment programmers. The agreements gave DIRECTV the right to distribute programming services owned by The Sci-Fi Channel, TNN: The Nashville Network, CMT: Country Music Television, The Family Channel, USA Network, and Turner Broadcasting. The pursuit of distribution agreements did not stop there, nor would they ever. The company was actively negotiating with other cable programmers, professional and collegiate sports leagues, and movie studios, part of its constant effort to offer satellite viewers more content than cable operators.

First Satellite Launch: 1993

As the deal making waged on and the operational aspects of DIRECTV's infrastructure gradually came together, a pivotal moment in the company's existence arrived before the end of the year. In December 1993, the company's first satellite was launched, ascending then resting 23,000 miles above the earth. Approximately five times stronger than traditional satellites and capable of transmitting up to eight times as many video signals, the company's first Hughes-built ''bird'' was soon ready to beam programming and information directly to a DIRECTV home receiving unit, its high-power capabilities requiring a dish, or antenna, measuring only 18 inches. All that remained for the company to become a revenue-generating enterprise was the completion of the 13 major software systems on Earth that controlled DIRECTV's programming, scheduling, and billing.

The date for DIRECTV's DBS service to begin was set for May 1, 1994. In preparation for the momentous event, agreements were reached with 2,000 dealers and 1,000 electronics stores, including Sears and Circuit City, to sell the equipment required for DIRECTV service. Agreements were in place for another 2,000 outlets, including Ward's and Best Buy stores, to sell the service beginning in the fall of 1994. By the end of 1995, Hartenstein wanted to have 8,000 retailers selling the company's pizza-sized satellite dishes. Hartenstein had other target numbers he was trying to reach as the DBS-1 satellite sat positioned in geosynchronous orbit, none more important than the projected break-even point for his pioneering company. According to the company's estimates, three million subscribers paying $30 in monthly subscription fees would push DIRECTV past the point of operating at a loss and usher in profitability. Hartenstein hoped to reach this threshold by late 1996 or early 1997. By 2000, Hartenstein projected there would be ten million DIRECTV subscribers.

Initially, DIRECTV's DBS service was sold in five markets. Expansion into seven states was completed by June 1994, setting up the coast-to-coast launch of DBS service in the fall of 1994. By the time the company rolled out national service, its broadcast capabilities had been bolstered considerably. The DBS-2 satellite was launched in early August 1994, increasing the company's broadcasting capacity to 40 channels of cable programming and 50 pay-per-view channels. A third satellite was launched in mid-1995, making DIRECTV's basic lineup roughly four times the size of cable's offering.

The sale of DIRECTV dishes was brisk at first, aided by the launch of DBS-1 just before the holiday season. The company boasted approximately 350,000 subscribers by the end of 1994, exceeding its expectations, and was gaining new subscribers at a rate of 3,000 per day. It was a promising start, but there was still much to accomplish before Hartenstein could claim a lasting hold on the broadcast market.

The obvious need was to gain as many new subscribers as possible to reach the point where the company was profitable. How to gain new subscribers proved to be a murkier question, posing a problem with no easy solution and sparking debate among industry analysts and satellite broadcasters alike. The dilemma centered on the long-term value of offering potential customers subsidies on the hardware required to receive DBS service. By reducing the cost of dishes, so the thinking went, more people would be willing to subscribe to satellite service. The greater the subsidies, however, the greater the operating losses became, as the difference between manufacturing costs and what the customer paid for the hardware widened. Considering that DIRECTV was backed by Hughes and General Motors, the company could absorb financial losses that other, less-endowed companies could not sustain, but the use of subsidies had another drawback, one perceived to be more menacing to a company's fortunes than escalating operating losses. Consensus maintained that if subscribers paid less up-front costs, they were likelier to later cancel their subscriptions, or "churn out," because they had made less of a financial investment in the service. Gaining new subscribers in this respect represented artificial growth, causing greater operating losses and a higher churn-out rate, which could render a DBS service provider financially moribund.

The catch-22 of subsidizing subscriber growth presented Hartenstein with a difficult challenge as he set out to increase DIRECTV's subscriber base. Nevertheless, he could take comfort in DIRECTV's stalwart industry position. Roughly a year after launching its service the company ranked as the largest competitor in the DBS television market, far ahead of its closest competitor, Primestar. By June 1995, DIRECTV had more than 500,000 subscribers scattered across the United States, with projections calling for the company to slip past the one-millionth-subscriber mark by the end of 1995. In early 1996, the company gained its first major partner when AT&T Corp. paid $137.5 million for a 2.5 percent stake in the company, kicking off a banner year in which one million new subscribers signed up for DIRECTV. By the end of 1996, revenues reached $621 million, but profitability still eluded the company.

Chasing Growth in the Late 1990s

DIRECTV performed remarkably well in its fourth year of operation, but the celebratory mood that should have pervaded company headquarters in El Segundo, California, was tempered by an anticlimactic air. During the year, the company signed up its three millionth subscriber, reaching the point of projected profitability, but 1997 ended with a loss. In other respects, the company was demonstrating enviable strength. DIRECTV had nearly one million more subscribers than its closest competitor, it controlled nearly 50 percent of the U.S. DBS market, and the company's revenues had more than doubled in 1997, reaching $1.28 billion. The cost of luring new subscribers, however, meant jeopardizing profitability. In an effort to stimulate demand, the company lowered the price of its dish and set-top box to $199, further distancing itself from the threshold of profitability. Although DIRECTV was recording robust growth, some analysts wondered whether the company would accumulate too much in operating losses while it hotly pursued new subscribers.

As the company entered 1998, the word from Hughes was that the company would sacrifice profits to gain new subscribers. One of the major factors prompting the decision was the expected implementation of digital compression technology by the cable industry. In early 1998, the cable industry was beginning to embrace the technology, which as it had for DBS operators, would increase capacity and picture quality. DIRECTV believed it needed to act fast before an important marketing advantage began to lose its strength. In a March 1998 interview with the *Los Angeles Business Journal,* Mike Smith, Hughes's chairman and chief executive officer, explained: "We have decided to postpone profitability in our DIRECTV business another year because we think it's better to lower our prices and add more subscribers while cable is still vulnerable. They haven't yet gone to digital . . . we are trying to take advantage of this window that we now have."

The actions of DIRECTV during the last years of the 1990s demonstrated its determination to sign up new subscribers. In March 1999, the company began a national retail and marketing promotion to new subscribers that included free installation and three months of free service. The offering helped DIRECTV sign up 120,000 new subscribers in March alone, leading to a record first quarter of 1999 during which more than 300,000 subscribers signed up. A bigger boost to the company's subscriber rolls arrived via acquisition. In January 1999, Hughes announced the acquisition of DIRECTV's major partner, United States Satellite Broadcasting, and DIRECTV's closest competitor, Primestar, as well as the purchase of two high-power satellites. After the deals were completed, DIRECTV's programming selection exceeded 200 channels and its subscriber count swelled to more than seven million.

By August 2000, DIRECTV had more than 8.5 million subscribers, trailing only cable behemoths AT&T and Time Warner in the number of multichannel video subscribers. According to company projections, DIRECTV expected to reach ten million subscribers by the end of the year. Although the company was close to turning a profit, some analysts were worried by slackening new subscriber growth, while other analysts offered a more optimistic perspective, pointing to potential growth that could witness DIRECTV catapulting past AT&T and Time Warner by 2005. As it had been since the company's inception, DIRECTV's future was clouded by numerous factors. However, few could deny the company's strident progress and its entrenched market position. If direct-to-home satellite television came to dominate the nation's media landscape, no company stood better poised than DIRECTV to reap a lion's share of the financial rewards.

Principal Subsidiaries

DIRECTV Latin America.

Principal Competitors

AT&T Broadband, LCC; Echostar Communications Corporation; Time Warner Inc.

Further Reading

Brown, Rich, "Dishing Up Full Power," *Broadcasting & Cable,* March 28, 1994, p. 48.

Colman, Price, "A Mixed Bag for DBS: While Subscribers and Revenue Are Growing, Industry Faces Variety of Challenges," *Broadcasting & Cable,* June 9, 1997, p. 41.

——, "No Laurel-Resting for DirecTV's Hartenstein," *Broadcasting & Cable,* November 3, 1997, p. 52.

Crespo, Mariana, " 'You Get More Eyeballs,' " *Financial World,* February 14, 1995, p. 94.

Dziatkiewicz, Mark, "The One to Watch," *America's Network,* June 15, 1995, p. 55.

"Eddy Hartenstein," *Satellite Communications,* July 1993, p. 26.

Fine, Howard, "Smith on Mission to Beat Cable with DirecTV," *Los Angeles Business Journal,* March 9, 1998, p. 3.

Gorchov, Jolie, "Satellite TV Gets Boost, but Cable Still Has an Edge," *Los Angeles Business Journal,* December 13, 1999, p. 8.

Green, Michelle Y., "The DirecTV System, How It Works," *Broadcasting & Cable,* May 31, 1999, p. 24.

——, "Sitting on Top of the World," *Broadcasting & Cable,* May 31, 1999, p. 4.

La Franco, Robert, "The Unlikely Mogul," *Forbes,* November 30, 1998, p. 52.

Maney, Kevin, "Revolution from on High," *Canadian Business,* June 1995, p. 81.

Mermigas, Diane, "Hughes Denies DirecTV Spinoff; Parent Company Seeks Acquisitions to Complement Its Satellite Service," *Electronic Media,* June 12, 2000, p. 3.

—Jeffrey L. Covell

EASTMAN
www.eastman.com

Eastman Chemical Company

100 North Eastman Road
P.O. Box 511
Kingsport, Tennessee 37662-5075
U.S.A.
Telephone: (423) 229-2000
Toll Free: (800) 327-8626
Fax: (423) 229-1351
Web site: http://www.eastman.com

Public Company
Incorporated: 1994
Employees: 14,736
Sales: $4.59 billion (1999)
Stock Exchanges: New York
Ticker Symbol: EMN
NAIC: 325131 Inorganic Dye and Pigment Mfg. (pt); 325188 All Other Basic Inorganic Chemical Mfg. (pt); 325199 All Other Basic Organic Chemical Mfg. (pt); 325211 Plastics Material and Resin Mfg.; 325221 Cellulosic Organic Fiber Mfg.; 32591 Printing Ink Mfg.; 325998 All Other Miscellaneous Chemical Product and Preparation Mfg. (pt); 541710 Research and Development in the Physical, Engineering, and Life Sciences

Founded in 1920 as a subsidiary of the Eastman Kodak Company, Eastman Chemical Company was spun off as an independent company by Kodak in 1994. Eastman Chemical produces a wide range of plastics, chemicals, and fibers and is a world leader in the production and recycling of polyester plastics. Since the mid-1990s the company has been engaged in a major globalization effort, making a number of key acquisitions worldwide and establishing a prominent e-commerce presence.

U.S. Chemical Production in the Wake of World War I

When World War I broke out in 1914, George Eastman watched the supply of essential materials arriving from European producers to his company, the Eastman Kodak Company, slow to a trickle. The ramifications were nearly disastrous. The company had grown dependent on European manufacturers for many of the raw materials required to sustain its operations, particularly photographic paper, optical glass, and gelatin, without which Eastman's photography empire would shrivel into insolvency. Also of great importance and in short supply during the war years were the numerous chemicals crucial to the photography company's production processes, including methanol, acetic acid, and acetone. As the war dragged on, Eastman's predicament grew increasingly severe, and film production at Eastman Kodak's manufacturing facilities in Rochester, New York, nearly ground to a halt.

Determined to ensure Kodak's future self-reliance, Eastman decided the most prudent solution was to develop an independent supply of chemicals. Accordingly, after the conclusion of the war, Eastman and other Kodak delegates began searching for a suitable location for a Kodak-owned and -operated chemical production facility. As Kodak employees were scouting the country, a resident of Kingsport, Tennessee, named J. Fred Johnson was conducting a nationwide search of his own, hoping to sell a half-built wood distillation plant to an interested party. Johnson, an employee of the Kingsport Improvement Company, was attempting to revitalize Kingsport's economy, which had thrived during the war but was limping along at the war's conclusion, bereft of the business generated by the manufacturing industries that had temporarily established operations in Kingsport for war-related work.

One company that had come to Kingsport during the war was the American Wood Reduction Company, which had contracted with the federal government to construct a wood distillation plant for making methanol and other related chemicals. Before the plant was finished, however, the war ended and American Wood Reduction cut its ties to Kingsport, leaving a lone watchman to stand guard over the partly constructed facility. After the retreat of American Wood Reduction, Johnson began his search for an industrial concern that could use the idle wood distillation plant.

By 1920 Kodak and Johnson had found each other, and a group of Kodak representatives led by Perley S. Wilcox, a future chairman of Kodak and an employee since 1898, arrived in Kingsport to examine the half-built wood distillation facility

Company Perspectives:

"With our intense focus on delivering improved performance, we expect to improve earnings as business conditions improve and the benefits of our cost reductions are realized. I firmly believe that the best days of Eastman are ahead of us. The industry has moved through the trough of the chemical cycle and the business climate worldwide is becoming more favorable to us. This growth, along with innovative efforts such as e-commerce, should produce significant value creation for all of us as shareowners."

—Earnest W. Deavenport, Jr., chairman and CEO

Johnson was eager to sell. Finding it to their liking, the Kodak group pushed for its acquisition, and later that year George Eastman authorized the purchase of the plant and surrounding acreage for $205,000. Wilcox was named director and general manager of the new company, becoming the first leader of Tennessee Eastman Corporation, a Kodak subsidiary.

Shortly after the construction of the wood distillation plant was finished, the solitary watchman who had guarded an architectural skeleton was replaced by more than 300 Tennessee Eastman employees, who were given the task of meeting Kodak's substantial chemical needs. Kodak's Rochester facilities required 40,000 gallons of methanol per month, in addition to other necessary chemicals such as acetic acid and acetone.

Tennessee Eastman delivered its first shipment of methanol to Rochester in July 1921. The company generated $35,000 in sales after its first year, but its total production fell short of Kodak's chemical needs for the next several years. In addition, the Kingsport plant was unprofitable and would remain so long after its production volume was raised to a sufficient level.

Product Diversification in the 1920s and 1930s

By the mid-1920s Tennessee Eastman was satisfying Rochester's monthly methanol needs, but weak profits continued to hound Tennessee Eastman for another decade. To improve profitability, the company began marketing the byproducts created from the Kingsport plant's distillation processes, including charcoal, tars, wood preservatives, and other process wastes. Charcoal powder and wood tar were combined to form a charcoal briquette that the company sold as cooking and household fuel, transforming the 300 railroad cars of charcoal dust the company produced each month into a money-making sideline business. Other byproducts from the Kingsport plant also were marketed, including coal tars and various derivatives of acetone (which were sold to sugar refineries), as well as lumber.

Process economy started Tennessee Eastman down the road toward profitability and provided a springboard for diversification into segments of the chemical industry exclusive of Kodak's needs. Sales in 1930 were $1.95 million, with acetic anhydride and lumber ranking as the company's two major products. During the 1930s, Tennessee Eastman began to make pivotal contributions to its parent company's Rochester facilities, beginning with its manufacture of cellulose acetate in 1930. Kodak had experimented with using cellulose acetate as a film base back in 1907, striving to replace flammable nitrocellulose with a nonflammable alternative. The company's innovation quickly became the industry standard.

Perhaps more important, Tennessee Eastman distinguished itself as a leader and pioneer in the chemical industry through its production of acetate yarn. An experimental acetate yarn plant had been constructed in 1928, and by 1931 the Kingsport-based facility had begun large-scale production, churning out 287,000 pounds of yarn that year alone. Within a decade, Tennessee Eastman's acetate yarn was recognized throughout the textile industry as the best quality yarn on the market, securing the company's economic stability for the next two decades and paving the way for the development of other mainstay products.

One year after large-scale production of acetate yarn had begun, Tennessee Eastman began producing Tenite cellulosic plastics, which were used for radio parts, toys, telephones, and automobile steering wheels. That year, 1932, also was the first year Tennessee Eastman's trade sales exceeded its sales to Kodak.

Reorganization: 1950–68

By 1940 Tennessee Eastman was recording nearly $30 million in annual sales, an exponential increase from the $1.95 million generated ten years earlier. The increase had been fueled primarily by the company's production of acetate yarn, which by this point was Tennessee Eastman's single major product, as it would be a decade later, when annual sales stood at $130 million. Kodak organized an additional chemical subsidiary in 1950, Texas Eastman Company, then formed Eastman Chemical Products, Inc., in 1953 to serve as the marketing arm for both Texas Eastman and Tennessee Eastman. Tennessee Eastman, meanwhile, had undergone a name change, switching its corporate title from Tennessee Eastman Corporation to Tennessee Eastman Company in 1951. Although the name change was minor, a significant development occurred contemporaneously that dramatically altered the company's future. During the early 1950s, Tennessee Eastman developed cellulose acetate filter tow, which was used in cigarette filters, giving the company a product that drove sales upward for the next half century and supplanted acetate yarn as its mainstay product.

With filter tow sales leading the way, Tennessee Eastman registered $244 million in annual sales in 1960, continuing to record exponential leaps in annual revenues decade by decade. In 1968 the Eastman Chemicals Division of Eastman Kodak Company was formed, bringing together the various chemical concerns within Kodak's corporate structure and unifying them as a division. When it was organized, the chemicals division included Tennessee Eastman, Texas Eastman Company, Carolina Eastman Company, Eastman Chemicals Products, Inc., and the following related marketing organizations: Holston Defense Corporation, Ectona Fibers Limited, Bay Mountain Construction Company, and Caddo Construction Company.

With this collection of companies banded together, annual sales generated by the division shot upward, swelling to $588 million in 1970, a revenue total derived in large part from the production of filter tow and polyester fibers. Late in the decade, the Eastman Chemicals Division introduced polyethylene terephthalate (PET) resin, used to make plastic containers. The

Key Dates:

1920: Tennessee Eastman Corporation is created as a subsidiary of Eastman Kodak Company.
1931: Tennessee Eastman begins large-scale production of acetate yarn.
1950: Texas Eastman Company is formed.
1951: Tennessee Eastman Corporation becomes Tennessee Eastman Company.
1954: Eastman begins producing polyethylene.
1968: Eastman Chemicals Division is formed.
1978: Eastman begins producing PET resin.
1990: Eastman Chemicals Division is reorganized as Eastman Chemical Company.
1994: Eastman Chemical Company is incorporated.
2000: Eastman announces that it will begin online marketing of its chemicals and polymers.

addition of PET to the division's product line helped annual sales exceed $2 billion by the beginning of the 1980s.

In 1990 Kodak reorganized its chemicals division, renaming it Eastman Chemical Company. Annual sales by this point exceeded $3.5 billion, ranking the company among the largest chemical concerns in the world. With large market shares in PET and cellulosics, Eastman Chemical entered the 1990s as the jewel of the Kodak empire. Kodak, on the other hand, was not faring as well. As the decade progressed, debt began to mount, and Eastman Chemical was put in the awkward position of supplying cash to its debt-heavy parent, a reversal of roles for the former captive chemical supplier that complicated its corporate priorities and hobbled its investments in chemical operations.

As a result, Kodak spun off its chemical subsidiary to Kodak shareholders on the first day of 1994, creating the tenth largest chemical company in the country. As part of the spinoff, Eastman Chemical was saddled with $1.8 billion in long-term debt. By the end of its first year as an independent company, however, Eastman Chemical had whittled its debt down by $600 million, reducing its ratio of debt to total capital from 63 percent to 48 percent during a 12-month span. Sales also continued to grow into the mid-1990s, surpassing the $5 billion mark for the first time in 1995.

Globalization in the 1990s

Eastman Chemical moved toward its future as an independent chemical supplier supported by four core product groups: container plastics, specialty polyester packaging plastics, coatings materials for paints and solvents, and filter tow. Like other major chemical companies, Eastman realized that international expansion was the only way to maintain a competitive edge into the next century. Overall, the U.S. chemical industry saw significant growth in exports in the first half of the 1990s, from $43 billion in 1991 to $64.7 billion in 1996, and Eastman was no exception. In 1994 approximately one-third of Eastman's $4.3 billion in total sales came from international markets; by 1997 foreign sales exceeded $1.8 billion and accounted for 39 percent of the company's total sales. Much of the increase was the result of increased production capacity, both at home and abroad. In 1996 and 1997, Eastman opened new container plastics manufacturing operations in Mexico and Spain; in 1998 it began production at plants in Argentina and Malaysia, and at two new plants in The Netherlands. Also in 1997, Eastman Chemical Ltd., Singapore took steps toward establishing a niche in the burgeoning Chinese market, investing several hundred million dollars into new facilities in the Special Economic Zone of Shenzhen, China.

Eastman's expansion plans ultimately got ahead of economic reality, however, and by 1997 the company found itself burdened with significant production overcapacity. This reversal of fortune was in part the result of decreased demand for the company's specialty and performance products, particularly in the United States and China. Increased competition, brought on by globalization and the struggle over emerging marketplaces, also contributed to the excess capacity. The subsequent lower prices and decreased volume were accompanied by rising raw material costs, and Eastman suffered steadily decreasing earnings from 1996 to 1998.

The company responded to this sudden downturn with an aggressive restructuring plan. It implemented a drastic cost-reduction program, pledging to cut $500 million in expenses between 1997 and 2000, and in 1999 it reorganized itself into two business segments, polymers and chemicals. In addition, by the end of 2000 the company divested itself of the propylene glycol segment of its fine chemicals division, to focus its attention on potentially more lucrative adhesives, inks, and coatings markets. Toward this aim, in 2000 the company announced its intention to acquire the hydrocarbon resins and part of the rosins resins concerns of Hercules, Inc.

In the late 1990s Eastman also made strides toward establishing Internet capability. The commodity nature of chemicals made them a logical fit for e-commerce, since they were subject to fairly regular international standards, which made the selling process relatively straightforward. Eastman was determined to take advantage of the new technology, and in October 2000 it announced a plan to make its chemicals and polymers available through online business-to-business relationships with existing customers, as well as through its web site and a number of virtual marketplaces.

This reorganization, along with the shift to e-commerce, made some downsizing inevitable, and Eastman's workforce was reduced by almost 2,000 employees between 1996 and 1999. By 1999, however, Eastman saw a slight increase in business for the first time in four years, and in 2000 it was able to announce a plan to increase its PET manufacturing capacity by 110,000 metric tons a year. By the end of the third quarter of 2000 the company was on a pace to exceed $5 billion in sales for the first time since 1995, although continually rising fuel prices and the general slowdown of the world's economy made the future far from certain.

Principal Subsidiaries

ABCO Industries, Incorporated; Lawter International, Inc.; McWhorter Technologies, Inc.; Genencor International, Inc. (50%); Primester (50%); Jager, Fabrik Chemischer Rohstoffe

GmbH & Co. (Germany); Eastman Chemical, Europe, Middle East and Africa, Ltd. (The Netherlands); Chemicke Zavody Sokolov (Czech Republic; 76%); Eastman Chemical Ltd. (Singapore).

Principal Divisions

Arkansas Eastman Division; Carolina Operations Division; Tennessee Eastman Division; Texas Eastman Division.

Principal Competitors

BASF Aktiengesellschaft; The Dow Chemical Company; Union Carbide Corporation.

Further Reading

Brister, Kathy, ''Information Technology Grows in Importance at Eastman,'' *Knoxville News-Sentinel,* March 4, 1999.

''Eastman Chemical,'' *Rubber World,* August 1995, p. 6.

''Eastman Growth Strategy Includes a Global Reach,'' *Chemical Marketing Reporter,* November 14, 1994, p. 24.

Hunter, David, ''Eastman's Deavenport in the Driver's Seat,'' *Chemical Week,* June 29, 1994, p. 36.

Kiesche, Elizabeth, ''Prospects for Success of Fresh Chemical Spinoffs Look Mixed,'' *Chemical Week,* January 5, 1994, p. 20.

McCall, Ron, *Eastman Chemical Company: Years of Glory, Times of Change,* Rochester: Eastman Kodak Company, 1990.

Miller, James P., ''Eastman Chemical Co. Is Developing Its Own Image,'' *Wall Street Journal,* November 14, 1994, p. B3.

Prince, Greg, ''Summer Vacation? No Way!,'' *Beverage World,* August 1991, p. 48.

Sparks, Debra, '' 'We Have to Show Them': There's a Lot Below the Surface at Eastman Chemical—Too Bad Wall Street Can't See It,'' *Financial World,* May 10, 1994, p. 37.

—Jeffrey L. Covell
—updated by Stephen Meyer

Echo Bay Mines Ltd.

10180 101st Street
Suite 1210
Edmonton, Alberta T5J 3S4
Canada
Telephone: (403) 429-5811
Fax: (403) 429-5899
Web site: http://www.echobay.com

6400 S. Fiddler's Green Circle
Suite 540
Englewood, Colorado 80111-4957
U.S.A.
Telephone: (303) 714-8800
Toll Free: (800) 395-4143
Fax: (303) 714-8994

Public Company
Incorporated: 1964
Employees: 1,212
Sales: US$210.4 million (1999)
Stock Exchanges: American Toronto Paris Brussels Zurich Frankfurt
Ticker Symbol: ECO
NAIC: 212221 Gold Ore Mining; 212222 Silver Ore Mining

Echo Bay Mines Ltd. is one of North America's largest gold mining concerns. Founded in 1964 as a high-risk silver mining outfit, Echo Bay has grown into one of the leading precious-metal mining operations in the world. Echo Bay is respected for its excellence in mining in remote and hostile regions. The company's mining expertise has made it a sought-after partner for joint ventures. Echo Bay has a history of turning a profit on risky enterprises that other mining groups have declined.

Into the Wild: 1960s

In the early 1960s a group of Edmonton entrepreneurs operating under the name Northwest Explorers saw an opportunity in Canada's northwest. A forgotten silver claim, a dormant mill, and a new railroad were the ingredients N.S. Edgar, E.R. Mead, and A.J. McBeth saw as the recipe for a fortune. The Edmonton businessmen devised a plan to finance and operate a silver mine near Canada's frigid Great Bear Lake. The venture centered around a silver deposit first discovered in 1935 by the Consolidated Mining and Smelting Company, later known as Cominco. Cominco had drilled two adits—gradually declining tunnels—in the mid-1930s, to check the ore grade and extent of the vein. Concluding that the Echo Bay claim would not be profitable, Cominco tabled the idea indefinitely.

The Northwest Explorers group, remembering the old Echo Bay claims, observed developments in the early 1960s that changed the picture. In 1960 the Eldorado mining operation, located five miles west of the Echo Bay site, shut down. Its facilities seemed destined to rust in the Arctic cold. Meanwhile, the decision to build the Pine Point Railway reduced the transportation problems associated with operating a mine so far north. Armed with this knowledge, and certain optimism, the Northwest Explorers raised the capital, optioned the property, and leased the Eldorado mill. In 1963 new surveys indicated that the mine could turn a profit, and, by October 1964, the Echo Bay mine at Port Radium was fully operative, milling 80 tons of silver ore per day. In 1965 Echo Bay averaged 52.6 ounces of silver per ton of ore, making it the richest silver mine in Canada. By 1966 new drilling indicated that the deposits were much more extensive than anyone had dreamed. Echo Bay bought the Eldorado mill and plant outright, and stepped up production.

Most silver producers mined the metal secondarily to another metal such as gold, copper, lead, or zinc. Echo Bay, however, was one of a handful of mining firms whose principal product at the time was silver. Industrial usage of silver as a conductor of electricity and in photographic films helped keep the metal in short supply and thus priced high. North American consumption was actually twice production. As a result, in the mid-1960s, Echo Bay was extremely profitable.

In 1967 International Utilities Corporation, a Philadelphia, Pennsylvania-based conglomerate, purchased a majority of Echo Bay stock, eventually holding three-fourths of the company's shares. International Utilities operated the company as a subsidiary, focusing on silver production at the Echo Bay mine.

Key Dates:

1935: Echo Bay silver deposit is discovered by Consolidated Mining and Smelting Company.
1964: Echo Bay begins full-scale mining operations at Port Radium.
1967: International Utilities Corporation purchases majority stock in Echo Bay.
1979: Echo Bay options rights to develop Lupin gold claim.
1982: Lupin mine begins operations; Port Radium site closes.
1986: Echo Bay acquires McCoy gold mine in Nevada.
1997: Alaska-Juneau mining operations are terminated.
1998: Lupin mine closes temporarily.
2000: Lupin mine reopens.

In 1969 Echo Bay experienced a decrease in profits as silver prices dropped and the favorable tax conditions for new mines ran out. Echo Bay's earnings were tied more closely to the price of silver than were the earnings of other companies that mined silver primarily as a byproduct of copper or of other metals. As a result Echo Bay stockpiled silver when prices were low, as in 1971, and mined lower grade ores when those prices were high. This strategy, along with cost efficiency efforts, insured a long life for the mine.

A New Gold Standard: The 1970s and 1980s

Throughout the 1970s Echo Bay remained a medium-sized silver-mining concern excavating the rich veins beneath the frozen earth at Port Radium. In 1975, however, an event occurred that drastically altered the company's make-up. The longstanding U.S. ban on private ownership of gold bullion was lifted, and the metal's price rocketed. The soaring price of gold, which eventually reached US$600 an ounce in 1981, sparked the interest of Echo Bay. In 1979 the company optioned rights to develop the Lupin gold claim from another Canadian mining company, Inco Limited.

The Lupin site was 56 miles south of the Arctic Circle, making it a high-cost operation; but Echo Bay's expertise in mining frozen wastelands had been sharpened through its years of experience at its Port Radium operation, and the company was optimistic it could turn a profit. Lupin's probable and possible reserves were about 2.7 million tons of ore, with a grade of 0.38 troy ounces per ton, giving the mine about a seven-year life expectancy. Financing was raised through a preferred stock and warrant issue, and preliminary planning anticipated active production by 1982. The cost of developing the mine was expected to be C$108 million. Mining leases and permits were purchased in 1980, and the free world's northernmost gold mine began operations on schedule in 1982.

The Lupin mine proved to be a good investment indeed. The mine averaged 156,000 troy ounces of gold during its first two years, making it Canada's third largest gold mine. Production gradually increased during the 1980s, averaging about 195,880 ounces per year in the latter half of the decade. New reserves were found, extending the mine's life. By 1990, the main shaft was deepened to about 4,000 feet, and Echo Bay anticipated production of about 190,000 ounces annually for the foreseeable future.

Operating a mine so far north had unique problems, transportation being the most severe. When the Lupin mine was constructed in the early 1980s, all the materials had to be shipped in by airplane, at great cost. Each winter, Echo Bay spent about US$3 million to build and maintain a 360-mile ice road, 340 miles of which was over frozen lakes. Between January and April, trucks delivered much of Lupin's supplies for the year, including some five million gallons of diesel fuel and 15 million pounds of chemicals, explosives, and other bulk materials. Some 700 to 900 roundtrips were made every winter between Lupin and Yellowknife, taking 24 hours each way. The ice road allowed Echo Bay to avoid the even higher cost of air freight. Although the cost of operating a mine so far north resulted in an ''Arctic premium'' of about 35 percent, the high grade of the z-shaped ore deposit at Lupin allowed the mine to operate profitably.

The opening of the Lupin mine in 1982 coincided with the closing of Echo Bay's flagship silver mine near Port Radium. After 19 years, the original Echo Bay silver operation was tapped out. Echo Bay Mines had been transformed from a silver miner to a gold miner, and with the transition came new anxieties. Gold mines generally traded on the open market at a much higher price-to-earnings ratio than silver mines or conglomerates; and Echo Bay's parent, International Utilities Corporation, feared a corporate raid. In 1983 International Utilities spun off Echo Bay's shares directly to its own shareholders, who benefited from the higher stock values of a publicly owned gold mine. The parent company, meanwhile, decreased the risk of a hostile takeover.

Echo Bay's success with the Lupin operation inspired the company to expand further into the gold-mining industry. In 1984 Echo Bay acquired the Copper Range Company from Louisiana Land and Exploration, for US$55 million. Echo Bay was interested by the Round Mountain gold mine in Nevada, which was 50 percent-owned by Copper Range. Two other gold mining firms—Homestake Mining Company and Case, Pomeroy & Company, Inc.—each owned a quarter of the mine. The Round Mountain mine used heap leaching, a process that allows cheap mineral recovery from low-grade ores. With this method, deposits previously disregarded can be mined profitably. Echo Bay Chairman Robert F. Calman told the *Wall Street Journal* in December 1984 that in buying Cooper Range Company, ''We've bought the expertise as well as the company.''

Further Expansion in the Late 1980s

Heap-leaching technology would prove invaluable to Echo Bay in future ventures. Simplified, the process begins with recovery of ore from the traditional open pit. The ore is then crushed into pebbles smaller than an inch in diameter, and placed on massive impermeable pads that extend for acres. The three-story-high heaped ore is then sprinkled with sodium cyanide for 100 days. The solution penetrates the ore, bonding with the gold and silver, which then runs off to a collection drain. The precious metal-pregnant solution is then pumped into tanks where it is concentrated by a carbon absorption and desorption process. Gold and silver are then removed from the concentrated solution by electrolysis and refined into doré bars—part silver, part gold with some impurities. The doré is then sent to a separate refinery for processing into pure bullion bars.

With its expertise in Arctic mining and heap-leach processing, Echo Bay set out on a program of exploration and acquisition. In late 1985 the company agreed to buy the Sunnyside gold and silver mine in Colorado from Standard Metals Corporation for US$20 million plus royalties. In 1986 Echo Bay bought several properties from Tenneco, including three gold mines in Nevada—Borealis, Manhattan, and McCoy—for US$130 million and royalties.

The McCoy mine turned out to be a jewel. Several months after it took over the operation, Echo Bay discovered a massive gold deposit one mile from the McCoy mine. Known as the Cove deposit, the discovery contained an estimated 1.2 million ounces of gold and 53 million ounces of silver. Later estimates assessed Cove's riches at 4 million ounces of gold and 250 million ounces of silver. Plans for a new mill, to be ready by 1989, were developed. Heap leaching began in 1988.

The combined McCoy and Cove mining complex covered 110 square miles, and in 1989 produced 246,800 gold equivalent ounces, which included silver value converted to gold ounces at the average market price ratio, twice the 1988 level. Both mines operated with open pits and underground ramps; they share milling and leaching facilities. By the end of 1989 Echo Bay had invested US$383 million in the acquisition and development of McCoy and Cove. The company expected to mine 350,000 gold equivalent ounces from the operation in 1990, at a cost of about US$240 per ounce.

In 1988 Echo Bay entered a joint venture with Silver King Mines and Pacific Silver Corporation. Echo Bay's Sunnyside mine in Colorado, Illipah mine in Nevada, Easy Junior and Pan development properties in Nevada, and Pacific Silver's Robinson and Golden Butte mines in Nevada would be operated by Silver King. The deal promised to improve Echo Bay's overall gold output in the long run while allowing the company to concentrate its own efforts on other projects. Subsequently, the operating partner became known as the Alta Gold Company.

In 1987 Echo Bay decided to expand the Round Mountain mine. The mill at the Manhattan mine, located 18 miles from Round Mountain, began processing Round Mountain's high-grade ores. Milling is preferred to heap leaching where an ore grade measures a certain richness because more gold can be milled out of the high grade ore than can be recovered by leaching. The complex, including the Manhattan operation, was expected to produce 440,000 ounces of gold in 1990. New reserves placed the mine's active life at 15 years at that rate.

In April 1988 Echo Bay Mines acquired significant interests in the Muscocho mining group of companies—consisting of Muscocho Explorations Ltd., Flanagan McAdam Resources Inc., and McNellan Resources Inc. The deal included the purchase by Echo Bay of C$26.5 million worth of newly issued common shares and C$23.5 million in convertible bonds. Echo Bay agreed not to increase its interests in the group to more than 33 percent for six years. Muscocho group's Magino and Magnacon properties in Ontario, and the Montauban mine in Quebec, represented Echo Bay's first participation in eastern Canadian mines.

The acquisition proved a major disappointment for Echo Bay, however. By mid-1989, Muscocho's Magino and Magnacon mines were far behind schedule. Echo Bay traded its one-third equity in Muscocho plus some cash and loans for 36 percent direct ownership of Magnacon and 50 percent of Magino; and Echo Bay also became the mines' operator. Although the Muscocho investment was a costly write-down for Echo Bay, the future of the two mines it retained from the deal was bright.

In February 1990 Echo Bay began operating its 70 percent-owned Kettle River gold mine in Washington state. The mine was expected to produce 110,000 ounces of gold annually, and the possibility of discovering additional reserves seemed excellent. Other promising ventures for Echo Bay's future included two major mine development properties in Alaska. The Alaska-Juneau mine was at one time the largest gold mine in North America. It was shut down during World War II. Echo Bay owned 85 percent of the mine and was preparing in 1990 to start large-scale production, expected to be about 365,000 ounces annually by 1993 or 1994. By 1990 Echo Bay also owned 50 percent of the Kensington mine located 45 miles north of the Alaska-Juneau property, and was studying the feasibility of starting operations there. The ore body at Kensington was considered especially rich, three times the grade at Alaska-Juneau. The company hoped to mine 200,000 ounces of gold per year at a cost somewhat lower than its other operations.

Gold Market Goes Bust

However, the early 1990s brought hard times to the world gold market, and the effects on the company's fortunes were nearly disastrous. The price of gold rose a mere one percent between 1989 and 1990, while mining expenses rose 11 percent, leaving Echo Bay with a net loss of US$59.7 million for fiscal 1990. After some crucial write-downs—including the Muscocho Group investment—the company entered 1991 determined to increase production by 12 percent. With worldwide gold production growth virtually at a standstill, and with economic prosperity in Asia opening up potential new markets, the company was able to see a small profit in 1991. However, the benefits of this aggressive strategy were only temporary, and 1992 brought decreased overall revenue and a net loss of $31 million.

Determined to jump-start its slumping business, Echo Bay sold six million of its common shares in July 1993, with the aim of increasing its operating revenue and freeing up resources for future investment. In 1994, after managing to cut production costs to US$199 per ounce, the company began actively pursuing new exploration opportunities overseas. In June it formed a joint venture with International Gold Resources to develop mining operations in Ghana; that same month it partnered with Santa Elina Gold Corp. to launch an exploration project in Brazil. In March 1995 it entered into an agreement with TVI to bid on the Kingking property in the Philippines. Echo Bay's efforts reflected a broader trend throughout the mining industry in the mid-1990s, as companies poured record amounts of money into international exploration projects, particularly in South America, Australia, and Southeast Asia. By

October 1996 Echo Bay had become the fourth largest spender in the industry.

Unfortunately, massive investment did not prove to be the cure for the company's problems, and in 1996 Echo Bay saw its revenues plummet to US$337.3 million—compared to US$360.7 million for 1995—while suffering a net loss of over US$175 million. Further exacerbating the company's financial woes were the continual difficulties involved with getting the Alaska-Juneau properties operational. A series of battles with the EPA over environmental issues had made it difficult for the company to obtain permits, and production costs were proving exceedingly high. By 1996 the company recognized that the expected yield of the mines would fall far short of original estimates, and in January 1997—after 12 years and over US$100 million invested—Echo Bay announced plans to terminate the Alaska-Juneau project.

By this time gold prices had fallen to an 18-year low, and Echo Bay was forced to scale back a number of its new operations. In April 1997 the company sold off its option in the Mexican Dolores property, which it had acquired the previous July, and in October it was compelled to decline to exercise its option on the Kingking project in the Philippines. In early 1998 it announced the temporary closing of the Lupin mine, a move that resulted in 650 layoffs. During this time the company reduced its overall workforce by one-third, and cut production by 25 percent. Fiscal 1997 was the worst in company history, bringing a net loss of US$420.5 million.

However, it appeared Echo Bay had gotten the damage under control; while the company continued to experience losses for the next two years, they were significantly less drastic—US$20.1 million in 1998, US$37.3 million in 1999. A number of key divestments, coupled with signs of improvement in the gold market, made it possible for Echo Bay to announce plans to reopen the Lupin mine by April 2000. In the third quarter of 2000 the company enjoyed net earnings of US$9 million, and seemed to have gotten back on an even keel.

Principal Competitors

Anglo American plc; Barrick Gold Corporation; Newmont Mining Corporation.

Further Reading

"Daring Pays Off for Company: Great Bear Lake Prospect Achieves," *Northern Miner*, November 24, 1966.

Gooding, Kenneth, "Mining Groups Spend Record Sums," *Financial Times* (London), October 23, 1996.

Heinzl, Mark, "Echo Bay Aims to Restore Golden Image," *Denver Rocky Mountain News*, January 7, 1996.

Henriques, Diana, "More Brass Than Gold?" *Barron's*, February 15, 1988.

Martin, Neil A., "Quest for Silver," *Barron's*, April 17, 1972.

McCartney, Laton, "Time for Gold?" *Town & Country*, March 1990.

Raabe, Steve, "Gold's Plunge Costly; Echo Bay Joins Cutback Club," *Denver Post,* January 7, 1998.

Rojo, Oscar, "Edmonton-Based Mining Company to Extend Global Reach," *Toronto Star*, June 13, 1994.

Rudnitsky, Howard, "Men Who Moil for Gold," *Forbes*, October 5, 1987.

Simon, Bernard, "Gold Miners Hit by Lackluster Price," *Financial Times* (London), March 7, 1991.

—Thomas M. Tucker
—updated by Stephen Meyer

FLEXTRONICS®

Flextronics International Ltd.

11 Ubi Road, #07-01/02
Meiban Industrial Building
Singapore 408723
Telephone: +65 844 3366
Fax: +65 448 6040
Web site: http://www.flextronics.com

Public Company
Incorporated: 1969 as Flextronics Inc.
Employees: 70,000
Sales: $6.4 billion (2000)
Stock Exchanges: NASDAQ
Ticker Symbol: FLEX
NAIC: 334413 Semiconductor and Related Device Manufacturing; 334418 Printed Circuit Assembly Manufacturing; 541420 Industrial Design Services

Flextronics International Ltd. claims to be the second largest electronic manufacturing services (EMS) provider in the world in terms of revenue, with estimated fiscal 2001 revenue of between $10 and $12 billion, behind industry leader Solectron Corp., with projected revenue of $15 billion. Through global expansion the company has more than 16 million square feet of facility space and some 70,000 employees worldwide. Flextronics expanded significantly by acquiring other manufacturers while taking advantage of the desire of original equipment manufacturers (OEMs) to outsource manufacturing and sell off their manufacturing facilities. In addition to manufacturing, Flextronics offers a full range of design services that enable it to create, test, and manufacture a product based on a customer's concept. Flextronics serves the manufacturing needs of customers in telecommunications, networking, computers, consumer electronics, and related industries.

Developing from ''Board Stuffer'' to Contract Manufacturer: 1969–92

Flextronics Inc. was founded in 1969 by Joe McKenzie to provide overflow manufacturing services to Silicon Valley companies that needed more printed circuit boards than they could produce in-house. The companies sent their overflow work to Flextronics, where McKenzie and his wife hand-soldered all the parts onto the boards and then returned the finished goods. This type of work was known as ''board stuffing.''

The business did well in the 1970s, and in 1980 Flextronics was sold to Bob Todd, Joe Sullivan, and Jack Watts. Todd became CEO and transformed the company from a board stuffer to a contract manufacturing firm. The company pioneered automated manufacturing techniques to reduce labor costs associated with board assembly. It introduced board-level testing to insure quality and in 1981 became the first American manufacturer to go offshore by setting up a manufacturing facility in Singapore.

Flextronics expanded its services in the 1980s and began delivering turnkey solutions in the middle of the decade. Based on customer specifications, Flextronics would handle everything from buying parts to manufacturing. The company also began offering computer-aided design (CAD) services, designing and blueprinting an entire printed circuit board based on a customer's idea. In 1987 the company was able to go public, but it was just three weeks before the stock market crashed.

Flextronics expanded to produce working, shippable products in the late 1980s. Its disk and tape subsystems were used in Sun Microsystems workstations. The Hayes modem was also a product that Flextronics helped assemble. The company built a global manufacturing base with factories located throughout Asia. Unfortunately, these factories relied on a high-volume U.S. market that virtually crashed during the economic recession of the early 1990s. As profits disappeared and losses mounted, survival of the company became paramount.

Since the Asian operations were still profitable, one option would have been to scale back or close the company's U.S. facilities. The high cost of closing a manufacturing facility, however, would have bankrupted the company. Instead, the Asian plants were spun off as a separate company and taken private in 1990 with the help of outside funding. The U.S. plants were subsequently closed.

Company Perspectives:

Headquartered in Singapore, Flextronics International is a leading provider of flexibility and speed in Electronics Manufacturing Services (EMS) to Original Equipment Manufacturers (OEMs) in the fast-growth communications, networking, computer, medical and consumer markets. Flextronics is a major global operating company with design, engineering and manufacturing operations in 28 countries and four continents. This global presence allows for manufacturing excellence through a network of global facilities situated in key markets that in turn provide its customers with the resources, technology and capacity to maximize productivity. Flextronics' ability to provide design and manufacturing services, coordinate innovative product design, provide a full spectrum of specialized services and IT [information technology] expertise, in conjunction with their global presence, establishes Flextronics as a top-tier EMS provider.

Growth Through Acquisitions: 1993–98

The new, private company—renamed Flextronics International Ltd.—had its headquarters in Singapore. Michael Marks became chairman in July 1993 and CEO in January 1994. The company had its initial public offering (IPO) in 1994, becoming a publicly traded company for the second time. Marks's strategy was to rebuild the company's U.S. presence. From 1992 to 1995 revenues nearly tripled to $237 million.

From 1993 to 1998, when Flextronics' revenues surpassed $1 billion (later restated to $2.3 billion to reflect acquistions), the company completed more than 12 acquisitions. It built a global infrastructure for high-volume manufacturing, expanded its purchasing and engineering capabilities, and increased its workforce from 3,000 to more than 13,000. At the core of Flextronics' international growth was its industrial park model. Located in low-cost regions of each major geographic area—including Mexico, Brazil, Hungary, China, and later in Poland and the Czech Republic—Flextronics' industrial parks brought suppliers onsite to decrease logistics costs, increase time-to-market, decrease shipping costs, and improve communication and quality. The co-location of manufacturing operations and suppliers in the industrial parks gave Flextronics greater operational flexibility and responsiveness to customer needs.

In 1994 Flextronics acquired nChip, which specialized in semiconductor packaging and multichip modules. In 1995 Microsoft picked Flextronics as its new turnkey contract manufacturer for its mouse. Among the products being discussed were wallet-size PCs and intelligent home devices linked to computers and other hardware.

In December 1996 Flextronics closed its contract electronic manufacturing plant in Richardson, Texas. The closure was part of the company's strategy to shutter its smaller plants in order to create larger campuses, or industrial parks, at other locations. Workers at the plant were offered jobs at Flextronics' San Jose, California facility. During the same year Flextronics acquired two companies in Hong Kong—the Astron Group and FICO Plastics Ltd.—and the Ericsson Business Networks production facility in Karlskrona, Sweden, which was finalized in April 1997.

In 1997 Flextronics completed a 150,000-square-foot expansion of its manufacturing and R&D facilities in San Jose, California, where its U.S. headquarters was located, giving it a total of 280,000 square feet in two buildings. Toward the end of the year a secondary stock offering of 1.5 million shares was expected to raise about $56 million. The company also expanded its global facilities, including an expansion of its plant in China from 210,000 square feet to 450,000 square feet, and built a new plant in Guadalajara, Mexico. By the end of 1997 Flextronics was ranked as the fifth largest contract manufacturer in the United States, up from tenth in 1995.

To better serve the wireless market, Flextronics and Dow Chemical Co. formed a joint venture called Intarsia Corp.—with Dow holding the majority interest—to produce thin-film integrated passive components. Flextronics expected to make use of Intarsia's capabilities to build and develop products for wireless communications OEMs.

Between March 1997 and mid-1998 Flextronics acquired seven manufacturing-related operations in Brazil, Hungary, Italy, Sweden, and the United States. As a result of these acquisitions, Flextronics' revenue more than doubled from $640 million in fiscal 1997 ending March 31 (subsequently restated to $1.5 billion), to $1.34 billion in fiscal 1998 (subsequently restated to $2.3 billion). Net income nearly doubled from $11.6 million (later restated to $43.6 million) to $22.4 million (later restated to $77.7 million).

More Acquisitions, Partnerships: 1998–2000

In 1998 Flextronics introduced a worldwide network of Product Introduction Centers (PICs), which were facilities that designed, prototyped, tested, and launched new products, thereby shortening critical time-to-market. Among the products designed and built by Flextronics were 3Com's Palm Pilot and the Microsoft mouse.

Hewlett-Packard selected Flextronics to be a primary manufacturer in Europe for its inkjet printers. Flextronics would supply printed circuit board assemblies and complete box assembly for the printers, which would be manufactured at the company's industrial park in Hungary.

By mid-1998 Flextronics had 2.6 million square feet of manufacturing space in 26 operation centers in Europe, the Americas, and Asia. Recent acquisitions included contract manufacturers Neutronics Holdings A.G., Conexao Informatica Ltd. of Brazil, and Altatron Inc. It also acquired DTM Products Inc., which produced injection molded plastics, and Energipilot A.B., which provided cables and engineering services.

Flextronics had aggressively gained manufacturing contracts among telecommunications and networking OEMs, including Ericsson A.B., Motorola Inc., Alcatel Alsthom, Bay Networks Inc., and Cisco Systems Inc. Telecommunications and networking products accounted for 46 percent of the company's revenue, followed by consumer goods (29 percent), computer products (12 percent), medical products (four per-

Key Dates:

1969: Company is founded in Silicon Valley as Flextronics Inc.
1980: Company is sold to new owners.
1981: Flextronics becomes the first American manufacturer to go offshore by setting up a manufacturing facility in Singapore.
1987: Flextronics goes public.
1990: The company goes private in a leveraged buyout and is reorganized as Flextronics International Ltd., with Singapore as its new base.
1994: Flextronics goes public for the second time.
1998: Annual revenue surpasses $1 billion in fiscal 1998 ending March 31, 1998.

cent), and others (nine percent). Having gained outsourcing contracts from computer OEMs Hewlett-Packard Co., Compaq Computer, and Intel, Flextronics expected computer products to account for 25 percent of its revenue in fiscal 1999. For the fiscal year ending March 31, 1999, Flextronics had revenue of $2.2 billion and net income of $60.9 million.

After letting up on acquisitions to consolidate its holdings, Flextronics announced in December 1998 that it would acquire the ABB Automation Products manufacturing plant in Vasteras, Sweden, which produced printed circuit boards and other electronic components. As a result, ABB would become a Flextronics customer, purchasing output from the plant's new owner.

In April 1999 Flextronics entered into a service partnership with Corio Inc., an application service provider. Under the agreement, Flextronics would host and maintain application software on its servers, while Corio would implement the software for their joint clients. This would enable clients to rent, rather than purchase, expensive enterprise resource planning (ERP) systems and help them meet capacity demands without big investments.

Also in April 1999 Flextronics announced that it would purchase a second manufacturing facility from Ericsson, this one located in Visby, Sweden. The purchase was part of a trend among contract manufacturers to acquire the manufacturing facilities of OEMs. Upon completion of the purchase Flextronics also announced a new global supply agreement with Ericsson. In June Flextronics strengthened its presence in Western Europe by acquiring Finnish telecommunications contract manufacturer Kyrel EMS Oyj for approximately $100 million in stock. Flextronics strengthened its relationship with Compaq when it won a new order to supply Compaq with printed circuit board assemblies for PC servers.

In October the company made a secondary stock offering of five million shares. Around this time it also expanded its manufacturing operations in Richardson, Texas, by leasing an additional 109,000 square feet, primarily to serve customer Lucent Technologies Inc. Then, in November 1999, Flextronics announced that it would purchase The Dii Group Inc. of Niwot, Colorado, for $2.4 billion in stock. It was the largest acquisition among contract manufacturers to date.

In January 2000 Flextronics was ranked third on *Industry Week's* list of "100 Best-Managed Companies." The company continued to acquire manufacturing facilities from OEMs, who were willing to divest them to concentrate on their core competencies. The acquisitions positively affected Flextronics' bottom line, as it reported its best quarter ever for the fiscal quarter ending December 31, 1999, when it had a 103 percent increase in quarterly revenue to $1.2 billion and a 117 percent increase in quarterly net income to $34.3 million. In January 2000 it acquired facilities in Rochester, New Hampshire, and Limerick, Ireland, from networking solutions provider Cabletron Systems for about $100 million.

In a move to increase its design capabilities, Flextronics appointed Nicholas Brathwaite to the new post of senior vice-president and chief technology officer. Brathwaite came to Flextronics in 1996 when the company acquired nChip, and he led the development of Flextronics' Product Introduction Centers (PICs). Flextronics planned to establish two or three more PICs in 2000, noting that more than half of the company's revenue was from products impacted by the centers.

In March 2000 Flextronics added more than 600,000 square feet of manufacturing space on the East Coast with the acquisition of four companies based in North Carolina's Research Triangle: Circuit Board Assemblers, Newport Technology Inc., EMC International, and Summit Manufacturing.

Flextronics also joined with Cadence Design Systems Inc. and Hewlett-Packard Co. to establish SpinCircuit Inc., an e-commerce company. SpinCircuit was an Internet gateway that would link printed circuit board (PCB) design engineers directly to suppliers of more than two million parts through its online catalog. SpinCircuit was intended to cut costs associated with PCB development and the selection of electronic components. Later in the year Flextronics and Cisco Systems partnered to integrate their supply chains via the Internet.

For fiscal 2000 ending March 31, Flextronics reported revenue of $4.3 billion (later restated to $6.4 billion), a 93 percent increase over the previous year. Net income nearly doubled to $120.9 million (later restated to $143.2 billion).

Flextronics made several acquisitions during 2000, with no end in sight. The largest was The Dii Group, completed in April 2000 for $2.4 billion, which gave Flextronics a manufacturing presence in Ireland, Germany, and the Czech Republic as well as additional PCB assembly capacity in China, Malaysia, Mexico, Austria, and the United States. Other acquisitions included Uniskor Ltd., the largest and fastest-growing EMS in Israel, for $20 million; enclosure maker Palo Alto Products International; Chicago-based Chatham Technologies Inc. for $590 million; Singapore-based JIT Holdings for $640 million; and plastics supplier Li Xin Industries Ltd. for about $69 million.

Major outsourcing contracts won in 2000 included a five-year agreement with Motorola Inc. with an estimated value of $30 billion in revenue. Motorola would outsource as much as 40 percent of its manufacturing operations affecting cell phones, two-way radios, set-top boxes, and other broadband cable products. Anticipating that consumer demand could fluctuate unpredictably, Motorola sought the greater flexibility offered by outsourcing the development and manufacture of communications-related products. As part of the agreement, Motorola made a $100 million equity investment in Flextronics that was convertible over time into 11 million shares of Flextronics stock, representing a three to five percent stake in the company.

Flextronics also continued to strengthen its manufacturing capabilities in Europe. It announced plans for an industrial park in Gdansk, Poland. For fiscal 1999 Europe accounted for 40 percent of Flextronics' revenue. The company's new Multek unit, acquired from The Dii Group, gained a 60,000-square-foot PCB manufacturing facility in Guadalajara, Mexico, with the purchase of Cumex Electronics S.A. de C.V.

In August 2000 Siemens signed an outsourcing agreement with Flextronics to build 33 million mobile telephones for Siemens by the end of 2003. Later in the year Flextronics purchased the Siemens operations in L'Aquila, Italy.

Around this time Flextronics acquired Chicago-based Chatham Technologies Inc. for about $590 million in stock. Chatham was a leading provider of integrated electronic packaging systems to the communications industry. Later in the year Flextronics would form a new enclosures business unit.

Flextronics' aggressive acquisitions strategy began to affect the company's bottom line in fiscal 2001. For the first quarter ending June 30, 2000, the company reported a $368.9 million loss. Without amortization and one-time charges, though, the company would have reported a $71.7 million profit.

In the meantime, Flextronics was anticipating aggressive growth over the next five years. According to *Business Week,* Chairman Michael Marks predicted Flextronics' revenue could grow to $50 billion in five years. Leading contract manufacturer Solectron Corp. was already on track to reach the $20 billion mark within a year. The electronic contract manufacturing industry was expected to grow at a 20 percent annual rate, and in the past four years the industry had more than doubled to $88 billion annually. Fueling this growth was the willingness of OEMs not only to outsource manufacturing, but also to sell their manufacturing facilities to contract manufacturers to achieve greater flexibility in meeting consumer demand.

Principal Divisions

Flextronics Design; Flextronics Enclosures; Flextronics Semiconductor; Flextronics Network Services; Multek; Flextronics Photonics.

Principal Competitors

Celestica Inc.; SCI Systems, Inc.; Solectron Corp.; Jabil Circuit, Inc.

Further Reading

Allen, Margaret, ''Flextronics to Close Plant,'' *Dallas Business Journal,* December 27, 1996, p. 1.

Barlas, Pete, ''Flextronics Eyes $60M from Stock Sale,'' *Business Journal,* September 29, 1997, p. 7.

''The Barons of Outsourcing,'' *Business Week,* August 28, 2000, p. 177.

Bishop, Amanda, ''Flextronics Expands Its Richardson Presence,'' *Dallas Business Journal,* November 12, 1999, p. 16.

Bruner, Richard, ''Flextronics Makes a Home in Hungary,'' *Electronic News (1991),* February 28, 2000, p. 10.

Bylinsky, Gene, ''Heroes of U.S. Manufacturing,'' *Fortune,* March 20, 2000, p. 192.

Caldwell, Bruce, ''Services Partnership—Corio, Flextronics to Offer Application Services to Small and Midsize Companies,'' *InformationWeek,* April 5, 1999, p. 99.

Demers, Marie Eve, ''SpinCircuit: Distribution's Next Frontier,'' *Electronic News (1991),* April 10, 2000, p. 14.

''Flexing Its Muscle,'' *Electronic News (1991),* October 18, 1999, p. 6.

''Flextronics Adding Ericsson Plant,'' *Electronic News (1991),* April 26, 1999, p. 36.

''Flextronics Adding on Facilities,'' *Electronic News (1991),* February 22, 1999, p. 34.

''Flextronics Buying Finland's Kyrel,'' *Electronic News (1991),* June 21, 1999, p. 62.

''Flextronics' Plastic Play,'' *Electronic News (1991),* September 4, 2000, p. 4.

''Flextronics to Buy ABB PCB Unit,'' *Electronic News (1991),* December 21, 1998, p. 22.

''Flextronics to Make HP Inkjet Printers in Europe,'' *Electronic News (1991),* June 15, 1998, p. 61.

Hersch, Warren S., ''Contract Manufacturer Spotlight—Flextronics Finds Niche in Telecom, Networking,'' *Computer Reseller News,* August 31, 1998, p. 115.

Kaiser, Rob, ''Motorola Makes Deal with Singapore-Based Electronics Manufacturer,'' *Knight-Ridder/Tribune Business News,* May 31, 2000.

King, Julia, ''Manufacturers Rent ERP Apps,'' *Computerworld,* April 5, 1999, p. 26.

Krause, Reinhardt, ''Microsoft in Hardware Push,'' *Electronic News (1991),* December 18, 1995, p. 1.

Kroll, Karen M., ''Taking Stock,'' *Industry Week,* January 10, 2000, p. 37.

Levine, Bernard, ''Boom Spurs Flextronics,'' *Electronic News (1991),* January 24, 2000, p. 4.

——, ''Celestica Completes $757.4M Offering,'' *Electronic News (1991),* March 13, 2000, p. 42.

——, ''Compaq, Flextronics Extend Relationship,'' *Electronic News (1991),* September 27, 1999, p. 49.

——, ''Contractors Design More,'' *Electronic News (1991),* February 14, 2000, p. 10.

——, ''Contractors Expand Again,'' *Electronic News (1991),* August 7, 2000, p. 17.

——, ''Contractors Tightening Their Grip,'' *Electronic News (1991),* November 29, 1999, p. 2.

——, ''Dow Chemical/Flextronics Form Passives Joint Venture,'' *Electronic News (1991),* December 22, 1997, p. 45.

——, ''Flextronics Deal Rocks EMS World,'' *Electronic News (1991),* June 5, 2000, p. 1.

——, ''Flextronics-Ericsson Visby Deal Complete,'' *Electronic News (1991),* July 12, 1999, p. 2.

——, ''Flextronics Sets Israeli Buy,'' *Electronic News (1991),* May 1, 2000, p. 60.

——, ''Is EMS the Final Answer?,'' *Electronic News (1991),* April 10, 2000, p. 2.

——, ''Multek Buys Mexican PCB House,'' *Electronic News (1991),* June 26, 2000, p. 54.

——, ''The Package,'' *Electronic News (1991),* January 24, 2000, p. 40.

McKernan, Ron, ''Contractors Charm the Street,'' *Electronic News (1991),* August 14, 2000, p. 44.

''More OEMs Sell Facilities to Contract Manufacturers,'' *Purchasing,* May 20, 1999, p. 84.

Roberts, Bill, ''Ready, Fire, Aim,'' *Electronic Business,* July 2000, p. 80.

Royal, Weld, ''Flextronics Looks Abroad,'' *Industry Week,* June 12, 2000, p. 14.

—David P. Bianco

Forstmann Little & Co.

767 Fifth Avenue
New York, New York 10153
U.S.A.
Telephone: (212) 355-5656
Fax: (212) 759-7059
Web site: http://www.forstmannlittle.com

Private Company
Founded: 1978
Employees: 20
Sales: $25 million (1998 est.)
NAIC: 52312 Securities Brokerage

Forstmann Little & Co. acquires or invests in high-quality, high-growth companies, allotting substantial amounts of its own capital, which is contributed by a small number of pension funds and wealthy individuals who are limited partners in the firm. It is a specialist in the technique known as the leveraged buyout, whereby a company is converted from public to private ownership, mostly by the use of borrowed funds. Between 1978 and 2000 the firm acquired businesses valued in excess of $16 billion. It invested almost $10 billion in 28 acquisitions and investments and delivered compound annual returns of 20 percent on subordinated debt and over 50 percent on equity after carried interest, according to its own analysis.

Leading LBO Player: 1980–86

Nicholas Forstmann was working for the leveraged buyout (LBO) firm Kohlberg Kravis Roberts & Co. (KKR) in 1977 when he suggested to his brother Theodore—who was working for older brother J. Anthony Forstmann's money-management company—that they form their own LBO firm. William Brian Little, another investment banker, joined them in forming Forstmann Little & Co. the following year, initially employing only one staffer, a secretary. Each founder had his specialty, with a 1987 article describing Nicholas as the numbers cruncher, Little as the dealmaker, and Theodore—the senior partner and dominant personality—as the man who corralled the investors. Their original stake was $400,000 from ten investors. The firm charged a modest management fee ranging from 0.5 to 1.5 percent of the investment and took a standard 20 percent of the profit after completion of the sale of acquired assets. By late 1983 the firm had raised $300 million from 30 limited partners, who consisted of pension funds and wealthy individuals. Pension-fund investors, in early 1987, included AT&T Corp., Boeing Co., Boise Cascade Corp., Eastman Kodak Co., General Electric Co., GTE Corp., and Minnesota Manufacturing and Mining Co.

In a leveraged buyout, a public company is purchased from stockholders by investors who generally put up only ten percent or less of the purchase price. The rest is raised by bank loans or subordinated debt—usually in the form of bond issues—with company assets as collateral. Payment on the debt and profit beyond that often comes from the sale of undervalued corporate assets. Another source of profit may come from taking the company public again. Between 1980 and 1983 Forstmann Little invested a total of $329 million in six companies. All but one were sold by the end of 1986, yielding annual return on equity ranging between 27 and 147 percent. ''Inflation was 14 percent, and interest rates were 8 percent,'' Ted Forstmann recalled to Dyan Machan of *Forbes* in 1998. ''You made a 6 percent gain just doing a deal.''

Forstmann Little's first high-profile transaction was its 1984 acquisition of Dr. Pepper Co. for $650 million. Dr. Pepper earned 8.5 times the original amount for its equity investors, according to one estimate. This spectacular gain—in less than three years—was partly due to high prices obtained from the separate sale of the company's core operation, its bottling plants, the Canada Dry subsidiary, and other assets, including a television station and a specialty textile company. Observers also credited a slash in corporate overhead and an annual 20 percent increase in the marketing budget for an appreciable rise in operating profits between 1984 and the sale of the core operation in 1986. Also in 1984, Forstmann Little purchased The Topps Co., Inc. for $98 million. After recapitalizing the firm and taking it public in 1987, the firm had—by 1990—earned $204 million and still owned 55 percent of the stock, which it sold the following year.

In 1985 Forstmann Little purchased 12 ITT Corp. divisions for $408 million and named the grouping FL Industries Inc.

Key Dates:

1978: Forstmann Little & Co. is formed.
1984: The firm makes its first large-scale acquisition, purchasing Dr. Pepper Co.
1990: The firm buys General Instrument Corp. and Gulfstream Aerospace Corp. for large sums.
1996: After turning around Gulfstream, the firm sells $1 billion worth of its stock.
2000: Forstmann Little owns or has investments in seven companies.

Unencumbered by the bureaucracy and paperwork of a public company, the electrical- and industrial-products firm's managers—13 of whom received equity stakes—closed several factories, improved customer service, and reduced inventory. When the business was sold in 1992, equity-fund partners profited at a 56 percent annual rate of return. But this gain was minor compared to the profit from the 1986 acquisition of Sybron Corp., a manufacturer of laboratory, dental, and medical products and specialty chemicals, for $335 million. Sold in 1988, this company yielded an annual equity fund return of 270 percent.

Investors took notice, and by the beginning of 1987 Forstmann Little's buyout fund of $1.4 billion was second only to KKR's $2 billion. By the end of the year this fund had grown to $2.7 billion.

Eschewing Junk Bonds: 1987–89

Forstmann Little's philosophy was to work hard at managing, as well as buying, its companies. The managers of the acquired company usually remained, with stakes—generally 20 percent collectively—in the resulting private firm. Forstmann Little general and limited partners supervised their investments by assuming positions on the acquired companies' boards and, if deemed necessary, pressing for strategic and personnel changes. In making acquisitions, the firm avoided relying on issues of high-yield but risky ''junk bonds'' to meet its needs for subordinated-debt financing. This put the finances of acquired companies on a sounder basis by reducing the debt load; moreover, the privately placed bonds—unlike junk bonds—did not have to be paid off until the company was sold. Investors in Forstmann Little's partnership fund for buying the subordinated debt of acquired companies therefore generally had to accept yields below market rate for this kind of investment. But participants in this fund received the option of taking a piece of the 37.5 percent equity stake in each buyout reserved for debt-fund investors on the same terms as the managers and equity-fund partners.

By the end of the 1980s Forstmann Little had acquired six more companies. By far the largest was Lear Siegler, Inc., a diversified manufacturer purchased in 1987 for $2.1 billion. In outbidding its rivals for Lear Siegler, the firm was aided by a temporary drying up of the junk-bond market following the disclosure of an insider trading scandal involving speculator Ivan Boesky. But this did not turn out to be one of the greatest deals for the firm. Forstmann Little eventually had to invest another $1 billion in Lear Siegler. Although it sold more than $1.5 billion of the company's assets by 1990, the firm was not able to cash in completely until the sale of Safelite Glass Corp.—formerly Lear Siegler's automotive-glass arm—in 1996. The sale brought in only about $300 million. Safelite filed for bankruptcy protection in 2000.

During the 1980s Forstmann Little claimed to achieve an average compounded annual return of 85 percent for equity-fund partners and 33 percent for subordinated-debt partners on completed transactions, after taking its own profit and fees. ''Forstmann Little,'' Anthony Bianco of *Business Week* concluded in 1992, ''thrived by paying reasonable prices for mature businesses with steady cash flow and a dominant position in industries less volatile than the economy as a whole.'' One observer pointed out, however, that the uncompleted deals at the time (by Forstmann's definition, a deal could not be considered completed until a company was either sold or taken public) included Lear Siegler and The Pullman Co., another poor-performing acquisition (in 1988) that filed for bankruptcy protection in 1994.

Ted Forstmann had long railed against the issuing of junk bonds to finance leveraged buyouts. In October 1988 the *Wall Street Journal* published a column in which he blamed junk bonds for ''debt that has virtually no chance of being repaid.'' His concern was far more than theoretical, for rivals such as KKR and Ronald Perelman's MacAndrews & Forbes Holdings were outbidding Forstmann Little for lucrative LBO deals by employing junk-bond financing. In the opinion of some observers the senior partner had developed an obsessive desire to outperform—and if not outperform, discredit—Henry Kravis, senior partner of KKR. But it was KKR that captured the prize in the frenzied bidding in late 1988 for RJR Nabisco Inc. In by far the largest LBO deal ever, KKR paid more than $25 billion for the company, thereby saddling it with crushing debt but earning a lot of money for grateful lawyers, investment bankers, and loan officers. The Forstmann Little founders entered the bidding but dropped out after concluding they could not finance a takeover without junk bonds. ''[Ted] Forstmann's antijunk diatribes had painted them into a corner,'' was the verdict of the authors of *Barbarians at the Gate,* the best-selling account of this episode.

LBO activity dropped sharply the following year, in the wake of at least $4 billion of junk-bond defaults and debt moratoriums. For the first time in the decade, Forstmann Little made no acquisitions. The bankruptcy of Drexel Burnham Lambert Inc. in 1990 and conviction of Michael Milken—its junk-bond chief—seemed to vindicate the firm's position, as did KKR's problems servicing the huge debt incurred by RJR Nabisco as a result of its buyout. Although Forstmann Little's investors were not happy to see their money sitting on the sidelines, the firm did not immediately relax its standards. ''I still don't think that winning is doing the deal no matter what,'' Ted Forstmann told Bianco in 1992. ''Winning is making money for your partners.'' Reportedly, he tried to assemble a new equity fund to revive companies ravaged by LBO debt but was rebuffed by prospective investors who felt he did not have the track record for such an undertaking.

Forstmann Little in the 1990s

By 1991, however, Forstmann Little, fortified by $2.8 billion in its existing funds, had adopted a riskier, more aggressive strategy. The acquisition of General Instrument Corp. for $1.75 billion and (with Allen E. Paulson) of Gulfstream Aerospace Corp. in 1990—a recessionary year—for $850 million involved technology enterprises with growth prospects but the need for major investment in research and technology. "With these companies, clearly there is more volatility in the numbers than we're used to," Nicholas Forstmann conceded to Bianco. The firm had so much money in its coffers, however, that it was able to take a conservative approach, financing the acquisitions with less debt and more equity than previously. In fact, the $285 million purchase of Department 56, Inc., a manufacturer and supplier of specialty giftware, in 1992 was made without any bank financing—the first self-financed transaction in the history of leveraged buyouts.

General Instrument, a large manufacturer and supplier of telecommunications equipment, was taken public in 1992 for nearly three times a share what Forstmann Little had paid. By the spring of 1994 the firm's investors had realized more than $1.6 billion in cash and current stock value for $202 million in equity. To avoid default, Gulfstream had to be recapitalized in 1993 by converting $450 million of subordinated debt to preferred stock, thereby eliminating $38 million in annual interest. Ted Forstmann then assumed chairmanship of the company himself, guiding it to three consecutive years of profit, including a record $47 million in 1996. In that year Gulfstream raised $1 billion from a public offering. Forstmann Little sold its remaining stake in the company for about $1 billion in 2000, bringing its total proceeds from its investment to about $2.8 billion.

Forstmann Little did not make another acquisition until late 1994, when it purchased Thompson Miniwax Holding Corp. for $700 million and 95 percent of Ziff-Davis Publishing Co. for $1.4 billion. It sold its stake in the latter less than a year later for $2.1 billion to Japan's Softbank Corp. Thompson Miniwax was sold to Sherman-Williams Co. at the end of 1996 for $830 million. In 1996 the firm acquired 97.5 percent of the shares of Community Health Systems, Inc., a for-profit hospital chain, for nearly $1.4 billion. This company made its initial public offering in 2000, selling about one-quarter of the outstanding stock for $243.75 million in gross proceeds.

Forstmann Little did not acquire a company in 1997 and only one—Yankee Candle Co.—in 1998. During this period more than $70 billion was committed by all institutions for leveraged buyouts, but Ted Forstmann thought prices had gone too high. "It's amateur hour . . . like the Italian restaurant business in New York," he told Machan. "The owner was headwaiter at a previous restaurant. That owner was headwaiter at another previous restaurant, etc." He added, "I don't do auctions. I would sooner take my pants off in public. . . . Price is about the fifth thing I consider. You steal the wrong company and you slowly go broke."

Forstmann Little's next major commitment, in 1999, was a $1 billion investment for a 12 percent stake in the telephone carrier McLeod USA Inc., which was operating in some 16 states, primarily west of the Mississippi. In 2000 the firm increased its stake in the telecommunications industry by investing $1.25 billion in NEXTLINK Communications, Inc., a national provider of broadband communications services in top 50 markets. NEXTLINK was renamed XO Communications in late 2000.

Forstmann Little's portfolio in late 2000 consisted of partial or entire ownership of the following seven companies: Capella Education Company; Community Health Systems, Inc.; McLeod USA Inc.; Metiom, Inc.; NEXTLINK Communications, Inc.; Webley Systems, Inc.; and Yankee Candle Company. All these acquisitions or investments had been made since 1996. The firm had seven general partners at the beginning of 1999, when Erskine Bowles, former White House chief of staff, joined the firm. At the same time Forstmann Little became affiliated with Carousel Capital, a private equity firm cofounded by Bowles. Little, who had retired in 1994, died in 2000.

Principal Competitors

Blackstone Group; DLJ Merchant Banking Partners; Hicks, Muse & Co. Inc.; Kohlberg Kravis Roberts & Co.; Thomas H. Lee Co.

Further Reading

Andrews, Suzanne, "Won't Someone Please Pay Attention to Teddy Forstmann?" *Institutional Investor,* February 1993, pp. 27–35.

Bianco, Anthony, "Gulfstream's Pilot," *Business Week,* April 14, 1997, pp. 65–69, 72, 74, 76.

——, "Look Who's Got the Last Laugh Now," *Business Week,* February 10, 1992, pp. 112–14.

Burrough, Bryan, and John Helyar, *Barbarians at the Gate,* New York: Harper & Row, 1990.

Darby, Rose, "Financial Buyers Return in Big Healthcare Deals," *Investment Dealers' Digest,* December 9, 1996, p. 32.

Deogun, Nikhil, and Stephanie N. Mehta, "McLeod USA Gets a $1 Billion Infusion," *Wall Street Journal (Europe),* August 31, 1999, p. 8.

Forstmann, Theodore, "Violating Our Rules of Prudence," *Wall Street Journal,* October 25, 1988, p. A26.

Fromson, Brett, "Dealmaker of the Decade," *Washington Post,* June 4, 1995, pp. H1, H5.

Henriques, Diana B., "Refilling Forstmann's War Chest," *New York Times,* December 15, 1994, pp. D1, D7.

Hylton, Richard D., "How KKR Got Beaten at Its Own Game," *Fortune,* May 2, 1994, pp. 104–07.

"Investors Loyal to Buyout Firm," *New York Times,* January 11, 1991, p. D8.

Machan, Dyan, "A Hero Among Barbarians," *Forbes,* July 6, 1998, pp. 132, 134.

Rothman, Andrea, "Ted Forstmann Doesn't Have to Say 'I Told You So,' " *Business Week,* March 5, 1990, pp. 77–78.

Spragins, Ellyn E., "Forstmann Little: Going Fast by Going Slow," *Business Week,* January 26, 1987, pp. 76–78.

—Robert Halasz

Fuller Smith & Turner P.L.C.

Griffin Brewery
Chiswick Ln. South
London, Chiswick W4 2QB
United Kingdom
Telephone: (+44) 20 8996-2000
Fax: (+44) 20 8995-0230
Web site: http://www.fullers.co.uk

Public Company
Incorporated: 1845
Employees: 2,344
Sales: £142.35 million (US$226.6 million) (2000)
Stock Exchanges: London
Ticker Symbol: FSTA
NAIC: 312120 Breweries; 722410 Drinking Places (Alcoholic Beverages); 721110 Hotels (Except Casino Hotels); 722110 Full Service Restaurants

While its larger U.K. competitors, such as Bass and Whitbread, are selling off their brewery operations to concentrate on managing the pub and hotel chains, leading regional brewer Fuller Smith & Turner P.L.C. happily juggles both sides of the British beer industry. Fuller Smith & Turner operates one of the United Kingdom's oldest brewery sites, the Griffon brewery on Chiswick Lane. The company's Fuller's Beer Company subsidiary produces a strong variety of ales, porters, and especially bitters, including the company's flagship London Pride and ESB (Extra Special Bitter) brands. Newer products include Organic Honey Dew, a beer made from organically grown ingredients, launched in 2000, and London Porter, initially an export-only beer, which was introduced to the U.K. market in the same year. Other brands include Chiswick Bitter, Red Fox, Jack Frost, and 1845. The company's total production neared 240,000 barrels in the company's 2000 fiscal year, with the company's own inns and pubs accounting for nearly 40 percent of sales. That business, operated under the Fuller's Inns subsidiary, is comprised of the company's more than 200 pubs and hotels, including more than 100 company-managed pubs, and a growing number of bars (which are exempt from the traditional opening-time restrictions placed on British pubs). The company's pubs operate under several brand concepts, including the Ale & Pie concept—each pub-restaurant features its own signature pie—and the Broadwalks bar-disco concept. The company has also seen strong success with the 1998 launch of its Fine Line concept, designed to appeal to the emerging 20-something segment and especially the rising number of affluent as well as female customers. The company also operates a string of hotels, including the mid-priced English Inn hotel brand. In all the Fuller's Inns operations accounted for nearly £85 million of the company's £142 million in 2000 sales. A third Fuller Smith & Turner subsidiary, Fuller's Wines, which operated a chain of 60 retail wine and spirits stores, was sold off to the Unwins chain in 2000. Traded on the London Stock Exchange, Fuller Smith & Turner continues to be controlled by the families behind the founding partnership, including Anthony Fuller, chairman, who holds some 14 percent of the company's stock, J.F. Russell-Smith, serving as president of the board of directors, and Michael Turner, who holds the company's managing director position.

Partnership in the 19th Century

Fuller Smith & Turner's Griffin brewery is the oldest brewery operating in London and one of the oldest brewery sites in the United Kingdom—the brewery dates back to the mid-1700s. The "modern era" of the Chiswick Lane site started when John Fuller took over the brewery's operation in 1829. Fuller's son John Bird Fuller then joined with partners Henry Smith and John Turner in 1845 to form the Fuller Smith & Turner partnership in order to exploit the brewery's production, and a number of brewery-owned pubs and inns.

As the next generation took over in the 1870s, with George Pargiter Fuller inheriting his father's share of the company, Fuller's had already established a reputation for its beers in its southern England area. The company's slogan "Fuller's Beers of Honest Repute" became a catchword of sorts in the 1890s, as the company began marketing itself—including using hot air balloons. In 1892, Fuller Smith & Turner took out a trademark on the Griffin Brewery's name, and incorporated a griffon into the company's logo.

Company Perspectives:

We aim to be the benchmark in retailing and brewing, delivering Quality, Service and Pride in everything we do.

The company expanded into new directions as the century reached an end. In 1894 Fuller Smith & Turner inaugurated the Drayton Court Hotel. That same year, the company opened its first off-license store, that is, a retail store devoted to sales of wine, spirits, and beer. While Fuller's remained a relatively small brewer, it began to achieve recognition at the beginning of the new century, and growing sales encouraged Fuller Smith & Turner to acquire a new brewery, the Beehive, in Brentford, in 1909. By then, the company had begun investing in a new fleet of steam-driven vehicles for transporting its beers, joining the brewery's stable of Shire horse-drawn wagons.

Fuller Smith & Turner exchanged its partnership status for that of a private limited corporation in 1929. During the 1930s, the company phased out its horse-drawn deliveries. The Shire horses, however, were to reappear in front of Fuller's carts in the late 1980s, bringing the company's products to special events and other company-sponsored activities. Meanwhile, the company built up its fleet of steam-driven trucks during the 1930s, which themselves began to be replaced by diesel engine trucks after World War II.

Remaining a Regional Independent for the 21st Century

In the 1950s, Fuller Smith & Turner branched out again, opening a new subsidiary, the Griffin Catering Company. While that subsidiary did not survive the end of the 20th century, restaurant service remained a fixture in many of the company's pubs and hotels. Fuller Smith & Turner was also finding success on more familiar territory. The award of the first place medal by the Brewers Exhibition of 1959 to the company's London Pride bitters established that brand as one of the U.K.'s favorite regional brews. London Pride became the company's flagship brand, generating the highest volume of sales. The following year, in 1960, Fuller Smith & Turner extended its lodgings portfolio with the opening of the Master Robert Motel.

The rising prominence of national and international brewers on the English beer scene prompted Fuller Smith & Turner to join in the formation of the CAMRA association. This ''Campaign for Real Ale'' encouraged public recognition of ale conditioned in traditional casks, such as Fuller Smith & Turner's ales, as opposed to the more industrial methods being put into use by the industry's growing giants. The CAMRA campaign helped spark growing consumer demand for the smaller, more traditionally brewed beers, such as those produced by Fuller Smith & Turner. Maintaining its commitment to its traditions, Fuller Smith & Turner nonetheless launched a program to modernize and expand its production facilities. Started in 1975, the renovation was completed at the end of the decade and the company inaugurated its new brewery facility in 1981.

By then, the company's beer labels were achieving greater peer recognition. The company's ESB (Extra Special Bitter) brand won the CAMRA Beer of the Year award in 1978—a distinction the brand achieved again in 1981 and 1985. London Pride took its turn as well, winning the CAMRA award in 1979. The company capped the decade with a new Beer of the Year, launching the Chiswick Bitter brand. In the mid-1990s, Fuller Smith & Turner marked its 150th anniversary with the launch of a new brand, the bottled conditioned ale 1845.

By then, the British brewing industry was feeling the full effects of the 1989 Beer Orders—legislation that placed into effect a cap on the number of pubs a single brewer was entitled to own. This legislation caused a long industry shakeout, as brewer's longtime dominant hold on the British pub scene began to slip. With a limit of just 2,000 pubs per brewer, large numbers of pub freeholds came onto the market. At the same time, a number of brewers began looking to exit their brewery operations in favor of refocusing themselves as pub and hotel operators. Such was the case with two of the United Kingdom's top brewers, Bass and Whitbread, both of which sold off their brewery operations to Belgium giant Interbrew at the turn of the century. Meanwhile, the regional brewing segment began to experience rising pressure to consolidate, in part in order to achieve greater economies of scale, in part in order to boost their share values. Fuller Smith & Turner, which by then counted as one of the largest of the independent regional brewers, was able to preserve its independence thanks to the continued control of the founding families of more than 60 percent of the company's stock.

Fuller Smith & Turner instead moved to heighten the brand awareness of its flagship London Pride brand, doubling its advertising spending to more than £1 million per year, and launching its first national television advertisement campaign. The success of this campaign, with its slogan, ''Whatever You Do, Take Pride,'' helped boost the company's production of that brand to more than 100,000 barrels in 1997. Total production topped 150,000 barrels the following year, aided by the back-to-back triumphs of the ESP brand as champion bitter at the World Beer Championships in Chicago in 1998 and 1999. The company was also making headway with its hotel concept, English Inn, which began to eclipse its other hotel offerings—the company Master Robert Motel was sold off in 2000.

Meanwhile, the company continued to launch new brand concepts. A new branded ale, Red Fox, which debuted in 1997, was joined by the launch of an organic beer, made with organically grown ingredients, called Organic Honey Dew, in 2000. The company was also seeing success with the opening of a new brand name concept for a chain of bars—which were exempt from the traditionally limited opening times of the United Kingdom's pubs—called the Fine Line. Designed to appeal to the young, affluent, and female markets in London, the Fine Line chain was quickly crowned with success, and won the award for Best Newcomer at the 1999 Retailer of the Year awards.

In 2000, Fuller Smith & Turner moved to refocus its operations around the dual core of its Fuller's Inns division—which included its pub, bar, and hotel operations—and its Fuller

Key Dates:

1654: Brewing begins in Chiswick.
1829: John Fuller joins Chiswick brewery.
1845: Fuller, Smith & Turner partnership is formed.
1872: Charles Pargiter Fuller inherits Fuller family share.
1892: Griffin Brewery name receives trademark.
1894: Company opens Drayton Court Hotel, launches first Fuller's Wine off-license store.
1929: Partnership is reincorporated as private limited company.
1959: Fuller Smith launches Griffin Catering Company subsidiary.
1960: Company opens Master Robert Motel.
1975: Fuller Smith begins modernization of brewery facilities.
1995: Company launches 150-year anniversary ale, 1845.
1997: Company launches Red Fox ale.
1998: Fine Line bar concept is introduced.
2000: Fuller Smith launches Organic Honey Dew, sells Fuller's Wine retail network to Unwins.

Brewing Company division. The company then moved to dispose of its Fuller's Wine chain, which by then had grown to a network of 60 retail stores. That operation was sold to rapidly growing Unwins in 2000 for £7.5 million. The sale added to the company's war chest as it began to seek further acquisitions. At the end of 2000, the company acknowledged its interest in picking up as many as 70 pubs from the Whitbread group as that company, after its acquisition by Interbrew, put up its 3,000-strong pub empire for sale at the end of the 20th century. At the same time, the company continued to pursue the expansion of its hotel holdings, with plans to open three new English Inn hotels in Kingston, Surry, Bristol, and London by mid-year 2001.

Principal Subsidiaries

Fuller's Inns; The Fuller's Beer Company.

Principal Competitors

Ann Street Group Limited; Bass PLC; Diageo Plc.; Greene King plc; Heineken N.V.; The Nomura Securities Co., Ltd.; Punch Taverns Group Ltd.; Scottish & Newcastle plc; Young & Co.'s Brewery, P.L.C.

Further Reading

Baker, Lucy, ''Fuller's Rules out Bid for Whitbread Estate,'' *Independent*, December 2, 2000, p. 19.
Blackwell, David, ''Fuller Favors Expanding Pubs,'' *Financial Times*, December 2, 2000.
Bowers, Simon, ''Fuller's Sees Opening in Whitbread Pub Sale,'' *Guardian*, December 2, 2000.
Reddall, Braden, ''Fuller's Takes Pride in Good Start to Year,'' *Reuters*, May 26, 2000.
Rose, Anthony, ''Down the Offie: A Brave New World,'' *Independent*, August 19, 2000, p. 16.
——, ''Fuller Smith & Turner,'' *Investor's Chronicle*, December 8, 2000.

—M.L. Cohen

Fyffes Plc

1 Beresford Street
Dublin 7
Ireland
Telephone: (+353) 1-809-5555
Fax: (+353) 1-872-6609
Web site: http://www.fyffes.com

Public Company
Incorporated: 1888 as E.W. Fyffe, Son and Co.; 1902 as Charles McCann Limited
Employees: 3,595
Sales: EUR 1.69 billion (US$1.79 billion) (1999)
Stock Exchanges: London
Ticker Symbol: FFY
NAIC: 111336 Fruit and Tree Nut Combination Farming

Fyffes Plc is one of the world's largest importers and distributors of fruits, ranking number five worldwide and number one in Europe. The company is also Europe's leading importer and distributor of bananas, which accounts for some 30 percent of its business. In addition to fruits, the company sources vegetables, flowers, and potted plants. Supporting the company's operations are its network of 100 storage, distribution, ripening, and other facilities, located primarily in Europe, a fleet of 17 company-owned or leased temperature-controlled ships, and its own land-based transportation fleet. Beyond its core Irish and U.K. base, Fyffes also has gained a strong share of the German, Dutch, French, Danish, Italian, and Spanish fruits and vegetable markets. Although the company's sales come primarily through its sourcing and distribution activities, Fyffes also has taken steps to secure a position for itself in the "new economy." In 1999, the company launched its worldoffruit.com web site and subsidiary, offering Internet-based business-to-business fruits and vegetables sourcing and information. That company is expected to go public early in the new century. In 2000, also, Fyffes has partnered with U.K. ingredients group Glanbia to launch the ingredientsnet.com business-to-business web site with a focus on food ingredients such as edible oils, fats, flour, and sugar. Fyffes is led by Chairman Neil V. McCann, grandson of one of the company's founders, and his sons Carl P., vice-chairman, and David V., CEO. The company posted sales of EUR 1.69 billion (US$1.79 billion) in 1999.

Going Bananas in the 1880s

The predecessor companies to Fyffes Plc both had their roots in the 19th century. Edward Wathen Fyffe was one of the first to bring commercial shipments of bananas to the United Kingdom in the 1880s. Fyffe had discovered the fruit while living on the Canary Islands, where he had accompanied his wife during her convalescence from tuberculosis. Fyffe decided that England was ripe for the exotic fruit and began commercial imports of bananas in 1888 through his company, E.W. Fyffe, Son and Co. Ten years later, Fyffe joined his company with another London-based green grocer supplier, Hudson Brothers, forming Fyffe Hudson & Co. Limited.

Fyffe Hudson continued to build up imports of bananas from the current and former British colonial islands. At the turn of the century, the company took a step to solve one of the largest difficulties in transporting bananas—preventing them from ripening during the voyage itself. A breakthrough in the banana industry came when it was discovered that maintaining bananas below a certain temperature inhibited the ripening process. At the turn of the century, Fyffe Hudson commissioned a ship outfitted with a cooling system developed by J & E Hall, and the company's first refrigerated vessel, the Port Morant, completed its maiden voyage between Avonmouth, England, and Kingston, Jamaica, in 1901.

That same year, Fyffe Hudson, which had been operating from its eastern England location, merged with the Liverpool-based Elder Dempster and Company, adding that company's western England port. The merger, which created the company Elders and Fyffes Limited, thus secured operations in England's two major ports serving shipping between the United Kingdom and its island colonies. The company went public, continuing to add to its fleet of ships and becoming a major importer in the English market.

Meanwhile, in Ireland, the other half of the future Fyffes Plc was making a name for itself in its own home market. The McCann family's involvement with fruit began in the 1890s,

Company Perspectives:

Fyffes' principal objectives are: To increase the Group's revenues and earnings based on the growing worldwide demand for fresh produce. To continually find better ways to work with its suppliers, increase efficiency and meet its customers' needs. To maximise the returns earned by shareholders on their investment. To provide interesting and fulfilling careers for its people.

when Charles McCann began packing apples in stone barrels for shipment to Canada. By 1902, McCann had raised enough funds to open his own green grocer's store in Dunkalk, Ireland. At the same time, McCann began a relationship with the newly merged young Elders and Fyffes company, becoming the first to sell the English company's bananas on the Irish market. While running a retail store, McCann also developed a significant wholesale business, becoming one of the principal distributors of fruits and vegetables in the company's County Armagh region.

In 1913, the United Fruit Company, later known as United Brands and then Chiquita Brands International, bought a controlling share of Elders and Fyffes' stock. The American company quickly acquired the rest of Elders and Fyffes, establishing itself as the United Kingdom's leading banana importer. Elders and Fyffes continued to operate under its own name, and in 1929 scored a marketing coup when it became the first company to place its own label on its fruit. The famed "Blue Label" soon became synonymous with bananas in the United Kingdom and inspired similar labeling practices across the world's fruits segments.

With the clout of its parent company behind it, Elders and Fyffes was able to build up its banana business to the extent that it had gained a de facto monopoly of banana imports to the United Kingdom. After the disruption of its business caused by World War II, Elders and Fyffes made the world's newsreels with its resumption of banana deliveries in 1945.

Yet, by the 1950s, Elders and Fyffes began to face increasing competition in its home markets. Among its new competitors was Geest Horticultural Products, which in the early 1950s decided to challenge Fyffes by launching banana growing operations in the Windward Islands. Geest succeeded in signing supply agreements with a number of the United Kingdom's rapidly growing supermarket groups, and it steadily imposed itself on the banana imports scene. By the mid-1960s, Elders and Fyffes had been forced to relinquish nearly half of the United Kingdom's banana market to Geest.

Elders and Fyffes also was seeing challenges from the Irish market. In 1956, Neil McCann, who had extended his father's Dunkalk business into the Dublin market, while adding banana ripening and distribution to its wholesale activities, joined with a number of other Irish wholesalers to form United Fruit Importers Limited, based in Dublin. Two years later, McCann joined with another group of wholesalers to form Torney Brothers & McCann Limited, which extended both companies' distribution and storage facilities in the Dublin area and expanded the two companies' distribution reach throughout Ireland.

In the mid-1960s, Torney Brothers & McCann and a number of other banana importers, ripeners, and distributors in the region—including Charles McCann Limited of Dunkalk and Red Diamond Limited of Cork—set up their own banana supply company, Banana Importers of Ireland (BII). The new company, founded in 1965, further undermined Elders and Fyffes' market share in Ireland as BII offered direct shipments to Ireland's ports, cutting the costs of bananas for BII's group of ripeners and distributors.

If Elders and Fyffes saw its overall market share shrinking, it was comforted by seeing that market undergo a strong expansion as consumer demand for bananas raised the fruit to one of the most popular in the U.K. market. Nonetheless, the company saw fit to diversify its operations in the early 1960s. The purchase of George Jackson & Co. Limited in 1964 gave Elders and Fyffes that midlands-based produce distributor's business, extending Elders and Fyffes' range of business and reducing its reliance on bananas for the first time. Four years later Elders and Fyffes bought George Monro Limited, which added that company's fresh fruit and vegetable distribution activities. The purchase led Elders and Fyffes to change its name to Fyffes Group Limited in 1969.

By then, Neil McCann had assumed leadership of Torney Brothers & McCann operations and steered the combination of that business with United Fruit Importers Limited. The merger of the two wholesalers groups created Fruit Importers of Ireland Limited (FII) in 1968. Under Neil McCann, FII began to consolidate much of the fruit importers market in Ireland, before turning to the greater U.K. market in the 1980s.

Big Banana for the 21st Century

Among FII's first acquisitions was that of Connolly Shaw Limited, which brought that company's importer rights to the Jaffa (Israel) and Cape and Outspan (both South Africa) fruit brands. The company extended its penetration into southern Ireland with the acquisition of Southern Fruit Suppliers Limited, based in Waterford, Ireland, in 1971. The following year, the company acquired Shell & Byrne Limited, adding that company's supplier relationship to the Five Star grocery chain, as well as its imports of apples and onions from the United States.

In 1973, FII completed two more significant acquisitions, adding the Kilkenny area to its operations with the purchase of Philip Lenehan Limited, then boosting its banana business with the purchase of Red Diamond Limited. A number of other acquisitions followed through the 1970s, including Munster Fruit and Produce Limited in 1974, extending the company into the Kerry and West Cork areas. In 1977, FII's subsidiary McCann Nurseries, which grew apples and tomatoes, formed the Green Ace Produce Group to pack and sell EEC-regulated apples and tomatoes.

Neil V. McCann succeeded his father as CEO in 1979 and stepped up FII's growth. In 1980, FII—still known as Fruit Importers of Ireland—merged operations with those of subsidiary Charles McCann Limited under a new holding company, known as FII Limited. The following year, the company sold 25 percent of its shares to an outside investor group, Development Capital Corporation, setting the gears in motion for the com-

Key Dates:

1888: Edward Fyffe begins commercial imports of bananas to the United Kingdom.
1890: Charles McCann begins apple exports.
1897: Fyffe forms Fyffe Hudson & Co.
1901: The company merges with Elder Dempster and Company to form Elders and Fyffes.
1902: Charles McCann opens store in Dunkalk.
1913: United Fruit Company acquires Elders and Fyffes.
1929: Fyffes introduces "Blue Label."
1956: United Fruit Importers Limited is formed.
1958: Torney Brothers & McCann is formed.
1965: Banana Importers of Ireland is created.
1968: Torney Brothers & McCann merges with United Fruit Importers Limited to form Fruit Importers of Ireland Limited (FII).
1969: Elders and Fyffes becomes Fyffes Group Limited.
1981: FII goes public.
1986: FII acquires Fyffes.
1989: Company name is changed to Fyffes Plc.
1996: Company acquires banana business from Geest Plc.
1999: Company acquires 50 percent of Capespan Holdings International.
2000: Company launches worldoffruit.com web site.

pany's public offering, completed in February 1981, on the Dublin stock exchange.

The public offering gave FII the capital to begin a series of acquisitions through the 1980s that helped it grow into one of the ten largest public companies in Ireland. Among the company's acquisitions for the decade were those of Uniplumo Limited, adding, in 1981, the importing, cultivation, and distribution, including retail operations, of house plants to the company's portfolio; the 1983 acquisition of Frank E. Benner, which added that Northern Ireland company's flowers, fruits, and vegetables trade; the acquisition of Daniel P. Hale & Co., based in Belfast, in 1984; and the acquisitions of Kinsealy Farms Limited and 50 percent of Gillespie & Co. in 1985.

FII's biggest score of the decade came in 1986 when it agreed to acquire the Fyffes operation from United Brands. The deal marked FII's first overseas acquisition, transforming it into one of the United Kingdom's premier fruit distribution groups. The transformed group also changed its name, becoming FII-Fyffes. The company renamed itself again, as Fyffes Plc, in 1990.

The company maintained its acquisition pace through the end of the 1980s and into the 1990s. Fyffes added Jack Dolan Limited and Sunpak Mayfield Fresh Produce Limited in 1988, Bernard Dempsey & Co. and J. Langan & Sons in 1989, and J. Grey & Son in 1990. Whereas these acquisitions remained centered primarily on the Irish and English markets, in the early 1990s Fyffes turned its sights on building a position for itself throughout Europe. The company added Erobanancanarias S.A., based in Spain, and Brdr. Lemcke A.S. of Denmark in 1993, followed by Velleman & Tas B.V. of The Netherlands, J.A. Kahl GmbH of Germany, Sofiprim S.A. of France, and finally Jamaica Banana Holdings Limited, all in 1994.

Not all of the company's acquisition attempts were successful: in 1992, Fyffes made an offer to buy out rival Del Monte for some US$500 million, an acquisition that would have catapulted the company to the top of the world's fruit distribution market. That offer was turned aside by Del Monte. Soon after, Fyffes itself became the object of a takeover offer, this time from another rival, Dole. Fyffes rejected this offer. Instead, with the war chest it had built up for the Del Monte acquisition attempt, Fyffes went shopping again. After picking up a new string of companies in 1995, including Angel Rey of Spain, International Fruit Company of The Netherlands, and J.W. Swithenbank Limited, the company joined with the newly formed Windward Isle Banana Company to acquire Geest's banana operations in 1996. This acquisition helped boost Fyffes into the world's top five fruit distribution companies, giving it two-thirds of the U.K. banana market, and a top share across Europe as well.

Neil V. McCann began to eye retirement, naming eldest son Carl P. McCann as Fyffes' vice-chairman, and younger son David V. McCann as chief executive officer. The younger generation continued the diversification moves of their father, as Fyffes sought to reduce its reliance on bananas. This was seen as especially important given increasing pressure from the United States to end a system of preferential tariffs that all but excluded so-called dollar bananas, grown in Latin America, from the European market, in favor of the more expensive bananas from the smaller plantations on the formerly European islands and colonies. The dispute, which later erupted into threats of an all-out trade war at the end of the decade, encouraged Fyffes to boost its distribution activities in other fresh fruit and vegetable markets, while the company also broadened its sourcing to include a good share of dollar bananas as well. Among the company's moves was the acquisition of a 50 percent share of South Africa's Capespan Holdings International, giving Fyffes a strong share of the fresh fruits market.

At the turn of the century, Fyffes turned toward the Internet, launching two web sites, worldoffruit.com, offering a business-to-business portal for fruit transaction and information, which went online in mid-2000, and ingredientsnet.com, a joint venture with the United Kingdom's Glanbia Group, offering similar business-to-business services to the food ingredients market. As more and more of the world's sourcing activity turned to the Internet, Fyffes' moves were seen as giving the company a strong position in the top ranks of the world's fresh fruit and vegetables distributors.

Principal Subsidiaries

Anaco International B.V. (The Netherlands; 50%); Angel Rey S.A. (Spain; 70%); Banana Importers of Ireland Limited (95%); Bernard Dempsey & Co Limited; Big River LLC (U.S.A.; 50%); Brdr Lembcke A.S. (Denmark; 50%); Daniel P Hale and Co Limited (U.K.); E & F Lines Limited (U.K.); Eurobanancanarias S.A. (Spain; 50%); FII Holdings Limited (U.K.); Frank E Benner Limited (U.K.); Gillespie and Company Limited (90%); Green Ace Producer Group Limited (92%); Greeve Citrus B.V. (The Netherlands; 50%); Hugh McNulty (Wholesale) Limited (50%); International Fruit Company B.V. (The Netherlands); J.A. Kahl

(GmbH & Co) Munich (Germany); J.W. Swithenbank Limited (U.K.; 50%); Jack Dolan Limited; James Lindsay & Son plc (U.K.); Kinsealy Farms Limited; Padwa Group Limited (U.K.); Peviani Spa (Italy; 50%); Sofiprim S.A. (France; 50%); Sunpak Mayfield Fresh Produce Limited; Uniplumo (Ireland) Limited (85%); Velleman & Tas B.V. (The Netherlands); W J Pearson & Sons Limited (U.K.).

Principal Competitors

Chiquita Brands International Inc.; C.H. Robinson Worldwide Inc.; Dole Food Company Inc.; Fresh Del Monte Produce Inc.; Savia, S.A. de C.V.; Sunkist Growers, Inc.; U.S.A. Floral Products, Inc.

Further Reading

Davies, Peter N., *Fyffes and the Banana: Musa Sapientum,* London: Athlone Press, 1990.

Grose, Thomas K., ''Two Sides of the Banana Split,'' *USA Today,* March 3, 1999, p. 3B.

Payne, Doug, ''Fyffes Enjoys Fruits of Growth,'' *European,* January 1, 1996, p. 28.

Roddam, Tony, ''Fyffes Marches Through Banana War Flak,'' *Reuters,* June 14, 1999.

Smith, Kevin, ''Fyffes Eyes Big Slice of Web Fresh Produce Trade,'' *Reuters,* January 13, 2000.

—M.L. Cohen

Geest Plc

Midgate House, Midgate
Peterborough PE1 1TN
United Kingdom
Telephone: (+44) 1775-761-111
Fax: (+44) 1775-763-009
Web site: http://www.geest.co.uk

Public Company
Incorporated: 1935 as Geest Horticultural Products
Employees: 7,884
Sales: £526 million (US$845.1 million) (1999)
Stock Exchanges: London
Ticker Symbol: GET
NAIC: 311991 Perishable Prepared Food Manufacturing

Geest Plc is a leading producer and distributor of fresh chilled foods to the U.K., Benelux, and French markets. The company's range of more than 1,400 products includes lines of ready meals, breads, pizzas, salads, whole produce and prepared fruits and vegetables, condiments, and other products found in supermarkets and convenience stores. The bulk of the company's sales are made through fresh prepared foods, which accounted for 75 percent of the group's 1999 sales of £526 million (US$845.1 million). The company has made strong investments, however, as well as a notable number of acquisitions and joint venture partnerships, to boost its activities in other fast-growing fresh convenience foods segments, such as salads (the company has a 46 percent market share for this segment in the United Kingdom) and stir-fry, dips, soups and sauces, pizza, and pasta. A major area of investment focus for Geest is the ready-meals market, a segment growing by some ten percent per year as changes in consumer attitudes, as well as steady increases in both the quality and variety of these foods, have combined with changes in consumer kitchen habits (in the United Kingdom, the average time spent on food preparation per day has dropped to just half an hour in the late 1990s, compared with one and one-half hours in the 1980s) to drive this category. The average consumer probably does not know Geest at all, however, as the company sells its products through the major supermarket chains, including Marks and Spencer's, Tesco, and Sainsbury's, its three largest customers in the United Kingdom, who in turn sell the company's products under their own brand names and labels. The majority of the company's sales are made in the United Kingdom; Geest's 1999 acquisition of Vaco, of Geel, Belgium, and a five-year supply contract signed with The Netherlands' Albert Heijn supermarket chain, however, have already raised sales in the Benelux countries to three percent of Geest's total sales. In 2000, the company also moved into the French market, notably with the acquisition of Cinquième Saison, a supplier of fresh salads to that country's major supermarket retailers. The company's expansion and focus on the fresh prepared food market has been led by chairman Ian Menzies-Gow since 1996.

From Flowers to Bananas: 1950s

The Geest name came to England in the 1930s from The Netherlands, when brothers John and Leonard van Geest left their family's flower-growing business to expand operations across the North Sea, opening a flower bulb import company in the United Kingdom. The van Geest family had been involved in flower growing and horticulture since the late 19th century. After helping to establish the family's operations in England, brother John van Geest left to start his own business. That company, founded in Lincolnshire in 1935 as Geest Horticultural Products, began growing its own flower bulbs for sale in the United Kingdom, rather than relying on Dutch imports.

Geest Horticultural Products began to see strong growth following World War II, particularly after it diversified into a new product area—that of importing and distributing fresh produce—in the late 1940s. Many of the company's products came from The Netherlands, such as its tomatoes, as that country began development of an extensive network of greenhouses that were to make it one of the world's leading hydroponics-based vegetable producers. The Geest catalog soon extended to cucumbers, melons, carrots, and other fruits and vegetables. The company was quick to develop a large degree of vertical integration, gaining control of nearly every aspect of its product

Company Perspectives:

Vision statement: To become the best fresh prepared food and produce company wherever we operate. We shall achieve this by excelling in service, quality, value and innovation to the delight of our customers. We shall grow in any geographic market where customer partnership and consumer demand can be developed.

offerings, including growing, shipping, handling, distribution, even manufacturing its own boxes and other logistics supports.

Until the 1950s, imports of bananas to the United Kingdom had been almost entirely under Ireland-based Fyffes' control. Geest, however, decided to challenge that company's dominance of the banana trade, as the fruit swiftly gained popularity among British consumers. Geest started its own banana import operations in the early 1950s, turning specifically to the countries in the Windward Islands chain—St. Lucia, St. Vincent, the Grenadines, Grenada, and Dominica—for their banana production. The company also played a major role in developing the banana industry on these islands and elsewhere in the Caribbean. Through its banana imports and its other produce interests, the company also was able to attract a number of the United Kingdom's largest supermarket chains to its growing customer lists. In the late 1950s, the company's banana imports had flourished, and the company even started its own shipping line, offering vacation cruises as well as cargo space for its banana imports. By the 1960s, Geest had successfully captured 50 percent of the U.K. banana market from Fyffes.

Prepared Foods Specialist for the 21st Century

Although Geest also became one of the United Kingdom's most prominent flower and bulb importers in the United Kingdom, it quickly became most identified with its banana business. Yet in the early 1970s, the company took its first step toward a diversification that later was to redefine the company entirely.

Geest's produce imports positioned it to move into a new product area. As the United Kingdom's chains of supermarkets developed, the country's consumer habits also were changing. Frozen foods and meals had become a mainstay of many kitchens, particularly as more and more women began joining the workforce. This trend in turn led to a need for many consumers for so-called ''timesaving'' foods, such as prepared meats and salads. Geest opened its first facility for producing prepared salads in Spalding in 1972. This diversification led the company to change its name to Geest Holdings Plc.

By the 1980s, consumer habits had sufficiently altered as to support a greater number of investments in the fresh prepared foods market. Geest began its own push into this category in the mid-1980s, when it took a listing on the London Stock Exchange. The listing, which enabled the Geest family to cash out on its holdings, also saw the company's name changed to simply Geest Plc. With this new access to investment capital, Geest began to step up its prepared foods holdings. In the late 1980s, the company acquired two new subsidiaries, Katies Kitchen, which added fresh pizza selections in 1988; and Bourne Salads, acquired in 1989, which increased the company's own salad production capacity. At the same time, Geest launched a new subsidiary, Spalding Ready Meals, which brought the company into a new—and fast-growing—category in 1988.

Geest entered the 1990s with still more acquisitions, including those of The Pasta Company in 1990, and Kent Salads and English Village Salads in 1991. The company's push into fresh prepared foods coincided with a downturn in its core banana import business. The early 1990s in fact saw Geest's banana business reeling from several natural and economic disasters. After bearing the brunt of a number of tropical storms and flooding, which wiped out parts of its banana production, the company also faced an outbreak of Black Sagitoka, which destroyed large portions of its banana crops. Coupled with these problems were a number of economic pressures, such as the fixing of new import quotas by the GATT treaty and an ensuing glut of bananas on the European market as producers rushed to get their bananas onto the continent before the new quotas took effect. The glut significantly decreased prices at a time when Geest, forced to seek its bananas from the so-called Dollar Banana producers of Latin America (which were not given the preferential import tariffs as banana producers in the former European colonies—a subject that was to erupt into a trade war in the late 1990s), was paying higher prices for its bananas.

If Geest's banana business was troubled, its fresh prepared foods business was taking off in the early 1990s. A new series of acquisitions, together with the launches of a number of new subsidiaries, continued to boost this segment of the company's operations toward the middle of the decade. Among the company's new subsidiaries and acquisitions were Abbeyvale Foods, Caledonian Produce, Spalding Soups & Sauces, the Bakery, and Spalding Dips & Dressings, all added or launched in 1993. The following year, the company acquired Spring Valley and South Africa Geest Foodservice, adding a new fresh tropical fruits imports component. These acquisitions and investments led Geest to sell off its underperforming Wholesales Market division in 1994.

Geest continued to develop its prepared foods business and also began to prepare a move from its United Kingdom base onto the European continent, when it created its Geest Foods Europe subsidiary in 1995. One year later, Geest made the next move in what had been the company's transformation, when it agreed to sell off its banana operations to a joint venture formed between Fyffes and a company set up among the Windwards Islands nations to take control of their own banana production for the first time. Shorn of its banana business, the trimmed down Geest was welcomed by the stock market, which quickly doubled the company's share price. Nonetheless, the company was soon the subject of takeover speculation, as larger food groups—such as Unilever and Hillsdown Holding—eyed increases in their own fresh prepared foods business.

This was because fresh prepared foods was making steady inroads in consumers' food purchases budgets. As the average time spent per day in food preparation dropped to just half an

Key Dates:

1930: John and Leonard van Geest start up flower bulb import business in United Kingdom.
1935: John van Geest launches Geest Horticultural Products.
1940s: Company begins produce imports.
1953: Company begins banana imports.
1959: Import shipping and cruise line is launched.
1972: Company opens salad preparation facility in Spalding; changes name to Geest Holdings.
1986: Geest Holdings goes public on the London stock exchange and changes name to Geest Plc.
1988: Company acquires Katies Kitchen; launches Spalding Ready Meals.
1989: Company acquires Bourne Salads.
1990: Company acquires The Pasta Company.
1991: Company adds Kent Salads and English Village Salads.
1993: Company adds Abbeyvale Foods, Caledonian Produce, Spalding Soups & Sauces, the Bakery, and Spalding Dips & Dressings.
1994: Company sells off Wholesale Market division.
1996: Company sells off Banana division.
1997: Company adds J. Pao & Sons Ltd., Geest Iberia, Savon Valley Foods, and Geest Tilbrook.
1999: Enzafruit joint venture is created; Cinquième Saison (France) is acquired.
2000: Alresford Salads is created.

hour in the United Kingdom, and renewed growth in the British economy was creating new numbers of overworked, but well-paid, workers, the fresh prepared foods categories were gaining more and more floor space in the United Kingdom's supermarkets. At the same time, changes in store opening rules—such as the ending of restrictions on Sunday openings—were making these foods more available to consumers than ever before. By the late 1990s, the various fresh prepared foods segments were growing an average of ten percent per year. Geest's position at the start of the trend had enabled the company to build up per-segment market share stakes of as much as 40 percent and more.

Meanwhile, Geest was adding to its holdings. In 1996, after the sale of the banana division, the company made its first acquisition on the European continent, of Vaco, a maker of fresh ready meals based in Belgium, giving it a wider access to the countries in the Benelux region. The company also reached an agreement with The Netherlands' Albert Heijn, a subsidiary of the world's number three retailer, Royal Ahold, to supply the Albert Heijn chain of 650 supermarkets with fresh ready meals.

Acquisitions continued to mark Geest's growth through the late 1990s as it sought to expand its production capacity as well as its variety of food products. In 1997 the company added J. Pao & Sons Ltd., Geest Iberia, Savon Valley Foods, and Geest Tilbrook. Taking a break over 1998, the company returned again to the expansion trail in 1999, adding France's Cinquième Saison (giving the company access to the French market for the first time), Wingland Foods, Yorkshire Fresh Salads, and the Fresh Snack Company. The company also formed the joint ventures Geest QV and Enzafruit Worldwide, which saw the company move its fresh fruit and produce operations out from under its full control—a move that some analysts saw as a prelude to the company's exit from these markets.

Geest's transformation into a leading fresh prepared foods company continued into 2000 as the company started up a new subsidiary, Alresford Salads, built up from facilities acquired from The Watercress Company. At the same time, Geest stepped up its investments in its production capacity, adding three new plants in the first half of the year. The company was heartened by continued gains in the fresh prepared foods market overall, especially as its own growth continued to outpace the food market in general. In addition, although the United Kingdom represented one of the largest single markets for fresh prepared meals, the trend toward decreasing food preparation time and increased acceptance of prepared foods was expected to take off on the European continent as well, giving Geest a lot to look forward to in the new century.

Principal Subsidiaries

Abbeyvale Foods; The Bakery; Bourne Salads; Caledonian; Cinquième Saison (France); English Village Salads; ENZAFRUIT Worldwide (50%); The Fresh Snack Company; Geest QV (50%); Katies Kitchen; Kent Salads; The Pasta Company; Saxon Valley; Spalding Ready Meals; Spring Valley (South Africa); Tilbrook; Vaco (Belgium); Yorkshire Fresh Salads.

Principal Competitors

Booker Plc; Chiquita Brands International Inc.; Dole Food Company Inc.; Fyffes Plc; Hazlewood Foods Plc; Hibernia Foods Plc; Hillsdown Holdings Ltd.; Northern Foods Plc; Unilever; Uniq plc.

Further Reading

Barrow, Rebecca, "Convenience Food Fattens Up Geest," *Daily Telegraph,* September 19, 1997.
Hughes, Chris, "Geest," *Independent,* September 15, 2000, p. 21.
Murray-West, Rosie, "Geest Gaining from the 'Ready Meal' Culture," *Daily Telegraph,* March 17, 2000.
Potter, Ben, "Geest Still Looks a Tasty Prospect," *Daily Telegraph,* October 15, 1999.
Stevenson, Tom, "A Slimmer, More Attractive Geest," *Independent,* March 22, 1996, p. 16.

—M.L. Cohen

genzyme

Genzyme Corporation

One Kendall Square
Cambridge, Massachusetts 02139-1562
U.S.A.
Telephone: (617) 252-7500
Toll Free: (800) 436-1443
Fax: (617) 252-7600
Web site: http://www.genzyme.com

Public Company
Incorporated: 1981
Employees: 3,800
Sales: $635.4 million (1999)
Stock Exchanges: NASDAQ
Ticker Symbols: GENZ (Genzyme General); GZMO (Genzyme Molecular Oncology); GZSP (Genzyme Surgical Products); GZTR (Genzyme Tissue Repair)
NAIC: 325412 Pharmaceutical Preparation Manufacturing (pt); 325414 Biological Product (Except Diagnostic) Manufacturing; 339112 Surgical and Medical Instrument Manufacturing (pt); 621511 Medical Laboratories

Genzyme Corporation is a leading biotechnology company that focuses on five business areas: therapeutics, diagnostic services, diagnostic products, pharmaceutical and fine chemicals, and tissue repair. Headquartered in Cambridge, Massachusetts, Genzyme is an industry leader in the development of biotherapeutical treatments for lysosomal storage disorders. The company has an extensive international distribution network and has gained approval for its products in more than 50 countries.

Enzyme Technology in the Early 1980s

In 1981, Henry Blair founded Genzyme to produce products based on enzyme technologies. With the help of venture capital funding, Blair acquired Whatman Biochemicals Ltd., which became Genzyme Biochemicals. In 1982, Blair acquired a British catalog business, Koch-Light Laboratories, a supplier of chemicals to the pharmaceutical industry. The pharmaceutical manufacturing arm of Koch Laboratories in 1986 became Genzyme Pharmaceutical and Fine Chemicals based in Haverill, England.

Despite these developments, Genzyme struggled until 1983, when Dutch-born Henri Termeer left Baxter Travenol (now Baxter International) to become company chairman at Genzyme. Termeer studied economics at the University of Rotterdam and earned an M.B.A. at the University of Virginia before joining Baxter in 1973. After undergoing two years of training in Chicago, Baxter assigned him to run its largest overseas sales organization in Germany. The position gave him valuable experience in managing a major business operation. By the time he joined Genzyme, Termeer was one of Baxter's executive vice-presidents. He was recruited to Genzyme by the venture capital firm Oak Investment Partners, which had substantial investments in the start-up company.

Termeer took a personal risk in moving to Genzyme, sacrificing half his salary and a comfortable lifestyle in southern California for forbidding office space in Boston's notorious Combat Zone—the city's red light district. The company employed only 11 people. On assuming the chairmanship, Termeer immediately began a search for investment capital. He also formed an advisory board, consisting of a group of eminent MIT scientists to identify promising new areas for product development. While many biotechnology companies worked to develop huge blockbuster drugs, Genzyme crafted a niche strategy focusing on less glamorous products that could be sold readily. This strategy proved to position the company well, even as it developed longer-term products.

Genzyme aggressively pursued its strategy first through developing expertise in engineering and modifying enzymes and carbohydrates. Enzymes are proteins that essentially act as catalysts for many cellular processes, whereas carbohydrates often coat proteins and govern their interactions with other substances or chemicals. The company's expertise in these areas yielded readily marketable products. Genzyme developed and marketed a product called cholesterol oxidase, including an enzyme that worked as the active agent in cholesterol tests.

In 1983, Termeer became president of Genzyme and in 1985 he was named chief executive officer. In 1986, Genzyme be-

Company Perspectives:

Today, Genzyme is accelerating the momentum created by our many past successes and preparing for significant growth in the years ahead. Our attention is directed at "building our strengths," enhancing our core resources and capabilities while concentrating on those areas where we can add the greatest value. This strategic focus enables us to achieve significant progress across all aspects of our business while positively influencing the lives of many patients.

came a public company with an initial public offering that raised $28.2 million. In the same year, the company opened a Japanese subsidiary financed by Japanese sales and built a manufacturing facility in Cambridge, Massachusetts, for the production of medical grade hyaluronic acid. Genzyme also raised $10 million to finance the development of Ceredase through a research and development limited partnership. Genzyme divested Koch-Light Laboratories in 1987. In 1988, the company, with partial funding from the Department of Trade & Industry, opened a pharmaceutical chemical plant in Haverville, United Kingdom, doubling Genzyme's manufacturing capacity. In addition, the company received U.S. Food and Drug Administration approval to market the antibiotic Clindamycin Phosphate for the treatment of serious hospital infections.

In 1989, Termeer acquired Integrated Genetics (IG) of Framingham, Massachusetts, a move that industry observers termed a masterstroke. Termeer's successful negotiations for the company stemmed from a coincidental meeting with IG Chairman Robert Carpenter. Both attended a reunion of Baxter alumni in Chicago, and the two alums accompanied one another on the return flight to Boston. Although mired in financial difficulty, IG possessed superior technology. In 1988, Termeer unsuccessfully bid for IG when its stock hovered at $5 per share. But Carpenter was willing to deal in 1989 after trying to sell out to a large pharmaceutical company. Several weeks after the airplane flight, Carpenter accepted Genzyme's offer for less than $3 a share in Genzyme stock, amounting to $31.5 million. The acquisition considerably strengthened Genzyme's expertise in molecular biology, protein chemistry, carbohydrate engineering, nucleic acid chemistry, and enzymology.

In the same year, Genzyme raised $39.1 million in a public stock offering and another $36.8 million through a research and development limited partnership to develop four hyaluronic acid (HA) based drugs to reduce the formation of postoperative adhesions. The company also formed its Genzyme Diagnostics Division. By the end of 1989, Genzyme reported revenues of $34.1 million.

The Early 1990s: Product Breakthroughs, Corporate Strategies

By far Genzyme's most lucrative, if not controversial, product was the drug Ceredase, approved by the U.S. Food and Drug Administration in 1991. The drug was the first effective treatment for Gaucher's disease, a rare but previously untreatable and potentially fatal genetic disorder. The illness, which afflicted about 20,000 people worldwide in the early 1990s, most commonly strikes Jews of East European descent. The victims of the disease lack a natural enzyme that metabolizes fats, causing lipids, or fatty substances, to mass in the liver, spleen, and bone marrow, resulting in a variety of crippling conditions and years of painful physical deterioration. Genzyme's scientists successfully produced the missing enzyme, which could be infused intravenously and consequently reverse the lipid buildup, allowing patients to live normal and active lives with few side effects.

Although Ceredase won praise as a life-saving treatment, it also drew criticism for being the most expensive drug ever sold, running on average $150,000 per patient a year. As a result, the drug became a vehicle for criticism of high drug prices. In 1992, the Office of Technology Assessment, a nonpartisan Congressional research agency, issued a report accusing Genzyme of pricing the drug so high that patients would have to exhaust their lifetime insurance to buy Ceredase for two or three years. The report noted that the real costs and risks of developing the drug were low because most of the work was done by government researchers. The federal agency stated that the pricing also raised serious questions concerning whether the government should participate in developing drugs with little or no control over their final pricing. Company Chairman and President Henri Termeer said the agency's report was flawed and that the high cost stemmed from the enormous expense of producing the product. To assuage criticism, Genzyme agreed to give Ceredase to patients whose insurance benefits ran out. Nevertheless, others also voiced complaints. Speaking on behalf of the National Organization for Rare Disorders, Abbey S. Meyers, the organization's president, stated in the *Wall Street Journal* on May 20, 1994 that "we were appalled" at Genzyme's pricing of Ceredase. This criticism was the latest in complaints about the exorbitant cost of biotechnology drugs. In Congressional hearings, patients had complained about the cost of the anemia drug erythropoietin, or EPO, from Amgen Inc., which cost between $4,000 and $6,000 a year, and Genentech Inc.'s human growth hormone at $12,000 to $18,000 a year. But Ceredase's price far surpassed either of these two drugs and quickly drove the issue onto the legislative agenda.

These criticisms aside, Ceredase was enormously expensive to make, relying on enzyme extraction from placentas from hospitals around the world. The harvesting of the material was done by a unit of the Institut Merieux of Paris. The production of a year's supply for the average patient required approximately 20,000 placentas equaling about 27 tons of material. In 1994, Genzyme supplied Ceredase to 1,100 patients. The drug's high price stemmed also from its applicability to only a small number of patients, placing the primary burden for paying the research costs and a return to investors on those being treated. Genzyme argued, moreover, that Ceredase differed from other drugs in a critical respect that influenced its price. Typically, drug prices were set to be competitive with existing treatments, including surgery and hospitalization, in spite of production costs. But since Ceredase was the only existing treatment for Gaucher's disease, the price reflected the drug's full production and marketing costs.

Genzyme's monopoly on Ceredase was protected under the Orphan Drug Act, passed in 1983 to give seven-year exclusive rights to drug companies that produce drugs for rare diseases (those afflicting less than 200,000 people). According to

Key Dates:

1981: Henry Blair founds Genzyme.
1983: Henri Termeer becomes Genzyme chairman.
1988: Genzyme opens pharmaceutical chemical facility in the United Kingdom.
1991: Ceredase gains FDA approval.
1994: Genzyme receives FDA approval to market Cerezyme; Genzyme Tissue Repair Division is formed.
1997: Genzyme acquires PharmaGenics, Inc. to create Genzyme Molecular Oncology.
1999: Genzyme Surgical Products is formed.

Termeer, the Act attracted the capital investment needed to research and develop the drug. In 1994, Genzyme received FDA approval to market Cerezyme, a genetically engineered replacement for Ceredase. The company also hoped to benefit from Orphan Act designation for various projects concerning cystic fibrosis, Fabry's disease, and severe burns.

By 1991, Genzyme raised nearly $100 million for research and development while retaining control over its equity and production rights, a stark contrast to many young biotechnology firms that had to sacrifice these assets to finance themselves. Nearly half the funds, $47.3 million, came from a public offering of Neozyme I Corp., formed by Genzyme in 1990 to research and develop six healthcare products. In 1992, the company formed Neozyme II to fund other Genzyme projects. The companies operated primarily as paper businesses to finance research and development projects and retain rights to the products. If the projects proved successful, Genzyme could buy the rights back.

In 1991, Genzyme also took IG laboratories—the genetic testing services business—public, raising another $14.1 million. Genzyme reported revenues of $121.7 million, more than double 1990 revenues of $54.8 million. In addition, Genzyme announced that it would build new corporate headquarters and manufacturing facilities in Boston on a 51-acre site along the Charles River. The company looked at sites in more than a dozen states, narrowing its choice to two in Massachusetts—Boston and Cambridge—both with international scientific reputations. These sites were close to Genzyme's current headquarters in Cambridge and close to large clusters of biotechnology companies. Boston's offer of a sizable state-owned parcel that could be quickly developed, plus many inducements, including breaks on city and state taxes and government assistance with site planning, road construction, utility rates, and others, clinched the deal. Regional economists hoped that Genzyme's $110 million facility would be one anchor of a thriving regional biotechnology industry, bringing thousands of new research and manufacturing jobs to raise the city and Massachusetts out of recession. Genzyme also ran a pilot production facility in Framingham, Massachusetts, and operations in The Netherlands, Japan, and England.

Continuing Diversification and Growth into the Mid-1990s

Genzyme's other corporate moves in 1991 included the selling of its interest in GENE-TRAK systems for $10 million and the acquisition of Genecore International's diagnostic enzyme business. The acquisition gave Genzyme worldwide diagnostic sales, production capacity, and inventory, as well as related patent and distribution rights. The company also established Genzyme, B.V., a European subsidiary in Naardan, Holland, to manage the development and regulatory approval of Genzyme's biotherapeutic products.

Genzyme's research achievements for 1991 included beginning clinical development of Thyrogen, a thyroid stimulating human hormone for use in the diagnosis and treatment of thyroid cancer. Genzyme also initiated clinical development of HAL-S synovial fluid replacement, a treatment for tissue damage resulting from arthroscopic surgery. In addition, Genzyme and Tufts University scientists jointly performed breakthrough analysis concerning the role of a key protein responsible for cystic fibrosis, a lung disease. In 1992, the researchers innovated a method to mass-produce this protein for the treatment of the disease by genetically altering mice with a human gene governing production of the protein and then harvesting it from fat globules in the mouse's milk. The discovery marked the first time that animal milk was used to produce proteins of this type.

In 1992, Genzyme developed technology to make purer and stronger pharmaceuticals and to simplify the pharmaceutical preparation process. Genzyme won FDA orphan drug designation for several treatments, covering Cystic Fibrosis Transmembrane Conductance Regulation (r-CFTR), Cystic Fibrosis Gene Therapy (CFGT), Thyrogen Cancer Agent, and Vianain Enzymatic Debridement Agent for treating severe burn patients. In 1994, the company received FDA approval to sell Cerezyme, the genetically engineered replacement for Ceredase.

By the early 1990s, Genzyme had become a large and thriving diversified company, in contrast to many biotechnology firms plagued by clinical failures, cuts in research, layoffs, and funding troubles. In 1994, Repligen Inc. of Cambridge, Massachusetts, announced layoffs of one-third of its staff after failing to find financial backing. Synergen Inc.'s stock plunged on news that its leading drug failed in clinical trials, compelling the Boulder, Colorado firm to cut more than half of its payroll. Glycomed Inc. of Alameda, California, eliminated 30 percent of its workforce to conserve cash. Cambridge Biotech Corp. of Worcester, Massachusetts, a once-leading biotech firm, filed for Chapter 11 protection. Signaling the industry's poor health, Oppenheimer Global Bio-Tech Fund, a specialty mutual fund for stock investors, announced that it was shifting investment strategy to focus on ''emerging growth'' stocks. With these reversals, investor confidence plummeted, causing financing to dry up and research projects to be dropped, and leaving many smaller firms vulnerable if their flagship drugs failed to pay off. To raise cash, several companies licensed their main products at minimal sale prices. Other companies canceled plans to add manufacturing capacity and sold facilities and leased them back. The main culprit for the industry's woes was a string of clinical failures, as some biotech firms prematurely initiated clinical studies to gain the broadest possible market exposure for their products. Still, in 1994 more than 100 biotechnology products were either in final Phase III clinical tests or awaiting FDA marketing approval.

Genzyme and other large biotechnology companies capitalized on the industry fallout by buying financially troubled firms and products at low prices. Genzyme aggressively began acquiring companies in the late 1980s as part of a broad strategy to minimize risk. Aside from the acquisitions of Integrated Genetics and Gencore International in 1992, Genzyme acquired Medix Biotech, Inc., a producer and supplier of monoclonal and polyclonal antibodies, immunoassay components, and immunodiagnostic services. In the same year, the company's U.K. subsidiary, Genzyme Limited, bought Enzymatix Limited of Cambridge, United Kingdom, which was integrated into Genzyme's Pharmaceutical and Fine Chemicals division. Genzyme also acquired Vivigen, a genetics testing laboratory in Santa Fe, New Mexico. In 1993, Genzyme acquired both Virotech of Russelsheim, Germany, a producer and distributor of in-vitro diagnostic kits, and Omni Res srl of Milan, Italy, a producer and seller of immunobiological products. Acquisitions in 1994 included a Swiss pharmaceutical concern, Sygena Ltd.; BioSurface Technology Inc., a developer of wound healing products; and TSI Inc., a former high-flying drug testing company that expanded too rapidly and posted major financial losses. The TSI acquisition was made by Genzyme Transgenics Corp., created by Genzyme in 1993 to promote and develop technology combining recombinant microbiology and experimental embryology to produce specialized proteins from animal milk. The TSI purchase made Genzyme Transgenics, 73 percent owned by Genzyme—the largest player in the emerging biotechnology market called ''pharming,'' the use of genetically altered farm animals to produce pharmaceuticals.

Genzyme's diversification moves generally received praise, but they also raised speculation that the company would face difficulty integrating the various operations. Moreover, despite the company's numerous acquisitions, its major revenue producer was still just one product, Ceredase/Cerezyme. Beyond this product, Genzyme's line of future drugs contained no blockbuster moneymakers, a strategy originally crafted by Termeer to minimize risk. Unlike many of its competitors, Genzyme had yet to experience any major disappointments in clinical trials on near-term drug development projects.

In 1995, Genzyme's next project, a range of hyaluronic acid (HA) products, also looked promising. Hyaluronic acid contains a polysaccharide found in a variety of human tissues that can be used to prevent postoperative adhesions following abdominal, gynecological, cardiac, and orthopedic surgery. Noting that hyaluronic acid could be used by virtually all surgeons, Genzyme predicted that the market for the drug would be about $1.3 billion, four times that for Ceredase. Unlike the Ceredase market, however, Genzyme faced several competitors for hyaluronic acid, including major pharmaceutical companies. Other products also were being developed to serve the same purpose. In addition, concerns arose that the product was unlikely to be universally effective in preventing postoperative adhesions, and thus the marketing of the drug would be split with competing products. Nevertheless, Termeer expressed confidence in the drug and said that Genzyme would beat competitors to the market by at least five years.

Genzyme's diversification also included a move into gene therapy. Although its leading product, Ceredase, and its genetically engineered successor, Cerezyme, proved highly effective, the company began working with scientists at the University of Pittsburgh and at IntroGene B.V., a biotech firm in Rijswijk, The Netherlands, to develop a gene therapeutic treatment to replace the drugs. The new therapy, if successful, would correct the enduring genetic defects responsible for Gaucher's disease. In addition, in 1995 Genzyme planned to spend $400 million to research and develop gene therapy to treat cystic fibrosis, the most common fatal hereditary disease in the United States. These moves stemmed in part from attempts to avoid obsolescence as the revolutionary developments in gene therapy, still mostly in the exploratory stage, threatened to bypass biotechnology developments.

By the mid-1990s, Genzyme continued to be well positioned to capitalize on emerging technologies and to minimize risk if several of its products failed. The company arose in 1981 to become one of the top five biotechnology companies in terms of sales. Nevertheless, the biotechnology field remained highly competitive, with numerous rivals in the United States and elsewhere, many of which had greater resources than Genzyme. With large pharmaceutical and biotechnology companies as competitors, the prospect loomed that these companies would develop more effective products and marketing strategies. Indeed, Genzyme's competitive pressures were most acute in the therapeutics field. Although no alternatives existed for Ceredase and Cerezyme, another company was attempting to make an alternative product using an enzyme in insect cells. Genzyme's hyaluronic acid products for postoperative adhesions faced competition from both HA-based and non-HA-based products. The company anticipated that the chief competitive factor would be the measure of acceptance by surgeons depending on product performance and price. Several academic and commercial enterprises were engaged in developing therapies to treat either the symptoms or the cause of cystic fibrosis. A number of groups were developing gene therapy approaches to the disease and received government approval to conduct limited human trials. Other organizations were investigating pharmacological and biological agents that would alleviate the symptoms of the disease. A leading biotech firm, Genentech Inc., had already received FDA marketing approval for its product, Pulmozyme. With these competitive elements, any one of these groups could develop gene therapy products or drug therapies before Genzyme, or obtain patent protection that would effectively bar the company from commercializing its technology. Nevertheless, Genzyme's aggressive strategy had paid off in the past and appeared to position the company well for future developments.

Resurgence of the Biotechnology Industry in the Late 1990s

In the second half of the decade Genzyme devoted increased attention to developing gene therapy programs for a wider range of diseases. In addition to continuing its search for better cystic fibrosis treatments, pledging an additional $400 million to its cystic fibrosis research programs in 1995, the company began exploring alternative genetic treatments for lysosomal storage disorders, notably Gaucher disease and Fabry disease. These alternative treatments were aimed at creating genetic material that would enable patients suffering from these disorders to generate deficient enzymes naturally. During this period the company also developed new therapies for Pompe disease (another lysosomal storage disorder), renal disease, and hypothyroidism in recovering cancer patients. Renagel, a kidney therapy designed to control blood phosphate levels in hemodialysis patients, was launched in 1999, and within one year was being used by more than 30,000 patients.

In the mid-1990s the company also deepened its involvement in cancer research. In 1995 Genzyme Transgenics was the first company to develop a monoclonal antibody in the milk of a transgenic goat. Through this process, which spliced human genetic material into the DNA of milk-producing mammals, researchers were able to produce recombinant human proteins for use in a range of disease therapies. Genzyme took further steps toward expanding its cancer research capabilities in 1996, when it reached an agreement with Imperial Cancer Research Technology Ltd. in the United Kingdom to establish a joint venture dedicated to researching cancer gene therapies. In 1997, the company created a new division devoted to studying cancer vaccines on the molecular level.

In the mid-1990s Genzyme undertook a radical corporate restructuring. The plan called for the eventual partitioning of the company's diverse interests into separate divisions, each of which would have its own "tracking stock." The move effectively established separate companies within the corporation. The realignment began in 1994 with the purchase of BioSurface Technology Inc., which Genzyme converted into a new division, Genzyme Tissue Repair. This new division brought together Genzyme's four existing tissue repair research projects and was launched with eight products in various stages of development and an initial investment of $26 million. At the same time, Genzyme's other research programs were brought together within a larger division, called Genzyme General.

The strategy behind Genzyme Tissue Repair involved the integration of three of Genzyme's specialties—enzymes and recombinant proteins, biomaterials, and cell culture techniques—to develop new approaches to skin grafts and cartilage restoration. Proceeding from advances made in Sweden over the previous seven years, Genzyme Tissue Repair began research on a new method of growing cartilage cells in 1995, and by 1997 its Carticel therapy was demonstrating success with patients suffering from damaged knees. At the same time the division also developed a skin graft product, Epicel, for use with burn victims.

In the wake of the successful integration of Genzyme Tissue Repair into the Genzyme Corporation, the company created a third division, Genzyme Molecular Oncology, in 1997, to study the potential uses of microbiological solutions in the development of a cancer vaccine. The Genzyme Surgical Products Division followed in 1999, with a mission to develop medical instruments and biomaterials for cardiovascular therapies and general surgical uses. In 2000 the company announced its plan to acquire Biomatrix, Inc., which eventually would become its fifth division, Genzyme Biosurgery. This diversification resulted in steady growth, culminating in record net earnings of more than $142 million for fiscal 1999.

Principal Subsidiaries

Genzyme Transgenics Corporation; IG Laboratories, Inc. (69%).

Principal Divisions

Genzyme Biosurgery; Genzyme General; Genzyme Molecular Oncology; Genzyme Surgical Products; Genzyme Tissue Repair.

Principal Competitors

Chiron Corporation; Genentech, Inc.; Johnson & Johnson.

Further Reading

Abate, Tom, "Biotech Firms Transforming Animals into Drug-Producing Machines; Transgenic Creatures Carry Human DNA That Produce Proteins," *San Francisco Chronicle*, January 17, 2000.

Alster, Norm, "Henri Termeer's Orphan Drug Strategy," *Forbes*, May 27, 1991, pp. 202–05.

Convey, Eric, "Genzyme Makes Move in New Direction," *Boston Herald*, January 23, 1996.

Diesenhouse, Susan, "Boston Over Cambridge in a Biotechnology Race," *New York Times*, December 25, 1991.

"Genzyme Buys PharmaGenics to Create Cancer Focus," *Pharmaceutical Business News*, February 7, 1997.

Hilts, Philip J., "U.S. Agency Criticizes High Price of Drug," *New York Times*, October 6, 1992.

Rosenberg, Ronald, "Genzyme's Plan to Beat Obsolescence," *Boston Globe*, January 8, 1995.

——, "New Competitor Looms for Cambridge Drug Maker," *Boston Globe*, April 29, 2000.

Schwartz, John, and Friday, Carolyn, "Beating the Odds in Biotech," *Newsweek*, October 12, 1992, p. 63.

Stecklow, Steve, "Genzyme Receives FDA Approval to Sell Cerezyme," *Wall Street Journal*, May 25, 1994.

Stipp, David, "Biotechnology Firms Find Themselves in Cash Crunch," *Wall Street Journal*, July 26, 1994, p. B10.

——, "Genzyme to Buy BioSurface, Merge It into a New Unit with Separate Stock," *Wall Street Journal*, July 26, 1994, p. B4.

——, "Stock Swap for TSI Set by Genzyme Transgenics Corp.," *Wall Street Journal*, June 16, 1994, p. B7.

Tanouye, Elyse, "What's Fair?: Critics Say Many New Drugs Are Priced Far Too High," *Wall Street Journal*, May 20, 1994, p. R11.

Zitner, Aaron, "Change in Drug Rules Expected; Senate Committee Said to Favor 'Fast Track' Approval Process," *Boston Globe*, June 12, 1997.

—Bruce P. Montgomery
—updated by Stephen Meyer

GKN plc

Post Office Box 55
Redditch, Worcestershire B98 0TL
United Kingdom
Telephone: (01527) 517715
Fax: (01527) 517700
Web site: http://www.gknplc.com

Public Company
Incorporated: 1900 as Guest, Keen and Co. Limited
Employees: 40,700
Sales: £4.64 billion (US$7.51 billion) (1999)
Stock Exchanges: London
Ticker Symbol: GKN
NAIC: 336350 Motor Vehicle Transmission and Power Train Parts Manufacturing; 332117 Powder Metallurgy Part Manufacturing; 336411 Aircraft Manufacturing; 336412 Aircraft Engine and Engine Parts Manufacturing; 321920 Wood Container and Pallet Manufacturing; 562110 Waste Collection; 562210 Waste Treatment and Disposal; 562920 Materials Recovery Facilities; 811112 Automotive Exhaust System Repair

Born out of the early 20th-century mergers of three companies, GKN plc has evolved into a global industrial giant centered on three main businesses: automotive components, industrial services, and aerospace. In the automotive sector, GKN is a world leading manufacturer of driveline systems and constant velocity joints, and is also one of the largest producers of powder metal and powdered metal components—notably those used in automobiles—in the world. Industrial services includes four main businesses: Chep, a joint venture offering pooling services for pallets, automotive crates, and containers; Cleanaway, another joint venture and the leading waste management and recycling firm in Europe; Interlake Material Handling, a U.S.-based supplier of racking systems used in warehouses and distribution centers; and Meineke Discount Muffler Shops, a U.S. franchised chain of shops specializing in muffler and other car repair. In aerospace, GKN manufactures helicopters, supplies aircraft propulsion systems and components, and offers engineering services to clients in the aerospace, automotive, rail, marine, and defense sectors. The global nature of the company's operations are quite evident in its geographical revenue breakdown: about 39 percent of revenues are generated in the United Kingdom, about 31 percent on Continental Europe, and about 27 percent in the Americas.

Development of the Predecessor Companies

Although the mergers that created GKN took place at the beginning of the 20th century, the companies out of which GKN evolved were considerably older. The group, however, has changed so much in the intervening years that there is little left of its original elements. They were essentially family companies and typical of the entrepreneurial spirit responsible for the United Kingdom's leading position in the iron and steel industry during much of the 19th century.

One segment of the story begins in 1759 when nine businessmen formed an iron-smelting works at Dowlais in southern Wales that was initially called Dowlais Iron Works. John Guest took over as works manager in 1767. When Guest died, his son Thomas succeeded him and he was followed in turn by his son Sir Josiah ''John'' Guest, an able entrepreneur, who raised the renamed Dowlais Iron Company to prominence and became its sole owner in 1851. Sir John Guest's wife, Lady Charlotte Guest, was one of the most striking characters to emerge in the company's formative years. After her husband's death in 1852 she ran the company for three years. In 1889 the company built a new integrated steel works on the coast at Cardiff, at which iron was produced from 1891 and steel from 1895.

The second strand of the tripartite merger is centered on Arthur Keen, who was responsible for the two mergers that created GKN. Keen went into business in 1856 with a U.S. businessman who had acquired the British patent rights for an automatic bolt-making machine. In 1864, the business went public as the Patent Nut & Bolt Company. Keen's requirement for steelmaking technology led to the amalgamation with the Dowlais Iron Company and the incorporation of Guest, Keen and Co. Limited in 1900.

Company Perspectives:

Our Vision: GKN is a global industrial company that is committed to growth and fosters entrepreneurship. We shall lead and excel in every market we serve.

Our Mission: Create, grow and manage dynamically, a focused group of industrial businesses. Create an environment that encourages our people to realise their maximum potential. Exceed our customers' expectations through innovation, quality and total service. Achieve operational excellence. Deliver sustained outstanding value to our shareholders.

The third element in the merger, Nettlefolds, was centered on the manufacture of custom woodscrews, and stemmed from a partnership comprising John Sutton Nettlefold and his brother-in-law Joseph Chamberlain, who in 1854 set up a woodscrew factory at Smethwick. The company flourished to become the leading screwmaker in the United Kingdom. In 1880 it took over the Birmingham Screw Company, and also registered as a public company, Nettlefolds Limited. Further diversification took place in 1887 when a wire-rods, steelhoops, bars, and wires plant was set up in Rogerstone, Newport.

1900s Through 1950s: Concentrating on Steel, Screws, and Fasteners

In 1902, Guest, Keen and Co. acquired Nettlefolds, linking companies with diverse activities in a bid to exploit the benefits of horizontal integration. The first chairman of the newly created company was Arthur Keen, under whom the business was consolidated. This consolidation, based upon steel, continued throughout the first half of the 20th century, with Guest, Keen, and Nettlefolds Limited moving into areas such as rolling, forging, pressing, stamping, and machining.

Arthur Keen died in 1915, to be succeeded by his son, Arthur T. Keen, who died in 1918. The company emerged from World War I still centered on steelmaking, fasteners, and coal mining, primarily aimed at the railway and construction markets.

In 1919 the Earl of Bessborough took over as chairman, and the company took the lead in the nut and bolt industry with the acquisition of F.W. Cotterill. The group continued on the acquisition trail with the takeover in 1920 of John Lysaght, which had subsidiaries involved in steelmaking and rerolling in the United Kingdom and Australia. This acquisition was particularly significant. With the Lysaght purchase came Joseph Sankey, which produced steel presswork, including wheels, chassis, and motor body parts, marking the group's entrance into the motor industry.

In 1920 Edward Steer, a member of the Nettlefolds family, became chairman, a position he was to hold until 1927 when H. Seymour Berry took over. After Berry's death following a riding accident in 1928, Sir John Field Beale headed the company. He was to preside over GKN during the Great Depression and the economic recovery of the 1930s.

In 1929 the steel industry was hit by the Great Depression, which resulted in a new wave of mergers. Three years later, the government introduced duties on imported steel to make domestic steel more attractive, and these moves, combined with rearmament in the latter part of the decade, provided the impetus for a further round of new investment in the industry.

Against this background, GKN continued to expand. In 1930 the group took over Exors. of James Mills, one of the world's largest manufacturers of bright steel bars, and entered the Swedish market with the acquisition of Aug. Stenman A.B., a Swedish manufacturer of hinges and fasteners. Four years later, the iron and steel operations of the Dowlais works, which had once stood at the forefront of the iron and steel industry, were transferred within the group to the Cardiff, Margam, and Port Talbot works of Guest Keen Baldwins Iron and Steel Company. This was a newly formed company created to acquire the heavy iron and steel operations of GKN Ltd. and Baldwins Ltd.

The company was expanding steadily under the chairmanship of Sir Samuel Beale, the younger brother of Sir John Field Beale. Sir Samuel Beale led GKN through World War II, and was to remain a director until 1957.

After the war, the Labour government set about economic reconstruction. The industry was asked to draw up a five-year plan for reorganization and modernization, to reverse the deterioration in its competitive position.

GKN expanded its iron-using and steel-using businesses, such as castings and pressings, to support the fast-expanding U.K. motor industry. J.H. Jolly took over as chairman in 1947, and in 1948, just three years before the nationalization of the steel industry, the group acquired Brymbo Steel Works in North Wales. In the same year it transferred its trading activities to two new companies. GKN (Midlands) took over the bolt and nut works at Darlaston and the screw works at Smethwick, while GKN (South Wales) Ltd. took over the rerolling works and wire and nail plants at Cardiff.

Then in 1951 came the much heralded and controversial Iron and Steel Act under which the three steelmaking companies, Brymbo, G.K. Baldwin, and John Lysaght, together with GKN (South Wales), were nationalized. Two years later Sir Kenneth Peacock took over as chairman.

Steel nationalization proved to be relatively short-lived, and with the return of the Conservative government the industry was denationalized in 1955. GKN bought back its four companies and at the same time Guest, Keen, Baldwins—which had been jointly owned with Baldwins and had been the group's largest source of steel supply—became a wholly owned subsidiary named Guest, Keen Iron and Steel Company.

1960s and 1970s: Major Transformation, Moving the Company into Defense and Auto Sectors

The group was still largely dependent on its original core businesses, but the 1960s were to see a transformation that gathered speed in the ensuing decades. During the 1960s, when the U.K. economy proved far less buoyant, GKN undertook major restructuring and reinforced its links with the growing motor industry, primarily through the acquisition of Birfield Ltd., which supplied components for the Austin-Morris mini. The group entered the defense-equipment market, winning an

Key Dates:

1759: Nine businessmen form an iron-smelting works in southern Wales called Dowlais Iron Works.
1767: John Guest becomes manager of Dowlais Iron Works, the beginning of the involvement of the Guest family in the business.
1851: The grandson of John Guest becomes sole owner of Dowlais Iron Company.
1854: John Sutton Nettlefold enters into a partnership to make custom woodscrews.
1856: Arthur Keen enters into a partnership to manufacture an automatic bolt-making machine.
1864: Keen's business goes public as the Patent Nut & Bolt Company.
1880: Sutton's business goes public as Nettlefolds Limited.
1900: Dowlais Iron Company and the Patent Nut & Bolt Company merge to create Guest, Keen and Co. Limited.
1902: Guest, Keen and Co. acquires Nettlefolds; the company changes its name to Guest, Keen and Nettlefolds Limited.
1920: Company acquires John Lysaght and with it, Joseph Sankey, maker of steel auto parts—marking GKN's entrance into the auto industry.
1951: The U.K. government nationalizes the steel industry, including GKN's steelmaking companies.
1955: The steel industry is denationalized and GKN buys back its steel companies.
1962: GKN enters the defense sector.
1966: Company acquires Birfield and its minority stake in Uni-Carden, maker of constant velocity joints.
1967: The company's steel operations, now called GKN Steel Company, are renationalized.
1974: One of the company's founding operations, the Dowlais plant, leaves the company orbit; GKN Chep, a joint venture pallet pooling service, is formed with Brambles Industries of Australia.
1981: GKN and Brambles join forces again to take over waste disposal firm Redland Purle, which is later known as Cleanaway.
1983: GKN acquires Meineke Discount Muffler Shops.
1986: Company adopts the name GKN plc; most of its remaining steel operations are divested.
1988: A minority stake in Westland, a U.K. helicopter maker, is acquired.
1994: GKN gains full control of Westland through a hostile takeover.
1995: Company makes its final exit from steelmaking.
1998: Company combines its armored vehicle operations with those of Alvis, in return for 29.9 percent stake in Alvis.
1999: GKN acquires Interlake Corporation.
2000: GKN and Finmeccanica of Italy merge their helicopter businesses into a 50–50 joint venture called AgustaWestland.

order for the FV432 armored personnel carrier for the British Army in 1962.

In 1967 the Labour government renationalized the steel businesses. Restructuring, which began in 1961 and was aimed at streamlining the businesses to make them more competitive, resulted in a series of subdivisions. The steel operations were the first to be restructured, with the creation of GKN Steel Company, which was nationalized in 1967.

The shake-up continued with the regrouping of its fastener, forgings, and castings, rolled and bright steel, building supplies and services, and engineering operations. GKN International Trading was created to deal with exports, and the group's overseas interests in Australia, New Zealand, South Africa, and Sweden were also reorganized. The group continued to expand in its traditional areas and to diversify, for example into gas-fired central-heating systems.

In 1963 GKN bought three suppliers of forgings to the motor industry: Ambrose Shardlow, in partnership with United Steel, Smethwick Drop Forgings, and Smith's Stampings. Three years later it took over the diversified Birfield Ltd., which brought with it a 39.5 percent stake in Uni-Cardan AG, a European automotive-components maker based in West Germany. GKN later raised its stake in Uni-Cardan to nearly 100 percent. The Uni-Cardan acquisition proved to be of primary significance to the group's strategy. Among Uni-Cardan's products were constant velocity joints, which permit the full transmission of torque from a car's engine to the wheels. These joints, originally designed for front-wheel-drive vehicles, were to play a crucial role in the growth of GKN's automotive business both at home and abroad.

In 1969 GKN unveiled a joint venture with Broken Hill Proprietary (BHP) of Australia to build a new steel complex at Westernpoint, Australia. The complex was constructed in two phases, the second of which was completed in 1978. The following year GKN sold its half interest to BHP.

In the 1970s GKN continued to increase its involvement in the automotive business and to build up its presence in distribution at home and abroad and its investment in service businesses. The decade also posed major problems. In the latter part of the 1970s the group's chairman Sir Barrie Heath, who took over from Sir Raymond Brookes in 1975, had to contend with hyperinflation, the oil crisis, and a collapse in demand for steel and automotive parts.

During the chairmanship of Sir Barrie, a management committee under Trevor Holdsworth undertook strategic restructuring to pull the company through, moving out of Australia and broadening the manufacturing base in the United States.

During the 1970s, GKN acquired a large number of small distribution companies, largely in the fastener and steel sectors. It later extended this strategy to automotive components, signaling a move into vehicle-parts and accessories distribution on a worldwide scale. The acquisitions continued on the steel and automotive sides, including Kirkstall Forge Engineering, the largest independent manufacturer of heavy-duty axles in the United Kingdom.

In 1974 the Brymbo Steel Works were returned to GKN by the then government-owned British Steel Corporation (BSC) in exchange for GKN Dowlais, in a deal which, while ending the group's long historical association with the Dowlais plant, gave it an internal source of supply. In the same year GKN took another significant step on the steel side with the purchase of Miles Druce & Company, making GKN the largest steel stockholder in the U.K. private sector. In 1974 GKN invested in the services sector with the formation of the United Kingdom's first national cargo-pallet hire pool, GKN Chep, with Brambles Industries of Australia.

In 1976, GKN stepped up its attack on the U.S. market with the formation of GKN Automotive Components Inc. to supply constant velocity—universal—joints for the new generation of front-wheel-drive cars. Within a year the group announced a further U.S. move, unveiling plans to set up a production plant, costing $50 million, in Sanford, North Carolina. Three years later, GKN announced that a second constant-velocity joint factory was to be built in North Carolina, in Alamance County, costing some $80 million. The two plants were commissioned in 1980 and 1981.

In 1977, the group was still stepping up investment in steelmaking and rerolling with the opening of a new rod mill and steel works in Cardiff, costing £52 million. It announced a £48 million rolling mill for Brymbo Steelworks.

The group's U.S. involvement was enhanced in 1979 with the acquisition of Parts Industries Corporation of Memphis, Tennessee, the fourth largest vehicle parts and accessories distributor in the United States. It raised its European profile in this area with the purchase from Unilever of Unigep Group of France and in the United Kingdom with the purchase of Armstrong Autoparts and Sheepbridge Engineering, both possessing large distribution chains.

The company sold off operations that did not fit into its strategy, which in 1979 included its 50 percent stake in John Lysaght (Australia) and the divestment of GKN Bolts and Nuts Ltd., one of the pillars of the company when it was formed in 1902. This sector had been suffering heavy financial losses.

The year 1979 also brought its frustrations. GKN had bid for Fitchell and Sachs, the largest supplier of car parts in West Germany, after taking a minority stake in 1976. After three years of patient negotiations, however, the bid was blocked by the West German courts.

At the end of the decade, GKN set about further restructuring which reflected the increasing importance of automotive components and the nonmanufacturing businesses. It was preparing for the 1980s, which were to prove another period of rapid change, under the initial chairmanship of Sir Trevor Holdsworth, who retired in 1988, and then of David Lees.

1980s: Major Moves into Industrial Services

The cold wind of recession hit the group in the early 1980s, and the decade started with a shock. GKN announced a loss of £1 million for 1980, the first since it was incorporated in 1902. Sir Trevor Holdsworth, who was responsible for fundamental changes to group strategy, set about slimming down and reshaping the group. Its workforce, for instance, had shrunk from 93,000 in 1980 to 38,000 when he retired. As the new structure evolved, the group moved out of steel, further internationalized through local investments and joint ventures, built up the automotive side, and developed industrial service businesses from its involvement in distribution.

The decade brought a series of sales and acquisitions, reflecting deep-rooted changes. In 1981 GKN and Brambles of Australia took a 50/50 interest in Redland Purle, the largest private-sector waste-disposal operator in the United Kingdom. The business is now known as Cleanaway Ltd. In the same year there was another major change when GKN and BSC merged their steel rerolling and associated businesses to create Allied Steel and Wire Ltd. In the following year, when the group became Guest, Keen and Nettlefolds plc, it won a large contract from the British Army for its Saxon armored personnel carrier.

In 1983, another strand of the business took shape with GKN and Costain of the United Kingdom merging their scaffolding and building-services operations to create GKN Kwikform, which became a market leader in the United Kingdom. That year the group expanded further in the United States with the acquisition of Meineke Discount Muffler Shops, one of the largest franchised exhaust-system fitters, while in the United Kingdom it set up a facility to produce fiberglass-reinforced road springs for commercial vehicles. Another success in the defense area came in 1984 when the group was awarded a contract for its Warrior tracked armored personnel carrier.

During 1984 and 1985, the group expanded its vehicle-parts-distribution businesses in the United States, and in Australia with the acquisition of Quinton Hazell Automotive. Viscodrive GmbH was created in West Germany to develop viscous drive-control units and a year later, in 1985, Viscodrive Japan and Translite were set up to market the units and composite leaf springs to the Japanese motor industry.

Another name change came in 1986 when the group became GKN plc, reflecting the move away from its original businesses. This change was underlined when in the same year the group sold its steel-stockholding operations and merged its engineering steels and forgings activities with BSC to form United Engineering Steels, with operating assets of about £600 million.

The group's international expansion continued apace. In 1986 and 1987, GKN made further European acquisitions in Spain and Italy, in the driveshaft and powder metallurgy areas, respectively. During 1987 it became a market leader in vending services following several acquisitions, and sold Allied Steel and Wire, which did not fit in with its strategy. In 1988 the group sold off the underperforming GKN Autoparts distribution business.

Also in 1988 the group hit the headlines by taking a 22.02 percent stake in Westland, the troubled U.K. helicopter and aerospace group. The deal roughly doubled the group's defense sales, which then accounted for about five percent of its £2 billion turnover.

It also forged an alliance with Jaguar cars. The two companies created a joint venture to supply all the major body pressings for the Jaguar/Daimler range of saloon and high-performance sports cars. In the United States GKN made some important changes, selling its imported-vehicle-parts distribution business and expanding the distribution of domestic-vehicle parts through the acquisition of Mid-America Industries.

In 1989 the group reported record pretax profits of £214.8 million, a far cry from the beginning of the decade. During that decade the group's emphasis had clearly shifted overseas. Sales of the U.K. subsidiaries in 1989 accounted for less than 37 percent of total sales of £2.7 billion against 68 percent a decade before. The transformation of GKN from its original businesses was quite apparent in the breakdown by sector at the end of the 1980s: the automotive side accounted for 61 percent of sales; industrial services, 35 percent; and defense, four percent.

1990s and Beyond: Strengthening a Three-Legged Structure

GKN suffered in the early 1990s as recession cut into automobile sales in the United Kingdom and elsewhere, including the major U.S. market. The company's defense operations also felt the effects of the economic downturn as the aerospace sector was hit particularly hard. Under the leadership of Lees, GKN once again responded aggressively during recession, further streamlining operations through a series of divestments. Along with more recently acquired businesses, such as vending and scaffolding, GKN also severed its ties to its remaining founding operations. The last of the fasteners operations were jettisoned, and in February 1995 the company's only tie to steelmaking, its 40 percent stake in United Engineering Steels, was sold off. GKN had recovered sufficiently by 1994 to take the bold—if widely criticized at the time—action of a hostile takeover of Westland, completed for approximately £557 million. By 1996 Westland had orders totaling £4 billion (US$6.2 billion) for its Lynx, SuperLynx, and EH101 helicopters. Other key moves during the first half of the decade included the extension of Chep into the lucrative U.S. market and the expansion of the automotive components business into the fast-growing markets of Asia and Latin America.

In late 1996 a jury in Charlotte, North Carolina, ruled against GKN and its Meineke subsidiary in a class-action lawsuit brought in 1993 on behalf of 2,500 franchisees and former franchisees of Meineke. The plaintiffs had charged that GKN and Meineke had defrauded them out of millions of dollars of payments that were earmarked for the chain's advertising fund. In March 1997 a federal judge set the damage award at US$591 million but this was reduced two months later to US$390 million. While it appealed, GKN was forced to take a provision of £270 million (US$436 million) in its 1996 accounts to cover the award, leading to a net loss for the year of £187 million (US$302 million). In August 1998, however, a U.S. appeals court overturned both the ruling and the damage award, freeing GKN to write back £248 million (US$413 million) in its 1998 accounts, swelling net profits that year to £567 million (US$941 million).

Meanwhile, in January 1997, Lees, in a possibly unprecedented move for GKN, ventured outside the company to find the person he hired that month as chief executive, Chung Kong Chow. Lees had decided to split the chairman and chief executive positions, and to remain nonexecutive chairman. Chow, a citizen of Hong Kong, had been chief executive of BOC Gases, the main division of the industrial gases group BOC.

In late 1997 Chow set a goal of increasing annual sales, which then stood at £3.38 billion (US$5.61 billion), by 40 percent over the next five years. Acquisitions were slated to fuel this growth in part, and one of the key areas for such growth was the company's powder metallurgy division, which was part of the automotive components operations. Using the technology of sintered metal, which involved the compressing of granules of iron and other materials, GKN was able to make light, strong auto parts—and there were applications outside the auto industry as well. After acquiring Sinter Metals in 1997, GKN made several more acquisitions in this field in 1998 and 1999, including six in the latter year alone. The most significant acquisition of the late 1990s came in February 1999, when the company acquired Interlake Corporation, based in Lisle, Illinois, for £348 million (US$570 million). Interlake brought to GKN not only a powdered metals firm called Hoeganaes Corporation but also Chem-tronics Inc., a maker of lightweight aircraft engine components that became part of GKN's aerospace unit, and Interlake Material Handling Inc., a manufacturer of racking systems used in warehousing that was added to the company's group of industrial services subsidiaries.

GKN also restructured its aerospace and defense operations in the late 1990s. In late 1998 the company combined its armored vehicle business with that of Alvis plc in return for a 29.9 percent stake in Alvis. In mid-2000 GKN reached a final agreement with Finmeccanica S.p.A. of Italy on a merger of their respective helicopter businesses into a 50–50 joint venture called AgustaWestland, which instantly became the number two helicopter maker in the world, trailing only the Boeing Company. Then in October 2000 GKN announced that it had agreed to acquire from Boeing a factory in St. Louis, Missouri, where fuselage and wing parts for certain Boeing military aircraft were made. In conjunction with this purchase, GKN said that it would combine all of its aerospace operations, with the exception of the AgustaWestland venture, under a newly created subsidiary called GKN Aerospace Services.

Already by 1999, GKN was approaching Chow's goal of a 40 percent revenue increase as sales reached £4.64 billion (US$7.51 billion), a 37 percent increase over 1997. Net income for 1999 stood at £358 million (US$579 million). Already considered the top U.K. engineering firm as a result of the market leading companies that comprised GKN's three legs, GKN under Chow's leadership was attempting to shed its reputation as an establishment firm run by engineers and accountants and adopt a more entrepreneurial culture and more growth-oriented focus. Chow was expected to pursue additional acquisitions to drive growth in the early 21st century.

Principal Subsidiaries

AUTOMOTIVE: GKN Automotive Ltd.; GKN Automotive International GmbH (Germany); GKN Automotive AG (Germany; 98.5%); GKN Hardy Spicer Ltd.; GKN Driveshafts Ltd.; GKN Automotive Umformtechnik GmbH (Germany); GKN Automotive Polska Sp. z o.o. (Poland); GKN Transmisiones

España SA (Spain); GKN Indugasa SA (Spain); GKN Automotive Inc (U.S.A.); GKN Viscodrive GmbH (Germany; 98.5%); Hoeganaes Corporation (U.S.A.; 80%); GKN Sinter Metals Inc. (U.S.A.); GKN OffHighway Systems Ltd.; GKN Wheels Nagbol A/S (Denmark); GKN Armstrong Wheels Inc (U.S.A.); Walterscheid Rohrverbindungstechnik GmbH (Germany); GKN Sankey Ltd.; GKN Autostructures Ltd.; GKN Sheepbridge Stokes Ltd.; GKN Squeezeform; GKN Sankey Ltd. INDUSTRIAL SERVICES: Chep South Africa (Pty) Ltd (South Africa); Meineke Discount Muffler Shops Inc. (U.S.A.); Interlake Material Handling Inc. (U.S.A.). AEROSPACE: GKN Westland Helicopters Ltd.; GKN Westland Industrial Products Ltd.; GKN Westland do Brasil Comércio e Representaçoes Ltda (Brazil); GKN Westland Aerospace Ltd.; GKN Westland Aerospace (Avonmouth) Ltd.; Aerospace Composite Technologies Ltd.; GKN Aerospace GmbH (Germany); GKN Westland-Sitec GmbH (Germany); GKN Aerospace Inc. (U.S.A.); GKN Aerospace Chem-tronics Inc. (U.S.A.); GKN Westland Aerospace Inc. (U.S.A.); GKN Westland Design Services Ltd.; Westland Systems Assessment Ltd.; GKN Westland Ltd.; GKN Westland Inc. (U.S.A.); CORPORATE: GKN (United Kingdom) plc; GKN Industries Ltd.; Ipsley Insurance Ltd (Isle of Man); GKN North America Inc. (U.S.A.); The Interlake Corporation (U.S.A.).

Principal Competitors

American Axle & Manufacturing Holdings, Inc.; Dana Corporation; Delphi Automotive Systems Corporation; Kaman Corporation; Magna International Inc.; MascoTech, Inc.; Midas, Inc.; Monro Muffler Brake, Inc.; Pacific Aerospace & Electronics, Inc.; United Technologies Corporation; Valeo S.A.

Further Reading

Barnett, Correlli, *The Audit of War: The Illusion and Reality of Britain As a Great Nation,* London: Macmillan, 1986.

''British Engineering: Good in Parts?,'' *Economist,* March 23, 1996, p. 62.

Burt, Tim, ''Dilemma of Divided Loyalties,'' *Financial Times,* March 23, 1994, p. 26.

——, ''GKN: David Lees' Long Goodbye,'' *Financial Times,* August 5, 1996, p. 7.

——, ''No Rush for Careful Patrician: Westland Was a One-Off Buy,'' *Financial Times,* August 24, 1995, p. 22.

''Confucius Rules at GKN,'' *Economist,* September 16, 2000, p. 76.

Foster, Geoffrey, ''GKN Changes Gear,'' *Management Today,* October 1984, pp. 50+.

GKN: Brief History of Guest, Keen & Nettlefolds, Redditch, U.K.: GKN, 1980.

Griffiths, John, ''Reshaping Helps GKN Recover Its Balance,'' *Financial Times,* August 10, 1989, p. 19.

Hill, Roy, ''The Reshaping of GKN,'' *Director,* March 1988, pp. 50+.

Jones, Edgar, *A History of GKN: Volume One: Innovation and Enterprise,* Basingstoke, U.K.: Macmillan, 1987.

——, *A History of GKN: Volume Two: The Growth of a Business,* London: Macmillan, 1990.

Kohli, Sheel, ''GKN's Chief Executive Looks East for Further Profit After Winning Over Business Elite of the West,'' *South China Morning Post,* November 16, 1997, p. 5.

Lister, David, ''Corporate Profile: GKN,'' *Times* (London), August 2, 1999, p. 22.

Lorenz, Andrew, ''GKN Hits Its Stride,'' *Management Today,* February 1997, pp. 36–40.

Marsh, Peter, ''Expansion, Expansion, Expansion, the Clarion Call to Rouse GKN,'' *Financial Times,* December 15, 1998, p. 27.

Nicoll, Alexander, ''Helicopter Makers' Moment of Truth Is Still to Come: Yesterday's Deal Between Agusta of Italy and Westland Heralds Further Consolidation in the Industry,'' *Financial Times,* March 19, 1999, p. 21.

Skapinker, Michael, ''An Uneasy Mix That May Need Reshuffling,'' *Financial Times,* March 9, 1987, p. 16.

''A Three-Legged Stool,'' *Financial Times,* May 16, 1990.

—Bob Vincent
—updated by David E. Salamie

Grede Foundries, Inc.

9898 West Bluemound Road
Milwaukee, Wisconsin 53202
U.S.A.
Telephone: (414) 257-3600
Fax: (414) 256-9399
Web site: http://www.grede.com

Private Company
Incorporated: 1940
Employees: 4,000
Sales: $600 million (1999 est.)
NAIC: 331511 Iron Foundries

Grede Foundries, Inc. is one of the largest foundry companies in North America. Grede specializes in casting parts from ferrous metals, which includes steel, gray iron, and ductile iron. The company makes components for several key industries, including the automotive industry and the compressor and pump industry, and makes parts for construction machinery and equipment, farm machinery and equipment, and for appliances, air conditioners, oil field equipment, and many other products. Some typical products Grede casts at its several foundries are axles, compressor parts, exhaust manifolds, spool valves, brake parts, water pumps, crankshafts, and various cases, carriers, and housings. The company provides its customers with design assistance, machining, sub-assembly, and custom packaging, beyond its basic service of manufacturing castings. Grede operates 12 foundries in the United States, located in Wisconsin, Michigan, Indiana, Kansas, Minnesota, Oklahoma, Kentucky, and South Carolina. The company operates one foundry in Tipton, England, and has a joint venture with a Mexican foundry to build a new plant in Monterrey, Mexico. In addition, Grede has been involved in a technology exchange program with the largest European independent foundry, the Swiss company Georg Fischer Foundries Group. Some of Grede's major customers include automakers Ford and DaimlerChrysler, General Electric Company, Rockwell International, J.I. Case Company, and Caterpillar Inc. The company is privately owned and still run by members of the Grede family. Grede Foundries Inc. was built up from a single Milwaukee foundry, and prospered even when other companies in the industry cut back. Growth was particularly strong in the 1990s, when the company's sales rose from $250 million to over $600 million by the end of the decade.

Early Years

Grede Foundries Inc. was put together out of foundries bought and expanded by an ambitious Milwaukee man, William J. Grede. Grede's introduction to the metal business seems to have come about when he took a job as a cookware salesman as he worked his way through college. The young Grede was peddling aluminum pots and pans beginning around 1914. By the time Grede was 23, in 1920, he had put aside enough money to buy a small iron foundry in a suburb of Milwaukee. He made only a modest down payment for Liberty Foundry, in Wauwatosa, Wisconsin, and his investment soon paid off. The foundry employed 40 people at the time Grede bought it, and in its first year under Grede's management, it produced 1,000 tons of gray iron castings. The foundry quickly expanded, adding on new facilities beginning in 1923. By 1930, the original plant had been added onto seven times.

Building on his success with Liberty Foundry, William Grede bought another foundry, in nearby Waukesha, Wisconsin, in 1927. Spring City Foundry was larger than Liberty had been in 1923, with 150 employees. It produced gray iron castings. In its first year under Grede's management, Spring City Foundry tripled its production.

The Great Depression began in 1929, but apparently Grede was able to keep his businesses afloat despite the economic downturn. Other area businesses were not as fortunate. In 1932, Grede entered into a venture with a struggling Milwaukee firm, Milwaukee Steel Foundry Company. Milwaukee Steel was a good-sized business, with 100 employees, but in the midst of the Depression, it was operating at only ten percent of capacity. Grede's management turned things around, and brought the company back to profitability.

William Grede was involved in three businesses—Liberty Foundry and Spring City Foundry, which he owned, and Milwaukee Steel Foundry. In 1940, Grede brought together the three foundries as one corporate entity. This was Grede Found-

Company Perspectives:

Grede Foundries, Inc. was founded in 1920 by William J. Grede. The Company specializes in ferrous metals: gray iron, ductile iron, and steel castings. Grede has helped our customers build the backbone of civilization by providing castings for many of the products they are famous for throughout the world.

ries, Inc. The new company benefited from centralized management, and from the sharp growth in the metal castings market with the outbreak of World War II. When the United States entered the war in 1942, the Milwaukee Steel division of Grede Foundries was producing at record levels. Grede Foundries added capacity to its steel castings division by acquiring another Milwaukee foundry, the Smith Steel Foundry Co.

Acquisitions and Expansion After World War II

William Grede continued to build his company after World War II. In 1947, Grede Foundries built a new foundry in the Upper Peninsula of Michigan. This was called Iron Mountain Foundry, in Kingsford, Michigan. It specialized in gray iron casting. It started out with 64 foundry workers, and gradually increased its capacity. Grede Foundries was producing gray iron castings and steel castings as its major products. But the company became interested in producing ductile iron, a new product that was more malleable than gray iron, and could be drawn out or hammered into thin pieces. Grede Foundries was at the forefront of the industry in producing ductile iron by 1950. In 1951, the company purchased a gray iron foundry in Reedsburg, Wisconsin, and converted this to a ductile iron facility.

After World War II, members of the next generation of the Grede family began joining the company. These were actually William Grede's two sons-in-law. Betty Grede married Walter Davis, an attorney, who eventually became vice-president and general counsel of Grede Foundries. Grede's other daughter, Janet, married Burleigh Jacobs. Jacobs began working for Grede Foundries in 1945, and in 1947 he took over management of the new foundry the company built in Kingsford, Michigan. By 1950, Jacobs was back in Milwaukee, heading the Milwaukee Steel division. He held many different positions in Grede Foundries before becoming president in 1960.

The company made several more acquisitions and expansions in the 1960s and 1970s. Grede moved beyond its Wisconsin/Michigan home grounds in 1966, buying Wichita Midwest Foundry, in Wichita, Kansas. This plant specialized in ductile iron, and later moved into making special silicon-molybdenum alloy iron castings. In the mid-1970s, Grede expanded its Iron Mountain Foundry division by entering into a unique relationship with General Motors Corp. The carmaker's Allison Division signed a contract with Grede to fund expansion of the Michigan plant and build a dedicated casting manufacturing line. General Motors paid for the production equipment in return for its exclusive use of Allison Division's parts. This gave the Allison Division quick turnaround on its orders, which had to be shipped as needed to its plant in Indianapolis. Grede benefited by having a secure buyer for its output.

One way Grede managed its growth was through careful marketing. The company's founder, William Grede, was described as an avid salesman, and his son-in-law and successor Burleigh Jacobs also believed marketing was key to keeping the company on track. Jacobs hired Jack Steele in 1966 as the company's full-time marketing director. Steele believed in careful planning, and in following up the financial impact of product changes. He instituted a program to mail Grede's customers a detailed questionnaire every 18 months. The feedback was used to analyze the past year's sales data, and help chart improvements for the future. Grede also marketed its products particularly to the top ten companies in the ten industries that made greatest use of iron and steel castings. Grede aimed high, hoping to be the number one supplier for each of these large customers. These were companies such as General Motors and Caterpillar—the well-known giants of American industry.

In the mid-1970s, Grede Foundries set up a new facility next to its existing Milwaukee Steel plant to specialize in short runs. This plant produced steel, gray iron, and ductile iron castings on special orders. It bought the land for this in 1974, paying $1.5 million for a parcel of real estate adjacent to Milwaukee Steel. By that time, Grede had grown to be one of the largest foundry companies in the United States. It built new corporate headquarters in 1975. Its total employment in Wisconsin alone was abut 1,200 people. Then in 1977, Grede bought another foundry in Kansas, the Hartmann Manufacturing Co. of Hutchinson, Kansas. This plant made gray iron castings, with an annual production capacity of 5,000 tons. The plant employed 110 people, and brought in over $2 million annually near the time of the sale to Grede. Grede had grown by the late 1970s to a complex of eight foundries in three states, with a total annual capacity of about 95,000 tons of iron and steel castings. Sales in the late 1970s were around $70 million and growing.

Persevering, Despite Poor Economic Conditions: 1980s

By 1980, Grede's sales stood at just under $100 million. The firm was not finished growing yet. It was already one of the largest foundry companies in the country, and it planned to put significant money back into its facilities to both increase production and keep the technology up to date. In 1981 the company announced that it would spend $34 million on upgrades and expansion at all its plants. The United States entered a recession beginning in the middle of 1981, and by 1982, the business downturn was threatening other players in the foundry industry. Due to the poor economic outlook, Grede delayed some of its upgrading. Because the company was still privately owned, it did not have to concern itself with wary investors, who expected short-term profits. The company instead continued to focus on its long-term goals, according to an interview with Burleigh Jacobs in the July 1989 *Foundry Management & Technology*. ''[We] can make business planning decisions based on the long haul,'' Jacobs told the magazine. ''We don't concern ourselves with daily changes in the price of our stock and quarterly profit reports as officers in publicly held companies do.'' So the company went ahead with its capital improvements, though at a slightly slower pace, and by 1984, when the business downturn seemed to be ending, the company was ready to make acquisitions again.

Key Dates:

1920: William Grede buys first foundry.
1940: Grede Foundries, Inc. is formed out of Grede's three Wisconsin foundries.
1960: Burleigh Jacobs, founder's son-in-law, becomes president.
1966: Grede buys foundry in Wichita.
1984: Company moves into the Southeast with purchase of South Carolina foundry.
1987: Bruce Jacobs becomes president.
1999: Grede's British branch takes over key DaimlerChrysler contract.

Sales passed the $100 million mark by 1984, and Grede looked around for smaller companies it could buy. In 1984, the company purchased the Roberts Foundry division of White Consolidated Industries, Inc., a plant located in Greenwood, South Carolina. Many of Grede's customers had moved southeastward, and this purchase gave the company its first plant in that area. The acquisition of Roberts was the first of a string of buys in the late 1980s. In 1986, Grede bought two foundries from the Eaton Corp. These were Perm Cast, in Cynthiana, Kentucky, and Vassar, in Vassar, Michigan. The Perm Cast plant gave Grede access to another market area with its mid-southern location, as did Vassar, located in the lower peninsula of Michigan, the heart of the auto industry. Closer to home, Grede bought a Fredonia, Wisconsin company, Fredonia Foundry, in 1988. Fredonia made castings by a process called the lost foam process, also known as the evaporative pattern casting process. This technology had received considerable industry interest in the 1980s, and it was Grede's first foray into this process. Then in 1989, Grede made a bid for a shuttered iron foundry in New Castle, Indiana, owned by Dana Corp. It was a large plant, with total production capacity of 30,000 tons of ductile iron castings. The acquisition of the New Castle plant gave Grede a ten percent boost in its total casting capacity.

Along with the investment in acquired facilities, Grede continued to pour money into improvements to its existing plants. During the latter half of the 1980s, the company spent over $90 million on technology upgrades. Much of the money went to new machinery, such as state-of-the-art molding machines, water cooling systems, and new furnaces. A significant investment also went to computerization of a broad array of plant processes. By the end of the 1980s, most of Grede's plants were equipped with computer-aided design and computer-aided manufacturing (CAD/CAM) systems. The technological upgrades worked to increase the company's manufacturing capacity, and in many cases, to speed manufacturing processes. Bruce E. Jacobs, son of Burleigh Jacobs and grandson of founder William Grede, became president of the company in 1987. By the end of the 1980s, Grede's annual sales were over $250 million, and the company was the second largest independent ferrous casting company in the United States.

The 1990s and Beyond

Recessionary conditions affected the foundry industry again in the early 1990s, but again, poor conditions had little impact on Grede. The company lost sales, and some plants ran at reduced capacity, but Grede was able to retain most of its workers. Grede began making a heavier investment in worker training in the early 1990s, as its plants became increasingly technologically sophisticated. The company paired up with a Milwaukee technical college to boost workers' literacy and English skills, and instituted specialized courses, such as a class to teach about spotting casting defects. Management personnel were also required to take college-level management courses, as training and retaining skilled workers became increasingly important to the successful operation of Grede's foundries.

The company had some export business, selling castings to the Far East and to European markets. In 1990 Grede became involved with a large European foundry company, the Swiss firm Georg Fischer Foundry Group. The Swiss firm wanted to expand into the U.S. market, and Grede became the company's exclusive North American trading partner. The principal benefit to both companies was an exchange of technology and information. Later in the 1990s Grede bought a foundry in the United Kingdom, giving it its first plant abroad.

By the mid-1990s, many foundry companies were facing difficulties as customers switched from using heavy iron and steel castings to lighter-weight components made from aluminum or magnesium. However, Grede continued to prosper. In 1995, Grede bought a steel foundry in St. Cloud, Minnesota, and converted it to a ductile iron shop. Grede used the new plant to make components for cars and farm equipment. Sales continued to grow, rising from $461 million in 1995 to a peak of $633 million in 1998. As competitors stumbled, Grede found more opportunities. In 1999, a foundry owned by one of Grede's chief competitors, Intermet Co., announced it would shut its doors, forcing DaimlerChrysler, a large customer, to look elsewhere for its parts. The Intermet foundry had made engine bedplates using compacted graphite iron (CGI), a lighter-weight iron. Intermet and another company had jointly developed the CGI technology. DaimlerChrysler then contracted with Grede's Tipton, England foundry to make the CGI bedplates. This was a coup for Grede, which only had the one European outpost.

In 2000, Grede began construction of a new foundry in Mexico, to be operated as a joint venture with a Mexican firm, Proeza S.A. de C.V. of Monterrey. The new foundry expected to sell ductile iron castings to the automotive industry, agricultural industry, and to construction customers worldwide. Grede continued as a family-owned business, with the founder's grandson in control. It had successfully grown to serve diverse markets, its customers major corporations in North America, Europe, and Asia. Even as some customers turned to lighter-weight components, Grede prospered and increased its production.

Principal Competitors

Intermet Corp.; Citation Corp.; Waupaca Foundry, Inc.

Further Reading

"Grede Acquires Foundry in Kansas," *Milwaukee Journal*, August 11, 1977.
"Grede Buys 8 Buildings from A-B," *Milwaukee Journal*, November 28, 1974.

Jensen, Dave, ''Manufacturers Enter Age of Re-Enlightenment to Retrain Work Force,'' *Business Journal-Milwaukee*, May 27, 1991, p. S22.

Kueny, Barbara, ''Continual Growth Assures Grede of a Bright Future,'' *Business Journal-Milwaukee*, May 28, 1990, p. X23.

Rogers, Robert C., and East, William R., ''Three Generations of Growth at Grede Foundries,'' *Foundry Management & Technology*, July 1989, pp. 30–41.

Weiss, Barbara, ''Grede Buys Roberts F'dy,'' *American Metal Market*, August 6, 1994, p. 1.

Wrigley, Al, ''DaimlerChrysler Taps UK Foundry,'' *American Metal Market*, December 27, 1999, p. 2.

——, ''Grede Foundries Buying ME Casting Plant,'' *American Metal Market*, May 24, 1995, p. 16.

—A. Woodward

Grupo TACA

Caribe Building, First Floor
San Salvador
El Salvador
Telephone: (503) 298-1560
Fax: (503) 298-3064
Web site: http://www.grupotaca.com

Private Company
Incorporated: 1931 as Transportes Aéreas Centro-Americanos
Employees: 4,000
Sales: $600 million (1999 est.)
NAIC: 481111 Scheduled Passenger Air Transportation; 481112 Scheduled Freight Air Transportation; 481212 Nonscheduled Chartered Freight Air Transportation; 48819 Other Support Activities for Air Transportation

Grupo TACA (Transportes Aéreas Centro-Americanos) is the third largest air carrier in Latin America. ''There has never been an airline quite like TACA anywhere in the world,'' writes aviation historian R.E.G. Davies. An amazing story of opportunistic success and derring-do in the pioneer days of Central American aviation, TACA has risen again to become a leading force in the region. Reformed from five national airlines, TACA boasts a fleet of 30 airplanes that fly to 39 destinations in 19 countries. It holds cooperative agreements with American Airlines and several smaller regional carriers. The company has been controlled by the Kriete family since the 1960s. TACA operates a large aircraft maintenance unit called Aeroman.

Opportunistic Origins

Lowell Yerex, a New Zealander, was educated in Indiana and flew for Canada's Royal Flying Corps in World War I. He was shot down in May 1918 and spent the rest of the war in a POW camp. After the war, he returned to the United States. He barnstormed for a brief time in a war surplus plane he had bought with money earned at a San Francisco shipyard.

In 1929, Yerex went south of the border to join Mexico's short-lived C.A.T. airline. In October 1931, he followed a prospector named Henson to Honduras where his partner, T.C. Pounds, had started the first airmail service. After three months of not getting paid for flying various ad hoc flying jobs, Yerex emerged as the sole owner of Pounds and Henson's Stinson Junior biplane.

This was the beginning of Transportes Aéreas Centro-Americanos, popularly known as TACA. Yerex won the Honduran airmail contract in February 1932, and with it the right to issue his own postal stamps (which cost about 50 cents per kilogram). TACA's mail service linked the capital of Tegucigalpa with provincial centers such as La Ceiba, Trujillo, and Juticalpa.

As Davies recounts in *Airlines of Latin America Since 1919,* Yerex worked out a very efficient forwarding system, charging different rates for cargo based on priority. His dedication also helped solidify his business prospects. For example, Yerex took a bullet in the eye while dropping pamphlets over a guerilla village, securing his relationship with the new Honduran Presidente, General Tiburcio Carias-Andino.

Going International in 1933

Success on the home front thus assured, Yerex began to expand. He bought his only Honduran competitor of any size, Empresa Dean, in 1933. TACA soon opened its first international route, connecting Tegucigalpa and San Salvador. Service was extended to Guatemala City and Managua in 1934. TACA acquired airlines in Guatemala (Compañia Nacional de Aviación, S.A.) and Nicaragua (Líneas Aéreas de Nicaragua, Empresa Palacios) in 1935, and Costa Rica (Empresa Nacional de Transportes Aéreas) in 1936.

However, the Nicaraguan operation lost its local contract in 1938. TACA bought Líneas Aéreas Nicaraguenses in 1939, putting it back in the airmail business there. For the next six years, TACA participated in an enormous airlift to support a gold mining operation called La Luz in the center of the Nicaraguan jungle.

Like most airlines in underdeveloped countries, TACA had to carve many of its own airfields out of the jungle. The mountainous terrain they encountered made the pilots' role even more challenging. In addition, the company operated 29 radio sta-

Company Perspectives:

GRUPO TACA has an aggressive growth and development strategy driven by a four part vision aimed at ensuring dominant revenue production, world class product integrity, a competitive well-prioritized cost structure, and programs to treat our people with the communication and compensation structures needed to maintain high morale and productivity. This "FOCUS PLAN," coupled with an aggressive and prudent growth strategy, today generates over $500 million in annual revenues and is expected to generate over $1 billion in annual sales within five years. Daily, more than 4,000 employees apply their knowledge and experience at every level to operate a complex air transport operation, thus allowing GRUPO TACA to face future challenges and penetrate new markets efficiently.

tions. TACA carried 90,000 passengers and 14,000 tons of cargo in 1941; freight accounted for 60 percent of revenues.

Most of these operations TACA acquired consisted of only two or three planes each, typically Ford or Fokker trimotors. TACA began to replace these with twin-engine Lockheed 14s in 1939. By 1940, TACA had accumulated 40 aircraft—up from just 14 in 1934—but only half as many pilots. TACA renamed its acquisitions along the following model: Compañía Nacional TACA de Guatemala, S.A. On August 25, 1939, a non-operating holding company, TACA, S.A., capitalized at $4 million, was registered in Panama City, although the group did not fly there until 1943. The El Salvador unit became a base for TACA's international operations.

Yerex, a citizen of the British Empire, founded British West Indian Airways (BWIA) separately from TACA in Trinidad in 1939. When he sold his controlling interest in TACA to American Export Lines, Inc. for $2 million on October 1, 1940, the deal brought the parties into conflict with Pan American, the influential U.S. airline led by Juan Trippe. Soon Guatemala's dictator, General Ubico, had forced TACA out of his country in favor of a Pan Am-backed startup. According to Davies, Yerex was paid pennies on the dollar for his assets there. Further, Pan Am overpowered American Export in the U.S. Congress and courts.

In 1942, Yerex entered a joint venture, Empresa de Transportes Aerovías Brasil, S.A., that promised significant opportunities for growth below the equator. Panama's TACA, S.A. became Inter-American Airways, S.A. on January 27, 1943, as Yerex was planning to sell off TACA and the newly formed BWIA. Seeking a solid U.S. connection with which to win rights to fly to Miami, on October 5, 1943 Yerex sold $2.25 million worth of Inter-American stock to a group of U.S. investors including the Maryland Casualty Company, Time Inc., and Transcontinental & Western Air Inc. (TWA), then controlled by Howard Hughes. Inter-American's name was changed to TACA Airways, S.A. in November 1943, and capitalization increased to $10 million.

TACA extended its route network to Lima, Peru, and formed subsidiaries in Venezuela and Colombia. To counter TACA's threat, Pan Am bought minority interests in a dozen state-owned airlines in the Caribbean and Central America. When Yerex shopped for more enthusiastic investors in Great Britain in 1945, TACA's board of directors replaced him as chairman with Benjamin Pepper of the Pennsylvania Railroad.

Postwar Decline

TACA's Colombian affiliate ceased operations in May 1947, after suffering several accidents and losing $4 million during the year. This removed a strategically important staging ground for TWA's assault on Pan Am, via TACA. By then, TACA only held a nine percent stake in Aerovías Brasil, and its influence along the Atlantic coast would only decline further.

TACA had opened a sales office in New York City. In January 1947, it moved this to Miami and appointed the Waterman Steamship Corporation its agent for the United States. Although Waterman helped TACA acquire a handful of DC-3 and DC-4 aircraft, the airline could not match the vigorous new wave of postwar competition. Paul Richter, a TWA executive, took over the chairmanship of TACA in September 1947.

TACA had acquired a 51 percent holding in a local San Salvador airline, Aerovías Latino-Americanos, in 1947. TACA's Honduran and Nicaraguan units were sold in February 1948. The next month, a new revolutionary government in Costa Rica impounded TACA's three planes in that country. TACA de Costa Rica had served routes ranging from San José to Panama. TACA was left with separated operations in just El Salvador and Venezuela.

In spite of these setbacks, Waterman acquired a 35 percent interest from TWA in February 1949. It injected $600,000 to keep the airline running and sold off the Venezuelan subsidiary. A new holding company was chartered as a Delaware corporation in New Orleans: the TACA Corporation. Its capital was listed as $200,000. El Salvador's TACA, S.A. became TACA International Airlines.

Waterman eventually sold its TACA shares to its own shareholders. Many were acquired by McLean Industries in May 1955, then by Southern Industries Corporation, in January 1956.

New Blood: 1960s–80s

Ricardo H. Kriete bought a controlling interest in the El Salvador operation in April 1961. The Kriete family saw annual revenues grow to about $15 million in the 1970s.

The company made El Salvador its base in 1983. TACA's AEROMAN aircraft maintenance unit was established at the same time. While political upheaval prompted many businesses to pull out of Central America in the 1980s, Roberto Kriete, Ricardo's grandson, invested millions in Grupo TACA.

Roberto Kriete met Federico Bloch at a Boston business school and made him TACA's president and CEO. The company's management team was eventually populated with former executives from Continental Airlines, Northwest Airlines, Continental, and Chase Manhattan Bank, giving it a unique, technically savvy, Anglo-Latino corporate culture. Kriete told *LatinFinance:* "We believe we are the best management team in the industry south of the border."

Key Dates:

1931: Lowell Yerex starts Transportes Aéreas Centro-Americanos (TACA) in Honduras.
1933: TACA begins its international expansion.
1940: Yerex sells control of TACA to American Export Lines.
1943: TWA buys into TACA.
1945: TACA's board forces Yerex out of chairman slot.
1949: Waterman Steamship Corporation buys control of TACA, charters it in New Orleans.
1961: Ricardo Kriete acquires controlling interest in TACA.
1983: TACA relocates headquarters to El Salvador.
1989: TACA acquires interests in five Central American airlines.
1997: Grupo TACA is unified under a common logo.
1998: TACA participates in a $4 billion order for Airbus aircraft.

Kriete and Bloch felt the group needed more mass to remain viable so in 1989 they began investing in five Central American flag carriers: TACA International of El Salvador, LACSA (Líneas Aéreas Costarricenses) of Costa Rica, AVIATECA (Compañía Guatemalteca de Aviación, S.A.) of Guatemala, TACA of Honduras, and NICA (Nicaraguenses de Avación) of Nicaragua.

Unified in the 1990s

The union of these airlines together created some needed economies of scale, but gathering them under one banner was an extended process not completed until 1997. A new corporate identity was unveiled in the same year: five stylized golden macaws flying in tight formation.

The group's focus on its home region and high frequency of flights helped its cargo business grow by more than 20 percent in 1997. TACA operated three dozen dedicated freighter flights a week between Central America and four U.S. airports: Miami, Los Angeles, Houston, and New Orleans. Perishable produce and textiles continued to make up a large part of its business; TACA had begun serving U.S. firms with manufacturing operations in Central America, such as Intel. TACA partnered with American Airlines, its Dallas sales agent, and competed with Delta Air Lines and Continental Airlines, which it accused of predatory pricing in its passenger business.

Grupo TACA joined other airlines in large aircraft purchases to get financing rates similar to those obtained by large U.S., European, and Asian carriers. The consortium leased six Airbus A320 aircraft in 1997 for $210 million. It then teamed with TAM of Brazil and LAN Chile in a 1998 order for 175 Airbus aircraft worth $4 billion. Grupo TACA accounted for $1.2 billion of the total. TACA also used ATR-42 turboprops to service its shorter, regional routes.

TACA promoted both southbound and northbound leisure travel. The airline partnered with the state of Louisiana, which provided promotional money and offered sales-tax rebates to tourists on jewelry, equipment, and furniture. Honduras and Costa Rica were the source of the most traffic to New Orleans.

The consortium's sales were more than $600 million in 1998. A new affiliate, TACA-Peru, was added in the fall of 1999. TACA began service to Montreal in October 2000. The carrier already served Toronto. Both flights originated in San Jose and stopped in El Salvador and Havana.

Principal Divisions

Cargo; Aeroman.

Principal Competitors

CINTRA; Continental Airlines, Inc.; Delta Air Lines, Inc.; UAL Corporation.

Further Reading

Anderson, Ed, "La. Luring Honduran Travelers; Joint Effort with Airline Credited for Increase," *Times-Picayune,* October 27, 1999, p. C1.
Barnett, Chris, "Airlines Told: Get in the Service Ballpark," *Journal of Commerce,* June 9, 1998, p. 7A.
Davies, R.E.G., *Airlines of Latin America Since 1919,* Washington, D.C.: Smithsonian Institution, 1983.
Wing, Lisa K., "The Sky's the Limit," *LatinFinance,* March 1999, p. 91.

—Frederick C. Ingram

Haggen Inc.

2211 Rimland Drive
Bellingham, Washington 98226
U.S.A.
Telephone: (360) 733-8720
Toll Free: (888) 424-4367
Fax: (360) 650-8235
Web site: http://www.haggen.com

Private Company
Incorporated: 1933 as Economy Food Store
Employees: 3,500
Sales: $560.0 million (1999 est.)
NAIC: 44511 Supermarket and Other Grocery (Except Convenience) Stores

Haggen Inc. owns a chain of supermarkets located in Washington and Oregon that operates under the names Top Food & Drug and Haggen. Regarded as an innovator in the grocery business, the company focuses on operating full-service supermarkets with numerous specialty departments, including floral, videotape rental, deli, dry cleaning, and banking. Of the company's 26 stores, 15 are "Tough On Prices" Top Food & Drug units and 11 are more upscale Haggen stores. The Haggen family owns the company.

First Store Opening in 1933

The Haggen grocery business began in 1933, in the trough of the Great Depression. Benett and Dorothy Haggen, along with Dorothy's brother, Doug Clark, invested $1,100 in a grocery store in Bellingham, Washington, 20 miles south of the Canadian border. The family's first store was called the Economy Food Store, which did well enough to justify a relocation to a larger site several years later. The new, larger store was called the White House Market, touting the slogan, "You may never be president but someday we'll see you in the White House." Despite the harsh economic climate, the Haggens' grocery store did reasonably well, luring a steady stream of customers from the Bellingham area. Significantly, one of the Haggens' attractions was an in-store baking operation established in 1941, the first hint of the full-service approach that would later define their company. By the end of World War II, the Haggens were ready to expand, with the White House providing the financial foundation for postwar growth.

In 1947, the Haggens built the Town and Country Shopping Center in Bellingham. The couple opened Haggen's Thriftway and shuttered the White House, spending the next several years building business at the new location. During this period, the family business was incorporated as Haggen Inc., the name under which it operated when expansion into a retail chain commenced 15 years after relocating to the Town and Country Shopping Center. By 1962, the company had opened a second grocery store in Everett, Washington, halfway between Bellingham and Seattle, to the south. Next, the company continued to move south with establishment of a store in Lynnwood, Washington, in 1967, the same year the name of the burgeoning chain was changed to Haggen's Foods.

As Haggen Inc. expanded, it did so by constructing its own stores, rather than acquiring existing stores or facilities used for other purposes. This was not an unusual method of expansion for supermarket companies during the 1960s, particularly in the relatively undeveloped, sparsely populated markets where Haggen Inc. was establishing stores. In later years, however, when expansion via acquisition became more common within the industry, Haggen Inc. continued to build its stores from the ground up, with only a few exceptions. The company's rate of growth was affected as a consequence, taking on a pace more measured than that of those competitors who added new units by purchasing existing stores. Growth was further slowed by the company's existence as a privately held concern, which meant it expanded without benefit of sizable infusions of cash from investors. Accordingly, as Haggen Inc. progressed, its success was determined by more than sheer size. Instead, astute management and innovation became benchmarks for the company's success, qualities that began to emerge as Haggen Inc. entered the 1970s and fell under the second generation of family management.

Expansion and Innovation in the 1970s

The Haggen Inc. chain grew to five stores in 1970 with the addition of two more stores in Lynnwood. The debut of the Lynnwood stores also marked the year Don Haggen and his

Company Perspectives:

For over 67 years, the Haggen family has built a tradition of quality and service and earned the trust of our customers.

brother Rick paired together to run the family business. Under the brothers' stewardship, which would endure for more than 25 years, Haggen Inc. became known as a successful innovator in the grocery business, establishing merchandising trends that were aped by much larger, higher-profile competitors. The brothers increased the number of stores to seven by 1977, all located in Washington. Two years later, they made their first memorable imprint on the supermarket industry. In 1979, the flagship Bellingham store was expanded greatly to 44,220 square feet, creating the company's first superstore, a format that would earn wide acceptance in the 1980s and 1990s by nearly all types of retailers. Inside the store, the essence of Haggen Inc. under the control of Rick and Don Haggen was on display. The store housed a service deli, a large wine department, a pharmacy, and a floral shop—ubiquitous features of supermarkets at the century's end, but novelties at the end of the 1970s. The creation of a full-service supermarket, particularly the store's floral department and the catering service operated by the deli, enabled Haggen Inc. to compete effectively with supermarket chains pursuing a more aggressive expansion strategy. By positioning itself as a service-oriented grocer—one of the first companies to do so—Haggen Inc. could compete on factors other than price, giving the company an edge over fast-growing chains benefiting from economies of scale.

The innovative Haggen brothers pioneered another marketing idea three years after their signal success with the Bellingham superstore. In 1982, they unveiled two massive warehouse stores east of Seattle in Snohomish and Wenatchee. The stores, which were expansions of existing stores, housed a variety of specialty departments that were based on the Bellingham superstore. During the first six months of operation, the stores recorded sales figures that by far outpaced the results registered before they were expanded, with sales at the Wenatchee store increasing more than 45 percent and sales at the Snohomish stores swelling by nearly 65 percent. Called Top Foods—"Top" being an acronym for "Tough On Prices"—the stores became the Haggen brothers' primary expansion vehicle for the future.

With the success of the store expansions in Bellingham, Snohomish, and Wenatchee, the Haggen brothers had discovered their niche in the grocery market. A Top Foods opened in Everett in 1984, a 71,000-square-foot store that ranked as the largest supermarket in the Pacific Northwest at the time. A flurry of store openings followed, as the company rolled out its proven market winner throughout the Puget Sound region. Between 1987 and 1994, Haggen Inc. opened eight Top Foods stores, adopting the new name Top Food & Drug in 1990.

Expansion in the 1990s

By 1994, there were 11 Top Food & Drug stores in operation and two Haggen stores, both in Bellingham. By this point in its development, Haggen Inc. ranked as the third largest grocery chain based in Washington. Revenues were expected to reach $350 million during the year, a total that would make Haggen Inc. the tenth largest privately owned company in the state. Size was not the company's hallmark, however. Rick Haggen, who served as president, and his brother Don Haggen, presiding as chairman and chief executive officer, preferred to tout service and innovation over size. The company claimed to be the first to open an in-store espresso shop, a Starbucks that opened in 1989 at the 45,000-square-foot Bellingham flagship store. It claimed to be the first supermarket to remain open 24 hours a day and the first grocer in the Pacific Northwest to display fish on ice, an idea the company imported from Europe. "We travel to Europe every couple years and around the United States to see what others are doing," Rick Haggen remarked in a June 24, 1994 interview with the *Puget Sound Business Journal.* "Also, we have valuable partnerships with other grocery companies that enable us to share ideas and marketing information. Those share groups have been a tremendous help to us," he added.

As Haggen Inc. entered the mid-1990s, expansion continued, driven by a successful format that been honed for decades and kept in check by prudent management careful not to overreach the company's capabilities. The company avoided entering the Seattle market, where competitors such as Quality Food Centers (QFC), upscale Larry's Markets, Albertson's, and Safeway saturated the metropolitan area. Instead, the company concentrated on less competitive battlegrounds, where its service-oriented stores stood in sharper contrast to the surrounding competition and where sites were easier to secure for its bricks-and-mortar method of expansion. New stores were scheduled for Stanwood, south of Seattle, and Kent, east of Seattle, as well as a third Haggen store in Bellingham. The company also planned to establish a presence in Portland, Oregon, its first step beyond Washington's borders. The Haggen brothers hoped to cluster four or five stores on the west side of Portland and then penetrate the east side, using its more upscale Haggen format to secure a hold in the metropolitan market. The first Portland store was slated for its debut in late 1995.

As Haggen Inc. entered the latter half of the 1990s, a greater emphasis was placed on expanding its upscale Haggen format, at least in proportion to the additions made to its chain during the 1980s. Between 1994 and mid-1999, the number of Top Food & Drug units increased from 11 to 15 and the number of Haggen units jumped from two to seven. The pace of expansion paled in comparison with the rate recorded by Haggen Inc.'s larger competitors, but the company made no apologies for its methodical growth. Instead of focusing on chain expansion and market share, the company concentrated on maximizing the efficiency of its chain, implementing new marketing programs, and enhancing the services it provided to customers.

The company's credo of improving service before expansion, a strategy espoused by the Haggen brothers for more than 25 years, was instilled in their successor. In December 1996, Rick and Don Haggen relinquished their respective posts of president and chief executive officer to Dale Henley, the company's senior vice-president and chief financial officer. For the first time in the company's history, day-to-day control over the Haggen franchise fell to a non-Haggen family member, although Rick and Don Haggen continued to exert their influence as co-chairmen.

Key Dates:

1933: First store opens in Bellingham, Washington.
1941: In-store bakery is opened.
1962: A second store is opened, signaling the development of a retail chain.
1970: Brothers Don and Rick Haggen take control of the company.
1979: Company's first superstore opens.
1982: First Top Food & Drug store opens.
1996: Nonfamily member Dale Henley is named president and chief executive officer.
1999: Plans are announced for an online shopping service.

Henley, like the Haggen brothers before him, professed a preference for building new stores from the ground up and pursuing a deliberate expansion strategy. Few industry observers chose to argue against the strategy. Haggen Inc. was recording impressive financial growth by concentrating in large part on the efficiency and performance of its existing stores. In 1998, revenues totaled $521 million, increasing substantially from the $433 million collected in 1997, yet the company had added only one new store in 1998.

Despite the vibrancy of the chain, Haggen Inc. was not without its share of concerns. The supermarket chains that embraced a growth via acquisition strategy were rapidly adding new stores and consolidating as the 1990s came to an end, making site selection difficult for the Bellingham-based company. The last years of the decade also saw the emergence of a new type of competitor, adding to the pressure already exerted by the larger supermarket chains. Companies such as Kirkland, Washington-based Homegrocer.com Inc., and Foster City, California-based Webvan Group Inc. represented a new breed of competitor, one that marketed groceries and a host of related items via the Internet for home delivery. Haggen Inc. found itself defending against the loss of sales to online shopping services, which eventually forced the company to develop a response to the threat of e-commerce grocers.

In late 1999, Haggen Inc. announced that it would unveil an online presence by 2000. The company's Internet efforts were overseen by Jeff Haggen, Don Haggen's son, who was promoted to the newly created position of vice-president of e-commerce. Jeff Haggen headed a small staff of three to five people to develop a presence for the company on the Internet, a foray that was defensive in nature. ''The number one reason to offer that service to our customers is they are being confronted with other options out there,'' Jeff Haggen was quoted as saying in the August 21, 2000 issue of *Supermarket News.* ''While we don't see a lot of market share being built in some of our smaller, micromarkets, it will prevent us from losing market share,'' he added. Haggen Inc. planned to offer store-pickup service through its online shopping service, as opposed to the delivery service offered by Homegrocer.com and several large supermarket chains. Testing of the company's online shopping service was under way in late 2000, by which time the company operated 15 Top Food & Drug units and 11 Haggen stores.

Principal Competitors

The Kroger Co.; Safeway Inc.; Albertson's Inc.

Further Reading

Alaimo, Dan, ''Haggen Premieres Two New Video Rental Units,'' *Supermarket News,* April 3, 1995, p. 45.
——, ''Rivals Driving Haggen to On-Line Sales Service,'' *Supermarket News,* August 21, 2000, p. 29.
''Haggen Shuffles Management,'' *Supermarket News,* February 17, 1997, p. 6.
Harper, Roseanne, ''Haggen Runs with Galloping Gourmet,'' *Supermarket News,* February 21, 2000, p. 45.
Kim, Nancy J., ''Haggen Readying an Online Grocery Service,'' *Puget Sound Business Journal,* December 10, 1999, p. 5.
——, ''Haggen Succeeds with Build, Not Buy, Approach,'' *Puget Sound Business Journal,* June 25, 1999, p. 31.
Law, Steve, ''Grocer Parks Cart in Portland,'' *Business Journal-Portland,* November 4, 1994, p. 1.
McCarrell, Pat, ''Haggen on Prowl for Existing Store Sites,'' *Puget Sound Business Journal,* June 27, 1997, p. 68.
Wolcott, John, ''Innovative Haggen Still Not Afraid to Upset Shopping Cart,'' *Puget Sound Business Journal,* June 24, 1994, p. 56.

—Jeffrey L. Covell

Harnischfeger Industries, Inc.

P.O. Box 554
Milwaukee, Wisconsin 53201-0554
U.S.A.
Telephone: (414) 486-6400
Fax: (414) 486-6747
Web site: http://www.harnischfeger.com

Public Company
Incorporated: 1884 as Pawling & Harnischfeger
Employees: 13,700
Sales: $2.04 billion (1998)
Stock Exchanges: OTC
Ticker Symbol: HRZIQ
NAIC: 333131 Mining Machinery and Equipment Manufacturing

Harnischfeger Industries, Inc. is a world leader in the manufacture, marketing, and servicing of mining equipment for both surface and underground operations. Until the year 2000, when it sold its Beloit Corporation subsidiary, Harnischfeger was also a major manufacturer of machinery for the pulp and paper industry. The company is represented in markets around the world, including Europe, Latin America, Australia, and Southeast Asia, and in South Africa, Canada, and the United States. Harnischfeger manufactures specialized equipment for underground mining of coal, as well as equipment for surface extraction of ores and minerals. A significant portion of the company's income comes from servicing mining equipment worldwide and providing spare parts. The company has a long history, punctuated in recent years by bankruptcy and near bankruptcy. After surviving a disastrous business downturn in the 1980s, the company made an impressive comeback, and then ended the 1990s in Chapter 11. Harnischfeger was forced to sell off its pulp and paper machinery manufacturing division to remain in business.

19th-Century Beginnings

Like many century-old American enterprises, Harnischfeger traces its origins to an industrious immigrant with a dream. In 1884 Henry Harnischfeger was working at a sewing machine company in Milwaukee. Born in Germany, Harnischfeger had worked previously as a locksmith, a machinist, and a machine maker. He was a foreman in the sewing plant when the company appeared about to go under. Forming a partnership with Alonzo Pawling, a pattern maker in the same plant, Harnischfeger launched a small machine and pattern shop in Milwaukee.

It was a modest beginning. The company had one milling machine, one drill press, one planer, and two lathes. After each snowstorm, someone had to shovel the flat roof so it would not collapse. Wind whistled in through the building's cracks. Milwaukee was bustling at the time, however, and before long Pawling and Harnischfeger's reputations as craftsmen brought business to their door. Located in the midst of many booming manufacturing companies on Walker's Point, Pawling and Harnischfeger soon were building machines for knitting, grain-drying, stamping, brick-making, and milking, as well as conducting their regular repair work. The company was called Pawling & Harnischfeger and was commonly known as P&H. Soon, the small shop was expanding.

Harnischfeger's dream was to build a line of machinery that the company could produce and market itself. His chance came in 1887 after a tragedy occurred at a nearby plant, when another manufacturer's overhead crane fell, killing a workman. An engineer at that plant, H.A. Shaw, designed a more durable, safer crane powered by three electric motors. P&H soon hired Shaw, and their first electric overhead crane was shipped in 1888. It was a risky investment for the small company, which had built a three-story brick plant and large foundry and hired more workers.

In 1892 Shaw left with his patent to form his own company, and 1893 saw the onset of a severe economic downturn. Struggling beneath debt and with little work, the foundry was kept in operation by an order from the Pabst Brewery for six grain-dryers. A few years later Shaw lost exclusive rights to manufacture the electric crane, and Pawling & Harnischfeger immediately jumped back into production. Adding a line of electric hoists—essentially, smaller versions of the crane—as well as electric motors and controls, the company was prospering by the turn of the century, with nearly 100 employees.

Company Perspectives:

Harnischfeger Industries, Inc.: A recognized global leader in the manufacture and service of capital machinery.

Growing Product Lines in the Early 20th Century

In 1903 a fire destroyed Harnischfeger's main shop; the following year the company built a new plant in West Milwaukee on land that had been purchased for expansion. Covering 20 acres, the plant was state-of-the-art at the time; it eventually became the world's leading manufacturer of overhead cranes. Soon after moving to the new facility, Harnischfeger began streamlining its operations and making the parts it had previously purchased from suppliers. Eventually the company designed, manufactured, and repaired every component of every product it sold, demonstrating self-reliance and accountability that brought repeat business from its customers.

Throughout the company's growth, Harnischfeger oversaw the business affairs while Pawling handled the engineering. Pawling's health declined in 1911, and he asked Harnischfeger to buy out his share of the business. Three years later, Pawling died and the company became Harnischfeger Corporation, retaining P&H as its trademark out of respect for its cofounder.

The heavy equipment industry is notoriously cyclical, alternating boom with bust. The year Pawling's health began to fail was a bust year. During those times, the company was saved by an order from J.I. Case Company for 1,000 gasoline tractor engines. The demand for cranes resumed in 1913, then skyrocketed with the start of World War I a year later.

In the meantime, Henry Harnischfeger was looking for other products to help even out the cycles of the heavy equipment market, and he eventually settled on excavating and mining equipment. After the war, the company's engineers designed the world's first gasoline-powered dragline, a truck-mounted machine that could lift, pile-drive, clam, and drag. They also created a backhoe and a shovel-type excavator mounted on crawlers. With ample applications in both mining and construction, the products were instantly successful, and Harnischfeger became well known in those industries throughout the world. The main plant was expanded to handle this manufacturing; by 1930 the number of employees had grown to 1,500.

This modest diversification, however, did not offset the effects of the Great Depression. There was no market for Harnischfeger products, and the company lost money every year from 1931 to 1939. Harnischfeger was forced to offer used equipment—returned because customers could not afford to keep it—at fire-sale prices just to raise cash. In 1937 and 1938 the company's workers struck and, eventually, formed a union.

Founder Henry Harnischfeger had died in 1930, and his son Walter became president. Despite the weak market demand, Walter Harnischfeger continued to innovate and improve the company's products. Harnischfeger replaced the rivets in its cranes with all-welded design and fabrication in the 1930s, creating cranes and excavators that were stronger, lighter, and less costly. Harnischfeger also sought more ways to diversify in the 1930s and 1940s, making welding machines, welding electrodes, diesel engines, and even prefabricated houses. Other Harnischfeger innovations changed the industry, while not exactly becoming household words. These included the electromagnetic brake and control system, Magnetorque, designed by Harnischfeger's engineers in 1946.

World War II rocked the world, but revived the American economy. By 1940 Harnischfeger's plant was operating at full capacity again, and it had spent millions on plant additions. The company's cranes lifted tanks and heavy artillery in defense plants, its hoists positioned planes on aircraft carriers, and its excavators dug foundations for new buildings. Despite the burgeoning demand, chronic material shortages, a lack of skilled workers, and increased government regulation made it a difficult time for the company.

Postwar Expansion

Harnischfeger hit its stride during the postwar industrial boom. From $29 million in sales in 1946, Harnischfeger grew steadily to $86 million by 1957, despite periodic economic downturns. New plants were built in Michigan, Illinois, and California, and plants were added and expanded in Milwaukee. Harnischfeger also had developed a market overseas, and companies were licensed abroad to build Harnischfeger cranes and excavators. Agreements were signed with Rheinstahl Union Brueckenbau of West Germany in 1952 and Kobe Steel, Ltd., of Japan in 1955.

Growth begets growth. In 1951 Harnischfeger borrowed $5 million to develop better products. In 1956 it joined the American Exchange, opening itself up to more shareholders. Previously, the company had been primarily a family-owned company, though listed on the Midwest Stock Exchange.

In 1959 Walter Harnischfeger became chairman of the company and his son, Henry, became president. During this period industries were becoming more complex, and Henry Harnischfeger felt challenged to choose between being an average competitor in several tough fields or the leader in two or three. Between 1964 and 1968, Harnischfeger streamlined its operations. The prefabricated home and diesel engine lines were dropped, and road-building equipment and welding product divisions were all dropped or sold. By the late 1960s Harnischfeger had two divisions. The Construction and Mining Division produced digging and lifting machines, such as electric and hydraulic excavators, and truck- and crawler-mounted cranes, while the Industrial and Electrical Division manufactured overhead cranes and hoists, as well as the electrical motors and controls needed to power them. The two divisions were run, essentially, as separate companies, with individuated engineering and marketing responsibilities.

From there, product lines were broadened and improved, especially for the larger products. Between 1969 and 1979 the average capacity of Harnischfeger's mining equipment doubled. In 1964 the company introduced stacker cranes to serve material handling markets. In 1967 it offered a new line of hydraulic backhoes and cranes for the booming hydraulic construction equipment market. Easier to operate and more mobile, these machines were very successful in the industry.

Key Dates:

1884: Milwaukee entrepreneurs Alonzo Pawling and Henry Harnischfeger go into business together, launching a small machine and pattern shop.
1914: Pawling dies; company is renamed Harnischfeger Corp.
1956: Company stock is listed on the American Exchange.
1971: Company stock is listed on the New York Stock Exchange.
1986: Harnischfeger acquires Beloit Corporation for $175 million.
1999: Company files for Chapter 11.
2000: Harnischfeger sells off Beloit division.

Global Company in the 1960s and 1970s

Harnischfeger's global presence also grew, with 25 percent of its production being exported in 1965 and 40 percent of American output being exported a decade later. The company's licensed overseas partners and subsidiaries continued to grow, the largest being Harnischfeger GmbH, based in Germany, with distribution in Europe, the Middle East, and North Africa.

The restructuring of the 1960s left the company well poised for growth in the 1970s. After the oil embargo of 1973, new coal reserves were opened and oil pipelines and mass transit systems were built, increasing sales of Harnischfeger machinery. Annual sales grew from $150 million in 1970 to $646 million in 1981, excluding nearly $200 million sourced from overseas licensees. The company's stock was listed on the New York Stock Exchange for the first time in 1971. The company continued to borrow funds to fuel growth, pouring nearly $200 million into upgrading its plants and equipment, as well as into research and development, between 1975 and 1980. In the late 1970s, however, economic recession and high interest rates hit the company hard. Unhappy with its balance sheet, Harnischfeger sought to bring its debt-equity ratio into better focus by lowering capital requirements and cutting production costs. In 1979 Harnischfeger's interest bills alone came to about $28 million, and debt was roughly 40 percent of total capital in 1980.

From Bust to Boom in the 1980s

The heavy equipment industry was hit hard by the recession, and Harnischfeger lost money for the first time since the end of the Depression in 1938. Harnischfeger also fell victim to political change abroad: the company had been about to ship a $20 million order to Iran when the Ayatollah Ruhollah Khomeini came to power, halting all trade between Iran and other countries. At the same time, the inflated deutsche mark was dulling the competitive edge of Harnischfeger's German subsidiary.

The recession spread across the globe and by 1981 had depressed many of Harnischfeger's primary markets. In 1982 sales dropped by a third, and the company reported a $77 million loss; staving off bankruptcy, the company went into technical default on some of its loan agreements. In 1983 sales fell to less than half of 1981 sales and the company lost another $35 million, some of the losses due to plant closings and discontinued product lines. The company's workforce plunged from 8,000 in 1979 to 3,800 in 1982. Harnischfeger was no longer concerned about growth; it was concerned about survival.

In 1982 Henry Harnischfeger became chairman and CEO, and the position of president was assumed by William Goessel, formerly of Beloit Corporation, a manufacturer of papermaking machinery headquartered in Beloit, Wisconsin. For the first time in its nearly 100 years, Harnischfeger's president was not a Harnischfeger. The year Goessel became president was one of the company's darkest, with some plants operating at less than 20 percent of capacity. In his first week on the job, Goessel was told the company would run out of cash in six weeks; then he learned that the company was in technical default on $175 million of debt. Goessel closed some operations, slashed the workforce, sold off excess inventory, and set about restructuring Harnischfeger's finances. He shifted the focus of operations from old technologies to computerized systems. The ailing construction equipment business, which had accounted for about half of Harnischfeger sales at one point, was sold.

The heavy equipment industry was going through vital changes at the same time, with the crane market shrinking while competition was increasing both at home and abroad. Leveraged buyouts and closings threatened several of the major construction crane manufacturers. In 1984 Harnischfeger announced that it would be buying virtually all of its construction cranes from Kobe Steel, which then owned about ten percent of Harnischfeger's stock. Family interest in Harnischfeger had been reduced to five percent. Between debt restructuring, public stock offerings, and cash from liquidations, Harnischfeger was able to pay its debts to private lenders by 1984 and report a profit that year. With the wolves gone from the door, at least until the ten-year notes came due in 1994, the company was again free to shift its focus back to growth.

The new focus was material handling. In 1983 sales of mining, construction, and material handling equipment and systems were about equal, but the automated factory systems market seemed to be booming. Many factories were modernizing and retooling, using computerized systems to upgrade efficiency in production lines. In 1984 Harnischfeger formed a new subsidiary—Harnischfeger Engineers—to tap this market; by year's end General Motors and Nabisco Brands were customers.

Automated material handling systems are computer controlled complexes of machinery that unload raw materials at the receiving dock, steer work through the factory, and send finished goods out for shipping. The systems include stacking cranes that retrieve parts in inventory and vehicles that are automatically guided by electric wires embedded in a factory floor. Harnischfeger seemed an unlikely competitor in the industry, but by the end of 1984 Harnischfeger Engineers was building a $5 million automated warehouse at a General Electric jet engine plant in Massachusetts.

One of the company's most notable milestones was the 1986 acquisition of Beloit Corporation. A manufacturer of pulp and papermaking machinery, Beloit was founded in 1858 and was also family run. The purchase was made for $175 million during a down cycle in the paper industry. About seven months later, at the onset of a boom in papermaking equipment and pulp and paper systems, the newly formed holding company, Harnischfeger Industries, sold a 20 percent stake in Beloit to Mitsubishi for $60 million. By 1988 Beloit was Harnischfeger's largest and most profitable unit, and by 1990 Beloit's sales were nearly $1.1 billion. It was a brilliant acquisition for Harnischfeger Industries and gave the parent company cash to reinvest in all its units.

Also purchased that same year was Syscon Corporation, for $92 million. This company provided software to the defense industry and was a leader in information systems integration. Harnischfeger's Systems Group—which included Syscon and Harnischfeger Engineers—was conceived as a counterbalance to the cyclical nature of mining equipment and papermaking machinery sales. Much of Syscon's work was with the U.S. Department of Defense, making it vulnerable to military cutbacks, but the company's work increasingly involved computer-based information systems designed to reduce paperwork and, therefore, could be of use in all federal departments as well as large companies. By 1990 Syscon was developing systems for the U.S. Departments of Labor and Education.

Harnischfeger was prospering in 1988, thanks to these acquisitions, the paper boom, and the improving climate in the mining industry. It was a record year, ending with doubled earnings. Two more common stock offerings were made in 1987 and 1988 to help bolster the balance sheet. In 1989 income from operations was up 65 percent over 1988. By 1990 roughly 60 percent of Harnischfeger's sales and earnings stemmed from papermaking machinery. Beloit equipment was used in producing 70 percent of the world's newsprint and writing and printing grade papers, as well as half of the world's tissues, towels, and napkins. Replacement parts for these machines was a thriving business as well.

Harnischfeger had clearly weathered its storms. The company announced in 1990 that it was shopping for new acquisitions. That same year, the paper cycle began a cyclical downturn. Although orders for papermaking machines dropped, a quarter of Beloit's paper machine manufacturing had been subcontracted to avoid the expense of expanding, so even with business decreasing, Beloit maintained presentable margins. Meanwhile, the Mining Equipment Division was still expanding, with sales of its massive electric-powered shovels growing nearly 20 percent in the first half of 1990. The poorest performing unit was still the material handling business, which supplied overhead cranes and hoists. Harnischfeger announced plans to buy a stake in Measurex Corporation in 1990, but not more than 20 percent due to a seven-year ''standstill'' agreement between the companies. A Cupertino, California company, Measurex made industrial process-control systems, primarily for the paper industry. Beloit and Measurex entered a joint agreement on marketing, sales, and development.

Tumultuous 1990s

William Goessel passed the reins to Jeffery T. Grade in 1991. Grade, then president, became CEO, and Goessel stayed on as chairman of the board. The paper slump continued and Beloit's paper machine orders suffered in 1992, hurt by industry overcapacity and a lingering global recession. Mining equipment sales were strong that year, while the material handling division had an increase in sales but a dip in operating profits. Stalled defense contracts hurt Syscon in 1992, but caused the company to broaden its commercial and federal agency business bases. Goessel retired as chairman in early 1993, and Grade became chairman and CEO.

Grade was by all accounts a dashing and flamboyant leader, who claimed to have been a fighter pilot in Vietnam, hero of dangerous night landings on aircraft carriers, who had been shot down deep in enemy territory and fought his way to safety. He was a notoriously flashy dresser, with three company cars and a company jet at his disposal. He enraged Wall Street by continually falling short of earnings expectations, a feat he accomplished for 14 out of 24 quarters while he was CEO. A profile in *Barron's* for July 12, 1999 revealed that Grade had no Navy record, and Grade revised his story to say that he had been a passenger on some practice flights while a college student enrolled in the Navy ROTC. By the time his false war record was exposed, Grade already had led Harnischfeger into bankruptcy.

Part of Harnischfeger's 1990s disaster came about because a string of acquisitions led to unwieldy debt. The company bought Joy Technologies in 1994, a company that made equipment for underground mining. This was a new area for Harnischfeger, but Grade's ultimate goal was to get into areas that would balance the dangerous cyclicity of its paper equipment and other product lines. In 1996, Harnischfeger bought an ailing British mining equipment firm, Dobson Park Industries, for $322 million. Neither Dobson nor Joy were doing particularly well, and Joy's slump caused it to close nine plants in 1996. Whereas Grade's predecessor William Goessel had cut Harnischfeger's debt as much as he could, Grade expanded it. The company's debt-to-overall-capital ratio climbed to 45 percent at the end of Grade's first year as CEO, up to 53 percent by 1997. That year Harnischfeger launched an unsuccessful hostile takeover bid for a machine-tool manufacturer, Giddings & Lewis, taking the company to court to force its board to consider the deal. Harnischfeger's stock began to fall in spite of record quarterly earnings, and Grade insisted Wall Street was overreacting to an announced year-end earnings shortfall. ''We are the global leaders in everything we do. . . . We haven't lost any customers; we haven't lost any market share,'' Grade insisted to the *Milwaukee Journal Sentinel* (May 22, 1997). Nevertheless, the company's stock slid as news came in of a disastrous deal the company had undertaken in Indonesia. Harnischfeger had sold the Singapore-based Asia Pulp & Paper four huge paper making machines, and the company was so eager to make the sale that it agreed to manage construction of the plants in Indonesia for which the machines were destined. This was not something Harnischfeger had done before, and soon complications forced sizable cost overruns, leading Asia Pulp & Paper to stall on payments. The Asian economic downturn of 1998 made the situation worse. A disastrous third quarter loss in 1998 led Harnischfeger to lay off 20 percent of its workforce. By January 1999, Harnischfeger's stock was ranked the worst-performing on the S&P 500. In May 1999, Jeffery Grade was out, and in June Harnischfeger filed for reorganization under Chapter 11 of the U.S. bankruptcy code. John Nils Hanson succeeded Grade and worked to put the company back together.

In 1998 Harnischfeger had sold off 80 percent of its material handling division to Chartwell Investments. The company's mining equipment division was still profitable, though far less so in 1998 than it had been in 1997, dropping from more than $200 million in operating profit to $82 million. The pulp and paper division, stung by the ongoing Indonesian fiasco, lost more than $368 million. To get out of bankruptcy, Harnischfeger put its pulp and paper division, Beloit Corp., up for sale. Beloit was sold off piecemeal in 2000, with proceeds going to the company's creditors. By late 2000, Harnischfeger had filed a plan to emerge from Chapter 11 as a pared-down company concentrating on the manufacture of mining equipment. Its two principal divisions were P&H Mining Equipment, for surface mining, and Joy Mining Machinery, making and servicing equipment for underground mining. The company's stock moved off the New York Stock Exchange and began trading over the counter. Even without its paper making equipment unit, Harnischfeger remained a large company with a strong global presence. It seemed possible that Harnischfeger could move on from its disastrous 1990s and prove itself all over again in the next century.

Principal Subsidiaries

Harnischfeger Corporation; Harnischfeger Engineers, Inc.; Syscon Corporation.

Principal Divisions

Joy Mining Machinery; P&H Mining Equipment; Mining Group.

Principal Competitors

Caterpillar Inc.; Bucyrus International, Inc.

Further Reading

''Back from the Brink,'' *Industry Week,* July 9, 1984, pp. 16–17.
Bettner, Jill, ''Digging Out,'' *Forbes,* June 18, 1984, pp. 110–11.
Briggs, Jean, ''Those Deadly Words—Too Soon,'' *Forbes,* October 27, 1980, p. 149.
Byrne, Harlan, ''Harnischfeger Industries, Inc.,'' *Barron's,* March 5, 1990, p. 53.
''A Centennial History of the Harnischfeger Corporation,'' Milwaukee: Harnischfeger Industries, Inc., 1984.
Daykin, Tom, ''Earnings Below Estimates for Wisconsin's Harnischfeger Industries,'' *Knight-Ridder/Tribune Business News,* September 12, 1996, p. 912B0346.
''A Failing Grade,'' *Business Week,* June 7, 1999, p. 42.
''Firm Plans to Buy Stake, Possibly 20%, of Measurex,'' *Wall Street Journal,* May 31, 1990, p. A4.
''From Old Tech to High-Tech,'' *Financial World,* November 14, 1984, p. 107.
Geer, John F., Jr., ''Dig It: Why Harnischfeger Has Been Buying into Underground Mining Equipment,'' *Financial World,* February 26, 1996, p. 52.
Goodman, Jordan, ''Scaling the Wall of Adversity,'' *Money,* May 1985, pp. 103–04.
''Harnischfeger Expects Lower Fiscal '93 Profit Than Analysts Predict,'' *Wall Street Journal,* January 14, 1993, p. B4.
Huber, Robert, ''Do You Want to Cook Hamburgers?,'' *Production,* December 1988, pp. 34–39.
''Huge Layoff at Harnischfeger,'' *Business Week,* September 7, 1998, p. 42.
Jerenski, Laura, ''The Naked Truth,'' *Forbes,* May 18, 1987, pp. 86–87.
Kirchen, Rich, ''Goessel Continues to Turn on the Juice at Harnischfeger,'' *Business Journal-Milwaukee,* March 19, 1990, p. 13.
Laing, Jonathan R., ''Grave Digger,'' *Barron's,* July 12, 1999, pp. 25–28.
Lank, Avrum D., ''Wis. Machine Tool Maker Rejects Harnischfeger Offer,'' *Knight-Ridder/Tribune Business News,* May 9, 1997, p. 509B1252.
Lazo, Shirley, ''Speaking of Dividends,'' *Barron's,* December 10, 1990, p. 64.
——, ''Speaking of Dividends,'' *Barron's,* March 14, 1988, p. 79.
McFadden, Michael, ''Prospering Merchants of Productivity,'' *Fortune,* December 10, 1984, p. 50.
''Measurex Corp.,'' *Insider's Chronicle,* July 30, 1990, p. 3.
''Measurex Corp.,'' *Wall Street Journal,* August 15, 1990, p. B2.
''Measurex Corp.,'' *Wall Street Journal,* October 15, 1990, p. A5.
Rose, Robert, ''Laden with Cash, Harnischfeger Seeks Acquisition,'' *Wall Street Journal,* March 19, 1990, p. B3.
Rottenberg, Dan, ''Adrenaline in the Rust Belt,'' *Business Month,* May 1990, p. 43.
Rudolph, Barbara, ''Construction, Mining, Rail Equipment,'' *Forbes,* January 2, 1984, pp. 190–93.
''Sale of Final Beloit Units Approved,'' *Pulp & Paper,* April 2000, p. 15.
Sharma-Jensen, Geeta, ''Harnischfeger Stock Falls After Firm Reports Record Profits,'' *Knight-Ridder/Tribune Business News,* May 22, 1997, p. 522B0916.
Siegel, Matt, ''The Worst Stock on the S&P 500,'' *Fortune,* January 11, 1999, p. 196.
''Stake in Measurex Increased to 14%,'' *New York Times,* August 28, 1990, p. D4.
''Supplier Companies,'' *Pulp & Paper,* December 1991, p. 129.
''13D Highlights,'' *Insider's Chronicle,* April 24, 1989, p. 2.
Wrubel, Robert, ''Harnischfeger: Paper Profits,'' *Financial World,* June 26, 1990, p. 16.

—Carol I. Keeley
—updated by A. Woodward

Homestake Mining Company

1600 Riviera Drive, 2nd Floor
Walnut Creek, California 94596-3569
U.S.A.
Telephone: (925) 817-1300
Fax: (415) 397-5038
Web site: http://www.homestake.com

Public Company
Incorporated: 1877
Employees: 1,250
Sales: $691.0 million (1999)
Stock Exchanges: New York Australia Toronto Basel Geneva Zurich
Ticker Symbol: HM
NAIC: 212221 Gold Ore Mining; 212222 Silver Ore Mining

Owner and operator of the oldest gold mine in the United States, Homestake Mining Company is an international gold mining company with substantial gold interests in Canada and Australia, as well as smaller interests in Chile. From the company's Homestake mine, which began producing gold in 1876, Homestake Mining has built a mining empire that has vaulted it past all competitors and ranked it as the premier gold producer in U.S. history.

The Race for Gold in the 1870s

In 1874, a U.S. Cavalry scouting party led by Lt. Col. George A. Custer inched its way through the deep valleys and steep ridges carved into the Black Hills of Dakota Territory, 15 years before the region became part of the country's 40th state, South Dakota. The expedition begun that year set in motion a cavalcade of events that in a few years would lead to Custer's Last Stand at Little Bighorn, the massacre of Sioux at Wounded Knee, the financial ascension of the powerful and wealthy Hearst family, and the founding of Homestake Mining Company, the country's preeminent gold producer. These were the effects of one definitive moment when Custer's troops spotted traces of gold in the mountainous and sparsely populated Black Hills, an ill-fated moment for Custer and the Sioux and a propitious one for the Hearst family and all those enriched by Homestake Mining's formation.

For a populace already tantalized by the riches gold could bring, no formal declaration was required, and word of the new discovery quickly spread throughout the western territories. Within months, settlers were pouring into the area, scouring the countryside for further confirmation of gold's existence in the region. With their arrival, small yet burgeoning communities were established, such as Deadwood, the local hotbed of entertainment for miners and prospectors, where Wild Bill Hickok and Calamity Jane met their end. As more settlers moved into the region, tensions between the Sioux and the region's new denizens mounted, touching off a war that led to Custer's death two years after his scouting party had discovered gold. Hostilities between the Sioux and U.S. forces did not end until the battle at Wounded Knee in 1890, by which time a more affirmative manifestation of the scouting party's discovery already had developed into a flourishing enterprise.

One fortune-seeker drawn by the news of gold in the Black Hills was a prospector named Moses Manuel, who in 1876 staked a claim that would become known as Homestake. Manuel's ownership of Homestake was fleeting, however, ending the following year when the mine was sold to a consortium of San Francisco investors led by George Hearst, father of publishing magnate William Randolph Hearst. Hearst and his backers paid Manuel $70,000 for the Homestake mine, and in return they received the largest gold mine in the United States: literally the mother lode of the Western Hemisphere. With the profits gleaned from his father's mine in southwest South Dakota, William Randolph Hearst would begin his meteoric rise, purchasing the *San Francisco Examiner* in 1887 and going on to build the world's largest publishing empire.

These were the effects of the frenzy for gold in South Dakota; lives were lost and fortunes were made, making for a quintessential chapter of life in the American frontier. Homestake Mining Company was incorporated in 1877. At the time, George Hearst and his syndicate likely had little idea of the magnitude of their purchase. The Homestake mine eventually

Company Perspectives:

Homestake has maintained a major role in the gold mining industry for over 120 years. Since 1990, the Company has produced 17 million gold and equivalent ounces. At the end of 1999, Homestake's share of proven and probable reserves amounted to 18.8 million ounces of gold and 110 million ounces of silver. Homestake operates both underground and open pit mines and uses a variety of mineral processing methods to extract gold, including conventional milling, heap leaching and roasting. The Company has received numerous industry awards for its superior record in the environmental, health and safety areas.

would supply the United States with the bulk of its gold for more than 100 years and would surpass competitors in becoming a prodigious force in the global gold industry.

Record Profits on the Eve of World War II

The mining company enjoyed the lucrative years of gold mining's heyday during the first half of the 20th century. The company prospered during this period, sending its miners deeper and deeper into the Homestake mine, where they located sizable deposits of gold enveloped in tons of ore. In 1935, the company recovered enough gold to register $11.39 million in net income, a record that would stand for nearly 40 years. One year before Homestake mine established its net income benchmark, the price of gold, set by the U.S. Treasury Department at a fixed amount per ounce, was raised from $20.67 an ounce to $35 an ounce, welcome news for gold producers like Homestake Mining. The price of gold, however, would remain at that price for roughly the next 40 years, fixed and unchanged as gold production costs rose.

As the years passed and production costs increased, the gap separating the cost to produce gold and the fixed price established by the government narrowed, coming inexorably together and threatening to make the country's largest gold mine a profitless hole in the ground. Homestake Mining's inability to increase or at least maintain its profit margin was a growing concern as the company entered the 1940s and the United States entered World War II.

America's entrance into World War II brought gold production to a halt, as miners and other workers were transferred to industries vital to the country's prosecution of the war. The Homestake mine remained closed for three years, reopening again in 1945, which, as it turned out, benefited the company, as much of its competition dissolved during this time. For gold mining companies with smaller producing mines than Homestake Mining, the years before the war had been difficult enough. When the government called a halt to gold production, many decided against reopening after the respite, leaving Homestake Mining in a more favorable market position than before the war. Competition, however, was not the company's most worrisome problem; the upward march of gold production costs continued to hamper profits. To reduce production costs, the company installed automated hoisting equipment, introduced television monitoring and short-wave communication equipment, and sought to double each miner's productivity, but these were temporary solutions to a perpetual problem. By 1951, one ounce of gold cost Homestake Mining $22.18 to produce, a total that was creeping dangerously close to the fixed $35 per ounce price paid by the federal government.

The Search for New Resources in the 1950s and 1960s

In response, Homestake began a diversification program in 1953, purchasing over the next four years uranium properties in Utah, Wyoming, and New Mexico. By the mid-1960s, the mining of uranium was contributing more than half of the company's $4.9 million in net income, quickly supplanting gold as the company's greatest money earner. The Homestake mine, however, still represented the largest gold-producing property in the Western Hemisphere, making Homestake Mining the largest producer of gold by far in the United States. Although the Homestake mine had been expanded, reaching depths of 6,800 feet by the mid-1960s, its profitability had plunged as well, falling in the face of rising production costs and an industrywide downturn. In the quarter century leading up to the mid-1960s, the number of gold mines in operation in the United States had plummeted precipitously from 9,000 to 600, while the cost of producing an ounce of gold had steadily risen from less than $20 to nearly $33. Operating income from the Homestake mine fell from $12.1 million in 1941 to $2 million in 1963, and dividends fell during the period from $4.50 a share to $1.60 a share.

To exacerbate matters, the amount of gold produced in 1963 represented the lowest peacetime level since 1884, further convincing Homestake Mining's management that the only viable solution lay in diversification away from gold production. In 1962, Homestake Mining entered into a joint venture with AMAX Gold to develop lead and zinc properties in southeast Missouri, then two years later entered into another joint venture to develop potash in Saskatchewan, Canada, which began production in 1968. The concerted movement toward diversification during the 1960s also brought Homestake Mining into Australia to produce and ship iron ore from Koolanooka, in western Australia, through its Homestake Iron Ore Company of Australia Ltd. subsidiary in 1966, and led to the formation of another subsidiary, Compania Madrigal, created to develop copper, lead, and zinc deposits in Peru in 1967. Also during this time, production began at Homestake's Buick lead and zinc mine in Missouri and silver production began at its Bulldog mine in Creede, Colorado, bolstering Homestake Mining's market presence in nongold mining businesses.

After 20 years of diversification into uranium, lead, zinc, and copper, Homestake Mining had become a much different company, a transformation readily borne out in its bottom line. By the early 1970s, uranium, lead, zinc, and silver production accounted for 75 percent of the company's profits, while the production of gold, formerly Homestake Mining's mainstay business, was increasingly becoming a break-even enterprise. The gold industry, however, was about to experience significant changes that would alter the focus of Homestake Mining's business, redirecting it once again back to gold. During the 1970s, the price of gold was freed from its fixed price of $35 an ounce, at last removing the formidable barrier that forced

Key Dates:

1876: Moses Manuel stakes claim at Homestake gold mine in Lead, South Dakota.
1877: Consortium of San Francisco investors, led by George Hearst, purchases Homestake.
1934: U.S. Treasury Department fixes price of gold at $35/ounce.
1942: U.S. Government orders mining companies to cease production of gold.
1945: Gold mines resume operations.
1953: Homestake begins uranium explorations.
1962: Homestake enters joint venture with AMAX Gold.
1980: McLaughlin gold mine is discovered.
1984: Homestake acquires Felmont Oil Corporation.
1989: Homestake sells off oil and natural gas interests.
1992: Homestake acquires International Corona Corporation.
2000: Homestake Mining announces intention to shut down original Homestake mining operations.

Homestake Mining to diversify its business. In response, gold production was reinvigorated throughout the country and gold producers, such as Newmont Mining Corporation and Kennecott Corporation, began developing large gold properties, forcing Homestake Mining to either wait for the competition to catch up or supplement its existing gold properties.

The company's management chose the latter, deciding, as Homestake Mining's president and chief executive officer declared in a speech before the New York Society of Security Analysts, "to reestablish and confirm [the company's] reputation as the United States' preeminent gold miner." Beginning in 1978, Homestake Mining launched an aggressive exploration program to find new gold deposits, which resulted in the discovery of the McLaughlin gold mine in California in 1980, a symbolic discovery made in the first year of a decade that would see Homestake Mining move back into gold and away from uranium, lead, zinc, and silver.

A New Golden Age: The 1980s

The McLaughlin mine took five years and $280 million to develop, but, when it finally did begin producing gold in 1985, it added significantly to Homestake Mining's annual total of gold production, which tripled during the decade. The company's gold reserves tripled as well during the 1980s. Nevertheless, uranium, lead, zinc, and a relatively new business area for the company—oil and natural gas—continued to contribute significantly to the company's annual revenue total. During the mid-1980s, these nongold businesses generated nearly half of the company's revenues, but by the end of the decade all would be divested, as Homestake Mining returned to its roots and became almost exclusively a gold producer and developer.

Homestake Mining had entered the oil business in 1980 through a joint venture with Hrubitz Oil Company. It then sought to strengthen and accelerate its position in the energy business with the 1984 acquisition of Felmont Oil Corporation. The company sold its interests in oil and natural gas in 1989, however, as it quickly began exiting its nongold related businesses. Uranium mining was terminated in 1990, the same year Homestake Mining's lead and zinc properties, organized as part of The Doe Run Company in 1986, were sold to Fluor Corporation, creating a much more focused corporate organization.

In 1991, Homestake Mining recorded its first full-year loss in nearly 50 years, losing $262 million in large part because of mining property write-downs, operational problems, and low gold prices. The following year, however, the company made the largest acquisition in its history when it purchased International Corona Corporation. With the acquisition of International Corona, Homestake Mining gained low-cost gold production properties, five million ounces of reserves, and gold development property in British Columbia. The write-down charges stemming from the acquisition totaled $176 million, $106 million of which was recorded in 1991, which accounted for a significant portion of the company's loss for the year.

Once acquired, International Corona was renamed Homestake Canada Inc., and then Homestake Mining initiated a corporatewide restructuring program to ease the absorption of the unit into Homestake Mining's organization. Nearly 200 jobs were eliminated, administrative and exploration offices were closed, and upper management positions were changed during the restructuring process, as the company prepared for the mid-1990s and beyond.

With its enormous wealth of gold production properties, Homestake Mining entered the mid-1990s still holding tight to its venerable position as America's leading gold producer. Although the company's gold production costs were high compared with the rest of the industry, the addition of International Corona's low-cost gold production properties raised hopes that Homestake Mining would continue to outdistance its competition as it headed toward its third century of business, still producing gold from its coveted Homestake mine.

International Expansion in the 1990s

In the mid-1990s Homestake began aggressively acquiring interests in a number of mining operations worldwide, many of which were in geographical regions that were previously unfamiliar to the company. In June 1995 it staked its first claim in Europe, when it reached an agreement with the Irish mining company Navan Resources to acquire a 50 percent share of Navan's holdings in the Chelopech mine in Bulgaria. In the same month Homestake bought a five percent stake in Zoloto Mining Ltd. of Russia, a deal that included a second option to obtain an additional 62 percent share. The company became extremely busy again in November 1996, when it entered into a joint project with Franc-Or Resources of France to begin explorations in French Guiana; that same month, Homestake purchased the Whiskey Gulch and Marshall Dome mines in Alaska. During this same period Homestake also made two key discoveries in Chile—the Manto Agua de la Falda and Jeronimo mines—that led to the creation of Agua de la Falda S.A., a joint venture with the state-owned Corporacion Nacional del Cobre Chile (Codelco), in 1996.

Homestake's most ambitious move came in December 1996, when it announced its intention to acquire the Santa Fe Gold

Corporation. The deal, worth $2.3 billion, would give Homestake the largest gold reserves in North America and place it second only to Barrick Gold Corporation of Canada in total North American production. What was intended as a friendly takeover quickly became a bidding war, however, when Newmont Mining Corporation submitted its own offer for Santa Fe. Although the move was not exactly unexpected, since Newmont had made an offer several months earlier, it did initiate a lengthy public relations battle between the two rivals, each determined to convince Santa Fe it was giving it the best deal. Newmont ultimately won out, finally signing a merger agreement with Santa Fe in March 1997 for $2.5 billion. The deal made Newmont the largest gold producer on the continent and second in the world to Anglo American of South Africa.

Undaunted, Homestake continued to expand as it approached the year 2000, acquiring the Plutonic, Lawlers, and Darlot mines in Western Australia in April 1998 and the Argentina Gold Corp. in April 1999. Homestake's Australian gold production more than tripled between 1993 and 1998, from 300,000 ounces to more than 900,000 ounces. By the year 2000 Homestake's Australian operations accounted for 39 percent of the company's total gold production, compared with 30 percent for its U.S. mines and 30 percent for its Canadian mines. Altogether, the company produced more than 2.4 million ounces in gold and equivalent amounts of silver in 2000. At the same time, production costs dropped steadily in the late 1990s, reaching a 20-year low of $192 per equivalent ounce in 1999.

Unfortunately, the late 1990s also saw a steady decline in the price of gold, with a drop of $109 per ounce in a four-year period. By July 1999 gold was selling for $253/ounce, its lowest price in 20 years. Homestake was forced to report a loss of $218.3 million for 1998, as total sales dropped almost $200,000 from the previous year. In an attempt to simplify its operations, so that it could refocus on its most profitable mines, Homestake began selling off many of the foreign interests it had acquired only a few years before. In July 1998 the company terminated its agreement with Franc-Or; in April 2000, it sold its Bulgarian interests to Gold Mines of Sardinia in exchange for stock. A particularly sad result of the downsizing came in September 2000, when the company, citing a significant reduction in ore quality, announced its intention to shut down the original Homestake Mine in Lead, South Dakota, by January 2002.

Principal Subsidiaries

Homestake Canada Inc.; Homestake Gold of Australia Limited; Minera Homestake Chile, S.A.; Homestake de Argentina S.A.

Principal Operating Units

Eskay Creek Mine (Canada); Williams and David Bell Mines (Canada; 50%); Ruby Hill Mine; Round Mountain Mine (50%); Homestake Mine; McLaughlin Mine; Marigold Mine (33.3%); Kalgoorlie Consolidated Gold Mines (KCGM) Pty. Ltd. (Australia; 50%); Plutonic Gold Mine (Australia); Darlot Gold Mine (Australia); Lawlers Gold Mine (Australia); Jeronimo (Chile; 51%); Agua de la Falda Mine (Chile; 51%); Veladero (Argentina; 60%).

Principal Competitors

Anglo American plc (U.K.); Barrick Gold Corporation (Canada); Newmont Mining Corporation.

Further Reading

Anderson, Scott, "Homestake Buys Big Rival," *Toronto Star,* December 23, 1997.

"Another Coin?," *Forbes,* March 1, 1965, p. 42.

Blackburn, Mark, "For Homestake, It's Okay to Be Dull," *New York Times,* January 27, 1980, p. F1.

"The Boom That Isn't," *Forbes,* June 15, 1972, p. 48.

Cook, James, "Nowhere to Go But Up," *Forbes,* November 12, 1990, p. 39.

"Gold Digs," *Newsweek,* May 25, 1964, p. 85.

"Gold from Lead," *Time,* March 11, 1966, p. 88.

"Gold Without Glitter," *Forbes,* December 1, 1962, p. 30.

Hall, William, "Swiss Set to Abandon Gold Standard," *Financial Times* (London), April 16, 1999.

"Homestake Mining Co.," *Wall Street Transcript,* August 5, 1985, p. 78,807.

"Homestake Mining Company," *Wall Street Transcript,* October 19, 1981, pp. 63,364.

"Homestake Mining Company," *Wall Street Transcript,* October 15, 1973, p. 34,675.

"Homestake Mining Corp.," *Wall Street Journal,* May 9, 1984, p. 44.

"Homestake Seeks Two Kinds of Gold," *Business Week,* April 23, 1984, p. 38.

"Homestake Winds Up with Red Ink in 1991," *American Metal Market,* February 24, 1992, p. 15.

Levine, Jonathan, "What's Pickens Really Panning for in Homestake?," *Business Week,* March 14, 1988, p. 42.

Loehwing, David A., "New Gold Rush," *Barron's,* June 18, 1973, p. 3.

"Luck vs. Judgment," *Forbes,* July 1, 1967, p. 49.

Palmer, Jay, "Golden Handcuff," *Barron's,* June 17, 1991, p. 16.

Sherman, Joseph V., "New Sourdoughs," *Barron's,* June 21, 1965, p. 3.

Sinton, Peter, "Gold Deal May Create Mining Giant," *San Francisco Chronicle,* December 10, 1996.

Smith, Kerri S., "Letter Blasts Newmont Gold Bid," *Denver Post,* February 11, 1997.

Viani, Laura, "Restructuring of Homestake to Save $25M," *American Metal Market,* August 24, 1992, p. 8.

—Jeffrey L. Covell
—updated by Stephen Meyer

Hub Group, Inc.

377 E. Butterfield Road, Suite 700
Lombard, Illinois 60148
U.S.A.
Telephone: (630) 271-3600
Fax: (630) 964-6475
Web site: http://www.hubgroup.com

Public Company
Incorporated: 1971
Employees: 1,600
Sales: $1.3 billion (1999)
Stock Exchanges: NASDAQ
Ticker Symbol: HUBG
NAIC: 48851 Freight Transportation Arrangement; 541614 Process, Physical Distribution, and Logistics Consulting Services

Hub Group, Inc. is America's leading intermodal transportation company. Intermodal transportation involves arranging for the transportation of freight using different types of conveyances, typically by rail and truck or truck and ship. Hub specializes in alleviating shippers' difficulties in coordinating different transport services. The company operates a network of over 30 transportation hubs, mostly covering the Midwest and the eastern United States, but extending also to the West and into Mexico. Hub Group is a significant partner with all the major U.S. railroads, and is a major revenue producer for them. Hub also brokers highway transportation through a wide variety of carriers. The company uses a sophisticated computer network to plan and track shipments and coordinate billing. Hub Group operates a subsidiary company, Hub Group Distribution Services, that offers clients an array of logistics services, coordinating transportation, warehousing, inventory management, set-up and assembly of products and displays, and other services, to businesses nationwide. Another Hub division specializes in providing transportation services to the automotive industry. The Hub Group provides international shipping expertise through a subsidiary, HLX. HLX coordinates international transport of goods for importers and exporters, planning and managing movement of goods from ship to their final inland destination. Hub Group was founded in 1971 and grew rapidly, finding itself on a list of the 500 fastest-growing companies regularly since the mid-1990s. Founder Philip Yeager and his son David are instrumental in managing the publicly owned company, and the Yeager family still controls a majority of Hub Group's stock.

Beginnings in the 1970s

Hub Group, Inc. was founded by Philip C. Yeager in Hinsdale, Illinois, in 1971. Yeager was a longtime employee of the Penn Central Railroad. He spent over ten years working with shippers, coordinating intermodal transportation between rail cars and trucks. But Yeager lost his job when Penn Central went bankrupt, and in 1971 he and his family moved to suburban Chicago. Yeager understood the difficulties shippers had working with railroads, and he wanted to use his expertise by becoming what was called at that time a third-party agent. The third party was the point of a triangle connecting the railroad and a highway shipper, who coordinated services between them. The third-party agent managed the movement of a load of goods from its origin to its destination, plotting the best and cheapest route and arranging for the pick-up and transfer of goods between rail and truck. Yeager's Hub City Terminal opened in April 1971, operating out of a cramped office in a side street in Hinsdale. Yeager and his wife ran the business with only a few employees. In its first year, Hub City moved 900 trailers, a modest success. The business grew quickly, expanding into neighboring markets.

Philip Yeager claimed in an interview with *American Shipper* from May 1991 that at first he did not expect more of Hub City than a ''nice family business.'' However, the company began to become a national presence in the mid-1980s, when Hub started to actively solicit business from *Fortune* 500 companies. It took some convincing to get large companies to pay attention to Hub at first, basically because they were unfamiliar with the advantages of intermodal shipping. Yeager explained that ''Many people had felt that intermodal was an inferior product and had to be sold at a discount. The fact is that it is just as good as truck, or even better in some lanes.'' Hub took this message to *Fortune* 500 companies, and eventually managed to

Company Perspectives:

Hub Group's mission is to provide world class logistics solutions that consistently exceed customer expectations.

get some big accounts. Hub's services made it easier for big companies to handle the railroads, which in Yeager's account were not well-equipped to coordinate transport between truck and rail. Yeager convinced major companies that they saved money and hassle by employing a third-party agent. Hooking the *Fortune* 500 accounts spurred Hub to rapid growth. By the early 1990s, *Fortune* 500 accounts made up about 35 percent of Hub's total business, and it was one of the fastest-growing segments of the company.

New Operations in the Late 1980s and Early 1990s

The company continued to be privately held by Yeager and his family. But it was more than the small family business Yeager had at first envisioned. Up from the mere handful of employees Hub started with, by 1990 it had 350 employees, working out of 35 locations. Local Hub offices were spread across the country, radiating out from the company's suburban Chicago center. Yeager's strategy for his staff was to offer a low salary but high commission. Productive workers could make a lot of money on top of the base salary. By the late 1980s, Hub began to diversify into several focused operating divisions. In 1989, the company added a division called Hub Highway Services. This coordinated the company's over-the-road trucking services. After a year in business, the Highway Services division brought in over $17 million. Hub Group as a whole had sales of $350 million in 1990. The Highway Services division expanded Hub beyond intermodal shipping into straight trucking, but the company found that this was difficult to coordinate from its many regional offices. Eventually Highway Services was operated out of a central office in Overland, Kansas. Highway Services grew to broker trucking services using a pool of over 3,000 carriers. At times Hub Highway Services kept track of the operation of 100,000 trucks simultaneously. By the mid-1990s, this division had grown to a $100 million business, serving major corporations such as Borden, Nabisco, Clorox, and Lever Brothers.

Hub Group made many other changes in 1990. It began operating a premium intermodal service division called Bantam, providing premium service between Chicago and Los Angeles. Bantam soon grew to cover seven major intermodal traffic corridors. The company also launched a subsidiary, Hub Group Distribution Services (HGDS), in 1990. HGDS offered door-to-door distribution of shipments for its clients. Hub Group also opened a subsidiary in Canada in 1990, and moved into the southern California market more aggressively by opening an office in San Diego.

The company also made a significant investment in information technology in 1990. Hub Group installed an electronic data interchange, or EDI, computer system that allowed it to link in real time with the computer systems of all the major railroads. Hub's regional offices were also tied together using the EDI system. The technology allowed the company instant access to information from the railroads, such as location of cars and receipt of billing. Hub was also directly connected to some of the banks that a number of its customers used for paying their bills. Hub used its data interchange system to manage one of its largest accounts, the logistics arm of the giant retailer Sears. Hub Group took on the Sears account in 1991, signing a contract with Sears Logistic Service to handle all that company's intermodal freight needs. This was a huge boon to Hub, because Sears made more than 70,000 intermodal shipments a year.

Hub Group was the first intermodal shipping agent to install an EDI system, and its technological prowess allowed the company to expand rapidly in the 1990s. By 1992, the company had become by its own account the nation's largest intermodal shipping agent. Sales ballooned, growing for example 30 percent between 1991 and 1992, and coming close to this in following years. As the company grew, and took on more and more distinguished clients, it targeted new markets. In 1992 Hub Group announced the formation of a new corporate division that would provide intermodal transportation services to the automotive industry. Hub did little business with automakers previously, but it saw the car market as a viable opportunity. The auto industry had changed the way it managed its parts and inventory during the 1980s, responding to competition from Japanese automakers. As the U.S. auto industry moved toward so-called just-in-time inventory management, it turned to third parties for logistics expertise. Hub Group hoped to get a piece of this. Also, Hub had moved recently to open units in Canada and in Mexico. As U.S. automakers moved parts across borders with increasing regularity, Hub felt it was in a good position to arrange intermodal transport for them.

Hub Group became increasingly attractive to large corporate customers as the company grew prominent in the early 1990s. Hub gained a major new client in 1993 when the giant detergent company Clorox Co. agreed to let Hub handle all its intermodal shipping for its cleaning products division. Clorox was looking for measures that would help it cut costs, and bargained that signing on with Hub would save it hundreds of thousands of dollars over the coming few years. In the early 1990s Hub also provided logistics services to major food makers Kraft General Foods and Nestlé, and close to 40 percent of Hub's clients were *Fortune* 500 companies. Because of Hub's state-of-the-art data management capabilities, it was able to offer sophisticated services to some of the nation's biggest companies. It provided completely "paperless" tracking of transactions, keeping tabs on what could be tens of thousands of shipments yearly for major corporations like Sears. Hub's data capabilities allowed the company to operate more efficiently, so that it could save itself money. Hub changed over in the mid-1990s to what it called a "two-way management" system for pick-up and delivery of freight, made possible by its computer technology. The two-way system meant that a trailer leaving Chicago for Los Angeles, for example, sent enough advance notification that a new load could be waiting for it when it unloaded its cargo on the West Coast. Before Hub instituted this system, less than 25 percent of its carriers were reloaded. With the advanced computer notification it had working by the mid-1990s, over 70 percent of its equipment got reloaded.

Hub Group also initiated a new international intermodal freight division in the mid-1990s. It launched a division called

Key Dates:

1971: Company founded by Philip Yeager in Hinsdale, Illinois.
1985: Company begins soliciting *Fortune* 500 accounts.
1989: Hub adds highway services division.
1990: Company installs sophisticated computer data exchange system.
1996: Hub Group goes public.

Hub Group International in 1994, and focused first on international shipments within North America. Soon after, Hub announced it was forming a joint venture with the Norton Lilly International Shipping Agency to move cargo over land for ocean carriers. The joint venture was christened HLX. Hub also acquired American President Distribution Services in 1996, the international intermodal business division of a major shipping company, American President Companies Ltd. Hub paid $8 million for American President's division, giving Hub access to 25 international accounts. American President Distribution was doing about $90 million of business annually. Hub's sales were over $750 million.

Public Company in the Late 1990s and Beyond

Hub Group grew enormously in the 1990s, expanding into new markets and increasing its sales by hefty percentages year after year. In March 1996 Hub Group went public, listing its stock on the NASDAQ. Its shares started out at $14, and a year later had zoomed up to over $27. The company had become much more broadly based than it had when it was a one-room third-party agent. By 1997 Hub offered a full array of logistics services, and arranged for air freight, international shipping, highway trucking, and comprehensive intermodal transportation services. Intermodal transport still accounted for the bulk of Hub's business, but the company planned to increase its share of revenue from other businesses in the coming years. Meanwhile, the company endeavored to improve its efficiency in its intermodal business. A shortage of equipment for truck-train transport had hampered intermodal's growth somewhat in the early 1990s. In 1999, Hub worked out an agreement with several major railroads to let it manage rail containers. Hub gained management of over 2000 railroad containers, with a provision to add up to 1,000 more over the next year. By using its computer network to keep track of them, Hub Group was able to reduce the time the rail containers stood empty between loads. This gave both Hub and the railroads much more efficiency in moving freight.

In 2000, Hub Group announced the installation of a new Internet-based computer system that let carriers arrange shipment details on line. Its logistics arm, HGDS, also found new business using the Internet. It began handling shipping needs of online retailers, especially in fulfilling bulky and heavy orders for such items as furniture and exercise equipment. HGDS offered more than just shipping. It also managed set-up and assembly of goods after delivery, pick-up of returned items, and other services.

Hub Group continued to boom in both sales and profits. Sales for fiscal 1999 were $1.3 billion, an increase of almost 15 percent over the previous year. Profits also rose appreciably, up more than 20 percent for the year. While Hub's revenue from its core intermodal transport business rose a small amount, the company made big strides in other areas. Its revenue from its logistics business was up almost 90 percent, and revenue from truck brokerage also increased by close to 20 percent. Hub seemed to be moving in the direction it had set itself when it went public. It was not only increasing its total business, but was growing quickly in non-intermodal areas. This made it a more balanced and comprehensive company.

Principal Subsidiaries

Hub Group Distribution Services; HLX.

Principal Divisions

Intermodal Shipping; Highway Brokerage; Supply Chain Solutions.

Principal Competitors

Landstar System; Exel Logistics Ltd.

Further Reading

Bonney, Joseph, "Hub Group Goes International," *American Shipper*, April 1994, p. 80.
——, "Hub Group Targets Automakers," *American Shipper*, May 1992, p. 26.
——, "Philip Yeager's Hub Group," *American Shipper*, May 1991, p. 62.
Bowman, Robert, "How Clorox Cleaned Up Its Piecemeal Use of Intermodal Services," *Distribution*, April 1993, p. 56.
Burke, Jack, "Intermodal Marketers Still Aspiring Logisticians," *Knight-Ridder/Tribune Business News*, August 15, 1993, p. 08150032.
Gillis, Chris, "Hub Group's Logistics Strategy," *American Shipper*, November 1996, p. 55.
"Hub Group Adjusts to Public Life," *American Shipper*, June 1997, p. 64.
"Hub Group Extends Premier Service Network," *Logistics Management & Distribution Report*, August 31, 1999, p. 33.
"Hub Group Reports Jump in Net Income," *American Shipper*, March 2000, p. 97.
"Hub Moves Intermodal to Internet," *Fleet Owner*, February 2000, p. 89.
"Hub + EDI = Growth," *Railway Age*, April 1992, p. 44.
Knee, Richard, "APC Sells Intermodal Marketing Unit," *American Shipper*, June 1996, p. 10.
"Making E-Commerce Shipping Simple," *Appliance Manufacturer*, February 2000, p. 82.
Yawn, David, "Hub Group Expects Growth Through New Contract," *Memphis Business Journal*, August 19, 1991, p. 9.

—A. Woodward

Icon Health & Fitness, Inc.

1500 South 1000 West
Logan, Utah 84321
U.S.A.
Telephone: (435) 750-5000
Fax: (435) 750-0209
Web site: http://www.iconfitness.com

Private Company
Incorporated: 1977 as Weslo Design International, Incorporated
Employees: 6,000
Sales: $1 billion (2000 est.)
NAIC: 33992 Sporting and Athletic Goods Manufacturing

Icon Health & Fitness, Inc. is the world's largest manufacturer of fitness and exercise equipment. Sold under the brand names Weslo, ProForm, HealthRider, Weider, IMAGE, JumpKing, Reebok, and NordicTrack, Icon products include treadmills, stationary bicycles, elliptical trainers, trampolines, strength machines, and related items. Icon sells its products using its own catalog, web sites for each of its brand names, and infomercials; through retailers including Sears, Wal-Mart, and Kmart; and through other marketing methods. Although the company originally sold just to home consumers, it now sells its equipment to commercial users such as health and fitness clubs. Icon thus is a major player in the world of fitness, a multibillion-dollar international industry.

Origins and Predecessor Firms

In 1977 two college students started a small import business that would eventually become Icon Health & Fitness. Longtime friends Scott Watterson and Gary Stevenson were majoring in business at Utah State University in Logan, Utah, when they and Bradley Sorenson incorporated Weslo Design International under Utah law. According to the company's incorporation papers, its original purpose was to "engage in wholesale and retail sales of clocks, furniture, marble, metals, insulation, and other raw materials and manufactured items, and to engage in export and import sales of such items, and to invest and make investments in real and personal property, and to engage in any business whatsoever . . .". After graduating from Utah State, the founders expanded their product line by selling wood-burning stoves. To balance the seasonal sales of the stoves, they began selling trampolines and minitrampolines, their entry into the exercise equipment field.

By 1983 the young company's annual sales had reached about $30 million, mostly from the sales of both kinds of trampolines and also exercise bicycles. At that point Stan Tuttleman, a Philadelphia businessman, bought 55 percent of Weslo, including all interests of Blaine Hancy, an early partner of Watterson and Stevenson.

Under Tuttleman's ownership, Weslo continued to grow, reaching 1988 annual sales of about $60 million. In 1988 Weider Health and Fitness acquired Weslo and ProForm and made them subsidiaries of the privately owned company founded by Ben and Joe Weider. Stevenson and Watterson continued to manage Weslo with stock options as an incentive. With new products such as motorized treadmills, Weslo's annual sales reached $202.4 million in 1991.

In 1993 the company began using television information commercials or infomercials to sell its products. Cofounder Scott Watterson in Icon's January 1996 newsletter said, "Where we once marketed our products exclusively to the retail trade, the introduction of infomercials opened doors for our company to successfully reach the consumer directly." Icon's first major infomercial demonstrated the benefits of the ProForm Crosswalk treadmill. By January 1995 Icon's direct marketing program included print, broadcast, and direct-mail operations.

Celebrities such as skater Peggy Fleming, baseball star George Brett, and NFL quarterbacks Roger Staubach and Steve Young eventually promoted Icon products in infomercials and various other formats.

The Formation of Icon Health & Fitness

Weider originally considered taking Weslo, Inc. and ProForm Fitness Products, Inc. public, but instead the owners decided to

Company Perspectives:

Icon Health & Fitness is the world's largest manufacturer and marketer of home fitness equipment.

sell the two subsidiaries to Bain Capital, a Boston-based investment firm headed by Mitt Romney, who had ties to Utah through his membership in The Church of Jesus Christ of Latter-day Saints. Weider initially received $159.3 million in cash while keeping 25 percent ownership. In addition to Bain Capital, the new owners included founders Stevenson and Watterson and other executives. They incorporated Icon Health & Fitness, Inc. on November 14, 1994 by combining Weslo; ProForm; Legend Products, Inc.; and American Physical Therapy Inc., a Weider division. Watterson became Icon's chairman and CEO, while Stevenson served as president and chief operating officer.

Product innovations continued to fuel Icon's growth in the mid-1990s. For example, in 1995 the company introduced ProForm Crosswalk treadmills with a trademarked Space Saver feature that allowed home users to store the Crosswalk vertically. In 1996 Icon added 25,000 square feet of office space to its Logan, Utah headquarters.

In 1996 Icon sold bonds to raise $82.5 million, most of which was used the following year to acquire HealthRider Corporation, a Salt Lake City company that sold a popular line of exercise equipment. Gary H. Smith and his wife, Helen, had in 1990 discovered the HealthRider machine designed by Doyle Lambert. After acquiring the patent rights, the Smiths incorporated ExerHealth Inc. in March 1991, with Gary Smith as the new company's president and CEO. In 1992 ExerHealth began using infomercials to sell its HealthRider, primarily to those at least 40 years old. The company added aeROBICRider and SportRider, two lower-priced versions of its original product, and added over 250 retail outlets in 33 states by 1996. In 1995 the firm began international sales by using LaForza Limited to distribute its products in Europe. With the addition of HealthRider's annual sales of $250 million in 1995, Icon's sales in 1996 reached about $1 billion.

Business in the Late 1990s and Beyond

In 1997 Icon acquired Hoggan Health Industries, a 20-year-old exercise equipment manufacturer. Unlike Icon, with its emphasis on home exercisers, Hoggan made equipment for institutional use in rehabilitation and fitness centers. Icon's annual sales were $836.2 million in fiscal 1997.

That same year Icon faced two challenges. First, in June 1997 the Federal Trade Commission (FTC) charged Icon and three other fitness equipment companies with false advertising that exaggerated their machines' fitness and weight-loss benefits. While denying any wrongdoing, Icon and the other companies admitted they could not back up any of their advertising claims. They all agreed to not make future claims without valid documentation. No fines or penalties were involved. The four companies settled quickly with the FTC to avoid expensive court actions. Also in 1997 Icon voluntarily recalled 78,000 ProForm R930 Space Save Riders after receiving reports of injuries due to the product's tendency to close into the upright storage position while being used. Icon cooperated in this recall with the Consumer Product Safety Commission, which worked with many other companies to prevent more injuries from similar products.

In the late 1990s NordicTrack, another leader in the exercise equipment industry, declared bankruptcy and then was purchased by Icon. Started in 1976 by Minnesota inventor Ed Pauls, NordicTrack had helped pioneer the fitness machine industry with its popular cross-country skiing device. In 1986 CML Group Inc. purchased NordicTrack, and sales continued to increase. From its peak sales of $477 million in 1993, NordicTrack declined to $267 million in 1997. Facing stiff competition from makers of a variety of equipment, NordicTrack started 125 permanent retail mall stores and set up 100 temporary mall kiosks, instead of just relying on its usual infomercials and other forms of direct marketing. That ''clumsy expansion was an invitation to disaster,'' said Jay Weiner in the December 14, 1998 *Business Week*. Faced with a saturated market, NordicTrack filed for Chapter 11 bankruptcy in November 1998. Icon Health & Fitness bid first to acquire NordicTrack, and in December 1998 NordicTrack announced its intent to be acquired by Icon. The Utah company paid $12 million for the Chaska, Minnesota-based firm, which by that time had closed its retail stores.

Although NordicTrack had declined as a business, its brand name remained popular. Icon used that reputation as it offered new NordicTrack brand products. By 2000 NordicTrack treadmills, ellipticals, recumbent bikes, and strength machines were available, some with small TV screens and Internet access.

In the late 1990s Icon began offering its products through licensing agreements with other firms. For example, in 1998 it signed an agreement with Reebok to produce home exercise equipment to be sold under the Reebok name. By 2000 it offered brand names NordicTrack, ProForm, and HealthRider under various licensing agreements. Meanwhile, Icon in 1998 introduced its new ProForm Club Series of commercial treadmills, which surprised the fitness industry since ProForm previously was sold just to home consumers.

At the end of its fiscal year ending May 31, 1999, Icon Health & Fitness recorded total annual sales of $710 million, down about five percent from its 1998 total of $749 million. It also had a net loss in 1999 of $7.8 million compared to a 1998 net loss of $9.5 million. In fiscal 1999, ''Icon chose to reduce its sales to longtime customers Service Merchandise, Venture Stores and Caldor, all of whom had credit problems,'' said Icon spokesperson Colleen Logan in a September 1, 1999 *Business Wire*. ''That choice, although it reduced the Company's topline sales, helped protect its financial position.''

Also in 1999 Icon introduced a web site for its recently acquired line of NordicTrack products. Cyber shoppers at www.nordictrack.com were invited to buy the company's products on a retail basis or through an online auction system. The interactive site also allowed people to type in personal data and then receive a health report with recommendations for better health.

By early 2000 Icon expanded its use of the Internet by introducing iFit.com, host to ''the world's first internet-controlled fitness equipment,'' according to a February 8, 2000

Key Dates:

1977: Weslo Design International, Incorporated is founded.
1988: Weider Health and Fitness, Inc. purchases Weslo and ProForm.
1990: Weider acquires Image Inc.
1991: Weider acquires JumpKing Inc.
1992: Weider acquires Legend Sporting Goods.
1993: A direct consumer sales campaign is started by using infomercials.
1994: Icon Health & Fitness, Inc. is created as a Delaware corporation; ProForm becomes registered as an ISO 9001 manufacturer.
1995: Icon acquires Image, Inc., a Utah corporation.
1997: Icon acquires HealthRider Corporation and Hoggan Health Industries.
1998: Icon licenses Reebok home exercise equipment; CML Group Inc. announces in December its sale of bankrupt NordicTrack to Icon.
1999: Icon completes a major financial restructuring to reduce its heavy debt load.
2001: Company announces its agreement to acquire Ground Zero Design of Colorado Springs.

Business Wire. This new technology allowed exercisers to plug their equipment into their computers and then use the iFit.com web site to select various programs that could adjust speed, incline, resistance levels, or weight levels to get the best workout. The iFit.com technology received several awards in 2000, including a Best Value honor from the Good Housekeeping Institute and the Most Innovative Product designation from The Sports Authority.

In 2000 Icon began designing and manufacturing eight models of scooters priced from $39 to $129. Icon distributed its more expensive scooters through Sears and also The Sports Authority, Dick's Sporting Goods, Oshman's, and other sporting goods stores. Scooters were first sold in early 1999 by other companies primarily to children, teenagers, and young adults. According to Huffy Vice-President Bill Smith in the *Sporting Goods Business* on October 11, 2000, about 50,000 scooters were sold in 1999, but he expected at least five million would be sold by the end of 2000.

Groundbreaking was held in August 2000 for a new Texas industrial park that Icon would occupy. Located in Mesquite in the Dallas-Fort Worth area, the Skyline Business Park would accommodate Icon's plans for a 400,000-square-foot distribution facility.

In December 2000 Icon announced it would not participate in the Super Show 2001 in Las Vegas. Described as the world's major trade show for sports equipment and fitness apparel, the Super Show had included Icon ever since it was first held in 1986. The show's general decline in the late 1990s and bad timing were two factors involved in Icon's decision, which was supported by spokepersons from both Sears and Dick's Sporting Goods.

Icon in January 2001 announced its acquisition of Ground Zero Design, a manufacturer of exercise equipment that had been founded in 1999. Based in Colorado Springs, Ground Zero planned to remain in Colorado Springs as an Icon division employing about 35 people. Icon purchased Ground Zero to help it enter the commercial market. ''Icon dominates the consumer business; virtually everything you see at Sears or Sam's Club is Icon under various brand names,'' explained Roy Simonson, Ground Zero's cofounder in the *Colorado Springs Gazette-Telegraph*. ''But they have no experience in the commercial market. They were looking for someone with fresh ideas already connected to the industry.'' Simonson designed what writer Steven Saint called Ground Zero's ''15-piece line of nontraditional training machines designed to follow the movement of the user's body rather than dictate a certain position or movement.''

At the start of the new millennium, Icon faced several challenges. It had to continue to find new customers, since most fitness machine owners would not consider purchasing a second fitness machine. Their customers were limited to middle or upper-class people or clubs that catered to such individuals. The good news was that the U.S. economy, although declining, remained basically healthy, so many could afford to purchase their products. Many overweight and unfit Americans had much to gain from treadmills, the main fitness product sold in the United States, and other devices that Icon offered. The fitness equipment industry praised Icon's high-tech innovations, one of the company's obvious strengths. Icon also benefitted from leadership continuity, for its cofounders Scott Watterson and Gary Stevenson remained in charge of leading their company into the 21st century.

Principal Divisions

JumpKing; ProForm; Weslo; NordicTrack; HealthRider; Image.

Principal Competitors

Brunswick Corporation; Cybex International; Guthy-Renker Corporation.

Further Reading

Agoglia, John, ''Icon Refinancing Is 'Critical' to Viability,'' *Sporting Goods Business*, October 11, 1999, p. 22.
——, ''Reverse Order: ProForm Jumps from Home to Club,'' *Sporting Goods Business*, April 15, 1998, p. 16.
Boulton, Guy, ''Shaping Up Business: Icon Health & Fitness Restructures to Shed Itself of Excessive Debt,'' *Salt Lake Tribune*, October 10, 1999, p. E1.
Cassidy, Hilary, ''Will Scooters Keep Rolling Along?'' *Sporting Goods Business*, October 11, 2000, pp. 22–24.
''Executive Focus: Gary H. Smith,'' *Deseret News*, June 6, 1993, p. M2.
''Fitness Industry Leader Releases TOP Brand Names for Licensing; Icon Health & Fitness Ready for Licensing Ventures,'' *Business Wire*, December 15, 2000.
''Fitness Leader Says No to the Super Show; Icon Health & Fitness Leaves Behind an Old Venue,'' *Business Wire*, December 15, 2000.
Grossman, Cathy Lynn, ''Treadmill Sales Outpace Ski, Ab Machines,'' *USA Today*, November 23, 1998, p. 01D.

Hawthorne, Kate, ''Pulling It All Together,'' *Marketeer*, May 1996, pp. 16–18.

''Icon Continues 21-Year Profit Streak; Receives Sears Order for 75,000 New Treadmills; Now Hiring for 250 Open Positions,'' *Business Wire*, September 1, 1999, p. 1.

''Icon Health & Fitness and iFit.com Awarded Retailer's Top Honors; Starting the Year Off Right, Icon and iFit.com Receive Major Awards in the First Quarter of 2000,'' *Business Wire*, May 22, 2000.

''Icon to Buy Ground Zero,'' *Salt Lake Tribune*, January 6, 2001, p. B4.

''iFit.com Works with Microsoft's Windows Media to Create World's First Internet Appliance for 'Body Surfing' the Web,'' *Business Wire*, February 8, 2000.

Knudson, Max B., ''ProForm, Weslo Health-Equipment Firms Sign a Deal to Boost Their Fiscal Fitness,'' *Deseret News*, November 15, 1994, p. D7.

Lee, Renee C., ''Mesquite Development Groundbreaking Today . . . ,'' *Fort Worth Star-Telegram*, August 24, 2000, p. 3.

''Logan's Icon Health Buys Hoggan Health,'' *Salt Lake Tribune*, February 19, 1997.

Lorenzi, Neal, ''Consumer Product Safety Commission Product Recalls,'' *Professional Safety*, September 1997, p. 12.

McEvoy, Christopher, ''FTC Cracks Down on Top Fitness Vendor,'' *Sporting Goods Business*, July 7, 1997, p. 42.

''NordicTrack Goes On-line; America's Number One Fitness Brand Launches High-Tech Outlet,'' *PR Newswire*, April 27, 1999, p. 1.

Rebello, Joseph, ''Bain Group to Buy Assets of Three Firms,'' *Wall Street Journal*, November 14, 1994, pp. A3, A6.

''Retail Entrepreneurs of the Year: Helen Smith, Gary Smith,'' *Chain Store Age*, December 1996, p. 94.

Retsky, Maxine Lans, ''Exercise Good Judgement When Developing Your Advertising,'' *Marketing News*, August 18, 1997, p. 5.

Saint, Steven, ''Maker of NordicTrack Buys Springs Firm,'' *Colorado Springs Gazette-Telegraph*, January 6, 2001, p. BUS1.

''Tailored for an LBO,'' *Mergers and Acquisitions*, November/December 1996, p. 26.

Villarosa, Linda, ''A Fitness Industry, with Gadgets Galore,'' *New York Times*, April 25, 2000.

Walden, David M., ''Icon Health & Fitness, Inc.,'' in *Centennial Utah: The Beehive State on the Eve of the Twenty-First Century,* Encino, Calif.: Cherbo Publishing Group, 1995, by G. Wesley Johnson and Marian Ashby Johnson, pp. 134–35.

Weiner, Jay, ''How Nordictrack Lost Its Footing,'' *Business Week*, December 14, 1998, p. 138.

—David M. Walden

Infosys Technologies Ltd.

Electronics City, Hosur Road
Bangalore 561 229
India
Telephone: +91-80-852-0261
Fax: +91-80-852-0362
Web site: http://www.inf.com

Public Company
Incorporated: 1981
Employees: 7,000
Sales: US$203.44 million (2000)
Stock Exchanges: NASDAQ Bangalore Mumbai National
Ticker Symbol: INFY
NAIC: 541511 Custom Computer Programming Services; 541512 Computer Systems Design Services

Infosys Technologies Ltd. is a software development company with headquarters in Electronics City, Bangalore, India, an area known as "India's Silicon Valley" for its concentration of high-tech multinational and Indian companies. Cofounded by Chairman and CEO N.R. Narayana Murthy, Infosys Technologies has accomplished a number of firsts for an Indian company, including becoming the first to be listed on an American stock exchange and the first to offer an employee stock option plan (ESOP). About 500 employees have become millionaires as a result of the company's ESOP. In 2000 the firm's international client base included 200 American firms, for which Infosys Technologies provided software for enterprise resource planning (ERP), Y2K compliance, electronic commerce, and other applications.

Early History: 1980s

Infosys Technologies Ltd. was founded in 1981 in Bangalore, India, by N.R. Narayana Murthy and seven other software engineers with a combined investment of about $1,000. One of eight children of an Indian village official, Murthy would emerge as the company's chairman and CEO. He became regarded as the most highly esteemed manager in India, due in part to his mathematical abilities and Western style of management. The company opened its first international office in the United States in 1987.

Favorable Business Climate: 1990s

Following a series of economic reforms in India in 1991, Infosys Technologies began to grow more rapidly. It became a public limited company in 1992, with an initial public offering (IPO) on three of nine Indian stock exchanges to follow in 1993. In 1993 it received ISO 9001/TickIT Certification, and in 1995 it established development centers across India.

By mid-1995 the firm had 900 employees and was worth $120 million, with about $20 million in annual revenue. In addition to its 400,000-square-foot facilities in Bangalore, the firm had offices in Boston, New York, and Maastricht in the Netherlands. In 1996 it established its European headquarters in the United Kingdom. Its main facility featured more than 1,000 networked workstations for use in creating software. The company had written the reservation system for Holiday Inns in the United States. Other customers included Reebok International, Nestlé S.A., and AT&T.

Infosys established headquarters in what has been called "India's Silicon Valley" because of its concentration of more than 100 foreign and domestic companies. The firm's main software development centers were in the southern Indian city of Bangalore in an area called Electronics City. Other high-tech companies with facilities there included Siemens and Hewlett-Packard. Such companies were attracted by the fact that none of the firms' workforces had to be unionized, software exports were not taxed in India, benefits were a relatively minor cost, and the profit potential was enormous. These cost-savings were first recognized by American multinationals in the 1980s.

India was able to provide these firms with highly trained computer programmers and software engineers. About 15,000 computer science majors graduated from universities in India every year. The Indian Institute of Science in Bangalore was equipped with the most advanced technology, and the govern-

Company Perspectives:

We are a world leader in providing IT [information technology] consulting and software services. We offer offshore-software services, such as application development, software maintenance, Internet consulting, and establishing software development centers in different parts of the world to provide high quality rapid time-to-market solutions at affordable prices.

Our solutions cover a wide range of business areas including e-commerce and e-business enabling, warehouse and inventory management, and customer management for industries including financial services, insurance, retail, telecommunications, utilities, and manufacturing.

ment supported the university system by providing millions of dollars for training.

Exponential Growth: Late 1990s

For fiscal 1998 ending March 31, Infosys Technologies reported net revenue of $68.33 million, a 73 percent increase over fiscal 1997. The company's growth was fueled by its offshore software development model and the branding of some of its services. Infosys Technologies offered its clients an offshore model, whereby the company would replicate the systems and infrastructure of its international clients in India. During fiscal 1998 the firm's market capitalization rose to about $770 million from $192 million at the end of 1997.

Four marketing offices were opened during fiscal 1998, including two in the United States and one each in Canada and Japan. The company had a total of 12 marketing offices, eight in the United States and four in other countries. During the year, the company gained 40 new clients. More than 70 percent of the company's revenue came from repeat business.

Initiatives launched during the year included offerings for engineering services, Internet and intranet solutions, and Enterprise Package Solutions. The company was also addressing Euro conversion issues. Technical staff increased during the year to 2,186 from 1,396 at the end of fiscal 1997. Total employees increased to 2,622 from 1,701.

The company expanded the decentralized development of software by commissioning the Infosys Towers facility at J.P. Nagar, Bangalore, during fiscal 1998. The development centers at Pune, Bhubaneswar, and Chennai were also expanded. The company also began construction on Infosys Park at Electronics City, Bangalore, to be completed by December 1999.

It was during fiscal 1998 that Infosys Technologies become one of some 20 companies in the world to reach Level 4 of the Capability Maturity Model (CMM) of the Software Engineering Institute (SEI) at Carnegie Mellon University. The certification covered fixed-price software development, maintenance, and re-engineering processes, which together contributed about 90 percent of the company's revenue. Obtaining the certification reflected the firm's commitment to meeting international quality standards.

In October 1998 Infosys Technologies held its third annual customer conference. The company used the conference to disseminate its best practices across its client base and to enhance the power of its global delivery model. Nearly 60 client representatives participated in this year's conference. The company stressed long-term relationships with its clients. In 1999 repeat business accounted for 90 percent of revenue, up from 83 percent in 1998.

The company's principal source of revenue, on a geographic basis, was North America, which accounted for 82 percent of revenue in both 1998 and 1999. Europe accounted for eight percent in both years, and India, approximately three percent. The rest of the world accounted for the remainder. During 1999 the company opened an office in Seattle and shifted a European office from Maastricht in the Netherlands to Frankfurt, Germany, giving it 13 marketing offices outside India, including nine in the United States.

That same year Infosys Technologies expanded the range of its services and was becoming a full service partner to its clients. Projects the company worked on included ERP projects, a loyalty management package utilizing Microsoft technologies, and a system and security architecture consulting study. Its Internet consulting and development group designed and built high-performance and secure infrastructure for electronic commerce. During fiscal 1999 Infosys Technologies added 39 new clients, including The Boeing Company, Paradyne Corporation, and AMP Inc.

Infosys Technologies was listed on the NASDAQ stock exchange on March 11, 1999. It was the first India registered company to become listed on an American stock exchange. Listing on the NASDAQ enabled Infosys Technologies to institute an employee stock option plan through the use of American Depository Receipts (ADRs), each of which was worth half a share. By mid-2000 the company had issued 4.16 million ADRs.

Moreover, listing on the NASDAQ was expected to help the company raise money to finance its drive to become a global company, grow through acquisitions, and enhance its image. It would help the company attract a high-quality workforce by offering employee stock options. Infosys Technologies had been hiring 800 to 900 new employees per year. The IPO raised $70 million, and in the months following the IPO the company's stock price rose 20 percent. According to *Business Week,* the company gained $1 billion in market capitalization on its first day on the NASDAQ. By the end of 1999 the stock was trading at $290 per share, a 15-fold increase over the IPO price.

At the beginning of 1999, most of the company's growth was expected to come from developing customized software. The company was also getting into Internet and intranet applications, enterprise resource planning (ERP) software, electronic commerce, and Euro conversion software.

During fiscal 1999 the company attained SEI CMM Level 5, the highest level assessed by the SEI for quality. It continued to build up its infrastructure by completing its new facility, Infosys Park, at Electronics City, Bangalore, which could accommodate up to 2,000 software and support personnel. At the beginning of 1999 it began construction of a new software development facility at Pune Infotech Park, Hinjawadi, Pune. The first phase of this facility would have capacity for 1,200 professionals. The

Key Dates:

1981: Infosys Technologies Ltd. is founded in Bangalore, India, by N.R. Narayana Murthy and seven other software engineers.
1987: Infosys opens its first U.S. office.
1992: Infosys becomes a public limited company in India.
1993: Company issues stock through public offerings on three stock exchanges in India.
1999: Infosys becomes the first India-based public company to be listed on an American stock exchange, the NASDAQ.

company also opened offices in Germany, Sweden, Belgium, and Australia.

In mid-1999 an integrated extranet developed by Infosys Technologies for longtime outsourcing partner Nordstrom Inc. went online. It used a Windows NT software application that enabled the Nordstrom Product Group to combine 20 spreadsheet applications into an integrated applications environment of databases linked over the Internet.

Other repeat business came from the firm's Y2K work. For example, Infosys Technologies had performed Y2K compliance work for insurer Aetna Inc. during 1999, using about 50 software programmers and engineers. At the beginning of 2000 Aetna contracted for an additional 300 Infosys employees to develop its electronic commerce initiatives in the areas of global healthcare and financial services. Using the Infosys offshore model, Aetna worked with the firm's U.S. office, which in turn conveyed information to programmers in India.

Infosys's Global Delivery Model enabled it to develop software collaboratively in different geographic locations. For example, a project's requirements might be outlined in the client's New York offices, with software development done in Bangalore, and deployment anywhere in the world. The time differences associated with different parts of the world enabled Infosys Technologies to provide 24-hour productive days and problem-solving.

As of February 2000 the company had a market capitalization of more than $20 billion. For fiscal 2000 ending March 31, Infosys Technologies reported revenue of $203.44 million, compared to $120.96 million in 1999, an increase of 68 percent. Net income rose from $17.45 million in fiscal 1999 to $61.34 million in fiscal 2000. A statement from CEO N.R. Narayana Murthy noted, ''Demand for e-commerce services, an area where the company has a proven track record, continues to drive our revenue growth.''

During fiscal 2000 Infosys Technologies made its first strategic investment in a leading-edge technology company, committing $3 million to Massachusetts-based EC Cubed, Inc., an application provider for business-to-business electronic commerce.

The company reported a net profit of $28.4 million in the first quarter ending June 30, 2000, compared to $13.6 million for the same period in 1999. Overall revenue rose to $83 million, compared to $48.2 million in 1999. These results exceeded analysts' expectations. One analyst predicted the company's profits would double in the next two quarters, due to surging exports, higher priced services, and a larger proportion of high-margin e-commerce work.

For the quarter ending June 30, 2000, Infosys said that e-commerce work made up nearly 29 percent of its total revenues, or $22.6 million, compared to nearly 19 percent in the quarter ending March 31, 2000, and 6.4 percent in the same quarter in 1999.

During the first quarter of fiscal 2001 Infosys Technologies increased its workforce by nearly 20 percent to 6,446 employees. The company was expected to grow to more than 7,500 employees by the end of fiscal 2001 (March 31, 2001). In issuing a ''buy'' rating, Merrill Lynch noted that many of Infosys Technologies' customers had asked the firm to increase its ''team size'' by 80 to 100 percent over the next year.

In August 2000 Infosys Technologies opened an office in Hong Kong to take advantage of the e-commerce activity there, especially in business-to-business applications. One analyst estimated that the Asia Pacific region would account for nearly 20 percent of global business-to-consumer and business-to-business electronic commerce by 2003. Opening the office was part of Infosys Technologies' strategy to expand its e-commerce business from the United States and Europe into the Asia Pacific region. Its clients have included Amazon.com, Blue Martini, Cephren, Cisco Systems, Dell Online (Japan), EC Cubed, preis24.com, and SAPMarkets.

With a growing client base, support from investors, and a reputation for quality, Infosys Technologies appeared likely to remain a leader in developing software systems and applications for the exploding global electronic commerce market.

Principal Competitors

Analysts International Corporation; Cambridge Technology Partners, Inc.; Computer Horizons Corp.; Computer Sciences Corporation; Cap Gemini America; Keane Inc.

Further Reading

''Focusing On: Software Application TCO,'' *Software Magazine,* February 2000, p. S1.

Girishankar, Saroja, ''Nordstrom Outsources to Develop Speed,'' *InternetWeek,* July 5, 1999, p. 16.

Greenemeier, Larry, ''Aetna Expands Offshore Outsourcing,'' *InformationWeek,* January 17, 2000, p. 87.

Harding, Elizabeth U., ''Frank Billone: The Price Is Right,'' *Software Magazine,* September 1999, p. 10.

''India Infosys Eyes Nasdaq Listing,'' *CNET News.com,* January 28, 1999, http://news.cnet.com/news/0-1007-200-337960.html?tag=st.ne.ni.rnbot.rn.ri.

''Indian Software Firm's Profit Seen to Double,'' *CNET News.com,* July 11, 2000, http://news.cnet.com/news/0-1003-200-2239297.html?tag=st.ne.1430735.

''Indian Software Firms Profiting,'' *CNET News.com,* October 11, 1998, http://news.cnet.com/news/0-1003-200-334116.html?tag=st.ne.ni.rnbot.rn.ni.

"India's IPOs: All That Glitters Isn't a Jewel," *Business Week,* December 20, 1999, p. 56.
"N.R. Narayana Murthy," *Business Week,* July 3, 2000, p. 36B.
"N.R. Narayana Murthy, Founder, Infosys Technologies, India," *Business Week,* June 14, 1999, p. 83.
Rauss, Uli, "India's Silicon Valley," *World Press Review,* July 1995, p. 36.
Smith, Greg, "RFPs Miss the Mark," *InformationWeek,* March 20, 2000, p. 67.

—David P. Bianco

International Flavors & Fragrances Inc.

521 West 57th Street
New York, New York 10019
U.S.A.
Telephone: (212) 765-5500
Fax: (212) 708-7132
Web site: http://www.iff.com

Public Company
Incorporated: 1909 as Morana, Inc.
Employees: 4,682
Sales: $1.44 billion (1999)
Stock Exchanges: New York
Ticker Symbol: IFF
NAIC: 311942 Spice and Extract Manufacturing; 325188 All Other Inorganic Chemical Manufacturing; 325199 All Other Basic Organic Chemical Manufacturing

International Flavors & Fragrances Inc. (IFF) has been a leader in the fiercely competitive flavor and fragrance industry since 1958, when it debuted under its present name. A strictly business-to-business operation, IFF routinely provides individually tailored fragrances for a host of products ranging from fine perfumes to deodorants to scents used in laundry detergents. Although fragrances traditionally have been the backbone of IFF's bottom line, flavorings operations have grown to comprise about 41 percent of sales. IFF's flavors are used in processed foods, beverages, confectionery products, baked goods, pharmaceuticals, oral care products, and other areas. A globally active firm, International Flavors & Fragrances has operations in more than 35 countries and generates nearly 70 percent of its revenues outside the United States—39 percent from Europe, Africa, and the Middle East; 16 percent in Latin America; and 13 in the Asia-Pacific region. The company claims to operate the world's largest research and development effort devoted to fragrances and flavors, spending more than $100 million each year to create new flavors and fragrances at 32 laboratories in 24 countries.

Early Years

International Flavors & Fragrances traces its origins back to the 1909 incorporation of Morana, Inc. in New York City. In 1920 Morana was taken over by a young man who would build the business into one of the foremost companies in the industry. Arnold Louis Van Ameringen arrived in the United States from Holland in 1917 on his way to represent a Dutch fragrance manufacturer known as Polak-Schwarz. Van Ameringen's job security, however, did not stand the test of distance. Before a year had passed he was fired for suggesting a now-common American practice—a profit-sharing plan for employees. Undaunted, Van Ameringen opened his own fragrance and flavor supply business the following year. After merging this firm into Morana, Van Ameringen decided in the mid-1920s to boost sales by persuading manufacturers of bar soaps and detergents to add fragrances to their products. Several adopted this suggestion and found that the new ingredient caused their sales to soar. Van Ameringen's business prospered along with theirs, growing large enough by 1929 to warrant merging the company with the operations of William T. Haebler, in whose honor he renamed the company Van Ameringen-Haebler, Inc.

American workers quickly recognized the new company as a good place to be employed. At Van Ameringen-Haebler, the boss had an open-door policy, and bonuses, always promptly paid, ranged between six and nine percent of annual salaries. Employees, especially the highly trained and hard-to-come-by perfumers, were encouraged to settle into the company for the long term. In return, Van Ameringen asked that absolute secrecy about formulas be maintained at all times to prevent competitors from copying original ideas. As a private concern, Van Ameringen also was able to keep the company's financial details under wraps.

Despite Van Ameringen's best efforts, however, secrecy was not always easy to maintain. In the unauthorized biography *Estée Lauder: Beyond the Magic,* author Lee Israel maintained that Van Ameringen was romantically involved with Lauder and that he was responsible for the "Youth Dew" fragrance that brought her such fame after its 1953 introduction. Israel also noted that Van Ameringen gave Lauder extended credit—

Company Perspectives:

At IFF, our goal is to be our customers' most valued resource for creative, consumer-preferred and technologically superior flavors and fragrances.

a favor that culminated in a corporate friendship that spanned several decades.

Van Ameringen-Haebler's sales in 1958 were $28.4 million, of which a scant ten percent came from the company's flavor formulas. In an effort to expand both manufacturing and marketing in this segment of the business, Arnold Louis Van Ameringen merged the company with a European manufacturer primarily concerned with flavors, offering broad access to the American fragrance market in return. Founded in The Netherlands in 1889 and called N.V. Polak & Schwarz's Essencefabricken, Van Ameringen's new partner was a company he knew well—the same one that had fired him in 1917.

Expanding in the Late 1950s and 1960s

The new venture, named International Flavors & Fragrances Inc., proved an instant success and immediately found such broad markets in the European food industry that new facilities in Holland, Switzerland, France, and Brazil were added to augment the company's older American factories. Within two years foreign manufacturers of cake mixes, pharmaceutical products, gelatin desserts, candies, and soft drinks were using IFF flavorings at a rate that brought the division's sales figures to 35 percent of the $34.2 million total in 1960.

It was clearly time to go public. Offered over the counter, the first shares went on sale in October 1961. At about the same time, Arnold Van Ameringen decided to step down as president so that he could devote himself to raising funds for mental health causes, although he continued to serve as chairman of the board until his death in 1966. Van Ameringen chose as his successor Henry Walter, the man who had been his trusted legal counsel for years.

A rather eccentric man, Walter was daring enough to brave Manhattan's rush-hour traffic on a bicycle and, even as the head of a fragrance company, to wear red suspenders brandishing hand-embroidered skunks. Although Walter could boast a law degree from Columbia University plus almost 30 years of legal practice, he had little knowledge of the fragrance and flavor business, which he often referred to as the ''sex and hunger trade.'' Nevertheless, Walter firmly took the IFF helm and made sure to imprint his own corporate style on his staff without delay. Just as Van Ameringen had done, Walter also made secrecy his top requirement. In one 1963 action, he chose to emphasize this mandate by suing the Cott Beverage Corporation—which had just employed a former IFF employee as their new director of research and information—maintaining that IFF's formulas for ginger ale and several other soda flavors had been usurped. The outcome of the case was never publicized, but the action itself was enough to convince employees that Walter meant business.

Other changes made the company more visible as an international concern. Walter made it a rule to use local workers in every foreign facility, allowing him to mention in the company's 1966 annual report that only four Americans were currently working in IFF's overseas plants. Being in closer touch with non-Americans also brought the company reliable information about local tastes in fragrances. The company learned that women in warmer climates preferred to use perfumes with a higher fragrance content (though not necessarily a stronger type) than their counterparts in cooler climates, and European men preferred aftershaves that were more highly scented than those used by American men. By the end of 1965 the close attention to cultural differences had paid off handsomely—fully 51 percent of sales came from overseas markets.

Walter allocated generous amounts of corporate income ($5.8 million in 1967) to flavor and fragrance research, and he himself made sure that few innovations in other companies escaped his notice. Especially interesting to him was a process of inking by microencapsulation invented by National Cash Register to replace messy carbons. A man quick to note the far-reaching potential of any industrial novelty, Walter soon licensed the process, and it was not long before IFF was producing scent strips for children's ''scratch-'n-sniff'' books and perfume samples for magazines. By mid-1966 these new products had stimulated demand enough to send a daily average of $60,000 worth of fragrance compounds flowing from the company's Manhattan headquarters. In addition, at the end of 1970 the fragrance markets for both toiletries and detergents had brought sales figures to $102.7 million, and such customers as Revlon, Procter & Gamble, and General Mills were relying heavily on IFF. Characteristically, Walter celebrated by allocating $8.4 million for the research that was keeping the company out in front of the competition.

Cutting Costs in the 1970s

If Henry Walter's big push during the 1960s had been expansion, his equally great ambition in the 1970s revolved around cost-cutting. The advertising budget, potentially very large in a company concerned with fragrances, could be kept to skeletal levels because IFF was a business-to-business concern, rather than a retail marketer. A few trade journal ads usually sufficed and were used for direct mail together with the company's annual report, the cost of which was pared to $1 per copy.

In 1970 S.J. Spitz, a veteran of the chemical industry, joined Walter's staff as chief operating officer. Spitz was well known for cost-cutting, and together he and Walter managed their 2,671-strong staff with economy and precision.

By 1973 the company's 50 salesmen (20 in the United States and 30 in Europe) were handling both flavors and fragrances and producing an average annual turnover of $3 million each. Even the perfumers came under new scrutiny. In most companies, perfumers were precious and carefully handled assets, but at IFF bonuses were cut to the bone, and there was now a new rule that employees leaving the company were barred from their share of profits, even if the money had been earned during their tenure. Complaints about the new regime left Walter unmoved. ''When a

Key Dates:

1909: Morana, Inc. is incorporated.
1920: Arnold Louis Van Ameringen merges his fragrance and flavor supply businesses into Morana.
Mid-1920s: Van Ameringen persuades makers of bar soaps and detergents to add fragrances to their products.
1929: Morana is merged with the operations of William T. Haebler to form Van Ameringen-Haebler, Inc.
1958: Company merges with Netherlands-based N.V. Polak & Schwarz's Essencefabricken to form International Flavors & Fragrances Inc. (IFF).
1961: Company goes public; Henry Walter succeeds Van Ameringen as head of IFF.
1985: Eugene P. Grisanti takes over as chairman and CEO.
2000: Richard A. Goldstein is named chairman and CEO; IFF acquires Bush Boake Allen Inc.

company gets beyond a certain point,'' he told *Dun's Review* in 1974, ''you cannot run it in the old paternalistic way.''

In the early 1970s IFF was secure in a fragrance division that was still producing 75 percent of the bottom line, and Walter was elated about the new popularity of men's toiletries as well as the growing profitability of air freshener products. The calm, however, was interrupted in 1973 by the oil embargo, which quadrupled prices of all oil-based ingredients and encouraged other suppliers to raise theirs to match.

By the end of the decade, despite a client list that included Lever Bros. and Colgate-Palmolive, it was impossible to ignore a fragrance market growth rate that had slowed, both domestically and overseas, from 16 percent to eight percent. In addition, tough competition was another cause for concern. By the late 1970s most top couturiers and cosmetics houses were at least assumed to be regular IFF customers. Their loyalty, however, was no guarantee of sales growth; these same clients usually invited several fragrance suppliers to submit samples for any new fragrance.

Developing the Flavor Business in the 1980s

Whereas all fragrance contracts were lucrative, a deal on a potentially expensive perfume could command a very high level of profit. Unwilling to compromise IFF's claims in this area, Walter gladly paid his chief perfumer, Bernard Chant, a 1982 basic salary of $230,000 plus bonus for supervising 40 staff members and dreaming up new ideas. But Chant's considerable creativity could not stem the ominous downward spiral. By 1980 sales figures reached $448.3 million, rising just one percent in 1981 to reach $451.1 million. The following year net sales sank to $447.9 million as a result of both a recession and a strong dollar overseas that affected the company's foreign markets.

Always a man who tied his company's developments to events in the outside world, Walter turned his attention to the growing world population and its burgeoning need for food. He noted that the agricultural industry was rising to the challenge with improved fertilizing techniques and freezing methods and, in other food service areas, the microwave oven was being used increasingly to bring food to the world's tables in record time. Walter also observed that such advances were not without their downside. The new fertilizers and freezers often came with high price tags, and the broadening spectrum of foods being produced frequently lacked flavor.

Once he had decided to concentrate on developing his share of the flavor market, Walter gave his experienced research team the green light. Thanks to the generous research budget ($30.6 million in 1980, rising to almost $35 million by 1985), IFF now reaped handsome dividends. The company made full use of the worldwide trend toward healthier eating and drinking by developing beverages that contained little or no caffeine, breads and pizzas with sharply reduced salt, and flavorful cheese products containing little or no fat. At the same time, new consumer interest in ethnic foods brought a need for complex flavoring blends, and a taste for more sophisticated and lower-fat desserts broadened the flavor market further. The flavor segment of IFF's business contributed a healthy 38 percent of total sales by the end of 1984.

Fragrance research also received close attention during these years. Henry Walter had long held the view that fragrances might carry the psychological benefit of mood elevation. As a first attempt to find answers, he had much earlier sponsored a study by leading sex experts Masters & Johnson, who were trying to determine the effect of fragrance on sexual behavior; he encouraged his scientists to find scents that might discourage overeating, relieve stress, or bolster sexual excitement.

In mid-1985 both CEO S.J. Spitz and Chairman Henry Walter decided to retire. Into the top spot stepped former Senior Vice-President Eugene P. Grisanti, a Harvard-trained lawyer with 24 years of experience with IFF. Grisanti got off to a brisk start. His first act was to streamline management by eliminating the position of CEO and giving the vice-presidents of the flavors and fragrance divisions more decision-making responsibility. Next, he instituted a teamwork concept among his New York- and Paris-based product development units, who were now encouraged to cut costs and effort by working closely together. Grisanti also carried on the Walter tradition of a generous research budget, which by 1990 had reached $54 million. Grisanti directed this money in part toward such ''bread-and-butter'' projects as the development of exactly the right beef-fat flavor for McDonald's low-cholesterol fries and in part toward innovative research into covering bad odors. By the end of 1992 IFF sales figures had reached $1.13 billion, up from $962.8 million in 1990, despite the recurrent recession that brought thousands of layoffs and forced consumers to compromise on important purchases. Sales and earnings growth continued through 1995, when revenues reached $1.44 billion and net income hit $248.8 million. The latter figure was more than triple that of 1985, when Grisanti had taken over. During the same period, IFF's stock quadrupled in price.

Stagnating Results in the Late 1990s

Revenues and earnings stagnated in the late 1990s, however, because of stiffening competition, pricing pressure from increasingly cost-conscious customers, and the effects of the Asian financial crisis and economic difficulties elsewhere. The latter hit particularly hard because of IFF's strong international base—about 70 percent of revenues were generated outside the United States. The company began restructuring, closing a plant in Union Beach, New Jersey, in 1997, then launching a global restructuring in mid-1999 that aimed to increase earnings by $15 million a year starting in 2000. An aroma manufacturing plant in Haverhill, England, was slated for closure along with additional operations in Brazil and the Philippines. About 200 employees, or five percent of the workforce, lost their jobs. In 1999, IFF took a pretax charge of $40.9 million in connection with the restructuring, resulting in net income for the year of $162 million, a significant drop from the $248.8 million figure of 1995. Research and development expenditures, meantime, reached an all-time high in 1999, $104 million—the largest in the industry. Near the end of 1999, Grisanti, under some pressure from the company board stemming from the company's continued lackluster performance, retired from the company. Board member Richard M. Furland, former president of pharmaceutical company Bristol-Myers Squibb Company, was named interim chairman and CEO.

As restructuring activities continued in 2000, IFF began participating in a consolidation drive that was sweeping the fragrance and flavors industry and was being propelled by the industry's slower growth and production overcapacity. In April the company acquired Laboratoire Monique Rémy, a firm based in France that was a leader in the production of natural raw materials for flavors and fragrances. In June, Richard A. Goldstein took over as chairman and CEO of IFF. Goldstein was a 25-year veteran of Unilever, reaching the position of president and CEO of Unilever United States, Inc. Goldstein had pursued some significant acquisitions in his position as head of Unilever's U.S. unit and, after just a few months at the helm of IFF, announced the company's first major acquisition in decades. In September IFF agreed to acquire Bush Boake Allen Inc. (BBA) for about $965 million, a deal that closed in November. The addition of BBA, which had 1999 sales of $499 million, vaulted IFF into the number one position worldwide in the flavors sector while bolstering its already top position in fragrances. Both BBA and IFF had strong global positions, with BBA giving IFF a significant presence in India for the first time. Meanwhile, in October, IFF announced another major reorganization in which the company adopted a new global structure. In place of the separation of fragrances and flavors into their own divisions, the company adopted a structure centering on the broad global units of business development and operations; the structure also included a matrix element in that there would also be a single regional manager for five geographic clusters: North America; Europe; Latin America; the Asia-Pacific region; and Central Asia, Africa, and the Middle East. Through this restructuring, IFF hoped to achieve annual cost savings of $25–$30 million by 2003; these savings were in addition to the $70 million in savings expected to accrue from the acquisition of BBA. Under bold new leadership, International Flavors & Fragrances appeared poised to return to the solid growth that had characterized the company from 1985 to 1995.

Principal Subsidiaries

International Flavors & Fragrances I.F.F. (Nederland) B.V. (Netherlands); Aromatics Holdings Limited (Ireland); IFF-Benicarlo, S.A. (Spain); International Flavours & Fragrances (China) Ltd.; Irish Flavours and Fragrances Limited (Ireland); International Flavours & Fragrances I.F.F. (Great Britain) Ltd. (U.K.); International Flavors & Fragrances I.F.F. (Italia) S.r.l. (Italy); International Flavors & Fragrances I.F.F. (Deutschland) G.m.b.H. (Germany); International Flavors & Fragrances I.F.F. (Switzerland) A.G.; International Flavors & Fragrances I.F.F. (France) S.a.r.l.; International Flavors & Fragrances (Hong Kong) Ltd.; International Flavors & Fragrances (Japan) Ltd.; International Flavors & Fragrances S.A.C.I. (Argentina); I.F.F. Essencias e Fragrancias Ltda. (Brazil); International Flavours & Fragrances (Australia) Pty. Ltd.; P.T. Essence Indonesia; International Flavors & Fragrances (Mexico) S.A. de C.V.; International Flavors & Fragrances I.F.F. (España) S.A. (Spain); ALVA Insurance Limited (Bermuda).

Principal Competitors

BASF Aktiegesellschaft; Bayer AG; Dragoco Gerberding and Co. AG; Firmenich S.A.; Givauden S.A.; Haarmann and Reimer GmbH; Heller Seasonings & Ingredients, Inc.; Kerry Group plc; McCormick & Company, Incorporated; Millennium Chemicals Inc.; Northwestern Flavors, Inc.; Quest International; Sensient Technologies Corporation; Takasago Perfumery Co.; T. Hasegawa Co. Ltd.

Further Reading

''A.L. van Ameringen Dies at 74; A Crusader for Mental Health,'' *New York Times,* January 5, 1966, p. 31.

Bary, Andrew, ''Take a Whiff: Why International Flavors & Fragrances Looks Tempting Right Now,'' *Barron's,* July 20, 1998, pp. 20, 22.

Commercial and Financial Chronicle, October 30, 1961, p. 1843.

''A Cook's Tour of IFF Operations with Marketer Hinrichs,'' *Industrial Marketing,* September 1970, p. 55.

Curan, Catherine, ''Perfume Company Banks on CEO's Nose for Business: International Flavors Hopes to Pace Flagging Industry,'' *Crain's New York Business,* June 26, 2000, p. 4.

Floreno, Anthony, ''F&F Financial Results Show There's Growth in Industry,'' *Chemical Market Reporter,* January 26, 1998, p. 17.

''IFF Shaking Inventory Blues,'' *Commercial and Financial Chronicle,* July 26, 1976, p. 2.

''IFF: The Sweet Smell of Success,'' *Forbes,* October 15, 1973, p. 34.

''International Flavors Elects Walter,'' *New York Times,* December 12, 1962, p. 13.

''International Flavors: Funding Far-Out Ideas for Future Growth,'' *Business Week,* November 12, 1984, p. 129.

''International Flavors Joins Big Board Today,'' *New York Times,* March 2, 1964, p. 41.

Israel, Lee, *Estée Lauder: Beyond the Magic,* New York: MacMillan, 1985.

Jacobs, Karen, ''International Flavors to Acquire Bush Boake Allen,'' *Wall Street Journal,* September 26, 2000, p. B12.

Karp, Richard, ''The Big 'If' at IFF,'' *Dun's Review,* March 1974, p. 52.

Lublin, Joann S., ''International Flavors Is Set to Name Unilever's Goldstein Chairman and CEO,'' *Wall Street Journal,* April 26, 2000, p. B2.

Margetts, Susan, ''Sex, Hunger—and IFF,'' *Dun's Review,* November 1969, p. 95.

McCoy, Frank, ''International Flavors Smells Like Money Again,'' *Business Week,* April 18, 1988, p. 70.

Mendelson, Alan Mark, ''Dollars from Scents,'' *Barron's,* March 31, 1980, p. 39.

Nemy, Enid, ''In the World of Fragrance, Reputations Rest on the Nose . . . ,'' *New York Times,* February 11, 1993, p. C2.
Ouellette, Jennifer, ''New IFF CEO Begins Path Back to Growth,'' *Chemical Market Reporter,* June 26, 2000, p. 24.
Roman, Monica, ''Beef-Fat Flavor May Not Sound Glamorous, But . . . ,'' *Business Week,* March 11, 1991, p. 70.
Smith, Lee, ''Adventures in the Sex and Hunger Trade,'' *Fortune,* August 9, 1982, p. 47.
''A Sweet Little Business,'' *Forbes,* October 1, 1963, p. 41.
''The Sweet Smell of Success,'' *Magazine of Wall Street,* August 3, 1968, p. 18.
''U.S. Charges 7 Firms Over $29 Million Cost to Clean Waste Site,'' *Wall Street Journal,* July 17, 1992, p. A6.

—Gillian Wolf
—updated by David E. Salamie

Interstate Bakeries Corporation

12 East Armour Boulevard
P.O. Box 419627
Kansas City, Missouri 64141-6627
U.S.A.
Telephone: (816) 502-4000
Fax: (816) 502-4155
Web site: http://www.irin.com/ibc

Public Company
Incorporated: 1930
Employees: 34,000
Sales: $3.52 billion (2000)
Stock Exchanges: New York
Ticker Symbol: IBC
NAIC: 311812 Commercial Bakeries (pt)

Interstate Bakeries Corporation is the largest independent baker in the United States, producing breads and cakes in more than 60 bakeries across the country. The company distributes its products under a wide range of brand names, including Sunbeam, Dolly Madison, Wonder, and Hostess. Founded in the 1930s, the company grew by acquiring other regional and national bakers. In the late 1970s, it was purchased by a failing computer leasing firm, whose financial difficulties troubled the company well into the 1980s. By the start of the 1990s, however, after more than a decade of modernization, Interstate had recovered to take the lead in its industry by buying out its largest competitor.

Origins and Expansion: 1930s–40s

Interstate, a company based in Kansas City, Missouri, was founded in 1930 by baker Ralph Leroy Nafziger. Nafziger came from a family of bakers, and he produced wholesale bread loaves packaged in a distinctive country-gingham wrapper, which were resold in grocery stores. Seven years after its incorporation, Interstate merged with another, much better established Kansas City baker, the Schulze Baking Company, Inc., which had been founded in 1893. This move was the first of a series of acquisitions and mergers that Interstate undertook over the course of the next several decades, as the bread baking industry changed from a highly fragmented field, made up of a large number of small, independent, local operations, to a more consolidated industry, with a few big producers of national brands.

Interstate's next acquisition came at the end of 1943, when the company bought the Supreme Baking Company of Los Angeles, whose plant it had previously rented. Seven years later, the company also bought the O'Rourke Baking Company of Buffalo, New York. With the purchases, Interstate sought to extend its geographic coverage into new areas.

The Postwar Cake Boom

Interstate's growth through acquisitions remained steady throughout the 1950s. In 1951, the company bought Mrs. Karl's Bakeries, located in Milwaukee. Three years later, the company moved aggressively into the cake baking industry, purchasing the Ambrosia Cake Company, the Remar Baking Company, and the Butter Cream Baking Company. Four years later, Interstate also acquired the Campbell-Sell Baking Company, based in Denver, Colorado. At the end of the decade, Interstate added to its cake franchise when it purchased the Kingston Cake Bakery, in Kingston, Pennsylvania.

In 1960, the company strengthened its standing in the Midwest when it acquired Cobb's Sunlit Bakery, of Green Bay, Wisconsin. Over the next two years, Interstate purchased the Schall Tasty Baking Company of Traverse City, Michigan, and the Sweetheart Bread Company. Other important acquisitions during the 1960s included Hart's Bakeries, Inc. After its long period of steady expansion, Interstate also undertook a consolidation of its operations, closing some plants. The company's Buffalo bakery, once owned by O'Rourke's Baking Company, was sold. In addition, Interstate closed its Butter Cream Baking Company plant and its Schall Tasty Baking Company factory. At the end of that year, the company's net sales reached $191 million, up from $124 million in 1959, through a period of steady growth.

Interstate began to expand again in the late 1960s. In March 1968, the company bought the Millbrook bread division of the National Biscuit Company. This division included seven bakeries, located in upstate New York, which produced bread, rolls, cakes, and doughnuts for distribution throughout the region. In addition, Interstate took possession of a fleet of about

Company Perspectives:

Baking has always been a simple business wrapped in a complex environment. The challenges to succeed in the past remain constant today . . . perfect the basics. Provide consumers with products that connect with their lifestyle; when they want them and where they want them; delivering consistent quality and value day-in and day-out.

Premium bread, cake and baked snack treats fill important roles in today's lifestyle. Interstate Bakeries Corporation is one of the nation's premium providers of fresh baked foods to consumers and has been for more than four generations. Our Company's focus is to guarantee high-quality, great-tasting and consistently fresh bread and cake for today's active families. It has been our focus for some time. Perfecting the basics is a continual process.

700 delivery vehicles in the acquisition. This brought Interstate's overall total of motor delivery trucks to about 4,000.

In August 1968, Interstate moved outside the baking industry for the first time, acquiring a food processor, the Baker Canning Company, and its subsidiaries, Shawano Farms, Inc. and the Shawano Canning Company, companies that canned peas, beans, and corn at three canneries in Wisconsin. Its products were sold mainly to institutions and were distributed through six warehouse facilities.

By the end of the 1960s, Interstate was baking bread in 30 different cities throughout the United States, in a total of 36 different plants. The company's regional strengths were in the Midwest, the West, and upstate New York. On July 25, 1969, Interstate changed its name to the Interstate Brands Corporation, to reflect the broader scope of its activities, which now included canning as well as baking. The company had become the third largest wholesale baker in America. Its best known products were the Butternut and Blue Seal bread brands, and Dolly Madison cakes, which were distributed across the country. Interstate sold its canning operation in 1974 and resumed acquisition of properties that fit in with its core line of business, baking. In December of that year, Interstate bought Nolde Brothers, Inc., for $500,000.

Hard Times in the 1970s

Then, in 1975, Interstate became the object of an acquisition itself. The company's unwanted suitor was founded in 1961 as the Data Processing Financial and General Corporation, based in Hartsdale, New York, a suburb of White Plains, where the International Business Machines Corporation (IBM) was located. Data Processing, which changed its name to DPF, Inc. in 1971, leased IBM computers to other businesses throughout the 1960s. In 1970, IBM introduced a new computer model, and DPF's equipment instantly became obsolete. The company lost $43 million over the next five years, until it finally got back on its feet in 1974 and began to look for a company to acquire that would allow it to diversify its activities, since the computer leasing field no longer seemed tenable, as IBM continued to step up its pace of new product introductions.

In 1975, DPF decided that Interstate Brands would be a good business to buy. ''We wanted a sober, solid, low-technology business,'' DPF's chairman later told *Forbes*. In June, DPF offered to buy 43 percent of the outstanding shares of Interstate. Immediately, the baker sued to block the acquisition, but its request was denied. Interstate Brands then, in turn, announced that it would purchase Farmbest Foods, a dairy products processor, from Philadelphia-based I.U. International Corporation. Interstate planned to issue a block of 375,000 shares of common stock to purchase Farmbest, which would have reduced the amount of stock DPF could control to only 37 percent of the total outstanding shares. DPF sued to block this move, and finally, after additional wrangling, DPF acquired Interstate for $37 million.

In the wake of this purchase, Interstate's headquarters were transferred to Hartsdale, New York. The company's new owners set out to wring greater profits out of its operations by upgrading facilities. ''Almost nothing had been done here in terms of capital enhancement of the business for some years; some areas needed nothing more than a Band-Aid, while some needed major surgery,'' one DPF executive told *Barron's*. To modernize Interstate's plants, DPF embarked on a program that saw 17 factories closed and 19 new properties purchased during the last five years of the 1970s.

As part of this program, Interstate announced in 1976 that it would undertake the construction of a new $5 million bakery in Montana. The following year, the company shed the Nolde Brothers subsidiary and purchased the Silver Loaf Baking Company. Other acquisitions during this time included the Eddy Bakeries division of General Host and Mrs. Cubbison's Foods, Inc., a bread stuffing maker.

On February 27, 1979, DPF fully completed its merger with Interstate. Two years later, the acquiring firm sold what was left of its computer operations to a group of former managers and changed the entire company's name to Interstate Bakeries Corporation. Although Interstate earned a $50 million tax break from the collapse of the computer outfit, ultimately, the bakery operations were left with a heavy financial burden to bear.

By the start of the 1980s, Interstate was operating 36 different plants, selling bread and cakes in 30 different markets. Seventy percent of the company's revenues came from bread, with 30 percent derived from cakes. Although sales of white bread had grown stagnant, as people became more health conscious, sales of variety breads, such as Interstate's Pritikin diet bread and Sun-Maid raisin bread, which carried a higher price tag and had a longer shelf life, had benefited from this trend.

In addition, Interstate looked to benefit from the general recession gripping the economy, since a poor economy, paradoxically, meant good news for bakers. As one Interstate executive explained to *Barron's*, ''Downturns in the economy always see people eating more bread than they might otherwise do.'' Interstate's cake business, which was supported through heavy advertising, offered higher profits than its bread sales and also was relatively immune from the effects of a poor economy, since, some analysts noted, people tended to keep treating themselves to sweets when they could not afford more expensive luxuries.

Key Dates:

1930: Interstate Baking Company is formed in Kansas City, Missouri.
1937: Interstate merges with Schulze Baking Company, Inc.
1943: Interstate purchases Supreme Baking Company of Los Angeles.
1954: Interstate acquires Ambrosia, Remar, and Butter Cream Cake Companies.
1969: Interstate changes name to Interstate Brands Corporation.
1975: DPF acquires Interstate Brands.
1981: Interstate Brands becomes Interstate Bakeries Corporation.
1987: IBC Holdings Corporation is formed; Interstate becomes private company.
1991: IBC Holdings becomes Interstate Bakeries again, goes public.
1995: Interstate acquires Continental Baking Company.

Back on Solid Ground by the Late 1980s

With the separation of Interstate's computer business from the core baking operations, Dale Putnam, head of Interstate's bakery division, was named chief executive officer of Interstate in January 1982. Putnam moved Interstate headquarters back to Kansas City, its historical base of operations. The company then looked to focus all of its attention on baking, as well as on improvements in two areas: plant efficiency and market penetration. Although the company had already spent $100 million upgrading its manufacturing facilities in the late 1970s, it planned to continue its efforts in this area, in hopes of increasing its profitability to a level consistent with that of its two largest competitors.

Despite these efforts, Interstate struggled in the early 1980s. The company was saddled with the financial consequences of DPF's failed computer business, the declining demand for white bread, its staple product, and stiff competition from other national bakers. A proposed merger with another independent baker, American Bakeries Company, never materialized, and Interstate was forced to close additional baking plants that were no longer profitable. In May 1983, Interstate closed out a four-year period of declining financial returns with a loss.

The bad news continued in 1984, as Interstate racked up $4.2 million in red ink. At that time, the company appointed a new president, Robert Hatch, a veteran of General Mills, who came on board just days before Interstate's bankers demanded payment on $36 million worth of loans. In an effort to get the company out of the shadow of its computer-leasing losses, Interstate took another $21 million writeoff and cashed in its $37 million pension fund to pay off the banks. "We're trying to put our financial house in order," noted B.J. Hinkle, Interstate's chief financial officer, in *Barron's*. Termination of the pension plan, Hinkle reported, has "given us time to slow down a little bit and evaluate our product line." The pension plan was replaced by another retirement package.

Interstate next decided to emphasize strong brand marketing, rather than relying on price to differentiate its products from those of its competitors. The company, therefore, increased its spending on advertising by two-thirds. Interstate also attempted to sell its western operations to the Good Stuff Food Company of Los Angeles for $55.1 million, but this deal ultimately was abandoned.

As Interstate moved into the late 1980s, its efforts to recover appeared to be bearing fruit. Sales of white bread had stabilized, and the company also began to introduce new products, such as coffee cakes, pecan rolls, pudding pies, and a wider variety of breads. To keep manufacturing efficiency high, Interstate shut down five plants and spent $109 million to modernize 27 others.

In addition, in 1986, the company also made a series of acquisitions, in the hope of filling in marketing gaps. In May, it purchased the Purity Baking Company, of Decatur, Illinois, which made Sunbeam breads, and in December, Stewart Sandwiches of Utah was brought into the Interstate fold. Stewart Sandwiches sold frozen and refrigerated products, such as roast beef and turkey sandwiches.

Interstate reported $13.4 million in earnings for the year ended May 1987. Later that year, the company continued its string of acquisitions, purchasing Landshire Food Products, Inc. and Stewart of Northern California, Inc., the partner of its earlier acquisition. In addition, Interstate bought the Langedorf cake and cookie operations of the Good Stuff Food Company.

Interstate's most significant financial move during 1987, however, was its withdrawal from the financial markets through a leveraged buyout. IBC Holdings Corporation (IBC) was formed to buy up all of Interstate's outstanding stock, and Interstate was taken private by its management, with the help of a group of investment banking houses, in September 1987.

Following this move, Interstate parent IBC made a major acquisition, purchasing the ten bakeries of the Merita/Cotton's Bakeries division of the American Bakeries Company for $132 million. Shortly after this purchase, the president of Merita, Charles A. Sullivan, moved over to take command of IBC, becoming president and CEO. With the contribution of the new Merita unit, and its own revitalized operations, IBC's sales grew strongly in the last years of the 1980s. The company reported sales of $855 million for 1988, which rose to $1.1 billion by May 1989.

In May 1991, IBC Holdings Corporation changed its name back to Interstate Bakeries Corporation, before the company once again went public, selling stock on the market in July 1991. Through this move, Interstate was able to raise $250 million to pay down its debts, which were holding down the company's profits, despite the company's increased efficiency and sales. With increased cash flow and reduced debt level, Interstate was able to decrease its expenditures on interest.

National Brand Recognition in the Late 1990s

In the early 1990s, Interstate saw the popularity of its main product, bread, increase, as the federal government put forth new dietary guidelines. The company sought to take advantage of this new demand by decentralizing its operations, so that local facilities could run as efficiently as possible. "With 31 bakeries across the country, you can't run a business from Kansas City," Sullivan asserted.

By the mid-1990s, this strategy had succeeded so well that Interstate was in a position to make a major acquisition. In early January 1995, the company announced an agreement to buy one of its primary competitors, the Continental Baking Company, for $330 million and 16.9 million shares of Interstate stock. Continental, owned by Ralston Purina, produced the widely popular lines of Wonder and Wonder Lite breads, as well as the snack cakes, donuts, pies, muffins, and cookies marketed under the Hostess name. As Continental's plants were located in parts of the country not yet tapped by Interstate, the company could look forward to becoming a greater national presence. Moreover, Interstate had positioned itself to become the largest player in the baking industry, with anticipated annual revenues in excess of $3 billion. Thus, despite its checkered financial history of the last several decades, Interstate appeared to be well on its way to robust health in the coming years of the 1990s.

With the acquisition of Continental Baking Company, Interstate became the largest producer of wholesale bread and cake in the country. The company wasted no time taking advantage of the name value of its recently acquired brands, launching an aggressive marketing campaign in January 1996. A key part of the strategy involved airing a series of national television advertisements, including the first Wonder Bread ads in almost ten years, which employed the slogan "Remember the Wonder." The company also reversed Continental's ill-advised policy of shrinking the size of Hostess snack cakes, restoring them to their original sizes—in some instances even making them larger—without raising prices. This concentrated brand building resulted in 1997 sales of more than $3 billion, an increase of 11.6 percent over the previous year. During this time the company also introduced a number of new products, including fat-free Wonder and Butternut breads and Hostess Lights.

The Continental purchase evoked a certain amount of apprehension, however, within the U.S. Justice Department. Wary of potential antitrust issues, the agency ordered Interstate to divest itself of one of its other holdings. The company quickly complied, agreeing to sell the Butternut Bakery in Chicago in January 1997. This sale was followed in 1998 by the removal of Weber's brand products from certain markets in southern California.

The divestiture order did not stop the company's expansion entirely, however. During this same period the company broadened its holdings to include a wider range of products in certain key markets. In March 1997 the company acquired the San Francisco Bread Company, famous for its line of hearth breads, and in January 1998 it purchased the John J. Nissen Baking Company of Biddeford, Maine, thereby strengthening its position as a leading baked good supplier in the Northeast. The Nissen purchase soon was followed by other acquisitions in the region, including Drake's and the My Bread Company in New Bedford, Massachusetts. This growth allowed the company to diversify its product line, while at the same time simplifying its distribution process. With sales in 1998 once again surpassing the $3 billion mark, Interstate spent almost $100 million on new operations, including a 280,000-square-foot facility in Biddeford, Maine, one of the largest showcase bakeries in the world, and a Toledo bakery with a capacity of 250,000 loaves of bread a day.

Interstate's fortunes took a sharp nose-dive in October 1998, however, when the company announced that its second quarter earnings would fall below expectations. The investment markets were not kind; on October 30 Interstate stock plunged 25 percent in just two hours, after attaining a year-long high of $34.375 only three weeks earlier. A year later the company's stock was still stranded at $22.75, far below analysts' expectations of $30. Although there were no actual buyout inquiries, the company, fearing a possible takeover, created a shareholder rights plan designed to discourage possible predators.

Interstate announced another dramatic financial drop in 2000, with net earnings of $89 million, down from $126 million the year before. Organized labor troubles and rising fuel prices, along with the unexpected flooding of the Rocky Mount, North Carolina Merita baking facilities, were blamed for the decline. The company also suffered a setback of a different sort in August 2000, when a San Francisco court awarded $126 million to 18 Wonder/Hostess bakery employees who had filed a racial discrimination suit against Interstate. Still, despite this series of disasters, the company headed into the next century with full confidence that its "Powerhouse Brands" would stimulate sales growth for years to come.

Principal Subsidiaries

Interstate Brands Corporation; Mrs. Cubbison's Food, Inc.; IBC Trucking Corporation.

Principal Divisions

Eastern Division; Central Division; Western Division.

Principal Competitors

The Earthgrains Company; Flowers Industries, Inc.; McKee Foods Corporation.

Further Reading

Kravets, David, "Wonder Bread Squeezed," *Associated Press,* August 3, 2000.

Mann, Jennifer, "Feeling the Heat: KC-Based Interstate Bakeries Looks to Turn Its Fortunes Around After a Rough Couple of Years," *Kansas City Star* (Mo.), August 29, 2000.

——, "A Tempting Target: Interstate Bakeries Cooks Up a Poison Pill to Ward Off Firms Intrigued by Low Share Price," *Kansas City Star* (Mo.), October 12, 1999.

Rudolph, Barbara, "Out of the Computer and into the Oven," *Forbes,* March 15, 1982, p. 56.

Simon, Ruth, "Putting the Yeast Back into Profits," *Forbes,* February 9, 1987, pp. 62, 64.

Troxell, Thomas N., Jr., "Yeasty Return," *Barron's,* March 1, 1982.

Weiss, Gary, "Making Dough," *Barron's,* December 3, 1984, pp. 30–34.

—Elizabeth Rourke
—updated by Stephen Meyer

J.P. Morgan Chase & Co.

270 Park Avenue
New York, New York 10017-2070
U.S.A.
Telephone: (212) 270-6000
Fax: (212) 270-2613
Web site: http://www.jpmorganchase.com

Public Company
Incorporated: 1968 as Chemical New York Corporation
Employees: 90,000
Total Assets: $705 billion (2001 est.)
Stock Exchanges: New York London
Ticker Symbol: JPM
NAIC: 522110 Commercial Banking; 522190 Other Depository Credit Intermediation; 522210 Credit Card Issuing; 522291 Consumer Lending; 523110 Investment Banking and Securities Dealing; 523120 Securities Brokerage; 523210 Securities and Commodity Exchanges; 523920 Portfolio Management; 523991 Trust, Fiduciary, and Custody Activities; 551111 Offices of Bank Holding Companies

J.P. Morgan Chase & Co. is the name adopted by the Chase Manhattan Corporation following its year-end 2000 acquisition of J.P. Morgan & Co. Incorporated. J.P. Morgan Chase is one of the largest financial institutions in the world encompassing global commercial banking services, including investment banking, wealth management, institutional asset management, and private equity, under the J.P. Morgan name; and a retail banking business known as Chase comprising regional consumer banking in the New York tri-state area and Texas, credit cards, mortgage banking, consumer lending, insurance, and middle-market banking. The creation of J.P. Morgan Chase brought together two of the most venerable names in banking, not to mention two famous historical figures associated with the two firms—J. Pierpont Morgan and David Rockefeller; it also was the culmination of a historical process full of mergers, most notably those on the Chase side that occurred in the 1990s. In 1991 two banking giants, Chemical Banking Corporation and Manufacturers Hanover Corporation, merged to form the number five bank in the United States under the Chemical Banking name. Then in 1996 Chemical Banking acquired Chase Manhattan, adopting the more prestigious Chase name and forming what was then the largest bank holding company in the country. The old Chase Manhattan itself was the product of a 1955 merger between the Bank of Manhattan Company, which was formed in 1799, and Chase National Bank, which traced its origins back to 1877.

Bank of Manhattan Company: 1799–1955

Chase Manhattan's earliest predecessor, the Manhattan Company, was formed in 1799, ostensibly to supply New York with clean water to fight a yellow fever epidemic. Its real purpose, however, was to establish a bank. Organized by Aaron Burr to challenge the supremacy of the Bank of New York and the Bank of the United States, the company had a charter in which Burr had surreptitiously inserted a clause authorizing it to engage in other businesses with any leftover capital. To no one's surprise, the company soon discovered that the water-supply operation would not require all of its resources, so the Bank of Manhattan Company was opened in 1799 at 40 Wall Street. The bank's first president was Daniel Ludlow.

In 1808, the year Daniel Ludlow resigned, the company was allowed to sell the water operation to the City of New York and devote its energy to banking. From that time onward, the Bank of Manhattan flourished. The bank introduced several innovative banking practices, among them, the method by which it had gained a charter. Its example spawned corruption among other groups who sought incorporation; the construction of canals during the 1820s and 1830s or the building of railroads in the 1850s and 1860s often became the pretext for procuring a bank charter that might not otherwise have been granted.

Since the bank had virtually no restrictions in its charter, it was able to loan money to a wide variety of patrons, including tradespeople, land speculators, and manufacturers as well as the New York state government. This open banking policy provided a great impetus for westward expansion in the United States during the mid- and late 19th century. By the turn of the

Company Perspectives:

Chase's Vision: We provide financial services that contribute to the success of individuals, businesses, communities and countries around the world. By creating solutions for our customers, opportunities for our employees and superior returns for our shareholders, we help each to achieve their goals.

century the Bank of Manhattan had established itself as one of the largest holders of individual depositor accounts. Its policy of providing personal banking services worked so well that, at the time of its merger with Chase in 1955, the Bank of Manhattan operated 67 branches throughout New York City and was widely regarded as one of the most successful and prestigious regional banks in America.

Chase National Bank: 1877–1955

The other part of Chase Manhattan, the Chase National Bank, was established in New York in 1877 and named after Salmon P. Chase, Secretary of the Treasury under Abraham Lincoln. It was not until 1911, however, when Albert Henry Wiggin took over the leadership of the bank, that Chase developed into a power on Wall Street. In 1905, at the age of 36, Wiggin became the youngest vice-president in the company's history. By 1911 he was president of the bank and by 1917 the chairman of its board of directors.

Chase was a relatively small bank when Wiggin took over, but he soon began to transform it into one of the largest in the world. He did this by expanding the bank's list of corporate accounts through the offer of more banking services, especially trust services. Wiggin helped to found Mercantile Trust in 1917 and in the same year organized Chase Securities Corporation to distribute and underwrite stocks and bonds. This affiliate soon became a major force in the equities markets. In addition, Wiggin established strong ties to big business by recruiting the bank's directors from the most influential companies in the United States.

Wiggin's greatest contribution to the bank was his arrangement of a series of mergers during the 1920s and early 1930s in which Chase absorbed seven major banks in New York City. The largest of those, the Equitable Trust Company, had more than $1 billion in resources when it was acquired in 1930. The eighth largest bank in the United States at the time, it was owned by John D. Rockefeller and led by Rockefeller's brother-in-law Winthrop Aldrich. Not long after the merger, Wiggin assumed the chairmanship of what was then the largest bank in the world.

In 1932, however, the leadership at Chase changed dramatically. Wiggin had used not only his own funds, but also those of the bank to engage in stock speculation, and that year was forced to resign. In the following years, Wiggin and several of his close associates were disgraced by a Congressional investigation that uncovered, among other transgressions, the use of affiliated companies to circumvent the laws restricting stock market transactions. Moreover, it was learned that during the stock market crash of 1929, Wiggin had made $4 million selling Chase stock short—and using bank funds to do so.

Winthrop Aldrich directed the bank's operations from the mid-1930s to the end of World War II, a period when Chase continued to expand and develop, becoming the first bank to open branches in both Germany and Japan after World War II. Aldrich knew, however, that Chase was hampered in its domestic development by the fact that all of its consumer branches were located in Manhattan. The bank had always concentrated on corporate and foreign business and ignored innovations such as branch banking, leaving it in a weak position to capitalize on the prosperity of middle-income Americans during the postwar boom. In 1955, Aldrich arranged a merger between Chase and the Bank of Manhattan, at the time the nation's 15th largest bank, but more importantly one with an extensive branch network throughout New York City.

Chase Manhattan, 1955–81: The David Rockefeller Era

From the time of the merger between Chase and the Bank of Manhattan, there was a new driving force behind the bank's activities: David Rockefeller. Rockefeller had joined Chase as the assistant manager of its foreign department after the war, becoming vice-president by 1949. In the early 1950s, he was head of the bank's metropolitan department; it was actually Rockefeller who advised Aldrich on the benefits of the merger with the Bank of Manhattan. With the merger complete, he was named executive vice-president and given the task of developing the largest bank in New York City. At the same time he was also appointed vice-chairman of the executive committee. In 1969, he became chairman of the board of directors, the same year the Chase Manhattan Corporation was incorporated and the Chase Manhattan Bank N.A. became its wholly owned subsidiary.

As the head of Chase Manhattan, David Rockefeller soon became a major international power broker. Never really interested in the day-to-day operations of the bank, he began to travel extensively, meeting with political and business leaders around the world. This high international profile led Rockefeller to use the bank in the service of what he regarded as desirable American foreign policy; by becoming one of the pillars of the U.S. foreign policy establishment, his influence on the Council of Foreign Relations and Trilateral Commission was very strong.

This close association between Chase and the prevailing U.S. political establishment inevitably drew the bank into controversy. In 1965, Chase's decision to purchase a major share in the second largest bank in South Africa provoked an intense campaign by civil rights groups to persuade institutions and individuals to withdraw their money from a firm that clearly supported the apartheid regime. In 1966, widespread protests were directed against the bank following Rockefeller's decision to open a Chase branch in Saigon. A strong supporter of U.S. involvement in the Vietnam War, Rockefeller traveled to the capital of South Vietnam to open the building personally; a sandstone fortress, it was designed to withstand mortar attacks and mine explosions.

David Rockefeller and Chase's foreign controversies continued into the 1970s. During this time, the shah of Iran had been

Key Dates:

1799: The Bank of Manhattan Company is founded.
1824: Chemical Bank is established.
1838: George Peabody forms a merchant bank in London.
1851: Hanover Bank begins business.
1853: Manufacturers National Bank is founded.
1854: Junius S. Morgan becomes a partner of Peabody in the London merchant bank and soon takes it over.
1861: Junius's son, J.P. Morgan, founds a New York sales and distribution office called J.P. Morgan & Co.
1864: J.S. Morgan renames the London merchant bank J.S. Morgan & Co.
1877: Chase National Bank is formed.
1895: J.P. Morgan consolidates his father's businesses under J.P. Morgan & Co.
1914: Manufacturers mergers with Citizens Trust Company and subsequently changes its name to Manufacturers Trust Company.
1929: Hanover merges with Central Trust Company to form the Central Hanover Bank and Trust Company.
1930: Chase acquires Equitable Trust Company, owned by John D. Rockefeller.
1933: The Glass-Steagall Act separates commercial and investment banking.
1935: J.P. Morgan spins off its investment banking arm as Morgan Stanley.
1954: Chemical merges with Corn Exchange Bank and Trust Company.
1955: Bank of Manhattan and Chase National merge to form Chase Manhattan Bank.
1959: J.P. Morgan merges with Guaranty Trust Company to form Morgan Guaranty Trust Company of New York.
1961: Manufacturers and Hanover merge to form Manufacturers Hanover Trust Company.
1968: Chemical New York Corporation is established as a bank holding company for Chemical Bank.
1969: Chase Manhattan Corporation is formed as a bank holding company, with Chase Manhattan Bank, N.A. becoming its main subsidiary; Manufacturers Hanover Corporation is created as a bank holding company, with Manufacturers Hanover Trust as its subsidiary; J.P. Morgan & Co. Incorporated is formed as a bank holding company, with Morgan Guaranty Trust as its principal subsidiary.
1987: Chemical acquires Texas Commerce Bankshares.
1989: The Federal Reserve grants J.P. Morgan permission to underwrite corporate debt securities, marking the firm's return to the U.S. investment banking sector.
1991: Chemical merges with Manufacturers Hanover, creating Chemical Banking Corporation.
1996: Chemical Banking acquires Chase Manhattan and adopts the Chase name.
1997: J.P. Morgan purchases 45 percent stake in American Century Investments.
1999: Chase acquires Hambrecht & Quist Group Inc.
2000: Chase acquires Robert Fleming Holdings Ltd.; Chase merges with J.P. Morgan to form J.P. Morgan Chase & Co.

the bank's best customer in the Middle East. Iran's $2.5 billion in deposits from oil profits amounted to approximately eight percent of Chase's total deposits in 1975. When the shah fell from power in 1979, it was Rockefeller who, along with Henry Kissinger—at that time the chairman of the firm's international advisory committee—persuaded the Carter administration to allow the shah into the United States. When Iran tried to retaliate by withdrawing its funds from Chase, Rockefeller succeeded in convincing the government to freeze all Iranian assets in U.S. banks, a move that led to the seizure of hostages at the American Embassy in Teheran.

The 1970s were a difficult time for the bank. Chase lost significant domestic business as regional banks lessened their dependence on Chase Manhattan for their own growth and expansion; their burgeoning resources made it less important that they go to the "banker's banker" for loans. In addition, Chase lost millions of dollars in bad loans to Latin American countries, which resulted in its being placed on the Federal Reserve's list of "problem banks"—ones that needed constant supervision. Although the company's foreign income increased from one-half to two-thirds of its total income during this time—to nearly $4 billion—the bank had a hard time competing with Citibank's aggressive expansion. Nevertheless, Chase remained the country's third largest bank, with 226 branches in New York City and 105 branches and 34 subsidiaries around the globe.

1980s: Battered by Bad Loans and Third World Debt Crisis

The 1980s ushered in a period of significant acquisitions for Chase. In 1984 the bank purchased Nederlandse Credietbank N.V., a Dutch bank headquartered in Amsterdam. The same year it purchased the Lincoln First Bank in Rochester, New York. In 1985, the bank bought six Ohio savings and loan institutions. In 1986, Chase acquired Continental Bancor.

In 1981, David Rockefeller retired from his position at Chase. Willard C. Butcher, his hand-picked replacement, had been president and CEO of Chase, and succeeded him as chairman of the board. Butcher took up where his predecessor left off; Chase maintained a very high profile in international finance, continuing to view itself as a worldwide power broker.

But the most important problem for Chase Manhattan in the 1980s was a series of bad loans that had no equal in quantity or magnitude in the bank's history. It started when Drysdale Government Securities defaulted early in 1982 on $160 million in interest payments to brokerage firms. Chase had acted as an intermediary for these deals, and thus was forced to pay $117 million of the interest Drysdale owed. Only a few months later, Penn Square Bank, N.A. collapsed after $2.5 billion in unsecured loans that it had made to oil and natural gas interests in Oklahoma went sour. Chase purchased some of those loans, but moved quickly to write off $161 million of them to prevent further financial damage. Chase had also been one of the most heavily exposed banks lending money to Third World countries. On February 20, 1987 Brazil announced that it would suspend payment on its foreign debt and threw the money-center banks into a panic. In May, Chase added $1.6 billion to its loan loss reserves. As a result, it posted a loss of $894.5 million for 1987—the worst year for American banking since the Great Depression.

Battered by the Third World debt crisis and faced with strong competition from insurgent regional banks, Chase Manhattan faltered in the late 1980s. Between 1986 and 1988, it reduced its workforce by ten percent, or about 6,000 employees. In 1988 the *New York Times* speculated that the venerable banking giant might be a takeover candidate because of its depressed stock price and prestigious name. Then, in 1989 and 1990 Chase suffered huge losses from commercial real estate loans, sinking the bank's finances to new lows. Reflecting the seriousness of the situation, the bank's board asked Butcher to retire a year early so that a new team could deal with the crisis.

Butcher's heir apparent during the turbulent late 1980s was his president and chief operating officer, Thomas G. Labrecque. Following a stint in the Navy, Labrecque had joined Chase in 1964 as a trainee, moving up the ranks until 1970 when he started working directly for Rockefeller on various troubleshooting assignments. He made his mark at Chase in 1975 with his work on the Municipal Assistance Corp., which helped bail New York City out of a financial crisis. Labrecque was also credited with convincing Chase's board in 1978 that the bank should expand its retail business—which by the 1990s would generate nearly half of the bank's revenues. In 1981 he was named president.

Restructuring in the Early 1990s

Industry observers noted that Labrecque's more well-known predecessors had emphasized Chase's worldwide position at the expense of a domestic operation which, with its various problems and scandals of the 1980s, seemed out of control. When Labrecque—virtually unknown outside of banking circles—took over as CEO in late 1990, his immediate task was to implement a restructuring plan intended to rein in control of Chase's operations and turn the bank's fortunes around. Like other banks struggling through those industry-wide difficult years, Chase cut costs, trimmed staff (another 6,000 by the end of 1991), and reduced operations. Labrecque also scaled back the bank's international presence by beginning to jettison its foreign retail banking subsidiaries; no longer would Chase aim to be a full-service world bank, such as its longtime rival Citicorp. Branch banking operations outside the New York area—in Arizona, Florida, and Ohio—were eliminated. Successful consumer lending operations were shorn up through such moves as the 1993 acquisition of consumer mortgage company Troy & Nichols, Inc. Overall, Chase intended to concentrate on three areas: regional banking in the New York tristate region; national consumer operations in credit cards, mortgages, and automobile loans; and international investment banking.

Chase also began at this time to focus more on technology, a particular strength of the man Labrecque chose as his president, Arthur F. Ryan, who had been in charge of the firm's consumer bank. The company initiated a $500 million program to upgrade its information processing systems. It also entered into the online home banking arena through alliances with Microsoft Corporation, Intuit Inc., America Online, and CompuServe.

Perhaps most importantly, Labrecque and Ryan embarked in 1992 on a program to transform Chase's corporate culture. In addition to efforts to bolster quality control and customer service, perhaps the most important addition to Chase's operations was that of teamwork; the bank had historically suffered from turf wars. As a result of these efforts, by 1994 cost-containment efforts had translated into an improvement in the bank's overhead efficiency ratio (noninterest expenses divided by revenues) from 75 percent to 60 percent. Following a net loss of $334 million in 1990, Chase enjoyed four successive years healthily in the black; 1991 showed $520 million in net income on net revenues of $3.35 billion, while 1994 showed $1.08 billion in net income on net revenues of $3.69 billion.

The question for Chase in the mid-1990s was whether all of Labrecque and Ryan's efforts had come soon enough to save the bank's independence. In the fiercely competitive environment of the times, Chase had actually lost ground; increasing consolidation engendered through a mind-boggling series of bank mergers from 1993 through 1995 had caused Chase's ranking among U.S. banks to fall from second to seventh in terms of total assets. Weakness in the price of its stock, reflecting ongoing investor skepticism, not only prevented Chase from strengthening itself through further acquisitions but also made the bank itself vulnerable to takeover. Moreover, the company's June 1995 announcement to lay off an additional 3,000 to 6,000 workers (or 8.5 to 17 percent of its workforce) by early 1996, further fueled takeover speculation.

Merging with Chemical in 1996

Finally, on August 28, 1995, the wait was over. Chemical Banking Corporation announced a merger with Chase Manhattan. The $10 billion stock swap transformed sixth largest Chase and fourth largest Chemical into the largest banking company in the United States with assets of nearly $300 billion. Although it was termed a merger of equals, it was technically an acquisition of Chase by Chemical even though the combined corporation adopted the more prestigious Chase name. In September 1995, the first round of executive positions was announced with more than half the positions going to Chemical executives. Chemical's takeover of Chase was consummated on March 31, 1996.

Chemical, like the Bank of Manhattan, was formed as an offshoot of a nonbanking entity. In 1823 the New York Chemical Manufacturing Company was established, then one year later it created a banking division called Chemical Bank. Following the passage of more liberal banking laws in 1838 as well as the expiration of the original charter of New York Chemical Manufacturing, Chemical Bank was reincorporated in 1844 as a bank only. By 1851 all of the chemical division's inventories and real estate holdings had been divested.

The depression of 1857 hit many banks hard, with 18 New York City banks closing in a single day. Chemical Bank earned the nickname ''Old Bullion'' during the crisis by continuing to redeem bank notes in specie for several days after all other financial institutions had started issuing paper loan certificates. In 1865 the bank acquired a national charter under the National Bank Act of 1865 as the Chemical National Bank of New York. Chemical grew rapidly during the final decades of the 19th century, entering the new century as one of the largest and strongest banks in North America.

Following a period of decline in the early 20th century marked by extremely conservative management, Chemical began diversifying in the 1920s under the leadership of Percy H. Johnston. He set up a trust department and engineered the bank's first merger, in 1920, with Citizens National Bank, a small but wealthy New York commercial bank. In 1923 Chemical established its first branch bank, and by decade's end had 12 branches in Brooklyn and Manhattan; the first overseas office, in London, was opened in 1929. That same year, the bank reincorporated as a state bank under the name Chemical Bank & Trust Company, then changed its name to Chemical Bank Trust Company following a merger with United States Mortgage and Trust Company. Chemical weathered the Great Depression through careful management of its assets. By 1946, when Johnston retired, Chemical had grown to become the seventh largest bank in the United States.

From 1946 to 1972, Chemical's assets rose from $1.35 billion to $15 billion. This growth stemmed largely from a series of mergers, starting in 1948 with a takeover of Continental Bank and Trust Company of New York. Eight mergers were consummated between 1951 and 1972, with the first major one being that with the Corn Exchange Bank and Trust Company in 1954. This merger brought Chemical 98 additional branches throughout New York City. A second major 1950s merger came in 1959 when Chemical merged with New York Trust Company, which had a large trust and wholesale banking business. In the early 1960s, Chemical began to expand into New York's suburbs, opening branches on Long Island and in wealthy Westchester and Nassau Counties. In 1968, following an industry trend, a bank holding company, Chemical New York Corporation, was formed to facilitate expansion into other financial areas.

The late 1960s and early 1970s saw Chemical significantly expand its international operations. In the 1970s the bank also diversified the services it offered to both corporate and individual customers. Among acquisitions during the decade were a finance company with branches in 11 states, two investment advisory firms, and a mortgage company, as well as the 1975 purchase of Security National Bank, which had a large Long Island branch network. Chemical also formed a real estate financing subsidiary and a wholesale bank in Delaware.

During the 1980s Chemical turned to interstate bank mergers as banking regulations continued to be liberalized. In 1987 the bank acquired Texas Commerce Bankshares in what was at the time the largest interstate banking merger in U.S. history. Texas Commerce was one of the largest bank holding companies in the Southwest and had the largest affiliate system in Texas. Two years later Chemical merged with Horizon Bancorp, a New Jersey bank holding company which was renamed Chemical Bank New Jersey.

Despite these interstate moves, Chemical entered the 1990s in a position similar to that of Chase Manhattan: suffering from the aftereffects of the crazed loan environment of the 1980s and the Third World debt crisis. Facing increasing competition, Chemical took the dramatic action of merging with Manufacturers Hanover Corporation in 1991 in the largest bank merger in U.S. history at the time. The new company, which took the name Chemical Banking Corporation, had assets of $135 billion, making it the number five bank in the country. In the years leading up to the merger with Chase Manhattan, Chemical closed redundant branches in New York, pulled out of the upstate New York and New Jersey markets, and bolstered itself in Texas with the purchase of the failed First City Bancorp in 1992 and Ameritrust Texas Corporation in 1993, becoming the leading corporate bank in Texas.

Manufacturers Hanover, for its part, had a history as long as that of Chase and Chemical and as filled with mergers. Manufacturers National Bank was formed in 1853 in Brooklyn and, after combining with Citizens Trust Company in 1914, changed its name to Manufacturers Trust Company. Hanover Bank, meantime, was established in New York in 1851, eventually merging with the Central Trust Company to form the Central Hanover Bank and Trust Company in 1929. Both Manufacturers Trust and Central Hanover grew through a slew of mergers and acquisitions, until the two banks joined forces in 1961 as the Manufacturers Hanover Trust Company. This bank became a subsidiary of a newly formed bank holding company, Manufacturers Hanover Corporation, in 1969.

Late 1990s: Consolidation and Further Takeovers

The new Chase Manhattan emerged from the 1996 Chase-Chemical merger as by far the leading New York area bank for both consumers and businesses as well as the second largest bank in Texas. On a national level, it was among the leaders in a number of areas, including private banking for the wealthy, corporate lending, credit cards, and new mortgage origination. In the immediate wake of the merger, Chase concentrated on eliminating duplicate operations, cutting 12,000 jobs in the process and a number of branches toward estimated annual cost savings of $1.7 billion. Leading the new Chase following the merger was Walter V. Shipley, who had been in charge of Chemical, while the head of the old Chase, Thomas G. Labrecque, was named president and COO. Another key figure was William B. Harrison, Jr., who was vice-chairman of Chase's lucrative corporate banking and trading operations.

In a replay of the past, Chase Manhattan almost immediately began feeling pressure to make additional acquisitions or to even effect another blockbuster merger in order to keep pace with the rapid consolidation of the financial services industry in the late 1990s as deregulation progressed ever further. The firm was in fact soon surpassed in asset size by Citigroup Inc., which was formed in 1998 from the merger of Citicorp and Travelers Group Inc., owner of the brokerage firm Salomon Smith Barney. Speculation centered on a deal with a major investment banking firm, such as Goldman Sachs Group Inc., Merrill Lynch & Co., Inc., or Morgan Stanley Dean Witter & Co., but Chase was unable to complete such a merger. In July 1999, Harrison succeeded Shipley as CEO of Chase Manhattan (becoming chairman as well in January 2000), and the new leader managed to complete some smaller, strategic deals. In December 1999 Chase acquired San Francisco-based Hambrecht &

Quist Group Inc. (H&Q) for about $1.35 billion. H&Q was a relatively small investment bank, with annual revenue of only about $373 million, but it specialized in a then-hot area: high-tech stock offerings. Two other smaller acquisitions also occurred in 1999, that of the mortgage business of Mellon Bank Corporation and the credit card portfolio of Huntington National Bank. Harrison's appointment was also seen as an impetus for the 1999 launch of Chase.com, a new operating unit that aimed not only to take the bank's traditional businesses into cyberspace but also to invest in new Internet ventures such as multibank consortia for online bill presentation and payment, trust services, and mortgage brokering.

Chase made a more substantial acquisition of an investment banking firm in August 2000 when it spent about $7.7 billion in cash and stock for Robert Fleming Holdings Ltd., a privately held British firm. By acquiring Fleming, Chase gained an enhanced presence in investment banking not only in Europe but also in Asia, where Fleming's corporate finance operation was doing quite well. Chase had its eye on even bigger game, however, and just one month after completing the takeover of Fleming, Chase announced that it was merging with J.P. Morgan & Co. Incorporated.

Brief History of J.P. Morgan

The famous House of Morgan traces its roots back to 1838 and the founding in London of a merchant banking firm by George Peabody. Junius S. Morgan became Peabody's partner in 1854, soon taking over the firm and renaming it J.S. Morgan & Co. in 1864. In the meantime, Junius's son, John Pierpont (J.P.) Morgan, had established a New York sales and distribution office called J.P. Morgan & Co. in 1861. J.P. Morgan inherited his father's businesses upon his death in 1890 and consolidated them five years later under J.P. Morgan & Co. Morgan played a key role in financing many of the businesses that turned the United States into an industrial power around that time, including General Electric Company, U.S. Steel, and AT&T. Taking on the role later played by the chairman of the Federal Reserve, Morgan was instrumental in pulling a group of bankers together to stave off the 1907 financial crisis. There was much criticism, however, for the power wielded by Morgan and his bank, particularly from the system of interlocking directorships that led Morgan partners to hold 72 directorships on the boards of 47 corporations—corporations that were worth $10 billion. A 1912 investigation into these interrelationships led to the passage of the Federal Reserve Act of 1913 and the Clayton Antitrust Act of 1914, the latter of which ended reciprocal directorships.

Following J.P. Morgan's death in 1913, his son, J.P. (Jack) Morgan, Jr., became the firm's senior partner. The company continued to thrive but the disastrous business practices of banks during the 1920s, which played a key role in the subsequent 1929 stock market crash, led to the enactment of new banking regulations in the early 1930s that changed the course of J.P. Morgan's history. The Banking Act of 1933, better known as the Glass-Steagall Act, separated commercial and investment banking. J.P. Morgan & Co. elected to pursue commercial banking and spun off its investment banking business as Morgan Stanley & Co. Incorporated in 1935.

In 1940 J.P. Morgan & Co. Incorporated was incorporated under New York State law. Two years later, the firm went public. Needing more capital and higher lending limits, J.P. Morgan merged with Guaranty Trust Company in 1959 to form Morgan Guaranty Trust Company of New York. Ten years later, a new bank holding company was formed called J.P. Morgan & Co. Incorporated, which had Morgan Guaranty as its principal subsidiary.

During the late 1960s and 1970s J.P. Morgan began venturing back into the investment banking sector but only outside the United States, where Glass-Steagall did not hold sway. Eventually, by the late 1980s, U.S. regulators began loosening the restrictions. The Federal Reserve gave J.P. Morgan permission to underwrite corporate debt securities in 1989, followed one year later by permission to underwrite equities. But J.P. Morgan's move back into investment banking progressed at a slow pace compared to its rivals, who were busily gobbling each other up. Working to build up a new investment banking operation from scratch, J.P. Morgan largely missed out on the great high-tech IPO boom of the late 1990s. At the same time, the company's asset management arm continued to focus on its traditional customers—the elite—meaning that it for the most part missed another boom of the 1990s: individual investing by the masses. Trying to make up for this shortfall, J.P. Morgan in 1997 purchased a 45 percent stake in American Century Investments, the fourth largest direct distributor of mutual funds in the United States.

The J.P. Morgan Chase Era Begins

At the end of 2000, Chase Manhattan acquired J.P. Morgan in a deal valued at about $32 billion. The newly named J.P. Morgan Chase & Co. boasted assets totaling $660 billion, ranking it behind only Citigroup and Bank of America Corporation among financial services firms. Douglas A. Warner III, the head of J.P. Morgan, was named chairman of J.P. Morgan Chase, while Harrison, Chase's head, was named president and CEO. The new banking giant had two main units: J.P. Morgan, comprising global commercial banking services, including investment banking, wealth management, institutional asset management, and private equity; and Chase, the consumer banking operations, including the bank branches in the New York area and in Texas, credit cards, mortgage banking, and consumer lending. Comparing the old Chase with the new J.P. Morgan Chase, the merger greatly reduced the relative size of the consumer operations, from which only about 27 percent of the revenue and 19 percent of the pretax earnings would now be derived. Looking to generate annual cost savings of $3 billion, J.P. Morgan Chase announced that it would be eliminating 5,000 jobs from its workforce, would consolidate the processing systems of its two predecessor firms, and would sell off $500 million in real estate. There was also speculation that, with the heart of the firm clearly on the commercial side, J.P. Morgan Chase might eventually divest some of its consumer businesses, such as credit cards and auto loans, which were being increasingly viewed as noncore operations.

Principal Operating Units

J.P. Morgan; Chase.

Principal Competitors

American Express Company; Bank One Corporation; Bank of America Corporation; The Bank of New York Company, Inc.; The Bear Stearns Companies Inc.; Capital One Financial Corporation; Citigroup Inc.; Credit Suisse First Boston; Deutsche Bank AG; Dime Bancorp, Inc.; First Union Corporation; FleetBoston Financial Corporation; General Electric Capital Corporation; Goldman Sachs Group Inc.; HSBC Holdings plc; Household International, Inc.; KeyCorp; Lehman Brothers Holdings Inc.; MBNA Corporation; Merrill Lynch & Co., Inc.; Morgan Stanley Dean Witter & Co.; UBS AG; Wells Fargo & Company.

Further Reading

Bennett, Robert A., ''Chase's Ambitious Agenda,'' *U.S. Banker,* April 2000, pp. 38–40, 42.

''Chase's Battle to Catch Up: A Shaken Superpower Seeks Its Role in Banking's New World,'' *Business Week,* April 9, 1984, pp. 74+.

Frank, Stephen E., ''Chase Dithers While Other Banks Move,'' *Wall Street Journal,* September 25, 1997, p. C1.

——, ''Chase Gives Its Two Top Officers Shared Power,'' *Wall Street Journal,* December 17, 1997, p. A3.

Gilbert, Alorie, ''Chase.com's Agenda,'' *Information Week,* May 15, 2000, pp. 42–44+.

Hansell, Saul, ''After Chemical Merger, Chase Promotes Itself As a Nimble Bank Giant,'' *New York Times,* September 3, 1996, p. D3.

——, ''Chemical Wins Most Top Posts in Chase Merger,'' *New York Times,* September 29, 1995, p. C1, C6.

——, ''A New Chase Tries to Lead: Will the Merged Bank Be Greater Than Its Parts?,'' *New York Times,* March 29, 1996, p. D1.

Harrison, William B., Jr., ''Chase Manhattan Names a New Chief Executive,'' *New York Times,* March 25, 1999, p. C1.

Holland, Kelley, ''A Chastened Chase: The Humbled Bank Starts to Revive—by Transforming Its Culture,'' *Business Week,* pp. 106–09.

Lipin, Steven, ''Joining Fortunes: Chemical and Chase Set $10 Billion Merger, Forming Biggest Bank,'' *Wall Street Journal,* August 28, 1995, pp. A1, A4.

Lipin, Steven, and E.S. Browning, ''Is New Chase the Bank of the Future?,'' *Wall Street Journal,* September 14, 2000, pp. C1, C4.

Lipin, Steven, et al., ''Blending Legends: Chase Agrees to Buy J.P. Morgan & Co. in a Historic Linkup,'' *Wall Street Journal,* September 13, 2000, pp. A1, A18.

Loomis, Carol J., ''It's a Stronger Bank That David Rockefeller Is Passing to His Successor,'' *Fortune,* January 14, 1980, p. 38.

——, ''The Three Year Deadline at 'David's Bank,' '' *Fortune,* July 1977, p. 70.

McGeehan, Patrick, and Saul Hansell, ''Chase Hopes Deal for Morgan Will Bring It Prestige,'' *New York Times,* September 14, 2000, p. C1.

McLean, Bethany, ''Chasing J.P. Morgan's Assets and Prestige,'' *Fortune,* October 2, 2000, p. 48.

Meehan, John, and Leah J. Nathans, ''Agony at Chase Manhattan: Can Incoming CEO Labrecque Keep the Bank Independent?,'' *Business Week,* October 8, 1990, pp. 32–36.

O'Brien, Timothy L., ''Chase Manhattan Planning to Lay Off 8.5% to 17% of Work Force by Early '96,'' *Wall Street Journal,* June 27, 1995, p. A3.

——, ''The Friendly Merger Banker: At Chase, the Chairman Tries to Make All Sides Winners,'' *New York Times,* June 22, 1999, p. C1.

——, ''Intuit to Unveil On-Line Pact with 20 Firms,'' *Wall Street Journal,* July 14, 1995, pp. A2, A5.

O'Brien, Timothy L., and Steven Lipin, ''In Latest Round of Banking Mergers, Even Big Institutions Become Targets,'' *Wall Street Journal,* July 14, 1995, pp. A3–A4.

Radigan, Joseph, ''Can the New Chase Dominate?,'' *U.S. Banker,* July 1997, pp. 42–44+.

Rea, Alison, and Lisa Sanders, ''Big Bank, Grand Ambition,'' *Business Week,* March 3, 1997, p. 79.

Rogers, David, *The Future of American Banking: Managing for Change,* New York: McGraw-Hill, 1993, 346 p.

Sapsford, Jathon, ''J.P. Morgan, Chase to Form Bank Behemoth,'' *Wall Street Journal,* September 14, 2000, pp. C1, C21.

Sapsford, Jathon, and Gregory Zuckerman, ''Chase Accord Leaves Investors Unconvinced: Hambrecht's Size Provokes Doubts About Potential,'' *Wall Street Journal,* September 29, 1999, p. C1.

Schifrin, Matthew, ''Chase Manhattan's Unsung Turnaround,'' *Forbes,* October 25, 1993, pp. 141–46.

Silverman, Gary, and Louise Lee, ''Chase: Building 'Brick by Brick,' '' *Business Week,* October 11, 1999, pp. 148–50.

Sorkin, Andrew Ross, ''Chase Will Pay $7.7 Billion in Cash and Stock for Fleming,'' *New York Times,* April 12, 2000, p. C4.

Timmons, Heather, et al., ''The Chase to Become a Financial Supermarket,'' *Business Week,* September 25, 2000, pp. 42–44.

Wilson, John Donald, *The Chase: The Chase Manhattan Bank, N.A., 1945–1985,* Boston: Harvard Business School Press, 1986, 432 p.

—updated by David E. Salamie

J Sainsbury plc

J Sainsbury plc

Stamford House
Stamford Street
London SE1 9LL
United Kingdom
Telephone: (020) 7695-6000
Fax: (020) 7695-7610
Web site: http://j-sainsbury.co.uk

Public Company
Incorporated: 1922 as J. Sainsbury Limited
Employees: 183,000
Sales: £16.27 billion (US$25.68 billion) (2000)
Stock Exchanges: London
Ticker Symbol: SBRY
NAIC: 445110 Supermarkets and Other Grocery (Except Convenience) Stores; 522120 Savings Institutions; 233110 Land Subdivision and Land Development

J Sainsbury plc, widely known in its home nation as Sainsbury's, is one of the largest operators of supermarkets in the United Kingdom. There are about 440 Sainsbury's stores in the United Kingdom, the largest of which stock more than 23,000 products; 40 percent of the items carry the Sainsbury's brand. The Sainsbury's chain was once the largest U.K. food retailer, but in the stiffly competitive 1990s Tesco PLC pulled into the lead while ASDA Group Limited, which was purchased by U.S. giant Wal-Mart Stores, Inc. late in the decade, began threatening to drop Sainsbury's to number three. J Sainsbury also owns nearly 170 supermarkets in the northeastern United States operating under the Shaw's and Star Markets names, while Sainsbury's Bank is a joint venture with the Bank of Scotland that runs in-store banks in the United Kingdom offering basic savings accounts, bonds, personal loans, mortgages, and other consumer-oriented financial products. In late 2000 the company was in the process of disposing of two other holdings: the Homebase chain of nearly 300 do-it-yourself (DIY) home centers located throughout the United Kingdom and an 80 percent stake in Sainsbury's Egypt, a chain of more than 100 supermarkets and neighborhood stores in and around Cairo. The founding Sainsbury family still maintains a 30 percent stake in the company.

Early History

Sainsbury's was off to a romantic but practical start in 1869 when two young employees of neighboring London shops met, married, and started a small dairy store in their three-story Drury Lane home. Mary Ann Staples, 19, had grown up in her father's dairy business. John James Sainsbury, 25, had worked for a hardware merchant and grocer. Their shop was a success from the start, as both John and Mary Ann had the business knowledge and capacity for hard work that it took to win the loyalty of the local trade. Their passion for order, cleanliness, and high-quality merchandise made the shop an inviting place, in contrast to the prevalent clutter of many tiny family-owned shops and the unsanitary conditions of the street vendors' stalls and carts.

Seven years later the Sainsburys opened a second shop in a newly developed section of town and moved into the upper portion of the building. Within a few years, they had opened several similar branches, planning to have a shop for each of their sons to manage. By the time their six sons were adults, the branches far outnumbered the family size. Yet caution has always been characteristic of Sainsbury expansion; they regularly passed up opportunities to buy groups or chains of stores, preferring to develop each new store independently.

The passion for high quality led them to a turning point in 1882, when they opened a branch in Croydon. They used advanced design and materials that had an elegance not attempted in the other shops and which made the store easy to keep clean. The walls, floor, and counter fronts were tiled, the countertops were marble slabs. Customers were seated on bentwood chairs. The store's cleanliness—still a rarity in food shops of that time—and elaborate decor helped attract more prosperous customers; it was an instant success. Several similar shops were added during that decade, while Sainsbury's also developed a less elaborate design for suburban branches opened during those years. In these, business could be done through open windows, as in the common market areas, but the design also attracted customers to come into the store to see a greater variety of food.

Company Perspectives:

Sainsbury's Supermarkets was established in 1869 by John James and Mary Ann Sainsbury and is Britain's longest standing major food retailing chain. The founders' principles and values guide us as strongly today as they did at the outset—to be the customer's first choice for food shopping by providing high quality, value for money, excellent service, and attention to detail.

In 1890, Sainsbury's moved its headquarters to Blackfriars, where it remained throughout the 20th century. The location provided easy access to wholesale markets and transportation. To obtain the best quality in food, Sainsbury's always kept in close touch with suppliers, and it controlled and distributed stock from a central depot until the 1960s.

Steady Growth in the Early 20th Century

By the beginning of the 20th century sons John Benjamin, George, and Arthur were working in the family business; they and other company employees were trained with equal care and attention to detail. Alfred and Paul went through the same training when they joined the company in 1906 and 1921, respectively. Frank, the third son, took up poultry and pork farming in 1902 and became a major supplier.

During this time, in terms of numbers, rivals seemed to be outdistancing Sainsbury's. Lipton's, the largest, had 500 stores. It took Sainsbury's another 14 years to open its 115th branch. But Sainsbury's continued to place the highest priority on quality, taking the time to weigh each decision, whether it meant researching suppliers for a new product, assessing the reliability of a new supplier, or measuring the business potential of a new site.

The outbreak of World War I slowed expansion plans even further. Rationing and shortages of food, particularly fresh produce, led to the creation of grocery departments selling jams, spices, potted meat, and flour—all bearing Sainsbury's own label. Women began attending the training classes at the Blackfriars headquarters, to replace the male employees who had left for military service. Some worked in the packing plant for Sainsbury-label foods; others served as salespeople in the stores.

Eldest son John Benjamin took much of the initiative in the interwar years, adding new grocery lines while retaining his father's insistence on high quality. By 1922 there were 136 branches, many of them along the new suburban rail lines, and the firm was incorporated as J. Sainsbury Limited. Mary Ann died in 1927 and her husband in 1928, leaving John Benjamin in charge. By this time, so much public attention accompanied branch openings that when Sainsbury's opened a branch in Cambridge, it published an apology in the local newspaper for the impact of a huge opening day crowd. Altogether, 57 new branches were opened between 1919 and 1929, and the gilded glass Sainsbury sign had become a universal symbol of a spacious, orderly interior displaying foods of the finest quality.

There was an apparent break with tradition in 1936 when Sainsbury's bought the Thoroughgood stores, a chain of nine shops in Britain's Midlands. However, the purchase was made with the same care and emphasis on quality that had distinguished all other Sainsbury branches. Stamford House, which had been built in 1912 as an extension of the headquarters at Blackfriars, was extended to provide more space for the centralized supply procurement and distribution that maintained quality control for all branches, which by this time numbered 244. Specially designed lightweight vans had replaced horse-drawn vehicles, further speeding deliveries.

World War II not only slowed Sainsbury's growth through shortages of food and labor, but also brought the stores into the line of fire. Some branches were totally destroyed; others were extensively damaged. Vehicles carrying mobile shops carried on trade as far as possible in the areas affected by the Blitz. Yet the evacuation of bomb-damaged areas made it impossible to continue the centralized procurement and distribution operation that had provided efficiency, economy, and standardization of products and services. Along with other wartime restrictions, this caused sales to dwindle to half the prewar level.

John Benjamin's sons Alan and Robert, who had shared the general manager's post since their father's retirement in 1938, became aware of the crucial role of communications during the trying days of this wartime decentralization. The *JS Journal,* begun in 1946 (and its sister publication, the *Employee Report,* begun in the late 1970s) exemplified the thorough job of reporting that kept staff members abreast of company developments and business conditions. Both publications have won national awards for excellence.

Postwar Recovery

Long before the last of the wartime restrictions were lifted in 1954, the brothers had begun an aggressive recovery program. Basic operations were recentralized to regain the economies of scale that kept prices down while retaining a substantial profit margin. Alan studied America's burgeoning supermarkets and opened the first self-service Sainsbury's in June 1950 in Croydon, where his grandfather had opened his "turning point" store nearly 70 years earlier.

Expansion in the 1950s often meant converting existing stores to supermarkets in addition to adding new outlets. In 1955, the 7,500-square-foot Sainsbury's at Lewisham was considered the largest supermarket in Europe. By 1969, Sainsbury supermarkets had an average of 10,000 square feet of space. Supermarkets and hypermarkets in the 1980s would triple that amount.

John Benjamin and Arthur were the only two of the founders' sons whose own sons joined the family business. Arthur's son James, who had joined the company in 1926, was named Commander of the Order of the British Empire for his accomplishments. He created new factory facilities at Sainsbury's headquarters in 1936 and also set up the Haverhill line of meat products.

John Benjamin's sons Alan and Robert, and Alan's son John, were also honored for their work. Alan was made Baron Sainsbury of Drury Lane in 1962, and his son John was made Baron Sainsbury of Preston Candover in 1989. Robert was knighted in 1967. Alan and Robert shared the presidency of

Key Dates:

1869: John James and Mary Ann Sainsbury open a small dairy store in their Drury Lane home.
1882: First branch outside London is opened in Croydon.
1922: Firm is incorporated as J. Sainsbury Limited.
1936: The Thoroughgood chain is acquired.
1950: First self-service Sainsbury's opens in Croydon.
1971: The period after the initial J is dropped from the company name.
1973: Company goes public as J Sainsbury plc.
1977: First Savacentre hypermarket opens.
1981: First Homebase home and garden center is opened.
1987: Sainsbury gains full control of the U.S. chain Shaw's Supermarkets.
1995: The Texas Homecare chain is acquired from Ladbroke Group.
1997: Sainsbury's Bank is launched.
2000: Sainsbury agrees to sell Homebase chain and Sainsbury's Egypt.

Sainsbury's, John was chairman, and Robert's son David was deputy chairman through the 1980s.

With typical caution, Sainsbury's did not actually use the word supermarket in its own communications until the late 1960s, even though it owned almost 100. Nonetheless, the company was at the forefront of new technology. In 1961, for example, Sainsbury's became Britain's first food retailer to computerize its distribution system. In the late 1980s, electronic cash registers at the checkout counter were replaced by scanners. Multibuy, a special feature of the scanning system, automatically applied a discount to multiple purchases of certain designated items. Spaceman, a microcomputer planning system, used on-screen graphics to plot the allocation of merchandise to specific shelf space in the stores. Electric funds transferred at the point of sale (EFTPOS), allowed customers to use debit cards to make purchases.

Diversifying in the 1970s and 1980s

Sainsbury's centenary, 1969, sparked a series of rapid changes. Alan's son, John, became chairman of a new management tier, which reported directly to the board of directors. Departmental directors were given greater responsibility for operating functions to strengthen the centralized control that had always been company policy. With ordering, warehousing, and distribution computerized, strict controls on the speeded-up activity were vital. Sainsbury's became a public company in 1973, two years after making a name change: the period after the initial J was dropped.

Personnel policies at Sainsbury's adhered closely to the principles established at its founding: thorough training, open communication, and continuing training on the job. The company recruited actively at schools and universities, preferring to "grow its own talent," but holding employees to high standards of performance. Along with other leading companies and the City University Business School, Sainsbury's conducted a practical management course, the Management M.B.A. Sainsbury's employees participated in profit sharing and share option schemes.

The company's community involvement was also active, taking many forms. John Sainsbury addressed the London Conference on saving the ozone layer early in 1989. The only retailer invited to take part in the conference and the associated exhibition, he presented details of the technological changes made in Sainsbury's aerosol products and plant operations to eliminate chlorofluorocarbons from their operations. Incubation of small start-up businesses, arts sponsorships, and grand-scale charity drives were other ongoing projects.

Forces within the grocery industry compelled Sainsbury's to begin a program of diversification within the retail category. Increased competition from discounters threatened to squeeze profit margins. Creeping market saturation and flat population growth combined to intensify competition as well. Sainsbury's began to make significant additions to its nonfood merchandise for the first time. The company's first petrol station, a convenience for shoppers, was opened in 1974 at a Cambridge store. To gain the economies of direct supplier-to-store deliveries, Sainsbury's formed a joint venture with British Home Stores in 1975, launching a chain of hypermarkets—huge stores combining grocery items and hard goods—called Savacentre; the first Savacentre opened in 1977 in Washington, Tyne and Wear. Sainsbury's retained control of all food-related operations, leaving nonfood lines to its partner until 1989, when Savacentre became a wholly owned subsidiary of Sainsbury's. Meanwhile, Sainsbury's opened a Savacentre hypermarket in Scotland in 1984.

Homebase, a chain of upscale DIY stores, was in the planning stage by 1979. Sainsbury's owned 75 percent of this joint venture, and Grand Bazaar Innovations Bon Marché, Belgium's largest retailer (later known as GIB Group), owned the remaining 25 percent. The partners opened their first Homebase home and garden center in 1981, and had expanded the chain to 76 locations by the mid-1990s.

Sainsbury's looked to overseas markets for growth opportunities as well. In 1983, the company began to amass shares in Shaw's Supermarkets, a New England supermarket chain founded in 1860. Shaw's heritage of carrying high-quality food at the lowest prices meshed well with the ideals of the British firm. Moreover, like Sainsbury's, Shaw's had also been at the forefront of computer technology. By 1987, Sainsbury's had completed the purchase of 100 percent of the 60 stores in Massachusetts, Maine, and New Hampshire, and had plans to open additional stores in that area.

Challenging Times in the Highly Competitive 1990s

The company boosted its holdings in the United States with the 1994 acquisition of a 50 percent voting stake and 16 percent nonvoting equity in Giant Food Inc., a Washington, D.C.-area chain with 159 stores. Sainsbury's increased its nonvoting equity to 20 percent in 1996 and was widely expected to purchase the remaining shares by the end of the decade, but Dutch retailer Royal Ahold N.V. stepped in during 1998 to acquire all of Giant Food.

Sainsbury's also developed a powerful private-label program. By the mid-1990s, its own-label products generated 66 percent of total sales. Three of the company's proprietary products in particular made headlines in the early 1990s. Novon, a laundry detergent introduced in 1992, marked Sainsbury's move into head-to-head competition with national brands. Within just six weeks of Novon's launch, the company's share of the detergents market doubled to 20 percent. In 1994, Sainsbury's changed the formulation and packaging of its own cola beverage, reintroducing it as ''Classic Cola.'' The budget-priced cola featured red cans with italicized letters and a stripe; ads promoted the drink's ''Original American Taste.'' Within just a few weeks, Classic Cola won 13 percent of Britain's total cola market, while sales of both Coca-Cola and Pepsi at Sainsbury stores plummeted. Not surprisingly, an incensed Coca-Cola demanded that Sainsbury's modify its packaging, claiming that the brands' similarity prevented customers from discerning between them. The supermarket chain acquiesced, but significantly decreased the rival brand's share of shelf space in stores.

Another highly successful, but less confrontational, private-label product also broke new ground for the category. In 1993, the company launched its own periodical, *Sainsbury's: The Magazine*. Like the publications it competed with, *Sainsbury's: The Magazine* featured illustrated pieces on fashion, health, and cooking, as well as national brand advertising. Sold only in Sainsbury's supermarkets, the magazine became ''the most successful new magazine venture in Britain in many years,'' according to a November 1994 *Forbes* article.

Under the leadership of Chairman, CEO, and great grandson of the founders David Sainsbury, who took over leadership from his cousin John in 1992, sales tripled from £3 billion in 1985 to £10.6 billion in 1994. During the early 1990s, however, Sainsbury's began losing ground to competitors ASDA, Safeway, and Tesco. Perhaps because of arrogance and complacency or the distractions of its forays into the U.S. market and the DIY sector, Sainsbury's core U.K. supermarket operations lost their edge in a number of areas, including price, customer service, and innovation. Customers began perceiving, rightly or wrongly, Sainsbury's as higher in price than the competition, as offering too many private label products in comparison to name brands, as having insufficient staff to help customers in the aisles, and as having longer checkout lines. Both Tesco and Safeway gained sales through the introduction of loyalty cards, a new marketing practice initially scorned by Sainsbury's and then belatedly embraced through the June 1996 launch of the Reward Card. In 1995 Tesco displaced Sainsbury's from its perch as the top grocery retailer in the United Kingdom. For the fiscal year ending in February 1996 Sainsbury's posted its first profit decline in 22 years.

Among management's first moves aimed at turning the company's fortunes around was a mid-1995 customer service initiative that involved the addition of more than 5,000 staff to man service counters, help customers in the aisles, and pack the groceries. Management changes were also afoot, including the replacement of the marketing director. On the DIY front, meantime, Sainsbury's completed the acquisition of the Texas Homecare chain from Ladbroke Group PLC in March 1995 for £290 million. Texas Homecare held 7.6 percent of the U.K. DIY market. With the acquired units slowly being converted to the Homebase brand, Homebase by the late 1990s became the number two DIY chain in the United Kingdom, trailing only B&Q, which was owned by Kingfisher plc. In August 1996 Sainsbury's gained full control of Homebase when it bought out its partner in the venture, GIB Group, for £66 million.

In a new attempt at innovation, Sainsbury's launched Sainsbury's Bank in February 1997, becoming the first supermarket firm to open a fully licensed retail bank. A joint venture 55 percent owned by Sainsbury and 45 percent by Bank of Scotland, Sainsbury's Bank initially offered telephone banking services in Sainsbury supermarkets, including two credit cards and two savings accounts. By early 1998 the new bank had 700,000 customer accounts with £1.5 billion on deposit and had begun offering personal loans and mortgages. A whole host of additional financial services were introduced over the new few years. Sainsbury's Bank was profitable for the first time in fiscal 2000.

During 1997 Dino Adriano, who had joined Sainsbury in 1964 as a trainee accountant and had previously served as chairman of Homebase, was named group chief executive. Then, in a historic development, David Sainsbury in May 1998 announced his retirement as chairman in order to take on a political appointment as minister for science in Tony Blair's administration. In July 1998 George Bull, who had been serving as chairman of Diageo plc, took over as chairman of Sainsbury, becoming the first nonfamily member to head the company.

Under the new leadership, Sainsbury's continued to struggle and faced a new threat from ASDA following its 1998 acquisition by U.S. retailing giant Wal-Mart Stores. While Tesco had largely replaced Sainsbury's as the U.K. supermarket chain known for quality—and had thereby become the first choice for most middle- and upper-middle-class shoppers—ASDA began emphasizing the everyday-low-price scheme of its new parent, quickly becoming the price leader and gaining both working class and middle class customers in the process. Sainsbury's seemed to be lost between these two rivals and their respective niches. One response to the ASDA insurgency was Sainsbury's ''low price guarantee'' launched in October 1999, which promised to match the lowest prices on 1,600 commonly purchased products, including name brand items. Sainsbury's also began adding nonfood items to its supermarkets' shelves, something its competitors had done several years previous. Needing funds to begin a store remodeling campaign, Sainsbury's cut 2,000 jobs from its workforce in 1999.

In contrast to the difficulties of the U.K. supermarket operations, Sainsbury's Shaw's and Homebase units were thriving. Shaw's was bolstered in June 1999 through the acquisition of Star Markets for US$476 million. Star Markets operated in the Greater Boston and Cape Cod areas. A venture into a new foreign territory began in March 1999 when Sainsbury purchased a 25.1 percent stake in Edge SAE, a retail food chain based in Cairo, Egypt. Six months later the stake was increased to 80.1 percent and the company was later renamed Sainsbury's Egypt.

Fiscal 2000 proved to be another difficult year for Sainsbury's. Profits fell 23 percent as the U.K. supermarkets operations suffered a significant profit decline that far outweighed the strong performance at Shaw's and Homebase. This prompted another management shakeup, and in March 2000 Peter Davis took over as chief executive from the retiring Adriano. Davis had most recently been chief executive at Prudential plc, the largest life insurance firm in England, and had served as marketing director at Sainsbury's from 1976 to 1986.

Within months of the appointment of Davis, Sainsbury's appeared to be moving more quickly and decisively to engineer a turnaround. Davis quickened the pace of restructuring in the U.K. supermarkets, aiming to overhaul the entire store network within three years, rather than the eight years outlined previously. A major cost-cutting campaign that aimed at reducing annual operating expenditures by £600 million was initiated. Perhaps most importantly, Davis was attempting to fashion a successful niche for Sainsbury's, aiming to tout the stores' quality and range of products and to not compete with Tesco and ASDA on price. This was a risky strategy but Davis had apparently concluded that competing on price played into his competitors' strengths.

As this restructuring was being launched, Sainsbury also began pulling back from its diversification program, intending to concentrate on turning around the U.K. supermarkets. In mid-2000 Sainsbury began shopping Homebase around, and in December of that year reached an agreement to sell the home improvement chain for £969 million (US$1.4 billion) in a complex three-way transaction. The Homebase chain itself was slated to go to Schroder Ventures, a U.K. private equity firm, while 28 development sites were to be purchased by Kingfisher, owner of the rival B&Q chain. Sainsbury would also reinvest £31 million in Homebase, resulting in a 17.8 percent stake. By retaining a stake, Sainsbury hoped to profit from a potential sale or IPO involving Homebase. Proceeds from the sale of Homebase were earmarked for the supermarket remodeling program and for upgrading Sainsbury's information technology systems as part of the efficiency drive.

Also in December 2000, Sainsbury announced that it had reached an agreement to sell its Egyptian supermarket chain to three Arab companies, who planned to remove the Sainsbury name from the stores. The venture was troubled from the start. Sainsbury had been the first international supermarket chain to enter the Egyptian market and was supported by the Egyptian government, but local supermarket owners were fearful of the new foreign competition and consumers began a boycott believing that Sainsbury would put local shops out of business. In October 2000 an outbreak of violence in the West Bank spread into Egypt when rumors that the Sainsbury chain was connected with Israel circulated, leading to the vandalizing of Sainsbury stores in Cairo. Sainsbury Egypt was also suffering mounting losses.

These disposals would reduce the company to the Sainsbury's chain in the United Kingdom, the increasingly successful Sainsbury's Bank, and Shaw's in the United States, the 12th largest U.S. food retailer with annual revenues of about US$4 billion. There was much speculation that Sainsbury would exit the U.S. market as well, but evidence to the contrary surfaced in November 2000 when the company agreed to purchase 18 Grand Union stores in Vermont and Connecticut. One further development in late 2000 was the announcement that Sainsbury would move its headquarters from the Stamford House complex at Blackfriars to Holborn Place in London. This development too was part of Davis's drive to make the company more efficient as the new site would be more modern and would enable a consolidation of a number of key staff within one location. It was becoming ever clearer that the new management at Sainsbury was quickening the pace of change and laying the foundation for a turnaround that would be quite remarkable.

Principal Subsidiaries

Sainsbury's Supermarkets Ltd.; J Sainsbury Developments Ltd.; Shaw's Supermarkets Inc. (U.S.A.); Sainsbury's Bank plc (55%).

Principal Competitors

ASDA Group Limited; Hannaford Bros. Co.; Safeway plc; The Stop & Shop Companies, Inc.; Tesco PLC.

Further Reading

Bagnall, Sarah, "How King of the Grocers Was Eased Off Its Throne: Arrogance and Complacency Blamed for Sainsbury's Decline," *Times* (London), May 9, 1996.

Beck, Ernest, "Britain's Ailing Sainsbury Faces Stark Choice," *Wall Street Journal,* October 25, 1999, p. A49I.

Bernoth, Ardyn, and Matthew Lynn, "Counter Attack: Profile—David Sainsbury," *Times* (London), January 14, 1996.

Brown-Humes, Christopher, "Humble Pie on Offer at Sainsbury," *Financial Times,* May 11, 1996, p. 5.

Buckley, Neil, "A Long Shopping List to Regain Lost Momentum: Sainsbury's Sales and Margins Have Caused Analysts Concern," *Financial Times,* November 2, 1995, p. 19.

——, "Super Service," *Financial Times,* June 16, 1995, p. 16.

Churchill, David, "How Precision Boosts Sainsbury's Productivity," *Financial Times,* January 11, 1982, p. 10.

Cope, Nigel, "Checking Out," *Management Today,* February 2000, pp. 66–71.

Davidson, Andrew, "Dino Adriano," *Management Today,* March 1999, pp. 62+.

De Jonquieres, Guy, and John Thornhill, "Family Still Minding the Store," *Financial Times,* July 1, 1991, p. 30.

East, Robert, *The Anatomy of Conquest: Tesco Versus Sainsbury,* Kingston Upon Thames, United Kingdom: Kingston Business School, 1997.

The First 120 Years of Sainsbury's, 1869–1989, London: Sainsbury's, 1989.

Hollinger, Peggy, "Politic Departure Ends Six Years in the Chair and Rings Down the Curtain on Six Generations of Sainsburys at the Helm," *Financial Times,* May 7, 1998, p. 24.

——, "The Poser for the Pragmatist at Sainsbury's," *Financial Times,* May 31, 2000, p. 30.

——, "Sainsbury: Supermarkets, Super Margins, Superseded," *Financial Times,* October 30, 1996, p. 25.

——, "The Vision to Overcome a Mountain of Problems," *Financial Times,* June 1, 2000, p. 28.

Hunt, Jonathan, "Sainsbury's: The Innovative Traditionists," *Chief Executive,* October 1985, pp. 12+.

JS 100: The Story of Sainsbury's, London: Sainsbury's, 1969.

Kennedy, Carol, *The Merchant Princes: Family, Fortune, and Philanthropy—Cadbury, Sainsbury, and John Lewis,* London: Hutchinson, 2000, 309 p.

——, "Public Company, Private Dynasty," *Director,* December 1992, p. 46.

Marcom, John, Jr., "Britain's Sainsbury to Buy Rest of Shaw's in a Cautious Approach to Growth in U.S.," *Wall Street Journal,* June 22, 1987.

Nicholas, Ruth, "Sainsbury Cola Gives in to Coke," *Marketing,* May 12, 1994, p. 1.

Parkes, Christopher, ''Fattened Up in Readiness for a New Boston Tea-Party: Sainsbury Set to Take Full Control of Shaw's,'' *Financial Times,* June 20, 1987, p. 8.

Raghavan, Anita, and Ernest Beck, ''Sainsbury Enters Talks to Sell Homebase Stores,'' *Wall Street Journal,* November 29, 2000, p. A23.

Rogers, David, ''Britain's Supermarkets: An Industry in Turmoil,'' *Supermarket Business,* August 1989, p. 37.

Stogel, Chuck, ''The Once and Future King?,'' *Brandweek,* May 8, 1995, p. 34.

Tait, Nikki, ''From High Road to Main Street,'' *Financial Times,* November 20, 1991, p. 20.

Urry, Maggie, ''Developing 'Softly Softly' Outside the Mainstream,'' *Financial Times,* May 20, 1988, p. 12.

Williams, B.R., *The Best Butter in the World: A History of Sainsbury's,* London: Ebury, 1994.

Wilsher, Peer. ''Housekeeping?,'' *Management Today,* December 1993, p. 38.

Zwiebach, Elliot, ''Sainsbury to Buy 50 Percent of Giant's Voting Stock,'' *Supermarket News,* October 10, 1994, p. 1.

—Betty T. Moore and April Dougal Gasbarre
—updated by David E. Salamie

Jetro Cash & Carry Enterprises Inc.

15-24 132nd Street
College Point, New York 11356
U.S.A.
Telephone: (718) 762-8700
Fax: (718) 762-8335
Web site: http://www.jetrord.com

Private Company
Incorporated: 1976
Employees: 2,000
Sales: $440 million (1999 est.)
NAIC: 42185 Service Establishment Equipment & Supplies Wholesalers; 42241 General Line Grocery Wholesalers

Jetro Cash & Carry Enterprises Inc. is a private company with two units: Jetro Cash & Carry, a wholesale grocery operation that operates cash-and-carry warehouses stocking a broad variety of items, including Jetro's own private-label ones; and majority-owned Restaurant Depot, a similar wholesale cash-and-carry operation with warehouses selling food, paper supplies, and tabletop items to restaurants nationwide. Jetro Cash & Carry differs from conventional wholesalers in not providing delivery of goods nor requiring a minimum order. In some ways it resembles a warehouse club, but it does not charge a membership fee and only accepts trade customers, not individuals. Restaurant Depot, with sales volume at about one-third of Jetro Cash & Carry's, functions in the same way. Jetro Cash & Carry Enterprises is a division of Jetro Holdings, Inc., which is owned in large part by Metro, a German retailer whose parent company is Swiss-based Metro Holding AG.

Jetro Cash & Carry: 1976–2000

Jetro Cash & Carry was founded in 1976 by private investors and soon spread its operations from New York City to California, New Jersey, Miami, and Philadelphia. By the mid-1980s the warehouse buying-club concept was well established. Like these enterprises, Jetro was housed in no-frills, bare-to-the-walls concrete floor and exposed ceiling facilities with merchandise piled high and sold at wholesale prices for the customer to take away. Unlike them, however, Jetro was open only to the trade (such as grocers, restaurateurs, and institutions) and charged no membership fee.

Jetro had revenues of $361 million in 1996. Any retailer or foodservice buyer who brought in a resale tax certificate in his or her name was entitled to obtain a Jetro customer membership card with no minimum purchase required. The company maintained 15 warehouses in 2000, of which four were in New York City. There were five more in California, with three in Los Angeles and one each in Oakland and South San Francisco. Jetro also had warehouses in Baltimore, Chicago, Jersey City, Miami, Philadelphia, and in Northborough, Massachusetts. The company maintained area offices in Atlanta, Chicago, Houston, Los Angeles, New York, and San Diego.

Jetro was distributing more than 11,000 products in 2000 at each of its locations. Product lines consisted of the following: automotive supplies; baked goods; barbecue accessories; beverages; bulk foods; candy; canned goods; chemical supplies; coffee/tea; convenience foods; cooking equipment; cookware; cutlery; dairy; delicatessen; foodservice equipment/supplies; frozen food; general merchandise; grocery; hardware; industrial wraps; light kitchen equipment; linens; meat and poultry; over-the-counter drugs; paper products; party supplies; pet supplies; plasticware; produce; refrigerated entrees; sanitary equipment and supplies; school supplies; seafood; serving equipment; small appliances; snack food; specialty/gourmet; stationery; tabletop/tableware; tobacco; toys; video; refrigeration equipment; heavy kitchen equipment; brewing equipment; and storage equipment. Its private-label offerings included groceries under the Red & White name.

The markets being served by Jetro Cash & Carry were convenience and discount stores, drug and health-and-beauty-aids stores, grocery stores, hardware stores and home centers, restaurants, and institutional accounts. The number of foodservice accounts served was about 50,000. Jetro also was providing shopping guides, store directories, and warehouse staff to assist customers in locating the products they needed, seven days a week. Its customers were small shopkeepers and res-

Company Perspectives:

Jetro Cash & Carry is the nation's leading wholesale grocer. Jetro introduces supermarket style wholesale shopping for retailers and institutional (foodservice) buyers throughout parts of the United States with over 11,000 products at each location at your disposal.

taurateurs turning up at its warehouses. ''We buy from manufacturers and make it available to them on a when-needed basis,'' CEO Stanley Fleishman told *Newsday* in 2000. ''Small grocery stores often have a tough time getting small quantities of product when they need them,'' he added. Fleishman said Jetro was providing a greater variety of product than most bulk-discount wholesalers. The company's slogan was, ''We are your one-stop warehouse for savings, selection and service, seven days a week.'' Metro purchased its stake in Jetro Holdings in 2000. Active in 18 countries, it was expecting much of Jetro's growth to come from the western United States.

Restaurant Depot: 1990–2000

Restaurant Depot was founded by Jerry Cohen in 1990 in Elmhurst, a community in New York City's borough of Queens. Like Jetro, it was a wholesaler with similarities to the warehouse clubs that were attracting a number of foodservice small businesses, such as ''ma and pa'' restaurants and small catering companies. Like these clubs, Restaurant Depot offered no credit or delivery service, fielded no salespeople or displays, and did not advertise in the mass media. To become a member required a resale or business license. In addition to low prices, Restaurant Depot offered the convenience and flexibility of buying in odd lots from day to day.

Restaurant Depot offered restaurateurs savings of up to 30 percent on more than 10,000 items, ranging from produce to paper goods and flatware. About half of these customers' savings came from eliminating trucking and delivery overhead, and the rest derived from high volume and a no-frills location with more than 55,000 square feet of selling space. These customers included delicatessen and coffee shop owners, as well as schools and other institutions. The staff was helpful in advising customers on the kinds of equipment and products they would need to open their own businesses. At this time Restaurant Depot also was open to the public, with Cohen describing housewives as constituting five to ten percent of the warehouse's business. Jeff Weinstein of the *Village Voice* visited the store in 1992, noting its ''elephantile'' shopping carts and bargains such as 24 eight-ounce bottles of San Pellegrino water for $12.95.

By the summer of 1994 Restaurant Depot was a division of Jetro. The Elmhurst warehouse had done so well, with sales volume of more than $100,000 a week, that the company began to open new outlets, including one in Pompano Beach, Florida. There were eight in early 1998, consisting, in addition to the ones in Elmhurst and Pompano Beach, of facilities in Baltimore; Chelsea, Massachusetts; Fountain Valley, California; Philadelphia; Plainview, Long Island; and South Hackensack,

Key Dates:

1976: Jetro Cash & Carry Enterprises is founded by private investors.
1990: Restaurant Depot is founded by Jerry Cohen.
1994: Restaurant Depot becomes a Jetro division.
2000: Metro, a German retailer, takes a majority stake in Jetro.

New Jersey. By this time the general public was no longer permitted entry; a free membership card was provided to those in the trade after presentation of a resale certification or tax-exempt number. Large orders could be called in and loaded onto trucks supplied by the customer. The Chelsea warehouse, a 52,000-square-foot facility a few blocks from the New England Produce Market, was aimed at Boston's restaurant industry and included a tabletop and restaurant equipment department, weekly product tastings, and food preparation demonstrations. Two years later, the warehouse manager said it had become a primary resource for start-up restaurants and smaller mom-and-pop operators.

Restaurant Depot opened another Long Island-based warehouse in 1998, in Bohemia, a Suffolk County community. The 36-foot-high, 44,000-square-foot building included a three-bay loading dock and a 6,000-square-foot built-in refrigerator/freezer. Like other company warehouses it was open seven days a week, although with limited hours on weekends. In this way a restaurateur who, for example, ran short of supplies on Saturday, could walk in and purchase needed goods on Sunday morning.

In early 2000 Restaurant Depot opened a new 45,000-square-foot warehouse in Pittsburgh, on the Allegheny River shore. Jetro's director of marketing claimed that, like the division's other warehouses, it would typically be able to sell its food products and restaurant equipment at 15 to 25 percent less than its competitors. By the fall of 2000, Restaurant Depot had opened five or six other warehouses, not counting the ones in Bohemia and Pittsburgh. In all there were at least 17 Restaurant Depot warehouses. Three were in California (Fountain Valley, Oakland, and San Diego), three in New Jersey (Kenilworth, Pennsauken, and South Hackensack), and three in New York (Bohemia, Elmhurst, and Plainview). Two were in Illinois (Alsip and Des Plaines) and two in Pennsylvania (Philadelphia and Pittsburgh). Others were in Baltimore, Chelsea, Milwaukee, and Pompano Beach. Customers consisted of convenience and grocery stores, restaurants, and institutional accounts. About 70,000 accounts were being served.

Restaurant Depot described itself in 2000 as selling a full range of fresh meat and produce, chicken and pork, frozen products, dry groceries, paper and cleaning supplies, beverages, and equipment. Its locations were being staffed by former restaurant owners, chefs, and foodservice specialists available for consultation. A monthly flyer of specials was being mailed to all registered customers. There was no minimum order.

Principal Competitors

Bozzuto's Inc.; Costco Wholesale Corp.; Di Giorgio Corp.; Krasdale Foods Inc.; Key Food Stores Cooperative Inc.; Harold

Levinson Associates; Penn Traffic Co.; Sam's Wholesale Clubs.

Further Reading

Anastasi, Nick, "Growing Restaurant Depot Chain Hungry for Suffolk," *Long Island Business News,* August 24, 1998, p. 3A.

Directory of Wholesale Grocers 2000, Tampa: Business Guides, Inc., 2000, pp. 366–67.

Donegan, Priscilla, "Wholesale Clubs: What the Fuss Is All About," *Progressive Grocer,* May 1988, pp. 94–96, 98, 101.

Gault, Ylonda, "Restaurateurs Find a 1-Stop Savings Site," *Crain's New York Business,* August 24, 1992, p. 5.

Long, Dolores, "Buying Clubs Take Off," *Restaurant Business,* June 10, 1986, pp. 338, 340, 342.

"Metro Set to Buy Jetro," *Eurofood,* March 30, 2000, p. 2.

Schooley, Tim, "Restaurant Depot to Open Supply Shop in Strip District," *Pittsburgh Business Times,* January 7, 2000, p. 1.

Shillington, Patty, "Warehouse Store Caters to Restaurants," *Miami Herald,* August 3, 1996, p. 70.

Smith, Samantha T., "Restaurant Warehouse to Open This Week," *Boston Business Journal,* January 2, 1998, p. 3.

"Top 100 Private Companies," *Newsday,* September 17, 2000, pp. C42, C44.

Weinstein, Jeff, "Demand and Supply," *Village Voice,* October 13, 1992, p. 54.

—Robert Halasz

Juno Online Services, Inc.

1540 Broadway, 27th Floor
New York, New York 10036
U.S.A.
Telephone: (212) 597-9000
Fax: (212) 597-9100
Web site: http://www.juno.com

Public Company
Incorporated: 1999
Employees: 263
Sales: $114.0 million (2000)
Stock Exchanges: NASDAQ
Ticker Symbol: JWEB
NAIC: 514191 Online Information Services

Juno Online Services, Inc., the company known for providing free, advertising-supported e-mail service, has yet to turn a profit since launching its service in April 1996. After building up its computer systems and related infrastructure, it began offering billable Internet access and enhanced e-mail in 1998. As of late 2000 Juno offered three levels of service. The company's basic service provides free Internet access and free e-mail. The next level is Juno Web, which provides priority access to the World Wide Web, free live technical support, more local access telephone numbers, and other features. The third and highest level, Juno Express, is a broadband service available in certain markets that employs DSL technology for high-speed Internet access. From a peak of more than seven million subscribers in 1999, Juno's subscriber base had dropped in late 2000 to approximately 3.4 million subscribers. Nevertheless, it was still the third largest dial-up Internet service provider (ISP) behind America Online, Inc. and EarthLink, Inc.

Building Subscriber Base with Free e-mail: 1995–98

Juno Online Services L.P. was established in June 1995 as a subsidiary of investment firm D.E. Shaw & Co. with a $20 million investment. Charles Ardai, then 25 years old, was president, and David E. Shaw was the company's chairman. Shaw was also CEO of D.E. Shaw & Co., where Ardai was employed as senior vice-president. It was reportedly Ardai who convinced Shaw that free e-mail would be a ''killer app'' around which to build an entire business. Within a month Juno announced it would provide free e-mail service that would be supported by advertising revenue. Another company, FreeMark Communications of Cambridge, Massachusetts, announced that it would offer a similar service by the end of 1995.

On April 22, 1996, Juno launched its free e-mail service. Customers would receive free e-mail in exchange for permitting advertising on their computer screens and providing demographic information about themselves. This information would be provided to advertisers, who could then target their advertising messages appropriately. Initial reaction was skeptical since the software was not downloadable over the Internet; Juno would send it on a disk via regular mail. Through an arrangement with AT&T Corp., Juno's service began with 200 points of presence, or local access telephone numbers, as well as a toll-free telephone number.

Juno began with 15 sponsoring advertisers, including Snapple and Land's End. Advertisers would pay Juno only for ads that were delivered to Juno subscribers. The company was seeking to have its software bundled with computers and had signed deals with two of the top ten PC makers by the April launch. FreeMark's competing e-mail service launched on May 6, 1996.

By June 1996 it was announced that WorldCom Inc., the fourth largest long-distance provider in the United States, would provide the fiber-optic network for Juno's e-mail service. In its first months Juno's service proved very popular and was expected to have a six-figure membership by the end of June. Juno spread the word about its service through traditional advertising methods, including ads in magazines, newspapers, and billboards.

Juno was attracting numerous advertisers as well. Advertisers could target their messages and be assured that they were at least seen, if not read. Since Juno's service was free, it was felt that customers would not abandon the service, as they were doing with paid services such as America Online (AOL) and CompuServe (which would ultimately be acquired by AOL).

Company Perspectives:

Juno is a leading provider of Internet-related services to millions of computer users throughout the United States. We offer several levels of service, ranging from basic dial-up Internet access—which is provided to the end user for free—to competitively priced broadband Internet access. Our strategy of offering several different service levels and our easy-to-use, intuitive software are designed to attract a broad spectrum of users, including the millions of people who are only now beginning to explore the Internet.

In September modem manufacturer U.S. Robotics agreed to include Juno software on CD-ROMs that were shipped with the company's modems. Juno also signed software distribution agreements with Blockbuster Video, the Sam Goody chain of music stores, mail-order music service BMG Direct, and the Billboard Music Guide.

Other companies also were offering free e-mail service. In September *PC Magazine* reviewed three services: Juno, Freemark Mail, and HotMail. Juno and Freemark were dial-up services, whereas HotMail was accessible from any computer with a Web browser. In a sense, HotMail was not actually free, because it required Internet access. The magazine found that Juno offered more features, allowing users to save messages as text files, save addresses to an address book, and import entire message folders. Its interface resembled Windows, and users could change fonts, text, and background colors. Mercury Mail was another company offering free e-mail.

By December 1996 Juno had 800,000 subscribers and about 30 advertisers. They included some large firms such as Ford Motor Co. and Miramax Films. For the year Juno reported revenue of about $100,000 and a net loss of $23 million, mainly due to operating expenses.

By mid-1997 Juno claimed to have 2.2 million users. Juno's 1997 advertising revenue was estimated at $4 million by research firm Jupiter Communications, and the company was spending more than that on membership growth, software, and market research. Freemark Mail had failed, and two other available services—HotMail and NetAddress—required Internet access. Juno's subscriber base climbed to 3.5 million by early 1998, then a reported 4.5 million by the end of March. The number of advertisers rose to more than 100. Juno signed a five-year, multimillion-dollar marketing deal with long-distance carrier LCI International Inc. for exclusive rights to advertise its phone services. One survey indicated that Juno's service was used by 14.7 percent of all Web and online users, compared with 6.1 percent for HotMail, which recently had been acquired by The Microsoft Network. For 1997 Juno reported revenue of $9.1 million and a net loss of $33.7 million.

Juno continued to actively defend its users from unwanted e-mail and vigorously prosecuted spammers (junk mail marketers). The company had adopted a ''zero-tolerance'' approach to unsolicited commercial e-mail in late 1997. In February 1998 it filed a lawsuit against five companies for allegedly forging Juno's domain name and making it appear that their unsolicited e-mail messages were coming from Juno. A similar suit was filed in May 1998 against a New York-based pornography spammer.

In April 1998 Juno introduced the Juno Advocacy Network, which was aimed at political lobbying and advocacy groups. Through the Juno Advocacy Network, such groups could reach Juno's subscribers with their messages based on congressional district, age, gender, hobbies, income, and other demographic data.

Offering More Services and Forming New Alliances: 1998–2000

Juno introduced premium service levels, for which customers paid subscription fees, in 1998. The first billable services were introduced on July 22, 1998. At the time Juno had 5.4 million users. In addition to basic free e-mail service, Juno began offering Juno Gold, an enhanced e-mail service that would allow users to attach files to e-mails, for $2.95 per month. Juno Web, the highest level of service, offered Internet access and full e-mail capabilities for $19.95 a month, a price comparable with other Internet service providers. Since the beginning of 1998 Juno had more than doubled its points of presence from 500 to 1,200 by purchasing dial-up access from a variety of providers, including Concentric Network, AT&T, Sprint, and WorldCom.

In December 1998 the Hartford Financial Services Group began advertising insurance services to Juno's 6.1 million members under a five-year agreement. Online queries could be answered with a quote within ten minutes. For 1998 Juno's revenue more than doubled to $21.7 million, but the company reported a net loss of $31.6 million.

In 1999 Juno formed marketing alliances with America Online and with WingspanBank.com, the Internet banking subsidiary of Bank One Corp. The agreement with WingspanBank .com gave it the exclusive right to market credit cards and certain banking services to Juno's e-mail subscribers, which had reached seven million by mid-1999. In a deal with America Online announced in August 1999, Juno would start offering a co-branded version of AOL's proprietary instant messaging service. Juno hoped that instant messaging would help attract people to its recently introduced online community, JunoLand.

Juno went public in May 1999 with an initial public offering (IPO) on NASDAQ at $13 a share. For the rest of the year the stock traded in a range between less than $10 and more than $27 before spiking to $87 a share in December 1999. After the first quarter of 2000, though, it was trading back in the $7 to $16 range and heading progressively lower to barely more than $2 a share in late 2000.

In mid-1999 Juno selected Rapp Collins Worldwide of New York to handle its $10 million direct response campaign. The campaign utilized direct response TV and direct mail. Juno's brand advertising was handled by DDB Worldwide. Both agencies were owned by Omnicom Group. By September Juno had about 7.2 million subscribers.

News Corp., which owned about 9 percent of Juno, announced in October 1999 that its News Digital Media subsid-

Key Dates:

1995: Juno Online Services is founded as a limited partnership.
1996: Juno rolls out free e-mail service in April.
1998: Juno begins offering billable services, including enhanced e-mail and Internet access.
1999: Juno becomes a publicly traded company; at the end of the year it adds Internet access to all levels of service and introduces broadband Internet access.

iary would supply Juno users with entertainment, news, sports, and business content through Juno's portal site, www.juno.com.

In December 1999 Juno launched version 4.0 of its software and expanded the functionality of all three service levels. Internet access was added to those levels that previously offered only e-mail. As with its free e-mail service, free Internet service was supported by advertisers. Juno Express was introduced as the company's highest service level. With Juno Express, customers in select markets could get high-speed broadband access to the Internet through a deal Juno made earlier in the year with Covad Communications, which operated one of the largest DSL networks. In May 2000 Juno announced that Juno Express was available in 22 U.S. markets. The company planned to roll out Juno Express over Covad's DSL network in new markets throughout the year. Juno Express was priced at $49.95 a month.

In offering free, ad-supported Internet access, Juno faced competition from several other free Internet service providers. The leader in the field was NetZero Inc., which was backed by a $144 million investment from Qualcomm Inc. Juno hoped to distinguish itself from other free providers by offering a range of billable services to which users could migrate after becoming more sophisticated. When one free Internet service provider, WorldSpy.com, ceased operations, Juno offered to pay it a fee for every WorldSpy subscriber that transferred to a Juno account. WorldSpy had about 260,000 subscribers when it went out of business in mid-2000. For 1999 Juno's revenue again more than doubled to $52 million, with a net loss of $55.8 million.

Until 2000, Juno's advertising had been handled by DDB Worldwide. Following a review in early 2000, Juno awarded its $20 million advertising account to Hampel/Stefanides in New York. The agency produced four 15-second spots to air on CNBC and Fox Network in the fourth quarter of 2000.

In February 2000 Juno teamed with Mail.com Inc. to launch Juno WebMail, a Web-based e-mail service that would utilize Mail.com's Web-based e-mail technology. Juno WebMail would enable Juno subscribers to send and receive e-mail from any computer connected to the Web, using their juno.com e-mail address.

Later in the year Juno announced that it would host a co-branded version of Mall.com, with the eponymous Austin, Texas-based company, on its shopping channel. Mall.com would be featured on Juno's home page, shopping pages, and product category pages, and Juno also would launch a marketing campaign to promote Mall.com to its members through pop-up and banner ads. More than 120 vendors were affiliated with Mall.com.

In June 2000 Juno filed a lawsuit against free Internet service provider NetZero and wireless telecommunications giant Qualcomm for allegedly violating its advertising technology patents. The lawsuit raised important issues regarding Internet-related patents, their enforceability, and whether they would stifle competition among companies seeking to offer free Internet access. Other major Internet-patent suits filed in 2000 included Amazon.com's suit against BarnesandNoble.com regarding its online ordering system and Priceline.com's suit against Microsoft regarding online purchasing.

With Juno's technology, subscribers logged on and downloaded their e-mail messages and receive ads. The connection was then terminated while users read their e-mail and viewed the ads offline. Juno's suit charged that Qualcomm's latest Eudora e-mail software violated Juno's patents in this area.

In October 2000 Juno formed an alliance with Activeworlds .com to provide real-time 3-D chat capabilities to Juno's 3.4 million subscribers. Meanwhile, Juno's stock was floundering, though the company had managed to secure a $125 million financing commitment from an unnamed private source. It also formed alliances with IBM, Time Warner, and Barnes & Noble in the second half of 2000.

The alliance with Time Warner was expected to give Juno access to Time Warner's broadband pipeline. Juno was the second company behind Road Runner to gain access to Time Warner's broadband cable network. The two companies, along with America Online, were to participate in a trial being conducted in Columbus, Ohio, to see if Time Warner's cable system could handle multiple ISPs. In order for Juno to gain full deployment over Time Warner's cable system—and thus offer cable Internet access to its members—Time Warner would have to restructure its exclusive arrangement with Road Runner. At the time Time Warner was under pressure from the Federal Communications Commission to provide open access to ISPs to gain approval for its pending merger with America Online.

Juno's partnership with IBM was announced in August 2000. Under the agreement free Internet access from Juno would be offered on IBM personal computers. The deal was part of Juno's strategy to reduce its subscriber acquisition costs, which were $45 million in the most recent quarter, to under $20 million in the current quarter. At the time Juno had about 3.4 million subscribers. About 730,000 Juno members were paying for billable services. For the second quarter of 2000, 62 percent of Juno's revenue came from billable services, and 38 percent came from ads and electronic commerce. The company continued to post losses, however.

Although unable to turn a profit since its inception, Juno and President Charles Ardai remained optimistic about the company successfully achieving maturity; and indeed, Juno again more than doubled its revenues in 2000, to $114 million. As 29-year-old Ardai told the *Standard* in September 2000, ''We're on the verge of an Internet mutation. The way people use the Net is going to explode—we're talking about Internet connectivity across devices we haven't even thought of. Who better than Juno to bridge those?''

Principal Competitors

America Online, Inc.; EarthLink, Inc.; NetZero Inc.; Microsoft Corporation.

Further Reading

Abercrombie, Paul, "Suit Claims Bay Area Firm Sent 'Spam,' " *Tampa Bay Business Journal,* February 6, 1998, p. 3.

"AOL Extends High-Speed Access Via GTE," *Content Factory,* July 28, 1999.

"Bank One Unit, E-mail Firm in Marketing Alliance," *American Banker,* July 21, 1999, p. 12.

"Briefly: Juno Spreads Out," *Telephony,* May 8, 2000.

Busch, Melanie, "WorldCom Inc. Provides Hardware for First Free E-mail Service to Be Offered," *Knight-Ridder/Tribune Business News,* June 4, 1996.

Charski, Mindy, "Free E-mail: A Viable Option for Careful Consumers," *PC World,* July 1997, p. 76.

Coulton, Antionette, "B of A Advertising Its Cards on E-mail Service," *American Banker,* June 9, 1998, p. 18.

Crum, Rex, "Juno Marches On," *Upside Today,* August 14, 2000, http://www.upside.com/Ebiz/398fl81a0.html.

"Free-mail," *Economist (US),* April 27, 1996, p. 71.

Fusaro, Roberta, "AOL, Juno Fend Off Spammers," *Computerworld,* January 11, 1999, p. 24.

Gabriel, Frederick, "Millionaires of Silicon Alley: David E. Shaw," *Crain's New York Business,* November 29, 1999, p. 49.

"Hample/Stefanides Wins Juno Account," *Adweek Eastern Edition,* May 1, 2000, p. 86.

Hogan, Mike, "Forget E-mail, Try Free Mail," *PC/Computing,* November 1996, p. 76.

"IBM Deal Helps Juno Get Subs," *ISP Business News,* August 21, 2000.

"Juno in Deal with U.S. Robotics," *Mediaweek,* September 2, 1996, p. 30.

"Juno Online Services, AT&T Team Up for Free E-mail Service Via the Net," *PC Week,* March 25, 1996, p. 59.

"Juno Online Taps Rapp for Direct Response," *Advertising Age,* July 5, 1999, p. 13.

"Juno Opens Review for $20 Mil Account," *Advertising Age,* February 14, 2000, p. 1.

"Juno Strategy Called into Question," *ISP Business News,* August 7, 2000.

"Juno Will Deliver for Fox Media," *Content Factory,* October 27, 1999.

Krause, Jason, "In Flat Market, ISP Says 'We're Not Dead Yet,' " *Standard,* September 11, 2000, http://www.thestandard.com/article/display/0,1151,18345,00.html.

Ladley, Eric, "Free ISP Broaches DSL Offerings," *ISP Business News,* May 8, 2000.

——, "Juno Charges Qualcomm, NetZero Violated Patent," *ISP Business News,* June 19, 2000.

"Mail.Com and Juno Launch Web-Based E-mail Service for Juno Subscribers," *Direct Marketing,* February 2000, p. 15.

McAdams, Deborah, "Juno Gains Access to TW Broadband Pipe," *Broadcasting & Cable,* August 7, 2000, p. 41.

Messina, Judith, "Delivering On-Line," *Crain's New York Business,* March 30, 1998, p. 3.

Moch, Chrissy, "Download: Time Warner Throws FCC a Bone," *Telephony,* August 7, 2000.

——, "Staking a Claim: Free ISPs Fight for Market Share in Wake of Consolidation Trend," *Telephony,* September 11, 2000.

Neelakantan, Shailaja, "Freemail," *Forbes,* August 12, 1996, p. 140.

"Newswire Roundup," *Adweek Eastern Edition,* August 28, 2000, p. 35.

Plotnikoff, David, "New Company Offers Free E-mail Service," *Knight-Ridder/Tribune Business News,* April 30, 1996.

Randall, Neil, "Free-mail: E-mail Services Meet Madison Avenue," *PC Magazine,* September 24, 1996, p. 44.

Riedman, Patricia, "Juno Advocacy Network Eyes Political Ad Dollars," *Advertising Age,* April 6, 1998, p. 35.

——, "Juno Bolsters Free E-mail Service with Internet Access," *Advertising Age,* July 20, 1998, p. 21.

Savage, Sean, "Free E-mail Available If You Don't Mind the Ads," *Knight-Ridder/Tribune Business News,* September 6, 1995.

"Short Takes: Hartford in Sales Deal with Web Dial-up Firm," *American Banker,* December 15, 1998.

Siegmann, Ken, "The Case of Ardai's Juno," *PC Week,* December 9, 1996, p. A3.

Spangler, Todd, "Juno Bids to Be a Top Consumer ISP Brand," *Internet World,* July 27, 1998, p. 38.

Taylor, Cathy, "You've Got Mail, But First a Word from Our Sponsor," *Mediaweek,* April 22, 1996, p. 14.

"3-D Chat Pact Formed," *Mediaweek,* October 9, 2000, p. 39.

"Trans World Entertainment Corp.," *Billboard,* September 4, 1999, p. 86.

"TW Signs Juno for Multiple ISP Trial," *Television Digest,* August 7, 2000.

"Under FCC Pressure, Cable Giants Test Open Networks," *ISP Business News,* August 7, 2000.

Vargas, Alexia, "Digital New York," *Crain's New York Business,* July 17, 2000, p. 14.

"VC Visions—On the Upswing," *Computer Reseller News,* October 23, 2000, p. 51.

Walsh, Mark, "Local Firms Join Instant Message Duel," *Crain's New York Business,* August 23, 1999, p. 3.

Wingfield, Nick, "Juno Offers Free E-mail Service to End-Users," *InfoWorld,* July 10, 1995, p. 10.

Young, Vicki M., "Juno Online, Mall.com in Joint Web Enterprise," *WWD,* June 20, 2000, p. 5.

—David P. Bianco

Kodansha Ltd.

12-21, Otowa 2-chome
Bunkyo-ku, Tokyo 112-8001
Japan
Telephone: (81) 3-3945-1111
Fax: (81) 3-3946-6200
Web site: http://www.kodanclub.com

Private Company
Incorporated: 1925 as Dai Nippon Yuben Kai Kodansha
Employees: 1,200
Sales: US$1.65 billion (1998)
NAIC: 51112 Periodical Publishers; 51113 Book Publishers; 51121 Software Publishers; 51211 Motion Picture and Video Production; 51212 Motion Picture and Video Distribution

Kodansha Ltd. is the largest publishing company in Asia. The company is run by a woman, Sawako Noma, which is highly unusual in Japan. Even more intriguing is the fact that a woman assumed the helm of Kodansha—albeit briefly—even before World War II. Moreover, Kodansha is a company dedicated to internationalism, awarding prizes for book publishing in Africa, and zealous in its commitment to aiding fledgling book publishers in Asia. It is the only book publishing company in Japan that has a subsidiary in the United States, Kodansha International/USA, responsible for translating Japanese literature, history, and art into English in order to broaden Western understanding of Japanese culture. Most extraordinary to a Westerner, accustomed to regarding Japanese culture as inimical to individualism, is the individualism of those who founded and led Kodansha, and who have left their imprint on the company.

The Early 20th Century: Seiji Noma's First Magazines

The company was founded by Seiji Noma, who noted in his autobiography that he was born at a time of great turmoil in Japanese history. By 1878, the year of his birth, the political upheavals occasioned by the clash between the Tokugawa shogunate and the imperialist forces who owed their allegiance to the mikado, or emperor, had been over for some years. The social and economic transformation of Japan, however, had only begun. Seiji Noma's family had sided with the shogunate and lost. The result was catastrophic for his parents and grandparents. The defeated *daimyos* (lords) ended by surrendering their fiefs to the state, and their *samurai* (retainers) found themselves deprived of their traditional offices and revenues. For the first time in their lives, *samurai* were on a par with everyone else and had to earn a living as best they knew how. Seiji Noma's *samurai* father, and his mother, a fencing expert, tried various livelihoods, with little success. Seiji Noma's mother and sister were determined to give him an education, however, and worked hard to pay for it.

Just as his mother's and sister's thrift made Noma into a respected teacher, and later a school inspector, so his wife would steer him toward a more responsible life. What he did have in common with other successful entrepreneurs, however, was boundless ambition and a restless drive to get ahead. In short, he was prepared to take risks. Thus, when a very prestigious administrative post at Tokyo University's law school was offered to him, he accepted. Even though he had little administrative experience, he eagerly left his secure and comfortable niche as a school inspector on the island of Okinawa. Even this did not satisfy him for long. He was delighted when the university yielded to the new craze for oratory—or debating—and allowed the establishment of a debating society in his home. He had a real flair for eloquent speech and never tired of reminding audiences how he enthralled his classes reciting from memory the heroic *kodan* (sagas) from Japan's medieval past.

The debating society gave Noma's ambition a new direction. He made up his mind to publish the monthly speeches of the students and professors, although he had not the slightest idea of how this could be done. He was flipping through the pages of a telephone book in 1910, spotted the name of the Dai Nippon Printing Company, went there immediately, and astonished the owners with his bold plans for a new magazine. This would be the origins of Kodansha Ltd.

It was surprising that Dai Nippon Printing agreed to collaborate with Noma in such a risky venture, and that they even granted him a modest salary as an editor of the magazine,

Company Perspectives:

Under the present leadership of Sawako Noma, Kodansha has set itself new goals in the ever changing media industry and continues to play a dominant role as a leader of Japanese book and magazine publishing.

Yuben, which was to be astonishingly successful. But success was far from easy.

Noma actually founded Dai Nippon Yuben Kai in 1909 to publish his magazine; a year later, the first issue of *Yuben* appeared. From then on, Noma shouldered the responsibilities of his administrative position during the day and his editing responsibilities at night; meanwhile, the publication costs of his new magazine exceeded his wildest imagination. Most of his time was spent less in editing than in trying to drum up money, an exhausting routine that would undermine his health. Noma was not satisfied with only one magazine, but sought to create another. His publishers were reluctant, gave up the rights to his first magazine, *Yuben,* and handed Dai Nippon Yuben Kai over to Noma, who became his own publisher.

It was to be the most difficult undertaking of his life, and Noma was not only a neophyte in this enterprise but was wholly without means. Moreover, he had to relinquish his solid position at the university to enter an unfamiliar business.

Although it was less than 50 years since Japan had opened up formally to the West, when the country had had no printing presses and traditional Japanese parchment was still used instead of paper, by 1920 Japan had not only caught up with the West in its printing methods but had overtaken all Western countries, except Great Britain, to become the second largest publisher of books in the world. Seiji Noma was interested in publishing magazines rather than books, but even in this realm there were formidable competitors, none more challenging than Jitsugyo no Nihon-sha, with as many as five magazines. With his wife, a former primary school teacher, Noma arduously learned each step of the publishing business. In the process, his young family became impoverished and heavily indebted while Seiji Noma was constantly obliged to haggle over prices with printers and book dealers. Only his faith in his product kept him from giving up.

Seiji Noma would establish another company, Kodansha, in 1911 to publish his second magazine, *Kodan Kurabu,* later renamed *Kodansha,* after the medieval *kodan,* of Japan. Noma's strong didactic streak now found an outlet in his new magazine. *Kodansha* would contain the stories of Japan's heroic past, a heroism in which Seiji Noma and his generation believed, and which had been fortified as a result of Japan's war against Russia in 1904. After a weak start *Kodan Kurabu* had turned out to be surprisingly popular. The stories appealed to the right audience—Japan's rapidly growing population of literate men and women. Illiteracy was wiped out by the 20th century, a tremendous achievement in any country, especially one in which illiteracy had been widespread only 50 years earlier.

By now, Noma had become a successful publisher, and between 1914 and 1923 five more successful magazines had been launched and Seiji Noma's publishing company was well on its way to becoming the leading magazine publisher in Japan. He was in many respects a typical Japanese employer of his generation—his employees worked long hours and were given only two days off each month, and he relied heavily on cheap labor in the form of adolescent boys. Yet few of his workers lost their jobs, even in the recession of the 1920s, and Noma built living quarters with recreational facilities for his young unmarried workers. With the catastrophic earthquake in Tokyo and Yokohama in 1923, Kodansha and Dai Nippon Yuben Kai turned out to be two of the few publishing companies in Japan—most of which were centered in Tokyo—to survive the earthquake intact. Seiji Noma was by then a very wealthy man, the "magazine king" of Japan and to his competitors, "the Mussolini of our magazine world." He was also a cosmopolitan man; he had a European wing built on to his mansion and he eagerly borrowed publishing ideas from the West. His idea for the highly successful magazine *Fujin,* launched in 1920, had sprung from his perusal of the American *Saturday Evening Post* and *Ladies Home Journal.* It would be a publication for everyone and include "all that was interesting and amusing, light and soothing." Hence not everything he published had to be educational, an impression his memoirs are at pains to convey.

In 1925, toward the end of his life, but still only in his 50s, Seiji Noma launched his eighth and most successful magazine, *Kingu* (from the English word "king"). Once again, the tone of *Kingu* was moralistic and educational. Yet it was phenomenally successful, with monthly sales of more than 1.5 million copies, the most successful magazine in modern Japanese history. Also in 1925, Noma merged his two publishing companies, Dai Nippon Yuben Kai and Kodansha. The merged company was incorporated as Dai Nippon Yuben Kai Kodansha (DNYKK).

Noma's last magazine venture, a children's publication, was far less popular, but by then, ten years before his death, he had become more interested in entering the highly competitive world of book publishing. Whereas the number of books the company published before World War II was very small, they sold very well and might have established DNYKK as a leading book publisher had it not been for Seiji Noma's untimely death at the age of 60 and the advent of World War II.

Whether or not Seiji Noma was as intensely patriotic as he himself suggests is difficult to ascertain. Of the many hardships encountered in the fiercely competitive world of Japanese publishing, censorship was one of them. In the 1930s, when Seiji Noma wrote his autobiography, government control of the press was absolute. Therefore, Noma's memoirs had to be deeply patriotic, even though censorship must have weighed heavily on him as a publisher.

Despite the Depression of the 1930s, Kodansha continued to produce 70 percent of all magazines in Japan. Understandably, nothing in Seiji Noma's memoirs hints at the growing militarization of Japan and of the intense pressure put on publishers to produce reading matter of a chauvinistic and militaristic character. Like all publishers, Noma had to conform. The year of his death, 1938, was also the year in which Japanese publishing began its steep decline that would end with the cessation of all publishing activity in Japan in 1945. These were harsh years for Japanese publishers. With Seiji Noma's death, his son Hasashi Noma would take the helm, only to die of an illness shortly afterward. Seiji Noma's widow, Sae Noma, was forced to take over. Her leadership of a major company was unprecedented in

Key Dates:

1878: Seiji Noma is born.
1909: Dai Nippon Yuben Kai is formed.
1911: Seiji Noma publishes *Kodan Kurabu* and launches a second company, Kodansha.
1920: *Fujin* is launched.
1925: Dai Nippon Yuben Kai merges with Kodansha.
1941: Sae Noma, Seiji Noma's widow, takes over the company.
1966: Kodansha America is formed.
1987: Sawako Noma becomes president.
1994: Kodansha author Kenzaburo Oe wins the Nobel Prize for literature.
1997: Sales peak at US$1.8 billion.

Japan, where women did not even have the right to vote. Like her husband, she was spirited and intelligent, but was growing old. With her only child dead, she adopted into the family the second husband of her dead son's widow, Shoichi Takagi, who thenceforth took the family name of Noma, becoming DNYKK's director in 1941. During this period, Dai Nippon Yuben Kai Kodansha became known increasingly by its nickname, Kodansha, and eventually the company was officially renamed Kodansha.

World War II was a time of enormous hardship for Japan's book publishers. Aside from having to deal with the military government's control of the press, there was also the extreme shortage of paper and the unpopular rationing system whereby the government determined the amount of paper to be allocated to each company. Naturally there was cooperation with the authorities. Kodansha's was no more marked than others; indeed, had the company not cooperated, it would have suffered the fate of two other prominent publishing companies, Kaizosha and Chuo Koronsha, which were forced to close down in 1944. Nonetheless, as the largest magazine publishing company, Kodansha's ''collaboration'' was perhaps the most visible.

Under the circumstances, it was noteworthy that any reputable publications saw the light of day during the war, as indeed they did. Nonetheless, the year 1945 marked the nadir of Japanese publishing, which was forced to a standstill because of the exhaustion of paper supplies.

The Revitalization of the Publishing Industry in Postwar Japan

Once press controls were lifted following Japan's surrender, however, the Japanese entrepreneurial spirit was far from dead. As early as September 1945, before the American occupation authorities had time to occupy the country, an enterprising publisher put out a booklet, minus front and back covers, entitled *Japanese American Conversation Handbook.* The fact that this paperback sold out perhaps testified less to the quality of the product than to the fact that the Japanese were starved for reading matter. With the coming of the Americans to Japan in December 1945, more specifically the Supreme Command of the Allied Powers under General Douglas MacArthur, Japanese censorship officially came to an end, only to be replaced by American censorship. The formerly stridently militaristic Japan Book Publishers Association now just as vehemently denounced Japan's ''collaborators'' during the war, most notably Kodansha Ltd. under Shoichi Noma's direction.

The charges of collaboration had the desired effect: in the first wave of three purges of civilian Japanese, Shoichi Noma was dismissed in 1946 as president of Kodansha. Even worse, nearly all the company's officials felt themselves under pressure to resign, leaving Kodansha a skeleton of its former self. Kodansha's competitors must have been secretly delighted by this turn of events and rumors abounded that Kodansha was nearing its end. But they underestimated a company that had survived the devastating earthquake of 1923 and the debilitating Depression of the 1930s. In 1946, the year Shoichi Noma was fired, Kodansha employees kept the firm going until Shoichi Noma's almost miraculous rehabilitation in 1949.

Shoichi Noma was another self-made man who, like his predecessor Seiji Noma, owed his good fortune to a good education—he graduated with a law degree from Tokyo University in the 1930s—as well as to his native talents and to key women in his life, most notably his friendship with Seiji Noma's widow and his marriage to Seiji Noma's widowed daughter-in-law, which led to his adoption into the Noma family. Made director of Kodansha in 1941, he became its president shortly before he was fired in 1946. Returning as president in 1949, he set forth—very like Seiji Noma—to modernize and reorganize the company, cost what it might. When he stepped down in 1981 in favor of his adopted son, Shoichi Noma had changed the face of Kodansha. Of the 34 magazines that Kodansha published in 1981, only *Fujin* was a survivor of the prewar era, and book publishing, tentatively begun before World War II, was now Kodansha's main business. Shoichi Noma was extremely successful perhaps because, like Seiji Noma, he had grand ambitions and was not easily satisfied; he wanted nothing less than to make his company a major force in the international publishing world.

The time was propitious for this. The Korean War had broken out in 1950 and lifted Japan out of the financial doldrums, resuscitating its industry. By the time the war ended, the publishing industry in Japan had recovered fully from the ravages of World War II. By then, Kodansha also was making a gradual recovery. Shoichi Noma had the same instinct as Seiji Noma for determining the right magazine to publish. In Shoichi Noma's case, the pivotal turnabout in his company's fortunes was the publication of the literary magazine *Gunzo,* which attracted some of Japan's finest modern writers. Shoichi Noma also showed himself to be a maverick by engaging in large-scale co-publishing projects with foreign publishers to produce such highly acclaimed and profitable book series as *Museums of the World* and *Sanctuaries of World Religions.* In fact, it was Shoichi Noma who first embarked on the mass publication of books in Japan, earning him the honorific ''Father of Japanese Publishing.'' Soon Kodansha was churning out 1,000 book titles a year. In 1963 Noma decided to try the market in the United States, a daring venture for a Japanese publisher. Unlike Japanese cars and televisions, very few Japanese books were being exported abroad. Kodansha International/USA in New York City would become one of Kodansha's most important and successful branches, churning out hundreds of titles on Japanese art, literature, and history in English translation. By 1980 Kodansha was the largest and most successful publishing company in Japan.

Shoichi Noma's innovations in the field of publishing were matched by his pioneering work in fostering international understanding. His brainchild, the Publishers' Organization for Cultural Exchange, was established to introduce Japanese culture abroad and to introduce foreign culture to Japan.

This was followed in 1979 with the establishment of the Noma Asia/African Scholarship, to enable promising Asians and Africans to study in Japan, and the Noma Award for Publishing in Africa, set up in 1980, was a prize for the best book written and published in Africa. The same year also saw the establishment of the Noma Literacy Prize, to go to the group or individual who has done most to combat illiteracy.

In 1981, Shoichi Noma retired in favor of his adopted son Koremichi Noma, who was president of Kodansha until his death in 1987. During this period Kodansha entered the audiovisual computer age with a broad range of videos and computer software and, like most Japanese publishing companies, expanded its array of comic books until in the 1990s the number of Kodansha's comic book titles reached almost 3,000.

Information Technology in the 1990s

With Koremichi Noma's untimely death, his widow Sawako Noma stepped in as president, the second woman leader in Kodansha's history. The university-educated, English-speaking Sawako Noma, mother of five children, continued her predecessors' strategy of strengthening Kodansha's global publishing position and furthering its humanitarian concerns.

The next decade saw tremendous growth for Kodansha, with sales reaching a peak of US$1.8 billion by 1997, an increase of 32 percent since Sawako Noma became company president. Much of this success resulted from the company's eagerness to explore emerging technologies as means of developing new products. In the early 1990s Kodansha became one of the few Japanese publishing companies to provide information about its book titles on the Internet, and in July 1997 it became the second Japanese publisher to offer online book ordering. In the later part of the decade Kodansha also participated in several joint ventures to promote innovation in electronic publishing. In 1998 it was one of 30 publishers in a consortium dedicated to marketing e-books through a network of satellite-linked computer terminals, which were situated in retail outlets throughout the country. The next year Kodansha introduced the FD Bookclub, a line of Web-based talking books for the hearing impaired. In the year 2000 the company joined eight other publishers in creating a virtual bookstore, with the aim of offering exclusively digital content products.

The *manga* sensation of the late 1990s also proved immensely profitable for Kodansha. *Manga*—the Japanese term for graphic novel—first became popular in Japan in 1959, with Kodansha's publication of *Weekly Shonen,* a serialized comic book. The form did not achieve widespread success in North America until several decades later, with the appearance of a number of animated films based on *manga* characters, most notably *Akira* and, in the last years of the decade, *Pokémon.* In the early 1990s Kodansha licensed the rights to *Akira* to Marvel subsidiary Epic Comics, authorizing them to create a comic book version of the story specifically geared toward the American audience. In 1996, at the height of the *manga* craze, the company cosponsored a competition in Japan calling for story and character ideas that might be adapted for publication or film. That same year, Kodansha launched a new business in North America dedicated to marketing Japanese-made animation software, and in 2000 the animated series Cardcaptor, an original Kodansha production that was immensely popular in Japan, premiered in the United States.

The shift into the electronic marketplace did not diminish Kodansha's reputation as a publisher of print literature. In 1993 Kodansha America started Kodansha Globe, a line of paperbacks devoted to a range of world cultures. In 1994 Kodansha author Kenzaburo Oe won the Nobel Prize for literature, and several of the publisher's titles were bestsellers throughout the decade. At this time Sawako Noma also introduced an extensive new series of company-sponsored literary awards, including prizes for excellent translations of Japanese works. In the United States Kodansha America dedicated increased attention to publishing the work of American writers in addition to expanding its line of English translations of Japanese works. On the domestic front, the company directed its focus to the growing women's magazine market, launching a series of successful new publications, including *Voce* and *Mine.* Although the company continued to contend with numerous challenges at decade's end, including copyright infringement in other Asian countries and a decline in reading among Japan's adolescent population, its proven ability to recognize new opportunities helped it maintain a prominent position in the Japanese—and international—publishing world into the 21st century.

Principal Subsidiaries

Kodansha Publishing Co., Ltd.; King Record Co., Ltd.; Kodansha International Ltd.; Kodansha International/USA, Ltd.; Kodansha Famous Schools, Inc.; The Nikkan Gendai Ltd.; Sansui-sha Publication Co., Ltd.; My Health Co., Ltd.; KBS (Kokusai Bunka Shuppan Ltd.); ASK Kodansha Co., Ltd.; Asmik Corporation; Kodansha Images; Kodansha Institute of Publication, Ltd.; Daiichi Shuppan Center Ltd.; IPEC, Inc.; Kodansha Scientific Ltd.; Scholar Publishers Inc.; Planning Editorial Center Ltd.; Daiichi-Tosho Storage Ltd.; Toyokuni Printing Co.; Daiichi Paper Co., Ltd.

Principal Competitors

Asahi Shimbun Publishing Company; Time Inc.; Times Publishing Limited.

Further Reading

Charle, Suzanne, "The Kay Graham of Japan's Media Industry," *New York Times,* January 11, 1999, Sec. C, p. 15.

Goozner, Merrill, "Manga Mania Heads for the U.S.: Comics Craze May Be the Next Japanese Export to Sweep America," *Chicago Tribune,* May 23, 1994.

Miyatake, Hisa, "Internet Making Crossroads in Japanese Business World," *Kyodo News International, Inc.,* February 10, 1995.

Noma, Seiji, *The Nine Magazines of Kodansha,* London: Methuen & Co., 1934.

—Sina Dubovoj
—updated by Stephen Meyer

KOSS CORPORATION

Koss Corporation

4129 North Port Washington Avenue
Milwaukee, Wisconsin 53212
U.S.A.
Telephone: (414) 964-5000
Fax: (414) 964-8615
Web site: http://www.koss.com

Public Company
Incorporated: 1953 as J.C. Koss Hospital Television Rental Co.
Employees: 250
Sales: $34.87 million (1999)
Stock Exchanges: OTC
Ticker Symbol: KOSS
NAIC: 33431 Audio and Video Equipment Manufacturing

Koss Corporation is the leading U.S. maker of stereo headphones. The company pioneered the stereo headphone in the 1950s. The product was invented by founder John Koss and his partner, Martin Lange. The name Koss became synonymous with quality headphones, before suffering market share loss to imported products. Koss products are manufactured in the United States, and include a complete line of headphones, from high-end equipment geared to serious audiophiles and music professionals to inexpensive gear sold at mass merchandisers such as Target and Kmart. The company also makes computer speakers under a licensing agreement, and licenses its name to several companies that sell electronic goods and speakers abroad. In recent years Koss has also moved into non-retail markets, selling its audio gear to the telecommunications industry, the aviation industry, and to the audio demonstration market. Diversification into related electronics areas in the 1980s proved disastrous for Koss, sending the company into bankruptcy. Koss emerged from Chapter 11 in 1985, and remained dedicated to its core product line. Over 80 percent of the company's sales come from stereo headphones. Koss is publicly traded over the counter. Over half its stock is owned by management and employees.

Audio Revolution

Koss Corporation became the premier manufacturer of stereo headphones after inventing the device for consumers in 1958. The stereo headphone was conceived by company founder John Koss and his partner Martin Lange, though the pair had no idea what a breakthrough they were making. John Koss was born in Milwaukee, Wisconsin, in 1930. After graduating from high school, he played in a jazz band. He married in 1952, and cash received as a wedding gift, intended for the couple's first sofa, became the foundation of a new business. This was the J.C. Koss Hospital Television Rental Co. Koss took the $200 gift and bought used televisions in Chicago, then rented them out to patients confined to Milwaukee hospitals. This business supported Koss and his family for several years. Koss began looking for new ideas, and eventually teamed up with Martin Lange, an engineer. They began marketing a device that allowed people to test their television tubes. Their next product was a winner, though only by accident. They came up with a new kind of compact record player and demonstrated it at a Wisconsin audio show in 1958. To attract attention to the device, the pair decided they needed a gimmick. They adapted a pair of headphones used by aviators in World War II to plug into the machine, so that buyers at the audio show could appreciate the stereo sound of the portable player. The record player did not garner many customers, but the headphones that went with it were the hit of the show. No one had previously devised a way to get a good, musical sound in stereo through a headset, and visitors to the audio show were apparently enchanted by the experience. Koss went into business manufacturing and marketing the headphones, and found eager customers nationwide. Classical music lovers appreciated the stereo effect, where the left and right ear hear different signals, just as in the concert hall. Moreover, the rock and roll era was coming into its own, and young people were listening to music louder and louder. With Koss headphones, people could turn the music up full volume, and not enrage their neighbors or bring the police.

A Profitable Niche in the 1960s and 1970s

Koss Corp. stumbled on its Stereophone more or less by accident, but the timing could not have been better. In the

Key Dates:

1953: Television rental business is launched by John Koss.
1958: Koss and partner debut stereo headphones.
1967: Koss Corp. goes public.
1979: Company hires new president to guide future growth.
1984: Koss Corp. files for Chapter 11 bankruptcy.
1985: Company emerges from bankruptcy.
1991: Michael Koss becomes CEO.
1997: Revenues approach $40 million.

1960s, the baby boom generation found headphones a necessary part of a stereo set, and sales increased rapidly. John Koss ran the company with few controls and little formal planning. The management hierarchy was simple, and Koss himself worked tirelessly to promote his product. Koss came up with clever billboards for the Milwaukee area, including the Mona Lisa in headphones. *Consumer Reports* magazine rated Koss headphones number one, and Koss was considered the leading name in headphones, with little serious competition. Koss stood for quality, and the company managed to squelch competition from cheap imports by offering a superior product. When a Japanese firm began selling an inexpensive $12 headphone set in the early 1960s, Koss raised its own prices, widening the gulf between the two. This worked. Koss also advertised heavily, not only with billboards but with radio and television spots. The company grew at roughly 15 to 20 percent annually in its early years, with after tax profit at around ten percent. The company went public as Koss Corp. in 1967, with sales at around $1 million. Koss built his family a luxurious home, and in 1968 started a profit-sharing program with his employees.

The company expanded internationally in the 1970s. By the mid-1970s, the company had an international sales office in London, a subsidiary plant in Italy, a marketing subsidiary in Canada, and a manufacturing facility in Ireland. The Koss brand controlled between 25 to 40 percent of the stereo headphone market worldwide. But international sales were sometimes troublesome for the company. Despite record sales in 1976, profits lagged because of poor exchange rates with foreign currencies. Koss eventually decided to shut down its Italian manufacturing plant because of recurring labor problems. Despite some bumps, the company continued to expand in the 1970s. In 1976 Koss began marketing its headphones through Sears, Roebuck and Co., and followed this with moves into other mass merchandisers. Previously, Koss had been an exclusively high-end product found mostly in audio stores. Koss continued to represent the higher end of the headphone market, and competed against cheaper products when it teamed with Sears.

The company had ridden the surge in youth culture and youth music in the 1960s and 1970s. But by the end of the 1970s, market conditions were not as promising. The baby boomers had grown up, and the stereo headphone market seemed to have matured. Sales in 1979 stood at $25 million. Koss Corp. was a profitable mid-sized company, one of the largest public companies in the Milwaukee area, and it had been built up by John Koss and his sons without professional management expertise. At the end of the 1970s, John Koss seemed unsure what to do with the company. He wanted it to grow and prosper, but he began to feel that he did not have the business background to steer the company to $50 million and beyond. In addition, he wanted to give up some of the day-to-day work and enjoy his success. Consequently, in 1979, Koss brought in James D. Dodson, an area executive with an air compressor manufacturer, to be president and chief operating officer. Koss knew Dodson from a Milwaukee business group. He believed that this experienced manager could lead the company to further growth through careful planning and standardized business practices, and this would be better than Koss's off-the-cuff and instinctive leadership style.

Into and Out of Bankruptcy in the 1980s

James Dodson signed a five-year contract with Koss Corp. in 1979, and quickly implemented changes. The management style changed to a more formal system, with communication by memo and things done according to written rules. Koss Corp. had a new long-term goal, which was to diversify away from stereo headphones into several related electronics areas. The company brought the Koss brand name to a line of speakers, and bought a Florida company, Calibron, that made VCR head cleaners and other similar products. The idea was to use the company's solid base in headphones to fund these newer ventures, and hopefully land a profitable niche in some related areas. Koss Corp. defined itself at the beginning of the 1980s as a company with three distinct business segments. The first was accessories, which included the core headphone line as well as "audio/video care products" including the VCR head cleaner. Components was the second segment, which included the company's new line of speakers. The third segment was called "Portable Personal Listening." This last was perhaps the most problematic for Koss Corp.

The company had come up with a portable cassette player and headphones around 1976, but decided not to produce it for fear of being undercut by cheap imports. But by 1981, Sony had put out its Walkman, which soon became virtually the generic name for portable cassette players. Koss moved quickly to get its device on the market, a portable player it called the Koss Music Box. The company contracted with a manufacturer in Taiwan to make the Music Box. The supplier ran into delays, and the Music Box did not make it onto store shelves in time for Christmas 1981. By the time Koss got the Music Box to market in February 1982, it was too late. The price of Sony's Walkman had dropped to $60, making the $90 Koss counterpart uncompetitive, and even cheaper knock-offs at half Sony's price were also widely available. Sales for Dodson's first two years had been good, reaching a record in 1981 of $25.2 million. But consumer demand for headphones dropped precipitately over 1983 and 1984, declining an estimated 50 percent. With the unsellable Music Box on its hands, Koss suffered. Its share of the U.S. headphone market had at its peak been an estimated 50 percent, but in the mid-1980s it plunged to around 25 percent. In May 1984 John Koss returned to the company, and Dodson left one month later. The company gave up on the Music Box, but it had gone heavily into debt paying its manufacturer in Taiwan. Sales for 1984 stood at $20 million, with a net loss of $6 million.

With a grim financial picture, Koss did all it could to cut expenses. It closed its European operations and dismissed many people domestically who were not absolutely essential. Koss got its domestic manufacturing workers to take a 30 percent pay cut, and John Koss himself cut his pay in half and sold his home. Koss negotiated a $1.2 million loan in the fall of 1984 in order to keep operating through the crucial holiday season. At the end of December, Koss filed for Chapter 11 bankruptcy protection. The company continued to operate while struggling to free itself of its $15 million in debt. The company brought in a new executive vice-president, James Dorman, to see Koss through the bankruptcy proceedings. With a much reduced staff, Koss put out a new line of headphones for the mass market, selling $10 to $20 sets at stores such as Target, Zayre, and Kmart. It also repackaged the high end of its line. The company negotiated with the banks in charge of its debt, and by the end of 1985, came up with a plan to pay off $9 million. Koss sold Calibron, the VCR head cleaner manufacturer it had bought under Dodson, as well as its Irish plant and another building. The company raised some more money through loans and, in December 1985, paid off the banks and emerged from bankruptcy.

The company recovered well from the bankruptcy, again firmly under family control, but with a stricter sense of management standards. With a smaller workforce, Koss learned to put out its products with more efficiency. The company instituted new policies, such as a goal of coming up with one new product idea or improvement of an existing product every six months. The financial goal of becoming a $50 million company seemed to have been put aside, and Koss determined to stick to its core product, headphones.

Sustaining a Niche in the 1990s and Beyond

In 1991 Michael J. Koss, son of founder John Koss, took over as president and chief executive officer. His brother Johnny Koss and his brother-in-law Michael Moore were also instrumental in leading the corporation. The company continued to focus its skills on making headphones, which it sold at prices ranging from $10 to $2,000 a pair in the early 1990s. The company came up with many innovative twists, such as headphones that changed color when exposed to light, and headphones designed specifically for use with computers by people playing computer games. Sales hovered around $25 million, reaching over $27 million in 1990, dropping to around $24 million in 1991, and then back up to $26 million in 1992. The company kept its management and workforce small, and improved its quality control system so that fewer headphones had to be scrapped or reworked at the end of the assembly process. Koss built up its brand name with mass-market outlets, while continuing to sell top-of-the-line, professional-quality equipment through audio and electronics retailers. In the early 1990s Koss also licensed its name to a Dutch company, which sold Koss brand electronics throughout North and South America.

Despite a consistent earnings record, the company did not have a big following on Wall Street, and its stock price was low in the early 1990s. Koss stock began to rise in the late 1990s. Koss had record sales in 1997 of almost $40 million, with a profit of roughly $4 million. The company had stiff competition from Sony and other Asian manufacturers, but because its products were made domestically by a relatively small workforce, it was able to respond quickly to new trends. Koss made headphones with enhanced features such as noise suppression, collapsible and cordless models, and headphones with interchangeable components. It licensed its name to makers of car speakers and stereos, and made headphone equipment for the telecommunications industry. At the same time, Koss put out a solid line of relatively low-priced headphones that gave the company strong holiday sales, as these were seen as a good gift item. At the end of the 1990s and into the 2000s, Koss seemed to have a solid base as a headphone manufacturer. Sales had reached all-time highs, and though they had dropped to less than $35 million for fiscal 1999, net income remained high. Without spreading itself into other electronics areas, the company continued to mine its niche, where it had high brand recognition and significant market share. Koss did not have plans to spread beyond headphones, and even curtailed its computer speaker business in 1998, converting it into a licensing arrangement with another maker. Its one core business line seemed likely to sustain Koss in coming years, as it responded nimbly to improved technology and found ways to sell its headphones through a wide range of retailers.

Principal Competitors

Sony Corporation; Matsushita Electric Industrial Co., Ltd.

Further Reading

Bednarek, David I., ''Koss Corp. May Be Suffering from Wall Street's Low Interest,'' *Milwaukee Journal*, September 1, 1991.

——, ''Once Ignored, Koss Stock Gets a Hearing on Wall Street,'' *Milwaukee Journal*, January 31, 1993.

Chilsen, Jim, ''Koss Rediscovers Success by Working 'Outside the Lines','' *Wisconsin State Journal,* April 19, 1998, pp. 1C–2C.

Daniell, Tina, ''Can Koss Rebound?,'' *Milwaukee Journal*, May 26, 1985, pp. 1, 4.

Dwyer, Kevin, ''The Koss Charm Shines Through Hard Times,'' *Business Journal-Milwaukee*, December 26, 1983, p. 6.

Hajewski, Doris, ''Stock Rises 47 Percent at Milwaukee's Koss Corp. on Earnings Report,'' *Knight-Ridder/Tribune Business News*, January 9, 1997, p. 109B0914.

Hartman, Curtis, ''All the Right Moves,'' *Inc.*, January 1988, pp. 68–76.

''Koss Plays a Different Tune,'' *Wisconsin Business*, February 1986, pp. 7–8.

Petzinger, Thomas J., ''Family Ties Help Koss Survive Tough Times,'' *Capital Times,* February 3, 1996, pp. 1B, 4B.

Randolph, Gordon L., ''Things Were Bad, But Look Good Now for Koss,'' *Milwaukee Journal Business News*, October 19, 1976, p. 12.

Tait, Nikki, ''Sound Way to Survive Among the Big Boys,'' *Financial Times*, November 24, 1998, p. 1.

—A. Woodward

L.L.Bean®

L.L. Bean, Inc.

Casco Street
Freeport, Maine 04033
U.S.A.
Telephone: (207) 865-4761
Toll Free: (800) 341-4341
Fax: (207) 552-6821
Web site: http://www.llbean.com

Private Company
Incorporated: 1934
Employees: 4,000
Sales: $1.07 billion (1999)
NAIC: 454110 Electronic Shopping and Mail-Order Houses; 451110 Sporting Goods Stores; 448140 Family Clothing Stores

L.L. Bean, Inc. is a leading U.S. catalog company and the largest catalog supplier of outdoor gear in the world. The L.L. Bean catalogs, a tradition since the company's founding, are the engine that drives company sales; in 1999 the company took in $854 million from catalog sales alone. The 1999 catalogs, 70 in all, offered approximately 16,000 different items, most tied to the pursuit of outdoor, active lifestyles. For the solitary fisherman or the busy baby boomer, the name L.L. Bean stands for quality, value, and enduring style—so much so that each year more than three million visitors make pilgrimages to the company's original retail store, in Freeport, Maine, to soak up the Bean ambiance and the Bean bargains. Retail sales for 1999 (including those for the L.L. Kids Store, adjacent to the flagship store; a second L.L. Bean Store in McLean, Virginia; ten factory outlet stores; and more than 20 independently owned retail stores in Japan) reached $206 million. The llbean.com e-commerce web site has been operational since 1996. L.L. Bean also enjoys a high reputation, among its corporate peers as well as its customers, for order fulfillment.

Early 20th-Century Origins: The Maine Hunting Shoe

The founder of the company was a 40-year-old Maine outdoorsman named Leon Leonwood Bean. Orphaned at age 12, Bean began to develop his entrepreneurial skills by doing odd jobs and by selling soap door-to-door. He also earned money by trapping. ''Although he was a natural salesman,'' according to Robert B. Pile in *Top Entrepreneurs and Their Businesses*, ''he was never really satisfied in one job and drifted about from place to place.'' Finally, Bean went to work for his older brother, Otho, in a Freeport dry goods store. There Bean sold overalls to manual laborers and earned $12 a week. His true love, however, was hunting and fishing in the Maine woods and streams, a love that would eventually lead to the development of one of the most popular and enduring products in American retailing.

Like most outdoorsmen in the early 1900s, Bean frequently suffered the problem of hiking with waterlogged boots. In 1912 he decided to add leather tops to a pair of ordinary rubber boots. He sought the services of a local shoemaker, and, after a few pairs of the boots had been sewn together, he penned a circular entitled ''The Maine Hunting Shoe.'' A model of early direct-mail advertising, the circular began: ''Outside of your gun, nothing is so important to your outfit as your foot-wear. You cannot expect success hunting deer or moose if your feet are not properly dressed.'' Bean mailed the letter to sportsmen from outside Maine who had purchased Maine hunting licenses and touted his original shoe as ''light as a moccasin, with the protection of a heavy hunting boot.'' He priced his product at $3.50 per pair and, to further entice his fellow hunters, offered a money-back guarantee.

Bean's marketing was flawless; however, his product was not. Of the 100 pairs of his Maine Hunting Shoes that were ordered and sent, 90 were returned because the tops had separated from the bottoms. Rather than give up his fledgling enterprise, though, Bean honored his guarantee and then borrowed $400 to redesign and perfect his boots (Bean also perfected his guarantee, making it unconditional and, in fact, the essence of Bean's customer service culture through the present day). His determination to satisfy himself and his customers paid off after he traveled to Boston to meet with representatives of the U.S. Rubber Company, who were able to fulfill his original design intentions. Bean redoubled his boot-making efforts and his commitment to the mail-order business, fortuitously in the same year that the U.S. Post Office began its parcel post service.

Company Perspectives:

The Golden Rule: "Sell good merchandise at a reasonable profit, treat your customers like human beings, and they will always come back for more."
—Leon Leonwood Bean, company founder

Bean's revamped footwear quickly became successful, and he soon expanded his marketing push into other states. A *Fortune* "Hall of Fame" article records that when another of Bean's brothers, Guy, became the town postmaster, Bean established his factory directly over the post office and facilitated the mailing process with a system of chutes and elevators. "He never lost his touch. Knowing that hunters from out of state often drove through Freeport in the middle of the night on their way to some hunting camp in the far wilds, Bean opened for business 24 hours a day. Night customers found a doorbell and a sign that read: 'Push once a minute until clerk appears.' "

1920s Through 1950s: Adding Retail Store, Expanding Product Line

Bean's name spread during the 1920s, due to word-of-mouth as well as print advertising and the founder's continuing innovations. In 1920 Bean opened a showroom store adjacent to his workshop, to accomodate the demands of visitors. In 1922 Bean reengineered the Maine Hunting Shoe by adding a split backstay to help eliminate chafing. Within two years, sales rose to $135,000 annually. In 1923 the company received welcome publicity when its boots were used to outfit the Macmillan Arctic Expedition. Two years later, the first full-sized catalog was mailed, featuring nonshoe apparel and sporting gear for the first time.

The catalog expanded again in 1927, adding fishing and camping equipment to the Bean line. Typical of the ad copy was the inducement: "It is no longer necessary for you to experiment with hundreds of flies to determine the few that will catch fish. We have done that experimenting for you." For years, in fact, Bean insisted on personally testing all of the products the company planned to sell. Perhaps this is why the Maine Hunting Shoe, as innovative as it was, proved to be simply the first in a string of classic Bean products, such as the Maine Guide Shirt, the Chamois Cloth Shirt, Bean Moccasins, the Zipper Duffle Bag, and Bean Cork Decoys. (The company also included high-quality non-Bean products, beginning with the Hudson Bay "Point" Blanket in 1927.)

During the Great Depression era, the mail-order house managed not only to survive but to thrive, passing the million-dollar mark in sales in 1937. According to Pile, "Bean invested nearly every dollar he made back into the business, with his eye on building it for the long term." The secret to L.L. Bean's success during these growth years was a threefold emphasis on quality products, fair pricing, and creating a timeless appeal to the Bean catalogs, which always featured paintings of outdoor Maine scenes and stories that underscored the strong link between Bean products and an outdoor lifestyle. In addition, Leon Leonwood instituted a postage-paid policy, further strengthening the company's reputation for catering to the customer. By the post-World War II era, both Beans, the man and the company, had become living legends. Moreover, the list of Bean customers was fast becoming a collection of legends itself, with Calvin Coolidge, Franklin Roosevelt, Jack Dempsey, John Wayne, and Ted Williams alternately figuring prominently.

In 1951 Bean, still at the helm as he approached 80, announced that the Freeport retail store would begin operating 24 hours a day, 365 days a year. Another important innovation during this decade was the introduction in 1954 of a women's department. Yet despite the now famous Bean name, as the company entered the 1960s its sales volume was not as high as might have been expected. Pile asserts that "dark clouds loomed on the horizon as [Bean] became older. . . . No longer did sales increase 25 percent or more each year; dollar volume actually began to flatten. Merchandise in the catalog and in the store was no longer up-to-the-minute and, even worse, orders were being slowly filled by part-time people who had little interest in doing the best possible job." The downhill course the company appeared to be on was steepened by the inception of other sports specialty marketers. This course was altered, however, following Bean's death in 1967 when ownership of the company fell to the Bean heirs. Only one was interested in management: Leon A. Gorman, grandson of the founder.

Late 1960s Through Early 1990s: Modernization and Substantial Growth

Gorman was first hired by the company in 1960. In 1967 he became president of a languishing business, with $3.5 million in annual sales and $65,000 in profits. Strong leadership and redirection were required and Gorman filled the need. His first decisions included expanding the advertising budget and demographic target group and making prices more competitive. He refrained from seeking growth through more retail outlets for fear of jeopardizing the catalog business. During his first full year as president, sales rose to nearly $5 million. The company had gotten back on track just in time to enjoy a huge recreation boom that was spreading across the country. By 1975 sales had reached $30 million and the company was employing more than 400 people. During the 1970s, the computerization of many business segments and the relocation of manufacturing to a new building further speeded the company's growth. In 1974 the company built near Freeport a 110,000-square-foot distribution center, which was expanded to 310,000 square feet in 1979.

Several trends contributed to Bean's substantial growth in the 1980s. Among them was the accidental, or perhaps inevitable, affiliation of the Bean label with prep culture and clothing. According to Milton Moskowitz, Lisa Birnbach's *Official Preppy Handbook,* tongue-in-cheek or not in its declaration of the Bean store as "nothing less than prep mecca," helped fuel a 42 percent rise in 1981 sales. A new health and fitness boom contributed to Bean's growth, as well as a surge in mail-order shopping. First-time Bean customers, nearly 70 percent of whom were women, increased rapidly during the 1980s. The company bolstered its retail space late in the decade, expanding the Freeport store by 40,000 square feet in 1989 and opening the first factory store in North Conway, New Hampshire, in 1988.

As the 1990s approached, however, the country experienced a serious recession; sales slowed, returns rose, and a 30 percent

Key Dates:

1912: Leon Leonwood Bean begins selling the Maine Hunting Shoe through direct mail.
1925: First full-sized catalog is mailed out, featuring nonshoe apparel and sporting gear.
1927: Fishing and camping equipment are added to the catalog.
1937: Annual sales exceed $1 million for the first time.
1954: A women's department opens at the Freeport retail store.
1967: Bean dies; Leon A. Gorman, grandson of the founder, takes over as president.
1988: First factory store opens in North Conway, New Hampshire.
1992: First international store opens in Tokyo, Japan.
1993: L.L. Bean offers its first line of children's clothing.
1996: Annual sales exceed $1 billion for the first time.
1997: L.L. Kids store opens, adjacent to the Freeport flagship store.
1999: The company launches its first affiliated brand, Freeport Studio.
2000: Second full-price L.L. Bean store opens in McLean, Virginia.

postal increase loomed on the horizon. For a time, Bean suffered along with the other major catalog marketers and was forced to lay off ten percent of its hourly and salaried workforce over a two-year period. In a 1992 *Forbes* article, Phyllis Berman placed the problem in a more serious context: "What went wrong? To some extent L.L. Bean is the victim of success. A whole generation is already outfitted with L.L. Bean leisurewear and camping equipment. Its durable, high quality clothing lines have spawned many imitators. Meanwhile, similar items turn up in discount stores. . . . Bean carried relatively few styles and introduced new products slowly. But today's trend-conscious and jaded consumers want variety and novelty."

Berman, who continued by questioning Gorman's management decisions, may have been premature in her analysis; by the end of 1992, the company's 80th anniversary, sales had risen by 18 percent to $743 million. The same year, L.L. Bean opened its first store in Japan, a ripe market that also contributed high year-end catalog revenues. A second Japanese store was added in July 1993; both were jointly owned by Seiyu and the Matsushita Electric Industrial Co. By 1997 there were 11 L.L. Bean Japan stores. Meanwhile, in the fall of 1993, L.L. Bean launched its first line of children's clothing.

Mid-1990s and Beyond: Countering Stagnant Sales with Numerous Initiatives

Sales continued to grow smartly through the 1995 fiscal year, reaching $976 million, although that figure was three percent below the company's target. In fact, for the remainder of the decade, revenues were essentially flat, increasing only to $1.08 billion in 1996 (the first time the billion dollar mark had been breached) and standing at $1.07 billion by 1999. Once again, L.L. Bean faced criticism for not changing with the times, both fashion-wise and otherwise. Particularly for women, the company's clothes were seen as "too" traditional and not fashionable enough. The company's venerable catalogs were being lost amid the myriad catalogs now being mailed out to every American. In addition, the number of retailers offering casual outdoor clothing was on the rise, including such names as American Eagle Outfitters, the Gap, and REI. On top of all that, international sales were hurt by the sluggish Japanese economy and by the late 1990s Asian financial crisis.

L.L. Bean responded aggressively to its latest challenge with a number of late 1990s and early 2000s initiatives. The company joined the e-commerce bandwagon in 1996 with the launching of online ordering via the llbean.com web site. That same year, a new state-of-the-art order fulfillment center was opened in Freeport, boasting 650,000 square feet of space and the capacity to process 27 million items per year. With the new line of children's clothing proving to be a great success, L.L. Bean opened an L.L. Kids store adjacent to the flagship retail store in Freeport, in 1997. This 17,000-square-foot store featured a number of special attractions, including a two-story waterfall, a trout pond, a hiking trail, and an electronic rock climbing wall. On the women's clothing front, L.L. Bean launched a new brand and a new catalog called Freeport Studio in 1999. The company's first affiliated brand, Freeport Studio featured more contemporary and fashion-forward casual clothes for baby boomer women. Finally, in 2000 L.L. Bean began what a number of industry analysts considered a long overdue expansion of its full-price retail stores. In July of that year, a 76,000-square-foot L.L. Bean store opened in McLean, Virginia, in a fancy suburban Washington mall.

This beginning of a potentially nationwide retail expansion was aimed at increasing overall sales as well as lessening the company's dependence on catalog sales, which comprised 85 percent of the total. Initial sales for the Freeport Studio venture were somewhat disappointing but perhaps not surprising given the extremely competitive nature of the women's clothing sector. It was nevertheless clear that L.L. Bean was once again attempting to update its image and its sales strategy through dramatic undertakings at the turn of the millennium, and it would take some time to determine whether the company could return to the strong growth of the 1980s and the mid-1990s.

Principal Competitors

American Eagle Outfitters, Inc.; Bass Pro Shops, Inc.; Cabela's Inc.; Coldwater Creek Inc.; The Coleman Company, Inc.; Columbia Sportswear Company; The Gap, Inc.; Gart Sports Company; Johnson Outdoors Inc.; Lands' End, Inc.; The North Face, Inc.; The Orvis Company Inc.; Recreational Equipment, Inc.; Speigel, Inc.; The Sports Authority, Inc.; The Sportsman's Guide, Inc.; The Timberland Company; Venator Group, Inc.; Wolverine World Wide, Inc.

Further Reading

Alpert, Mark, "Yuppies Want More Than Most Catalogues Offer," *Fortune,* October 22, 1990, p. 12.
Bean, L.L., *My Story: The Autobiography of a Down-East Merchant,* Freeport, Me.: 1962, 104 p.
"Bean Sticks to Its Backyard," *Economist,* August 4, 1990, p. 57.

Berman, Phyllis, "Trouble in Bean Land," *Forbes,* July 6, 1992, pp. 42–44.

Bonnin, Julie, "In L.L. Bean Store, the Catalog Fantasy Lives," *Minneapolis Star Tribune,* December 13, 1993, p. 1E.

Brown, Tom, "Worried About Burnout? Try Fly Fishing," *Industry Week,* January 17, 1994, p. 29.

Cyr, Diane, "Lean Times for Bean," *Catalog Age,* March 1998, pp. 1, 24.

"For Your Information," *Minneapolis Star Tribune,* February 23, 1993, p. 8D.

Gorman, Leon A., *L.L. Bean, Inc.: Outdoor Specialties by Mail from Maine,* New York: Newcomen Society in North America, 1981, 23 p.

Hamilton, Martha M., "L.L. Bean Gets a Bigger Tent," *Washington Post,* July 29, 2000, p. E1.

"Leon A. Gorman," *Chain Store Age Executive,* December 1992, p. 57.

Llosa, Patty de, "The National Business Hall of Fame (Leon Leonwood Bean)," *Fortune,* April 5, 1993, pp. 112, 114.

Montgomery, M.R., *In Search of L.L. Bean,* Boston: Little, Brown, 1984, 242 p.

Moskowitz, Milton, et al, "L.L. Bean," in *Everybody's Business: A Field Guide to the 400 Leading Companies in America,* New York: Doubleday, 1990.

Murphy, Edward D., "Bean Expansion Banks on Kids," *Portland Press Herald,* July 27, 1997, p. 1F.

——, "L.L. Bean Agrees to $750,000 in Fines," *Portland Press Herald,* August 31, 2000, p. 1A.

——, "L.L. Bean Going National with Retail Stores," *Portland Press Herald,* May 22, 1999, p. 1A.

——, "L.L. Bean Pulling Out of Sales Slump," *Portland Press Herald,* December 16, 1999, p. 1A.

——, "A New Style for Bean's," *Portland Press Herald,* June 28, 1998, p. 1A.

Pile, Robert B., "L.L. Bean: The Outdoorsman Who Hated Wet Feet," in *Top Entrepreneurs and Their Businesses,* Minneapolis: Oliver Press, 1993, pp. 29–43.

Port, Otis, and Geoffrey Smith, "Beg, Borrow—and Benchmark," *Business Week,* November 30, 1992, pp. 74–75.

Rosenfield, James R., "In the Mail: L.L. Bean," *Direct Marketing,* February 1992, pp. 16–17.

Sly, Yolanda, "Bean's Looks to Broaden Market: Catalog Giant Opens D.C. Area Mall Store," *Bangor Daily News,* July 28, 2000.

Sterngold, James, "Young Japanese Like Rugged American Look of L.L. Bean," *Minneapolis Star Tribune (New York Times),* March 4, 1993, p. 6E.

Symonds, William C., "Paddling Harder at L.L. Bean," *Business Week,* December 7, 1998, p. 72.

Tedeschi, Mark, "LL.Business," *Sporting Goods Business,* August 7, 1997, p. 51.

Tucker, Frances Gaither, Seymour M. Zivan, and Robert C. Camp, "How to Measure Yourself Against the Best," *Harvard Business Review,* January/February 1987, pp. 8–10.

Vannah, Thomas M., "A Most Bucolic Business," *New England Business,* May 1990, pp. 64, 63.

—Jay P. Pederson
—updated by David E. Salamie

Lawson Software

380 St. Peter Street
St. Paul, Minnesota
U.S.A.
Telephone: (651) 767-7000
Toll Free: (800) 477-1357
Fax: (651) 767-7141
Web site: http://www.lawson.com

Private Company
Incorporated: 1975
Employees: 2,000
Sales: $313 million (2000 est.)
NAIC: 511210 Software Publishers

Throughout its 25-year history, Lawson Software has remained focused on providing businesses with software applications for core functions such as finance, human resources, supply chain management, and procurement. With the advent of e-commerce and the World Wide Web in the 1990s, Lawson moved quickly to add relevant components to its suite of business applications and make its software accessible with a web browser. As the year 2000 drew to a close, Lawson remained ahead of the curve by partnering with application service providers (ASPs) to host its software for use by client companies.

Providing Software for Core Business Functions: 1975–89

Lawson Software was founded in 1975 in Minneapolis, Minnesota, by William Lawson, chairman of the board; Richard Lawson, CEO; and John Cerullo, chief technology officer. The two Lawsons were brothers with an interest in software programming, and Cerullo was a former senior programmer for Control Data and the U.S. Department of Defense. The company initially provided custom mainframe software for Burroughs and IBM installations. Its mission was to provide packaged business applications for its customers, based on the latest technology. Over the years the company broadened its platform support, adding products for the IBM System/38 in 1981, IBM AS/400 in 1988, Unix in 1990, and Microsoft Windows NT in 1998.

Over the years Lawson gained experience in mainframe, midrange, and open systems computing. The company fully embraced open systems technology in 1985 and effectively made transitions in computer platforms as new technologies emerged: from mainframe and mid-range systems to client/server environments and, in the 1990s, to web-enabled applications.

Remaining Focused on Software for Back-End Applications: 1990–95

At the beginning of the 1990s Lawson began producing software applications for the Unix platform and continued to support IBM's AS/400. Demand was strong, and Lawson enjoyed a 55 percent increase in its Unix-based applications business from 1991 to 1992, while its AS/400 business grew by more than 25 percent. Overall revenue for 1992 increased more than 22 percent to $37.6 million, compared to $30.8 million in 1991. Packaged software accounted for $31.8 million of Lawson's 1992 revenue, virtually all of it from sales to U.S. firms. At the time Lawson's principal competitor was Oracle Corporation.

In 1993 Lawson introduced its Open Enterprise Release, which included multilevel client/servers applications for accounting, human resources (HR) management, distribution management, materials management, and its Universe environmental system. The Open Enterprise Release of the Universe environmental system allowed Lawson applications to be configured in different ways to support a flexible client/server model. Customers could chose from Windows, Motif, or Macintosh graphical user interfaces (GUIs), and the system could be used on character-based terminals as well. The Open Enterprise Release included several modules with an average price per module of $24,000, that supported the AS/400 as well as several Unix platforms.

In 1994 Lawson's revenue rose to $70.2 million from $44.8 million in 1993. Software sales accounted for $58.5 million of Lawson's 1994 revenue. During the year the company increased its workforce from 400 to 580 employees.

In 1995 Lawson began tailoring its Open Enterprise applications for specific vertical markets, the first of which was healthcare. Lawson worked with healthcare companies and healthcare

Company Perspectives:

For more than a quarter of a century, Lawson has delivered leading-edge business management solutions that offer unsurpassed performance, reliability and cost-effectiveness. Lawson focuses on Fortune 2000 organizations, delivering 360 degree e-business solutions to service industries such as healthcare, retail, professional services, public sector, financial services, and telecommunications.

professionals to develop customized financial, HR, and materials management application software specifically for the healthcare industry, including integrated delivery networks, hospitals, long-term care facilities, and health maintenance organizations (HMOs). Tailored applications would help customers reduce implementation costs by as much as 15 percent, according to one analyst.

Lawson also introduced Open Enterprise Desktop to better integrate desktop applications with its client/server suite. Open Enterprise Desktop created a single environment for desktop applications and the Lawson Enterprise line. Priced at $200 per desktop and sold in bundles of five, it was available for Unix servers and for Windows 3.1, Windows NT, and OS/2 clients.

Other new products introduced in 1995 included the Lawson Employee Information Center, a kiosk component developed for the HR module of its Open Enterprise system. The kiosks would allow employees to query the system for personal and company information without having to go through the HR department.

Incorporating New Technologies in Upgraded Applications: 1996–2000

In 1996 Lawson introduced workflow capabilities for its Open Enterprise 6.1 that would allow users to move from application to application without leaving the Lawson desktop. Workflow processes could be defined at any of three levels: the desktop, the workgroup, or the enterprise. The new capabilities gave enterprises the scalability and flexibility they needed to cope with business process changes.

Lawson planned to release Version 7.0 of Open Enterprise in June 1996, which would include Internet capabilities made possible by licensing Java from Sun Microsystems Inc. Prior to that, Lawson came out with its Open Enterprise Webpage Generator, an application that let users of Lawson's Open Enterprise application complete an order using standard web browsers. It allowed companies to develop and access web forms that were created using HTML (hypertext markup language). The company's customers could then use a web browser to view a form and fill out a purchase order. The Open Enterprise Webpage Generator was made available for free to companies using Lawson's Open Enterprise 6.1.

Instead of releasing its new suite as Version 7.0 in mid-1996, Lawson re-branded its Open Enterprise applications suite as the Lawson Insight Business Management System. It was initially released for Unix and AS/400 platforms, with beta testing being conducted for Windows NT in 1996 and 1997. Insight featured four distinct application sets: financials, human resources, procurement, and supply chain management. New enhancements included three-tier workflow capabilities for the desktop, the workgroup, and the enterprise, and Internet/intranet ordering capabilities. In addition, Lawson added an activity-based management component that could be accessed by any of the four applications. Pricing for Insight began at $150,000 and depended on the number of users; general release was set for September 1996.

After announcing a partnership with Netscape Communications in September 1996, Lawson bundled Netscape's Navigator web browser and FastTrack Server with its Insight Business Management System. As a result, Insight users would be able to integrate hypertext and hyperlinks into their business applications. Bundling the browser and server gave Lawson's customers a solution for accessing and managing their business processes over the Internet or a corporate intranet.

Toward the end of 1996 Lawson took the lead over its competitors in Java-enabled applications by releasing six World Wide Web "Service Centers": Employee Service Center, Supervisor Service Center, Procurement Service Center, Customer Information Center, Vendor Information Center, and Financial Information Center. The centers worked with Lawson's Insight suite and tied various application functions together with a simplified browser interface. The service centers were built around Java-enabled applications, a technology that IT (information technology) managers needed to justify building out nationwide corporate intranets. Lawson was ahead of competitors SAP AG, PeopleSoft, and Oracle, who expected to introduce their Java-enabled applications in mid-1997. For 1996 Lawson's revenue surpassed $100 million, and the company had 960 employees.

In 1997 Lawson continued developing browser client enhancements to its Insight Business Management System. CEO William Lawson told *InfoWorld,* "We will integrate with the browser in a much more profound way. And by making our software web-deployable, we've made something unusual." The company felt that the new architecture, which provided Insight users with direct access to applications through a front-end web browser, required a new name and called it Self-Evident Applications (SEA). Key elements of the new architecture included personalized web pages and an HTML-based interface that enabled system administrators to deploy Java applets. All of Lawson's future software would be based on this new model. For 1997 Lawson reported revenue of $166 million.

For 1998 Lawson continued to focus on two vertical markets, healthcare and retail. It targeted mid-size companies and did not plan to follow competitors such as PeopleSoft into the larger arena of enterprise resource planning (ERP) software. By mid-year, though, Lawson began bundling its suite of business applications for finance, human resources, and distribution with an Oracle database and Hewlett-Packard Co. NetServers, thus making it a mid-size competitor in the ERP marketplace.

Lawson also sought to make its software more accessible to non-technical business executives. It introduced Lawson Insight PI (Performance Indicator), an add-on to its Insight system that

Key Dates:

1975: Lawson Software is founded in Minneapolis, Minnesota, by William Lawson, Richard Lawson, and John Cerullo.
1990: Lawson adds software products for the Unix platform.
1993: Lawson introduces its Open Enterprise Release for client/server systems.
1995: Lawson begins targeting vertical markets, the first of which is healthcare.
1996: Lawson re-brands and significantly upgrades Open Enterprise as the Lawson Insight Business Management System.
1997: Lawson develops new software architecture called Self-Evident Applications.
1998: Lawson adds software products for Windows NT.
1999: Lawson releases Insight 2 Business Management System.

let users retrieve information from the system without having to build a data warehouse. Insight PI extracted relevant data, based on pre-selected performance indicators, from an intelligent data warehouse containing information from Lawson's software. Each version of Insight PI was designed for a specific corporate user, such as a CEO, CFO, or COO.

Lawson rolled out Windows NT versions of its Insight business applications in April 1998 at its annual user conference. In this respect Lawson lagged behind some of its competitors, showing a reluctance to move to NT. Lawson also unveiled its Strategic Ledger, which let companies capture and analyze data at more levels, and announced consulting partnerships with Ernst & Young and Arthur Andersen.

In mid-1998 Lawson began marketing SuiteExpress to companies with less than 2,000 employees and revenue between $25 million and $400 million. SuiteExpress for Human Resources bundled a new version of the company's Insight Human Resources Process software suite with Oracle's Oracle8 database running under Windows NT on Hewlett-Packard NetServers. With this bundled product Lawson was competing with larger vendors such as SAP AG and PeopleSoft Inc. for middle market companies. Lawson planned to introduce similar bundled systems for its other applications in finance, procurement, and supply chain management.

ERP support for remote or handheld devices was a new trend in 1998. Lawson added support for PalmPilot and Windows CE devices to its Insight Performance Indicator modules, thus allowing remote users to capture company data or receive alerts under certain conditions.

Lawson began targeting new vertical markets in 1998, introducing software targeted to the public sector market. The insurance and professional services industries were two additional markets for which the company began tuning its software. Lawson also expanded internationally, opening sales offices in Amsterdam and Munich in 1998. The company had a presence in 14 countries and planned to open an office in Australia in 1999. Its Insight business suite added support for the euro currency in 1998, and Lawson introduced Insight Human Resources software for companies in the United Kingdom, France, Germany, and the Netherlands for delivery by January 1999. Approximately 90 percent of Lawson's business came from U.S. firms, mainly in retail and healthcare.

In October 1998 Lawson introduced its SEA Designer Suite for use with its Insight business system. The Designer Suite included three modules—Form Designer, Report Designer, and Chart Designer—that let non-technical users easily customize forms, charts, and reports. Later in the year Lawson delivered several new components for its Insight PI data warehouse and analysis suite. The company had gained more than 80 customers for PI since it was introduced earlier in the year. Lawson claimed that the role-based PI system could anticipate 80 percent or more of the questions for a particular job description.

In 1999 Lawson released several new products, including Lawson Insight Franchise Management, a web-deployable software package that managed retail franchisee contracting and billing. The package could be integrated with Lawson's financials and supply chain management software applications. Another new product called Open Components Solution was a set of object-oriented development tools that would make it easier to customize Lawson's applications. The tools would allow "all things Lawson to be accessed by all things Windows," according to a company spokesperson. Lawson also made its complete line of applications accessible via Lotus Notes through an integration of its Insight suite with Lotus Domino.

Lawson's most significant new product, though, was Insight II, the next generation of its business management applications suite. Lawson's Insight 2 Business Management System included a new feature, Strategic Ledger, which further simplified data analysis for non-technical users. Strategic Ledger allowed for real-time financial analysis, reporting, and strategic planning and let users pull and analyze data from outside systems in real time. All of the Insight II modules were based on a new object-oriented component architecture dubbed "Bobjects," or Business Objects, and all were accessible through a standard web browser.

Toward the end of 1999 Lawson introduced Insight II Workforce Analytics and Insight II Customer Relationship Management (CRM) modules. Workforce Analytics could store and extract data from Lawson's accounting and HR applications to provide an analysis of a company's compensation, turnover, and staffing. Lawson's CRM component marked the company's entry into the CRM market and was scheduled for release in 2000. The CRM applications would be available for general business use and for Lawson's target vertical markets: healthcare, retail, and professional services. Other Insight II components added in 1999 included Candidate Self-Service and Recruiter Self-Service, which Lawson acquired and integrated into its Insight II HR software suite.

In the second half of 1999 Lawson offered a bundled payroll solution called Fast HR/Payroll Solution. It included IBM's Project Office project-management tool to track the software implementation and report on its progress and was available for Windows NT and Unix systems running an Oracle or Informix

Corp. relational database. The package was offered as a standalone application for internal use or as a hosted service through application service providers (ASPs) USinternetworking Inc. and Shared Medical Systems Corp. The Fast HR/Payroll Solution was priced from $450,000 to $600,000, depending on the number of users and the level of service required. Around the same time Lawson also offered a bundled solution that included financials and HR software for small to mid-size retail chains in cooperation with IBM and Microsoft Corporation.

Other developments in 1999 included the launch of a web portal called Insight II SEAport, which extended Lawson's web-based self-service applications. The SEAport suite was based on Lawson's Self-Evident Applications (SEAs). It let users create a customized ''Webtop'' that integrated various sources of information, including Lawson applications, messaging, and Internet content. In launching its own web portal, Lawson was following the lead of its competitors. Web portals enabled companies to feed information to their employees based on their role or function.

In 1999 Lawson announced plans to go public the following year, but it remained a private company throughout 2000. Jay Coughlan, named president and COO of Lawson in early 2000, confirmed for *Minneapolis-St. Paul City Business* that the company wanted to go public for a variety of reasons, including the fact that it mostly competed with public companies and that it wanted to use stock options to attract and retain employees. For fiscal 1999 Lawson had revenue of $270 million and 1,700 employees worldwide. During the year the company moved from Minneapolis to new headquarters in St. Paul.

Lawson was attracted to the CRM market and had software in beta testing early in 2000. However, the company finally decided to package CRM software developed by Siebel Systems Inc., one of the top CRM vendors, rather than develop its own software. The market for CRM software, which tracked customer contacts and included sales force automation, was projected to grow from $2 billion in 2000 to more than $10 billion by 2003, a much faster growth rate than was projected for the overall ERP market.

A major initiative for 2000 was the LawsonTone program. Instead of purchasing Lawson software for internal use, companies could join the LawsonTone program and access the software through a participating ASP. By the end of July Lawson had signed up 22 ASP partners to host its software, and in October another 20 joined for a total of 42 partners. Each ASP partner was expected to add value through its industry-specific expertise.

Lawson also began shipping components of its Collaborative Commerce Suite, which included e-commerce applications, in the first half of 2000. The suite included six e-commerce solutions: Trade Communication Services, which managed customer payments and contacts; Payment Server Integrator, which accepted payments and routed them directly to back-office applications; Site Builder, a set of development and integration tools for building web sites; Auction System, which allowed customers to host online auctions; E-Resource Management, which consolidated directory-type information for sharing throughout the enterprise; and Mail Server, a system-to-user communication system that included automatic e-mail notifications based on workflow processes.

For fiscal 2000 ending May 31, Lawson reported revenue of $306 million, an increase of 15.7 percent over 1999. International revenue increased 41.5 percent, and three of the company's new vertical markets—professional services, financial services, and telecommunications—experienced triple-digit growth. Revenue from the retail market grew by 33.3 percent.

In November 2000 Lawson announced an upgrade to its Insight system, called the Lawson.insight 8 Series. It was scheduled for delivery in January 2001 and included software suites for financial, human resources, supply chain management, analytic, enterprise relationship management, and e-commerce applications.

For the future Lawson appeared committed to making its software applications available to companies through the hosted services of ASPs and BSPs (business service providers). While it planned to continue to support its traditional client/server customers, the company said it would phase out Windows applications that required it to go in and install software at a customer's site. A new initiative announced in December 2000, called Lawson@Business Server Provider, was indicative of the direction Lawson was heading. The initiative was aimed at ASPs and BSPs and would enable them to get to market faster, secure more market share, and create competitive barriers to entry. The first delivered component of Lawson@Business Server Provider was Multi-tenancy, a unique technology solution that allowed ASPs and BSPs to securely host multiple customers on a single set of Lawson applications. Meanwhile, the company continued to sign more ASPs and BSPs to its LawsonTone program.

Principal Competitors

SAP AG; Oracle Corporation; PeopleSoft Inc.; System Software Associates Inc.; Siebel Systems, Inc.; J.D. Edwards & Co.; Great Plains Software Inc.; Baan Co.

Further Reading

''ASP Pulse,'' *Computer Reseller News,* July 31, 2000, p. 83.

Bowen, Ted Smalley, ''Lawson Building Credibility in ASP Arena,'' *InfoWorld,* February 7, 2000, p. 16.

——, ''Lawson Reveals CRM Offerings, Claims Close Integration,'' *InfoWorld,* December 6, 1999, p. 30.

Busse, Torsten, and Pardhu Vadlamudi, ''SAP, Lawson Develop Internet Connectivity for Client/Server Applications,'' *InfoWorld,* March 11, 1996, p. 36.

Colkin, Eileen, ''Better HR Apps,'' *InformationWeek,* September 6, 1999, p. 101.

Emigh, Jacqueline, ''Lawson Unveils @BSP Platform for ASPs/BSPs,'' *ZDNET,* December 14, 2000, http://www.zdnet.com/sp/stories/news/0,4538,2664876,00.html.

Frye, Colleen, and Deborah Melewski, ''Lawson Software,'' *Software Magazine,* July 1995, p. 120.

Gilbert, Alorie, ''Lawson Set to Debut CRM Package,'' *InformationWeek,* November 29, 1999, p. 30.

——, ''Targeted Data Extraction Boosts Analysis,'' *InformationWeek,* October 18, 1999, p. 109.

Gildred, Tom, ''Who's Who in the Middle Market ERP Space?,'' *San Diego Business Journal,* May 15, 2000, p. 29.

Gray, Lloyd, ''Filling a Data Prescription,'' *PC Week,* December 14, 1998, p. 92.

——, ''Lawson Eyes Middle Market,'' *PC Week,* June 8, 1998, p. 56.

——, ''Lawson Hops Continents with Business Software,'' *PC Week,* August 3, 1998, p. 46.

——, ''Lawson Shows Web Interface,'' *PC Week,* May 26, 1997, p. 8.

Greenberg, Ilan, ''ISVs Bolster Human Resource Applications,'' *InfoWorld,* September 11, 1995, p. 12.

——, ''Lawson Begins Vertical Apps Push with Health Care Line,'' *InfoWorld,* June 5, 1995, p. 32.

——, ''Lawson Looks to Collect on Web Bet,'' *InfoWorld,* February 3, 1997, p. 9.

Hodges, Judith, and Deborah Melewski, ''Lawson Software, Minneapolis,'' *Software Magazine,* July 1993, p. 126.

Holt, Stannie, ''Lawson Aims for Design Simplicity,'' *InfoWorld,* October 12, 1998, p. 61.

——, ''Lawson Aims to Ease with Customizing Tools,'' *InfoWorld,* February 22, 1998, p. 69.

——, ''Lawson Banks on Tool for Financial Analysis,'' *InfoWorld,* March 22, 1999.

——, ''Lawson Ships Data-Analysis Tool, Adds Raft of International Features,'' *InfoWorld,* August 10, 1998, p. 57.

Holt, Stannie, and Martin LaMonica, ''ERP Vendors Join the Ranks of Web Portal Sites,'' *InfoWorld,* May 31, 1999, p. 17.

Howle, Amber, ''Hosted-Software Model Holds Future for ASPs,'' *Computer Reseller News,* March 6, 2000, p. 53.

Kerstetter, Jim, ''Lawson Eases App Distribution,'' *PC Week,* February 17, 1997, p. 8.

——, ''Lawson Justifies Intranets with Java-Enabled Apps,'' *PC Week,* October 21, 1996, p. 8.

——, ''Lawson Sweetens Application Pot,'' *PC Week,* July 22, 1996, p. 27.

——, ''Lawson Targets NT, Tighter Web Links,'' *PC Week,* February 24, 1997, p. 61.

''Lawson Customers Testify to Benefits,'' *Modern Materials Handling,* March 31, 2000, p. 29.

''Lawson Extends Global Service Provider Market Leadership,'' *Business Wire,* December 13, 2000.

''Lawson Integrates Desktop Apps,'' *InfoWorld,* July 31, 1995, p. 16.

''Lawson Links to Lotus Notes,'' *InfoWorld,* February 8, 1999, p. 65.

''Lawson Moves to Client/Server with Open Enterprise Release,'' *Software Magazine,* July 15, 1993, p. 68.

''Lawson Plans IPO, Keeps Manageable Focus,'' *Chain Store Age Executive with Shopping Center Age,* June 1999, p. 104.

''Lawson Role-Plays,'' *PC Week,* July 27, 1998, p. 6.

''Lawson Software,'' *Chain Store Age Executive with Shopping Center Age,* February 1999, p. 66.

''Lawson Software,'' *Chain Store Age Executive with Shopping Center Age,* August 1999, p. 78.

''Lawson Software,'' *Chain Store Age Executive with Shopping Center Age,* October 1999, p. 116.

''Lawson Software,'' *Chain Store Age Executive with Shopping Center Age,* April 2000, p. 94.

''Lawson: Unix Port Not Hurting AS/400 Sales,'' *Software Magazine,* January 1993, p. 14.

''Lawson Wins $2.4 Million Deal,'' *PC Week,* July 13, 1998, p. 74.

Maselli, Jennifer, ''Lawson Adding Features to Software,'' *Information Week,* November 13, 2000, http://www.informationweek.com/story/IWK20001113S0009.

——, ''Lawson Targets Vertical Markets,'' *Information Week,* November 20, 2000, p. 44.

Metzler, Melissa, ''New Headquarters Express Firm's Culture,'' *Minneapolis-St. Paul City Business,* August 4, 2000, p. S36.

Munn, Roderick W., ''Lawson Insight,'' *HRMagazine,* November 1997, p. 49.

Niemela, Jennifer, ''Jay Coughlan,'' *Minneapolis-St. Paul City Business,* May 5, 2000, p. S8.

Pender, Lee, ''Lawson Adds E-Com Suite to ERP,'' *PC Week,* March 13, 2000, p. 26.

——, ''Lawson CRM Suite: Buy over Build,'' *PC Week,* December 6, 1999, p. 10.

——, ''Lawson Offers Insight to Execs,'' *PC Week,* March 22, 1999, p. N12.

——, ''Lawson Will Standardize ERP Tools,'' *PC Week,* March 1, 1999, p. 10.

——, ''Vendors Heed Cries for Easier ERP Installation,'' *PC Week,* March 15, 1999, p. 10.

Pickering, Wendy, ''Lawson Draws Vertical Financial Line,'' *PC Week,* May 29, 1995, p. 29.

——, ''Open Enterprise Gains Workflow,'' *PC Week,* February 5, 1996, p. 27.

Piven, Joshua, ''ERP Vendors Caught in Web of Their Own Making,'' *Computer Technology Review,* October 1999, p. 1.

Reilly, Mark, ''Lawson Ditches Plans for New Sales Software,'' *Minneapolis-St. Paul City Business,* July 21, 2000, p. 1.

——, ''Lawson Plans Front-End Market Entry,'' *Minneapolis-St. Paul City Business,* January 21, 2000, p. 10.

''Siebel Teams with Lawson,'' *Washington Business Journal,* April 14, 2000, p. 41.

Songini, Marc L., ''Lawson Hones E-Business Application'' *Computerworld,* November 27, 2000, http://www.computerworld.com/cwi/story/0,1199,NAV47_STO54331,00.html.

——, ''Lawson Readies Release of Applications Upgrade,'' *Computerworld,* November 21, 2000, http://www.computerworld.com/cwi/story/0,1199,NAV47_STO54272,00.html.

Spooner, John G., and Mark Hammond, ''ERP Coming to Handhelds,'' *PC Week,* June 15, 1998, p. 1.

Stedman, Craig, ''Lawson, PeopleSoft Tread into Analysis,'' *Computerworld,* October 25, 1999, p. 8.

——, ''Lawson Sticks to Its Own Turf,'' *Computerworld,* April 20, 1998, p. 24.

Stein, Tom, ''Big Strides for ERP,'' *InformationWeek,* January 4, 1999, p. 67.

——, ''Customized Applications—Lawson Lets Users Tailor Their Forms,'' *InformationWeek,* October 12, 1998, p. 138.

——, ''ERP Overhaul for Lawson,'' *InformationWeek,* March 22, 1999, p. 42.

——, ''ERP Points to Portals,'' *InformationWeek,* May 31, 1999, p. 26.

——, ''Information Retriever—Lawson Add-On Eases Data Access,'' *InformationWeek,* March 16, 1998, p. 102.

——, ''Lawson Rolls out Windows NT Apps,'' *InformationWeek,* April 13, 1998, p. 24.

Tiazkun, Scott, ''ERP Players Move into Niche Areas,'' *Computer Reseller News,* March 15, 1999, p. 14.

——, ''New Insight: Vendor to Release New Suite,'' *Computer Reseller News,* November 22, 1999, p. 3.

Vadlamudi, Pardhu, ''Lawson Bundles Web Server,'' *InfoWorld,* September 23, 1996, p. 16.

——, ''Lawson C/S Suite to Gain Three-Tier Workflow Tools,'' *InfoWorld,* February 12, 1996, p. 40.

——, ''Lawson Plans Customized Versions of 7.0 C/S Suite,'' *InfoWorld,* May 6, 1996, p. 40.

—David P. Bianco

Lazard LLC

121 Boulevard Haussmann
75382 Paris, Cedex 08
France
Telephone: (+33) 1 44 13 01 11
Fax: (+33) 1 44 13 01 00
Web site: http://www.lazard.com

Private Partnership
Incorporated: 1848 as Lazard Frères
Employees: 2,700
Sales: US$512 million (1998 est.)
NAIC: 523110 Investment Banking and Securities Dealing

Lazard LLC is one of the last of the world's leading private investment banking firms, and one of the world's top ten mergers and acquisitions specialists. With the strength of the Lazard brand name—representing some 150 years at the top of its profession, and often mentioned in the same sentence with such global heavyweights as Morgan Stanley and Goldman Sachs—Lazard LLC is in the process of reinventing itself for the 21st century. Formerly three separate and autonomous firms—Lazard Frères & Co. LLC; Lazard Brothers & Co., Limited; Lazard Frères & Cie—each bearing the Lazard name but devoted to their respective New York, London, and Paris locations, the company, led by Michel David-Weill, a fourth generation Lazard family member, has taken steps to merge the three houses into a single corporate and cultural entity, with the Paris office as its headquarters. The move, begun in 2000 and expected to take up to three years to complete, is designed to help Lazard compete in a rapidly changing global investment banking marketplace, which has seen the rise of a few so-called "superbanks" capable of overseeing the wave of multibillion dollar mega-mergers that have marked the world's corporate landscape in the 1990s and early 2000s. Lazard, which does as much as half of its business in the mergers and acquisitions market, nevertheless intends to remain steadfast to its tradition of modest size and private status, offering full-service, client-oriented banking, investment, and other financial services. In 2000, however, Lazard was under attack; outside investors, such as French financier Vincent Bolloré, not only gained significant footholds in Lazard's ownership, but also placed pressure on the company to simplify its corporate structure. The loss of former heir-apparent (and David-Weill son-in-law) Edouard Stern, followed by the departure of rainmaker Stephen Rattner, raised succession issues for Lazard as it struggled to meet the challenges of the new global investment banking climate.

From Merchants to Merchant Bankers in the 1850s

The Lazard dynasty began modestly enough, as three brothers from France's Alsace region—Alexandre, Elie, and Simon—left their native country to settle in New Orleans in 1848. There, the Lazard brothers founded the Lazard Frères (which means "brothers" in French) dry goods store. A year later, Lazard Frères & Co. followed the rest of the world's fortune seekers to the gold rush in San Francisco. The company quickly expanded its business from its range of dry goods to include banking and merchant banking services, as well as exchange services for the foreign currencies market.

This last activity encouraged the company to return to France, where the Lazards opened a second office in Paris in 1852. The Paris office, which initially counseled the French government on its gold purchases, quickly focused on its financial advisory business. Lazard Frères et Cie, as the Paris branch was named, began working closely with France's government and the Banque de Paris, establishing itself as the preeminent investment banker in the French capital.

In the late 1850s, another member of the Lazard family, Alexandre Weill, cousin to the three Lazard brothers, left France to join his cousins in the United States. The family business continued to grow, adding new services to its financial portfolio, including arbitrage services, making the shift away from its dry goods business complete by the 1870s. By 1876, Lazard Frères had abandoned all of its other activities to focus solely on its financial services business. The following year, the partners opened a third office, in London, in order to be present in that financial center. The London office adopted the name Lazard Brothers & Co.

Company Perspectives:

Lazard is dedicated to our cornerstone enterprise: financial advice and transaction execution on behalf of our clients. The firm's resources are concentrated on these activities, and our bankers are free to devote a rare level of expertise to their clients full-time.

Originally a unified company, the Lazard financial empire developed into a multiheaded organization during the later years of the 19th century. Precipitating the change in the company was the rise to control of Alexandre Weill, who, as the only member of the four partners to have male children, supplied the heirs to the family's financial empire. Weill's decision to move the San Francisco office to New York—placing the company at the heart of that booming financial center—prompted discord among his cousins and set the scene for a segmentation of the three company branches. Lazard Frères & Co. opened its New York office in 1880 and quickly carved a place for itself among the top Wall Street investment banking firms.

Each of the three Lazard offices concentrated on its local market, placing the company's name at the center of the three main financial centers of the day. The lack of a rapid means of communication among the offices meant that each conducted its own business independent of the others and, at the same time, developed its own corporate cultures and its own partnership organizations. The Weill family, which initially took over operations of the Paris branch, maintained their ownership of the branch offices, however, and continued to receive the largest share among any of the other partners. These latter were, in fact, only partners in name: while each of the Lazard partners received a share of the company's profit pool—the amount was later determined from the Paris office—they did not in fact receive any equity in the company.

The separation into distinct houses took place at the turn of the 20th century. In 1908, the London office became a separate company, which was a prelude to the company leaving, in large part, the Lazard/Weill family's control. This move was forced upon the company by the British government in 1919, when the Bank of England enacted new rules prohibiting ownership of banks in the United Kingdom by foreign companies. Lazard Brothers came under the control of S.P. Pearson & Sons, when the Weill family sold nearly half of its stake in the London office. Pearson eventually built up its ownership of Lazard Brothers, reaching some 80 percent of that company's shares, in the 1930s. Pearson maintained its position in Lazard Brothers until the end of the 20th century, when it agreed to sell its stake back to the Weill family.

The Weills continued to control the New York and Paris branches; during the initial decades of the century, the Paris office was led by David David-Weill (who added the hyphen to the family name), Alexandre Weill's grandson. David David-Weill then transferred leadership of the company to his son Pierre. The outbreak of World War II, however, forced Pierre David-Weill to flee Paris and Europe for the United States, where he took over control of the New York office. David-Weill was joined by André Meyer, as both were named resident partners of Lazard Frères & Co. in 1943. In Paris, Lazard Frères & Cie ceased operations under the Nazi occupation.

The devastation of the European financial scene during the war caused the focus of Lazard's activity to shift to its New York office. The rebuilding of much of the European and world's economies helped promote Wall Street as the world's financial capital, and Lazard established itself among the top financial services firms. Helping to solidify the company's reputation was the arrival of Felix Rohatyn in 1948. Rohatyn, who left the company only in 1997 to become the U.S. Ambassador to France, forged a reputation as one of the era's great dealmakers, building Lazard into one of the market's top mergers and acquisitions specialists. With Meyer and Rohatyn at the lead of the New York office, Lazard Frères & Co. became the strongest of the three Lazard houses.

Piecing Together an Empire for the 21st Century

Meanwhile, a new generation of the David-Weill family was preparing to make its mark on the family-owned company. In the 1950s, Pierre's son, Michel David-Weill, joined Lazard Frères & Cie, which had been devastated by the war years. Michel David-Weill succeeded in turning around that company by the end of the decade, re-establishing the Lazard name as the preeminent name in investment banking in Paris. In 1961, Michel David-Weill, who inherited the family's controlling share of the Lazard empire, was named as a general partner of New York-based Lazard Frères & Co.

The 1970s saw the balance of power shift within the global Lazard empire—which by then included offices worldwide. The failing health of André Meyer gave David-Weill an opportunity to take over direction of the New York branch as well as the Paris branch, uniting the two formerly separate offices under the same chief for the first time since the beginning of the century. Michel David-Weill was named senior partner of Lazard Frères & Co. in 1977.

Meanwhile, in London, the third member of the Lazard investment family was struggling against a new wave of competitors entering the British financial markets in the 1970s. Struggling to keep up in its market, Lazard Brothers finally sought help in the form of a merger with another company. This move, however, was blocked by the other two members of the Lazard group.

The Lazard Brothers crisis served to open up an opportunity for David-Weill to buy back some of the shares in the London office from Pearson. In 1984, David-Weill set up Lazard Partners, a private limited U.S. partnership, joining his own and related Lazard shares into the new vehicle. Pearson in turn contributed its holdings in Lazard Brothers, taking a 50 percent share of Lazard Partners, which then gained 100 percent control of the London office. Although the deal did not yet give David-Weill outright control over the London Lazard branch, it did bring together the three branches into a more cooperative, globally operating network.

David-Weill's timing was right. While the Paris branch was reaping the benefits of the French wave of nationalizations

Key Dates:

1848: Lazard Frères is founded in New Orleans.
1849: Lazard Frères moves to San Francisco.
1852: Lazard Frères & Cie is opened in Paris.
1856: Alexandre Weill joins company.
1876: Company focuses on banking activities.
1877: Lazard Brothers is opened in London.
1880: Lazard Frères moves to New York.
1908: Lazard Brothers separates from other branches.
1919: Company sells a 45 percent stake to S.P. Pearson & Sons.
1932: Pearson gains 80 percent of Lazard Brothers.
1943: Amid the upheaval of World War II, Pierre David-Weill and André Meyer flee France and join the New York office.
1948: Felix Rohatyn joins company as partner.
1950: Michel David-Weill joins Lazard Frères & Cie.
1961: David-Weill is named general partner of Lazard Frères & Co.
1977: David-Weill is named senior partner of Lazard Frères & Co.
1984: Lazard Partners is formed.
1989: David-Weill is named head of Lazard Brothers.
1995: Lazard Capital Markets is formed.
1996: Single profits pool is created for three Lazard firms.
1997: Lazard Asset Management takes over all Lazard asset management operations.
1999: David-Weill buys out Pearson stake.
2000: All Lazard operations are combined under Lazard LLC's direction.

of its banking industry, which Lazard Frères et Cie helped coordinate, David-Weill had correctly recognized the growing globalization of the international marketplace, as mergers and acquisitions began to cross borders, a trend that especially picked up in the 1990s. Meanwhile, Lazard had shunned, in large part, the wave of leveraged buyouts that washed across the financial world during the 1980s, thereby avoiding the fall-out as the world economy slumped in the late 1980s and early 1990s.

At the end of the 1980s, David-Weill was named senior partner at the Lazard Brothers branch, marking the first time since the beginning of the century that one person held the leadership position in all three Lazard firms. The move toward formally uniting the three branches under a single management only came slowly, however.

In the mid-1990s, the three Lazard firms took a number of steps toward unification. Among these was the creation of Lazard Capital Markets, which was formed as a single globally operating entity providing underwriting services to Lazard clients in all three branches. More significantly, the three offices began a common profits pool from which to pay its partners. David-Weill himself decided the amount partners were to be paid. The move was not well received by the company's partners, given that the New York office generated twice the amount of profits of either the London or Paris offices. The company lost a number of its partners, particularly a number of its brightest stars, who were tempted away by the promise of better compensation at one of the newly emerging investment banking giants.

Lazard found itself caught up in a new trend. As mergers and acquisitions specialists became involved in a series of ''mega-mergers,'' which in turn were creating a new breed of huge, globally operating companies, the banking firms themselves began to take on scale to meet their new clients' needs. The emergence of giants such as Morgan Stanley Dean Witter and Goldman Sachs and others had come to dwarf the three individual Lazard houses. Lazard, which had long ranked among the top tier mergers and acquisitions houses, found itself slipping in the ranks, and even dropped out of the top ten entirely in 1997.

In that year, the three Lazard firms took a new step toward their own in-house merger, when the New York-based Lazard Asset Management absorbed the other Lazard companies' asset management operations. Lazard, however, continued to find difficulty in recruiting—and even keeping—the industry's top banking stars. The retirement of Felix Rohatyn, who was named the U.S. Ambassador to France in 1997, shook up the company. Lazard was equally shaken by the defection of Edouard Stern—David-Weill's son-in-law and probable successor—who left the company that same year. Rohatyn's, and Stern's, replacement as top rainmaker was Steven Rattner, a former journalist who had gained an international reputation as a top deal-maker during the 1990s. Rattner, named CEO of Lazard Frères & Co., was credited with helping to clarify some of Lazard's operations, such as revealing the amount paid to each partner, while also convincing Michel David-Weill to cut his own 15 percent share of the New York office's profits back to just ten percent in an effort to appease disgruntled New York partners.

Rattner did not remain with Lazard for long. His own political ambitions (he was popularly tipped for a role in the presidential cabinet in the event of a win by Al Gore) brought him to step back from active management of Lazard in 1999, before leaving the company altogether in 2000. By then, however, David-Weill had used his own funds to buy out Pearson's share of Lazard Partners, giving him majority control of the three pieces of the Lazard empire.

In 2000, David-Weill announced his decision to rejoin the pieces to create a single, globally operating entity, Lazard LLC. Based in the company's traditional Paris headquarters, the newly united Lazard hoped to regain some of its former luster in the world's international market. The company remained dedicated to its modest size and, especially, to its status as one of the few remaining private partnership companies in the industry—a position that enabled the company to provide a higher degree of discretion to its clients.

Although David-Weill had succeeded in uniting his family's empire under his control, he nevertheless faced a new outside threat, when both Swiss investment firm Warburg USB and French multibillionaire investor Vincent Bolloré built up significant positions in firms that indirectly owned parts of the Lazard company. Warburg and Bolloré both began to place pressure on David-Weill to simplify the company's organizational structure, widely described by observers as "Byzantine," but which also was credited with helping the company to avoid the risks of a hostile takeover in an investment climate that promised increasing consolidation moves in the new century.

Principal Subsidiaries

Lazard Frères & Co. LLC; Lazard Brothers & Co., Limited; Lazard Frères & Cie; The Caliburn Partnership (Australia); Lazard & Co. GmbH (Germany); Lazard AB Stockholm; Lazard Asia (H.K.) Ltd (Hong Kong); Lazard Asia Limited (South Korea); Lazard Asia Ltd (China); Lazard Asia Ltd (Singapore); Lazard Asset Management; Lazard Asset Management (Deutschland) GmbH (Germany); Lazard Asset Management (U.K.); Lazard Asset Management Egypt; Lazard Asset Management Pacific Co. (Australia); Lazard Brothers & Co., Limited (U.K.); Lazard Canada Corporation; Lazard Capital Markets (France); Lazard Capital Markets (U.K.); Lazard Freres & Cie (France); Lazard Freres & Co. LLC; Lazard Freres K.K. (Japan); Lazard India; Lazard Japan Asset Management (K.K.); Lazard Sp. Z.O.O. (Poland); Lazard Vitale Borghesi S.P.A. (Italy); Lazard, Asesores Financieros S.A. (Spain).

Principal Competitors

The Bear Stearns Companies Inc.; Daiwa Securities Group Inc.; Deutsche Bank AG; FMR Corp.; The Goldman Sachs Group, Inc.; Lehman Brothers Holdings Inc.; Merrill Lynch & Co., Inc.; Morgan Stanley Dean Witter & Co.; The Nomura Securities Co., Ltd.; Paine Webber Group Inc.; Salomon Smith Barney Holdings Inc.; UBS Warburg.

Further Reading

Cave, Andrew, "Lazard Men Quit and Go Private," *Daily Telegraph,* March 1, 2000.

Gledhill, Dan, "Lazard Bows to Rival's Pressure," *Independent on Sunday,* October 1, 2000, p. 1.

Lenzner, Robert, "Assault on the House of Lazard," *Forbes,* September 4, 2000.

Owen, David, "Adapting to Change Not Easy for an Icon," *Financial Times,* November 10, 2000.

Reed, Stanley, "The Leadership Question at Lazard Frères," *Business Week,* June 21, 1999, p. 170.

Washington, Sharon Walsh, "Lazard to Combine Global Offices," *Washington Post,* June 8, 1999, p. E03.

—M.L. Cohen

M&F Worldwide Corp.

35 East 62nd Street
New York, New York
U.S.A.
Telephone: (212) 572-8600
Fax: (212) 572-8400

Public Subsidiary of MacAndrews & Forbes Holdings Inc.
Incorporated: 1902 as MacAndrews & Forbes Co.
Employees: 311
Sales: $95.9 million (1999)
Stock Exchanges: New York
Ticker Symbol: MFW
NAIC: 311942 Spice and Extract Manufacturing; 551112 Offices of Other Holding Companies

M&F Worldwide Corp. is a holding company that, through its wholly owned subsidiary Pneumo Abex Corporation, is the world's largest producer of licorice flavors. About 70 percent of its licorice sales are to the worldwide tobacco industry for use as flavoring and moistening agents in the manufacture of American-blend cigarettes, moist snuff, and chewing and pipe tobacco. M&F Worldwide also sells licorice flavors to confectioners, food processors, and pharmaceutical manufacturers for use as flavoring or masking agents. In addition, the company sells licorice-root residue as a garden mulch and produces natural flavors and plant products from roots, berries, spices, and botanicals for use in food, tobacco, and pharmaceutical products. The company's predecessor, MacAndrews & Forbes Co., was the second company acquired by Ronald O. Perelman, who went to on to build a multibillion-dollar business empire under the names MacAndrews & Forbes Holdings Inc. and Mafco Holdings Inc. Headquartered in the same Manhattan mansion where Perelman lives and administers MacAndrews & Forbes Holdings, M&F Worldwide was, in 2000, 32 percent owned by Perelman through Mafco Holdings.

A Century of Licorice Production: 1870–1970

The licorice plant grows wild in a belt of Eurasia running along the 40th parallel north and was exploited by ancient civilizations from Egypt to China for the root, which yields a sweetening agent with nearly 50 times the saccharinity of cane sugar. Two Scots, Edward MacAndrew and William Forbes, traveled to Turkey in 1850, where they established the firm of MacAndrew & Forbes. Within a short time they built a licorice-extracting factory in Sochia. In 1870 James C. MacAndrew, David Forbes, and Alexander Geddes established an American firm by the same name in Newark, New Jersey, where they built another such factory. The firm became MacAndrews & Forbes Co. in 1902, following the purchase of Mellor & Rittenhouse Co., a licorice-extracting firm with a plant on the Delaware River in Camden, New Jersey. The merged company closed its Newark facility and moved to this location.

MacAndrews & Forbes was now the world's largest producer of licorice and licorice products for the rapidly growing tobacco industry. It became a subsidiary of James Buchanan Duke's American Tobacco Co. in 1904 and also had a Baltimore plant by 1911, when the U.S. Supreme Court dissolved the union on antitrust grounds and required the sale of said plant to J.S. Young Co. MacAndrews & Forbes had assets of $16.3 million and a net profit of $1.94 million in 1920. By the end of this decade it had added boxboard, wallboard, insulation board, and fire-extinguishing agents as products derived from licorice-root residue. The company also had a subsidiary producing carpets and rugs in Gloucester, New Jersey, Greece, and China. Company sales rose as high as $12.66 million in 1927. During the Depression, MacAndrews & Forbes remained profitable even though annual sales dipped below $6 million, but it disposed of its carpet-and-rug business. The company also moved its headquarters from Camden to New York City.

MacAndrews & Forbes's sales reached a peak of $15.82 million in 1951. In addition to the sales of licorice extract from the Camden plant to the American tobacco market, it was supplying about 60 percent of the licorice products needed for the European market. Its only U.S. competitor was J.S. Young, and more Americans were smoking cigarettes than ever before. The tobacco industry used relatively more licorice in the other forms of tobacco consumption than in cigarettes, and perhaps this was the reason that sales and profits slipped during the 1950s. Certainly the company did not have to fear competition in its field, because extracting and processing licorice called for

Key Dates:

1870: A MacAndrew & Forbes firm is founded in Newark, New Jersey.
1902: As MacAndrews & Forbes Co., the operation moves to Camden, New Jersey.
1967: Two Philadelphia textile manufacturers take control of the company.
1980: Leveraged-buyout entrepreneur Ronald Perelman acquires a controlling share of the company.
1986: The company purchases a French licorice-extraction firm.
1995–97: Through a complex series of maneuvers, this company becomes M&F Worldwide, a publicly traded company.

years of experience. In 1952 nearly one-third of the firm's employees had been on its payroll for at least 25 years.

In 1963 MacAndrews & Forbes began selling licorice-root mulch to the public, under the name Right Dress, within a 200-mile radius of Camden. Insulation-board manufacturing ended in 1965, and the following year the company acquired the Philadelphia paperboard-coating facilities of the International Paper Co. Sales and profits were stagnant, but this posed no danger under ultraconservative management. Indeed, the company's rock-solid finances attracted suitors, among them Raymond Perelman, a Philadelphia entrepreneur, and two Philadelphia textile manufacturers, Samuel Rosenman and Lawrence Katz. Rosenman and Katz purchased about 25 percent of the stock—a controlling interest—in 1967 and assumed management of the company, moving its headquarters to Philadelphia.

At this time MacAndrews & Forbes was processing roughly half the world's total annual crop of 35,000 to 40,000 tons of licorice root. Rosenman and Katz purchased M.F. Neal & Co., Inc. of Richmond, Virginia, to sell a variety of other natural flavoring agents to the tobacco industry. They also bought Wilbur Chocolate Co. of Lititz, Pennsylvania, a producer of cocoa mixes and chocolate coatings with annual sales of $21 million, for $5.7 million in 1968. Their main interest, however, was to use the company's cash to move back into the textile field. In 1968 they opened a plant in McBee, South Carolina, for the manufacture of polyester textured yarn and knitted fabrics. Two paperboard machines were shut down in 1968, and the remaining one was sold in 1973 for about $6.5 million.

Organizational Changes: 1975–95

Of MacAndrews & Forbes's 1975 sales, chocolate accounted for 42 percent, textiles for 30 percent, and flavors (the most profitable item) for 28 percent. With the fading of the brief polyester boom, the textile division lost $1 million the following year and the company disposed of it in 1977, when total sales came to $110.06 million. Rosenblum and Katz frequently traveled to Iran to search for licorice root and dined at the palace of the shah of Iran. Following the shah's fall in 1978, they sought to sell the business. An offer from Ronald Perelman, however, was most unwelcome (probably because of previous differences with his father) and in 1979 they sold their shares to Richard and Burton Koffman for $8.6 million. Perelman persisted in seeking the company, and in 1980 purchased what amounted to a 22 percent share from the Koffmans for nearly $10 million.

This purchase was made through Perelman's first acquisition, Cohen-Hatfield Industries, Inc., a jewelry company. Cohen-Hatfield then acquired the rest of the company in a tender offer for $34 million. Cohen-Hatfield next merged with MacAndrews & Forbes to form MacAndrews & Forbes Group Inc., which moved to New York City. This company acquired Technicolor Inc., a processor of color film, in 1982, for $105 million. The following year Perelman offered to buy the 62.5 percent of MacAndrews & Forbes Group that he did not own for $52.7 million. Nine separate shareholder suits sought to block the transaction in court on the grounds that the price was too low, but in vain. Following approval of the offer in 1984, MacAndrews & Forbes Group was privatized as a subsidiary of MacAndrews & Forbes Holdings Inc., a newly formed, closely held company owned by Perelman. To raise the cash for the purchase, the holding company sold low-grade, high-yield "junk" bonds to clients of Drexel Burnham Lambert Inc.

MacAndrews & Forbes Co. continued in existence as a flavors operation, the jewelry segment being discontinued in 1985 and the chocolate division being sold in 1986 for $40.5 million. The company maintained a 45 percent share in an Iranian licorice-extraction plant and purchased from Pakistani merchants any licorice root that came over the border from strife-torn Afghanistan. Nevertheless, seeking to reduce dependence on such chancy sources, Perelman sent buyers to Russia, Iraq, eastern Turkey, and western China to negotiate long-term contracts for supplies at low cost. He extended the company's wholesale market to Europe in 1986 by purchasing a French operation, Extraits Vegetaux et Derives, S.A., which had its own extraction plant and an established continental distribution network. A *Business Week* article reported in 1986 that the MacAndrews & Forbes licorice business was five times larger than it had been in 1979. According to *Institutional Investor,* which in 1989 called Perelman the richest man in the United States, earnings tripled between 1980 and 1988, when they reached $20 million on sales of more than $100 million. Also according to the magazine, the company was valued at $350 million by Wall Street (although an internal MacAndrews & Forbes memo scoffed at that sum, describing it as the work of "someone [who] must be smoking licorice root").

Public Company: 1995–2000

In 1995 Perelman acquired Abex Inc., a producer of flight- and engine-control systems and hydraulic pumps for aircraft. This company was merged into a subsidiary of Mafco Holdings Inc., save for the aerospace division, which became Power Technologies Inc., a publicly traded company. The aerospace business was sold in 1996 for $201.1 million. Later in 1996 Power Technologies acquired Flavors Holdings Inc. for $180 million. This Perelman entity included the licorice business, which was then a subsidiary of Flavors Holdings named Mafco Worldwide Corp. Through a series of transactions, Mafco Worldwide merged with and into Pneumo Abex Inc., a previously indirect, wholly owned subsidiary of Abex incorporated in 1988. Pneumo Abex became a subsidiary of Flavors Holdings. Power Technologies was renamed M&F Worldwide in 1997. There was method behind these convoluted transactions and reshufflings, since the complicated Perelman empire of holding and operating companies was, according to Leah Nathans Spiro of *Business Week,* ''a clever structure that yields tax, financial, and management benefits.''

M&F Worldwide added a Chinese subsidiary and joint venture in 1998 with a factory in Xianyang. In 1999, foreign suppliers of the company were obtaining bales of licorice root that originated mainly in Afghanistan, Azerbaijan, China, Pakistan, Syria, Turkey, Turkmenistan, and Uzbekistan. Four suppliers of the root met 55 percent of the company's purchases that year. At the end of 1999 M&F had on hand about a two-year supply of the root, which had an indefinite retention period when kept dry. The company also was purchasing licorice extract produced by others for use as a raw material, primarily in China and Turkmenistan. M&F was shredding the root to matchstick size at its facilities in Camden, Xianyang, and Gardanne, France, and then extracting licorice solids from the shredded root with hot water. After filtration and evaporation, the concentrated extract was being converted into powder, semifluid, or blocks, depending on the customer's requirements. Licorice root residue was still being sold as a garden mulch under the Right Dress name.

Non-licorice flavoring agents and plant products were being produced in Richmond, where unprocessed spices, herbs, and plant products, principally chilies, sage, cassia (cinnamon), cocoa-bean shells, dried palmetto berries, goldenseal root, slippery elm bark, and many other natural products were being cleaned, ground, or cut. Customers included tobacco and confectionery producers, both in the United States and abroad.

M&F believed that it was manufacturing more than 70 percent of the worldwide licorice flavors sold to end-users in 1999. About 71 percent of its licorice sales went to the worldwide tobacco industry, with Philip Morris Companies Inc. alone accounting for about 30 percent of company sales. Net sales came to $95.9 million in 1999, and net income to $19.1 million. The company's long-term debt was $49 million at the end of the year. In mid-2000, M&F had about $124 million of tax-loss carryforwards inherited from Power Control Technologies and available to be used to offset future federal income taxes payable. Perelman owned 32 percent of the stock through Mafco Holdings Inc. Although no longer chairman of the board (as he was from 1995 to 1997), he remained chairman of the executive committee of the board. James P. Maher, who previously held executive positions in other Perelman entities, was president, chairman, and CEO of the company.

In November 2000 Perelman proposed that M&F Worldwide purchase Mafco Holdings' 83 percent stake in Panavision Inc. This manufacturer of motion picture and television cameras and lenses lost money on sales of $202.8 million in 1999, mainly because of heavy interest payments on long-term debt of nearly $500 million arising from a complex 1997–98 recapitalization in which Mafco Holdings gained its controlling share. Perelman proposed that M&F Worldwide pay at least $190.3 million, or $26 a share, in cash and stock for Panavision. This was the amount that Mafco Holdings paid for the shares, but the stock was trading at only about $6 a share in late 2000. An M&F shareholder filed suit to prevent the purchase, charging that the proposal constituted ''unfair self-dealing and breach of fiduciary duties.''

Principal Subsidiaries

Boam Produce (Europe) Est. (Lichtenstein; 45%); Concord Pacific Corporation; EVD Holdings Inc.; EVD Holdings S.A. (France); Extraits Vegetaux et Derives, S.A. (France); Flavors Holdings, Inc.; Mafco Establishment (Lichtenstein); Mafco Weihai Green Industry of Science and Technology Co. Ltd. (China; 50%); PCT International, Inc.; Pnemo Abex Corporation; Rishmoc Produce & Export Co. (Iran; 45%); Xianyang Concord Natural Products Co. Ltd. (China).

Principal Competitors

Bush Boake Allen Inc.; Givaudon-Roure Flavors Corp.; McCormick Flavor Group Inc.

Further Reading

Bary, Andrew, ''Perelman's Price,'' *Barron's,* November 20, 2000, p. 45.

Dunkin, Amy, ''This Takeover Artist Wants to Be a Makeover Artist, Too,'' *Business Week,* December 1, 1986, p. 110.

Fisher, Daniel, ''Sweet Deal,'' *Forbes,* August 9, 1999, p. 136.

Hack, Richard, *When Money Is King,* Los Angeles: Dove Books, 1996.

MacAndrews & Forbes Company, *The Story of Licorice,* New York: McAndrews & Forbes Company, 1952.

''MacAndrews Plans to Divest Itself of Textile Business,'' *Wall Street Journal,* December 23, 1977, p. 8.

Marcial, Gene G., ''Has Ron Perelman Spotted a Pearl?,'' *Business Week,* June 26, 1995, p. 126.

Meyers, William, ''How Ron Perelman Became the Richest Man in America,'' *Institutional Investor,* May 1989, pp. 143–46.

NacManie, Miron, ''MacAndrews & Forbes Co.,'' *Wall Street Transcript,* October 27, 1969, pp. 18,353–54.

Norris, Floyd, ''Perelman's Plan: Take Profits While Public Owners Suffer,'' *New York Times,* November 24, 2000, p. C1.

''Perelman Offers to Buy Remainder of MacAndrews,'' *Wall Street Journal,* September 26, 1983, p. 2.

''Pulp Mill Updates Licorice Plant,'' *Chemical Engineering,* April 10, 1967, p. 120.

Spiro, Leah Nathans, ''The Operator,'' *Business Week,* August 21, 1995, p. 56.

''Whetting America's Taste for Licorice,'' *Business Week,* June 7, 1952, p. 114.

—Robert Halasz

Mannesmann AG

Mannesmannufer 2
D-40213 Düsseldorf
Germany
Telephone: +49 (0) 211 820-0
Fax: +49 (0) 211 820-1846
Web site: http://www.mannesmann.com

Public Subsidiary of Vodafone Group Plc
Incorporated: 1890 as Deutsch Österreichische Mannesmannröhren Werke Aktiengesellschaft
Employees: 31,000
Sales: EUR 23.27 billion (1999)
Stock Exchanges: Frankfurt Milan
Ticker Symbol: MMN
NAIC: 51331 Wired Telecommunications Carriers; 513322 Cellular and Other Wireless Telecommunications

Mannesmann AG is a leading German telecom provider. Its D2 unit operates the country's largest mobile phone service; its ground-based telephone network, Mannesmann Arcor, is second only to government-sponsored Deutsche Telekom. Mannesmann developed from a steel tube manufacturer into a highly diversified, globally focused group of companies involved in machinery and plant construction, industrial drive and control systems, electrical and electronic engineering, automotive technology, and its traditional area, steel tube production. Telecommunications has emerged as the company's sole focus, however. Vodafone Group plc acquired 99 percent of the company in February 2000.

Origins

The history of Mannesmann began five years before the company's founding with a major technical achievement. In 1885, the brothers Reinhard and Max Mannesmann invented a rolling process for the manufacture of thick-walled seamless steel tubes, the so-called cross-rolling process, at their father's file factory in Remscheid. Introducing the invention, they founded tube mills between 1887 and 1889 with several different business partners, in Bous on the Saar (in the Bohemian Komotau), in Landore, Wales, and at home in Remscheid. The machine building industry was unable to supply the necessary plant for the application of the rolling process, and the iron and steel industry was not able to provide the necessary supplies of high-quality semi-finished products. As a result, numerous other inventions had to be made and long years of experiments passed before the initial difficulties in the industrial exploitation of the new process were overcome.

In 1890, a technical breakthrough was achieved with the brothers' invention of the pilger rolling process. The name was taken from the analogous Luxembourg Echternach pilgrims' procession, as during the rolling process the prepierced thick-walled steel ingot was moved forward and backward and turned at the same time in order to be stretched into a thin-walled tube. The combination of the pilger and the cross-rolling processes became known as the Mannesmann process. On July 16, 1890, the tube and pipe mills existing on the Continent were folded into Deutsch Österreichische Mannesmannröhren Werke Aktiengesellschaft, which had its headquarters in Berlin. Reinhard and Max Mannesmann formed the first board of management but left it in 1893. In that year the company headquarters was moved from Berlin to Düsseldorf, at that time the center of the tube and pipe industry.

From about this time, seamless medium-sized steel tubes were successfully produced and sold worldwide at a profit, by far surpassing rival products in quality. It was thus possible to reduce the loss of more than 20 million marks, which had accumulated during the company's first years of business, and, eventually, to pay the first dividend in 1906.

The success of Mannesmann's tubes alarmed competitors grouped in associations and syndicates. Feeling their very existence threatened, they stopped supplies of large and small tube sizes, for which seamless production was not yet possible, to dealers selling Mannesmann tubes. To be able to supply a complete range of products, Mannesmann built a factory for the production of longitudinally welded tubes in the second half of the 1890s; the company also acquired shares in companies involved in tube and rolled steel trading and pipeline construction.

Company Perspectives:

Since its merger with Vodafone, Mannesmann has been market leader in the global telecommunications business. The Vodafone Group has holdings in 25 countries on five continents.

Mannesmann's position in the export business, which was important from the beginning of the company, was consolidated and expanded by the acquisition of the British Mannesmann tube mill in Landore, Wales, which had been founded by the Mannesmann and Siemens families but had never overcome its start-up problems, and by the founding of a Mannesmann tube mill with its own electrical steelworks in Dalmine, Italy. Since the turn of the century, branch offices undertaking storage and direct sales business, sometimes with tube processing workshops and pipeline construction capacities, were set up in cooperation with well-established companies all over the world, especially in South America, Asia, and South Africa.

Except for the works in Dalmine and Bous, which operated their own small steelworks, Mannesmann continued to be dependent on supplies of semi-finished products from third parties; even Bous had to buy scrap and pig iron. With the tendency toward horizontal integration by means of increasing numbers of cartels and vertical integration in the formation of vertically structured coal and steel groups that mined their own ore and coal, produced pig iron and crude steels, and converted them to finished products, this dependence on suppliers began to endanger Mannesmann's existence. Accordingly, the company's foremost strategic goal became to achieve self-sufficiency in semi-finished products and thus to enable the company to determine price, quality, and the actual delivery period. In the process, iron ore and pit or hard coal mines, a lime works, a factory for the production of refractory materials, and finally, in 1914, a plate rolling mill with an open hearth steelworks at Huckingen on the Rhine were acquired. Plans for the expansion of the steelworks and the construction of blast furnaces were thwarted by the outbreak of World War I.

In the period that followed, the company was forced to employ emergency labor, to cope with changes in its range of products, and to make up for the loss of export business, which formerly had accounted for 60 percent of sales. The British Mannesmann Tube Company, with its works in Landore and Newport, was lost. The Italian subsidiary in Dalmine had to be sold under duress. The loss of the works on the Saar and in Bohemia could only be avoided by allowing French and Czechoslovakian companies to participate.

This was not a time to shape and realize long-term corporate strategies. In the ten-year period beginning in 1914, day-to-day problems required full attention. At the end of the war, plants had to be replaced completely or were, upon instant transfer to peacetime production, no longer usable.

Export contacts were reestablished, and machinery in the remaining works was replaced and expanded to compensate for the loss of production capacity. Although Mannesmann's major steelworks had not yet been built, this construction plan was by no means abandoned. Measures were carried out that efficiently supplemented the existing installations. The mining division was strengthened by the acquisition of another pit coal mine and of a coal trading company with its own inland fleet. The works harbor at Huckingen was expanded to accommodate seagoing vessels, and the works area was enlarged by the purchase of further land.

In November 1925, Mannesmann turned down the offer to take part in the formation of what was at the time the largest German coal and steel group, Vereinigte Stahlwerke AG, and decided to maintain its independence even in those difficult times. This decision resulted in the creation of a company-owned semi-finished product manufacturing unit. In 1927, Mannesmann began to build a blast furnace, the Thomas steelworks, and auxiliary plants and shops. Despite a few strikes, a general lockout, and delays caused by harsh winter weather, expansion proceeded so quickly that as early as May 1929 two blast furnaces, each producing 800 tons a day, the sinter plant, and the Thomas steelworks with four converters holding 30 tons each, went into operation. The steelworks already had numerous facilities that, not only in terms of technology but also in terms of safety standards and regard for the environment in general, were ahead of their time. With the blast furnace and the Thomas steelworks, the company integrated the ore and pit coal mines on one side with the steel and rolling mills on the other and completed its development into a fully vertically structured coal and steel group, typical of the Ruhr industry until the 1970s. Mannesmann thus became independent of outside suppliers of semi-finished products and was able to make full use of the advantages offered by the combination of mining and steelmaking.

To promote sales, the domestic marketing organization was made more efficient by the establishment of warehousing companies. Shareholdings in trading, production, and assembly businesses in many European and overseas countries were acquired. The Landore works lost during the war was recovered. Holdings in a company for the construction of power supply plants in Berlin and in a pipeline construction firm in Leipzig were acquired, to promote Mannesmann's tube sales. The latter two participations marked the beginning of new activity for Mannesmann that developed into a group of companies operated by Mannesmann Anlagenbau AG. The participation in the family-owned Maschinenfabrik Gebr. Meer in Mönchengladbach, founded in 1872, which had for many years successfully constructed rolling mills for the manufacture of seamless tubes and tube processing machines, did not represent an attempt to diversify, but resulted from the fact that the company could no longer design and build its own rolling mills as it had done since 1886. Since the task was now assigned to others, Mannesmann intended to make sure that new designs were not made accessible to competitors.

Technical developments in the period before the outbreak of World War II were characterized by the successful solution of problems in the manufacture of tubes of high-alloy stainless steel and the successful application of the extrusion process and the introduction of a new rolling mill for the manufacture of thick-walled seamless steel tubes. At the same time, the semi-finished and heavy plate product lines were extended, with the contribution of newly acquired companies. The Depression and the ensuing economic boom, further invigorated by government

Key Dates:

1890: Mannesmann is formed to produce seamless steel tubes.
1927: Facilities to make semi-finished steel products are built.
1952: Plants are started in Brazil, Canada, and Turkey.
1968: Mannesmann diversifies into hydraulics.
1981: First electronics firm is acquired.
1990: Mannesmann heads D2 cellular phone consortium.
1995: Traditional businesses are sold off in favor of telecoms.
1999: Mannesmann spends US$42 billion on telecom acquisitions.
2000: Vodafone Group plc acquires Mannesmann.

job-creating schemes, both affected the company. The production and sale of all Mannesmann products were governed by national, European, and international cartels, from the mid-1920s until the end of World War II.

The outbreak of World War II hit the company during a phase of plant replacement. The Bous works and its staff were moved to Düsseldorf. Production remained essentially unchanged but, to a far greater extent than in World War I, the works replaced their conscripted workforce with unskilled workers, women, civilian foreign workers, and prisoners of war.

All works were bombed several times and suffered varying degrees of damage. With the Allies approaching, the plants were vacated and as far as possible protected against plunder by emergency crews. By order of the Allies, Mannesmann was liquidated and in 1952 divided into three independent groups of companies, one of them Mannesmann AG. By 1955, Mannesmann AG had absorbed the other two and more or less reestablished its former unity. Mannesmann was the first group in the coal and steel industry to be split up into independent smaller groups, convene a general meeting of shareholders, pay a dividend, have its shares quoted at the stock exchange, increase its share capital, issue a loan, and regain its former structure.

The Czechoslovakian works were lost, and the Bous works, reintegrated in the 1930s, were confiscated again and later brought into a French company in which Mannesmann's stake rose from 40 to 51 percent in 1959 and, finally, to 100 percent in 1985. The British Mannesmann company already had been sold in the 1930s.

Global After World War II

Even before the company's future was definitely settled, it again began to build up extensive activities abroad. Between 1952 and 1955, Mannesmann founded its own steel and tube mills in Brazil, Canada, and Turkey, establishing its presence in several important markets. Although the Canadian joint venture was divested in the early 1970s, the Turkish joint venture, small at the start, was repeatedly enlarged. Companhia Siderúrgica Mannesmann S.A. in Belo Horizonte developed into the Brazilian group of companies that supplied Mannesmann products and services, in particular to the South American markets. Its range of products and services included rolled and drawn high-grade and special steel products, steel wires and welding rods, steel tubes, steelworks and rolling mill machinery and equipment, compressors, excavators, plastics injection molding machines, hoists, hydraulic systems, and components for industrial drive and control systems. The group ran its own ore mines and had eucalyptus plantations for charcoal production. Its marketing was carried out by an independent trading company, Mannesmann Comercial S.A., of Sao Paolo.

Other participations—for example, in companies producing irrigation systems, forage silos, agricultural tractors and engines, and plastics tubes and pipes—turned out to be less successful. As their future prospects began to look unpromising, they eventually were given up. The traditional coal and steel companies, on the other hand, were since the 1960s exposed to growing international competition. In many countries, new large, low-cost plants were constructed that aimed at the world market. International competition, frequently government-supported, threatened to eliminate European producers.

With investment expenses rising steeply, it was doubtful whether Mannesmann would in the future be able to compete worldwide in tubes, rolled steel, and tube processing. The existing excess production capacity for steel tubes, rolled steel products, and pit coal left very little hope for continuing with satisfactory profits. As a traditional coal and steel group, Mannesmann's outlook was not promising.

Nevertheless, by the end of the 1960s, Mannesmann had broken from tradition and was looking for new ways to secure its future. Domestic ore mining came to a complete halt and coal mining interests were brought together in a unified company, the Ruhrkohle AG.

Leading Hydraulics in the 1970s

The gradual acquisition of G.L. Rexroth GmbH between 1968 and 1975 reflected the new trend of development. From modest beginnings, the company was expanded and internationalized to become the world leader in hydraulics. In addition to hydraulic components and systems, the company's range of products and services included pneumatics and linear motion technology, electric servo drives, gears, and couplings. Rexroth marked the beginning of the restructuring of the Mannesmann group. This first step was successful and pointed the way forward for the company.

In 1970, Mannesmann and Thyssen agreed on a division of labor; Mannesmann took over tube production and tube laying from Thyssen and transferred its own rolled steel production and sheet processing activities in Germany to Thyssen. The new Mannesmannröhren Werke became the world's largest producer of tubes. Despite capacity reduction and concentration on the most efficient plants, further drastic restructuring became necessary as market conditions turned out to be worse than even the most pessimistic forecasts had anticipated. When losses reached almost DM 1 billion in 1986–87, the situation became temporarily very grave.

By 1988, the worst problems had been overcome. Structural adjustment, however, which, at the semi-finished products level, led to cooperation with other long-established steelworks, was not yet completed. Cross-border cooperation between the European tubemakers was one way to preserve the European tube industry. Two forward-looking strategies at Mannesmannröhren Werke were participation in a company for the production of hydride stores for the storage and transportation of hydrogen and development of purest gases and in a company producing automotive components with manufacturing facilities in a converted former steelworks.

With the acquisition of Demag AG, a well-established group with a rich and eventful history, Mannesmann strengthened its activities in machinery and plant construction during the first half of the 1970s. By the middle of the decade, about 30 percent of the company's external sales was coming from these divisions.

Electronic in the 1980s

At the beginning of the 1980s, Mannesmann gained access to the growing electronics markets by acquiring Hartmann & Braun in 1981 and Kienzle Apparate GmbH in 1981 and 1982. Hartmann & Braun was an international company in the field of measurement, control, and automation engineering, with subsidiaries in Germany, in other European countries, and overseas. The change of emphasis in Mannesmann's range of products toward the processing industry, with its higher growth potential, proved successful. Mannesmann's second acquisition in this field, Kienzle, operated in data processing and supplied electronic systems for motor vehicles. Mannesmann previously had entered data processing both as a user and through its successful development of printers. Kienzle enabled Mannesmann to operate in the center of data processing. Originally, Kienzle supplied only the German market; later it became international and established sales operations in other countries, some with local partners.

The acquisition of a majority holding in Fichtel & Sachs AG in 1987 and in Krauss Maffei AG in 1989 enabled Mannesmann to consolidate its leading position in the machinery and plant construction sectors. A key motive for the acquisition of Krauss Maffei was the possibility of expanding Demag's plastics machinery activities and thus ensuring, according to the standard set by Mannesmann, lasting success in world markets. Most of Krauss Maffei's other divisions—process engineering technology, transport technology, foundry technology, automation technology, surface treatment technology, and defense technology—offered good growth potential.

Following the Fichtel & Sachs investment, the group's total activities constituted, in addition to the highly cyclical plant business, a less cyclical mass market products business with closer proximity to consumers. In the latter business, foreign sales were gaining an increasing importance. In most of their fields of activity, the Mannesmann companies were of a size that enabled them to carry out the necessary development work, produce at competitive cost, and maintain extensive sales and service organizations.

Telecoms in the 1990s

In 1990, Mannesmann again broke new ground. Believing that in a highly developed economy the service sector would grow at an above-average rate and that telecommunications would be a particularly promising service, a consortium headed by Mannesmann tendered for the license to construct and operate the private D2 cellular telephone network. The acceptance of the bid submitted by Mannesmann Mobilfunk GmbH was of major importance to Mannesmann. It provided the company with an opportunity to enter the service sector.

The change in Mannesmann's corporate structure was reflected clearly in the sales breakdown. In 1968, coal, steel, and tubes accounted for half of sales, and machinery and plant construction for 16 percent. Twenty years later, the situation was very different: in 1989, machinery and plant construction and electrical and electronic engineering together accounted for 53 percent of sales and tube mills accounted for only 22 percent. At the same time overall sales had quintupled, rising from DM 4.4 billion in 1968 to DM 22.3 billion in 1989. In 1990, the 100th year of its corporate history, Mannesmann was a broadly diversified capital goods producer occupying a leading position in most of its fields of activity.

The 1990s brought several challenges, however. Commenting on the company's situation, Mannesmann's Chairman Werner Dieter paraphrased a quote from German folklore: "Before he provides the remedy, God makes you sweat, and right now we are sweating quite a lot." For the first time since it was founded, in fact, Mannesmann was about to lose money on operations. Net profits hit a high of US$315 million in 1989, dropped to half of that in 1991, and fell to break-even in 1992.

The problem that was afflicting Mannesmann also was hurting much of German industry during this time: uncompetitively high wages, a distended workforce, and an overdependence on recession-hit markets in Germany and throughout Europe. German industrial wage rates climbed nearly 50 percent higher than those in the United States and Japan, and Mannesmann was pricing itself out of business. The tubing business from which the company grew became the conglomerate's least healthy division in the early 1990s, losing an estimated US$40 million in 1992. Moreover, Mannesmann's auto parts, construction equipment, machine tool controls, and plant construction businesses all lost money in 1992. The only successes during this period came from the company's factory crane and conveyor business; Mannesmann was the largest supplier of such equipment in the world, with US$1.2 billion in sales in 1992.

The company did, however, have the financial resources to help adapt to these economic problems. Under Dieter's leadership, Mannesmann determined a financial strategy that would lead to recovery. First, the company began shifting Mannesmann's engineering work from high-cost Germany to the lower-cost, highly competitive United States. Toward that end, the company acquired Rapistan, a Michigan-based leading conveyor belt company. It also opened a large factory in Kentucky to produce automotive shock absorbers. Another move Mannesmann believed would help it through this time involved entering into the cellular technology market, and it established a new division to oversee such operations. Although high start-up costs for the division contributed to a fall in net earnings, Dieter predicted that the system would be making money by 1995.

In 1994, Mannesmann returned to profitability with net income of DM 340 million after a loss of DM 513 million the previous year. Operating profits and sales also increased. Mannesmann credited its machinery and plant construction, automotive technology, and telecommunications divisions with the success. In an unusual turn of events for the leader of Mannesmann, however, Dieter came under investigation in 1994 for alleged fraud. Specifically, charges surfaced that he had used his position to channel lucrative orders from Mannesmann's Rexroth GmbH subsidiary to Hydrac GmbH, a components company owned by his family. It also was alleged that the components were sold by Hydrac at inflated prices. Dieter was replaced, and in 1995 he stepped down from the company's supervisory board, even though a review commissioned by Mannesmann could not conclude that he had in fact defrauded the company. Dieter had overseen Mannesmann's return to profitability, and it remained for the company's new leader to take the company forward into the 21st century.

Mid-1990s Transformation

A complete transformation of Mannesmann began in 1995, when the conglomerate began selling off operating companies en masse. Within three years, it shed 39 businesses with combined annual sales of more than US$4 billion. The company still had 50 subsidiaries after the divestitures.

A number of telecommunications acquisitions took place in the same time period. Mannesmann bought an 8 percent stake in Omnitel Pronto Italia, a unit of Olivetti S.p.A., in 1995. The next year, it bought rights to Deutsche Bahn's fiber optic network for US$525 million. Mannesmann controlled D2, which had become Germany's largest provider of mobile phone service by August 1997.

The company worked quickly to enter markets throughout Europe. In September 1997, Mannesmann announced that it was paying US$600 million for a 25 percent interest in a joint mobile/land line phone venture with Olivetti based in The Netherlands. Mannesmann committed to paying another US$700 million by 2000 to raise its shareholding to 49.9 percent. It also was entering the Austrian market and already owned a stake in a British Telecommunications-led venture in France called Cegetel.

The German market for fixed-line telephone service was opened to competition in January 1998. Mannesmann Arcor, a joint venture with the Deutsche Bahn railroad, soon became a leading independent provider.

Income rose dramatically after the restructuring, and investors loved it. Mannesmann's share price rose 78 percent in 1998. Vodafone made its first overtures to a takeover late in the year. About this time, Chief Financial Officer Klaus Esser told *Business Week,* "There will be a time when 50 percent or more of our asset base is in telecoms, but we are not a telecom company." He became Mannesmann's CEO in May 1999; within a year of this, Mannesmann indeed would be exclusively a telecom company.

In January 1999, Mannesmann agreed to buy a controlling interest in Omnitel and its fixed-line affiliate, Infostrada, for US$7.8 billion. Olivetti, then launching a US$33 billion takeover bid for Telecom Italia, was eager to hand off the units to raise cash and to allay antitrust concerns.

At the same time, Vodafone plc bought AirTouch, acquiring stakes in the Cegetel and D2 joint ventures, making it a partner with Mannesmann. It also owned a stake in the number three German mobile phone company, E-Plus, however, making it a competitor.

Mannesmann spent US$46 billion acquiring telecom companies in 1999. It paid US$1.2 billion for the "o.tel.o" phone company in May. In September, Mannesmann announced that it would spin off its telecom unit from the engineering and automotive units.

When (in October 1999) Mannesmann acquired the British mobile phone company Orange from Hong Kong-based Hutchison Whampoa Ltd. for US$33 billion (a considerably overvalued poison pill, in the eyes of some analysts), it prompted a takeover bid from Vodafone. Esser may have believed that Mannesmann's ownership of Orange would have prevented Vodafone from launching its bid because of antitrust concerns. Regulators indicated, however, that Vodafone would merely have to divest itself of the Orange unit in the event of a merger.

Mannesmann CEO Esser cast about the continent for partners to help him fend off the aggressor. Deals with Vivendi and others were rumored but never materialized. Even the promising November rollout of wireless Internet service in Italy and Germany was not quite enough to cinch shareholder loyalty.

Mannesmann shareholders ultimately accepted the Vodafone offer, giving the British company 99 percent ownership in exchange for Vodafone shares. The value of Vodafone stock simply had run up too high to refuse. Indeed, 40 percent of Mannesmann's shareholders, many of them institutional investors, also held stock in Vodafone—giving them the prospect of both stocks being devalued if the deal fell through. When finally sealed in February 2000, it was worth US$185 billion—50 percent more than Vodafone's original offer.

Bosch and Siemens bought Mannesmann's Atecs (Engineering and Automotive) unit, which had been slated for an IPO, in April 2000. In October 2000, Enel S.p.A., Italy's national electricity provider, agreed to buy Mannesmann's Infostrada S.p.A. fixed-line telephone business for EUR 12 billion. Infostrada had three million voice customers and was Italy's largest fixed-line operator. It had lost EUR 89 million on revenues of EUR 726 million in 1999.

Principal Subsidiaries

Cegetel SA (France; 15%); Mannesmann Arcor AG & Co. (81.8%); Mannesmann Datenverarbeitung GmbH; Mannesmann Eurokom GmbH; Mannesmann Mobilfunk GmbH (65.2%); Mannesmann o.tel.o GmbH; Omnitel Pronto Italia SpA (Italy; 55.2%).

Principal Divisions

Mannesmann Arcor; Mannesmann D2; Mobilfunk; Omnitel.

Principal Competitors

British Telecommunications PLC; Deutsche Telekom; France Telecom SA; ThyssenKrupp AG.

Further Reading

''Dieter Leaves Mannesmann,'' *American Metal Market,* March 1, 1995, p. 2.

Ewing, Jack, ''The Playing Field Tilts in Deutsche Telekom's Favor,'' *Business Week,* European Business, February 22, 1999, p. 27.

Ewing, Jack, and Stanley Reed, ''Can Mannesmann Wriggle Away?,'' *Business Week,* Industrial/technology edition, January 17, 2000, pp. 52–54.

Fuhrman, Peter, ''Struggling to Adapt,'' *Forbes,* April 26, 1993, p. 102.

''Inquiry Inconclusive on German Executive,'' *New York Times,* June 23, 1995, p. D2.

''The Inside Stories,'' *Datamation,* June 15, 1988, p. 116.

Lanchner, David, ''Failed Message,'' *Institutional Investor,* April 2000, pp. 53–61.

Linsenmeyer, Adrienne, '' 'If There's a Seat at the Bar, Take It,' Says Mannesmann's Dieter. 'If Not, Knock Someone Off,' '' *FW,* July 23, 1991, p. 24.

''Mannesmann Group Revenues Decline,'' *American Metal Market,* December 16, 1986, p. 3.

''Mannesmann in Black,'' *New York Times,* May 6, 1995, p. 18.

Miller, Karen Lowry, and Stephen Baker, ''The Right Call?,'' *Business Week,* November 30, 1998, p. 142.

Morais, Richard C., ''Making Up for Lost Time,'' *Forbes,* November 21, 1994, p. 122.

''Old Dogs, New Tricks: Mannesmann,'' *Economist,* October 5, 1985, pp. 71f.

''Producer Prices for Steel Pipe Seen Stabilizing; Mannesmann: End to 'Structural' Crisis Not in Sight,'' *American Metal Market,* September 7, 1987, p. 7.

Regan, James G., ''Mannesmann to Buy 51% VDO Adolf Stake,'' *American Metal Market,* October 25, 1991, p. 4.

Tagliabue, John, ''Mannesmann Joins Forces with Olivetti,'' *New York Times,* September 8, 1997, p. D2.

Wessel, Horst A., *Kontinuität im Wandel 100 Jahre Mannesmann 1890–1990,* Gütersloh: Mannesman AG, 1990.

—Horst A. Wessel and Beth Watson Highman
—updated by Frederick Ingram

Maritz Inc.

1375 North Highway Drive
Fenton, Missouri
U.S.A.
Telephone: (636) 827-4000
Fax: (636) 827-5505
Web site: http://www.maritz.com

Private Company
Incorporated: 1894 as E. Maritz Jewelry Manufacturing Company
Employees: 6,500
Sales: $2.20 billion (2000)
NAIC: 541611 Administrative Management and General Management Consulting Services

Maritz Inc. represents a group of companies that provide marketing research, travel, and performance improvement services to corporate clients. The company's performance improvement division designs and implements employee incentives programs that help corporate clients improve employee satisfaction and productivity. The company's market research arm conducts custom-designed research studies that provide corporate clients with information concerning profitability and market share. The company's travel services division handles travel and related services for corporate clients. Maritz Inc. operates globally through a host of subsidiaries and through approximately 240 offices in Europe and North America.

Beginnings As a Jewelry Wholesaler

Maritz Inc. exited the 20th century as an entirely different type of company than the one that entered the 20th century. It was a transformation driven by necessity and hastened by crisis, a change in direction that Edward Maritz could not have foreseen when he founded the E. Maritz Jewelry Manufacturing Company in 1894. Maritz was 31 years old when he began distributing jewelry and engraved watches. As a wholesaler, he served jewelers in the metropolitan areas surrounding Kansas City and St. Louis, a territory that expanded to include the southern and western United States by 1900. Over the course of the next 20 years, Maritz established himself as one of the country's leading wholesale jewelers, a reputation that was galvanized in 1921 when he became a major importer of Swiss watch movements. Maritz sold the Swiss-movement watches to retailers under his own trade names, Merit, Record, and Cymrex. The 1920s also saw Maritz add general lines of silverware and diamond jewelry to his product selection, as his wholesale catalogs reached a customer base that stretched from coast to coast.

The years of robust growth and expansion ended in 1929, a year that spelled disaster for the nation and tragedy for the Maritz family. Edward Maritz died in 1929, passing away on the eve of the Great Depression. The economic strife quickly destroyed the legacy of success Maritz had built during 35 years of business, leaving his son, James A. Maritz, with the unenviable task of trying to perpetuate a family business that had been stripped of its customers. As jewelry retailers shuttered their stores, wholesalers collapsed as well, but James Maritz refused to yield. He found a new market for his father's jewelry and watches and, by so doing, created a new business that would develop into a multibillion-dollar dynasty for generations of Maritz family members.

To keep his father's business financially afloat, Maritz approached business executives, the individuals who managed large national corporations. He offered to sell the companies watches and jewelry at wholesale prices, which the companies could give to employees as service awards. The new spin on an old family business worked. Maritz found a receptive audience and the basis for a new type of company. The watches and jewelry could be used not only as service awards—given to employees at retirement or after 20 years of service, for instance—but also as bonuses to salespeople, a particularly difficult profession during the decade-long economic turmoil. The company's first major success in its new guise came as such, as part of a nationwide sales incentive campaign launched by a St. Louis hat manufacturer in 1930. The hat manufacturer's salespeople were presented with the first Maritz Prize Book, a catalogue containing the items available for reaching particular sales goals. The results confirmed success, with sales exceeding the hat manufacturer's expectations and establishing Maritz as a pioneer in the field of sales incentives.

Company Perspectives:

Our mission is to help our clients improve their performance in critical areas such as sales, marketing, quality, customer satisfaction, and cost reduction by influencing the behavior of our clients' customers, employees, and channel partners. Emphasizing excellence and value, we will create, develop, and implement the best possible action plans for our clients through a unique combination of our worldwide resources that includes marketing services, employee involvement processes, and travel services. We will offer these services worldwide through our operating companies and their associates, either separately or in combination.

The decision to cater to corporate customers rather than jewelry retailers more than saved the Maritz family business from near-certain doom: it created a business capable of recording financial growth during the economically devastating 1930s. After World War II, the company, operating as Maritz Sales Builders, was firmly and exclusively devoted to the incentives business. The company moved into a new headquarters facility in 1950 and began building a network of outposts geared toward serving its corporate clientele. Annual sales reached $5 million as several Maritz Sales Builder sales offices were opened across the country during the mid-1950s. An important acquisition was completed during this time as well, steering the company into what would later become one of its core businesses. A small travel agency in Detroit was purchased, enabling the company to offer group travel as part of its incentives program. The Detroit travel agency became the foundation of Maritz Travel Company, one of the three pillars that would support Maritz Inc. at the century's end.

Full Range of Corporate Services: 1960s

As the company entered the 1960s, it began to realize the range of opportunities that were available in the industry it had helped to create. An in-house creative department was established in 1959, giving the company the capability to produce its own prize book, media, and awards. In 1961, the company adopted the name Maritz Inc. and began developing plans for a new headquarters office in St. Louis County, Missouri, a home the company would occupy into the 21st century. The company's foray into coordinating travel proved to be a boon to business, securing the Maritz name in the record books of the travel industry. Over a four-day period in October 1964, the company helped bring more than 6,000 dealers from 50 countries to the World's Fair in New York City, a U.S. record at the time for a single travel agency in a single week. Aside from making the company a historical footnote, the development of Maritz Travel Company showed the gains that could be made by diversifying. Energized by such evidence, the company's executives decided in the 1960s to pursue growth through acquisition, a strategy that would accelerate expansion and flesh out its motivation services.

During the 1970s, Maritz Inc. hit its stride, recording impressive growth that made the company an international enterprise. In 1973, another core business was added to the company's fold with the acquisition of a small research firm. The acquisition signaled the company's entry into the market research business, a venture that formed the foundation for Maritz Marketing Research Company. Maritz Inc. also opened a travel office in Hawaii in 1973, ushering in an era of geographic expansion. Two years later, the company established Maritz U.K., its first overseas operation. Maritz Travel Company followed suit, establishing subsidiaries in England and Spain, which were complemented by field offices in Jamaica, Nassau, Switzerland, and Italy. By 1982, the company had added two more international subsidiaries, Maritz Deutschland GmbH and Maritz France S.A., which were grouped with Maritz U.K. to form Maritz European Operations.

By the end of the 1980s, steady expansion and the occasional strategic diversification had created one of the largest privately owned companies in the country. In 1989, Maritz Inc.'s revenues eclipsed $1 billion for the first time, with profits reaching $38.5 million. It was a record year for the company, with the bulk of its financial might coming from its two major divisions, corporate travel and motivation programs. These two divisions, which shared the spotlight with the company's other primary division, market research, suffered from poor performance as Maritz Inc. entered the 1990s. Consequently, the entire organization faltered, leaving company officials to pine for a return to 1989's record-setting financial results.

Difficulty in the 1990s.

At the time of the company's early 1990s malaise, the third generation of the Maritz family was in control, led by William Maritz. Total profits began a three-year plunge after 1989, falling to $11.4 million by 1992, a decline the company attributed to the recessive economic conditions and the ''lingering effects of the Persian Gulf War,'' according to a July 20, 1992 *St. Louis Business Journal* article.

Despite the disappointing results, the company ranked as the national leader in the incentives industry, far ahead of its closest rivals, Carlson Cos. and Business Incentives. Further, its Maritz Marketing Research division was performing remarkably well, enjoying a record year in 1992 that produced $64 million in revenue, making it the sixth largest research operation in the country. By 1992, there were signs that the company was beginning to arrest its financial slide, as the recessive economic conditions lessened in intensity. In the fall of 1992, Maritz Inc. signed an agreement with Ford Motor Co. to help the car manufacturer boost productivity and cut costs, a deal believed to be worth $100 million over a three-year period.

The company's wilting profitability regained its vitality by 1993, but before the telling financial results could be tabulated another form of strife beset the organization. In mid-1993, a feud erupted within the Maritz family, pitting William Maritz against his sister, Jean Maritz Hobler, who owned 20 percent of the family business. The trouble began when Jean Maritz Hobler informed her brother that the Hobler side of the family wanted to sell its interest in the company, which triggered a debate over the value of the Hoblers' holding. William Maritz cited a 1986 buy-sell agreement that valued the 20 percent stake at $39.4 million, a figure Jean Maritz Hobler deemed too low. She hired a financial advisory firm for a different appraisal. The

Key Dates:

1894: Edward Maritz begins distributing watches and jewelry.
1929: James Maritz enters the employee incentives business.
1950: Exclusively committed to employee motivation programs, the company begins to expand.
1973: Profits reach $38.5 million before beginning a three-year decline.
1989: Revenues surpass $1 billion for first time.
1994: Company resolves year-long valuation dispute between CEO William Maritz and his sister, Jean Maritz Hobler, over the latter's 20 percent stake in the company.
2000: Heybridge, an electronic-commerce subsidiary, is formed.

financial advisory firm set the value at $81 million, creating a $41 million gulf that separated brother and sister. ''This is war,'' William Maritz told the *St. Louis Business Journal* in a July 26, 1993 interview. ''If we give in to their demands,'' he added, ''it would dilute the value of the 320 management stockholders who also worked to build this company.''

The family battle took place in the company boardroom. Jean Maritz Hobler used her votes to banish two board members and replaced them with individuals sympathetic to her cause. She relinquished her seat on the board and handed it to her son, Peter Hobler. William Maritz responded by increasing the number of Maritz Inc. directors from seven to nine members and appointed his sons to the new seats. Jean Maritz Hobler's husband, Wells Hobler, a former Maritz Inc. employee, was declared ''a retiree not in good standing,'' making him ineligible for the perquisites customarily granted to retirees in good standing. The heated exchange endured for roughly a year, eventually ending in compromise in June 1994 when the company announced it would buy back the Hobler family's shares for a reported $60 million over the ensuing five years. William Maritz offered his perspective on the rift in the company's 1994 annual report (although privately held, Maritz Inc. made a practice of publishing annual reports). ''Privately held companies periodically must go through wrenching readjustments among family owners,'' he wrote. ''Maritz Inc. has done this, and now begins its second 100 years with a clear picture of its potential, its goals and its ownership.''

With ownership consolidated on William Maritz's side of the family, the company entered its second century of business hoping for a return to growing profits. When business had grown sluggish during the first years of the decade, the company remained optimistic, setting a goal of $2 billion in revenue and $58 million in earnings by 1997. As the company entered the mid-1990s, it appeared to be progressing toward its financial goals. In 1996, the company posted earnings of $25.2 million on revenue of $1.8 billion, marking the second consecutive year that profits had increased. The company's travel operations, which ranked as the fifth largest in the United States, had fully recovered from the downturn during the recession and served as the sole source of travel for 35 corporations. The incentives side of the family business was also performing admirably, thanks in large part to the company's persistent pursuit of innovation. Although the company had suffered from a typical weakness of family management—becoming embroiled in a rift among family members—Maritz Inc. had avoided becoming complacent, a frequent flaw of companies in their third and fourth generation of family management. Some of the programs conducted by Maritz Performance Improvement were more than 35 years old, but the company continually added new technology and new features to its programs to keep them on the cutting edge of personnel development systems.

During the latter half of the 1990s, Maritz Inc. surged past its revenue goal amid organizational changes that reshaped the company for the 21st century. In 1997, after spending five years developing a telephone marketing and research operation, the company sold the division, called Maritz Teleservices, to Matrixx Marketing Inc. Although Teleservices only represented 2.5 percent of the company's $2 billion in revenue, the division accounted for more than one-third of its St. Louis-based staff. The following year, Steve Maritz was named chief executive officer, representing the fourth generation of Maritz family management.

As Maritz Inc. prepared for business in the 21st century, considerable attention and resources were being paid to developing Internet-related businesses. Between 1999 and 2000, the company established more than 400 web sites, enough for the company to seriously contemplate entering the web development business. The Internet represented an opportunity for incentives businesses to operate tracking, promotions, and reward redemption electronically, greatly strengthening the link between employees and their company's incentives program. Maritz Inc. seized such an opportunity. After an ambitious year of web site development the company formed an electronic commerce subsidiary, Heybridge, which began operating in April 2000. Through Heybridge, Maritz Inc. planned to expand beyond its customer base of large national corporations and reach small and mid-market companies. ''Maritz traditionally has not catered to these clients,'' the company's director of corporate administrations told the *St. Louis Business Journal* on July 31, 2000. The company's Internet strategy applied to each of its major, divisions—travel, employee incentives, and research—lending a modern look to a company approaching its 110th anniversary. As the company moved forward, its entrenched market position and decades of experience fueled confidence that the Maritz family dynasty would continue to thrive in the decades ahead.

Principal Subsidiaries

Maritz Performance Improvement Company; Heybridge; Maritz Marketing Research Inc.; Maritz Travel Company; eMaritz Inc.

Principal Divisions

Performance Improvement; Marketing Research; Travel Services.

Principal Competitors

American Express Company; Carlson Wagonlit Travel; J.D. Power and Associates.

Further Reading

Bye, Connie, ''150 Largest Privately Held Companies,'' *St. Louis Business Journal,* March 27, 2000, p. 29A.

Desloge, Rick, ''Maritz's Profit Hits $25.2 Million,'' *St. Louis Business Journal,* August 12, 1996, p. 1A.

——, ''Maritz Declares 'War' on Sister: Family $41 Million Apart on Buyout of Hoblers' Stake,'' *St. Louis Business Journal,* July 26, 1993, p. 1.

——, ''Maritz Notches $100 Million Deal with Ford,'' *St. Louis Business Journal,* September 14, 1992, p. 1.

——, ''Persian Gulf War, Recession Pound Earnings at Maritz Inc.,'' *St. Louis Business Journal,* July 20, 1992, p. 1.

Geer, Carolyn T., ''Prenuptial for Business Partners,'' *Forbes,* December 5, 1994, p. 166.

Lerner, Howard, ''Maritz, Landing Real Estate Investors Bet on Gambling,'' *St. Louis Business Journal,* March 14, 1994, p. 1A.

—Jeffrey L. Covell

Media General

Media General, Inc.

333 E. Franklin Street
Richmond, Virginia 23219
U.S.A.
Telephone: (804) 649-6000
Fax: (804) 649-6066
Web site: http://www.media-general.com

Public Company
Founded: 1879 as Dispatch Co.
Employees: 8,200
Sales: $795.4 million (1999)
Stock Exchanges: American
Ticker Symbol: MEG-A
NAIC: 51111 Newspaper Publishers; 51312 Television Broadcasting

Media General, Inc. is a diversified media company with interests in daily and weekly newspapers, broadcast television, and newsprint production, mostly in the southern and eastern United States. In December 2000 the Richmond, Virginia-based company purchased Spartan Communications for $605 million, underscoring its long-term goal of remaining a top media player in the Southeast. Investor ''Super'' Mario Gabelli owns approximately 27 percent of the company. An additional 11 percent of the company is owned by the founding Bryan family, which controls the board of directors.

From Family-Run Newspaper to Media Conglomerate: 1879–1969

The precursor to Media General began in 1879 as the Dispatch Co., which published the *Richmond Dispatch* and was run by the Bryan family. In 1896 the Bryans bought the *Richmond Leader,* and seven years later they merged it with a competing newspaper to create the *News Leader.* In 1937 the company started an AM radio outlet in Richmond. In 1949 an FM radio station was also launched. The FM station reached a larger area but had a much smaller audience, especially in its first few decades when FM technology was in its infancy.

By 1940 the company's newspapers had the widest circulation in Virginia, and the Dispatch Co. changed its name to Richmond Newspapers Inc. During the 1950s and 1960s the *News Leader* was known for its conservative editorials that strongly supported segregation, and some critics blamed it for splitting Richmond along racial lines. In 1964, the company began an $8.3 million three-year modernization program. New technologies were rapidly changing the way newspapers could be produced, and Richmond decided to take advantage of them. The company bought computer typesetting equipment, new presses, and photocomposition machinery, which set advertising on photographic film instead of in type. The equipment was expected to save $300,000 to $400,000 a year. The company also added a 42,780-square-foot, five-floor addition to its main office.

By the mid-1960s the Richmond area had grown to about 1.2 million people, and the company's newspapers were read by 90 percent of the community's households—the highest rate of readership in a major U.S. media market. With a circulation of 275,000, Richmond Newspapers not only had the highest newspaper circulation in Virginia, but was 34th in the United States. The *Times-Dispatch* had 12 news bureaus. The AM radio station was reaching a million listeners during the day by the late 1960s, and nearly 500,000 at night. The firm also owned both daily newspapers in Winston-Salem, North Carolina, and a cable television system in Virginia.

In 1966 the company went public and set about transforming itself from a small newspaper publisher into a media conglomerate. That year it bought a 52.2 percent interest in the Tribune Co. for $17.5 million, plus an exchange of stock. Based in Tampa, Florida, this media company had 1965 revenues of $18.9 million and owned the *Tampa Tribune* and the *Tampa Times,* as well as radio stations WFLA AM and FM and the television station WFLA. The television station, an NBC affiliate that began airing in 1955, was the fastest growing part of the operation, with income jumping from $416,000 in 1961 to $1.4 million in 1965. Its broadcasts had a 75-mile radius and reached 1.7 million people. Furthermore, Tampa was one of the fastest growing cities in the United States and was considered a good environment in which to build a media business.

Company Perspectives:

Our mission is to be a leading provider of high-quality news, information and entertainment services in the Southeast by continually building our position of strength in strategically located markets.

In 1969 Media General, Inc. was formed as a public holding company for Richmond Newspapers and the Tribune Co. Media General then bought an additional 29 percent of the Tribune Company's stock for $9 million. Alan S. Donnahoe, a former statistician and research director who had been with Richmond Newspapers since 1950, was appointed president of Media General. In 1970 the new company bought New Jersey's *Newark News* and Garden State Paper's newsprint recycling plants from Richard B. Scudder for $50 million in Media General stock. The newspaper soon was closed for a year by an extended strike, however, and when it reopened it was severely weakened. The *Newark News* lost $3 million in five months before Media General closed it down. The company's loss was mitigated by the fact that it had earlier sold the Sunday edition to the rival *Newark Star-Ledger* for $20 million. Media General also kept $8 million worth of the *News*'s presses.

Garden State Paper's reprocessing mills in California, New Jersey, and Chicago sold recycled newsprint to 160 newspapers and had patents on its recycling processes. Its cash flow was $27 million in 1970, growing to $32 million in 1971. With recycling becoming increasingly popular, it was expected to continue that growth rate. The recycling plant was so successful that some industry analysts felt that it was the paper plant, not the newspaper, that Media General had been after in the deal.

The 1970s and 1980s: On the Threshold of the Information Age

One of the primary functions of the company's computers and phototypesetters was preparing the *News Leader*'s financial section. In 1971 the company decided that it could use that data to start a strictly financial newspaper. The *Financial Daily* was printed weekday afternoons in Richmond and flown to major cities along the East Coast. It included financial data on 9,000 securities and 4,000 stocks, as well as news centering on financial interests. When the printers union struck over wages and control of the automated typesetting equipment, Donnahoe bought more computers and the automated printing proceeded.

The *Financial Daily* continued to lose money, however; it lost $1.5 million during its first months of operation. Although the company spent $300,000 on an ad campaign for the *Financial Daily* and mailed 400,000 subscription offers, it found only 2,500 people interested in the $165 per year subscription. Rather than continue to support the newspaper, hoping it would eventually break even, Donnahoe soon decided to turn it into the *Financial Weekly,* lowering the price to $50 a year. When the daily paper went to a weekly format, management transferred the automated printing techniques to the other Richmond newspapers. About 200 printers were replaced by 140 clerks, who were paid an average of $50 a week less than the printers.

Impressed with the $750,000 per year the new automation saved in production expenses, the company spent $24 million to automate the Tampa newspapers. It also began selling financial data to money managers, though the *Financial Weekly* was still losing money in 1973. Garden State Paper was contributing 20 percent of Media General's revenue, and in mid-1973 the firm announced plans to boost its recycling capacity 25 percent to 325,000 tons a year.

In the mid-1970s advertising fell and newsprint costs rose. Many newspaper chains were pinched by these trends, but Media General was able to profit because of its newsprint recycling operations. Not only did it hold down its own costs, but the firm made money selling newsprint to such customers as the *New York Times,* the *Washington Post,* and the *Los Angeles Times.* Garden State Paper accounted for about 40 percent of Media General's $170 million in total revenues. The biggest user of waste paper was the residential construction market, which used tons of fiberboard made from recycled paper. Demand from a home-building boom led to a doubling of the price of waste newsprint in 1973 and 1974, and to ensure Garden State's supply, Media General bought one of the biggest waste paper dealers in New York and signed contracts with several West Coast brokers.

In 1977 Media General, along with Knight-Ridder Newspapers, Inc. and Cox Enterprises, Inc., built a $125 million newsprint mill in Dublin, Georgia. The mill had an annual capacity of 156,000 tons, of which Media General took 20,000. Media General earned $18 million in 1978 on sales of $243.7 million. In 1980 the firm bought Golden West Publishing Corp., a chain of weekly newspapers in southern California, for $8 million. It bought another weekly newspaper publisher, Highlander Publications, for $12.7 million.

In 1982, with afternoon newspapers in steep decline throughout the United States, Media General stopped publication of the *Tampa Times* evening paper. It also sold WFLA AM and FM to John Blair & Co. for $14 million. Cable television was becoming a huge market, however, and Media General won a 15-year cable franchise in affluent Fairfax County, Virginia, near Washington, D.C. The cable system was a $120 million investment. In 1982, newspapers and publishing accounted for 42 percent of company profits, newsprint accounted for 45 percent, and broadcasting accounted for 13 percent.

Also in 1982, Media General bought William B. Tanner Co., a Memphis-based media buying service, for $36 million. The Tanner Co. served 200 large advertisers and about 6,000 broadcast outlets. In 1983, William Tanner was charged with income tax fraud, mail fraud, and accepting kickbacks, and federal law enforcement agents searched Tanner's premises for documents relating to the charges. Consequently, Tanner stepped down, and Media General took direct control of the company, renaming it Media General Broadcast Services. Tanner eventually pleaded guilty and went to jail, but Media General was cleared of any wrongdoing. Nevertheless, the broadcast unit was seriously hurt by the episode. Sales plummeted, and Media General Broadcast began losing between $2 million and $6 million a year.

In 1983 Media General bought television stations in Jacksonville, Florida, and Charleston, South Carolina. In 1984 Don-

Key Dates:

1879: Bryan family forms Dispatch Co.
1896: Dispatch Co. acquires *Richmond Leader.*
1903: *Richmond Leader* merges with rival newspaper to form *News Leader.*
1937: Dispatch Co. establishes its first AM radio station.
1940: Dispatch Co. is renamed Richmond Newspapers Inc.
1964: Richmond Newspapers begins three-year modernization program.
1966: Richmond Newspapers goes public and acquires a majority interest in the Tribune Co.
1969: Media General, Inc. is formed as a holding company for Richmond Newspapers and the Tribune Co.
1982: *Tampa Times* stops publishing evening edition.
1992: *News Leader* ceases publication.

nahoe, who was 68, retired and was succeeded by James S. Evans, who joined the firm in 1973 as a vice-president. Revenue for 1984 was $507.8 million.

In 1985 the company ceased publication of the afternoon *Winston-Salem Sentinel.* Its sister paper, the profitable morning *Journal,* expanded its coverage, started a new weekly business section, and absorbed most of its staff. Also in 1985, Media General acquired 40 percent of Garden City Newspapers Inc., the troubled newspaper publisher that the firm hoped to turn around.

After the stock market crash of 1987 a group of investors led by Hollywood producer Burt Sugarman bought about ten percent of Media General's stock. In 1988 the group offered first $1.57 billion and then about $2 billion for the company shares they did not already own. Media General management was able to refuse the takeover offer because the company had been created with two kinds of stock. The owners of the Class B stock, mostly the company's management, were given veto power over any takeover attempts. Sugarman challenged the legality of the A and B structure, but a judge upheld it, and, in the end, Sugarman sold his stake back to Media General for $100 million. Of this, $44 million was in cash and $56 million was represented by interest in the Pomona, California paper mill.

In 1988, the company sold Media General Broadcast Services to its management. Broadcast was still losing money, and Media General took a charge against earnings to cover the sale. In 1989, five Media General insiders sold about 50 percent of their stake in the company. The five said that they were selling for tax purposes, but some industry analysts felt that the move was related to a downturn in advertising and media, as well as the recent loss of the Pomona paper mill. The company also sold its recently acquired weekly newspapers at Highlander Publications and Golden West Publishing. The company made $20.7 million in 1989 on sales of $595 million.

Newsprint operations accounted for 47 percent of company profits in 1987. Although in 1990 the company decided to sell Garden State's recycling mill in Garfield, New Jersey, as part of a strategy to concentrate on its communications properties, management soon changed its mind and took the mill off the auction block before it was sold. The company had a difficult year in 1991, losing $62 million, in part due to a decline in sales prompted by the recession and in part due to a sharp increase in capital expenditures. The recession hampered advertising sales at the company's own newspapers and also hurt sales of recycled newsprint, since other newspapers were printing fewer pages. The recession seriously hurt the debt-laden Garden City Newspapers, and Media General wrote off its investment and took a $78.3 million charge against earnings.

In May 1992 publication of the 104-year-old Richmond *News Leader* ceased. An afternoon paper, its circulation had sunk to less than 100,000, while the morning *Times-Dispatch* was thriving. The *News Leader* was merged into the *Times-Dispatch,* and 44 of the two newspapers' 1,100 employees were laid off.

A New Strategy for the 1990s

With newsprint costs rising steadily throughout the early 1990s—prices rose 40 percent over the course of 1994—CEO J. Stewart Bryan III felt it was time to narrow the company's focus. In 1995 Media General embarked on a series of acquisitions and divestitures designed to redirect the company's energy into its holdings in the Southeast. The first major deal occurred in September of that year, when Media General purchased 27 Virginia newspapers, four of which were dailies, from Worrell Enterprises, Inc. In July of the following year the company reached a merger agreement with Park Acquisitions, Inc. worth more than $700 million. The purchase gave Media General 28 new daily and 82 new weekly newspapers, in addition to ten new TV affiliates. With this expansion of its regional broadcasting operations, the company now owned 22.1 percent of the television market in the Southeast. In all, over the course of 18 months Media General spent more than $1 billion buying and selling media outlets, doubling its holdings in the region in the process. The company also suffered a net loss of more than $10 million in 1997.

Not all of the company's shareholders supported Bryan's new business strategy. In early 1998 Mario Gabelli, a money manager based in Rye, New York, whose group controlled more than $290 million of Media General's Class A stock, requested an opportunity to nominate new members to the company's board. In Gabelli's opinion, the company needed to halt its acquisitions and capitalize its cable holdings to get back into the black. The Bryan family still owned the majority of Media General's Class B stock, however, which gave it greater power in board decisions, and Gabelli's request was ultimately denied. In certain respects, Bryan's strategy seemed to be working; Media General's stock reached an all-time high in March 1998.

The company continued to keep busy throughout the following year. In June 1998 it sold off its Kentucky newspapers, acquired in the Park Acquisitions deal, for $254.8 million, and in July it reorganized its publishing division to establish a stronger focus on community newspapers in Virginia and North Carolina. In April 1999 it sold its Fairfax County cable TV holdings to Cox Enterprises for $1.4 billion, officially exiting the cable industry. Much of this money was reinvested the following December, when Media General purchased Spartan Communications for $605 million. The acquisition added 13 South Carolina television stations to the company's holdings, ten of which were CBS affiliates—making Media General the second largest CBS affiliate in the country.

Immediately following the Spartan Communications purchase, Mario Gabelli entered the scene once again, with a proposal to establish a new rule that would prevent Media General from making acquisitions worth more than $25 million without the unanimous approval of the board. He petitioned to have this proposal included in the next proxy statement to the shareholders; the board's majority refused his request. In February 2000 Gabelli again attempted to nominate two new members to the board, but because his letter of intent failed to explain his interests in the nomination, as required in the company's bylaws, his nominations were once again ignored. In May 2000, all nine of the company's current directors were reelected.

Media General once again ran into hard times toward the end of 2000, when its third quarter earnings fell below expectations, causing a dip in the company's stock. The acquisition of Spartan Communications, however, had increased Media General's share of the region's broadcast television market to 30 percent, and its long-term goal of becoming a major media outlet in the Southeast remained firmly in place heading into the 21st century.

Principal Competitors

Cox Enterprises, Inc.; Gannett Co. Inc.; Knight-Ridder Newspapers, Inc.

Further Reading

''After 104 Years, Richmond Newspaper Closes,'' *New York Times,* May 31, 1992.

Cuff, Daniel F., ''A Jolt to Media General Image,'' *New York Times,* September 15, 1983.

Day, Kathleen, ''Media General to Add TV Stations, Papers; Richmond Firm Agrees to $110 Million Deal,'' *Washington Post,* July 23, 1996.

Dorfman, John R., ''Five Media General Insiders Sell Close to 50% of Shares,'' *Wall Street Journal,* May 8, 1989.

Harris, Roy J., ''Barris Industries, Giant Group Offer $1.57 Billion to Buy Media General,'' *Wall Street Journal,* March 1, 1988.

Jackson, Cheryl, ''Media General, Owner of Tampa Tribune in Fla., to Emphasize Southeast,'' *Tampa Tribune,* February 12, 1998.

''Media General's Fortunate Misfortune,'' *Business Week,* November 25, 1972.

''Media General to Start a Financial Newspaper,'' *Wall Street Journal,* May 17, 1971.

Mencke, Claire, ''How Newspaper Publishers Are Coping with Sky-High Paper Prices,'' *Investor's Business Daily,* February 22, 1995.

''The Old Newspaper Man,'' *Forbes,* January 15, 1976.

Rayner, Bob, ''Media Company Rejects Dissident Shareholder's Bid,'' *Tampa Tribune,* February 23, 2000.

''Richmond Newspapers Presses Ahead,'' *Barron's,* January 16, 1967.

Sloan, Jim, ''Media General Executive Vows to Protect Corporation's Turf,'' *Tampa Tribune,* February 13, 1997.

—Scott Lewis
—updated by Stephen Meyer

Mity Enterprises, Inc.

1301 West 400 North
Orem, Utah 84057
U.S.A.
Telephone: (801) 224-0589
Toll Free: (800) 327-1692
Fax: (801) 224-6191
Web site: http://www.mitylite.com

Public Company
Incorporated: 1987 as Mity-Lite, Inc.
Employees: 506
Sales: $47.49 million (2000)
Stock Exchanges: NASDAQ
Ticker Symbol: MITY
NAIC: 33721 Office Furniture Manufacturing (Including Fixtures)

Mity Enterprises, Inc. designs, manufactures, and sells a variety of high quality institutional furniture. Its multipurpose line includes several sizes and shapes of lightweight but durable folding-leg tables and a variety of folding and stacking chairs. The company also sells cluster furniture for use in high-density settings, auditorium seating, dispatch seating, big and tall seating, healthcare seating, and a line of lightweight lecterns. Its customers include churches (its original market), hotels, call centers, police and emergency dispatch centers, schools, universities, government agencies, and nursing homes. Mity Enterprises sells products in the United States and other nations under the trade names Mity-Lite, Domore, DO3, JG, Corel, CenterCore, and Broda. A public corporation, Mity has been featured in multiple years on the *Forbes* and *Business Week* lists of ''Best Small Companies'' and ''Hot Growth Companies,'' respectively.

Getting Started

Gregory Wilson, Mity-Lite's founder, earned his undergraduate economics degree from Brigham Young University and then his M.B.A. in finance from Indiana University in 1973 before gaining experience with several companies. He worked for Ford Motor Company, Stereo Optical Company, Skyline Industries, Bridgers and Paxton Consulting Engineers, and Heath Engineering. He helped Little Giant Ladder Company design its products and commence manufacturing. Beginning in 1981, Wilson started and operated four furniture making companies that sold a variety of products such as boat seats and church pews.

In 1987 Wilson started Mity-Lite after a man from The Church of Jesus Christ of Latter-Day Saints asked him to design a new lightweight table for use in church cultural halls. The church purchasing agent, who had previously bought products from Wilson, said he was tired of buying particle board tables that had to be replaced frequently. He also said some Mormon women wanted lighter tables that would not cut their fingers.

Consequently, Wilson and his partner Wayne Swensen and designer Brent Bonham sought advice from the aerospace industry on how to build better folding tables. With that input, the newly organized Mity-Lite used high-impact ABS plastic, the same material used in football helmets and car bumpers, to start building light but durable tables. Its new tables weighed about half that of the competitors' particle board and plywood tables. A company video showed Mity-Lite tables left unharmed after being jumped on and abused with sledge hammers, while competitors' tables collapsed or were severely damaged.

Although Mity-Lite tables cost about twice as much as competitors' models, the company in Orem, about 40 miles south of Salt Lake City, soon grew and prospered. From four employees in 1987, the firm by early 1990 had grown to a staff of 45 and claimed about five percent of the folding-table market. In 1990 Mity-Lite also started recording its international sales, then representing about $50,000.

Expansion in the 1990s

In April 1994 the company completed its IPO by selling one million shares to raise $5.3 million. The company in 1994 employed 90 workers at its 40,000-square-foot facility in Orem. There the firm produced 35 varieties of lightweight tables, along with table carts, table cloths, table skirting, and skirt clips. In 1994 Mity-Lite also began shipping its new Polyflex Stacking Chairs.

Company Perspectives:

The Company's strategy for future growth includes continued penetration into the domestic and international niche markets, introducing complementary products such as stacking and folding chairs, staging, and partitions into its existing distribution system, as well as acquiring synergistic businesses, and cost effectively enhancing its manufacturing process.

Mity-Lite in 1994 sold its products in all 50 states and several other nations, aided by a sales office in Swindon, England. Its customers included hundreds of local churches, all Utah colleges or universities, and the Hilton hotel chain. *Forbes* in its November 7, 1994 issue ranked Mity-Lite as number 12 in its annual listing of the nation's top 200 small companies. At that time its five-year average return on equity was 39.8 percent, and its earnings per share had increased 71 percent over the past five years.

In 1997 Gregory Wilson spoke at a World Trade Association of Utah meeting about the challenges of expanding internationally. Wilson admitted that Mity-Lite was overconfident after its success in the United States and Canada. In its first effort outside North America, Mity-Lite faced some difficulties in England. For example, the firm had to change from a telephone contacting system that had proved successful in North America to using local distributors.

Cultural differences were part of the problem in expanding to England, said Stan Pool, Mity-Lite's vice-president of sales and marketing. He reported that instead of relying on selling its products to American colleges and universities, in England the company learned to emphasize sales to small student clubs.

Acquisitions and Other Developments in the Late 1990s and Beyond

In 1997 Mity-Lite acquired 49.9 percent of the stock of DO Group Inc. for $750,000 cash and a loan of $1 million to a DO Group subsidiary. Located in Elkhart, Indiana, DO Group had initiated this deal when it approached Mity-Lite after its 1994 IPO. ''An opportunity to work with a company like Mity-Lite is one we just could not pass up,'' said DO Group Chairman Dennis Kebrdle in a March 6, 1997 *Deseret News* article. ''We believe combining our well established Domore and DO3 product lines with the dynamic business management systems at Mity-Lite will provide significant growth opportunities for both companies.''

The following year Mity-Lite announced that its partially owned affiliate DO Group had acquired some of the assets of Corel Corporate Seating, a producer of many kinds of chairs, and JG Auditorium Seating, a manufacturer of a wide range of auditorium seating and lecture products. DO Group said it would integrate both companies into its Elkhart, Indiana plant.

Also in 1998, Mity-Lite's continued success earned it a Utah Best Practices Award from Arthur Andersen in the category of ''exceeding customer expectations.'' Founder Gregory Wilson said his company hired an independent research firm to track Mity-Lite's customer satisfaction by conducting annual surveys of 500 customers. Between 96 and 98 percent of those responding said they were satisfied, and 92 percent said they would buy Mity-Lite products again. Word-of-mouth advertising from such satisfied customers really helped Mity-Lite, for Wilson reported in a October 7, 1998 *Deseret News* article that, ''Fifty percent of our leads are from customer referrals, and they have a high closing rate.''

Mity-Lite again expanded in November 1998 by acquiring all outstanding stock of Broda Enterprises Inc. of Waterloo, Ontario, for $2.5 million. Broda made healthcare seating and accessories used mainly in nursing homes and other long-term facilities. Its main product was the 785 Tilt Recliner Chair that allowed many positions for the user while making it easier for care givers. These chairs provided some mobility to patients who otherwise would remain bedridden. The company in its 2000 annual report estimated that there were 28,000 nursing homes in the United States and Canada, the main markets for its Broda products.

In February 1999 Promus Hotel Corporation named Mity-Lite as a preferred supplier of folding tables and stacking chairs. This was a major contract, for Promus owned or managed over 2,000 American and international hotels, including Hampton Inns, Doubletree Hotels, Homewood Suites, Red Lion, Embassy Suites, and Harrison Conference Centers.

On April 9, 1999 Mity-Lite through two of its wholly owned subsidiaries acquired certain assets and debts of The CenterCore Group, Inc. in a bank foreclosure. For about $5.3 million, its C Core, Inc. subsidiary purchased CenterCore's inventory, machinery, accounts receivable, and intellectual property rights. BOCCC, Inc., another Mity-Lite subsidiary, purchased CenterCore's outstanding subordinated debt obligations for $500,000 cash.

A few months later Mity-Lite announced it planned to expand its 70,000 square feet of office and production space by another 30,000 square feet. With its growth rate averaging about 25 to 30 percent every year since its 1987 start, Mity-Lite definitely needed more room to expand.

The firm sold most of its products in the United States. International sales brought in just 7.8 percent, 11 percent, and 11.3 percent of total net sales in fiscal years 1998, 1999, and 2000 respectively. The exception to that pattern was that more than 50 percent of its healthcare seating products were sold in Canada. Mity-Lite also sold products in Mexico, Brazil, Venezuela, Peru, Argentina, Columbia, Dominican Republic, England, France, Jordan, United Arab Emirates, Hong Kong, China, Korea, Taiwan, Singapore, and Malaysia.

On March 31, 2000 Mity-Lite announced its agreement to acquire the remaining 50.1 percent of DO Group's stock in exchange for about $2.2 million in cash and 41,000 shares of Mity-Lite shares. DO Group's customers, including police departments, 911 emergency centers, air traffic control operations, large corporations, the U.S. Postal Service, and the Federal Aviation Administration, purchased products sold with the Domore, DO3, JG, and Corel trade names. Following the completed acquisition of the DO Group, Mity-Lite on April 6, 2000

Key Dates:

1987: Gregory Wilson starts Mity-Lite in Utah.
1994: Mity-Lite completes its IPO on the NASDAQ.
1997: Company acquires a minority equity interest in DO Group, Inc.
1998: Company acquires Broda Enterprises Inc.
1999: Mity-Lite acquires CenterCore; firm's board of directors approves a three-for-two stock split; SwiftSet line of folding chairs is introduced; company delivers its one millionth table.
2000: Company completes its acquisition of DO Group, Inc.; MLI Acquisition, Inc. is created as a wholly owned subsidiary; Mity Enterprises, Inc. is organized as a holding company.

merged its two wholly owned subsidiaries DO Group and C Core into a new subsidiary called DO Group, Inc.

Business Week recognized Mity-Lite's success by listing it for the second year in the list of the ''Hot Growth Companies.'' The magazine ranked Mity-Lite number 99 in 1999 and number 93 in its 2000 listing. ''Making the list for the second time in two years is a great honor,'' said Mity-Lite CEO Gregory L. Wilson in a press release dated June 15, 2000. ''Only 30 other companies repeated from last year's list.''

On June 14, 2000 Mity-Lite introduced its new trademarked Summit Lectern Series. This line of five models of one-piece lecterns in several colors were lightweight, durable, easy to set up, and came with a 12-year warranty.

In 2000 Mity-Lite continued its good financial performance of the 1990s. Its net sales increased steadily from $9.9 million in fiscal 1994 to $15.4 million in 1996, $25.3 million in 1998, $29.5 million in 1999, and $47.5 million in fiscal 2000, ended March 31. The firm's net income also grew, from $1.1 million in 1994 to $4.7 million in 2000. Mity-Lite's annual report for 2000 stated the company had no long-term debt.

Mity-Lite's growth was reflected in its new physical plant. In 2000 it constructed a 30,000-square-foot manufacturing and office building on nine acres of land purchased next to its Orem, Utah facility that had 70,000 square feet. With an annual growth rate of 25 to 30 percent since its start in 1987, Mity-Lite definitely needed the extra space.

With its acquisitions, new product lines, and a new building, Mity-Lite shareholders on August 17, 2000 voted to approve the organization of Mity Enterprises, Inc. as a parent public company overseeing three wholly owned subsidiaries: Mity-Lite, Inc.; Broda, Inc.; and DO Group, Inc. Still under the helm of Gregory L. Wilson, its board chairman, president, and chief executive officer, the reorganized corporation seemed well positioned in late 2000 for future growth and contributions to the commercial furniture industry.

Principal Subsidiaries

DO Group, Inc.; Broda, Inc.; Mity-Lite, Inc.

Principal Competitors

Steelcase Inc.; Virco Manufacturing Corporation; Palmer-Snyder, Inc.; McCourt Manufacturing, Inc.; Midwest Folding Products; Krueger International, Inc.; Falcon Products, Inc.; SICO; Southern Aluminum, Inc.; U.S. Industries, Inc.; Bevis Custom Furniture, Inc.; Globe Business Furniture; Artco-Bell Corporation; Shelby Williams Industries, Inc.; Clarin, a Greenwich Industries division; Meco Corporation; Technion; Interior Concepts; Hamilton Sorter; Haworth Inc.; Herman Miller, Inc.; Knoll Group Inc.; Kimball International, Inc.; Neutral Postures; Hon Industries Inc.; U.S. Prison Industries; Invacare Corporation; L.P.A. Medical Inc.; Graham-Field Inc.; Maple Leaf Wheelchair Manufacturing Inc.; Sunrise Medical Inc.; Hillenbrand Industries Inc.; Winco Inc.; Homecrest Industries Incorporated.

Further Reading

''DO Group Acquires Portion of 2 Seating Firms' Assets,'' *Deseret News*, July 15, 1998, p. B3.
Haddock, Sharon M., ''Orem Company Expands Line with Acquisition,'' *Deseret News*, March 6, 1997, p. D7.
Knudson, Max B., ''4 Utah Small Businesses Among Top 200 in U.S.,'' *Deseret News*, October 23, 1994, p. B3.
Kratz, Gregory P., ''Delighting Customers Pays Off,'' *Deseret News*, October 7, 1998, p. B5.
''Mity-Lite Sells European Sales Office to Briton,'' *Deseret News*, April 5, 1995, p. B7.
Pusey, Roger, ''Global Marketing Called Mixed Bag,'' *Deseret News*, September 12, 1997, p. B7.
——, ''Mity-Lite Makes Tables Manageable,'' *Deseret News*, August 7, 1994, p. M1.
Williams, Lane, ''Innovative Portable-Table Firm Trying to Top the Competition,'' *Deseret News*, March 21, 1990, p. D8.

—David M. Walden

Musicland Stores Corporation

10400 Yellow Circle Drive
Minnetonka, Minnesota 55343
U.S.A.
Telephone: (952) 931-8000
Fax: (952) 931-8300
Web site: http://www.musicland.com

Public Company
Incorporated: 1977 as The Musicland Group, Inc.
Employees: 15,900
Sales: $1.89 billion (1999)
Stock Exchanges: New York
Ticker Symbol: MLG
NAIC: 451220 Prerecorded Tape, Compact Disc, and Record Stores; 451211 Book Stores; 454110 Electronic Shopping and Mail-Order Houses

The leading specialty retailer in the United States of prerecorded music, movies, and audio and video accessories, Musicland Stores Corporation operates more than 1,300 stores in 49 states, Puerto Rico, and the United Kingdom. These include approximately 650 Sam Goody stores (selling prerecorded home entertainment products, primarily in suburban shopping malls); 400 Suncoast Motion Picture Company stores (selling video, DVD, and movie-related products, primarily in metropolitan shopping malls); around 75 Media Play superstores (selling books, music, videos, software, and other products in select large-to-mid-size markets); and some 200 On Cue stores (selling a variety of entertainment products in small town markets). Each of these stores also has a sister e-commerce site, offering another sales channel to the company's customers. As 2001 began, Musicland was in the process of being acquired by Best Buy Co., Inc., a leading operator of consumer electronics superstores.

Early Years, Featuring Many Owners

Musicland began humbly in 1956 with a single outlet near downtown Minneapolis. One of the founders, Terry Evenson, had opened his first music store in his hometown of Cloquet, Minnesota, while still a teenager some eight years earlier. Following a college education he helped fund by leading a dance band, Evenson served in the Korean War. He then resettled in Minneapolis and launched the Musicland business with partner Grover Sayre, a former member of his band. The partnership had grown to a chain of 15 stores by 1964, at which time Evenson and Sayre decided to sell their interest.

His entrepreneurial streak still alive, Evenson founded a sizeable chain of greeting card stores, which he ultimately sold to Hallmark. Sayre, on the other hand, remained with Musicland until 1981. From 1964 until 1968, Musicland was the property of two St. Louis Park, Minnesota, brothers, Amos and Dan Heilicher. Veterans of record distribution since the 1930s, the Heilichers had supplied Evenson with prerecorded music since his early days in Cloquet. Musicland expanded rapidly to 48 stores under their management before the private concern merged with Pickwick International, a music and book production, distribution, and merchandising corporation based in New York with 300 retail outlets. The Heilicher brothers remained in the Twin Cities to head Musicland's distribution and retailing divisions.

Then in 1976, according to Mike Langberg, "Amos Heilicher had a falling out with other members of the Pickwick board and sold his stake in the company." The year after the break, packaging giant American Can (since renamed Primerica to reflect its diversification into financial services and other industries) purchased Pickwick for $102 million (Pickwick's revenues for the year ending April 30, 1976, totaled $264.9 million). At this juncture Musicland appeared a clear leader in record retailing, with approximately 230 stores. In 1977 Musicland was incorporated as the Musicland Group, Inc.

Unfortunately for Primerica, wrote Langberg, "the purchase of Pickwick was a classic case of bad timing. The recorded music business lurched into a long slide after 1978, while Primerica—with little knowledge of retailing in its top executive ranks—poured money into acquisitions of smaller record store chains and opening of new stores." Some of the slide was due to the flash-in-the-pan music phenomenon of disco. The greatest factor, though, was likely the changing demographics

Company Perspectives:

As the leader in the entertainment retailing industry, we are embracing new tech-savvy strategies which will enhance and integrate our online and in-store presence to increase customer loyalty, customer retention and, thus, revenue. Our annual cash flow, upwards of $100 million, enables us to implement new strategic plans to build sales, and improve service in our stores and online. Our consumer-centric vision will provide customers with access to products when and how they want it. Our plans are geared to benefit consumers and investors.

of record buyers: baby boomers were no longer primarily teenagers, the largest record-buying group by age, but part of an older crowd fast approaching middle age.

1980s: Eugster's Turnaround, an IPO, Then an LBO

From 1979 to 1983, Ted Deikel (best known for his leadership of Minnesota-based mail-order firm Fingerhut) managed Musicland and Primerica's other retailing concerns. Deikel's foremost task was to restructure Pickwick and return it to profitability. It was to Jack W. Eugster, hired in 1980 by Deikel, that the arduous job of reshaping an overexpanded Musicland fell. A former Dayton Hudson and Gap Stores retailing executive, Eugster took several predictable steps over the next few years, including closing more than 100 poorly located or unprofitable outlets and centralizing distribution to just two (rather than the previous 18) warehouses. In addition, he sought savings by taking the tiniest and least obvious of measures, including switching off back room store lights and shaving the number of paper bag sizes offered to the customer.

Eugster's greatest contribution came with the introduction of a computerized inventory system that, according to Christopher Palmeri, was ''the standard in the record retailing business.'' Called Retail Inventory Management (RIM), the two-way system tracked every individual item that left the St. Louis Park warehouse by means of a bar code similar to those for supermarket products. Computerized registers at each retail outlet then scanned the bar codes at the point of sale and relayed the information back to headquarters. The final step in the process involved a computer model that forecasted the optimum levels for all music and video products on a store-by-store basis.

In 1985, because of RIM and Eugster's other managerial improvements, Musicland was back in the black. The transition had been complex and costly, though, for from 1981 to 1984 virtually all of the company's nonretail operations (i.e., wholesale distribution and record production) were curtailed, even while American Can continued to buy up and merge smaller record chains into Musicland. Nonetheless, flush with revenues of $327.5 million and profits of $8.8 million, the subsidiary entered 1986 both comfortable in the knowledge that it was the nation's largest music retailer and hungry for further expansion. In May of that year, plans to acquire California-based Record Bar / Licorice Pizza, a 60-store joint enterprise, for $13 million were announced. When completed, the deal would bring Musicland's tally of stores to 512. Other major developments included the launch of Musicland's first for-sale video specialty store; debuting as Paramount Pictures before being renamed Suncoast Motion Picture Company, Musicland's movie division saw sales grow to nearly seven percent of all corporate revenues within its first year. Then, in August, American Can announced its plans for an initial public offering of Musicland stock.

The offering was postponed until February 1987, when 19 percent of Musicland was sold by parent company American Can (that same year, American changed its name to Primerica), the newly public firm dubbed the Musicland Group, Inc. The IPO was particularly well received due to Musicland's dominant market position and a new upsurge in record-buying among the 30- and 40-something crowd. Consonant with this trend, Sam Goody, with its more upscale image and emphasis on new age, jazz, and classical music, made its Twin Cities debut a year later. A discount record chain begun during the Great Depression, Sam Goody was bought by American Can back in 1978. Within ten years, the chain had expanded from 28 to 190 stores, most located either on the West or East Coasts. Next to the original Musicland chain, Sam Goody had become a primary contributor to the company's overall revenues of more than half a billion.

Retailing trends, market dominance, high hopes for video sales, and other positive indices within Musicland's divisions prompted Eugster and a group of fellow investors committed to the company's long-term growth (including the Donaldson, Lufkin & Jenrette investment group) to pursue a daring highly leveraged buyout (LBO) in August 1988. When the ink was dry on the $410 million deal, Musicland's new management had decreased Primerica's ownership stake from 81 percent to just 20 percent and also reduced Primerica's role to that of passive investor. As part of the transaction, a new entity called Musicland Stores Corporation was incorporated, which acquired the Musicland Group, Inc. Following the LBO, Musicland continued its program of aggressive expansion, solidly outdistancing such competitors as Trans World Music, Wherehouse Entertainment, and Tower Records.

1990s: Recovering from a Near-Death Experience

In July 1990 the company entertained plans of going public, believing it could raise as much as $96 million in interest-free capital. With the Iraqi invasion of Kuwait in August and the subsequent downturn in the stock market, however, the plan was scrapped. Due to the economic recession, Musicland saw its sales soften and profits stall along with those of other music retailers. ''In late November [1991],'' according to a January 1992 *Minneapolis Star Tribune* article, ''some industry observers speculated that Musicland was hitting rough times when it ended negotiations to buy New York City-based Record World Inc., a chain of 80 music stores, from Chemical Banking Corp.'' Such speculation was quelled in February 1992, however, when Musicland extricated itself from LBO financing pressures by taking the company public in an enormously successful offering. A follow-up *Minneapolis Star Tribune* article from that month cited Ken Salmon, an analyst with C.L. King & Associates. According to Salmon, Musicland's Wall Street appeal, despite both significant internal and external economic pressures, was that: ''It's bigger and slightly better in

Key Dates:

1956: Terry Evenson and Grover Sayre open the first Musicland store near downtown Minneapolis.
1964: The now 15-store chain is sold to Amos and Dan Heilicher.
1968: Having grown to 48 stores, Musicland is merged with Pickwick International.
1977: American Can acquires Pickwick; Musicland, with 230 stores, is incorporated as the Musicland Group, Inc.
1978: American Can acquires the Sam Goody chain, which is later made part of Musicland.
1980: Jack W. Eugster is hired to head up Musicland.
1986: Musicland launches a video-for-sale chain, Paramount Pictures, which is later renamed Suncoast Motion Picture Company.
1987: American Can changes its name to Primerica and sells 19 percent of Musicland to the public through an IPO.
1988: Musicland is taken private, as Musicland Stores Corporation, through a $410 million highly leveraged buyout.
1992: Musicland goes public again through another IPO; the Media Play and On Cue formats debut; sales top the $1 billion mark.
1995: Company begins converting Musicland stores to Sam Goody outlets.
1999: E-commerce sites are launched, one each for the four store formats.
2000: Musicland agrees to be acquired by Best Buy Co. for $685 million.

everything—whether it's sales per square foot or operating margins—than any other music company out there. It was not an LBO under stress.''

Following the offering, Musicland topped the $1 billion mark in sales in 1992 and redefined itself as a conservatively capitalized company. In addition, holdings by the chief outside investors—Primerica, Donaldson, and Equitable—were cut by 30 to 60 percent. The largest remaining stockholder among the three, Donaldson, saw its interest drop from about 25 percent to 17 percent. In November 1992 Musicland reaffirmed its market-driving reputation by opening its first Media Play store in a suburban strip center in Rockford, Illinois. A 40,000-square-foot prototype (later Media Plays ranged up to 50,000 square feet) competitive with such discounters as Wal-Mart and such multimedia retailers as Borders Group, the store was part of a new program to capitalize on the emerging trend of integrated media. ''In the new megastore,'' wrote Palmeri, ''customers are encouraged to browse. There is a kids' play section, easy chairs in the travel book section, a café in the center of the store.'' Musicland expanded its portfolio of store formats further through the 1992 launch of On Cue, with the first unit opening in Fairmont, Minnesota. The On Cue format was similar to Media Play's in its range of products, though not in the selection nor in the store size, and was designed as a freestanding outlet for smaller markets, with populations of 25,000 to 40,000.

The early returns on Media Play were astoundingly good, with the original store achieving sales of $10 million in its first full year. Musicland then launched an aggressive program of expansion, opening 89 Media Play stores and 153 On Cue stores from 1992 through 1995. Meanwhile, the company's mall stores, which were not faring as well as the nonmall units, began to be reorganized. In 1995, the Musicland stores began to be converted to Sam Goody outlets. Among the rationales for this move was the ability to promote and manage one store identity rather than two as well as the feeling that the Musicland name was limited in that it implied that only music was sold there. The conversion was completed by 1997.

In November 1995 Musicland announced plans to sell a 30 percent stake in Suncoast in order to pay down debt and fund expansion of Media Play and On Cue, but the plan was scuttled in early 1996 because of a lack of enthusiasm from Wall Street. The company needed cash because its growth strategy had faltered and its stock price had fallen precipitously. At the same time that the music industry was going through a sales slump, music retailers were facing brutal competition from both consumer electronics category killers Best Buy and Circuit City and big discount merchandisers, including Target, Kmart, and Wal-Mart. All of these chains were aggressively expanding their sales of music and videos by drastically cutting prices, in some cases below cost. Media Play was supposed to represent Musicland's own category killer but because of these competitors, who were in a better financial and operational position to maintain the low prices, Media Play was unable to gain an edge by undercutting them. With sales at the mall stores also suffering from the new competition, Musicland's overall sales were failing to increase at the pace needed to maintain previous profit levels. The company began closing underperforming stores, taking charges for this purpose and for the writing down of goodwill associated with the 1988 LBO. The company's poor performance, coupled with the charges, led to net losses of $135.8 million in 1995 and $193.7 million in 1996.

For most of 1996 and 1997, Musicland teetered on the verge of bankruptcy, a fate that befell a number of other music retailers during this period. The company closed more than 100 stores, including 19 Media Play outlets, and scaled back its expansion plans. It also shut down its St. Louis Park distribution center, with operations there shifted to a huge new facility that had opened in Franklin, Indiana, in March 1995. Needing a strong 1997 Christmas selling season to cement its recovery, Musicland delivered in part by placing emphasis on the new DVD format, selling $1 million worth of DVDs during the week of December 14 to 20 alone. Sales of DVDs for all of 1997 were $50 million. Also helping was a resurgence in sales of music video, fueled primarily by the popular group Hanson. Consequently, Musicland returned to the black in 1997, posting net income of $14 million on sales of $1.77 billion. Results for the following year were even better: $38 million in profits on revenues of $1.85 billion.

A cautious return to expansion came in 1999, when 39 stores were added, most of them either Media Play or On Cue outlets, with On Cue becoming the fastest growing format. That year, the company also ventured into e-commerce for the first time, launching sites for each of its four main brands: Media Play, On Cue, Sam Goody, and Suncoast. The sites were launched through an advertising campaign dubbed ''We Got Dot.'' For 1999, Musicland reported record sales of $1.89 billion and record profits of $58.4 million.

Online revenues during the first quarter of 2000 had already reached $1.9 million, although the e-commerce initiative was thus far a money-losing one. In October 2000, Musicland purchased a 20 percent stake in an 18-store retail chain called Golf Galaxy, which was privately owned and based in Minneapolis. This venture into sporting goods seemed somewhat odd, although the company had once owned the Dunhams sporting goods chain before selling it following the 1992 IPO. Throughout 2000, Musicland was dogged by a lagging stock price, in spite of its seeming recovery from the dark days of the mid-1990s. One reason for the lack of investor enthusiasm was the uncertain future of the music industry, specifically in light of the rampant downloading of music over the Internet that had been made popular by Napster and other online music services. Nevertheless, Musicland was itself preparing its web sites to deliver downloaded music if the demand arose and if it became feasible to do so at a profit.

Meanwhile, by late 2000, the company was still saddled with $260 million in long-term debt and needed another year of strong earnings to retire the bulk of it. A different avenue for expunging the debt arose, however, in the form of a company takeover. In early December 2000 Musicland agreed to be acquired by crosstown rival Best Buy Co. for $425 million in cash and the assumption of the company's debt. Best Buy planned to retool some of Musicland's store formats and was particularly interested in gaining a presence within shopping malls by revamping the Sam Goody format through the addition of such consumer electronics goods as MP3 players, cellular products, and gaming items. Having conquered the nation's major markets, Best Buy also coveted the access to the smaller markets that would be gained through ownership of the On Cue chain. For Musicland, becoming part of Best Buy would give it access to more capital and could spark an acceleration in its growth.

Principal Subsidiaries

The Musicland Group, Inc.; Media Play, Inc.; MG Financial Services, Inc.; MLG Internet, Inc.; Musicland Retail, Inc.; On Cue, Inc.; Request Media, Inc.; Suncoast Group, Inc.; Suncoast Motion Picture Company, Inc.; Suncoast Retail, Inc.; TMG Caribbean, Inc.; TMG-Virgin Islands, Inc.

Principal Competitors

Amazon.com, Inc.; Barnes & Noble, Inc.; Best Buy Co., Inc.; Books-A-Million, Inc.; Borders Group, Inc.; BUY.COM INC.; Circuit City Group; Columbia House Company; Hastings Entertainment, Inc.; Kmart Corporation; MTS, Incorporated; Target Corporation; Trans World Entertainment Corporation; Wal-Mart Stores, Inc.; Wherehouse Entertainment, Inc.

Further Reading

Apgar, Sally, ''Musicland Exec, Calling Old Name 'Limiting,' Says Mall Outlets to Be Sam Goody Stores,'' *Minneapolis Star Tribune,* April 28, 1995, p. 1D.

——, ''Musicland Plans Stock Offering to Add Stores and Pay Off Debt,'' *Minneapolis Star Tribune,* January 17, 1992, pp. 1D, 4D.

——, ''Musicland Stores Corp. Draws Rave Reviews As It Makes Debut Appearance on Wall Street,'' *Minneapolis Star Tribune,* February 27, 1992, pp. 1D, 7D.

——, ''Out of Tune: With Its Growth Strategy Faltering and Stock Languishing, Musicland Stores Corp. Is Looking at Making Some Changes,'' *Minneapolis Star Tribune,* January 15, 1996, p. 1D.

Calamba, Shella, ''Smaller Works Better: Musicland Aims Its On Cue Stores at Populations of 10,000 to 30,000,'' *Minneapolis Star Tribune,* June 19, 1995, p. 1D.

Cochran, Thomas N., ''Musicland Stores Corp.,'' *Barron's,* August 20, 1990, p. 45.

Coleman, Calmetta Y., ''Musicland's Efficiency Drive Produces Upbeat Results,'' *Wall Street Journal,* July 20, 1999, p. B4.

Dravo, Ed, ''Music Bland,'' *Financial World,* January 21, 1997, p. 86.

''DVD Keeps Musicland from Going OOB,'' *Discount Store News,* February 9, 1998, pp. 6, 102.

Feldman, Amy, ''Somebody's Eating My Lunch,'' *Forbes,* December 4, 1995, p. 166.

Forster, Julie, ''Perfect Pitch,'' *Corporate Report-Minnesota,* June 1999, p. 10.

Gillespie, Scott, ''Musicland Defers Payments, Keeps Closing Stores,'' *Minneapolis Star Tribune,* February 14, 1997, p. 1D.

Goddard, Connie, ''Musicland to Open 10 ''Full-Media' Stores Around U.S.,'' *Publishers Weekly,* August 9, 1993, pp. 18–19.

Goldstein, Seth, ''Jack Eugster: The Billboard Interview,'' *Billboard,* July 3, 1999, pp. 70+.

Hisey, Pete, ''Media Play Tries Second Take,'' *Discount Store News,* July 15, 1996, p. 1.

Kennedy, Tony, ''Musicland Posts a Loss for the Second Quarter Despite Rise in Revenues,'' *Minneapolis Star Tribune,* July 15, 1993, p. 2D.

——, ''Musicland's Best-Seller,'' *Minneapolis Star Tribune,* October 12, 1993, p. 1D.

——, ''Musicland Stores Will Expand in Minnetonka,'' *Minneapolis Star Tribune,* August 4, 1993, p. 3D.

Koshetz, Herbert, ''Move to Acquire Pickwick Is Made by American Can,'' *New York Times,* January 20, 1977, p. 57.

Kurschner, Dale, ''The Day the Music Died: When Is Musicland Going to File for Bankruptcy?,'' *Corporate Report-Minnesota,* December 1996, pp. 38–42, 44–46.

Langberg, Mike, ''Musicland Plans Initial Public Offering,'' *St. Paul Pioneer Press & Dispatch,* November 10, 1986.

——, ''Musicland Plays Sweet Tune of Growth,'' *St. Paul Pioneer Press & Dispatch,* June 8, 1987.

Levy, Melissa, ''Musicland Began with a Minneapolis Store,'' *Minneapolis Star Tribune,* December 8, 2000, p. 1D.

Mehler, Mark, and Geoff Mayfield, ''Management in Leveraged Buy of Musicland,'' *Billboard,* February 20, 1988, pp. 1, 78.

Moore, Janet, ''A Global Growth Strategy: Best Buy Made Itself Huge and Profitable by Building a Nationwide Chain of Electronics Superstores,'' *Minneapolis Star Tribune,* December 8, 2000, p. 1D.

——, ''Musicland Traveling the Comeback Trail,'' *Minneapolis Star Tribune,* May 8, 1998, p. 1D.

''Musicland Buyout Approved: Deal Valued at $410 Million,'' *Billboard,* September 10, 1988.

''Musicland's Big Picture: More Video Sales,'' *Corporate Report-Minnesota,* July 1990, p. 18.

Paige, Earl, ''Acquisition of Calif. Chain Near Completion: Musicland, Record Bar Ink $13-Million Deal,'' *Billboard,* May 3, 1986, p. 3.

——, ''Musicland, MCA Expose Promo Options,'' *Billboard,* November 28, 1992, p. 63.

Palmeri, Christopher, ''Media Merchant to the Baby Boomers,'' *Forbes,* March 15, 1993, pp. 66, 70.

Pedersen, Martin, ''Musicland's New Multimedia Store Tune,'' *Publishers Weekly,* April 12, 1993, p. 22.

"People: Sam Goody," *New York Times,* December 13, 1977, Sec. 3, p. 5.

Pokela, Barbara, "Musicland Hits Different Note with Area's First Sam Goody," *Minneapolis Star Tribune,* November 21, 1988.

Ramstad, Evan, "Best Buy Makes Two Acquisition Pacts," *Wall Street Journal,* December 8, 2000, p. B8.

Reilly, Patrick M., "Musicland Plans Media Medley in Superstores," *Wall Street Journal,* July 26, 1993, pp. B1, B4.

—Jay P. Pederson
—updated by David E. Salamie

新世界發展有限公司
New World Development Company Limited

New World Development Company Limited

30th Floor, New World Tower
18 Queen's Road Central
Hong Kong
Telephone: (852) 2523 1056
Fax: (852) 2810 4673
Web site: http://www.nwd.com.hk

Public Company
Incorporated: 1970
Employees: 16,500
Sales: HK$20.54 billion (US$2.63 billion) (2000)
Stock Exchanges: Hong Kong
Ticker Symbol: 0017
NAIC: 233210 Single Family Housing Construction; 233220 Multifamily Housing Construction; 233110 Land Subdivision and Land Development; 233310 Manufacturing and Industrial Building Construction; 234110 Highway and Street Construction; 234120 Bridge and Tunnel Construction; 234920 Power and Communication Transmission Line Construction; 452110 Department Stores; 483112 Deep Sea Passenger Transportation; 485113 Bus and Other Motor Vehicle Transit Systems; 513310 Wired Telecommunications Carriers; 513322 Cellular and Other Wireless Telecommunications; 514191 On-Line Information Services; 531120 Lessors of Nonresidential Buildings (Except Miniwarehouses); 531312 Nonresidential Property Managers; 541330 Engineering Services; 561612 Security Guards and Patrol Services; 721110 Hotels (Except Casino Hotels) and Motels; 722110 Full-Service Restaurants

Since its founding in 1970, New World Development Company Limited has been a leader in Hong Kong's bustling commercial and residential development market. The company also has become the largest private property developer in mainland China since its entrance into that market in 1991. Among the company's properties are 17 hotels in Hong Kong, China, and Southeast Asia, most of which operate under the Renaissance or Courtyard brand. As a conglomerate, however, New World Development is much more than just a property company. It owns a 60 percent stake in New World Infrastructure Limited (NWI), which has its own listing on the Hong Kong Stock Exchange. NWI is involved in infrastructure projects in Hong Kong, Macau, and China, helping to build roads, bridges, water treatment and power plants, cargo handling facilities, and communications networks. New World Services Limited, 51 percent owned by New World Development, provides construction and engineering services, manages facilities and other properties, offers security services, operates bus lines and ferry services, and provides environmental, waste disposal, cleaning, pest control, laundry, information technology, and elder-care services. New World Development also is involved in telecommunications and information technology through 88 percent stakes in New World Telephone Limited, which operates a fixed, fiber-optic-based telephone network with more than 900,000 subscribers in Hong Kong; and New World PCS Limited, operator of a mobile phone service in Hong Kong with 620,000 subscribers. The company also operates department stores in Hong Kong and China. As of 2000, about 8 percent of net sales was generated from rental income, 9 percent from property sales, 36 percent from construction and engineering, 11 percent from hotel and restaurant operations, four percent from infrastructure operations, 14 percent from telecommunications services, and the remaining 18 percent from other operations.

Founded in 1970

The founders of New World Development were Dr. Cheng Yu-tung, the current company chairman, and the late Young Chi-wan. In 1970 they joined up to merge their holdings in the colony's commercial and residential property market.

Both men started their careers in Hong Kong's jewelry trade. Cheng Yu-tung, who proceeded during the 1960s to become managing director of the Chow Tai Fook Jewellery Company, had already by the 1950s begun investing in Hong Kong's real estate market. As chairman of many commercial property firms, and as vice-chairman of Hang Lung Bank from 1970, Cheng was well placed in the Hong Kong business community. So was Young Chi-wan. As principal founder and, eventually, general manager of Miramar Hotel & Investment Company, the worldwide hotels group, Young had amassed among his other posi-

Company Perspectives:

It is important that all of us, however old or young, have a mindset that enables us to capture all the opportunities that changes in the world are bringing to us. A mindset that is characterized by creativity and initiative, harnessed by focus and discipline. In our company, this mindset is requisite and indelible.

As economic cycles come and go, we have conquered the challenges and maximised the opportunities. Our solid foundations and the mindset that we possess will firmly position our company for growth.

tions the chairmanship of Yeung Chi Shing Estates and King Fook Gold and Jewellery Company.

In 1970, the two men linked their vast commercial and residential property holdings. Their aim was to acquire first-class rental properties with the development for sale and rental of prime commercial and residential sites in mind. The steadily increasing population of Hong Kong, and the shortage of land on which it might live and work, made the development of such commercial and residential sites potentially lucrative. In addition, Cheng and Young recognized Hong Kong's mounting importance as an international financial center, with increasing inflows of foreign investment to the colony providing for different residential and commercial property needs.

New World Development was incorporated in Hong Kong on May 29, 1970, as a private limited company. The company's first chairman was Dr. Ho Sin-hang, the former chairman of Hang Seng Bank, one of the colony's leading financial institutions. Ho, who served as chairman of the company until 1981, brought a number of his business associates to the new property concern. Cheong Liang-yuen, then vice-chairman of the newly created New World Development, had been a director of Hang Seng Bank, as well as of the Hong Kong and Shanghai Hotels Company. He brought with him considerable expertise in Hong Kong's property development and management market. Lee Quo-wei, appointed managing director of New World Development, had served as the general manager of Hang Seng Bank. In 1972, he was appointed a fellow of the Institute of Bankers in London. Among the other executives who joined New World Development as directors from the Hang Seng board were Tang Shiu-kin, Dr. Ho Tim, and Michael Sandberg, who was later knighted for his contribution to Hong Kong's business life.

It was not long before the company's board elected to float the property concern on the Hong Kong stock market. In June 1972, New World Development became a quoted company when the board issued 96.75 million shares at HK$2 each. With the funds raised, New World Development financed the building of the New World Centre in central Hong Kong, complete with a shopping mall and commercial and residential properties. The first phase of the project, which included the New World Hotel, was completed in 1978, with phase two reaching completion two years later with the opening of the Regent Hotel.

To facilitate construction work of its real estate projects, the company acquired in 1972 a 51 percent equity stake in Shun Fung Ironworks, for around HK$7.6 million. This was followed in 1973 by the purchase of a controlling interest in Hip Hing Construction Company Limited and, the following year, by the acquisition of a 55 percent equity stake in Young's Engineering Company Limited.

Adverse market conditions in 1974, precipitated by poor market conditions worldwide, prompted New World Development to increase its interests in the hotel trade. The company already had a stake in Miramar Hotel & Investment Company through the involvement of Chi Wan Young. In 1976, the company acquired the Kai Tak Land Investment Company Limited, which, under the name it adopted in 1985, New World Hotels (Holdings) Limited, became the subsidiary that handled all hotel operations, both directly owned hotels and managed hotels.

Another 1976 acquisition was that of Timely Enterprises Corporation Limited, which owned the American International Tower at 18 Queen's Road Central. New World Development subsequently moved its headquarters into this building, which in 1980 was renamed New World Tower.

Diversifying Further in the 1980s

Also in 1980, New World Development purchased a 75 percent stake in Mei Foo Investments. This gave the company access to extensive residential properties in Hong Kong, 48,000 square feet of retail commercial space, and 16,000 square feet of space for use by schools.

Infrastructure servicing contracts from the Hong Kong government were included in the range of business New World Development was completing at this time. In 1982, the company was awarded a contract to develop three massive projects under the colony's Home Ownership and Private Sector Participation Scheme. A year earlier, the company won a contract from the U.S. government to redevelop six prime sites in exchange for a lease to rent key properties for development by New World Development.

In 1983, the continuing effects of worldwide recession, and the resulting dampening effect on Hong Kong's property market, led the company to diversify into shipping. New World Development purchased a 60 percent interest in the Hong Kong Islands Line Company, which operated cargo services across the Atlantic. This business was sold subsequently, in February 1989. Even so, by 1985, New World Development had purchased a 39 percent stake in the Hong Kong-based Asia Terminals Limited, the largest container freight station and cargo distribution center in southeast Asia. Phases one and two of the terminal site were opened in 1987. Increased business by the cargo handling operation led to the construction of phases three and four as well. The second airport planned for Hong Kong, in the colony's port vicinity, convinced New World Development to plan a phase five addition to the terminal, a 13-story container complex, with a total of 5.2 million square feet of space (it opened in 1994).

The year 1984 saw the start of New World Development's most ambitious project yet: the construction of the Hong Kong Convention and Exhibition Centre, with its ultramodern facilities providing space for international gatherings on a waterfront site in Wanchai. Commissioned by the Trade Development Council, the complex was opened in November 1988. More than 853 events of varying size, involving both international and local

Key Dates:

1970: New World Development Company Limited is founded.
1972: Company goes public through a listing on the Hong Kong Stock Exchange.
1976: Company acquires Kai Tak Land Investment Company Limited, which is later renamed New World Hotels (Holdings) Limited.
1978: The first phase of the New World Centre is completed.
1988: The Hong Kong Convention and Exhibition Centre, developed by the company, opens.
1989: The company begins taking on infrastructure projects in China; Ramada International Hotels is acquired.
1990: New World Hotels is taken public.
1991: Company enters the Chinese property development sector.
1993: Company is awarded a license to operate a fixed telecommunications network in Hong Kong, marking its entrance into the telecom field.
1995: Hotel management operations are consolidated into a new entity, Renaissance Hotel Group N.V., which is taken public; company forms New World Infrastructure (NWI) to consolidate all its infrastructure projects in Hong Kong and China; NWI is taken public.
1997: New World Telephone launches its PCS cellular service in Hong Kong; New World Services Limited is created as an umbrella organization for all of New World's services businesses; New World sells its stake in Renaissance Hotel Group as well as its interest in all hotel properties located outside Hong Kong, China, and Southeast Asia.
1998: New World Services begins operating bus routes in Hong Kong, soon followed by ferry services.
1999: The company's China property arm, New World China Land Limited, is taken public.

Hong Kong participants, were held at the convention center in 1989 alone. Finding occupants for the residential properties in the luxurious convention center was, however, a slow process. A 70 percent occupancy rate was attained by the end of 1990, with about 310 units leased. In the meantime, a new hotel opened at the complex in July 1989. Called New World Harbour View Hotel, it offered a commanding view of Victoria Harbour.

New World Development began in 1986 to develop more than 1,100 residential units on Lantau Island. Construction was carried out in partnership with the Hong Kong Resort Company, with whom New World Development had established a joint venture. In the same year, New World Development entered another partnership with Caltex Petroleum Corporation of the United States to redevelop the oil company's depot in Tsuen Wan. This turned the site into Riveria Gardens, a residential estate of 6,200 flats with commercial facilities.

A further joint venture agreement was signed at the time with the Canton Railway Corporation of Kowloon. This called for more than 1,400 residential units to be developed, with commercial facilities, in the vicinity of the Light Rail Transit System in Tuen Mun, which came to be known as Pierhead Garden.

In 1987, the success of the Lantau Island development convinced New World Development to construct additional residential properties, in conjunction with the Hong Kong Resort Company. On the infrastructure side, the company entered a joint venture agreement with the colony's Mass Transit Railway to develop the Sai Wan Ho site situated above the Sai Wan Ho station on Hong Kong Island.

In 1988, New World Development took a 24 percent interest in the Gammon/Nishimatsu consortium behind the building of the four-kilometer Tate's Cairn Tunnel, to run from Siu Lek Yuen in Shatin to Diamond Hill. The consortium gained a 30-year franchise to run the first private sector tunnel in Hong Kong. Opened in May 1991 in a bid to ease traffic congestion in East Kowloon, initial traffic estimates for the tunnel began at 100,000 vehicles daily. In 1988, New World Development purchased a one-third interest in Asia Television, one of the two television license holders in the colony. The television station subsequently underwent an extensive restructuring, complete with job cuts and capital investment programs. Satisfied with progress on this front, New World Development in 1989 raised its stake in Asia Television to 50 percent. In January 1989, meanwhile, Henry Cheng, son of the cofounder Cheng Yu-tung, was named managing director.

In late 1989, New World Development increased its presence in the hotel trade by acquiring Ramada International Hotels & Resorts, the world's third largest hotel chain, for US$540 million. In a separate agreement, an affiliate of Prime Motor Inns agreed to operate Ramada hotels in the United States, while the Hong Kong company retained control of all Ramada Renaissance properties in the United States and all Ramada properties outside that important market. In July 1990, Prime Motors Inns sold its rights to operate the U.S. Ramada hotels to the Blackstone Group of New York. In early 1990 New World Development sold 14 Ramada properties in the United States to reduce the bank financing necessary for the original acquisition.

Restructuring, Telecommunications, Focusing on China: 1990s and Beyond

Also in 1990, New World Hotels was taken public, with New World Development maintaining a controlling, majority stake. New World Hotels owned and/or managed a number of hotels in Hong Kong, including the Regent of Hong Kong, New World Hotel, Hotel Victoria, the Grand Hyatt Hong Kong, and New World Harbour View Hotel. Aside from its interests in Hong Kong, the company managed six hotels in China, including the Jing Guang New World Hotel in Beijing and the Yangtze New World Hotel in Shanghai, opened in 1990.

The company had been active in China since it developed its first hotel there in 1980. The June 4, 1989 Tiananmen Square massacre, in which Chinese soldiers fired on pro-democracy activists in Beijing, scared off most foreign investors. New World ventured, however, that China's economic reform program would continue and that the bloodshed presented a buying opportunity. In June 1990 New World Development signed two investment contracts with the Guangzhou municipal government to develop the 26.5-kilometer Guangzhou ring road and the 600,000-kilowatt Zhujiang thermal power station. The company also moved into the property development field in China for the first time in 1991 when it entered into a joint venture with the Guangzhou municipal government to develop a project called Fortune Garden. New World Development continued to take on new projects in southern China in 1992, including the Shenzhen-Huizhou Expressway and a portion of the Beijing-Zhuhai Expressway. The company was steadily increasing its investment in China and did not redomicile itself like other Hong Kong-based firms had in advance of the fast approaching 1997 handover of Hong Kong to China; tying the company's future to China, New World's leaders did not fear the Chinese takeover, but were instead focusing on the opportunities that were arising from the increasing standard of living in the giant mainland nation. Whereas the company had a relatively small, by Hong Kong standards, land bank of six million square feet at home, it had quickly, by the early 1990s, become the largest private landowner in China, with more than 25 million square feet.

New World Development entered 1993 with interests in property development and investment, hotels, facilities management, container terminals, infrastructure projects, and television. The company began laying the groundwork for another diversification, this time into telecommunications services. With the monopoly status of Hong Kong Telecom slated to end in mid-1995, New World Development in 1993 was awarded a license to operate a fixed telecommunications network in Hong Kong once the market was opened to competition. A new subsidiary was formed called New World Telephone Limited, which began offering international direct dialing services during the 1996 fiscal year. New World Telephone next moved to enter the burgeoning cellular telephone market, gaining a Personal Communications Service (PCS) license in Hong Kong in 1996. The following year, the company launched its PCS service and quickly became the leading PCS cellular operator in Hong Kong.

Another 1993 development was the establishment of New World Department Store Limited to create a department store chain that could complement the company's shopping facilities in Hong Kong and China. By 2000, there were New World Department Stores in Hong Kong and in eight mainland cities. On the hotel front, three new hotels bearing the New World name were opened in Manila, Ho Chi Minh City, and Shenyang, China, during 1994. The following year, the hotel management operations of New World Development, including those of Ramada and New World International, were consolidated into a new entity, Renaissance Hotel Group N.V. New World then conducted an IPO of Renaissance stock with a listing on the New York Stock Exchange, emerging from the transaction with a 34.8 percent stake in Renaissance. New World completed restructuring moves in other areas as well in 1995. The company formed New World Infrastructure Limited to consolidate all of its infrastructure projects in Hong Kong and China. In October 1995 New World Infrastructure also was taken public, on the Hong Kong Stock Exchange. New World Development retained a 66.5 percent stake. The company also created an investment fund called New World China Homeowner Development Company Limited, which took over responsibility for the company's interests in public housing developments on the mainland. New World held a 57 percent interest in the US$500 million fund, with the remainder sold to private investors. Through these moves, New World hoped to take on a more modern management structure, to make its various activities be more transparent to outsiders, and to bring in additional partners and investors to take on some of the burdens of the massive capital expenditures that were required.

During 1997, the year of the handover of Hong Kong to China, New World Development created a new subsidiary, which was initially 72 percent owned by the company, called New World Services Limited. Included within this new umbrella organization were all of New World's services businesses, including construction, electrical and mechanical engineering, property and facility management (including the management of the Hong Kong Convention and Exhibition Centre), and security services. Also in 1997 came the formation of New World Enterprise Holdings Limited, a US$1 billion fund that New World planned to use to invest in companies in China, notably unprofitable state-run enterprises, with the intention of helping them reform and modernize themselves. Initial major investments included a drugstore chain in Kunming, China; the largest maker of ceramic glass panels in China; and Beijing AutoTech Service Company Limited, a player in the auto after-sales service market in China. New World divested itself of its non-Asian hotel holdings in yet another 1997 development. It sold its stake in Renaissance Hotel Group to Marriott International Inc. for US$491 million, as well as its interest in all hotel properties located outside Hong Kong, China, and Southeast Asia for US$80 million. Around this same time, New World Infrastructure expanded into water treatment plants in China and Macau through the establishment of a joint venture with Suez Lyonnaise des Eaux S.A., one of the largest water companies in France.

In 1998 New World Services (NWS) formed a joint venture with U.K.-based FirstGroup plc called New World First Bus Services Limited, which was 74 percent owned by NWS. The venture was awarded the franchise to operate 88 Hong Kong bus routes formerly operated by China Motor Bus Co. NWS soon bought out its joint venture partner. In 1999 NWS established New World First Ferry Services to operate ferry services in the inner harbor of Hong Kong and beyond, including a ferry service to Macau. New World Infrastructure, meantime, expanded into the development of telecommunications networks.

In July 1999 the company's China property arm, New World China Land Limited, was taken public with a listing on the Hong Kong Stock Exchange. New World retained a 70 percent stake. By that time, the company's Chinese development activities included 68 projects with a total floor area of 246.4 million square feet. The bulk of these projects involved building low-cost residential housing in major Chinese cities—including Wuhan, Shenyang, Tianjin, and Huizhou, a sector in which the company had been involved since 1994.

For the fiscal year ending in June 2000, New World Development reported that revenues had increased by 17 percent over the previous year but that net profits had fallen by 84 percent. The profit drop was attributed in large part to interest payments that stemmed from the heavy debt load the company had incurred through its expansion activities of the 1990s. Even with the company's heavy investments in China, about 90 percent of its earnings were being generated from property, hotel, and construction operations in Hong Kong. While waiting for a payoff from its early commitment to the mainland, New World Development in the early 1990s was likely to focus on debt reduction strategies, including the sale of New World Telephone and the divestment of New World Development's stake in Hong Kong's Regent Hotel, as well as completion of an initial public offering of a stake in New World Services.

Principal Subsidiaries

Addlight Investments Limited (56%); Billionoble Investment Limited (60%); Billion Huge (International) Limited (70%); Billion Park Investment Limited (57%); Birkenshaw Limited; Blanca Limited; Broadway-Nassau Investments Limited (51%); Care & Services Company Limited (51%); Cheong Sing Company Limited; City Team Development Limited (81%); Extensive Trading Company Limited (51%); Far East Engineering Services Limited (51%); Fook Hong Enterprises Company Limited; General Security (H.K.) Limited (51%); Gold Queen Limited; Grand Hyatt Hong Kong Company Limited (64%); Hang Bong Company Limited; Hip Hing Construction Company Limited (51%); Hong Kong Island Development Limited; Hong Kong Island Landscape Company Limited (51%); Hong Kong New World Department Store Company Limited; International Property Management Limited (51%); Island Sauna Company Limited; Kin Kiu Enterprises Limited; King Lee Investment Company Limited; Kleaners Limited (51%); New China Steam Laundry Company Limited (51%); New World Finance Company Limited; New World Hotel Company Limited (64%); New World Telephone Limited (88%); NWD (Hotels Investments) Limited (64%); New World PCS Limited (88%); Paterson Plaza Properties Limited; Peterson Investment Company Limited; Pollution & Protection Consultant Limited (51%); Pollution & Protection Services Limited (51%); Polytown Company Limited (51%); Pontiff Company Limited; Tai Yieh Construction & Engineering Company Limited (51%); Trident Engineering Company Limited (51%); True Hope Investment Limited (60%); Try Force Limited (60%); Urban Parking Limited (51%); Urban Property Management Limited (51%); Vibro (HK) Limited (50%); Wai Hong Cleaning & Pest Control Company Limited (51%); Waking Builders Limited (51%); Young's Engineering Company Limited (51%); Bianchi Holdings Limited (Jersey); New World China Land Limited (Cayman Islands; 70%); NW China Homeowner Development Limited (Cayman Islands; 70%); New World Infrastructure Limited (Cayman Islands; 60%); New World Services Limited (Cayman Islands; 51%); Dalian New World Plaza International Co., Ltd. (China; 62%); Fung Seng Real Estate Development (Shanghai) Co., Ltd. (China; 56%); Guangzhou Metropolitan Properties Co., Ltd. (China); Guangzhou New World Properties Development Co., Ltd. (China); Guangzhou Xin Yi Development Limited (China; 64%); New World (Shenyang) Property Development Limited (China; 63%); New World (Tianjin) Development Co., Limited (China); Ningbo New World Department Store Limited (China; 98%); Ningbo Firm Success Consulting Development Company Limited (China); Shanghai Juyi Real Estate Development Co., Ltd. (China; 56%); Shenyang New World Development Store Limited (China; 90%); Sichuan New World Danshen Base Industrial Co., Ltd. (China; 51%); Tianjin New World Department Store Limited (China); Wuhan New Eagle Development Co., Limited (China; 67%); Wuxi New World Department Store Limited (China); Pacific Ports Company Limited (Bermuda; 60%); New World Enterprise Holdings Limited (British Virgin Islands); New World First Bus Services Limited (British Virgin Islands; 51%); New World First Holdings Limited (British Virgin Islands; 51%).

Principal Divisions

Property; Telecommunications and Technology; Services; Infrastructure.

Principal Competitors

Cheung Kong (Holdings) Limited; Cheung Kong Infrastructure Holdings Limited; China Resources Enterprise, Limited; CITIC Pacific Ltd.; Guangdong Investment Limited; Hang Lung Development Company, Limited; Henderson Land Development Company Limited; Hysan Development Company Limited; Jardine Matheson Holdings Limited; Shanghai Industrial Holdings Limited; Shangri-La Asia Limited; Sun Hung Kai Properties Limited; The Wharf (Holdings) Limited.

Further Reading

''Blueprint for a Brave New World,'' *Financial Times,* August 14, 1995, p. 15.

Chan, Biddy, and Teo Chian Wei, ''Spinoffs Buoy New World Development,'' *Asian Wall Street Journal,* November 8, 1996, p. 5.

Condon, Bernard, ''Capitalist Roader: Cheng Yu-tung Goes West,'' *Forbes,* October 20, 1997, pp. 228–29+.

Davies, Simon, ''Making a Long Term Bet,'' *Asian Business,* July 1993, p. 16.

Guyot, Erik, and Chow, Lotte, ''New World Development to Invest More Than $400 Million in China,'' *Wall Street Journal,* October 13, 1995.

Hock, Tan Lee, ''New World Seeks Growth Abroad,'' *Asian Finance,* March 15, 1991, pp. 46, 48–50.

''Land in the Bank,'' *Far Eastern Economic Review,* March 9, 1989, p. 90.

Levander, Michelle, ''New World Development Is Still Struggling to Recover,'' *Asian Wall Street Journal,* October 31, 2000, p. 15.

Marchand, Christopher, ''Brave New World,'' *Far Eastern Economic Review,* May 4, 1989, p. 85.

Sender, Henny, ''China Savvy,'' *Far Eastern Economic Review,* April 22, 1993, pp. 64–67.

Murphy, Kevin, ''New World Patiently Profits in China,'' *International Herald Tribune,* January 11, 1996, p. 11.

Prystay, Cris, ''New World Develops Potential by Focusing on Housing in China,'' *Asian Wall Street Journal,* April 27, 1998, p. 3.

Rabano, Belinda, ''New World Unit Applies to List in Hong Kong,'' *Asian Wall Street Journal,* June 17, 1999, p. 11.

Stein, Peter, ''The New Game: Hong Kong's Tycoons Now Bet Their Future on China's Big Market,'' *Wall Street Journal,* July 1, 1997, pp. A1+.

Taylor, Michael, ''Boom with a Queue,'' *Far Eastern Economic Review,* August 22, 1991, pp. 48–49.

——, ''Four Pillars,'' *Far Eastern Economic Review,* August 22, 1991, pp. 49–51.

Wong, Jesse, ''For Chengs, Ramada Deal Is Gutsy Move,'' *Wall Street Journal,* July 20, 1989.

Yoshihashi, Pauline, and Lebow, Joan, ''Ramada to Sell Hotels for $540 Million to Hong Kong Firm and Prime Motor,'' *Wall Street Journal,* April 19, 1989.

—Etan Vlessing
—updated by David E. Salamie

Newport News Shipbuilding Inc.

4101 Washington Avenue
Newport News, Virginia 23607
U.S.A.
Telephone: (757) 380-2000
Toll Free: (800) 753-8790
Fax: (757) 380-4713
Web site: http://www.nns.com

Public Company
Incorporated: 1886 as Chesapeake Dry Dock & Construction Co.
Employees: 17,300
Sales: $1.86 billion (1999)
Stock Exchanges: New York
Ticker Symbol: NNS
NAIC: 336611 Ship Building and Repairing

Newport News Shipbuilding Inc. is the largest non-government-owned shipyard in the United States and the only one in the United States capable of building and servicing a full range of nuclear-powered and conventional ships for both defense and commercial service. The largest employer in Virginia, the company has expanded nationwide, building, over its more than 100-year history, more than 700 vessels, including many that have taken part in the great historical events of 20th century American history, from the days of President Theodore Roosevelt's Great White Fleet to the battles of World War II and on into the nuclear age.

19th-Century Origins

Newport News Shipbuilding was founded in 1886 at one of the most favorable shipping locations in the United States. The yard owes its existence to Collis P. Huntington, one of the business partners who founded the Central Pacific Railroad and drove it eastward through the Sierras to form the nation's first transcontinental rail line. After his successes in California, Huntington returned east and was instrumental in building the Chesapeake & Ohio Railroad from Richmond to the town named for him in West Virginia. Then he turned his sights to develop Newport News as the carrier's eastern terminus. He was president of the Old Dominion Land Co. which laid out lots to start the development of the town. Coal and grain facilities were built and Huntington then sought to found a drydock there.

Commenting on the yard's location, Huntington later noted that "It was my original intention to start a shipyard plant in the best location in the world, and I succeeded in my purpose. It is right at the gateway of the sea. There is never any ice in the winter, and it is never so cold but you can hammer metal out of doors."

The drydock was opened April 29, 1889, and the maritime press hailed it as the "wonder of the age." The first shipbuilding job was a reconstruction project, but the contract for Hull No. 1, the tug *Dorothy,* was signed in 1890. After many years of service that tug would eventually return to the yard in 1974 and be dedicated as a permanent exhibit in 1976.

According to the official history, William Tazewell's *Newport News Shipbuilding: The First Century,* Huntington protested to the Secretary of the Navy in 1890 about competition from the Norfolk Navy Yard, a harbinger of many such disputes over government versus private shipbuilding in the future. Newport's first successful bids for construction of naval vessels, three gunboats, followed in 1893. The navy was pleased with the work and the yard was awarded more contracts for battleship construction. In this period the yard was also doing considerable commercial work, including the construction of cargo ships, passenger vessels, bay and river steamers, and tugs. In 1899, contracts for new vessels exceeded $10.5 million and 4,500 men were employed at the yard. Dry Dock No. 2 opened in 1901, the first of several expansions that continued into the 1990s.

Newport News was a company town in all respects, and Huntington personally underwrote financial losses in the early days. Huntington was said to be one of the largest, if not the largest, landholders in the country, and ran his vast interests from his New York office until his death in 1900. Ownership of the Newport News company then passed to Collis's son Archer Milton Huntington, a scholar, poet, and philanthropist with little interest in the shipyard.

Company Perspectives:

Newport News Shipbuilding is one of the top ten defense companies and the premier shipbuilder in the United States. We design, build, and maintain the most sophisticated ships in the world—nuclear-powered aircraft carriers and submarines. Our goals for the future are simple: To strengthen and grow our leadership position in our core defense businesses, to effectively manage technology insertion and systems integration, to become the life cycle manager for our products and to deliver superior value and performance to our shareholders and customers.

Thus, after Huntington's death, the man most instrumental in guiding the shipyard was Homer L. Ferguson, a former navy officer and student of naval architecture and marine engineering, who came on board at the yard in 1905 and was made assistant superintendent of hull construction. Ferguson would become president of the company in 1915, serving in that capacity until 1946, when he was named chairman of the board. During his tenure at Newport News, he successfully steered the company through a long period that included two wars and the Great Depression.

In 1907 President Roosevelt dispatched the Great White Fleet on a round-the-world voyage to demonstrate U.S. sea power. Seven of the fleet's 16 battleships had been built at Newport News. The shipyard was also soon to demonstrate its adaptability; when all-big-gun ships became the standard for naval warfare, the company built six of these "dreadnought" ships, most of which saw service as late as World War II. The yard's adaptability was recognized frequently in later years. It built its first five submarines in 1905, and in 1934 the navy turned to the yard for the first aircraft carrier designed for such service. Most construction, however, continued to be for merchant shipping, among which were barges used in construction of the Panama Canal.

There were boom conditions at the yard during World War I, when the company built 25 destroyers and the last battleship launched until World War II. Moreover, Newport News reconditioned the liner *Leviathan* for use as a troopship. After wartime projects were completed, there was a period in which no more naval work and few commercial contracts were available. The company took whatever work it could find and diverged into other manufacturing.

The disarmament treaties of the 1920s resulted in scrapping a number of warships, but the gathering war clouds of World War II saw a revival of shipbuilding. According to a *Fortune* magazine article of 1936, although 49 U.S. shipyards had been closed since 1920, Newport News became stronger due to "the ablest management in the business" under Ferguson.

In addition to its shipbuilding in this period, the company repaired locomotives; built an aqueduct, a bridge, and an office building; manufactured traffic lights, transmission towers, and 9,000 freight cars; and produced a variety of other equipment. Perhaps the most spectacular of all non-shipbuilding work was the fabrication of the largest turbines in the world for the Dnieprostroi Dam in the Soviet Union. After World War II, the company entered the atomic energy field, fabricating assemblies for nuclear reactors.

In 1940, Archer Huntington sold the shipyard to a syndicate of underwriters. Rumors of a sale had been circulating for years, and once the company was again thriving after the Great Depression, Archer regarded the time as right for a sale. The book value of the plant and property was reported at $17.79 million and its replacement value was around $29 million. The group of investors reportedly purchased Newport News for $18 million and the company went public, trading shares on the New York stock exchange.

Also during this time, the navy ordered seven carriers and four cruisers from Newport News, the beginning of a string of orders as a world war again seemed imminent. Newport News set up a subsidiary, North Carolina Shipbuilding Co. in Wilmington, North Carolina, to help handle the crush of wartime business. Vessels built there included 126 "Liberty" cargo ships before it was closed at the end of the war. Employment at Newport News rose to a high of 31,000 in 1943, with more than 50,000 at the Wilmington subsidiary.

However, the exultation felt by management and employees at the close of the war they helped win was tempered by uncertainty of the future. In the lean days that followed, the yard performed ship conversions and repair work. But with the development of jet aircraft, existing carriers were inadequate and the navy began planning supercarriers. After the outbreak of the Korean War the yard was awarded a contract for the first of several new supercarriers, the *Forrestal.*

Post-World War II Growth

A memorable day in the yard's history came on February 8, 1950, when the keel assembly for the *United States,* the largest passenger ship ever built in the nation, was laid. Launched in the summer of 1951, it was the world's fastest passenger ship and the first built at the yard in ten years. Also, in the fall of 1950, the yard fabricated the last turbines for the Grand Coulee Dam in the state of Washington.

In 1951 William E. Blewett, Jr., became the shipyard's eighth president. A forceful leader, Blewett decided to shift the company's focus into the field of nuclear power, a move praised more than 30 years later by another company president, Edward J. Campbell, as "easily the most significant of the last 45 years." By 1956, the company's Atomic Power Division had more than 200 employees, and a new subsidiary, the Eastern Idaho Construction Co., was formed to set up a reactor test station near Arco, Idaho. Engineers worked there with the navy's Bureau of Ships, planning for atomic-powered supercarriers. The age of the supertankers had also arrived, and on August 7, 1958, the largest tanker yet built in the United States, the *Sansinena,* was launched at the yard.

The advent of nuclear power brought numerous changes to Newport News, with new sections devoted to quality inspection, health physics, controlled material handling, and lead shielding. Since its earliest days the yard had an active apprenticeship program, and now it added classes and lectures about the new science of atomic propulsion.

Key Dates:

1886: Newport News is founded by Collis P. Huntington.
1893: Company is awarded its first U.S. Navy contract.
1951: New president, William Blewett, Jr., steers company into nuclear power.
1968: Tenneco Inc. acquires Newport News.
1982: Newport News is awarded $3.1 billion U.S. Navy contract.
1994: Company reenters commercial market.
1996: Spinoff from Tenneco is completed.
1999: Further pursuit of commercial work is abandoned.

In 1959 the yard launched its first nuclear powered submarine, the *Shark,* the first submarine built by Newport News in more than 50 years. The *Enterprise,* the world's first nuclear-powered carrier, was launched on September 24, 1960. The *Robert E. Lee,* christened December 18, 1959, was the first of 14 Polaris-class subs built at the yard. A new subsidiary, Newport News Industrial Corp., was set up to engage in specialized work on land-based nuclear power plants.

The 1960s brought several challenges to Newport News. The Equal Employment Opportunity Commission charged in 1966 that the company was discriminating against its African-American employees. Although the company denied the charge, it entered into an agreement to accelerate promotions of African Americans and also began hiring greater numbers of women for jobs previously held only by men.

Tenneco Era of Ownership Begins in 1968

Moreover, by the fall of 1967, Newport News faced serious financial problems, as aerospace giants were moving into shipbuilding, leaving Newport News dangerously undercapitalized to compete. The yard reported a loss of nearly $3.5 million in the first half of 1968, a decisive factor in merger negotiations that the company began pursuing. In September 1968, Tenneco Inc., of Houston, Texas, acquired Newport News for approximately $123 million.

In the course of restructuring Newport News, Tenneco encountered strong opposition from organized labor and the Occupational Health and Safety Administration (OSHA). Eventually, the employees gained representation by the United Steelworkers Union. OSHA levied a fine of $766,190 on the shipyard, citing 617 cases of deficient medical care, unsafe working conditions, and excessive noise. It was reportedly the largest fine OSHA had ever imposed on any company.

In the wake of such problems, Wall Street analysts advised Tenneco to sell Newport News, warning that the division would require costly modernization and reorganization. But Tenneco officials recognized the shipyard's potential, especially after plans for a 600-ship navy were announced in 1981. Indeed, the navy depended on the yard for all kinds of ships; it was chosen as the lead yard in designing the *Los Angeles* class of attack subs, launched on April 6, 1974. Moreover, the company continued to overhaul and refuel Polaris subs on a regular schedule and converted several into improved Poseidon missile systems. Conversion and repairs remained a staple and the company's manufacturing operations were steady. In fact, the business backlog at Newport News had reached $1.4 billion by the end of 1971, and employment had risen to 27,500 by 1972.

However, while revenues rose year to year, profits failed to keep pace, as the company was faced with a profit squeeze due largely to the costs of plant expansions and labor. Indeed, the building of more modern ships, particularly the nuclear-powered vessels, proved a necessarily time-consuming process, as designs were changed mid-construction, and workers often found themselves idle while their co-workers completed other aspects of construction.

Also a major dispute between the yard and the U.S. Navy developed over the costs of building nuclear ships. The navy's Admiral Rickover continuously disputed costs, accusing Newport News of being unable to do its job properly. Newport News, in turn, accused the navy of being unable to properly finance its fleet. This dispute reached a climax in 1975, when the shipyard temporarily halted work on a cruiser. The yard threatened to get out of the business, but its claims against the navy were finally settled out of court when Deputy Defense Secretary William P. Clements, Jr., realizing that the situation had gotten out of hand, sought negotiations. A settlement was reached, and the relationship between the shipbuilder and the navy was mended.

During this time, with the navy representing a 93 percent share of the company's operating revenues, Newport News decided to attract more commercial business. The company constructed the new North Yard, where the liquefied natural gas carrier *El Paso Southern* was launched in 1977, followed by other supertankers. While the company enjoyed record revenues in 1975 through 1977, the commercial market for oil tankers declined dramatically in the face of a worldwide oil crisis, and eventually Newport News's revenues declined similarly.

During this time, a new Newport News president, Edward J. Campbell, was named, and he promptly set about turning the company around. Faced with declining profits, outmoded facilities, pending lawsuits, and even a substantial strike by ship designers and production workers, Campbell had his work cut out for him. Lawsuits and strikes were eventually settled, and Campbell focused on a program for improving conditions at the yards.

His efforts paid off; for the first time, company revenues topped the billion dollar mark in 1981 and profits rose to $82 million. In 1983 the company posted record sales and income for the fourth straight year, with profits of $150 million and employment at 29,000. At the end of 1982, the navy awarded Newport News a $3.1 billion contract for the fifth and sixth Nimitz-class carriers, reportedly the biggest contract ever awarded a shipbuilder, and guaranteeing work into the 1990s. Moreover, an improved modular construction method was developed, employing computer technology that cut man hours and eliminated errors. In fact, the Tenneco annual report for 1984 reported that "Improvements in earnings over the last five years are a direct result of innovative engineering concepts in modular construction and incentive-based contracts with the U.S. Navy."

1990s: A Decade of Change

Newport News reentered the commercial cargo ship market in a big way in October 1994 when it signed a $150 million tanker contract with Eletson Corp., a major Greek shipping company. Newport News said the contract was the first commercial construction contract from an international ship owner won by an American yard since 1957. ''After almost 40 years of eating the dust of low-cost Korean, Japanese and West German yards, U.S. shipbuilders are suddenly back in world markets with a bang,'' a *Forbes* magazine reporter noted, adding that ''work rule changes, greatly improved modular construction techniques, and a remorseless attack on overhead costs have helped builders like Newport News, long dependent on big navy contracts for their living, to capitalize on . . . wage differentials.''

Other commercial construction contracts brought so much business that Newport News abandoned a bid to build tankers for a Canadian consortium, citing time and space constraints. At the end of 1994, the company had work under contract extending into 2002. Moreover, a letter of intent between Newport News and the United Arab Emirates was signed in December 1994 to establish a new shipbuilding and repair company in Abu Dhabi. The shipyard was to be an equity investor and manage the Abu Dhabi Ship Building Co., which would construct and repair military and commercial vessels. During this time, W.R. (Pat) Phillips was named chairman and chief executive officer of the shipyard and William P. Fricks was promoted to executive vice-president and chief operating officer.

Navy work still comprised the majority of the yard's business in 1994, when the company was awarded a $3 billion contract to build the Nimitz-class aircraft carrier *Ronald Reagan.* The christening of the last Los Angeles-class vessel *Cheyenne* came in April 1995. Due to cutbacks in the defense budget, however, the yard entered into a bitter contest with the Electric Boat Division of General Dynamics Corporation, of Groton, Connecticut, for the contract to design and build the navy's new attack submarines.

Tenneco approved a $68 million World-Class Shipbuilding Project in December 1994, to upgrade the yard's steel fabrication facilities, a step the company expected would dramatically reduce costs for future ship construction. Newport News also began a $29 million project to extend the yard's largest dry dock, allowing for simultaneous construction of carriers and large commercial ships.

Still, operating income for 1994 was $200 million, compared with $225 million in 1993, and revenues also decreased slightly from $1.9 billion to $1.8 billion. While the *New York Times* reported that several analysts were predicting that Tenneco would divest itself of Newport News, Tenneco Chairman and CEO Dana G. Mead maintained that the corporation had no such plans. In its 1994 annual report, company officials stated that the shipyard would continue to pursue additional U.S. Navy contracts in its core business of new ship construction, refueling and overhaul, and nuclear engineering. However, they said the yard also would continue working to diversify through commercial shipbuilding and foreign military sales, and by ''increasing sales of technological expertise.''

After 46 years of service at Newport News, company Chairman William R. Phillips retired in October 1995, which paved the way for the promotion of William P. Fricks. Fricks assumed command at a pivotal juncture in Newport News's history. The January 1994 decision to pursue commercial work represented a difficult transition for a company that exclusively relied on U.S. Navy contracts. Fricks inherited the daunting task of achieving the company's stated goal of reducing its reliance on Navy work to 60 percent of revenues by 2000. His job was made that much more difficult by the uncertain relationship between Newport News and its parent company, Tenneco. Speculation concerning Tenneco's divestiture of Newport News continued as the transition in leadership was underway. In January 1996, the rumors became closer to fact when Tenneco confirmed that it might spinoff Newport News as part of its sweeping restructuring program aimed at shedding non-core businesses. Eventually, Tenneco chose to take such a course when it announced its merger with El Paso Energy Corp. In December 1996, Tenneco shareholders approved the merger and the spin off of Tenneco's automotive parts and packaging businesses and its Newport News subsidiary as separate companies. Once again, Newport News operated as an independent company.

As Newport News embarked on a new era, it also reopened a chapter of its earlier history in commercial work. In September 1997, the company christened the *American Progress,* the first commercial ship built by Newport News in nearly two decades and the first U.S.-built double-hull oil tanker constructed according to the standards mandated by the U.S. Pollution Act of 1990. Triggered by the 1989 Exxon *Valdez* oil spill, the law stipulated that all ships carrying petroleum products in U.S. coastal waters be double-hull vessels by 2015, which gave birth to Newport News's ''Double Eagle'' program. The *American Progress* was the first of nine tankers scheduled to be built by Newport News, but the foray into the commercial sector soon faltered. The Double Eagle program suffered from higher than anticipated costs and anemic demand for newer, higher-profit-margin tankers. By 1998, the company had decided to stop pursuing commercial shipbuilding contracts, a failed diversification punctuated by the somber June 1999 christening of the tanker *Brenton Reef,* the last of the six tankers the company built for commercial customers. ''Somebody asked me,'' Fricks remarked in a June 18, 1999 interview with *Knight-Ridder/Tribune Business News,* '' 'Would you do it over?' and I said 'No.' ''

The discouraging exit from the Double Eagle program was just one of the difficult events Fricks had to contend with in 1999. Newport News was the target of two hostile takeovers in 1999, one from Litton Industries Inc. and another from General Dynamics Corporation, both of which Fricks was able to fend off. The company also had to withstand a four-month strike by more than 9,000 of its steel workers that commenced in April 1999, which coincided with the loss of an acquisition target, Avondale Industries Inc., to rival suitor Litton Industries.

Despite the setbacks that marred the latter half of the 1990s, Newport News entered the 21st century with optimism, focused on its core defense products, aircraft carriers and submarines. In 2000, construction of the aircraft carrier *USS Ronald Reagan* was nearly complete, with the christening ceremony scheduled for March 2001. Hopes were buoyed also by the shipyard's return to building submarines, namely four Virginia-class submarines. Construction of the first two submarines, *SSN 774* and *SSN 775,* was underway as the company entered the new century. Construction of *SSN 776* and *SSN 777* was scheduled to begin in 2001.

Principal Subsidiaries

Continental Maritime Industries, Inc.; Newport News Shipbuilding and Dry Dock Company.

Principal Competitors

Litton Industries, Inc.; Todd Shipyards Corporation; General Dynamics Corporation.

Further Reading

Banks, Howard, "The New Newport News," *Forbes,* August 7, 2000, p. 122.

Cosco, Joseph, "Down to the Sea in Ships," *Journal of Business Strategy,* November-December 1995, p. 48.

Dinsmore, Christopher, "Tenneco Executive Confirms Chance of a Spin Off of Newport News Shipbuilding," *Knight-Ridder/Tribune Business News,* January 31, 1996, p. 1310183.

Huber, Lisa, "Tenneco Nears Decision on Virginia Shipyard," *Knight-Ridder/Tribune Business News,* March 20, 1996, p. 3200244.

Jones, Kathryn, "Tenneco's Plan May Reap $1 Billion," *New York Times,* December 14, 1994, p. D4.

Krewatch, Mark, "Tenneco-Era Virginia Shipyard Workers Look to Future with Hope," *Knight-Ridder/Tribune Business News,* December 9, 1996, p. 1209B0942.

Phalon, Richard, "Back in the Game," *Forbes,* December 5. 1994, pp. 58–60.

Schmitt, Eric, "Two Submarine Makers Vie for a $60 Billion Project," *New York Times,* May 17, 1995, p. A1.

Sheanm, Tom, "Newport News, Va., Finishes Last Oil Tanker in Private Contract," *Knight-Ridder/Tribune Business News,* June 18, 1999, p. OKRB9916912E.

Shorrock, Tim, "Virginia Yard Homes in on Five-Ship Contract," *Journal of Commerce,* May 17, 1995, p. B8.

Tazewell, William L., *Newport News Shipbuilding: The First Century,* Newport News, Va.: The Mariner's Museum, 1986.

"Va. Yard Wins Federal Aid to Design LNG Tanker," *Journal of Commerce,* June 2, 1995, p. B8.

—William O. Craig
—updated by Jeffrey L. Covell

NOKIA

Nokia Corporation

Keilalahdentie 4
FIN-02150 Espoo
Finland
Telephone: (358) 9 18 071
Fax: (358) 9 656 388
Web site: http://www.nokia.com

Public Company
Incorporated: 1865
Employees: 55,000
Sales: EUR 19.77 billion (US$19.93 billion) (1999)
Stock Exchanges: Helsinki Stockholm London Frankfurt Paris New York
Ticker Symbol: NOK
NAIC: 334210 Telephone Apparatus Mfg.; 334220 Radio and Television Broadcasting and Wireless Communications Equipment Mfg.; 334290 Other Communications Equipment Mfg.; 334419 Other Electronic Component Mfg.

Nokia Corporation is the world's largest manufacturer of mobile phones, with a worldwide market share of about 27 percent, far surpassing the number two player, Ericsson, which has about 17 percent. About two-thirds of the company's net sales are generated by the Nokia Mobile Phones business group. Nokia's other main business group is Nokia Networks, which is responsible for about 30 percent of net sales. Nokia Networks is a leading global supplier of infrastructure for mobile, fixed, broadband, and Internet Protocol (IP) networks. With a sales network that spans 130 nations, Nokia Corporation generated more than half of its sales in Europe, a quarter in the Americas, and about 22 percent in the Asia-Pacific region. Over the course of its more than 135 years in business, the company has evolved from a concentration in pulp, paper, and other basic industries to a focus on telecommunications.

19th-Century Origins

Originally a manufacturer of pulp and paper, Nokia was founded as Nokia Company in 1865 in a small town of the same name in central Finland. Nokia was a pioneer in the industry and introduced many new production methods to a country with only one major natural resource, its vast forests. As the industry became increasingly energy-intensive, the company even constructed its own power plants. But for many years, Nokia remained an important yet static firm in a relatively forgotten corner of northern Europe. Nokia shares were first listed on the Helsinki exchange in 1915.

The first major changes in Nokia occurred several years after World War II. Despite its proximity to the Soviet Union, Finland has always remained economically connected with Scandinavian and other Western countries, and as Finnish trade expanded Nokia became a leading exporter.

During the early 1960s Nokia began to diversify in an attempt to transform the company into a regional conglomerate with interests beyond Finnish borders. Unable to initiate strong internal growth, Nokia turned its attention to acquisitions. The government, however, hoping to rationalize two underperforming basic industries, favored Nokia's expansion within the country and encouraged its eventual merger with Finnish Rubber Works, which was founded in 1898, and Finnish Cable Works, which was formed in 1912, to form Nokia Corporation. When the amalgamation was completed in 1966, Nokia was involved in several new industries, including integrated cable operations, electronics, tires, and rubber footwear, and had made its first public share offering.

In 1967 Nokia set up a division to develop design and manufacturing capabilities in data processing, industrial automation, and communications systems. The division was later expanded and made into several divisions, which then concentrated on developing information systems, including personal computers and workstations, digital communications systems, and mobile phones. Nokia also gained a strong position in modems and automatic banking systems in Scandinavia.

Oil Crisis, Corporate Changes: 1970s

Nokia continued to operate in a stable but parochial manner until 1973, when it was affected in a unique way by the oil crisis. Years of political accommodation between Finland and the Soviet Union ensured Finnish neutrality in exchange for

Company Perspectives:

Nokia is a leading international communications company, focused on the key growth areas of wireline and wireless telecommunications. Nokia is a pioneer in digital technology and wireless data communications, continuously bringing innovations to the highly competitive and growing telecommunications markets. Nokia is also actively involved in international R&D cooperation, including the development of the standards for third generation mobile telephony.

lucrative trade agreements with the Soviets—mainly Finnish lumber products and machinery in exchange for Soviet oil. By agreement, this trade was kept strictly in balance. But when world oil prices began to rise, the market price for Soviet oil rose with it. Balanced trade began to mean greatly reduced purchasing power for Finnish companies such as Nokia.

Although the effects were not catastrophic, the oil crisis did force Nokia to reassess its reliance on Soviet trade (about 12 percent of sales) as well as its international growth strategies. Several contingency plans were drawn up, but the greatest changes came after the company appointed a new CEO, Kari Kairamo, in 1975.

Kairamo noted the obvious: Nokia was too big for Finland. The company had to expand abroad. He studied the expansion of other Scandinavian companies (particularly Sweden's Electrolux) and, following their example, formulated a strategy of first consolidating the company's business in Finland, Sweden, Norway, and Denmark, and then moving gradually into the rest of Europe. After the company had improved its product line, established a reputation for quality, and adjusted its production capacity, it would enter the world market.

Meanwhile, Nokia's traditional, heavy industries were looking increasingly burdensome. It was feared that trying to become a leader in electronics while maintaining these basic industries would create an unmanageably unfocused company. Kairamo thought briefly about selling off the company's weaker divisions, but decided to retain and modernize them.

He reasoned that, although the modernization of these low-growth industries would be very expensive, it would guarantee Nokia's position in several stable markets, including paper, chemical, and machinery productions, and electrical generation. For the scheme to be practical, each division's modernization would have to be gradual and individually financed. This would prevent the bleeding of funds away from the all-important effort in electronics while preventing the heavy industries from becoming any less profitable.

With each division financing its own modernization, there was little or no drain on capital from other divisions, and Nokia could still sell any group that did not succeed under the new plan. In the end, the plan prompted the machinery division to begin development in robotics and automation, the cables division to begin work on fiber optics, and the forestry division to move into high-grade tissues.

Rise of Electronics: 1980s

Nokia's most important focus was development of the electronics sector. Over the course of the 1980s, the firm acquired nearly 20 companies, focusing especially on three segments of the electronics industry: consumer, workstations, and mobile communications. Electronics grew from ten percent of annual sales to 60 percent of revenues from 1980 to 1988. In late 1984 Nokia acquired Salora, the largest color television manufacturer in Scandinavia, and Luxor, the Swedish state-owned electronics and computer firm. Nokia combined Salora and Luxor into a single division and concentrated on stylish consumer electronic products, since style was a crucial factor in Scandinavian markets. The Salora-Luxor division was also very successful in satellite and digital television technology. Nokia purchased the consumer electronics operations of Standard Elektrik Lorenz A.G. from Alcatel in 1987, further bolstering the company's position in the television market to the third largest manufacturer in Europe. In early 1988 Nokia acquired the data systems division of the Swedish Ericsson Group, making Nokia the largest Scandinavian information technology business.

Although a market leader in Scandinavia, Nokia still lacked a degree of competitiveness in the European market, which was dominated by much larger Japanese and German companies. Kairamo decided, therefore, to follow the example of many Japanese companies during the 1960s (and Korean manufacturers a decade later) and negotiate to become an original equipment manufacturer, or OEM, to manufacture products for competitors as a subcontractor.

Nokia manufactured items for Hitachi in France, Ericsson in Sweden, Northern Telecom in Canada, and Granada and IBM in Britain. In doing so it was able to increase its production capacity stability. There were, however, several risks involved, those inherent in any OEM arrangement. Nokia's sales margins were naturally reduced, but of greater concern, production capacity was built up without a commensurate expansion in the sales network. With little brand identification, Nokia feared it might have a difficult time selling under its own name and become trapped as an OEM.

In 1986 Nokia reorganized its management structure to simplify reporting efforts and improve control by central management. The company's 11 divisions were grouped into four industry segments: electronics; cables and machinery; paper, power, and chemicals; and rubber and flooring. In addition, Nokia won a concession from the Finnish government to allow greater foreign participation in ownership. This substantially reduced Nokia's dependence on the comparatively expensive Finnish lending market. Although there was growth throughout the company, Nokia's greatest success was in telecommunications.

Having dabbled in telecommunications in the 1960s, Nokia cut its teeth in the industry by selling switching systems under license from a French company, Alcatel. The Finnish firm got in on the cellular industry's ground floor in the late 1970s, when it helped design the world's first international cellular system. Named the Nordic Mobile Telephone (NMT) network, the system linked Sweden, Denmark, Norway, and Finland. A year after the network came on line in 1981, Nokia gained 100 percent control of Mobira, the Finnish mobile phone company that would later become its key business interest as the Nokia Mobile Phones

Key Dates:

1865: Nokia Company is founded as a maker of pulp and paper.
1898: Finnish Rubber Works is founded.
1912: Finnish Cable Works is formed.
1915: Nokia shares are first listed on the Helsinki exchange.
1967: Nokia merges with Finnish Rubber Works and Finnish Cable Works to form Nokia Corporation.
1979: Mobira Oy is formed as a mobile phone company.
1981: The first international cellular system, the Nordic Mobile Telephone network, comes on line, having been developed with the help of Nokia.
1982: Nokia acquires Mobira, which later becomes the Nokia Mobile Phones division.
1986: Company markets internationally the first Nokia mobile telephone.
1993: The first Nokia digital cellular phone hits the market.
1998: Nokia surpasses Motorola as the world's number one maker of mobile phones.

division. Mobira's regional sales were vastly improved, but Nokia was still limited to OEM production on the international market; Nokia and Tandy Corporation, of the United States, built a factory in Masan, South Korea, to manufacture mobile telephones. These were sold under the Tandy name in that company's 6,000 Radio Shack stores throughout the United States.

In 1986, eager to test its ability to compete openly, Nokia chose the mobile telephone to be the first product marketed internationally under the Nokia name; it became Nokia's ''make or break'' product. Unfortunately, Asian competitors began to drive prices down just as Nokia entered the market. Other Nokia products gaining recognition were Salora televisions and Luxor satellite dishes, which suffered briefly when subscription programming introduced broadcast scrambling.

The company's expansion, achieved almost exclusively by acquisition, had been expensive. Few Finnish investors other than institutions had the patience to see Nokia through its long-term plans. Indeed, more than half of the new shares issued by Nokia in 1987 went to foreign investors. Nokia moved boldly into Western markets; it gained a listing on the London exchange in 1987 and was subsequently listed on the New York exchange.

Crises of Leadership, Profitability in the Late 1980s and Early 1990s

Nokia's rapid growth was not without a price. In 1988, as revenues soared, the company's profits, under pressure from severe price competition in the consumer electronics markets, dropped. Chairman Kari Kairamo committed suicide in December of that year; not surprisingly, friends said it was brought on by stress. Simo S. Vuorileto took over the company's reins and began streamlining operations in the spring of 1988. Nokia was divided into six business groups: consumer electronics, data, mobile phones, telecommunications, cables and machinery, and basic industries. Vuorileto continued Kairamo's focus on high-tech divisions, divesting Nokia's flooring, paper, rubber, and ventilation systems businesses and entering into joint ventures with companies such as Tandy Corporation and Matra of France (two separate agreements to produce mobile phones for the U.S. and French markets).

In spite of these efforts, Nokia's pretax profits continued to decline in 1989 and 1990, culminating in a loss of US$102 million in 1991. Industry observers blamed cutthroat European competition, the breakdown of the Finnish banking system, and the collapse of the Soviet Union. But, notwithstanding these difficulties, Nokia remained committed to its high-tech orientation. Late in 1991, the company strengthened that dedication by promoting Jorma Ollila from president of Nokia-Mobira Inc. (renamed Nokia Mobile Phones Ltd. the following year) to group president.

Leading the Telecommunications Revolution: Mid-1990s and Beyond

Forbes's Fleming Meeks credited Ollila with transforming Nokia from ''a moneylosing hodgepodge of companies into one of telecommunications' most profitable companies.'' Unable to find a buyer for Nokia's consumer electronics business, which had lost nearly US$1 billion from 1988 to 1993, Ollila cut that segment's workforce by 45 percent, shuttered plants, and centralized operations. Having divested Nokia Data in 1991, Nokia focused further on its telecommunications core by selling off its power unit in 1994 and its television and tire and cable units the following year.

The new leader achieved success in the cellular phone segment by bringing innovative products to market quickly with a particular focus on ever-smaller and easier-to-use phones featuring sleek Finnish design. Nokia gained a leg up in cellphone research and development with the 1991 acquisition of the United Kingdom's Technophone Ltd. for US$57 million. The company began selling digital cellular phones in 1993.

Ollila's tenure brought Nokia success and with it global recognition. The company's sales more than doubled, from Fmk 15.5 billion in 1991 to Fmk 36.8 billion in 1995, and its bottom line rebounded from a net loss of Fmk 723 million in 1992 to a Fmk 2.2 billion profit in 1995. Securities investors did not miss the turnaround: Nokia's market capitalization multiplied ten times from 1991 to 1994.

In late 1995 and early 1996, Nokia suffered a temporary setback stemming from a shortage of chips for its digital cellular phones and a resultant disruption of its logistics chain. The company's production costs rose and profits fell. Nokia was also slightly ahead of the market, particularly in North America, in regard to the shift from analog to digital phones. As a result, it was saddled with a great number of digital phones it could not sell and an insufficient number of analog devices. Nevertheless, Nokia had positioned itself well for the long haul, and within just a year or two it was arch-rival Motorola, Inc. that was burdened with an abundance of phones it could not sell—analog ones—as Motorola was slow to convert to digital. As a result, by late 1998, Nokia had surpassed Motorola and claimed the top position in cellular phones worldwide.

Aiding this surge was the November 1997 introduction of the 6100 series of digital phones. This line proved immensely popular because of the phones' small size (similar to a slim pack of cigarettes), light weight (4.5 ounces), and superior battery life. First introduced in the burgeoning mobile phone market in China, the 6100 soon became a worldwide phenomenon. Including the 6100 and other models, Nokia sold nearly 41 million cellular phones in 1998. Net sales increased more than 50 percent over the previous year, jumping from Fmk 52.61 billion (US$9.83 billion) to Fmk 79.23 billion (US$15.69 billion). Operating profits increased by 75 percent, while the company's skyrocketing stock price shot up more than 220 percent, pushing Nokia's market capitalization from Fmk 110.01 billion (US$20.57 billion) to Fmk 355.53 billion (US$70.39 billion).

Not content with conquering the mobile phone market, Nokia began aggressively pursuing the mobile Internet sector in the late 1990s. Already on the market was the Nokia 9000 Communicator, a personal all-in-one communication device that included phone, data, Internet, e-mail, and fax retrieval services. The Nokia 8110 mobile phone included the capability to access the Internet. In addition, Nokia was the first company to introduce a cellular phone that could be connected to a laptop computer to transmit data over a mobile network. To help develop further products, Nokia began acquiring Internet technology companies, starting with the December 1997, US$120 million purchase of Ipsilon Networks Inc., a Silicon Valley firm specializing in Internet routing. One year later, Nokia spent Fmk 429 million (US$85 million) for Vienna Systems Corporation, a Canadian firm focusing on Internet Protocol telephony. Acquisitions continued in 1999, when a further seven deals were completed, four of which were Internet-related. Meanwhile, net sales increased a further 48 percent in 1999, while operating profits grew by 57 percent; riding the late 1990s high tech stock boom, the market capitalization of Nokia took another huge leap, ending the year at EUR 209.37 billion (US$211.05 billion). Nokia's share of the global cellular phone market increased from 22.5 percent in 1998 to 26.9 percent in 1999, as the company sold 76.3 million phones in 1999.

Nokia's ascendance to the top of the wireless world by the end of the 1990s could be traced to the company being able to consistently, over and over again, come out with high-margin products superior to those of its competitors and in tune with market demands. The continuation of this trend into the 21st century was by no means certain as the increasing convergence of wireless and Internet technologies and the development of the third generation of wireless technology (which followed the analog and digital generations and which was slated to feature sophisticated multimedia capability) were predicted to open Nokia up to new and formidable competitors. Perhaps the greatest threat was that chipmakers such as Intel would turn mobile phones into commodities just as they had previously done with personal computers; the days of the $500 Nokia phone were potentially numbered. Nevertheless, Nokia's 25 percent profit margins were enabling it to spend a massive US$2 billion a year on research and development and continue to churn out innovative new products, concentrating on the various standards being developed for the third generation wireless networks.

Principal Subsidiaries

Nokia Matkapuhelimet Oy; Nokia Mobile Phones Inc. (U.S.A.); Nokia Networks Oy; Nokia GmbH (Germany); Nokia UK Limited; Nokia TMC Limited (South Korea); Beijing Nokia Mobile Telecommunications Ltd. (China); Nokia Finance International B.V. (Netherlands).

Principal Operating Units

Nokia Networks; Nokia Mobile Phones; Nokia Venture Organization; Nokia Research Center.

Principal Competitors

Alcatel; Telefonaktiebolaget LM Ericsson; Harris Corporation; Kyocera Corporation; Lucent Technologies Inc.; Matsushita Communication Industrial Co., Ltd.; Mitsubishi Electric Corporation; Motorola, Inc.; NEC Corporation; Nortel Networks Corporation; Oki Electric Industry Company, Limited; Koninklijke Philips Electronics N.V.; Pioneer Corporation; Qualcomm Incorporated; Robert Bosch GmbH; Samsung Group; Sanyo Electric Co., Ltd.; Siemens AG; Sony Corporation; Tellabs, Inc.; Toshiba Corporation.

Further Reading

Baker, Stephen, and Kerry Capell, "The Race to Rule Mobile," *Business Week,* February 21, 2000, pp. 58–60.

Baker, Stephen, Roger O. Crockett, and Neil Gross, "Nokia: Can CEO Ollila Keep the Cellular Superstar Flying High?," *Business Week,* August 10, 1998, pp. 54–60.

Berkman, Barbara N., "Brainstorming in the Sauna," *Electronic Business,* November 18, 1991, pp. 71–74.

——, "Sagging Profits Spark Identity Crisis at Nokia," *Electronic Business,* March 4, 1991, pp. 57–59.

Burt, Tim, and Greg McIvor, "Land of Midnight Mobiles: A Former Toilet-Paper Maker from Finland Has Become the World's Largest Manufacturer of Mobile Phones," *Financial Times,* October 30, 1998, p. 18.

Edmondson, Gail, Peter Elstrom, and Peter Burrows, "At Nokia, a Comeback—and Then Some," *Business Week,* December 2, 1996, p. 106.

Fox, Justin, "Nokia's Secret Code," *Fortune,* May 1, 2000, pp. 161–64+.

Furchgott, Roy, "Nokia Signals Desire for Higher Profile," *ADWEEK Eastern Edition,* June 12, 1995, p. 2.

Guth, Robert A., "Nokia Fights for Toehold in Japan's Cell-Phone Market," *Wall Street Journal,* June 26, 2000, p. A26.

Heard, Joyce, and Keller, John J., "Nokia Skates into High Tech's Big Leagues," *Business Week,* April 4, 1988, pp. 102–103.

Jacob, Rahul, "Nokia Fumbles, But Don't Count It Out," *Fortune,* February 19, 1996, pp. 86–88.

La Rossa, James, Jr., "Nokia Knocks on U.S. Door," *HFD—The Weekly Home Furnishings Newspaper,* February 10, 1992, pp. 66–67.

Lemola, Tarmo, and Raimo Lovio, *Miksi Nokia, Finland,* Porvoo, Sweden: W. Sööderströöm, 1996, 211 p.

Lineback, J. Robert, "Nokia's Mobile Phone Unit Is Ringing Bells," *Electronic Business Buyer,* June 1994, pp. 60–62.

Meeks, Fleming, "Watch Out, Motorola," *Forbes,* September 12, 1994, pp. 192–94.

"Not Finnished Yet," *Economist,* February 9, 1991, p. 73.

Salameh, Asad, "Nokia Repositions for a Major Cellular Marketing Initiative," *Telecommunications,* June 1992, p. 43.

Silberg, Lurie, "A Brand Apart," *HFD—The Weekly Home Furnishings Newspaper,* September 5, 1994, pp. 54–55.

Williams, Elaine, "100-Year-Old Nokia Experiences Fast-Growth Pains," *Electronic Business,* June 26, 1989, pp. 111–14.

—April D. Gasbarre
—updated by David E. Salamie

Northland Cranberries, Inc.

800 First Avenue South
Wisconsin Rapids, Wisconsin 54495
U.S.A.
Telephone: (715) 424-4444
Fax: (715) 422-6800
Web site: http://www.northlandcran.com

Public Company
Incorporated: 1987
Employees: 950
Sales: $236.8 million (1999)
Stock Exchanges: NASDAQ
Ticker Symbol: CBRYA
NAIC: 111334 Berry (Except Strawberry) Farming; 311421 Fruit and Vegetable Canning; 311411 Frozen Fruit, Juice, and Vegetable Manufacturing

Northland Cranberries, Inc. is the world's largest cranberry grower and a major cranberry processor and marketer. It owns 25 cranberry marshes, principally in its home state of Wisconsin. It also owns cranberry growing properties in Massachusetts and in Canada. It markets cranberries and cranberry juice products under the Northland brand name, and also supplies cranberries to private label cranberry juice manufacturers. It also sells juice under the Seneca brand, as well as the TreeSweet, Awake, and Orange Plus brands. The company owns extensive cranberry processing plants in Wisconsin, and operates juice bottling and packing facilities in New York, North Carolina, and Wyoming.

From Limited Partnerships to Public Company

Northland Cranberries, Inc. began as a small group of limited partnerships of Wisconsin cranberry growers. The partnerships were engineered by John Swendrowski, who became the president and chief executive officer of the company. Before the mid-1980s, however, Swendrowski knew little about cranberries. He was a loan officer for a Wisconsin bank, and before that he had been an English teacher and football coach at a Catholic high school. Swendrowski played football briefly for the University of Wisconsin, and went on to teaching and coaching in Wisconsin Rapids, Wisconsin. He eventually found the pay too low and, when he was in his 30s, began looking for ways to supplement his income. Swendrowski's first entrepreneurial venture was a truck-leasing business. A bank offered to buy up the truck-leasing enterprise after a few years, and Swendrowski ended up taking a job at the bank. He became a loan officer for the Wood County Bank, where he was soon put in charge of loans to cranberry growers. In the 1980s, many Wisconsin cranberry growers were older farmers with only small parcels of land devoted to the crop. If younger family members were not interested in taking on the cranberry land, it was hard to sell it. Most farmers only grew cranberries as a sideline, and the crop was restricted by complex government regulations controlling wetlands. Swendrowski learned that cranberries could be a valuable crop, and growers could benefit by getting together on a larger scale. Hence he decided to put together limited partnerships to buy up cranberry marshes. These partnerships raised capital to improve the berry stock as well as install and maintain the hydraulics in the fields. By 1987, Swendrowski had formed five limited partnerships. That year he decided to embark on a new business strategy. Leaving the bank, he consolidated the five partnerships as a publicly traded company, incorporated as Northland Cranberries, Inc. Swendrowski became president and CEO, and he owned close to 40 percent of the total stock.

The company was on track for growth. It began buying up more cranberry marshes so it could increase its production. All the company's crop went to one buyer for its first several years, Ocean Spray Cranberries, Inc. Ocean Spray was a Massachusetts cooperative made up of over 700 cranberry growers. It sold its juices and cranberry products under the Ocean Spray brand name, which was by far the biggest name in the market. Northland worked under contract to Ocean Spray, so that it had a guaranteed buyer and expected relatively stable income. By 1988, Northland had become the single largest cranberry grower in Wisconsin. Its sales rose from around $4.6 million in 1987 to more than $11 million four years later. The company put profits back into the ground, buying up more marshland whenever possible. By 1990 the young company had already increased its acreage by over 30 percent. In 1991 it ventured out

Company Perspectives:

Northland Cranberries, Inc. is an integrated grower, processor and marketer of cranberries, cranberry products and other fruit beverages and concentrates. Publicly-owned since 1987, Northland is recognized as the world's largest cranberry grower and a major U.S. beverage company.

of Wisconsin for the first time, leasing cranberry bogs on Nantucket Island, Massachusetts.

Expectations for the cranberry industry were high because of favorable reports in the 1980s and 1990s about the health benefits of the fruit. Studies in the 1980s seemed to show that the high acid content of cranberry juice was good for kidney function, and the juice was also high in vitamin C. Ocean Spray was a powerful marketer, and cranberries began to transform from a seasonal crop used mostly in sauce for holiday turkeys to more of an everyday healthy juice or food. Northland quickly became profitable, with pretax earnings increasing from $185,000 in its first year to $1.5 million by 1991. The company was the only publicly traded entity in the cranberry market, since Ocean Spray was a cooperative. One other grower, A.D. Makepeace, was a public company, but its stock was almost entirely in the hands of family members. Northland's stock did well, perhaps because any investor wanting access to the cranberry market had only one place to go.

Parting Ways with Ocean Spray

In mid-1992, Northland Cranberries announced that it was ending its exclusive relationship with Ocean Spray. The giant cooperative had bought all the company's previous crop, providing stability to the growing young company. But Northland had come to be a bigger player in the market. Its crop had increased by 240 percent since the company's inception, and Northland felt it could negotiate a better deal for its berries by leaving the Ocean Spray cooperative. Ocean Spray offered less money per barrel than Northland found it could get elsewhere, and Ocean Spray delayed payment on a crop for as long as 15 months. Northland therefore agreed to sell its 1993 crop to two independent fruit processors, at a price hike of almost 20 percent per barrel over what Ocean Spray was offering. It divided its crop equally between Cliffstar Corp., of Dunkirk, New York, and Clement Pappas & Co., based in Seabrook, New Jersey.

The company continued to do well as an independent grower. In 1994, Northland invested $5 million into the construction of a new facility for receiving, processing, storing, and packaging its berries. Northland for the first time put its fresh berries on the market under the Northland name. This was the company's first push into marketing. It managed to get its bagged cranberries into supermarkets across the country. The next year Northland introduced its Northland brand cranberry juice blends. It began marketing the juice in its home state of Wisconsin, offering five flavors of mixed juices, including Cranberry Raspberry and Cranberry Cherry. Northland's products were made from 100 percent juice, something that set its line apart from Ocean Spray's. Cranberry juice alone is too sour to be consumed straight, but Northland sweetened it by mixing it with lighter juices such as apple and grape. Ocean Spray, by contrast, featured juices mixed with sweeteners and diluted with water. This became the key marketing difference between the two brands.

Northland President John Swendrowski called the move to pushing its own juice a vertical integration strategy that went ''from marsh to market,'' in a June 1997 interview in *Beverage Industry*. All aspects of the company's business grew in the mid-1990s. In 1994, Northland acquired another 286 acres of marshland in Wisconsin, and after several more acquisitions in Wisconsin and Massachusetts, the company ranked as the largest cranberry grower in the world. In 1996 Northland reached an agreement with a German drink company to sell its cranberry juice concentrate in Europe. The German concern, Rudolf Wild GmbH, worked to develop European markets for cranberry products, which were not well known there. Northland also began experimenting with growing the berries abroad. It developed test fields in Ireland, and looked at Poland as another possible area suitable for growing cranberries.

By 1997, Northland had 2,548 acres planted with cranberries, and it owned over 24,000 other acres of support land. It provided 12 percent of the North American cranberry supply, and it also had excellent facilities for processing the fruit. It had its own state-of-the-art processing plant in Wisconsin Rapids, and also held bottling contracts with two other juice companies, to help with nationwide distribution. Marketing was the third leg of its ''marsh to market'' strategy, and Northland began concentrating its energies there. It had begun pushing its Northland cranberry juice blends in supermarkets in Wisconsin, offering a single 64-ounce size. The brand did well, bringing in around $12 million in less than two years on the market. In 1997, one year sooner than planned, Northland began a national rollout of its juices. It backed the wider distribution with advertising on radio, television, and in print. Northland's ads aimed to inform consumers that its products were 100 percent juice, whereas market leader Ocean Spray made juice drinks, a separate category, that contained only about 27 percent juice. Northland's juices carried the National Cancer Institute's 5-A-Day seal, meaning that a glass of the juice counted as one of the five fruits and vegetables the institute recommended for an optimum daily diet. The company also swung a deal with the Ladies Professional Golf Association, making Northland the ''Official Juice of the LPGA'' for three years. The company hoped to follow a five-year plan that would leave it a worldwide cranberry growing and marketing entity, close on the heels of Ocean Spray.

By 1998, Northland's line of cranberry juice was available in 80 percent of supermarkets nationwide. Its market share climbed, matched by a fall in Ocean Spray's. The company moved more aggressively into juice marketing by making significant acquisitions. In 1998 Northland spent over $30 million to buy up the juice division of Seneca Foods Corp. Northland had previously had a bottling contract with Seneca. The company acquired Seneca's bottling and packaging plants in Dundee, New York; Mountain Home, North Carolina, and Jackson, Wyoming, as well as a warehouse facility in Eau Claire, Wisconsin, and a grape receiving station in Portland, New York. Northland got the exclusive rights to the Seneca brand name, and rights to three other

Key Dates:

1987: John Swendrowski forms company out of group of limited partnerships.
1993: Northland leaves Ocean Spray cooperative.
1995: Northland introduces its own branded juice line.
1998: Company acquires juice division of Seneca Foods.

brands: TreeSweet, Awake, and Orange Plus. Northland also acquired Minot Food Packers, Inc., in 1998. Minot packed juices for private labels, and Northland already had significant sales to private label manufacturers. The company hoped to build on its private label business, and it was also able to move into the manufacturing of cranberry sauce for the first time. Another new direction for Northland was the foodservice business, which it entered in 1998. Northland began offering its Northland line of cranberry juices to foodservice customers such as hospitals, schools, and restaurants, and marketed other juices to institutions under the brand name Meadow Valley.

Difficult Conditions in the Late 1990s and After

As a result of all its increased business, sales climbed markedly, more than doubling between 1997 and 1998. Profits too rose sharply, increasing from $2.9 million in 1997 to $5.6 million in 1998. Northland's founder and CEO Swendrowski declared in 1999 that the company was meeting its financial targets, and that it would probably continue to grow, though there was an oversupply of cranberries. In fact record-breaking crops in 1997, 1998, and 1999 left the cranberry market in disarray as prices fell. Both Northland and Ocean Spray rethought their juice marketing positions. Ocean Spray came up with a 100 percent juice line, Wellfleet Farms, while Northland considered moving into the dilute juice-drink market. The 100 percent juice that Northland had championed was a faster growth category than the dilute line, but the cost of making it was also higher. The low price for cranberries made business conditions very difficult. Ocean Spray, already cutting employees to hold down costs, hired a consultant in 1999 to scope out possibilities of a merger. Faced with an Ocean Spray that might become part of a giant drink company such as PepsiCo or Coca-Cola, Northland also began considering a merger. The company hired a consultant in late 1999 to help it come up with strategies for maintaining profitability.

Early in 2000, Northland announced the sale of its private label juice business. This segment had been contributing about $43 million in sales, and the company let it go for around $28 million. The buyer was Cliffstar Corp., one of the two companies who had first bought Northland's berry crop after its split from Ocean Spray. Northland hoped to concentrate on its Northland and Seneca brands after letting the private label business go. Later that year, Northland declared that it wanted to sell some of its juice brands in order to raise cash. Low cranberry prices continued to dismay the company. The bad news of a third quarter loss sent its stock to an all-time low. By the fourth quarter of 2000, the company's board of directors had come up with some restructuring moves. Northland planned to close down or sell its bottling plant in Bridgeton, New Jersey. After it sold its private label business to Cliffstar, it had more bottling capacity than it could use, so the New Jersey plant was scheduled to shut down. Northland's board also formulated a plan to hand over much of its sales and marketing support for its Seneca and Northland brand juices to an outside company, Crossmark. Crossmark was a large company with expert management knowhow. By outsourcing its marketing, Northland hoped to save $1 million annually. Northland reorganized its existing marketing team, and let go approximately 20 employees. Faced with a mounting credit crunch because of continuing poor prices for cranberries, Northland also acknowledged that sale of part or all of the company was possible.

Principal Competitors

Ocean Spray Cranberries, Inc.; Apple & Eve, Inc.

Further Reading

"Buyer Sues Northland Over Sale of Private Juice Label," *Wisconsin State Journal*, September 9, 2000.

"Cranberries Rot, So Does the Stock," *Business Week*, December 19, 1994, p. 42.

"Cranberry Grower Ends Pact with Ocean Spray," *Wisconsin State Journal*, June 15, 1992.

Hajewski, Doris, "Northland Cranberries Deal Falls Through, Lower Earnings Expected," *Knight-Ridder/Tribune Business News*, April 25, 1997, p. 425B0959.

Holleran, Joan, "100% Northland," *Beverage Industry*, June 1997, p. 40.

"The Juice Is Loose," *Fortune*, February 17, 1997, p. 162.

Khermouch, Gerry, "Cranberry Leaders May Evolve Lines," *Brandweek*, April 12, 1999, p. 6.

Martin, Chuck, "Northland Stock May Prove Fruitful," *Milwaukee Journal*, May 13, 1990.

"Northland Cranberries Looking to Raise Cash," *Capital Times* (Madison, WI), July 20, 2000.

"Northland Cranberries to Sell Juice Concentrate in Europe," *Capital Times*, February 9, 1996.

"Northland Increases Market Share," *Wisconsin State Journal*, November 29, 1997.

"Northland, Ocean Spray Alliance Possible," *Wisconsin State Journal*, September 11, 1999.

"Northland to Buy Juice Division," *Supermarket News*, September 14, 1998, p. 63.

"A $19 Million Cranberry Deal," *Wisconsin State Journal*, August 6, 1994.

Phalon, Richard, "The Big Money in Bitter Berries," *Forbes*, June 10, 1991, pp. 77–79.

"Wisconsin Rapids, Wis.-Based Cranberry Company Reaps Doubled Income," *Knight-Ridder/Tribune Business News*, October 22, 1999, p. OKRB99295061.

"Wisconsin Rapids, Wis.-Based Cranberry Grower to Explore Sale, Merger," *Knight-Ridder/Tribune Business News*, March 8, 2000, p. ITEM00088065.

—A. Woodward

Outokumpu Oyj

Riihitontuntie 7B
Espoo FIN-02201
Finland
Telephone: +358-9-4211
Fax: +358-9-421-3888
Web site: http://www.outokumpu.com

Public Company
Incorporated: 1932
Employees: 11,972
Sales: $2.92 billion (1999)
Stock Exchanges: Helsinki
Ticker Symbol: OUTV1
NAIC: 212234 Copper Ore and Nickel Ore Mining (pt); 212231 Lead Ore and Zinc Ore Mining; 331111 Iron and Steel Mills (pt); 331411 Primary Smelting and Refining of Copper; 331421 Copper Rolling; 332813 Electroplating; 42183 Industrial Machinery and Equipment Wholesalers (pt)

Outokumpu Oyj is a diversified metals company involved in the exploration and mining, smelting and refining, and fabrication of copper, zinc, nickel, and stainless steel. The company's mining activities are conducted in Finland, Norway, Australia, Chile, and Ireland. Ranking as the largest manufacturer of copper products in the world, Outokumpu Oyj is the only company in its industry that operates major copper products facilities in North America, Europe, and Asia. Aside from copper, the company's other core business is stainless steel. Outokumpu Oyj controls 10 percent of the European market for rolled stainless steel and 4 percent of the global market. The company also accounts for 3 percent of the world's zinc production and 4 percent of its nickel production.

Origins

The Finnish word "outokumpu" can be translated as "mysterious" or "strange hill," a reference to a specific hill in eastern Finland where both Outokumpu Oyj and Outokumpu, the community that developed around the company, were located. Local lore held that the "strange hill" in the wooded hills of eastern Finland contained valuable mineral deposits. Local prospectors needed no further encouragement to begin scrutinizing the outokumpu, their interest piqued by the promise of hidden wealth. From as early as 1725, samples from the hill were sent to the national College of Mines for analysis, but all hopes were dashed when scientific examination revealed that the prospectors had discovered iron pyrite, more commonly known as "fool's gold." In fact, the fabled hill did contain hidden wealth, but it took until the early 19th century for the value of the subterranean treasure to be identified.

In 1908, a discovery was made 40 miles outside of Outokumpu that triggered the formation of Outokumpu Oyj. A massive metallic boulder was found, prompting further analysis. Tests revealed that the giant orb contained valuable copper ore, carried, scientists theorized, by the movement of ice sheets during the most recent Ice Age. The glacial pattern of movement directed scientists northwest of the metallic boulder, toward the mysterious hill in Outokumpu. In 1910, test drilling at the hill confirmed the existence of a substantial copper ore deposit, leading to the establishment of a mining operation that formed the foundation for Outokumpu Oyj.

To add value to the ore at the hill, a small smelter was constructed alongside the mining operation, as preparations immediately commenced to turn the site into a commercial concern. Outokumpu Oyj experienced a somewhat fitful start to its business life, its birth giving rise to a divisive struggle over control. Finnish businessmen battled with government officials, with each side claiming ownership of the copper resources. The contentious debate was exacerbated by the hovering presence of foreign mining companies, who sniffed opportunity and tried to insinuate themselves into the picture. Operationally, the mining and smelting operations suffered at first from an insufficient number of employees with the technical acumen to solve problems that arose. When a certain aspect of the operations failed to work properly, the only recourse in many instances was to keep making adjustments until the problem was solved. It was a slow, sometimes painstaking, process, but eventually lessons were learned. By 1914, the company's first shipment was made: 60 metric tons of copper ingots sold in St. Petersburg, Russia.

Over time, the operational aspects of the smelting and mining operations improved, but the thorny question of owner-

Company Perspectives:

Outokumpu is a versatile metals group operating worldwide. In its business, Outokumpu focuses on base metals production, stainless steel, copper products and technology. In its traditional areas of core competence, Outokumpu is recognized as one of the industry leaders. This position is also the one from which the Group derives its mission: Our task and mission is to put our expertise as both a producer and technology supplier to use in responsible metals production and thus to contribute to meeting the world's need for metals. In all business operations, Outokumpu underscores the crucial importance of its customers, good profitability and responsibility for the environment. The Group's core values also emphasize continuous improvement of competence as an essential prerequisite to securing competitiveness.

ship persisted. The individual responsible for solving this fundamental dilemma was Dr. Eero Makinen, the most influential figure during Outokumpu Oyj's development. Dr. Makinen joined the company as a 32-year-old mining engineer in 1918. Among his numerous contributions to the company, perhaps none was more important than his persistent effort to lend stability to the organization. During its first decade of existence, the company struggled in vain to secure private capital from Finnish sources, which left the company vulnerable to the covetous interests of foreign parties. In order to stave off a hostile takeover, Dr. Makinen argued strongly for government intervention, believing ownership by the Finnish state would end the threat of foreign mining concerns. Dr. Makinen prevailed, convincing the Finnish State to assume ownership of Outokumpu Oyj in 1924. It was not until 1932, however, that the company was formally incorporated.

From its outset, Outokumpu Oyj was an export-driven company, relying heavily on supplying unprocessed ore and smelted ore to neighboring nations. During the 1920s, for instance, the company sold raw ore to Germany and refined copper to Sweden. The company's first appreciable surge of growth occurred during the late 1920s and early 1930s, when Finland's rapid industrialization propelled the company much closer to the forefront of technology. The paucity of technical expertise, which had hobbled Outokumpu Oyj's progress during its first years in business, no longer was a problem. Evidence of the greatly improved technological sophistication of the company's engineers was on display in 1935, when Outokumpu Oyj constructed what was then the largest electric copper smelter in the world. Located near Finland's eastern border in Imatra, the smelter was moved in 1944 to distance the valuable facility from the looming threat of Soviet troops. Dismantled and then rebuilt near Finland's west coast, the massive smelter found a permanent home in Harjavalta, the site of Outokumpu Oyj's greatest achievement.

Flash Smelting and Postwar Diversification

At Harjavalta in the late 1940s, Outokumpu Oyj's scientists and engineers developed a new process of extracting metal from its ore. Called flash smelting, the closed extraction process captured nearly all of the sulfur-rich gases from the smelting furnace. Developed by Petri Bryk and John Ryselin, flash smelting was regarded as the most significant metallurgical breakthrough of the 20th century, an appraisal that had not changed by the century's end. The success of flash smelting, which later was licensed to other metallurgical companies, eventually led to the formation of an Outokumpu Oyj technology division. To aid in the development of further metallurgical innovations, the company relied on its metallurgical lab, first established in Pori in 1942. The formation of a full-scale metallurgical lab and the widespread acceptance of flash smelting testified to the evolutionary leap the company had achieved in the technical aspects of its business. The early days of solving problems by trial-and-error had given way to world-recognized sophistication in metallurgical science, securing a lasting market position for Outokumpu Oyj during the latter half of the 20th century.

As the company's expertise blossomed, so too did the scope of its business. Initially, the company vertically integrated its copper operations by taking control over the various processing stages of the copper ore mined at Outokumpu. Such vertical integration brought the company closer to the end-user, or "downstream," enabling it to reap profits and to better control costs along the downstream stages of copper processing. In 1940, for example, the company began producing copper semi-products in Pori. The facilities in Pori had already begun producing a number of non-ferrous alloys by the late 1940s, but, unlike with copper, the company did not possess the raw materials to produce the other alloys. Consequently, the company was forced to purchase the basic materials from other companies, an arrangement that did not suit Outokumpu Oyj officials. The company resolved to develop its own sources for the raw materials it needed, leading to the formation of an exploration department in 1951. Not long after the hunt for new ore deposits began, the mining and production of other metals commenced. Outokumpu Oyj would no longer exist as a copper-only company.

The company's quest for self-sufficiency recorded its first success several years after the creation of an exploration department. In 1954, a deposit of nickel-bearing pyrrhotite ore was found in Kotalahti, ushering the company into the nickel production business. A nickel plant, completed by 1960, was constructed in Harjavalta, where Outokumpu Oyj's engineers were able to incorporate flash smelting technology into nickel production. Also in 1954, the company opened its Vihanti mine, which added zinc to its growing portfolio of metals. Next, cobalt and sulfur production fell under Outokumpu Oyj's purview, with the company's decade of diversification ending in 1959, when a chromite deposit discovered in northern Finland led Outokumpu Oyj into steel production.

As the company diversified its involvement in metal production, it also strengthened and expanded its network of sales offices. Outokumpu Oyj's initial focus on export markets endured throughout the 1930s, but the company redirected its efforts inward during subsequent years, as it focused on meeting domestic metal demands. In the 1950s, however, the company began focusing on export sales with renewed vigor. Sales representatives were established in Norway, Sweden, and Denmark during the decade, as the company's steadily increasing capacity necessitated a larger customer base. By 1964, as was true during the company's formative years, export sales exceeded domestic sales.

Outokumpu Oyj's physical expansion beyond Finland's borders was not limited to its marketing functions only. Although the

Key Dates:

1914: First shipment of metal is made.
1924: Finnish government assumes ownership of Outokumpu Oyj.
Late 1940s: Flash Smelting is developed.
1951: An exploration department is established.
1976: Stainless steel plant in Tornio goes online.
1988: Outokumpu Oyj debuts on the Helsinki Stock Exchange.
2000: AvestaPolarit is created through the merger of Outokumpu Steel and Avesta Sheffield.

company was beginning to greatly expand and diversify its exploration efforts, by the 1960s it could no longer supply its refining operations with enough ore by relying exclusively on Finnish sources. Outokumpu Oyj's production capacity had increased to the point where foreign sources of ore were required to keep the company's facilities operating at optimal efficiency. To answer the call for a greater supply of ore, the company brokered several extended purchase agreements with overseas mines. Not long after securing these agreements, the company demonstrated its penchant for self-reliance by forming an international department in 1974 to foster its own exploration and development efforts overseas. Because of these efforts, the company secured stakes in mining operations in Canada and Norway.

The 1950s and 1960s were years of aggressive expansion, time spent building the infrastructure and assembling the resources to support a multinational mining, refining, and production organization. The years of steady growth set the stage for what promised to be a profitable decade ahead, when the sprawling yet integrated mining operations would find full expression. The 1970s proved to be a difficult decade, however, witnessing the company's first annual losses in 40 years. The oil embargo during the early 1970s caused production costs to escalate, a pattern aped by labor costs. Instead of being a decade of progress, the 1970s forced Outokumpu Oyj into its shell, restricting capital improvements substantially. With the exception of a new stainless steel plant in Tornio that became operational in 1976, Outokumpu Oyj made no capacity expansions during the decade, choosing to wait until a more stable economic climate returned.

A Mining Giant Takes Shape in the 1980s

The 1980s brought Outokumpu Oyj a return to prosperity and expansion. Much of the growth occurred on the international front, as the company significantly strengthened its presence overseas. The roster of company-controlled sales offices overseas grew to include facilities in the United States, the Netherlands, Singapore, Japan, Italy, Mexico, Switzerland, Chile, and elsewhere, accounting for one-third of Outokumpu Oyj's total sales by the early 1990s. The company grew via acquisition during the 1980s as well, purchasing an Ohio-based fabricator of zirconium copper in 1983 and a Wisconsin-based producer of specialty alloy wire in 1985. Other important additions included the purchase of a controlling interest in Tara Mines in Ireland and the acquisition of the Viscaria copper mine in Sweden.

Domestically, one of the most significant developments during the 1980s concerned Outokumpu Oyj's ownership. Since the 1960s, the company had offered employees the option of retiring with full pension benefits at the age of 52. In the 1980s, company officials feared the payment of pension benefits in the coming years could trigger a financial crisis. As a precaution, Outokumpu Oyj offered shares in the company to those Finnish employees who were eligible for pension benefits, hoping such employees would accept an ownership stake in exchange for their benefits. Nearly all of the employees agreed to the proposal. The crisis was averted and, in October 1988, Outokumpu Oyj shares debuted on the Helsinki Stock Exchange.

As Outokumpu Oyj prepared for the 1990s, an exhaustive reorganization occurred that altered the relationship among the company's scores of businesses. During the late 1980s, centralized management was shelved, replaced by a more autonomous organization that ceded authority to individual business units. Many of the company's subsidiaries and divisions were restructured as independent corporations, enabling the organization as a whole to react more nimbly to changing market conditions.

During the 1990s, Outokumpu Oyj sharpened its focus on its core metal businesses. Between 1993 and 1996, the company invested in a major expansion and modernization program that increased the copper smelting capacity at Harjavalta by three-fifths and doubled the company nickel smelting capacity. Although copper and nickel were important metals, particularly copper, Outokumpu Oyj was recording its greatest profit gains with its stainless steel businesses. By the late 1990s, the consistently strong performance of stainless steel convinced management to direct much of the company's capital resources toward strengthening its involvement in stainless steel. In December 1999, Outokumpu Oyj executives decided to launch a major expansion program at Tornio. The project, expected to double capacity, was scheduled to be completed by 2002. The most significant event concerning Outokumpu Oyj's involvement in stainless steel occurred in 2000, when the company's steel businesses merged with the Avesta Sheffield Group, owned by Sweden-based Avesta Sheffield AB. The merger created AvestaPolarit, the second largest stainless steel producer in the world. AvestaPolarit, 55 percent-owned by Outokumpu Oyj, generated more than EUR 3 billion in annual sales, supported by facilities in Finland, Sweden, the United Kingdom, and the United States.

Principal Operating Units

Stainless Steel; Copper Products; Metals Production; Mining; Technology.

Principal Competitors

Mitsui Mining & Smelting Company, Limited; Kennecott Utah Copper; Inco Limited.

Further Reading

"Outokumpu Gets Export Tax Review," *American Metal Market,* November 14, 2000, p. 10.
"Tracing Our Roots," http://www.outokumpu.com/group/backgr.htm.

—Jeffrey L. Covell

Peet's Coffee & Tea, Inc.

1400 Park Avenue
Emeryville, California 94608
U.S.A.
Telephone: (510) 594-2100
Fax: (510) 594-2180
Web site: http://www.peet.com

Public Company
Incorporated: 1966
Employees: 1,500
Sales: $67.8 million (1999)
Stock Exchanges: NASDAQ
Ticker Symbol: PEET
NAIC:31192 Coffee and Tea Manufacturing; 45299 All Other Specialty Food Stores; 42199 Other Miscellaneous Durable Goods Wholesalers

Founded in Berkeley, California, in the mid-1960s, Peet's Coffee & Tea, Inc. encompasses 57 retail stores (38 in northern California) and a mail-order and online channel selling 33 types of coffee and assorted teas. By late 2000, it was launching its first effort to appeal to a national audience and was preparing for an initial public offering (IPO). The IPO, held on January 25, 2001, met with resounding success, raising $24.6 million for the company. Peet's sales profile is unique: roughly 15 to 20 percent of its sales come from brewed coffee as compared to 85 percent at other mass-market coffee houses. Online, instore, and mail-order sales of beans and teas account for the remainder of its sales. From the start, the company has prided itself on the excellence of its beans and the immediacy of its service. Peet's roasts coffee to order six days a week and schedules orders received each day for roasting and shipping the day after. Peet's consciously appeals to a college-educated clientele in the 25- to 45-year-old bracket. A third of Peet's customers buy beans only, a third buy drinks, and a third buy some of each.

The Founding of Peet's: 1966

Peet's Coffee & Tea came into being in 1966, when good coffee meant vacuum-packed percolator grind. For the preceding decade, national coffee brands had been debasing their product, incorporating an ever-higher proportion of cheap, tannic robusta coffee beans. Meanwhile, Arthur Peet, a Dutch immigrant with a passion for European-style dark roasts, had begun importing arabica coffee beans, which yield the strong, oily brews favored by Europeans, in the 1950s. Peet had grown up in the family's coffee and tea business in Alkmaar, Holland. After World War II, he worked in the tea trade in Indonesia.

In the mid-1960s in San Francisco, Arthur Peet began brewing his own blend of dark roast beans, which he sold at his first retail store at Walnut and Vine Streets in North Berkeley. Although some dismissed his dark-roasted coffee as tasting ''burnt,'' the brew caught on with students, artists, writers, and musicians, and the outfit quickly became known as a small, premium purveyor of quality beans with a devoted group of followers, who accorded it cult-like status.

It would be five years before Peet's opened its second store in Menlo Park and nine more before it opened its third outlet on Domingo Avenue in Berkeley in 1980. From the start, Peet's emphasized quality over quantity and the roasting of fine beans rather than the creation of coffee shops. In fact, it deliberately focused on the sale of whole beans for home consumption and guaranteed delivery of its beans fresh from the roasting facility. It was as happy to have its customers order its coffee by mail and brew their own morning cup at home as to have them come in and buy a cup of ready-made. This commitment continued throughout the 1980s and 1990s. ''I still consider us a specialty roaster more than a beverage bar,'' Jerry Baldwin, who took over ownership of Peet's from Arthur Peet in 1984, was quoted as saying in a 1999 *San Francisco Chronicle*. Peet's coffee beans and teas were never vacuum-packed and were shipped within 24 hours of being roasted to order. In the store, coffee was made fresh every half hour, and no beans were allowed to stand for more than seven days.

Peet's and Starbucks in the 1970s and 1980s

In 1984, the year espresso machines made their appearance, Jerry Baldwin bought Peet's, adding it to a portfolio that included Caravali, a wholesale coffee brand, and a small Seattle chain known as Starbucks. Inspired by Peet's, Baldwin and his

Company Perspectives:

Peet's Coffee & Tea is a super-premium coffee roaster with a focus on delivering the freshest, deep roasted beans for home and office enjoyment. The company is dedicated to providing a personalized and superior experience for its customers to enjoy quality coffee, tea, and related products. Peet's is a privately-held company committed to strategically growing its successful online, mail-order, and retail business products while maintaining a unique culture and focus on customer satisfaction.

two partners, Gordon Bowker and Zev Siegl, had pulled together $8,000 in cash and loans in 1971 to found Starbucks. That was when Baldwin first met Peet; in 1971, he and his partners traveled to Berkeley to learn about Peet's coffee before Arthur Peet would sell it to them for use at Starbucks. When they returned to Seattle, they served Peet's coffee for the next 18 months at their new store in the Pike Place Market. That store, designed to be more of a coffee and tea outlet than a café—just like Peet's—did not at the time offer espresso or muffins, or even any place to sit down. Coffee was poured free into porcelain cups for tasting, and while the customer paused to drink, Baldwin and his staff bombarded him or her with information about coffee. Sales of fresh-roasted beans and teas exceeded the owners' expectations that first year, totaling $49,000. In 1972, Starbucks opened its second store near the University of Washington, and a third store followed soon after.

In 1987, Baldwin sold off Starbucks, which then had only six stores, to Howard Schultz, a former Peet's employee who had left Peet's in 1986 to start his own coffee company, Il Giornale. Baldwin's reason for selling off Starbucks was that it would never be as good as Peet's. The deal included a noncompete agreement, which expired in 1992, the year that Starbucks went public and began its astronomic expansion worldwide.

Peet's expansion during the 1970s and 1980s was conservative by comparison. The company opened stores sporadically—one or two every year, all within northern California—and its marketing strategy was low-key. The decision to keep the company small and local was in part a conscious reflection of maintaining Alfred Peet's tradition. Baldwin emphasized quality over quantity and word-of-mouth publicity, which supported the company's message of quality with "a whisper rather than a shout." But Baldwin himself favored a small approach to business, based upon his own early dislike of the bureaucratic world. A native of San Francisco, Baldwin started out his work life as a bellhop and doing inventory for clothing stores. After completing a stint in the army, he took time off and traveled to Hawaii, then went to work for Boeing in 1969 as a programmer for government contracts such as the Concorde. Eventually he left the corporate world to become an English teacher. However, while Baldwin admittedly did not like the corporate atmosphere for its bureaucracy, he acknowledged in a 1999 *Boston Globe* article that his time at Boeing gave him some idea of his capabilities.

Accelerating Expansion in the Mid-1990s

Peet's growth picked up somewhat in 1994 after the company received a $6 million private placement from the San Francisco investment firm Hambrecht & Quist. The money allowed Peet's to open a 60,000-square-foot roastery in Emeryville, which had the capacity to supply 150 stores. Stores at this time and throughout the remainder of the 1990s averaged $1.2 million in sales annually. They cost about $350,000 to $400,000 to open, outfit, and decorate in the company's coffee-inspired colors, but each was run autonomously by its manager and reflected the style of the neighborhood in which it was located.

By 1996, sales at Peet's approximately 30 stores, which by then sold coffee, tea, scones, and muffins, and a variety of brewing accessories and equipment, totaled about $40 million. In comparison, Starbucks brought in $696.5 million from its more than 1,100 stores in the United States, Canada, Japan, and Singapore. The two regarded themselves as friendly competitors with distinct orientations. Then, in 1997, with the spread of coffee shops still on the rise, Peet's caught the expansion bug. Plotting a national expansion that included opening 10 to 15 new stores annually until there were several hundred Peet's across the country, Baldwin aimed to establish a national presence for his high-end company. "My goal is for Peet's to stay independent," he said in a 1999 *New York Times* article. "To do that, we're forced to grow. Peet's would be more vulnerable in a single market than in multiple markets." Expansion would also protect Peet's against a potential regional economic downturn.

New shops were planned to open primarily in cities where Peet's mail-order business already had a solid following. Although 45 percent of Peet's mail-order business came from southern California, Peet's had a sizable clientele nationwide (an estimated $1 million in online sales alone in 1998), due in large part to the relocation of students and other Californians who missed their Peet's brew. Some in the business world expressed concern that the conservative Peet's could never catch up with Starbucks and faced a significant hurdle in finding affordable real estate in markets where the recent multitude of coffee and bagel chains had pushed prices up. Others expressed concerns about Baldwin's tightly controlling management style and the fact that, even as the company prepared for expansion, two top executives had recently left the company, and it was without a president and chief executive. In 1997, Chris Mottern replaced Samuel Salkin as president and chief executive officer.

Retired Arthur Peet himself was of the opinion that the move to expand should have occurred in the early 1990s when Starbucks began its successful growth campaign. However, Baldwin remained optimistic about carving out a market as the number two coffee chain with what he deemed the best products and execution in the industry. Peet's first growth move was to employ a Starbucks-type maneuver, opening its Pasadena store across from one of Starbucks' busiest shops in 1997.

But even as Peet's looked to a national market, it remained insistent upon not becoming so large that individual stores lost their neighborhood feel or that the company replaced quality with consistency as some of its competitor chains had. Most employees were part-time, but all received benefits. In order to avoid problems with theft and poor performance, servers were interviewed twice, and all were offered stock options. Peet's also remained committed to putting money back into the communities it served both at home and overseas. The company supported Coffee Kids, an international nonprofit organization dedicated to improving the life of children and families in

Key Dates:

1966: Arthur Peet opens the first Peet's store in North Berkeley.
1971: Peet's opens its second store in Menlo Park; Jerry Baldwin and partners open the first Starbucks outlet in Seattle's Pike Place Market, selling Peet's coffee.
1975: Peet's opens a third store in Berkeley.
1984: Baldwin's group buys Peet's Coffee & Tea.
1987: Peet's owners sell the Starbucks chain to Howard Schultz.
1994: Peet's opens a 60,000-square-foot roastery in Emeryville.
1995: Peet's opens its first store outside the Bay Area; Peet's begins to supply Au Bon Pain bakery cafés with coffee.
1997: Peet's opens its first store outside northern California; Chris Mottern replaces Salkin as president and chief executive officer.
1999: Peet's enters the Boston market; first Chicago store opens.
2001: Shares of Peet's rise 17 percent on first day of NASDAQ trading.

coffee-growing communities, and sponsored an annual seven-day bike ride to raise funds for HIV- and AIDS-related medical care and public awareness. All stores upheld Peet's longtime tradition of serving drinks free on Christmas and the anniversary of its opening, a day when employees donated their tips to a local nonprofit organization and Peet's then matched the amount raised up to $1,000 per store. Customer loyalty was encouraged with programs such as ''Peet's Customer of the Week'' promotion, the winner of which received complimentary coffee.

By 1999, Peet's had close to 50 stores, had expanded into the Chicago and Portland, Oregon, areas, and was set to enter the Boston market where heavy mail-order business had indicated the area was ripe for a new coffee establishment. ''We believe that limited and selective additions of new store sites, rather than broad scale site development, will better support our brand position,'' the company said in an article online. Boston coffee drinkers has been introduced to Peet's in 1995 when Au Bon Pain began to serve Peet's coffee in its stores. Peet's discontinued supplying Au Bon Pain with its coffee in 1998 because, according to Peet's, coffee was kept on the burners too long. Starbucks, which had opened its first store in Boston in 1994, and bought out the Coffee Connection, a Boston institution, in 1995, welcomed the addition of Peet's. ''It elevates awareness of coffee in the market, and that tends to be a positive thing,'' said Donna Peterson, Starbucks's marketing manager for the New England region, in a 1999 *Boston Globe* article. Plans for the Boston market called for stores with a café atmosphere, including laptop plug-ins, and for a lighter roast to accommodate East Coast taste in coffee.

Peet's also adopted a more aggressive approach toward marketing its coffee on the West Coast in 1999. It partnered with Host Marriott to establish Peet's kiosks at the San Francisco International Airport. ''The opening of these kiosks represents a wonderful opportunity to introduce Peet's to visitors to the Bay Area and to help build brand awareness in markets like Los Angeles and Chicago,'' Baldwin was quoted as saying in a 1999 company newswire. Other moves to update the company included providing high-speed Internet access for linking its 56 stores with corporate headquarters. In 2000, Peet's contracted with an online advertising agency to launch an interactive promotional campaign designed to raise coffee drinkers' awareness of the importance of freshness in quality coffee. This campaign led immediately to a significant increase in online revenue.

With Americans buying 450 million cups of coffee a day and spending $18 billion a year at the start of the 21st century, and coffee houses becoming the boardrooms of the nation, Peet's arranged for its January 2001 IPO of 3.3 million shares of common stock. The sale would lower Baldwin's share of the company from 31 percent to about 15 percent. Some thought it a bad time for an offering. In fact, Peet's posted a net loss of $2.5 million on total revenue of $39.2 million for the first six months of 2000, compared to a net gain of $100,000 on revenue of $31.2 million for the first six months of 1999. However, Baldwin insisted that Peet's would be able to ride the wave of coffee enthusiasm created by rival Starbucks and others. As Baldwin saw it, Peet's timing was perfect. Peet's would step in with its better product and reap the rewards of selling to an already educated public ready to graduate to super-premium coffee.

Principal Competitors

Caribou Coffee Company, Inc.; Coffee People; Diedrich Coffee; Gevalia; Green Mountain Coffee, Inc.; Seattle's Best Coffee; Starbucks Corporation.

Further Reading

Donker, Anne, ''On a Coffee Family Tree an Older Branch Sprouts Anew,'' *New York Times*, August 22, 1999, Section 3, p. 4.
Emert, Carol, ''A Wake-Up Call for Peet's,'' *San Francisco Chronicle*, April 30, 1997, p. B1.
Gaines, Judith, ''Up the Latte of Success,'' *Boston Globe*, July 5, 2000, p. D1.
Gellene, Denise, ''Another Cup of Coffee?,'' *Los Angeles Times*, February 20, 1997, p. D1.
Julian, Sheryl, ''Peet's 'Cupper Brings His Brew to Town,'' *Boston Globe*, July 19, 1995, p. 73.
Resende, Patricia, ''Business People: Baldwin Aims to Restart a Coffee Legacy,'' *Boston Herald*, December 12, 1999, p. 46.

—Carrie Rothburd

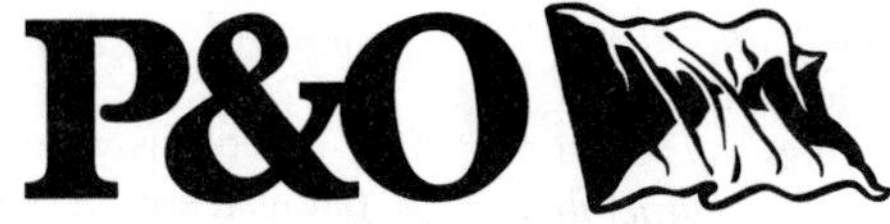

The Peninsular and Oriental Steam Navigation Company

79 Pall Mall
London SW1Y 5EJ
United Kingdom
Telephone: (0207) 930 4343
Fax: (0207) 930 8572
Web site: http://www.p-and-o.com

Public Company
Incorporated: 1840
Employees: 62,674
Sales: £6.14 billion (US$9.92 billion) (1999)
Stock Exchanges: London Frankfurt Hong Kong Sydney Tokyo
Ticker Symbol: PO
NAIC: 483111 Deep Sea Freight Transportation; 483112 Deep Sea Passenger Transportation; 488310 Port and Harbor Operations; 488320 Marine Cargo Handling; 493110 General Warehousing and Storage; 493120 Refrigerated Warehousing and Storage

The Peninsular and Oriental Steam Navigation Company (P&O) began as a shipping company. It was founded at the crucial period for the shipping industry of transition from sail to steam. Many companies were founded at this time, only to fail quickly in the early days of steam. P&O, along with Cunard, is one of the few survivors of the steamship pioneers and has outlasted its competitors through a mixture of caution, shrewdness, ruthlessness, and good luck.

P&O remained primarily a shipping company for the first 140 years of its existence. In the mid-1970s it began to diversify to become a major international group of more than 250 companies, involved not only in freight and passenger shipping but also in housebuilding, large construction projects, property, and numerous service activities. Another shift occurred in the late 1990s and early 2000s, however, when P&O divested a number of operations to focus on ports, ferries, and other logistics activities. P&O is the most internationally diverse port operator with activities at 50 ports in 19 countries on every continent. It is the largest ferry operator in the United Kingdom and is a major provider of business-to-business logistics in Europe. P&O's container shipping business is conducted through P&O Nedlloyd, a joint venture between P&O and Royal Nedlloyd N.V. that is one of the three largest container carriers in the world.

Mail Carrying Beginnings

The founding of P&O traditionally dates from the awarding of the contract by the Admiralty for the carriage of the mail between England and the Iberian Peninsula in August 1837.

In 1815 Brodie McGhie Willcox opened a shipping agency and brokers' office in Lime Street, London, and employed Arthur Anderson as clerk. Anderson was made a partner in 1822. In 1826 Willcox and Anderson were appointed London agents for the Dublin and London Steam Packet Company, an aggressive and highly successful steam packet company that ran between the two cities in its name. This connection brought together the three founders of P&O—Willcox, Anderson, and Richard Bourne, a man of great financial acumen.

In the early days, Willcox and Anderson ran small sailing vessels to Spain and Portugal. This trade forced them to take sides in the 1833 civil war in Portugal and shortly afterward in the Carlist uprising in Spain. In both cases they chose the winners and the fledgling company was granted trading facilities and official favors from the grateful Spanish and Portuguese royal families. They attempted in 1834 to float the Peninsular Steam Navigation Company but were soon in financial difficulties.

It was the contract to carry the mails to the Iberian Peninsula, awarded to Bourne rather than to Willcox and Anderson, that enabled the company to survive and develop into a giant. Mail contracts guaranteed a regular income and provided P&O with steady income for decades. The existing mail packet ships were inefficient and corrupt. P&O undertook to reach Lisbon in 84 hours, compared with up to three weeks for the mail packets, for the sum of £30,000 a year—significantly less than the packets. The first run ended in disaster when the *Don Juan* was wrecked off the Spanish coast, but the company's reputation was enhanced by the daring rescue of the mails and £21,000 in cash.

Company Perspectives:

Throughout its 150 years P&O has been a premier British shipowner, and in its time the largest in the world. It has flown the same quartered flag, embodying the royal colours of Portugal and Spain, from its very beginnings. And it all started with a handful of paddle-steamers and a contract to carry mails—the first application of the technology ushered in by the Industrial Revolution to bring frequency and regularity to international communication. Carrying mails remained P&O's preoccupation for its first hundred years, and thereby the Company made a major contribution to a revolution in world politics and commerce.

Expanding to the East: Mid-19th Century

In 1840 the company was awarded a contract to take the mails to Alexandria, the key staging post in the carriage of mails to India. This contract heralded the start of rapid company growth, beginning with the purchase of two large ships, the *Great Liverpool* and the *Oriental.*

In December 1840 the company was incorporated by royal charter under its present name of the Peninsular & Oriental Steam Navigation Company, with authorized capital of £1 million, and Willcox and Anderson as joint managing directors. Despite the absence of a mail contract at this stage and the East India Company's monopolistic hold on this trade, P&O was obliged to set up a regular steamship service to India within two years.

Prevented by the East India monopoly from operating out of Bombay, the most convenient port of call, P&O set about organizing a service between Suez, Aden, Point de Galle, and Calcutta to link up with its service between England and Egypt. Before the opening of the Suez Canal, passengers to India had to disembark at Alexandria and endure an arduous and often unsafe journey by carriage across the desert to the Red Sea, where they joined another ship. P&O actively encouraged the construction of a railway across Egypt and, to secure supplies, ran farms and repair yards en route.

P&O's first voyage to India was carried out in 1842 by the *Hindostan,* its largest ship to date. This ambitious undertaking necessitated the setting up of coal and supply stations at intermediate points along the route and of arrangements for the overland part of the journey. The greater speed and reliability of P&O's service in comparison with that of its rival, the East India Company, eventually won P&O access to Bombay.

In 1844 Anderson introduced the novel concept of leisure cruising to Victorian Britain. The first cruises took place in the Mediterranean Sea and involved shore excursions to Malta, Smyrna, Constantinople, Jaffa, and Egypt. The Crimean War of the mid-1850s put a stop to cruising until the 1880s, when it was taken up by other companies. P&O only reentered this business in 1904 with the conversion of a liner, the *Rome,* into a cruise ship, the *Vectis.*

Meanwhile, P&O pressed further east and built more ships. In 1845 the *Lady Mary Wood,* the first P&O steamship to travel to Singapore, completed the journey in 41 days (sailing ships could take up to a year to complete this journey) before opening a service between Ceylon and Hong Kong. The company's steamers took silk out of and opium into China. Its first connection with Australia was made in 1852 and with Japan in 1859.

Problems were looming on the horizon, however. Substantial increases in coal prices played havoc with operating costs. The Crimean War brought great disruption to services; in 1855 one-third of P&O tonnage was in the Black Sea transporting men, horses, supplies, and equipment. The 1869 opening of the Suez Canal was also a mixed blessing. P&O's ships' draft and breadth were inappropriate for the canal, and the company's regional offices and dockyards became redundant after the canal opened, as it became more economical to send ships back to England for repairs. Passengers still had to be transferred overland across Egypt for a decade or more after ships that could use the canal had been built, because the Post Office took years to be convinced it was safe for the mails. Other companies were not thus restricted, and within a couple of years the company's income was falling by £100,000 a year.

It was at this stage that a new regime took the helm. In 1854 Willcox resigned as managing director but remained on the board and became chairman from 1858 until his death in 1862. He was succeeded by Anderson, who remained chairman until his death in 1868. Thomas Sutherland became chairman in 1872 at the relatively young age of 38. At the age of 18, Sutherland had become a P&O office boy. He had spent a dozen years of impressive service in Hong Kong and upon taking charge of the company was faced with the burden of cutting expenditure and of rebuilding the fleet.

Sutherland gradually turned P&O's fortunes around. By 1884 P&O's fleet contained 50 ships, only six more than in 1870, but the ships of 1884 had almost double the gross tonnage of 1870. The end of the 19th century was a period of calm for British shipping generally. Consolidation of the empire was under way and ships were increasing in size, speed, and comfort to the extent that Bombay could be reached from England within 15 days.

Expanding Through Acquisition: Early 20th Century

In 1910 P&O bought the Blue Anchor Line, a company that specialized in the carriage of emigrants and general cargo from the United Kingdom to Australia and of Australian wool on the return journey. Until this point, P&O had concentrated on first-class passenger trade. This purchase gave P&O an interest in all classes of passenger traffic.

The process of expansion by acquisition accelerated. In 1914 Sutherland masterminded secret negotiations leading to the merger of P&O and British India Steam Navigation Company (BI). BI was Britain's largest shipping company, with 131 vessels totaling 598,203 gross registered tons (grt), compared with P&O's 70 ships of 548,654 grt. BI's routes complemented those of P&O; it was strong in the Indian Ocean, the Persian Gulf, and Southeast Asia, but rarely ventured west of Suez. There was no change of company name following the merger, but until the 1950s P&O and BI shared the same board of directors.

At this point, after leading P&O for more than 40 years, 78-year-old Thomas Sutherland retired and handed over the reins to

Key Dates:

1840: The Peninsular and Oriental Steam Navigation Company is incorporated by royal charter.
1842: P&O makes its first voyage to India.
1869: The opening of the Suez Canal forces the company to rebuild its fleet and economize.
1914: P&O acquires British India Steam Navigation Company.
1923: A series of further acquisitions increases the company fleet to 500 vessels.
1960: P&O takes full control of Orient Lines.
1965: P&O and three other U.K. shipping companies form Overseas Containers Ltd. (OCL); the company also begins operating roll-on/roll-off ferries.
1971: Company is reorganized into five divisions: bulk cargo, passenger, general cargo, a general holding company, and European and air transport.
1974: Princess Cruises is acquired; diversification begins with the acquisition of Bovis, a construction company.
1986: P&O becomes the sole owner of OCL, which is renamed P&O Containers Ltd.
1996: P&O merges its containers business with that of Royal Nedlloyd N.V. to form P&O Nedlloyd Ltd.
1997: Bovis Homes is spun off.
1999: P&O sells off Bovis Construction, Earls Court and Olympia, and the bulk of its investment property portfolio.
2000: Company demerges its cruise line unit as P&O Princess Cruises plc.

James Lyle Mackay, Lord Inchcape, chairman of BI. The change at the top coincided with the outbreak of World War I, during which the merchant fleet had to contend with torpedoes, submarines, airstrikes, and mines. By the end of 1914, 100 ships of the enlarged P&O fleet had been requisitioned.

At the outbreak of war, the tonnage of the P&O fleet was greater than 1.1 million grt. More than 500,000 grt were lost during hostilities, but by the war's end the P&O fleet stood at more than 1.5 million grt. This expansion was achieved by an aggressive program of acquisition to prepare P&O for the postwar era. In 1916 P&O acquired the New Zealand Shipping Company and Federal Steam Navigation Company, prominent in the frozen food trade from New Zealand to the United Kingdom. In 1917 it acquired interests in the Union Steamship Company of New Zealand; the Hain Steamship Company, which had worldwide tramping interests; and James Nourse Ltd., which operated between India and the West Indies. P&O bought the Orient Line in 1918 and the Khedivial Mail Line in 1919. In 1920 P&O bought Britain's oldest steamship company, the General Steamship Navigation Company, founded in 1824. By 1923, when P&O bought the Strick Line, the P&O fleet was composed of 500 vessels.

The first ten postwar years were prosperous for P&O: the war had created a backlog of trade; passenger traffic picked up briskly; and emigration from Britain, Australia, and New Zealand reached new highs. The growth of foreign competition was loosening the hold of British ships in many markets, however. Building and operating costs were rising rapidly, and there was a ship surplus. These problems were exacerbated by the civil war in China, which badly hurt P&O's trade, and the Wall Street crash of 1929, which heralded the start of the Great Depression of the 1930s. P&O encountered severe financial difficulties, necessitating salary cuts of ten percent in 1931. By 1932 P&O was unable to pay a dividend to its shareholders.

Alexander Shaw, Lord Inchcape's son-in-law, became chairman in 1932. He inherited a modern fleet with which to combat the crisis. This fleet included the most successful vessel of the decade, the 20,000-ton *Viceroy of India,* which was completed in 1929. This ship was quieter than its predecessors, traveled at 19 knots, and brought a new level of luxury to sea travel, including the first onboard indoor swimming pool.

As the 1930s progressed, international politics again disrupted the merchant shipping market. In 1935, following Mussolini's invasion of Ethiopia, nine BI ships were requisitioned to support League of Nations sanctions. In 1937 Japan began eight years of undeclared war on China. These events, plus growing uncertainty in Europe, disordered supplies and routes. Nevertheless, business improved and Alexander Shaw—now Lord Craigmyle—retired in 1938, two years after restoration of the company's dividend.

Shaw was succeeded by Sir William Crawford Currie, who remained as chairman until 1960. World War II began. The *Rawalpindi* was requisitioned in August 1939, only to be lost three months later. The pace of requisitioning accelerated, and by Easter 1940 all of BI's 103 ships, composed of 55 passenger ships and 48 cargo ships, were under official direction. P&O contributed 16 troop carriers, which transported more than one million troops during the conflict.

In 1939 the fleet of the P&O group contained 371 vessels totaling 2.2 million grt. During the course of the conflict, 182 vessels, equivalent to 1.2 million grt, were destroyed. P&O itself lost more than 40 percent of its fleet in tonnage terms. Elsewhere within the group, Hain lost all 24 of its cargo vessels; Nourse lost seven vessels; BI lost 45; and one quarter of Union Line and 85 percent of Strick Line was destroyed.

Emphasizing Cargo and Cruising in the Postwar Era

A steep rise in shipbuilding prices and increased foreign competition, particularly from developing countries, characterized the immediate postwar period. The postwar era also saw the end of the British Empire; India regained its independence in 1947, causing a rapid decline in the number of steady passengers, such as soldiers, civil servants, and their families.

P&O responded to the new situation by refocusing its activities on cargo. By 1949 P&O's cargo fleet had been rebuilt to its prewar levels, whereas the passenger fleet was at only 60 percent of its 1939 strength. P&O also began its involvement with the tanker market in the late 1950s and by the mid-1960s P&O was the main independent tanker operator in the United Kingdom.

International politics intervened briefly again in 1956 with the Suez Canal crisis and the closure of the canal. The canal was crucial to the company's U.K./Far East and U.K./Australian routes. Longer voyages and the fear of war, however, led to higher returns and a short-term stimulus for P&O.

Despite the threat to passenger shipping from the growth of civil aviation, the passenger business was not neglected, and in the mid-1950s two new prestigious passenger ships were ordered—the 2,050-berth *Oriana* for the Orient Line, launched in 1959, and the 2,250-berth *Canberra,* launched in 1960. In May 1960 P&O bought the remainder of Orient Line, and briefly renamed its passenger operation P&O Orient Lines.

The 1960s were difficult years for shipping. P&O suffered from the general shipping slump and competition from the growth of flags of convenience—ships usually were registered or flagged in the country of ownership, but certain flags attracted ships by offering financial or legal advantages and became known as "flags of convenience." The company also entered new areas of business during this decade. In 1961 the abolition of national service marked the end of BI ships as troop carriers and the beginning of a program of educational cruises. In 1963 P&O, now chaired by Sir Donald Anderson, concluded a long-term agreement with Anglo-Norness Shipping Company, the world's major tanker and bulk shipping operator, to market its fleet of bulk and combination carriers. In 1965, through Ranger Fishing, which was sold in 1974, P&O entered the freezer trawler business. Through North Sea Ferries, P&O bought and operated its first roll-on roll-off vessels—cargo ships or ferries on or off which cars, trucks, and trailers drive directly.

The most important development of all, however, was P&O's pioneering role in containerization, one of the most important changes in shipping in the 20th century. P&O was at the forefront of the containerization revolution through the creation of Overseas Containers Ltd. (OCL), which was formed in 1965 by four British shipping companies—P&O, Alfred Holt, British and Commonwealth, and Furness Withy. Sir Andrew Crichton was seconded from the P&O board as OCL chairman.

In March 1969 OCL's first fully cellular container service began between the United Kingdom and Australia. Initially a lossmaker, OCL gradually became a success, and in 1986 P&O bought that part of OCL that it did not already own, changing the name to P&O Containers Ltd.

Reorganization and Diversification: 1970s and 1980s

In 1971 Ford Geddes became P&O chairman. He took charge of a group composed of 127 companies whose profits had fallen to £4.9 million, from £12.6 million in 1969. Geddes immediately set about a thorough overhaul of P&O's structure. The company was divided into five divisions: bulk cargo, passenger, general cargo, a general holding company, and European and air transport. This rationalization led to the disappearance of old names such as Hain and Nourse, BI, General Steam, and many others.

The effects of the rationalization were slow to filter through, and P&O increasingly cast around for opportunities in other sectors. In the early 1970s the property market was booming, encouraging P&O to make a bid for the construction company Bovis. The bid stirred up serious opposition within P&O, based in part on resistance to diversification but, mostly, on a belief that the bid was pitched too high. This led to the resignation of Geddes in November 1972. He was replaced by the third Lord Inchcape as non-executive chairman, with Alexander Marshall as managing director. P&O's purchase of Bovis went through in 1974 at about half the price of the original offer.

Competition from air travel caused the withdrawal of regular liner passenger services, with the final scheduled trip to the Far East taking place in 1969. Passenger business now consisted of the ferry service and cruises. In 1974 P&O bought Princess Cruises, which then formed the cornerstone of P&O's extensive U.S. cruise business, augmented by the 1988 purchase of Sitmer Cruises.

Lord Inchcape became chief executive in 1978 and initiated another reorganization. This entailed the sale of all interests in the North Sea and the U.S. oil and gas industry acquired in the 1960s, the dismantling of the energy division, and a reduced role for general cargo and the bulk division. During the period 1974–80, the number of ships in the P&O fleet fell from 178 to 89. Because of the introduction of much larger ships, however, total tonnage fell by only 3 to 4 percent, standing at 2.45 million grt in 1981.

By the late 1970s Lord Inchcape was searching for younger talent for the board. His eye alighted on Jeffrey Sterling, a City financier who had built up his own group of companies based on the Sterling Guarantee Trust. Sterling joined the board in 1980.

Shortly afterward a hostile bid for the company was received from Trafalgar House, the owner of Cunard and also a competitor in the construction business. The bid was referred to the Monopolies and Mergers Commission, which allowed it to proceed in early 1984. This interlude gave Jeffrey Sterling, who became chairman in November 1983, time to organize P&O's defense, however, and the bid was not renewed.

In 1985 P&O merged with Sterling's Sterling Guarantee Trust (SGT). This deal brought the group numerous nonshipping interests, including Town and Country Properties; the ownership and management of the Earls Court and Olympia exhibition centers; the catering company Sutcliffes; a security company called Sterling Guards; various other service-related concerns; and Buck & Hickman, a maker and distributor of tools. In 1986 P&O bought Stock Conversion, a major property company, then the following year purchased European Ferries, which had activities in ferries, property, and ports.

Focusing on Ferries, Ports, and Logistics in the 1990s and Beyond

Acquisitions continued in the early 1990s. In 1991 P&O purchased a half-share in Laing Properties, another major property concern. That same year, P&O acquired the bulk of the Ellerman cargo shipping business from Cunard, giving it more than a quarter of the British share of container trades between Australasia and Europe, 100 percent of the United Kingdom-Australasia run, and 15 percent of the Europe-South Africa trade. In late 1993, P&O made its first large investment in China since 1949 by purchasing a 25 percent stake in the Shekou Container Terminal in southern China for about US$40 million. P&O began managing the terminal at the start of 1994. Further investments in China followed. Meantime, a number of the nonshipping companies gained through the purchase of SGT were divested in 1993, including Sutcliffes, Sterling Security, and Buck & Hickman.

Pressure for restructuring increased in the mid-1990s as P&O's ferry operations suffered from the new competition from Eurotunnel, the channel tunnel between Britain and France that opened in 1994 and soon gained 40 percent of the market for car and freight crossings. Other P&O businesses, including containers, bulk shipping, and property, also were struggling; on the positive side, the company's cruise lines were experiencing rapid growth, so much so that Princess Cruises ordered the construction of the world's largest cruise ship, *Grand Princess,* which made its maiden voyage in 1998 weighing 108,900 tons.

Meantime, restructuring commenced in the other sectors, starting in late 1996 when P&O merged its containers business with that of Royal Nedlloyd N.V. of The Netherlands to form P&O Nedlloyd Ltd., a 50–50 joint venture that instantly became one of the world's largest container shipping companies with annual revenues of US$4 billion. In 1997 P&O spun off Bovis Homes, a housebuilding unit, as a separate, publicly traded firm. P&O the following year formed another joint venture, this one involving the company's short sea routes on the English Channel—the routes in competition with Eurotunnel—which were merged with those of Stena Line AB of Sweden, forming P&O Stena Line (Holdings) Ltd. The new entity was 60 percent owned by P&O. Through the merger, the two partners hoped to reduce their operating costs by about £75 million a year and thereby improve their competitive position. A third joint venture was formed in July 1998 when P&O merged its bulk shipping operations with those of the China steel group Shougang to form Associated Bulk Carriers Ltd., which was incorporated in Hong Kong and was 50 percent owned by P&O. In April 2000, however, P&O bought out its partner and announced that it would spin off the subsidiary through an IPO. But unfavorable market conditions scuttled the public offering that had been planned for Oslo.

The divestment drive continued in 1999 and 2000. During the former year, P&O sold off Bovis Construction, Earls Court and Olympia, its Australian services operations, and the bulk of its investment property portfolio. Most of the rest of the investment property was sold off in 2000. Having already reduced itself to cruises, ferries, ports, and logistics, P&O took the further step in October 2000 of demerging its cruise line unit as P&O Princess Cruises plc, which was listed on the London and New York stock exchanges. P&O also planned to sell off its bulk shipping unit, Associated Bulk Carriers, and float its containers business, the P&O Nedlloyd joint venture, when market conditions had sufficiently improved. Thus the future of P&O was to be centered on the management of ports, the operation of ferries, and the providing of logistics for the business-to-business supply chain. At the dawn of the 21st century, the P&O units operating in these areas were growing, fueled by increasing e-commerce, world trade, and tourism as well as consolidation in the industry. Although it had jettisoned its more glamorous cruise line activities, P&O appeared to have a bright future in the lower profile but equally profitable logistics sector.

Principal Subsidiaries

PORTS, FERRIES, AND LOGISTICS: Century Group Pty. Ltd. (Papua New Guinea); International Terminal Operating Co. Inc. (U.S.A.); Larne Harbour Ltd.; Pacific Cold Storage Inc. (U.S.A.); P&O Australia Ltd.; P&O Australia Ports Pty. Ltd.; P&O Cold Logistics Ltd. (Australia); P&O European Ferries (Irish Sea) Ltd.; P&O European Ferries (Portsmouth) Ltd.; P&O Ferrymasters Ltd.; P&O Maritime Services Pty. Ltd. (Australia); P&O New Zealand Ltd.; P&O North Sea Ferries B.V. (Netherlands); P&O North Sea Ferries Ltd.; P&O Polar Australia Pty. Ltd.; P&O Ports Ltd. (Australia); P&O Ports (Europe) Ltd.; P&O Scottish Ferries Ltd.; P&O Trans European (Holdings) Ltd.; P&O Trans European Ltd.; P&O Trans European GmbH (Germany); Three Quays International Ltd.; Nhava Sheva International Container Terminal Ltd. (India; 95%); Container Terminals Australia Ltd. (79.9%); P&O Stena Line (Holdings) Ltd. (60%); Asian Terminals Inc. (Philippines; 53.4%); Terminales Rio de la Plata S.A. (Argentina; 53.1%); Southampton Container Terminals Ltd. (U.K.; 51%); Partrederiet International Offshore Services ANS (Norway; 50%); PT Kuala Pelabuhan Indonesia (50%). CARGO SHIPPING: Associated Bulk Carriers Ltd. (Hong Kong); P&O Nedlloyd Container Line Ltd. (50%); P&O Nedlloyd B.V. (Netherlands; 50%); P&O Nedlloyd Ltd. (50%); Roadways Container Logistics Ltd. (50%). PROPERTY: P&O Developments Ltd.; P&O Properties International Ltd.; P&O Properties Inc. (U.S.A.); TCD North Inc. (U.S.A.); Technology Park/Atlanta Inc. (U.S.A.; 94.4%); Vector Investments Ltd. (50%); Boston Wharf Company (U.S.A.); Charlwood Alliance Holdings Ltd.; Chelsea Harbour Ltd.; P&O Property Holdings Ltd.; P&O Properties Ltd.; P&O Shopping Centres Ltd.; P&O Properties Boston Inc. (U.S.A.); Maxxiom Ltd. (50%).

Principal Competitors

A.P. Moller; APL Limited; Crowley Maritime Corporation; CSX Corporation; Eurotunnel Group; Evergreen Marine Corporation (Taiwan) Ltd.; Hanjin Shipping Co., Ltd.; Hutchison Whampoa Limited; Mitsui O.S.K. Lines, Ltd.; Neptune Orient Lines Limited; Nippon Yusen Kabushiki Kaisha; Sea Containers Ltd.; Stolt-Nielsen S.A.

Further Reading

Apthorp, Brian, *Surgeon P&O: A Personal Account of Three Voyages in the Light White Ships of the P&O Steam Navigation Company,* Hong Kong: Joplin Trading Company, 1985.

Cable, Boyd, *A Hundred Year History of the P&O,* London: Ivor Nicholson and Watson, 1937.

Divine, David, *These Splendid Ships: The Story of the Peninsular and Oriental Line,* London: Frederick Muller Limited, 1960.

Dyer, Geoff, "P&O Seeks to Dispel Gloom," *Financial Times,* January 19, 1996, p. 20.

Haws, Duncan, *The Ships of the P&O, Orient, and Blue Anchor Lines,* Cambridge: Stephens, 1978.

Hewitt, Garth, "Oil and Troubled Waters: P&O's Turbulent Turnaround," *International Management,* December 1980, pp. 26+.

Howarth, David, and Howarth, Stephen, *The Story of P&O,* London: Weidenfeld and Nicholson, 1986.

Jowit, Juliette, ''Floating a Glamorous Princess to Lift Sister Out of Shade,'' *Financial Times,* February 4, 2000, p. 24.

——, ''P&O Ports Enter the Spotlight As Cruise Ships Set Sail,'' *Financial Times,* August 15, 2000, p. 23.

Kirk, R., *The Postal History of the P&O Service to the Peninsula,* London: London Royal Philatelic Society, 1987.

McCart, Neil, *P&O's Canberra,* London: Kingfisher Railway Publications, 1989.

——, *Twentieth Century Passenger Ships of the P&O,* Wellingborough: Stephens, 1985.

Padfield, Peter, *Beneath the House Flag of the P&O,* London: Hutchinson, 1981.

Parker, John G., ''Honing P&O's Interests,'' *Traffic World,* February 14, 2000, pp. 35–36.

Prada, Paulo, ''P&O to Spin Off Its Cruise Unit, Plans London, Big Board Listings,'' *Wall Street Journal,* February 4, 2000, p. A12.

Rabson, Stephen, and Kevin O'Donoghue, *P&O: A Fleet History,* World Ship Society, 1988.

Rose, Matthew, and Charles Goldsmith, ''Two Ferry Operators Look to Compete with Eurotunnel by Merging Operations,'' *Wall Street Journal,* October 7, 1996, p. B13I.

—Debra Johnson
—updated by David E. Salamie

PepsiCo, Inc.

700 Anderson Hill Road
Purchase, New York 10577-1444
U.S.A.
Telephone: (914) 253-2000
Fax: (914) 253-2070
Web site: http://www.pepsico.com

Public Company
Incorporated: 1965
Employees: 118,000
Sales: $20.37 billion (1999)
Stock Exchanges: New York Chicago Swiss Amsterdam Tokyo
Ticker Symbol: PEP
NAIC: 311411 Frozen Fruit, Juice, and Vegetable Manufacturing; 311919 Other Snack Food Manufacturing; 311821 Cookie and Cracker Manufacturing; 311930 Flavoring Syrup and Concentrate Manufacturing; 312111 Soft Drink Manufacturing; 312112 Bottled Water Manufacturing

PepsiCo, Inc. is one of the world's top consumer product companies with many of the world's most important and valuable trademarks. Its Pepsi-Cola Company division is the second largest soft drink business in the world, with a 21 percent share of the carbonated soft drink market worldwide and 29 percent in the United States. Three of its brands—Pepsi-Cola, Mountain Dew, and Diet Pepsi—are among the top ten soft drinks in the U.S. market. The Frito-Lay Company division is by far the world leader in salty snacks, holding a 40 percent market share and an even more staggering 56 percent share of the U.S. market. In the United States, Frito-Lay is nine times the size of its nearest competitor and sells nine of the top ten snack chip brands in the supermarket channel, including Lay's, Doritos, Tostitos, Ruffles, Fritos, and Chee-tos. Frito-Lay generates more than 60 percent of PepsiCo's net sales and more than two-thirds of the parent company's operating profits. The company's third division, Tropicana Products, Inc., is the world leader in juice sales and holds a dominant 41 percent of the U.S. chilled orange juice market. On a worldwide basis, PepsiCo's product portfolio includes 16 brands that generate more than $500 million in sales each year, ten of which generate more than $1 billion annually. Overall, PepsiCo garners about 35 percent of its retail sales outside the United States, with Pepsi-Cola brands marketed in about 160 countries, Frito-Lay in more than 40, and Tropicana in approximately 50. As 2001 began, PepsiCo was on the verge of adding to its food and drink empire the brands of the Quaker Oats Company, which include Gatorade sports drink, Quaker oatmeal, and Cap'n Crunch, Life, and other ready-to-eat cereals.

When Caleb D. Bradham concocted a new cola drink in the 1890s, his friends' enthusiastic response convinced him that he had created a commercially viable product. For 20 years, ''Doc'' Bradham prospered from his Pepsi-Cola sales. Eventually, he was faced with a dilemma; the crucial decision he made turned out to be the wrong one and he was forced to sell. But his successors fared no better and it was not until the end of the 1930s that Pepsi-Cola again became profitable. Seventy years later, PepsiCo, Inc. was a mammoth multinational supplier of soft drinks, juices, and snack food. PepsiCo's advance to that level was almost entirely the result of its management style and the phenomenal success of its television advertising.

Ups and Downs in the Early Years

Doc Bradham, like countless other entrepreneurs across the United States, was trying to create a cola drink similar in taste to Coca-Cola, which by 1895 was selling well in every state of the union. On August 28, 1898, at his pharmacy in New Bern, North Carolina, Bradham gave the name Pepsi-Cola to his most popular flavored soda. Formerly known as Brad's Drink, the new cola beverage was a syrup of sugar, vanilla, oils, cola nuts, and other flavorings diluted in carbonated water. The enterprising pharmacist followed Coca-Cola's method of selling the concentrate to soda fountains; he mixed the syrup in his drugstore, then shipped it in barrels to the contracted fountain operators who added the soda water. He also bottled and sold the drink himself.

In 1902 Doc Bradham closed his drugstore to devote his attention to the thriving new business. The next year, he pat-

Company Perspectives:

PepsiCo's overall mission is to increase the value of our shareholder's investment. We do this through sales growth, cost controls and wise investment of resources. We believe our commercial success depends upon offering quality and value to our consumers and customers; providing products that are safe, wholesome, economically efficient and environmentally sound; and providing a fair return to our investors while adhering to the highest standards of integrity.

ented the Pepsi-Cola trademark, ran his first advertisement in a local paper, and moved the bottling and syrup-making operations to a custom-built factory. Almost 20,000 gallons of Pepsi-Cola syrup were produced in 1904.

Again following the successful methods of the Coca-Cola Company, Bradham began to establish a network of bottling franchises. Entrepreneurs anxious to enter the increasingly popular soft drink business set themselves up as bottlers and contracted with Bradham to buy his syrup and sell nothing but Pepsi. With little cash outlay, Pepsi-Cola reached a much wider market. Bradham's first two bottling franchises, both in North Carolina, commenced operation in 1905. By 1907, Pepsi-Cola had signed agreements with 40 bottlers; over the next three years, the number grew to 250 and annual production of the syrup exceeded one million gallons.

Pepsi-Cola's growth continued until World War I, when sugar, then the main ingredient of all flavored sodas, was rationed. Soft drink producers were forced to cut back until sugar rationing ended. The wartime set price of sugar—5.5 cents per pound—rocketed after controls were lifted to as much as 26.5 cents per pound in 1920. Bradham, like his rivals, had to decide whether to halt production and sit tight in the hope that prices would soon drop, or stockpile the precious commodity as a precaution against even higher prices; he chose the latter course. But unfortunately for him the market was saturated by the end of 1920 and sugar prices plunged to a low of two cents per pound.

Bradham never recovered. After several abortive attempts to reorganize, only two of the bottling plants remained open. In a last ditch effort, he enlisted the help of Roy C. Megargel, a Wall Street investment banker. Very few people, however, were willing to invest in the business and it went bankrupt in 1923. The assets were sold and Megargel purchased the company trademark, giving him the rights to the Pepsi-Cola formula. Doc Bradham went back to his drug dispensary and died 11 years later.

Megargel reorganized the firm as the National Pepsi-Cola Company in 1928, but after three years of continuous losses he had to declare bankruptcy. That same year, 1931, Megargel met Charles G. Guth, a somewhat autocratic businessman who had recently taken over as president of Loft Inc., a New York-based candy and fountain store concern. Guth had fallen out with Coca-Cola for refusing the company a wholesaler discount and he was on the lookout for a new soft drink. He signed an agreement with Megargel to resurrect the Pepsi-Cola company, and acquired 80 percent of the new shares, ostensibly for himself. Then, having modified the syrup formula, he canceled Loft's contract with Coca-Cola and introduced Pepsi-Cola, whose name was often shortened to Pepsi.

Loft's customers were wary of the brand switch and in the first year of Pepsi sales the company's soft drink turnover was down by a third. By the end of 1933, Guth bought out Megargel and owned 91 percent of the insolvent company. Resistance to Pepsi in the Loft stores tailed off in 1934, and Guth decided to further improve sales by offering 12-ounce bottles of Pepsi for a nickel—the same price as six ounces of Coke. The Depression-weary people of Baltimore—where the 12-ounce bottles were first introduced—were ready for a bargain and Pepsi-Cola sales increased dramatically.

Guth soon took steps to internationalize Pepsi-Cola, establishing the Pepsi-Cola Company of Canada in 1934 and in the following year forming Compania Pepsi-Cola de Cuba. He also moved the entire American operation to Long Island City, New York, and set up national territorial boundaries for the bottling franchises. In 1936, Pepsi-Cola Ltd. of London commenced business.

Guth's ownership of the Pepsi-Cola Company was challenged that same year by Loft Inc. In a complex arrangement, Guth had organized Pepsi-Cola as an independent corporation, but he had run it with Loft's employees and money. After three years of litigation, the court upheld Loft's contention and Guth had to step down, although he was retained as an adviser. James W. Carkner was elected president of the company, now a subsidiary of Loft Inc., but Carkner was soon replaced by Walter S. Mack, Jr., an executive from the Phoenix Securities Corporation.

Mack established a board of directors with real voting powers to ensure that no one person would be able to wield control as Guth had done. From the start, Mack's aim was to promote Pepsi to the hilt so that it might replace Coca-Cola as the world's best-selling soft drink. The advertising agency Mack hired worked wonders. In 1939, a Pepsi radio jingle—the first one to be aired nationally—caught the public's attention: "Pepsi-Cola hits the spot. Twelve full ounces, that's a lot. Twice as much for a nickel, too. Pepsi-Cola is the drink for you." The jingle, sung to the tune of the old British hunting song "D'Ye Ken John Peel," became an advertising hallmark; no one was more impressed, or concerned, than the executives at Coca-Cola.

In 1940, with foreign expansion continuing strongly, Loft Inc. made plans to merge with its Pepsi-Cola subsidiary. The new firm, formed in 1941, used the name Pepsi-Cola Company since it was so well-known. Pepsi's stock was listed on the New York Stock Exchange for the first time.

Sugar rationing was even more severe during World War II, but this time the company fared better; indeed, the sugar plantation Pepsi-Cola acquired in Cuba became a most successful investment. But as inflation spiraled in the postwar U.S. economy, sales of soft drinks fell. The public needed time to get used to paying six or seven cents for a bottle of Pepsi which, as they remembered from the jingle, had always been a nickel. Profits in 1948 were down $3.6 million from the year before.

In other respects, 1948 was a notable year. Pepsi moved its corporate headquarters across the East River to midtown Man-

Key Dates:

1898: Pharmacist Caleb D. Bradham begins selling a cola beverage called Pepsi-Cola.
1905: Bradham begins establishing a network of bottling franchises.
1923: Bradham's company goes bankrupt.
1928: Roy C. Megargel reorganizes the firm as the National Pepsi-Cola Company.
1931: Company again goes bankrupt and is resurrected by the president of Loft Inc., Charles G. Guth.
1933: The size of Pepsi bottles is doubled, increasing sales dramatically.
1936: Pepsi-Cola Company becomes a subsidiary of Loft.
1939: First national radio advertising of the Pepsi brand.
1941: Loft and Pepsi-Cola merge, the new firm using the name Pepsi-Cola Company.
1964: Diet Pepsi debuts; Mountain Dew is acquired from Tip Corporation.
1965: Pepsi-Cola merges with Frito-Lay to form PepsiCo, Inc., with the two predecessors becoming divisions.
1967: Frito-Lay introduces Doritos tortilla chips to the national U.S. market.
1977: PepsiCo acquires Taco Bell.
1978: PepsiCo acquires Pizza Hut.
1981: Frito-Lay introduces Tostitos tortilla chips.
1986: The Kentucky Fried Chicken (KFC) chain is acquired.
1997: Taco Bell, Pizza Hut, and KFC are spun off into a new company called Tricon Global Restaurants.
1998: PepsiCo acquires Tropicana Products for $3.3 billion.
1999: Pepsi Bottling Group is spun off to the public, with PepsiCo retaining a 35 percent stake.
2000: PepsiCo reaches an agreement to acquire the Quaker Oats Company for $13.4 billion.

hattan, and for the first time the drink was sold in cans. The decision to start canning, while absolutely right for Pepsi-Cola and other soft drink companies, upset the franchised bottlers, who had invested heavily in equipment. However, another decision at Pepsi-Cola—to ignore the burgeoning vending machine market because of the necessarily large capital outlay—proved to be a costly mistake. The company had to learn the hard way that as canned drinks gained a larger share of the market, vending machine sales would become increasingly important.

1950s: The Steele and Crawford Era

Walter Mack was appointed company chairman in 1950, and a former Coca-Cola vice-president of sales, Alfred N. Steele, took over as president and chief executive officer, bringing 15 other Coke executives with him. Steele continued the policy of management decentralization by giving broader powers to regional vice-presidents, and he placed Herbert Barnet in charge of Pepsi's financial operations. Steele's outstanding contribution, however, was in marketing. He launched an extensive advertising campaign with the slogan "Be Sociable, Have a Pepsi." The new television medium provided a perfect forum; Pepsi advertisements presented young Americans drinking "The Light Refreshment" and having fun.

By the time Alfred Steele married movie star Joan Crawford in 1954, a transformation of the company was well underway. Crawford's adopted daughter, Christina, noted in her best-seller *Mommie Dearest:* "[Steele had] driven Pepsi into national prominence and distribution, second only to his former employer, Coca-Cola. Pepsi was giving Coke a run for its money in every nook and hamlet of America. Al Steele welded a national network of bottlers together, standardized the syrup formula . . . , brought the distinctive logo into mass consciousness, and was on the brink of going international." In fact, Pepsi-Cola International Ltd. was formed shortly after Steele's marriage.

Joan Crawford became the personification of Pepsi's new and glamorous image. She invariably kept a bottle of Pepsi at hand during press conferences and mentioned the product at interviews and on talk shows; on occasion she even arranged for Pepsi trucks and vending machines to feature in background shots of her movies. The actress also worked hard to spread the Pepsi word overseas and accompanied her husband, now chairman of the board, on his 1957 tour of Europe and Africa, where bottling plants were being established.

Steele died suddenly of a heart attack in the spring of 1959. Herbert Barnet succeeded him as chairman and Joan Crawford was elected a board member. Pepsi-Cola profits had fallen to a postwar low of $1.3 million in 1950 when Steele joined the company, but with the proliferation of supermarkets during the decade and the developments in overseas business, profits reached $14.2 million in 1960. By that time, young adults had become a major target of soft drink manufacturers and Pepsi's advertisements were aimed at "Those who think young."

Al Steele and Joan Crawford had been superb cheerleaders, but a stunt pulled in 1959 by Donald M. Kendall, head of Pepsi-Cola International, is still regarded as one of the great coups in the annals of advertising. Kendall attended the Moscow Trade Fair that year and persuaded U.S. Vice-President Richard Nixon to stop by the Pepsi booth with Nikita Khrushchev, the Soviet premier. As the cameras flashed, Khrushchev quenched his thirst with Pepsi and the grinning U.S. Vice-President stood in attendance. The next day, newspapers around the world featured photographs of the happy couple, complete with Pepsi bottle.

1960s and 1970s: The Pepsi Generation, Diversification

By 1963, Kendall was presiding over the Pepsi empire. His rise to the top of the company was legendary. He had been an amateur boxing champion in his youth and joined the company as a production line worker in 1947 after a stint in the U.S. Navy. He was later promoted to syrup sales where it quickly became apparent that he was destined for higher office. Ever pugnacious, Kendall has been described as abrasive and ruthlessly ambitious; beleaguered Pepsi executives secretly referred to him as White Fang. Under his long reign, the company's fortunes skyrocketed.

Pepsi-Cola's remarkable successes in the 1960s and 1970s were the result of five distinct policies, all of which Kendall and his crew pursued diligently: advertising on a massive, unprecedented scale; introducing new brands of soft drinks; leading the industry in packaging innovations; expanding overseas; and, through acquisitions, diversifying their product line.

The postwar baby boomers were in their mid- to late teens by the time Kendall came to power. ''Pepsi was there,'' states a recent company flyer, ''to claim these kids for our own.'' These ''kids'' became the ''Pepsi Generation.'' In the late 1960s Pepsi was the ''Taste that beats the others cold.'' Viewers were advised ''You've got a lot to live. Pepsi's got a lot to give.'' By the early 1970s, the appeal was to ''Join the Pepsi people, feelin' free.'' In mid-decade an American catchphrase was given a company twist with ''Have a Pepsi Day,'' and the 1970s ended on the note ''Catch the Pepsi Spirit!''

The Pepsi Generation wanted variety and Pepsi was happy to oblige. Company brands introduced in the 1960s included Patio soft drinks, Teem, Tropic Surf, Diet Pepsi—the first nationally distributed diet soda, introduced in 1964—and Mountain Dew, acquired from the Tip Corporation, also in 1964. Pepsi Light, a diet cola with a hint of lemon, made its debut in 1975, and a few years later Pepsi tested the market with Aspen apple soda and On-Tap root beer. The company also introduced greater variety into the packaging of its products. Soon after Kendall's accession, the 12-ounce bottle was phased out in favor of the 16-ounce size, and in the 1970s Pepsi-Cola became the first American company to introduce one-and-a-half and two-liter bottles; it also began to package its sodas in sturdy, lightweight plastic bottles. By the end of the decade, Pepsi had added 12-pack cans to its growing array of packaging options.

The company's expansion beyond the soft drink market began in 1965 when Kendall met Herman Lay, the owner of Frito-Lay, at a grocer's convention. Kendall arranged a merger with this Dallas-based snack food manufacturer and formed PepsiCo, Inc. Herman Lay retired soon thereafter but retained his substantial PepsiCo shareholding. The value of this stock increased dramatically as Frito-Lay products were introduced to Pepsi's nationwide market. At the time of the merger, key Frito-Lay brands included Fritos corn chips (created in 1932), Lay's potato chips (1938), Chee-tos cheese-flavored snacks (1948), Ruffles potato chips (1958), and Rold Gold pretzels (acquired by Frito-Lay in 1961). Doritos tortilla chips were introduced nationally in 1967. The addition of Frito-Lay helped PepsiCo achieve $1 billion in sales for the first time in 1970. That same year, the corporation moved into its new world headquarters in Purchase, New York.

During the 1970s, Kendall acquired two well-known fast-food restaurant chains, Taco Bell, in 1977, and Pizza Hut, in 1978; naturally, these new subsidiaries became major outlets for Pepsi products. But Kendall also diversified outside the food and drink industry, bringing North American Van Lines (acquired in 1968), Lee Way Motor Freight, and Wilson Sporting Goods into the PepsiCo empire.

Overseas developments continued apace throughout Kendall's tenure. Building on his famous Soviet achievement, he negotiated a trade agreement with the U.S.S.R. in 1972; the first Pepsi plant opened there two years later. Gains were also made in the Middle East and Latin America, but Coca-Cola, the major rival, retained its dominant position in Europe and throughout much of Asia.

1980s Highlighted by the Cola Wars

By the time PepsiCo greeted the 1980s with the slogan ''Pepsi's got your taste for life!,'' Kendall was busy arranging for China to get that taste too; production began there in 1983. Kendall put his seal of approval on several other major developments in the early 1980s, including the introduction of Pepsi Free, a non-caffeine cola, and Slice, the first widely distributed soft drink to contain real fruit juice (lemon and lime). The latter drink was aimed at the growing 7-Up and Sprite market. Additionally, Diet Pepsi was reformulated using a blend of saccharin and aspartame (NutraSweet). ''Pepsi Now!'' was the cry of company commercials, and this was interspersed with ''Taste, Improved by Diet Pepsi.'' On the Frito-Lay side, meantime, the Tostitos brand of crispy round tortilla chips was introduced in 1981.

In 1983 the company claimed a significant share of the fast-food soft drink market when Burger King began selling Pepsi products. A year later, mindful of the industry axiom that there is virtually no limit to the amount a consumer will buy once the decision to buy has been made, PepsiCo introduced the 3-liter container.

By the mid-1980s, the Pepsi Generation was over the hill. Kendall's ad agency spared no expense in heralding Pepsi as ''The Choice of a New Generation,'' using the talents of superstar Michael Jackson, singer Lionel Richie, and the Puerto Rican teenage group Menudo. Michael Jackson's ads were smash hits and enjoyed the highest exposure of any American television commercial to date. The company's high profile and powerful presence in all of the soft drink markets—direct results of Kendall's strategies—helped it to weather the somewhat uncertain economic situation of the time.

On only one front had Kendall's efforts failed to produce satisfactory results. Experience showed that for all its expertise, PepsiCo simply did not have the managerial experience required to run its subsidiaries outside the food and drink industries. A van line, a motor freight concern, and a sporting goods firm were indeed odd companies for a soft drink enterprise; and Kendall auctioned off these strange and ailing bedfellows, vowing never again to go courting in unfamiliar territories.

With his house in excellent order, the PepsiCo mogul began to prepare for his retirement. He had bullied and cajoled a generation of Pepsi executives and guided them ever upward on the steep slopes of Pepsi profits. But he had one last task: to lead PepsiCo to victory in the Cola Wars.

Hostilities commenced soon after the Coca-Cola Company changed its syrup recipe in the summer of 1985 and with much fanfare introduced New Coke. Pepsi, caught napping, claimed that Coca-Cola's reformulated drink failed to meet with consumer approval and pointed to their own flourishing sales. But serious fans of the original Coke were not about to switch to Pepsi and demanded that their favorite refreshment be restored. When blindfolded, however, it became manifestly apparent that these diehards could rarely tell the difference between Old Coke, New Coke, and Pepsi; indeed, more often than not, they got it wrong. In any event, the Coca-Cola Company acceded to the public clamor for the original Coke and remarketed it as Coca-Cola Classic alongside its new cola.

Some advertising analysts believed that the entire ''conflict'' was a clever publicity ploy on the part of Coca-Cola to demonstrate the preeminence of its original concoction (''It's the Real Thing!''), while introducing a new cola—allegedly a Pepsi taste-alike—to win the hearts of waverers. More interesting perhaps than the possible differences between the colas were the very real differences in people's reactions. Four discrete fields were identified by Roger Enrico and Jesse Kornbluth in their book, *The Other Guy Blinked: How Pepsi Won the Cola Wars:* the totally wowed (possibly caffeine-induced); the rather amused; the slightly irritated; and the distinctly bored.

The latter group must have nodded off in front of their television sets when Pepsi took the Cola Wars beyond the firmament. ''One Giant Sip for Mankind,'' proclaimed the ads as a Pepsi ''space can'' was opened up aboard the U.S. space shuttle *Challenger* in 1985. Presumably, had a regular can been used, Pepsi-Cola would have sloshed aimlessly around the gravity-free cabin. This scientific breakthrough, together with the almost obligatory hype and hoopla, and more mundane factors such as the continued expansion in PepsiCo's outlets, boosted sales to new heights, and Pepsi's ad agency glittered with accolades. The debate persisted, at least within Coke and Pepsi corporate offices, as to who won the Cola Wars. The answer appeared to be that there were no losers, only winners; but skirmishes would inevitably continue.

Late 1980s and Early 1990s: Focusing on International Growth and Diversification

D. Wayne Calloway replaced Donald M. Kendall as chairman and chief executive officer in 1986. Calloway had been instrumental in the success of Frito-Lay, helping it to become PepsiCo's most profitable division. The new chairman realized that his flagship Pepsi brand was not likely to win additional market share from Coca-Cola, and focused his efforts on international growth and diversification.

Calloway hoped to build on the phenomenal success of the Slice line of fruit juice beverages, which achieved $1 billion in sales and created a new beverage category within just two years of its 1984 introduction. From 1985 to 1993, PepsiCo introduced, acquired, or formed joint ventures to distribute nine beverages, including Lipton Original Iced Teas, Ocean Spray juices, All Sport drink, H2Oh! sparkling water, Avalon bottled water, and Mug root beer. Many of these products had a ''New Age'' light and healthy positioning, in line with consumer tastes, and higher net prices. In 1992, PepsiCo introduced Crystal Pepsi, a clear cola that, while still a traditional soda, also tried to capture the momentum of the ''New Age'' beverage trend.

In the restaurant segment, PepsiCo's 1986 purchase of Kentucky Fried Chicken (KFC) and 1990 acquisition of the Hot 'n Now hamburger chain continued its emphasis on value-priced fast foods. But the company strayed slightly from that formula with the 1992 and 1993 purchases of such full-service restaurants as California Pizza Kitchen, which specialized in creative wood-fired pizzas, Chevys, a Mexican-style chain, East Side Mario's Italian-style offerings, and D'Angelo Sandwich Shops.

Pepsi lost a powerful marketing tool in 1992, when Michael Jackson was accused of child molestation. Although the case was settled out of court, Pepsi dropped its contract with the entertainer. The firm launched its largest promotion ever in May 1992 with the ''Gotta Have It'' card, which offered discounts on the products of marketing partners Reebok sporting goods, Continental Airlines, and the MCI long distance company telephone. The company also launched a new marketing (or, as the company phrased it, ''product quality'') initiative early in 1994, when it announced that packaged carbonated soft drink products sold in the United States would voluntarily be marked with a ''Best if Consumed By'' date.

Although Pepsi had commenced international expansion during the 1950s, it had long trailed Coca-Cola's dramatic and overwhelming conquest of international markets. In 1990, CEO Calloway pledged up to $1 billion for overseas development, with the goal of increasing international volume 150 percent by 1995. At that time, Coke held 50 percent of the European soft drink market, while Pepsi claimed a meager 10 percent. But Pepsi's advantage was that it could compete in other, less saturated segments. The company's biggest challenge to expanding its restaurant division was affordability. PepsiCo noted that, while it took the average U.S. worker just 15 minutes to earn enough to enjoy a meal in one of the firm's restaurants, it would take an Australian 25 minutes to achieve a similar goal. Pepsi still had other options, however. In 1992, for example, the company forged a joint venture with General Mills called Snack Ventures Europe which emerged as the largest firm in the $17 billion market. By 1993, PepsiCo had invested over $5 billion in international businesses, and its international sales comprised 27 percent, or $6.71 billion, of total annual sales.

In January 1992, Calloway was credited by *Business Week* magazine with emerging from the long shadow cast by his predecessor ''to put together five impressive years of 20 percent compound earnings growth, doubling sales and nearly tripling the company's value on the stock market.'' Calloway also worked to reshape PepsiCo's corporate culture by fostering personal responsibility and a decentralized, flexible management style.

Mid-to-Late 1990s: The Enrico Restructuring

Calloway, who was battling prostate cancer, retired as CEO in April 1996 and was replaced by Roger A. Enrico, who became chairman as well later in the year (Calloway died in July 1998). Since joining Frito-Lay's marketing department in 1971, Enrico had stints heading up both Pepsi-Cola and Frito-Lay before becoming head of the restaurants division in 1994. He engineered a quick turnaround of the struggling chains by changing the overall strategy, for example adopting more franchising of units rather than company ownership. Under Enrico, the marketing of new concepts was also emphasized, with one notable success being the introduction of stuffed-crust pizza at Pizza Hut.

After taking over leadership of PepsiCo, Enrico quickly faced major problems in the overseas beverages operations, including big losses that were posted by its large Latin American bottler and the defection of its Venezuelan partner to Coca-Cola. PepsiCo ended up taking $576 million in special charges related to international writeoffs and restructuring, and its international arm posted a huge operating loss of $846 million, depressing 1996 profits. Among the moves initiated to turn around the international beverage operations, which faced brutal competition from the entrenched and better organized Coca-Cola, was to increase emphasis on emerging markets, such as India, China, Eastern Europe, and Russia, where Coke had a less formidable presence, and to rely less on bottling joint ventures and more on Pepsi- or franchise-owned bottling operations.

Another area of concern was the restaurant division, which had consistently been the PepsiCo laggard in terms of performance. Enrico concluded that in order to revitalize the beverage division and to take advantage of the surging Frito-Lay, which already accounted for 43 percent of PepsiCo's operating profits, the restaurants had to go. Hot 'n Now and the casual dining chains were soon sold off, and in January 1997 PepsiCo announced that it would spin off its three fast-food chains into a separate publicly traded company. The spinoff was completed in October 1997 with the formation of Tricon Global Restaurants, Inc., consisting of the Taco Bell, Pizza Hut, and KFC chains. The exit from restaurants removed one obstacle facing Pepsi in its battle with Coke: that most large fast-food chains had been reluctant to carry Pepsi beverages, not wanting to support the parent of a major competitor. Consequently, Coke held a huge market share advantage over Pepsi in the fast-food channel. Pepsi subsequently made some inroads, for example, in 1999 sealing a ten-year deal with the 11,500-plus-outlet Subway chain.

Enrico placed more emphasis, however, on building sales of Pepsi in its core supermarket channel. In this regard, he launched an initiative called "Power of One" that aimed to take advantage of the synergies between Frito-Lay's salty snacks and the beverages of Pepsi-Cola. This strategy involved persuading grocery retailers to move soft drinks next to snacks, the pitch being that such a placement would increase supermarket sales. In the process, PepsiCo would gain sales of both snacks and beverages while Coca-Cola could only benefit in the latter area. Power of One harkened back to the original rationale for the merger of Pepsi-Cola and Frito-Lay. At the time, the head of Pepsi, Kendall, had told Frito-Lay's leader, Herman W. Lay: "You make them thirsty, and I'll give them something to drink." The promise of this seemingly ideal marriage had never really been achieved, however, until the Power of One campaign, which in 1999 helped increase Frito-Lay's market share by two percentage points and boosted Pepsi's volume by 0.6 percent.

In the meantime, Enrico was active on a number of other fronts. The company in 1997 nationally launched the Aquafina bottled water brand, which quickly gained the number one position in a fast-growing sector. In a move into the nonsalty snack category, Frito-Lay acquired the venerable Cracker Jack brand that year, and subsequently bolstered the brand through renewed advertising, a new four-ounce-bag package, the addition of more peanuts, the inclusion of better prizes, and the strength of Frito-Lay's vast distribution network. In August 1998 PepsiCo opened up another front in its ongoing war with Coca-Cola by acquiring juice-maker Tropicana Products, Inc. from the Seagram Company, Ltd. for $3.3 billion in cash—the largest acquisition in PepsiCo history. Coca-Cola had been the owner of Tropicana's arch-rival, Minute Maid, since 1960, but Tropicana was the clear world juice leader, led by the flagship Tropicana Pure Premium brand. Tropicana had a dominating 41 percent share of the fast-growing chilled orange juice market in the United States. The brand was also attractive for its growth potential; not only were sales of juice growing at a much faster rate than the stagnating carbonated beverage sector, there was also great potential for brand growth overseas. Psychologically, the acquisition also provided PepsiCo with something it very much needed: it could boast of holding at least dominant position over Coca-Cola.

In 1999 PepsiCo divested itself of another low-margin, capital-intensive business when it spun off Pepsi Bottling Group, the largest Pepsi bottler in the world, to the public in a $2.3 billion IPO. PepsiCo retained a 35 percent stake. PepsiCo was now focused exclusively on the less capital-intensive businesses of beverages and snack foods.

On the beverage side, Enrico, who had gained a reputation as a master marketer, spearheaded a bolder advertising strategy for the flagship Pepsi brand. In 1999, Pepsi-Cola was the exclusive global beverage partner for the movie blockbuster *Star Wars, Episode 1: The Phantom Menace.* The company also revived the old "Pepsi Challenge" campaign of the 1970s with the new Pepsi One diet drink facing off against Diet Coke. Pepsi's "Joy of Cola" advertising campaign was gaining accolades and in 2000 captured renewed attention following the signing of a string of celebrities to endorsement deals, including singer Faith Hill and baseball stars Sammy Sosa and Ken Griffey, Jr. Pepsi also greatly increased the number of vending machines it had planted around the United States, making a renewed push to gain on Coke in another area where the arch-enemy had long dominated.

By the end of 1999, after three and one-half years at the helm, Enrico had clearly turned PepsiCo into a stronger, much more focused, and better performing firm. Although revenues were more than one-third lower due to the divestments, earnings were higher by more than $100 million. Operating margins had increased from 10 percent to 15 percent, while return on invested capital grew from 15 percent to 20 percent. Net debt had been slashed from $8 billion to $2 billion. During 1999, Steve Reinemund was named president and COO of PepsiCo. Reinemund had headed Pizza Hut from 1986 to 1992 then was placed in charge of Frito-Lay. In the latter position, he oversaw a division whose sales increased 10 percent per year on average and whose profits doubled. During his tenure, Frito-Lay's share of the U.S. salty snack sector jumped from 40 to 60 percent.

Turning Acquisitive in the Early 21st Century

In October 2000 Enrico announced that he intended to vacate his position as CEO by the end of 2001 and his position as chairman by year-end 2002. Reinemund was named the heir apparent. Also that month, PepsiCo reached an agreement to acquire a majority stake in South Beach Beverage Company, maker of the SoBe brand. Popular with young consumers, the SoBe drink line featured herbal ingredients and was the fastest growing brand in the burgeoning noncarbonated alternative beverage sector.

An even more tempting target soon attracted PepsiCo's attention: the powerhouse Gatorade brand owned by the Quaker

Oats Company. Gatorade held an astounding 83.6 percent of the U.S. retail market for sports drinks and was the world leader in that segment with annual sales of about $2 billion. PepsiCo entered into talks with Quaker about acquiring the company for about $14 billion in stock, but by early November the two sides had failed to reach an agreement. Coca-Cola and Groupe Danone quickly came forward to discuss acquiring Quaker. Coke came exceedingly close to signing a $15.75 billion takeover agreement, but the company's board pulled the plug on the deal at the last minute. Danone soon bowed out as well. At that point, PepsiCo reentered the picture, and in early December the firm announced that it agreed to acquire Quaker Oats for $13.4 billion in stock. This appeared to be quite a coup for PepsiCo as it would not only bring on board the valuable Gatorade brand and make PepsiCo the clear leader in the fast-growing non-carbonated beverage category, it would also add Quaker's small but growing snack business, which included granola and other bars as well as rice cakes. Quaker's non-snack food brands—which included the flagship Quaker oatmeal, Life and Cap'n Crunch cereals, Rice-a-Roni, and Aunt Jemima syrup—did not fit as neatly into the PepsiCo portfolio but were highly profitable and could eventually be divested if desired. In conjunction with the acquisition announcement, Enrico said that upon completion of the merger, he and the head of Quaker, Robert S. Morrison, would become vice-chairmen of PepsiCo, Morrison would also remain chairman, president, and CEO of Quaker, and Reinemund would become chairman and CEO of PepsiCo, thereby accelerating the management transition. At that same time, PepsiCo's CFO, Indra Nooyi, who was the highest ranking Indian-born woman in corporate America, would become president and CFO. It seemed likely that this new management team would take PepsiCo to new heights in the early 21st century and that the company would continue to be a more and more formidable challenger to arch-rival Coca-Cola.

Principal Divisions

Frito-Lay Company; Pepsi-Cola Company; Tropicana Products, Inc.

Principal Competitors

Borden, Inc.; Cadbury Schweppes plc; Campbell Soup Company; Chiquita Brands International, Inc.; The Coca-Cola Company; ConAgra Foods, Inc.; Cott Corporation; Groupe Danone; General Mills, Inc.; Golden Enterprises, Inc.; Keebler Foods Company; Kraft Foods, Inc.; Nestlé S.A.; Ocean Spray Cranberries, Inc.; The Procter & Gamble Company.

Further Reading

''Boards of Pepsi-Cola and Frito-Lay Approve Merging As PepsiCo,'' *Wall Street Journal,* February 26, 1965, p. 8.

Bongiorno, Lori, ''The Pepsi Regeneration,'' *Business Week,* March 11, 1996, pp. 70+.

Byrne, John A., ''PepsiCo's New Formula,'' *Business Week,* April 10, 2000, pp. 172–76+.

Cappelli, Peter, and Harbir Singh, ''Do Pepsi and Oatmeal Mix?,'' *Wall Street Journal,* December 5, 2000, p. A26.

Collins, Glenn, ''PepsiCo Pushes a Star Performer,'' *New York Times,* November 3, 1994, pp. D1, D8.

Collins, Glenn, and Stephanie Strom, ''Can Pepsi Become the Coke of Snacks?,'' *New York Times,* November 3, 1996.

De Lisser, Eleena, ''Pepsi Has Lost Its Midas Touch in Restaurants,'' *Wall Street Journal,* July 18, 1994, p. B1.

Deogun, Nikhil, ''Pepsi Challenge: Can Company's Brass Mute Flashy Culture and Make Profits Fizz?,'' *Wall Street Journal,* August 8, 1997, pp. A1+.

——, ''PepsiCo to Buy Quaker for $13.4 Billion,'' *Wall Street Journal,* December 4, 2000, pp. A3, A8.

——, ''PepsiCo to Reorganize U.S. Operations,'' *Wall Street Journal,* June 2, 1997, p. A3.

——, ''Revamped PepsiCo Still Needs to Conquer Wall Street,'' *Wall Street Journal,* July 27, 1998, p. B4.

Deogun, Nikhil, Betsy McKay, and Jonathan Eig, ''PepsiCo Aborts a Play for Quaker Oats,'' *Wall Street Journal,* November 3, 2000, p. A3.

Dietz, Lawrence, *Soda Pop: The History, Advertising, Art, and Memorabilia of Soft Drinks in America,* New York: Simon and Schuster, 1973, 184 p.

Duncan, Amy, ''Pepsi's Marketing Market: Why Nobody Does It Better,'' *Business Week,* February 10, 1986.

Enrico, Roger, and Jesse Kornbluth, *The Other Guy Blinked: How Pepsi Won the Cola Wars,* New York: Bantam, 1986, 280 p.

Fisher, Anne B., ''Peering Past Pepsico's Bad News,'' *Fortune,* November 14, 1983, pp. 124+.

Frank, Robert, ''PepsiCo's Critics Worry the Glass Is Still Half Empty,'' *Wall Street Journal,* September 30, 1996, p. B4.

Gibney, Frank, Jr., ''Pepsi Gets Back in the Game,'' *Time,* April 26, 1999.

''Gulp, Munch & Merge,'' *Forbes,* July 15, 1968, pp. 20–21.

''Herman W. Lay of PepsiCo,'' *Nation's Business,* September 1969, pp. 88–89, 92–95.

''Holders of Pepsi-Cola and Frito-Lay Approve Proposal for Merger,'' *Wall Street Journal,* June 9, 1965, p. 8.

Kraar, Louis, ''Pepsi's Pitch to Quench Chinese Thirsts,'' *Fortune,* March 17, 1986.

Lousi, J.C., and Harvey Z. Yazijian, *The Cola Wars,* New York: Everest House, 1980, 386 p.

Mack, Walter, and Peter Buckley, *No Time Lost,* New York: Atheneum, 1982, 211 p.

Martin, Milward W., *Twelve Full Ounces,* New York: Holt Rinehart, 1962, 136 p.

McCarthy, Michael J., ''Added Fizz: Pepsi Is Going Better with Its Fast Foods and Frito-Lay Snacks,'' *Wall Street Journal,* June 13, 1991, pp. A1+.

McKay, Betsy, ''Juices Up: Pepsi Edges Past Coke and It Has Nothing to Do with Cola,'' *Wall Street Journal,* November 6, 2000, pp. A1+.

McKay, Betsy, and Jonathan Eig, ''PepsiCo Hopes to Feast on Profits from Quaker Snacks,'' *Wall Street Journal,* December 4, 2000, p. B4.

McKay, Betsy, and Nikhil Deogun, ''PepsiCo's Enrico to Pass CEO Baton to His Number Two by End of Next Year,'' *Wall Street Journal,* October 4, 2000, p. B1.

''PepsiCo—More Than Just 'Pepsi,' '' *Financial World,* November 4, 1970, pp. 5, 26.

''Pepsi's Sitting on Trop of the World After Making Juicy Deal with Seagram,'' *Beverage World,* August 15, 1998, p. 14.

Reeves, Scott, ''The Pepsi Challenge,'' *Barron's,* August 11, 1997, pp. 17–18.

Rothman, Andrea, ''Can Wayne Calloway Handle the Pepsi Challenge?,'' *Business Week,* January 27, 1992.

Sellers, Patricia, ''If It Ain't Broke, Fit It Anyway,'' *Fortune,* December 28, 1992, pp. 49+.

——, ''PepsiCo's New Generation,'' *Fortune,* April 1, 1996, pp. 110–13+.

——, ''Pepsi Opens a Second Front,'' *Fortune,* August 8, 1994, pp. 70–76.

——, "Why Pepsi Needs to Become More Like Coke," *Fortune,* March 3, 1997, pp. 26–27.

Sparks, Debra, "Will Pepsi Take the Wall Street Challenge?," *Financial World,* April 8, 1996, pp. 26–29.

"Steady Gains for PepsiCo," *Financial World,* March 1, 1972, pp. 7, 19.

Stoddard, Bob, *Pepsi: 100 Years,* Los Angeles: General Publishing Group, 1997, 207 p.

"Wayne Calloway's Nonstop Cash Machine," *Forbes,* September 7, 1987.

"Who Acquired Who?," *Forbes,* April 1, 1967, p. 69.

Zellner, Wendy, "Frito-Lay Is Munching on the Competition," *Business Week,* August 24, 1992, pp. 52–53.

—April Dougal Gasbarre
—updated by David E. Salamie

Pez Candy, Inc.

35 Prindle Hill Road
Orange, Connecticut 06477
U.S.A.
Telephone: (203) 795-0531
Fax: (203) 799-1679
Web site: http://www.pezcandy.com

Private Company
Incorporated: 1953 as Pez-Haas Inc.
Employees: 200
Sales: $21 million (1999 est.)
NAIC: 31134 Nonchocolate Confectionary Manufacturing

Pez Candy, Inc. is the United States manufacturer and marketer of Pez candy. Pez is unique among candies because it is a combination candy and toy. The candy itself is fruit flavored and brick-shaped, designed to be inserted into a dispenser. The dispenser is a plastic rectangle topped with a head shaped like any of various fanciful characters. Some dispensers tie in with holidays, such as a witch for Halloween and Santa Claus for Christmas. The company often designs dispensers to tie in with blockbuster movies, as it did when it featured a series of character heads from *Star Wars.* The company has designed many Pez dispenser heads based on licensed Disney characters, as well as cartoon characters such as Porky Pig, Popeye, and the Teenage Mutant Ninja Turtles. Since the company began marketing the dispensers in 1955, it has produced hundreds of models. In the 1990s, the dispensers became the object of avid collectors. Pez Candy, Inc. manufactures the candy at its facility in Orange, Connecticut, while the dispensers are made in Hungary, China, and Slovenia. Pez candy enjoyed a heyday in the 1960s and 1970s. The company was more or less dormant in the 1980s, doing no advertising. The candy was rediscovered in the 1990s, and a mania for collecting the old dispensers fueled interest in the product.

Antecedents in Europe

The unusual candy named Pez was invented around 1927 by Eduard Haas III, the scion of a distinguished Austrian family of baking powder manufacturers. Eduard Haas I was a physician who seemed to have invented or at least pioneered baking powder, advocating it as a superior leavening that made pastries and cakes light enough even for patients suffering from stomach complaints. Haas's baking powder was one of many of the doctor's obsessions. Not all were so benign. He died suddenly as a result of medical experiments he performed on himself. His son, Eduard Haas II, had just begun his own medical career when his father died. Forced to support his family, the son left medicine and became a grocer, marketing his grandfather's baking powder as well as pre-measured cake mixes. It was his son, Eduard Haas III, who propelled the baking powder business to greater heights, and along the way developed Pez. Eduard Haas III used newspaper ads to market the cake mixes and baking powder he made by his grandfather's recipe. When he was just 18, in 1915, Haas III was granted a trademark for Hasin cake mix and a slogan proclaiming its health benefits. The Haas products, invented by a doctor, had a reputation for wholesomeness, and before World War I, Haas had distributed millions of recipe booklets and baking tips throughout Austria. The family business had become a thriving concern. The company faced difficulties following World War I, but was eventually operating three branch factories, and producing baking powder, cake mix, vanilla, blancmange powder, and Quittin, a substance that helped jams set.

Eduard Haas III was described by contemporaries as a health fanatic. He enjoyed sucking peppermints, finding them calming and refreshing. He considered sucking mints a vastly superior habit to smoking tobacco. Peppermints at the time were made by adding peppermint oil to boiled sugar, and they were sold through apothecaries. Haas had the idea of using his company's equipment to manufacture peppermints through a cold-press process, so that the costly peppermint flavoring oil would not evaporate. Haas set his company's chemists to experimenting some time in the early 1920s, and soon had a product that allegedly impressed friends and factory visitors so much that they begged to know where they could purchase it. Haas then set about finding a way to make the mints so that they would not have to be packed by hand. Using existing equipment that was designed to make effervescent drink cubes, Haas came up with the classic brick-shaped tablet. He named it Pez, based on the German word for peppermint, Pfefferminz.

Company Perspectives:

An integral part of the American scene for approximately 50 years, PEZ Candy continues to be enjoyed by generations of Americans. PEZ was first marketed as a compressed peppermint candy over 70 years ago in Vienna, Austria. The name PEZ was derived from the German word for peppermint . . . PfeffErminZ. Today, over 3 billion Pez Candies are consumed annually in the U.S.A. alone. With great tasting flavors and collectable dispensers, PEZ is more than just a candy . . . it's the pioneer of ''interactive candy'' that is both enjoyable to eat and fun to play with.

Pez soon spread across Europe, advertised by attractive ''Pez Girls.'' It was touted as an alternative to smoking, or at least a breath freshener for use after smoking. It was not a children's candy, but an adult product. One early slogan translates as ''Smoking prohibited. PEZing allowed.'' Pez was first sold in pocket-sized tins.

After World War II, the Haas Austrian factories had to be rebuilt, and some Haas products, including baking powder and blancmange mix, were temporarily prohibited. Pez though, survived. In 1948, Haas applied for a patent for a new kind of Pez container. This was a little rectangular box with a hinged lid, meant to mimic a cigarette lighter. This Pez box made its debut in Austria in 1949, and a U.S. patent for the device was granted in 1952.

U.S. Company Launched

Pez was known throughout Europe, and the name Pez was allegedly English, a claim that allowed Haas to sidestep rigorous Austrian packaging requirements. But the sweet was not sold in the United States. While economies across Europe were in ruins, the U.S. was booming. Consequently, in 1953 Eduard Haas III recruited an Austrian man of Czech heritage, Curt Allina, who had been raised in the United States, to head up an American marketing arm for Pez. Pez-Haas, Inc. was incorporated in 1953, with offices in New York. The company sold Pez candy through East Coast distributors, marketing it as a sophisticated adult treat. The early flavors were peppermint, lemon, and chlorophyll mint. The candy began its U.S. push with vigorous claims to its healthfulness. Pez was supposed to be good for your nerves, to restore confidence and self-esteem lost to bad breath, to stave off hunger pangs and so allow consumers to lose weight, and to stimulate the circulatory and respiratory systems and fight infections. The cigarette lighter-shaped dispenser was not only a trick to play on smokers asking for a light, but it was hygienic, allowing Pez users to give the candy to friends without touching it. As an item for adults, Pez was marketed at a much higher price than other candies. Candy bars in 1953 cost five cents, and Pez sold for 25 cents for a dispenser and two refills. But Pez did not catch on in the United States like Haas had hoped. By 1955, plans were underway to convert Pez to a genuine children's product. Instead of the strong peppermint and other adult flavors such as coffee and eucalpytus, Pez-Haas, Inc. began selling fruit flavors including orange and wild cherry. That same year saw the first toy-like dispensers. These were unlike the later headed dispensers, in that the whole body of the figure was molded. By 1957, the design was simplified to the head-only format. The first licensed character was the sailor cartoon character Popeye, who headed a Pez dispenser in 1958.

By 1960, all marketing of Pez in the United States was directed at children, and the old adult flavors and cigarette lighter-style dispenser were no longer available. The company ran television commercials on children's shows and offered children special premiums, such as a toy gun that shot Pez pellets, if they mailed in Pez wrappers and a small amount of cash. Pez was a success in the United States, soon selling beyond the East Coast and reaching the entire country. The company contracted with Disney to license its popular movie characters for Pez dispenser heads, and came up with a succession of original designs as well. The company moved its headquarters four times in the New York City area in the 1950s and 1960s, until it built a new facility in Orange, Connecticut, in 1974. The new headquarters also included a manufacturing facility. The dispensers continued to be manufactured abroad, in Austria, Yugoslavia, Portugal, and Hong Kong, but after the Connecticut plant was finished, the candy was made in the United States. Haas Foods continued to make and sell Pez candy and many other products in Europe, and Pez-Haas Inc. had exclusive rights to the U.S. market. By the start of the 1970s, the American company accounted for about 25 percent of Haas Foods' total worldwide sales and more than 50 percent of worldwide Pez sales.

Quiet Times in the 1970s and 1980s

Pez had taken off in the United States soon after it changed from an adult product to a candy aimed at children. It reached a nationwide market by the 1960s, and was associated with scores of popular movie and cartoon characters, from Peter Pan to Frankenstein. By the time the company moved to Connecticut in 1974, advertising had been pared down. The company mostly ran print ads in candy industry journals and did not try to appeal directly to children, as it had earlier. The company investigated working with McDonald's in the 1970s, to make Pez dispensers as a give-away item with the restaurant's children's meals, but the scale of the production was too large for Pez to handle. The company persisted as a relatively small player in the candy market. In 1979, Curt Allina, who had built Pez-Haas up from its beginning in 1953, was abruptly terminated. In the 1980s, the company released fewer new dispenser designs than it had previously, though it continued to find tie-ins to licensed characters. The 1980s saw a series of Warner Brothers cartoon character Pez dispensers, the cartoon cat Garfield, and the Smurfs, among others. But the company kept a low profile. In the late 1980s, the company name changed from Pez-Haas Inc. to Pez Candy, Inc., to indicate that it sold only Pez, and not other Haas products.

Resurgence in the 1990s

By the early 1990s, Pez Candy, Inc. had done virtually no advertising for about ten years. Although the company continued not to advertise, its namesake product still got talked about. The 1986 film *Stand By Me* mentioned Pez, when one character claimed the candy as his favorite food. Similar placements in movies and television multiplied in the 1990s, as Pez was

Key Dates:

1927: Eduard Haas III's Austrian food company begins marketing Pez in Europe.
1953: American company Pez-Haas, Inc. markets Pez in the United States.
1955: Pez is recast as a children's candy instead of adult mint.
1974: Pez Candy moves to Orange, Connecticut, begins U.S. candy production.
1992: Episode of the popular television series ''Seinfeld'' involving Tweety Pez highlights craze for Pez among adults.

rediscovered as a nostalgia item. Pez was mentioned on the popular television show ''Murphy Brown'' and on Jay Leno's ''Tonight Show'' in the early 1990s. A 1992 episode of ''Seinfeld,'' one of the most popular television shows of the 1990s, featured a sub-plot dedicated to a Tweety Bird Pez dispenser. All the media attention sparked sales for Pez. The company expanded its Connecticut plant in the early 1990s to handle the mounting demand. Sales for 1992 were $18 million.

By the mid-1990s, collecting old Pez dispensers had become a noticeable nationwide mania. By 1996, Pez collectors held several conventions, each drawing hundreds of people. Rare dispensers were sold for hundreds, sometimes thousands, of dollars. Collectors launched newsletters and web sites, and compiled detailed timelines and product lists of the dispensers. Pez was even indirectly responsible for the birth of one of the most successful Internet companies, eBay Inc. The girlfriend of eBay founder Pierre Omidyar was a Pez collector, and she had the idea of an online source for trading Pez dispensers. Thus eBay was born, and it soon became one of the Web's most trafficked spots. Pez Candy, Inc. was not directly involved in any of the fervor surrounding its products, but without doing any advertising, Pez claimed tremendous name recognition.

By the end of the 1990s, Pez Candy, Inc. seemed to be moving to take fuller advantage of its popularity. In 1999, the company made an arrangement with the fast-food chain Jack-In-The-Box to sell ''Jack''-head Pez dispensers at its restaurants for $1.99 each. This was Pez Candy's first successful foray into the children's meal premium market. Jack-In-The-Box was a relatively small chain, with 1,450 units compared to over 12,000 for McDonald's in the United States. Competition between McDonald's, Burger King, Taco Bell and other fast-food chains for enticing toys was intense, and Jack-In-The-Box hoped to win some attention by offering Pez. Pez Candy's president Scott McWhinnie noted in an April 12, 1999 article in *Nation's Restaurant News* that Pez was indeed designed for children three and up, but the candy currently had an immense adult following.

The Jack-In-The-Box promotion was followed in 2000 by a deal with Parlux Fragrances Inc. of Fort Lauderdale, Florida, to market Pez-brand perfumes and bath products. Parlux made fragrances for adults, such as a Perry Ellis brand scent, and it did not anticipate putting out grape Pez perfume. It licensed some of Pez's generic dispensers, such as a clown, policeman, and bride and groom, and hoped to put out its new scents in ''Pez-inspired'' containers, according to the *Wall Street Journal* of January 7, 2000. The agreement with Parlux, which was to run for five years, was clearly trading on the Pez brand's popularity and high name recognition with adults. Sales for Pez Candy, Inc. stood at an estimated $21 million by the end of the 1990s, not a huge increase since the beginning of the decade. But the company seemed ready to take its popularity a step farther, forging innovative marketing agreements. The product seemed to be going back toward its original marketing in a way—not as a hygienic breath mint but as something adults clearly craved.

Principal Competitors

Ferrara Pan Candy Co.; Nestlé USA, Inc.

Further Reading

Carrns, Ann, ''Eau de Plastic Clown? Perfume Company Cuts Deal with Pez,'' *Wall Street Journal*, January 7, 2000, p. B1.
Cheng, Kipp, ''eBay,'' *Adweek*, June 28, 1999, p. IQ/42.
McCarthy, Michael J., ''The PEZ Fancy Is Hard to Explain, Let Alone Justify,'' *Wall Street Journal*, March 10, 1993, pp. A1, A8.
''Pez de Resistance,'' *People Weekly*, December 2, 1991, p. 123.
Sauerwein, Kristina, ''Sweet Dreams,'' *Entertainment Weekly*, July 26, 1996, p. 10.
Spector, Amy, '' 'Jack' Pez Dispenser, McD's Furby Signal Intensifying Toy Wars,'' *Nation's Restaurant News*, April 12, 1999, p. 1.
Vigoda, Ralph, ''Pez Candy Dispensers Become Hot Collector's Item,'' *Knight-Ridder/Tribune Business News*, June 6, 1996, p. 6050171.
Welch, David, *Collecting Pez*, Murphysboro, Ill.: Bubba Scrubba Publications, 1994.

—A. Woodward

Pfizer Inc.

235 East 42nd Street
New York, New York 10017-5755
U.S.A.
Telephone: (212) 573-2323
Fax: (212) 573-7851
Web site: http://www.pfizer.com

Public Company
Incorporated: 1900 as Charles Pfizer & Company Inc.
Employees: 50,900
Sales: $27.3 billion (1999 pro forma)
Stock Exchanges: New York Boston Cincinnati Midwest Pacific Philadelphia London Paris Brussels Zurich Swiss
Ticker Symbol: PFE
NAIC: 325412 Pharmaceutical Preparation Manufacturing; 325411 Medicinal and Botanical Manufacturing; 325413 In-Vitro Diagnostic Substance Manufacturing; 325414 Biological Product (Except Diagnostic) Manufacturing; 325611 Soap and Other Detergent Manufacturing; 325620 Toilet Preparation Manufacturing; 541710 Research and Development in the Physical, Engineering, and Life Sciences

Pfizer Inc. is one of the leading research-based healthcare companies in the world. Following its June 2000 takeover of Warner-Lambert Company, Pfizer was organized into four groups: Pfizer Pharmaceuticals Group, Warner-Lambert Consumer Group, Pfizer Animal Health Group, and Pfizer Global Research and Development. Among the prescription drugs marketed by Pfizer Pharmaceuticals with annual revenues exceeding $1 billion are Norvasc, for the treatment of hypertension and angina; Lipitor, a cholesterol reducer; Zoloft, an antidepressant; Zithromax, an oral antibiotic; Diflucan, an antifungal product; and Viagra, the famous treatment for erectile dysfunction. Warner-Lambert Consumer markets a number of leading consumer brands, including such over-the-counter healthcare mainstays as Benadryl, Sudafed, Listerine, Visine, Rolaids, and Ben Gay; in the confectionery area, Trident, Dentyne, Certs, and Halls; Schick and Wilkinson Sword shaving products; and Tetra fish food. Pfizer Animal Health is a world leader in medicines for pets and livestock. On the development side, Pfizer Global R&D spends $4.5 billion a year shepherding candidates through the product pipeline, which at any one time can include more than 130 possible new products. R&D efforts also are aided by the 250 alliances that Pfizer has formed with academia and industry.

Pfizer's Early History

In 1849 Charles Pfizer, a chemist, and Charles Erhart, a confectioner, began a partnership in Brooklyn to manufacture bulk chemicals, Charles Pfizer & Company. While producing iodine preparation and boric and tartaric acids, Pfizer pioneered the production of citric acid, a product Pfizer continues to market to soft drink companies, using large-scale fermentation technology. By the end of the 19th century, Pfizer was producing a wide range of industrial and pharmacological products and had offices in New York and Chicago. In 1900 the company was incorporated in New Jersey as Charles Pfizer & Company Inc.

While Pfizer technicians became experts in fermentation technology, across the ocean Sir Alexander Fleming made his historic discovery of penicillin in 1928. Recognizing penicillin's potential to revolutionize healthcare, scientists struggled for years to produce both a high quality and large quantity of the drug. Experimentation with production became an imperative during the Nazi air raids of London during World War II. In a desperate attempt to solicit help from the community of American scientists, Dr. Howard Florey of Oxford University traveled to the United States to ask the U.S. government to mobilize its scientific resources.

Because of its expertise in fermentation, the government approached Pfizer. Soon afterward, Dr. Jasper Kane from the company laboratory began his own experiments. Initially using large glass flasks, Dr. Kane's experimentation then led to deep-tank fermentation. Later, the company announced its entrance into large-scale production with the purchase of an old ice plant in Brooklyn. Refusing government money, the company paid the entire $3 million for the purchase and within four months

Company Perspectives:

Our Mission: We will achieve and sustain our place as the world's premier research-based health care company. Our continuing success as a business will benefit patients and our customers, our shareholders, our families, and the communities in which we operate around the world.

John McKeen (future chairperson and president) had converted the ancient plant into the largest facility for manufacturing penicillin in the world.

Early production, however, was not without its difficulties. The first yields of penicillin required constant supervision, and yet quality and quantity remained low and inconsistent. In one of those inexplicable quirks of history, however, a government researcher browsing in a fruit market in Peoria, Illinois, discovered a variant of the ''Penicillium'' mold on an overripe cantaloupe. Using this variant, production suddenly increased from ten units per millimeter to 2,000 units per millimeter. By 1942 Pfizer divided the first flask of penicillin into vials for the medical departments of the Army and Navy; this flask was valued at $150,000. Mass production began in 1944, when Pfizer penicillin arrived with the Allied forces on the beaches of Normandy on D-Day. Meantime, in June 1942, Pfizer reincorporated in Delaware and went public with an offering of 240,000 shares of common stock.

Even as the government controlled production of the drug for the sole use of the Armed Forces, the public, aroused by miraculous results of penicillin, asked Pfizer to release the drug domestically. In 1943 John L. Smith, Pfizer president, and John McKeen, against the explicit regulations of the federal government, supplied penicillin to a doctor at the Brooklyn Jewish Hospital. Dr. Leo Lowe administered what was thought of as massive dosages of penicillin to several patients and cured, among others, a child suffering from an acute bacterial infection and a paralyzed and comatose woman. Smith and McKeen, visiting the hospital on Saturdays and Sundays, were witness to penicillin's curative effects on the patients.

Postwar Expansion for Pfizer: Terramycin and Beyond

Nevertheless, it was not until the end of the war when the federal government realized its mistake in restricting production of the drug. In 1946 Pfizer purchased Groton Victory Yard, a World War II shipyard, in order to renovate it for mass production of the new publicly accessible medicine. This marked Pfizer's first official entrance into the manufacturing of pharmaceuticals. In a few years the five-story building, equipped with 10,000 gallon tanks, produced enough penicillin to supply 85 percent of the national market and 50 percent of the world market. In 1946 sales already had reached $43 million.

Competition from 20 other companies manufacturing penicillin soon resulted in severe price reductions. The price for 100,000 units dropped from $20 to less than two cents. Furthermore, although the company could boast ownership of fermentation tanks ''exceeded in size only by those in the beer industry,'' Pfizer's bulk chemical business decreased as former customers began establishing production facilities of their own. Pfizer's instrumental role in developing antibiotics proved beneficial to society, but a poor business venture.

All this was to change drastically under the new direction of President John McKeen. In 1949 McKeen, whose career at Pfizer began the day after he graduated from the Brooklyn Polytechnic Institute in 1926, was elevated to president and, later, chair of the company. Already responsible for increasing sales by an impressive 800 percent between 1939 and 1950, McKeen's business acumen became even more evident during the marketing campaign for Terramycin, which was launched in 1950. In the postwar years, pharmaceutical companies searched for new broad-spectrum antibiotics useful in the treatment of a wide number of bacterial infections. Penicillin and streptomycin, while helping to expand the frontier of medical knowledge, actually offered a cure for only a limited number of infections. Pfizer's breakthrough came with the discovery of oxytetracycline, a broad-range antibiotic that soon would prove effective against some 100 diseases.

The drug's remarkable capture of a sizable portion of the market was not due entirely to its inherent curative powers. Rather, it was McKeen's ability to promote the new drug that actually propelled Pfizer into the ranks of top industry competitors. McKeen's first accomplishment was the timely decision to market the antibiotic under a Pfizer trademark. Thus Terramycin, the drug's chosen name, launched Pfizer into its first ethical drug campaign. Lacking the resources other pharmaceutical companies had to promote their drugs, McKeen announced the ''Pfizer blitz,'' whereby the company's small sales force used an unusual array of marketing strategies.

For the first time, the company circumvented traditional drug distributing companies and began selling Terramycin directly to hospitals and retailers. Pfizer's minuscule detail force (pharmaceutical salespeople) would target one small region at a time and promote their product to every accessible healthcare professional. The sales force left generous samples of the drug at every sales call, sponsored golf tournaments, and ran noisy hospitality suites at conventions. Surprised at the success of this tiny band of salespeople, which eventually would grow into a 4,000-person army, industry competitors reluctantly increased their own sales forces and, similarly, began promoting their products directly to physicians.

Taking the calculated risks of insulting the entire medical community, Pfizer ran lavish advertisements in the conservative *Journal of the American Medical Association.* The ad was greeted with a large degree of reservation and threatened the drug industry's abhorrence of ''hard sell'' marketing. In an unprecedented move, the company had paid a prohibitive $500,000 to run the multipage ad. In two years the entire Terramycin campaign cost $7.5 million, and Pfizer became the largest advertiser in the American Medical Association's journal.

After 12 months on the market, Terramycin's sales accounted for one-fourth of Pfizer's total $60 million in sales. Yet problems with the company's advertising strategy were to surface soon. In 1957, while promoting a new antibiotic called Sigmamycin, a Pfizer advertisement used the professional cards

Key Dates:

1772: Henry Nock founds the business that eventually becomes Wilkinson Sword.
1849: Charles Pfizer and Charles Erhart found Charles Pfizer & Company.
1866: Parke-Davis is founded in Detroit by Hervey C. Parke and George S. Davis.
1870s: Dr. Joseph Lawrence develops the original formula for Listerine.
1877: Wilkinson Sword begins making straight razors.
1881: Lawrence sells his formula to Jordan Wheat Lambert, who founds Lambert Pharmacal Company.
1886: William R. Warner founds William R. Warner & Company.
1899: Several major U.S. gum producers merge to form American Chicle.
1900: Charles Pfizer & Company Inc. is incorporated in New Jersey.
1916: Warner & Co. acquires Richard Hudnut Company, a cosmetics firm.
1921: Colonel Jacob Schick invents the Magazine Repeating Razor, forerunner of the Schick Injector razor.
1942: Pfizer goes public.
1944: Pfizer begins mass production of penicillin, primarily for the war effort.
1950: Pfizer launches Terramycin, an antibiotic; Warner & Co. is renamed Warner-Hudnut, Inc.
1955: Warner-Hudnut merges with Lambert Pharmacal to form Warner-Lambert Company.
1962: Warner-Lambert acquires American Chicle.
1970: Charles Pfizer & Company is renamed Pfizer Inc.; Warner-Lambert acquires Schick and Parke, Davis.
1984: Agouron Pharmaceuticals, Inc. is founded.
1989: Pfizer launches Procardia XL.
1992: Pfizer launches Novasc, Zoloft, and Zithromax.
1993: Warner-Lambert acquires Wilkinson Sword.
1995: Pfizer acquires the animal health unit of SmithKline Beecham.
1997: Warner-Lambert launches Lipitor through a marketing alliance with Pfizer.
1998: Pfizer divests its Medical Technology Group; Pfizer launches Viagra.
1999: Pfizer begins comarketing Celebrex; Warner-Lambert acquires Agouron Pharmaceuticals.
2000: Pfizer acquires Warner-Lambert.

of eight physicians to endorse the drug. John Lear, science editor of the *Saturday Review,* denounced this advertisement in a scathing attack. Not only were the names of the eight physicians fictitious, Lear claimed, but the code of Pharmaceutical Manufacturers Association prohibited soliciting endorsements from physicians. Moreover, Lear used the Pfizer ad to underscore and criticize what he saw as a trend toward the overprescription of antibiotics, exaggerated claims on drug effects, and concealment of possible side effects.

Pfizer was quick to defend their advertisement. The company upheld the reputability of the ad agency, William Douglas McAdams Inc., a highly respected firm responsible for the Sigmamycin campaign. While defending the drug and the clinical reports supporting the drug's efficacy, Pfizer admitted that the business cards were purely symbolic and, therefore, fictitious and, as a result, may have been misleading. The company accordingly changed the campaign.

John Lear's final attack on Pfizer expressed an unspoken industry complaint. Not only was it disturbing that such ''hard sell'' tactics should actually prove successful, but so was Pfizer's status in the industry; as the company's recent past was in bulk chemical production, it was a relative newcomer to the industry of ethical drugs. Lear argued that the young company should have shown respect for the industry's formal and restrained method of conducting business. Pfizer, however, was not intimidated by the industry's attitude toward its advertising campaign; it was interested in claiming and maintaining a share of the market. If it meant breaking tradition, it was clear Pfizer was not going to hesitate.

Aside from its modern marketing campaigns, Pfizer was very successful at developing a diversified line of pharmaceuticals. Whereas many companies concentrated their efforts on developing innovative drugs, Pfizer generously borrowed research from its competitors and released variants of these drugs. Although all companies participated in this process of ''molecular manipulation,'' whereby a slight variance is produced in a given molecule to develop greater potency and decreased side effects in a drug, Pfizer was particularly adept at developing these drugs and aggressively seizing a share of the market. Thus the company was able to reduce its dependence on sales of antibiotics by releasing a variety of other pharmaceuticals.

At the same time Pfizer's domestic sales increased dramatically, the company was quietly improving its presence on the foreign market. Under the methodical directive of John J. Powers, head of international operations and future president and chief executive officer, Pfizer's foreign market expanded into 100 countries and accounted for $175 million in sales by 1965. It would be years before any competitor came close to commanding a similar share of the foreign market. Pfizer's 1965 worldwide sales figures of $220 million indicated that the company might possibly be the largest pharmaceutical manufacturer in the United States. By 1980 Pfizer was one of only two U.S. companies among the top ten pharmaceutical companies in Europe, and the largest foreign healthcare and agricultural product manufacturer in Asia.

Pfizer's crowning success to its unorthodox business procedures involved McKeen's quest for diversification through acquisition. While competing companies within the industry preferred to keep $50–$70 million in savings, Pfizer not only kept a meager $25 million in cash, but was the only major pharmaceutical to use common equity to borrow capital. ''Not to have your cash working is a sort of economic sin,'' McKeen candidly stated. Between 1961 and 1965 the company paid $130 million in stock or cash and acquired 14 companies, including manufacturers of vitamins, antibiotics for animals, chemicals, and Coty cosmetics.

McKeen defended this diversification strategy by claiming that prodigious growth had decreased overall profits while competitors, on the other hand, had neither grown nor profited from their conservative investments. Furthermore, Pfizer's largest selling drug, Terramycin, generated only $15–$20 million a year and thus freed the company from a dependence on one product for all its profits.

In 1962 Pfizer allotted $17 million for research and that same year McKeen announced plans for his "five by five" program, which included $500 million in sales by 1965. Obviously, sales would not come from new pharmaceuticals, but from the company's accelerated rate of acquisitions.

McKeen never actually saw the company reach this goal during his presidency. In 1964 sales did surpass $480 million, but the following year Powers replaced McKeen as chief executive officer and president and inherited a company with almost half its sales generated from foreign markets and wide product diversification from 38 subsidiaries.

For the next seven years Powers continued to preside over the company's comfortable profits and sizable growth. In the absence of McKeen's style of conducting business, Powers directed Pfizer toward the more conservative and methodical approach of manufacturing and marketing pharmaceuticals.

Powers also guided the company in a new direction with an increased emphasis on research and development. With increased funds allocated for research in the laboratories, Pfizer joined the ranks of other pharmaceutical companies searching for the innovative and, therefore, profit making, drugs. Vibramycin, an antibiotic developed in the 1960s, was very profitable; by 1981 it generated sales of $250 million.

Emphasizing R&D at Pfizer in the 1970s and 1980s

In 1970 the company changed its name to the more modern-sounding Pfizer Inc. In the early 1970s Edmund Pratt, Jr., stepped in as company chairman and Gerald Laubach took over as Pfizer president. Although company assets reached $1.5 billion and sales generated $2 billion by 1977, Pfizer's overall growth was much slower through the period of the late 1970s and early 1980s. Increased oil prices caused comparable increases in prices for raw materials; low incidents of respiratory infections slowed sales for antibiotics; and even a cool summer in Europe reduced demands for soft drinks and, consequently, the need for Pfizer citric acids. All of these factors contributed to the company's slow rate of growth.

In light of this, the two new top executives significantly changed company strategy. First, funds for research and development reached $190 million by 1981; this marked a 100 percent increase in funding from 1977. Second, Pfizer began a comprehensive licensing program with foreign pharmaceutical companies to pay royalties in exchange for marketing rights on newly developed drugs. This represented a noticeable change from the years Powers supervised international operations. Under his directive, Pfizer chose to market its own drugs on the foreign market and establish joint ventures or partnerships only if no other option was available.

The two new drugs—one called Procardia, a treatment for angina licensed from Bayer AG in Germany for its exclusive sale in the United States, and the other called Cefobid, an antibiotic licensed from a Japanese pharmaceutical company—promised to be highly profitable items. Furthermore, drugs discovered from Pfizer's own research resulted in large profits. Sales for Minipress, an antihypertensive, reached $80 million in three years, and Feldene, an anti-inflammatory, generated $314 million by 1982.

By 1983 sales reached $3.5 billion and Pfizer was spending one of the largest amounts of money in the industry on research ($197 million in 1983). Pratt, in a final move to shed Pfizer of its former idiosyncracies, began selling some of its more unprofitable acquisitions.

Interestingly, one Pfizer product acquired through a company acquisition in the 1960s experienced a market rediscovery during the 1980s. Ben Gay, a well established liniment marketed for relief of arthritis pains through the late 1970s, found new patrons in the health-conscious 1980s. Discovering that sales for Ben Gay were increasing when marketed as a fitness aid, Pfizer began an advertising campaign by employing athletic superstars to endorse the drug. This campaign cost the company $6.3 million in 1982.

By 1989, Pfizer operated businesses in more than 140 countries. Net sales that year were $5.7 billion, but net income declined. Research and development expenditures had quadrupled during the 1980s, and Pfizer planned to continue investing heavily in research and development. Procardia XL was launched in 1989, and Diflucan, an antifungal agent, received Food and Drug Administration (FDA) approval. Globally, Pfizer chalked up $150 million in sales—in 14 countries—of its Plax dental rinse.

Blockbuster Introductions Marking the 1990s for Pfizer

Pfizer headed into the 1990s with numerous drugs in development, including preparations in the areas of anti-infectives, cardiovasculars, anti-inflammatories, and central nervous system medications. Net sales in 1990 reached $6.4 billion. Procardia rapidly became the most widely prescribed cardiovascular drug in the United States. Research and development costs rose 20 percent, in keeping with Pfizer's determination to invest heavily in new drugs.

Pfizer International launched 37 new products worldwide in 1990. The company's antifungal drug, Diflucan, became the world's leading drug of its kind during this time. Sales of Pfizer's newest products accounted for 30 percent of all pharmaceutical sales, up from 13 percent in 1989.

Pfizer entered the decade facing controversy about heart valves produced by Shiley, Inc., a Pfizer subsidiary. In 1990, 38 fractures of implanted valves were reported. Pfizer instituted a policy of compensating those with fractured valves. Shiley was sold later in the decade to Sorin Biomedica S.p.A., a subsidiary of Fiat S.p.A., for $230 million.

In 1992, Pfizer received final FDA approval for Norvasc, used in treating angina and hypertension. Zithromax, an antibiotic developed to treat outpatient pneumonia, tonsillitis, and pharyngitis, also hit the market that year after FDA approval, as did the antidepressant Zoloft. By the late 1990s, all three of these drugs had reached blockbuster status—achieving annual sales of more than $1 billion. Net sales in 1992 were $7.2 billion, with a net income of $811 million, and research and development expenses hit $863 million. Pfizer's chairperson and CEO of 19 years, Ed Pratt, retired and was succeeded by William C. Steere, Jr.

Although the early 1990s were marked by a wave of mergers and acquisitions in the global pharmaceuticals industry, Pfizer declined to join in, and was instead content to build its product pipeline organically rather than through acquisition. By 1995, in fact, the R&D budget hit $1.3 billion. The one major acquisition that the company did complete during this period came not in the area of human pharmaceuticals but in the animal health realm. In 1995, Pfizer spent $1.45 billion for the animal health unit of SmithKline Beecham plc, the largest acquisition in Pfizer history. The purchase transformed the company's Animal Health Group into one of the largest providers of medicines for both livestock and pets, with remedies for more than 30 species, including anti-infectives, antiparasitics, anti-inflammatories, and vaccines.

Not content with its own rich product pipeline, Pfizer entered into a series of partnerships whereby it comarketed drugs developed by smaller pharmaceutical firms, firms that were attracted by Pfizer's powerful sales force. In 1997 Pfizer helped Warner-Lambert bring Lipitor, a cholesterol-lowering pill, to market. Lipitor soared to the top of the anticholesterol niche in the United States, achieving sales of $865 million in 1997 and $2.2 billion in 1998. Another 1997 introduction of a comarketed drug was Aricept, which was developed by Japan's Eisai and quickly became the leading drug prescribed to treat the symptoms of Alzheimer's disease.

Focusing ever further on pharmaceuticals, Pfizer in 1998 sold its Medical Technology Group in four separate transactions: Valleylab was sold to U.S. Surgical Corporation for $425 million; AMS to E.M. Warburg, Pincus & Co., LLC for $130 million; Schneider to Boston Scientific Corporation for $2.1 billion; and Howmedica to Stryker Corporation for $1.65 billion. These transactions, however, were overshadowed that year by Pfizer's introduction of Viagra, a pill for treating male impotence, or what the company called ''erectile dysfunction.'' By far the most famous of the new ''lifestyle drugs,'' Viagra was an instant blockbuster: more than 350,000 prescriptions were written in the first three weeks, and sales for 1998 totaled $788 million; sales exceeded $1 billion in 1999. Less than a year after the launch of Viagra, Pfizer began comarketing Celebrex, which had been developed by G.D. Searle & Co., then a unit of Monsanto Company. Celebrex, the first of a new category of pain drugs called Cox-2 inhibitors, was approved for the treatment of arthritis pain and inflammation. The new drug became the most successful pharmaceutical launched in U.S. history, with 19 million prescriptions written in the first 12 months; sales during 1999 alone exceeded $1.4 billion.

Having participated in three record-setting launches in the late 1990s, Pfizer was one of the fastest growing drug companies in the world in revenue terms. Sales increased from $11.31 billion in 1996 to $16.2 billion in 1999. The overall growth for the 1990s was even more impressive as revenues increased 284 percent from the 1989 total of $4.2 billion. During this same period, Pfizer increased its R&D budget sixfold, reaching nearly $2.8 billion by 1999, or more than 17 percent of sales—among the top levels in the industry.

The company was not without its problems, however, particularly as a series of setbacks beset its drug development efforts. Trovan, an antibiotic that Pfizer hoped would be a blockbuster, ran into trouble during clinical studies following reports that it killed some patients. Development stopped on an experimental drug for diabetic nerve damage. Zeldox, an antipsychotic drug, and Relpax, a migraine treatment, saw their development delayed. In addition, sales of Viagra suffered at least a temporary setback following reports that some users of the drug had died of heart attacks. It was with this somewhat shaky product pipeline as a backdrop that Pfizer entered into a battle for control of Warner-Lambert in late 1999, a battle that Pfizer won early the following year.

Early Histories of Warner and Lambert

Warner-Lambert Company was the product of the 1955 merger of Warner-Hudnut, Inc. and the Lambert Pharmacal Company. Warner was founded in the late 19th century by William R. Warner, a Philadelphia pharmacist who had earned a fortune by inventing a sugar coating for pills. In 1886 he formed William R. Warner & Company and began making drugs. In 1908, several years after Warner's death, the company was acquired by Gustavus A. Pfeiffer & Company, a patent medicine company from St. Louis. Pfeiffer retained the Warner company name, moved its headquarters to New York, and began a series of acquisitions that included Richard Hudnut Company, a cosmetics firm acquired in 1916, and the DuBarry cosmetic company. By the 1940s, some 50 companies had been acquired during the Warner company's history.

Elmer Holmes Bobst arrived at Warner in 1945, already a veteran executive of the pharmaceutical industry and a multimillionaire. As president of Hoffmann-La Roche's U.S. office, he had proved instrumental in acquiring for the Swiss company a large share of the U.S. drug market. Many observers were surprised that Bobst accepted the position at Warner; he was then 61 years old, wealthy, and could have settled into a comfortable retirement.

Nevertheless, when Gustave A. Pfeiffer, Warner's chairperson and the only surviving member of the original founding family, approached Bobst with an offer of the presidency, he accepted. Nearly 30 years earlier, Bobst had been asked to join Warner as the head of its pharmaceutical division but declined when the Pfeiffer family refused to sell Bobst any of the company stock (the family held all the common stock). By the mid-1940s, however, Bobst had proved his abilities, and Pfeiffer readily offered the job on Bobst's terms; Bobst was hired and allowed to purchase 11 percent of the common stock. By 1955, Bobst's holdings were worth more than $3 million.

What Bobst inherited with his new position was a family-operated company suffering from an aging product line and antiquated facilities. Although the Hudnut cosmetic line accounted for most of the company's $25 million in sales, that product line was barely turning a profit. In an effort to improve the image of the cosmetics production, Bobst renamed the firm Warner-Hudnut in 1950.

Bobst's managerial style was well suited to the company's policy of growth through acquisition. Moreover, his experience with high-level industry and political affairs enabled him to hire a new management team of accomplished executives and public figures. Successful investment bankers, business executives, and political officials were brought in, notably Anna Rosenberg, the company's manager of industrial and public relations, who was once the U.S. assistant secretary of defense, and Alfred Driscoll, later Warner's president, who had served as governor of New Jersey for seven years.

In 1952, Bobst made his first major acquisition, purchasing New Jersey Chilcott Laboratories, Inc. Chilcott earned its reputation as a manufacturer of ethical drugs in large part through its development of Peritrate, a long-acting ''vasodilator,'' which enlarged constricted blood vessels. Three years later Bobst arranged a merger between his company and Lambert Pharmacal.

Lambert Pharmacal's history is tied to that of the oral antiseptic Listerine. Dr. Joseph Lawrence developed the original formula for Listerine in the 1870s. Lawrence sold his formula in 1881 to Jordan Wheat Lambert, who founded the Lambert Pharmacal Company to make and sell Listerine. The product became widely popular, particularly under the advertising strategy of Gordon Seagrove, who joined Lambert in 1926 after leaving his job as a calliope player in the circus. Seagrove made Listerine a household staple by promoting its ability to cure halitosis, sore throats, and dandruff. The advertising copy for one magazine ad depicted a man encouraging a woman to continue massaging Listerine into his head, with the tagline ''Tear into it, Honey—It's Infectious Dandruff!''

Bobst had met the president of Lambert, Edward Williams, at a meeting of the American Foundation for Pharmaceutical Education, and the two decided that their operations, each producing different but reputable products, would complement one another. Bobst was particularly interested in gaining access to Lambert's well-organized distribution network, which incorporated modern marketing techniques previously unavailable at Warner-Hudnut's. Furthermore, Williams brought a strong background in the management of pharmaceutical companies, enhancing Bobst's accomplished executive team, which had little experience in the pharmaceutical industry. When Warner and Lambert merged in 1955 to form Warner-Lambert Company, former governor Alfred Driscoll was named president of the new company.

Growing Through Acquisition: Warner-Lambert in the 1960s and 1970s

The new company quickly outgrew its New York headquarters and so relocated to Morris Plains, New Jersey, a suburb of New York City, in 1956. Acquisitions were soon to follow. Warner-Lambert acquired Emerson Drug, maker of Bromo-Seltzer, in 1956. Six years later, the company acquired American Chicle, maker of Chiclets and other chewing gums, for about $200 million in stock. American Chicle had been formed in 1899 through the merger of several major U.S. gum producers. Many industry analysts criticized the high price paid for American Chicle; in 1962, the company's net income for the year was less than $10 million. By 1983, however, after expanding into foreign markets, Chiclet sales were reaching the $1 billion mark. Ward S. Hagan, chairperson of American Chicle, called its gum and mint business ''the largest in the world.''

Meanwhile, the success of Peritrate, the drug that had come to Warner-Hudnut through that company's purchase of Chilcott Laboratories, was the cause of some controversy. Peritrate proved useful in a wider application of treatments than originally allowed, and the FDA approved of Peritrate's ''new drug'' usages in 1959. Over the next several years, however, Warner embarked on a controversial Peritrate advertising campaign. Appearing in several medical journals, including the *Journal of the American Medical Association,* ten-page ads advocated the use of Peritrate not only for the treatment of angina, but as a ''life-prolonging'' prophylactic for all cardiac patients. The advertisement, based on the results of one study, was released at a time when the FDA had initiated an increasingly aggressive policy of evaluating claims for drug effectiveness. Even as the director of the study refuted the advertisement claims, Warner-Lambert executives stood by the claims for the effectiveness of their drug. By 1966, however, when an estimated 56 percent of the 3.1 million people afflicted by heart disease used Peritrate, the government, under the directive of the FDA, seized a shipment of the drug, bringing charges against the company's unapproved advocacy of an even wider usage for the drug.

Concurrently, Listerine continued to increase in popularity under its new ownership; by 1975, the oral antiseptic held a sizable portion of the $300 million market. Warner-Lambert continued to invest heavily in advertising for Listerine. For years, Listerine had been advertised as a preventive measure against colds and sore throats, and, during the Asian flu epidemic of 1957, Bobst personally placed an ad in *Life* magazine promoting Listerine's ability to resist the sickness. The company's advertising agency had rejected the ad earlier, since its claims were unsubstantiated, but the promotion resulted in sales increases of $26 million for the year.

By 1975, the Federal Trade Commission (FTC) had begun to investigate the Listerine advertisements. The FTC disputed the cold prevention claims of Listerine as insupportable and ordered the company to embark on a disclaimer ad campaign amounting to $10 million, a figure equal to the company's average annual advertising expenditure between 1962 and 1972. The FTC argued that only corrective disclaimers could educate the consumer, and, in 1978, the Supreme Court upheld the FTC's order.

During the 1970s and 1980s, Warner-Lambert made several acquisitions, including cough drop manufacturer Smith Brothers, American Optical, and Schick Shaving. The latter, which was acquired in 1970, traced its origins to the 1920s when Colonel Jacob Schick, inspired by the repeating rifle, invented the Magazine Repeating Razor, which eventually was redubbed the Schick Injector razor.

Warner-Lambert also acquired Parke, Davis & Co. in 1970. The company was founded in Detroit in 1866 as Parke-Davis by Hervey C. Parke and George S. Davis. Among the numerous medical innovations marking the history of Parke, Davis were the 1938 development of Dilantin, which became the drug of choice for the treatment of epilepsy; the 1946 introduction of the first antihistamine, Benadryl; and the 1949 discovery of chloromycetin, a broad-spectrum antibiotic.

The acquisition of Parke, Davis met with some resistance. The Antitrust Division of the Justice Department launched an investigation of the proposed merger. According to the chair of the House Judiciary Committee, the merger would raise "serious problems" because it had the potential to limit competition and create a monopoly. Upon approval, the merger would result in combined revenue of $1.7 billion and would rank the new company among the 100 largest industrial companies in the United States.

On November 12, 1970, the Justice Department announced that it would not challenge the merger despite the Antitrust Division's recommendation to the contrary. The department referred the matter to the FTC, which held concurrent authority to enforce the Clayton Act. A day later, the merger was completed. By 1976, however, the FTC ordered the company to sell several units of its Parke, Davis subsidiary that produced specified drugs. Those units producing thyroid preparations, cough remedies, cough drops and lozenges, normal albumin serum, and tetanus immunoglobulin would have to be sold to restore competition in those product lines.

Satisfied with the FTC's actions, S. Burke Giblin, chair and CEO of Warner-Lambert at the time of the ruling, nevertheless faced several other challenges in the ensuing years. In 1976, Warner-Lambert disclosed figures to the Securities and Exchange Commission (SEC) concerning illegal payments abroad, announcing that more than $2.2 million "in questionable payments" had been uncovered in 14 of the 140 countries in which Warner-Lambert conducted business.

Only months later an explosion at an American Chicle plant in Queens, New York, killed six people and injured 55. After a year of investigation, a grand jury indicted the company and four of its officials on charges of reckless manslaughter and criminally negligent homicide. The charges were based on reports that the fire department had warned the company about the explosive potential of magnesium stearate dust used as a gum-machine lubricant. Contending that the charges were "outrageous" and unwarranted, company executives appealed the case. In 1978, a state judge dismissed the charges, citing "crystal clear and voluminous evidence" that the company had tried to eliminate the danger of an explosion. The following year, however, the New York State court's appellate division voted to restore the indictments. Finally, in 1980, the state's highest court once again dismissed all charges in connection with the explosion.

Another controversy involved Warner-Lambert's Benylin cough syrup product, which was made available without a prescription in 1975. In response to questions regarding the cough syrup's effectiveness, the FDA ordered the drug back on a prescription-only status, and, after seven years of deliberation, a settlement finally was reached in which the FDA approved the reinstated over-the-counter sale of the drug.

In 1978, Warner-Lambert purchased Entenmann's Bakery for $243 million in cash. By 1982, Entenmann's had become Warner-Lambert's most profitable consumer division, with sales reaching $333 million and an annual growth rate of 19 percent. During this time, however, a rumor was started that Entenmann's profits were supporting the Reverend Sun Myung Moon's Unification Church. Since the source of the rumor was said to have come from Westchester County in New York, Warner-Lambert took out an ad in the county newspaper denying the alleged connection. Nevertheless, the rumor continued to circulate and actually received a large amount of publicity in the Boston, Massachusetts area. It was reported in some places that Entenmann's delivery and sales staff were being harassed, and one Rhode Island church urged a boycott of the baked goods. When sales growth began to slip, Warner-Lambert mailed a letter to 1,600 churches in New England describing Entenmann's history as a family-owned business for 80 years before it was purchased. As Entenmann's profits continued to slip, Warner-Lambert sold the bakery to General Foods for $315 million in 1982.

The late 1970s had proved financially unstable for Warner-Lambert. Profit margins were off by 40 percent in 1979, the majority of revenues came from the sale of consumer goods, and the company was considered a potential takeover candidate. One critic characterized it a "floundering giant." That year, Ward S. Hagan replaced Bobst as chairperson, while Joseph D. Williams assumed the chief executive office. Hagan and Williams then embarked on a restructuring program with the goal of revitalizing the pharmaceutical operations and trimming unprofitable and noncore businesses.

Restructuring and Refocusing on Core Areas in the 1980s and 1990s

Five unprofitable subsidiaries, including American Optical and Entenmann's, were divested between 1982 and 1986, providing Warner-Lambert with capital of nearly $600 million. At the same time, such company programs as the "Total Production System" aimed to increase productivity by cutting downtime, reducing paperwork, and creating a more flexible work environment. Hagan and Williams closed or consolidated 24 plants in foreign and domestic locations, while reducing the company labor force by almost half, from 61,000 to 32,000. Research for new drugs at the Parke, Davis division was supported by a 20 percent increase in budgetary funds during 1983 to $180 million.

Despite its improved financial condition, Warner-Lambert came under criticism, particularly for its 1982 purchase of IMED Corp., a small hospital supply manufacturer. Many found Warner-Lambert's $468 million purchase, 23 times IMED's earnings, exorbitant. IMED was the market leader, with 35 percent of sales in the hospital supply field and continued annual sales growth of 50 percent. The company, however, was beset with problems. IMED's executives apparently concentrated on short-term sales goals, at the expense of new product development. In fact, a management conflict between IMED's manufacturing and research and development executives caused many important employees to resign in frustration. In 1986, Warner-Lambert sold IMED and some of its affiliates to the Henley Group, Inc. for $163.5 million.

Williams, who was given the additional duties of chairperson during Warner-Lambert's turnaround period, was able to report that return on equity had increased from 9 to 32 percent from 1979 to 1986, as sales diminished through divestments and profits held fairly steady. Investing in research and development and luring industry talent from competing companies, Williams hoped to develop and increase sales of high-margin prescription drugs, such as Lopid, a cholesterol-reducing drug that received positive publicity in the late 1980s. A trend among consumers toward treatment without medication, however, as well as swelling support for reform of the healthcare industry—and the attendant possibility of price controls—caused uncertainty among ethical drug producers. Business also was threatened by a late 1980s recession and discounting in the consumer goods segment.

In anticipation of these potentially adverse market forces, a new chairperson and CEO, Melvin R. Goodes, announced yet another reorganization of Warner-Lambert late in 1991. The plan called for a 2,700-person layoff, reorganization of the global management scheme, and consolidation of operations into two groups: pharmaceuticals and consumer products. Goodes also began to concentrate the company's marketing efforts on three primary geographic markets: North America, Europe, and Japan. The company invested $1.3 billion in advertising and promotion and $473 million in research and development, apparently banking on its consumer goods, which still constituted 60 percent of annual sales in 1992.

That year, Warner-Lambert became the fourth company to enter the competitive and controversial market for transdermal nicotine patches. Its prescription smoking cessation device, branded Nicotrol, was strongly promoted through direct consumer advertising, and the product enjoyed early success. Sales, however, quickly declined in 1993; Warner-Lambert's late entry into the segment, chronic product shortages, a lower than expected success rate, side effects, and, especially, reports that some users had suffered heart attacks, all led to declines in sales.

In 1993, the company became the first to win approval from the FDA for a drug (Cognex) that retarded the progression of Alzheimer's disease. Warner-Lambert also formed joint ventures with Glaxo Holdings plc and Wellcome plc to orchestrate the movement of the companies' drugs from prescription to over-the-counter and generic markets. Another development in 1993 was the acquisition of Wilkinson Sword, a maker of shaving products and toiletries and a business that fit well alongside Schick. Wilkinson Sword traced its origins back to 18th-century London, where in 1772 Henry Nock began making guns and bayonets. James Wilkinson, a son-in-law of Nock, soon became a partner in the enterprise and then inherited the company in 1805. Wilkinson's son Henry joined the firm and expanded the business into sword making. The manufacturing of straight razors began in 1877.

The critical drug development front showed only mixed results for Warner-Lambert in the early 1990s. Lopid, whose sales had peaked at $556 million in 1992, went off patent in January 1993, resulting in significant and immediate generic competition and plummeting sales. Meantime, sales of Cognex were disappointing. Neurontin, which had been approved for the treatment of epilepsy, also got off to a slow start, although by 1998 sales had hit a solid $514 million. Sales of Accupril, a cardiovascular drug, were $175 million in 1994; by 1998 sales had increased to $454 million. In the OTC realm, Warner-Lambert helped the newly merged Glaxo Wellcome plc bring Zantec 75 heartburn treatment to market in 1996. The alliance ended in 1998, however, when Warner-Lambert bought the U.S. and Canadian rights to the product, which that year achieved sales of $168 million.

Two key pharmaceutical introductions marked 1997. Following its approval by the FDA in December 1996, Lipitor was launched in February of the following year. This drug was used to reduce cholesterol levels and proved to work faster and more effectively than other available remedies. As a result, Lipitor became the blockbuster pharmaceutical long sought by Warner-Lambert and was in fact the first prescription drug to achieve $1 billion in worldwide sales in its first year on the market. Sales in 1998 reached $2.19 billion.

The other 1997 launch, Rezulin, also got off to a fast start—posting $750 million in 1998 sales—but then ran aground. Launched in March 1997 as a breakthrough treatment for the most common kind of diabetes, type 2 diabetes, Rezulin was by March 1999 the subject of an FDA investigation into its safety, after 30 people in the United States who were taking the drug died after developing liver problems. The FDA at first allowed the drug to continue to be sold with a change in the labeling requiring strict monitoring of liver function. In 2000, however, Rezulin was pulled from the market.

The Rezulin setback and the lack of any blockbusters in the pipeline that were close to market provided the impetus for Warner-Lambert's acquisition of Agouron Pharmaceuticals, Inc. for about $2.1 billion in stock in May 1999. Agouron had been founded in 1984 by several University of California at San Diego scientists who pioneered in computer-aided drug design. The method employed by Agouron involved first understanding the structure of disease-causing proteins in the body and then using computers to design pharmaceuticals that can inhibit the proteins' activity. Agouron had been focusing its development efforts in the areas of oncology and virology, and its first product was Viracept, one of the so-called protease inhibitors being used to treat HIV/AIDS. Viracept was soon considered the top drug in its class because it was more convenient to use and had slightly fewer side effects; sales thereupon totaled $530 million in 1998. Agouron's product pipeline was filled with promising new drugs, including treatments for cancer, macular degeneration (which affects the eyesight), and the common cold, in addition to more AIDS therapies.

Pfizer's Takeover of Warner-Lambert in 2000

Goodes retired from his position as CEO and chairman of Warner-Lambert in May 1999, with the company's president, Lodewijk J.R. de Vink, taking on Goodes's titles as well. In early November of that year, as drug industry consolidation was continuing, Warner-Lambert agreed to a nearly $70 billion merger with American Home Products Corporation (AHP). Pfizer, not wanting to lose its 50 percent of the revenues from the sale of the blockbuster Lipitor—with sales nearing $4 billion per year—and seeking to bolster its product pipeline through the addition of Agouron, stepped in within hours with a hostile bid exceeding AHP's offer. Warner-Lambert attempted to fend Pfizer off, even bringing in a third party, the Procter & Gamble Company (P&G), to discuss a three-way deal with

P&G and AHP. P&G soon dropped out of the picture when its stock price plummeted on news of the talks. Finally, in early February 2000, Pfizer and Warner-Lambert reached agreement on what was initially an $84 billion merger, ending the largest hostile takeover action in U.S. history. AHP received a breakup fee of $1.8 billion, which was believed to be the largest such payment ever made.

The merger was completed in June 2000 in what ended up being a $116 billion stock swap. The combined company retained the Pfizer Inc. name, with the consumer product lines of the two firms combined within a unit called Warner-Lambert Consumer Group. The FTC forced the firms to complete a number of relatively minor divestitures. The new Pfizer boasted pro forma 1999 revenues of $27.3 billion, making it the world's number two drug company, trailing only Aventis. The company had the industry's largest R&D budget, totaling $4.7 billion in 2000, as well as what was generally considered to be the industry's top sales and marketing operation. In terms of prescription drugs, Pfizer now marketed eight products with annual sales in excess of $1 billion. The Warner-Lambert Consumer Group was a leading marketer of OTC healthcare, confectionery, and shaving brands, with 1999 pro forma revenues of $5.5 billion. The Pfizer Animal Health Group was the world leader in medicines for pets and livestock, with 1999 sales of $1.3 billion. William C. Steere continued at the helm of Pfizer in the initial months following the merger, but was slated to retire in early 2001 and be replaced by the company's president and COO, Henry McKinnell. The company veteran, who joined Pfizer in 1971, was faced with the challenges of integrating the staffs and cultures of Pfizer and Warner-Lambert, healing whatever wounds might be left over from the bruising takeover battle, and restoring investor confidence in the company's product pipeline. McKinnell was aiming to achieve annual cost savings of $1.6 billion by 2002 through the elimination of redundant activities and the centralizing of such operations as the two companies' distribution systems. Two major product launches were anticipated to occur in 2001: Zeldox, an antipsychotic drug, and Relpax, a migraine treatment.

Principal Operating Units

Pfizer Pharmaceuticals Group; Pfizer Global Research and Development; Animal Health Group; Warner-Lambert Consumer Group.

Principal Competitors

Abbott Laboratories; American Home Products Corporation; Aventis; Bayer AG; Bristol-Myers Squibb Company; Colgate-Palmolive Company; Eli Lilly and Company; Glaxo Wellcome plc; Johnson & Johnson; Merck & Co., Inc.; Novartis AG; Roche Holding Ltd.; Schering-Plough Corporation; SmithKline Beecham plc.

Further Reading

Alger, Alexandra, "Viagra Falls," *Forbes,* February 7, 2000, pp. 130–32.

Barrett, Amy, "The Formula at Pfizer: Don't Run with the Crowd," *Business Week,* May 11, 1998, pp. 96–97.

Baum, Laurie, "A Powerful Tonic for Warner-Lambert," *Business Week,* November 30, 1987, pp. 144, 146.

Benway, Susan Duffy, "Just What the Doctor Ordered: 'Restructuring' Revives Warner Lambert," *Barron's,* December 30, 1985, pp. 35+.

Bradford, Stacey L., "Sweet Dreams: Gum and Mints May Help Warner-Lambert Become a Bigger Success in Drugs," *Financial World,* October 21, 1996, pp. 44–45.

Byrne, Harlan S., "Warner-Lambert: On the Mend," *Barron's,* January 2, 1995, pp. 19–20.

Campanella, Frank W., "Healthy Turnaround: Warner-Lambert Is Poised for an Earnings Recovery," *Barron's,* February 1, 1982, pp. 35+.

Davenport, Caroline H., "Glowing Prospects: New Products Will Keep Pfizer Growing at a Healthy Clip," *Barron's,* December 22, 1980.

"Did Warner-Lambert Make a '$468 Million Mistake'?," *Business Week,* November 21, 1983, pp. 123+.

Gibson, W. David, "R&D = Rx for Growth: That's Warner-Lambert's New Corporate Formula," *Barron's,* February 20, 1984, pp. 13+.

Hayes, John R., "Pill Selling 101," *Forbes,* November 21, 1994, p. 64.

Hensley, Scott, "Pfizer Appoints McKinnell to Top Posts," *Wall Street Journal,* August 11, 2000, p. B10.

LaBell, Fran, "Fat Extenders in Salad Dressings," *Food Processing,* May 1992, p. 64.

Langreth, Robert, "Behind Pfizer's Takeover Battle: An Urgent Need," *Wall Street Journal,* February 8, 2000, p. B1.

——, "Pfizer's Warner-Lambert Purchase Contains Big Prize: Pipeline of Biotechnology Unit Agouron Is Stuffed with Potential Blockbusters," *Wall Street Journal,* April 24, 2000, p. B4.

——, "Pfizer, Warner-Lambert Agree on Terms," *Wall Street Journal,* February 7, 2000, p. A3.

Langreth, Robert, and Michael Waldholz, "Pfizer Pins Multibillion-Dollar Hopes on Impotence Pill," *Wall Street Journal,* March 19, 1998, p. B1.

Loynd, Harry J., *Parke-Davis: The Never-Ending Search for Better Medicines,* New York: Newcomen Society in North America, 1957.

Lubove, Seth, "Failure Focuses the Mind," *Forbes,* November 8, 1993, pp. 76–78.

Mahar, Maggie, "Legal Heartbreak?: Pfizer Faces Huge Liability If It Loses a Key Lawsuit," *Barron's,* April 2, 1990, pp. 8+.

Mines, Samuel, *Pfizer: An Informal History,* New York: Pfizer, 1978.

O'Reilly, Brian, "The Pills That Saved Warner-Lambert," *Fortune,* October 13, 1997, pp. 94–95.

"Pfizer: Counting on 'Spare Parts' to Keep Up Its Momentum," *Business Week,* January 9, 1984, pp. 109+.

"Pfizer Joins with Other Drug Makers on Price Control," *Chemical Marketing Reporter,* February 1, 1993, p. 7.

"Pfizer Wins U.S. FDA Approval for Norvasc," *European Chemical News,* August 17, 1992, p. 23.

Pratt, Edmund T., Jr., *Pfizer: Bringing Science to Life,* New York: Newcomen Society of the United States, 1985.

Rodengen, Jeffrey L., *The Legend of Pfizer,* Ft. Lauderdale, Fla.: Write Stuff Syndicate, 1999.

Roman, Monica, "Pfizer Finally Sees Its Payoff," *Business Week,* July 1, 1991, pp. 86+.

——, "Pfizer's Pipeline Is Full, But Will the Drugs Flow Fast Enough?," *Business Week,* September 11, 1989, pp. 74+.

Rundle, Rhonda L., and Waldholz, Michael, "Warner-Lambert Agrees to Buy Agouron," *Wall Street Journal,* January 27, 1999, p. A3.

Schroeder, Michael, "Heart Trouble at Pfizer," *Business Week,* February 26, 1990, pp. 47+.

Starr, Cynthia, "First-Ever Alzheimer's Drug Brings Some Hope to Millions," *Drug Topics,* October 11, 1993, pp. 16–18.

Stipp, David, "Why Pfizer Is So Hot," *Fortune,* May 11, 1998, pp. 88–90, 92, 94.

Tanner, Ogden, *Twenty-Five Years of Innovation: The Story of Pfizer Central Research,* Lyme, Conn.: Greenwich Publishing, 1996.

''Turning Warner-Lambert into a Marketing Conglomerate,'' *Business Week,* March 5, 1979, p. 60.

''Warner-Lambert: Reversing Direction to Correct Neglect,'' *Business Week,* June 15, 1981, pp. 65+.

Weber, Joseph, ''Curing Warner-Lambert—Before It Gets Sick,'' *Business Week,* December 9, 1991, pp. 91, 94.

Weber, Joseph, et al., ''The New Era of Lifestyle Drugs,'' *Business Week,* May 11, 1998, pp. 92+.

Zipser, Andy, ''Beyond Shiley: A Vote for Pfizer,'' *Barron's,* May 27, 1991, pp. 28+.

—Marinell Landa and April Dougal Gasbarre
—updated by David E. Salamie

R.R. Donnelley & Sons Company

77 West Wacker Drive
Chicago, Illinois 60601-1696
U.S.A.
Telephone: (312) 326-8000
Fax: (312) 326-8543
Web site: http://www.rrdonnelley.com

Public Company
Incorporated: 1890
Employees: 34,000
Sales: $5.18 billion (1999)
Stock Exchanges: New York Pacific Chicago
Ticker Symbol: DNY
NAIC: 323117 Book Printing; 323119 Other Commercial Printing; 51121 Software Publishers; 514191 Online Information Services

The largest commercial printing company in North America and a dominant player in the world communications arena, R.R. Donnelley & Sons Company began as a tiny print shop more than a century ago. In the decades since its first printing job, Donnelley has printed catalogues, magazines, books, telephone directories, and encyclopedias; in the late 20th century the company diversified its printing services to capitalize on the seemingly endless possibilities of the Internet and electronic business products. With sales of over $5 billion and 40 manufacturing facilities around the globe, Donnelley is the printer of choice for eight of the top ten U.S. publishers, providing one-stop printing services from projects numbering in the dozens to the millions in virtually any format.

Modest Beginnings: 1860s to 1890s

In 1864 Richard R. Donnelley, a 26-year-old saddlemaker's apprentice from Hamilton, Ontario, moved to Chicago. There he established a print shop, called Church, Goodman, and Donnelley—Steam Printers, which became a modest success. When the shop's building and presses were destroyed in the Chicago fire of 1871, leaving Donnelley virtually penniless, he borrowed $20 for a trip to New York, where he managed to get new presses completely on credit. Nevertheless, it took Donnelley nearly two years to get the printing plant fully operational again.

Donnelley was a perfectionist who paid particular attention to both the artistic aspects of printing as well as the trade's scientific developments. His approach resulted in a high quality of printing that won the firm many customers. In a move that proved fortuitous, Donnelley began printing telephone books in 1886, a market that grew astronomically with the importance of the telephone. The firm also pioneered the printing of mail-order catalogues, beginning with such local firms as Sears, Roebuck & Company. In 1890, under the aggressive leadership of Richard's son Thomas E. Donnelley, the firm was incorporated as R.R. Donnelley & Sons. By 1897 the company was so successful it expanded into larger quarters in another building. After the turn of the century, Donnelley began printing encyclopedias.

Printing Advances and Success with Magazines: 1900s–30s

Although becoming increasingly mechanized, printing was still very much a craft executed by hand before World War I. Donnelley often hired his employees right out of grade school, putting young workers through the Apprentice Training School he began in 1908, one of the first industrial training programs in the United States. Employees worked their way up through each department, learning all aspects of the printing business.

In 1921 Donnelley opened a printing plant in Crawfordsville, Indiana. The plant was built by local workers, who then helped install the equipment, and were offered jobs and training in how to use it. In 1928 Donnelley began printing one of the first of a new wave of national, mass marketed magazines, entitled *Time.* The following year, the onset of the Great Depression was disastrous for the printing industry, and magazine and newspaper circulations plummeted. However, with contracts such as *Time* magazine Donnelley was able to stay in business.

In 1934 magazine circulations began to increase again. Donnelley foresaw the demand for a larger format for magazines, printed on coated paper, as well as the industry's need to produce these new magazines on tight deadlines. Thus the company began

Company Perspectives:

R.R. Donnelley serves a broad range of customers who use words and images to inform, educate, entertain, and sell. We have the technical know-how, the digital infrastructure, the reliability, the financial strength, and the customer relationships to go anywhere and do anything to gets words and images in the hands of the right *people, in the* form *they prefer, with the* personalization *they respond to, at the* speed *they require. Our distinctive capabilities to* manage *and* distribute *words and images help our customers succeed.*

developing the materials and expertise to produce such magazines at a reasonable cost. Donnelley engineers combined a rotary press with smaller printing cylinders and a high-speed folder to increase production from 6,000 to 15,000 impressions an hour. Donnelley researchers, working with ink manufacturers, developed a heat-set process for instantly drying ink at these speeds, using a gas heater built right into the printing press. During this time, the publishers of *Time* magazine had been considering the development of a picture magazine. Shortly after they heard about Donnelley's new high-speed printing methods they awarded the firm the contract to publish the new *Life* magazine, the first issue of which came out in 1936.

World War II and Postwar Boom: 1945–59

World War II, with its paper shortages and government-imposed restrictions on commercial printing, was a difficult time for those in the business. After the war, however, printing boomed and soon became a $3 billion-a-year industry. New technologies promised to revolutionize printing, including phototypesetting and electronic scanners for platemaking. Donnelley, already the biggest commercial printer in the United States and continuing to grow, quickly invested in such technologies as they came out.

Donnelley went public in 1956 to raise capital for further expansion. By that time the company had over 160 presses, many of them huge and modern, using over 1,000 tons of paper and 20 tons of ink a day. The firm employed 7,500 people; Crawfordsville alone had 1,600 employees. Representing a rare exception in the printing industry, most Donnelley employees did not belong to a union. About 90 percent of Donnelley's executives and supervisors were graduates of the Apprentice Training School and were either college graduates who had gone through a training program or had come up through the ranks. The firm's turnover remained low.

The company's magazine printing business was its most profitable, and such nationally distributed periodicals as *Time, Life, Look, Sports Illustrated, Farm Journal, National Geographic,* and *Fortune* accounted for about half of sales. Donnelley's huge mail-order catalogues for Sears, Roebuck & Co. and Marshall Field's accounted for about 17 percent of sales. Donnelley printed over 1,000 telephone directories for subscribers throughout much of the country, accounting for about 13 percent of sales. It also printed encyclopedias, including *World Book, Encyclopedia Britannica,* and *Compton's,* as well as corporate reports, the Bible, and other religious publications. Donnelley engaged in less glamorous printing as well, such as booklets, pamphlets, menus, and the labels for packages and cans.

Donnelley mailed so many publications every day that the U.S. Post Office had employees working in the company's plants to supervise the vast mailings. Major plants, with floor space totaling nearly three million square feet, were located in Chicago; Willard, Ohio; and Crawfordsville and Warsaw, Indiana. The firm continued its role as a research and development leader in the industry, spending about $1.6 million a year. In addition to designing mechanical equipment and improving printing materials, Donnelley worked to keep up with cutting-edge electronic and photographic technology. Looking for new technologies was imperative as the costs of labor, material, and equipment were all rising, while intense competition kept prices down.

Having gone public, Donnelley grew by a total of 50 percent between 1954 and 1959, with record sales of $130.1 million in 1959. Despite a depressed economy, sales reached $149.8 million in 1961, with Time Inc. accounting for 29 percent.

Changing Times: 1960s–70s

During the mid-1960s, however, Donnelley's profits leveled off. The firm recovered by 1968 as magazine sales, which accounted for 41 percent of sales, broke out of a slump. By that point Donnelley's hardcover publishing had increased to represent 22 percent of sales while retail catalogues also stood at 22 percent. Printing technology changed rapidly in the late 1960s as photocomposition, computerized justification, and electronic scanning were changing the way plates were readied, and high-speed offset printing also changed the process. In 1968 Donnelley bought an RCA Videocomp, which set 4,500 characters of type per second using a cathode ray tube. One Donnelley manager estimated that the machine could set as much type as every hot-metal typesetter in the Midwest. Simultaneously, the firm created a separate photocomposition and electronics division which employed computer programmers and electronic communications specialists instead of production staff.

As type became easier to set, however, the popular magazine market was shrinking. *Look* folded in 1971, taking $15 million of Donnelley's business with it; then *Life* cut circulation from 8.5 million to 5.5 million. As a result of these losses, Donnelley laid off 700 people, soon cutting an additional 400 people to keep its costs down. Despite its losses, however, the firm made $24 million in 1971 on sales of $340 million. With magazines suffering, most of Donnelley's growth came from catalogues and directories. To keep pace, the firm opened a plant in Lancaster, Pennsylvania, in 1972, exclusively for the printing of phone books for the mid-Atlantic states. To further offset mass market magazine losses, Donnelley worked to win jobs producing special interest periodicals, printing 24 such periodicals for Ziff-Davis Publishing alone.

In 1972 *Life* magazine stopped publishing entirely, resulting in a $3 million charge against earnings and further layoffs. Donnelley also lost its contracts with *Fortune* and *American Home.* Fortunately, the company found new customers in *Esquire* magazine, and signed ten-year contracts with *Glamour* and *Mademoiselle,* and a five-year contract with *U.S. News &*

Key Dates:

1864: Richard R. Donnelley establishes print shop in Chicago.
1871: Great Chicago Fire destroys Donnelley's shop and presses.
1873: Rebuilt printing shop is back in business.
1886: Company begins printing telephone directories.
1890: Business incorporates as R.R. Donnelley & Sons.
1908: Donnelley establishes Apprentice Training School.
1921: Company opens plant in Crawfordsville, Indiana.
1928: Company begins printing *Time* magazine.
1936: Company begins printing *Life* magazine.
1945: Donnelley realizes large profits from World War II and turns to the future.
1968: Company purchases RCA Videocomp, a revolutionary new typesetter.
1972: *Life* folds; Donnelley picks up *Esquire, Mademoiselle, Glamour,* and *U.S. News & World Report.*
1974: Company begins focusing on short-run printing.
1987: Metromail Corp. is acquired.
1994: Donnelley goes digital with state-of-the-art computerized technology.
1996: Donnelley, with sales of $5 billion, is ranked the number one U.S. printer by *American Printer.*
1999: Company announces alliance with Microsoft for electronic bookstore.
2000: Company expands electronic capabilities with several new web-based programs.

World Report. Donnelley's conservative financial practices helped it weather the storm. The firm paid low dividends on its earnings, had net working capital of $90 million, and only $3 million in long-term debt.

In 1974 the firm began shifting away from high quality four-color extended runs, which had accounted for most of its work until then. Numerous small publishers were appearing, and others were moving toward smaller initial press runs to cut down on remainders and the costs of storage. Publishers instead wanted the ability to quickly reprint books that sold out their first edition; Donnelley was determined to change accordingly. Over the next few years the company installed a short-run plant in Crawfordsville, for producing college, professional, and trade books, and doubled capacity at its Willard, Ohio, plant. In the late 1970s the firm began building a state-of-the-art plant in Harrisonburg, Virginia, to offer overnight delivery to publisher warehouses on the East Coast.

Serving Clients Both Large and Small: 1980s

In the early 1980s, Donnelley increased its shift toward small press runs. It began an aggressive telemarketing campaign in which it contacted numerous small publishers, trying to change its image as a printing house for larger clients only. As a result, by 1983, Donnelley had between 600 and 700 book publishers as customers, and short-run books accounted for nearly 50 percent of unit sales.

Sales grew rapidly, reaching $2.2 billion in 1986. The following year Donnelley purchased Metromail Corp. for $282.6 million. Metromail provided lists to direct-mail marketers, and, as Donnelley already printed and distributed catalogues for direct-mail marketers, the acquisition was expected to complement Donnelley's existing business. It also moved into financial printing, opening a Wall Street financial printing center shortly before the stock market crash of October 1987.

In the late 1980s, Donnelley's expansion went into overdrive, culminating with the purchase of Meredith/Burda Printing for $570 million. Donnelley was also moving rapidly into such information services as computer documentation, with sales of $190 million by 1989 out of total sales for the year of $3.1 billion. The firm used electronic printing techniques and information from Metromail to help its clients gear advertising and editorial content toward different audiences. Furthermore, Donnelley was entering the markets for printing books for children, professional books, and quick-printing, with the purchase of 25 percent of AlphaGraphics, a high-end quick-printing chain.

The firm pushed expansion so hard because it believed ever-evolving technologies gave it an opportunity to capture large chunks of business from smaller companies that could not afford to keep up. Donnelley's moves into cutting-edge technology were not always successful, however; in 1984 it had made a premature, ill-fated attempt to move into electronic shopping.

Highs and Lows: 1990–96

With the U.S. economy in recession in 1991, the firm's net income declined about nine percent to $205 million. The following year, however, profits bounced back to $234 million and sales rose to nearly $4.2 billion. During this time, the company acquired Combined Communication Services, a trade magazine printer, and American Inline Graphics, a specialty, direct-mail printer. The firm also continued its expansion outside the United States, opening new offices and plants in the Netherlands, Scotland, Mexico, and Thailand. In addition, Donnelley increased its presence in electronic media and online services.

Such successes helped to partly offset losses in Donnelley's traditional markets. In early 1993 Sears ceased publication of its 97-year-old catalogue, which Donnelley had printed since its inception. Consequently, Donnelley laid off 660 employees, took a $60 million charge against earnings, and closed its historic Lakeside Press plant. A few months later, the company announced it would begin printing the *National Enquirer* and *Star* tabloids. These publications opted to use Donnelley because its advanced printing processes allowed for tighter deadlines and turnaround times of less than 40 hours.

In 1994 Donnelley scored several coups, including exclusive contracts with HarperCollins and *Reader's Digest,* a 51 percent stake in Editorial Lord Cochrane SA, South America's largest printing firm, as well as the development of a new state-of-the-art digital book production system first put into use in the Crawfordsville plant. Under a new program christened Donnelley Digital Architecture, the company was able to shift most printing jobs into digital form and shorten the entire publishing process, from proofing to final printing and binding. The next innovation, print-on-demand publishing, was initiated in a new 60,000-square-foot plant in Memphis, Tennessee, and accommodated print runs from mere hundreds to millions. Hoping to set a new standard for the industry, Donnelley wanted its customers to know that any print run, of any size, could be created and printed in record time.

Sales for 1994 climbed over 11 percent to just under $4.9 billion, and the following year the company acquired International Communications & Data, a direct-marketing information and list service provider; LAN Systems Inc., a systems integration company; and Corporate Software Inc., a leading reseller of business software. In the latter deal, Donnelley merged its Global Software Services division with Corporate Software, forming a new company called Stream International Inc., of which Donnelley retained an 80 percent interest.

The middle and late 1990s were also a time of concentrated international expansion, with Donnelley increasing its presence in Chile, China, India, and Poland, with operations in 21 countries. By the end of 1995 sales reached $6.5 billion, a 33 percent climb due in part to the company's global expansion. A slowdown came in the first quarter of 1996, however, when sales fell below expectations. Rather than adopt a wait-and-see posture, Donnelley announced restructuring plans which included closing its bindery in Scranton, Pennsylvania, while pouring millions into newer technologies and upgrades in other printing facilities. Despite taking some major writedowns during the year for its reorganization, Donnelley was still ranked the number one printing company in the United States by *American Printer* for 1996, and brought in sales of just over $5 billion.

Ending One Century, Beginning Another: 1997 to 2000

In 1997 came a major transition with the appointment of a new chairman and CEO, William L. Davis, formerly of the St. Louis-based Emerson Electric Company. Davis replaced longtime CEO John Walter, who had left to become the new head of AT&T. The year also saw the departure of the company's legal and financial services subsidiary, Donnelley Enterprise Solutions Inc., which was spun off as a public company. Over the next few years Donnelley was intent on integrating its three print management segments into a cohesive whole while investing millions in the latest digital printing innovations and business solution products. ''We recognize that our customers have a growing need to communicate effectively across a broad range of media to succeed,'' Chairman and CEO Davis told *Graphic Arts Monthly*'s Lisa Cross in a January 2000 article. A major step in this direction was the company's deal with Microsoft Corporation to produce and maintain an electronic bookstore, offering Internet clients hundreds of thousands of electronic book titles; while the acquisition of Omega Studios, a Texas-based desktop publishing service, was another coup for its evolving e-commerce solutions and services sector.

R.R. Donnelley & Sons had literally done it all in the printing industry, and was well prepared for the 21st century. The company offered ''traditional'' forms of printing, but its mounting investments in Web- and Internet-based publishing were consistently paying off with a growing roster of both domestic and international clients.

Principal Subsidiaries

AlphaGraphics; American Inline Graphics; Combined Communications Services; Meredith/Burda Printing; Metromail Corp.

Principal Competitors

Banta Corporation; Cadmus Communications Corporation; Moore Corporation Ltd.; Quad/Graphics Inc.; Quebecor Printing Inc.; World Color Press Inc.

Further Reading

Cross, Lisa, ''Print's Hot Prospects in the Digital Economy,'' *Graphic Arts Monthly*, January 2000, p. 50.

''Donnelley Invests in Print-on-Demand,'' *Graphic Arts Monthly*, October 1994, p. 98.

''Donnelley Recovers from *Life*'s Death,'' *Financial World,* May 16, 1973, p. 10.

''Donnelley's Global Information Play,'' *Mergers & Acquisitions*, January-February 1996, p. 53.

Hilts, Paul, ''Donnelley's Digital Production Vision: R.R. Donnelley and Sons Invited Book Publishers to Come to Crawfordsville to See the Future of Printing,'' *Publishers Weekly*, August 22, 1994, p. 24.

——, ''Donnelley, Microsoft Team to Expand eBook Business,'' *Publishers Weekly*, November 8, 1999, p. 11.

Kellman, Jerold L., ''Donnelley: A Big Printer Looks to Small Publishers and Short Runs,'' *Publishers Weekly,* January 14, 1983, p. 44.

''R.R. Donnelley & Sons Co.; Presses Shift to High Speed at Commercial Printer,'' *Barron's,* January 29, 1990, p. 59.

''R.R. Donnelley & Sons Set to Register Profits Gain,'' *Barron's,* September 25, 1972, p. 27.

''R.R. Donnelley Sees Another Bright Chapter in Continuing Success Story,'' *Barron's,* April 4, 1960, p. 28.

Roth, Jill, ''Top 100-Plus: The Listing,'' *American Printer*, July 1996, p. 29.

Taylor, Sally, ''Donnelley Is Bullish on the Book,'' *Publishers Weekly*, August 7, 1995, p. 318.

Waltz, George H., *The House That Quality Built,* Chicago: The Lakeside Press, 1957.

—Scott M. Lewis
—updated by Nelson Rhodes

Raytheon

Raytheon Company

141 Spring Street
Lexington, Massachusetts 02421
U.S.A.
Telephone: (781) 862-6600
Fax: (781) 860-2172
Web site: http://www.raytheon.com

Public Company
Incorporated: 1922 as American Appliance Company
Employees: 105,300
Sales: $19.84 billion (1999)
Stock Exchanges: New York Chicago Pacific
Ticker Symbol: RTNA; RTNB
NAIC: 336414 Guided Missile and Space Vehicle Manufacturing; 334511 Search, Detection, Navigation, Guidance, Aeronautical, and Nautical System and Instruments Manufacturing; 334220 Radio and Television Broadcasting and Wireless Communications Equipment Manufacturing; 334290 Other Communications Equipment Manufacturing; 334418 Printed Circuit Assembly (Electronic Assembly) Manufacturing; 336411 Aircraft Manufacturing

Raytheon Company is the third largest defense contractor in the United States, trailing only the Boeing Company and Lockheed Martin Corporation. Among the company's key defense products are missile defense systems, including the Patriot and Hawk ground-based missile systems; offensive missiles, including the Tomahawk, TOW, and Stinger; and radar, infrared, and other electronic systems for surveillance, reconnaissance, targeting, navigation, and other purposes. Raytheon has pioneered in the conversion of defense technologies into commercial products handled by Raytheon Commercial Electronics, such as marine electronic equipment, broadband wireless communications products, and infrared night vision systems for automobiles. Raytheon Aircraft Company is the number one maker of business and special mission aircraft in the world; this subsidiary, however, had been placed for sale in 2000. The sale of the company's aircraft unit would complete a divestiture program launched in the late 1990s that transformed Raytheon from an industrial conglomerate to a company focused solely on defense and commercial electronics.

Beginnings in Radio Tubes

Raytheon was founded in 1922 when a civil engineer named Laurence Marshall was introduced to an inventor and Harvard physicist named Charles G. Smith by Dr. Vannevar Bush. Marshall proposed a business partnership with Smith and Bush after hearing that Smith had developed a new method for noiseless home refrigeration using compressed gases and no moving parts. Marshall raised $25,000 in venture capital from investors and a former World War I comrade and incorporated the partnership in Cambridge, Massachusetts (near Bush's employer, the Massachusetts Institute of Technology), as American Appliance Company.

Marshall and Smith never developed their refrigeration technologies for the market, but instead shifted their attention to vacuum tubes and other electronic devices. In 1924 Marshall made a three-month tour of the United States to study the pattern of growth in the electronics market. Noting rapidly growing consumer demand for radios, Marshall negotiated the purchase of patents for the S-tube, a gas-filled rectifier that converted alternating current (AC) used in households to the direct current (DC) used in radio sets (ironically, the technology had been developed by Smith and Bush some years earlier while they worked for the American Research and Development Corporation). Up to that time, radios ran on an auto storage battery called the A battery and a high-voltage B battery, which were costly, cumbersome, messy, and relatively expensive to replace.

In 1925, shortly before S-tube production began, a firm in Indiana laid claim to the American Appliance company name. The partners decided to change their corporate moniker to Raytheon Manufacturing Company. Despite the fact that *raytheon* is Greek for ''god of life,'' the name actually was chosen for its modern sound. By 1926, Raytheon had become a major manufacturer of tube rectifiers and generated $321,000 in profit on sales of $1 million.

Company Perspectives:

From its early days as a maker of radio tubes, its adaptation of World War II radar technology to invent microwave cooking, and its development of the first guided missiles, Raytheon has successfully built upon its pioneering tradition to become a global technology leader.

Today, Raytheon is focused on its core businesses: defense and commercial electronics and business aviation and special mission aircraft. Each provides the company with the capabilities it needs to build on its strength as an innovator and to prosper in a highly competitive global economy.

Virtually all the tubes produced by Raytheon were used in radio sets whose design patents were held by RCA. In 1927 RCA altered its licensing agreements with radio manufacturers to stipulate that the radios could be built only with new rectifier tubes (called Radiotrons) manufactured by RCA. Raytheon was, in effect, denied access to its markets. The company was forced to switch to the production of radio-receiving tubes, a field in which more than 100 companies were engaged in fierce competition.

Marshall's response to operating in this difficult environment was to diversify. Raytheon acquired the Acme-Delta Company, a producer of transformers, power equipment, and electronic auto parts. Profits resulting from new products were immediately put back into research and development to improve products, particularly in industrial electronics and microwave communications.

Marshall also sought the support of the National Carbon Company (a division of Union Carbide Corp.) during this difficult period. In 1929, National Carbon took a $500,000 equity position in Raytheon and held an option to buy the remaining portion of the company for an additional $19.5 million. National Carbon knew that Raytheon rectifier tubes had originally replaced its B battery business and also was convinced that its battery distribution would do well handling replacement tubes marked Eveready-Raytheon. Although the cooperative project was unsuccessful, National Carbon's investment carried Raytheon through the Great Depression. National Carbon allowed its option to acquire Raytheon to lapse in 1938.

Moving into Defense Contracting During World War II

With world war looming in 1940, U.S. President Franklin Roosevelt and British Prime Minister Winston Churchill authorized the joint development of new radar technologies by American and British institutions. Through the Radiation Laboratory at the Massachusetts Institute of Technology, Raytheon was chosen to develop the top-secret British magnetron, a microwave radar power tube. The technology would provide the range and clearer images required for successful detection and destruction of enemy planes, submarines (when they surfaced), and German warships. The new device had more than 100 times the power of previous microwave tubes and was cited as one of the Allies' top secrets. Britain, however, needed the United States' manufacturing capacity. In June 1941 Raytheon also won a contract to deliver 100 radar systems for navy ships.

Workers produced 100 magnetrons a day until plant manager Percy Spencer discovered a method, using punch presses, to raise production to more than 2,500 a day. Spencer's ingenuity won Raytheon an appropriation of $2 million from the U.S. Navy for the construction of a large new factory in Waltham, Massachusetts. By the end of the war, Raytheon magnetrons accounted for about 80 percent of the one million magnetrons produced during the war. By 1944, virtually every U.S. Navy ship was equipped with Raytheon radar. The company became internationally known for its reliable marine radar. The company also offered complete radar installations, with the help of subcontractors, and developed tubes for the VT radio fuse, a device that detonated fired shells when it sensed they were near solid objects. Over the course of the war, Raytheon's sales increased 55 times, from $3 million in 1940 to $168 million in 1945.

Raytheon was fortunate to be involved in a high-growth area of defense industry. When the war ended, companies specializing in high-technology military systems suffered less from cuts in the postwar defense budget than aircraft or heavy-vehicle manufacturers, or shipbuilders. In large part as a result of the war, Raytheon emerged as a profitable and influential, but still financially vulnerable, electronics company.

During the spring of 1945 Raytheon's management formulated plans to acquire several other electronics firms. As part of a strategy to consolidate independent component manufacturers into one company, in April the company purchased Belmont Electronics for $4.6 million. Belmont, located in Chicago, was a major consumer of Raytheon tubes and was developing a television for the commercial market. That October, Raytheon acquired Russell Electric for $1.1 million and entered merger negotiations with the Submarine Signal Company. Sub-Sig, as the company was known, was founded in Boston in 1901 as a manufacturer of maritime safety equipment, including a depth sounder called the fathometer. Sub-Sig manufactured a variety of sonar equipment during the war and, like Belmont, was a major Raytheon customer. When the two companies agreed to merge on May 31, 1946, it was decided that Sub-Sig would specialize in sonar devices and that Raytheon would continue to develop new radar systems.

Despite Raytheon's strengthened position as a result of the mergers, the company faced severe competition in both the sonar and radar markets from companies such as General Electric, RCA, Westinghouse Electric, and Sperry. Belmont, which planned to bring its television to market in late 1948, suffered a crippling strike during the summer and, as a result, lost much of its projected Christmas business. Unstable price conditions the following spring created further losses from which the subsidiary was, in large part, unable to recuperate.

Laurence Marshall, though a superb engineer, was generally regarded as a poor manager. His inability to effect positive changes within the company led him to resign as president in February 1948. The following December he resigned as CEO, but he remained chairman of the board until May 1950, when he resigned after failing to gain support for a proposed merger with International Telephone & Telegraph. Charles F. Adams, a for-

Key Dates:

1922: American Appliance Company is founded.
1925: Company changes its name to Raytheon Manufacturing Company and begins making tubes for radios.
1940: Raytheon is chosen to develop magnetrons, a tube used in microwave radar systems, marking the company's entrance into defense technology.
1941: U.S. Navy contracts with Raytheon on the delivery of 100 ship radar systems.
1950: Raytheon's Lark missile comes to the fore when it successfully intercepts and destroys a test drone.
1965: Amana Refrigeration is acquired.
1967: Company introduces the first countertop microwave under the Amana name.
1976: Production of the Patriot missile defense system begins.
1980: Company acquires Beech Aircraft.
1993: Company acquires the corporate jet unit of British Aerospace.
1995: E-Systems Inc. is acquired.
1997: Raytheon acquires the defense businesses of Texas Instruments Inc. and Hughes Electronics Corporation; its home appliances unit is divested.
2000: Raytheon Engineers & Constructors is sold to Morrison Knudsen Corporation.

mer financial advisor who joined Raytheon in 1947, assumed Marshall's responsibilities.

The sudden resumption of military orders after the outbreak of the Korean War in June 1950 greatly benefited Raytheon, as Defense Department contracts enabled the company to develop new technologies with initially low profitability. That year, a "Lark" missile equipped with a Raytheon-designed guidance system made history when it intercepted and destroyed a Navy drone aircraft. Raytheon's advanced research center, called Lab 16, was designed to develop the Sparrow air-to-air and Hawk surface-to-air missiles. Raytheon became a partner in Selenia, a joint venture with the Italian firms Finmeccanica and Fiat, which was established to develop new radar technologies. Raytheon's association with Selenia afforded it an opportunity to work with the Italian rocket scientist Carlo Calosi.

Raytheon's Belmont operation was re-formed in 1954, but two years later all radio and television operations were sold to the Admiral Corporation. Raytheon continued, however, to develop new appliances, such as the Radarange microwave oven. In 1956 Charles Adams hired Harold S. Geneen, a highly innovative and dynamic manager, as executive vice-president. Three years later, however, Geneen left Raytheon to become chief executive of ITT. Richard E. Krafve (who once headed the Ford Motor Company's Edsel project) enjoyed only a short tenure as Geneen's successor; he disagreed frequently with Adams and was apparently unable to gain the respect of engineers. Thomas L. Phillips, manager of the Missile Division, replaced Krafve.

In 1956 and 1957, Raytheon and Minneapolis-Honeywell jointly operated a computer company called Datamatic. Raytheon soon sold its interest to Honeywell when Datamatic failed to compete effectively against IBM. Raytheon's joint venture projects with Italian companies continued to expand, however. D. Brainerd Holmes, a former director of the American manned space flight program, joined Raytheon in 1963 to manage the company's military business, reporting to Phillips.

Diversifying in the 1960s and 1970s

Raytheon's top managers began to recognize weaknesses in the company's organizational structure perhaps as early as 1962; Raytheon, they decided, had become too dependent on government contracts. So in 1964 Adams and Phillips, who had become chairman and president, respectively, conceived a plan that aimed to diversify the company's operations. Raytheon acquired Packard-Bell's computer operations and a number of small electronics firms. In 1965 Raytheon acquired Amana Refrigeration Company. Although Raytheon had invented the microwave oven 20 years earlier, it needed Amana to commercialize the technology. (Spencer had accidentally discovered microwave cooking in 1945 when a candy bar in his pocket melted as he stood near an operating magnetron tube; the company began selling commercial refrigerator-sized Radaranges in 1947, then five years later started selling, with limited success, expensive consumer models through a licensing deal with Tappan Stove Company.) In 1967 Raytheon helped launch a domestic revolution when it introduced the first countertop microwave under the Amana name, featuring 100 volts of power and priced at just less than $500. That same year, Caloric Corporation, a major manufacturer of gas ranges and appliances, was acquired as well. By the end of the decade, Raytheon had absorbed a number of additional companies, including the E.B. Badger Co., Inc., a designer and builder of petroleum and petrochemical plants; United Engineers and Constructors, a designer and builder of power plants; textbook publisher D.C. Heath & Company; and a geological survey company called the Seismograph Service Corporation.

Raytheon's association with Selenia became strained in 1967. Raytheon's directors concluded that its Italian partners were unwilling to reform the operations of Selenia and Elsi (a jointly operated electronics firm). They voted to sell Raytheon's share of the companies to its partners and end their association with Calosi. Nevertheless, the defense department in 1967 selected Raytheon as the prime contractor for the new SAM-D surface-to-air missile. Renamed the Patriot in honor of the nation's bicentennial, the missile entered full-scale production in 1976. Initially designed as a defense against high-tech aircraft, the Patriot was upgraded about ten years later with the capability to intercept and destroy short-range ballistic missiles.

The goal of reducing Raytheon's proportion of sales to the government from 85 percent to 50 percent was achieved on schedule in 1970. But, while Raytheon's sales continued to rise, profits began to lag. Intracompany discussions determined that, with the exception of D.C. Heath, Raytheon should dispense with its marginally performing educational services units. In 1972, after several relatively small acquisitions, Raytheon purchased Iowa Manufacturing Company (later called Cedarapids, Inc.), a producer of road-building equipment.

When Charles Adams retired as chair in 1975, Tom Phillips was elected the new chairman and chief executive officer.

Brainerd Holmes was promoted to president. Raytheon's financial performance during the mid-1970s was impressive: from 1973 to 1978 sales and profits grew at annual rates of 15 percent and 26 percent, respectively. Acquisitions in the latter years of the decade included Switchcraft, Inc., an electronics manufacturer, and Glenwood Range and Modern Maid gas range producers. The laundry products and kitchen appliance divisions of McGraw-Edison, which included the popular Speed Queen brand name, were added in 1979. The company's retained earnings were placed in high-yielding money market accounts until needed to finance acquisitions.

In 1977 Phillips tried to acquire Falcon Seaboard, an energy resources company involved primarily in strip mining coal, but withdrew the offer when favorable terms could not be reached. Instead, Phillips entered into negotiations to acquire Beech Aircraft, a leading manufacturer of single- and twin-engine aircraft. Raytheon acquired Beech in February 1980 for $800 million. The new affiliate recorded annual losses in each of the ensuing seven years, finally turning a profit in 1988.

At this time Raytheon's business with the government consisted mainly of radar systems, solar systems, communications equipment, and the Hawk, Sparrow, Patriot, and Sidewinder missiles, all of which totaled less than 40 percent of Raytheon's sales. Raytheon was now more widely exposed to commercial computer and consumer markets, but these markets had become unexpectedly competitive, leading Raytheon management to reconsider its trend of moving away from stable military contracts.

Raytheon's Data Systems division, created in 1971 through the merger of the company's information processing and display units, established a small market by manufacturing terminals for airline reservation systems. Raytheon failed, however, to integrate Data Systems effectively with a word processing subsidiary called Lexitron, which it acquired in 1978. As the computer products market expanded, Data Systems found itself unable to compete. After mounting losses, the division was sold to Telex in 1984. In January 1986 Raytheon acquired the Yeargin Construction Company, a builder of electrical and chemical plants, and the following October it acquired the Stearns Catalytic World Corporation, an industrial plant maintenance company.

When Brainerd Holmes retired on May 31, 1986, as he reached the traditional retirement age of 65, he was succeeded as president by R. Gene Shelley, who himself retired in July 1989 and was replaced by Dennis J. Picard. Picard succeeded Tom Phillips as chairman and chief executive of Raytheon in 1990, and Max E. Bleck rose to president.

Focusing on Defense and Commercial Electronics: 1990s and Beyond

While other major defense contractors moved to convert to civilian interests in the wake of post-Cold War defense budget cuts, Raytheon planned to buttress its position within its four main business segments: defense and commercial electronics, aircraft products, energy and environmental services, and major appliances. In 1992, Picard announced a new five-year plan. Its goals included increasing foreign military sales from 20 percent to 40 percent of total defense revenues; doubling energy and environmental services' $1.7 billion in sales; doubling Beech's $1.1 billion in sales; and increasing appliance sales by 60 percent.

The versatile Patriot missile—Raytheon's single most important product in the early 1990s—was considered pivotal to an increase in the company's overseas sales. From the end of the Gulf War until late in 1994, Raytheon received nearly $2.5 billion in orders for the missiles from overseas customers. The corporation's environmental and energy service was consolidated to form Raytheon Engineers & Constructors International Inc. (RECI), one of the world's largest engineering and construction groups, in 1993. The acquisitions of Harbert Corp., Gibbs & Hill, and key segments of EBASCO Services, Inc. that year were intended to help boost RECI's annual sales. The corporate jet unit of British Aerospace plc also was purchased that year for $387.5 million. The acquisition helped expand Beech's penetration of the business aircraft market. An extensive overhaul of the appliance segment, including downsizing, consolidation, and the 1994 acquisition of UniMac Companies, helped increase that division's sales and profits. Raytheon, meantime, exited from the publishing field with the 1995 sale of D.C. Heath to Houghton Mifflin Co. for $455 million.

The end of the Cold War and the resulting defense budget cuts ushered in a wave of mergers and consolidations in the defense industry by the mid-1990s. Raytheon was a key participant in this trend and also worked to rationalize its defense businesses. In early 1995 the company created Raytheon Electronic Systems from the merger of its Missile Systems Division and Equipment Division. Later that year Raytheon acquired Dallas-based E-Systems Inc. for more than $2.3 billion, gaining a leading developer of military intelligence communications systems. In 1996 Raytheon added two of Chrysler Corporation's defense businesses in a deal valued at about $475 million. The Chrysler units acquired were its electrospace systems operation, which was involved in satellite communications, secure communications, and electronic warfare systems; and its airborne-technologies operation, which modified commercial aircraft for use by the armed forces and by heads of state, often equipping the planes with high-tech signal-jamming and encoding equipment. Both of these units complemented the activities of E-Systems and, therefore, were consolidated into the newly named Raytheon E-Systems.

Raytheon's appetite was not yet sated, and in fact grew in 1997, when the company acquired the defense business of Texas Instruments Inc. for $2.9 billion in July and the defense business of Hughes Electronics Corporation, a subsidiary of General Motors Corporation, for $9.5 billion in December. The Texas Instruments deal brought to Raytheon a number of complementary operations, including laser-guided weapons systems, missiles, airborne radar, night vision systems, and electronic warfare systems. The Hughes defense unit was a leading supplier of advanced defense electronics systems and services. These latest acquisitions propelled Raytheon into the top three among defense contractors and into the top position in defense electronics. They also led to a marked increase in revenues, from $12.33 billion in 1996 to $19.53 billion in 1998. Following the completion of the Hughes transaction, Raytheon consolidated its defense businesses—Raytheon Electronic Systems, Raytheon E-Systems, and the Texas Instruments and Hughes units—into a new operation called Raytheon Systems Company. In connection with this restructuring and a smaller restructuring of Raytheon Engineers & Constructors, Raytheon took a $495 million restructuring charge in 1997 for a plan that by 1999 eliminated more than 14,000 jobs from the workforce and closed about 28 facilities in the United States. In December 1997, the company also created a new subsidiary called Raytheon Systems Limited, which was based in the United Kingdom and was formed to develop products for export from that country.

By this time it was clearly evident that Raytheon had made a marked shift in strategy, placing a greater emphasis on its defense businesses, alongside the commercial electronics applications that developed out of the defense operations. The divestment of additional noncore operations was further evidence of this trend, with the divestments also helping to hold down the company's mounting debt load, which exceeded $10 billion by the end of 1997 thanks to the defense acquisitions. In 1997 Raytheon sold its home appliance, heating, air conditioning, and commercial cooking operations to Goodman Holding Co. for $522 million. That same year, the company sold its Switchcraft and Semiconductor divisions in separate transactions totaling $183 million. Divestments continued in 1998, including the sale of the firm's commercial laundry business for $334 million. Operations now consisted of the defense units, Raytheon Commercial Electronics, Raytheon Aircraft Company, and Raytheon Engineers & Constructors. In December 1998 Daniel P. Burnham, a vice-chairman of AlliedSignal, Inc., took the helm at Raytheon as president and CEO. Picard remained chairman until August 1999, when Burnham took on that title as well.

Late in 1999 Raytheon revealed that it had uncovered pervasive management and financial problems in its defense electronics operations that forced it to cut its earnings projections for the fourth quarter and all of 2000. The company was over budget or behind schedule on more than a dozen Pentagon contracts, and other projects, both in the United States and overseas, were being delayed at the contract stage itself, including several billion-dollar deals involving Patriot missiles. With earnings down, Raytheon would be unable to pay down its $9.5 billion debt as quickly as it hoped. For the year, net income stood at $404 million, less than half the $844 million figure of the previous year. Meantime, late in 1999 the company launched a further restructuring, with additional job cuts, the closure or amalgamation of ten plants, and a charge of $668 million. To flatten the organizational structure, Raytheon Systems Company was reorganized into several smaller units: Electronic Systems; Command, Control, Communication and Information Systems; Raytheon Technical Services Company; and Aircraft Integration Systems. On the positive side for 1999, Raytheon contracted with the United Kingdom to develop a $1.3 billion high-tech radar surveillance system called Airborne Stand-Off Radar. That year also saw the sale of the Cedarapids subsidiary for $170 million.

As it worked to fix the problems in its defense operations, Raytheon was awarded a couple more large contracts in August 2000. The U.S. Army awarded a joint venture partnership of Raytheon and Lockheed Martin a $1.24 billion production contract on the Javelin Antitank Weapon System, which the partners first began producing in 1997. In addition, Lockheed Martin selected Raytheon for the design, development, and manufacture of three radar systems for the Theater High Altitude Area Defense System, a $4 billion missile defense system contracted for by the U.S. Army. Raytheon's portion of the project amounted to $1.3 billion. Meantime, Raytheon's ongoing series of divestitures were nearing their conclusion. In July 2000 Raytheon Engineers & Constructors was sold to Morrison Knudsen Corporation for more than $800 million. Later in the year it was reported that Raytheon Aircraft Company was being shopped around. The sale of the aircraft unit essentially would focus Raytheon exclusively on defense and commercial electronics. Once again, these further divestments were in part aimed at slashing the burdensome debt load, which had crept back up over the $10 billion mark by late 2000. Raytheon would need to rein in this debt load and clear up its other financial problems if it wished to return to or surpass the steadily, if unspectacularly, profitable years that preceded the major 1997 acquisitions.

Principal Subsidiaries

Raytheon Aircraft Company; Raytheon Systems Limited (U.K.).

Principal Operating Units

Electronic Systems; Command, Control, Communication and Information Systems; Raytheon Technical Services Company; Aircraft Integration Systems; Raytheon Commercial Electronics.

Principal Competitors

BAE Systems; The Boeing Company; Bombardier Inc.; Emerson Electric Co.; European Aeronautic Defence and Space Company EADS N.V.; General Electric Company; Gulfstream Aerospace Corporation; Harris Corporation; Litton Industries, Inc.; Lockheed Martin Corporation; Matra-BAE Dynamics; Northrop Grumman Corporation; Textron Inc.; United Technologies Corporation.

Further Reading

Banks, Howard, "Rocket Science Isn't Easy: Among Big Defense Contractors, Raytheon Is the Best of the Breed. That Ain't Saying Much," *Forbes,* November 1, 1999, pp. 79–80.

Hughes, David, "Raytheon Targets Growth Within Four Core Groups," *Aviation Week & Space Technology,* March 1, 1993, pp. 52–53.

Jones, Steven D., and Anne Marie Squeo, "Raytheon Expects to Post Charge for Sale of Unit for $800 Million," *Wall Street Journal,* April 17, 2000, p. B4.

Lipin, Steven, and Gabriella Stern, "GM Unveils Sale of Hughes Defense Arm to Raytheon Co. in $9.5 Billion Accord," *Wall Street Journal,* January 17, 1997, p. A3.

Lipin, Steven, and Jeff Cole, "Raytheon to Acquire E-Systems for $64 a Share, or $2.3 Billion," *Wall Street Journal,* April 3, 1995, p. A3.

Michaels, Daniel, "European Missile Firm Targets Raytheon," *Wall Street Journal,* August 1, 2000, p. A18.

——, "Raytheon Searches for a Buyer for Aircraft Unit," *Wall Street Journal,* October 18, 2000, p. A4.

Patron, Edward B., "Righting Raytheon," *Financial World,* March 25, 1996, pp. 34–36.

Robinson, Edward, "Raytheon Gets Streamlined," *Fortune,* June 7, 1999, pp. 32, 36.

Schriener, Judy, ''Blasting Off for Peacetime Targets,'' *ENR,* April 18, 1994, pp. 24–28.

Scott, Otto J., *The Creative Ordeal: The Story of Raytheon,* New York: Atheneum, 1974.

Smith, Geoffrey, ''Raytheon's Strategy: Guns and Lots More Butter,'' *Business Week,* November 6, 1992, p. 96.

Smith, Geoffrey, and Victoria Murphy, ''Reality Bites at Raytheon,'' *Business Week,* November 15, 1999, pp. 78, 80, 82.

Squeo, Anne Marie, ''Raytheon Hits Snags on Pentagon Work,'' *Wall Street Journal,* October 12, 1999, p. A3.

——, ''Raytheon to Take $668 Million in Charges: Firms Cites Financial Snags in Defense Electronics,'' *Wall Street Journal,* October 13, 1999, p. A3.

Suhrbier, Robin, ''Raytheon Pushes Single Brand,'' *Business Marketing,* January 1994, pp. 4, 40.

Therrien, Lois, ''Raytheon May Find Itself on the Defensive,'' *Business Week,* May 26, 1986, pp. 72+.

Wilke, John R., and Jon G. Auerbach, ''U.S. Puts Strings on Raytheon Purchase,'' *Wall Street Journal,* October 1, 1997, p. A3.

—April Dougal Gasbarre
—updated by David E. Salamie

Rhodia SA

26, quai Alphonse Le Gallo
92512 Boulogne-Billancourt Cedex
France
Telephone: +33 1 55 38 40 00
Fax: +33 1 55 38 44 43
Web site: http://www.rhodia.com

Public Company
Incorporated: 1998
Employees: 26,257
Sales: EUR 5.53 billion (US$5.2 billion) (1999)
Stock Exchanges: Euronext Paris New York
Ticker Symbol: RHA
NAIC: 325412 Pharmaceutical Preparation Manufacturing; 325212 Synthetic Rubber Manufacturing; 325110 Paint and Coating Manufacturing; 325611 Soap and Other Detergent Manufacturing; 31311 Fiber, Yarn, and Thread Mills; 311942 Food Extracts (Except Coffee, Meat) Manufacturing

One of the world's leading specialty chemicals companies, Rhodia SA—the former chemicals and fibers & polymers units of Rhône-Poulenc (now Aventis) spun off in 1998—is repositioning itself for the 21st century. The company's global operations, with nearly 150 manufacturing facilities in more than 25 countries and sales in more than 150 countries, produce chemical products in six primary divisions. The Industrial Products division produces rubber, silicon, paint, paper, and construction materials, such as reinforced concrete. In the Consumer Products division, the company produces an array of food additives; ingredients for cosmetics, soaps, and other bath and beauty products; and products for laundry and other detergents. The company's Organics division produces ingredients for pharmaceutical products (the company is the world's leading producer of acetylsalicylic acid and second largest producer of paracetamol) as well as perfumes and other synthetic products. The company's Services and Specialties division creates rare earth-based and other products for diverse uses, such as catalytic converters and materials for the automobile industry. Rhodia's Polyamide division creates textiles, threads, plastics, and fibers for a wide variety of uses, ranging from automobile engine and other parts to materials for sportswear and other clothing. Since 2000 Rhodia has been dismantling its sixth division, the Polyester division, as the company has begun a process of selling off its French and Brazilian polyester production facilities. At the same time, Rhodia has boosted its global reach with the acquisition of Albright & Wilson, a leading British chemicals group, which is expected to add some EUR 1.2 billion to the company's annual sales (which topped EUR 5.5 billion in 1999). Rhodia is quoted on both the Euronext Paris and New York stock exchanges.

Founding a French Chemicals Empire in the 19th Century

When Rhodia S.A. was created in 1998, it already boasted nearly 150 years of history. The company's origins follow two threads dating back to the middle of the 19th century. The first of these was the founding of a small factory producing dyes, tanning agents, and other products for textile companies based in the Lyon region of France in 1956. That company's founders, Marc Gilliard and Jean Marie Cartier, later joined with Pierre Monnet of Switzerland, whose company, Pierre Monnet et Cie, founded in 1868, specialized in synthetic dyes based on tar and other materials. The newly enlarged company became Gilliard, Monnet et Cartier, keeping the city of Lyon as the location of its headquarters.

By then, the second of the two threads that were eventually to become the chemicals and manufacturing giant Rhône Poulenc—which would emerge as France's largest company in the 20th century—had already established its own modest origins. In 1858, Etienne Poulenc bought an apothecary in Paris, adding his name to the billing to form the company Wittmann et Poulenc Jeune. Poulenc quickly turned to producing his own products, branching out into chemicals and supplies for the nascent photographic industry, as well as adding apothecary and pharmaceutical products. With the entry of his brothers into the firm, Poulenc's company was renamed Poulenc Frères, before becoming a public company in 1900. At the time, the

Company Perspectives:

Using the core skills and technologies of Rhodia worldwide, we will grow and succeed by building profitable businesses that satisfy the evolving needs of our customers, challenge our employees, serve the public, and establish our company as a recognized and respected market leader.

company expanded its name to become Les Etablissements Poulenc Frères.

Both Poulenc Frères and Gilliard, Monnet et Cartier were at the forefront of developments in what was rapidly becoming the modern era of medicine and medical treatment. At the end of the 19th century, the Gilliard, Monnet et Cartier company, which had begun more and more to invest in the research, development, and production of new chemical products, chose to emphasize its growing interest by changing its name to the Société Chimique des Usines de Rhône in 1895. The company also went public at this time.

Meanwhile, among Poulenc Frères' accomplishments were a number of significant breakthroughs, such as its introduction of arsenobenzol, one of the earliest successful treatments of the hitherto incurable syphilis. Around this time, Société Chimique des Usines de Rhône reinforced its concentration on its own chemical and pharmaceutical products when it exited its original textile dyes market. At this time, Société Chimique des Usines de Rhône also introduced a new brand name to denote a number of its chemical products—Rhodia.

World War I gave both companies a vast testing ground for their pharmaceutical products, as they developed new drugs and compounds to treat the wounds of the French war casualties. After the war, the Société Chimique des Usines de Rhône attempted to enter a new market, that of perfume manufacturing. For this venture, the company used the Rhodia brand name. Facing pressure, however, from its German competitors, which had already begun to dominate the chemicals industry in Europe by then, Société Chimique des Usines de Rhône decided to refocus its production entirely on specialty chemicals by the 1920s.

The end of that decade saw the birth of what was to become not only France's leading chemicals company, but the largest among all French companies. In 1928, the Société Chimique des Usines de Rhône and Les Etablissements Poulenc Frères merged to form the Société des Usines Chimiques Rhône Poulenc. Shortly after, the company became the first French company to begin mass production of the revolutionary new drug penicillin, discovered in 1928.

An Independent Chemicals Giant for the 21st Century

The period following World War II marked an era of steady growth for Rhône Poulenc, as the company established not only its French dominance, but a worldwide reputation as well. The company's operations expanded throughout the world, including the United States, where the company established the subsidiary Rhodia Inc. The U.S. operations only took the name of the French parent in 1978, when it became Rhône Poulenc Inc.

During this period, Rhône Poulenc actively pursued a program of growth by acquisition, making a number of significant purchases to help consolidate the French chemicals and pharmaceuticals industry, including the 1956 addition of Theraplix, first established in 1931. In 1961, the company changed its name, becoming Rhône Poulenc S.A. The 1960s saw another addition to the company in the form of the acquisition of the Institut Mérieux. By the end of the decade, Rhône Poulenc had solidified its leadership in the French market and had built up a position as the number three chemicals group in Europe.

If Rhône Poulenc's post-World War II growth had mirrored that of the French economy, the company continued to follow the same pattern as the French and worldwide economies slipped into a prolonged recession in the 1970s. Suffering from the ailing economic situation, Rhône Poulenc also made a number of strategic errors, such as granting the United States marketing rights for its highly successful drug Thorazine to rival SmithKline. Most important, Rhône Poulenc had long enjoyed its position behind France's high tariff barriers, effectively barring its international competition. The tariff barriers were taken away in the 1970s, and Rhône Poulenc suddenly found itself in head-to-head competition with an array of foreign companies, including several giant American and German chemicals and pharmaceuticals firms.

By the end of the decade, Rhône Poulenc was struggling and, in the early 1980s, posted losses of more than US$500 million. At the time, the public company came under a new attack; the rise to control of the Socialist government under François Mitterand had been won in part because of its promise to nationalize a number of key French industries. Mitterand made good on that promise in 1982, when Rhône Poulenc was taken over by the French government. Placed in charge of the newly nationalized company was Loïk Le Floch-Prigent, who was given the task of restructuring the ailing group. Le Floch cut back on the number of employees, eliminated a number of the company's struggling business units and subsidiaries, and by the mid-1980s had succeeded in bringing Rhône Poulenc back into the black.

Le Floch—who went on to head the French-owned oil company Elf—turned over the leadership of the rejuvenated Rhône Poulenc to Jean-René Fourtou in 1986. Fourtou continued Le Floch's transformation of the company, slashing some 20 subsidiaries, while going on an international spending spree to add 30 new companies, including the agricultural chemicals division of Union Carbide in 1986, Germany's Nattermann, and the industrial chemicals business from Stauffer in 1987. Fourtou's attention had turned especially to the United States, where Rhône Poulenc had picked up some 18 acquisitions.

In 1990, the big got bigger when the French government gave Rhône Poulenc 35 percent of the country's number three pharmaceuticals group, Roussel-Uclaf. In that same year, Rhône Poulenc merged its own pharmaceuticals operations with that of the United States' Rorer—developer of Maalox and other drugs—to form Rhône Poulenc Rorer, in which Rhône Poulenc held some two-thirds of the shares. Meanwhile, Rhône

Key Dates:

1856: Gilliard and Cartier company is founded.
1858: Wittmann et Poulenc Jeune is founded.
1868: Pierre Monnet et Cie is founded.
1895: Gilliard, Monnet et Cartier is reformed as Société Chimique des Usines.
1900: Les Etablissements Poulenc Frères is formed.
1902: Rhodia trademark and brand name is first used.
1928: Poulenc and Société Chimique des Usines merge to form Rhône Poulenc.
1948: U.S. subsidiary Rhodia Inc. is formed.
1956: Théraplix is acquired.
1961: Company name is changed to Rhône Poulenc S.A.
1967: Institut Mérieux is acquired.
1978: Rhodia Inc. changes name to Rhône Poulenc Inc.
1982: Rhône Poulenc is nationalized.
1991: U.S. drugs unit is merged with Rorer to form Rhône Poulenc Rorer.
1993: Rhône Poulenc is privatized.
1998: Rhône Poulenc (soon to be renamed Aventis) combines chemicals and polymers units to form Rhodia S.A., which is later spun off as a public company.
1999: Rhodia acquires Albright & Wilson; Aventis sells its shares in Rhodia.
2000: Rhodia acquires U.S.-based chemicals firm ChiRex.

Poulenc itself was teaming up with rival Merck & Co. to develop a series of children's vaccines in the early 1990s. The company also was pursuing its expansion in the booming Asian economies with the series of new factories serving the plastics and chemicals industries.

The company by then was able to look forward to a return to the private sector, as a new government led by Jacques Chirac promised to reverse the nationalization policies of the exiting Mitterand-led government. Rhône Poulenc was returned to the private sector in 1993. The company next began to expand into new areas of development, particularly the growing market for biotechnology products, techniques, and equipment. In 1993, Rhône Poulenc bought 37 percent of Applied Immune Sciences. The following year, the company acquired Fisons, a manufacturer of treatments for asthma and allergic reactions based in the United Kingdom.

After Rhône Poulenc and Merck joined together to spin off their animal healthcare products operations into the new company Merial, the French chemicals and pharmaceuticals giants prepared to get even bigger. The increasing globalization of the world's marketplace caused Rhône Poulenc to seek out a partner with which to counter the expansion moves of its largest U.S. and European competitors. The company found that partner in the German company Hoechst AG, as the two companies announced their intentions to merge to form Aventis in 1999.

As part of the process leading to the Aventis merger, Rhône Poulenc decided to spin off two of its divisions, its Chemicals division and its Fibers & Polymers division, to form a new separate company, Rhodia S.A. Rhodia S.A. was created in 1998 and some 30 percent of Rhodia was sold on the Paris and New York stock exchanges in 1999. Placed in charge of Rhodia was CEO Jean-Pierre Tirouflet, who led Rhodia on a restructuring of the assets inherited from Rhône Poulenc. Among the company's divestitures was its titanium dioxide operations, sold off in 1997, and the company began to prepare for an exit from the polyester market, shutting down a number of its European polyester production facilities. Meanwhile, the company unveiled an ambitious investment program to support its expansion drive in the Asia Pacific region. As Tirouflet told *Chemical Week,* the new company started business with "a business portfolio that's more balanced and able to withstand cycles."

The year 1999 marked a turning point for the company, as parent Rhône Poulenc sold off its position, setting Rhodia free as an independent company. In that year, also, Rhodia made a bold expansion move when it won a takeover battle for the United Kingdom's Albright & Wilson. That company, founded in 1851 and, from the late 1970s to mid-1990s, a subsidiary of Tenneco Inc. of the United States, had grown into one of the world's largest producers of phosphates and other phosphorus-based products, with sales of more than EUR 1.2 billion. The company's purchase price was an estimated US$850 million.

In July 2000, Rhodia once again made acquisition headlines when it reached agreement to purchase ChiRex, a U.S.-based fine chemicals specialist. That acquisition, for a price of nearly US$550 million, established Rhodia as a world leader in that fast-growing chemicals specialty. The company's debt ratio topped 130 percent with the acquisition, pushing down the company's stock price, however, so Rhodia might have placed itself in a delicate position. As the specialties chemicals industry continued to consolidate at the beginning of the new century, industry observers began to question whether Rhodia's low stock price might not make it an attractive target for a takeover attempt.

Principal Divisions

Consumer Products; Organics; Industrial Products; Services and Specialties; Polyamide.

Principal Competitors

Bayer AG; Ciba Specialty Chemicals Corporation; Clariant Ltd.; Imperial Chemical Industries PLC; SKW Trostberg AG.

Further Reading

David, Christian, "Jean-Pierre Tirouflet, génie de la finance monté en graine," *L'Expansion,* October 7, 1999, p. 22.
Halpern, Nathalie, "Rhodia lance une OPA sur l'americain ChiRex pour 3.8 milliards de francs," *Les Echos,* July 25, 2000, p. 9.
Hunter, David, "Rhodia Works on Its Winners," *Chemical Week,* November 11, 1998, p. 96.
Young, Andrew, "Rhodia Wins Battle for Albright," *Reuters,* May 13, 1999.

—M.L. Cohen

Rich Products Corporation

1150 Niagara Street
Buffalo, New York 14213
U.S.A.
Telephone: (716) 878-8000
Fax: (716) 878-8765
Web site: http://www.richs.com

Private Company
Incorporated: 1965
Employees: 7,000
Sales: $1.5 billion (1999 est.)
NAIC: 311412 Frozen Specialty Food Manufacturing; 311514 Dry, Condensed, and Evaporated Dairy Product Manufacturing; 311612 Meat Processed from Carcasses; 311712 Fresh and Frozen Seafood Processing; 311813 Frozen Cakes, Pies, and Other Pastries Manufacturing; 311822 Flour Mixes and Dough Manufacturing from Purchased Flour; 711211 Sports Teams and Clubs

Rich Products Corporation entered the 21st century as one of the leading frozen food manufacturers in the United States. Selling its more than 2,000 products largely to the foodservice and in-store bakery sectors, the company specializes in toppings, icings, desserts, cake mixes, breads, rolls, sweet goods, doughs, Italian specialties, seafood, and barbecue meats. Rich Products pioneered the nondairy industry with a soybean-based whipping cream, and later became known for Coffee Rich, a cream substitute used in coffee. The rights to these products have been licensed to Suiza Foods Corporation. Another alliance is with Sara Lee Corporation, whereby Rich provides sales, marketing, and distribution for all Sara Lee in-store bakery goods. The production facilities of Rich Products include ten plants in the United States and five located elsewhere, namely Canada, Mexico, South Africa, India, and China. Privately owned by the Rich family since its founding, Rich Products also owns a number of nonfood businesses, including three minor league baseball teams—the Buffalo Bisons, Wichita Wranglers, and Jamestown Jammers—and the Palm Beach National Golf and Country Club located in West Palm Beach, Florida.

Roots in Nondairy Innovation

Robert E. Rich, Sr., first learned about product substitution during World War II through the War Food Administration. After the war, he put that knowledge to use and directed a laboratory team to search for a vegetable-based replacement for whipped cream. His product was to be based on soybeans. In 1945 Rich was on his way to visit a distributor on Long Island and packed some of his soybean-based whipping cream in dry ice for the long train ride from Buffalo, New York. He had intended just to keep the cream cool, but it was frozen solid when he arrived in Long Island. When Rich mashed the frozen mass, he found that it still whipped up beautifully. The discovery launched the beginning of a frozen nondairy products industry.

Rich's innovation, named Rich's Whip Topping, was lauded as "the miracle cream from the soya bean." This was 1945, when the frozen food industry was burgeoning. Rather than marketing to supermarkets, Rich targeted his product to the foodservice sector, reasoning that restaurants, schools, hospitals, and other cost-conscious operators seemed a likely audience for the product. Rich quietly built solid markets, carving a niche that remains unchallenged.

During its early years, Rich continued to create variations on its Whip Topping. In the 1950s the company came out with the first commercial line of frozen cream puffs and eclairs. Its next innovation came in 1961 with the development of Coffee Rich, the nation's first frozen nondairy creamer. Since its introduction, Coffee Rich has dominated the market, claiming a 90 percent share into the 1980s. The product was also ahead of its time in health considerations: along with Whip Topping, Coffee Rich is the only 100 percent cholesterol-free, low-fat cream product distributed nationally. As soybean oil is low in saturated fats, Coffee Rich meets American Heart Association guidelines where most other nondairy creamers fail because they are made from high-fat tropical oils.

In the 1960s Rich Products began marketing frozen dough. While supermarkets wanted the aroma of fresh baked goods

Company Perspectives:

The Rich Mission strives to set new standards of excellence in customer satisfaction and to achieve new levels of competitive success in every category of business in which we operate. We will achieve this by working together as a team to: Impress Our Customers. *Provide exceptional service to our external and internal customers the first time and every time.* Improve, Improve, Improve! *Continuously improve the quality and value of the goods we produce and services we provide.* Empower People. *Unleash the talents of all our Associates by creating an environment that is safe, that recognizes and rewards their achievements, and encourages their participation and growth.* Work Smarter. *Drive out all waste of time, effort and material—all the barriers and extra steps that keep us from doing our jobs right.* Do The Right Thing! *Maintain the highest standards of integrity and ethical conduct and behave as good citizens in our communities.* Think Outside The Box. *Challenge the status quo and look for opportunities to make breakthrough innovations in Products, Processes, & Services.*

tempting shoppers, it was too much trouble for them to set up expensive bakeries on their facilities, and frozen dough met their needs perfectly. In the early 1960s, Rich began construction on a nondairy plant in Fort Erie, Ontario, just across the Niagara River from Rich's Buffalo headquarters. This plant is still in operation, producing both frozen dough and nondairy products. By the mid-1980s, Rich was operating what was the world's largest frozen dough plant in Murfreesboro, Tennessee. The dough—for breads, rolls, and pastries—was sold to supermarket chains throughout the country. Rich Products Corporation was incorporated in 1965. In 1969 Rich acquired Elm Tree Baking Company in Appleton, Wisconsin, adding frozen baked goods to its product line.

Aggressive Expansion in the 1970s and 1980s

The 1970s were marked by spurts of growth for Rich. To keep up with product demand, Rich had to expand its production capabilities rapidly. During this time, Rich acquired nine plants, including Federal Bakers Supply in Garfield, New Jersey, and L.K. Baker Company in Columbus, Ohio. Other operations were purchased in Winchester, Virginia, and Claremont and Fresno, California. Rich also purchased Palmer Frozen Foods, a regional frozen bakery goods producer and distributor in eastern Pennsylvania.

Rich also expanded its product line to seafood specialties, soup bases, and gravy mixes. As late as 1975, however, about 71 percent of Rich's revenues were still coming from nondairy replacement products. The expansion into seafood began in 1976 with the acquisition of SeaPak Corporation, which had plants in Brunswick, Georgia, and Brownsville, Texas.

Rich launched an aggressive campaign of growth through acquisition that saw its sales quadruple over the next eight years. Acquisitions included the H.J. Heinz Company's frozen dessert plant in Lake City, Pennsylvania, contributing cream pies and cakes to Rich's line, and PREAM, a nondairy coffee powder, from Early California Foods of Los Angeles. By 1982 company sales were at $400 million, and sales of nondairy replacement products accounted for about half of those revenues.

Succeeded by his son, Robert Rich, Jr., as president of the company, Rich, Sr., remained chairman. Together they developed an unusual acquisition strategy, giving preference to other father-and-son companies. Rich, Sr., contended that all the company's takeovers were friendly and that most of their acquisitions' owners stayed on afterward. Other acquisitions in the 1980s included the former Lloyd J. Harris plant, a Saugatuck, Michigan-based pie producer, and Casa Di Bertacchi Corporation of Vineland, New Jersey, a producer of frozen Italian pasta and meat specialties purchased in 1982.

In 1980 the company introduced a process, called Freeze Flo, that allowed products to remain soft while frozen, spurring the development of products such as frozen pie fillings that could be eaten right out of the freezer. The process took seven years and nearly $5 million to develop. By 1983 the company held 39 patents and was bringing in $2.5 million a year in licensing to 50 companies, mostly overseas. Rich incorporated Freeze Flo into many of its own new products, such as Rich's Grand America Ice Cream, the only ice cream on the market that can be shipped and stored at zero degrees Fahrenheit.

In 1983 Rich acquired Nashville's Tennessee Doughnut Company and Antoinetta's Frozen Italian Specialties of Harleysville, Pennsylvania. The company also purchased the Class AAA Buffalo Bisons baseball franchise, based in Rich's headquarters city. The team went on to set new minor league attendance records into the 1990s, becoming the best-drawing minor league baseball team in the nation. In 1984 Rich acquired a second baseball franchise, the Class AA Wichita (Kansas) Wranglers.

In 1986 Rich entered into a joint venture with J.R. Wood Inc., of Atwater, California. Together they launched Rich Fruit Pak, a frozen fruit processing plant in Escalon, California. The company formed Rich Communications Corporation in 1987. This served as the parent company to a pair of Western New York radio stations: WGR-AM Newsradio 550 and WGR-FM "97 Rock." These stations supplied the area with broadcasts of the NFL Buffalo Bills, the NHL Buffalo Sabres, and the Bisons. In 1988 Rich's frozen food line added barbeque and specialty meats with the acquisition of Byron's, Inc., of Gallatin, Tennessee.

These additions notwithstanding, the company's plan to expand via acquisition of family-owned food companies was slowed when the numerous leveraged buyouts of the 1980s pushed prices too high. Rich avoided the large debts that were often necessary to complete such transactions. Acquisitions slowed, and Rich concentrated on in-house development of a technology to make cholesterol-free frozen foods.

Expanding Internationally in the 1990s

In 1990, in its 32nd acquisition since 1969, Rich acquired the Blue Bird Baking Company, a major producer of pies and cakes. Having virtually reached its operating capacity, Rich planned to increase the capacity in six of its nine bakery manufacturing plants by 35 percent in order to make room for new

Key Dates:

1945: Robert E. Rich, Sr., makes the discovery that leads to the introduction of Rich's Whip Topping.
1961: Coffee Rich nondairy creamer is introduced.
1965: Rich Products Corporation is incorporated.
1969: Frozen baked goods are added to the product line.
1976: Company expands into frozen seafood with the acquisition of SeaPak Corporation.
1980: Company introduces Freeze Flo, a process that allows products to remain soft while frozen.
1982: Casa Di Bertacchi, producer of frozen Italian specialties, is acquired.
1983: Company expands outside food with the purchase of the Buffalo Bisons minor league baseball team.
1988: Company expands into barbecue and specialty meats through the purchase of Byron's, Inc.
1998: Rich swaps the rights to its retail nondairy product line for the Jon Donaire specialty dessert business of Suiza Foods.
1999: J.W. Allen, maker of frozen cakes, bakery mixes, and icings, is acquired.

products. Rich launched a multimillion-dollar capital expenditure plan that included plant expansions and renovations in California, Ohio, Wisconsin, Pennsylvania, Tennessee, and Virginia. In the spring of 1990, Rich built a $17 million research and development center.

In 1992 Rich acquired the Seneau Baking Company of Marlborough, Massachusetts, which became Rich Marlborough, a state-of-the-art bakery products manufacturing plant. The company also acknowledged the strength of its Mexican market that year by opening a broker's office in Guadalajara, joining the Rich offices in Monterrey and Mexico City. Whipped toppings, fruit fillings, glazes, and Better Creme icings were some of the company's best-sellers in Mexico. By that time, Rich also had offices in Japan, Singapore, Australia, and the United Kingdom.

International expansion continued in 1993 with the establishment of Rich Products of South Africa, which began making and distributing frozen dough products. The following year the company purchased a manufacturing plant in Toluca, Mexico, in order to begin making frozen dough in that nation. Also in 1994 Rich Products formed a third baseball franchise in Jamestown, New York, the Jamestown Jammers, which became a Class A affiliate of the Detroit Tigers playing in the New York-Penn League.

Growth outside the United States was key to meeting a new company goal of increasing revenues by 25 percent per year. By 1995, the year the company celebrated its 50th year in business, sales had reached $1 billion. That year, Rich expanded its manufacturing capacity in the United States through the opening of a nondairy products plant in Niles, Illinois. The company also expanded into the Indian market that year through a joint venture with Kwality Foods, the largest maker of ice cream in India. Called Rich Kwality Products Ltd., the venture was established to make nondairy products for distribution in India. Rich Products also established a joint venture with UFM of Thailand called Rich Products Manufacturing (Thailand) Co., Ltd. for the manufacture of frozen dough products. Back home, Rich entered into an alliance with Sara Lee Corporation in 1997, whereby Rich began marketing Sara Lee frozen cake and dessert products to in-store bakeries.

During 1998 Rich expanded in China through the establishment of a wholly owned subsidiary that opened a new state-of-the-art nondairy facility in Suzhou, China. This plant was particularly important for increasing production, and distribution throughout Asia, of the newly introduced Rich's Gold Label Whip Topping, which quickly became the leading nondairy topping in the region. In mid-1998 Rich Products entered into an asset swap with Suiza Foods Corporation, a leading fresh milk and dairy food company based in Dallas. Rich granted Suiza the world rights (except India and Israel) to market and sell its retail refrigerated and frozen creamer lines, which included the Coffee Rich, Farm Rich, Poly Rich, and Rich Whip brands. Rich retained ownership of both the brands and the plants where the products were made. In return, Rich received from Suiza control of the Jon Donaire line of fully prepared frozen desserts. The Jon Donaire line was marketed to the foodservice and in-store bakery sectors, which fit in with Rich's strategic direction involving a de-emphasis of retail sales. Owing to the firm's product line expansion over the decades, less than 5 percent of Rich's sales were generated by its line of nondairy whipped toppings and creamers by the time of the asset swap.

William G. Gisel, Jr., was named to the new position of chief operating officer of Rich Products in 1999. Gisel had joined the company in 1982 with a position in the legal department, then eventually became a key player in Rich's international expansion. In 1996 he was named president of Rich Products Food Group. As COO, Gisel became the highest ranking nonfamily member in company history. Remaining chairman and president of the company were Robert Rich, Sr., and Robert Rich, Jr., respectively. Meanwhile, a third generation of Rich family members were reaching management positions at the family-controlled firm, including three children of Rich, Jr.

There were a number of additional developments in 1999 that also helped set the stage for the company at the dawn of the 21st century. The pie plant located in Saugatuck, Michigan, was sold. Major improvements were made to two company plants: the nondairy plant in Buffalo and a bakery facility in Hilliard, Ohio, where the industry's highest capacity donut production line was installed through a multimillion-dollar project. Then, in late 1999, Rich Products acquired J.W. Allen & Co., a family-owned firm based in Wheeling, Illinois. J.W. Allen produced about 400 products at its plants in Wheeling and in Morristown, Tennessee, including frozen cakes, bakery mixes, and icings. The products were primarily marketed to in-store bakeries. The addition of J.W. Allen's $110 million in annual sales would increase Rich Products' revenues to more than $1.5 billion. As it looked toward the new century with no intention of being acquired itself or of going public, Rich Products Corporation was seeking additional overseas expansion opportunities, venturing into e-commerce through an initiative where clients could purchase such products as Byron's barbecue sauce, and pursuing the development of new products, most notably a new line of specialty drinks, including fruit smoothies, nutritional drinks, and coffee-based concoctions.

Principal Subsidiaries

Rich-SeaPak Corporation; Casa Di Bertacchi Corporation; J.W. Allen & Co.; Byron's, Inc.

Principal Divisions

Food Service Division; Bakery/Deli Division; International Division.

Principal Competitors

Diageo plc; H.J. Heinz Company; Kraft Foods, Inc.; Nabisco Holdings Corp.; Nestlé S.A.; The Pillsbury Company; The Quaker Oats Company; Sara Lee Corporation; Unilever.

Further Reading

Anzalone, Charles, "Robert Rich Sr. and His Non-Dairy Dynasty," *Buffalo News,* Buffalo Magazine, April 30, 1995, p. M6.

Cone, Edward, "The Best-Laid Plans," *Forbes,* July 24, 1989.

Cooke, James Aaron, "How Rich Products Went Global," *Logistics Management and Distribution Report,* September 1998, pp. 48–53.

Crispens, Jonna, "New Products Priority in Rich Project," *Supermarket News,* February 25, 1991.

Fink, James, "Gisel Thrives in Expanded Role at Rich Products," *Business First of Buffalo,* February 7, 2000, p. 4.

Garrison, Bob, "Rich Tradition," *Refrigerated and Frozen Foods,* December 1999, pp. 16–18+.

Greenberg, Jonathan, "All in the Family," *Forbes,* April 25, 1983.

Howard, Theresa, "Robert Rich Sr.," *Nation's Restaurant News,* January 1995, p. 166.

Lahvie, Ray, "Rich Products Acquires Seneau Baking Company," *Bakery Production and Marketing,* July 24, 1992.

Linstedt, Sharon, "Hiding Behind the Bakery Door: Rich Products Supplies Thousands of Items to Food Service Industry," *Buffalo News,* October 24, 1999, p. B20.

——, "Rich Licenses Rights to Three Products," *Buffalo News,* July 17, 1998, p. A1.

Malchoff, Kevin, "Frozen Food and Foodservice: The Perfect Match," *Frozen Food Digest,* July 1991.

"Rich Furthers Growth Plans with Seneau Baking Purchase," *Nation's Restaurant News,* July 8, 1992.

"Rich Products Opens Mexico City Office," *Nation's Restaurant News,* January 27, 1992.

Riddle, Judith, "Rich Products Expanding Non-Dairy to Guadalajara," *Supermarket News,* February 17, 1992.

Rosenbaum, Rob, "Freeze Flo Success Grounded in Skills of Rich Researchers," *Business First of Buffalo,* October 28, 1985.

Schroeder, Richard, "How Rich Forsook the Cow for the Soybean," *Buffalo News,* March 26, 1995, p. B14.

——, "1,700 Products, $1 Billion in Sales: That's the Profile of Rich Products in Its 50th Year," *Buffalo News,* March 26, 1995, p. B13.

Thayer, Warren, "Bob Rich on His Father, ECR, and Frozens' Future," *Frozen Food Age,* June 1995, p. 1.

Williams, Fred O., "Rich Products Acquires Competitor in Midwest," *Buffalo News,* November 9, 1999, p. E5.

—Carol Keeley
—updated by David E. Salamie

The Riese Organization

162 West 34th Street
New York, New York 10001
U.S.A.
Telephone: (212) 563-7440
Fax: (212) 613-1929
Web site: http://www.rieserestaurants.com

Private Company
Founded: 1953
Employees: 1,500
Sales: $150 million (2000 est.)
NAIC: 53112 Lessors of Nonresidential Buildings; 72211 Full-Service Restaurants; 722211 Limited-Service Restaurants

The Riese Organization is composed of a group of private corporations—perhaps 200 or more—that owns and operates restaurants and real estate, primarily in the New York City area. It includes National Restaurants Management, Inc., the corporation that formerly served as a holding company. The Riese Organization owns and operates about 110 eating places in New York, including franchises of such fast-food chains as Dunkin' Donuts, Pizza Hut, Kentucky Fried Chicken, and Roy Rogers. Holding leases on many of the busiest sites in Manhattan in terms of pedestrian traffic, its existence is based on the hoary adage that the three most valuable factors in real estate are ''location, location, and location.''

From One Luncheonette to Several Restaurant Chains: 1940–80

Irving and Murray Riese were born in Harlem, sons of Russian immigrants who were on welfare during the Depression. Irving went to work in his teens as a dishwasher at a Bronx ice cream parlor, bequeathing his job to Murray when he ''graduated'' to soda jerk. At the time, Murray recalled in a 1975 *New York Times* interview, ''We had to work about 9 out of 15 hours in a split-shift day at 35 cents an hour.'' Some of the staff went on strike to eliminate the split shift, he added, and ''I was one of the militants. We finally received about $500 in back pay, which [in 1940] we used to open a luncheonette'' in midtown Manhattan. The money was applied to a down payment on the purchase price of about $8,500.

In 1945 the Riese brothers sold the luncheonette for about $38,500. The profit was used to launch a program of buying troubled restaurant properties and then refurbishing and reselling them. ''We would buy and sell 20 to 25 restaurants in one month,'' Murray Riese recalled to Pamela G. Hollie of the *New York Times* in 1983. The brothers estimated that they had bought and sold at least 1,000 restaurants, coffee shops, drugstores, and nightclubs. Murray Riese explained to her how they got the money for further investments in these words: ''Let's say you sell apple pies. You buy the pie today and sell it today. You sell the pies for more than they cost and you have 60 days to 90 days to pay. You have a float. It pays to be in business just because of the float.''

This way of doing business ended in 1953, when federal tax authorities ruled that the Riese brothers were really real estate brokers and thus could not claim that their profits from selling restaurants were capital gains entitled to a lower rate of taxation unless these properties were held for three years rather than six months. The brothers then began to develop their own restaurants for the long term, leasing prime Manhattan real estate for the purpose of operating such restaurants or to sublease the sites to other businesses. Murray acted as the dealmaker and money man, while Irving concentrated on restaurant operations and marketing. In 1962 the brothers, through their National Restaurants Management, Inc., purchased Childs, a chain of restaurants operating in the red that had 19 locations and annual sales of about $10 million. National Restaurants, which was operating 30 units—many under the Cobb's Corner name—paid more than $2 million for the chain. Since they needed $1 million for the purchase and their bank would lend them no more than $500,000, the Riese brothers split the acquisition in two and borrowed $500,000 each. Within six months, they had made enough money by subleasing Childs properties to pay off the mortgage.

In 1967 the Riese brothers purchased a controlling share of Longchamps, Inc., a chain of higher-end city restaurants, including its flagship on the ground floor of the Empire State Building. They soon sold most of their Longchamps stock but in

Company Perspectives:

The Riese Organization will be making a high profile mark on the Manhattan restaurant scene well into the next century. That's good news not only for New York's largest independently-owned restaurant employer ... it's good news for all of New York!

1971 paid $8 million for an Upper East Side Longchamps; Luchow's, a landmarked downtown German restaurant; and the Autopub, Riverboat, and Downbeat restaurants. The Rieses were believed to be operating at this time eating places with a total gross of about $45 million a year, including a large number on 42nd Street, concentrated in both the Times Square and Grand Central Terminal areas.

With annual sales of about $80 million in 1972, the organization was said to be the nation's largest privately owned restaurant entity. It was operating about 150 restaurants at the time, and National Restaurants was the largest privately held restaurant operator in New York. In 1973 The Riese Organization acquired 22 of the 35 Schrafft's restaurants for an estimated $3 million. Like Childs and Longchamps, Schrafft's was a chain familiar to New Yorkers, yet all three (plus six Mayflower Donuts shops acquired in 1975) were seen by the Rieses as tired concepts, and they disappeared in favor of new formats at the same sites. ''We got the idea of treating restaurant properties as theaters,'' Murray Riese told Glenn Fowler of the *New York Times* in 1990. ''When a show closes you don't tear down the theater. You look for a new attraction.'' By 1975 the Riese Organization's stable included 35 outlets of the Brew Burger chain first developed by the brothers in 1972. In 1979 the organization acquired its first franchise, Beefsteak Charlie's. (The Rieses had been offered a McDonald's outlet in the early 1970s but passed on the opportunity.)

Thriving on Franchising in the 1980s

The Riese Organization subleased 15 Chock Full O'Nuts coffee shop sites in 1983 and was operating 20 of these counter-seat eateries as a franchisee by the end of the year. The Riese brothers—and Murray's son Dennis—were now in charge of about 250 restaurants, about half of them franchised fast-food outlets, serving an estimated 500,000 people a day, with 8,000 employees and annual sales of more than $200 million, of which revenue from restaurants and real estate were roughly equal. Most of these units were serving lunch to Manhattan office workers and shoppers, and many of them were soon to be marshaled into clusters that the organization called ''food courts.'' In Pennsylvania Station, for example, under a single lease with a single kitchen, the Rieses were running a fast-food outlet, doughnut shop, and bar. After the organization's $12 million purchase in 1983 of the United Artists Building at Seventh Avenue and West 49th Street, it lined the ground floor with its eating places.

The Riese brothers rode herd over their empire from minimally furnished headquarters in a dreary six-floor building on West 34th Street, so close to many of the units that Murray's son Dennis—now president and chief operating officer—could visit up to 25 a day. ''Inside'' man Irving continued to arrive at 5:30 in the morning and work till mid-evening, while ''outside'' partner Murray also put in long hours. Special telephone lines connected headquarters to each eating place and each one to the others, enabling a quick exchange of supplies or labor. The Rieses rarely contracted for help; staffers priced and printed 50 different menus each day, and when the brothers decided to change formats at a given location, a small team of painters and carpenters was sent out to prepare the site quickly for a new opening.

The Riese brothers are credited with originating the food court concept in 1983, the same year the organization signed franchise agreements to open 30 new Roy Rogers and 25 Godfather's Pizza outlets by 1988. This format called for units of different franchisers to be adjacently placed—although sometimes on separate floors—at the same location, with a single kitchen preparing food for each operation. Ordinarily, fast-food franchisers forbade, or at least discouraged, franchisees to combine such operations with other ones, especially competing ones. With their control of large pieces of Manhattan real estate—including all four corners of some major intersections and licenses to run 28 franchised operations in New York City, most of them on an exclusive basis—The Riese Organization was in a position to make its own rules. One Riese-operated Broadway site had as many as nine franchised eateries under one roof. The Marriott Corp., which then owned the Roy Rogers chain, sued the Rieses to keep them from combining a Godfather's Pizza and Haagen-Dazs outlet with a Roy Rogers unit in Times Square but lost the case.

''Mavericks with a reputation for arrogance and renowned in the world of franchising as tough negotiators,'' Milford Prewitt of *Nation's Restaurant News* wrote in 1996, ''the Rieses blatantly bent some of their franchisers' rules and often balked at certain franchising fees.'' Dennis Riese looked at it differently, telling Prewitt that the franchisers ''came into Manhattan with the same bias they had in the rest of the country. That is, that they were in control, and like 99 percent of their franchisees my father and uncle were supposed to turn over a check and sign their life away with a handshake. . . . For most franchisers, this was probably the only place in the country where this little franchisee was rubbing their face in the dirt.''

Franchised Haagen-Dazs, Famous Amos, and David's Cookies gourmet-snack outlets required little space, making them ideal for Penn and Grand Central locations. Agreements were signed to open franchised units for Church's Fried Chicken (1984), Nathan's Famous (1987), and Tad's Steaks (1988). The Rieses also were promoting their own sit-down restaurants. Three Charley O's units, aimed at young professionals, were doing large bar business in 1984. Eight J.J. Mulligan's featured hearty food in a publike ambience. The six Lindy's featured delicatessen-type dishes. Brew Burger was proving a disappointment, but when the chain was terminated, other company-owned or franchised units usually moved in at the same location.

In 1989 The Riese Organization controlled about 300 restaurants in Manhattan and on Long Island—about half of them in clusters—and had an estimated $332 million in annual sales.

Key Dates:

1940: Irving and Murray Riese open their first restaurant.
1953: The Rieses reorganize their business due to a federal tax ruling.
1962: The brothers, who own 30 eateries, purchase the 19-unit Childs chain.
1972: With about 150 units, the organization is said to be the nation's largest privately owned restaurant entity.
1979: The organization acquires its first franchise operation, Beefsteak Charlie's.
1989: The Riese empire of about 300 restaurants includes 28 franchise operations.
1999: The organization's chief entity files for bankruptcy operation; it emerges from bankruptcy the following year.

That year an investment group headed by the organization purchased 107 Houlihan's and Darryl's restaurants for more than $225 million. The acquisition gave the organization operation of 35 concepts, from dinner-house franchises such as Beefsteak Charlie's and Houlihan's to fast-food units franchised from Dunkin' Donuts, Kentucky Fried Chicken, Pizza Hut, and Nathan's Famous. The organization was offering advertising space almost anywhere in its outlets, including menus, walls, above the bars, and even on the clothing of the serving staffers.

Decline and Bankruptcy in the 1990s

But The Riese Organization then began to falter, in part because of the death of Irving Riese in 1990 but mainly because of the recession that began that year and lasted into 1992. To finance expansion of its food courts, the Riese brothers had in 1988 borrowed $140 million from the Bank of Tokyo-Mitsubishi Trust Co., using 14 properties as collateral. This debt increasingly hung over the organization's head, although a five-year restructuring was arranged in 1993. To cut costs, the company reduced the number of its units and leased properties, but in the process they also reduced their revenues, and hence the cash flow needed to pay the debt.

Dennis Riese, who left the organization in 1988 to strike out on his own, returned to his position in 1991. He trimmed the number of units to 250 and began investigating the development of new restaurant concepts. ''We have discovered that though franchised brands bring you more revenues, they do not bring you more profits,'' he later explained to Prewitt. ''The biggest problem [in midtown and downtown Manhattan] with fast food is that it is too dependent on lunch. Breakfast is nonexistent, and there is no such thing as dinner and you need all three dayparts with these rents you have to pay.'' In 1994 he formed Riese Capital Corp. to make loans to restaurateurs and to provide management and purchasing experience. This new company also opened Martini's, an upscale Italian restaurant, and The Java Shop, a coffee bar, in midtown Manhattan. Dennis Riese assumed full command of the reins of The Riese Organization on the death of Murray Riese in 1995.

Dennis Riese once again tweaked the sensibilities of franchisers in 1992, when he started operating food courts under The Riese Organization's own brand name, Riese Restaurants. T.G.I. Friday's sued to terminate its franchise at six of ten Riese-operated units for displaying the Riese Restaurants logo in concert with other franchised units assembled into food courts. Once again, however, it was The Riese Organization that prevailed. By 1998 the logo was present on the doors and windows of virtually all of the organization's eating places, with an accompanying list of every brand in its portfolio. Dennis Riese scored another win in 1995, when Carlson Cos. failed in litigation that claimed he was in violation of a franchise agreement with T.G.I. Friday's and sought to expel him from the system. When the owners of Rockefeller Center did not renew an expiring Lindy's lease in 1994, Riese refused to make way for an eatery with a karaoke-style ''Television City'' concept, staying put on the site for another 16 months. The Riese Organization also was engaged in a bitter dispute with Local 100 of the Hotel Employees and Restaurant Employees International Union in the late 1990s. Riese conceded that he had closed unionized locations and reopened them as new concepts without a bargaining agreement, but denied that this was a union-busting tactic. He reached a three-year agreement with the local in 1999.

To prevent foreclosure of its 14 loan-collateral properties, The Riese Organization paid off $68 million in debt owed to Bank of Tokyo-Mitsubishi Trust in 1997. To do so, it sold four of the properties to Vornado Realty Trust for $26 million, which provided new mortgages for the other ten and bought out the half-ownership in all 14 that was held by Irving Riese's two daughters. All of these properties were in the area of the West 30s near Herald Square, Madison Square Garden, and Pennsylvania Station.

National Restaurants Management filed for Chapter 11 bankruptcy protection in 1999, listing $8.7 million in assets and about $140.7 million in liabilities, including a $117.8 million loan that the Tokyo bank sold to Natrest Funding Inc. (or ALGM LLC) in 1998 for about 33 cents on the dollar. The Riese Organization subsidiary, which Riese said was unaffiliated legally with the parent organization, emerged from bankruptcy a year later, having paid ALGM only $2 million and meeting all other unsecured claims for about two cents on the dollar. The settlement also included the sale and leaseback of the United Artists Building and a midtown Broadway building. The restructuring also allowed Riese to buy out his two cousins' stake in National Restaurants Management, which accounted for about two-thirds of the organization's revenues in fiscal 1999 (the year ended in April 1999). The Riese Organization was running about 110 restaurants in New York City in 2000. Its sales were an estimated $150 million in fiscal 2000.

Principal Subsidiaries

DR One Corp.; National Restaurants Management, Inc.; Riese Capital Corp.

Principal Competitors

Ark Restaurants Corp.; Sbarro Inc.

Further Reading

Brennan, Denise M., ''The Rieses Add More Pieces,'' *Restaurant Business,* May 20, 1984, pp. 114, 116, 122, 124, 128.

Fowler, Glenn, ''Irving Riese, 71, a Restaurateur Specializing in Fast-Food Outlets,'' *New York Times,* December 11, 1990, p. B16.

''From Quick Lunch to Quick Millions,'' *Business Week,* October 23, 1971, p. 126.

Frumkin, Paul, ''Riese Exits Chap. 11,'' *Nation's Restaurant News,* August 21, 2000, pp. 4, 6.

——, ''Riese's NRMI Arm, NYC's Top Chain Operator, Files for Ch. 11,'' *Nation's Restaurant News,* July 19, 1999, pp. 1, 115.

Gabriel, Frederick, ''Riese Dynasty Faces the Loss of 14 Properties,'' *Crain's New York Business,* May 12, 1997, pp. 1, 33.

Gault, Ylonda, ''Riese, Back Within Fold, Sets Bold Plan,'' *Crain's New York Business,* June 8, 1992, pp. 3, 36.

Hollie, Pamela G., ''The Family That Feeds New York,'' *New York Times,* October 30, 1983, Sec. 3, p. 4.

Prewitt, Milford, ''Irving & Murray Riese,'' *Nation's Restaurant News,* February 1996, p. 126.

——, ''Riese Branches Out with Launch of Capital Corp.,'' *Nation's Restaurant News,* May 23, 1994, pp. 7, 50.

——, ''Riese Organization: Stalled Fast-Food Sales Turn Former NYC Empire into a Receding Power,'' *Nation's Restaurant News,* January 1998, pp. 146, 148.

——, ''Riese Sells Off Prime NYC Properties in Debt Refinancing,'' *Nation's Restaurant News,* July 21, 1997, pp. 3, 91.

——, ''Riese, Union End 3-Year Battle,'' *Nation's Restaurant News,* February 8, 1999, pp. 3, 77.

——, ''Unions Embrace New Tactics vs. Operators; Riese, Local 100 Battle Reflects Growing Trend,'' *Nation's Restaurant News,* May 12, 1997, pp. 1, 4, 159.

''Rieses Expand Brew Burger Chain,'' *New York Times,* December 14, 1975, Sec. 8, p. 6.

Thomas, Robert, Jr., ''Murray Riese, 73, Restaurateur Who Developed the Food Court,'' *New York Times,* July 21, 1995, p. B7.

—Robert Halasz

Roland Corporation

1-4-16 Dojimahama, Kita-ku
Osaka 530-0004
Japan
Telephone: (+81) 6 6345-9800
Fax: (+81) 6 6345-9792
Web site: http://www.roland.co.jp

Public Company
Incorporated: 1972
Employees: 845
Sales: ¥61.19 billion (US$850.0 million)
Stock Exchanges: Tokyo Osaka
Ticker Symbol: 7944
NAIC: 339992 Musical Instrument Manufacturing

Roland Corporation is one of the world's leading designers and manufacturers of electric musical instruments, focused on keyboards and synthesizers, sound modules, effects processors, electronic drums, recording equipment, and amplifiers. Through its Edirol subsidiary, Roland also produces and markets equipment for desktop music applications. The company's BOSS subsidiary produces guitar effects and rhythm machines, while its Rodgers subsidiary produces organs for the home and professional market. The company operates factories in Hosoe, Takaoka, Isaji, Miyakoda, and Matsumoto in Japan. Worldwide, Roland operates a network of joint-venture and subsidiary sales offices, including subsidiaries in the United States, the United Kingdom, Germany, Italy, France, and Canada. The company also operates a small number of Roland Music Schools in Japan. Led by founder and Chairman Ikutara Kakehashi, and by President and COO Katsuyoshi Dan, Roland Corporation is home to one of the world's best-known music brands. International sales accounted for more than 70 percent of the company's sales, which topped ¥61.19 billion (US$850 million) in the year 2000.

Creating 20th-Century Music History

Roland Corporation was founded by Ikutara Kakehashi in Osaka, Japan, in 1972, with just ¥33 million in capital. Yet Roland's greatest capital was to prove Kakehashi himself. Kakehashi's involvement in the music industry had begun in the 1950s, when he began building guitar amplifiers. Kakehashi finished his first amplifier in 1959, designed for the Hawaiian guitar sound popular in the late 1950s and early 1960s in Japan.

Kakehashi formed his first company soon after, incorporated as Ace Electronics. This company—which, at its beginning, consisted solely of Kakehashi himself—produced a variety of musical instruments, including organs, under the Ace Tone brand name. Yet Kakehashi's first successful product turned out to be a rhythm machine, introduced in 1964. Dubbed the FR-1 Rhythm Ace, this rhythm machine was one of the first to feature preset rhythms programmed to provide musicians with the popular beats of the day. The Rhythm Ace was not only successful in Japan, but also saw a degree of international success as the decade progressed.

Ace Tone continued to improve on the Rhythm Ace design, while introducing other new products, such as organs incorporating the company's rhythm machine technology. In the late 1960s, famed organ maker Hammond approached Kakehashi with an offer to merge the two companies and place Kakehashi at the head of a new Hammond Japan unit. Kakehashi agreed, and led the development of the Hammond Piper, one of that brand's most successful organ designs.

In the early 1970s, disagreements between Kakehashi and Hammond, and the financial takeover of Ace Tone, led Kakehashi, then 42 years old, to leave Hammond and set up his own company. Because Ace Tone had been hampered internationally by pronunciation problems (including its confusion with the compound acetone), Kakehashi determined to find a name that would be pronounced the same everywhere in the world. He settled on Roland—despite the fact that the name was less easily pronounced in Japanese. Roland Corporation was officially incorporated on April 18, 1972.

Pronunciation problems or no, Kakehashi's new company was to create one of the world's most important musical instruments brands. Working out of a house in Osaka, Japan, Kakehashi was joined by six former Ace Electronics employees. Kakehashi set about designing the company's first product, which was to be a drum machine based on the Rhythm Ace design. With no resources to begin production, Kakehashi took

Company Perspectives:

Ever since 1972 when the company was founded, Roland's mission has been to create sounds that people would like to hear. During those early days, we determined that the silicon chip would be the key element in developing new musical instruments producing superb sounds and conveying every nuance of the player's musical expression. Our prominent market position today owes much to the extensive use of leading-edge technologies over the years. Because our range of innovative products have always been quick to incorporate the most sophisticated computer and semiconductor technologies, Roland has been able to make a real difference by bringing people and music closer.

Pushing forward with our business to mark our 30th anniversary, we are now expanding our original mission by going into multimedia, adding another dimension to our founding brief of "Creating music that touches hearts." The possibilities of electronic musical instruments are limitless as we continue to discover new technological breakthroughs and introduce exceptional products. This is how we, with the cooperation of the Roland worldwide family, can best spread the joy of musical creation in the world and achieve corporate excellence.

his design—a simple drawing—on the road. By the end of the trip, Kakehashi had lined up orders for some 200 rhythm machines, dubbed the TR-77. Kakehashi called in to tell his employees to find a factory and start production.

The company opened its own factory the following year, in Hamamatsu, which was later to become Roland's worldwide headquarters. The company also opened two sales offices, in Tokyo and Osaka. Its product list was also beginning to grow. While the company later established itself as a top keyboard maker, it initially decided to avoid head-to-head competition in the overcrowded market for electric keyboards, still largely dominated by organ designs at the time. Instead, Kakehashi sought more unique products, and began producing an effects unit, the RE-100 tape delay. Featuring a longer tape than competitors, the RE-100 was notable primarily for inspiring its successor, the RE-201 Space Echo, which became one of the seminal guitar effects of the 1970s and became one of the company's best-selling products, remaining in production for more than 16 years.

While the Space Echo was inspiring musicians, Roland itself was inspired by the new musical currents of the 1970s. The use of synthesizers in popular music had begun to take off in the early part of the decade, and Kakehashi quickly sought to add the Roland name to the ranks of the world's synthesizer makers. Rather than build the huge expensive modular synthesizers favored by such names as Moog, Arp, and EML, Roland began designing its own synthesizer, but on a smaller scale. In 1973, the company debuted its SH-1000, the first synthesizer produced in Japan. Where a Moog synthesizer cost as much as $5,000 or more, the SH-1000 cost less than $1,000.

The SH series inspired a long string of successes in the 1970s, culminating in the highly popular SH-101, which sold more than 50,000 units after its launch in 1981. The company also continued to improve its rhythm machine designs, producing the first programmable rhythm machines, including the CR-78, the first musical instrument to include a microprocessor in its design. Other successes for the company included its EP-30 electric piano, the first to provide a touch-sensitive keyboard, and the company's JC series of guitar amplifiers, which debuted in 1975. At that time, the company, which had already established joint-venture subsidiaries in the United States and Australia, launched a new brand, called BOSS, for its growing range of guitar effects designs. Supporting the company's growth was the opening of a new factory in Takaoka, Hamamatsu, in 1977.

Adding the Techno Beat in the 1980s

The rise of Disco and New Wave in the late 1970s and late 1980s, respectively, brought a steadily increasing demand for synthesizers, rhythm machines and effects, and helped propel Roland to the leading ranks of musical instruments manufacturers. The start of the 1980s saw the release of a new series of Roland products which were to prove pivotal to the creation of a new form of popular music in that decade. The release of the TR-808 drum machine in 1980 went largely unnoticed at the time. With its analog oscillators, the TR-808 seemed quickly out of date as a new generation of drum machine, using samples of real drums, began to take over the market. The TR-808 remained in production for just a few months. The following year, it was followed by another device, the TB-303 Bassline, a bass synthesizer with built-in sequencer designed to operate in tandem with the TR-606 Drumatix. Yet these devices failed to spark popular imagination as well.

The company saw greater success with its synthesizers, which included 1978's introduction of the Jupiter series, providing some of the earliest of the polyphonic synthesizers. The Jupiter series gave Roland a new hit in 1981, when it launched the Jupiter-8. The Jupiters were quickly joined by the Juno series, the first Roland units to feature DCOs (digital controlled oscillators), replacing the VCOs (velocity controlled oscillators) that had been the industry standard. The DCO provided tighter tuning control than the analog oscillators.

The success of the Jupiters, Junos, and other instruments enabled Roland to expand in the early 1980s. The company moved into new international markets, through a series of joint venture companies set up in the United Kingdom, Canada, Germany, and Denmark in 1981. Roland continued to pursue its expansion through joint ventures in the mid-1980s, moving into New Zealand, Italy, and Taiwan.

In the 1980s, Roland was one of the leading forces in the creation and adoption of the MIDI standard, which enabled musical instruments to communicate with each other. The company's first MIDI-based instruments were released in 1982, and by the mid-1980s all of the company's products were capable of sending and receiving MIDI data.

By then, new musical currents were beginning to appear in the United States and the United Kingdom. The creation of these new forms of music—called rap, hip hop, and, later, techno—was made possible in large part by such units as the TR-808 and TB-303, which at the time could be bought for next

Key Dates:

1972: Company is founded in Osaka, Japan; production of TR-77 begins.
1973: SH-1000 is launched; Hamamatsu factory opens.
1976: BOSS brand is introduced.
1978: Company creates U.S. joint venture subsidiary.
1981: Joint venture subsidiaries in the United Kingdom, Canada, Denmark, and Germany are formed.
1987: Roland acquires S.I.E.L. in Italy, which is renamed Roland Europe.
1988: Company launches Rodgers Instrument Corporation.
1989: Company goes public on Osaka exchange.
1994: Roland Audio Development Corp. (USA) and Edirol Corporation North America are created.
1996: Roland Europe is listed on Milan stock exchange.
1999: Roland Corporation receives listings on the first sections of the Tokyo and Osaka stock exchanges.

to nothing. Roland itself had meanwhile moved entirely into the digital era, adding such innovations as its RD-1000 digital piano, in 1986, and the D-50 digital synthesizer in 1987.

In 1987, Roland expanded again. In that year, the company bought up S.I.E.L. S.p.A, based in Italy, which had been producing synthesizers and organs. The company took over S.I.E.L.'s operations, renamed the company as Roland Europe S.p.A. in 1988, and released a new series of products for the European market, including the E-10 and E-20 Intelligent Synthesizers. Roland Europe went public on the Milan stock exchange in 1996. On the Japanese market, the company introduced the Musi-kun Desktop music systems, one of the earliest computer-based music production systems. Also in 1988, Roland set up a new subsidiary operation for production of organs, largely for the home market. The Rodgers Instrument Corporation, established in the United States, began supplying organs to the Japanese market in 1989 as well.

Roland went public in 1989, listing on the Osaka stock exchange's second section. The following year the company's line of HP digital pianos debuted, boosting the company to the top ranks of the home digital piano market; meanwhile Roland saw continued success of its D series of digital synthesizers, which topped the 300,000-unit mark in 1990. At that time, the company created a new U.S. subsidiary, Roland Audio Development Corp., which then turned its attention to designing and manufacturing amplifier systems.

Music Brand Leader in the 21st Century

The growing use of computers and computer production for music production and music making took Roland into new directions as well. In 1994, the company set up a new subsidiary, Edirol, in order to develop products for the computer music market, including sound cards and modules, MIDI interfaces, and software. Two years later, Roland debuted its VS-880 Digital Studio Workstation, which provided a professional-quality hard-disk recording and production system. The VS series was a great success for the company, selling more than 150,000 units by the end of the decade. The company, which had largely shifted rhythm machine development to its BOSS subsidiary, instead began to perfect a new generation of digital drums, starting in 1992 and culminating in the launch of the V-drums, one of the first to become acceptable for use by professional drummers.

Throughout the 1990s, Roland had also produced a highly successful range of MIDI-based sound modules, which provided high-quality instrument sounds, beginning with the launch of the SC-55 Sound Canvas in 1992. Meanwhile, Roland continued to develop its own technologies for the creation and reproduction of sound, including Structured Adaptive Synthesis (SA) and Composite Object Sound Modeling (COSM), which enabled Roland's instruments to achieve truer approximations of real instrument sounds, while also opening up new perspectives for the creation of new sounds.

As the 1990s concluded, Roland found itself gaining ever-increasing fame—not just from its new instruments and products, but from its early products as well—as new generations of music makers adopted and adapted the company's now legendary analog synthesizers and rhythm machines. Entering the 21st century, Roland and Chairman Ikutara Kakehashi remained committed to the company's heritage of developing musical instruments to shape the music of the future. Helping to ensure the company's growth was a conversion of its stock listing to the Tokyo and Osaka stock exchanges' first sections in 1999. In 2000, Ikutara Kakehashi's contribution to the music industry was recognized when he was added to the Hollywood Rock Walk's Hall of Fame.

Principal Subsidiaries

Roland Corporation U.S. (U.S.A.); Edirol Corporation North America (U.S.A.); Roland Canada Music Ltd.; Roland Brasil Ltda. (Brazil); Roland Corporation Australia Pty. Ltd.; Roland Corporation (NZ) Ltd. (New Zealand); Roland (U.K.) Ltd.; Edirol Europe Ltd. (U.K.); Roland Elektronische Musikinstrumente GmbH (Germany); Roland France SA; Roland Scandinavia as (Denmark); Roland Benelux N.V. (Belgium); Intermusica Ltd. (Hungary); Roland (Switzerland) AG; Musitronic AG (Switzerland); Roland Austria GmbH; Roland Italy S.p.A.; Roland Electronics de España, S.A. (Spain); Roland Portugal S.A.; Roland Taiwan Enterprise Co., Ltd.; Rodgers Instruments LLC (U.S.A.); Roland Audio Development Corp. (U.S.A); Roland Europe S.p.A. (Italy); Roland Taiwan Electronic Music Corp.

Principal Competitors

Baldwin Piano & Organ Company; Casio Computer Co., Ltd.; Fender Musical Instruments Corporation; Gibson Musical Instruments; Harman International Industries, Incorporated; Korg, Inc.; Sony Corporation; Yamaha Corporation.

Further Reading

''Roland Chairman Inducted into Hollywood Hall of Fame,'' *Kyodo World News Service*, February 7, 2000.
''Roland Europe to Launch Flotation,'' *Financial Times*; May 31, 1996.
Youngblood, Paul, ''Roland in the 20th Century: 30 Years of Innovation,'' *Roland Users Group*, Winter 2000.

—M.L. Cohen

The Royal Bank of Scotland Group plc

The Royal Bank of Scotland Group plc

42 St. Andrew Square
Edinburgh EH2 2YE
United Kingdom
Telephone: (0131) 556 8555
Fax: (0131) 556 8535
Web site: http://www.royalbankscot.co.uk

Public Company
Incorporated: 1727 as The Royal Bank of Scotland
Employees: 92,900
Total Assets: £306 billion (US$480 billion) (2000)
Stock Exchanges: London
Ticker Symbol: RBOS
NAIC: 522110 Commercial Banking; 522210 Credit Card Issuing; 522220 Sales Financing; 522291 Consumer Lending; 522292 Real Estate Credit; 523920 Portfolio Management; 524113 Direct Life Insurance Carriers; 524126 Direct Property and Casualty Insurance Carriers; 524210 Insurance Agencies and Brokerages; 551111 Offices of Bank Holding Companies

The Royal Bank of Scotland Group plc ranks as the leading Scotland-based banking group and the number three bank in the United Kingdom, after HSBC Holdings plc and Lloyds TSB Group plc. The group's founding bank, the Royal Bank of Scotland, was established in 1727 and was the second bank started in Scotland (the Bank of Scotland had been founded in 1695). The Royal Bank of Scotland and National Westminster Bank (NatWest), which Royal Bank acquired in 2000, are the group's two main retail banking brands and offer a full range of banking services for personal, business, and corporate customers. The group also owns Ulster Bank, which operates in both Northern Ireland and the Republic of Ireland, and Rhode Island-based Citizens Financial Group, which is the number two bank in New England, after FleetBoston Financial Corporation. Other key holdings include Direct Line, the largest provider of automobile insurance in the United Kingdom, offering life insurance as well and selling directly to consumers by telephone and via the Internet; and Coutts & Co. and Adam & Company, both of which are private banks.

Royal Bank's 18th-Century Origins

After one failed attempt, the Royal Bank of Scotland was established on May 31, 1727. The first attempt to establish the bank came in the late 17th century when Scotland tried to improve its economic position with the so-called Darien scheme. The Darien scheme was a plan to establish a Scots trading colony, designed along the lines of England's London East India Company, in Panama. With a population of only around 1.1 million at the end of the 17th century, Scotland could not hope to raise the requisite capital alone, so the scheme's architects relied on England for the bulk of their subscriptions. English investors, however, withdrew their money at the last minute when the English government realized that a successful Scottish venture could jeopardize the position of the London East India Company. Forced to finance the venture alone, the Scots raised £238,000 for the enterprise. Unfortunately, the entire sum was lost when the venture collapsed in 1699 due to difficulties with the heat, the Spanish, and outbreaks of fever.

The failure was devastating to Scotland, which had lost a quarter of its liquid assets in the disaster. Feelings ran so high against England for its lack of support that when the two countries were joined by the 1707 Act of Union, the English government deemed it wise to agree to pay compensation. The government provided for an ''Equivalent'' of £398,085 (and ten shillings) to cover the Darien losses and other debts, and allowed for an ''Arising Equivalent,'' which would be a percentage of tax revenue. Because only £150,000 of the promised money was actually available in cash, many Scottish creditors were given debentures bearing interest at 5 percent. Little of this interest actually materialized, however, until 1719, when an act was passed establishing an annual fund of £10,000 to be raised by Scotland's customs and excise.

Organizations such as the Society of the Subscribed Equivalent Debt arose in both Scotland and England to aid in collecting the interest due, to buy more debenture stock, and to issue loans to members based on the value of their holdings. In 1724 these organizations were joined and regularized by Parliament to create the Equivalent Company. By 1727 this company, which was essentially acting as a bank to its members, chose to take the next logical step and officially become a bank. It was impossible to do so in England, where the Bank of England's

Company Perspectives:

We aim to be recognised as the best performing financial services group in the United Kingdom. In striving towards that aim we are mindful of the responsibilities to shareholders, customers, employees, and the communities in which we operate.

Achieving our aim while successfully balancing these responsibilities is the primary challenge. We believe that we can best respond to this challenge by remaining independent.

monopoly was firmly fixed, but the field was open in Scotland, where the monopoly of the Bank of Scotland, established by an act of the Scots Parliament in 1695, had expired in 1716. The Equivalent Company was granted a charter for banking on May 31, 1727, and was incorporated as the Royal Bank of Scotland.

The new bank opened in Edinburgh on December 8, 1727, with an authorized capital of £111,347 and a governor, a court of directors, and a staff of eight: a cashier, a secretary and his clerk, an accountant and his clerk, two tellers, and a messenger. It was a modest beginning but the new bank received a welcome boost in the form of £20,000 from the government, which chose that occasion to finally honor a commitment undertaken as part of the 1707 Act of Union, which provided for that sum to be lent out at interest for the development of Scottish fisheries and general manufacturing.

The Royal Bank learned to compete well against the Bank of Scotland and other banks as they were subsequently established. Circulation wars were an especially popular way of discomfiting the competition. At the time official government-backed banknotes did not exist; each bank issued its own, and a favorite ploy was to amass as many of a rival's banknotes as possible and present them for payment all at once, causing frequent embarrassment and occasional temporary closures. Before long, however, an efficient countertactic was mounted when competitors demanded redemption of banknotes be paid entirely with sixpences. Eventually the practice died out.

Although the tricks may have been discontinued, the rivalry among competing banks remained. By the later 18th century the struggle for dominance shifted to Glasgow, Scotland's second largest city, which was rapidly gaining prominence as a center for industry and commerce. Smaller banks had already sprung up there to satisfy new demand, and the big two, the Royal Bank and the Bank of Scotland, both Edinburgh-based, soon reacted to the threat of more competition. The Royal's first Glasgow branch opened in 1783 and the bank became deeply involved in the city's booming industries: the cotton trade, steam ships, sugar, and tobacco. Before long the Royal dominated the financial market in Glasgow; indeed, by the 1810s the bank's Glasgow trade eclipsed its business in Edinburgh.

Facing Increased Competition in the 19th Century

By the early 19th century a new threat faced the Royal and its arch-rival the Bank of Scotland. As large banking institutions whose clients tended to be big companies and very wealthy individuals, the two were perceived—and accurately so—as being removed from the interests of the general public. The average small customer's banking needs were served by small private banks which in turn banked with the Royal or the Bank of Scotland. The system, which struck many as unsatisfactory, was changed with the arrival in 1810 of the new Commercial Bank of Scotland, which billed itself as "the Bank of the Citizens." The new bank did well, having built up a branch network in Scotland of 30 banks by 1831, when it was granted a Royal Charter of Incorporation. The Commercial's success was watched with interest, and other, similar banks soon appeared, most notably the National Bank of Scotland, incorporated in 1825.

Increased competition notwithstanding, the Royal continued to thrive as the 19th century progressed. As its success in Glasgow had proved, the bank was keenly aware of the opportunities afforded by the expansion of industry: in 1826 it financed Scotland's first steam-powered railway, the first of several successful transport ventures. As the bank prospered it also expanded. By 1836 five new outlets had been established in Dundee, Paisley, Perth, Rothesay, and Dalkeith. The Royal Bank began a policy of aggressive acquisition, taking over many new branches after the 1857 failure of the Western Bank of Scotland and in 1864 acquiring the Dundee Banking Company, which had been founded in 1763. The Royal Bank also expanded its operations into England in 1874.

The Scottish banking community was shocked in 1878 when the City of Glasgow Bank spectacularly crashed: although the incident worked to the big banks' advantage (they divided the unfortunate bank's branches between them), it highlighted the need for limited liability and for a bank's accounting practices to be audited by independent, professional accountants. The Royal Bank was already protected on the first score under the terms of its charter, but the Commercial and the National made haste to register under the Companies Act to prevent a similar misfortune befalling them.

Turning More Acquisitive in the 20th Century

The Royal increased its presence in England in the early 20th century. In 1924 the bank acquired Drummonds Bank, a small but highly regarded London bank (whose clients had included George III and Beau Brummel) originally founded in 1717 by an expatriate Scotsman. Six years later the Royal acquired the Bank of England's West End Branch and also Williams Deacon's Bank, whose branch network in Manchester and the northwest provided the Royal with its first English presence outside the capital. The trend toward acquisition continued in 1939 with the addition of another private London bank, Glyn, Mills & Co. This bank and Williams Deacon's continued to operate under their own names as subsidiaries, and together with their parent the Royal Bank were known as the Three Banks Group. As the bank grew it took advantage of technology. At this time the Royal Bank introduced telephones, typewriters, adding machines, and teleprinters. After World War II the bank founded a residential banking college to train staff for an increasingly sophisticated financial world.

By 1959 banking trends clearly favored consolidation. Scottish banks needed to match the financial might of their English counterparts if they were to be able to accommodate the needs of growing Scottish industry and commerce. Accordingly, the National and Commercial banks merged to form the National Commercial Bank of Scotland, and in 1966 further strengthened

Key Dates:

1692: Coutts & Company is organized.
1727: The Royal Bank of Scotland is founded.
1810: Commercial Bank of Scotland is established.
1825: National Bank of Scotland is founded.
1829: Manchester and Liverpool District Banking Company is founded.
1833: National Provincial Bank of England is organized.
1834: London and Westminster Bank is formed.
1836: London and County Bank is established; Ulster Bank is founded.
1864: Royal Bank acquires Dundee Banking.
1874: Royal Bank expands into England for the first time.
1909: London and Westminster merges with London and County to form London County and Westminster Bank.
1917: London County acquires Ulster Bank.
1918: National Provincial Bank merges with Union of London and Smiths Bank to form National Provincial and Union Bank of England; London County and Parr's Bank merge to form London County Westminster and Parr's Bank.
1920: National Provincial and Union acquires Coutts & Company.
1923: London County is renamed Westminster Bank Ltd.
1924: Royal Bank acquires Drummonds Bank; Manchester and Liverpool District Banking is renamed District Bank; National Provincial and Union Bank is renamed National Provincial Bank.
1930: Royal Bank makes two acquisitions: the Bank of England's West End Branch and Williams Deacon's Bank.
1939: Royal Bank acquires Glyn, Mills & Co.; Royal Bank, Williams Deacon's, and Glyn, Mills comprise the Three Banks Group.
1959: National Commercial Bank of Scotland is formed from the merger of the National Bank of Scotland and Commercial Bank of Scotland.
1962: National Provincial Bank acquires District Bank.
1968: National Provincial Bank, District Bank, and Westminster Bank announce that they will merge to form National Westminster Bank Plc (NatWest).
1969: Royal Bank and National Commercial merge to form the new Royal Bank of Scotland; National and Commercial Banking Group is formed as a holding company for Royal Bank and its English concerns.
1970: Glyn, Mills, Williams Deacon's, and National Bank are merged as Williams & Glyn's Bank; NatWest opens for business.
1979: National and Commercial Banking Group is renamed the Royal Bank of Scotland Group plc; NatWest gains U.S. presence with purchase of National Bank of North America.
1985: Royal Bank Group establishes Direct Line; two group subsidiaries, Williams & Glyn's and Royal Bank of Scotland, are merged under the latter name.
1987: NatWest's investment banking arm, County NatWest, underwrites a stock offering for an employment agency, leading to the Blue Arrow affair.
1988: Royal Bank Group acquires Rhode Island-based Citizens Financial Group and enters into an alliance with Banco Santander of Spain. NatWest acquires First Jersey National Bank.
1989: NatWest acquires New Jersey-based Ultra Bancorp, with U.S. holdings organized as National Westminster Bancorp.
1996: NatWest Bancorp is sold to Fleet Financial Group.
2000: Royal Bank acquires NatWest.

their position by acquiring the English and Welsh branches of the National Bank. Three years later, however, the National Commercial Bank merged with the Royal Bank. A new holding company was formed called National and Commercial Banking Group Ltd., which included the Scottish side, the Royal Bank of Scotland, and the English concerns, Glyn, Mills & Co., Williams Deacon's, and the National Bank. In 1970 the latter came together as Williams & Glyn's Bank Ltd.

Greatly strengthened by the amalgamation, the group was ideally placed to take full advantage of the two watershed economic events of the 1970s. In 1971 the regulatory Bank of England eased restrictions on Scottish banks operating in England, allowing the Royal Bank to compete freely for the first time. The range of financial services that banks could provide was also substantially broadened. Perhaps even more significantly, the rise of the North Sea oil industry in the 1970s proved an unprecedented boom to the Scottish economy and especially to banks, such as the Royal, which were quick to recognize the tremendous potential of the new industry. Taking advantage of its newfound strength, the bank expanded its foreign interests, establishing branches in New York and Hong Kong and opening representative offices in Chicago, Houston, Los Angeles, and San Francisco. At decade's end, the group's holding company was renamed the Royal Bank of Scotland Group plc.

Diversifying and Expanding in the 1980s and 1990s

The 1980s began with the group vulnerable to a takeover. The group's board took the initiative late in 1980 of seeking a merger itself with a British bank having a large overseas presence. Talks began with Standard Chartered Bank, leading to the announcement of a merger in early 1981. Hongkong and Shanghai Banking Corporation came forward with a rival bid within days, setting off a bidding war. The bids were referred to the Monopolies and Mergers Commission, which in January 1982 ruled against both of them. In the wake of this decision, the holding company was given a full-time executive team for the first time and in 1985 the group's clearing bank subsidiaries, Williams & Glyn's Bank and Royal Bank of Scotland, were merged as Royal Bank of Scotland.

The group also adopted a more aggressive program of expansion and diversification. In 1985 the bank created the Royal Bank of Scotland Group Insurance Company Limited, a telephone-based general insurance business. The subsidiary, soon renamed

Direct Line, proved a runaway success, becoming the largest motor insurer in the United Kingdom. It soon offered household and life insurance. In 1988 the Royal acquired the Rhode Island-based Citizens Financial Group, the fifth largest bank in New England, and promptly set upon a course of aggressive expansion. By late 1995, following the acquisition of a number of banks in the region, Citizens had established major presences in Connecticut and Massachusetts in addition to its home state of Rhode Island. It became the third largest commercial bank in New England with the April 1996 purchase of First New Hampshire Bank, which had been a subsidiary of Bank of Ireland. Following this transaction, Bank of Ireland held a 23.5 percent stake in Citizens.

The tremendous success of Direct Line and Citizens led to speculation in the early 1990s that the Royal would sell one or both of these subsidiaries, but the rumored divestments did not occur. In fact the subsidiaries played a fundamental role not only in keeping profits high but also in protecting the group from fluctuations: if one sector of the Royal Bank's business were to suffer a reverse, the others could carry the group for a time. Meanwhile, under the new leadership of George Mathewson, who became chief executive in 1992, Royal Bank in 1993 acquired Adam & Company, an Edinburgh-based private bank that had been founded ten years earlier.

Although Royal Bank described itself as "conservative," it was by no means fearful of creating and exploiting new opportunities. Its innovative use of technology was second to none in U.K. banking. In 1994 the bank introduced a 24-hour, seven-days-a-week telephone banking service, Direct Banking. Perhaps the bank's biggest coup, however, was its creation of the Inter-Bank On-Line System (IBOS), a sophisticated cross-border banking system whereby funds could be transferred nearly instantaneously from the United Kingdom to IBOS member banks in Europe. The project grew out of a 1988 alliance with the Spanish Banco Santander and as of 1994 there were 3,500 IBOS branches in five countries, with many more planned.

With astonishing rapidity the Royal diversified into new financial services, products, and initiatives. In 1994 the bank pioneered its "finance shops," which offered an extensive realm of mortgage and savings products to customers. The bank also placed a new emphasis on credit card services, making this an independent operation. Also, the Royal established a specialist group to finance public sector projects in 1994. The bank also captured an increasing share of the U.K. mortgage lending market, traditionally the province of the building societies (the rough equivalent of U.S. savings and loan associations).

Expansion and innovation continued in the second half of the 1990s. In 1996 the Royal Bank formed an independent offshore bank called Royal Bank of Scotland International. Direct Line expanded into roadside assistance insurance and in November 1999 acquired Green Flag, making Direct Line Rescue the number three roadside assistance specialist in the United Kingdom with nearly three million customers. In 1997 Royal Bank entered into joint ventures with food retailer Tesco PLC and Richard Branson's Virgin Group, with both ventures specializing in branded personal finance products. That same year Royal Bank began offering online banking over the Internet. The group also acquired Angel Train Contracts Limited, a rolling stock leasing firm.

In the United States, Royal Bank regained full ownership of Citizens in September 1998 when it purchased Bank of Ireland's minority holding. The following year Citizens acquired the commercial banking business of State Street Corporation, then in January 2000 Citizens acquired Boston-based UST Corp. With $28 billion in assets overall, half of which were held by Citizens Bank of Massachusetts, Citizens Financial Group was one of the 40 largest banks in the United States and held the number two position in New England—although it was much smaller than the leader, FleetBoston Financial Corporation, whose assets exceeded $190 billion.

To further expand its share of the mortgage lending market, Royal Bank pursued the acquisition of a U.K. building society, a move that had long been expected. It reached an agreement in 1998 to acquire Birmingham Midshires for £630 million but the society pulled out of the deal in order to accept a higher offer from Halifax plc. Midshires had to pay Royal Bank £5 million to gain its release from the deal. Somewhat audaciously, the Royal pursued an acquisition of the much larger Barclays Bank in 1999, during a period when that bank was without a chief executive, but this initiative was rebuffed. Later in 1999, however, the Royal Bank Group commenced a prolonged takeover battle with longtime rival Bank of Scotland, the prize being London-based National Westminster Bank. Royal Bank ended up on the winning side and acquired NatWest in March 2000.

NatWest's District Bank Roots

National Westminster Bank Plc (NatWest) was created in 1970 by the merger of three major banks all established in the early 19th century: the District Bank, the National Provincial Bank, and the Westminster Bank. The District Bank was first established in 1829 in Manchester as the Manchester and Liverpool District Banking Company, with a starting nominal capital of £3 million. The company planned to create a banking network for northwest England by opening new branches and acquiring smaller banks, and within five years had opened 17 branches.

By 1840, however, Manchester and Liverpool District Banking was forced to write off over £500,000 in bad debts—a huge sum at the time—due to management misjudgment, slowing the firm's acquisitions and expansion for the next few years. In addition, the bank was closely associated with England's textile industry; the company suffered during the cotton famine of the 1860s caused by the North's blockade of Southern ports during the American Civil War. Judicious acquisitions, however, helped the bank weather this particular storm.

At the beginning of 1885, the bank, recovered from its previous losses, opened an office in London. As customer deposits increased and astute commercial credit policies and management were put to work, the bank began a moderate expansion program that lasted until the outbreak of World War I. After a five-year hiatus, the company was caught up in the postwar boom and opened 130 new branches between 1919 and 1924. In the latter year, the bank shortened its name to District Bank.

Relatively unscathed by the worldwide depression of the late 1920s and early 1930s, the bank continued its expansion program, and immediately after World War II decided to create a network of branches throughout the country. In 1935 District Bank merged with the County Bank, a Manchester-based entity, increasing its paid-up capital to almost £3 million and kicking off its nationwide expansion. This strong-growth strategy continued unabated up to and following World War II until District Bank's acquisition by National Provincial Bank in 1962.

NatWest's National Provincial Bank Roots

National Provincial Bank of England was organized as a joint-stock company in 1833. At the time, the Bank of England had exclusive statutory power to issue bank notes within a 65-mile radius of London. Although the bank's administrative offices were in London, it decided to open its branches outside the 65-mile radius so that the bank could issue its own notes. From the beginning National Provincial lived up to its name, serving provincial customers throughout England. The bank was without a national competitor for about 60 years.

The first branch of National Provincial Bank was opened on January 1, 1834, in Gloucester. Like the District Bank, the company planned to establish new branches and acquire smaller banks, and by 1835 had opened 20 new offices. By the mid-1860s, National Provincial had acquired more than a dozen small banks and had established 122 branches and sub-branches throughout England and Wales. It finally opened a London banking office in 1866, recognizing that a presence in the world's financial capital was worth the sacrifice of its note-issuing privilege.

The bank continued to grow rapidly. At the dawn of the 20th century, the company had about 250 offices in England and Wales and approximately £3 million in capital. After World War I, the company began an accelerated acquisition-and-merger strategy. The most important of its mergers during this time came in 1918, a merger with the Union of London and Smiths Bank, itself the product of the amalgamation of two of the most venerable banking institutions in England, which added 230 branches to National Provincial's growing financial network. This merger created National Provincial and Union Bank of England, which was renamed National Provincial Bank in 1924.

Although National Provincial's growth had been interrupted by World War I, the bank vigorously renewed its acquisition program after the war. Sheffield Banking Company, Northamptonshire Union Bank, Guernsey Banking Company, Bradford District Bank, and Coutts & Company, all acquired between 1919 and 1924; North Central Finance (later Lombard North Central), acquired in 1958; and Isle of Man Bank, purchased in 1961, were a few of the significant purchases made by National Provincial. In 1962 District Bank was bought by National Provincial to create a company with over £1.4 billion in assets and 2,100 branches, although the two banks maintained their separate identities and independent operations.

NatWest's Westminster Bank Roots

Westminster Bank was organized in 1834 as the London and Westminster Bank, the first joint-stock bank in London. This firm was the first bank established under the auspices of the Bank Charter Act of 1833, which allowed joint-stock banks to be founded in London. For various reasons, the press, private banking concerns, and the Bank of England were so hostile to the Bank Charter Act that London and Westminster's management was primarily concerned with defending the company's right to exist rather than setting up an extensive branch network. As a result, the bank opened only six London branches in its first three years and no additional offices were established until nearly 20 years later.

London and Westminster made its first acquisition in 1847, when it bought Young & Son. In about 1870 it acquired Unity Joint-Stock Bank, and mergers with Commercial Bank of London and Middlesex Bank had been arranged in 1861 and 1863, respectively. By 1909 London and Westminster had opened or acquired 37 branches in and around London. Yet, despite this expansion effort, the bank felt the effects of competition from provincial banks such as Lloyds and Midland. These two banks had already established large regional branch networks and were quickly encroaching upon the London market. In order to meet this challenge, London and Westminster merged in 1909 with the influential and prestigious London and County Bank, which was founded in 1836 and had 70 offices citywide and almost 200 in rural counties. The resulting entity was named the London County and Westminster Bank.

In 1913, the bank formed a subsidiary, London County and Westminster Bank (Paris), which opened branches during and after World War I in Bordeaux, Lyons, Marseilles, Nantes, Brussels, and Antwerp. The bank itself also established offices in Barcelona and Madrid during the same time. In 1917, bank officials decided to acquire the 1836-founded Ulster Bank (which continued to operate separately), with 170 branches throughout Ireland, and in 1918 bought Parr's Bank, with over 320 offices throughout England. These purchases made London County Westminster and Parr's Bank (which became simply Westminster Bank Ltd. in 1923) the fifth largest bank in England.

During the economic difficulties of the late 1920s and early 1930s, the bank kept tight centralized control over the continental branch of the business to avoid the dangers of too rapid an expansion in unfamiliar markets, but this policy stunted Westminster's international operations. It did mean that the bank escaped the bad debts and currency fluctuations that plagued many other banks between the world wars, allowing the domestic side of the business to grow steadily. At the time of the merger with National Provincial in 1968, Westminster had 1,400 branches in England alone.

Emergence of NatWest and International Expansion: 1970s and 1980s

The merger of National Provincial and Westminster Bank, announced in early 1968, shocked the British public and banking community. In the late 1960s, the Bank of England tried to rationalize the banking industry through a policy known as competition and credit control, which aimed to put banks on a more equal and competitive footing and to improve control of the nation's money supply. Although the Bank of England indicated a willingness to allow mergers as part of the rationalization process, no one had seriously believed it would permit mergers among the largest and most influential banks.

The District Bank, National Provincial, and Westminster Bank were fully integrated in the new firm's structure, while Coutts & Company (a 1920 National Provincial acquisition), Ulster Bank, and the nonbanking subsidiaries continued as separate operations. Duncan Stirling, chairman of Westminster Bank, became NatWest's first chairman. In 1969 David Robarts, former chairman of National Provincial, assumed Stirling's position. The new company, National Westminster Bank, opened its doors for business on January 1, 1970.

In the late 1970s and early 1980s, following a massive restructuring and rationalization, NatWest began a concerted effort to expand its international operations. In 1975 NatWest expanded into Scotland, opening offices in Edinburgh, Glasgow, and later Aberdeen to support its participation in North Sea fuel projects. Under the direction of Robin Leigh-Pemberton, who became chairman in 1977, the company purchased the National Bank of North America in New York in 1979. By that year, NatWest had also extended its bases of operation in France and Belgium, had opened offices in West Germany, and had established overseas representatives in Australia, Bahrain, Canada, Greece, Hong Kong, Japan, Mexico, Singapore, Spain, and the Soviet Union.

Thomas Boardman replaced Robin Leigh-Pemberton as chairman of NatWest in 1983 when the latter was appointed governor of the Bank of England. Boardman and Tom Frost, who became NatWest's CEO in 1987, continued to transform NatWest from a domestic banking institution into an international financial organization, Part of the plan included forming NatWest Investment Bank through the acquisition of a medium-sized stock exchange jobber and a broker. NatWest also expanded its American subsidiary, NatWest USA, by acquiring First Jersey National Bank in 1987 and Ultra Bancorp, another New Jersey-based bank, in 1989. These acquisitions gave the newly named National Westminster Bancorp 285 branches throughout the Northeast and $20 billion in assets. Despite its reputation for caution, NatWest remained intent throughout the 1980s on building its American subsidiary into a superregional bank that might someday challenge the traditional dominance of the New York money-center banks.

The bank lived up to its reputation for caution, however, with its handling of the Third World debt crisis. In June 1987 it added £246 million to its reserves, becoming the first British bank to follow the lead of the American money-center banks by limiting its exposure to Third World loans.

Late 1980s and Early 1990s: Blue Arrow and Other Travails

NatWest's good name was tarnished, however, in December 1988, when the Department of Trade and Industry (DTI) began to investigate the role played by the bank's investment banking subsidiary, County NatWest, in an acquisition by the employment agency Blue Arrow. In 1987 County NatWest underwrote a stock offering for Blue Arrow to raise cash for the deal, but the results were disappointing. County NatWest was left with an interest in a 13.5 percent stake in Blue Arrow. It concealed that substantial interest by dividing the stake between itself, its own market-making arm, County NatWest Securities, and the Union Bank of Switzerland (UBS), to which it granted an indemnity against losses.

These moves were made in secret, however, to spare County NatWest the public embarrassment of a failed offering. But after the October stock market crash opened the Blue Arrow wound even further, its actions could no longer be concealed. In December 1987, County NatWest made a payment to UBS to release the indemnity, purchased County NatWest Securities' holding, and announced that it held a total stake of 9.5 percent in Blue Arrow.

The DTI released the results of its investigation in July 1989, sharply criticizing County NatWest's actions. In failing to report its stake in Blue Arrow, it said, County NatWest violated a law requiring any party holding a 5 percent or greater interest in a company to report that fact in a timely fashion. This served to deceive both regulators and the financial markets about the true value of Blue Arrow stock. Although the DTI report did not criticize him, Lord Boardman announced that he would retire from the bank in September, five months ahead of schedule, and two of NatWest's deputy chief executives and another senior director also resigned. Lord Alexander, the former head of the British government body overseeing corporate takeovers, became chairman on October 1, 1989.

The Blue Arrow affair continued to dog NatWest into the early 1990s. Three former executives of County NatWest were convicted in February 1992 of misleading the market by disguising the failure of the rights issue, but these convictions were later overturned upon appeal. In 1992 the DTI launched another investigation to determine whether NatWest officials had engaged in obstructive actions to impede the first inquiry, but no improprieties were found. The inquiry did, however, lead to the resignation of Frost, who stepped down from his chief executive post in March 1992 in order to devote his full attention to the investigation. His successor was Derek Wanless.

NatWest faced other difficulties during this period. In 1989 profits were dampened by provisions against possible losses on loans to less developed countries. The following year, a similar result came from an increase in U.K. loan losses. In 1991 NatWest was forced to take a bad debt charge of £1.88 billion (US$3.3 billion), an increase of 63 percent over the previous year, leading to a reduction in pretax profits of 78 percent, to £110 million (US$192 million). Adding to the gloom was the bombing of NatWest's headquarters by the Irish Republican Army in 1991.

Restructuring moves were initiated, including the reduction of the U.K. branch network from 3,000 to 2,800 and the trimming of its workforce in the United Kingdom by about 10,000 between 1989 and 1991. Also in 1991, NatWest merged its various international private banking units within the prestigious Coutts & Co. The following year, NatWest Markets was formed from the combination of the bank's corporate banking and investment banking arms, including County NatWest. Additional job cuts were undertaken, with the workforce reduced by another 7,000 employees in 1992 and 4,000 in 1993. Several noncore operations were divested: share-registrar services in the United Kingdom, retail banking in France and Australia, equity operations in Japan, and credit card merchandising in the United

States. There were also some new initiatives, most notably NatWest Life, a venture launched in 1993 to sell life insurance at the bank's branches.

Late 1990s: NatWest's Final Years of Independence

Through this restructuring and by getting its bad loan portfolio under control, NatWest returned to solid profitability in the mid-1990s, posting record pretax profits of £1.7 billion for 1995. Its total assets of £169 billion made NatWest the number two bank in the United Kingdom, after HSBC Holdings. Late in 1995 NatWest reached a decision to sell NatWest Bancorp. The bank had managed to engineer a turnaround of the long-troubled U.S. unit but, with banking industry consolidation proceeding at a feverish pitch in the United States, NatWest Bancorp would need to grow considerably larger to remain competitive. NatWest decided instead to sell out while acquisition prices were on the rise. In May 1996, then, NatWest Bancorp was sold to Fleet Financial Group, Inc. for £2.3 billion (US$3.6 billion). It was estimated that NatWest's return on its 16-year investment in the U.S. retail banking market was a disappointing 1 percent.

In the wake of the sales of NatWest Bancorp and NatWest Espana, also jettisoned in 1996, NatWest made four major acquisitions in a 12-month span. The bank acquired two investment banking firms, the U.S.-based Gleacher & Co. and J.O. Hambro Magan & Co., which was active throughout Europe. Also purchased were Greenwich Capital Markets Inc. and Gartmore PLC, a fund manager. All of these firms became part of NatWest Markets, which was being positioned to become one of the world's leading investment banks. NatWest was rocked in February 1997, however, by the revelation of hidden trading losses at NatWest Markets, whose chief executive soon resigned. NatWest's stock took a beating from these developments and from the disclosures that NatWest had approached Abbey National plc about a merger but had been rebuffed and then had initiated talks with U.K. life insurance firm Prudential plc regarding a consolidation, with these discussions falling through. Investors were becoming increasingly concerned about a lack of a clear strategy at NatWest and a perception of poor management. In a retrenchment aimed at focusing renewed attention on its core U.K. market, NatWest subsequently sold its equities businesses in Europe, the United States, and Asia, including Gleacher and Hambro Magan. Its failed foray into international investment banking led to a writeoff of £441 million (US$730 million) in 1997, helping to drop pretax profits to £975 million (US$1.6 billion).

In April 1999 David Rowland became chairman of NatWest following the retirement of Lord Alexander. Rowland had previously served as chairman of Lloyd's from 1993 to 1997. In yet another bid at expanding through a major acquisition, NatWest in September 1999 reached an agreement to acquire Legal & General Group PLC, a major U.K. insurance and pension-fund company, for nearly £11 billion (US$18 billion). Through this deal, NatWest aimed to greatly enlarge its insurance operations and gain additional opportunities for cross-selling financial products to its core banking customers. Unfortunately, the offering price was widely believed to be too high, and NatWest's share price almost immediately fell sharply. This left NatWest open to predators itself. Less than three weeks after announcing its proposed acquisition of Legal & General, Bank of Scotland came forward with a £20.85 billion (US$34.24 billion) hostile takeover bid of NatWest, despite the fact that the prey was twice the size of the predator.

In early October, Wanless was ousted from the chief executive slot, with Rowland taking over that position and his right-hand man, Ron Sandler, who had only recently left Lloyd's where he had been chief executive, being named chief operating officer. Attempting to fend off the unwanted Scottish advance, NatWest announced later in October that as part of its defense against the bid it would cut 1,000 jobs and sell off four businesses: Ulster Bank, Greenwich NatWest, Gartmore, and NatWest Equity Partners, a venture capital unit. NatWest planned to focus on retail, corporate, and private banking. In November, however, Royal Bank of Scotland stepped into the fray with a hostile takeover bid of its own, offering £20.7 billion (US$34 billion) in cash and stock for NatWest and setting off a prolonged and sometimes bitter takeover battle. With its more extensive operations in England, Royal Bank had an advantage over Bank of Scotland in the amount of cost savings it could conceivably wring out of a merger with NatWest. Finally, in February 2000, NatWest's board gave in and recommended to the company's shareholders that they accept the Royal Bank offer, which closed in March.

Royal Bank in the New Century

Moving quickly in the wake of its long sought-after acquisition of a major English bank, Royal Bank of Scotland soon sold off Gartmore and NatWest Equity Partners. Royal Bank expected to achieve annual cost savings of £1.22 billion (US$1.96 billion) from the integration of NatWest and began the process of slashing 18,000 NatWest jobs over a three-year period, including 9,000 in 2000 alone. Although NatWest no longer existed as an independent firm, the NatWest name lived on in the retail banking arena, giving Royal Bank two main U.K. retail banking brands. NatWest's corporate banking units, however, were integrated into those of Royal Bank, which was now one of Europe's largest banks in corporate financing. Royal Bank would also be operating two separate private banks, Coutts and Adam, with no plans for merging the two. The bank's management team, led by deputy chairman George Mathewson and chief executive Fred Goodwin, set an ambitious goal of surpassing Lloyds TSB Group and HSBC Holdings as the largest and most profitable bank in the United Kingdom. Toward this goal, further major acquisitions at home seemed unlikely, leading Royal Bank to remain alert for opportunities to further develop its successful Citizens unit in the United States and to expand in continental Europe.

Principal Subsidiaries

Angel Train Contracts Limited; The Royal Bank of Scotland plc; Adam & Company Group PLC; Citizens Bank of Rhode Island (U.S.A.); Citizens Bank of Connecticut (U.S.A.); Citizens Bank of Massachusetts (U.S.A.); Citizens Bank New Hampshire (U.S.A.); Coutts & Co.; Direct Line Insurance plc; Direct Line Financial Services Limited; Isle of Man Bank Limited; Lombard North Central PLC; National Westminster Bank Plc; Privilege Insurance Company Limited; RBS Advanta; RBS Mezzanine Limited; RBS Trade Services Limited; Royal Bank

Development Capital Limited; Royal Bank Insurance Services Limited; Royal Bank Insurance Services (Independent Financial Advisers) Limited; Royal Bank Invoice Finance Limited; Royal Bank Leasing Limited; Royal Scottish Assurance plc (70%); RoyScot International Finance B.V. (Netherlands); RoyScot Trust plc; Style Financial Services Limited; Tesco Personal Finance Limited (50%); The Royal Bank of Scotland (Gibraltar) Limited (50%); The Royal Bank of Scotland International Limited (Jersey); The Royal Bank of Scotland Trust Company (Jersey) Limited; The Royal Bank of Scotland Trust Company (Guernsey) Limited; The Royal Bank of Scotland Trust Company (I.O.M.) Limited (Isle of Man); The Royal Bank of Scotland (Nassau) Limited (Bahamas); Ulster Bank Limited; Virgin Direct Personal Finance Limited.

Principal Divisions

Royal Bank of Scotland-Retail; NatWest Retail; Wealth Management; Retail Direct; Corporate Banking & Financial Markets; Direct Line; Ulster Bank; Citizens (USA).

Principal Competitors

Abbey National plc; Alliance & Leicester plc; Bank of Scotland; Barclays PLC; FleetBoston Financial Corporation; HSBC Holdings plc; Halifax plc; Lloyds TSB Group plc; Northern Rock plc.

Further Reading

Ashby, J.F., *The Story of the Banks,* London: Hutchinson & Company, 1934, 283 p.

''The Blue Arrow Affair: The Buck Stops Where?,'' *Economist,* March 7, 1992, pp. 23+.

Bray, Nicholas, ''NatWest Chooses a Cautious Offensive,'' *Wall Street Journal,* February 28, 1992, p. A5A.

——, ''Reorganized NatWest Picks Up Steam, Heads Uphill,'' *Wall Street Journal,* December 15, 1994, p. B4.

Calian, Sara, ''Stodgy NatWest's Makeover Gets an Approving Nod from Investors,'' *Wall Street Journal,* February 7, 1997, p. A14.

Checkland, S.G., *Scottish Banking: A History, 1695–1973,* Glasgow: Collins, 1973, 785 p.

''County NatWest: Anatomy of a Cover-Up,'' *Economist,* January 28, 1989, pp. 78+.

Gapper, John, ''Losing Lots of Layers,'' *Financial Times,* June 8, 1993, p. 16.

Graham, George, ''The Awful History of Unhappy Banking Acquisitions in the United States,'' *Financial Times,* December 20, 1995, p. 20.

——, ''NatWest Bids Farewell to an Albatross: A Foray into the United States That Has Ended in a Costly Retreat,'' *Financial Times,* December 23, 1995.

——, ''NatWest Ponders Conundrum of Cash in Pocket,'' *Financial Times,* February 15, 1996, p. 27.

——, ''Strong Will Takes the Helm As Storms Threaten,'' *Financial Times,* September 9, 1998, p. 28.

Graham, George, and Mark Nicholson, ''A Scottish Aggressor: Royal Bank's Chairman Has Fulfilled a Long-Held Ambition to Capture an English Rival,'' *Financial Times,* February 12, 2000, p. 13.

Graham, George, and Nicholas Denton, ''Opportunity to Fulfil Ambition for Expansion: A Look at NatWest's Reasons for Buying Gartmore,'' *Financial Times,* February 20, 1996, p. 19.

Gregory, T.E., *The Westminster Bank Through a Century,* Oxford University Press, 1936.

''Growth in Mortgage Lending Helps Royal Bank Double to Pounds 201m,'' *Financial Times,* May 12, 1994.

Hamilton, Kirstie, ''NatWest's Double Act Falls Out of Favour,'' *Management Today,* October 1997, pp. 38–40, 43–44.

Healey, Edna, *Coutts and Co., 1692–1992: The Portrait of a Private Bank,* London: Hodder & Stoughton, 1992, 488 p.

Leighton, J.A.S.L., *Smiths the Bankers, 1658–1958,* London: National Provincial Bank, 1958, 337 p.

''Lord Boardman Banking on Discretion,'' *Director,* January 1989, pp. 54+.

Maccoll, Fiona, *The Key to Our Success: A Brief History of the NatWest Group,* London: National Westminster Bank, 1996, 16 p.

Melcher, Richard A., ''How NatWest Plans to Stretch Its String of Successes,'' *Business Week,* July 6, 1987, p. 46.

Munro, Neil, *The History of the Royal Bank of Scotland, 1727–1927,* Edinburgh: R. & R. Clark, 1928, 416 p.

''NatWest and the Bank of England: An Apology,'' *Economist,* January 23, 1993, p. 76.

''NatWest Groupies,'' *Economist,* December 16, 1995, p. 74.

Plender, John, ''Called to Account: Bank of Scotland's Opportunistic Bid for NatWest Highlights the Longstanding Weakness of the Larger Bank,'' *Financial Times,* September 25, 1999, p. 11.

Portanger, Erik, ''NatWest Recommends Royal Bank Bid,'' *Wall Street Journal,* February 14, 2000, p. A19.

——, ''Royal Bank of Scotland Advisers Use Novel 'Club' to Beat Rival in Fight for National Westminster,'' *Wall Street Journal,* February 15, 2000, p. C20.

Portanger, Erik, and Anita Raghavan, ''Bidding Battle Brews for Britain's NatWest,'' *Wall Street Journal,* September 27, 1999, p. A27.

——, ''NatWest Plans $16 Billion Move into Insurance: Bank Is in Late Discussions to Buy Legal & General in Big Effort to Expand,'' *Wall Street Journal,* September 3, 1999, p. A6.

''The Puzzling International Approach of NatWest,'' *Euromoney,* July 1981, pp. 141+.

''RBS Doubles Profits and Weighs Purchase,'' *Independent,* May 12, 1994.

Reed, Richard, *National Westminster Bank: A Short History,* London: National Westminster Bank, 1989.

Reed, Stanley, and Heidi Dawley, ''A Raid on the Staid,'' *Business Week,* October 11, 1999, p. 60.

''Royal Bank Expands in US with $140m Buy,'' *Financial Times,* June 14, 1994.

''Royal Bank Is Set to Expand IBOS System,'' *Herald,* January 21, 1994.

The Royal Bank of Scotland: A History, Edinburgh: Royal Bank of Scotland, 1997, 51 p.

The Royal Bank of Scotland, 1727–1977, Edinburgh: Royal Bank of Scotland, 1977, 56 p.

''Royal Takes Over Another US Bank,'' *Scotsman,* July 6, 1994.

''The Scottish Play,'' *Economist,* October 2, 1999, pp. 79–80.

''Where Diversity Helps Balance the Books,'' *Financial Times,* May 11, 1994.

Willman, John, ''RBS Refocuses NatWest on Customer Service,'' *Financial Times,* November 15, 2000, p. 34.

Withers, Hartley, *National Provincial Bank, 1833 to 1933,* London: Waterlow & Sons, 1933, 90 p.

—Robin DuBlanc
—updated by David E. Salamie

Royal Doulton plc

Minton House, London Road
Stoke-on-Trent, Staffordshire ST4 7QD
United Kingdom
Telephone: (01782) 292292
Fax: (01782) 292099
Web site: http://www.royal-doulton.com

Public Company
Incorporated: 1854 as Doulton & Co.
Employees: 6,000
Sales: £190.3 million (US$307.6 million) (1999)
Stock Exchanges: London
Ticker Symbol: RDN
NAIC: 327112 Vitreous China, Fine Earthenware, and Other Pottery Product Manufacturing; 327212 Other Pressed and Blown Glass and Glassware Manufacturing; 421220 Home Furnishing Wholesalers; 442299 All Other Home Furnishings Stores

Royal Doulton plc is one of the world's best-known fine china companies, designing and producing high-quality tableware and giftware under the popular brand names of Royal Doulton, Minton, Royal Albert, Caithness Glass, and Holland Studio Craft. The company operates five ceramic factories, four of which are in England and the other in Indonesia, and two glass factories in Scotland. Its products are marketed in more than 80 countries, with non-U.K. sales accounting for more than half the total and sales in the United States amounting to nearly 30 percent. In addition to its commercial product lines available in higher-end specialty shops and department stores—including the company's own retail outlets, which include some 360 stores and concessions within department stores—Royal Doulton also has accepted commissions to produce unique china service for royalty, wealthy individuals, embassies, luxury hotels, and England's House of Lords.

19th-Century Origins

The history of Royal Doulton may be traced to the early 19th century, when John Doulton began an apprenticeship at London's Fulham Pottery, one of the most important of the early commercial potteries in England. Becoming an accomplished potter known for his hard work and innovation, Doulton found employment in Lambeth, along the south bank of the Thames River, at a small pottery business owned by Martha Jones, who had inherited it from her late husband. In 1815, Jones asked Doulton and another employee, John Watts, to enter into a partnership with her, and the three founded a business called Jones, Watts and Doulton.

Producing utilitarian salt glaze and stoneware ceramics, stone jars, bottles, and flasks in its early years, the company eventually expanded its line to include mugs and jugs modeled in the likenesses of Napoleon and the Duke of Wellington, bottles for beer, gallipots (ointment pots), and blacking bottles. As a laboring child, Charles Dickens was said to have pasted labels on thousands of Doulton blacking bottles. Among product lines that became central to the history of Royal Doulton was the Toby jug, or beverage mug, first produced in the early 18th century. This jug was designed to represent a seated male figure, stout and smiling, with the spouts at either side of the mug's rim serving as points on the character's tricorn hat. Figurines were another important product line, and Doulton became known for the quality and attention to detail of its figurines. The earliest recorded figurative work produced by the company is attributed to John Doulton, who made a flask depicting Queen Caroline around 1820.

Five of John Doulton's sons joined him in the family business, but the second son, Henry, took his father's place in the pottery. Henry had become a master potter, learning all aspects of the business from the production stages through management, and he played an important role in product development and in improving working conditions at the Lambeth pottery. In the 1840s Henry Doulton established the world's first factory for making stoneware drainpipes, a significant development that helped England achieve improvements in healthcare by providing more sanitary conditions through the provision of piped water. As the pipe business continued to thrive, Henry opened an art studio in the early 1870s where he encouraged and employed talented artists. Meantime, the company was incorporated in 1854 as Doulton & Co.

Company Perspectives:

The Royal Doulton group owns an internationally recognised stable of brands, with a large number of outstanding products. It is continuing to build on the clear brand positioning that has already been established.

Henry also became known for his interest in the welfare of workers, a rare concern at a time when industrialists capitalized on cheap labor. Potteries generally were hazardous places during this time, as arsenic was used in painting and lead in glazing. Workers often succumbed to a debilitating lung disease then known as "potter's rot." In addition, laborers had to carry an enormous amount of weight, lifting several tons of materials from depths of eight to ten feet. To help workers with this burden, Henry Doulton obtained a mechanical hydraulic lifting device to help eliminate some of the manual labor. He also encouraged scientific research to determine more modern and safe methods of production.

In 1877 Henry Doulton bought a factory at Burslem in Stoke-on-Trent, a city known as The Potteries and home of English bone china. Other famous potters located here included Wedgwood, Minton, Beswick, and Royal Adderly. Indeed, the area became the center for potters, given its wealth of raw materials including clay for earthenware, coal to heat the kilns, as well as lead and salt for glazing. The established potters in this area initially were annoyed when Doulton moved in on their territory, and they predicted doom for the newcomer. Henry Doulton summed their attitude up thus: "In their view we Southerners know little about God and nothing at all about potting."

Through persistence and careful investment in staff and plant, Henry Doulton did succeed. The company's early success came from earthenware, decorated in the limited colors available from lead glaze at that time. This expansion into tableware design and decoration began in 1877, when Henry Doulton entered into a partnership with and later bought out Pinder & Bourne Company, a medium-sized producer of earthenware tableware. Later, Doulton's art director John Slater and manager John C. Bailey encouraged Henry to pursue the idea of using bone china in production, a material that could be painted with more and brighter colors. By 1884, Henry Doulton had given his consent to the new medium, and the success of the results attracted to Doulton an outstanding team of modelers, decorators, and painters.

By the late 1880s, the company and its products had become internationally famous. In 1885 Henry was honored for his achievements, receiving the Albert Medal of the Society of Arts for his "encouragement in the production of artistic pottery." Only one Albert Medal was awarded each year, and previous recipients had included the poet Alfred, Lord Tennyson and Sir Rowland Hill, honored for his creation of the penny postage system. Henry's greatest honor, perhaps, came in 1887, when Queen Victoria awarded him knighthood; he was the first potter ever to be distinguished in this fashion. When Sir Henry Doulton died in 1897, he left behind a company that had diversified and established itself as one of the leaders in its field.

Becoming "Royal" Doulton in the 20th Century

Sir Henry Doulton's son, Henry Lewis Doulton, who had been made a partner in the firm in 1881, became a leader at the company. In 1901, four years after his father's death, he received on behalf of the company the Royal Warrant of King Edward VII and was granted permission to add the word "Royal" to the Doulton name—a great and rare honor. As chairman and managing director, Henry Lewis Doulton guided the company through a difficult recession and period of war between 1900 and 1920.

Regarding product development, Henry Lewis Doulton was particularly interested in experimental glaze processes that produced unique, rare color effects. One such glaze, Rouge Flambé, a dramatic red and black glaze, remained unique to Royal Doulton, with a secret formula known only to three or four people in the company into the 1990s. The company also introduced new lines of character jugs, figurines, and decorative and utility china on earthenware and bone china bodies, and their popularity continued to grow. The character jugs represented a continuation of the beverage mugs of the 19th century and gained popularity in the 1930s when they were produced to represent famous characters from English songs, literature, and history.

In America, Royal Doulton became known as the finest English china. Indeed, Royal Doulton's presence in the American market was an important part of the company's growth and success. In 1945, a subsidiary, Royal Doulton USA Inc., was formed to help in the sales and marketing of the products in the United States.

Family leadership in the company continued. Ronald Duneau Doulton, a cousin of Henry Lewis Doulton, became one of the first directors of the business when it changed to a limited company, known as Doulton & Co. Limited, in January 1899. Lewis John Eric Hooper, son of Henry Lewis's sister, joined Royal Doulton in 1902. Under Eric's guidance much scientific research into the physical and chemical behavior of ceramic materials was carried out and new technology was developed and installed. His nephew, Orrok Sherwood Doulton, joined the company in 1935 and became director. Under his leadership, Royal Doulton captured the Queen's Awards for Industry, Technological Innovation, and Outstanding Export Performance.

In 1960, Doulton & Co. introduced English Translucent China, a medium it pioneered and from which the costly ingredient of calcined bone had been eliminated. Through this new product, which became known as Royal Doulton Fine China, the company was able to offer the qualities associated with fine bone china at a modest cost to consumers.

Acquisitions and the Pearson Interregnum: 1968–93

The year 1968 saw the first series of acquisitions by Doulton & Co. It first purchased the world-renowned Minton China, a company founded by Thomas Minton in 1793. Minton dominated the industry during the middle of the 19th century and the company's innovations included the acid gold decorating process, the majolica-type body, the pâte-sur-pâte relief decoration technique, encaustic tiles, and Parian statuary. In the same year, Doulton acquired Dunn Bennett, a company founded in 1876 when Thomas Wood-Bennett joined his father-in-law William Dunn to begin potting, concentrating on hotelware. In 1969,

Key Dates:

1750: Royal Crown Derby, maker of fine porcelain products, is established.
1793: Minton China is founded.
1815: Jones, Watts and Doulton is founded in London.
1854: Company is incorporated as Doulton & Co.
1877: Doulton purchases a factory in Stoke-on-Trent.
1884: Doulton begins using bone china in its production.
1890: Beswick is established as maker of table and ornamental ware.
1896: Tablewear maker Royal Albert is founded.
1897: Webb Corbett is formed to make English full-lead crystal.
1899: Firm changes to a limited company, under the name Doulton & Co. Limited.
1901: Company is granted permission to add ''Royal'' to the Doulton brand name.
1961: Caithness Glass is founded in Scotland.
1968: Doulton acquires Minton China.
1969: Doulton makes two further acquisitions: Webb Corbett and Beswick; Caithness Glass begins making paperweights.
1972: Pearson PLC purchases Doulton & Co., merging Doulton with its other pottery brands, including Royal Crown Derby and Royal Albert.
1986: Holland Studio Craft is founded as a producer of collectible cold-cast resin sculptures.
1993: Pearson spins off Royal Doulton plc as publicly traded company.
1996: Royal Doulton acquires Holland Studio and Caithness Glass.
1998: Major restructuring is launched.
1999: Waterford Wedgwood plc acquires a 15 percent stake in the company.
2000: Royal Crown Derby is sold to a management-led group.

Webb Corbett and Beswick became part of the Royal Doulton group. Webb Corbett was founded in 1897 to make English full-lead crystal; Beswick traced its history to 1890, when James Wright Beswick and his son began producing both table and ornamental ware. The hand-cut crystal of Webb Corbett later would be rebranded under the Royal Doulton name.

Orrok Sherwood Doulton's sons, Mark and Michael, both joined the company. Michael Doulton joined the company in 1970, working under a fictitious name while learning the different aspects of pottery production. Starting in 1976 he began acting as traveling ambassador for the company and with the formation of the Royal Doulton International Collectors Club, a group dedicated to the collection and preservation of Royal Doulton products, he served as honorary president beginning in 1980. Although the Doulton family remained an important and integral part to running the business, leadership extended outside the family in later years.

The greatest merger in the history of ceramics came in 1972, when Pearson PLC purchased Doulton & Co. Pearson had a controlling interest in Allied English Potteries and combined the two tableware groups under the Royal Doulton Tableware name. Pearson's emergence in the pottery industry came about almost by accident. Originally, the Pearson empire was concerned mainly with construction engineering and the development of oil fields. But after investing money into a struggling business called Booth's pottery during the 1920s, Pearson eventually became the controlling shareholder. Then, 20 years later, Pearson began increasing their pottery interests. In 1944, the company bought Colclough's of Longton, a business founded in 1893 that made moderately priced bone china teaware. Pearson combined its Booth pottery with that of Colclough's, forming a new entity called Booth and Colclough. In 1952, Pearson acquired the Lawley Group, a company controlling a national chain of specialist china and glass retailers and pottery manufacturers, including Ridgway and Adderly. Seven years later they purchased Swinnertons and Alcock, Lindley and Bloor, manufacturers of redware pots. Other names joining the group were Royal Crown Derby, Royal Albert, and Paragon. Royal Crown Derby, a luxury brand, traced its roots back to 1750 and founder William Duesbury; it was the oldest surviving maker of English porcelain. Founded in 1896, Royal Albert was a tableware maker whose ''Old Country Roses,'' introduced in 1962, was one of the best-selling bone china patterns of all time.

In 1974, Royal Doulton revived the concept of its original Lambethware, creating a casual tableware with a country charm and practicality, being oven and freezer proof and unaffected by detergent or the dishwasher. Royal Doulton Tableware Limited grew to represent approximately one-third of the entire British tableware industry.

Also during the period of ownership by Pearson, Royal Doulton management focused on achieving a greater degree of efficiency at its facilities. From 1987 to 1990, the company spent £10 million (approximately US$16.4 million) annually to automate and mechanize its factories, resulting in even finer quality and manufacturing flexibility. The company maintained a dozen factories producing all types and grades of product at that time.

Independent But Struggling: Mid-1990s and Beyond

Pearson began focusing more on its media interests in the 1990s and divested many of its other holdings. Royal Doulton plc was thus spun off from Pearson in December 1993 and was listed on the London stock exchange; according to analysts, the company had a market value of between £150 million and £200 million at the time.

Under the leadership of Stuart Lyons, Royal Doulton returned to a strategy of acquisition in its initial years as a newly independent company. During 1996 the firm acquired Holland Studio Craft and Caithness Glass, the latter for £5.5 million. Holland Studio had been founded in 1986 as a producer of collectible cold-cast resin sculptures. Among the subjects of these sculptures were dragons, wizards, frogs, bears, and pigs. Established in Scotland in 1961 as a maker of art glass, Caithness Glass expanded into paperweights in 1969 and soon gained a world-class reputation for the production of high-quality abstract paperweights. Another development in 1996 was the start-up of production at a new manufacturing plant in

Indonesia. With sales of fine china stagnant, this new facility was key to the company's strategy of expanding production of casual tableware for two of the company's core export markets, the United States and Japan. The new facility also was designed to counter the effects of high U.K. labor costs. Overall sales were flat in 1996, increasing just four percent to £251.8 million.

The situation at the company soon worsened. Lyons resigned suddenly in May 1997, after 12 years at the helm, following a failed acquisition of a large U.S. fine china company whose identity was not revealed. The botched takeover cost Royal Doulton £1.6 million in advisers' fees. Further acquisitions were put on hold as the new chief executive, Patrick Wenger, a 37-year company veteran, concentrated on turning around the company's core business. A restructuring was launched that included a workforce reduction of 330 because of the closure of its St. Mary's factory in Stoke-on-Trent as well as a restructuring of the group into six product divisions—tableware, giftware and collectibles, crystal and glass, hotel and airlines, prestige products, and licensing—each headed by its own managing director. Saddled with too much inventory, Royal Doulton drastically reduced its range of products, cutting the number of tableware patterns from 320 to 120 during 1997. Extraordinary charges totaled £11.6 million in 1997, leading to a net loss of £1.8 million for the year. Turnover, meantime, barely increased, resting at £252.2 million.

Continued inventory overstocking, production overcapacity, and high debt levels combined with the economic turmoil in Asia to further batter Royal Doulton in 1998. In the midst of a year in which sales declined 5.3 percent to £238.8 million (US$396.1 million), Hamish Grossart was appointed nonexecutive chairman in May. Grossart was an accountant by training who had gained a reputation as a corporate turnaround artist. Within months of his appointment, he was serving as acting chief executive following the involvement of Wenger in a serious automobile accident in Australia in November that left him unable to return to his management duties. In December, Royal Doulton announced a fundamental restructuring program involving the cutting of a further 1,200 jobs (or nearly one-fifth of the remaining workforce), the consolidation of three warehouses into one, a temporary closure of most of the company's U.K. factories, a further writedown of inventory, and the closure of some underperforming retail outlets. Overall, the company was aiming to reduce the number of product lines it produced from 48,000 to fewer than 20,000 over the four years that Grossart estimated it would take to complete a turnaround. Needing to modernize its product styles, it also was working to speed up the development of new concepts, attempting to reduce the time from design to market from two years to six months. Charges related to the restructuring added up to £47.7 million, resulting in a net loss for 1998 of £45 million.

In August 1999 a secondary stock offering raised £31.3 million. This fresh infusion of cash helped Royal Doulton reduce its net indebtedness from £43.6 million to £17.8 million over the course of 1999. The company was far from a turnaround, however, as sales declined a further 20 percent, to £190.3 million (US$307.6 million). About £11 million of the reduction represented sales that were lost because of interruptions in deliveries caused by the bungled implementation of new warehouse software being installed to meet Y2K compliance. Other reasons for the sales decline were the continued economic problems in Asia and the closure of an additional 61 underperforming retail outlets, including both stores and concessions within department stores. A further threat emerged in November 1999 when arch-rival Waterford Wedgwood plc acquired a 15 percent stake in Royal Doulton on the open market for £11.1 million. Waterford termed the transaction a "strategic investment" and not a prelude to an outright bid, but nevertheless declined to rule out a future bid if a rival takeover company emerged. For 1999, Royal Doulton posted a net loss of £34.6 million (US$55.6 million), including a restructuring charge of £9.1 million.

At the beginning of 2000, Wayne Nutbeen was promoted to chief operating officer, taking over day-to-day management duties from Grossart, who remained chairman. Nutbeen had worked for Waterford Wedgwood from 1988 to 1996, when he was hired away by Royal Doulton to head up the company's Australian subsidiary (Nutbeen, in fact, had been in the accident in Australia that ended the career of Wenger). Nutbeen then became head of Royal Doulton's North American operations at the beginning of 1999. Disposals marked the first six months of 2000. The head office in Stoke-on-Trent was sold. In addition, the venerable Royal Crown Derby porcelain subsidiary was sold to a management-led group for £16.5 million as the company continued to scale back its exposure to the higher ends of the market (Royal Doulton would, however, continue to distribute the brand). These moves helped cut pretax losses for the six months to June 30 from the £14.4 million figure of the previous year to £1.3 million. Sales were down 3 percent, a vast improvement over the year-earlier result. Although it was too early to declare the consummation of a turnaround, and a takeover by Waterford or some other firm was still a distinct possibility, Royal Doulton clearly had made much progress on its road to recovery.

Principal Subsidiaries

Royal Doulton (UK) Limited; PT Doulton Multifortuna (Indonesia; 70%); Caithness Glass Limited; China Millers Limited (50%); Royal Doulton Australia Pty. Limited; NV Royal Doulton (Europe) SA (Belgium); Royal Doulton Canada Limited; Royal Doulton Hong Kong Limited; Royal Doulton Japan KK; Royal Doulton Benelux B.V. (Netherlands); Royal Doulton USA Limited.

Principal Competitors

Corning Incorporated; Dansk, Inc.; Department 56, Inc.; Fitz and Floyd, Silvestri Corporation Inc.; Lenox, Incorporated; Mikasa, Inc.; Noritake Co., Limited; Oneida Ltd.; Spode Limited; Tiffany & Co.; Villeroy & Boch AG; Waterford Wedgwood plc.

Further Reading

Doulton, Michael, *Discovering Royal Doulton,* Shrewsbury: Swan-Hill Press, 1993.

Eyles, Desmond, *Royal Doulton, 1815–1965,* London: Hutchinson, 1965.

Fallon, James, "Parent to Spin Off Royal Doulton," *HFD—The Weekly Home Furnishings Newspaper,* August 9, 1993, p. 44.

Gosse, Edmund, *Sir Henry Doulton: The Man of Business As a Man of Imagination,* London: Hutchinson, 1970.

Litchfield, Michael, ''Crown Derby in Sale Shock,'' *Staffordshire Sentinel,* June 7, 2000.

——, ''Nutbeen to Take Over at Royal Doulton,'' *Staffordshire Sentinel,* November 29, 1999.

Neiss, Doug, ''Royal Doulton Expands with Efficiency,'' *HFD—The Weekly Home Furnishings Newspaper,* April 30, 1990, p. 94.

Pretzlik, Charles, ''Doulton to Cut 1,200 Jobs As Sales Slip,'' *Financial Times,* December 11, 1998, p. 21.

Shenker, Israel, ''From the Villages of Stoke-on-Trent: A River of China,'' *Smithsonian,* March 1989, pp. 131–38.

Spicer, Lorne, ''Hard Times Send Ceramics Maker Royal Doulton to Auction House,'' *Financial Mail* (London), November 22, 1999.

Stanistreet, Andrew, ''Action Plan Heralds New Era at Doulton,'' *Staffordshire Sentinel,* July 27, 1999.

Turpin, Andrew, ''Royal's Roving Rescuer,'' *Director,* October 1999, p. 118.

Wolffe, Richard, ''Royal Doulton Chief to Stand Down,'' *Financial Times,* May 29, 1997, p. 27.

——, ''Royal Doulton to Lose 330 Jobs,'' *Financial Times,* August 1, 1997, p. 11.

—Beth Watson Highman
—updated by David E. Salamie

Ruhrgas AG

Huttropstrasse 60
45138 Essen
Germany
Telephone: (49) 201-184-4464
Fax: (49) 201-184-4351
Web site: http://www.ruhrgas.de

Private Company
Incorporated: 1926 as AG für Kohleverwertung
Employees: 8,874
Sales: US$7.34 billion (1999)
NAIC: 221210 Natural Gas Distribution; 486210 Pipeline Transportation of Natural Gas; 333618 Other Engine Equipment Manufacturing; 234910 Water, Sewer, and Pipeline Construction

Ruhrgas AG is Germany's largest natural gas distribution company. The rise in the company's fortunes has paralleled the massive growth in the use of natural gas in Europe since World War II. With the discovery of new natural gas reserves in northern Germany, Siberia, and the North Sea in the 1950s and 1960s, along with growing public awareness of the environmental importance of burning cleaner fuels, natural gas emerged as a leading alternative to other fossil fuels. During the period of German reintegration, Ruhrgas was a major player in the transformation of East Germany's centralized energy industry into a competitive market. The opening of borders in the former Soviet Bloc allowed Ruhrgas to further expand its pipeline networks, linking Germany to valuable natural gas reserves in the East. Even with the appearance of rival concerns like Wingas in the 1990s diminishing the company's market share, Ruhrgas remained the industry leader through its aggressive exploration of emerging energy sources in the North Sea, the Baltic region, and Eastern Europe. Although the company is officially part of the Ruhrgas Group, the name Ruhrgas AG generally is recognized to refer to the corporation as a whole.

The Development of Fuel Technologies

Natural gas is a hydrocarbon mixture consisting, in large part, of methane. Although natural gas has been used for fuel in China for at least 3,000 years, it was unknown in Europe before its discovery in England in 1659. Natural gas is used primarily for space heating, manufacturing processes, and power generation. Until the early 1960s, natural gas tended to be seen as an unwelcome byproduct of oil production. Since long-distance transportation was difficult or expensive, many producing companies did not bother to separate the gas and sell it commercially. They simply burned or ''flared'' it off near the wellhead. Many of the world's oil fields were lit at night by these natural gas waste flares.

Most of the early advances in natural gas technology occurred in the United States, where natural gas is produced in abundance. The invention of leakproof pipe-coupling in 1890 is regarded as the beginning of modern long-distance pipeline transportation of natural gas. From the late 1920s, further developments in pipeline technology and the construction of ten major transmission systems eventually made natural gas cheaper to transport and affordable to U.S. consumers. By the 1930s, natural gas was rapidly replacing other energy sources as a home-heating material in the United States.

The development of the natural gas industry in Europe was much slower. The economic dislocations of the 1930s and World War II also slowed the development of the European industry. As late as 1965, only 1 percent of German energy needs was met by natural gas and few residential customers heated their homes with it. Coal-derived artificial gases and other materials dominated the industrial market, and oil and coal dominated home heating.

Early History of Ruhrgas

Ruhrgas has its earliest antecedents in a number of artificial gas producing and selling firms in the Ruhr, Germany's most important industrial area, which today encompasses Essen, Dortmund, and several other cities. Coal-derived gases predominated; the area is at the center of a rich coal deposit.

Company Perspectives:

Natural gas is a popular energy, not only in Germany but throughout Europe. It is economical, environmentally friendly and convenient. All current energy forecasts predict that natural gas's share in energy supplies will continue to increase. In Germany, this share is already over 21 percent and is to rise to 28 percent by 2020.

For us, one of the leading gas companies in Europe, this positive market potential is, however, not the only crucial factor deciding the success of the company. Gas companies are facing the challenge of continuing to be successful in a business environment which is undergoing radical change and where both energy policy and the energy industry are being liberalized.

Competition will intensify. Furthermore, gas has to defend itself against rival energies, above all, heating oil. Gas-to-gas competition also requires efficient company structures and customer-oriented corporate strategies.

We have a good starting position in the opening European gas market: We are the largest gas importer in Europe and one of the big European gas suppliers. We are on our way to becoming an integrated European gas transmission company with downstream involvement (e.g. investments in municipal utilities), upstream participations (e.g. in Gazprom of Russia) and growing involvement in Europe. With flexibility, a willingness to change and new ideas, we are shaping the further development of our core business and allied gas activities.

The first German gasworks, for street lighting, was built in Hannover in 1825, but Ruhrgas's home city of Essen did not have its own gasworks, Essener Gas A.G., until 1856. Although artificial gas became popular for manufacturing processes and municipal street lighting, it was less competitive with oil and petroleum products for heating purposes throughout most of the 19th century. The abundant coal of the Ruhr made artificial gas especially attractive to businesses. By 1900, the German gas industry was producing 1.2 billion cubic meters annually.

The first commercial German natural gas deposits were discovered in bore holes at Neuengamme in 1910. Between 1911 and 1919, when the source failed, small quantities from these deposits were used industrially in Hamburg. Coal-derived gases would continue to dominate the German market for another 50 years.

In 1926 Vereinigte Stahlwerke A.G. and Stinnes-Zechen set up a new gas transportation company, the A.G. für Kohleverwertung, in Essen. The directors envisaged a system for selling surplus gas to customers throughout the entire country. The following year, the company signed a contract to transport gas to the city of Hannover. On May 30th, 1928 the company was renamed Ruhrgas AG.

By 1929 Ruhrgas had secured a supply contract with the city of Cologne, had built a 180-kilometer pipeline from Hamm to Hannover, and had planned a pipeline to Frankfurt. During the early 1930s gas supply contracts were concluded with Düsseldorf and with a number of industrial concerns, including the Adam Opel motorworks. By 1936 Ruhrgas was delivering two billion cubic meters of coke-derived gas along a 1,128-kilometer-long network.

In 1938 the Deilmann company found natural gas near Bentheim in north Germany. The well was large and the flow took weeks to control, but it was another six years before a 75-kilometer pipeline was built to carry this gas to chemical works in Hüls.

In 1942 Ruhrgas was prospering, with deliveries of more than three billion cubic meters over a pipeline network of 1,644 kilometers. Although crews worked to repair frequent bomb damage, Allied bombing took a heavy toll, and gas deliveries fell drastically. At times only three out of 51 cokeries on the pipeline network were capable of supplying gas.

The Emergence of Natural Gas After World War II

After the war Ruhrgas recovered more quickly than many German concerns. By 1946, 98 percent of its pipeline network was restored but deliveries were only one billion cubic meters, one-third of the volume reached during wartime peak levels. Two years later, Ruhrgas and Thyssengas were exporting gas to The Netherlands. In 1951, with demand greater than supply, Ruhrgas was delivering gas at levels significantly higher than its 1942 record levels. The company's pipeline network had reached 2,000 kilometers and the company employed 1,043 workers.

In 1954 Ruhrgas began to take natural gas from the Bentheim field and began to demonstrate to its customers that this fuel, with estimated reserves of 20 to 30 billion cubic meters in West Germany alone, could be of the same quality as coal-derived gas. In 1956 a new company, Erdgasverkaufs-Gesellschaft of Münster, was organized to market the newly discovered natural gas of north Germany. Within four years the Dutch firm NAM discovered the Slochteren field in The Netherlands, then the largest natural gas find in Europe.

From 1965 onward, even larger offshore discoveries in the North Sea in Dutch, British, Norwegian, and Danish sectors made it clear that Europe had large reserves of commercially exploitable natural gas. Europeans began to adapt American pipeline technology to bring it ashore and distribute it over long distances. Cheap natural gas won many new industrial and municipal customers. During the same period, Soviet technicians found huge natural gas reserves in Siberia. The Soviet government realized that new technology made its gas exportable to Europe as a lucrative hard-currency earner.

Natural gas looked like the fuel of the future, but through most of the 1960s coke-derived gas transport remained the primary business of Ruhrgas as it extended its pipeline network through the most populous regions of West Germany. Although in 1965 natural gas supplied only a small portion of the country's energy, it already represented 10 percent of Ruhrgas's total deliveries of seven billion cubic meters. The company entered into large-scale supply contracts with Dutch and other gas production companies to ensure that it would be able to meet the booming demand. Supply contracts of 20 or 25 years' duration were normal in the industry.

Key Dates:

1910: Natural gas deposits are discovered at Neuengamme.
1926: Vereinigte Stahlwerke AG and Stinnes-Zechen form AG für Kohleverwertung.
1928: AG für Kohleverwertung is renamed Ruhrgas AG.
1929: Ruhrgas establishes supply contract with the city of Cologne.
1938: Natural gas deposits are discovered near Bentheim.
1942: Ruhrgas's annual deliveries rise to three billion cubic meters.
1946: Postwar pipeline reconstruction is 98 percent completed.
1956: Erdgasverkaufs-Gesellschaft, a gas marketing company, is formed.
1970: Ruhrgas signs agreement with Soyuzneftexport for purchase of Soviet natural gas.
1973: Norwegian natural gas agreement is reached with Phillips Petroleum for the annual purchase of five billion cubic meters of natural gas.
1981: Ruhrgas signs contract with Soyuzgasexport for the construction and financing of a new pipeline between Germany and the Soviet Union.
1995: Ruhrgas Energie Beteiligungs-Aktiengesellschaft (RGE) is formed.
2000: Memorandum of Understanding on environmental protection is established between Ruhrgas and Gazprom.

From 1965 to 1968, 371 kilometers of extensive new pipelines were built in cooperation with Thyssen and other companies to transport north German and Dutch natural gas, first to Mannheim and then to south Germany.

In 1969 Ruhrgas and the Soviet agency Soyuzneftexport negotiated the sale of Soviet gas. Although the talks coincided with Chancellor Brandt's new *Ostpolitik* or initiative to improve West Germany's relations with the Soviet Union and other Communist neighbors to its east, they worried the country's American allies. On February 1, 1970 an agreement was reached, providing for the yearly sale of three billion cubic meters of Soviet natural gas to Ruhrgas. The deal also provided for the export of badly needed pipe to the Soviet Union by the German industrial firm Mannesmann AG and financing by a consortium of German banks.

By 1970 natural gas already represented 70 percent of Ruhrgas's deliveries of 18 billion cubic meters along its 4,991-kilometer pipeline network. In February 1971 it reached an agreement with the Italian company SNAM to deliver gas from Aachen to the Swiss border along a pipeline now known as the Trans Europe Natural Gas Pipeline.

Increased quantities of natural gas were purchased under agreements with the Soviet Union. A 1974 contract provided for an annual delivery of 9.5 billion cubic meters until the year 2000. Ruhrgas, however, knew that it needed to diversify its supply sources. In 1973 it headed a buying consortium that negotiated a contract with Phillips Petroleum of the United States to buy an annual five billion cubic meters of Norwegian natural gas from the Ekofisk field in the North Sea.

By 1975, natural gas represented 89 percent of Ruhrgas's annual delivery of 27 billion cubic meters. The company entered further consortia to buy Norwegian gas. French companies also wanted access to Soviet natural gas. In June 1976 Gaz de France joined with Ruhrgas to form Mittel-Europäische-Gasleitungsgesellschaft (MEGAL GmbH), a pipeline company, to transport Soviet gas from the German-Czech border to the French border.

In September 1977 gas from the Norwegian Ekofisk field began to flow through a new subsea pipeline to the German port of Emden in fulfillment of a contract between Phillips Petroleum and a consortium led by Ruhrgas, which included Gasunie of The Netherlands and Gaz de France. Ruhrgas's share of the gas was 50 percent.

In November 1981 Ruhrgas took the controversial step of signing an agreement with the Soviet gas export agency Soyuzgasexport to help build and finance a huge new gas pipeline from the Soviet Union. For the obvious needs of diversification, Ruhrgas sought and contracted with a number of other countries to supply its needs. Ruhrgas continued to exercise options for increased deliveries from The Netherlands. In 1991 the company signed an agreement with the Dutch company Gasunie for the supply of an additional 100 billion cubic meters up to the year 2013. In addition, Ruhrgas was developing facilities at the German port of Wilhelmshaven for the import of liquefied natural gas (LNG) from Algeria, Nigeria, and other far-flung sources.

In September 1982 Ruhrgas joined a consortium including Thyssen, Gasunie, and Gaz de France to buy natural gas through an 850-mile undersea pipeline from the Norwegian Statfjord field. The line connected with the Ekofisk pipeline that had been delivering gas to the north German port of Emden since 1977. In 1985 this pipeline became operational. The company announced in August 1990 that it intended to make Norway a more important supply source. The same year, Ruhrgas and the other German importers exercised their option under the 1986 Troll Agreement with Norway and seven Norwegian North Sea gas producers to increase their imports from 8.5 billion cubic meters a year to 13.5 billion cubic meters per year beginning in 1993. Ruhrgas would take about 80 percent of this annual increase. Two new undersea pipelines were planned.

In the early 1990s 24 percent of Germany's natural gas came from domestic sources, 32 percent from the former Soviet Union, 28 percent from The Netherlands, and only 15 percent from Norway. Denmark provided just one percent of the total. In recognition of Norway's importance, Ruhrgas launched a major public relations effort in Norway, sponsoring scholarships for Norwegian students in Germany and German-Norwegian history conferences.

Through the 1980s the German gas industry was able to expand its residential market steadily at an annual rate of 300,000 households per year, as more German household consumers switched from oil- and coal-based heating systems to natural gas. By 1990 about 33 percent of West Germany's households had gas-fired central heating. In 1990 gas demand in West Germany reached an all-time high of 68.6 million tons of coal equivalent (tce).

Expanding European Energy Markets in the 1990s

The unification process that began in November 1989 connected the western German gas industry with the markets in the former East Germany, where gas demand was 9.5 million tce units and represented only 8.7 percent of East German energy consumption. A large gas supply infrastructure was already in place but 40 percent of deliveries were to power plants and 35 percent to industry. Only four percent went to private households.

This market opportunity was enhanced greatly by the realization that much of East German industry was an ecological disaster area. Heavy dependence on brown lignite coal and coal-derived gas meant that pollution levels were far above the levels considered acceptable in West Germany and other European Community countries.

Concern about the environment gave a huge boost to Ruhrgas and other natural gas companies as they stressed the environmental advantages of their product. Studies by the German Environmental Protection Agency showed that natural gas was the cleanest fossil fuel and interfered less with the environment than any other source of energy. It was moved by buried pipelines, almost no pollution or waste heat was produced by its conversion into a secondary energy source and, finally, natural gas-fired plants emitted hardly any uncombusted matter such as soot.

In the past, the German government had to balance these advantages against the fact that Germany's coal reserves remained vast. In the former West Germany alone, they were estimated at 25,000 million tons and unified Germany was second in the world after the former Soviet Union in the production of lignite brown coal. Government policy had provided subsidies to keep delivery systems in working order in the event of an energy crisis, but the ''green'' vote and the environmental crisis were compelling an increased emphasis on natural gas.

By December 1989 Ruhrgas had signed an extensive cooperation agreement with Schwarze Pumpe (Black Pump), the East German energy group. The agreement provided for contracts at all levels and envisaged the connection of the two countries' gas supply grids.

By the middle of 1990, the Erdgasversorgungsgesellschaft (EVG), a subsidiary of Ruhrgas and Verbundnetz Gas AG (VNG), a company originally under Schwarze Pumpe's authority and responsible for the country's gas supply network, began to build a 300-mile connecting pipeline through Thuringia and Saxony at a cost of DM 600 million. Ruhrgas agreed to supply VNG with two billion cubic meters of natural gas when the pipeline was completed in 1992.

In June 1990 Ruhrgas purchased 35 percent of VNG from Treuhandanstalt, the East German privatization agency. Another ten percent was purchased by the West German company BEB. In September 1991 the remaining shares in VNG were divided up among the East German cities and several European energy companies, giving them access to the East German gas network. Wintershall AG, a subsidiary of BASF with 15 percent of VNG, and British Gas, with 5 percent of VNG and an interest in several former municipal and local networks, announced plans for aggressive new investment and competition. Wintershall said it would challenge Ruhrgas's traditional market dominance with new pipelines.

In 1990 Ruhrgas sold 510 billion kilowatt hours of gas, 98 percent of which was natural. With a commanding position in the German gas industry and ownership of its own highly complex transmission system of pipelines, compressor stations, underground storage, and other facilities, Ruhrgas had become a national institution.

As the end of 1992 and the European single market drew nearer, Ruhrgas argued for a communitywide, market-oriented nonregulatory energy policy. Ruhrgas believed this philosophy, which had guided German energy policy, would ensure future success in the expanding European market.

In 1994 Ruhrgas AG established two holding companies: Ruhrgas Energie Beteiligungs-Aktiengesellschaft (RGE), which assumed control over shares in 26 utilities throughout Germany and Europe, and Ruhrgas Industries GmbH, which was responsible for pipeline and equipment design, manufacturing, and construction. After the reorganization the company expanded its interests over a wider territory. In March 1998 it reached an agreement with ROMGAZ to acquire natural gas supplies in Romania, and in June of the same year it founded Ruhrgas Austria AG, with the purpose of building its client base beyond the Vararlberg and Tyrol regions.

The late 1990s also witnessed increased natural gas extraction in the North Sea. In 1997 Ruhrgas purchased stakes in the Elgin/Franklin natural gas fields via its U.K. subsidiary. That same year it came to agreement with BP Gas Marketing Ltd. for 15 billion cubic meters of natural gas through the year 2013. In 1998 the Interconnector, the first gas pipeline between the United Kingdom and Europe, was inaugurated. Ruhrgas purchased a 5 percent stake in the pipeline, later increasing its share to 10 percent. This investment, coupled with already existing transport deals with the Belgian transit company Distrigaz, helped make Ruhrgas the only German company with a long-term agreement for the transport of natural gas between the British and German markets.

Ruhrgas participated in a number of environmental initiatives throughout the latter part of the decade. In 1997 the company entered into a Joint Implementation agreement with OAO Gazprom in Russia. A strategy promoted by the United Nations, Joint Implementation was a means of promoting climate protection through ''cross-border'' cooperation. In response to this arrangement, the two companies received a European Better Environment Award in 1998. In June 2000 the companies fortified their compact with a new Memorandum of Understanding, the purpose of which was to devise cost-effective ways to reduce greenhouse gases. New measures included repairs to pipelines in the Vladimir region of Russia, the pursuit of a more economical means of gas dehydration, and a lowering of fuel consumption in compressor stations. The overall goal of the project was to reduce carbon dioxide emissions by 4.5 million tons a year.

During this time Ruhrgas also investigated new ecological applications for natural gas use. In May 2000 the company participated in a joint project with other leading energy companies in the construction of 15 innovative, low-energy homes, with the intent of reducing carbon dioxide emission through the use of clean-burning appliances.

By 1999, Ruhrgas had controlling interests in more than 10,000 kilometers of pipeline, which were transporting 586 billion kwh (kilowatt hours) of natural gas. The company continued to derive gas supplies from diverse sources, with 35 percent coming from Russia, 22 percent from Norway, 18 percent from The Netherlands, and 5 percent from Denmark and the United Kingdom. Meanwhile, domestic production of natural gas stood at 20 percent. In addition, the company had more than 1,600 billion cubic meters of natural gas under contract through the year 2030, giving it the largest supply base in Europe. Estimates from that same year showed that 43 percent of all German homes, and 75 percent of new homes, were heated with natural gas.

The opening of new markets and the increase in competition also left Ruhrgas vulnerable to takeover. In November 2000 rival energy company Eon, the second largest utility in Germany, announced its intention to purchase 17 percent of Ruhrgas AG, in addition to the 18 percent it already owned through its shares in Ruhrkohle. While Eon's interest in Ruhrgas hinged on its desire to have an active role in shaping the gas company's policy, by year's end it remained to be seen what impact the proposed acquisition might have on Ruhrgas's activities throughout the continent.

Principal Subsidiaries

Ruhrgas Energie Beteiligungs-Aktiengesellschaft (RGE); Ruhrgas Industries GmbH; NETRA GmbH Norddeutsche Erdgas Transversale & Co. Kommanditgesellschaft (44.3%); Etzel Gas-Lager Statoil Deutschland GmbH & Co. (74.8%); Ruhrgas UK Exploration and Production Ltd.; GasLINE-Telekommunikationsnetzgesellschaft deutscher Gasversorgungsunternehmen mbH & Co. Kommanditgesellschaft; Ruhrgas Austria AG.

Principal Competitors

N.V. Nederlandse Gasunie; RWE-DEA Aktiengesellschaft für Mineraloel und Chemie; VEBA Oel AG.

Further Reading

Davis, Michael, ''Texas Gets European Gas Dispute; Marathon Case Belongs in State Court, Panel Says,'' *Houston Chronicle,* June 13, 1997.

Gas Today and Tomorrow, Essen: Ruhrgas, 1991.

Harnischfeger, Utta, ''Eon Attempts to Seize Ruhrgas,'' *Financial Times (FT.com),* November 14, 2000.

—Debra Johnson
—updated by Stephen Meyer

Russell Reynolds Associates Inc.

200 Park Avenue
New York, New York 10166-0002
U.S.A.
Telephone: (212) 351-2000
Toll Free: (888) 772-6200
Fax: (212) 370-0896
Web site: http://www.russellreynolds.com

Private Company
Incorporated: 1969
Employees: 740
Sales: $230.6 million (1999)
NAIC: 541612 Human Resources and Executive Search Consulting Services

Russell Reynolds Associates Inc. is one of the world's leading providers of executive recruiting services, with 35 offices in the United States and other countries around the world by the year 2000. Teams of professionals provide expertise in more than 40 industry, functional, and geographic specialties. On average, the firm conducts more than 3,000 recruiting assignments a year, at levels ranging from chief executive and outside directors to senior managers in all management functions. Nearly half of these are for positions based outside the United States.

Quick Rise to the Top Echelon: 1969–77

A Yale graduate, Russell Reynolds was a commercial banker with Morgan Guaranty Trust Co. for nine years before joining an executive recruiting firm in 1966 and established his own firm in 1969, using his background and banking connections to advantage. He was fortunate—or shrewd—enough to launch his enterprise during a period (1967–77) when the annual number of executives hired worldwide through search firms rose from 4,000 to 16,000. This was attributed to several factors, including the decline of ''old boy'' networks in an era demanding specialized knowledge and experience; the growth of multinational corporations, requiring the casting of a wider net to fill positions around the world; and a talent gap arising from the low birth rate of the Depression years.

Russell Reynolds Associates was a ''white shoe'' firm that distinguished itself from run-of-the-mill ''headhunters'' by an air of class, exemplified by young, aggressive Ivy Leaguers in pinstriped suits and monogrammed shirts. (''These guys all wear suspenders and cookie-cutter suits,'' a rival later grumbled to Joann S. Lublin of the *Wall Street Journal.*) Staffers were expected to make contacts at cocktail and dinner parties and to share inside information with their colleagues. Russell Reynolds's image extended to its Park Avenue office, which in 1984 sported a Steinway baby grand piano in the reception area and a Winston Churchill painting in one of the meeting rooms. Correspondence with clients was sent by messenger rather than through the mail.

Russell Reynolds Associates' first customer was the brokerage and investment banking firm Oppenheimer & Co., which was still a client in 1977, when Reynolds told Reba White of *Institutional Investor,* ''About 80 percent of our assignments is repeat business.'' As a member of the Association of Executive Recruiting Consultants, Russell Reynolds Associates subscribed to a code of ethics that forbade competing assignments, approaching an employee of a client firm, working with a member of a client firm without prior approval by the firm's managers, or making false statements for ''research'' purposes. In practice this meant that a member firm hired by a client could not recruit an executive working for that client for at least two years. Russell Reynolds was the first executive search firm to successfully establish a business predominantly based on retainers paid in advance and credited against the eventual tab, rather than on a contingency basis with a commission on each position filled.

By 1975 the firm's executive searches included 25 for chief executives and presidents (including those of subsidiaries). Russell Reynolds Associates had revenues of nearly $6 million in 1976, with some 44 percent from the financial field, 30 associates, and an administrative staff of more than 50. There were offices in Chicago, Houston, London, and Los Angeles. A Paris office was added in 1977, when company revenues reached $6.7 million. By this time junior partners at Russell Reynolds were being hired at $35,000 to $40,000 a year, with the possibility of $60,000 in two years. Salaries reached as high

Company Perspectives:

At Russell Reynolds Associates, our commitment to assisting our clients in building their human capital base is reflected in our single, seamless global approach, one in which industry expertise is central to exceeding client expectations. More than 40 specialized industry and functional practice groups provide our clients with in-depth market knowledge on both multinational and local levels. And our "one firm" collaborative culture, in which a shared, global proprietary database is an essential tool, means that we can deliver results with the speed that today's marketplace demands.

as $200,000 to $250,000, and Reynolds himself was earning $350,000.

Russell Reynolds Associates was now one of the world's "Big Six" executive recruiters, which in 1977 accounted for 27 percent of all such searches, including more than half of all searches involving positions paying at least $100,000 a year and bearing the titles of chief executive, chief operating officer, or executive vice-president. All were said to use the same three-stage process: first, drawing up a profile of the executive wanted; next, finding three to six individuals who most closely fit the profile; last, landing the individual chosen by the client. The first phase alone often took much time, as the recruiting firm sought to understand the requirements of the position to be filled and the corporate culture of the client, in the interests of a compatible match. Next, after a suitable profile was drafted, the recruiting firm turned to its research department, which housed closely guarded data banks of 50,000 to 100,000 or more names. Some of these names came by combing periodicals or directories; others, from unsolicited resumes; still more, from staffers who had filled out "contact forms" after meeting someone who seemed to be a prospect. Dozens of candidates might then be approached and screened—without disclosing the actual job and company—before a culled-down list would be given to the client, usually ranked by desirability. At this point the recruiter would commence what one called "shuttle diplomacy" to bring the client and candidate together.

Prosperity and Problems: 1979–92

By the 1980s no-raiding rules were being honored more in the breach than the observance. "Flexibility" became the watchword as big executive search firms like Russell Reynolds Associates told their clients that while they would not raid personnel within a division, they would henceforth not consider other divisions of a client firm off-limits. Their argument was that their revenues were in danger of shrinking because too many clients were taking unfair advantage of the rule by hiring each of the Big Six search firms at least once every two years to fill a relatively low-fee position in order to keep all the other personnel off-limits.

Russell Reynolds Associates added a Washington, D.C. office in 1979 and a San Francisco office in 1980. It ranked fourth among U.S. executive recruiters in the latter year, with $17.6 million in revenues. The firm opened its first Asian office, in Hong Kong, in 1981, and added offices in Boston, Dallas, and Madrid the same year. In 1984 it opened offices in Singapore and Sydney. By that year the company's annual revenues had reached $36 million. Most of the 29 managing directors were earning at least $150,000 a year. These were heady days for Russell Reynolds, with after-tax profit margins estimated at 15 percent a year. The company moved its headquarters to the Pan Am Building and opened offices in Frankfurt, Melbourne, and Tokyo in the mid-1980s. Oriental rugs sprouted on the floors of its offices. In keeping with the founder's emphasis on image, a barber was hired to give New York employees a free haircut each week. An associate explained to John A. Ryan of *Forbes,* "Russ sweats the details, worrying whether the receptionist in Dallas chews gum."

Following the stock market crash of October 1987, the financial community underwent severe retrenchment, especially in New York City, where this sector lost 45,000 jobs in three years. Russell Reynolds Associates, which was receiving one-third of its business from financial firms, reduced its number of employees in the United States by 8 percent in 1990. That year, of the company's global revenues of $93 million, the U.S. total stagnated at $54.5 million. The next year was even worse, and by early 1992 some 15 to 20 percent of U.S. staff had been let go in the last 18 months, according to an industry newsletter. By the end of 1992 Russell Reynolds had chosen to expand its international business rather than move into other types of consulting, opening offices in Milan, Brussels, and Edinburgh. A Toronto office was added in 1993, the year that Russell Reynolds left the firm. Hobson Brown, Jr., who was already president, succeeded him as chief executive.

Renewed Impetus: 1993–2000

The increased pace of international banking and global business in the 1990s proved most advantageous to Russell Reynolds Associates. It was the top recruiting firm in Great Britain in 1994, with $16.4 million in revenues. Among its British clients was National Westminster Bank plc, for whom it found staffers for its investment banking operation in the United States. Another was the London office of Bankers Trust Co. Because this bank insisted that no search firm working for one of its offices recruit executives from another office, the firm kept its hands off Bankers Trust's New York operation. Russell Reynolds had, at this time, 24 investment banking recruiters in New York, London, and Tokyo, and 13 more in Brussels, Frankfurt, Hong Kong, Madrid, Milan, Paris, Singapore, Sydney, and Toronto. Most of these recruiters were specialists knowledgeable about the talent available in a particular area, such as derivatives or capital markets.

In New York, Russell Reynolds Associates was—to a greater degree than its rivals—trying to persuade its Wall Street clients to allow the firm to meet all of its needs for elite personnel, bypassing line managers if necessary. Morgan Stanley & Co. already had done so in the early 1980s, and Lehman Brothers became the second in 1990. Whenever a senior-level job became open at Lehman, the firm's operating committee gave the assignment to Russell Reynolds. In return, Lehman received volume discounts on recruiting fees. *Institutional Investor* rated Reynolds first in 1993 among recruiters in Wall

Key Dates:

1969: Russell Reynolds founds his eponymous firm.
1977: The firm is one of its field's Big Six, with $6.7 million in annual revenues.
1984: The firm's annual revenues reach $36 million.
1993: Russell Reynolds is the leading recruiter on a revived Wall Street.
1999: Reynolds is the fastest growing of the major executive search firms.

Street revenue ($31 million), Wall Street searches (570), and Wall Street recruiting professionals (39).

An unusual 1994 search by Russell Reynolds Associates was a well-publicized one to replace cofounder Ben Cohen as chief executive officer for Ben & Jerry's Homemade Inc., the Vermont ice cream maker. Ben & Jerry's, which received 22,500 applications by first conducting a ''Yo! I Want To Be Your CEO!'' essay contest, hired the firm to winnow a dozen finalists from 500 being considered. (The entry that came in the form of a squawking parrot probably did not make the cut.)

A more reliable source of new business in the 1990s was the healthcare field, which in 1995 accounted for about ten percent of Russell Reynolds Associates' revenues. A staff of 20 based in seven of the firm's offices completed more than 300 searches in this field during 1993 and 1994, spread evenly between the United States, Europe, and the Asia/Pacific region. The average such search was taking four months. Clients paid a retainer ranging between $100,000 and $200,000, with this sum subtracted from the commission, which was 35 percent of the hired executive's first-year cash compensation.

Russell Reynolds Associates received $130 million in revenue in 1994, of which financial services was believed to account for nearly half. Three managing directors in the financial services sector resigned that year to start their own firm. One of the three told Alex Markels of the *Wall Street Journal* that the firm had become ''more institutionalized'' since the founder's departure. Russell Reynolds opened offices in Hamburg, Mexico City, and Menlo Park, California, that year. A Warsaw office was added in 1995, a Shanghai office in 1996, and five offices—in Amsterdam, Buenos Aires, Calgary, Copenhagen, and Sao Paulo— were added in 1997. That year the firm won an award from the International Women's Forum in recognition of its leadership initiative and achievement in the advancement of women.

In 1999 Russell Reynolds was the fastest growing of the large executive search firms. Its revenues rose 22 percent that year, to $230.6 million, of which U.S. revenues increased to $123.1 million, 32 percent more than the 1998 total. It was believed that more than 70 percent of this sum represented repeat business with existing clients. A Munich office opened in 2000. Russell Reynolds staffers were providing expertise in such specialties as industry concentrations in financial services, technology, and healthcare; regions such as Eastern Europe and Japan; functional specialties such as nonexecutive directors and financial officers; and assessment of human capital and its alignment with business challenges.

Principal Competitors

Boyden Associates Inc.; Egon Zehnder International Inc.; Heidrick & Struggles; Korn/Ferry International; Spencer Stuart & Associates.

Further Reading

Byrne, John A., ''How to Leverage Style,'' *Forbes,* June 4, 1984, pp. 164–65.
Carey, David, ''Ascent of the Headhunter,'' *Institutional Investor,* May 1994, pp. 86–93.
Day, Kathleen, ''Global Perspective Aids Search for Pharmaceutical Executives,'' *Washington Post,* April 10, 1995, Washington Business Sec., p. 11.
''Don't Call Us, We'll Call You,'' *Economist,* March 28, 1992, pp. 78–79.
''How Success Cramps the Headhunters' Style,'' *Business Week,* May 5, 1980, pp. 66, 69.
Markels, Alex, ''Russell Reynolds Loses Three Officials Who Resign to Form Their Own Firm,'' *Wall Street Journal,* August 29, 1995, p. B7.
Meyer, Herbert E., ''The Headhunters Come Upon Golden Days,'' *Fortune,* October 9, 1978, pp. 100–02, 104, 106, 110.
Shao, Maria, ''The New Emperor of Ice Cream,'' *Boston Globe,* February 2, 1995, pp. 35, 46.
Temes, Judy, ''Layoffs Lop Heads at Headhunting Firms,'' *Crain's New York Business,* January 7, 1991, p. 4.
White, Reba, ''Headhunting in Wall Street,'' *Institutional Investor,* February 1977, pp. 32–33.

—Robert Halasz

Sanrio Company, Ltd.

6-1, Ohsaki 1-Chome
Shinagawa-ku
Tokyo 141-8603
Japan
Telephone: (+81) 3 37798111
Fax: (+81) 3-3779-8054
Web site: http://www.sanrio.co.jp/english

Public Company
Incorporated: 1960 as Yamanashi Silk Center Co., Ltd.
Employees: 1,008
Sales: ¥139.18 billion (US$1.26 billion) (2000)
Stock Exchanges: Tokyo
NAIC: 339932 Game, Toy, and Children's Vehicle Manufacturing; 713110 Amusement and Theme Parks; 511120 Periodical Publishers; 511130 Book Publishers; 512110 Motion Picture and Video Production; 512131 Motion Picture Theaters (Except Drive-Ins); 722110 Full-Service Restaurants; 451120 Hobby, Toy, and Game Stores

Japan's Sanrio Company, Ltd. is helping to make the world a cuter place. The company designs, manufactures, markets, and distributes a vast range of gifts, greeting cards, and other products—ranging from toasters to luxury cars to condominiums—bearing the likeness of one or more of dozens of company-created characters with names like Pochacco, Winkipinki (a character whose birthday is described by the company as ''the day the tulips bloom in the garden''), Chippy Mouse, and My Melody. By far the most popular of Sanrio's characters, however, is Hello Kitty, which has inspired some 26,000 products and rivals Mickey Mouse as one of the top contemporary cartoon characters. Hello Kitty represents some 5,000 of the 15,000 available Sanrio products. The Hello Kitty character accounts for about half of Sanrio's annual sales, which topped ¥139 billion (US$1.2 billion) in 2000. Although Hello Kitty and other characters have helped Sanrio gain worldwide notoriety, more than 90 percent of the company's sales are generated in Japan, where the company operates a restaurant chain and movie theaters; produces movies, television series, and video games; publishes books and magazines; and operates two amusement theme parks—the Hello Kitty-dedicated Puroland, and Harmonyland, located in Oita, Kyushu. Sanrio also owns or franchises a chain of more than 2,500 retail stores, located principally in Japan but including more than 200 stores in the United States. Sanrio, trading on the Tokyo Stock Exchange, is run by founder, President, and CEO Shintaro Tsuji.

Bringing Cuteness to the World in the 1960s

Sanrio Company, Ltd. began business in 1960 as Yamanashi Silk Center Co. But founder Shintaro Tsuji, who had raised ¥1 million to launch his company, had ambitious plans for building what the company called ''the Social Communication Business.'' Built around the Japanese culture's tradition of gift-giving, Tsuji's company quickly turned to producing the gifts themselves. In 1962 the company began decorating its gift products with Strawberry, the first of what was to become a long string of company-designed characters. The Strawberry character enabled Tsuji to take his company's products overseas, finding success in the United States. The success of the character—which was able to capitalize as well on such worldwide hits as the Beatles' ''Strawberry Fields Forever''—inspired the company to open a retail store in San Francisco, dubbed the Strawberry Shop. Strawberry also inspired the company to begin production and publication of its own newspaper, *Strawberry Newspaper.*

The company opened a new retail store concept in Tokyo in 1971, the Gift Gate store. Two years later, the company changed its name to Sanrio Company, Ltd. In that year, the company began production of a new magazine, *Shi to Meruhen* (*Poetry and Fairytales*). The company also was preparing the launch of what was to become its greatest success, even becoming an icon in its country.

In 1974, the company introduced two new characters, Patty and Jimmy. These characters were joined by another new character, a pink and white, somewhat expressionless, cat with a box behind its ear. Dubbed ''Hello Kitty,'' the new character initially was marketed toward young girls, especially at the ages

Company Perspectives:

The "Social Communication" Business: Everybody wants to spend their days being happy. It is a common wish of just about anyone on the face of the Earth. But just what is happiness? As the old saying goes, "No man is an island." Humans need each other. We help each other to survive, to live a meaningful life. We trust and depend on our companions. We strive to get along with one another. Perhaps that is what happiness is . . . And who are our "companions"? For a start, there are those closest to home: Mother, father, children, brother, sister, lover. . . . Then, there are our schoolmates, our work mates . . . If one looks broadly enough, our circle of companions encompasses all of humankind. In order to get along with one another, we need to respect and to love. And the expression of respect and love is the basis of Sanrio's "Social Communication" business. Ever since Sanrio's establishment in 1960, this philosophy has been the core of our business, which ranges from the design and sale of social communications gifts and greeting cards, to publishing, production and distribution of the Strawberry Newspaper, to the planning and operation of theme parks. The common thread running through all our various businesses is the idea of giving "from the heart" and "of the heart." Whether one is sad, down, happy, or whatever. . . . We want to help people share these important feelings with one another. This is the reason for our business. And it is a business of which we are very proud.

of five and six, who were still too young to adopt "older" Barbie or other dolls of that type. Yet Hello Kitty quickly proved to be a hit far beyond its original target audience.

As with all of its characters, Sanrio marketed Hello Kitty on nearly every product imaginable as well as on even the most unimaginable products. By the end of the century, Sanrio had placed the Hello Kitty character on more than 15,000 products, including a condominium complex built in celebration of Hello Kitty's 25th anniversary. Licensees brought Hello Kitty to such diverse products as toasters, telephones, watches, and even specially designed automobiles, as Hello Kitty quickly became as ubiquitous a cartoon icon as Mickey Mouse in Japan. With Hello Kitty, Sanrio had tapped into the Japanese mania for "kawai" or cuteness, a quality that sometimes sufficed as a product's primary marketing tool. But Sanrio also was to find the Hello Kitty image easily exportable, particularly in the United States, where the vagaries of trendiness were to legitimize the cat for a whole new generation of teenagers and even older consumers.

While Hello Kitty came to represent half of Sanrio's annual sales, the company continued to produce new characters and new products, as well as to branch out into other industries. In 1974, Sanrio created a subsidiary in the United States, Sanrio Communications, Inc., which began producing animated films for the U.S. market, as well as handling distribution of Sanrio's products. In 1975, the company launched a new magazine, *Strawberry News.* That same year, the company released its first commercial animated feature film, called *Little Jumbo.*

Until the mid-1970s, Sanrio's characters were featured on products manufactured by Sanrio itself. In 1976, however, Sanrio began to build on the success of the Hello Kitty character, signing the first of a long series of licensing agreements to add Hello Kitty and many of its other characters to products such as credit cards and toys included in McDonald's children's meals. In that year, also, the company set up a new subsidiary, Sanrio, Inc., based in San Jose, California, to oversee its U.S. development. The Sanrio Communications company was reorganized as a subsidiary under Sanrio, Inc. The company later moved its U.S. headquarters to San Francisco. Meanwhile, Sanrio also was achieving recognition for its film production, winning the Academy Award for Best Documentary Film for 1978 for the Sanrio-produced *Who Are the Debolts and Where Did They Get 19 Kids?* The company also released the film *The Glacier Fox* in 1978.

Expansion in the 1990s

Sanrio continued to produce new characters and the products and toys to feature them. In 1975, the world met such characters as My Melody, Robby Rabbit, and Little Twin Stars. The end of that decade saw the appearance of Giga Chibiko Gang (the Milky Way Gang) and Sanrio's own version of the Snow White crew, Seven Silly Dwarfs. The early 1980s brought a host of new characters as Sanrio stepped up the pace of its launches, with such names as Mellotune in 1981, Zashikibuta in 1983, and Dachonosuke and Little Wonder Story in 1985.

Sanrio also followed the somewhat standard approach to international growth established by many Japanese companies. After building up its first overseas business in the U.S. market, the company next turned to the European market, more difficult to master because of the different languages and cultures. The company first moved into Europe in 1980, opening up a branch office in western Germany to prepare the company's introduction into the European market. Then, in 1983, Sanrio set up a full-fledged European subsidiary, choosing Hamburg, Germany, to form Sanrio GmbH. Back in the United States, meanwhile, Hello Kitty's popularity reached still greater heights when it was named UNICEF's child ambassador to the United States. In that year, also, the company began to produce and sell videos, as the new media began to go mainstream in technology-hungry Japan.

In the late 1980s and early 1990s, Sanrio pursued further international expansion. The company started up a subsidiary for the vast Latin America market in Brazil in 1987. At the beginning of the 1990s, Sanrio's expansion target widened to include the huge and dynamic Asian market. In 1990, the company established the subsidiary Sanrio Far East Co., Ltd. Two other subsidiaries were opened in the first half of the 1990s, in Taiwan in 1992 and in Hong Kong in 1994. If older generations in many of the Asian countries had been somewhat hostile to Japanese culture in the previous 50 years, new generations of children and teenagers eagerly embraced the country's love of kawai, especially Hello Kitty.

Back home, however, Sanrio was building toward its, and Hello Kitty's, biggest success. The company founded its own amusement park, Puroland, in 1990. Dedicated to Hello Kitty, the amusement park quickly began to attract surprising numbers of

Key Dates:

1960: Company is founded as Yamanashi Silk Center Co., Ltd.
1962: Strawberry character is introduced.
1969: Strawberry Shop is opened in San Francisco.
1971: Company opens first Gift Gate store in Japan.
1973: Company changes name to Sanrio Company, Ltd.
1974: Company launches Hello Kitty; forms Sanrio Communications in Los Angeles.
1976: Company begins licensing of characters; forms Sanrio Inc. in San Jose.
1983: Company establishes West German subsidiary.
1987: Company establishes Brazilian subsidiary.
1990: Company opens Puroland theme park; establishes Sanrio Far East, Ltd.
1991: Company opens Harmonyland theme park.
1992: Company establishes Taipei subsidiary.
1994: Company establishes Hong Kong subsidiary.
1999: Hello Kitty celebrates 25th anniversary.

adults as the Hello Kitty phenomenon began to break out of the children's market to become a cult icon throughout the whole of Japanese society. With the Japanese economy dipping into a deep recession for the first time in some 40 years, consumers eagerly adopted Hello Kitty and other Sanrio characters, perhaps in a mass display of nostalgia for a simpler, less stressful period in history. At the same time, Sanrio, which had counted young girls as its primary market, had its first crossover success with the introduction of its frog-shaped character Keroppi in 1988. That success inspired the company to create a series of other ''gender-neutral'' characters, helping the company gain increasing popularity in the young boys market as well.

Puroland was followed quickly by the opening of a second Sanrio-based theme park, Harmonyland, featuring characters from across the Sanrio spectrum, which opened in 1991. As the recession in Japan reached crisis proportions, Sanrio's characters—and the products they were designed to support—helped boost the company to the top ranks in Japan. In 1994, Hello Kitty was named child ambassador for UNICEF for Japan, another diamond in the character's crown. Although Sanrio faced competition from such new arrivals as Nintendo's Mario Bros. and Bandai's Pokémon characters, as well as such fads as the Tamagutchi virtual pets, Hello Kitty continued its long-running reign as queen of cuteness in that country. In the United States and other parts of the world, meanwhile, Hello Kitty also was transcending age barriers and generation gaps, being adopted—often tongue in cheek—as a fashion statement among teenagers and even older consumers.

The economic crisis in other parts of the Asian world also helped to spur on the Hello Kitty craze in such countries as Thailand, Singapore, and Taiwan (where riots broke out among people waiting in line for McDonalds' Hello Kitty promotion). In the meantime, Japan and Sanrio geared up for the celebration of Hello Kitty's 25th birthday, in 1999. That occasion was marked by the launch of two of the most unusual Hello Kitty licensed products. The first, offered by Daihatsu Motor Co., was a car featuring such ''standard'' equipment as Hello Kitty door locks, dashboard, and upholstered seats. The second was condominium apartments, sold by Itochu Housing, decorated according to the Hello Kitty theme. The Hello Kitty craze, which had only just begun to gather momentum in many parts of the world, promised Sanrio a leading role in the world's cuteness market for the 21st century.

Principal Subsidiaries

Sanrio Communication World Co., Ltd.; Sanmare Co., Ltd.; Sanrio Far East Co., Ltd.; Sanrio Enterprise Co., Ltd.; Sanway Co., Ltd.; Kokoro Co., Ltd.; Harmonyland Co., Ltd.; Sanrio, Inc. (U.S.A.); Sanrio G.m.b.H. (Germany); Sanrio do Brasil Comerico e Representacoes Ltda.; Sanrio Taiwan; Sanrio [Hong Kong] Company Limited.

Principal Competitors

4Kids Entertainment, Inc.; Andrews McMeel Universal; Applause Enterprises, Inc.; Bandai Co., Ltd.; Hasbro, Inc.; Arvel Enterprises Inc.; Mattel, Inc.; Nintendo Co., Ltd.; Russ Berrie and Company, Inc.; The Walt Disney Company.

Further Reading

Huang, Annie, ''Hello Kitty Frenzy,'' *Dallas Morning News,* August 19, 1999, p. 1D.
Ikenberg, Tamara, ''A Cool Cat,'' *Newsday,* November 15, 2000, p. B31.
Parker, Ginny, ''Japan Specializes in Cute,'' *Minneapolis Star Tribune,* December 16, 1999, p. 33A.
Parry, Richard Lloyd, ''Hello Kitty,'' *Independent,* October 28, 2000, p. 1.
Wong, Martin, ''I Was a Cat,'' *Yolk,* September 30, 1995.

—M.L. Cohen

The Santa Cruz Operation, Inc.

400 Encincal Street
Santa Cruz, California 95060
U.S.A.
Telephone: (831) 425-7222
Fax: (831) 427-5448
Web site: http://www.sco.com

Public Company
Incorporated: 1979
Employees: 810
Sales: $148.9 million (2000)
Stock Exchanges: NASDAQ
Ticker Symbol: SCO
NAIC: 511210 Software Publishers

Founded in 1979 as a Unix consulting company, The Santa Cruz Operation, Inc. (SCO) became a leader in providing Unix operating systems in the 1980s and 1990s. As an operating system, Unix faced heavy competition from MS-DOS in the 1980s and Windows NT in the 1990s, not to mention OS/2 in the early 1990s. SCO remained committed to developing Unix systems for Intel-based PCs and later for network servers. Its close relationship with Microsoft Corporation led it to adopt a Windows-friendly strategy, uncommon among Unix providers. SCO introduced Tarantella network management software in 1996, which provided for web-based management and deployment of server-based applications. With the release of Tarantella Enterprise II in December 1999, SCO was moving away from its Unix server operating systems toward server-based applications and browser-based client services. In 2000 the company announced that it was selling its two Unix divisions to Caldera Systems Inc. and planning to change its name to Tarantella Inc.

Introducing Unix Operating Systems in the 1980s

The Santa Cruz Operation, Inc. (SCO) was founded in 1979 by Doug and Larry Michels as a Unix system porting and consulting company. Larry Michels, who had spent the past ten years as vice-president and director of TRW's Advanced Product Laboratory in Los Angeles, was SCO's president. His son Doug, a recent graduate of the University of California at Santa Cruz, was executive vice-president. From 1979 to 1984 the company evolved into a provider of Unix operating systems. An alternative to other operating systems such as MS-DOS, Unix was developed originally by AT&T engineers and was designed to handle several tasks at once.

In 1983 Microsoft entered into an exclusive agreement with SCO to exchange Unix technology. That year SCO delivered the first packaged Unix operating system that ran on Intel-powered PCs. Called the SCO Xenix System V, it provided small businesses with an affordable business-critical computing system. As Intel developed more powerful processors throughout the 1980s, SCO introduced new versions of its Unix operating system to run on them. These new versions also had the ability to run applications developed on earlier versions, a feature known as ''upward compatibility.''

With the support of AT&T, SCO and Microsoft unveiled Xenix System V for the AT&T 6300 and IBM PC XT and compatible computers at the Unix Expo in New York City in 1985. According to *PC Week,* Xenix was a Microsoft version of Unix designed to be used on a microcomputer. AT&T wanted to establish Unix System V as the common operating system for workstations connected to mainframes. In 1987 Microsoft and SCO introduced Xenix System/V 386 to run on Intel's 80386 chip. The system would be sold by both Microsoft and SCO with different packaging.

In 1986 SCO introduced SCO Professional, a software package that contained a Xenix version of DOS standard Lotus 1-2-3 for spreadsheet applications, and SCO FoxBASE, which provided the functionality of dBASEII for database applications. By making these industry-standard DOS applications available on Xenix, SCO hoped to attract new users to its operating system. Also in 1986 SCO established its first European headquarters with the acquisition of Logica Ltd. in the United Kingdom.

In 1987 SCO hosted its first annual SCO Forum conference, which has been held each summer on the campus of the University of California at Santa Cruz, overlooking Monterey Bay. In October 1987 AT&T and Sun Microsystems announced a new alliance to refine and improve Unix. That led to the establish-

Company Perspectives:

Our mission is to create, market, and support the server software that system builders choose for networked business computing. SCO believes that server-based network computing, which is based on Internet and web technologies, enables businesses to dramatically improve their customer information flow and business transaction efficiencies. Companies that adopt a server-based network computing model can understand their customers better, reach wider potential markets, bring products to market faster, and improve their overall customer satisfaction levels. With server-based computing and SCO products and services, IT [information technology] professionals can immediately leverage their existing investments, deploy applications faster, and dramatically cut the cost of systems administration and management.

ment of the Open Software Foundation, a consortium of computer makers whose goal was to set software standards for the Unix operating system.

SCO's revenue doubled each year from 1984 to 1987, as the company put its efforts into marketing its Xenix system to businesses. More applications for the Xenix operating system were being written by third-party developers. The system offered multi-tasking, multi-user capabilities. By the end of fiscal 1987 SCO's share of the Xenix market had grown from 12 percent in January 1986 to more than 40 percent, with an installed base of 60,000 systems. SCO was offering Xenix at the retail level, while its competitors were focusing on original equipment manufacturers (OEMs). To promote Xenix to multi-user work groups, SCO hosted numerous conferences, taught classes covering how to use Xenix and how to sell it, and issued numerous press releases and publications. Its bimonthly technical bulletin, *Discover,* sometimes ran more than 30 pages.

SCO was able to complete its second round of venture capital financing in 1987, with funds from Accel Partners, Citibank Investment Management Fund, and the Fleming American Fund. Investors controlled about 10 percent of SCO. For fiscal 1987 ending September 30, SCO posted revenue of $27.1 million. Profits were about $500,000, and the company had a large workforce of about 500 employees.

In October 1987 SCO claimed that it beat IBM in a race to develop Xenix operating systems for IBM's PS/2 Models 50, 60, and 80. The SCO Xenix 286 and SCO Xenix 386 were the only operating systems to take full advantage of the Intel 80286 and 80386 chips in IBM's new product line. A year later SCO announced a Xenix 386 upgrade that offered several new features found in AT&T's System V/386 release 3.2, which merged AT&T's Unix System V with Microsoft's Xenix. The new features included mouse and video graphics array (VGA) support, more communications protocols, and an extended multiscreen feature that allowed users to open more than one window on a terminal.

SCO announced its integrated software solution for Xenix in 1988. Its Office Portfolio program would integrate stand-alone business applications under a common user interface, allowing information to be copied and moved between applications. Several applications could run at once. Applications included in Office Portfolio included SCO Professional, which was an improved Lotus 1-2-3 spreadsheet program, and SCO FoxBase+, a dBASE III Plus work-alike program. In October 1988 Sun Microsystems entered into a strategic alliance with SCO to port its applications to run under Unix on the Sun-3 family of workstations.

In early 1989 Microsoft, which had been focusing on developing the OS/2 operating system for IBM PCs, announced that it would invest in SCO. For an estimated $20 million Microsoft took a 20 percent equity position in SCO. Noting the slow pace of acceptance for OS/2, analysts interpreted the investment as an indication of Unix's potential as a desktop operating system. Later in the year Hewlett-Packard Co. signed an agreement to market and incorporate the SCO Unix operating system into its 386-based Vectra PCs, which would allow the HP computers to handle Unix-based multi-user applications.

In 1989 SCO introduced Open Desktop, the first 32-bit graphical user interface (GUI) for UNIX systems running on Intel processor-based computers. When it was announced at the Uniforum in March 1989, Open Desktop was positioned as a Unix equivalent of OS/2's Extended Edition. Open Desktop began shipping in September 1989.

Becoming Unix System Market Leader for Desktop PCs: 1990s

In 1990 Lotus Development Corporation filed lawsuits against SCO and Borland International, the maker of Quattro Pro. The suit against SCO alleged that SCO Professional copied virtually all Lotus 1-2-3 commands and menus. SCO filed a countersuit asking for a judgment of copyright non-infringement. In mid-1991 SCO and Lotus reached an out-of-court agreement, whereby SCO would remove its SCO Professional spreadsheet from the market and recommend SCO Professional users migrate to Lotus 1-2-3 for Unix System V.

In 1990 SCO joined with AT&T and Intel to announce a binary compatibility specification for different versions of Unix systems running on Intel's 80386 and 80486 processors. The new specification was expected to resolve incompatibilities among versions of Unix that ran on high-end Intel platforms. The new specification was regarded as a step toward a single Unix system that would allow the development of shrink-wrapped Unix applications on a scale comparable with applications available for DOS, Windows, and OS/2. Sales for fiscal 1990 were $118.9 million, an increase of 43 percent over the previous year.

By 1991 SCO was clearly the market leader in providing Unix systems for PCs. SCO accounted for an estimated 65 percent of all Unix shipments for Intel-based machines in 1989. By 1991 SCO claimed there were some 350,000 SCO Unix 386 and predecessor SCO Xenix 286 systems running worldwide. The two main market opportunities for Unix at the time were minicomputer replacement and the advent of distributed computing in large companies.

By mid-1991 SCO had grown to 1,300 employees. Following a reorganization into four business units, SCO cut about 65 positions at its headquarters in Santa Cruz as well as at its

Key Dates:

1979: The Santa Cruz Operation, Inc. (SCO) is founded by Larry Michels and his son, Doug Michels, as a Unix consulting company.
1983: SCO enters into an agreement with Microsoft Corporation to exchange Unix technology and delivers the first packaged Unix operating system for Intel-powered PCs.
1989: Microsoft invests $20 million in SCO; SCO introduces Open Desktop, the first 32-bit graphical user interface (GUI) for Unix systems running on Intel processor-based computers.
1993: SCO becomes a publicly traded company on NASDAQ; Larry Michels resigns as president.
1994: SCO introduces Global Access, the first commercial product to use Mosaic; Alok Mohan is hired as CFO, then becomes president and COO.
1995: SCO acquires UnixWare and related technology from Novell Inc.
1996: SCO introduces Tarantella network management software.
1998: Doug Michels is promoted to president and CEO.
2000: SCO announces the sale of two divisions to Caldera Systems Inc. and plans to change company name to Tarantella Inc.

offices in Toronto, Canada, and London, England. The four business units were the Distributed Corporate Computing Unit, which would oversee SCO's work on the Advanced Computing Environment (ACE) initiative; the General Business Systems Unit, which included SCO's operating systems; the Business Systems Unit, which included SCO's applications software; and the Services Unit, which included SCO's consulting, training, and support services. For fiscal 1991 ending September 30 SCO reported revenue of $137.8 million.

The ACE initiative was formed in April 1991 to develop a standard open operating system for microcomputers and workstations. It included Microsoft, SCO, and DEC, among other companies. In November 1991 SCO cut another 110 positions, many of them involved with developing the ACE-RISC workstation platform. SCO planned to focus its development efforts on the already popular Intel platform. By May 1992 SCO and Compaq Computer had left the ACE consortium.

In cooperation with Microsoft, SCO introduced the Microsoft LAN Manager for Unix Systems, which was an enhanced version of the Microsoft LAN Manager for DOS and OS/2. Responding to a competing Unix initiative called Univel Inc., which was a joint venture between Novell Inc. and Unix System Laboratories Inc., SCO licensed Novell's Netware transport protocols to provide better integration between SCO Unix operating systems and Novell's Netware. The license would give SCO users direct access to NetWare networks and enable SCO to compete against Univel and other Unix suppliers.

Facing increased competition for Unix market share from Univel and SunSoft, which was the software arm of Sun Microsystems Inc., SCO introduced a major upgrade to Open Desktop in 1992. Open Desktop accounted for 61 percent of the desktop Unix operating system market. With Microsoft's Windows NT operating system expected later in 1993, Unix vendors were forming alliances to compete more effectively against the new Windows operating system for networks. Unix Systems Laboratories (USL) agreed to provide SCO with application development technologies to allow software developers to create common application source code for USL and future SCO Unix operating systems.

In November 1992 SCO won a contract from the U.S. Department of Defense to provide Unix operating systems and networking products for up to 70,000 workstations for the Air Force. The potential value of the contract was estimated to be $100 million.

Achieving Profitability and Going Public: 1992–93

Fiscal 1992 was SCO's first profitable year in its 12-year history. It reported revenue of $163.7 million. After that SCO went public on the NASDAQ in 1993, selling six million shares at $12.25 each on May 26. The company felt it was important to be a public company to compete better with Microsoft, Sun Microsystems, and others for a share of the *Fortune* 500 market, where IT managers preferred doing business with a public company. Before the company went public, though, President and CEO Larry Michels resigned in the wake of allegations of sexual harassment. In March 1993 Swedish-born Lars Turndal, head of SCO's European operations since 1988, was named to succeed Larry Michels as president and CEO. Doug Michels became executive vice-president and chief technical officer. In April the lawsuit against Larry Michels was settled.

In March 1993 SCO acquired British software vendor IXI Ltd., which formed the basis for SCO's Cambridge development center. With the release of Windows NT in 1993, six former Unix competitors formed an alliance called Common Open Software Environment (COSE). Members of the alliance included SCO, Hewlett-Packard, Unix System Laboratories, IBM, Univel, and SunSoft.

Reorganizations and Acquisitions Under New Management: 1994–2000

In 1994 SCO introduced Global Access, the first commercial product to use Mosaic, which was a new graphical user interface for Internet access and the forerunner of the Netscape Web browser. At the time four companies were licensed by the National Center for Supercomputing Applications at the University of Illinois at Champaign-Urbana to develop third-party applications using Mosaic. Also in 1994 SCO co-hosted the First International Conference on the World Wide Web in Geneva, Switzerland.

In May 1994 SCO hired Alok Mohan, formerly with NCR, as its chief financial officer (CFO). In December Mohan would be elected to SCO's board of directors and become president and chief operating officer, replacing president Lars Turndal. Mohan later became SCO's CEO in July 1995 and would serve until April 1998, when he was named chairman of the board.

The company also announced that it would scale back its attempts to diversify and refocus on its core Unix products. Toward the end of the year it shipped the next generation of its operating system, code-named Everest, to 1,000 beta testers for possible release in mid-1995. In December 1994 SCO acquired British-based software developer Visionware Ltd. for $14.8 million and established an office in Leeds, England. The acquisition would help SCO develop Windows-to-Unix connectivity tools. SCO's Windows-friendly strategy was designed to prevent Unix users from migrating *en masse* to Windows NT.

In 1995 SCO gained support from IBM for its Open Server Unix network operating system through a sales and marketing agreement. SCO would gain improved distribution through the agreement, and IBM would benefit from the popularity of SCO's products. IBM would provide service and support for SCO's Open Server software products across IBM's new multiprocessor server line, the PC Server 720. SCO also created a new product division, the Client Integration Division, which joined Visionware Ltd. and IXI Ltd. to develop software to provide Unix-based Windows integration. The division's first product was Wintif 95, an emulation package that provided a Windows 95 interface for Unix servers. SCO also hoped that Open Server 5.0, previously code-named Everest, would be more attractive to systems managers than Windows NT.

Also in 1995 SCO began developing a new server operating system, code-named Voyager, that would focus on telecommunications applications and support technology such as switching and PBX. Server products based on the new system were expected in 1996 and 1997.

Later in 1995 SCO acquired Novell Corporation's UNIX system source technology business as well as its UnixWare 2 operating system. In exchange, Novell received 6.1 million shares of SCO stock and would continue to receive Unix royalties. SCO planned to merge Open Server 5.0 with UnixWare 2 to create a standard high-volume Unix operating system for release in 1997. As part of the deal, Hewlett-Packard would take the lead in developing a next-generation 64-bit implementation of Unix that would combine HP-UX, SCO Unix, and UnixWare, along with NetWare services.

In 1996 SCO launched the Big E Initiative to establish a standard UNIX system for high-volume Intel processor-based servers in business enterprises. Following the acquisition of UnixWare, SCO announced that it would support both Open Server and UnixWare as separate products throughout 1996. The company then planned to merge both operating systems into a single platform, the UnixWare/OpenServer operating system, which would provide full backward compatibility with both UnixWare and Open Server applications. SCO released UnixWare 2.1 in February 1996. Also in February SCO and Hewlett-Packard unveiled their 64-bit operating system, called Summit 3D. SCO planned to license the technology to OEMs. SCO's goal was to unify some of the 17 versions of Unix currently on the market. SCO also gained support from hardware vendors who pledged to make SCO UnixWare their volume operating system for enterprisewide servers.

With the acquisition of Novell's Unix business, SCO controlled the source code used by 90 percent of all Unix suppliers, according to *InformationWeek.* The company was looking at four product areas for future growth: Internet products, layered technologies, Windows integration products, and new Unix licensing agreements.

SCO announced its SCO Internet Family at the 1996 Internet World trade show and planned to ship a version of SCO Unix with integrated Internet functions before 1997. In December 1996 SCO announced Tarantella network management software, which provided centralized deployment and management of server-based applications across the web. Tarantella would allow network administrators to distribute applications across multiple Unix servers, which could then be accessed by any Java-enabled web browser.

SCO again reorganized in 1997, laying off 10 percent of its workforce, or 120 employees. It also combined its product development groups into one engineering and marketing division and planned to distribute software electronically over the Internet. The company already was consolidating its products through the development of Gemini, the new operating system that would combine Open Server and UnixWare. A beta version of Gemini was introduced in August 1997, fulfilling SCO's promise to unify its Unix offerings. SCO had spent more than $50 million to develop Gemini and Tarantella, which would be the company's two most important products for fiscal 1998.

In 1998 SCO delivered the UnixWare 7 operating system, the most advanced server operating system for Intel processors. SCO offered five editions: UnixWare Base Edition, priced at $795; Messaging Edition, priced at $2,295; Intranet Edition; Departmental Edition; and Enterprise Edition, priced at $4,995. Among the products bundled with various editions were Netscape's directory, messaging, and enterprise web servers; network and systems management tools from Computer Associates International Inc.; and RealNetworks' multimedia streaming technologies.

SCO launched the Data Center Initiative in 1998 to establish a standard Unix system for Intel processor-based servers in the data center. Hardware vendors supporting the initiative included Compaq, Data General, ICL, and Unisys.

Project Monterey, initially involving SCO and IBM, was begun in 1998 to develop a high-volume enterprise Unix system. Its goal was to establish a single product line to run on systems ranging from entry-level servers to large enterprise environments. In April 1999 Compaq joined Project Monterey, which also included Sequent Computer Systems. As Doug Michels told the *San Jose Mercury News,* ''Project Monterey came out of trying to understand how the world is changing as Intel is introducing its 64-bit chip, Itanium, which is a pretty radical shift. It's still a ways away.'' In November 1999 Oracle Corporation joined Project Monterey.

In April 1998 Doug Michels was promoted to president and CEO, and Alok Mohan was named chairman of the board. Also in 1998 Novell announced that it would sell its 6.1 million shares of SCO.

New Directions: 1999–2000

At the end of 1999 it was clear that SCO was moving away from UnixWare to focus more on Web and application hosting.

The release of Tarantella Enterprise II software in December 1999 signaled SCO's first big step away from its UnixWare server operating system toward server-based applications and browser-based client services. In March 2000 SCO reorganized into three divisions: Server, Tarantella, and Professional Services. Then, in August 2000, SCO announced that it would sell its Server Software Division and Professional Services Division to Caldera Systems Inc. of Orem, Utah. Caldera was a leader in providing Linux operating systems for business. The acquisition would enable Caldera to combine Linux and UNIX server solutions and services into the first comprehensive Open Internet Platform, which would provide customers with a single scaleable platform.

Under the terms of the sale, SCO would receive a 28 percent interest in Caldera, Inc., a new holding company formed to acquire the divisions, and $7 million in cash. SCO would keep its Tarantella Division as well as the SCO Open Server revenue stream and intellectual properties. SCO would gain two seats on the board of directors of Caldera, Inc., one of which would be filled by Doug Michels. Forum2000, scheduled for August 20–23, 2000, would be cohosted by Caldera Systems and SCO. Later in the year SCO announced that it expected the sale of its two divisions to Caldera would close in the second quarter of fiscal 2001, with the delay attributed to regulatory processes. In preparation for the sale, SCO reduced its workforce by 19 percent, laying off 190 employees and leaving it with a workforce of about 810. In a related development, IBM canceled Project Monterey in September 2000 and planned to integrate its technology into its own version of Unix, called AIX.

For fiscal 2000 ending September 30, SCO reported revenue of $148.9 million compared with $223.6 million for fiscal 1999, a decline of 33 percent. For fiscal 2000 SCO reported a net loss of $57 million, which included a one-time charge of approximately $16.5 million, compared with net income of $16.9 million in fiscal 1999. The company attributed the losses to Y2K-related slowdowns, while analysts noted that the company's UnixWare was being hurt by Linux, which could offer the same value for less money.

As calendar year 2000 drew to a close, SCO was anticipating completing the sale of two divisions to Caldera and benefiting from the future synergy between the Unix system and Linux product lines. Through a private placement of common stock and warrants SCO raised $13.1 million to finance continued development of its Tarantella business. Following the sale of its two divisions SCO planned to change its name to Tarantella Inc. and leverage its technology to take advantage of the mostly untapped market for web-enabled applications.

Principal Competitors

Citrix Systems Inc.; Microsoft Corporation; Sun Microsystems Inc.; Novell Inc.; International Business Machines Corporation.

Further Reading

Aragon, Lawrence, "SCO Contract Could Hit $100 Million," *Business Journal,* November 30, 1992, p. 1.

Barrier, Michael, "How a California Software Firm Is Trying to Open up the Personal Computer's Future," *Nation's Business,* March 1992, p. 14.

Bellamah, Pat, "Xenix System-V Exploits Full Processing Power of 386 Chip," *PC Week,* July 28, 1987, p. 1.

Berinato, Scott, "SCO Taking Tarantella to NT," *PC Week,* December 13, 1999, p. 20.

Berst, Jesse, "SCO Wants to Make Friends of Windows Buyers," *PC Week,* February 13, 1995, p. 104.

Brennan, Laura, "SCO Targets Unix Strategy for NetWare," *PC Week,* January 20, 1992, p. 8.

"California-Based Software Firm Santa Cruz Operation Gets Back on Track," *Knight-Ridder/Tribune Business News,* November 15, 1999.

Cassell, Jonathan, "SCO Enhances Unix Operating System," *Electronic News (1991),* July 13, 1992, p. 13.

——, "USL to Provide Technology to Fight Microsoft Windows NT," *Electronic News (1991),* September 7, 1992, p. 22.

Cassell, Jonathan, et al., "Is ACE Consortium in the Hole As Compaq, SCO Throw in Cards?," *Electronic News (1991),* May 4, 1992, p. 1.

Cone, Edward F., "Speaking the Same Language," *Forbes,* April 3, 1989, p. 10.

Cunningham, Cara A., "SCO Considers IPO After Profitable Year," *PC Week,* August 31, 1992, p. 16.

——, "SCO Ships Version 2.0 of Its Open Desktop," *PC Week,* July 6, 1992, p. 25.

——, "SCO Upgrades Open Desktop to Stem Rising Competition," *PC Week,* May 18, 1992, p. 6.

——, "Vendor Wagons Circle Around SCO UnixWare," *PC Week,* April 29, 1996, p. 41.

Davis, Dwight, and Rick Whiting, "Building a PC/Workstation Software Bridge," *Electronic Business,* July 8, 1991, p. 49.

Deckmyn, Dominique, "SCO Makes ASP Dash with Client System," *Computerworld,* March 6, 2000, p. 24.

——, "SCO Reorganizes, Expects Low Sales," *Computerworld,* March 27, 2000, p. 32.

——, "SCO's CEO Says Unix Sell-Off Is 'Right Deal,' " *Computerworld,* August 14, 2000, p. 24.

DeMocker, Judy, "SCO Ties NCs to Unix; Tarantella Serves Apps to Thin Clients," *InfoWorld,* December 9, 1996, p. 1.

Eskow, Dennis, and Andrew Ould, "Lotus Guns for Borland, SCO in Wake of Copyright Victory," *PC Week,* July 9, 1990, p. 1.

Foley, John, "Can SCO Run Unix?," *InformationWeek,* March 25, 1996, p. 57.

Foley, Mary Jo, "SCO Sharpens Focus, Realigns Execs to Stem Losses," *PC Week,* August 23, 1993, p. 175.

Gage, Deborah, "SCO Intensifies Unix/Windows Integration Efforts," *Computer Reseller News,* September 11, 1995, p. 83.

Garvey, Martin J., "Compaq Joins Unix Effort," *InformationWeek,* April 12, 1999, p. 26.

Gill, Philip J., "Unix Punch for PCs," *Datamation,* February 1, 1991, p. 26.

Glitman, Russell, "Latest Unix Spec Clears the Stage for Compatibility," *PC Week,* August 27, 1990, p. 4.

Graziano, Claudia, "SCO Ships UnixWare 7, Gains Partners," *PC Week,* March 16, 1998, p. 20.

Grossman, Evan, "Show Marks Key Unix Alliances," *PC Week,* March 6, 1989, p. 4.

Harbaugh, Logan, "Three Clustering Solutions for Intel-Based Systems," *InformationWeek,* June 5, 2000, p. 104.

Harding, Elizabeth U., "PC Unix Granddaddy Learns New, Distributed Tricks," *Software Magazine,* March 1994, p. 104.

"HP Enters RISC Station Server Market," *Electronic News,* September 11, 1989, p. 32.

Kang, Cecilia, "Santa Cruz, Calif.-Based Software Maker Suffers from Y2K Bug Bites," *Knight-Ridder/Tribune Business News,* March 21, 2000.

Lattig, Michael, "Project Monterey Partners Predict Renaissance for Unix," *InfoWorld,* August 23, 1999, p. 18.

Leach, Norvin, ''SCO Acquires British Software Maker IXI,'' *PC Week,* March 8, 1993, p. 149.

——, ''SCO Breaks Out Open Desktop OS,'' *PC Week,* May 24, 1993, p. 57.

——, ''SCO Files for Public Offering,'' *PC Week,* April 12, 1993, p. 145.

——, ''SCO Fine-Tunes Windows Focus in Rebound Attempt,'' *PC Week,* September 4, 1995, p. 27.

Leone, Genevieve, ''As Software Industry Stocks Drop, SCO Hones Its 'Clever' Edge in Unix,'' *Business Journal-San Jose,* March 27, 1989, p. 13.

Litman, Jonathan, ''DOS Mainstays Mirrored for Xenix Use,'' *PC Week,* February 1, 1986, p. 3.

Lyons, Daniel J., ''Push Is on to Get Xenix Out of the Lab and into the Office,'' *PC Week,* October 6, 1987, p. 183.

Mace, Scott, ''SCO Brings Internet Access to PCs,'' *InfoWorld,* March 7, 1994, p. 47.

Mateyaschuk, Jennifer, ''Novell to Sell Stakes in Corel and SCO,'' *InformationWeek,* July 6, 1998, p. 121.

McCarthy, Vance, ''Layoffs at SCO Flag Problems for ACE Group,'' *PC Week,* November 11, 1991, p. 129.

McHugh, Josh, ''Watch Out for Sharks!,'' *Forbes,* October 20, 1997, p. 290.

''Microsoft LAN Manager for Unix Systems,'' *Software Magazine,* November 15, 1991, p. 85.

Morrissey, Jane, ''SCO Steels for Competition,'' *PC Week,* December 21, 1992, p. 99.

Nash, Jim, ''Reorganization, Cuts in Works at SCO,'' *Business Journal,* May 16, 1994, p. 1.

Nicholls, Bill, ''Operating System Updates,'' *Byte.com,* September 7, 2000.

O'Malley, Christopher, ''Bringing Unix to PCs: Doug Michels, Santa Cruz Operation Inc.,'' *Personal Computing,* July 1989, p. 83.

Ould, Andrew, ''SCO Cuts 65 Employees As Part of Reorganization,'' *PC Week,* June 10, 1991, p. 126.

——, ''Win Over SCO Strengthens Lotus' Hand in Borland Suit,'' *PC Week,* June 24, 1991, p. 163.

Pallatto, John, ''Unix Developers Band Together for Solidarity,'' *PC Week,* May 24, 1993, p. S3.

Panettieri, Joseph C., ''SCO Gets Help,'' *InformationWeek,* April 3, 1995, p. 106.

Patch, Kimberly, ''Companies Tap Mosaic for Internet Services,'' *PC Week,* March 28, 1994, p. 53.

Petreley, Nicholas, ''Down to the Wire,'' *InfoWorld,* January 10, 2000, p. 74.

Picarille, Lisa, ''Sun Spurs Software Vendors' Migration to the Unix Market,'' *PC Week,* October 3, 1988, p. 13.

Pontin, Jason, ''SCO Embarks on New Unix Course,'' *InfoWorld,* October 16, 1995, p. 39.

——, ''SCO Set to Counter Windows NT Growth with Everest Upgrade,'' *InfoWorld,* May 8, 1995, p. 18.

Porter, Patrick L., ''For Unix, It's Now or Never,'' *Software Magazine,* October 1996, p. 107.

Quindlen, Ruthann, ''Microsoft Heeds Godfather's Advice, Stays Alive in Unix Fray,'' *PC Week,* February 27, 1989, p. 67.

Russell, Joy, ''SCO Fulfills Promise to Unify Unix Offerings,'' *InternetWeek,* September 1, 1997, p. 45.

Safi, Quabidur R., ''Santa Cruz Operation's SCO Unix Deserves Its Place in the Sun,'' *PC Week,* August 9, 1993, p. 81.

Sandler, Corey, ''AT&T Shows Off Xenix System V at Univ Expo,'' *PC Week,* September 24, 1985, p. 3.

Scannell, Ed, and Dan Neel, ''Caldera and SCO Make Multiplayer Trade,'' *InfoWorld,* August 7, 2000, p. 16.

''SCO Gets New Management Team,'' *Software Magazine,* March 1993, p. 14.

''SCO Lays off 120,'' *Computerworld,* June 9, 1997, p. 30.

Shaffer, Richard A., ''A Winner from Santa Cruz,'' *Personal Computing,* September 1988, p. 61.

Stoll, Marilyn, ''Software Firms Sing the Praises of Integration,'' *PC Week,* April 26, 1988, p. 123.

Sussman, Ann, ''SCO Beats IBM to Market with Xenix for PS-2s,'' *PC Week,* October 20, 1987, p. 5.

''26: The Santa Cruz Operation,'' *Software Magazine,* June 15, 1991, p. 46.

Van Name, Mark L., et al., ''The Santa Cruz Operation Inc.,'' *PC Week,* July 2, 1990, p. 79.

Vaughan, Jack, ''SCO Finds New Foes,'' *Software Magazine,* May 1995, p. 96.

Vijayan, Jaikumar, ''Clustering Goes Mainstream,'' *Computerworld,* August 31, 1998, p. 47.

Wagner, Mitch, ''SCO Raises Cluster Bar,'' *InternetWeek,* August 23, 1999, p. 8.

Well, Nancy, and Cara Cunningham, ''SCO's UnixWare Gets Backing for Data Center,'' *InfoWorld,* March 2, 1998, p. 36.

Willett, Shawn, ''SCO Launches Unix Operating Systems for Intel-Based Servers,'' *InfoWorld,* May 17, 1993, p. 12.

Wirthman, Lisa, ''SCO, HP Try Hand at a Unified Unix,'' *PC Week,* February 19, 1996, p. 6.

——, ''SCO Ships First UnixWare Since Novell Purchase,'' *PC Week,* February 19, 1996, p. 25.

——, ''SCO Takes Wares to Web,'' *PC Week,* August 26, 1996, p. 6.

——, ''SCO to Cut Its Work Force,'' *PC Week,* June 16, 1997, p. 155.

——, ''SCO to Launch Gemini,'' *PC Week,* August 18, 1997, p. 6.

——, ''SCO Unix Family Calls Web Home,'' *PC Week,* May 6, 1996, p. 15.

Zachman, William, ''Pact Heralds Approach of Shrink-Wrapped Unix,'' *PC Week,* September 10, 1990, p. 10.

—David P. Bianco

Santa Fe International Corporation

2 Lincoln Centre, Ste. 1100 5420 LBJ Fwy.
Dallas, Texas 75240-2648
U.S.A.
Telephone: (972) 701-7300
Fax: (972) 701-7777
Web site: http://www.sfdrill.com

Public Subsidiary of SFIC Holdings (Cayman) Inc.
Incorporated: 1946 as Santa Fe Drilling Company
Employees: 4,800
Sales: $614.2 million (1999)
Stock Exchanges: New York
Ticker Symbol: SDC
NAIC: 213111 Drilling Oil and Gas Wells

Santa Fe International Corporation is one of the world's leading offshore drilling contractors. The company has the world's largest fleet of heavy-duty harsh-environment jackup rigs, mobile rigs that jack down their legs on the sea floor so that the hull of the rig is elevated above the surface of the water. Santa Fe also operates semisubmersible rigs, land rigs, and one platform rig. Semisubmersible rigs operate on top of the water and include machinery and drilling equipment on decks supported by the buoyancy of submerged barges. Land rigs operate onshore. Platform rigs are made up of pieces of self-contained drilling equipment. When this equipment is assembled on an offshore platform, it forms a platform drill. The company drills both within the United States and internationally in countries such as Kuwait, Azerbaijan, Egypt, Indonesia, Saudi Arabia, and Venezuela. Headquartered in Dallas, Texas, Santa Fe also offers drilling-related services, such as platform-rig maintenance, incentive drilling, and drilling engineering. The company was founded by J.D. ''Joe'' Robinson, a California drilling superintendent, in 1946. The Kuwait Petroleum Company purchased Santa Fe in 1981. SFIC Holdings (Cayman) Inc., a wholly owned subsidiary of the Kuwait Petroleum Company, owns about 39 percent of the company. Santa Fe went public in 1997, with a secondary offering in 2000.

A New Venture in 1946

Crude oil production was at an all-time high during World War II when oil was needed to fuel the war. To meet the high demand for oil, most oil companies maintained their own drilling departments. However, when the war ended in 1945, the world had more oil than it needed. Many oil companies closed their drilling departments, which were extremely costly to maintain. They decided instead to outsource their drilling to independent contractors, drillers with equipment who could be paid on a per-day basis.

J.D. ''Joe'' Robinson, a drilling superintendent at Union Oil Company in Santa Fe, California, anticipated the company he worked for would follow suit and shut down its drilling department and outsource their drilling. Robinson planned to capitalize on the situation. He planned to start his own drilling company and make an offer to purchase Union's rigs. He would then bid on Union's drilling. Robinson's plan succeeded. On December 19, 1946, Santa Fe Drilling Company was incorporated. Robinson and 61 drillers he had worked with put up $250,000 of their own money and secured loans for another $600,000. They offered Union $750,000 for their eight rigs, and Union agreed. Santa Fe had about $100,000 left over for operating expenses.

Santa Fe set up shop in Union's former drilling headquarters in Santa Fe, California, but later relocated to Dallas, Texas. During its first years in business, the company kept careful watch over its expenses. Included in the purchase of Union's equipment and office space was a warehouse that contained several gallons of orange paint. ''Not wanting to waste anything, the paint went on rigs, office windows, frames, awnings, signs, and anything else in need of paint.'' Santa Fe became known for its orange equipment.

In 1947 the company began drilling wells in California. The following year Santa Fe landed its first international job—drilling a well in Venezuela. A few years later, Santa Fe embarked on its first desert job in the neutral zone between Kuwait and Saudi Arabia. Teams of drillers were hired to work in Tunisia, Iran, and Kuwait. The company was in full swing.

Company Perspectives:

At Santa Fe International Corporation, our mission is to provide premier quality international drilling and energy services and maximize long-term shareholder value by offering our customers and associates the highest competitive standards of personnel, equipment, and operational performance with uncompromising safety standards and business ethics.

Over the past 50 years, we have earned a reputation for delivering what we promise. Our strength is our ability to execute—which is made possible by the workforce, management team, and systems developed over the past half century. We believe our ability to provide labor, know-how and equipment anywhere in the world and consistently conduct safer and more efficient drilling operations sets us apart from our competitors.

In support of our fleet of drilling rigs, we provide services encompassing design and construction of new rigs, upgrade and modification of existing units, as well as oil field related management services.

Expansion in the 1950s and 1960s

Throughout the next few decades, Santa Fe expanded its fleet and territory as quickly as possible, while striving to maintain a high safety record and offer its customers high-quality service. By 1954, Santa Fe had 21 land rigs operating in the United States, Europe, North Africa, South America, and the Middle East. Around the same time, the company began drilling offshore. Santa Fe won a contract in Trinidad to use a land rig hooked up to a jackup barge that would enable it to drill oil offshore.

The company realized, however, that if it wanted to capitalize on offshore drilling, it needed to design rigs suited for this purpose. In 1957 Santa Fe unveiled Blue Water No. 1, its first semisubmersible rig. Blue Water No. 1 enabled the company to drill the first well ever drilled by a semisubmersible rig in the Gulf of Mexico. Two years later, Santa Fe landed a contract for Blue Water No. 2, an enhanced version of Blue Water No. 1. To increase its cash flow, in 1963 Santa Fe entered into a joint venture with the Kuwait Drilling Company.

Despite its ambitious expansion, however, Santa Fe knew that the drilling business was precarious at best. The drilling industry was highly competitive and vulnerable to fluctuations in oil and natural gas prices, political turmoil and war in international countries, unfavorable weather conditions, and the extraordinarily high cost of repairing and replacing rigs. The company knew that consolidation was the key to its future success.

In 1981, Santa Fe was acquired by the Kuwait Petroleum Corporation (KPC). KPC was founded in 1980 to help manage Kuwait's growing oil endeavors. The company quickly become a world leader in the oil industry. Its aim was to protect Kuwait's oil reserves and maximize its revenue. After the acquisition, Santa Fe became a wholly owned subsidiary of KPC.

New Rigs and an IPO in the 1990s

Santa Fe believed it could find a niche in the drilling industry in which it would offer services in areas with extremely harsh weather conditions such as winds of up to 100 mph and waves as high as 38 feet. Meeting this demand, however, required the construction of rigs that could stand up to such fierce weather conditions and drill effectively in spite of them.

In 1991 Galaxy I, one of the largest harsh-environment jackup rigs in the world, was delivered to Santa Fe. Galaxy I was built for Santa Fe by Keppel Fels of Singapore. Galaxy II, a $150 million, enhanced version of Galaxy I, was delivered to Santa Fe in 1998 under a five-year contract. The heavy-duty rig earned Santa Fe approximately $130,000 a day.

Santa Fe went public in 1997 and sold 35 million shares of common stock. The proceeds from the initial public offering went to KPC (which now held 69 percent of Santa Fe) to help finance its exploration and production in Kuwait. During the same year, Santa Fe announced an agreement with U.K.-based Amoco Exploration Company to provide a new heavy-duty, harsh-weather rig—Galaxy III—for drilling operations in the U.K. sector of the North Sea. Keppel Fels, the company that constructed Galaxy I and II, also constructed Galaxy III. "This is a momentous occasion for Santa Fe," said Steve Garber, Santa Fe's president and chief executive officer. "Building a new rig of this caliber is a powerful signal not only of our position in the marketplace, but of the strength of the demand in our industry. We are extremely pleased to expand our long-standing relationship with Amoco through this new addition to our rig fleet."

Galaxy III reached its destination in the North Sea on December 5, 1999. The new rig was transported from Keppel Fels in Singapore aboard the Transshelf, a heavy-lift ship. Moving such a large rig was not easy, and the journey took 61 days. With the addition of Galaxy III, Santa Fe operated six of the industry's 17 heavy-duty, harsh equipment jackup rigs.

Around the same time, Santa Fe also landed a three-year contract for a 3,000 horsepower land rig in Kuwait. The $19.5 million rig was larger than any other land rig operating in the Middle East. The rig was named Santa Fe Rig 180 and was equipped with three mud pumps and five diesel engines. Garber commented on the Rig 180 in a company press release: "The addition of Rig 180 to our fleet, coupled with the recent completion of four new land rigs in Venezuela, each with a term contract, reinforces Santa Fe's confidence in land drilling activities in the major international oil provinces. We have been engaged in land rig operations in the Middle East for forty-seven years and are one of the largest drillers in the area."

In mid-2000 Santa Fe completed its second public offering of 30 million shares via its immediate parent SFIC Holdings (Cayman) Inc, a wholly owned subsidiary of KPC. As with the first public offering, Santa Fe did not receive the proceeds from the offering; instead, KPC used the proceeds to fund other ventures. After the second public offering, SFIC owned about 44.5 million shares or 39 percent of Santa Fe's stock.

Key Dates:

1946: J.D. ''Joe'' Robinson founds Santa Fe Drilling Company.
1947: Santa Fe begins drilling wells in California.
1948: Company drills its first international well in Venezuela.
1951: Santa Fe drills its first desert well in the Middle East.
1957: Company unveils Blue Water No. 1, its first semisubmersible rig.
1968: Company is renamed Santa Fe International Corporation.
1981: Santa Fe is acquired by the Kuwait Petroleum Corporation (KPC).
1991: Santa Fe receives Galaxy I, a large, harsh-environment jackup rig.
1997: Santa Fe launches its first public offering.
1998: Galaxy II is delivered to Santa Fe.
1999: Galaxy III reaches its destination in the North Sea.
2000: Santa Fe launches its second public offering.

Drilling in 2000 and Beyond

In 1999 the drilling industry—vulnerable to many uncontrollable factors, including the demand for oil and fluctuations in oil prices—suffered a downturn that affected Santa Fe. That year the company posted a net income of $149.8 million on revenues of $614.2 million, down from its 1998 net income of $287.1 million, posted on revenues of $811.3 million. The company attributed the slip in sales to a sluggish year for the drilling industry as a whole and the cost of new equipment.

In 2000, the company believed that if oil and gas prices remained at or around current levels, the offshore drilling market would improve somewhat in the near future. Santa Fe President and CEO Steve Garber indicated that in the future the company planned to solidify its niche as a harsh-weather driller and would focus on drilling in ''deep, difficult, and remote'' places. To reach this goal the company was designing a new, high-tech semisubmersible rig. ''We are convinced that in the long-term demand for high quality rigs aimed at the deep water field development market will be strong and we intend to be in a good position to take advantage of that demand,'' said Garber. Also in 2000, Santa Fe had bid to construct and operate a new winterized rig on a man-made island in the northern Caspian region of Kazakhstan.

Principal Subsidiaries

Sphere Supply.

Principal Competitors

Ensco International; Noble Drilling Corporation; R & B Falcon Corporation; Transocean Sedco Forex, Inc.

Further Reading

Chubb, Courtney, ''Santa Fe's Triumphant New York Offering Unlikely to Herald Wave of Similar Deals,'' *Oil Daily,* June 12, 1997.
''Fels Ships Oil Rig to the U.S.,'' *Straits Times,* August 27, 1998.
''Santa Fe International Corp. SDC,'' *Energy Alert,* August 1998.
''Santa Fe, Snyder Announce Merger,'' *Energy Daily,* January 15, 1999.

—Tracey Vasil Biscontini

Severn Trent PLC

2297 Coventry Road
Birmingham, West Midlands B26 3PU
United Kingdom
Telephone: (44) 121-722-4000
Fax: (44) 121-722-4800
Web site: http://www.severn-trent.com

Public Company
Incorporated: 1989
Employees: 11,095
Sales: £1.63 billion (1999)
Stock Exchanges: London
Ticker Symbol: SVT
NAIC: 221310 Water Supply and Irrigation Systems; 221320 Sewage Treatment Facilities; 551112 Offices of Other Holding Companies; 551114 Corporate, Subsidiary, and Regional Managing Offices; 562111 Solid Waste Collection; 562112 Hazardous Waste Collection; 562119 Other Waste Collection; 562212 Solid Waste Landfill; 562221 Hazardous Waste Treatment and Disposal; 924110 Administration of Air and Water Resource and Solid Waste Management Programs

As the fourth largest non-government-owned water company in the world, Severn Trent PLC supplies water and sewerage services to eight million domestic and industrial consumers across the British Midlands. In the mid-1990s, its service area encompassed 8,000 square miles, reaching from Gloucestershire to Humberside, mid-Wales to Rutland. Water supply became the primary activity of Severn Trent, the successor company to the state-owned Severn Trent Water Authority, when it was privatized—along with the rest of the water industry—in 1989. Privatization improved the company's profits, but also exposed it to controversy over such issues as executive salaries and environmental stewardship. Since becoming a PLC, Severn Trent also has diversified into several related areas, including waste management, water technology services, and the creation of software systems for a variety of industrial applications. The company also has reached beyond the boundaries of its home market, becoming involved in a number of consulting and operational activities abroad.

The Birth of Modern Water Management in 19th-Century Britain

The harnessing of water resources in Britain began during the Industrial Revolution, when rapidly expanding urban centers demanded more water than local rivers and lakes could provide. In the Severn Trent region, the principal city of Birmingham was among the first to develop modern water management. In the 19th century water was brought to the city via an aqueduct dependent on gravity from the Elan Valley reservoirs in rural Wales. Other cities in the region, notably Derby, Nottingham, and Leicester, brought water from the Peak District in Derbyshire.

In these early days, water projects—the province of either private companies or local authorities—were regulated in the sense that each project required an act of parliamentary approval to proceed. Since each proposal was considered in isolation of the others, however, water supply across the nation was haphazard and inefficient. The major cities were comparatively well served, as were smaller settlements lucky enough to lie along the route from a water source to a city, but many areas had no water provision at all. As early as 1869 the problems inherent in such an unplanned system were recognized, and the Royal Commission on Water Supply raised the suggestion of regional planning. No action was taken, however, until 1924, when the Ministry of Health established Regional Advisory Water Committees to coordinate development and operation.

Privatization and the Water Act of 1973

Successive acts of Parliament solidified the central government's involvement with water supply, culminating in the Water Act of 1973, which put an end to the network of individual suppliers and created ten regional Water Authorities in England and Wales. The far-reaching act also encompassed river management and sewage disposal, operations hitherto entirely separate from water supply, bringing all three related operations under common management.

Company Perspectives:

The principle of environmental leadership lies at the heart of our business strategy. It is not just a matter of demonstrating high environmental standards in the operations that we carry out; environmental leadership enables us to provide customers with practical and innovative services that address the environmental challenges of modern society.

During the 1980s Britain's Conservative government instituted a wide-ranging policy of privatizing public utilities and services. This policy soon affected the water industry, and as a result the Severn Trent Water Authority became Severn Trent PLC in 1989. After privatization, however, the former water authorities, as monopoly providers of an essential utility, remained subject to government regulatory control. The Office of Water Services (Ofwat) set a ceiling on the rates the water companies could charge their customers. Severn Trent and the other providers also were required to meet standards regarding water purity and pollution control stipulated by both the United Kingdom and the European Community. It would be difficult to determine which issue—pricing or environmental quality—attracted more controversy after Severn Trent was privatized.

Public Relations Problems in the Early 1990s

In the 1990s the privatized water industry as a whole came under attack for its pricing policies, and Severn Trent certainly took its share of the criticism. It frequently was alleged that Severn Trent's profits were disproportionately benefiting shareholders rather than being recycled back to customers. The cost of water to the average domestic consumer in the Severn Trent region increased 69 percent from 1989 to 1994—during a period when Severn Trent's profits were steadily rising. The company stoutly defended its policies, however, citing the vast capital outlay required to achieve environmental standards mandated by both London and Brussels.

Environmental issues certainly did not receive adequate attention when the industry was in the public sector: Severn Trent and the other former authorities inherited an antiquated, ecologically hazardous infrastructure in urgent need of upgrading. Severn Trent invested heavily in improvements to the system, and continued to do so through a ten-year program, begun at privatization, that was estimated to cost £5 billion. Critics maintained, however, that the investment burden was being unfairly shouldered by consumers when it should have been borne by Severn Trent, whose healthy profits proved it perfectly capable of doing so. Further, it was alleged that the required capital outlay, much of which was expended in the first few years after privatization, was mitigated in the company's favor by two factors. First, the government's debt write-off was designed to ease the water authorities' financial obligations. Second, the cost of improvements was substantially lower than expected due to very favorable deals made during the economic recession of the early 1990s. Furthermore, critics argued that Severn Trent's financial commitments were actually significantly lower than those of the other former authorities. Because the Severn Trent region is landlocked, the company thus was saved the formidable expense of cleaning up beaches and treating sewage disposed of in the sea.

The company responded to such criticism by stating that the costs of necessary improvements were so onerous that they had to be shared by the consumer. Severn Trent also claimed that its charges were the second lowest among the country's water companies and that it had not raised water rates beyond the maximum allowed by the industry regulator, Ofwat. Finally, the company attributed its higher profits at least partially to the rigorous and successful cost-cutting program it had initiated since privatization.

Nevertheless, one outraged journalist at the *Birmingham Post* responded: ''If the commercial minds at Severn Trent were to be troubled by conscience, they would be asking themselves this: how the financial rewards can have been reaped so richly from privatization and the environmental responsibilities so grossly neglected.'' Severn Trent pointed to several improvements it had made since privatization in response to environmental concerns, including the reservoir Carsington Water and a complete overhaul, at a cost of £70 million, of the Frankley Water Treatment Works. The company also cited encouragingly high compliance rates with quality standards: 99.8 percent in drinking water purity, and 99.0 percent with effluent standards. Severn Trent was convicted of six pollution offenses in 1993, however, making it the fourth worst offender in the United Kingdom for dumping waste into rivers.

The company was widely suspected of incompetence if not malfeasance in a 1994 incident in Worcestershire, for example, when a pollution scare left 35,000 homes without water for a few days. A Shropshire waste disposal firm known as Vitalscheme dumped—without, Severn Trent emphasized later, the knowledge or permission of the water company—a chemical cocktail of industrial solvents into its sewerage works. The pollutant flowed 80 miles down the River Severn, undetected for several days, until it reached drinking water supplies and consumers reported evil-smelling, foul-tasting water. Several people became ill. Severn Trent reacted quickly to the complaints, warned consumers against drinking the water, traced the pollution to its source, took steps to remedy the situation, and subsequently voluntarily paid £25 compensation to each household affected. Nonetheless, the incident damaged Severn Trent's reputation. Some alleged that the company, even if not actually compliant in the original dumping, was deficient in detecting the pollutant and reckless in precipitately assuring consumers that the water was again safe to drink. Severn Trent set up its own independent enquiry into the affair, led by Professor Kenneth Ives, and decided to prosecute Vitalscheme. The Ives report found that, ''Severn Trent responded with great speed and efficiency to the emergency, thanks to well prepared emergency planning.'' The long-term health effects of the chemicals, if any, were unknown.

Severn Trent's image also suffered from the financial arrangements surrounding Chairman John Bellak's early retirement in 1994. Most customers and some shareholders were already disgruntled with the massive increases in executive salaries after privatization. Severn Trent was by no means unique in boosting its top executives' pay—it was a common practice among Britain's privatized industries—but critics questioned the necessity

Key Dates:

1924: British Ministry of Health establishes Regional Advisory Water Committee.
1973: The Water Act creates ten regional water authorities in England and Wales.
1974: Severn Trent Water Authority is formed.
1989: Severn Trent Water Authority is incorporated as Severn Trent PLC.
1991: Severn Trent acquires Biffa Waste Services.
1998: Severn Trent Services is formed.
2000: Severn Trent purchases UK Waste from Waste Management Inc. (U.S.A.).

for raising the chairman's salary a total of 241 percent, from a 1989 level of £51,000 to the opulent 1994 figure of £174,000. The controversy came to a head when Bellak (who had enjoyed some very lucrative share options in addition to his increased salary) received £500,000 in compensation for being requested to retire a few years early. Severn Trent's customers and shareholders and a group of 50 members of Parliament condemned the deal and repeatedly demanded an explanation for Bellak's departure. Tempers were not improved by the subsequent revelation that Richard Ireland, Bellak's replacement, was garnering £100,000 for a work schedule that equated to attending less than one meeting per week. Ireland responded that he would, in fact, be devoting two days a week to his job.

Severn Trent's noncore business activities were by contrast free from controversy. The company became a major player in the waste management industry with its 1991 purchase, for £212 million, of Biffa Waste Services, the fourth largest firm of its kind in Britain and the tenth largest in Europe. Biffa operated a threefold business in the United Kingdom and Belgium: collection, whereby it disposed of other companies' waste materials; landfills, a rapidly growing area; and liquid waste management, handled through liquid treatment plants. Biffa's financial returns were somewhat disappointing, but this was due not to the subsidiary's actual performance—its productivity and potential were sound—but rather to the financing scheme by which it was purchased. Severn Trent bought Biffa through Eurobonds with an extremely high interest rate (the annual interest bill was some £24 million) and this adversely affected profits. Independent financial commentators agreed with Severn Trent that once it came out from under its financing cloud, Biffa would prove a credit to the company.

Severn Trent Systems was the computer software arm of the company. The business arose almost tangentially from Severn Trent's own need to process the volumes of information necessary for running a major utility. Customers' needs and specifications, billing, costs of labor and materials, resource management, regulatory and environmental requirements—all such data needed to be processed quickly and accurately. At first in conjunction with IBM and later on its own—after it had purchased the U.S.-based Computer Systems and Applications—Severn Trent developed systems appropriate to its needs. Having established the groundwork, it was a logical next step to market the experience to other, similar organizations. Severn Trent Systems offered a highly complex and sophisticated range of computer services encompassing work management systems, customer information and complaints systems, systems specific to industry types, and professional consulting services in an array of procedural and technical areas. The company's clients in the utility industries included Western Reserves, which supplied Kansas City, Missouri, with gas and electricity; London Electricity; Houston Lighting and Power Co.; Sydney Electricity; and the City of Seattle Water Department.

Severn Trent Technologies developed and marketed purification technology. The subsidiary Capital Controls was in the chlorine, ozone, and ultraviolet disinfection business, while Stoner Associates specialized in pipe network computer modeling and served the water, gas, and oil industries. Severn Trent Technologies operated in the U.S. and European markets and was investigating opportunities in China.

Severn Trent Water International Ltd. operated on numerous levels: as a water management consultant, a provider of water and wastewater technology, an operations contractor, and a water utility manager/operator. The company's most significant operations were centered in the United States, Mexico, and Belgium. In the United States, Severn Trent had contracts to operate more than 150 water and wastewater treatment plants. The acquisitions of the American companies AM-TEX and McCullough Environmental Services helped to increase Severn Trent's penetration of the market.

In 1994, Severn Trent received a ten-year contract to provide an array of water and wastewater services to a quarter of Mexico City. Included in the project were the installation of 250,000 water meters, the development of customer billing services, and operation and maintenance of secondary water distribution and sewerage systems.

In Belgium, Severn Trent operated through its 20 percent interest in Aquafin, a designer and builder of sewers and wastewater treatment facilities whose influence was spreading throughout the northern part of the country. The Belgian arm of Biffa provided extensive waste management services. In addition, Severn Trent acquired Cotrans in 1994, through which the company entered the municipal contracts market, responsible for the collection of domestic and industrial waste. Severn Trent Water International also was actively pursuing interests in Germany, Puerto Rico, Swaziland, Mauritius, and India.

Severn Trent's post-privatization diversification program proved more successful than many such programs initiated by the other former water authorities. Expansion seemed likely and promising for the company. For the foreseeable future, however, the majority of Severn Trent's profits were expected to derive from its primary function as a U.K. supplier of water and wastewater services. In this area of its business, Severn Trent had been hounded by controversy. As a monopoly supplier of an essential utility, Severn Trent's position was in some ways an unenviable one: struggling to balance the sometimes conflicting needs of the environment, customers, and shareholders.

Nevertheless, in late 1994, the company announced that its operating performance and profits continued to improve and that it remained committed to achieving, in the words of Chairperson Ireland, ''the right balance between the interests of our shareholders and our customers.'' Toward that end, the company allocated a total of £47.5 million for improving customer service and reducing the impact of tariffs on customers. As a result, Severn Trent's domestic customers received a £4 reduction in their bills during 1995–96. Moreover, a similar reduction was expected for 1996–97.

Into the 21st Century: Further Steps Toward Unregulated Business

As the year 2000 approached, the company continued its aggressive pursuit of new opportunities in the unregulated business arena, while striving to maintain its role as a leading water provider in the United Kingdom. At times, however, the effort to run a profitable water utility in England's tightly regulated market seemed like a losing battle. The severe drought that hit most of Europe in the summer of 1995 delivered yet another series of negative blows to Severn Trent's public image. The dry season exposed the weak infrastructures of the newly privatized English water companies, whose inefficient management practices and poorly maintained pipe networks resulted in continually unreliable service. The problem was exacerbated by the revelation that Severn Trent had seen big profits during this same period, further undermining the public's, as well as the government's, faith in the company.

Eventually The Office of Water Services decided to impose stricter control over the company's profitability. In November 1999 Ofwat issued a determination compelling Severn Trent to reduce customer costs by 14.1 percent in April 2000 and to implement additional reductions of 1 percent each of the following two years. In response to subsequent lost revenues, which were estimated to exceed £115 million the first year alone, the company felt obligated to carry out a radical restructuring of its regulated water business. Intent on cutting £52.5 million in costs, the company closed several plants and laid off 1,100 employees. Even after this streamlining, however, Severn Trent Water saw lower profits between the 1998–99 and 1999–2000 fiscal years, with an overall growth in sales of only 3.1 percent, by far the least aggressive of the company's various businesses. By contrast, Severn Trent Services experienced a sales increase of 63.4 percent during the same period, while Biffa's sales rose by 17.5 percent.

Toward decade's end, Severn Trent paid increasing attention to growth potential outside the water industry. In 1999–2000, the company's nonregulated divisions were responsible for 42 percent of total revenue and employed more than half of the Severn Trent workforce. The company made a number of key acquisitions during this period, the most significant of which was the purchase of UK Waste in June 2000, which made Biffa Waste Services the largest waste management concern in the United Kingdom. The company also added 24 new labs to Severn Trent Services in 2000, with the intent of becoming a major provider of lab analysis and onsite monitoring in the United States. At the same time the company introduced a new line of telecommunications products for small and medium-sized businesses, which it offered through Severn Trent Talks, in association with TCI; created Severn Trent Energy, a gas and electric utility division; and began marketing an innovative new water meter with no moving parts.

In spite of this apparent shift toward its unregulated interests, Severn Trent was determined to remain a leading water provider into the 21st century. Some favorable press in the late 1990s helped rebuild public confidence in the company. In September 1999 it was included in the Dow Jones Sustainable Group Index, and in 2000 the company received a top ranking in the Environment Index of Corporate Environmental Engagement. That same year, Severn Trent was the only water company in England invited to participate in the World Business Council for Sustainable Development. With the movement toward utility deregulation in other European countries Severn Trent began to recognize growth potential for its water business outside of its traditional territory, and in February 2000 it officially entered the Italian water market with the purchase of Ecotecnica.

Principal Subsidiaries

Severn Trent Water Ltd.; Biffa Waste Services Ltd.; Severn Trent Water International Ltd.; Severn Trent Industries Ltd.; Severn Trent Systems Ltd.; Severn Trent Services Inc. (U.S.); Stoner Associates (U.S.); Aquafin N.V. (Belgium; 20%); Severn Trent Property Ltd.; Charles Haswell and Partners Ltd.

Principal Competitors

Hyder PLC; Suez Lyonnaise des Eaux (France); United Utilities PLC.

Further Reading

Butler, Daniel, ''A Chance They Mustn't Waste,'' *Accountancy,* June 1993, pp. 34–35.

Callus, Andrew, ''Water Water Everywhere But Any Profits?,'' *Reuters Company News,* November 24, 2000.

''Dry Britain Turns Heat on Water Firms,'' *Agence France-Presse,* August 21, 1995.

''£500,000 Severn Trent Payoff to Ex-Chairman Infuriates Shareholders,'' *Independent,* July 30, 1994.

''Homes and Trade Hit As MP Demands Action on River Pollution,'' *Birmingham Post,* April 19, 1994.

Jones, Matthew, and Andrew Taylor, ''Severn Trent Warns of Impact of Climate Change,'' *Financial Times* (U.K.: *FT.com*), November 28, 2000.

Leathley, Arthur, ''Labour Steps Up Campaign Over Utility Chiefs' Pay,'' *Times* (London), January 7, 1995, p. 2.

''The Lex Column: Severn Trent,'' *Financial Times,* June 15, 1994.

''Outrage As Water Bills Rise 9pc,'' *Birmingham Post,* February 24, 1994.

''Pollution Scare Hits Water for Thousands,'' *Birmingham Post,* April 16, 1994.

''Public Left to Clean Up the Mess,'' *Birmingham Post,* July 8, 1994.

''Severn's Clear Message of Commitment,'' *Investors Chronicle,* February 4, 1994.

''Severn Trent Hunting for Chemical Cocktail Solution,'' *Birmingham Post,* May 5, 1994.

''Severn Trent in the Top Four of River Polluters,'' *Birmingham Post,* March 7, 1994.

''Severn Trent Managers Attacked Over Profits,'' *Birmingham Post,* December 18, 1993.

''Severn Trent's Dirty Washing,'' *Birmingham Post,* July 6, 1994.

''Severn Trent Takes Legal Action Over Chemical Spillage,'' *Times* (London), June 15, 1994.

''Severn Water 'Approved' Contamination,'' *Independent,* April 24, 1994.

''Tapping a Well of Riches,'' *Birmingham Post,* February 24, 1994.
Turncocks to Ozone: A Brief History of Severn Trent Water, Birmingham, England: Severn Trent Water Ltd., 1994.
''UK Company News: Severn Trent Held to 4 Percent Rise,'' *Financial Times,* June 15, 1994.
''Water Boss Earns £100,000 for One Meeting a Week,'' *Birmingham Post,* July 8, 1994.
''Water Company's List of Shame,'' *Birmingham Post,* July 26, 1994.
Wilsher, Peter, ''British Water Makes Waves Overseas,'' *Management Today,* October 1993, pp. 86–90.

—Robin DuBlanc
—updated by Stephen Meyer

Siebel Systems, Inc.

2207 Bridgepointe Parkway
San Mateo, California 94404
U.S.A.
Telephone: (650) 295-5000
Toll Free: (800) 647-4300
Fax: (650) 295-5111
Web site: http://www.siebel.com

Public Company
Incorporated: 1993
Employees: 6,000
Sales: $790.9 million (1999)
Stock Exchanges: NASDAQ
Ticker Symbol: SEBL
NAIC: 511210 Software Publishers

Siebel Systems, Inc. began in sales force automation software, then expanded into marketing and customer service applications, including customer relationship management (CRM). From the time it was founded in 1993, the company grew quickly. Benefiting from the explosive growth of the CRM market in the late 1990s, Siebel Systems was named the fastest growing company in the United States in 1999 by *Fortune* magazine. With the growth of electronic commerce, Siebel formed strategic alliances and made several acquisitions to provide e-business solutions for CRM and related areas. One secret to Siebel's success has been its ability to form alliances; as of late 2000 the company had more than 700 alliance partners. Revenue for 2000 was expected to surpass the $1 billion mark.

Providing Software for Sales Force Automation and Customer Relationship Management: 1993–97

Siebel Systems, Inc. was founded in 1993 by Thomas M. Siebel and Patricia House. Siebel served as the company's chairman, CEO, and president, and House was the firm's marketing vice-president. Previously, Siebel had served as CEO of Gain Technology, a multimedia software firm that merged with Sybase Inc. at the end of 1992. Prior to that he held a number of executive management positions at Oracle Corporation, where he and Pat House met in 1986. At Oracle, Tom Siebel developed the software to run Oracle's product marketing division.

When Siebel Systems was founded, there were some 400 vendors serving the emerging market for sales force automation software. Most of the products being offered were electronic contact managers. As Tom Siebel wrote in *Forbes ASAP,* "We thought that if we could build robust software systems that enabled large organizations to apply information technology and communication technology to establish and manage customer relationships across the range of interactive channels—field sales, telesales, telemarketing, the Web, resellers, and customer service—we might create a viable business."

Siebel hired software engineer William Edwards, former head of the engineering department at document software company Frame Technology Corp., to oversee software development. Guided by his own market research, Siebel established broad guidelines for the new sales force automation software that he wanted: make the software scaleable, so that it worked as well for a 50-person sales force as for a 5,000-person sales force; make it work in several languages and currencies; and make it customizable, so that it would work for companies in different industries.

Siebel's sales force automation software allowed teams of sales people to analyze, access, and act on a centralized collection of detailed information about competitors and clients. In 1994 Siebel released the Siebel Sales Information System, priced between $3,500 and $6,500 per seat, for companies with large sales forces. It ran on the Windows NT operating system and would be co-marketed by Microsoft Corporation and Siebel. Among the company's early clients were Charles Schwab & Co., Cisco Systems Inc., Andersen Consulting, and Compaq Computer Corporation. Charles Schwab joined Siebel's board of directors in October 1994 and bought a 2.5 percent interest in the company. Andersen Consulting's managing partner, George Shaheen, also joined Siebel's board, with Andersen Consulting taking a 10 percent stake in the company in 1995. By 1997 Andersen employed 300 technicians who specialized in installing Siebel software for its clients.

Company Perspectives:

Siebel Systems, Inc. was founded in 1993 to address the growing need of organizations of all sizes to acquire, retain, and better serve their customers. Today, Siebel Systems is the world's leading provider of eBusiness application software, with more than 6,000 employees who operate in more than 30 countries and 100 offices around the world.

By 1995 Siebel Systems had $8 million in revenue. It shipped the initial release of Siebel Sales Enterprise software in April 1995. At the end of the year the company introduced version 2.0, which added new sales management tracking and reporting capabilities, including a new executive information system that displayed real-time sales forecast and "opportunities" data. Priced at $1,750 per user, version 2.0 also automatically converted currencies and allowed users to generate quotes.

For 1996 revenue jumped to $39 million. In June 1996 the company went public. A number of enabling technologies were just becoming more widely available, including replication technology, high-performance relational databases, Windows, 32-bit processing, object-oriented programming, multimedia capabilities, and high-bandwidth communications, among others. Siebel was expanding beyond sales force automation (SFA) software into software for customer service and marketing.

Siebel made two acquisitions in September and October 1997: InterActive WorkPlace Inc., which specialized in intranet-based business intelligence software, for $15 million in stock, and Nomadic Systems Inc., which focused on the pharmaceutical industry, for $11 million in stock. For 1997 Siebel's revenue rose to $120 million.

Acquisitions and Alliances Accelerating Growth: 1998–2000

In 1998 Siebel launched the Siebel Certified Consultants program. By the end of 2000 Siebel had more than 400 consulting partners who would recommend and install Siebel solutions for their clients. Siebel acquired Scopus Technology Inc. for about $460 million in stock in 1998. Scopus specialized in software for customer service, field service, and call center applications, and formed the basis for a new business unit at Siebel. Following the acquisition Siebel would have 900 employees and more than 500 customers. Siebel was now considered the market leader in sales force automation software, ahead of competitors Vantive Corp., Aurum Corp. (a subsidiary of The Baan Co.), and Clarify Corp. Tom Siebel predicted that his company, along with SAP America Inc. and Oracle, would emerge as the top three companies in the enterprise relationship management system market. According to one 1998 survey, the market for sales force automation (SFA) software would grow to $6 billion in 2003, from about $600 million in 1993. *Sales & Marketing Management* estimated the market for SFA software at $1 billion in 1998 and projected it to grow to $3 billion by 2000.

Siebel continued to pursue its strategy of forming alliances with other companies and adding new features to its SFA software. In October 1998 Siebel formed a partnership with Active Software, which would make connectors to integrate Siebel's software with packages from SAP, Oracle, PeopleSoft, and Baan. Siebel also began shipping Siebel Marketing Enterprise software, which integrated data mart technology from Sagent Technology Inc. and included more than 60 marketing analysis tools.

In 1998 SFA software was evolving into the broader arena of customer relationship management (CRM), or enterprise relationship management (ERM), as it was also known. Siebel was able to offer not only SFA software, but also call center solutions and a variety of other front-office applications that would help businesses better manage their customer relationships.

Siebel 99, introduced at the end of 1998, represented a significant upgrade. It included not only a variety of new tools, but also offered access from the Web as well as from a Windows CE handheld device. Among the new features incorporated into Siebel 99 were a sales coaching tool, a presentation generator, an automatic expense reporting tool, and new analysis tools. The coaching feature, which helped call center operators handle service and support calls, was based on technology acquired from Scopus Technology.

For 1998 Siebel saw its revenue rise 89 percent to $391.5 million, while net income rose 135 percent to $55.7 million. Tom Siebel told *InfoWorld,* "We're the fastest growing company in the history of the application software business." At the end of the year Siebel had about 1,400 employees and had operations in 24 countries.

In early 1999 Siebel stepped up its branding campaign by launching a web portal, offering free software, and announcing Siebel Sales for Workgroups for release later in the year. The web portal, www.sales.com, offered a range of free information and services for sales personnel. Siebel also was distributing a free version of its Siebel Sales 5.0 module for individual users. In addition, the company advertised its name by having the free software module bundled with certain Compaq computers. Siebel dubbed its initiative to reach individual sales professionals and small and mid-sized companies "Siebel Everywhere."

Through an alliance with Siebel, management consulting firm Keane Inc. announced that it would launch its customer relationship management (CRM) practice and offer packaged applications from Siebel. Keane estimated that the alliance would result in $75 million in CRM-related consulting and software revenue in 1999.

During the year several high-ranking executives from rival SAP America defected to Siebel. They included Paul Wahl, former CEO of SAP America, who became president and COO of Siebel in May 1999, and Jeremy Coote, former SAP American president, who became Siebel's vice-president of North American operations. Following the appointment of Wahl as president, Tom Siebel would continue as the firm's chairman and CEO. Toward the end of 1999 SAP America filed a lawsuit against Siebel Systems for predatory hiring practices, claiming Siebel hired 27 former SAP executives during the year.

Other alliances formed in 1999 included an agreement with enterprise resource planning (ERP) vendor J.D. Edwards to offer Siebel's SFA software modules with Edwards's flagship

Key Dates:

1993: Siebel Systems, Inc. is founded by Thomas Siebel and Patricia House.
1995: Siebel delivers Siebel Sales Enterprise software for sales force automation.
1996: Siebel becomes a publicly traded company.
2000: Revenue surpasses the $1 billion mark.

OneWorld ERP suite. Siebel also began bundling Microsoft's SQL Server 7.0 database as an option and offered low-priced upgrades as an incentive for customers to drop Oracle's database platform in favor of Microsoft's product. At the time Siebel and Oracle were going head-to-head for leadership in the SFA and CRM applications markets.

Siebel formed an alliance with Great Plains Software Inc. to deliver a suite of front- and back-office applications. Great Plains' back-office applications included accounting, financial, and manufacturing packages. Under the agreement the new suite would add Siebel's front-office applications covering sales, marketing, and e-business functionality. The combination would allow users to complete sales transactions over the Web, for instance. Great Plains delivered the first component of its new package in November 1999 as the Sales and Marketing Series of Great Plains Siebel Front Office, with customer service and call-center applications to follow in 2000. The suite was aimed at small and mid-sized businesses.

The market for CRM solutions exploded in 1999 and was projected to reach $16.8 billion by 2003. In mid-1999 competitor Oracle Corporation announced that it was creating a dedicated sales group for CRM solutions that would be headed by Craig Brennan, a former Siebel implementation leader. Siebel, for its part, claimed that it would surpass Oracle in applications revenue in 1999. Siebel also added web-conferencing and document-sharing capabilities provided by ActiveTouch Inc. to its sales.com portal. Meanwhile, the number of vendors offering SFA and CRM solutions had declined from around 400 in 1993 to about 40 in 1999, with further consolidation likely.

CRM competitors SAP, SAS Institute Inc., and Siebel all signed agreements with Dun & Bradstreet in mid-1999 to incorporate D&B's data on 50 million businesses with their CRM software. A new trend emerging in mid-1999 involved application service providers (ASPs) adding CRM applications to their hosted services. Siebel formed a relationship with ASP Corio Inc. to allow Corio to host Siebel's full suite of CRM applications. Corio integrated the Siebel applications with PeopleSoft's enterprise resource planning (ERP) suite to provide clients with a complete hosted service.

Toward the end of 1999 Siebel and IBM agreed to jointly develop and market Siebel's CRM applications, while Siebel agreed to tune its applications for IBM platforms. The agreement was another sign that the market for CRM applications was surpassing the market for ERP applications. Whereas ERP applications focused on cutting costs, CRM applications were designed to drive revenue by giving sales forces the tools they needed to win and retain customers. The explosive growth of the Web and e-commerce was making customer loyalty a fleeting concept. The new emphasis would be on customer service, aided by CRM applications, to win and retain customers. Siebel faced competition from ERP vendors who were adding CRM applications to their offerings, such as ERP vendor PeopleSoft Inc., which acquired CRM vendor Vantive Corp. in 1999.

At the end of 1999 Siebel was recognized as the fastest-growing technology firm in the United States in the annual survey, Technology Fast 500, which was conducted by accounting firm Deloitte & Touche. From 1994 to 1998 Siebel's sales increased 782,978 percent, according to the survey. During the year Siebel's stock was added to the NASDAQ 100 index, and Siebel was named the fastest-growing company in the United States by *Fortune* magazine.

At the end of 1999 Siebel acquired OnTarget Inc., a provider of consulting services and training programs for sales and marketing organizations, for about $250 million in stock. OnTarget, whose markets included high-tech, telecommunications, and professional services companies, would become a wholly owned subsidiary of Siebel.

Siebel also completed a number of Internet-related alliances. It joined forces with procurement vendor Ariba Inc. to integrate the two companies' software applications to better link buyers and sellers over the Internet. Ariba specialized in business-to-business e-commerce solutions. Another strategic alliance with BroadVision Inc. would result in integrating BroadVision's personalized e-business applications with Siebel Front Office applications. Both companies committed joint development, sales, and marketing resources to the venture.

Just before the end of 1999 Siebel spun off sales.com as an independent, private company, backed by $27 million in funding from Siebel and venture capital firms Seqouia Capital and U.S. Venture Partners. Siebel would not have a controlling interest in the company, but its executives would sit on the board of sales.com. Sales.com was subsequently folded back into Siebel toward the end of 2000, with company officials citing the difficulty in raising capital for dot.com companies in general as the reason for the action.

For 1999 Siebel reported revenue of $790.9 million and net income of $122.1 million. For 2000 Siebel was poised to become a major provider of e-commerce infrastructure software, and sales were projected to reach the $1 billion mark. During the year 2000 Siebel would continue to make acquisitions, form strategic partnerships, and continue its rapid growth.

In January 2000 Siebel acquired Paragren Technologies Inc., a specialist in marketing automation software. The acquisition added marketing features that were lacking in Siebel's product portfolio. Paragren's One-by-One suite pulled customer data from data warehouses and applications, then used that data to segment customers. It could then build personalized marketing campaigns around those segments and track and analyze campaign performance. Siebel planned to integrate One-by-One to allow sales and service personnel to access data generated by marketing campaigns and customer responses.

During the year Siebel entered into strategic alliances with several companies to strengthen its e-business solutions.

Among the companies involved were Aspect Communications Corp., American Management Systems, i2 Technologies Inc., Manugistics Group Inc., and Avaya, a Lucent Technologies company. Siebel also entered into a global strategic alliance with management consulting firm PricewaterhouseCoopers.

The company also expanded its alliances with IBM, Compaq, Great Plains, J.D. Edwards, and other companies. In February 2000 Siebel announced that IBM would deploy Siebel eBusiness Applications on a global basis across its multichannel, customer-facing infrastructure to unite field sales and service, marketing and call center professionals, web sites, and business partners.

Siebel also introduced a new series of wireless eBusiness applications to provide field sales and service professionals with real-time wireless access to customer data. In March 2000 Siebel formed an alliance with Palm Inc., a 3Com Corporation company, to jointly market and sell handheld eBusiness solutions. As part of the alliance Siebel would integrate its eBusiness solution with the Palm Address Book, Calendar, and To-Do applications. Other wireless initiatives included a strategic alliance with Sprint PCS to market and sell nationwide access to Siebel eBusiness Applications over the Sprint PCS Wireless Web for Business. Later in the year Siebel announced a worldwide strategic alliance with Nokia Corporation to use the Nokia WAP (wireless application protocol) Server to provide wireless access to Siebel eBusiness Applications.

In April 2000 Siebel began shipping Siebel eBusiness 2000. This new package would allow companies to manage sales, marketing, and customer service across all communication channels and points of customer contact, including the Web, call center, field sales and service, and reseller channels. The MidMarket Edition of Siebel eBusiness 2000 began shipping in July.

Siebel subsequently acquired OpenSite Technologies Inc., a provider of web-based e-commerce solutions, for $542 million in stock. OpenSite products would be branded Siebel Dynamic Commerce and would be included in Siebel's e-commerce product line. They would be used to support business-to-business online auctions and exchanges. In July Siebel acquired MOHR Development Inc., a privately held provider of sales training and consulting services for the financial services, manufacturing, and technology markets. MOHR solutions and expertise would be incorporated into Siebel Multichannel Services.

Later in the year Siebel acquired OnLink Technologies Inc. for about $609 million in stock. Siebel planned to integrate OnLink's technology with Siebel eBusiness Applications to strengthen its position in e-commerce. Siebel further strengthened its e-commerce position by acquiring Toronto-based Janna Systems Inc. for stock worth approximately $1.1 billion. Janna was a well-known provider of e-business solutions for the financial services industry.

As 2000 drew to a close, it was clear that Siebel had successfully made the transition of CRM to the Web. It offered a suite that combined CRM, PRM (partner relationship management), and EAI (enterprise application integration) with personalization tools that helped organizations manage, synchronize, and coordinate sales, marketing, and customer service across all communication channels and points of contact. The firm's revenue for 2000 would easily surpass the $1 billion mark.

Principal Subsidiaries

OnTarget Inc.

Principal Competitors

Oracle Corporation; SAP America Inc.; Vantive Corporation (subsidiary of PeopleSoft Inc.); SalesLogix Corporation; Clarify Corporation (subsidiary of Nortel Networks); SAS Institute Inc.; E.piphany Inc.; Broadbase Software Inc.

Further Reading

''Appointment: Ex-SAP Exec Wahl Tapped to Head Siebel,'' *InfoWorld,* May 17, 1999, p. 20.

Bekker, Scott, ''Siebel: CRM Faces Challenges Adapting to New Market Dynamic,'' *ENT,* September 22, 1999, p. 26.

Booker, Ellis, ''Siebel Offers Free App to Build CRM Sales,'' *InternetWeek,* March 8, 1999, p. 16.

Bowen, Ted Smalley, ''CRM Comes to Midmarket,'' *InfoWorld,* November 8, 1999, p. 20.

Brewer, Geoffrey, ''Tom Siebel Is Bulking Up,'' *Sales & Marketing Management,* September 1998, p. 56.

Bull, Katherine, and Michael Vizard, ''Selling Siebel: CEO Thomas M. Siebel Explains Why Demand for Front-Office Applications Will Outpace ERP by the Year 2000,'' *InfoWorld,* November 30, 1998, p. 1.

Bunish, Christine, ''Q & A: Siebel Ponders SFA Future,'' *Business Marketing,* June 1998, p. 16.

Burt, Jeffrey, ''Siebel Leads Way for Enterprise Software,'' *eWeek,* July 24, 2000, p. 32.

Callaghan, Dennis, ''Siebel Expands Offerings with Janna,'' *eWeek,* September 25, 2000, p. 36.

Carr, David F., ''Siebel's Web Move: Portal for Salespeople,'' *Internet World,* March 15, 1999, p. 18.

Delevett, Peter, ''San Jose Mercury News, Calif., Wiretap Column,'' *Knight-Ridder/Tribune Business News,* December 1, 2000.

Gilbert, Alorie, ''Front-Office Integration with ERP,'' *InformationWeek,* November 8, 1999, p. 105.

——, ''Siebel Strengthens Sales.Com,'' *InformationWeek,* August 16, 1999, p. 36.

Girard, Kim, ''Merger Could Bring Call Center/Sales Integration,'' *Computerworld,* March 23, 1998, p. 44.

Gonsalves, Antone, ''SAP, SAS and Siebel Tap D&B Database,'' *PC Week,* August 23, 1999, p. 33.

——, ''Siebel Systems Riding High,'' *PC Week,* April 24, 2000, p. 25.

Gray, Lloyd, and John S. McCright, ''Focusing on the Customer,'' *PC Week,* November 30, 1998, p. 3.

''Great Plains Expands Partnership with Siebel Systems,'' *Canadian Corporate News,* September 18, 2000.

Greenberg, Ilan, ''Siebel's Sales Goes Global,'' *InfoWorld,* December 11, 1995, p. 32.

——, ''Users Buying into Sales Automation,'' *InfoWorld,* October 17, 1994, p. 32.

Grygo, Eugene, ''E.piphany Aims to Raise Stakes in CRM Market,'' *InfoWorld,* July 24, 2000, p. 12.

Harding, Elizabeth U., ''CRM Tools Manage Your Most Important Asset—Customers,'' *Software Magazine,* April 2000, p. 10.

Holt, Stannie, ''J.D. Edwards, Siebel to Integrate Products,'' *InfoWorld,* May 17, 1999, p. 5.

——, ''Siebel Delivers Sales Solutions,'' *InfoWorld,* March 1, 1999, p. 12.

——, ''Siebel Release Pumps Up the Functionality,'' *InfoWorld,* November 23, 1998, p. 3.

Howle, Amber, ''Keys to the Kingdom,'' *Computer Reseller News,* June 12, 2000, p. 78.

''Keane, Siebel Launch Practice,'' *PC Week,* May 10, 1999, p. 41.

Kean, Virginia, ''Siebel Aims to Become the Industry's Relationship Guru,'' *Insurance & Technology,* November 1998, p. 65.

Longwell, John, ''Tom Siebel: The Serviceman,'' *Computer Reseller News,* November 13, 2000, p. 149.

Mateyaschuk, Jennifer, ''Front-Office Play,'' *InformationWeek,* August 30, 1999, p. 18.

——, ''Siebel and Internet Companies Grab Top Slots on Fast 500 List,'' *InformationWeek,* November 22, 1999, p. 18.

McHugh, Josh, ''The Hardwiring of a Salesman,'' *Forbes,* May 19, 1997, p. 248.

Moore, Mark, ''Upgrades Spruce Up Sales-Force Automation,'' *PC Week,* December 4, 1995, p. 18.

Mulqueen, John T., ''Siebel to Pick Up Scopus,'' *InternetWeek,* March 9, 1998, p. 87.

Pender, Lee, ''CRM Makes It to the Big Time,'' *Computer Reseller News,* November 1, 1998, p. 14.

——, ''SFA Vendors: Tight Race, Big Profits,'' *Computer Reseller News,* July 13, 1998, p. 107.

''Prebuilt Data Mart,'' *InformationWeek,* October 19, 1998, p. 40.

''SAP America Alleges Executive Raiding,'' *Philadelphia Business Journal,* November 12, 1999, p. 3.

Scannell, Ed, and Dan Briody, ''IBM, Siebel Seal Customer Software Pact,'' *InfoWorld,* November 1, 1999, p. 12.

''Siebel Broadens ERP Integration,'' *InfoWorld,* October 26, 1998, p. 67.

''Siebel Outgrows Its Competition,'' *San Francisco Business Times,* November 19, 1999, p. 11.

''Siebel Reports Strong Sales in First Quarter,'' *Business Journal,* April 21, 2000, p. 30.

''Siebel's OpenSite Acquisition Closed,'' *San Francisco Business Times,* May 26, 2000, p. 10.

''Siebel Systems, Inc. to Acquire Janna Systems Inc.,'' *Canadian Corporate News,* September 12, 2000.

Siebel, Thomas M., ''Cyberhouse Rules,'' *Forbes ASAP,* November 27, 2000, http://www.forbes.com/asap/2000/1127/096.html.

Siebel, Thomas M., and Pat House, *Cyber Rules: Strategies for Excelling at E-Business,* New York: Doubleday, 1999.

''Siebel to Acquire OnTarget,'' *InfoWorld,* November 22, 1999, p. 3.

''Siebel to Buy OpenSite,'' *San Francisco Business Times,* April 21, 2000, p. 10.

''Supersalesman Siebel,'' *Business Week,* January 10, 2000, p. 78.

Sweat, Jeff, ''Better Links for Buyers and Sellers over the Internet,'' *InformationWeek,* November 15, 1999, p. 40.

——, ''CRM Vendors Move into Small-Business Market,'' *InformationWeek,* December 13, 1999, p. 213.

——, ''CRM Vendors Post Heady Numbers,'' *InformationWeek,* January 31, 2000, p. 121.

——, ''Focus on Customer Service Fuels CRM Boom,'' *InformationWeek,* February 14, 2000, p. 87:

——, ''Lucent Spin-Off Partners with Siebel for CRM,'' *InformationWeek,* July 3, 2000, p. 36.

——, ''Siebel Acquisition and Alliance Bolster Front-End Suite,'' *InformationWeek,* January 24, 2000, p. 35.

——, ''Siebel Adds BroadVision to String of Internet Alliances,'' *InformationWeek,* November 22, 1999, p. 34.

——, ''Siebel and Interact Shift Gears on Net Ventures,'' *InformationWeek,* October 30, 2000, p. 38.

——, ''Siebel Branches Out—Vendor Targets Sales Professionals,'' *InformationWeek,* March 1, 1999, p. 30.

——, ''Siebel 99,'' *InformationWeek,* December 20, 1999, p. 56.

——, ''Siebel Sales and Profits Soar,'' *InformationWeek,* October 30, 2000, p. 193.

——, ''Siebel Takes Big E-Business Steps,'' *InternetWeek,* April 24, 2000, p. 70.

Sweat, Jeff, and Eileen Colkin, ''Front-Office Vendors Defy Apps Market Slump,'' *InformationWeek,* February 1, 1999, p. 117.

Tiazkun, Scott, ''Great Plains, Siebel Forge Partnership,'' *Computer Reseller News,* July 19, 1999, p. 34.

——, ''Steps Up Siebel Rivalry—Oracle Dedicates Unit to CRM Sales Efforts,'' *Computer Reseller News,* July 19, 1999, p. 3.

——, ''Tom Siebel—Siebel,'' *Computer Reseller News,* November 8, 1999, p. 98.

Warner, Melanie, ''Confessions of a Control Freak,'' *Fortune,* September 4, 2000, p. 130.

——, ''Oracle and Siebel's Software Hardball,'' *Fortune,* October 16, 2000, p. 391.

Whiting, Rick, ''Siebel to Offer SQL Server Package,'' *InformationWeek,* July 5, 1999, p. 32.

—David P. Bianco

SKANSKA

Skanska AB

Klarabergsviadukten 90
SE-111 91 Stockholm
Sweden
Telephone: +46-8-753-88-00
Fax: +46-8-755-12-56
Web site: http://www.skanska.com

Public Company
Incorporated: 1887 as AB Skånska Cementgjuteriet
Employees: 45,063
Sales: SKr 79.13 billion (US$9.28 billion) (1999)
Stock Exchanges: Stockholm
Ticker Symbol: SKA.B
NAIC: 233320 Commercial and Institutional Building Construction; 234120 Bridge and Tunnel Construction; 233210 Single Family Housing Construction; 233220 Multifamily Housing Construction; 233310 Manufacturing and Industrial Building Construction; 234920 Power and Communication Transmission Line Construction; 234990 All Other Heavy Construction

After helping to build Scandinavia, Skanska AB is ready to help build the rest of the world. The Stockholm, Sweden-based company is one of the world's top ten international construction and related services companies, and one of the top five construction companies in the United States. Although the Scandinavian countries and the United States form the company's largest markets, Skanska is actively pursuing its expansion elsewhere, particularly in Poland, Russia, and other Eastern European countries; the United Kingdom; and in Latin America, starting with its 1999 acquisition of Argentina's largest construction company, SADE. Skanska participates in nearly every construction and property development segment, from residential building to large-scale public works projects, including bridges and projects such as the Öresund link between Denmark and Sweden, which opened in 2000, and stadiums, such as the Houston NFL stadium, a project worth some US$350 million. Skanska also has made a specialty of sorts in the construction of telecommunications and Internet infrastructure projects, such as the construction of a high-speed fiber optic network for RNC Corporation started in 1999. While operating in more than 50 countries, Skanska has pursued a policy of establishing for itself a "local" presence in its markets, combining acquisitions with organic growth to build a position as a domestic player in each new market. In 1999, Skanska, which trades on the Stockholm stock exchange, posted more than SKr 79 billion (US$9.28 billion) in revenues, with net income of SKr 4.3 billion (US$500 million). Skanska is led by President and CEO Claes Björk.

Cementing Start in the 19th Century

Skanska had its start in the late 19th century as a manufacturer of cement-based decorative building elements, used for dressing up Sweden's churches and other public buildings. The company was founded as AB Skånska Cementgjuteriet (or Scanian Pre-Cast Cement) by Rudolf Frederik Berg in 1887. Yet Berg's background as an engineer soon expanded the company's field of operations beyond decorative elements and into the construction arena itself. By the end of its first year, Skanska had begun producing materials for general construction, such as concrete blocks and other cement-based fittings. But the company also joined in construction projects itself, building upon its expertise in working with concrete.

Although Skanska remained interested in the general construction market, it also became known for its prowess in various construction specialties, such as bridge building, where the company specialized in erecting concrete bridges. The budding telecommunications industry also provided an opportunity for Skanska—and marked the company's first international contract. By 1897, Skanska had begun to handle large-scale orders for its concrete fittings. This led to a contract with the United Kingdom's National Telephone Company to supply some 100 kilometers (approximately 60 miles) of hollow concrete blocks used for supporting telephone cables. Skanska was to use this and other similar orders to develop itself as one of the leading telecommunications infrastructure specialists in Scandinavia—and elsewhere in the world.

Company Perspectives:

Mission: Skanska's mission is to develop, build and maintain the physical environment for living, traveling and working. By combining its resources in these fields, the Group can offer clients attractive, cost-effective and thus competitive solutions.

Vision: Skanska shall be a world leader—the client's first choice—in construction-related services and project development.

The British order led the company to seek further foreign contracts. A new large-scale order came at the beginning of the new century, when Tsarist Russia sought to replace the wood-based sewer system then in place in the city of St. Petersburg and throughout the Russian empire. Skanska won the contract to produce the concrete pipes that provided the basis of Russia's modern sewer system and opened its first non-Scandinavian facility in St. Petersburg in 1902.

Skanska's Scandinavian home base remained its primary market, however, and over the next three decades, Skanska was able to claim credit for building much of the modern infrastructure in Sweden, Norway, Denmark, and Finland as the company established itself as one of the region's largest construction companies. Among the company's most significant projects during this time was its construction of Sweden's first asphalt road, completed in 1927 in Borlänge in the country's central region. Skanska's completion of the Sandö bridge in 1943 gave it another triumph: at 264 meters, the Sandö bridge gained fame as the world's longest concrete-based arch-span bridge—a distinction held until the 1960s.

Building an International Construction Business for the 21st Century

Skanska began to focus more and more on its international growth following World War II. The company marked a milestone with the introduction of its Allbetong method. Using this system, Skanska was able to produce prefabricated elements for large-scale construction projects, such as apartment buildings and others. Manufactured in Skanska's factories, the elements were then put into place using construction cranes. The Allbetong method helped cut down on the time and labor involved in a construction project and played a pivotal part in Skanska's international development, as the company turned more and more to markets beyond its Scandinavian base.

Helping to fuel the company's expansion was its listing on the Stockholm stock exchange in 1965. Following the listing, Skanska stepped up its international growth, moving into new markets in Africa and the Middle East. After securing a strong position for itself in these markets by the late 1960s, Skanska returned closer to home, entering Poland and the Soviet Union in the early 1970s. Among the company's major projects in the Eastern European markets during this period was its construction of the Forum Hotel in Warsaw, which featured 750 rooms and also marked the first turnkey hotel project completed by Skanska outside of its Swedish home base.

Skanska also began to move into the United States, one of the world's largest construction markets. As elsewhere, Skanska sought to foster its international expansion by creating a local presence in each of the markets it hoped to serve. For this the company pursued a number of acquisitions, including Slattery, active on the East Coast, and Sordoni, later renamed Sordoni Skanska and placed under the Skanska USA subsidiary. The company was then able to pursue an organic growth strategy in its new markets through its local subsidiary companies.

By the early 1980s, Skanska's international business had risen to become a significant percentage of its sales. As an acknowledgment of this, the company simplified its name, abandoning the full AB Skånska Cementgjuteriet name after nearly 100 years to become Skanska AB in 1984. Over the following decade, Skanska continued to expand its international business, placing itself among the world's top ten internationally operating companies (a ranking that excludes certain Japanese construction companies that focus wholly on the Japanese market), as well as occupying a major position in the U.S. market.

The company's U.S. position was strengthened with the addition of Barclay White Inc., based in Philadelphia, Pennsylvania. Barclay White had long played a prominent role in that state's construction industry. Founded in 1913, the company originally focused on the greater Philadelphia region, where it completed projects for such clients as Midvale Steel Company, Swarthmore College, Bryn Mawr College, Friends Hospital, and Friends Central School. Major clients in the 1950s and 1960s included SmithKline, Penn Fruit Co., Merck Sharp & Dohme, Continental Can, and General Motors. After adding construction management services at the beginning of the 1970s, the company took itself private. During that decade, and into the building boom years of the 1980s, Barclay White tripled in size, as it took on such projects as the Franklin Institute Futures Center, Bell of Pennsylvania's Corporate Computer Center, the corporate headquarters for State Farm Insurance, and others. By the late 1990s, Barclay White's revenues had topped US$300 million.

By the mid-1990s Skanska had succeeded in imposing itself as one of the top U.S. construction companies, winning such contracts as a large share in the US$380 million extension of Boston's Central Artery. Back home, the company was preparing to fulfill one of its longtime plans. In 1994, Skanska, as majority shareholder in the Sundlink consortium, won the contract to build the bridge portion of the Öresund bridge and tunnel link between Sweden and Denmark, marking the first permanent physical link between the European continent and the Scandinavian region.

Skanska had been involved in some of the earliest plans to link the two countries across the Öresund channel. The first proposals to build a tunnel crossing had appeared in the late 1800s. Skanska, joining with Danish construction group Hojgaard & Schultz, launched its own proposal in the 1930s to build a road, rail, and bicycle bridge across the Öresund. World

Key Dates:

1887: Rudolf Frederik Berg founds AB Skånska Cementgjuteriet.
1897: Company receives first foreign contract.
1902: Company establishes production facility in St. Petersburg. 1927: Company completes first asphalt-paved road in Sweden.
1952: Allbetong method of prefabricated construction is introduced.
1965: Company lists on Stockholm stock exchange.
1974: Company completes first turnkey hotel project outside of Sweden.
1984: Company changes name to Skanska AB.
1994: Skanska acquires Beers Construction Company.
1995: Company wins contract to build Öresund link between Denmark and Sweden.
1999: Company acquires A.J. Etkin (U.S.A.); Gottleib Group (U.S.A.); SADE (Argentina).
2000: Skanska acquires Exbud (Poland) and IPS (Czech Republic).

War II intervened with further consideration of the project. As the Scandinavian economies once again began to grow in the 1950s, Skanska and Hojgaard & Schultz again joined together to present a bridge and tunnel proposal. Yet indecision about the project persisted for another 30 years. Finally, in 1991, the Danish and Swedish governments reached an agreement to build a toll-based bridge and tunnel link between the two countries. Bids were accepted, and in 1995, Skanska, as part of the Sundlink consortium, which included Germany's Hoctief, Hojgaard & Schultz, and fellow Danish company Monberg & Thorsen, won the contract to build the bridge portion of the Öresund link. Construction was completed and the link opened to traffic in 2000.

By the time it had signed the Öresund contract, Skanska already had completed a major move to enhance its U.S. presence, when it acquired Beers Construction Company in 1994. The Beers acquisition gave Skanska a significant presence in Beers's primary Southeast market, where the company had built up a position as one of the leading construction companies in the area, with operations across Florida, Georgia, North and South Carolina, Virginia, and Tennessee, and with a presence in more than 17 additional states across the country. Beers had been founded in Georgia by two Frenchmen in 1905 as Southern Ferro Concrete Company, specializing in fireproof construction projects using reinforced concrete. Harold W. Beers joined the company in 1907 as senior engineer, then gave his name to the company in 1935. Beers's Atlanta base placed it in position to participate in the phenomenal growth of that city, which saw Atlanta rise to one of the South's largest urban centers by the 1990s. The company was involved in the construction of a number of Atlanta landmark structures, including the Southern Bell Headquarters building and others. After developing expertise in hospital construction in the 1970s and 1980s, Beers expanded its operations into the sports world, where it became one of the region's leading arena construction contractors. After completing the Georgia Dome in the early 1990s, Beers, now a part of Skanska, won contracts to build a substantial part of the Atlanta Olympic Games infrastructure, including the Centennial Olympic Stadium, later renamed Turner Field. In 1999, Beers won the contract to build the Houston Stadium, which was set to become the largest NFL stadium upon completion in 2002.

In Scandinavia, Skanska ran into a hurdle after it acquired a majority share of Scancem, the region's largest cement producer, which held a near-monopoly on cement production in Scandinavia. Skanska was forced to divest itself of the Scancem holding in 1998. In 1999, the company beefed up a number of its international operations, including in the United States, with the acquisitions of A.J. Etkin Construction Company, renamed Etkin Skanska, and the Gottleib Group. Skanska also entered the South American market for the first time, acquiring Argentina's largest construction group, SADE Ingenieria y Construcciones S.A., as the beachhead for Skanska's expansion throughout Latin America.

Closer to home, Skanska continued to pursue its expansion in Eastern Europe. After acquiring a majority share in Poland's largest construction company, Exbud, in April 2000, Skanska added a controlling share of IPS Praha a.s., the largest construction company in the Czech Republic. Meanwhile, the company was pursuing expansion in a number of new areas, including enhancing its telecommunications and Internet infrastructure arm and boosting its operations in facilities management. Skanska also began to divest itself of a series of noncore operations—such as its shareholding in real estate group Piren AB and bearings manufacturer Aktiebolaget SKF, as well as a number of its real estate holdings, such as properties in London, sold to Sun Life for some US$60 million at the beginning of 2000. The shedding of these assets was part of Skanska's commitment to rebuilding its identity beyond a pure construction group to becoming a full-scale international construction services provider.

Principal Subsidiaries

Barclay White Inc. (U.S.A.); Costain Group; Flexator; Heinz Essmann GmbH; Industriventilation Produkt; Poggenpohl Group (Germany); SADE Ingenieria y Construcciones S.A. (Argentina); Skanska AS (Norway); Skanska Danmark A/S (Denmark); Skanska Etkin Construction (U.S.A.); Skanska Europe AB; Skanska International AG (Switzerland); Skanska Oy (Finland); IPS Praha a.s. (Czech Republic; 66%); Skanska UK; Skanska Project Development and Real Estate; Skanska BOT AB; Skanska Oresund AB; Skanska Projektutveckling och Fastigheter AB; Skanska Projektutveckling Sverige AB; Skanska Services; SCEM Reinsurance S.A. (Luxembourg); Skanska Facilities Management; Skanska Financial Services AB; Skanska Forsakrings AB; Skanska IT Solutions AB; Skanska Teknik AB; Skanska Sweden; Skanska Industrial Construction; Skanska International Civil Engineering AB; Skanska Prefab AB; Skanska Road Construction; Skanska Sverige AB; Skanska Underground Construction and Bridges; Skanska (USA) Inc.; Beers Construction Co.; Koch Skanska Inc.; Slattery Skanska Inc.; Sordoni Skanska Construction Co.

Principal Competitors

AMEC plc; Autostrade-Concessioni e Costruzioni Autostrade S.p.A; Bechtel Group Inc.; Bilfinger + Berger Bau AG; Bouygues S.A.; Bovis Lend Lease; Centex; Colas S.A.; Eiffage S.A.; Fluor Corporation; Flour Daniel Inc.; HOCHTIEF A.G.; Louis Berger Group Inc.; Philipp Holzmann Group; Schneider Electric S.A.; Technip; Turner Corp.; Vinci; WS Atkins Plc.

Further Reading

Austin, Tony, ''Internet Helps Build Skanska Q1 Profit,'' *Reuters,* May 2, 2000.

Malmsten, Nina, ''Skanska Sets Sights on Czech, Hungary Builders,'' *Reuters,* May 25, 2000.

''Skanska Still Interested in Buying Czech IPS,'' *Reuters,* May 25, 2000.

''Skanska to Sell off Scancem Stake Following Merger Ruling,'' *European Report,* November 14, 1998.

—M.L. Cohen

building the global e-Future

Softbank Corp.

24-1, Nihonbashi-Hakozakicho
Chuo-ku
Tokyo 103-8501
Japan
Telephone: (03) 5642-8005
Fax: (03) 5641-3401
Web site: http://www.softbank.co.jp

Public Company
Incorporated: 1981 as Japan Softbank
Employees: 6,865
Sales: ¥423.22 billion (US$3.99 billion) (2000)
Stock Exchanges: Tokyo
Ticker Symbol: 9984
NAIC: 523910 Miscellaneous Intermediation; 551112 Offices of Other Holding Companies

Softbank Corp. is a holding company whose primary interest is the Internet. The company holds stakes in more than 400 Internet companies, serving as one of the leading Internet-oriented venture capital firms. Among Softbank's key Internet holdings are stakes in Yahoo! Inc., Yahoo Japan Corporation, E*Trade Group Inc., and Morningstar Japan K.K. Other holdings include Nasdaq Japan, Inc., trade show operator Key3Media Group Inc., and a 49 percent stake in Aozora Bank Ltd., the former Nippon Credit Bank Ltd., which failed in late 1998 and was then bought from the Japanese government by a Softbank-led consortium in September 2000. Softbank was founded and led by Masayoshi Son (rhymes with ''lone''), a self-promoting 24-year-old whose rapid rise earned him the nickname ''the Bill Gates of Japan.'' Son possessed a rare combination of character traits as an inventor, businessman, and ''consummate salesman.'' Although he hailed from a country that was not often distinguished for encouraging entrepreneurship, the editors of *Business Week* ranked him one of the best entrepreneurs of 1994. Originating as a wholesaler of PC software, Softbank by the early 1990s had branched out into computer magazine publishing and computer trade shows, as well as becoming a notable software venture capitalist. The firm's shift to the Internet began in 1996 with the purchase of a controlling interest in one of the Web pioneers, Yahoo!

1980s Entrepreneurial Origins

Son was born in 1957 to Japanese citizens of Korean descent. By his own account, his early years were characterized by second-class citizenship and poverty. In a 1992 interview with Alan M. Webber of the *Harvard Business Review,* he acknowledged that, like many other Koreans in Japan, his entire family had assumed a Japanese surname, Yasumoto, in order to better assimilate into society. Son's family was able to move out of a squatter town and into the middle class by the time he reached the age of 13. At 16, Son traveled to the United States to attend high school.

The youngster flourished in his new environment, resuming his Korean surname and breezing through three grades to graduate from his California high school within a couple of weeks. Son attended Holy Names College for two years, then transferred to the University of California at Berkeley. It was there that, with the help of some professors of microcomputing, he made his first $1 million at the age of 19 by developing a pocket translator. Son sold the patent for his device to Sharp Corp., which marketed it as the Sharp Wizard. By the time he was 20, Son had earned another million importing used video game machines from Japan.

Although Son realized that it would be relatively easy to launch a business in the United States, the budding entrepreneur also knew that the Japanese culture tended to produce employees who were likely to be more loyal and work harder than their American counterparts. Consequently, he decided to return to his homeland upon his graduation from college. He spent the next 18 months researching 40 different business options ranging from software development to hospital management. Using a matrix, Son ranked each one against 25 of his own ''success measures.'' He described a few of these to Webber in the *Harvard Business Review* interview: ''I should fall in love with [the] business for the next 50 years at least,'' ''the business should be unique,'' and ''within 10 years I wanted to be number one in that particular business.'' The field he chose—whole-

Company Perspectives:

Vision: Softbank aims to leverage the power of the digital information revolution to make knowledge available to people no matter who or where they are and, by doing so, to foster the realization of a better life for all.

saling personal computer (PC) software—met the majority of his criteria. At the time, most software developers did not have the capital to promote their products to hardware manufacturers, and most hardware manufacturers and retailers did not have software to run on their machines. Son hoped to carve out a profitable niche as a liaison between the two groups.

At first, his 1981-formed company, Japan Softbank, was more spectacle than substance. Using a combination of previously earned and borrowed funds, Son purchased one of the biggest display areas available at a 1981 consumer electronics show in Tokyo. Having absolutely no product to offer, Son called all 12 of the software vendors he knew at the time and offered to display their wares at his booth *gratis.* Not surprisingly, many jumped at the opportunity. Although his exhibit, which featured a large banner proclaiming a ''revolution in software distribution,'' caught many attendees' attention, most already had their own contacts with software vendors. The show earned the fledgling entrepreneur only one contact; luckily, it was with Japan's foremost PC retailer, Joshin Denki Co. Son negotiated exclusive rights to purchase software for the chain, then parlayed that top-notch industry connection into exclusive contracts with other firms, including Hudson Software, the country's largest vendor. Over the course of its first year in business, Japan Softbank's monthly sales mushroomed from US$10,000 to US$2.3 million. By 1983, the company served over 200 dealer outlets.

By that time, Son was already pursuing additional business interests in the broader field he called ''computing infrastructure.'' He first diversified into publishing in 1982. His first two magazine titles, *Oh!PC* and *Oh!MZ,* lost hundreds of thousands of dollars in their inaugural months due to lack of interest. But Son feared that if he dropped these sidelines clients would smell trouble, so instead he revamped the layout and threw the weight of an expensive television advertising campaign behind the project. By the early 1990s, the flagship *Oh!PC* enjoyed a circulation of about 140,000 and had become the forerunner of a stable of 20 Softbank-published periodicals, including the Japanese edition of *PC Magazine,* launched in 1989. Writing for *Forbes* in 1992, Andrew Tanzer noted that ''the magazines rather shamelessly promote products Son distributes,'' an accepted practice in Japan. By the early 1990s, the division had also put out over 300 computing books and become Japan's leading publisher of high-tech magazines.

A lengthy bout with hepatitis sidelined Son from 1983 through 1986. Although he gave up Japan Softbank's presidency during this period, Son kept tabs on the company via computer and telecommunications equipment installed in his hospital room. His prolonged recuperation apparently gave him time to conjure up new ideas. Upon his return to Japan Softbank's helm, Son invented a ''least-cost routing device'' that came to form the basis of the company's DATANET telephone data division. The idea evolved when Japan's telephone monopoly, Nippon Telegraph & Telephone Corp. (NTT), was joined by three new common carriers—DDI Corporation, Teleway Japan, and Japan Telecom—in 1986. Although they offered lower long-distance rates, the inconvenience of dialing the three newcomers' additional four-digit prefixes deterred many customers from signing on. Son's computerized invention, which he described as about ''the size of two cigarette packs,'' would automatically choose the cheapest carrier and route, then dial the appropriate number. Periodic online updates kept the routers' rate information current. Japan Softbank offered the devices free to telephone customers and made money by collecting royalties on common carriers' increased billings. In the early 1990s, Son expanded the business by offering routers installed in new telephones and fax machines.

Early 1990s: Venture Capitalist and Corporate Matchmaker

Son renamed his company Softbank Corp. in 1990. Seeking ways to invest his profits—and perhaps to erect a bulwark against getting bypassed in the distribution chain—Son soon earned renown as a venture capitalist and corporate ''matchmaker.'' Early deals paired U.S. software vendors with Japanese partners who modified American computer applications for sale in Japan. Softbank made commissions on the matchmaking, then distributed the newly modified products.

The ''marriages'' got bigger in the early 1990s. In 1991, Son arranged two major computer networking alliances that combined the resources of a coterie of well-known rivals. The lead company in the first venture was BusinessLand Inc., a top systems integrator in the United States. It owned 54 percent of the US$20 million venture, appropriately named BusinessLand Japan Co. Softbank held another 26 percent of the equity, while Toshiba Corp., Sony Corp., Canon Inc., and Fujitsu Ltd. each controlled 5 percent. Unlike its California-based majority partner, BusinessLand Japan eschewed the retail market in favor of corporate customers. While some analysts observed that the new venture's Japanese participants would give it a leg up on pre-existing competitors such as America's Electronic Data Systems (EDS), IBM Corp., and Digital Equipment Corp., others noted a conflict of interest in having computer manufacturers among BusinessLand Japan's investors. In fact, the venture failed and was liquidated within a year.

Nonetheless, Son had no trouble convincing many of those same corporations to invest in a second endeavor that same year, Novell Japan Ltd., in which Novell took a 54 percent stake. Softbank held 26 percent of the new company, while hardware manufacturers NEC, Toshiba Corp., Fujitsu Ltd., Canon Inc., and Sony Corp. each chipped in four percent of the equity. Although each of the latter five partners produced its own version of the networking system, all were compatible. The coalition sold network operating systems, peripherals, cables, transceivers, boards, and other network-related products. Since, according to Son's estimate, less than 5 percent of Japan's PCs were networked in 1990, the allies expected to make Novell's NetWare the industry standard there. Son predicted that the Japanese computer networking industry would ''grow like

Key Dates:

1981: Masayoshi Son founds Japan Softbank as a wholesaler of PC software.
1982: Company diversifies into publishing.
1989: Company launches the Japanese edition of *PC Magazine.*
1990: Company is renamed Softbank Corp.
1994: Softbank is taken public; the trade show division of Ziff Communications is acquired.
1995: Company purchases 17 computer trade shows, including Comdex, from Interface Group.
1996: Ziff-Davis Publishing Co. is acquired; Softbank gains a controlling stake in Yahoo! Inc., which goes public later in the year; an 80 percent stake in memory board maker Kingston Technology Company is acquired.
1999: Softbank transforms itself into a holding company focusing on the Internet; stake in Kingston Technology is divested.
2000: Ziff-Davis is sold off; ZD Events is spun off as Key3Media Group, with Softbank retaining a significant stake; ZDNet is sold to CNET Networks; the Nasdaq Japan Market, partially owned by Softbank, is launched; a Softbank-led consortium purchases Nippon Credit Bank, Ltd., which is renamed Aozora Bank Ltd.; Softbank's stock plunges 90 percent as the Internet stock bubble bursts.

hell'' in a 1992 interview for the *Harvard Business Review.* This prediction came true: by 1994, Novell Japan Ltd. boasted US$130 million in annual sales.

That same year, Son engineered what *Business Week* called a ''sweeping alliance'' involving Cisco Systems Inc., Fujitsu Ltd., Toshiba Corp., and a dozen other Japanese firms. The partners anted up a total of US$40 million to fund the launch of Nihon Cisco System, which planned to distribute internetworking systems in Japan.

Although he was widely hailed as a ''whiz kid,'' Son was not infallible. Within just six months in 1991, he allegedly lost US$10 million in a bungled online shopping venture. Systembank, a joint venture with Perot Systems, was intended to provide systems integration for large Japanese corporations. According to a February 1995 article in the *New York Times,* Systembank was ''quietly disbanded.'' In 1994, Son convinced NTT to invest US$200,000 in a ''video on demand'' alliance. The proposed interactive system would allow subscribers to request movies and other media at their leisure. Son boldly predicted that the joint venture would have ten million customers by the turn of the century. But NTT, which had a similar agreement with Microsoft Corporation, did not plan to have the necessary infrastructure (i.e., fiber optic cable to households) ready for another five to ten years, which pushed back Son's anticipated timetable substantially.

Son's first postgraduate American venture, Softbank Inc., was formed in 1993 with the cooperation of Merisel Inc., Phoenix Technologies Ltd., and telemarketer Alexander and Lord. The new subsidiary planned to distribute software through the interactive Softbank On-Hand Library service. Softbank Inc.'s vice-president, Meg Tuttle, described the demo disks as ''adware.'' Reviewer Steve Bass of *PC World* ''fell in love'' with the US$10 CD-ROMs, which allowed users to ''test-drive'' over 100 programs, then order and pay for the selected software online. Several big-league computer companies, including Apple Computer, IBM, and Ingram Micro, had already launched similar promotions. But other analysts and competitors nixed the idea. For example, David Goldstein, president of Channel Marketing, told *PC Week*'s Lawrence Aradon that offering software on compact disks would become ''the Edsel of the computer industry.'' The venture's direct competition with one of Softbank's most important consumer groups, software retailers, broke what Steve Hamm of *PC Week* called one of Son's golden rules: ''don't compete with clients or suppliers.'' By early 1995, in fact, a number of industry analysts pronounced the venture defunct for that very reason.

Mid-1990s: Expanding into ''Digital Information Infrastructure''

Son took Softbank Corp. public in 1994 in an offering that valued the company at US$3 billion. The founder retained a 70 percent interest in his company. Coming off the late 1994 loss of a bidding war for the U.S. magazine publishing operations of Ziff Communications Co., Son acquired that firm's trade show division for US$202 million. The subsidiary's name was changed from ZD Expos to Softbank Expos. Early in 1995, Softbank made a major addition to that interest with the US$800 million purchase of a package of 17 computer trade shows from Sheldon Adelson's Interface Group. The acquisition, which was financed with at least US$500 million in debt and a new offering of Softbank Corp. shares, nearly doubled Softbank's U.S. operations.

The acquisition included the Las Vegas Comdex show, which was characterized in a 1995 *Wall Street Journal* article as ''a huge draw in the computer industry.'' Launched in 1979, Comdex attracted 195,000 attendees and 2,200 exhibitors to its November 1994 show. Although the event remained popular, its high prices had come under criticism. Some major exhibitors, including Compaq, Packard Bell, Oracle, and Seagate Technologies, had already opted out of the show by the time Softbank took over. Son expressed confidence that he could revitalize the event without a total revamp, citing the fact that exhibit space for the 1995 show was already 90 percent booked by the previous spring. Expansion plans for the new businesses included the first French Softbank Expo in 1995 and the premier Japanese and British Comdexes in 1996.

Son's aggressive approach to acquisitions continued in 1996. In February Softbank was able to secure Ziff-Davis Publishing Co., which Son had failed to acquire in late 1994, through a US$1.8 billion purchase price, paid to Forstmann Little & Co. (the firm that had outbid it the first time around). Ziff-Davis was the leading publisher of computer and high-tech magazines in the United States and had a several-years-long relationship with Softbank involving licensing deals to publish Japanese versions of Ziff computer magazines, including *PC Magazine.*

Son's expansion into trade shows and publishing was part of his aim to become the world's leading provider of ''digital information infrastructure.'' Along these lines were two additional 1996 developments. In 1995 Softbank had already purchased a five percent stake in Yahoo! Inc., initially the provider of a directory for the Internet before evolving into the premier Internet portal. In April 1996 Softbank increased this stake to a controlling 37 percent, marking the firm's first major investment in the Internet; later in 1996 Yahoo! was taken public. Son was aggressive not only with acquisitions but also in exploiting synergies between his burgeoning holdings. For example, the new Ziff-Davis magazine title *Internet Life* was recast as *Yahoo! Internet Life;* positioned as the ''*TV Guide* of the Internet,'' this title's advertising rate base reached 200,000 by the end of 1996. Softbank and Yahoo! also set up a joint venture called Yahoo Japan Corporation, 60 percent owned by Softbank, which created a Japanese-language version of Yahoo! that quickly became the most visited web site in Japan. Consummated in September 1996 was the US$1.51 billion purchase of an 80 percent stake in Kingston Technology Company, a privately held maker of PC memory boards based in Fountain Valley, California. The acquisitions and investments in Softbank, Ziff-Davis, Yahoo!, and Kingston were part of a clear and rapid expansion outside of Japan, concentrating on the world's key technology market, that of the United States. Yet another 1996 development, meanwhile, was centered on Japan as Softbank entered the field of digital satellite broadcasting through the establishment of Japan Sky Broadcasting Co., Ltd., a joint venture with Rupert Murdoch's News Corporation Limited.

Softbank's spectacular series of acquisitions resulted in the doubling of net sales from fiscal 1996 to fiscal 1997, from ¥171.1 billion (US$1.61 billion) to ¥359.74 billion (US$2.9 billion), and a 94 percent jump in pretax profits, from ¥15.98 billion (US$150.3 million) to ¥29.57 billion (US$238.3 million). At the same time, long-term debt used to fund the company's expansion was ballooning, reaching ¥595.03 billion (US$4.79 billion) by the end of fiscal 1997. Concern about the debt load, coupled with slower sales growth and falling margins, as well as allegations of improprieties in the company's financial disclosures (which were widely disseminated in a best-selling book in Japan called *Inside Revelation: Softbank's Warped Management,* whose publisher, Yell Books, was sued by Softbank), sent Softbank's stock plunging from ¥8,450 in early 1997—its peak for the year—to a low of ¥1,670 by November of that year. Another setback for Softbank in 1997 was a serious dilution of its initial 50 percent stake in Japan Sky Broadcasting when Sony Corporation and Fuji TV joined the venture followed by the merging of it with a competitor, Japan Digital Broadcasting Services. Softbank's stake was reduced to 11.4 percent.

To raise some much needed cash, Son began seeking listings for some of his subsidiary companies. In November 1997 Yahoo Japan was taken public on the Japanese over-the-counter market, with Softbank keeping a 51 percent stake. Then in April 1998, 26 percent of stock in the renamed Ziff-Davis Inc. was sold through an IPO on the New York Stock Exchange, raising US$400 million. Prior to its listing, Ziff-Davis was given ownership of Softbank's exhibits operations, which were initially called ZD Comdex and Forums Inc. but were soon renamed ZD Events Inc., as well as ZDNet, a web site featuring online versions of a number of Ziff-Davis publications. Meantime, Softbank's stock began trading on the first section of the Tokyo Stock Exchange in January 1998.

Late 1990s and Beyond: Emphasizing the Internet

The late 1990s saw Softbank increase its investments in the Internet significantly, during what would eventually be viewed as the Internet stock bubble. By mid-1999, Softbank had significant stakes in Yahoo!, Yahoo Japan, ZDNet, community-oriented portal GeoCities, e-commerce ''superstore'' Buy-com Inc., consumer loan specialist E-Loan Inc., and online broker E*Trade Group Inc. Through joint ventures, Softbank had helped establish several more Japanese versions of successful American web sites, including E-Loan Japan, E*Trade Japan, GeoCities Japan, and Morningstar Japan, the latter a venture with Morningstar Inc. that set up a web site providing Japanese financial news and market analysis. Although not all of Son's Internet investments were successful, he was able to ride the US$338 million he had invested in Yahoo! to spectacular heights. Yahoo!'s soaring stock price led Softbank's investment to be worth more than US$10 billion by mid-1999. Overall, the US$2 billion that Son had invested in 100 Internet companies was worth more than US$17 billion by this time. In March 1999 Ziff-Davis created a tracking stock for ZDNet and sold 16 percent of the unit to the public through an IPO. In the topsy-turvy world of the Internet stock bubble, by mid-1999 ZDNet had a market capitalization greater than that of Ziff-Davis, despite Ziff-Davis's 84 percent stake in ZDNet.

In June 1999 Softbank Corp. transformed itself into a holding company focusing on the Internet. The finance-oriented Internet holdings, including E*Trade and Morningstar Japan, were combined within a new subsidiary called Softbank Finance Corporation. Softbank's technology services related to e-commerce were bundled within Softbank Technology Corp., which was taken public in July 1999 on the Japanese OTC market. That same month, Softbank sold its stake in Kingston Technology back to the company's founders for US$450 million, in a move to divest non-Internet assets. Also in July, Softbank began exploring strategic options related to Ziff-Davis, including the possible sale of the company in what would be a further concentration on the Internet. One month earlier, Softbank joined with the National Association of Securities Dealers (NASDAQ) to create a joint venture called NASDAQ Japan, Inc. to set up a Japanese version of the NASDAQ Stock Market. In June 2000 the NASDAQ Japan Market commenced operations with eight listed companies.

In early 2000 Softbank began selling off Ziff-Davis piecemeal, initially planning to retain ZDNet. In April 2000 the magazine unit was sold for US$780 million to a partnership headed by Willis Stein & Partners, L.P., emerging as Ziff Davis Media Inc. The ZD Events unit was spun off to shareholders as a new company called Key3Media Group, Inc., in which Softbank retained a sizeable stake. ZDNet would have then become a standalone, publicly traded company 45 percent owned by Softbank. But CNET Networks Inc., ZDNet's archrival, stepped in with a takeover offer, which was accepted, resulting in a US$1.6 billion-in-stock acquisition later in 2000.

By February 1999, Son's emphasis on the Internet had helped send his company's share price soaring to ¥60,667 (US$592). At that point, Softbank's market value was US$190 billion. By late November, the share price had plunged more than 90 percent to ¥5,970 (US$53.87). The company's market value dropped by US$172 billion in just nine months, reaching US$17.9 billion. During this precipitous decline, Softbank was forced to abandon plans to sell shares in five of its main subsidiaries: Softbank E-Commerce Corp., Softbank Finance, Softbank Media & Marketing Corp., Softbank Broadmedia Corporation, and Softbank Networks Inc. Later in 2000, faced with continued stock market doldrums, Softbank put the brakes on joint ventures in Europe with News Corporation and Vivendi, both of which aimed at creating European versions of U.S. Internet companies. In September 2000, a Softbank-led consortium purchased Nippon Credit Bank, Ltd., which had collapsed in late 1998, from the Japanese government for US$932 million. Softbank held a 49 percent stake in the bank, which was renamed Aozora Bank Ltd., as Softbank became the first nonfinancial company to enter the Japanese banking sector. Both Nasdaq Japan and Aozora Bank were viewed by Son as underpinnings of a new financial infrastructure in Japan that might foster the development of the Internet-centered economy—and in turn, Softbank—by remedying the chronic shortage of capital faced by the nation's venture firms.

It was clear that Son remained one of the most innovative businesspeople in Japan, if not the world. The severe decline in his company's stock price during 2000, however, left the future rather clouded. Investors found Softbank's vast array of holdings in more than 600 companies, most of which were not publicly traded, confusing. The technology bear market made further IPOs problematic. Without question there were valuable holdings in the Softbank portfolio, most notably Yahoo! and Yahoo Japan (the latter's stock had risen 6,000 percent from its IPO in November 1997 to late 2000). Son also believed that the downturn in Internet stocks actually presented him with opportunities to make additional investments at bargain-basement prices.

Principal Subsidiaries

Softbank E-Commerce Corp.; Softbank Finance Corporation; Softbank Media & Marketing Corp.; Softbank Broadmedia Corporation; Softbank Networks Inc.; Softbank Technology Corp. (63%); Yahoo Japan Corporation (51.2%); NASDAQ Japan, Inc. (43%); Aozora Bank Ltd. (49%); Softbank Inc. (U.S.A.); Softbank Venture Capital (U.S.A.); Softbank International Ventures (U.S.A.); Softbank Korea Co., Ltd.; Softbank China Holdings Pte. Ltd.

Principal Competitors

Accel Partners; CMGI, Inc.; Flatiron Partners; Fujitsu Limited; idealab!; Internet Capital Group, Inc.; Kleiner Perkins Caufield & Byers; Safeguard Scientifics, Inc.; Sequoia Capital; Trinity Ventures; Vulcan Northwest Inc.

Further Reading

"After the Party," *Economist,* May 18, 1996, p. 65.

Aragon, Lawrence, "Off and Running," *PC Week,* March 14, 1994, p. A1.

Bass, Steve, "Hot Picks for the Home Office," *PC World,* March 1995, p. 241.

"The Best Entrepreneurs," *Business Week,* January 9, 1995, p. 112.

Bickers, Charles, "Japan's Mr. Internet: Softbank's Bold Moves Cause Ripples in Japan Inc.," *Far Eastern Economic Review,* July 29, 1999, pp. 11–12.

Bremner, Brian, "Is Softbank Sinking? Don't Bet on It," *Business Week,* April 24, 2000, p. 144.

——, "Why Softbank Is Shouting 'Yahoo!,' " *Business Week,* September 7, 1998, p. 48.

Bremner, Brian, and Amy Cortese, "Cyber-Mogul: to Conquer the Net, Masayoshi Son Takes to the High Wire," *Business Week,* August 12, 1996, pp. 56–62.

Bremner, Brian, and Linda Himelstein, "Softbank's Cyber Keiretsu," *Business Week,* April 5, 1999, p. 24.

Bulkeley, William M., Jim Carlton, and Norihiko Shirouzu, "Japanese Firm to Buy Comdex Computer Show," *Wall Street Journal,* February 14, 1995, p. A3.

Burke, Steven, "$20 Million Joint Venture Gives BusinessLand Foothold in Japan," *PC Week,* June 11, 1990, p. 119.

Butler, Steven, "Empire of the Son: The Bill Gates of Japan Controls a Huge Chunk of the Internet," *U.S. News and World Report,* July 5, 1999, pp. 48, 50.

Desmond, Edward W., "Japan's Top Technology Investor Takes a Hit," *Fortune,* September 8, 1997, pp. 150–52.

Gilley, Bruce, Chester Dawson, and Dan Biers, "Internet Warrior on the Defensive," *Far Eastern Economic Review,* November 16, 2000, pp. 54+.

Hamilton, David P., "Comdex Owner Doesn't Plan to Alter Show," *Wall Street Journal,* February 21, 1995, p. A13B.

Hamilton, David P., and Norihiko Shirouzu, "Softbank to Buy Memory Board Maker," *Wall Street Journal,* August 16, 1996, p. A3.

Hamm, Steve, "The Rising Son," *PC Week,* April 10, 1995, p. A1.

"Heat Turns Up on the Rising Son," *Financial Times,* November 13, 1997, p. 39.

Holyoke, Larry, "Japan's Hottest Entrepreneur Hits the U.S.," *Business Week,* February 27, 1995, p. 118G.

Ip, Greg, and Bill Spindle, "NASDAQ Plans to Set Up a New Stock Market in Japan: Softbank to Invest in Proposed Project," *Wall Street Journal,* June 16, 1999, p. A19.

Landers, Peter, "Prodigal Son: For 'Japan's Bill Gates,' Last Year Was Daunting. Can Masayoshi Son Come Back?," *Far Eastern Economic Review,* January 22, 1998, pp. 42+.

Lipin, Steven, "Persistence Pays Off in Second Sale of Ziff-Davis," *Wall Street Journal,* December 29, 1995, p. C1.

——, "Ziff-Davis Unit of Forstmann Set to Be Sold," *Wall Street Journal,* November 9, 1995, p. A3.

McCartney, Laton, "The Rising Son," *Upside,* April 1997, pp. 108–110.

Moffett, Sebastian, "The Entrepreneur: Softbank's Masayoshi Son Builds an Unconventional Empire," *Far Eastern Economic Review,* November 7, 1996, p. 206.

——, "A Whole New Ballgame," *Far Eastern Economic Review,* July 4, 1996, p. 70.

Ono, Kazuyuki, "Fortunate Son: A One-of-a-Kind Success Story," *Tokyo Business Today,* October 1995, pp. 26+.

Patch, Kimberly, " 'Virtual Shopping' Via CD-ROM," *PC Week,* July 12, 1993, p. 6.

Pollack, Andrew, "A Japanese Gambler Hits the Jackpot with Softbank," *New York Times,* February 19, 1995, sec. 3, p. 10.

Shirouzu, Norihiko, and David P. Hamilton, "Softbank's Buying Spree May Be Hard Act to Follow," *Wall Street Journal,* August 19, 1996, p. B4.

Smith, Dawn, "Demo Disk Double-Take," *Marketing Computers,* October 1993, pp. 18–19.

Spindle, Bill, "Japan's Softbank Hits Some Rough Road," *Wall Street Journal,* October 17, 1997, p. A16.

Strom, Stephanie, ''Its Own Stock Battered, Softbank Abandons Spin-off Plan,'' *New York Times,* August 2, 2000, p. C4.

Sugawara, Sandra, ''Masayoshi Son Was Among the First to Flout Japan's Business Establishment,'' *Washington Post,* May 9, 1999, p. H1.

Tanzer, Andrew, ''Hot Hands,'' *Forbes,* May 11, 1992, p. 182.

Umezawa, Masakuni, ''The New Golden Age of Wireless,'' *Tokyo Business Today,* November 1994, pp. 10–12.

Webber, Alan M., ''Japanese-Style Entrepreneurship: An Interview with Softbank's CEO, Masayoshi Son,'' *Harvard Business Review,* January–February 1992, pp. 93–103.

Weinberg, Neil, ''Overreaction,'' *Forbes,* February 9, 1998, pp. 47–48.

Weinberg, Neil, and Amy Feldman, ''Bubble, Bubble . . . ,'' *Forbes,* March 11, 1996, p. 42.

—April D. Gasbarre
—updated by David E. Salamie

Energy to Serve Your World℠

The Southern Company

270 Peachtree Street, N.W.
Atlanta, Georgia 30303
U.S.A.
Telephone: (404) 506-5000
Fax: (404) 506-0455
Web site: http://www.southernco.com

Public Company
Incorporated: 1947
Employees: 32,949
Sales: $11.59 billion (1999)
Stock Exchanges: New York Pacific Cincinnati Philadelphia Boston Midwest
Ticker Symbol: SO
NAIC: 221111 Hydroelectric Power Generation; 221112 Fossil Fuel Electric Power Generation; 221113 Nuclear Electric Power Generation; 221119 Other Electric Power Generation; 221121 Electric Bulk Power Transmission and Control; 221122 Electric Power Distribution

The Southern Company is a utility holding company whose principal subsidiaries provide power in Alabama, Georgia, Florida, and Mississippi. Nonutility assets include Southern Electric International, which markets technical services, Southern Company Energy Marketing, a joint venture with Vastar, and The Southern Investment Group, which seeks new business opportunities. With the gradual deregulation of the utilities industry in the 1990s, Southern Company expanded its holdings into New England, New York, the Midwest, and California, making it the largest power producer in the country. In addition, Southern now owns power generating operations in Europe, Hong Kong, the Philippines, and South America.

The Early 20th Century: Dams and Mergers

The Southern Company traces its roots to a group of entrepreneurs in Alabama and Georgia. Alabama's early power industry was led by James Mitchell and Thomas Martin. Mitchell worked for the Thomson-Houston Company, a predecessor of General Electric, and later built power plants and railroads in Brazil. After leaving Brazil he met with the United Kingdom's financial community and then came to the southern United States, where he scouted sights for hydroelectric installations. Eventually he decided to build a dam on the Cherokee Bluffs site along Alabama's Tallapoosa River.

Seeking to acquire the necessary land, in November 1911 Mitchell met Thomas Martin of Tyson, Wilson & Martin, a law firm handling the title work for hydroelectric developers along the Tallapoosa. Mitchell's technical expertise and access to U.K. capital meshed with Martin's legal training and local knowledge, and the two decided to join forces.

After the Cherokee Bluffs site became embroiled in a lawsuit brought by the owner of a waterwheel plant nearby, Mitchell and Martin turned to a site on the Coosa River at Gadsden, Alabama. The Gadsden site was owned by William P. Lay who in 1906 had organized the Alabama Power Company to dam the river. Lay had been unable to secure capital and readily agreed to join with Mitchell and Martin on the project.

Others also were planning hydroelectric projects along the Coosa and Tallapoosa Rivers. To prevent ruinous competition, Mitchell and 14 investor groups joined in the Alabama Traction, Light and Power Company, Ltd., a holding company organized in Canada to attract U.K. investment. Through Alabama Traction, Light and Power Mitchell raised British capital for Lay's dam. Built by engineer Eugene Adams Yates, Lay Dam was completed in 1914.

At this time Alabama Traction, Light and Power also was acquiring small hydroelectric power companies already in existence. During 1912 and 1913 it bought a 10,000-kilowatt steam electric plant in Gadsden, Alabama, and a 2,000-kilowatt hydroelectric plant at Jackson Shoals, Alabama. By 1913 the company was supplying electricity to Talladega and Gadsden.

Alabama Power Company, the operating subsidiary of Alabama Traction, Light and Power, expanded rapidly, but World War I depleted British capital and left Alabama Power overextended. Unable to meet his obligations Mitchell went to

Company Perspectives:

OUR BUSINESS IS ENERGY. We supply it. To millions of people. To large energy users in regions with significant growth. In the Southeast. In California. In New England. And in other targeted areas throughout the United States. In China and the Philippines. In Germany and other European Union countries. And in South America and the Caribbean.

We're big. Nearly 50,000 megawatts big. That's among the biggest. We generate more electricity than anyone else in the United States.

We know what we're doing. That's clear in our growth. And in our success as one of the world's largest suppliers of energy. We are among the best in reliability, customer satisfaction and costs. And in making electricity cleaner.

We're successful. Our strategy is working. Our growth is exceeding our goals. We're doing what we said we would do.

the United Kingdom and convinced bondholders to defer interest payments and authorize the sale of new bonds and preferred stock.

James Mitchell died in 1920 and was replaced as president by his lawyer partner Tom Martin. Martin helped Alabama Power grow by buying up small electric systems, sponsoring industrial development, and pushing rural electrification. He remained a force in the southern power industry through the 1950s.

Georgia's first hydroelectric project was built by S. Morgan Smith. In the 1870s Smith had invented a water turbine that won wide acceptance in Pennsylvania grist mills. Later he adapted his turbine to hydroelectric purposes and built a facility for clients at Appleton, Wisconsin. Around 1900 he began looking for a major city where he could build his own facility. Eventually he organized the Atlanta Water & Electric Power Company and dammed up the Chattahoochee River 17 miles north of Atlanta.

Smith died in 1903, so his sons Elmer and Fahs finished the dam, ran the S. Morgan Smith Company, and took over the Atlanta Water & Electric Power Company. They expanded the operation, built new plants, and sold turbines to other power projects, often taking an equity share in the new ventures as payment for their product.

Another person working on hydroelectric power in Georgia was A.J. Warner. Warner and investors formed the North Georgia Electric Company and built a dam, transmission lines, and an office building in the Atlanta area.

Soon after completing the dam the company fell on economic hard times. To strengthen cash flow, Warner worked out a deal with Elmer Smith in which Smith would buy Warner's electricity and sell it in Atlanta through the newly organized Atlanta Power Company. Despite the new business Warner's situation continued to worsen, and in 1910 Fahs Smith bought North Georgia Electric at a foreclosure sale.

Harry Atkinson, a young banker, also was active in the electric power industry in Georgia. In 1883 the Georgia Electric Light Company of Atlanta had received a franchise to supply the city. Georgia Electric Light of Atlanta got off to a poor start and became heavily indebted to the Thomson-Houston Company. In 1891 Atkinson and a group of Boston financiers gained control of the company and reorganized as the Georgia Electric Light Company.

Despite Atkinson's failures in sidelines such as shipping and railroads, Georgia Electric Light grew. With attorney Jack Spalding, Atkinson conducted a series of acquisitions, mergers, and consolidations. In 1912 he gathered a variety of Georgia utilities, including the Smith brothers' North Georgia Electric, into the Georgia Railway and Power Company. Most of the leading lights of the Georgia power industry sat on Georgia Railway and Power's board, and the company was the natural predecessor of Atkinson's Georgia Power Company, which in 1927 consolidated most of the state's remaining electric power companies.

Consolidation in the 1920s and 1930s

Steps toward the union of Alabama and Georgia Power began in 1924 when Tom Martin and Eugene Yates created Southeastern Power & Light Company, a holding company whose purpose was to amalgamate and integrate utilities throughout the state. Southeastern's first acquisition was Alabama Power, then owned by Alabama Traction, Light and Power of Canada. In 1925 Martin began negotiations with Georgia Railway and Power. A union seemed advantageous for both companies. The Georgia company needed new capital and supplementary power for dry seasons when rivers ran low. Southeastern was seeking new markets. In 1926 Southeastern acquired all the common stock of Georgia Railway and Power, which subsequently became Georgia Power Company.

Southeastern also acquired smaller utilities. In 1926 it bought properties in Augusta, Columbus, Macon, and Rome, Georgia, and amalgamated them into Georgia Power. The same year it acquired disparate electric properties in South Carolina, northwest Florida, and eastern Mississippi. The South Carolina properties became the South Carolina Power Company, the Florida operations became the Gulf Power Company, and the Mississippi properties became the Mississippi Power Company.

Martin's general manager, Yates, led the move toward technical interconnection. Southeastern also set up a wholesale power division to help convert factories from steam to electric power. Among early industrial converts were textile mills and coal mines.

The late 1920s saw electrical consolidation on a national scale. In 1929 a New York holding company called Commonwealth & Southern acquired all of Southeastern Power and Light's utilities. Commonwealth & Southern's chairman was a merger and acquisitions man named B.C. Cobb. In addition to the Southeastern properties, Commonwealth & Southern had a variety of Midwestern utilities and one other southern one, the Tennessee Electric Power Company, whose service area was contiguous to Southeastern's.

With the acquisition, Southeastern's president, Tom Martin, became president of Commonwealth & Southern. Cobb and Martin did not get along, nor at least initially did the northern

Key Dates:

1912: Harry Atkinson forms Georgia Railway and Power Company.
1914: Construction of Lay Dam at Gadsden, Alabama, is completed.
1924: Thomas Martin and Eugene Yates create Southeastern Power and Light Company.
1926: Southeastern Power and Light acquires Georgia Railway and Power.
1929: New York holding company Commonwealth and Southern acquires all of Southeastern's utilities.
1947: Securities and Exchange Commission approves the formation of The Southern Company.
1982: Southern Energy is formed.
1998: Southern Energy joins Vastar to form Southern Company Energy Marketing (SCEM).
1999: Environmental Protection Agency files civil action suit against Alabama Power and Georgia Power.
2000: Southern Company participates in Alabama Direct FuelCell Demonstration Project.

and southern subsidiaries of Commonwealth & Southern. Within two years, Martin returned to the presidency of Alabama Power.

In 1932 Cobb retired and was replaced by Wendell Willkie. Willkie had been the company's general counsel and would later run for president of the United States. The Great Depression had caused a drop in industrial production and thus a drop in industrial consumption of electricity. Willkie needed to increase consumption and cut costs. To increase consumption, he pushed the sale of electric appliances. To reduce costs, he made draconian cuts in wages and personnel. Despite his efforts, the company lost money in the mid-1930s.

Willkie also had to face the Tennessee Valley Authority (TVA) and the Public Utility Holding Company Act of 1935, both of which threatened Commonwealth & Southern. In 1933 Congress created the TVA, chartered to develop surplus power from navigation and flood control dams. The TVA competed directly with the southern subsidiaries of Commonwealth & Southern. These subsidiaries and other utilities sued to question the TVA's constitutionality but lost. Commonwealth & Southern sold Tennessee Electric Power to the TVA for $78 million in 1939, and in 1940 it sold sections of Alabama Power, Georgia Power, and Mississippi Power to the authority.

The Public Utility Holding Company Act of 1935 was written in response to the abuses of utility financiers such as Samuel Insull and Howard Hopson. The act permitted only contiguous and integrated systems and thus called for divestiture of some of Commonwealth & Southern's subsidiaries. Court challenges, negotiations, and World War II delayed dissolution until 1947 when the Securities and Exchange Commission (SEC) approved the creation of The Southern Company, comprising Alabama Power, Georgia Power, Mississippi Power, and Gulf Power. The company had to sell South Carolina Power to South Carolina Electric & Gas Company.

Postwar Expansion

The Southern Company's first president was Eugene A. Yates, former general manager of Southeastern Power & Light. Tom Martin, still a power in the organization, backed him.

The Southern Company lacked certain facilities. Among Yates's first acts was the creation of Southern Company Services, which ran power pooling operations, provided engineering for major projects, furnished pension and insurance services, and contributed staff services such as accounting and internal auditing. First owned jointly by the four operating subsidiaries, Southern Company Services became a directly owned subsidiary in 1963. Other housekeeping chores Yates was faced with included the sale of gas and transportation businesses, as required by the SEC.

The postwar years saw an increase in demand for power and a consequent increase in the need for capital. Southern made its first sale of common stock—1.5 million shares—in December 1949.

In 1950 The Southern Company acquired Birmingham Electric Company (BECO), which had long been pursued by Tom Martin. BECO's owner, the Electric Bond & Share Company of New York, put it up for sale in 1950 after the SEC ordered Electric Bond & Share to divest its holdings.

Also in 1950 Yates became chairman of The Southern Company, and Eugene McManus, president of Georgia Power, was promoted to president of the holding company. McManus gained nationwide attention for taking a new, friendlier approach in government-utility relations. He offered to supply municipalities and rural electric cooperatives at cost and he ended opposition to government hydroelectric projects.

In the mid-1950s The Southern Company became involved in a conflict-of-interest controversy. The Eisenhower administration had challenged the industry to provide 600,000 kilowatts for the Atomic Energy Commission's (AEC) southern installation. The Southern Company and Middle South Utilities proposed a plant that would sell electricity to the TVA, which in turn would sell it to the AEC. The Southern Company-Middle South venture won the contract but was dropped after it was discovered that a First Boston Corporation investment banker, working temporarily with the Bureau of the Budget, also had advised the utilities. In the end, the city of Memphis, Tennessee, built a municipal power plant to take up the load.

The late 1950s marked the beginning of a dramatic period of capital construction. In 1956 the company organized Southern Electric Generating Company (SEGCO), as a cooperative venture between Georgia Power and Alabama Power. With no coal deposits of its own, Georgia Power wanted a power plant in Alabama where it could be close to the source of energy and not pay rail costs; Alabama Power was attracted by economies of scale. Built on the Coosa River near Wilsonville, Alabama, and completed in 1962, the plant consisted of four 250,000-kilowatt units as well as two fully mechanized coal mines.

At the same time that SEGCO was gearing up, Tom Martin of Alabama Power was pushing for a series of dams on Alabama's Coosa and Warrior Rivers. The extensive project, which eventually provided 852,525 kilowatts of energy, took ten years and $245 million to build.

In January 1957 McManus left the presidency and was elected vice-chairman. Harllee Branch, president of Georgia Power, became president of The Southern Company. When Yates died in October 1957, McManus became chairman of the board. Branch's tenure was a long and satisfying one. As president and, later, chairman he served until June 1971. In Branch's first year, Georgia Power paid $11 million to acquire Georgia Power and Light, which served 38,000 customers in southern Georgia.

The 1960s were a time of construction, expansion, and profits. Sales, income, and dividends all increased yearly. Between 1960 and 1969 sales rose from $317 million to $666 million, net income went from $46 million to $94 million, and dividends rose from 70 cents to $1.15 per share.

By the late 1960s The Southern Company was showing the fruits of its huge building campaign. In 1969 it had 21 steam-electric plants and 30 hydroelectric power projects. Of the system's capacity, 81 percent came from steam-electric plants and 19 percent from hydroelectric dams. Overall, 31 percent of capacity had been constructed in the previous five years. The late 1960s also marked the beginning of a nuclear construction program.

In 1969 Harllee Branch, who had been president and chairman, retired as president in favor of Alvin W. Vogtle, Jr. The following year Vogtle became chief executive officer in anticipation of Branch's retirement as chairman.

The energy crisis of the early 1970s left The Southern Company virtually unscathed. At that point 84 percent of its electricity was generated by coal-fueled steam-electric plants and only 7.5 percent of the system's energy came from oil or natural gas.

Two concerns the company did have at this point were cleanliness of coal in an increasingly environmentally conscious nation and the availability of capital at a time when the company was spending more than $1 billion annually on construction. In the late 1970s a series of rate disputes between Southern's subsidiary Alabama Power and the Alabama Public Service Commission depressed earnings and caused the subsidiary to leave some jobs vacant and the parent to freeze its dividend payment.

The early 1980s saw a return to growth. In January 1982 The Southern Company formed Southern Electric International Inc. to market The Southern Company's technical expertise to utilities and industrial concerns. Large building programs also were continued. In 1984 The Southern Company announced that it would spend $7.1 billion over three years to complete seven generating plants including two nuclear units at the Vogtle site near Augusta, Georgia.

As the decade came to a close, Southern, like many utilities, found that its nuclear building program was over budget. In 1985 Southern had pledged not to pass through to ratepayers any more than $3.56 billion, which was then its share of the $8.35 billion estimated total cost of the Vogtle plant, which also had several smaller utilities as investors. Southern said any amount above that cap would be charged to its shareholders. When the estimated price of the project increased by $522 million in 1986, Southern posted a charge of $229 million against 1987 earnings. Problems with construction costs and regulators led to a series of disappointing earnings years and stagnant dividends.

In March 1988 The Southern Company acquired Savannah Electric & Power Company of Savannah, Georgia, for approximately 11 million common shares, exchanging 1.05 Southern shares for each Savannah Electric common share, a stock transaction valued at $239.3 million. Later that year the U.S. Attorney General's office in Atlanta began investigating Southern's tax accounting practices for spare parts. In 1989 it also began investigating whether executives at Gulf Power had made illegal political contributions. In 1989 Gulf Power pleaded guilty to conspiring to make political contributions in violation of the Public Utility Holding Company Act and impeding the Internal Revenue Service in its collection of income taxes. In accordance with the plea agreement, Gulf Power paid a fine of $500,000.

The year 1990 brought another disappointment as Georgia regulators refused to allow Southern to charge customers for a portion of its investment in the Vogtle nuclear plant. On a positive note, Southern agreed to sell a unit of Georgia Power's Scherer Plant to two Florida utilities for $810 million and formed Southern Nuclear Operating Company to provide services for nuclear power plants. Also in 1990, the Attorney General's office dropped its investigation of Southern's spare parts accounting practices.

The 1990s: The Global Age of Energy

The Energy Policy Act of 1992 inaugurated the era of deregulation in the utilities industry. By encouraging competition in the nation's regional power markets, the new laws compelled major utilities to expand and diversify to survive. Southern Company responded aggressively to deregulation, both at home and abroad. In 1998 it merged with Houston-based Vastar to form Southern Company Energy Marketing, with the purpose of exploring possible acquisitions in Texas and the Southwest. That same year, Southern purchased generating facilities in New England, New York, and California. While Southern Company's regulated utilities in the Southeast continued to perform well throughout the 1990s, expansion into the unregulated market transformed the company into the nation's largest supplier of electricity by decade's end, when it could claim nearly 50,000 megawatts of power generation.

Southern Company also led the charge into the rapidly growing world energy market. It obtained its first overseas holding with the purchase of a 50 percent stake in Bahamian utility Freeport Power in 1992. This initial expansion was followed in 1994 with acquisitions in Trinidad and Tobago and in 1995 with the purchase of South Western Electricity in Great Britain. In 1996 Southern Company negotiated an agreement with Hong Kong billionaire Gordon Y.S. Wu to take over 80 percent of Consolidated Electric Power Asia (CEPA), gaining complete control of the company the following year. Under Southern's ownership, CEPA's earnings rose from $68 million in 1998 to $175 million in 1999. Sual, a 1,218 megawatt coal-burning generating facility in the Philippines, was up and running by the end of the decade. Southern Company was also the first American utility to break into the German market with its 1997 purchase of a 25 percent share of Bewag. In 1999 Southern established a marketing operation in Amsterdam, with the goal of exploring potential growth areas in central Europe. Southern Company's European earnings reached $170 million by 1999.

The 1990s also saw increased friction between the Environmental Protection Agency and the major utilities. The Clean Air Act Amendments of 1990 imposed stricter standards on the reduction of harmful emissions from generating plants, establishing annual emissions reduction goals and requiring utilities plants to cease making repairs on outdated coal-burning facilities that lacked adequate pollution control equipment. In 1999, the EPA filed a civil action suit against seven major utilities, including Southern Company, for alleged noncompliance with these regulations. The companies also were cited for emitting illegal levels of smog-causing nitrogen oxides and sulfur dioxide. If found guilty of these violations, Southern Company could be required to pay millions of dollars in penalties.

In spite of these allegations, Southern Company had taken measures in the 1990s to establish itself as an industry leader in the reduction of harmful emissions. Over the course of the decade, Southern reduced its nitrogen oxide emissions by more than 20 percent, and its sulfur dioxide emissions by 30 percent, all while increasing production of electricity by 20 percent. The company devoted more than $4 billion over the course of the decade to environmental protection measures, including the country's largest electric vehicle leasing program for its employees. Southern Company also volunteered for the Department of Energy's Climate Challenge Program to reduce Carbon Dioxide. While coal-burning power plants still accounted for 78 percent of Southern's energy production in the year 2000, the company had pledged to reduce that figure to 60 percent by the year 2010, and 45 percent by 2020. In 2000 Southern Company participated in the Alabama Direct Fuel Cell Demonstration Project, an effort to develop cleaner power generation through electrochemical technology.

Much of Southern Company's future success overseas would depend on the stability of the Asian economy. By the year 2000, however, it was clear that the company's assertive business strategies had given it an edge in the competition over international energy markets. While increased investor interest in technology stocks in the late 1990s decreased the market share of the major utilities, Southern Company's continued commitment to aggressive domestic growth throughout the decade helped make it the leading provider of electric power in the United States.

Principal Subsidiaries

Alabama Power Company; Consolidated Electric Power Asia (Hong Kong); Georgia Power Company; Gulf Power Company; Mississippi Power Company; Savannah Electric and Power Company; Southern Energy, Inc.; Southern Company Energy Marketing, L.P. (60%); Southern Company Services, Inc.; Southern Nuclear Operating Company, Inc.; Western Power Distribution (U.K.; 49%).

Principal Competitors

Enron Corp.; Entergy Corporation; Tennessee Valley Authority (TVA).

Further Reading

Burnett, Richard, "Power Player: An Atlanta-Based Utility Giant Prepares for Deregulation and a Move into Florida," *Orlando Sentinel* (Fla.), March 2, 1997, p. H1.

Carter, Janelle, "Clean Air Law Sparks Suits: DOJ Targets Utilities with Coal-Burning Plants," *Associated Press,* November 3, 1999.

Crist, James F., *They Electrified the South,* Atlanta, Ga.: The Southern Company, 1981.

Quinn, Matthew C., "Southern Wins Race to Asia: Acquisition Will Turn It into World's Largest Independent Power Company," *Atlanta Journal and the Atlanta Constitution* (Ga.), October 10, 1996, p. F01.

—Jordan Wankoff
—updated by Stephen Meyer

Taylor Woodrow plc

4 Dunraven Street
London W1Y 3FG
United Kingdom
Telephone: (020) 7629 1201
Fax: (020) 7493 1066
Web site: http://www.taywood.co.uk

Public Company
Incorporated: 1921
Employees: 7,963
Sales: £1.5 billion (US$2.43 billion) (1999)
Stock Exchanges: London
Ticker Symbol: TWOD
NAIC: 233210 Single Family Housing Construction; 233220 Multifamily Housing Construction; 233110 Land Subdivision and Land Development; 531120 Lessors of Nonresidential Buildings (Except Miniwarehouses)

Taylor Woodrow plc is a major U.K.-based home builder and property developer and lessor. The company's home building activities take place on an international basis through the development of single-family housing developments, apartment and condominium complexes, and golf course communities in the United Kingdom, the United States, Canada, Spain, and Australia. On the property development side, Taylor Woodrow builds, manages, and leases office buildings, office and industrial parks, shopping centers, and high-rise residential complexes in the United Kingdom and Canada. The company also operates a smaller-scale construction business that provides selective construction services to selected clients.

Founding of Company by a Teenager in the 1920s

Frank Taylor, the founder of Taylor Woodrow, was a shopkeeper's son who became a tycoon and a peer of the realm. He was born in Hadfield, near Glossop, Derbyshire, in 1905. His family lived in a small house with the front room converted into a fruit shop; by the age of 11, Frank was operating the business alone.

While Frank was still a teenager the family moved to Blackpool (in northwestern England) and his father set himself up as a fruit wholesaler. Frank learned the business by working for a rival wholesaler. By 1921 his father decided to buy a house, but he was unable to secure a loan. Sixteen-year-old Frank offered the following arrangement: he would put up £30, his father £70, and the bank, with whom Frank had negotiated, a £400 loan. Frank proposed to build two houses with the money, including one for his uncle. In the end, Frank with his family sold the newly completed houses, realizing a handsome profit.

Frank soon began building small developments of 20 to 30 houses. His plan was to make enough money to open a fruit wholesale business in California, but his early successes persuaded him to remain in the construction industry.

After a few years in business, government authorities realized that Frank was still a minor and ruled that his land and property deals were illegal. Frank's uncle Jack agreed to serve as his adult partner, but Jack's sole contribution was the addition of his surname, Woodrow, to the company's title.

In 1930, Frank Taylor moved his business to London where he purchased some marshy land near a proposed factory. After arranging another loan, he installed a pumping station to drain the land and built houses for the new factory's employees. He sold 50 houses in the first week at an average cost of £450 each. The estate, Grange Park, took three years to complete and contained 1,200 homes. By 1934, Taylor Woodrow's profits were £54,000 and the firm was building estates throughout the home counties and southern England.

The company went public the following year with a capitalization of £400,000. Taylor, the managing director, then established a housing and apartment development company on Long Island, New York. Returning to London, Taylor purchased 100 acres of land along the Grand Union Canal and built new company headquarters; the offices were designed so that they could be converted into houses if extra funds were needed.

In 1937 the company entered the construction and civil engineering field through the formation of Taylor Woodrow Construction Limited. Although civilian business for the new

Company Perspectives:

We are an international leader in housing, property and value added construction support.

We are committed to delivering a world class business by providing creative solutions for the built environment.

subsidiary got off to a slow start, Taylor Woodrow received contracts, shortly before World War II, from the war office to build military installations. After war was declared, the company constructed gunnery camps, antitorpedo boat gun emplacements, land and sea defense works, hospitals, factories, caissons, and an aerodrome. When schedules were threatened because most of the workforce had been enlisted, Taylor hired laborers from Ireland, a technically neutral country. With workers and government contracts in plentiful supply, the company expanded dramatically. Among wartime acquisitions were the 1942 purchase of Greenham Plant Hire Co. and other firms involved in the supply of machinery and materials to the construction industry; these acquisitions formed the basis for subsidiaries that later were known as Greenham Trading and Greenham Construction Materials.

Postwar Overseas Expansion

After the war, many buildings had to be replaced and demobilization created a demand for new homes. In concert with other builders, Taylor Woodrow funded the research and design of Arcon, a prefabricated housing system. The Ministry of Works ordered 43,000 of these units.

In spite of the amount of work available in Britain, Taylor Woodrow had grown so large that it needed to expand overseas. In a joint venture with Unilever, the company extended operations into West Africa where it erected Arcon tubular steel frames to which walls of a variety of local materials could be added. In 1947, Taylor Woodrow (East Africa) was formed to build 127 miles of oil pipeline in Tanganyika. For three years, company teams constructed pipeline, erected a sawmill, and built prefabricated houses; but, dissatisfied with the project's central management, Taylor Woodrow withdrew.

The West African, South African, American, and United Kingdom projects were more successful. In Africa, the company built entire towns, from housing to sewers and breweries; in the United States, the firm continued its apartment complexes; in Britain, Taylor Woodrow erected factories and added bridge and tunnel construction and opencast coal mining to its activities. In 1953 the company established Taylor Woodrow (Canada) Ltd. and also purchased a controlling interest in Monarch Mortgage and Investments Ltd., a property development firm that owned land, apartment complexes, stores, and houses in the Toronto area. Monarch also had its own construction company.

Also in the postwar era, Taylor Woodrow built several energy plants in England, including the Battersea Power Station and another near Castle Donington. It completed the world's first full-scale nuclear power station at Calder Hill in 1955. In conjunction with other companies, Taylor Woodrow also built the Hinkley, Sizewell, and Heysham nuclear power stations.

In 1964, having already entered the property investment field in Canada, Taylor Woodrow did the same at home with the formation of Taylor Woodrow Property Company Limited. This firm was charged with purchasing land for development, with the developed property, such as office buildings and industrial parks, to be held in ownership as rental properties.

The company received the prestigious Queen's Award for Industry in 1966 for its development of a new pile driver, the Pilemaster. The firm also designed the first spherical prestressed concrete pressure vessels, initially used for a power station at Wylfa. Among major construction projects undertaken during the 1960s were the Miraflores earth-filled dam in Colombia and the Hong Kong Ocean Terminal, which opened in March 1966. The latter included what at the time was the largest shopping center in Asia.

Steadily Successful in the 1970s and 1980s

The building slump in Britain during the 1970s did not create any serious problems for Taylor Woodrow since it was operating very successfully in developing countries, particularly in the Middle East. In Oman, Taylor Woodrow built the first modern hospital, the first television studio, and Medinat Qaboos, a new township located near Muscat that included more than 1,000 homes. The company also was very active in Dubai. There, Taylor Woodrow was involved in a massive development, a little more than three-quarters of a square mile in area, that included dry docks, ship repair shops, and harbor works. The new docks were opened for business in February 1979 by the queen of England.

Back home, Taylor Woodrow's most prominent endeavor was the beginning of work on a massive redevelopment of London's crumbling Dockland, located near the Tower of London. Called St. Katharine Docks, the massive development was located on 25 acres, ten of which were water, and was envisioned to include a multifunctional array of properties: a major hotel, restaurants, office buildings, residential housing, schools, and recreation facilities, including a yacht club and marina. Although Taylor Woodrow Property was awarded a contract for developing St. Katharine Docks in 1969, the actual construction of what eventually became a world famous redevelopment complex continued, through several phases, into the 21st century.

Profits rose steadily throughout the 1970s, reaching £24 million by 1979. That year, Frank Taylor resigned as managing director and became life president; already knighted, he was elevated to the peerage in 1982 and assumed the title Baron Taylor of Hadfield.

Taylor Woodrow's three-pronged array of operations—property, housing, and construction—held it in good stead through the 1980s as profits peaked at £117 million in 1989. In the area of housing developments, the company was finding particular success in Canada and in Florida and California in the United States. Highlighting the construction sector was Taylor Woodrow's participation in the consortium that began building the Channel Tunnel in 1986. The engineering feat was completed in 1993. In 1988 Taylor Woodrow augmented its prop-

Key Dates:

1921: Frank Taylor builds two houses at the age of 16 and sells them at a profit.
1930: Taylor moves his business to London and begins developing Grange Park, a 1,200-home development.
1935: Taylor Woodrow becomes a public company.
1937: Company enters the construction and civil engineering field through the formation of Taylor Woodrow Construction.
1942: Firms involved in the supply of machinery and materials to the construction industry are acquired; they later form the basis for Greenham Trading and Greenham Construction Materials units.
1953: Taylor Woodrow (Canada) Ltd. is established and a controlling interest in Monarch Mortgage and Investments Ltd. is purchased.
1955: Company completes the world's first full-scale nuclear power station at Calder Hill.
1964: Firm enters the property investment field in the United Kingdom, through the formation of Taylor Woodrow Property Company.
1969: Taylor Woodrow Property is awarded a contract for developing St. Katharine Docks.
1993: A consortium that includes Taylor Woodrow completes construction of the Channel Tunnel.
1999: Company announces that it will focus on housing and property and deemphasize construction.
2000: Company exits from a number of construction activities and sells off Greenham Construction Material and Greenham Trading; Taylor Woodrow acquires the shares of Monarch Development it does not already own.

erty portfolio through the purchase of 1.85 million square feet of commercial space and 58.5 acres of undeveloped land from the Warrington-Runcorn Development Corporation for £77.1 million. As the decade ended, Frank Gibb retired as chairman and chief executive of the company. Peter Drew, who had led the development of St. Katharine Docks, became chairman while Tony Palmer took over as chief executive.

Restructuring in the 1990s

The early 1990s brought a reversal of fortunes stemming from a severe downturn in the construction contracting sector, a deep recession in the U.K. housing market, and a collapse of U.K. commercial property prices. After the company posted losses in 1991, Drew retired as chairman in early 1992. Colin Parsons, who had headed the successful Canadian subsidiary Monarch Development, took over as chairman. Under the leadership of Parsons and Palmer, Taylor Woodrow managed a quick turnaround, returning to profitability in 1992. Substantial restructuring efforts included the merger of the U.K. and international construction divisions and the withdrawal from unprofitable general building work in the United Kingdom. About 2,000 employees were cut from the company payroll. On the strength of a booming North American housing market and an improving U.K. commercial property market, Taylor Woodrow enjoyed steadily rising turnover and profits through the mid-1990s, with sales reaching £1.29 billion (US$2.14 billion) and net income hitting £56.2 million (US$92.7 million) by 1997.

Executive turnover revisited the company in the late 1990s. In early 1997 John Castle became the first chief executive to come from outside the group. He left, however, after just six months because of reported ''incompatibilities.'' Parsons took over on an interim basis, until Keith Egerton was named chief executive in November 1997, having previously headed Taylor Woodrow Property. The following summer Parsons retired from the company board and was replaced as chairman by Robert Hawley, a former chief executive of British Energy plc.

Parsons and Hawley initiated another round of restructuring at the company, having determined that the firm's future lay in housing and property. In 1999 the construction division was downsized into a ''focused provider of value added construction support.'' The construction workforce was reduced by about 250. A further contraction of the construction operations came the following year when the company announced plans to exit from foundation engineering, precast concrete products, and most other civil engineering work. Next, Taylor Woodrow divested Greenham Construction Materials and Greenham Trading. Meantime, in May 2000, the company spent about C$206 million (£88.8 million) to acquire the shares of Monarch Development it did not already own. This move fit in with the company's strategy of building its core housing and property businesses worldwide. The purchase also enabled Taylor Woodrow to consolidate its North American operations into one management structure. Having completed an exit from heavy construction, Taylor Woodrow hoped that its upscale housing developments and its massive property investments, such as the 2000 proposal for a £100 million leisure and residential development in Gateshead called Baltic Quay, would insulate it from any recessions that might arise in the early 21st century.

Principal Subsidiaries

HOUSING: Taylor Woodrow Capital Developments Limited; Taywood Homes Limited; Taylor Woodrow (Australia) Pty. Limited; Taylor Woodrow Holdings Pty. Limited (Australia); Taylor Woodrow Holdings of Canada Limited; Monarch Construction Limited (Canada); Monarch Development Corporation (Canada); Taylor Woodrow Finance (Ireland); Taylor Woodrow Homes, Inc. (U.S.A.); Taylor Woodrow Homes Florida, Inc. (U.S.A.); Taylor Woodrow, Inc. (U.S.A.); Taylor Woodrow Investments, Inc. (U.S.A.); Monarch Holdings (USA), Inc.; Monarch Homes of Florida, Inc. (U.S.A.). PROPERTY DEVELOPMENT AND INVESTMENT: Taylor Woodrow Chippindale Properties Limited; Taylor Woodrow Developments Limited; Taylor Woodrow Property Company Limited; Clipper Investments Limited; Pennant Investments Limited; St. Katharine by the Tower Limited; Monarch Construction Limited (Canada); Monarch Development Corporation (Canada). CONSTRUCTION: Taylor Woodrow Construction Limited; Taylor Woodrow Projects (M) Sdn Bhd (Malaysia).

Principal Competitors

Barratt Developments PLC; Beazer Group plc; The Berkeley Group plc; Bryant Group plc; George Wimpey PLC; John Laing plc; Persimmon plc; Redrow Group plc; Wilson Bowden plc.

Further Reading

Cheeseright, Paul, "Profits Up at Taylor Woodrow," *Financial Times,* March 10, 1989, p. 30.

Dickson, Tim, "Tackling the Decline at Taylor Woodrow," *Financial Times,* March 31, 1992, p. 23.

Jenkins, Alan, *Built on Teamwork,* London: Heinemann, 1980.

——, *On Site, 1921–1971,* London: Heinemann, 1971.

—updated by David E. Salamie

Thomas Nelson, Inc.

501 Nelson Place
Nashville Tennessee 37214-1000
U.S.A.
Telephone: (615) 889-9000
Toll Free: (800) 933-9673
Fax: (615) 889-5225
Web site: http://www.thomasnelson.com

Public Company
Founded: 1798 as Thomas Nelson and Sons
Employees: 850
Sales: $261.8 million (2000)
Stock Exchanges: New York
Ticker Symbol: TNM
NAIC: 51113 Book Publishers; 42212 Stationery and Office Supplies Wholesalers

Thomas Nelson, Inc.—with roots dating to 1798—is the world's largest publisher of Bibles and Bible-related materials. Through its Word Publishing division, it also publishes works by some of the most prominent contemporary Christian writers, including Billy Graham, Dr. James C. Dobson, Max Lucado, Dr. Robert Schuller, Chuck Swindoll, and Barbara Johnson. In addition, it markets a variety of gift and stationery products as well as games, audio- and videotapes, CD-ROMs, and e-books. Lebanese immigrant Sam Moore acquired the venerable Thomas Nelson name in 1969. He and his family still own approximately 25 percent of the company.

Spreading the Good Word, Bible Publishing: 1952–82

Thomas Nelson of Edinburgh, Scotland, founded Thomas Nelson and Sons when he published *The Pilgrim's Progress* in 1798. His son perfected the rotary press in 1850, and in 1854 the firm opened a U.S. office in New York City. In 1885 the company published an English revision of the King James Version of the Bible. In 1901 it published the American Standard Version. With sales of the Bible central to its business, the firm built a Bible bindery in 1946 in Camden, New Jersey. In 1952 Thomas Nelson published a Revised Standard Version of the Bible.

A man important to the future of Thomas Nelson began selling Bibles door-to-door while studying economics at the University of South Carolina in the 1950s. A Christian Lebanese immigrant to the United States, Sam Moore went on to work at Chase Manhattan Bank for a couple of years. However, he left the bank to begin his own Bible-selling company called Royal Publishers, Inc. in Nashville in 1959. He raised capital and used it to buy Bibles and to hire college students, whom he trained in door-to-door selling methods.

Once his firm expanded out of the Nashville area, Moore began publishing Bibles himself. In 1961 he took Royal public. The firm prospered and began to gain attention in the world of religious publishing. In 1969 a major opportunity presented itself when British interdenominational Bible publisher Thomas Nelson and Sons approached him about running its U.S. operations. Instead, Royal Publishing bought them. The $2.6 million purchase price included the Nelson name, its Bible printing plates, and its U.S. distribution network. The firm did not have a printing plant, and Moore continued his practice of subcontracting print jobs.

The purchase of Thomas Nelson and Sons made Moore's firm, now called Thomas Nelson, Inc., the largest Bible-publishing company in the United States. In 1976 the firm published the Bicentennial Almanac, which sold 600,000 copies at $20 each. In 1978 it built a new distribution center in Nashville. In the mid-1970s Moore spent $4 million having 150 scholars revise the Bible. In 1982 this revision project resulted in the New King James Version of the Bible, which sold so well that it made Thomas Nelson the largest Bible-publishing company in the world. Its principal market was a growing network of Christian bookstores throughout the United States.

New Authors

In 1983 the firm won an important new author when Moore persuaded Robert H. Schuller, already known for his books and television preaching, to let Thomas Nelson publish his

Company Perspectives:

We are a diverse team of editors, marketers, sales associates, accountants, designers, and countless other employees, working together to improve the lives of customers. We are developing new media and methods to serve the Christian community in all its diversity. Fulfilling with passion a mission ''to honor God and serve people.''

As we stand on the brink of our third century of service, we rededicate ourselves to following in the footsteps of the godly young bookseller and publisher whose name we proudly bear.

We are Thomas Nelson.

next book, *Tough Times Never Last, but Tough People Do!* Moore shuttled Schuller around on a private jet during a three-week book-signing tour, arranged for publicity in local papers, and helped the book become a bestseller. It eventually sold over 500,000 hardcover copies, many of them out of secular bookstores.

Also in 1983, Thomas Nelson bought a 240,000-square-foot bindery and printing press located near Kansas City, Kansas. Moore felt Thomas Nelson could print its own Bibles and increase its profits. Given its success in religious publishing, the firm decided to diversify into the secular publishing market as well. Nelson paid $2 million for New York publisher Dodd, Mead & Co., which owned the U.S. rights to Agatha Christie's 67 mystery novels and other properties. Both of these acquisitions proved to be mistakes. The U.S. dollar soared in value in 1984 and 1985, making printing inexpensive overseas. Nelson's competitors printed Bibles in Britain and the Far East and inundated the United States with Bibles selling at prices that Thomas Nelson could not match. In addition, the New York publishing business proved very different than publishing in Nashville, and Nelson management soon realized that they did not know how to succeed as a secular New York publisher. The firm lost $5.4 million in 1986 on sales of $72 million, and by then had amassed $40 million in debt.

The firm laid off about half of its workforce of 600. It sold Dodd, Mead and its printing plant and went back to contracting out its printing. The moves saved the company, and by 1988 it was profitable again and looking to diversify. This time, however, it stayed closer to home. The firm realized that the Christian bookstores it sold its Bibles to made about half of their money from selling photo albums, prayer journals, and other gift items, as well as from cassettes of Christian music. Thomas Nelson quickly moved into these markets. Early tapes included Barbra Streisand singing Christmas carols and Johnny Cash reading the Bible. Although Nelson's products were similar to those of its rivals, who had a head start in this market, the firm got its products into stores because of its relationships with the bookstores' buyers—and because it offered greater discounts than its competitors. Gift and music sales only totaled $1.4 million in 1989, but they quickly grew, reaching $8 million in 1990.

Music and Other New Business Opportunities in the 1990s

Thomas Nelson earned $4.3 million in 1990 on sales of $74 million. By 1991 the firm had sold more than 22 million copies of its New King James Version, and had reduced its debt to $12.5 million. In late 1992, Thomas Nelson bought Word, Inc., a gospel music and inspirational book publishing company previously owned by Capital Cities/ABC, for $72 million in cash. The purchase virtually doubled the size of the company. It strengthened Nelson's music business by bringing it several successful singers, including Grammy winner Amy Grant. Nelson's book business benefited from the addition of bestselling authors Billy Graham and Pat Robertson. Just as importantly, Word's distribution complemented Nelson's. Word sold well internationally and had a strong direct marketing presence. The purchase left the firm with only one serious competitor in Christian book publishing, Zondervan Publishing House, owned by Rupert Murdoch's News Corp.

With ''traditional values'' and Christianity increasingly visible and powerful in the United States, Thomas Nelson felt it could now sell large numbers of its products in the mainstream mass market. Nelson had already gotten its King James Bibles into Wal-Mart and Kmart, and, with the acquisition of Word and the growth of Christian music, the firm was now able to place other products in mass market outlets as well. It began by convincing retailers to increase their offering of religious goods, such as Christian-themed children's books and Bibles, during the Christmas season. When these offerings proved successful, the stores gradually added Christian pop music, card games, and calendars. In January 1995, Thomas Nelson began showing a 4.5 minute promotional video in 440 Sam's Club stores. In it, Christian author and preacher Max Lucado advertised ''A Time with God,'' a book, audio, and video package containing Bible verses accompanied by music by Thomas Nelson's music talent. This strategy proved successful; by 1995 Wal-Mart had expanded its Christian product line in 300 of its 2,100 stores.

Despite the pop-styling of most contemporary Christian music and the increased visibility of Christian issues in the United States, few mainstream radio stations would play Christian music. To get around this limit on its exposure, Thomas Nelson decided to build its own broadcast business. In 1994 it bought the Morningstar radio network in Texas, whose 39 stations had already been playing a lot of Christian music. Within a year, Thomas Nelson expanded the network to 105 affiliates and announced plans to enlarge it further. Perhaps aided by this radio exposure, consumer demand for Christian music continued to increase. In the mid-1990s, Blockbuster Entertainment stores doubled the shelf space they devoted to Christian cassettes and compact discs. By 1995, over a quarter of Christian music was sold through secular stores. Thomas Nelson hoped to sell half of its Christian music through secular retailers, though some industry analysts believed the genre would never achieve that kind of widespread popularity.

In 1994 Thomas Nelson bought Pretty Paper Inc. for 115,000 shares of common stock. Pretty Paper, which had sales of $5.6 million in 1993, became a wholly owned subsidiary. The purchase strengthened the company's line of gift items and its gift-item distribution network. Among other products, Pretty

Key Dates:

1798: Thomas Nelson publishes *The Pilgrim's Progress* in Edinburgh, Scotland.
1854: Thomas Nelson opens office in New York City.
1885: Thomas Nelson publishes Revised King James Bible.
1952: Thomas Nelson publishes Revised Standard Version of Bible.
1959: Sam Moore founds Royal Publishers, Inc.
1961: Royal goes public.
1969: Royal Publishers acquires U.S. branch of Thomas Nelson, adopts Thomas Nelson name.
1982: Thomas Nelson publishes New King James Version of Bible.
1992: Thomas Nelson acquires Word, Inc., a gospel music and inspirational book firm, for $72 million.
1994: Company acquires Morningstar radio network and Pretty Paper Inc.
1997: Thomas Nelson exits the music business, selling its Word Entertainment unit to Gaylord Entertainment Company.

offered two collections of gift stationery, ''Out in the Country'' and ''Potting Shed,'' both of which sold strongly. Thomas Nelson also sold gift products based on licensed cartoon characters from Looney Tunes and Paddington Bear.

With revenue moving forward on all fronts, the firm made $11.7 million in 1995 on sales of $265.1 million. That year Nelson and Word published 11 books that made it to the top-20 Christian Booksellers Association Hardbound Bestsellers' List, more than any other publisher. The growth of Christian publishing had created entire new genres, such as the Christian thriller, in which characters underwent personal transformations without the sex and violence found in most mainstream thrillers. In 1995, Word sold hundreds of thousands of copies of such books by Pat Robertson and Charles Colson.

Thomas Nelson founded a new division called Royal Media, which included the Morningstar Radio Network and the Royal Magazine Group. The magazine group published four magazines: *Aspire,* which covered lifestyle issues and celebrities and was sold on newsstands; *A Better Tomorrow,* which was geared toward older readers; *Release,* which covered Christian recording artists and targeted those working in the Christian music industry; and *Release Ink,* which did the same for the Christian book industry. The Morningstar Radio Network had grown to 138 stations in 130 cities. Its digital programming was delivered by satellite 24 hours a day and consisted of two programming formats: adult contemporary Christian music and what the firm called ''High Country.'' Nelson announced that it was considering a move into cable TV as well.

The firm's record and music division continued to expand, reaching sales of $89.7 million in 1995. Thomas Nelson acquired the Maranatha! Music catalog of printed and recorded music products and signed a long-term agreement with Maranatha covering future product development. Maranatha specialized in a sub-genre called ''praise and worship music'' in which Thomas Nelson formerly had a weak presence. Despite its successful diversifications, Thomas Nelson continued to depend on the Bible as the mainstay of the company's offerings; in 1995 Thomas Nelson published more than 1,200 different Bibles and Bible-related products.

Thomas Nelson in the 21st Century

The trend toward political conservatism in the United States was a major factor in Thomas Nelson's continued success through the mid-1990s. Industry-wide revenue on Christian merchandise reached $2.7 billion in 1993, compared to $1 billion in 1980, and analysts at the time were predicting that sales would exceed $8 billion within ten years. The increased role of mass merchants in the sale of Christian-themed books and music also played a significant role in this growth. Chain retailers including Wal-Mart, Kmart, and Walden Books were responsible for 15 percent of Thomas Nelson's total sales by 1995, up from two percent in 1990. By this time over half of Thomas Nelson's revenue came from book sales, while an additional 37 percent was earned in the music division. The company also retained its position as a leading Bible publisher in the 1990s, controlling over 35 percent of the U.S. market.

However, Bible sales had become stagnant by the mid-1990s, showing only three percent growth over the previous decade. Intent on bolstering this traditional mainstay of its business, Thomas Nelson began planning a new edition of its Contemporary English Version of the Bible in 1995. At the same time it started looking for ways to expand its music and gift divisions. Toward this end, in September 1995 the company acquired C.R. Gibson, the stationery and gift company, for $67 million. In April 1996 Thomas Nelson reached an agreement with Huffy Service First to help merchandise the company's new Stepping Stones line of baby products. The company also launched a number of new magazines during the mid-1990s, in an attempt to keep pace with the nation's expanding Christian readership.

Unfortunately, a sluggish retail market reversed the company's fortunes in 1996. Low sales, coupled with a high number of returns, resulted in a loss for the company for fiscal 1996, and the company's stock value dropped 50 percent from its September 1995 high of $26.25. In addition to a weakened retail industry, analysts cited mismanagement of the music club division, along with a glut of new magazine titles, as key factors in Thomas Nelson's losses. To make matters worse, Bible sales dropped 9 percent in 1996, as a glut of new publishers and editions, catering to increasingly specialized readerships, resulted in an oversaturation of the market.

Following a first quarter loss of $1.4 million for fiscal 1997, the company was forced to downsize its operations, selling its Word Entertainment music unit to Gaylord Entertainment in early 1997. The $110 million sale helped ease the financial pressure, and by the following year Thomas Nelson had once again become profitable. Out of the music business, the company began looking for new ways to expand its book and gift divisions. In May 1998 it reached a licensing agreement with Media Arts Group Inc. to help market gift products, and in May

1999 Thomas Nelson Gifts Canada established a distribution partnership with Word Entertainment Canada. With revenues increasing steadily over the latter part of the decade, the company was poised to make a major acquisition, purchasing Nashville-based Routledge Hill Press, publisher of *Life's Little Instruction Book* by H. Jackson Brown, Jr., and *America's Dumbest Criminals*, in December 1999. Keeping pace with the information age, Thomas Nelson also became the first Christian publisher to launch electronic book versions of its titles, releasing 17 of its bestsellers online in October 2000.

Principal Divisions

Thomas Nelson Publishers; Word Publishing; J. Countryman; Caribe Betania Editores; Thomas Nelson Gifts; Tommy Nelson; Nelson Bibles; Nelson Word Direct.

Principal Competitors

Courier Corporation; HarperCollins Publishers Inc. (Zondervan Publishing division); The Reader's Digest Association, Inc.

Further Reading

Caravajal, Doreen, ''The Bible, a Perennial, Runs into Sales Resistance,'' *New York Times*, October 28, 1996.

Chithelen, Ignatius, ''A Brush with the Devil,'' *Forbes,* August 19, 1991, pp. 61–62.

Fiorini, Phillip, ''For Bible Publisher, Sky's the Limit,'' *USA TODAY*, March 7, 1995.

Rotenier, Nancy, ''The Gospel According to Sam Moore,'' *Forbes,* April 12, 1993, pp. 122–23.

Sharpe, Anita, ''Heavenly Niche,'' *Wall Street Journal,* February 6, 1995, pp. A1, A5.

—Scott M. Lewis
—updated by Stephen Meyer

Toyota Motor Corporation

1, Toyota-cho
Toyota City, Aichi 471-8571
Japan
Telephone: (81) 565-28-2121
Fax: (81) 565-23-5800
Web site: http://www.global.toyota.com

Public Company
Incorporated: 1937 as Toyota Motor Co., Ltd.
Employees: 214,631
Sales: $119.66 billion (2000)
Stock Exchanges: Tokyo New York
Ticker Symbol: TM
NAIC: 42111 Automobile and Other Motor Vehicle Wholesalers; 332311 Prefabricated Metal Building and Component Manufacturing; 336111 Automobile Manufacturing; 336112 Light Truck and Utility Vehicle Manufacturing; 33612 Heavy Duty Truck Manufacturing; 336211 Motor Vehicle Body Manufacturing (pt); 336312 Gasoline Engine and Engine Parts Manufacturing; 336322 Other Motor Vehicle Electrical and Electronic Equipment Manufacturing (pt); 33633 Motor Vehicle Steering and Suspension Components (Except Spring) Manufacturing; 33634 Motor Vehicle Brake System Manufacturing (pt); 33635 Motor Vehicle Transmission and Power Train Parts Manufacturing; 336399 All Other Motor Vehicle Parts Manufacturing (pt)

Toyota Motor Corporation was Japan's largest car company and the world's third largest by the year 2000. The company was producing almost five million units annually in the late 1990s and controlled 9.8 percent of the global market for automobiles. Although its profits declined substantially during the global economic downturn of the early 1990s, Toyota responded by cutting costs and moving production to overseas markets. The company represented one of the true success stories in the history of manufacturing, its growth and success reflective of Japan's astonishing resurgence following World War II.

The Emergence of Japanese Automobile Manufacturing in the 1930s and 1940s

In 1933 a Japanese man named Kiichiro Toyoda traveled to the United States, where he visited a number of automobile production plants. Upon his return to Japan, the young man established an automobile division within his father's loom factory and in May 1935 produced his first prototype vehicle. General Motors and Ford already were operating assembly plants in Japan, but U.S. preeminence in the worldwide automotive industry did not deter Toyoda.

Since Japan had very few natural resources, the company had every incentive to develop engines and vehicles that were highly fuel efficient. In 1939, the company established a research center to begin work on battery-powered vehicles. This was followed in 1940 by the establishment of the Toyoda Science Research Center (the nucleus of the Toyota Central Research and Development Laboratories, Inc.) and the Toyoda Works (later Aichi Steel Works, Ltd.). The next year Toyoda Machine Works, Ltd. was founded for the production of both machine tools and auto parts.

As Japan became embroiled in World War II, the procurement of basic materials for automobile manufacturing became more and more difficult. At one point Toyoda was manufacturing trucks with no radiator grills, brakes only on the rear wheels, wooden seats, and a single headlight. Pushing toward the limits of resource conservation as the course of the war began to cripple Japan's economy, the company started piecing together usable parts from wrecked or worn-out trucks in order to build "recycled" vehicles.

When the war ended in August 1945 most of Japan's industrial facilities had been wrecked, and the Toyoda (or Toyota as it became known after the war) production plants had suffered extensively. The company had 3,000 employees but no working facilities, and the economic situation in Japan was chaotic. But the Japanese tradition of dedication and perseverance proved to be Toyota's most powerful tool in the difficult task of reconstruction.

Company Perspectives:

We believe the potential for growth in our industry is extremely promising. Today, only about one-third of the world's population enjoys the benefits of motor transport, while the remaining two-thirds do not have access to the convenience of automotive transport. Huge growth is in store for our industry in the emerging economies. Therefore, tremendous potential exists for quantitative expansion.

In addition, there is also room for qualitative growth, for adding value and improving the quality of the driving experience. Along with continuing initiatives to improve conventional vehicle functions, two major opportunities, already emerging, are intelligent transportation systems, ITS, and in-vehicle mobile terminals. ITS will route traffic more smoothly, reduce the risk of accidents, and make cars more fun to drive. Mobile terminals will bring a major leap forward in the types of information drivers and passengers can access on the road.

In view of this growth potential, we will continue to place emphasis on maintaining our position as a leading automobile manufacturer.

Postwar Challenges and Innovations: The Birth of the Small Car

Just as the Japanese motor industry as a whole was beginning to recover, there was mounting concern that American and European auto manufacturers would overwhelm the Japanese market with their economic and technical superiority. Japan's automakers knew that they could no longer count on government protection in the form of high import duties or other barriers as they had before the war.

Since American manufacturers were concentrating their efforts on medium-sized and larger cars, Toyota's executives thought that by focusing on small cars the company could avoid a head-on market confrontation. Kiichiro Toyoda likened the postwar situation in Japan to that in England. ''The British motorcar industry,'' he said, ''also faces many difficulties, but its fate will be largely determined by how strongly American automakers feel they should concentrate on small cars.'' It was January 1947 when Toyota engineers completed their first prototype for a small car: its chassis was of the backbone type (never used before in Japan), its front suspension relied primarily on coil springs, and its maximum speed was 54 miles per hour. After two years of difficulties the company seemed headed for success.

This was not to be accomplished as easily as expected, however. Two years later, in 1949, Toyota suffered its first and only serious conflict between labor and management. Nearly four years had passed since the end of the war, but Japan's economy was still in poor shape: goods and materials of all kinds were in short supply, inflation was rampant, and people in the cities were forced to trade their clothing and home furnishings for rice or potatoes to survive. That year the Japanese government took measures to control runaway inflation in ways that severely reduced consumer purchasing power and worsened the already severely depressed domestic automotive market. Japanese auto manufacturers found themselves unable to raise the funds needed to support their recovery efforts, for the new governmental policy had discontinued all financing from city banks and the Reconstruction Finance Corporation.

Under these conditions the company's financial situation deteriorated rapidly. In some months, for example, the company produced vehicles worth a total of ¥350 million while income from sales reached only ¥250 million. In the absence of credit sources to bridge the imbalance, Toyota soon was facing a severe liquidity crisis. In large part because of wartime regulations and controls, Toyota had come to place strong emphasis on the production end of the business, so that in the early postwar years not enough attention had been paid to the proper balance between production and sales. The Japanese economy at that time was suffering from a severe depression, and because the Toyota dealers were unable to sell cars in sufficient quantities, these dealers had no choice but to pay Toyota in long-term promissory notes as inventories kept accumulating.

Finally, Toyota was unable to meet its regular payroll. Delayed payments were followed by actual salary reductions and then by plans for large-scale layoffs—until April 1949, when the Toyota Labor Union went on strike. Negotiations between labor and management dragged on with the union leaders bitterly opposed to any layoffs. As a result, Toyota was compelled to reduce both production and overhead. Workers staged demonstrations to press their demands, and all the while Toyota kept falling further into debt, until the company finally found itself on the verge of bankruptcy.

Production dropped to 992 vehicles in March 1949, to 619 in April, and to 304 in May. Crucial restructuring efforts included a proposal to incorporate Toyota's sales division as a separate company, leading eventually to the formation of Toyota Motor Sales Company Ltd. in April 1950. Toyota Motor Sales Company handled all domestic and worldwide marketing of Toyota's automotive products until July 1982, when it merged with Toyota Motor Company.

In the meantime, discussions between labor and management finally focused on whether to admit failure, declare bankruptcy, and dissolve the company, or to agree on the dismissal of some employees and embark upon a rebuilding program. In the end management and labor agreed to reduce the total workforce from 8,000 to 6,000 employees, primarily by asking for voluntary resignations. At the management level, President Kiichiro Toyoda and all of his executive staff resigned. Kiichiro, Toyota's founder and a pioneer of the Japanese automotive industry, died less than two years later.

Not long after the strike was settled in 1950, two of the company's new executives, Eiji Toyoda (now chairman of Toyota Motor Corporation) and Shoichi Saito (later chairman of Toyota Motor Company), visited the United States. Seeking new ideas for Toyota's anticipated growth, they toured Ford Motor Company's factories and observed the latest automobile production technology. One especially useful idea they brought home from their visit to Ford resulted in Toyota's suggestion system, in which every employee was encouraged to make suggestions for improvements of any kind. On their return to Japan, however, the two men inaugurated an even more vital policy that remained in

Key Dates:

1918: Sakichi Toyoda establishes Toyota Spinning & Weaving Co., Ltd.
1933: Automobile Department is created within Toyoda Automatic Loom Works.
1935: First Model A1 passenger car prototype is completed.
1937: Toyota Motor Co., Ltd. is formed.
1950: Toyota Motor Sales Co., Ltd. is established.
1956: Toyota creates the Toyopet dealer network.
1957: Toyota Motor Sales, U.S.A., Inc. is formed.
1962: Toyota Motor Thailand Co., Ltd. begins operations.
1982: Toyota Motor Company and Toyota Motor Sales merge to form Toyota Motor Corporation.
1995: Hiroshi Okuda becomes company president.
1997: The Prius, Toyota's first ''eco-car,'' is launched.
1998: Toyota acquires majority share in Daihatsu Motor Co., Ltd.

force at Toyota through the 1990s: the continuing commitment to invest in only the most modern production facilities as the key to advances in productivity and quality. Toyota moved quickly and aggressively in the 1950s, making capital investments in new equipment for all of the company's production facilities. Not surprisingly, the company began to benefit from the increased efficiency almost immediately.

Along with improvements in its production facilities, Toyota also worked to develop a more comprehensive line of vehicles to contribute toward the growing motorization of Japanese society. During 1951, for example, Toyota introduced the first four-wheel-drive Land Cruiser. Moreover, as the domestic demand for taxis rapidly increased, production of passenger cars also rose quickly, from 50 units per month to 250 units per month by 1953.

In production control, Toyota introduced the ''Kanban'' (or ''synchronized delivery'') system during 1954. The idea was derived from the supermarket system, where ''consumers'' (those in the later production stages) took ''products'' (parts) from the stock shelves, and the ''storekeepers'' (those in the earlier production stages) replenished the stock to the degree that it was depleted. The Kanban system became the basis for Toyota's entire production system.

By the early 1950s, just as Toyota had anticipated, the Japanese market was crowded with vehicles from the United States and Europe. It soon became apparent that to be competitive at home and abroad, Toyota would not only have to make additional investments in manufacturing facilities and equipment, but also undertake a major new research and development effort. This was the reasoning behind Toyota's decision in 1958 to build a full-scale research center for the development of new automobiles (which also was to become Japan's first factory devoted entirely to passenger-car production). Toyota also began to offer a more complete line of products. Beginning with the Crown model, introduced in 1955, Toyota quickly expanded its passenger-car line to include the 1,000-cubic-centimeter Corona, then added the Toyo-Ace (Japan's first cab-over truck) and a large-sized diesel truck.

Throughout these years Toyota also was working hard on another important, if less conventional, approach to adapting itself to the rapid motorization of Japan, brought about by a remarkable increase in national income. When, for example, Toyota Motor Sales was capitalized at ¥1 billion, 40 percent of that amount (¥400 million) was immediately invested to establish an automobile driving school in an effort to help citizens acquire driver's licenses. Through this and similar efforts, Toyota made a major contribution to Japan's growing motorization in the years following 1965, a trend that was to lead to a mass domestic market for automobiles.

In 1955, ten years after its defeat in World War II, Japan became a member of the General Agreement on Tariffs and Trade (GATT); but automobiles remained one of Japan's least competitive industries in the international arena. Toyota, foreseeing the coming age of large-scale international trade and capital liberalization in Japan, decided to focus on lowering its production costs and developing even more sophisticated cars, while at the same time attempting to achieve the highest possible level of quality in production. This was a joint effort conducted with Toyota's many independent parts suppliers and one that proved so successful that ten years later, in 1965, Toyota was awarded the coveted Deming Prize for its quality-control achievements. That was also the year that the Japanese government liberalized imports of foreign passenger cars. Now Toyota was ready to compete with its overseas competitors—both in price and quality.

In subsequent years Japan's gross national product expanded rapidly, contributing to the impressive growth in auto sales to the Japanese public. The Toyota Corolla, which went on sale in 1966, quickly became Japan's most popular family car and led the market for autos of its compact size. Toyota continued to make major investments in new plants and equipment to prepare for what it believed would be a higher market demand. In 1971 the government removed controls on capital investment. In the wake of this move, several Japanese automakers formed joint ventures or affiliations with U.S. automakers.

Two years later, the 1973 Middle East War erupted and the world's economy was shaken by the first international oil crisis. Japan, wholly dependent upon imports for its oil supply, was especially affected. The rate of inflation increased and demand for automobiles fell drastically. Yet, in the face of the overall pessimism that gripped the industry and the nation, Toyota's chairman Eiji Toyoda proposed a highly aggressive corporate strategy. His conviction was that the automobile, far from being a ''luxury,'' had become and would remain a necessity for people at all levels of society. As a result, Toyota decided to move forward by expanding the company's operations.

The 1973 oil crisis and its aftermath were valuable lessons for Toyota. The crisis demonstrated the necessity for a flexible production system that could easily be adapted to changes in consumer preferences. For example, Toyota did away with facilities designed exclusively for the production of specific models and shifted instead to general-purpose facilities that could be operated according to changes in market demand for the company's various models.

Environmental Awareness in the 1970s

In December 1970 the U.S. Congress passed the Muskie Act, which set limits on automobile engine emissions. In the United States the enforcement of this law was eventually postponed, but in Japan even stricter laws were promulgated during the same time with no postponement of enforcement deadlines. When the Muskie Act was first proposed, automakers all over the world were opposed to it. They argued that it would actually prohibit the use of all internal combustion engines currently used, and they requested that the enforcement of the law be postponed until new technology, able to meet the law's requirements, could be developed.

Notwithstanding these developments, Toyota moved forward on its own to develop a new generation of cleaner and more fuel-efficient engines. After studying all the feasible alternatives—including catalytic systems, rarefied combustion, rotary engines, gas turbine and battery-powered cars—Toyota settled on the catalytic converter as the most flexible and most promising and succeeded in producing automobiles that conformed to the world's toughest emissions-control standards. (Meanwhile, imported cars were given a three-year grace period to conform to Japan's strict emissions-control standards.)

International Growth in the 1980s

In 1980 Japan's aggregate automobile production was actually better than that of the United States. In the same year, Toyota ranked second only to General Motors in total number of cars produced. Although Toyota made efforts over the years to improve the international cooperation between automakers, in such ways as procuring parts and materials from overseas manufacturers, Japan's successes in the world auto market nonetheless resulted in the Japanese automobile industry becoming a target of criticism.

Shoichiro Toyoda, president of Toyota during the middle and late 1980s, possessed a solid understanding of American culture. Toyoda reportedly believed that Toyota's future success depended in part on the way it handled public relations with the United States, a nation that he perceived to be extremely bitter about losing trade battles with Japanese industry. By means of intense advertising and controlled public relations under Toyoda's direction, Toyota tried to elevate the principle of free competition in the minds of the American people. At the same time, Toyoda carefully committed his company to greater international cooperation in both technological and managerial areas.

In 1984, for example, Toyota entered into a joint manufacturing venture with American giant General Motors called New United Motor Manufacturing, Inc. (NUMMI). This state-of-the-art facility allowed Toyota to begin production in the United States cautiously at a time of increasing protectionism, as well as learn about American labor practices. At the same time, it provided General Motors with insight into Japanese production methods and management styles. The plant was slated to build up to 50,000 vehicles a year. In the fall of 1985, moreover, Toyota announced that it would build an $800,000 production facility near Lexington, Kentucky. The plant, which was expected to begin assembling 200,000 cars per year by 1988, created approximately 3,000 jobs.

By the end of the 1980s, Toyota's position as a powerful, exceptionally well-run car company was nearly unassailable. After a decade of prodigious growth, the company stood atop the Japanese automobile industry and ranked number three worldwide, a position it had held since 1978 and strengthened in the ensuing years. By the beginning of the 1990s, Toyota commanded an overwhelming 43 percent of the Japanese car market, and in the United States it sold, for the first time, more than one million cars and trucks. Aside from these two mainstay markets, Toyota was solidifying its global operations, particularly in Southeast Asia, and carving new markets in Latin America, where the burgeoning demand for cars promised much growth. Toyota also spearheaded the Japanese automobile industry's foray into the luxury car market, leading the way with its Lexus LS400 luxury sedan, which by the mid-1990s was outselling market veterans BMW, Mercedes-Benz, and Jaguar.

Despite these favorable developments, all of which pointed toward further growth and underscored the car company's vitality, Toyota's management continued to strive for improvements. In 1990, for example, when the company was posting enviable financial results and its manufacturing processes provided a model for other companies to follow, Shoichiro Toyoda eliminated two layers of middle management, effected substantial cuts in the company's executive staff, and reorganized Toyota's product development. With the highest operating margin of any carmaker in the world, Toyota was a formidable competitor.

Toyota had little control over external forces, however, and as the 1990s progressed, a global economic downturn brought the prolific growth of Japan's largest car manufacturer to a halt. The recession stifled economic growth throughout the world, while a rising yen made Japanese products relatively more expensive in overseas markets. Toyota's profits declined for four consecutive years between 1991 and 1994, falling to the lowest level in more than a decade. Midway through Toyota's net income slide, the company gained new leadership when Totsuro Toyoda succeeded his brother in September 1992. Under Totsuro Toyoda's stewardship, a cost-cutting program was enacted that reduced expense account budgets 50 percent, limited travel expenditures, and eliminated white-collar overtime. Toyoda also continued the trend toward moving production to less expensive overseas markets by ordering the construction or expansion of six assembly plants in Great Britain, Pakistan, Thailand, Turkey, the United States, and Japan.

As Toyota's profit decline continued, however, the mounting losses persuaded Toyoda to intensify his cost-cutting measures. Design changes in the company's vehicles coupled with reductions in manufacturing and distribution costs saved Toyota ¥150 billion in 1993, and another ¥100 billion in savings was expected to be realized in 1994. That same year, the fourth consecutive year of negative net income growth, Toyota recorded ¥125.8 billion in consolidated net income, a little more than a quarter of the total posted in 1990, when the company earned ¥441.3 billion.

"The New Global Business Plan": 1995 and Beyond

When Hiroshi Okuda was promoted to company president in 1995 his chief ambition was to revitalize Toyota's standing in the global marketplace. In June he unveiled Toyota's New Global Business Plan, which placed renewed focus on innovation and international expansion. Okuda's targets were clearly defined: to raise production to six million vehicles a year; to increase Toyota's international market share to 10 percent; and to increase its share of the domestic market to 40 percent. He believed the first two goals would be achieved through the construction of new manufacturing plants in foreign markets, along with an increased emphasis on the "localization" of parts production. The purpose of localization was to reduce the time and expense involved with shipping components across great distances, enabling Toyota to increase its overall automobile production and devote greater resources to research and development. By widening the scope of operations in Toyota's overseas locations, Okuda envisioned a more streamlined, cost-effective manufacturing process. Furthermore, the stimulation of local economies was an effective public relations tool, enhancing the value of the Toyota brand name in foreign markets.

Okuda wasted no time putting his vision into practice. In 1995 Toyota announced its intention to set up a manufacturing operation in Indiana, in the hope of becoming a major participant in North America's highly competitive large truck market. In 1997 the company opened new plants in Canada and India, and in December it announced plans to build a second European plant in Valenciennes, France, to begin production of a new line of cars specifically designed for the European consumer. The year 1997 also saw increased production in Toyota's Thailand operations, with a total output of 240,000 vehicles. In 1998 the company also raised its export levels from the Thailand plants to 20,000 units, with most of the vehicles destined for the Australian and New Zealand markets. That same year, the company opened a new operation in Brazil, and in 1999 it began construction of a transmission production plant in the Walbrzych Special Economic Zone in Poland, which would begin exporting the parts to Toyota's manufacturing centers in France, Turkey, and the United Kingdom by 2002.

One of the most promising automobile markets to open up in the late 1990s was in China. By March 1998 Toyota already had stakes in four Chinese parts manufacturing plants, one of them a wholly owned subsidiary. The company took a more significant step in November 1998, when it established the Sichuan Toyota Motor Co., Ltd., Toyota's first vehicle production plant in China. A joint venture with the Sichuan Station Wagon Factory and Toyota Tsusho Corp., the new plant was scheduled to begin manufacturing coaster-class buses by 2001.

Okuda also assumed an aggressive approach to Toyota's role in the domestic market. In late 1996 he made drastic cuts to Toyota's vehicle prices in Japan, a move that incensed the competition. In August 1998 Toyota extended its hold over the domestic market with the purchase of a majority stake in Daihatsu. The company also implemented a number of environmental initiatives during this period, both at home and abroad. In July 1999 it inaugurated an initiative that aimed to eliminate all landfill waste by 2003, and in 2000 it introduced stricter environmental regulations in its U.S. manufacturing plants, which actually went beyond the current EPA standards.

One of the most radical innovations to arise from Okuda's revolution was the Prius, Toyota's first hybrid car. Launched in October 1997, the Prius combined a highly efficient gas engine with a self-regenerating electric motor, reducing carbon dioxide emissions by half. Although initial estimates showed that production would have to surpass 200,000 vehicles a year for the Prius to turn a profit, by March 1998 demand was already surpassing supply, and the future of the eco-car on the domestic market looked promising. Prius finally hit the U.S. and European markets in late 2000, amid increased fuel prices and mounting concerns over global warming.

Although a weakened euro caused Toyota to suffer losses in Europe toward the end of the 1990s, the new operation in France, scheduled to begin production in 2001 at a rate of 150,000 vehicles a year, was expected to reverse this trend. The company also experienced strong sales in the United States and Japan during this time, and in 2000 Toyota's total worldwide production exceeded five million vehicles for the first time ever.

Principal Subsidiaries

Toyota Motor Sales, U.S.A., Inc.; Toyota Motor Thailand Company Limited; Daihatsu Motor Co., Ltd. (51%); New United Motor Manufacturing, Inc. (U.S.A.; 50%); Toyota Motor Credit Corporation (U.S.A.); Hino Motors, Ltd.

Principal Competitors

Ford Motor Company; General Motors Corporation; Honda Motor Co., Ltd.

Further Reading

Butler, Steven, "Toyota Puts It on the Line: Stung by Recession, the Auto Maker Embarks on Deep Cost Cutting," *U.S. News and World Report,* August 23, 1993, p. 47.

Higgins, James V., "Toyota Is Ready to Lead a New Japanese Wave," *Detroit News* (Mich.), August 30, 1995, p. B1.

Kamiya, Shotaro, with Thomas Elliott, *My Life with Toyota,* Toyota City: Toyota Motor Sales Co., 1978.

Pollack, Andrew, "Toyota Profit Declines for a Fourth Year; Loss Had Been Feared; Future Called Brighter," *New York Times,* August 26, 1994, p. C2.

Spindle, William, "Toyota Retooled: Profits and Global Output Are Up, and New Models Are on the Way," *Business Week,* April 4, 1994, p. 54.

Sugawara, Sandra, "Toyota Steps on the Gas: A Leaner, Tougher Company Gambles on Global Leadership with New 'Eco-Car,' " *Washington Post,* December 14, 1997, p. H1.

Taylor, Alex, "A Back-to-Basics U-Turn in Japan," *New York Times,* August 26, 1994, p. C1.

Williams, G. Chambers, III, "Electric/Gasoline Car Is on the Road to U.S.," *Fort Worth Star-Telegram* (Tex.), January 2, 1999, p. 1.

—Jeffrey L. Covell
—updated by Stephen Meyer

Ube Industries, Ltd.

12-32, Nishi-Honmachi, 1-chome
Ube, Yamaguchi 755-8633
Japan
Telephone: (0836) 31-1122
Fax: (0836) 21-2252
Web site: http://www.ube-ind.co.jp

Public Company
Incorporated: 1942
Employees: 4,785
Sales: ¥514.78 billion (US$4.86 billion) (2000)
Stock Exchanges: Tokyo Osaka Nagoya
NAIC: 325211 Plastics Material and Resin Manufacturing; 325212 Synthetic Rubber Manufacturing; 325222 Noncellulosic Organic Fiber Manufacturing; 325411 Medicinal and Botanical Manufacturing; 325412 Pharmaceutical Preparation Manufacturing; 327310 Cement Manufacturing; 327320 Ready-Mix Concrete Manufacturing; 332312 Fabricated Structural Metal Manufacturing; 333220 Plastics and Rubber Industry Machinery Manufacturing; 333511 Industrial Mold Manufacturing; 333513 Machine Tool (Metal Forming Types) Manufacturing; 336399 All Other Motor Vehicle Parts Manufacturing; 421520 Coal and Other Mineral and Ore Wholesalers; 541710 Research and Development in the Physical, Engineering, and Life Sciences

Ube Industries, Ltd. is one of the largest chemical companies in Japan. Once devoted primarily to the mining and industrial applications of coal, Ube converted itself into a diversified chemical concern in the 1960s, as coal's importance as a raw material declined. Just over 40 percent of net sales are derived from the company's chemicals and plastics group, which manufactures petrochemicals, nylon resins, pharmaceuticals, industrial chemicals, and other products. Ube is the world's third largest producer of caprolactam, a raw material used in the manufacture of nylon. A little more than 38 percent of sales come from the construction materials group, whose products include cement, ready-mixed concrete, and building materials. Research and development, marketing, and distribution activities connected with cement are handled through joint ventures with Mitsubishi Materials Corporation. Key products for the machinery and metal products group, which generates 16 percent of net sales, include die-casting machines, injection-molding machines, and aluminum wheels for automobiles. Ube continues to be involved in the coal industry, with additional activities in dielectric ceramics, electric power, and medical equipment.

Origins in Coal and Related Industries

Ube Industries was formed in 1942 when four companies located in and around Ube City in Yamaguchi Prefecture merged under the impetus of a government order. The oldest of these was the Okinoyama Coal Mine, which was founded in 1897 by Yusaku Watanabe. Watanabe was noteworthy for his belief, particularly farsighted at the time, that coal was not just a fuel but a potential source of industrial raw materials. He also believed that the health of his company was inextricably linked to the overall development of the Ube area, a philosophy that the company adopted for the long term.

The second of the four companies to be founded was the Ube Shinkawa Iron Works, which was established in 1914 and manufactured coal-mining machinery. Ube Cement Production, Ltd., which used as its primary raw material limestone found near the Okinoyama mine, was founded in 1921. Lastly, Ube Nitrogen Industry, Ltd. was established in 1933, when the Japanese nitrogen fixation industry was still in its infancy. The company started out synthesizing ammonia and sulfuric acid from coal, and in 1936 it began producing nitric acid and distilling gasoline from the low-temperature carbonization of coal.

The four companies were clearly interdependent. In 1944 Ube Industries added to its position as one of Japan's leading coal-mining concerns by acquiring Nippon Kogyo's anthracite

Company Perspectives:

UBE's corporate vision for the 21st century can be summarized in the phrase: "Working with science to create a future that supports comfortable lifestyles." This represents UBE's commitment to creating a comfortable society in the future, by pursuing diversified businesses and producing a wide variety of products. UBE ensures that its activities serve the Earth's environment; for industrial and social infrastructure; for health and life; for the automobile society; for daily living; and for the local community. And all and each of those activities are converged on the ultimate target: "creating better lifestyles."

mine at Sanyo. The branch of the company's operations to be most affected by World War II was the nitrogen fixation plant. Ammonia, a major ingredient in both fertilizers and explosives, was a strategically important chemical, and the Ube plant was the nation's fourth largest producer. Demand for its products ran high during the course of the war, and its importance made it a likely target for U.S. bombers. Just after midnight on July 2, 1945, 100 B-29s from the 20th Air Force destroyed the Ube nitrogen plant almost completely; it was not rebuilt until after the war.

Rebuilding after Japan's defeat was not the only challenge that faced Ube Industries in the postwar years. The coal-mining industry began dying a slow death as crude oil gradually replaced coal as the nation's principal source of energy and the chemical industry's main raw material. For Ube, still heavily reliant on its coal operations, it meant diversification or dying along with the coal trade. In 1955 the company bolstered its cement production capacity by opening the Isa Cement Factory at Mine City, just outside Ube City. It also branched into producing urea and caprolactam, raw materials from which nylon is made, at a new plant in Ube City.

Diversifying in the 1960s and 1970s

In 1958 coal still accounted for 30 percent of the company's sales. In 1960, however, Ube began in earnest a 15-year process of phasing coal out of its operations, when it started using oil as its main source of raw materials. From there, it entered the burgeoning field of petrochemicals, beginning with plastics. In 1964 the company began producing low-density polyethylene at a new plant in Chiba Prefecture. It also added to its cement business by opening a factory at Kanda in Fukuoka Prefecture. Over the next ten years, it would invest roughly ¥200 billion in weaning itself from its traditional reliance on coal. Half of this sum would go into chemical and petrochemical production, and one-third into cement production.

This process of diversification and divestiture came to a head in the late 1960s and early 1970s. In 1967 Ube marked the 70th birthday of the Okinoyama mine by closing it down, cutting its oldest link with its corporate past. It also built a new chemical plant at Sakai in Osaka Prefecture. The next year, it added a polypropylene plant to the Sakai facility. In 1970 the company shut down its last remaining major source of coal, the Sanyo anthracite mine. In 1971 it added a synthetic-rubber factory to its plant at Chiba. Ube's sales composition figures for 1972 show that coal had disappeared entirely as a source of revenue; cement accounted for 46 percent of sales, fertilizers and caprolactam for 29.9 percent, machinery for 12.1 percent, and petrochemical products for 12 percent. The company had become Japan's fourth largest chemical concern, and its caprolactam output accounted for ten percent of the world's supply.

Ube reshaped itself into a fully diversified chemical concern during these years, and it did so organically, suggesting that it had not forgotten the interdependence that had made the merger between its four original companies so logical. Not only did it own the means of manufacture; it controlled the raw materials and the means of transportation and distribution as well. For instance, its cement plant at Isa took limestone mined from a nearby quarry, processed it, and sent the clinkers to Ube City, where they were turned into cement using kilns made by Ube's machinery subsidiary. The finished product was then distributed using Ube's own cement carriers, which were constructed by other Ube subsidiaries, Kasado Dockyard and Ube Dockyard, the carriers using engines made by Ube Machinery Works. Similar interrelationships marked the company's other manufacturing operations as well. In 1974 Ube built a 30-kilometer industrial highway between Mine City and Ube City. The company added a 1,020-meter bridge spanning Ube City's harbor to the highway in 1982. The Ube-Mine Industrial Highway cost ¥15 billion, but increased the efficiency of Ube's transportation operations.

Whatever pride Ube took in its busy journey from coal mine to conglomerate must have been short-lived, however. The oil price shocks of the 1970s plunged the Japanese chemical industry into a severe depression. Its primary raw material, once cheap and plentiful, now became scarce and prohibitively expensive. Ube fared no better than its competitors; sales fell off and profits dropped by nearly half just between 1974 and 1975. Coal once again became a viable raw material for Japanese chemical companies, and Ube was at least fortunate in that it had not disposed of all of its coal storage and processing facilities. It did not reopen the Okinoyama and Sanyo mines, however. Instead, it began importing coal from Australia and, later, the United States.

A slump in business naturally resulted in an industry-wide excess in production capacity. Despite general overcapacity in cement production, Ube acquired a 46 percent interest, later expanding it to a majority stake, in Okinawa-based Ryukyu Cement from Kaiser Cement and Gypsum, a subsidiary of U.S. conglomerate Kaiser Industries, for $7 million in 1976. In 1979 the Ministry of International Trade and Industry ordered Ube to shut down its urea plant at Ube City because of industry-wide overcapacity for that chemical.

Business from overseas helped fill the breach caused by difficulties at home. In 1978 Ube established a sales subsidiary in the United States, Ube America. It also received an order to build an ammonia plant in China, which it filled as a partner in a joint venture with the chemical company Marubeni. The plant used a heavy residual gasification process invented by Texaco.

Key Dates:

1897: Okinoyama Coal Mine is established.
1914: Ube Shinkawa Iron Works is founded.
1923: Ube Cement Production, Ltd. is formed.
1933: Ube Nitrogen Industry, Ltd. begins operations.
1942: The above four companies are amalgamated to form Ube Industries, Ltd.
1944: Company purchases an anthracite mine at Sanyo.
1955: Company branches into the production of urea and caprolactam, raw materials for nylon.
1964: Production of polyethylene begins.
1967: The Okinoyama mine is closed.
1970: The Sanyo anthracite mine is shut down.
1984: Company enters the pharmaceutical field through venture with Takeda Chemical.
1986: Ube and Marubeni form ATC, a joint venture to produce polypropylene compounds for bumpers and dashboards.
1989: Ube establishes A-Mold Corp. as a U.S. manufacturer of aluminum wheels.
1992: Ube Machinery, Inc. is formed in the United States to manufacture injection-molding and die-casting machines.
1993: Joint venture Thai Caprolactam Public Co., Ltd. is established.
1994: Company gains full control of Productos Quimicos del Mediterraneo, S.A., a Spanish producer of caprolactam.
1995: Ube and Mitsui Petrochemical Industries merge their polypropylene businesses into a joint venture, Grand Polymer Co., Ltd.
1997: Ube and Mitsubishi Materials form a joint venture, Ube-Mitsubishi Cement, to merge the cement-related marketing and logistics operations of the two firms.

In 1982, Ube received a contract to build a cement plant in the United Arab Emirates for a local company, Ajman Cement.

Joint Ventures During the 1980s and 1990s

The 1980s and 1990s were marked by a number of joint ventures for Ube, many of them with foreign companies and involving some kind of technical cooperation—technological innovation was an area in which the Japanese chemical industry had traditionally been weak. Its alliances with domestic rivals were often formed for the sake of diversification, a useful strategy in an industry just pulling out of a severe slump. In 1984 Ube joined with Marubeni and Massachusetts-based Wormser and formed Ube Wormser to produce and market Wormser fluidized-bed combusters in Japan. It also formed UM Technopolymer with Mitsubishi Petroleum, and Chiba Riverment and Cement with Kawasaki Steel. Ube entered the pharmaceutical field that year when it joined with Takeda Chemical to produce and market vitamin supplements.

In 1986 Ube and Marubeni tried to tap into the U.S. automotive plastics market when they set up ATC Inc., a joint venture to produce polypropylene compounds for bumpers and dashboards. ATC was 60 percent-owned by Ube, and based in Nashville, Tennessee, near the proposed site for General Motors' Saturn subcompact car plant. Ube made a significant move toward future diversification that year when it built a new research facility in Ube City, to develop new biotechnical, electronic-material, pharmaceutical, agricultural-chemical, biochemical, and ceramics technologies. A further move into the supply of automotive parts came in 1989 when Ube established A-Mold Corp. as a manufacturer of aluminum wheels.

More joint ventures marked the end of the decade, as well. In 1989 Ube and Finnish chemical company Kemira formed Kemira-Ube to manufacture hydrogen peroxide at an Ube plant in Ube City using a process developed by Kemira. Ube was to use half of the hydrogen peroxide to be produced to manufacture nylon and other products, and the other half was targeted for sale on the Japanese market. Ube also entered into a joint venture with the Japanese drug company Sankyo, in which drugs developed by Ube would be taken to clinical trials, produced, and then marketed by Sankyo. In 1990 Ube and Swiss chemical company Ems-Chemi formed UBE-EMS Yugen Kaisha to manufacture lactam, a base material used in certain kinds of plastics. Ube also entered into a joint venture with Rexene, a Dallas-based chemical company, to manufacture amorphous poly-alpha-olefin—a substance used in adhesives—in Japan using Rexene technology, and market it in the Far East and Pacific Rim.

After expanding rapidly in the heady bubble years of the late 1980s, Ube was saddled with overcapacity problems in many of its operations in the 1990s. The pronounced economic difficulties that beset Japan throughout the decade led Ube to restructure its operations, including a workforce reduction of 950 announced in March 1994; to pursue additional joint ventures; and to increasingly move production out of Japan to counter the effects of the strong yen. In the latter area, key moves were made in the production of caprolactam. In August 1993 Ube entered into an agreement with Thai Petrochemical Industry Co. and Marubeni to form Thai Caprolactam Public Co., Ltd., a joint venture charged with building a caprolactam plant in Thailand; production at the new plant began in the spring of 1997. In December 1993 Ube took a 30 percent stake in Productos Quimicos del Mediterraneo, S.A. (PQM), a producer of caprolactam based in Spain that was a subsidiary of British Petroleum Co. Ube gained full control of PQM during 1994. Around this same time, Ube, Thai Petrochemical, and Nissho Iwai Corporation formed a joint venture called Ube Nylon (Thailand) Ltd. to build a plant in Thailand for the production of nylon 6, a widely used nylon compound synthesized from caprolactam. These moves gave Ube a three-pronged global structure for the production of caprolactam and nylon, with factories in Japan, Europe, and Southeast Asia. They also solidified the company's position as the world's third largest producer of caprolactam. A third area of overseas expansion for Ube's chemical operations was that of synthetic rubber, and in December 1995 Ube once again joined with Thai Petrochemical and other partners to form a manufacturing joint venture; this latest start-up was called Thai Synthetic Rubber Co., Ltd., and it began full-scale production of synthetic rubber for marketing throughout Southeast Asia in January 1998.

Ube also created ventures to manufacture products in China. In early 1995 the company joined with Sumitomo Corporation and firms in Hong Kong and China to establish a joint venture concentrating on the manufacture of cement. With the steady rise of the yen, Ube reached a decision to stop making magnesium in Japan, and in 1995 formed Nanjing Ube Magnesium Co., Ltd. to begin producing magnesium in China. This was yet another joint venture, with the partners being China-based Nanjing Huahong Magnesium Industry Corp. and two Japanese trading firms, Kanematsu Corporation and Mitsui & Co., Ltd. Another development in 1995 was the merger of the polypropylene businesses of Ube and Mitsui Petrochemical Industries into a joint venture called Grand Polymer Co., Ltd., which began its existence as the number three producer of polypropylene in Japan.

Meantime, the company set up another manufacturing subsidiary in the United States in 1992. Based in Ann Arbor, Michigan, Ube Machinery, Inc. began operations during the 1996 fiscal year. The firm specialized in the assembly of injection-molding and die-casting machines and became an integral part of Ube's machinery and engineering unit. In the pharmaceutical area, Ube completed construction of its first bulk pharmaceutical production plant, which was located in Ube City, in 1995. Initially, the company focused on making pharmaceuticals for major drugmakers on a contract basis. By early 1997, however, Ube had plans to begin making an antiallergenic agent and an antihypertensive agent of its own devising. Needing additional production capacity, it completed construction of a second pharmaceutical plant at Ube City in early 1998. In June 1997 Ube became the first corporation in Japan to offer a stock option plan to its management and senior employees.

The cement industry in Japan remained particularly sluggish in the late 1990s. Although Ube had been able to improve the performance of its cement operations through restructuring and facility upgrades, the outlook still appeared bleak. In December 1997, therefore, Ube entered into an agreement with Mitsubishi Materials Corporation to form a joint venture, Ube-Mitsubishi Cement, to merge the cement-related marketing and logistics operations of the two firms. The new venture started off as the number two cement company in Japan in terms of market share.

Throughout its busy years of dealmaking in the 1990s, Ube was struggling to contain the inflated load of debt it had been saddled with since the collapse of the 1980s economic bubble. Compounding the company's difficulties was the fall of the Japanese economy into recession in the late 1990s coupled with the financial crisis that erupted in east Asia, with the downturn in Thailand of particular concern given Ube's significant investments there. Ube's difficulties were plainly evident in the results for the 1999 fiscal year, when net sales fell 14 percent and net income dropped 33 percent. To attempt to reverse its fortunes, Ube launched 21-UBE, a three-year management plan, in April 1999. The company's operations were organized into five operating segments: Chemicals & Plastics, Construction Materials, Machinery & Metal Products, Coal, and Corporate Research & Development (one year later the Coal segment was combined with some other operations to form a new segment called Energy & Environment). Each of these segments were to be run in a quasi-independent manner, with each responsible for achieving clear-cut goals and objectives. Within these segments, those operations that were unable to achieve or sustain a sufficient level of profitability were to be slated for divestment or closure. Previously, Ube had tolerated lossmaking operations under an emphasis on strength through diversification. Among the financial goals of 21-UBE was the reducing of interest-bearing debt from ¥609.1 billion to less than ¥500 billion and an increase in pretax profit from ¥2.97 billion to ¥33 billion.

While adopting this more modern, bottom-line oriented management style, Ube Industries also needed to determine whether, in order to achieve its goals, it could continue its policy of promoting the economic and social well-being of its home base. Ube had a longstanding commitment to a cluster of small cities on the southern tip of Honshu, which gave it a distinctly provincial air. Fully 70 percent of its employees and 80 percent of its capital spending were concentrated in this area. True to founder Yusaku Watanabe's vision of the inseparable relationship between the company and the community that surrounds it, Ube Industries had over the course of its history embarked on long-term development projects for the Ube area that included building new schools, hospitals, and high-tech research facilities, and expanding Yamaguchi-Ube Airport to accommodate direct flights to major domestic and international destinations. Ube subsidiaries had also operated golf courses, hotels, and a television station in the area. This commitment to a local community, whatever its overall merits, ran counter to the globalization philosophy that dominated early 21st-century business culture; as Sojiro Kita noted in *Nikkei Weekly,* Ube would perhaps be forced to sever its deep geographical bonds in the name of shareholder value enhancement, the dominant business tenet at the turn of the millennium.

Principal Subsidiaries

Ube Film, Ltd.; Ube Cycon, Ltd.; ATC Inc. (U.S.A.); Meiwa Plastic Industries, Ltd.; Ube Ammonia Industry, Ltd.; Ems-Ube, Ltd.; Productos Quimicos del Mediterraneo, S.A. (Spain); Ube Agri-Materials, Ltd.; Ube America Inc. (U.S.A.); Ube Electronics, Ltd.; Ube Shipping & Logistics, Ltd.; Kanto Ube Concrete Co., Ltd.; Daikyo Kigyo Co., Ltd.; Hagimori Industries, Ltd.; Ube Board Co., Ltd.; Ube Material Industries, Ltd.; Yamaishi Metal Co., Ltd.; Ube Machinery Corporation, Ltd.; Ube Techno Eng. Co., Ltd.; Ube Steel Co., Ltd.; Shin Kasado Dockyard Co., Ltd.; Fukushima, Ltd.; A-Mold Corp. (U.S.A.); A-Mold Sales International L.L.C. (U.S.A.); Ube Machinery Inc. (U.S.A.); U-Mold Co., Ltd.; Ube C&A Co., Ltd.; Ube Realty & Development Co., Ltd.; Ube International (U.S.A.), Inc.; Ube Corp. USA Inc.

Principal Operating Units

Chemicals & Plastics; Construction Materials; Machinery & Metal Products; Energy & Environment; Corporate Research & Development.

Principal Competitors

Asahi Chemical Industry Co., Ltd.; Husky Injection Molding Systems Ltd.; Kuraray Co., Ltd.; Mitsubishi Chemical Corporation; Mitsui Chemicals, Inc.; Nagase & Company, Ltd.; Sumitomo Chemical Company, Limited; Sumitomo Osaka Cement Co., Ltd.; Taiheiyo Cement Corporation.

Further Reading

''Company of the Month: Ube Industries, Ltd.,'' *Oriental Economist,* September 1973.

''Company of the Month: Ube Industries, Ltd.,'' *Oriental Economist,* November 1974.

Kita, Sojiro, ''Altering Focus from Diversity to Value,'' *Nikkei Weekly,* June 12, 2000, p. 14.

Murano, Takanao, and Hiroshi Hakamata, ''Cement Heavyweights Forming New Bonds: Latest Venture Joins Mitsubishi, Ube in No. Two Company,'' *Nikkei Weekly,* December 29, 1997, p. 8.

''Ube Industries, Ltd.,'' *Oriental Economist,* September 1982.

—Douglas Sun
—updated by David E. Salamie

UUNET

22001 Loudoun County Parkway
Ashburn, Virginia 20147
U.S.A.
Telephone: (703) 206-5600
Toll Free: (800) 488-6384
Fax: (703) 206-5601
Web site: http://www.uu.net

Wholly Owned Subsidiary of WorldCom Inc.
Incorporated: 1987 as UUNet Technologies Inc.
Employees: 7,000
Sales: $3.5 billion (1999)
NAIC: 514191 Online Information Services

Founded in 1987, UUNET is recognized not only as the first commercial Internet service provider (ISP), but it is also the world's leading Internet carrier. The company provides a comprehensive range of Internet services to more than 70,000 business customers worldwide, including Internet access, web hosting, remote access, virtual private networking (VPN), managed security, and multicast services, among others. It owns and operates one of the most widely deployed IP networks in the world, with more than 2,500 POPs (points of presence, or primary Internet connections) providing Internet connectivity in more than 100 countries. UUNET's parent company, WorldCom Inc., is one of the world's largest telecommunications companies.

A Pioneering Internet Service Provider: 1987–94

UUNet Technologies Inc. (UUNET) was founded in 1987, and in 1988 it sold the first commercial connection to the Internet. For the next several years UUNET would be a pioneering Internet service provider (ISP) and offer innovative services. In 1992 UUNET developed the first commercial application—layer firewall services for IP (internet protocol) networks. In 1993 UUNET began offering T-1 connections to the Internet. In 1994 UUNET designed and installed the first virtual private network (VPN) service, the Virtual Private Data Network (VPDN) product family. The company also began offering web hosting services by joining forces with electronic publisher Interse Corporation to provide companies with a turnkey solution for putting their businesses on the Internet. The service included a T-1 connection, offered at two different speeds, from UUNET, and Interse's World Wide Web server. Interse would also build the company's home page using HTML (hypertext markup language) and design an interactive, multi-tiered, and graphical presentation. In 1994 John Sidgmore became UUNET's CEO and president. He was formerly president and CEO of CSC Intelicom.

Providing Internet Access and Other Services to Corporate Customers: 1995–97

In early 1995 Microsoft Corporation was busy preparing its Microsoft Network (MSN), which would be offered with the release of Windows 95. UUNET provided Microsoft with a dedicated TCP/IP network that would allow MSN users to have dial-up access to both MSN and the Internet. UUNET would provide MSN users with a variety of high-speed service options, including ISDN and 28.8K bps (bits per second) modem access. Microsoft planned to offer full access to the Internet by the end of 1995. At the time UUNET had 25 points of presence and planned to have 100 connections in place within a few months. According to one analyst, UUNET was a good choice for Microsoft, because it had more expertise than telephone carriers about Internet protocol network management. Microsoft also took a minority interest in UUNET, with the funds to be used to expand UUNET's 25-city dial-up network, and also gained a seat on UUNET's board of directors.

UUNET completed its initial public offering (IPO) in May 1995. The stock was priced at $14 a share and raised more than $50 million. Two other ISPs—Netcom On-Line Communications Services Inc. and Performance Systems International (PSINet)—also had their IPOs that month, and all were well received by Wall Street. By July UUNET's stock was trading in the $45 range. Although none of the companies had shown a profit, investors were betting on their potential for explosive revenue growth in the coming year. At the time of UUNET's IPO, Microsoft owned about 15 percent of the company. As it

Company Perspectives:

UUNET's objective is to be the leading supplier to businesses and professionals of complete communications solutions using Internet-related technologies. To reach that goal, UUNET is constantly expanding its high-performance network infrastructure, developing and enlarging its suite of value-added products and services, building and leveraging relationships with strategic partners, and expanding operations worldwide.

turned out, UUNET's revenue for 1995 was $94 million, compared to $12.4 million in the previous year.

While UUNET had a smaller network than competitor Netcom On-Line Communications Services Inc., UUNET was focused on the corporate market, while Netcom was targeting the consumer market. The corporate market for Internet access was expected to grow more quickly, with the consumer market set to explode toward the end of the 1990s. The corporate market gave UUNET higher revenue streams, bigger margins, and a more reliable customer base. UUNET also offered premium services, such as network management and security, for which it could charge more. UUNET's corporate clients included America Online and AT&T as well as Microsoft, for whom it built Internet backbones. UUNET was not ignoring the consumer market, though, and most ISPs were pursuing a hybrid business model for both the corporate and consumer markets. UUNET was in the process of building out its network and adding points of presence.

In May 1995 UUNET introduced its Internet firewall and an encryption system for sending private data over public networks. The package included LanGuardian, a hardware-based encryption system, and Gauntlet, an application gateway firewall. It would allow workgroup users to create a virtual private network (VPN) over the Internet, thus facilitating collaborative development.

Later in the year UUNET introduced T-3 and SMDS (Switched Multimegabit Data Services), with pricing for the T-3 service starting at $5,000 per month. T-3 service was initially available in seven U.S. cities. The SMDS option was a public-switched data offering from the regional Bell operating companies (RBOCs), which allowed users to connect to UUNET's Internet backbone for around $1,500 a month.

UUNET's two principal services were leased-line connections for businesses under its AlterNet program and dial-up access through its AlterDial program. AlterDial was expected to have 130 points of presence by the end of 1995.

In November 1995 UUNET and Premenos Corporation entered into an alliance to build a system for electronic data interchange (EDI) over the Internet. EDI was seen to be a key element in business-to-business electronic commerce. Premenos produced a popular EDI software suite that enabled confidentiality, data integrity, user authentication, and built-in security.

In 1996 UUNET began offering more services related to electronic commerce over the Internet. They included end-to-end security, FTP (File Transport Protocol) hosting, dedicated servers that companies could lease for processor-intensive tasks such as graphics applications or web-based compilation, and improved reporting capabilities. By early 1996 UUNET was refocused on the corporate market, letting other ISPs such as America Online and CompuServe concentrate on consumers. With 1995 revenue of $94 million, UUNET was the largest player in the industry.

New Owners for UUNET: 1996

At the end of April 1996 it was announced that MFS Communications Inc. would acquire UUNET for $2 billion in stock. MFS Communications paid a 37 percent premium over market value for UUNET, making 40 of UUNET's 700 employees who owned UUNET stock millionaires. MFS Communications was based in Omaha, Nebraska, and offered local and long distance telephone service in New York and nationwide. It had built fiber-optic cable connections to 7,400 buildings in key financial districts in the United States and Europe. Together, the two companies would be able to offer end-to-end voice, data, and Internet services. Following the announcement UUNET extended its AlterDial service to 92 international cities.

In mid-1996 UUNET picked up GTE as a corporate customer when GTE introduced GTE Internet Solutions, which used UUNET's existing network to offer Internet access service in 250 cities in 46 states. At the time GTE was the largest local telephone service provider in the United States. Its Internet access service would be offered to consumers for $19.95 a month. At the same time UUNET formed an alliance with USConnect Inc. that would combine UUNET's national network with USConnect's systems integration expertise. The partnership would provide businesses with a single source for integrating their LANs with the Internet.

Later in 1996 UUNET became the first major commercial ISP to offer web hosting services for Windows NT 4.0. UUNET's hosting service included a personalized domain name for the customer, servers housed at UUNET with guaranteed power backup, constant web site monitoring, daily tape backups, monthly server traffic reports, and third-party audit services. UUNET priced the service at $3,000 a month, with a $5,000 start-up fee for the dedicated server. If clients required assistance with web site design, UUNET referred them to third-party content developers who were part of the Team UUNET program. UUNET first offered web hosting services in 1994 using the Unix platform and claimed to have more than 800 customers.

Web hosting was one service that ISPs could offer to distinguish themselves from their numerous competitors. In late 1996 UUNET began offering another service, ExtraLink, a package of extranet services that would enable companies to share information with customers and suppliers over a virtual private network (VPN). A related service, called ExtraLink Remote Access, allowed remote workers to access the corporate network without a large bank of modems.

Key Dates:

1987: Company is founded as UUNet Technologies Inc.
1988: UUNET sells the first commercial connection to the Internet.
1992: UUNET develops the first commercial application—layer firewall services for IP (internet protocol) networks.
1993: UUNET begins offering T-1 connections to the Internet.
1994: UUNET begins offering web hosting and virtual private network (VPN) services.
1995: UUNET completes its initial public offering (IPO).
1996: UUNET is acquired by telecommunications service provider MFS Communications Company, Inc., which is bought by WorldCom, Inc. later in the year.
1998: UUNET becomes the first Internet service provider (ISP) to offer commercial DSL (direct subscriber line) services.

For 1996 UUNET's revenues were estimated to be $216 million. Before the end of the year WorldCom Inc. acquired MFS Communications for approximately $12 billion in stock. Sidgmore remained CEO of UUNET and became vice-chairman and chief operating officer (COO) of WorldCom.

Prospering Under WorldCom: 1997–2000

With WorldCom as its parent company, UUNET was able to offer a pioneering service guarantee in early 1997. The company guaranteed uptime of more than 99.9 percent for intranet and business-to-business services. The guarantee applied to sites that were connected to one another by the UUNET network. It covered more than 300 locations in the United States and 500 in Europe and Asia.

UUNET also received $300 million from WorldCom to upgrade its Internet backbone in the United States and quadruple its capacity. Company officials estimated that the load on UUNET's backbone doubled every quarter, which meant the company would need to increase its capacity tenfold within a year and a hundredfold within two years. UUNET expected to have to spend about $300 million a year on network expansion for the next four or five years. UUNET's main ISP customers at the time were Microsoft, GTE, and EarthLink, with America Online also leasing a small portion of UUNET's network.

At the Internet World show in March 1997, UUNET announced it would offer global web hosting facilities to help multinational companies overcome the problem of narrow bandwidth between continents. UUNET planned to provide local web hosting through peer web service providers in Canada, Germany, the United Kingdom, and Taiwan. UUNET also announced the availability of IDSL technology, a combination of ISDN and DSL developed with MFS Communications and Ascend Communications Inc., that would provide small and medium-size businesses with direct connections to the Internet at a low cost. IDSL, which offered high-speed Internet access over standard phone lines, would first be deployed by the regional Bell operating companies (RBOCs), starting in California.

With the ISP market evolving and businesses demanding better quality and faster throughput, the large Internet backbone providers—including UUNET and Sprint—announced they would no longer carry traffic for mid-size ISPs free of charge. In some cases, the traffic-exchange agreements would be terminated, while in other cases the mid-size ISPs would be charged a fee. Costs were expected to be passed along to the consumer.

To further ensure that its Internet traffic reached its destination, UUNET introduced a Shadow Support Program that provided a secondary T-1 or T-3 line to businesses. Network administrators could then redirect traffic if there was a line outage or other problem, thus avoiding an interruption of service. At the time of the announcement, UUNET had been dealing with a growing number of customer complaints after two UUNET hubs in Los Angeles and Tyson's Corner, Virginia, failed.

In mid-1997 UUNET announced it would begin offering an Internet fax service by the end of the year. Called UUFax, the service was based on technology developed with software maker Open Port Technology Inc. and remote access hardware provider Ascend Communications Inc. Instead of sending faxes as analog traffic over telephone lines, UUFax would turn faxes into IP packets and deliver them via UUNET's global Internet backbone. By sending faxes over the Internet, companies could save the cost of a long-distance call.

In September 1997 UUNET acquired NLnet, the leading ISP in the Netherlands. NLnet's 45 points of presence there provided comprehensive local-dial access throughout the country. At the time the Netherlands was one of the top five countries for Internet usage on a per capita basis. With the acquisition UUNET had nearly 1,000 points of presence in the United States, Canada, Europe, and the Asia-Pacific region.

Also in September UUNET introduced multicast services for mass Internet broadcasting. Called UUCasting, the service allowed content providers to send only one stream of audio, video, or text data to UUNET, which would then deliver the content to large numbers of users. The service utilized 60 Cisco System routers that were dispersed throughout the UUNET network. UUCasting was the first commercially available multicasting service to give Internet content providers a way to reach hundreds of thousands of users without having to invest in their own T-3 lines. UUCasting became available in December 1997.

Later in the year UUNET became the first ISP to offer OC-3 service. The program, called OCDirect, was introduced at the 1997 Networld+Interop trade show. It would provide users with 155 mbps (megabytes per second) direct access to UUNET's Internet backbone, the fastest speed currently available and faster than anything being offered by other ISPs. OCDirect was only offered in the San Francisco Bay area, Washington, D.C., and New York City, mainly to ISP resellers, large web-hosting services, and large corporate users.

In November 1997 UUNET and BellSouth Corporation began offering 56K-bps dial-up services to provide faster access to the Internet and corporate LANs. UUNET's 56K bps access was immediately available through 415 points of presence, to be expanded to 500 POPs by the end of 1997. AT&T was the first to provide 56K bps service, starting in October 1997 and available in 11 U.S. cities. BellSouth's 56K bps service would be offered in four Southern cities. Following the adoption of the V.90 standard for 56K bps modems in February 1998, UUNET upgraded 300,000 of its dial-up access ports in more than 700 U.S. points of presence by mid-1998, with an additional 200,000 upgrades planned by the end of the year.

Following the acquisition by WorldCom of three other ISPs—ANS Communications Inc., CompuServe Network Services, and GridNet International—WorldCom announced it would consolidate them with UUNET and reorganize into two main divisions: UUNET WorldCom, which would emphasize packaged services, and WorldCom Advanced Networks, which would provide Web hosting, intranet and extranet, VPN, and data security services. UUNET Worldcom would be headed by Mark Spagnolo, UUNET's president and COO, while WorldCom Advanced Networks would be headed by former CompuServe Network Services president Peter Van Kamp. Both would report to John Sidgmore, WorldCom's vice-chairman and UUNET's CEO. The reorganization was necessitated in part by the need to stop providing overlapping Internet services from the different ISPs WorldCom had acquired, and also in part by its pending acquisition of MCI. Following the reorganization UUNET WorldCom would have about 3,000 employees and WorldCom Advanced Networks about 1,700 employees.

In August 1998 UUNET became the first ISP to offer a service-level agreement (SLA) that guaranteed customers 100 percent end-to-end network availability. To qualify companies had to have at least one-year contracts for frame relay, dedicated 56K-bps, T-1, T-3, or OC-3 Internet access services. UUNET also provided other SLAs covering problems with installation and transmission delays.

In November 1998 WorldCom closed its acquisition of MCI Corporation for $40 billion. John Sidgmore became vice-chairman of MCI WorldCom and remained CEO of UUNET.

In 1999 UUNET increased the capacity of its national network backbone from OC-12 to OC-48, quadrupling network speed from 644Mb/s to 2.4Gb/s. With more than 60,000 miles of OC-48 in its backbone, UUNET was attempting to stay ahead of increasing demand for Internet bandwidth. The company also upgraded its UUCast service by increasing the number of supporting router ports from 500,000 to one million and by offering transmission speeds up to OC-3 (155 mbps).

In 1999 UUNET began offering a managed global VPN service called UUsecure. The service, which would be available in 14 countries by the end of 1999, included network design, construction, management, and monitoring. Managed global VPN services represented a newly developing market, but competing services were already being offered by companies such as IBM, AT&T Corp., GTE Corporation, and Equant Network Services.

A mid-1999 survey of ISPs by *Data Communications* magazine revealed that UUNET was the largest, serving 178 of the 500 largest domains. UUNET was also ranked the best overall ISP and received the magazine's User's Choice Award. In 1999 the company expanded its DSL service, which it introduced in 1998, to include more than 1,000 points of presence in 850 cities. It also reasserted its presence in the web hosting market, expanding its hosting centers in San Jose, California, and Washington, D.C., and announcing plans to build seven others, which would give UUNET a total of 15 UUhost Data Centers. The overall web hosting market was projected to grow from $4.4 billion in 1999 to $14.4 billion in 2003, according to The Yankee Group.

For 2000 UUNET planned to upgrade its U.S. network to OC-192 (ten gbps, or gigabytes per second) using Juniper Networks Inc.'s new M160 routers. The company also began targeting small businesses, offering them a turnkey set of Internet services. Dubbed Business Essentials and Business Essentials Plus, the packages included the services and equipment most often needed by small businesses to use the Internet.

Later in 2000 UUNET established a Latin American regional headquarters in Sao Paulo, Brazil. UUNET's parent company, WorldCom, held a controlling interest in Embratel, Brazil's former state-owned long distance company. UUNET planned to take advantage of Embratel's infrastructure and presence in Brazil to enter the ISP market there, then expand throughout Latin America. At the time UUNET operated in 114 countries and served more than 70,000 businesses around the world.

For the future it was likely that UUNET would continue to expand globally and develop new services to maintain its leadership position as an ISP. For example, the company announced it would offer a bundled group of services called Access Choice, which was aimed at remote users and offered them wired as well as wireless access. While some new services would be developed internally, others might come from acquisitions made by UUNET's parent company, WorldCom. For example, WorldCom acquired Intermedia for $6 billion in 2000, which added Intermedia's web hosting subsidiary Digex to its group of companies. Tapping the resources of its parent company, UUNET was also well-positioned to build out its network, to increase the number of data centers it operated for web hosting and co-location services, and generally to invest $2–$3 million a day in its infrastructure.

Principal Competitors

PSINet Inc.; AT&T Corp.; Cable & Wireless plc; Exodus Communications Inc.; Qwest Communications International Inc.; GTE Corporation; Global Crossing Ltd.

Further Reading

Aragon, Lawrence, "On the Road," *PC Week,* March 6, 1995, p. A1.

Balderston, Jim, "GTE, UUNET Merge Internet Services," *InfoWorld,* July 15, 1996, p. 12.

Bucholtz, Chris, "Manageable Multicasting," *Telephony,* September 29, 1997, p. 8.

Davey, Tom, "ISPs Are Feeling the Heat," *PC Week,* December 9, 1996, p. 125.

——, "Shakeout Online," *InformationWeek,* June 30, 1997, p. 69.

Davis, Jessica, "UUNET Raises the Bar on Net Access Speeds," *InfoWorld,* October 13, 1997, p. 9.

"Dial W for Windfall," *Time,* September 9, 1996, p. 51.

Dunlap, Charlotte, ''Internet Service Providers,'' *Computer Reseller News,* June 3, 1996, p. 118.
——, ''UUNET Adds Win NT Web Hosting,'' *Computer Reseller News,* September 16, 1996, p. 65.
''EDI Software Made Simpler,'' *Industry Week,* December 4, 1995, p. 55.
Foley, Mary Jo, ''Microsoft Adds Internet Components to MSN,'' *PC Week,* January 16, 1995, p. 10.
Frazier, Lynne, ''GTE Unveils Internet Access Service via UUNET,'' *Knight-Ridder/Tribune Business News,* July 15, 1996.
Garner, Rochelle, ''Run for the Roses,'' *PC Week,* May 15, 1995, p. A1.
Gerwig, Kate, ''UUNET Extends Global Reach,'' *InternetWeek,* September 8, 1997, p. 16.
——, ''UUNET Plants Multicast Flag,'' *InternetWeek,* September 29, 1997, p. 18.
——, ''UUNET Widens Pipe, Offers Customers Tiered Access,'' *InternetWeek,* October 20, 1997, p. 54.
——, ''WorldCom's Plans to Integrate Face Users' Scrutiny,'' *InternetWeek,* May 11, 1998, p. 9.
Gunn, Angela, ''AlterDial,'' *PC Magazine,* October 10, 1995, p. 140.
Gupta, Udayan, ''Web Wonders Are Wooing Wall Street,'' *InformationWeek,* June 26, 1995, p. 138.
Humphrey, Sara, ''They've Got a Ticket to Ride,'' *PC Week,* October 23, 1995, p. N1.
Johnston, Margaret, ''UUNET Lays out Big Plans for Colocation Services Market,'' *InfoWorld,* November 15, 1999, p. 78C.
Jones, Jennifer, and Cathleen Moore, ''Juniper Router Speeds Traffic Between Hubs,'' *InfoWorld,* April 3, 2000, p. 16.
Kanellos, Michael, ''UUNET, USConnect Forge Net Alliance,'' *Computer Reseller News,* July 15, 1996, p. 45.
Knowles, Anne, ''UUNET Suite Tightens Security,'' *PC Week,* May 29, 1995, p. 14.
Ladley, Eric, and Bruce Sullivan, ''You Two Better Play Together Nicely!,'' *ISP Business News,* September 11, 2000.
LaPolla, Stephanie, ''New UUNET Service Delivers Net Faxing,'' *PC Week,* July 14, 1997, p. 19.
——, ''UUNET and MCI Eye Global Access,'' *PC Week,* March 10, 1997, p. 31.
——, ''UUNET Branches Out,'' *PC Week,* July 7, 1997, p. 10.
——, ''UUNET Investing $300 Million to Upgrade Internet Backbone,'' *PC Week,* March 3, 1997, p. 33.
——, ''UUNET Props up Backbone with New Shadow Support,'' *PC Week,* June 2, 1997, p. 27.
Leon, Mark, ''Cable Company Makes Deal with Big Implications for 'Net,'' *InfoWorld,* May 6, 1996, p. 10.
Mannes, George, ''Omaha's MFS Communications to Buy D.C. Area Internet Firm UUNET Technologies,'' *Knight-Ridder/Tribune Business News,* May 1, 1996.
''The Microsoft Factor,'' *Forbes,* August 14, 1995, p. 182.
Moeller, Michael, ''UUNET Extends AlterDial Internet Access,'' *PC Week,* May 27, 1996, p. 43.
Moltzen, Edward F., ''UUNET Going Public, Expects to Reel in $42 Million,'' *Computer Reseller News,* April 24, 1995, p. 41.
Moozakis, Chuck, ''UUNET Adds Speed, Capacity to Its IP Multicast Service,'' *InternetWeek,* April 19, 1999, p. 23.
Moran, Susan, ''Newsmaker,'' *Internet World,* June 29, 1998, p. 8.
Niccolai, James, ''MFS and UUNET Announce xDSL Services,'' *InfoWorld,* December 16, 1996, p. 12.
Perez, Juan Carlos, ''UUNET Eyes Latin American Market,'' *InfoWorld,* September 18, 2000, p. 68.
Poole, Jackie, ''Midrange ISP Prices Climb,'' *InfoWorld,* May 5, 1997, p. 10.
''Premenos, UUNET in Internet Alliance, *American Banker,* November 10, 1995, p. 15.
Quinton, Brian, ''UUNET Adds Muscle to Backbone,'' *Telephony,* April 19, 1999.
Rendleman, John, ''ISPs Roll out Audio, Video Hosting,'' *PC Week,* December 15, 1997, p. 10.
——, ''Telecom Providers Move Ahead with 56K,'' *PC Week,* November 24, 1997, p. 125.
——, ''UUNET Has the 'Essentials,' '' *eWeek,* June 5, 2000, p. 30.
——, ''UUNET Renews Hosting Focus with New Centers,'' *PC Week,* August 9, 1999, p. 53.
Rodriguez, Karen, ''UuNet, Interse Introduce Services to Help Companies Gain Internet Presence,'' *InfoWorld,* November 28, 1994, p. 56.
Rodriguez, Karen, and Jason Pontin, ''Microsoft, UuNet Team up to Give Windows 95 Users Internet Access,'' *InfoWorld,* January 16, 1995, p. 6.
Rogers, Amy, ''John Sidgmore,'' *Computer Reseller News,* November 16, 1998, p. 143.
Rooney, Paula, ''UUNET Expands Hosting Services, Adds Security,'' *PC Week,* January 22, 1996, p. 60.
——, ''UUNET, Sidgmore Tie up Business on the Internet,'' *PC Week,* February 26, 1996, p. 43.
Schroeder, Erica, ''MFS-UUNET Merger Talks Bode Well for Online Users,'' *PC Week,* May 6, 1996, p. 116.
Semilof, Margie, ''John Sidgmore,'' *Computer Reseller News,* November 17, 1997, p. 139.
Spangler, Todd, ''Two Executives Get New Roles at Revamped UUNET,'' *InternetWorld,* May 11, 1998, p. 8.
Thyfault, Mary E., ''UUNET Guarantees Total Network Availability,'' *InformationWeek,* August 10, 1998, p. 32.
''UUNET Ahead on DSL,'' *InformationWeek,* July 19, 1999, p. 20.
''UUNET Guarantees Service,'' *Computerworld,* August 10, 1998, p. 12.
''UUNET Plans $1.2 Billion Build-out,'' *ISP Business News,* May 1, 2000.
''UUNET Pumps up Backbone,'' *InternetWeek,* April 3, 2000, p. 10.
''UUNET Rolls out T-3 Internet Connection,'' *PC Week,* September 11, 1995, p. 3.
''UUNET's IPO Millionaires,'' *Forbes,* October 7, 1996, p. S50.
''UUNET Upgrades to 56K Standard,'' *Internet World,* June 29, 1998, p. 32.
Wagner, Mitch, ''UUNET Readies ISDN Hybrid,'' *Computerworld,* March 10, 1997, p. 1.
——, ''UUNET to Offer Uptime Guarantee,'' *Computerworld,* February 3, 1997, p. 2.
Wallace, Bob, ''MCI WorldCom Offers Outsourced Global VPNs,'' *Computerworld,* May 24, 1999, p. 68.
——, ''UUNET's Bundle Offers Wired and Wireless Services,'' *InformationWeek,* October 9, 2000, p. 202.
——, ''UUNET to Build, Expand Data Centers for $100M,'' *Computerworld,* August 9, 1999, p. 14.
Walsh, Jeff, ''ISPs Offer Bevy of Business Network Services,'' *InfoWorld,* December 16, 1996, p. 6.
——, ''UUNET Hosts on Windows NT,'' *InfoWorld,* September 9, 1996, p. 53.
Weil, Nancy, ''Owning the Net,'' *InfoWorld,* March 20, 2000, p. 36.
Williams, David, ''Top 25 ISPs,'' *Data Communications,* June 7, 1999, p. 28.

—David P. Bianco

Value City Department Stores, Inc.

3241 Westerville Road
Columbus, Ohio 43224
U.S.A.
Telephone: (614) 471-4722
Fax: (614) 478-2253
Web site: http://www.valuecity.com

Public Company
Incorporated: 1991
Employees: 15,700
Sales: $1.67 billion (2000)
Stock Exchanges: New York
Ticker Symbol: VCD
NAIC: 44821 Shoe Stores; 44819 Other Clothing Stores

Value City Department Stores, Inc. operates several chains of off-price department stores. Its largest is the 120-unit Value City chain. Value City stores are unique in offering a huge array of discounted goods in a vast space. Stores are typically between 80,000 and 100,000 square feet, about three times larger than most other off-price competitors. Items at Value City retail for at least 30 to 40 percent below regular department store prices. The stores sell men's, women's, and children's apparel, housewares, sporting goods, and other items. Much of the merchandise is purchased directly from manufacturers, and other goods are bought as overstock or from liquidations of other merchants. The stores offer leading brands as well as moderate and budget-priced lines. Value City also runs a chain of discount shoe stores called DSW Shoe Warehouse. Its roughly 60 stores sell brand-name shoes at lesser prices. Value City also runs the Massachusetts-based discount chain Filene's Basement, and the St. Louis-based Grandpa's chain. The company was formerly an operating division of Schottenstein Stores Corporation (SSC), a private firm run by members of the Schottenstein family. Schottenstein Stores was well known as a liquidator, specializing in buying up failing regional department stores. Value City is still led by a member of the Schottenstein family, and family members control about 60 percent of the firm's stock.

Early Years

In 1991 Value City Department Stores was spun off from Schottenstein Stores Corporation (SSC). SSC began as a single store in Columbus, Ohio, opened by Ephraim Schottenstein in 1917. Schottenstein's family emigrated from Lithuania and settled in Columbus in the late 1800s. Ephraim was apparently in the clothing business as early as 1909, and soon after he opened his store, E.L. Schottenstein Department Store. Ephraim Schottenstein had four sons, Saul, Alvin, Leon, and Jerome, and a daughter, Selma. The children all grew up working in the family store. One brother in particular, Jerome, was credited with orchestrating much of the growth of the corporation in later years. By the time Jerome was a teenager, he was taking trips to New York and making buying decisions for the store. Jerome became an executive in Schottenstein Stores in 1946. By the early 1950s, the Schottenstein retail empire encompassed only the original Schottenstein store and several furniture stores. But at that time the company began to get involved in the liquidation business, bidding on the merchandise of failing area stores. From liquidating merchandise, the company moved to acquiring bankrupt businesses. In 1963, Schottenstein Stores acquired a failing store in Dayton, Ohio, called Concord City, and the next year it bought another struggling store, Elyria City, in Elyria, Ohio. Then in 1966 the Schottenstein family acquired a store named Value City, in Independence, Ohio. The family business continued to buy up bankrupt stores, and it gave them all the Value City name. This name conveyed the prime message of the stores, which was to sell at budget prices.

Growth As a Liquidator in the 1970s and 1980s

Jerome Schottenstein became president of Schottenstein Stores Corp. in 1972. He went on to become an almost legendary figure in retailing: he was expert at buying liquidated merchandise, and equally astute at turning around failing stores. The Value City chain grew in the 1970s by taking over floundering regional chains and reopening them profitably. Some were closed and reopened under the Value City name, while others SSC funded and gave management assistance in exchange for a percentage of the business. SSC turned around bankrupt chains such as Valley Fair/Widmann in New Jersey

Company Perspectives:

Value City is striving at all levels to become the industry leader in all measures of performance. Management recognizes that achieving these goals requires a commitment to customers and to all associates. Success depends on attracting and retaining quality people. Training, development and recruiting are the highest priorities.

and Levine's in Texas. Most of the company's operations centered in the Midwest, in relatively small towns within 250 miles of Columbus. The company owned extensive real estate in and around Columbus, Ohio, where the firm was headquartered. But Jerome Schottenstein sometimes roamed far afield in looking for juicy liquidations. In the early 1980s he bought and sold the discontinued product line of flamboyant and bankrupted car maker John DeLorean. Schottenstein also sold overstocked Fiat cars. He was involved in the operation of an air freight company in Singapore, though he had never been to Singapore. While most of the Value City stores operated in relatively small towns such as Lima, Ohio, Schottenstein Stores Corp. also bought chains in big cities, such as Wieboldt's, in Chicago. By the early 1980s, Schottenstein Stores was still tightly controlled by the Schottenstein family. The Value City chain had grown to around 35 stores, and it pulled in about $250 million annually. The company's furniture division, Value City Furniture, was one of the leading furniture retailers in the country. SSC also ran a chain of lawn and garden stores in the Philadelphia area; a drug and beauty aid chain; a chain of auto supply stores, and it also had a 50 percent interest in two mall-based apparel chains, Silverman's and American Eagle. The entire Schottenstein retail enterprise was estimated to bring in $600 million a year.

Public Company in the 1990s

The Value City chain expanded through the Midwest in the late 1980s. It opened nine stores in 1989, and then six more in 1990, bringing the total to 53 stores in 11 states. Sales and earnings rose annually in the late 1980s. Sales of $537.8 million in 1990 were over 25 percent higher than the year previous, and operating profits too rose more than 20 percent. In mid-1991, Schottenstein Stores Corp. announced that it would take its Value City division public, offering a 25 percent stake in the business. The money raised would be used to retire debt. Value City's initial public offering went over well. Off-price retailing was seen as a smart trend, and Value City found eager investors. The stock price quickly rose by almost 90 percent, and the company soon declared a 2-for-1 stock split. The Schottenstein family still owned three-quarters of the new company's stock, giving it controlling power, and Jerome Schottenstein led Value City as chairman. His son Jay was vice-chairman and chief operating officer.

Jerome Schottenstein died in March 1992 of cancer at age 66. His son Jay, then 37, became chairman and CEO of Value City Department Stores, Inc. Jay had worked for SSC since 1976, and had been vice-chairman since 1986. He had worked closely with his father, and been responsible for much of the day-to-day business. Under his leadership, the Value City chain continued to expand as anticipated. Amid a generally flat retailing environment, Value City posted sales and earnings gains, and the company continued to open new stores. In 1992 it acquired a chain of 15 Gee Bee stores based in Johnston, Pennsylvania. Gee Bee was a struggling chain picked up by SSC in 1990. Value City took over the stores and converted most of them into Value Cities. The Value City formula seemed to make it stand out even as the market filled with other discount chains such as Marshall's, T.J. Maxx, and Filene's Basement. A writer for *Discount Store News* described Value City stores in an October 5, 1992 article as ''an off-price, value-driven mall, a collection of specialty stores, under one roof.'' The stores were so big, and with such a variety of merchandise, that they attracted shoppers from all income levels. While some of the goods were genuinely inexpensive, some of the bargains Value City offered were top-of-the-line brand name items including men's suits and raincoats. These sold for hundreds of dollars, which was still hundreds of dollars less than department stores charged. Thus it was not just consumers on tight budgets who were attracted to the stores. A native of Columbus familiar with the store described shopping there in a September 28, 1992 *Forbes* article as ''more like a sport than ordinary shopping.'' He claimed it was currently trendy among the city's affluent to dig for bargains at Value City.

Given the success of its IPO and its apparently excellent retailing strategy, the chain laid plans for major growth. Already by early 1993, the Value City chain boasted 79 stores and sales of around $870 million; management foresaw hitting the $1 billion mark soon. Over the next ten years, management planned to open a minimum of five to seven stores a year, and company planners expected sales to eventually hit $2 billion.

Yet by 1995 the story was a little different. Apparel, which accounted for about two-thirds of Value City's sales, was stagnant, and company analysts struggled to come up with a corrective strategy. The company had problems getting a new distribution center up and running, the market was considered flat in any case, and exceptionally warm weather in the fall of 1994 further depressed apparel sales. This led to a steep drop in earnings. The company looked at ways to make its stores friendlier, to advertise more effectively, and to move more goods from the back room onto the selling floor. Company executives reiterated that Value City had a great retail strategy. The firm's senior vice-president told the *Daily News Record* on November 3, 1995 that the chain was depending on its buyers being ''sharper and closer to need'' in order to get Value City cooking again. Despite difficulties, the chain continued to expand, moving mostly eastward. It opened stores in Atlanta, Georgia, and Charlotte, North Carolina, in 1995, and in 1996 opened nine stores total, including stores in New Jersey and Washington, D.C. Though the chain had long been suited to smallish towns, it expanded in Chicago and in suburbs of Philadelphia and St. Louis. All the stores the chain opened were not the same. The merchandise mix was specifically targeted to certain buying groups. A Paramus, New Jersey store, for example, was filled with pricier and more sophisticated goods, while others in less trendy urban markets were designated as ''moderate'' or ''budget'' stores overall. The chain's advancement continued as the firm bought up struggling regional merchants. Its new Philadelphia stores, for instance, were remodeled from units of a chain called Clover.

Key Dates:

1917: Ephraim Schottenstein opens first store.
1946: Jerome Schottenstein joins Schottenstein Stores as executive.
1966: Schottenstein Stores buys Value City store, and utilizes this name for subsequent purchases and resuscitations of bankrupt stores.
1991: Value City is spun off from Schottenstein Stores Corp. as public corporation.
1992: Jerome Schottenstein dies; son Jay takes over as CEO of Value City.
2000: Value City buys Filene's Basement chain.

By the late 1990s, Value City had grown to a chain of over 90 stores. But the growth had come at a cost. By 1997, Value City was in a slump that had lasted for many months and sent earnings spiraling down. Same-store sales growth was under 1 percent monthly, and inventory piled up. In late 1997 Value City hired a turnaround artist, Martin P. Doolan, to take over as president and chief executive, temporarily setting aside Jay Schottenstein and former president George Iacono. Doolan brought in a team of new executives, and set to work refocusing Value City's apparel buying. Some stores were slated for renovations, which included wider aisles, new carpeting and signs, and a way of grouping goods by category rather than brand name. The company also began offering more services to its customers, such as automated teller machines in the stores and promotional incentives to its store credit card holders, and upped the discount its employees received on purchases, from 10 to 20 percent.

By the fourth quarter of 1998, the company had survived its red ink period. Doolan had refocused the store on branded goods, and he attributed that shift to the company's returning fortunes. What Doolan called ''good brands'' had grown over his tenure from 15 percent of sales to over 60 percent. Most stores were renovated. The chain had halted its new store openings for fiscal 1998, but resumed its expansion with several new openings in the Southeast in 1999. Sales for 1998 reached $1.16 billion, and the company also made a new acquisition, buying up a shoe retailer called Shonac Corp. in May. A year later, the picture looked even better. Earnings increased dramatically, and the firm made several more strategic acquisitions. Value City took over eight stores from the Crowley's chain, which was in bankruptcy proceedings, giving it five stores in Detroit and three in Connecticut. Later in 1999, Value City acquired the inventory of the bankrupt Starter Corp., a maker of athletic outerwear. Value City also purchased a chain of 14 discount stores in the St. Louis area, Grandpa's. The company planned to reopen them as Grandpa's Value City.

In 2000, Value City paid $16.1 million in cash and stock for the Filene's Basement chain. Filene's Basement was a rival discounter which had had its IPO at the same time as Value City's. The Wellesley, Massachusetts-based chain had at first been quite successful, growing to over 50 stores. However, by 2000 Filene's Basement had started to shut its stores and enter bankruptcy proceedings. Value City intended to sell off one part of the purchase, a chain of warehouse stores called Aisle 3 Filene's operated, and to revive Filene's under new management. Value City began reopening some of the shuttered Filene's within months of the purchase, and it claimed it could bring the chain back to profitability within a year. With steadily growing sales and a stabilized earnings picture, Value City in the early 2000s seemed to be furthering its earlier pattern of success. It continued to expand across the country, using its tested strategy of buying up other bankrupt regional chains.

Principal Subsidiaries

Filene's Basement Corp.; Base Acquisition Corp.

Principal Competitors

Melville Corp.; TJX Co.

Further Reading

Arlen, Jeffrey, ''Value City: Orchestrating Off-Price,'' *Discount Store News*, May 3, 1993, p. A18.
''At Value City, Off-Price Retailing Is the Tradition,'' *Discount Store News*, July 25, 1983, p. 22.
''From Value City to Ann Taylor: Winners and Losers in This Year's New Issues,'' *WWD*, December 5, 1991, p. 20.
Gebolys, Debbie, ''Value City Lays Out Its Plans for a Turnaround,'' *WWD*, December 10, 1997, p. 5.
Koselka, Rita, ''The Schottenstein Factor,'' *Forbes*, September 28, 1992, pp. 104–05.
Lisanti, Tony, ''Value City a Sign of Retail Vitality,'' *Discount Store News*, October 5, 1992, p. 8.
Markowitz, Arthur, ''SSC: Powerful Retailer Besides Liquidator,'' *Discount Store News*, July 11, 1983, p. 5.
Palmieri, Jean E., ''Schottenstein Speaks Softly, But Carries a Big Pencil,'' *Daily News Record*, November 8, 1996, p. 4.
''Parent Takes Value City Public,'' *Discount Store News*, May 20, 1991, p. 1.
Phillips, Jeff, and Jackson, William, ''Schottenstein Empire Passes to Son, Jay,'' *Business First-Columbus*, March 16, 1992, p. 1.
Rurberg, Sidney; ''Schottenstein: It's All in Knowing When to Cure, When to Pull the Plug,'' *WWD*, July 14, 1983, p. 6.
Ryan, Thomas J., ''Crowley Milner Liquidating, Will Sell Eight Units to Value City,'' *Daily News Record*, February 8, 1999, p. 20.
——, ''Rx for Sagging Sales: Customer-Friendly Stores and Prices,'' *Daily News Record*, November 3, 1995, p. 3.
''Value City,'' *Fortune*, March 23, 1992, p. 109.
''Value City Aim: Absorb Gee Bee,'' *Discount Store News*, May 4, 1992, p. 1.
''Value City Chief Dead at 66,'' *Discount Store News*, April 6, 1992, p. 3.
''Value City Goes in the Black,'' *WWD*, October 12, 1998, p. 25.
''Value City Keeps Up the Pace,'' *Discount Store News*, November 18, 1996, p. 4.
''Value City Profits Soar 92.5%,'' *WWD*, November 30, 1999, p. 15.
''Value City to Acquire Filene's Basement for $16.1 Million,'' *Wall Street Journal*, February 4, 2000, p. B6.
Young, Vicki M., ''Value City Completes Filene's Basement Deal,'' *WWD*, March 22, 2000, p. 11.

—A. Woodward

VILLAGE VOICE MEDIA

Village Voice Media, Inc.

36 Cooper Sq.
New York, New York 10003
U.S.A.
Telephone: (212) 475-3300
Fax: (212) 475-8473
Web site: http://www.villagevoice.com

Private Company
Incorporated: 1985 as Stern Publishing
Employees: 500
Sales: $80 million (2000 est.)
NAIC: 51111 Newspaper Publishers

Village Voice Media, Inc. operates seven weekly ''alternative'' newspapers in large U.S. markets. Named after its flagship, New York City's *Village Voice*, the company also publishes similar papers in Los Angeles, Seattle, St. Paul, Cleveland, Nashville, and Orange County, California. Village Voice Media was formed in January 2000 to buy out Stern Publishing, which had owned the *Voice* since 1985 and had purchased all but one of the other papers in the late 1990s. Funds for the buyout came from investment firm Weiss, Peck & Greer and members of Stern management. Weiss, Peck & Greer also owns the 68-paper Lionheart Newspapers chain and Regent Communications, which operates 29 radio stations. Village Voice Media is headed by former Stern President and *Voice* publisher David Schneiderman.

Roots

The company's origins date to 1955, the year that the *Village Voice* was founded in New York City's Greenwich Village. Long a haven for artists, writers, and other bohemian types, Greenwich Village was also home to three World War II veterans who got together to start a news weekly that would speak to the values of the Village's residents. Dan Wolf had worked as a freelance writer of encyclopedia articles and had also done some editing. Ed Fancher was a practicing psychologist who had earlier written for his college newspaper. Author Norman Mailer, a friend of Wolf's, completed the trio by matching Fancher's $5,000 to help fund the startup. Wolf, Fancher, and Mailer each were considered 30 percent owners, with Mailer's lawyer receiving a 10 percent stake in exchange for drawing up the corporate papers. After a small number of staffers were hired and ramshackle office space was rented, work on a debut issue began.

The first *Village Voice*, 12 pages long, hit the streets on October 26, 1955, selling for five cents at various locations in Lower Manhattan. Only about a fourth of the 10,000 copies printed were actually sold. From the beginning the *Voice* included news articles, comprehensive entertainment listings, and reviews of Off-Broadway plays, books, movies, and more. Mailer, originally expecting to sit on the sidelines, decided to begin writing a weekly column in early 1956. The erratically written, frequently controversial column proved short-lived, and after several stormy months the author returned to being a mostly silent partner, though he would later make contributions on an occasional basis.

When a second infusion of cash was needed, Mailer and Fancher each invested another $10,000, with new partner Howard Bennett also contributing funds. At the same time, Mailer's lawyer dropped out of the partnership. Later, Bennett would sell his stake to Whitey Lutz.

The majority of the paper's original writers were unpaid, but the *Voice* was able to attract talented people because it offered them an open forum for their views. Editor Wolf, who had no real previous experience in such a role, brought respect for writing to the job from his own background, and allowed his writers unusual freedom in the pages of the publication. At times several different viewpoints would appear on a subject in the same issue, with each staffer given his or her chance to express their thoughts. The use of four-letter words, then almost unheard of, was also tolerated.

The *Voice*'s finances remained shaky throughout the late 1950s, even as the paper stayed on its path of representing the alternative voices of Greenwich Village. Noted left-leaning jazz commentator Nat Hentoff joined the paper during this time, beginning an association that would endure for more than 40 years. Offbeat cartoonist Jules Feiffer also began working for the *Voice*, beginning his own long-term association with the

Company Perspectives:

Our immediate goal is to maintain and even enhance the editorial quality of our newspapers. Our larger goals are to increase the pace of acquisition of alternative newspapers around the country, utilize the power of these brands in their local markets, to grow a substantial Internet presence and exploit opportunities in the radio market through cross-ownership and cross-promotion.

paper which led to wide syndication of his work by the mid-1960s. Articles were published that covered such subjects as the luminaries of the Beat Generation, civil rights activist Martin Luther King, Jr. and avant garde composer John Cage, in addition to the daily events of the Village.

The paper also started its own awards ceremony to honor Off-Broadway theater productions. The first one was held in the summer of 1956, with the awards dubbed the ''Obies,'' after the initials of the words ''Off Broadway.'' The paper's support of this alternative theater movement was crucial to its survival, and helped raise awareness of it far beyond the often obscure performance spaces in which it was presented. A number of performers who won Obies later graduated to mainstream acceptance, including James Earl Jones (whose father worked at the *Voice* as a janitor), Roy Scheider, George C. Scott, Hal Holbrook, Ruby Dee, and many others.

In 1959, just after weekly circulation broke the 10,000 mark, the *Voice*'s offices moved from their original loft location to the corner of Christopher Street and Seventh Avenue. The paper was now winning awards from the New York Press Association, and was becoming nationally known as a voice of alternative culture. By this time the newsstand price had doubled, to ten cents an issue.

Profitability in the Early 1960s

During the first seven years of its existence, the paper had lost more than $60,000. It had been able to survive only by tapping its initial investors for more funds, in particular relying upon Ed Fancher's inheritance. Both Fancher and Wolf took very little in salaries, relying on Wolf's wife's earnings and Fancher's psychology practice to support themselves. But the *Voice* was earning wide renown for its position on the left side of the political spectrum, its uncompromising editorial freedom, and its extensive coverage of New York's underground culture. Subscription requests trickled in from every corner of the globe, and the mainstream media began to acknowledge the *Voice*'s importance, with stories appearing in *Mademoiselle, Newsweek,* and the *New York Times.* In 1962 an anthology of *Voice* articles was published by Doubleday.

The paper achieved profitability purely by luck, however. In December 1962 the typographical union representing the staffs of several major daily New York newspapers went on strike, and other papers' staffs walked out in sympathy—shutting down the city's main sources of news. The strike lasted more than three months, and in the interim *Voice* sales shot up to 40,000 copies a week, with coverage of city news boosted to fill the void left by the big papers. Once the dailies returned to operation this number declined to 25,000, but it was still nearly double what pre-strike circulation had been. The increase in earnings from sales and advertising was significant, and finally brought a profit to the paper's owners. For the first time, *Voice* writers would also be paid, if only a nominal amount.

A second, month-long union strike in 1965 boosted circulation back up to 41,000, a number that did not drop off afterwards. Subsequently, several of New York's seven daily papers folded or consolidated operations, and by the end of 1967 the *Voice* was up to 90,000 readers. Advertising content nearly tripled during this same two-year period, with between 40 and 48 pages of ads running per issue in 1967. The *Voice*'s stature was growing, with space now being purchased by such established publications as the *New York Times* and the *New Yorker.* Surveys showed that the *Voice*'s readership was highly educated and earning more than the average U.S. household. Circulation in the Village was roughly unchanged from earlier years, but now the majority of readers came from outside the area, with a third not from New York at all. The paper's ad campaigns, created in-house, touted it as ''American's Weekly Newspaper of Non-Conformity,'' among other taglines.

Growth in sales spurred a growth in staff, and the *Voice*'s headquarters were expanded in 1968, and then moved in 1970 to University Place in the East Village. The late 1960s was a prime period for the *Voice*, with extensive coverage of the local, national, and international turmoil that was taking place. Writers such as Jack Newfield and Marlene Nadle covered events, with critics Andrew Sarris and Robert Christgau reviewing the film and music scenes.

A competitor appeared in late 1965 in the form of the monthly *East Village Other.* It was founded with the help of *Voice* mainstay John Wilcock, who was later fired because of his work for the rival. Other new alternative papers in the Village followed, as did hundreds across the country. Few survived for more than a handful of years, however.

In 1969 the *Voice* became the target of protests after it refused to run ads for a gay dating service. After considering the issue, the paper reversed its decision. The *Voice* was now publishing many classified ads for escort services and unlicensed massage parlors, generally considered fronts for prostitution. Although these were temporarily banished in the early 1970s, they would return with a vengeance in the 1980s and 1990s.

Sale to Taurus Communications

In the late 1960s the *Voice*'s owners began to get offers to purchase the paper. In January 1970 a deal was finalized for the newly formed Taurus Communications, controlled by New York City Councilman and Vanderbilt family heir Carter Burden, to purchase 80 percent of the *Voice*'s stock. The price was approximately $3.5 million. Wolf and Fancher retained complete editorial control, but Bartle Bull, minority shareholder in Taurus, was named president of the Village Voice Company in 1971. Following the sale the paper's writers demanded better pay, and they were given raises.

In 1973 the *Voice* purchased a printing company, Textmasters, Inc., and began using it to print the paper. The

Key Dates:

1955: *Village Voice* is founded in New York City's Greenwich Village.
1959: Offices move to larger space on Christopher Street and 7th Avenue.
1962: New York newspaper strike boosts *Voice* circulation, brings paper its first profits.
1970: *Voice* is sold to Taurus Communications, led by Vanderbilt heir Carter Burden; business relocates to East Village.
1973: Printing company Textmasters, Inc. is acquired.
1974: *Voice* merges with *New York Magazine*; founders Daniel Wolf and Ed Fancher are forced out.
1977: Rupert Murdoch purchases New York Magazine Co.
1985: The *Voice* is sold to Stern Publishing.
1988: *7 Days* entertainment weekly is launched by Stern; the venture folds two years later.
1994: Stern buys *LA Weekly*, then creates *Orange County Weekly* as a sister paper.
1997: *City Pages* and the *Reader* of Minneapolis-St. Paul are bought; *Reader* is shut down.
1997: *Seattle Weekly* and *Eastsideweek* are purchased; the latter is merged into the *Weekly.*
1997: *Cleveland Free Times* is acquired.
1997: *Long Island Voice* is launched, then later folded due to lack of growth.
2000: Stern Publishing is purchased in management buyout led by Weiss, Peck & Greer; the business is renamed Village Voice Media, Inc.

following summer Burden shocked the staff when he announced that he was merging the *Voice* with trendy, slick, upscale-oriented *New York* magazine, published by Clay Felker. Taurus Communications became a wholly owned subsidiary of the New York Magazine Co. in the deal.

Despite initial claims that the *Voice* would change very little, in July Wolf and Fancher were given their walking papers by Felker, now acting as *Voice* publisher. Ross Wetzsteon was named executive editor. Several months later Wolf, Fancher, Mailer, and Lutz, still owners of 20 percent of the *Voice*, sued New York Magazine, the *Voice*, and its owners for breach of contract and dereliction of fiduciary duties. With fears that the *Voice*'s staff might walk out in support, Felker gave them substantial raises as a preemptive move. An out-of-court agreement was reached with the minority shareholders in April 1975 that gave them $485,000 for their stake. During the months after Felker's ascension, several key *Voice* staffers had left or were fired, and as time went by more followed. Discussions among the former *Voice* editors and ex-staffers about starting a new paper were held, but the project eventually fell apart.

During this period the paper's cover price and ad rates were raised dramatically, and Felker brought in more of his own people to run the *Voice*. The new publisher's goal was a national publication, one which could compete with the likes of San Francisco's *Rolling Stone Magazine.* Milton Glaser redesigned the *Voice*'s look, and New York-centric articles and events listings were hidden deeper inside the paper. New editor Tom Morgan came on board in the summer of 1975, and a national advertising staff was set up. In early 1976 the biweekly national edition was rolled out. Though its first issue sold 80,000 copies, circulation soon dropped off, and it was folded within six months. Editor Morgan was out in September 1976, with Marianne Partridge taking his place.

Acquisition by Murdoch: 1977

Despite increased revenues from the *Voice* due to its higher cover price and ad rates, the New York Magazine Company was not doing well. The failed national edition had cost some $200,000, and an attempt by Felker to launch a new California-based magazine ate up further profits. In January 1977 Australian press magnate Rupert Murdoch bought 50.02 percent of the New York Magazine Company, giving him a controlling stake. He subsequently acquired the rest of the company from Clay Felker. One of his first moves was to fire editor Partridge, but he relented under pressure from the paper's staff. However, two years later she was replaced by David Schneiderman.

Although many *Voice* employees feared that the paper's quality would continue to slide under the owner of grocery store tabloids like the *Star,* Murdoch's tenure actually brought it closer to its original form. As with the previous purchase, the acquisition by Murdoch led to a number of personnel changes, but he largely let the paper run itself. The staff, which had flirted with unionization before, finally voted to organize. Circulation now stood at a steady 150,000, and remained there for the next several years.

Murdoch, who also owned the *New York Post,* chose to put the *Voice* up for sale in 1985 when the FCC held up his purchase of a New York radio station pending sale of one of his New York papers. He found a buyer in Leonard Stern, heir to the Hartz Mountain pet food company and owner of extensive real estate holdings. Stern had previously purchased the Felker-edited *New York Express,* but quickly folded it when he discovered it was unprofitable. He gave Murdoch $55 million for the *Voice*, pledging he too would be a hands-off owner.

Stern kept David Schneiderman on as editor, then bumped him up to president of Stern Publishing in 1987. The company was working on a new weekly, to be called *7 Days,* which would focus on entertainment in New York City. Dubbed "an uptown *Village Voice*" by Stern, the new magazine debuted in March 1988, reaching circulation of 80,000 by the summer. After two years of struggling to find its niche in a crowded field, *7 Days* was put up for sale, its circulation dropping and with no profits in sight. When no buyers expressed interest, Stern folded the publication. The *Voice*, meanwhile, continued to do well. Its back pages had resumed featuring lurid classified ads for escort services and phone sex lines, many now featuring full-color, suggestive photos. By some accounts, this was the most profitable part of the paper, and one for which it was now sometimes best known.

Acquisitions and Free Distribution

In the mid-1990s Stern looked again to expansion. In October 1994 the company bought the alternative *LA Weekly,* later creating a spinoff called the *Orange County Weekly.* The two West Coast publications were distributed free, and this attracted more readers, allowing their publisher to charge higher advertising rates. The *Voice*'s circulation had not grown much since the mid-1970s, and in the spring of 1996 Stern Publishing announced that it too would become a free paper. The move created a surge in demand, and circulation grew to 223,000 within a year.

In the spring of 1997 Stern made another acquisition, that of the Minneapolis/St. Paul-based *City Pages.* Shortly afterward a competitor, the *Twin Cities Reader,* was also acquired, and then folded. The free weekly *City Pages* had circulation of 100,000 at the time of acquisition, with the paper's length and its circulation numbers rising following the demise of the *Reader.*

The same scenario was played out in Seattle soon after, with the purchase of the *Seattle Weekly* and *Eastsideweek* followed by the absorption of *Eastsideweek* into the former. At the same time Stern was making plans to launch the *Long Island Voice,* which was targeted at the upscale suburban population east of Manhattan. In November, the five-year-old *Cleveland Free Times* was also acquired. Negotiations to buy a Santa Barbara, California alternative paper fell through.

In late 1999 Leonard Stern announced that Stern Publishing would go on the block. He cited his children's lack of interest in carrying on the business as one reason for the move. In January 2000 a consortium led by investment group Weiss, Peck & Greer and members of Stern management acquired the company for an estimated $160 million. Weiss, Peck & Greer had previously purchased control of the *Nashville Scene,* a weekly alternative paper, and owned a chain of small newspapers through its Lionheart Holdings LLC subsidiary. The investment firm, founded in 1970, also owned Regent Communications, which operated a chain of 29 radio stations. Weiss, Peck & Greer was itself owned by Robeco Group of Europe.

After the sale, Stern Publishing was renamed Village Voice Media, and the *Nashville Scene* was incorporated into its holdings. *Voice* publisher and Stern President Schneiderman was named CEO. His place at the *Voice* was later taken by Judy Miszner, former sales and marketing vice president for Stern. The money-losing *Long Island Voice* was not long for the world, and was folded by its new owners early in the year. CEO Schneiderman predicted further acquisitions, as well as development of related Internet businesses and cross-promotion with Weiss, Peck & Greer's radio station chain.

Though it was a relatively new company, Village Voice Media was heir to a long and storied history. Its flagship publication had seen changes over the years, but it was still the leading news and entertainment weekly for the downtown New York scene. Ownership of similar publications in other major markets also gave the company a leading position in the U.S. alternative news weekly field. Consolidation of this segment of the publishing world was ongoing, and it appeared likely that new acquisitions would continue to expand the company's portfolio.

Principal Subsidiaries

Village Voice; LA Weekly; Seattle Weekly; City Pages; Orange County Weekly; Cleveland Free Times; Nashville Scene.

Principal Competitors

Gannett Co., Inc.; The Hearst Corporation; Knight Ridder; MediaNews Group, Inc.; New Times, Inc.; Pulitzer, Inc.

Further Reading

Abrams, Bill, "Murdoch Will Sell the *Village Voice* to Stern of Hartz—Controversial Chief of Firm That Produces Pet Food to Pay $55 Million," *Wall Street Journal,* June 21, 1985.

Bates, Eric, "Chaining the Alternatives," *Nation,* June 29, 1998, p. 11.

Belsky, Gary, "Magazine Business Takes Toll on Stern," *Crain's New York Business,* April 2, 1990, p. 2.

Ciolli, Rita, "*Village Voice* Tries Suburbia/Manhattan Weekly Starts a Long Island Edition," *Newsday,* April 15, 1997, p. B3.

Ellison, Michael, " 'We Give the Guy His Say and Rip His Balls Off': That Pillar of the US Anti-Establishment, the *Village Voice* Is Up for Sale," *Guardian,* October 4, 1999.

Frankfort, Ellen, *The Voice,* New York: William Morrow and Company, 1976.

Green, Cynthia, "The King of Hartz Mountain Polishes His Image," *Business Week,* July 15, 1985, p. 124.

Jones, Tim, "Publisher Puts *Village Voice* on the Market," *Chicago Tribune,* September 24, 1999.

McAuliffe, Kevin Michael, *The Great American Newspaper,* New York: Charles Scribner's Sons, 1978.

Moses, Lucia, "VV Group: Going Once, Going Twice, It's Gone!," *Editor & Publisher,* January 10, 2000, p. 4.

Moss, Linda, "Hotshot Publisher Faces Test at 7 Days," *Crain's New York Business,* August 1, 1988, p. 1.

Stokes, Geoffrey, ed., *The Village Voice Anthology (1956–1980),* New York: William Morrow and Company, 1982.

Tran, Hung, "Industry Focus: Weiss Peck & Greer Looks to Make Local Newspapers New Again," *Buyouts,* January 24, 2000.

Wax, Alan J., "Lack of Ads Blamed for Lost *Voice,*" *Newsday,* January 6, 2000, p. A45.

—Frank Uhle

Walbridge Aldinger Co.

613 Abbott Street
Detroit, Michigan 48226-2521
U.S.A.
Telephone: (313) 963-8000
Fax: (313) 963-8123
Web site: http://www.walbridge.com

Private Company
Incorporated: 1916
Employees: 459
Sales: $800 million (2000 est.)
NAIC: 23331 Manufacturing and Industrial Building Construction; 23332 Commercial and Institutional Building Construction; 23594 Wrecking and Demolition Contractors; 23411 Highway and Street Construction; 23493 Industrial Nonbuilding Structure Construction

Walbridge Aldinger Co. is one of the 50 largest construction companies in the United States. The Detroit, Michigan-based firm has a long and distinguished history of building structures in the Motor City, ranging from concert halls and stadiums to the ''People Mover'' monorail. The company has had a highly fruitful relationship with the auto industry over the years, completing numerous major projects, including Chrysler Corporation's headquarters building in Auburn Hills, Michigan and many manufacturing facilities. Company subsidiaries also perform work in Canada, Mexico, and the United Kingdom, as well as in other American and overseas locations. Walbridge Aldinger provides design, engineering, and project management services, in addition to performing final construction. The privately held firm was purchased by John Rakolta in 1945 and is currently headed by his son John, Jr.

Beginnings

Walbridge Aldinger was founded in 1916 by two Detroit, Michigan contractors who sought to form a company that would be large enough to handle the many projects the growing city and its nascent auto industry were generating. George B. Walbridge had served as a colonel in the U.S. Army Corps of Engineers and had moved to Detroit in 1914 as vice-president of the New York-based construction firm George F. Fuller Company. His partner, Albert H. Aldinger, was a banker of German extraction who had previously founded a Canadian construction firm.

The new company quickly began to take on major assignments. Early buildings included Detroit's Orchestra Hall (1920); the Women's Colony Club (1924); Ford's Dearborn plant (1925); Olympia Stadium (1927); and the United Artist Building (1928). The next few years saw the city's WWJ Broadcasting studios and the University of Michigan's women's dormitories completed, among many others. In 1945 Walbridge and Aldinger sold the company to 23-year-old John Rakolta and a partner.

Over the succeeding decades, the company came to concentrate on work for the automobile industry. One notable project was the Chevrolet Technology Center, completed in 1954. John Rakolta continued to run the company throughout these years, and as he grew older he began grooming his son to take over. John, Jr., started working for the family business following completion of a degree in civil engineering, and in 1975 the 28-year-old began to take the reins from his father, assembling a new management team with John senior's blessings. He was named company president in 1979.

John Rakolta, Jr., adopted a more aggressive approach than his father had, boosting revenues from $50 million in 1975 to $80 million in 1979. The company's earnings at this time were still primarily derived from contracts with carmakers. At the start of the 1980s, the expanding Walbridge Aldinger moved its headquarters from Detroit to the suburb of Livonia.

One idea Rakolta had for growing the business was diversification into the commercial construction industry. Attempts to develop this area from within were made, but the key event came in 1984 when Walbridge Aldinger purchased a financially troubled Detroit-area commercial contractor named Darin & Armstrong. The acquisition more than doubled the company in size and also gave it a branch in Florida that operated throughout the southeastern United States. Rakolta's eye was increas-

Company Perspectives:

Our success as innovators in the construction industry is based upon a devotion to providing the best construction-related services that exceed our customers' expectations. We achieve this through a responsive team of experienced professionals with a ''Commitment to Excellence'' towards one common goal—A satisfied and valued client. It is this motivation which allows Walbridge Aldinger to stay on the cutting edge, providing commercial customers with the best possible services at the lowest possible cost. Our reputation as a leader in the industry is based on our greatest asset, our people and their ability to provide a variety of contract services: Integrated Program Management, Full-Service Turn-Key, Process Engineering and Technical Services, Construction Management, General Construction Contracting, and Design/Build.

ingly on cultivating clients outside of Michigan, with new projects soon under way in Florida, California, and elsewhere. Highlights of the 1980s included the Spaceship Earth building at the Epcot Center in Florida, the Ford Hermosillo Stamping Plant in Mexico, and Detroit's People Mover monorail system. The company also built three auto plants in Canada during the decade in partnership with Ellis-Don Ltd. of Toronto.

Heading into the 1990s

In 1989 the company's headquarters were moved back to Detroit when a 100,000-square-foot building was acquired from U.S. Mutual Savings & Loan, after that company ran out of funds to complete a renovation of the structure. Walbridge Aldinger completed the work at a cost of some $9 million and moved 100 of its employees into the space. A parking structure also was built across the street for their use. The move was attributed in part to the company's desire to attract more minority employees, as African Americans made up a much larger percentage of Detroit's population than Livonia's. Another motive was simply that the company was investing in the city in which it had been founded.

John Rakolta, Jr., was a strong booster of Detroit, which had seen its fortunes decline as economically advantaged residents fled to the suburbs and many once-proud buildings came to be abandoned in the downtown area. Rakolta and his wife, Terry, had earlier joined the Detroit Heritage Fund, a group of prominent local citizens who banded together in an attempt to revive the city's renowned London Chop House restaurant. The Rakoltas were active in conservative political causes as well, John as a fundraiser for the Republican Party and Terry with a campaign to protest the excessive doses of sex and violence served up by television programs such as ''Married with Children.'' Her efforts to organize boycotts of advertisers garnered much national media attention.

The 1990s started off well for the company, with Walbridge Aldinger completing the 44-story, $250 million One Detroit Center building in 1991. It was the city's first major new office structure since the five-tower Renaissance Center had been built in the mid-1970s. Work also was underway on the $700 million Chrysler Technology Center in Auburn Hills, Michigan. The company's docket consisted of approximately 60 percent auto industry-related construction, 30 percent commercial building, and ten percent public projects. Walbridge Aldinger was now one of the top two contractors in the state of Michigan, second only to Barton Malow of Southfield. Annual revenues stood at $550 million, more than ten times the 1975 figure.

The early 1990s saw a decline in revenues, however, as the economy slowed and building projects were scaled back. Walbridge Aldinger, again seeking to branch out, made its first bid on a Michigan Department of Transportation project, the $42 million Blue Water Bridge Plaza expansion in Port Huron. Before it could submit a bid, the company was required to undergo an 18-month certification process.

In 1993 Walbridge Aldinger was named the construction manager for Chrysler Corporation's newly announced world headquarters, which would be located near the automaker's Technology Center. In 1995 a strategic alliance was formed with Brown & Root, Inc. of Texas, called Walbridge Brown & Root International L.L.C. The new entity was charged with seeking international contracts for auto industry construction projects. Brown & Root, a subsidiary of Halliburton Co., operated internationally in the fields of engineering and construction, working for a wide range of clients, including governments, oil companies, and the chemical industry. The joint venture's first project was a Chrysler plant in Venezuela.

In 1997 Walbridge Aldinger won a contract with Toyota Motor Manufacturing of West Virginia to build a $400 million engine plant there. The project would require hiring some 700 workers, with completion scheduled for the following year. The U.S. construction industry was now returning to good health, with the Clinton era economic boom loosening up purse strings for new projects. Employment of construction workers also was up, and it was sometimes becoming difficult to find enough skilled workers for the many projects that were coming in. Detroit had legalized casino gambling during the decade, and several major players in that industry began racing to complete lavish facilities in the downtown area. The Detroit Lions and Detroit Tigers athletic teams also were making plans for new stadiums, and the company was involved with these projects as well. In the case of the Lions' stadium, Walbridge Aldinger and Perini Building Co. of Southfield were tapped initially to lay the groundwork for construction, but before actual work could commence they were dropped from the project, resulting in a severance payment to both companies.

In 1998 Walbridge Aldinger was rehired to work on the Lions' stadium, and the company also won a contract to demolish the landmark Hudson's department store building, an 88-year-old, 22-story structure that had been closed since 1983. A new Ford plant in India was completed during the year as well. Annual revenues reached a new high of $615 million.

1998 ISO 9001 Certification Paving Way for a Bright Future

The year 1998 also saw Walbridge Aldinger receive ISO 9001 certification. The International Organization of Standard-

Key Dates:

1916: Company is founded in Detroit by George B. Walbridge and Albert H. Aldinger.
1925: Company builds Ford Motor Company's new Dearborn, Michigan auto plant.
1945: John Rakolta and a partner acquire control of the company.
1954: Chevrolet Tech Center complex is completed.
1975: John Rakolta, Jr., begins to take over operations from his father.
1981: Company headquarters is moved from Detroit to neighboring Livonia.
1984: Acquisition of builder Darin & Armstrong doubles size of company.
1989: Headquarters is moved back to Detroit.
1991: Company's tallest building to date, 44-story One Detroit Center, is completed.
1994: Chrysler Tech Center is completed.
1996: Chrysler world headquarters building is finished.
1998: Company is first U.S. general contractor to receive ISO 9001 certification.
2000: Work begins on $550 million Compuware headquarters building.

ization in Geneva, Switzerland, had issued the standards, which prescribed construction techniques that improved efficiency and productivity while reducing costs. Walbridge Aldinger put its employees through extensive training and the company underwent a 16-month assessment to receive the certification, which gave it an advantage in procuring contracts with major clients, including the big three automakers.

The following year Walbridge Aldinger won a $50 million bid to build portions of an access road to Detroit's Metro Airport. Since 1991 the company had performed $142 million worth of work at the site, building parking structures, roads, and a hangar. The new access road, which connected the southern end of the airport with two major public thoroughfares, would be three miles long when finished. On May 15, 1999, the company performed the largest continuous concrete pour in history, using 150 concrete trucks carrying 2,333 separate loads. The 950-foot-long, 150-foot-wide section of concrete roadway was four feet thick. The decision to pour it continuously was dictated by the road's proximity to the airport's runways and the need to minimize disruption to travelers.

The year 2000 saw the company once again off the Lions' stadium project, this time because of a dispute with project manager Hammes Co. and clashes with the football team over costs. Co-contractor Barton Malow also withdrew. A major new assignment in Detroit was in the offing, however. Computer software and consulting giant Compuware was making plans to move from suburban Farmington Hills to the downtown area, and Walbridge Aldinger was brought in to manage the $550 million, 16-story project. The company was hired by developer REDICO, which was to build the structure and then lease it to Compuware. In March 2000 REDICO's president died, however, and Compuware decided to fund the project itself. This resulted in a series of delays while the design underwent further development. Meanwhile, Compuware's stock value was falling precipitously, and some speculated that the project might be downsized if the slide was not reversed. Nonetheless, in the late fall of 2000 a tentative beginning was made at the building site in downtown Detroit. Completion was projected for June 2003.

Throughout its 80-plus-year history, Walbridge Aldinger had taken on some of the largest and most challenging construction projects in the Detroit area, as well as in Florida, Canada, California, and abroad. The company's reputation for efficiency and quality was bringing in a continuous stream of work, especially from the automakers that had long been its bread and butter. The recently expanded commercial contracting business also was yielding many projects. As the 21st century dawned, the company's revenues were at record levels, and its future looked bright.

Principal Subsidiaries

Belding Walbridge; Walbridge Contracting, Inc.; Walbridge-Canada; Walbridge de Mexico; Walbridge Tilbury Ltd. (U.K.); Walbridge International.

Principal Competitors

Barton Malow Co.; Bechtel Group, Inc.; Clark Enterprises, Inc.; Fluor Daniel, Inc.; Foster Wheeler Corp.; Halliburton Co.; Jacobs Engineering Group, Inc.; Parsons Corp.; Peter Kiewit Sons Inc.; Turner Corporation; Washington Group International, Inc.; The Whiting-Turner Contracting Co.

Further Reading

Ankeny, Robert, "Firms Losing Stadium Work to Split $1.2M," *Crain's Detroit Business,* September 22, 1997, p. 7.

Barkholz, David, "Walbridge's Rakolta: Building on Success," *Crain's Detroit Business,* January 29, 1990, p. 1.

Cronan, Carl, "Walbridge Working Toward ISO Registry," *Business Journal,* June 18, 1999, p. 3.

"Detroit's New 'Taj Mahal,' " *Engineering News-Record,* October 18, 1991, p. 22.

Fricker, Daniel G., "Compuware Redesign Hinders Its Detroit Site," *Detroit Free Press,* October 12, 2000.

Gargaro, Paul, "Top 15 Contractors' Revenue Up 68% Since '91," *Crain's Detroit Business,* March 3, 1997, p. 12.

Goodin, Michael, "Walbridge Gets Chrysler HQ Contract," *Crain's Detroit Business,* April 12, 1993, p. 1.

——, "Walbridge to Bid for Blue Water Project," *Crain's Detroit Business,* May 6, 1991, p. 15.

Grogan, Tim, and Angelo, William J., "Three Years of Double-Digit Growth Have General Builders Soaring," *Engineering News-Record,* May 31, 1999, p. 113.

Mercer, Tenisha, "'97 Numbers Show Local Construction Boom Continuing," *Crain's Detroit Business,* March 2, 1998, p. 17.

Roush, Matt, "Construction Industry Expects Profits to Shrink," *Crain's Detroit Business,* April 29, 1991, p. 3.

"Walbridge Aldinger," *Constructor,* January, 1992.

Waldsmith, Lynn, "Field of Dreams: Will John Rakolta, the CEO of Walbridge Aldinger, Be Called Up to Tiger Stadium?," *Corporate Detroit,* October 1991, pp. 41–42.

Wernle, Bradford, "U.S. Construction Firms Eye Canada," *Crain's Detroit Business,* August 28, 1989, p. 3.

—Frank Uhle

Wells Fargo & Company

420 Montgomery Street
San Francisco, California 94163
U.S.A.
Telephone: (415) 411-4932
Toll Free: (800) 411-4932
Fax: (415) 677-9075
Web site: http://www.wellsfargo.com

Public Company
Incorporated: 1968 as Wells Fargo Bank, N.A.; 1983 as Norwest Corporation
Employees: 114,000
Total Assets: $263 billion (2000)
Stock Exchanges: New York Chicago
Ticker Symbol: WFC
NAIC: 522110 Commercial Banking; 522210 Credit Card Issuing; 522220 Sales Financing; 522291 Consumer Lending; 522292 Real Estate Credit; 522298 All Other Nondepository Credit Intermediation; 523110 Investment Banking and Securities Dealing; 523120 Securities Brokerage; 523920 Portfolio Management; 523991 Trust, Fiduciary, and Custody Activities; 524210 Insurance Agencies and Brokerages; 551111 Offices of Bank Holding Companies

Wells Fargo & Company is a diversified financial services company, ranking as the seventh largest bank holding company in the United States as of 2000. The company's community banking operations serve nearly 11 million customers through more than 3,000 bank branches (or what the company calls ''stores'') in 23 states, most of which are in the western United States—Ohio being the easternmost state of operation. Wells Fargo is the nation's number one home mortgage lender, with more than 1,200 ''stores'' serving all 50 states. The company is one of the top ''cross-sellers'' of financial services in the country, offering credit cards, personal loans, wealth management services, and insurance (the firm is the nation's second largest crop insurer). Business-oriented services include commercial banking services, lending, investment banking, venture capital, and equipment leasing. Wells Fargo is one of the leaders in the realm of online banking, having become the first major financial services firm to offer Internet banking back in 1995.

The Wells Fargo of the early 21st century is the product of more than 1,500 mergers over a nearly 150-year history. The bank has three main predecessors, however. In 1998 Norwest Corporation acquired the original Wells Fargo & Company and adopted the acquiree's name. Norwest's history originates in 1929 when several Midwest banks joined forces within a banking cooperative called Northwest Bancorporation, which was known as Banco. During the 1980s, Banco diversified into other areas of financial services, its affiliates reorganized, and Banco changed its name in 1983 to Norwest. Fifteen years later it acquired the original Wells Fargo. Wells traces its origins to a banking and express business formed in 1852 to exploit the economic opportunities created by the California gold rush. The banking operation split off from the express business in 1905. Throughout its colorful history, the company provided innovative services to its customers and demonstrated an ability to weather economic conditions that ruined its competitors. In 1996 Wells Fargo acquired Los Angeles-based First Interstate Bancorp in a major takeover. First Interstate first emerged as a separate company in 1957 as a spinoff of the banking interests of Transamerica Corporation called Firstamerica Bancorporation. Four years later the company was renamed Western Bancorporation, and in 1981 it adopted the First Interstate name. As it traced its origins to Transamerica, First Interstate had a lineage dating to 1904, when A.P. Giannini opened the Bank of Italy in San Francisco.

Norwest's Early History

During the generally prosperous 1920s, the nation's agricultural sector did not share in the good times. Many smaller banks that had overextended credit to farmers ran into serious trouble. In the Upper Midwest alone, 1,500 banks became insolvent from 1920 to 1929. It was with this backdrop that in early 1929, just months before the stock market crash, two banking associations were formed in the Twin Cities of Minnesota: Northwest Bancorporation and the First Bank Stock (later known as First Bank System Inc. and then U.S. Bancorp). The Northwest

Company Perspectives:

Wells Fargo was founded on the American frontier 148 years ago to satisfy a fundamental human need—to connect one customer to another and one market to another by transporting goods, services and funds fast and securely across great distances. We're still doing it today. Our vision—satisfying all our customers' financial needs—is built on that same process—connecting. That's the "next stage" of the new Wells Fargo.

cooperative, known more simply as Banco, initially included Northwestern National Bank of Minneapolis and several other Midwestern banks. Banco acquired stock in the affiliated banks and served as a mutual protection association for the beleaguered banks. Another 90 banks joined Banco in its first year of operation and by 1932 there were 139 affiliates.

During the Great Depression, numerous additional banks failed, another 700 in the Upper Midwest by 1932. None of the Banco members went under—and no depositor lost any savings—because the group was able to move liquidity around the system and in some cases, inject new capital into troubled banks. The number of members did decline, however, as some units in the group merged while others were sold off. Membership fell to 83 by 1940, then to 70 by 1952.

One of Banco's strategic advantages in the long run was its ability to operate in multiple states. The McFadden Act of 1927 had prohibited banks from operating branches across state lines. Banco was one of three major banks (the others being First Bank System and First Interstate Bancorp) that was allowed to conduct interstate banking under a grandfather clause in the 1927 act. This advantage was tempered somewhat by the emergence of bank holding companies in the late 1960s, but under the holding company arrangement, a subsidiary bank in one state was a separate entity from a subsidiary bank in another state. Prior to the 1970s, the affiliated members of Banco were largely autonomous. But during that decade, Banco began adopting a more unified structure in terms of systemwide planning, marketing, data processing, funds management, and loan syndication. By the end of the decade, Banco consisted of 85 affiliates in seven states: Minnesota, Wisconsin, Iowa, Nebraska, South Dakota, North Dakota, and Montana. Total assets had reached $11 billion, ranking Banco as the 20th largest bank in the United States. Banco was also active on the international banking scene through its lead bank, Northwestern National, which controlled Canadian American Bank, a merchant bank with offices in Winnipeg, London, Nassau, and Luxembourg.

Declining Fortunes, Then Turnaround: 1980s

Banco was beset by a series of major setbacks in the early 1980s. The troubles actually began in late 1979 when Richard H. Vaughan, the president and CEO, died by electrocution when he touched an electrical wire that had fallen during a storm. This set off a management crisis. Chester Lind stepped in as a caretaker leader until a more permanent successor could be found. In October 1981 John W. Morrison was named chairman and CEO. The new leader began centralizing the still loosely knit confederation. In 1982 the 80-odd affiliates began to be grouped into eight regions reporting to a corporate vice-chairman. Plans were also laid to unify all the affiliates and Banco itself under a new name. The change occurred in 1983, when Northwest Bancorporation became Norwest Corporation. Tellingly, the new name did not include "bank" or some variant thereof because Morrison aimed to create a diversified financial services company. To that end he had engineered the acquisition of Dial Corporation in September 1982 for $252 million. Based in Des Moines, Iowa, Dial had more than 460 offices in 38 states offering consumer loans for everything from cars to sailboats. It was considered one of the top consumer finance firms in the country and had a $1 billion consumer loan operation. Dial was renamed Norwest Financial Services Inc. in 1983.

While these restructuring initiatives were being carried out, the bank suffered another blow during the 1982 Thanksgiving weekend when the downtown Minneapolis headquarters burned to the ground. It would be six years before Norwest would be able to move into its new quarters at the Norwest Center, during which time the corporate staff was scattered around 26 different sites in the city, leading to numerous logistical difficulties. Meanwhile, with the farm economy going into a tailspin starting in 1981, Norwest began feeling the effects because it had a heavy farm loan portfolio—$1.2 billion, or seven percent of its overall loan portfolio. Norwest had another $1.2 billion in loans in foreign markets, which caused additional problems in the early 1980s as Norwest, like most U.S. banks, had made many bad loans overseas. As a result, Norwest saw its nonperforming loans increase 500 percent from 1983 to 1984, to more than $500 million. Further trouble came from the bank's mortgage unit, Norwest Mortgage Inc., which had been quickly built into the second largest holder of mortgages in the United States. In the summer of 1984 Norwest Mortgage lost nearly $100 million from an unsuccessful effort to hedge its mounting interest-rate risk on adjustable-rate mortgages. The loan losses and the mortgage debacle led to a drop in net income from $125.2 million in 1983 to $69.5 million in 1984.

In August 1984 the head of Norwest Mortgage was fired because of the hedging losses. By early 1995 substantial portions of Norwest Mortgage were divested, including operations involved in servicing mortgages and buying mortgages from other lenders for resale. The unit now focused strictly on originating mortgages. In the wake of Norwest's poor performance in 1984, Morrison resigned and was replaced by Lloyd P. Johnson, former vice-chairman of Security Pacific Corp. Johnson soon brought on board Richard M. Kovacevich, who was hired away from Citicorp to become vice-chairman and CEO of Norwest's banking group in early 1996 (he was named to the additional posts of president and COO of Norwest Corp. in January 1989). The new managers began slashing away at Norwest's bloated bureaucracy. They drastically curtailed the bank's agricultural and international loan portfolios, the former being reduced to $400 million by early 1989, the latter to $10 million. By December 1988, the nonperforming loan total stood at just $150 million. To help prevent future calamities, Norwest instituted tighter lending criteria.

On the banking side, Kovacevich continued the process of standardizing the operating methods of the various Norwest

Key Dates:

1852: Henry Wells and William G. Fargo form Wells, Fargo & Company to provide express and banking services to California.
1860: Wells Fargo gains control of Overland Mail Company, leading to operation of the western portion of the Pony Express.
1866: "Grand consolidation" unites Wells Fargo, Holladay, and Overland Mail stage lines under the Wells Fargo name.
1904: A.P. Giannini creates the Bank of Italy in San Francisco.
1905: Wells Fargo separates its banking and express operations; Wells Fargo's bank is merged with the Nevada National Bank to form the Wells Fargo Nevada National Bank.
1923: Wells Fargo Nevada merges with the Union Trust Company to form the Wells Fargo Bank & Union Trust Company.
1928: Giannini forms Transamerica Corporation as a holding company for his banking and other interests.
1929: Northwest Bancorporation, or Banco, is formed as a banking association.
1954: Wells shortens its name to Wells Fargo Bank.
1957: Transamerica spins off its banking operations, including 23 banks in 11 western states, as Firstamerica Corporation.
1960: Wells Fargo merges with American Trust Company to form the Wells Fargo Bank American Trust Company.
1961: Firstamerica changes its name to Western Bancorporation.
1962: Wells again shortens its name to Wells Fargo Bank.
1968: Wells converts to a federal banking charter, becoming Wells Fargo Bank, N.A.
1969: Wells Fargo & Company holding company is formed, with Wells Fargo Bank as its main subsidiary.
1981: Western Bancorporation changes its name to First Interstate Bancorp.
1982: Banco acquires consumer finance firm Dial Corporation, which is renamed Norwest Financial Service the following year.
1983: Banco is renamed Norwest Corporation.
1986: Wells Fargo acquires Crocker National Corporation.
1988: Wells Fargo acquires Barclays Bank of California.
1995: Wells Fargo becomes the first major financial services firm to offer Internet banking.
1996: Wells Fargo acquires First Interstate for $11.3 billion.
1998: Norwest acquires Wells Fargo for $31.7 billion and adopts the Wells Fargo name.
2000: Wells Fargo acquires First Security Corporation.

banks, increased marketing efforts, and expanded the services offered. He also began seeking acquisitions, particularly aiming to bolster Norwest's presence in key cities; in 1986, for example, Norwest acquired Toy National Bank of Sioux City, Iowa, which had assets of $145 million. At the same time came the pruning of some rural operations, including eight banks in southern Minnesota and seven branches in South Dakota. Later in the decade, opportunities to expand outside the group's traditional seven-state banking region began to arise as the barriers to interstate banking began to be dismantled. In 1988 Norwest entered rapidly growing Arizona for the first time through the purchase of a small bank near Phoenix. Norwest ended the 1980s fully recovered from its early-decade travails and ranking as one of the nation's most profitable regional banking companies and the 30th largest bank overall, with assets in excess of $25 billion. Net income stood at $237 million for 1989.

Norwest's Acquisitive 1990s

Acquisitions continued in the early 1990s. By early 1991 Norwest had 291 bank branches in 11 states, having moved into Indiana, Illinois, and Wyoming. In April 1990 Norwest paid $173 million for Sheboygan-based First Interstate of Wisconsin, a $2 billion concern. Also acquired was a troubled S&L in Norwest's home state, First Minnesota Savings Bank. The largest purchase yet came in 1992 when Norwest paid about $420 million in stock for United Banks of Colorado Inc., a bank based in Denver with total assets of $6.3 billion. Norwest Financial grew through acquisition as well, with the 1992 purchase of Trans Canada Credit, the second largest consumer finance firm in Canada. By the end of 1992 Norwest had total assets of $44.56 billion, more than double the figure of 1988. At the beginning of 1993, Johnson handed over his CEO position to Kovacevich.

Expansion of the banking operation into New Mexico and Texas came in 1993 through the acquisition of First United Bank Group Inc. of Albuquerque for about $490 million. First United had assets of $3.8 billion. Between January 1994 and June 1995, Norwest made an additional 25 acquisitions, including several in Texas, making it the most active acquirer among bank holding companies. In 1995 Norwest Mortgage became the nation's leading originator of home mortgages following the acquisition of Directors Mortgage Loan Corp., a Riverside, California-based lender with a residential mortgage portfolio of $13.1 billion. The following year Norwest Mortgage became the biggest home-mortgage servicer as well through the $600 million purchase of the bulk of the mortgage unit of the Prudential Insurance Co. of America. Meanwhile, in May 1996 Norwest Financial completed the purchase of $1 billion-asset ITT Island Finance, a consumer finance company based in San Juan, Puerto Rico. About one-quarter of Norwest Corp.'s earnings were generated by Norwest Financial in the mid-1990s, with another 12 percent coming from Norwest Mortgage. The traditional community banking operations—which extended to 16 states by 1995—accounted for only about 37 percent of the total. By year-end 1995, Norwest had total assets of $72.13 billion, making it the 13th largest bank holding company in the nation. Net income, which was nearing the $1 billion mark, had grown at a compounded annual rate of 25 percent over the previous eight years.

One of the keys to Norwest's success in the retail banking sector following the arrival of Kovacevich was the emphasis on relationship banking. His focus was on smaller customers, checking account depositors and small businesses, and he aimed to build relationships with them that would lead to cross-selling of other financial services—an auto loan, a mortgage, insurance, a mutual fund, and so on. To do so required the maintenance of an extensive network of bank branches staffed by well-trained tellers and bankers. This ran counter to the mid-1990s trend in the industry away from expensive branch banking and toward impersonal ATMs and Internet banking—the latter of course making cross-selling difficult. It was also in this cross-selling that the main units of Norwest—the retail bank, the finance company, and the mortgage company—fit and worked together. Another key to Norwest's success was its focus on these three key areas; although it did have other operations, such as a successful venture capital unit, the bank was not moving into such areas as investment banking, unlike numerous other banks, and it was not attempting to compete with large New York securities firms.

By the end of 1997, Norwest had become the 11th largest bank in the United States with total assets of $88.54 billion. With bank branches in 16 states, Norwest had the largest contiguous bank franchise in the nation. Its strongest markets were in Minnesota, Texas, Colorado, and Iowa. Having only entered the Texas market a few years previous, Norwest had built up a $10 billion presence there by buying 33 bank and trust outfits. Norwest Mortgage was national in scope, while Norwest Financial covered all 50 states, along with additional operations in Canada, the Caribbean, and Central America. Net income had reached $1.35 billion by 1997. Norwest had grown into this position of strength without completing any of the blockbuster mergers that shook up the banking industry in the 1990s, but in June 1998 the bank joined in the consolidation frenzy when it agreed to acquire Wells Fargo & Company.

Wells Fargo in the 19th Century: Banking, Express, Stagecoaches

Soon after gold was discovered in early 1848 at Sutter's Mill near Comona, California, financiers and entrepreneurs from all over North America and the world flocked to California, drawn by the promise of huge profits. Vermont native Henry Wells and New Yorker William G. Fargo watched the California boom economy with keen interest. Before either Wells or Fargo could pursue opportunities offered in the West, however, they had business to attend to in the East. Wells, founder of Wells and Company, and Fargo, a partner in Livingston, Fargo and Company, were major figures in the young and fiercely competitive express industry. In 1849 a new rival, John Butterfield, founder of Butterfield, Wasson & Company, entered the express business. Butterfield, Wells, and Fargo soon realized that their competition was destructive and wasteful, and in 1850 they decided to join forces to form the American Express Company.

Soon after the new company was formed, Wells, the first president of American Express, and Fargo, its vice-president, proposed expanding their business to California. Fearing that American Express's most powerful rival, Adams and Company (later renamed Adams Express Company), would acquire a monopoly in the West, the majority of the American Express Company's directors balked. Undaunted, Wells and Fargo decided to start their own business while continuing to fulfill their responsibilities as officers and directors of American Express.

On March 18, 1852, they organized Wells, Fargo & Company, a joint-stock association with an initial capitalization of $300,000, to provide express and banking services to California. Financier Edwin B. Morgan was appointed Wells Fargo's first president. The company opened its first office, in San Francisco, in July 1852. The immediate challenge facing Morgan and Danforth N. Barney, who became president in 1853, was to establish the company in two highly competitive fields under conditions of rapid growth and unpredictable change. At the time, California regulated neither the banking nor the express industry, so both fields were wide open. Anyone with a wagon and team of horses could open an express company and all it took to open a bank was a safe and a room to keep it in. Because of its late entry into the California market, Wells Fargo faced well established competition in both fields.

From the beginning, the fledgling company offered diverse and mutually supportive services: general forwarding and commissions; buying and selling of gold dust, bullion, and specie (or coin); and freight service between New York and California. Under Morgan's and Barney's direction, express and banking offices were quickly established in key communities bordering the gold fields and a network of freight and messenger routes was soon in place throughout California. Barney's policy of subcontracting express services to established companies, rather than duplicating existing services, was a key factor in Wells Fargo's early success.

In 1855, Wells Fargo faced its first crisis when the California banking system collapsed as a result of overspeculation. A run on Page, Bacon & Company, a San Francisco bank, began when the collapse of its St. Louis, Missouri, parent was made public. The run soon spread to other major financial institutions, all of which, including Wells Fargo, were forced to close their doors. The following Tuesday Wells Fargo reopened in sound condition, despite a loss of one-third of its net worth. Wells Fargo was one of the few financial and express companies to survive the panic, partly because it kept sufficient assets on hand to meet customers' demands rather than transferring all its assets to New York.

Surviving the Panic of 1855 gave Wells Fargo two advantages. First, it faced virtually no competition in the banking and express business in California after the crisis; second, Wells Fargo attained a reputation for dependability and soundness. From 1855 through 1866, Wells Fargo expanded rapidly, becoming the West's all-purpose business, communications, and transportation agent. Under Barney's direction, the company developed its own stagecoach business, helped start and then took over the Overland Mail Company, and participated in the Pony Express. This period culminated with the "grand consolidation" of 1866 when Wells Fargo consolidated under its own name the ownership and operation of the entire overland mail route from the Missouri River to the Pacific Ocean and many stagecoach lines in the western states.

In its early days, Wells Fargo participated in the staging business to support its banking and express businesses. But the character of Wells Fargo's participation changed when it helped start the Overland Mail Company. Overland Mail was organized in 1857 by men with substantial interests in four of the leading express companies—American Express, United States Express, Adams Express, and Wells Fargo. John Butterfield, the third founder of American Express, was made Overland Mail's president. In 1858, Overland Mail was awarded a government contract to carry the U.S. mail over the southern overland route from St. Louis to California. From the beginning, Wells Fargo was Overland Mail's banker and primary lender.

In 1859 there was a crisis when Congress failed to pass the annual post office appropriation bill and left the post office with no way to pay for the Overland Mail Company's services. As Overland Mail's indebtedness to Wells Fargo climbed, Wells Fargo became increasingly disenchanted with Butterfield's management strategy. In March 1860 Wells Fargo threatened to foreclose. As a compromise. Butterfield resigned as president of Overland Mail and control of the company passed to Wells Fargo. Wells Fargo, however, did not acquire ownership of the company until the consolidation of 1866.

Wells Fargo's involvement in Overland Mail led to its participation in the Pony Express in the last six of the express's 18 months of existence. Russell, Majors & Waddell launched the privately owned and operated Pony Express. By the end of 1860, the Pony Express was in deep financial trouble; its fees did not cover its costs and, without government subsidies and lucrative mail contracts, it could not make up the difference. After Overland Mail, by then controlled by Wells Fargo, was awarded a $1 million government contract in early 1861 to provide daily mail service over a central route (the Civil War had forced the discontinuation of the southern line), Wells Fargo took over the western portion of the Pony Express route from Salt Lake City to San Francisco. Russell, Majors & Waddell continued to operate the eastern leg from Salt Lake City to St. Joseph, Missouri, under subcontract.

The Pony Express ended when transcontinental telegraph lines were completed in late 1861. Overland mail and express services were continued, however, by the coordinated efforts of several companies. From 1862 to 1865 Wells Fargo operated a private express line between San Francisco and Virginia City, Nevada; Overland Mail stagecoaches covered the route from Carson City, Nevada, to Salt Lake City; and Ben Holladay, who had acquired Russell, Majors & Waddell, ran a stagecoach line from Salt Lake City to Missouri.

By 1866, Holladay had built a staging empire with lines in eight western states and was challenging Wells Fargo's supremacy in the West. A showdown between the two transportation giants in late 1866 resulted in Wells Fargo's purchase of Holladay's operations. The "grand consolidation" spawned a new enterprise that operated under the Wells Fargo name and combined the Wells Fargo, Holladay, and Overland Mail lines and became the undisputed stagecoach leader. Barney resigned as president of Wells Fargo to devote more time to his own business, the United States Express Company; Louis McLane, Wells Fargo's general manager in California, replaced him.

The Wells Fargo stagecoach empire was short lived. McLane had reached an agreement with a railroad group that failed. Although the Central Pacific Railroad, already operating over the Sierra Mountains to Reno, Nevada, carried Wells Fargo's express, the company did not have an exclusive contract. Moreover, the Union Pacific Railroad was encroaching on the territory served by Wells Fargo stagelines. Ashbel H. Barney, Danforth Barney's brother and cofounder of United States Express Company, replaced McLane as president in 1868. The transcontinental railroad was completed in the following year, causing the stage business to dwindle and Wells Fargo's stock to fall.

Central Pacific promoters, led by Lloyd Tevis, organized the Pacific Express Company to compete with Wells Fargo. The Tevis group also started buying up Wells Fargo stock at its sharply reduced price. In October 1869 William Fargo, his brother Charles, and Ashbel Barney traveled to Omaha, Nebraska, to confer with Tevis and his associates. There Wells Fargo agreed to buy the Pacific Express Company at a much-inflated price and received exclusive express rights for ten years on the Central Pacific Railroad and a much needed infusion of capital. All of this, however, came at a price: control of Wells Fargo shifted to Tevis.

Ashbel Barney resigned in 1870 and was replaced as president by William Fargo. In 1872 William Fargo also resigned to devote full time to his duties as president of American Express. Lloyd Tevis replaced Fargo as president of Wells Fargo, and the company expanded rapidly under his management. The number of banking and express offices grew from 436 in 1871 to 3,500 at the turn of the century. During this period, Wells Fargo also established the first transcontinental express line, using more than a dozen railroads. The company first gained access to the lucrative East Coast markets beginning in 1888; successfully promoted the use of refrigerated freight cars in California; had opened branch banks in Virginia City, Carson City, and Salt Lake City by 1876; and expanded its express services to Japan, Australia, Hong Kong, South America, Mexico, and Europe. In 1885 Wells Fargo also began selling money orders.

Early 20th Century: Independently Run Wells Fargo Bank

In 1905 Wells Fargo separated its banking and express operations. Edward H. Harriman, a prominent financier and dominant figure in the Southern Pacific and Union Pacific railroads, had gained control of Wells Fargo. Harriman reached an agreement with Isaias W. Hellman, a Los Angeles banker, to merge Wells Fargo's bank with the Nevada National Bank, founded in 1875 by the Nevada silver moguls James G. Fair, James Flood, John Mackay, and William O'Brien to form the Wells Fargo Nevada National Bank.

Wells Fargo & Company Express had moved to New York City in 1904. In 1918 the government forced Wells Fargo Express to consolidate its domestic operations with those of the other major express companies. This wartime measure resulted in the formation of American Railway Express (later Railway Express Agency). Wells Fargo continued some overseas express operations until the 1960s.

The two years following the merger tested the newly reorganized bank's, and Hellman's, capacities. In April 1906 the San Francisco earthquake and fire destroyed most of the city's business district, including the Wells Fargo Nevada National

Bank building. The bank's vaults and credit were left intact, however, and the bank committed its resources to restoring San Francisco. Money flowed into San Francisco from around the country to support rapid reconstruction of the city. As a result, the bank's deposits increased dramatically, from $16 million to $35 million in 18 months.

The Panic of 1907, begun in New York in October, followed on the heels of this frenetic reconstruction period. The stock market had crashed in March. Several New York banks, deeply involved in efforts to manipulate the market after the crash, experienced a run when speculators were unable to pay for stock they had purchased. The run quickly spread to other New York banks, which were forced to suspend payment, and then to Chicago and the rest of the country. Wells Fargo lost $1 million in deposits weekly for six weeks in a row. The years following the panic were committed to a slow and painstaking recovery.

In 1920, Hellman was very briefly succeeded as president by his son, I.W. Hellman II, who was followed by Frederick L. Lipman. Lipman's management strategy included both expansion and the conservative banking practices of his predecessors. In late 1923, Wells Fargo Nevada National Bank merged with the Union Trust Company, founded in 1893 by I.W. Hellman, to form the Wells Fargo Bank & Union Trust Company. The bank prospered during the 1920s and Lipman's careful reinvestment of the bank's earnings placed the bank in a good position to survive the Great Depression. Following the collapse of the banking system in 1933, the company was able to extend immediate and substantial help to its troubled correspondents.

The war years were prosperous and uneventful for Wells Fargo. In the 1950s, Wells Fargo President I.W. Hellman III, grandson of Isaias Hellman, began a modest expansion program, acquiring two San Francisco Bay-area banks and opening a small branch network around San Francisco. In 1954 the name of the bank was shortened to Wells Fargo Bank, to capitalize on frontier imagery and in preparation for further expansion.

1960s: Expanding Overseas and in California

In 1960, Hellman engineered the merger of Wells Fargo Bank with American Trust Company, a large northern California retail-banking system and the second oldest financial institution in California, to form the Wells Fargo Bank American Trust Company, renamed Wells Fargo Bank again in 1962. This merger of California's two oldest banks created the 11th largest banking institution in the United States. Following the merger, Wells Fargo's involvement in international banking greatly accelerated. The company opened a Tokyo representative office and, eventually, additional branch offices in Seoul, Hong Kong, and Nassau, as well as representative offices in Mexico City, Sao Paulo, Caracas, Buenos Aires, and Singapore.

In November 1966, Wells Fargo's board of directors elected Richard P. Cooley president and CEO. At 42, Cooley was one of the youngest men to head a major bank. Stephen Chase, who planned to retire in January 1968, became chairman. Cooley's rise to the top had been a quick one. From a branch manager in 1960 he rose to become a senior vice-president in 1964, an executive vice-president in 1965, and in April 1966 a director of the company. A year later Cooley enticed Ernest C. Arbuckle, the former dean of Stanford's business school, to join Wells Fargo's board as chairman.

In 1967 Wells Fargo, together with three other California banks, introduced a Master Charge card (now MasterCard) to its customers as part of its plan to challenge Bank of America in the consumer lending business. Initially 30,000 merchants participated in the plan. Credit cards would later prove a particularly profitable operation.

Cooley's early strategic initiatives were in the direction of making Wells Fargo's branch network statewide. The Federal Reserve had blocked the bank's earlier attempts to acquire an established bank in southern California. As a result, Wells Fargo had to build its own branch system. This expansion was costly and depressed the bank's earnings in the later 1960s. In 1968 Wells Fargo changed from a state to a federal banking charter, in part so that it could set up subsidiaries for businesses such as equipment leasing and credit cards rather than having to create special divisions within the bank. The charter conversion was completed August 15, 1968, with the bank renamed Wells Fargo Bank, N.A. The bank successfully completed a number of acquisitions during 1968 as well. The Bank of Pasadena, First National Bank of Azusa, Azusa Valley Savings Bank, and Sonoma Mortgage Corporation were all integrated into Wells Fargo's operations.

In 1969 Wells Fargo formed a holding company—Wells Fargo & Company—and purchased the rights to its own name from the American Express Corporation. Although the bank always had the right to use the name for banking, American Express had retained the right to use it for other financial services. Wells Fargo could now use its name in any area of financial services it chose (except the armored car trade—those rights had been sold to another company two years earlier).

1970s: Rapid Growth

Between 1970 and 1975 Wells Fargo's domestic profits rose faster than those of any other U.S. bank. Wells Fargo's loans to businesses increased dramatically after 1971. To meet the demand for credit, the bank frequently borrowed short-term from the Federal Reserve to lend at higher rates of interest to businesses and individuals.

In 1973 a tighter monetary policy made this arrangement less profitable, but Wells Fargo saw an opportunity in the new interest limits on passbook savings. When the allowable rate increased to 5 percent, Wells Fargo was the first to begin paying the higher rate. The bank attracted many new customers as a result, and within two years its market share of the retail savings trade increased more than two points, a substantial increase in California's competitive banking climate. With its increased deposits, Wells Fargo was able to reduce its borrowings from the Federal Reserve, and the one-half percent premium it paid for deposits was more than made up for by the savings in interest payments. In 1975 the rest of the California banks instituted a 5 percent passbook savings rate, but they failed to recapture their market share.

In 1973, the bank made a number of key policy changes. Wells Fargo decided to go after the medium-sized corporate and consumer loan businesses, where interest rates were higher.

Slowly Wells Fargo eliminated its excess debt, and by 1974 its balance sheet showed a much healthier bank. Under Carl Reichardt, who later became president of the bank, Wells Fargo's real estate lending bolstered the bottom line. The bank focused on California's flourishing home and apartment mortgage business and left risky commercial developments to other banks.

While Wells Fargo's domestic operations were making it the envy of competitors in the early 1970s, its international operations were less secure. The bank's 25 percent holding in Allgemeine Deutsche Credit-Anstalt, a West German bank, cost Wells Fargo $4 million due to bad real estate loans. Another joint banking venture, the Western American Bank, which was formed in London in 1968 with several other American banks, was hard hit by the recession of 1974 and failed. Unfavorable exchange rates hit Wells Fargo for another $2 million in 1975. In response, the bank slowed its overseas expansion program and concentrated on developing overseas branches of its own rather than tying itself to the fortunes of other banks.

Wells Fargo's investment services became a leader during the late 1970s. According to *Institutional Investor,* Wells Fargo garnered more new accounts from the 350 largest pension funds between 1975 and 1980 than any other money manager. The bank's aggressive marketing of its services included seminars explaining modern portfolio theory. Wells Fargo's early success, particularly with indexing—weighting investments to match the weightings of the Standard and Poor's 500—brought many new clients aboard.

By the end of the 1970s Wells Fargo's overall growth had slowed somewhat. Earnings were only up 12 percent in 1979 compared with an average of 19 percent between 1973 and 1978. In 1980 Richard Cooley, now chairman of the holding company, told *Fortune,* "It's time to slow down. The last five years have created too great a strain on our capital, liquidity, and people."

1980s: Concentrating on California

In 1981 the banking community was shocked by the news of a $21.3 million embezzlement scheme by a Wells Fargo employee, one of the largest embezzlements ever. L. Ben Lewis, an operations officer at Wells Fargo's Beverly Drive branch, pleaded guilty to the charges. Lewis had routinely written phony debit and credit receipts to pad the accounts of his cronies and received a $300,000 cut in return.

The early 1980s saw a sharp decline in Wells Fargo's performance. Richard Cooley announced the bank's plan to scale down its operations overseas and concentrate on the California market. In January 1983, Carl Reichardt became chairman and CEO of the holding company and of Wells Fargo Bank. Cooley, who had led the bank since the late 1960s, left to revive a troubled rival. Reichardt relentlessly attacked costs, eliminating 100 branches and cutting 3,000 jobs. He also closed down the bank's European offices at a time when most banks were expanding their overseas networks.

Rather than taking advantage of banking deregulation, which was enticing other banks into all sorts of new financial ventures, Reichardt and Wells Fargo President Paul Hazen kept things simple and focused on California. Reichardt and Hazen beefed up Wells Fargo's retail network through improved services such as an extensive automatic teller machine network, and through active marketing of those services.

In 1986, Wells Fargo purchased rival Crocker National Corporation from Britain's Midland Bank for about $1.1 billion. The acquisition was touted as a brilliant maneuver by Wells Fargo. Not only did Wells Fargo double its branch network in southern California and increase its consumer loan portfolio by 85 percent, but the bank did it at an unheard of price, paying about 127 percent of book value at a time when American banks were generally going for 190 percent. In addition, Midland kept about $3.5 billion in loans of dubious value.

Crocker doubled the strength of Wells Fargo's primary market, making Wells Fargo the tenth largest bank in the United States. Furthermore, the integration of Crocker's operations into Wells Fargo's went considerably smoother than expected. In the 18 months after the acquisition, 5,700 jobs were trimmed from the banks' combined staff and costs were cut considerably.

Before and after the acquisition, Reichardt and Hazen aggressively cut costs and eliminated unprofitable portions of Wells Fargo's business. During the three years before the acquisition, Wells Fargo sold its realty-services subsidiary, its residential-mortgage service operation, and its corporate trust and agency businesses. Over 70 domestic bank branches and 15 foreign branches were also closed during this period. In 1987, Wells Fargo set aside large reserves to cover potential losses on its Latin American loans, most notably to Brazil and Mexico. This caused its net income to drop sharply, but by mid-1989 the bank had sold or written off all of its medium- and long-term Third World debt.

Concentrating on California was a very successful strategy for Wells Fargo. But after its acquisition of Barclays Bank of California in May 1988, few targets remained. One region Wells Fargo considered expanding into in the late 1980s was Texas, where it made an unsuccessful bid for Dallas's FirstRepublic Corporation in 1988. In early 1989 Wells Fargo expanded into full-service brokerage and launched a joint venture with the Japanese company Nikko Securities called Wells Fargo Nikko Investment Advisors. Also in 1989, the company divested itself of its last international offices, further tightening its focus on domestic commercial and consumer banking activities.

1990s: Emergence of the New Wells Fargo from Combination of Wells Fargo, First Interstate, and Norwest

Wells Fargo & Company's major subsidiary, Wells Fargo Bank, was still loaded with debt, including relatively risky real estate loans, in the late 1980s. However, the bank had greatly improved its loan-loss ratio since the early 1980s. Furthermore, Wells continued to improve its health and to thrive during the early 1990s under the direction of Reichardt and Hazen. Much of that growth was attributable to gains in the California market. Indeed, despite an ailing regional economy during the early 1990s, Wells Fargo posted healthy gains in that core market. Wells slashed its labor force—by more than 500 workers in 1993 alone—and boosted cash flow with technical innovations.

The bank began selling stamps through its ATMs, for example, and in 1995 was partnering with CyberCash, a software startup company, to begin offering its services over the Internet.

After dipping in 1991, Wells's net income surged to $283 million in 1992 before climbing briskly to $841 million in 1994. At the end of 1994, after 12 years of service during which Wells Fargo & Co. investors enjoyed a 1,781 percent return, Reichardt stepped aside as head of the company. He was succeeded by Hazen. Wells Fargo Bank entered 1995 as the second largest bank in California and the seventh largest in the United States, with $51 billion in assets. Under Hazen, the bank continued to improve its loan portfolio, boost service offerings, and cut operating costs. During 1995 Wells Fargo Nikko Investment Advisors was sold to Barclays PLC for $440 million.

Late in 1995 Wells Fargo began pursuing a hostile takeover of First Interstate Bancorp, a Los Angeles-based bank holding company with $58 billion in assets and 1,133 offices in California and 12 other western states. Wells Fargo had long been interested in acquiring First Interstate, whose origins began with the founding in 1904 of the Bank of Italy in San Francisco by A.P. Giannini. After expanding his empire to the financial center of New York but being blocked from consolidating his various financial ventures, Giannini in 1928 formed a holding company, the Transamerica Corporation, which began business with $1.1 billion in assets and both banking and nonbanking activities. From the 1930s through the mid-1950s, Transamerica made a number of acquisitions of banks and other financial corporations throughout the western United States, creating the framework for the later First Interstate system.

The Bank Holding Company Act of 1956 placed new restrictions on companies such as Transamerica. Therefore, in 1957, Transamerica's banking operations, which included 23 banks in 11 western states, were spun off as Firstamerica Corporation. Transamerica pursued its insurance and other operations. Firstamerica changed its name to Western Bancorporation in 1961. Western expanded steadily in the 1960s, both domestically and overseas, ending the decade with assets of more than $10 billion. The bank's financial services network grew through the 1974 founding of the Western Bancorporation Mortgage Company and the 1979 formation of Western Bancorp Venture Capital Company.

In June 1981 the company changed its name to First Interstate Bancorp. The First Interstate name became a systemwide brand for most of the company's banks, thus promoting greater public recognition of the company and internal consistency. During the 1980s, in addition to acquiring more banks, First Interstate jumped into new areas of financial services as the deregulation of the banking industry progressed. In 1983 the First Interstate Discount Brokerage was set up to provide bank customers with securities and commodities support. In 1984 the bank branched into merchant banking with the purchase of Continental Illinois Ltd. and equipment leasing with the acquisition of the Commercial Alliance Corporation of New York; and broadened its mortgage banking activities by acquiring the Republic Realty Mortgage Corporation. In 1986 and 1987, First Interstate made a bold $3.2 billion attempt to hostilely take over the ailing Bank of America, but the bid was successfully defeated.

First Interstate ran into its own troubles in the late 1980s and early 1990s stemming from bad real estate loans and the severe recession in California. The bank posted losses in the hundreds of millions for 1987, 1989, and 1991. Consequently, First Interstate concentrated on rebuilding and rejuvenating its existing operations rather than acquiring new ones. A number of noncore unprofitable subsidiaries were jettisoned, including the equipment leasing unit, a government securities operation, and most of the wholesale banking unit. Rumors of a takeover of First Interstate were rife in the early 1990s before the bank recovered fully by mid-decade under the leadership of Joe Pinola and William Siart.

Despite First Interstate's healthier condition, and with the banking industry consolidation in full swing, Wells Fargo made a hostile bid for First Interstate in October 1995 initially valued at $10.8 billion. Other banks came forward as potential ''white knights,'' including Norwest, Bank One Corporation, and First Bank System. The latter made a serious bid for First Interstate, with the two banks reaching a formal merger agreement in November valued initially at $10.3 billion. But First Bank ran into regulatory difficulties with the way it had structured its offer and was forced to bow out of the takeover battle in mid-January 1996. Talks between Wells Fargo and First Interstate then led within days to a merger agreement. When completed in April 1996, following an antitrust review that stipulated the selling off of 61 bank branches in California, the acquisition was valued at $11.3 billion. The newly enlarged Wells Fargo had assets of about $116 billion, loans of $72 billion, and deposits of $89 billion. It ranked as the ninth largest bank in the United States.

Wells Fargo aimed to generate $800 million in annual operational savings out of the combined bank within 18 months, and immediately upon completion of the takeover announced a workforce reduction of 16 percent, or 7,200 positions, by the end of 1996. The merger, however, quickly turned disastrous as efforts to consolidate operations, which were placed on an ambitious timetable, led to major problems. Computer system glitches led to lost customer deposits and bounced checks. Branch closures led to long lines at the remaining branches. There was also a culture clash before the two banks and their customers. Wells Fargo had been at the forefront of high-tech banking, emphasizing ATMs and online banking, as well as the small-staffed supermarket ''branches,'' at the expense of traditional branch banking. By contrast, First Interstate had emphasized personalized relationship banking, and its customers were used to dealing with tellers and bankers not machines. This led to a mass exodus of First Interstate management talent and to the alienation of numerous customers, many of whom took their banking business elsewhere.

The financial performance of Wells Fargo, as well as its stock price, suffered from this botched merger, leaving the bank vulnerable to being taken over itself as banking consolidation continued unabated. This time, Wells Fargo entered into a friendly merger agreement with Norwest, which was announced in June 1998. The deal was completed in November of that year and was valued at $31.7 billion, with Norwest acquiring Wells Fargo and then changing its own name to Wells Fargo & Company because of the latter's greater public recognition and the former's regional connotations. Norwest also agreed to relocate the headquarters of the new Wells Fargo to San Francisco based on the bank's $54 billion in deposits in California versus $13 billion in Minnesota. The head of Wells Fargo, Paul Hazen, was named chairman of the new company, while the head of Norwest, Richard Kovacevich, became president and CEO. The new Wells Fargo started off as the nation's seventh largest bank with $196 billion in assets, $130 billion in deposits, and 15 million retail banking, finance, and mortgage customers. The banking operation included more than 2,850 branches in 21 states from Ohio to California. Norwest Mortgage had 824 offices in 50 states, while Norwest Financial had nearly 1,350 offices in 47 states, ten provinces of Canada, the Caribbean, Latin America, and elsewhere.

The integration of Norwest and Wells Fargo proceeded much more smoothly than the combination of Wells Fargo and First Interstate. A key reason was that the process was allowed to progress at a much slower and more manageable pace than that of the earlier merger. The plan allowed for two to three years to complete the integration, while the cost-cutting goal was a more modest $650 million in annual savings within three years. Rather than the mass layoffs that were typical of many mergers, Wells Fargo announced a workforce reduction of only 4,000 to 5,000 employees over a two-year period.

Continuing the Norwest tradition of making numerous smaller acquisitions each year, Wells Fargo acquired 13 companies during 1999 with total assets of $2.4 billion. The largest of these was the February purchase of Brownsville, Texas-based Mercantile Financial Enterprises, Inc., which had $779 million in assets. The acquisition pace picked up in 2000 with Wells Fargo expanding its retail banking into two more states: Michigan, through the buyout of Michigan Financial Corporation ($975 million in assets), and Alaska, through the purchase of National Bancorp of Alaska Inc. ($3 billion in assets). Wells Fargo also acquired First Commerce Bancshares, Inc. of Lincoln, Nebraska, which had $2.9 billion in assets, and a Seattle-based regional brokerage firm, Ragen MacKenzie Group Incorporated. In October 2000 Wells Fargo made its largest deal since the Norwest-Wells Fargo merger when it paid nearly $3 billion in stock for First Security Corporation, a $23 billion bank holding company based in Salt Lake City, Utah, and operating in seven western states. Wells Fargo thereby became the largest banking franchise in terms of deposits in New Mexico, Nevada, Idaho, and Utah; as well as the largest banking franchise in the West overall.

Following completion of the First Security acquisition, Wells Fargo had total assets of $263 billion. Its strategy echoed that of the old Norwest: making selective acquisitions and pursuing cross-selling of an ever-wider array of credit and investment products to its vast customer base. Under Kovacevich's leadership, Wells Fargo was posting smart growth in revenues and profits and was the envy of the banking industry for the smooth way in which it had completed the Norwest-Wells Fargo merger as well as its knack for integrating smaller banks. Although there was speculation that the next ''stage'' for Wells Fargo might involve a major merger with an eastern bank that would create a nationwide retail bank or a merger that would bring the bank one of the two other things it did not have—a global presence and a large investment banking arm—Kovacevich seemed content with the concentration on western U.S. banking and the broader finance and mortgage operations. Wells Fargo was more profitable than most of the ''megabanks'' that had formed in the 1990s, with the reason perhaps lying in its more modest ambitions.

Principal Subsidiaries

Norwest Bank Minnesota, N.A.; Norwest Limited, L.L.C.; Norwest Venture Partners VI, LP; WFC Holdings Corporation; Wells Fargo Bank, N.A.

Principal Competitors

Bank One Corporation; Bank of America Corporation; Citigroup Inc.; Fifth Third Bancorp; Firstar Corporation; General Electric Capital Corporation; Golden State Bancorp Inc.; Golden West Financial Corporation; Household International, Inc.; J.P. Morgan Chase & Co.; KeyCorp; National City Corporation; The PNC Financial Services Group, Inc.; Sanwa Bank California; The Sumitomo Bank, Limited; U.S. Bancorp; UnionBanCal Corporation; Washington Mutual, Inc.; Zions Bancorporation.

Further Reading

Acello, Richard, ''The Boy Wonder Banker Relaxes—Just Briefly,'' *San Diego Daily Transcript,* January 6, 1995, p. 1.

Asher, Joseph, ''Golden Jubilee for Two Holding Companies in Twin Cities,'' *ABA Banking Journal,* June 1979, pp. 102–04.

Bailey, Jeff, and Richard Gibson, ''Branching Out: Two Minnesota Banks Illustrate the Pitfalls of Interstate Networks,'' *Wall Street Journal,* July 26, 1985.

Beebe, Lucius M., and Charles M. Clegg, *U.S. West: The Saga of Wells Fargo,* New York: E.P. Dutton, 1949, 320 p.

Bradford, Stacey L., ''Norwest Passage,'' *Financial World,* January 21, 1997, pp. 41–43.

Bryan, Robert, ''First Interstate: California's Restless Giant,'' *Bankers Monthly,* October 1986, pp. 23+.

Byrne, Harlan S., ''Norwest Corp.: Earnings Surge at Bank Company's Consumer, Mortgage Operations,'' *Barron's,* October 26, 1992, pp. 31–32.

——, ''On the Money: Norwest Corp. Has Been Making the Right Moves,'' *Barron's,* January 5, 1987.

Carlsen, Clifford, ''Wells Fargo Hitches Wagon to Commerce on the Net,'' *San Francisco Business Times,* December 16, 1994, p. 6.

Carlton, Jim, ''Wells Fargo Discovers Getting Together Is Hard to Do: Efforts to Merge Operations with First Interstate Result in Alienated Customers,'' *Wall Street Journal,* July 21, 1997, p. B4.

Carson, Teresa, et al., ''Wells Fargo May Have Bagged a Bargain in Crocker,'' *Business Week,* February 24, 1986, p. 35.

DePass, Dee, ''Norwest Goes West: $31.4 Billion Buys New Name, Home,'' *Minneapolis Star Tribune,* June 9, 1998, p. 1A.

——, ''Norwest Officially Acquires Wells Fargo,'' *Minneapolis Star Tribune,* November 3, 1998, p. 1D.

——, ''Norwest Scouts Carefully Looking for the Right Deal,'' *Minneapolis Star Tribune,* December 22, 1997, p. 1D.

——, ''U.S. Bancorp, Norwest Grow in Different Ways,'' *Minneapolis Star Tribune,* December 22, 1997, p. 1D.

Eisenstein, Paul A., ''Turnaround at Norwest,'' *United States Banker,* January 1989, pp. 38+.

Ellis, James E., '' 'It's Not Sexy, but It's Sure,' '' *Business Week,* April 2, 1990, pp. 96–97.

Engen, John R., ''The Acquiring Mind of Richard Kovacevich,'' *Corporate Report-Minnesota,* October 1995, pp. 28–30+.

"First Interstate Breathes Again," *United States Banker,* February 1993, pp. 34+.

Glater, Jonathan D., "The Big Bank That Thinks Small: Norwest Targets 'Little Guys,' " *Washington Post,* January 8, 1995, p. H1.

Himelstein, Linda, and Kathleen Morris, "Why Wells Fargo Is Circling the Wagons," *Business Week,* June 9, 1997, pp. 92–93.

Hungerford, Edward, *Wells Fargo: Advancing the American Frontier,* New York: Random House, 1949, 274 p.

Iwata, Edward, "How to Make a Merger Work: Dick Kovacevich Is Successfully Piloting the New Wells Fargo," *San Francisco Examiner,* August 10, 1999, p. C1.

King, Ralph T., Jr., and Steven Lipin, "Wells Fargo Sets Big Cuts in California After Merger: Pact with First Interstate Could Take Heavy Toll in Branches, Personnel," *Wall Street Journal,* January 24, 1996, p. A3.

King, Ralph T., Jr., Timothy L. O'Brien, and Steven L. Lipin, "California Dream: A Chance to Cut Costs Drives Wells Fargo Bid for First Interstate," *Wall Street Journal,* October 19, 1995, pp. A1+.

Knecht, G. Bruce, "Banking Maverick: Norwest Corp. Relies on Branches, Pushes Service—and Prospers," *Wall Street Journal,* August 17, 1995, pp. A1+.

Kover, Amy, "Dick Kovacevich Does It His Way," *Fortune,* May 15, 2000, pp. 299–300+.

Levine, Thomas B., et al., "Two California Banks Riding Different Waves," *Business Week,* May 9, 1988, p. 127.

Loomis, Noel M., *Wells Fargo: An Illustrated History,* New York: Clarkson N. Potter, 1968, 340 p.

Milligan, John W., "The Fight for First Interstate," *United States Banker,* March 1996, pp. 32–36, 38–40.

Moody, Ralph, *Wells Fargo,* Boston: Houghton Mifflin, 1961, 184 p.

Mullen, Liz, "Banking on Independence," *Los Angeles Business Journal,* March 14, 1994, pp. 14+.

Murray, Matt, "Norwest, Wells Fargo Agree to a Merger," *Wall Street Journal,* June 9, 1998, p. A2.

"Norwest: Hurtling into Innovative Services," *Business Week,* May 28, 1984, pp. 78–79.

O'Donnell, Thomas C., "A 'Loyal Number Two' Takes Charge," *Forbes,* September 29, 1980, pp. 46+.

Racine, John, "How First Interstate Beats the California Blues," *American Banker,* January 11, 1995, pp. 4+.

Roosevelt, Phil, "King of the Cross-Sell: Richard Kovacevich Wants to Turn Wells Fargo into a Perpetual-Motion Machine," *Barron's,* October 11, 1999, pp. 20, 23.

Rose, Sanford, "They're Still Pioneering at Wells Fargo Bank," *Fortune,* July 1976, p. 122.

St. Anthony, Neal, "From Go-Go to Cut-Cut: Norwest, Growing Fast but Spending a Lot, Now Focuses on Controlling Costs," *Minneapolis Star Tribune,* August 5, 1994, p. 1D.

——, "Norwest Corp. Knows How to Grow," *Minneapolis Star Tribune,* August 13, 1990, p. 1D.

Schafer, Lee, "Executive of the Year: Lloyd P. Johnson," *Corporate Report-Minnesota,* January 1991, pp. 28+.

Sinton, Peter, "Bungles Bruise Wells Fargo: Merger Woes Hurt Once Sterling Reputation," *San Francisco Chronicle,* June 26, 1997, p. D1.

——, "Wells Fargo Wagon Rolls On," *San Francisco Chronicle,* March 25, 1996, p. B2.

Somasundarum, Meera, "Norwest, Banking Giant, Seeks Gains by Stressing Services for Customers," *Wall Street Journal,* December 10, 1996, p. B11A.

Timmons, Heather, "Can the Wells Fargo Wagon Roll Alone?," *Business Week,* October 23, 2000, p. 144.

"Waving Good-bye to Wells Fargo," *Business Week,* August 1, 1994, p. 36.

Weiner, Steve, " 'The Wal-Mart of Banking,' " *Forbes,* March 4, 1991, pp. 62, 65.

"Wells Fargo's Fight to Hold the West," *Business Week,* June 14, 1982, pp. 90+.

Wells Fargo Since 1852, San Francisco: Wells Fargo & Company, 1988.

Wilson, Neill C., *Treasure Express: Epic Days of the Wells Fargo,* New York: Macmillan, 1936.

Winther, Oscar O., *Via Western Express and Stagecoach,* Stanford, Calif.: Stanford University Press, 1945, 158 p.

Zuckerman, Sam, "A New Stage for Wells' Hazen," *San Francisco Chronicle,* November 4, 1998, p. D2.

—Dave Mote
—updated by David E. Salamie

WestJet Airlines Ltd.

35 McTavish Place NE
Calgary, Alberta T2E 7J7
Canada
Telephone: (403) 735-2600
Toll Free: (877) 937-8538
Fax: (403) 571-5367
Web site: http://www.westjet.com

Public Company
Incorporated: 1994
Employees: 1,400
Sales: C$203.57 million (US$140.7 million) (1999)
Stock Exchanges: Toronto
Ticker Symbol: WJA
NAIC: 481111 Scheduled Passenger Air Transportation; 481112 Scheduled Freight Air Transportation; 481211 Nonscheduled Chartered Passenger Air Transportation

WestJet Airlines Ltd. brought the Southwest Airlines model of no-frills short hops to Canada. Following four years of success in the west of the country, in 2000 the airline brought low-cost flights to a new hub near Toronto. WestJet's strategy closely mirrors that of Texas-based Southwest Airlines Co. Its fleet included about 20 or so Boeing 737 jets in 2000. More than two million passengers flew the airline in 1999.

A Mid-1990s Start-Up

Clive Beddoe was born in England in 1947. He emigrated to western Canada and, as president of the Hanover Group, Beddoe made a fortune developing commercial real estate in the Calgary area. He also owned a small private technical school called Career College.

According to *Canadian Business,* in 1994 Beddoe bought Western Concord Manufacturing Ltd., which brought him into the flying business. The company's executive air travel bills were totaling C$3,000 a week. He bought a twin engine Cessna 421 and flew it himself, saving thousands on fuel costs and pilot fees.

Further, he leased the plane to other businesses via local charter operation Morgan Air Services Co. Ltd. Morgan Air President Tim Morgan and investors Don Bell and Mark Hill joined Beddoe in the idea of starting their own discount airline. Hill wrote the original business plan, later becoming the director of strategic planning, while Morgan and Bell were named vice-presidents in charge of operations and customer service, respectively. Beddoe would be chairman and CEO.

Much to its credit, the group consulted Morris Air founder David Neeleman for advice. He had sold his successful Salt Lake City-based airline to Southwest Airlines Co. in 1993. He had also developed a computer reservations system, One Skies, which he sold to Hewlett-Packard. Neeleman agreed to provide 5 percent of the start-up capital himself and helped attract other investors. Ronald Greene of Renaissance Energy Ltd. joined them; Beddoe was also a major investor. By the spring of 1995 the group had more than $8.5 million in capital accumulated. The new company was named WestJet Airlines Ltd. in May 1995.

In January 1996, Research Capital Corp. helped place $20 million in stock with other private investors, the largest of which was the Ontario Teachers' Pension Plan Board. WestJet had become one of the most heavily capitalized airline start-ups in decades.

Still, the odds appeared stacked against the company. No scheduled airline had yet successfully competed against the market leaders, Air Canada and Canadian Airlines (also based in Calgary). (Canada 3000 Airlines Ltd. and Royal Airlines both were charter operations.) In the first place, fluctuations in the cost of fuel, an airline's largest expense, could devastate a small operation. In addition, Western Canada's lack of large population centers seemed to preclude the need for another airline.

However, WestJet's plan was to expand the market, much as Southwest had done in the United States, by lowering fares to the point that a new class of travelers could afford to fly. Beddoe called it the ''VFR'' market—''visiting friends and relatives.'' As such, WestJet would compete with cars and buses as much as planes.

Company Perspectives:

Though our geographical service areas may changes as we grow, our strategy and commitment to our business plan will not. We remain dedicated to maintaining low costs throughout our operations and to ensuring constant, consistent, and manageable growth. We also remain committed to integrating technology to ensure efficiency and excellence in customer service; to ensuring our people are supported and empowered by their company; and to maintaining the WestJet culture that has become a trademark and is paramount in our success.

Controlling costs was critical to WestJet's plan. The airline started out with cheaper labor than that of the established, unionized carriers. In fact, the CEO drew no salary at all. *Canadian Business* noted that Beddoe paid for his office furnishings out of his own pocket. Stock purchase and profit sharing plans helped provide extrinsic motivation, and the company fostered a casual and upbeat working environment. Such a corporate culture was regarded as necessary for good customer service.

WestJet relied on energetic, motivated employees to perform fast turnarounds. As at Southwest, flight crew and even executives were said to help tidy up the cabins between flights. WestJet also avoided carrying large amounts of debt, although it did buy its own well-used jets rather than lease new ones. The first had an average age of 23 years.

As might be expected, many of the perks of the big airlines were missing. WestJet offered no paper tickets, in-flight meals, frequent flier program, or airport lounges. It had only one class of seating and was not a member of any of the computer reservation systems used by most airlines and travel agents.

Commercial flight operations began with three planes on February 29, 1996. Vancouver, Kelowna, Calgary, Edmonton, and Winnipeg were the first cities served; several were added in the first year.

WestJet's fares were often more than 50 percent less than those of other airlines. The formula worked amazingly well. In its first six months, WestJet logged a profit of $2.5 million, surely one of the most successful airline launches ever.

Crisis in 1996

In September 1996, Canadian transport officials found WestJet's maintenance record-keeping program inadequate and forced the carrier to suspend operations. The grounding cost the carrier C$300,000 a day and stranded many passengers. It was the kind of a blow that could easily bankrupt a fledgling airline, especially given the broad suspicion of budget carriers that followed the ValuJet crash in the Florida Everglades earlier that year. Beddoe later told *Canadian Business,* ''I felt as if the company we had put so much toil and energy into was crashing down on top of me, and there was nothing I could do.'' The shutdown lasted 17 days.

In fact, WestJet did recover, and quickly. In its first fiscal year, which lasted ten months, the airline managed a small profit on C$37.3 million in revenues. It carried 760,000 passengers in its first full year.

WestJet had already added another plane to its fleet, bringing the total to four. WestJet operated Boeing 737s, the small airliner Southwest Airlines used to pioneer in its widely copied strategy for connecting underserved markets. It also would not keep routes open if enough demand were not there. (It did offer ''Limited Addition'' temporary service to a few destinations in Manitoba and Alberta.) Often, though, the entrance of WestJet doubled or quadrupled the existing traffic on a route. A typical fare was C$39 between Calgary and Edmonton.

WestJet began operating charters in October 1997. Its first client was a major tour operator; soon the airline was regularly flying to Las Vegas on a chartered basis. The company also began carrying cargo in the fall of 1997. Early in 1998, WestJet explored the possibility of a marketing agreement with Air Canada.

Pretax profits were C$12.4 million on revenues of C$125.9 million in 1998. The airline carried 1.7 million passengers and ended the year with more than 600 employees, or ''Westjetters.''

Steven Smith, formerly president of Air Ontario (a subsidiary of Air Canada), became WestJet president and CEO in March 1999. Beddoe remained chairman. (Neeleman had left to launch Jet Blue, another well-capitalized budget airline in New York City.)

The fleet was up to 11 aircraft by the middle of 1999. By this time, the company had paid out $3 million in profit sharing disbursements. About 86 percent of employees owned stock in the company.

WestJet went public on the Toronto Stock Exchange in July 1999. *Canadian Business* noted that its IPO was such a success that the company's market capital was soon valued at $375 million, five times greater than that of Canadian Airlines. The company's simple profitability in a troubled industry made WestJet stock attractive. Proceeds from the IPO were earmarked towards buying new planes and building a new hangar and headquarters.

In December 1999, Air Canada agreed to buy Canadian Airlines. The combined airline would be the world's tenth largest and would have an 80 percent share of the domestic market. Air Canada soon announced plans to reduce its domestic capacity by 15 percent.

Heading East in 2000

By 2000, WestJet had 1,100 employees. In interviews, company executives stressed the importance of not expanding too quickly lest the vital relationship between employee and customer be strained.

Nevertheless, Air Canada's takeover of Canadian Airlines and the prospect of other start-up airlines filling the void in the east prompted WestJet to accelerate its expansion plans. In the spring of 2000, the company announced plans to compete in the

Key Dates:

1994: Clive Beddoe and partners discuss starting a budget airline.
1995: Calgary businessmen invest millions in venture.
1996: WestJet flies first scheduled routes; survives 17-day grounding, imposed by Canadian transport officials for inadequate record-keeping.
1997: Charter and cargo services are added to repertoire.
1999: Steven Smith is named CEO; WestJet goes public.
2000: WestJet expands into eastern Canada.

eastern half of Canada—Air Canada's home turf. At a time when WestJet's fleet contained 15 old Boeing 737s, the carrier ordered 20 new ones to provide capacity for the expansion.

In March 2000, WestJet opened a hub in Hamilton, three dozen miles from Toronto. Several eastern markets, including Ottawa, were added within a couple of months. Fares were as little as one-sixth those charged by Air Canada.

According to *Canadian Business,* entrepreneur Ken Rowe had been planning to launch his own low-fare airline, dubbed CanJet Airlines, at Hamilton. Though he was reported to have changed his mind rather than challenge the more-established, better-funded WestJet; CanJet did in fact begin flying in September 2000.

Air Canada was also planning to base its own discount airline (Air Canada Lite) at Hamilton. Some doubted the state carrier could succeed where Delta Air Lines, US Airways Inc., and Continental Airlines Inc. had failed. Even United Air Lines, Inc., the largest airline in the world, lost $200 million trying to create a low-cost unit to compete with Southwest. ''The biggest risk for us,'' quipped Smith, ''is that eastern Canadians won't like low fares.''

Smith resigned in September 2000, purportedly due to differences in management style with Beddoe, who resumed the roles of president and CEO. Beddoe told the *National Post* that Smith did not fit in with WestJet's corporate culture and, as a result, its energy and drive were threatened. Smith denied Beddoe's charges that he was ''militaristic'' and ''dictatorial.''

Just about all of the statistics that were used to measure an airline's financial performance (traffic counts, load factors, revenues, earnings) continued to rise for WestJet in 2000. During its peak season in August, it filled nearly 90 percent of its seats. The same month, WestJet stock reached a value of $29, nearly three times its initial price. Although a number of competitors, old and new, were also adding capacity to the market, WestJet looked towards an ambitious future. It held options or orders for 94 aircraft to be delivered between 2000 and 2008.

Principal Competitors

Air Canada, Inc.; Air Transat Inc.; CANADA 3000 Airlines Ltd.; CanJet Airlines; Royal Aviation Inc.

Further Reading

Alam, Masud, ''Plane Truths: More Airlines, More Choices,'' *Toronto Star,* September 14, 2000.

Baglole, Joel, ''Fledgling Is Taking On Air Canada—WestJet, a Southwest Clone, Plans Make-or-Break Bet on Nationwide Service,'' *Wall Street Journal,* April 24, 2000, p. A26.

Cattaneo, Claudia, ''WestJet CEO Fired to Head Off Revolt: WestJet Founder Feared Defections by Key Executives,'' *Financial Post,* September 26, 2000, p. C1.

Collison, Melanie, ''WestJet's Clive Beddoe Is CEO of the Year,'' *Alberta Venture,* December 1999, p. 41.

''The D-Word, Diversity, Is Reshaping the Business Scene in Calgary,'' *Report on Business Magazine,* August 1998, http://www.robmagazine.com/archive/98ROBaugust/html/calgary.html.

Fitzpatrick, Peter, ''Wacky WestJet's Winning Ways: Passengers Respond to Stunts That Include Races to Determine Who Leaves the Airplane First,'' *National Post,* October 16, 2000, p. C1.

Flint, Perry, ''WestJet Defies the Odds,'' *Air Transport World,* June 1999, pp. 82–83.

Jang, Brent, ''Go East, WestJet, But Be Wary,'' *Globe and Mail,* September 14, 2000, p. B17.

McMurdy, Deirdre, ''Flying Around Air Canada,'' *Maclean's,* September 25, 2000.

Moorman, Robert W., ''WestJet Business Plan Appears Unaffected by CEO's Dismissal,'' *Aviation Week & Space Technology,* October 9, 2000.

Verburg, Peter, ''Air Contrarian,'' *Canadian Business,* August 27, 1999, p. 24.

——, ''The Little Airline That Could,'' *Canadian Business,* April 1997, pp. 34–40.

——, ''Reach for the Bottom,'' *Canadian Business,* March 6, 2000, pp. 42–48.

Wright, Lisa, ''Fired WestJet CEO Takes the High Road As Offers Flow In,'' *Toronto Star,* Bus. Sec., September 13, 2000, p. 3.

—Frederick C. Ingram

Wm. Morrison Supermarkets PLC

Hilmore House, Thornton Rd.
Bradford, West Yorkshire BD8 9AX
United Kingdom
Telephone: +44-1274-494-166
Fax: +44-1274-494-831
Web site: http://www.morrisons.plc.uk

Public Company
Incorporated: 1899 as William Morrison (Provisions) Ltd.
Employees: 23,294
Sales: £2.99 billion (US$4.79 billion) (2000)
Stock Exchanges: London
Ticker Symbol: MRW.L
NAIC: 445110 Supermarkets and Other Grocery (Except Convenience) Stores

Wm. Morrison Supermarkets PLC is holding its own in the battle for the British supermarket customer, despite its relatively small size and regional focus. England's fifth largest supermarket group, behind the national giants Sainsbury, Tesco, Safeway, and Wal-Mart-owned Asda, Morrison remains somewhat concentrated on its traditional northern England region, despite moves during the late 1990s to open stores in the country's southern regions. Morrison operates 107 stores, some 80 of which include gasoline stations. More than 30 Morrison supermarkets also feature branch banking in a partnership arrangement with Midland Bank. Morrison stores stock some 20,000 items; Morrison's private labels account for more than half of all sales. The stores feature a ''Market Street'' concept, with specialty shops, including fishmongers, butchers, pizza, and baked goods, and American shops—selling doughnuts and hotdogs—providing a High Street shopping experience to Morrison's largely suburban customers. Morrison boasts to be the sole grocer in the United Kingdom that offers the same prices in all of its stores. The company also produces most of its own products, through its Farmers Boy and Wm. Morrison Produce subsidiaries, enabling it to keep its prices—and costs—low. Morrison is led by 70-year-old Chairman Ken Morrison, son of the founder. The Morrison family owns 40 percent of the company, worth about £900 million. With no clear successor in sight, the company has not ruled out a future takeover by one of its larger rivals.

Wholesale Origins at the Turn of the 20th Century

William Morrison began his career selling eggs and butter wholesale, founding William Morrisons (Provisions) Ltd. in 1899. Soon after, Morrison opened a stall in Bradford, England's market, and then added stalls in other nearby markets. By the 1920s, Morrison's business had flourished enough to allow him to open his own retail stores, offering counter service, in the early 1920s. Morrison's operation remained a small, Bradford-area focused business throughout Morrison's lifetime—the company's warehouse was in the garage behind the family's home. Morrison had six children, the youngest of whom, Ken, the only boy, was born when Morrison was already 57 years old.

The younger Morrison was already working for his father by the age of five, running deliveries and later stocking goods in the warehouse. While his father encouraged Ken Morrison to study for a different future, Morrison joined the army at the age of 18. In 1950, with his health failing, William Morrison offered the family business to his son. Morrison joined the company that same year, telling the *Independent:* ''I decided to make a go of it.''

Ken Morrison approached the grocer's trade with a new perspective. Rather than the small, urban center shops run by his father, Morrison saw the future in larger-scale supermarkets, particularly in ex-urban and suburban locations. At the same time, improvements in packaging, and increasing branding of grocery products were occurring, coupled with a growing trend toward self-service shopping. Taking over as company chairman in 1956, Ken Morrison steered the family company into the newly developing supermarket industry, placing prices on all of its goods and adding checkout lines, a first for the Bradford area.

Company Perspectives:

The very best for less.

Morrison next turned his attention to opening new stores. In 1962, he bought an abandoned theater in Bradford and converted it into a supermarket. Once transformed, the theater offered some 5,000 square feet of retail space and a parking lot for the company's increasingly mobile customers. The success of that store encouraged Morrison to begin opening new stores. In 1967, the company backed its expansion with a public offering on the London Stock Exchange. Morrison's focus remained on its northern England region, and by the late 1970s, the company had succeeded in establishing itself as the region's top supermarket and one of the top chains in the country.

At the end of the 1970s, Morrisons, while continuing to open new stores, began to make acquisitions of other stores. These included the ten-store chain of Whelans Discount supermarkets, purchased from JJB Sports head David Whelan in 1979. In 1981, the company made a new expansion with the acquisition of the Mainstop grocery store group. The company's roots in wholesale selling proved central to generating profits while maintaining low prices, as Morrison operated its own subsidiaries to provide products, packaging, and distribution to its stores. Meanwhile, the company's format—a Market Street concept that reproduced the feel of the stalls and small shops of a typical High Street around the periphery of the Morrison store—appealed to customers.

Going National for the 21st Century

The company's growth during the 1980s brought it to more than 50 stores by the beginning of the 1990s. Meanwhile, the failing British economy of the late 1980s and early 1990s was bringing pressure on the company. Its competitors were leading a consolidation of the industry, through a wave of takeovers and acquisitions that created four giant supermarket chains—Asda, Safeway, Tesco, and Sainsbury. Morrison's competitors also began wooing customers with a series of promotions, loyalty cards, and other services, such as extended store hours, as well as launching aggressive ad campaigns. Morrison resisted temptation to join its rivals in this expensive competition.

Instead, the company clung to its discount formula and its insistence that all of its stores exhibit the same prices. Where its competitors' prices varied from store to store depending on their locations, Morrison's single-price formula contributed in winning customer loyalty. Nonetheless, Morrison bowed to some of its competitors' pressure when in 1993 it agreed to extend its store opening hours to include Sundays. The result of this move, however, was an increase in annual sales and profits.

Despite these moves, the company still faced a withering competitive climate and a continued economic crisis. By 1995, for the first time in 20 years, the company posted no new-store openings. Yet Morrison did not rest for long. With 81 stores by mid-decade, Morrison needed to continue building scale in order to compete with its giant competitors. The company returned to new store openings, including a growing number of superstores, modeled after the French hypermarket concept that extended traditional grocery lines into a wide variety of consumer goods. Morrison opened four superstores in 1996, while converting several other stores, during a £100 million expansion program.

The company's expansion also took it into new territory—for the first time, the company began opening stores outside of its traditional northern stronghold, moving into the highly competitive southern regions of England. While these moves raised eyebrows, the company's new stores—which shared Morrison's commitment to its single-price policy—quickly proved to be among the company's top revenue generators.

In 1997, Morrison reached an agreement with Midland Bank to bring banking into its supermarkets, matching its competitors. Yet, as the larger supermarket groups lavished spending on services such as home delivery and Internet shopping, Morrison remained steadfast on its no-frills, low-price formula to help it compete. At the same time, Morrison stepped up the pace of its store portfolio expansion, opening or buying ten more stores in 1998. Aiding the company's profits was the opening of a second distribution facility in Cheshire in 1998, which helped the company control its transportation costs.

The company faced an entirely new level of competition when global retailing giant Wal-Mart announced its acquisition of the Asda supermarket group. That chain's traditionally strong presence in the northern regions of England caused many analysts to fear for Morrison's future. Indeed, by then Morrison was one of the few remaining regional players in a market now entirely dominated by national supermarket groups, while the entry of Wal-Mart in the United Kingdom promised to force new globalization moves among that country's largest supermarket groups.

Yet Morrison, which continued its own steady national expansion, continued to buck the trend, even showing steady profit and sales growth in the late 1990s. The company's control of its supply and distribution left it less vulnerable to the price wars raging elsewhere in the sector. Stepping up this end of its business, Morrison completed a new investment program in its Farmers Boy subsidiary with an opening of a new 180,000-square-foot processing facility. At the same time, the company continued to acquire stores, including three superstores from Cooperative Retail Services, based in London. Celebrating its 100th anniversary in 1999, the company opened its 100th Morrison supermarket. By mid-2000, the company had completed a new round of store openings and acquisitions, bringing its total store holdings to close to 110 stores.

Ken Morrison, nearing 70 years old, remained at the helm of the company as chairman. Yet the succession of the company began to be called into question. Despite having turned over the managing director's position to John Dowd in 1997, Morrison's hands-on approach to his father's company remained an important factor in the firm's ability to compete in the crushing British supermarket climate. Morrison continued to insist at the turn of the company's second century that he would remain with the

Key Dates:

1899: William Morrison starts William Morrison (Provisions) Ltd.
1925: Business begins retail counter service.
1950: Ken Morrison joins company.
1956: Ken Morrison is named chairman.
1958: Company opens first self-service store.
1962: First self-service supermarket is launched.
1967: Company is listed on London stock exchange.
1979: Wm. Morrison Supermarkets acquires Whelan Discount stores.
1981: Company acquires Mainstop supermarket chain.
1993: Company extends store opening hours to Sunday.
1997: In-store Midland Bank branches are added.
1998: Second distribution facility in Cheshire is opened.
1999: Company celebrates 100th anniversary and 100th store opening.
2000: Morrison Supermarkets opens 180,000-square-foot facility for Farmers Boy subsidiary.

company, as he told the *Daily Telegraph*, ''as long as I am enjoying it.''

Principal Subsidiaries

Farmers Boy Ltd.; Farock Insurance Company Ltd.; Holsa Ltd.; Neerock Ltd.; Wm. Morrison Produce Ltd.

Principal Competitors

ASDA Group Limited; Boots Company Plc; Budgens Plc; Greggs Plc; Iceland Group Plc; J Sainsbury Plc; John Lewis Partnership Plc; Marks & Spencer Plc; Safeway plc; Somerfield Plc; Tesco Plc.

Further Reading

Herbert, Ian, ''The Proof Is in the Pudding,'' *Independent*, September 29, 1999, p. 1.
Rankine, Kate, ''Plain Speaking, Plain Selling, Plain Sailing,'' *Daily Telegraph*, July 29, 2000, p. 31.
Wootliff, Benjamin, ''Morrison Wins with Shoppers,'' *Daily Telegraph*, September 22, 2000.

—M.L. Cohen

Young & Co.'s Brewery, P.L.C.

The Ram Brewery
Wandsworth
London SW18 4JD
United Kingdom
Telephone: (+44) 20 8875 7000
Fax: (+44) 20 8875 7100
Web site: http://www.youngs.co.uk

Public Company
Incorporated: 1890 as Young & Co.'s Brewery Limited
Employees: 1,815
Sales: £91.7 million (US$145.9 million) (2000)
Stock Exchanges: London
Ticker Symbol: YNGA
NAIC: 312120 Breweries; 722410 Drinking Places (Alcoholic Beverages); 722110 Full Service Restaurants; 721110 Hotels (Except Casino Hotels)

Small but feisty Young & Co.'s Brewery, P.L.C. (better known as Young's) consists of the oldest continuously operating brewery in England as well as a chain of 200 pubs and hotels. Brewing a variety of some 20 house label lager beers, ales, stouts, and bitters, but also producing a limited number of wine and spirits labels, Young's also brews under contract to a number of national and international brands and distributors, including Bass and Whitworth. Such third-party brewing contracts help to boost production output in its Wandsworth brewing facility while helping to reduce its own operating costs. Nonetheless, the company has been hampered throughout the 1990s by under-production; the company has seen its production drop to as low as 60 percent of total capacity. The company's chain of pubs and hotels feature Young's' own beer labels as well as third-party labels; many of its pubs and restaurants include full restaurant service. Traded on the London stock exchange for more than a century, Young's has resisted a growing insistence toward consolidation within Britain's regional brewing industry, which has seen declines in the face of the rising clout of national and international brewing companies. Nonetheless, the company is pursuing a strategy of individual and small group purchases, including the November 2000 acquisition of 17 pubs from fellow brewer Smiles Holdings Plc. With some 34 percent of voting stock controlled by the Young family—including John Young, chairman—the company has also resisted pressure from its minority shareholders to simplify its shareholding structure. Much of the company's voting stock remains unlisted, as part of a three-tier share structure, leaving the Young family's control more or less unchallenged. In its fiscal year ended in April 2000, Young's' sales, which reached £91.7 million, reflected a 26 percent rise in production, including a five percent gain in production of the company's own labels.

More Than 400 Years of Brewing

The Ram Brewery remained England's oldest continuously operating brewery at the start of the 21st century. The company that grew up around the Ram Brewery's ales, stouts, and lagers, later built up an extensive portfolio of public houses and hotels that themselves reflect much of English history. Brewing on the Ram Brewery's premises most likely extended beyond 500 years of history, but the earliest records of a commercial brewery at the site date back to the year 1581. At the time, the brewery was owned and operated by one Humphrey Langridge, who was listed as the brewer at the Ram Inn in Wandsworth. The Ram Brewery remained in the Langridge and related Cripps family for more than 90 years.

The Draper family bought the brewery in 1672. Operated at first by brothers Somerset and Humphrey Draper, the brewery was kept in the Draper family until 1763, when it was sold to Thomas Tritton. Tritton operated the Ram Brewery until his death in the mid-1780s. Tritton's son, George Tritton, took over the brewery and kept it in the family until the beginning of the 1830s.

By then, the Tritton family had come into contact with the Young family. The establishment in 1803 of the Surrey iron railway—originally featuring wagons pulled by horses—provided a link between Wandsworth and Croyden. George Tritton became one of the shareholders in the project, and was joined by Florance Young, who manufactured brewing equipment. The relationship between the Trittons and Youngs deepened when Young's son, Charles Allen Young, joined with Anthony Bainbridge to purchase the Ram Brewery from the Tritton family in 1831.

Company Perspectives:

Young's is Britain's oldest brewery and one of the best known and best loved in the world. It produces a stunning variety of ales, stouts and lagers, which have won countless prizes, including three world championships.

Yet the Young family's initial participation in the brewery nearly ended in disaster; a year after Young and Bainbridge acquired the brewery, much of it burned. The partners quickly rebuilt their business, however, and began the first of a series of modernization efforts, installing a steam engine in the brewery in 1835. The Ram Brewery was able to step up its production of ales, stouts, and porters, in order to supply a growing number of customers—both the company's own customers and those of other pubs.

Like most of England's brewers, Young and Bainbridge kept its own public houses as retail outlets for its products. The company's earliest pub was the one attached to the brewery itself. Originally called the Ram, later renamed as the Brewery Tap, the pub most likely dated back to the 1670s, and was definitely in existence by the 1690s. Under the Tritton family, the Ram had acquired another outlet for its brewery products, the Dog and Fox at Wimbledon. The Dog and Fox—which had been in existence since at least the early 1600s—included eight rooms and other amenities, and was transferred to Young and Bainbridge in 1834. By then, Young and Bainbridge had also acquired another lease, to the Duke of Devonshire, originally assigned to the Ram in 1827 and then given to Young and Bainbridge in 1832. This pub, which initially served only beer, was granted a spirits license in the late 1850s. The company purchased the pub outright in 1925.

Young and Bainbridge went about acquiring other pubs, whether on a leased, purchased or freehold basis, for its growing production. In 1848, the company added the lease to another pub, the Windmill, which had been in operation since the late 1600s. Young and Bainbridge bought another pub in 1857, the Duke's Head, located in Wallington, which had been in operation since as early as the 1720s and which had been supplied with the company's beers since 1832.

Not all of the company's pubs came complete with 200-year histories: in 1864, Young and Bainbridge added the newly built Duke of Cambridge, located on the growing Battersea district of London. In order to support its growing network of publican houses, Young and Bainbridge installed a second steam engine in their brewery in 1867. The following decade the company built a new pub, called the Alexandra, for the expanding Wimbledon district. The company began construction of the Victorian-style building in 1876. Several years later, the company once again faced disaster, when in 1882 a fire destroyed much of the brewery and the Ram Inn. Young and Bainbridge carried on, however, rebuilding in 1883.

The following year saw changes in the company's leadership. The transfer of the company to Charles Florance Young, son of the founder, and the exit of the Bainbridge family from the brewery's interests, led to the ending of the Young and Bainbridge association and the founding of Young's in 1884. The company was formally incorporated as Young & Co.'s Brewery Limited in 1890. Young then took the company public in 1898.

Guarding the Tradition for the 20th Century

Young's continued adding leases, freeholds, and purchases of pubs into the 20th century. At the turn of the century, the company acquired the freehold to the Windmill, replacing its former lease on the property. In another transaction, in 1925, the company purchased one of its earliest leased properties, the Duke of Devonshire. Also, after acquiring the freehold to the Alexandra pub in Wimbledon in 1923, Young's began an extensive remodeling of the site, which was completed in 1927. The company continued to look to add more pubs to its network. In 1929, the company bought the freehold to the Spread Eagle, in London, which had originally opened in 1858 and then expanded by adding a number of adjoining buildings.

In the 1930s, the Alexandra received yet more attention, when Young's acquired the adjoining property and added it to the pub. At the same time, the company was granted the lease to a land site in the quickly developing town of Greenford, just outside of London, as the city's infrastructure of road and rails began to bring industrialization to the outlying areas. Development of the property ran into snags, however, and the company was not able to open its pub on the site until 1937. A mix-up in the application forms for the operating license also resulted in the pub receiving the name The Bridge—even though the pub was located nowhere near to a bridge.

The bombing of London during World War II also brought devastation to Young's when many of the company's properties, and especially the brewery itself, suffered major damage. By the end of the war the company was faced with rebuilding its cask shed and repairing the damage to the Ram Inn.

In the 1950s, Young's continued to expand its operations. While other breweries, such as Guinness and Bass, operated at the national and even international scale, Young's remained committed to its status as one of England's preeminent regional brewers. Nonetheless, the company's beers, stouts, ales, and porters attracted growing numbers of foreign customers. Meanwhile, Young's strengthened its list of pubs and hotels, adding the Holly Lodge, a small hotel located near to the Windmill. In 1958, the company added the Marquess of Anglesey, a site operated as a coffee house or pub since the mid-1600s. Helping the company in its expansion was the listing for sale of it's a shares for the first time in 1955. The A shares were the first to grant voting rights to shareholders, joining the unlisted B shares—entirely held by the Young family—and the previously listed non-voting shares. This three-tier structure later became the target of criticism; however, the method allowed the Young family to raise capital, while maintaining control of the company that bore the family's name.

A new generation of the Young family took the company's lead in 1962, when John Allen Young was appointed chairman. The great-great-great grandson of the company's founder quickly made his mark on the company—which he continued to lead into the 21st century—by instituting a policy of promoting draft beers in all of the company's growing list of pubs. The

Key Dates:

1581: Humphrey Langridge operates the Ram Brewery.
1672: Draper family buys Ram Brewery.
1763: The Drapers sell brewery to Thomas Tritton.
1786: Tritton's son, George Tritton, inherits brewery.
1831: Charles Allen Young and Anthony Bainbridge acquire Ram Brewery.
1884: Young and Bainbridge dissolve partnership; Charles Florance Young inherits brewery.
1890: The business is incorporated as Young & Co.'s Brewery Limited.
1898: Company is listed on the London Stock Exchange.
1945: Brewery is partially destroyed by bombing.
1955: Company offers Class A voting rights stock
1962: John Allen Young becomes chairman; company acquires Foster-Probyn Ltd.
1973: Company acquires Cockburn & Campbell Ltd.
1981: Queen Elizabeth II celebrates company's 150th anniversary.
1984: Young's builds new £5 million brewhouse.
1991: Company acquires HH Finch Ltd.
1999: John Allen Young resigns as chairman.
2000: Company acquires 17 pubs from Smiles Holdings Ltd.

importance of the company's export sales and its sales to pubs beyond its company-owned circuit was underscored, however, by the acquisition of bottling company Foster-Probyn Ltd., one of the largest bottlers in England in 1962.

As consumer tastes changed during the 1960s and 1970s, expanding beyond a traditional thirst for beers to include wines and other drinks, Young's saw a new opportunity to diversify their beverage range. In 1973, the company acquired wine merchant Cockburn & Campbell, which had been in existence since the turn of the 19th century. Celebrating its own 150th anniversary in 1981, Young's' importance in British brewing history was recognized by a visit to the Ram Brewery from the Queen of England.

The company expanded its brewing operations in 1984, building a £5 million brewhouse. The new facilities also included new equipment—some of the company's equipment had already been in use for more than a century. The company also continued to acquire single pubs, such as the Lamb Tavern in 1985. The Lamb was arguably the oldest pub in London—since it was located on the site of the Londinium Basilica, originally built by the Romans in the year 50. The Lamb itself dated from around the beginning of the 1800s, and had been independently run up until its acquisition by Young's The company carried out an extensive renovation of the Lamb in 1987 and instituted a no-smoking rule, making the Lamb the first no-smoking pub in the company's network.

At the start of the 1990s, Young's moved into a new direction when it began building hotels. While the company had operated hotels and inns as a traditional part of its network of pubs, the new strategy more forthrightly committed the company to the hotel business. The first such hotel was added to its Greenford pub site and called the Bridge Hotel.

The following year, Young's moved up the ranks of England's largest regional brewers when it agreed to acquire the pub operations from HH Finch Ltd. These acquisitions, which included Dirty Dick's, a pub in operation since 1804, became part of an overall industry trend toward consolidation. The United Kingdom's many regional brewers, hampered by the recession of the early 1990s and the lasting economic downturn of the British economy in general, had begun to seek mergers in order to cut down on high operating costs. Others, including Young's, sought to boost their production closer to capacity by adding contracts to brew beers for third-party brands. Among Young's' customers were Bass and Whitbread.

By the mid-1990s, Young's had built up a network of more than 150 pubs and hotels, serving some 20 internationally recognized and award-winning brands. The company continued to introduce new brands, such as the successful Double Chocolate Stout, and the bitter, Dirty Dick's, both launched in 1997. In the late 1990s, the company dodged attempts from a minority shareholder, investment group Guinness Peat, to force the company to streamline its shareholding structure and give its minority shareholders more voting rights. The company refused, yet nonetheless granted a number of concessions, including the retirement of John Allen Young, aged 77, to a position as executive chairman, and the resignation of Young's brother Thomas from the company's board of directors.

Analysts continued to call for a consolidation of the United Kingdom's regional brewing industry. Largely protected from a possible takeover, but suffering from low production levels that saw its brewery operating at just 60 percent capacity, Young's itself began to consider stepping up its acquisition pace. In 1998, the company was among those in the lead to acquire the 132-pub chain of tenanted pubs operated by Oxford-based brewer Morells. That deal never came through, however. Instead, the company continued to piece together small-scale acquisitions, such as the purchase of the freehold for the Fox & Hounds, a 170-year-old Ale House near Sloane Square in London, completed in 1998.

At the beginning of 2000, the company acquired four new pubs, including the Court House, in Dartford, Kent, from the Whitbread group; the Red Lion in Radlett, Hertfordshire, and the Cock Inn, in Boughton Monchelsea, Kent, both from pub operator Crowded House; and the Ship, in West Sussex, which had been independently operated. At the same time, Young's opened a new pub, the Bar Verve, in Slough, Berkshire.

The company boosted its holdings again in November 2000 when it reached an agreement to acquire 17 pubs from Bristol brewer Smiles Holdings Plc. The purchase, for £5.8 million, raised Young's' pub holdings to 200. Meanwhile, the company was said to be interested in acquiring properties from international brewing giant Interbrew, as the Belgium-based group was faced with shedding assets following its acquisitions of both Bass and Whitbread. Despite the continued expansion of its pub network, Young's remained committed to its position as one of the United Kingdom's most prominent regional brewers.

Principal Subsidiaries

Foster-Probyn Ltd.; Cockburn & Campbell Ltd.

Principal Competitors

Ann Street Group Limited; Bass PLC; Diageo Plc.; Fuller Smith & Turner P.L.C.; Greene King plc; Heineken N.V.; The Nomura Securities Co., Ltd.; Punch Taverns Group Ltd.; Scottish & Newcastle plc.

Further Reading

Baker, Lucy, ''Young's Eager to Soak up Interbrew Disposals,'' *Independent*, November 17, 2000, p. 19.

German, Clifford, ''Young Resigns As Brewery Boss,'' *Independent*, June 4, 1999, p. 22.

Osborn, Helen, *Inn & Around London: A History of Young's Pubs,* London:

Pretzlik, Charles, ''Young's on List to Bid for Rival,'' *Daily Telegraph*, July 18, 1998.

Rivlin, Richard, ''Drooping Brewers,'' *Sunday Telegraph*, November 15, 1998, p. 7.

—M.L. Cohen

INDEX TO COMPANIES

Index to Companies

Listings in this index are arranged in alphabetical order under the company name. Company names beginning with a letter or proper name such as Eli Lilly & Co. will be found under the first letter of the company name. Definite articles (The, Le, La) are ignored for alphabetical purposes as are forms of incorporation that precede the company name (AB, NV). Company names printed in bold type have full, historical essays on the page numbers appearing in bold. Updates to entries that appeared in earlier volumes are signified by the notation **(upd.)**. Company names in light type are references within an essay to that company, not full historical essays. This index is cumulative with volume numbers printed in bold type.

INDEX TO INDUSTRIES

Index to Industries

ACCOUNTING

ADVERTISING & OTHER BUSINESS SERVICES

AEROSPACE

AIRLINES

AUTOMOTIVE

BEVERAGES

BIOTECHNOLOGY

CHEMICALS

CONGLOMERATES

CONSTRUCTION

CONTAINERS

DRUGS/PHARMACEUTICALS

ELECTRICAL & ELECTRONICS

ENGINEERING & MANAGEMENT SERVICES

ENTERTAINMENT & LEISURE

FINANCIAL SERVICES: BANKS

FINANCIAL SERVICES: NON-BANKS

FOOD PRODUCTS

FOOD SERVICES & RETAILERS

HEALTH & PERSONAL CARE PRODUCTS

HEALTH CARE SERVICES

HOTELS

INFORMATION TECHNOLOGY

INSURANCE

LEGAL SERVICES

MANUFACTURING

MATERIALS

MINING & METALS

PAPER & FORESTRY

PERSONAL SERVICES

PETROLEUM

PUBLISHING & PRINTING

REAL ESTATE

RETAIL & WHOLESALE

RUBBER & TIRE

TELECOMMUNICATIONS

TEXTILES & APPAREL

TOBACCO

TRANSPORT SERVICES

UTILITIES

WASTE SERVICES

GEOGRAPHIC INDEX

Geographic Index

Germany

Hong Kong

Hungary

India

Indonesia

Iran

Ireland

Israel

Italy

Italy *(continued)*

Japan

Korea

Kuwait

Luxembourg

Lybia

Malaysia

Mexico

New Zealand

Nigeria

Norway

Oman

Philippines

Poland

Portugal

Qatar

Russia

Saudi Arabia

Scotland

Singapore

South Africa

South Africa *(continued)*

South Korea

Spain

Sweden

Switzerland

Taiwan

Thailand

The Netherlands

Turkey

United Arab Emirates

United Kingdom

United Kingdom *(continued)*

United States

United States *(continued)*

United States *(continued)*

United States *(continued)*

United States *(continued)*

United States *(continued)*

Venezuela

Wales

Zambia

NOTES ON CONTRIBUTORS

Notes on Contributors

BIANCO, David P. Freelance writer.

BISCONTINI, Tracey Vasil Pennsylvania-based freelance writer, editor, and columnist.

COHEN, M. L. Novelist and freelance writer living in Paris.

COVELL, Jeffrey L. Freelance writer and corporate history contractor.

DINGER, Ed. Freelance writer and editor based in Brooklyn, New York.

HALASZ, Robert. Former editor in chief of *World Progress and Funk & Wagnalls New Encyclopedia Yearbook*; author, *The U.S. Marines* (Millbrook Press, 1993).

INGRAM, Frederick C. South Carolina-based business writer who has contributed to *GSA Business, Appalachian Trailway News,* the *Encyclopedia of Business,* the *Encyclopedia of Global Industries,* the *Encyclopedia of Consumer Brands,* and other regional and trade publications.

MEYER, Stephen. Freelance writer living in Missoula, Montana.

MOZZONE, Terri. Minneapolis-based freelance writer specializing in corporate profiles.

RHODES, Nelson. Freelance editor, writer, and consultant in the Chicago area.

ROTHBURD, Carrie. Freelance writer and editor specializing in corporate profiles, academic texts, and academic journal articles.

SALAMIE, David E. Part-owner of InfoWorks Development Group, a reference publication development and editorial services company.

UHLE, Frank. Ann Arbor-based freelance writer; movie projectionist, disc jockey, and staff member of *Psychotronic Video* magazine.

WALDEN, David M. Freelance writer and historian in Salt Lake City; adjunct history instructor at Salt Lake City Community College.

WOODWARD, A. Freelance writer.